Central Themes

Strategic Leadership	Implementation	E-ship	Joint Ventures	International Expansion	Resource-Based View	Industry Change	Ethics	Chapters Primary/Secondary
X	X				X			**1** / 4, 5, and 12
X	X			X	X		X	**2** / 6, 10, and 11
X		X			X		X	**2** / 5, 11 and 12
X		X		X	X			**3** / 4, 6 and 12
X	X		X	X	X			**3** / 4, 5 and 12
	X			X	X	X		**4** / 2, 6, and 8
		X		X		X	X	**4** / 6, 8 and 12
X	X				X	X		**5** / 3, 4, and 12
X		X			X			**5** / 3, 4, and 12
			X	X	X	X		**6** / 3, 4, and 8
	X				X	X		**6** / 3, 4, and 8
X				X	X	X	X	**7** / 6, 8, and 10
	X	X	X		X			**7** / 3, 4, and 12
	X		X	X	X		X	**8** / 3, 4, and 6
	X	X	X	X	X			**9** / 6, 7, and 11
	X	X	X	X	X			**9** / 5, 8, and 11
X				X	X	X	X	**10** / 6, 7, and 12
	X	X			X			**10** / 3, 6, and 12
X	X			X	X			**11** / 3, 6, and 8
	X			X	X	X		**11** / 3, 4, and 6
X	X	X			X		X	**12** / 3, 5, and 11
X	X	X		X			X	**12** / 3, 6, and 11
X	X			X			X	**13** / 8, 10, and 11
X	X						X	**13** / 2, 3, and 11

A DYNAMIC DIFFERENCE.

A Dynamic Difference

The intent of **Strategic Management: A Dynamic Perspective** is to deliver a comprehensive yet accessible book that presents both enduring and emerging topics in Strategic Management. We use a fresh approach that takes a dynamic perspective of competitive environments and firms, allowing for an integrated view of internal and external drivers of competitive advantage, a tight link between strategy formulation and implementation, and an explicit integration of the role of strategic leadership (at many levels of management) in formulating and implementing strategy.

This work was borne out of feedback from colleagues and our experience in classrooms and organizations that strategy must anticipate and accommodate change, require simultaneous attention to formulation and implementation, and incorporate the role of strategic leadership throughout the strategy process. In addition, traditional views of strategy tend to be biased to a view that industry structure drives performance, or that unique firm characteristics are the source of advantage. In this book we take a much more integrated and holistic view of the competitive environment and help students see the interdependence of firms and environments. These aspects of the dynamic nature of strategy formulation and implementation have been integrated from start to finish in the student experience.

Our treatment of the process of strategic management—managing the firm's strategy formulation and implementation over time—**allows us to bring *management* back into strategy**. By returning strategic leadership into the teaching strategy, students at all levels can more readily see themselves as instrumental in the strategic management process.

Mason Carpenter   Wm. Gerard Sanders

Strategic Leadership

What is it?

Strategic Leadership is the role that top- and middle-managers play in strategy formulation and implementation.

Why is it important?

Strategic Leadership is important in regards to dynamic strategy because managers are often the key sources of dynamic capabilities that allow firms to compete in turbulent and rapidly changing competitive environments. The benefits are two-fold:

1. Students can better see how the strategic tone is set at the top but that successful implementation is dependent on individuals like themselves.

2. The instructor has an opportunity to talk about the personalities of the executives involved in the cases they use, and how those personalities may play out in strategy formulation and implementation.

Where do I find it?

Strategic Leadership is first introduced in Chapter 1 *(Introducing Strategic Management)* on page 7, and then it is more fully developed in Chapter 2 *(Leading Strategically Through Effective Vision and Mission)*. All chapters also include discussions of leaders in action.

Dynamic Perspectives on Strategy

What is it?

Dynamic perspectives on strategy give students a means of connecting the dots between internal resources and capabilities, ever- and increasingly rapid-changing external conditions, and firm and industry survival and profitability.

Why is it important?

Taking a dynamic perspective on strategy allows students to see that change is inevitable in strategy, but it can occur rapidly or slowly.

Where do I find it?

1. Chapter 6, *Crafting Business Strategy for Dynamic Contexts*, speaks directly to dynamic approaches to strategy and translates recent path-breaking research on dynamic perspectives into concepts and models students can use.

2. Using the "Strategy Diamond," which is introduced in Chapter 1 (Exhibit 1.4) on pages 11–15, students are taught to seek internal coherence and consistency in changing external environments.

Reviewers

Many people were involved in reviewing the manuscript, the book design, the case selection, and our teaching package. All deserve special thanks.

Yusaf Akbar, *Southern New Hampshire University*

Peter Antoniou, *California State University at San Marcos*

Ram Baliga, *Wake Forest University*

Kunal Banerji, *Florida Atlantic University*

Pamela Barr, *Georgia State University*

Tim Blumentritt, *Marquette University*

Ingvild Brown, *George Mason University*

F. William Brown, *Montana State University*

Patricia Buhler, *Goldey-Beacom College*

Aruna Chandra, *Indiana State University*

Jim Combs, *Florida State University*

Joseph Coombs, *University of Richmond*

Kevin Cooper, *Cal Poly at San Luis Obispo*

Wade Danis, *Georgia State University*

Ajay Das, *Baruch College*

James Davis, *University of Notre Dame*

Robert DeFillippi, *Suffolk University*

Scott Droege, *Mississippi State University*

David Dudek, *University of Hartford*

Jo Ann Duffy, *Sam Houston State University*

Linda Edelman, *Bentley College*

Teri Elkins, *University of Houston*

William Enser, *University of Tennessee*

Charles Fishel, *San Jose State University*

Michael Frew, *Oklahoma City University*

Marianne Gauss, *LaSalle University*

Nicholas Georgantzas, *Fordham University*

Drew Harris, *Longwood University*

Donald Hatfield, *Virginia Tech*

Bruce Heiman, *San Francisco State University*

Scott Henley, *Oklahoma City University*

Theodore Herbert, *Rollins College*

Glenn Hoetker, *University of Illinois*

R. Kabaliswaran, *New York University*

Hyungu Kang, *Central Michigan University*

Marios Katsioloudes, *Saint Joseph's University*

Edward Levitas, *University of Wisconsin at Milwaukee*

Scott Marshall, *Portland State University*

Robert McGowan, *University of Denver*

Gerry McNamara, *Michigan State University*

Arlyn Melcher, *Southern Illinois University at Carbondale*

John Mezias, *University of Miami*

Grant Miles, *University of North Texas*

Patricia Nemetz Mills, *Eastern Washington University*

Rex Mitchell, *California State University at Northridge*

Jeffrey Nystrom, *University of Colorado at Denver*

Clifford Perry, *Florida International University*

Joseph Peyrefitte, *University of Southern Mississippi*

Steven Phelan, *University of Nevada at Las Vegas*

Gerhard Plaschka, *DePaul University*

Douglas Polley, *Saint Cloud State University*

Annette Ranft, *Florida State University*

Violina Rindova, *University of Maryland*

David Robinson, *Texas Tech University*

Michael Russo, *University of Oregon*

James Schaap, *University of Nevada*

Joseph Schenk, *University of Dayton*

Anurag Sharma, *University of Massachusetts*

Roy Suddaby, *University of Iowa*

Gordon Walker, *Southern Methodist University*

Edward Ward, *Saint Cloud State University*

Marvin Washington, *Texas Tech University*

John Watson, *Saint Bonaventure University*

Gwendolyn Whitfield, *Pepperdine University*

Robert Wiggins, *University of Memphis*

Duane Windsor, *Rice University*

Robert Wiseman, *Michigan State University*

Diana Wong, *Eastern Michigan University*

Mary Zellmer-Bruhn, *University of Minnesota*

The Interdependence of Formulation and Implementation

What is it?

Students will walk away from this material with a clear understanding that formulation and implementation are interdependent, and that effective formulation takes implementation details into account early in the strategy process.

Why is it important?

Executives often say, "I would rather have a mediocre strategy with great implementation than a great strategy with mediocre implementation."

Where do I find it?

The interdependence of formulation and implementation is most clearly illustrated in the "How Would *You* Do That?" feature. This pedagogic tool is located in every chapter, and is supported with end-of-chapter activities and material in the *Instructor Manual*. Examples of this feature can be found in Chapter 1 on pages 16–17 (JetBlue), Chapter 2 on pages 26–27 (Tritec), and in Chapter 6 on pages 170–171 ([yellow tail]).

Mason Carpenter

Professor Carpenter has a B.S. in Business Administration from California State University (Humboldt) and University of Copenhagen, Denmark, and an M.B.A. from California State University (Bakersfield). He also completed graduate studies in enology at the University of Bordeaux, France. Before obtaining his Ph.D. in strategy at the University of Texas, Austin, he worked in banking, management consulting, and software development. His research concerns corporate governance, top management teams, and the strategic management of global firms, and is published in *Strategic Management Journal, Academy of Management Journal, Academy of Management Review, Academy of Management Executive, Journal of Management,* and *Human Resource Management.* He serves on the editorial boards of the *Academy of Management Journal, Academy of Management Review, Journal of Management, Journal of Strategic Management Education,* and *Organization Science.* He was also voted Professor of the Year by M.B.A. students, and identified as one of the most popular professors in the *BusinessWeek* M.B.A. poll. He recently received the Larson Excellence in Teaching award from the School of Business, and the University of Wisconsin's Emil H. Steiger Distinguished Teaching Award.

Wm. Gerard Sanders

Professor Sanders is an associate professor and the Department Chair in Organization Leadership and Strategy at the Marriott School of Management at Brigham Young University. He earned a Ph.D. in strategic management from the University of Texas at Austin. In 1996, Professor Sanders joined the faculty at BYU, where he teaches strategic management. He has also been a visiting professor at Penn State University. His research is in the area of corporate governance and its affects on firm strategy and performance. He has published extensively in the *Academy of Management Journal, Strategic Management Journal, Journal of Management, Human Resource Management,* among other outlets. His work on the effects of stock option pay has been featured in such outlets as the *New York Times,* the *Economist, BusinessWeek, CFO,* and on National Public Radio's Marketplace. Professor Sanders is on the Editorial Board of the *Academy of Management Journal.* In 2001 he received the Marriott School's J. Earl Garrett Fellowship and in 2003 he was designated a University Young Scholar. Prior to entering graduate school, Dr. Sanders spent twelve years in industry managing the acquisitions and financing of large portfolios of commercial real estate.

STRATEGIC MANAGEMENT
A Dynamic Perspective

CONCEPTS AND CASES

Mason A. Carpenter
University of Wisconsin-Madison

Wm. Gerard Sanders
Brigham Young University

PEARSON

Prentice Hall

Upper Saddle River, New Jersey 07458

Library of Congress Cataloging-in-Publication Data

Carpenter, Mason Andrew
    Strategic management : a dynamic perspective : concepts and cases/Mason Carpenter, Wm. Gerard Sanders.
        p. cm.
    Includes bibliographical references and index.
    ISBN 0-13-145353-X (hardcover : alk. paper)
    1. Strategic planning.   2. Industrial management.   I. Sanders,
Wm. Gerard. II. Title.
HD30.28.C3772 2007
658.4′092—dc22
                                                 2005037878

Senior Acquisitions Editor: David Parker
VP/Editorial Director: Jeff Shelstad
Senior Development Editor: Ronald Librach
Development Editor: Gina Huck
Editorial Assistant: Denise Vaughn
Marketing Manager: Anne Howard
Associate Director, Production Editorial: Judy Leale
Permissions Coordinator: Charles Morris
Production Manager: Arnold Vila
Creative Director: Maria Lange
Interior Design: Solid State Graphics
Cover Design: Solid State Graphics
Cover Photos: Dan Loh/AP World Wide Photos; FP Photo/Jeff Christensen/Newscom; Chris Hondros/Getty Images
Illustration (Interior): Matrix
Photo Development Editor: Amy Ray
Director, Image Resource Center: Melinda Reo
Manager, Rights and Permissions: Zina Arabia
Manager, Visual Research: Beth Brenzel
Manager, Cover Visual Research & Permissions: Karen Sanatar
Image Permission Coordinator: Nancy Seise
Photo Researcher: Diane Austin; Terry Stratford
Composition: BookMasters, Inc.
Project Management: BookMasters, Inc./Jennifer Welsch
Printer/Binder: RR Donnelley–Willard
Typeface: Minion 10/12

Credits and acknowledgments borrowed from other sources and reproduced, with permission, in this textbook appear on appropriate page or on page 431.

Pearson Education LTD.
Pearson Education Singapore, Pte. Ltd
Pearson Education, Canada, Ltd
Pearson Education–Japan

Pearson Education Australia PTY, Limited
Pearson Education North Asia Ltd
Pearson Educación de Mexico, S.A. de C.V.
Pearson Education Malaysia, Pte. Ltd

10 9 8 7 6 5 4 3 2 1
0-13-145353-X

DEDICATION

My work on this book is dedicated to my wife Lisa, and to our boys Wesley and Zachary.

—MAC

This book is dedicated to my family—my wife Kathy, and our children Ashley, Adam, and Noelle—for providing the patience and support necessary to complete this project.

—WGS

BRIEF CONTENTS

CONTENTS

8 Looking at International Strategies 212

PART SIX　　　　**CASE STUDIES: PULLING IT ALL TOGETHER**

Acknowledgments

We wrote this book to improve the student and faculty experience with learning and teaching about strategic management. As we take the perspective of practicing managers, it is fitting that we first acknowledge the students, faculty, and managers who were directly and indirectly engaged in developing *Strategic Management: A Dynamic Perspective*. This includes our own students and colleagues at the University of Wisconsin-Madison and Brigham Young University, the many executives and managers we have consulted with and brought into our classes, and those we worked with in our travels as we developed this book over the past 4 years.

Although we had a specific vision for the book, we can't take full credit for all the content that supports that vision. In particular, we want to acknowledge the contributions of the many researchers whose work helps managers understand and cope with the challenges of crafting and implementing strategies in changing times. You will see their work cited throughout the text, and we encourage you to read the original studies (including our own) upon which the content of this book is based. We also want to acknowledge the many managers whose views and daily challenges helped us develop a theoretically rigorous, yet practically relevant and readable approach to strategic management. At many points along the way these colleagues challenged us with observations like, "That's nice, but how would you do that?" and forced us to continually refine our writing to connect the dots—from concept to action—so to speak.

Out of this group of researchers and managers, one team deserves particular note. This would be Don Hambrick at Penn State University and Jim Fredrickson at the University of Texas at Austin. These talented and prolific researchers and award-winning teachers have been leading the bandwagon to put managers back into strategy, and have been exceptional mentors to both of us. You can see their imprint in our early research, in the managerial orientation of our textbook, and in the strategy diamond that ties all the chapters together. This strategy diamond will endure long after they are done writing; it will create a rich and relevant learning environment for students of strategy, and it will provide managers a tool for thinking through and answering in the affirmative, "Yes, I really have a strategy!"

Finally, we thank our team at Prentice Hall for making the book a reality. We wanted a publisher who shared and supported our vision and high aspirations for the next generation of undergraduate and MBA strategy textbooks. We determined that Prentice Hall was a leader in product development and, most important, in selling those products once developed and published. After all, that is the message of our book—the interdependence of strategy formulation and implementation in dynamic contexts. We both reflected on the quality of our interactions with our new publisher's representatives and it was clear that Prentice Hall's reps were the best we had seen on our respective campuses. This combination of editorial, marketing, and sales excellence sealed the deal for us.

1

Introducing Strategic Management

Part One
Strategy and
Strategic
Leadership in
Dynamic
Times

After studying this chapter, you should be able to:

1. Understand what a *strategy* is and identify the difference between business-level and corporate-level strategy.

2. Understand why we study *strategic management*.

3. Understand the relationship between *strategy formulation* and *implementation*.

4. Describe the determinants of *competitive advantage*.

5. Recognize the difference between the *fundamental* view and the *dynamic* view of *competitive advantage*.

▶ **1962**
Wal-Mart's
first store opens in
Rogers, Arkansas.

▶ **1970–1971**
Wal-Mart goes public in 1970.
Its first stock split occurs the
following year
(market price: $47.00).

A TALE OF TWO STORES

Sears' Early Dominance

The Sears versus Wal-Mart saga provides a striking example of strategy in action.[1] Sears was started as a catalog business in 1891, and through a combination of marketing savvy and a broad array of product offerings, sales grew briskly. With a vision of bringing the manufactured wonders of the world to the common people, the Sears Roebuck catalog offered everything from "guaranteed cures for stupidity" to products once available only to the social elite. To exploit its rapid growth, Sears soon took control of the production and distribution of its product offerings by establishing a network of factories that it either owned or financed.

Sears applied its catalog retail model to on-premise retailing in 1924, and from that point on, Sears dominated the retail industry for more than 50 years. At about the same time, General Robert E. Wood

► 1990–1991
Wal-Mart's stock splits for the ninth time (market price: $62.50). The company enters the international market for the first time with the opening of Club Aurrera in Mexico City.

1995   2000

left competitor Montgomery Ward to lead Sears, where he would put in place the structures, systems, processes, people, and culture that would guide—and bind—Sears' strategy and actions far into the future.

Wood came to Ward, and then to Sears, as a graduate of West Point (Class of 1900). He had been in charge of logistics and supply during the building of the Panama Canal and had served as quartermaster general of the U.S. army in World War I. Upon discharge from the service, he joined Montgomery Ward as vice president in charge of merchandising. Wood was fascinated with census data, and it was his interest in and understanding of demographic and economic statistics that gave him insights into the deep changes taking place in the structure of the U.S. and Latin American markets.

Under Wood's leadership, Sears set the standard for competition in retailing with a business model that combined large and varied inventories of goods, product-line breadth, and distribution through both large-scale catalog operations and mall-based retail outlets, all supplied by a vast network of company-owned or company-controlled factories. Key players, including also-ran competitors Montgomery Ward and JCPenney, believed that the Sears way was the only way to compete in the industry. "There is no better illustration of what a business is and what managing means," declared a leading management guru, and during the 1960s, *Fortune* dubbed Sears "the paragon of retailers. It is number one in the United States, and number two, three, four and five."

As sales approached 1 to 2 percent of the country's gross domestic product in the 1960s and 1970s, Sears sought to dig deeper into America's pocketbook by moving into other businesses, including banking (Discover credit cards), investment (Dean Witter), and real estate services (Coldwell Banker), and investing further in an insurance business (Allstate) established in 1931.

Wal-Mart's Entry In 1973, however, just as Sears was crowning its success (and the legacy of General Woods) with the opening of its new corporate headquarters in the world's tallest building, Chicago's Sears' Tower, an even longer shadow on the future of retailing was being cast by Sam Walton's much more modest building in Bentonville, Arkansas—home of the first Wal-Mart store and now corporate headquarters of Wal-Mart Stores Inc.

Sam Walton opened the first Wal-Mart Discount City store in 1962, after having run a successful Ben Franklin retail franchise for 20 years. Walton had grown up in the Depression and viewed hard work and thrift as a way of life. In building Wal-Mart, Walton brought these values to the company's culture, along with his never-say-never attitude and his against-the-odds management mentality. Although Target and Kmart also started operations in 1962, it would be the Wal-Mart strategy, fueled by Walton's passion to keep prices lower than those of his competitors, that redrew the map of global retailing. By 1970, the Wal-Mart chain had expanded to 30 stores in Arkansas, Missouri, and Oklahoma. Early expansion plans targeted rural areas with populations between 5,000 and 25,000. "Our key strategy," explained Walton, "was to put good-sized stores into little one-horse towns which everybody else was ignoring."

On the downside, Walton's geographical strategy meant that Wal-Mart had to build its own warehousing, transportation, and delivery systems from scratch. But because real estate and labor were less expensive in Wal-Mart's targeted U.S. locations, these investments actually lowered purchasing and carrying costs, and Walton passed the savings on to his customers in the form of lower prices. Wal-Mart built large warehouses so that it could buy in bulk, and the company-owned trucking fleet, which carried inventory from suppliers to storage and from storage to stores, further cut costs by moving inventory quickly from supplier to customer. Faced with dizzying growth in the 1980s, Wal-Mart then invested nearly $500 million in a state-of-the-art computerized inventory-management system that permitted managers to treat inventory as if it were all stored in one giant virtual warehouse (think of this concept as a forerunner of Amazon.com). By extending the technology to vendors, Wal-Mart not only strengthened its supplier relationships, but also shifted some of its carrying and distribution costs to vendors.

The paths of Sears and Wal-Mart crossed in the mid-1980s. At Sears, management was finding it increasingly difficult to balance the complex and competing needs of its hodgepodge of nonretail businesses like Allstate Insurance. The focus on nonretail businesses caused management to neglect retail operations, burdening the company with many outdated and unprofitable stores. On the retail side, one symptom of this neglect was Sears' slowness in adopting new information technologies. Also, its large investments in wholly owned production operations had made the once mighty retailer a lumbering dinosaur. Increased competition and declining market share would soon cause some industry analysts to sound the death knell for Sears, and over the next two decades the company steadily divested itself of its nonretail operations. The last of these, Sears' gargantuan credit-card operation, was sold to CitiGroup in late 2003 for $32 billion, and the company was, once again, a "pure" retailer.

Meanwhile, as Sears struggled to become leaner and more focused, Wal-Mart was systematically perfecting and expanding its powerful and highly profitable retailing model, primarily through its original Wal-Mart stores and, later, through its Sam's Warehouse Clubs and aggressive international expansion. As you can see in Exhibits 1.1 and 1.2, Sears' struggles vis-à-vis Wal-Mart were clearly visible—ranging from simple measures of firm size to overall profitability and market capitalization. Today, Wal-Mart is the largest retailer in the world, and the Wal-Mart model has become the dominant business model in worldwide retailing. It is interesting to see, however, that Wal-Mart's expansion globally has not been uniformly successful. For instance, it trails Carrefour in France, Tesco in the United Kingdom, and ALDI in Germany.

Sears, meanwhile, has made several unsuccessful efforts to turn itself around, and retail-industry experts have suggested that its best hope may be to plow the proceeds from the sale of its credit-card division back into its outdated retailing operations. Perhaps the most recent irony in the Sears saga is its acquisition by Kmart in 2005— within one year of Kmart's emergence from bankruptcy.

Why are some firms incredibly successful while others are not? And why is it that once they're successful, so few can sustain a high level of success? Although Sears was clearly once a very successful firm, even a half century of unrivaled success couldn't prevent Wal-Mart from taking over its position as the world's number-one retailer. In this text, we'll introduce you to the concepts that you'll need to answer questions about gaining and sustaining success in the world of business competition. ∎

Exhibit 1.1 Two Retailers at a Glance

	Sears	Wal-Mart
Year founded	1891	1962
Stores, 1980	864	600
Stores, 2004	2,026	5,289
Revenues, 1980	$25,194 million	$1,643 million
Revenues, 2004	$36,100 million	$285,222 million
Net profits, 1980	$606 million (2.4% return on sales)	$55 million (3.3% return on sales)
Net profits, 2004	($507) million (−1.4% return on sales)	$10,267 million (3.6% return on sales)
Market capitalization, 1980	$4.8 billion	$1 billion
Market capitalization, 2004	$12.2 billion	$200.2 billion

Sources: "Sears, Roebuck & Co.," Hoover's (accessed August 4, 2005); "Wal-Mart Stores Inc.," Hoover's (accessed August 4, 2005); Wal-Mart Stores Inc., 2004 Annual Report (accessed August 4, 2005).

Exhibit 1.2 Sears and Wal-Mart: A Financial Comparison

Source: Adapted from D. C. Hambrick and J. W. Fredrickson, "Are You Sure You Have a Strategy?" Academy of Management Executive 15:4 (2001), 48–59.

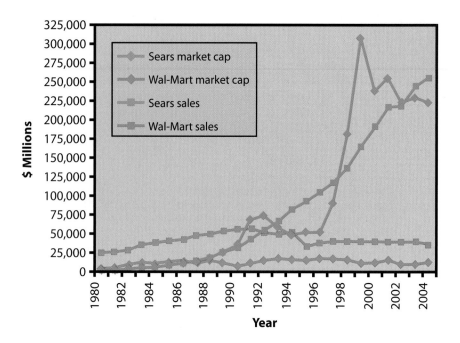

THREE OVERARCHING THEMES

As you've probably gathered from the topic of this book—*strategic management*—a firm's performance is directly related to the quality of its strategy and its competency in implementing it. You also need to understand that concerns about strategy preoccupy the minds of many top executives. Their responsibility is to see that the firm's whole is ultimately greater than the sum of its parts—whether these parts are distinct business units, such as Sears' retail operation and Allstate Insurance, or simply the functional areas that contribute to the performance of one particular business, such as Wal-Mart's massive distribution centers and retail operations. Good strategies are affected by and affect all of the functional areas of the firm, including marketing, finance, accounting, and operations. Thus, we'll also introduce you to the concepts and tools that you'll need to analyze the conditions of a firm and its industry, to formulate appropriate strategies, and to determine how to go about implementing a chosen strategy.

Three themes that run throughout this book are critical to developing competency in the field of strategic management:

1. ***Firms and industries are* dynamic *in nature.*** In recent years, theories and research have emerged on issues regarding dynamic markets and the importance of developing dynamic capabilities to create value. Our first theme, then, is the dynamic nature of both firms and their competitive environments. It's easy, for instance, to look at a financial snapshot of Wal-Mart and understand the competitive position that it commands in its industry. But we need to see Wal-Mart not as a snapshot but as an ongoing movie. Wal-Mart's current position wasn't the result of a single strategic decision but rather the product of many decisions made over time. Wal-Mart's current stock of resources and capabilities weren't always available to the firm; they had to be developed dynamically. For instance, its choice of remote locations required it to develop exceptional capabilities in logistics and supply-chain management. And as tempting as it is to use hindsight to see some of Wal-Mart's competitors as inept, they didn't sit idly by while Wal-Mart ascended to the top of the *Fortune* 500. For pedagogical simplicity, we first introduce some basic concepts in strategic management and then move on to discuss the concepts and tools that managers use to think of strategy in dynamic terms.

2. ***To succeed, the* formulation *of a good strategy and its* implementation *should be inextricably connected.*** Unfortunately, many managers tend to focus on formulating a plan of attack and give too little thought to implementing it until it's too late. Likewise, they may similarly give short shrift to the importance of strategic leadership in effectively bridging strategy formulation and implementation. In fact, research suggests that, on average, managers are better at formulating strategies

than they are at implementing them. This problem has been described as a "knowing–doing gap."[2] Effective managers realize that successfully implementing a good idea is at least as important as generating one. To implement strategies, the organization's leaders have numerous levers at their disposal. Levers such as organization structure, systems and processes, and people and rewards are tools that help strategists test for alignment—that is, the need for all of the firm's activities to complement each other and support the strategy.

3. ***Strategic leadership is essential if a firm is to both formulate and implement strategies that create value.*** Strategic leaders are those responsible for formulating firms' strategies—as a consequence of their hierarchical status in management this is their responsibility. In addition, strategic leadership plays two critical roles in successful strategy implementation, and it's important to highlight them here so that you can incorporate them into your own assessment of a strategy's feasibility as well as ensure that you include these roles in your implementation plans. Specifically, strategic leadership is responsible for (1) making substantive implementation-lever and resource-allocation decisions and (2) developing support for the strategy from key stakeholders.

WHAT IS STRATEGIC MANAGEMENT?

Strategic management is the process by which a firm manages the formulation and implementation of its strategy. But we still need to ask ourselves: What is the *goal* of strategic management? What does "having a *strategy*" mean? Even if we're pretty sure that we have a strategy and a goal for it, how do we know whether we have a good strategy or a bad one?

strategic management Process by which a firm incorporates the tools and frameworks for developing and implementing a strategy

The Strategic Leader's Perspective

In the hit 2002 movie *My Big Fat Greek Wedding*, a proud Greek father (and businessman) challenges anyone who'll listen: "Say any word, and I'll tell you how the root of that word is Greek."[3] He's right about the word *strategy*, which is derived from the Greek *strategos*. Roughly translated, it means "the general's view," and thinking about military ranks and responsibilities is a good way to focus on the difference between the general's view and that of some lower-level officer. The primary responsibility of a lower-level officer might be supply logistics, infantry, or heavy armored vehicles. Thus, lower-level officers may not be too concerned with the overall plan because of their attention to detail in specific areas of responsibility. The general, however, must not only understand how *all* of the constituent parts interrelate, but must use that understanding to draw up a plan that will lead to victory— a strategy. In the business context, the idea of strategy, therefore, suggests a big-picture perspective on the firm and its context. We call this holistic view of the organization the *strategic leader's perspective.*

The success of a military strategy depends not only on the quality of the general's planning and the vision behind it, but also on the execution of the strategy by the forces under the general's command. In business settings, likewise, a strategy is of little use if it is not well executed. In addition, the quality of a strategy is often dependent on the leader's soliciting and utilizing the advice of other senior and midlevel leaders. In other words, a good leader can't afford to devise a strategy in isolation from the lower-level leaders who are responsible for executing it.

The ideas of strategy need not focus exclusively on military analogies just because the root of the word is from this context. You can see ideas analogous to the difference between the general's view and the lower-level officer's view in sports, education, personal life, and business. The important thing about the Greek derivation of the word *strategy* is that the big-picture perspective is fundamentally different from the detail of operational tactics.

In business, strategy requires a big-picture perspective. Up to this point, most of your business courses have probably focused on important but limited aspects of business. Indeed, most business-education classes are devoted to specialized areas of study on specific functional areas, such as finance or marketing. In strategic management, however, we're concerned with an overall, holistic view of the firm and its environment and the ways in which such a view determines the competitive decisions that businesspeople have to make. For this reason, when studying strategic management we generally take the perspective of the strategic leader. Recognize, however, that strategies often emerge from bottom-up processes and from fortuitous circumstances that the leader could not have anticipated. The strategic leader's perspective does not mean to suggest that plans are formulated in some linear fashion by a single leader. Rather, the strategic leader's perspective is the holistic consideration of the business and its environment rather than the myopic focus on a single functional area.

Why Study Strategy?

You may wonder why it is important to study strategy when your career is unlikely to begin at the level of strategic leadership. By the end of the chapter, the answer to this question should be obvious. But, by way of overview, it is important to understand that top executives are not lone wolves when it comes to devising and implementing strategy. They rely on lower-level managers to collect and analyze data regarding competition and commercial opportunities. Likewise, the better employees understand the firm's strategy, the better they'll be able to make choices that are consistent with it. It's critical, therefore, that managers at every level understand the firm's strategy and work toward implementing its strategic initiatives.

What Is Strategy?

strategy Central, integrated, externally focused concept of how the firm will achieve its objectives

The idea of "strategy" means different things to different people (and a lot of these ideas aren't particularly accurate).[4] In fact, experts in the field have formulated various definitions of *strategy*. We've adopted the simple and direct definition offered by Donald C. Hambrick and James W. Fredrickson, who define **strategy** as the central, integrated, externally oriented concept of how a firm will achieve its objectives.[5] A strategy thus encompasses the pattern of actions that have been taken and those that are to be taken by an organization in pursuing its objectives.[6]

Because firms are attempting to sell products or services to potential customers, an implication of strategy in this context is that the firm is attempting to gain an advantage over other potential providers of those products and services. Virtually all firms face some level of competition. A strategy helps a firm accomplish its objectives in the face of competition. Strategy is not, however, necessarily a zero-sum game in which one firm wins and one loses. In many instances, firms cooperate in some aspects of business and compete in others.

Exhibit 1.3 outlines the strategic management process that you will be exploring and applying throughout this textbook. From the exhibit, you can see how vision, goals and objectives, internal and external analysis, and implementation levers can be used to help formulate and implement strategy. Strategy outlines the means by which a firm intends to create unique value for customers and other important stakeholders.[7] This definition of strategy is important because, as you will see later, it forces managers to think holistically and dynamically about what the firm does and why those activities consistently lead customers to prefer the firm's products and services over those of its competitors.

Business Strategy Versus Corporate Strategy

In studying strategy, you'll find it useful to distinguish between strategic issues at the *business level* and those at the *corporate level*. Some firms are focused sharply on their *business* strategy: They compete in only one or very few industries. Other firms compete in many industries. The opening vignette on Sears and Wal-Mart paints a picture of two firms that have similar core businesses (retailing) but have pursued vastly different corporate strategies—Wal-Mart has stuck with retailing, whereas Sears diversified into many unrelated industries, including insurance and stock brokerage services, before later divesting itself of these unrelated businesses. Some firms, such as General Electric (GE) or Vivendi, are called *conglomerates* because they're so diversified that it's difficult to pigeonhole them into any specific industry.

Consider the two largest competitors in the aircraft-engine industry. The largest is GE, with $11 billion in aircraft-engine sales; the second largest is Rolls-Royce PLC, with ap-

Exhibit 1.3 The Strategic Management Process

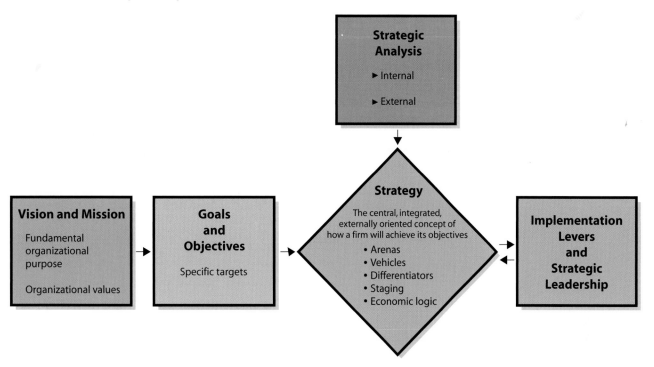

Source: Adapted from D. C. Hambrick and J. W. Fredrickson, "Are You Sure You Have a Strategy?" Academy of Management Executive 15:4 (2001), 48–59.

proximately $6.6 billion in total sales. Rolls-Royce gets most of its revenue—approximately 72 percent—from this industry. (The firm no longer makes luxury cars; the operation was parceled off to BMW and Volkswagen in 1998.) In contrast, GE is involved in hundreds of businesses, including such diverse enterprises as manufacturing light bulbs, medical devices, and commercial jet engines; providing home mortgages; broadcasting (it owns NBC); and operating self-storage facilities. It derives less than 10 percent of its revenue from aircraft engines. Within this industry, of course, both GE and Rolls-Royce face the same competitive pressures, such as determining how to compete against such rivals as Pratt & Whitney (the third-largest firm in the industry). In managing its portfolio of businesses, GE faces strategic issues that are less relevant to Rolls-Royce.

Business Strategy   What sort of issues are these? **Business strategy** refers to the ways a firm goes about achieving its objectives within *a particular business.* In other words, one of GE's business strategies would be how it pursues its objectives within the jet engine business. This strategy may encompass such things as how it competes against Rolls-Royce for contracts from Boeing and Airbus, how it cooperates with other suppliers of technology it uses in designing its engines, and the decision to ramp up scale in an effort to reduce its costs. When Wal-Mart managers decide how to compete with Sears for consumer dollars, they, too, are engaged in business strategy. Business strategy, therefore, focuses on *achieving a firm's objectives within a particular business line.*

> **business strategy** Strategy for competing against rivals within a particular industry

Increasingly, business strategy also takes into account the changing competitive landscape in which a firm is located. Two critical questions that business strategy must address are (1) how the firm will achieve its objectives *today,* when other companies may be competing to satisfy the same customers' needs, and (2) how the firm plans to compete *in the future.* In later chapters, we'll focus specifically on issues related to business strategy.

Corporate Strategy   **Corporate strategy** addresses issues related to three fundamental questions:

> **corporate strategy** Strategy for guiding a firm's entry and exit from different businesses, for determining how a parent company adds value to and manages its portfolio of businesses, and for creating value through diversification

1. ***In what businesses will we compete?*** In the 1970s and 1980s, for instance, Sears chose to branch out of retailing into credit cards, stock brokerage, and real estate,

whereas Wal-Mart remained focused on the retail business. GE managers address corporate-strategy questions when deciding whether the firm should enter a new business. AT&T's past attempts to reorganize itself as distinct divisions with separate ownership—which is the same thing as deciding that the corporate parent should *not* compete simultaneously in all of these businesses—is a matter of corporate strategy.

2. ***How can we, as a corporate parent, add value to our various lines of business?*** At GE, for instance, senior management might be able to orchestrate synergies and learning across its commercial- and consumer-finance groups. Sears once thought that it could provide one-stop shopping at retail outlets for everything from tools to life insurance. Thus, corporate strategy also deals with *finding ways to create value by having two or more owned businesses cooperate and share resources*.

3. ***How will diversification or our entry into a new industry help us to compete in our other industries?*** Sears managers thought that one-stop shopping would benefit all of its ventures by increasing the number of customers inside its retail stores. More recently, Wal-Mart has found that diversification into the grocery business segment of retailing has increased retail foot traffic and boosted sales of nongrocery retail products.

STRATEGY FORMULATION AND IMPLEMENTATION

strategy formulation Process of developing a strategy

strategy implementation Process of executing a strategy

Earlier we defined *strategy* as the central, integrated, externally oriented concept of how a firm will achieve its objectives. **Strategy formulation** is the process of *deciding what to do*; **strategy implementation** is the process of performing all the activities necessary *to do what has been planned*.[8] Because neither can succeed without the other, the two processes are iterative and interdependent from the standpoint that implementation should provide information that is used to periodically modify business and corporate strategy. Our opening vignette demonstrates the nature of this interdependence. Wal-Mart formulated an initial strategy that called for it to compete as a discount retailer in rural markets. As the company grew, it found that in order to implement this strategy, it had to invest heavily in organizational structure, systems, and processes. Ironically, these early steps in strategy implementation enabled Wal-Mart to reformulate and execute the strategy that has propelled the company to its dominant position as the low-cost leader of its industry.

The Wal-Mart example also shows how good strategies represent solutions to complex problems. They help to solve problems *external* to the firm by enabling the production of goods or services that both beat the competition and have a ready market. They solve problems *internal* to the firm by providing all employees, including top executives, with clear guidelines as to what the firm should and should not be doing.

Strategy Formulation

So now we know that strategy formulation means deciding what to do. Some strategies result from rational and methodical planning processes based on analyses of both internal resources and capabilities and the external environment. Others emerge over time and are adopted only after an unplanned pattern of decisions or actions suggests that an unfolding idea may unexpectedly lead to an effective strategy. Sometimes the recognition of a strategically good idea is accidental, but corporate innovation and renewal are increasingly the products of controlled experiments and the opportunistic exploitation of surprise.[9]

During its early years, for instance, the chipmaker Intel was consciously focused on the design and manufacture of dynamic, random-access memory chips (DRAMs), and through the 1970s and early 1980s virtually all of the firm's revenue came from DRAMs. Intel's participation in the DRAM market was intentional and planned virtually from the moment of its founding. By 1984, however, 95 percent of the company's revenue came from the microprocessor segment of the industry. Ironically, Intel's participation in this segment of the industry was not planned by senior management. Rather, it evolved from an experimental venture to make processors for Busicom, a Japanese maker of calculators.[10] Unbeknownst and unforeseen by top management was the fact that market demand was shifting dramatically from DRAMs to microprocessors. Only through the Busicom experiment—and

You might be more familiar with Rolls-Royce's automobiles than its jet engines. The fact is, however, that Rolls-Royce PLC no longer even makes luxury automobiles. The company's core business is now jet engines. Jet engines generate 72 percent of its revenues.

Intel's willingness to follow the signals this experiment sent them in terms of market-demand shifts—was the firm able to dramatically change its business strategy. To this day, Intel officials give credit for the firm's dominance in the microprocessor market to a strategy that emerged originally from a lower-level management initiative—one that, at the time, wasn't greeted with unanimous enthusiasm by senior management.[11]

Since their lucky foray into the microprocessor market, Intel managers have obviously focused on effective strategies for maintaining the firm's advantages in the segment while at the same time promoting experiments and exploiting surprises like Busicom to keep abreast of significant underlying market-demand shifts.

The Strategy Diamond and the Five Elements of Strategy Good strategy formulation means refining the elements of the strategy.[12] Remember, first of all, not to confuse *part* of a strategy—for example, being a low-cost provider or first mover in an industry—for strategy itself. Being a low-cost provider or first mover may be part of a strategy, but it's not a complete strategy.

As we noted earlier, a strategy is an integrated and externally oriented concept of how a firm will achieve its objectives—how it will compete against its rivals. Thus, a strategy consists of an *integrated set of choices*. These choices can be categorized as five related elements of strategy based on decisions that managers make regarding *arenas, vehicles, differentiators, staging,* and *economic logic*. We refer to this constellation of elements, which are central to the strategic management process outlined in Exhibit 1.3, as the *strategy diamond*. Most strategic plans focus on one or two such elements, often leaving large gaps in the overall strategy. Only when you have answers to your questions about *each of these five elements* can you determine whether your strategy is an integrated whole; you'll also have a better idea of the areas in which your strategy needs to be revised or overhauled. As Exhibit 1.4 shows, a good strategy diamond considers five key elements in order to arrive at specific answers to five questions:

1. *Arenas:* Where will we be active?
2. *Vehicles:* How will we get there?
3. *Differentiators:* How will we win in the marketplace?
4. *Staging:* What will be our speed and sequence of moves?
5. *Economic logic:* How will we obtain our returns?

Exhibit 1.4   The Business Strategy Diamond

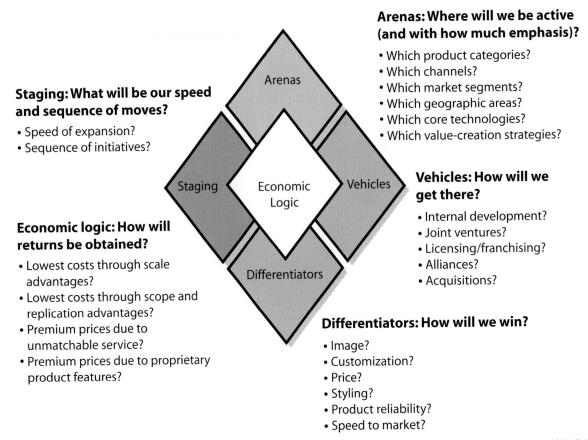

Arenas: Where will we be active (and with how much emphasis)?

- Which product categories?
- Which channels?
- Which market segments?
- Which geographic areas?
- Which core technologies?
- Which value-creation strategies?

Staging: What will be our speed and sequence of moves?

- Speed of expansion?
- Sequence of initiatives?

Vehicles: How will we get there?

- Internal development?
- Joint ventures?
- Licensing/franchising?
- Alliances?
- Acquisitions?

Economic logic: How will returns be obtained?

- Lowest costs through scale advantages?
- Lowest costs through scope and replication advantages?
- Premium prices due to unmatchable service?
- Premium prices due to proprietary product features?

Differentiators: How will we win?

- Image?
- Customization?
- Price?
- Styling?
- Product reliability?
- Speed to market?

Source: Adapted from D. C. Hambrick and J. W. Fredrickson, "Are You Sure You Have a Strategy?" Academy of Management Executive 15:4 (2001), 48–59.

Let's take a closer look at each of these elements.

arena Area (product, service, distribution channel, geographic markets, technology, etc.) in which a firm participates

Arenas   By **arenas**, we mean areas in which a firm will be active. Decisions about a firm's arenas may encompass its products, services, distribution channels, market segments, geographic areas, technologies, and even stages of the value-creation process. Unlike vision statements, which tend to be fairly general, the identification of arenas must be very specific: It will clearly tell managers what the firm should and should not do. In addition, because firms can contract with outside parties for everything from employees to manufacturing services, the choice of arenas can be fairly narrowly defined for some firms.

For example, as the largest U.S. bicycle distributor, Pacific Cycle owns the Schwinn, Mongoose, and GT brands and sells its bikes through big-box retail outlets and independent dealers, as well as through independent agents in foreign markets. In addition to these arena choices, Pacific Cycle has entirely outsourced the production of its products to Asian manufacturers. In outsourcing shoes and apparel lines, Nike follows a similar strategy in terms of arenas. One key difference, however, is that Nike, through its Nike Town retail outlets, has also chosen a direct retail presence in addition to its use of traditional retail distribution channels.

vehicle Means for entering new arenas (e.g., through acquisitions, alliances, internal development, etc.)

Vehicles   **Vehicles** are the means for participating in targeted arenas. For instance, a firm that wants to go international can achieve that objective in different ways. In a recent drive to enter certain international markets (such as Argentina), Wal-Mart has opened new stores and grown organically—meaning that it developed all the stores internally as opposed to by acquisition. Elsewhere (namely, in England and Germany), Wal-Mart has purchased existing retailers and is in the process of transferring its unique way of doing business to the acquired companies. Likewise, a firm that requires a new technology could

Pacific Cycle, based in Madison, Wisconsin, has carefully chosen the arenas in which it does business. The company designs and markets 10 different brands of bicycles, which it sells to big-box retailers and independent bike dealers around the world. Pacific Cycle does not actually manufacture any of the bikes itself, however. It outsources all of this work to companies in China and Taiwan instead.

develop it through investments in R&D. Or, it could opt to form an alliance with a competitor or supplier who already possesses the technology, thereby accelerating the integration of the missing piece into its set of resources and capabilities. Finally, it could simply buy another firm that owns the technology. In this case, then, the possible vehicles for entering a new arena include acquisitions, alliances, and organic investment and growth.

Differentiators **Differentiators** are features and attributes of a company's product or service that help it beat its competitors in the marketplace. Firms can be successful in the marketplace along a number of common dimensions, including *image, customization, technical superiority, price,* and *quality and reliability.* Toyota and Honda have done very well by providing effective combinations of differentiators. They sell both inexpensive cars and cars with high-end, high-quality features, and many consumers find the value that they provide hard to match. However, even though the best strategies often combine differentiators, history has shown that firms often perform poorly when they try to be all things to all consumers. It's difficult to imagine, for instance, a single product that boasts both state-of-the-art technology and the lowest price on the market. Part of the problem is perceptual—consumers often associate low quality with low price. Part of it is practical—leading-edge technologies cost money to develop and command higher prices because of their uniqueness or quality.

There are two critical factors in selecting differentiators:

■ ***These decisions must be made early.*** Key differentiators rarely materialize without significant up-front decisions, and without valuable differentiators, firms tend to lose marketplace battles.

■ ***Identifying and executing successful differentiators means making tough choices— tradeoffs.*** Managers who can't make tough decisions about tradeoffs often end up trying to satisfy too broad a spectrum of customer needs; as a result, they make too many strategic compromises and execute poorly on most dimensions.

Audi provides an example of a company that has aligned these two factors successfully. In the early 1990s, Audi management realized that its cars were perceived as low-quality, high-priced German automobiles—obviously a poor position from which to compete. The firm decided that it had to move one way or another—up market or down market. It had to do one of two things: (1) lower its costs so that its pricing was consistent with customers'

differentiator Feature or attribute of a company's product or service (e.g., image, customization, technical superiority, price, quality and reliability) that helps it beat its competitors in the marketplace

perceptions of product quality or (2) improve quality sufficiently to justify premium pricing. Given limited resources, the firm could not go in both directions—that is, produce cars in both the low-price and high-quality strata. Audi made a decision to invest heavily in quality and image; it invested significantly in quality programs and in refining its marketing efforts. Ten years later, the quality of Audi cars has increased significantly, and customer perception has moved them much closer to the level of BMW and Mercedes. Audi has reaped the benefits of premium pricing and improved profitability, but the decisions behind the strategic up-market move entailed significant tradeoffs.[13]

Differentiators are what drive potential customers to choose one firm's offerings over those of competitors. The earlier and more consistent the firm is at defining and driving these differentiators, the greater the likelihood that customers will recognize them.

staging Timing and pace of strategic moves

Staging Staging refers to the timing and pace of strategic moves. Staging choices typically reflect available resources, including cash, human capital, and knowledge. At what point, for example, should Wal-Mart have added international markets to its strategy? Perhaps if the company had pursued global opportunities earlier, it would have been able to develop a better sense of foreign-market conditions and even spread the costs of entry over a longer period of time. However, by delaying its international moves, the company was able to focus on dominating the U.S. market, which is, after all, the largest retail market in the world. Despite mixed results overseas, Wal-Mart is the undisputed leader in global retailing and has recently increased its emphasis on international markets as the basis for future growth.[14]

Staging decisions should be driven by several factors: resources, urgency, credibility, and the need for early wins. Because few firms have the resources to do everything they'd like to do immediately, they usually have to match opportunities with available resources. In addition, not all opportunities to enter new arenas are permanent; some have only brief windows. In such cases, early wins and the credibility of certain key stakeholders may be necessary to implement a strategy.

Consider the case of the 2002 Winter Olympic Games. In June 1995, the International Olympic Committee (IOC) awarded the 2002 Winter Olympic Games to Salt Lake City, Utah. Complications arose, however, when reports surfaced in late 1998 that some individuals associated with the Salt Lake Olympic Committee (SLOC), the group responsible for securing the winning bid and managing the event, had bribed IOC members in order to bring the Games to their community. The Justice Department alleged that prior to the selection of Salt Lake City, two top members of SLOC had paid $1 million in cash and gifts to members of the IOC to secure the designation. Some of these payments allegedly went toward the funding of U.S. college educations for IOC delegates' children. Other funds paid for their first-class travel or lavish gifts. The scandal forced the ouster or resignation of several IOC officials and led to reforms that included a new international ethics code. It also resulted in a complete restructuring of the SLOC management team.

In 1999, Mitt Romney, a partner with Bain Capital (and now governor of Massachusetts), was hired to save the Winter Olympics. He reports that one of the first things his management team discovered upon agreeing to take over was that there was a $379-million deficit on an original budget of $1.5 billion (by comparison, the previous Winter Olympics in Nagano, Japan, spent $2.8 billion to stage the Games). One source of budget woes was that most major sponsors had reneged on their pledges of support. For instance, the CEO of one perennially strong sponsor of the Olympics reportedly quipped that "any CEO who signs up to sponsor these Winter Games should be fired." Romney realized that without major advertisers, the project was doomed to failure, and unfortunately, the previous management of SLOC had forfeited all credibility with potential advertisers. To reestablish credibility, Romney's team set out to rack up some key early wins. To achieve this goal, they determined to do three things: cut operating expenses, install a new management team, and land their first new advertising commitment. Once those three objectives had been accomplished, the new SLOC gained significant credibility with large advertisers and eventually succeeded in implementing its turnaround strategy. In fact, when the games were over and all the bills were paid, SLOC finished with a $100-million surplus. And the IOC, which only a few years earlier was threatening to move the games away from Salt Lake City, praised the leadership of SLOC and their efforts by noting, "The Salt Lake City Games were undoubtedly great Games . . . [that] left a wonderful legacy for the city and were financially a huge success."[15]

Economic Logic **Economic logic** refers to how the firm will earn a profit—that is, how the firm will generate positive returns over and above its cost of capital. Economic logic is the "fulcrum" for profit creation. Earning normal profits, of course, requires a firm to meet all of its fixed, variable, and financing costs, and achieving desired returns over the firm's cost of capital is a tall order for any organization. In analyzing a firm's economic logic, think of both costs and revenues. Sometimes economic logic resides primarily on the *cost* side of the equation. Southwest Airlines, for example, can fly passengers for significantly lower costs per passenger mile than any major competitor. At other times, economic logic may rest on the firm's ability to increase the customer's willingness to pay premium prices for products (in other words, prices that significantly exceed the costs of providing enhanced products).

economic logic Means by which a firm will earn a profit by implementing a strategy

When the five elements of strategy are aligned and mutually reinforcing, the firm is generally in a position to perform well. The discussion in the box entitled "How Would You Do That? 1.1" demonstrates how you would apply the strategy diamond to the highly successful airline JetBlue. High performance levels, however, ultimately mean that a strategy is also being executed well, and we now turn to strategy implementation.

Strategy Implementation Levers

Whatever the origin of a strategic idea, whether it was carefully planned from the outset or evolved over time by means of luck or experimentation, successful strategies are dependent on effective implementation. As discussed earlier in the chapter, *strategy implementation* is the process of executing the strategy—of taking the actions that put the strategy into effect and ensure that organizational decisions are consistent with it.[16] The process of implementation also encompasses the refinement, or change, of a strategy as more information is made available through early implementation efforts. The goal of implementation is twofold:

- To make sure that strategy formulation is comprehensive and well informed

- To translate good ideas into actions that can be executed (and sometimes to use execution to generate or identify good ideas)

In sports, a coach's play-calling is only as good as the excellence with which the players execute it. Likewise in business: The value of a firm's strategy is determined by its ability to carry it out. "Any strategy," says Michael Porter, one of the preeminent writers on the subject, ". . . is only as good as its execution."[17] Adds Peter Drucker, one of our most prolific writers on management: "The important decisions, the decisions that really matter, are strategic. . . . [But] more important and more difficult is to make effective the course of action decided upon."[18]

Strategy implementation is studied in college courses, and it's the subject of hundreds of books in business school libraries. We don't intend to supplant the results of all of this study, but we do want you to focus on the implications of a very basic fact: *The processes of strategy formulation and strategy implementation are inextricably linked.* The five elements of strategy, for instance, are related to both formulation and implementation. Good implementation means that an organization coordinates resources and capabilities and uses structure, systems, processes, and strategic leadership to translate an intended strategy to bottom-line results. Throughout the text we help you to see the relationship between formulation and implementation. Chapter 2 introduces you to the role of strategic leadership, and Chapter 11 drills down much deeper into our implementation framework. At this point, and in order to help you consider the complexity of implementing a strategy, we introduce you to just the basic ideas of strategic leadership and implementation.

The Five Elements of Strategy at JetBlue

To experience how you might apply the strategy diamond, let's consider a recent entrepreneurial success story. The major U.S. airlines lost over $7 billion between 1998 and 2002. David Neeleman, however, confounded the experts when he decided that despite the industry's horrendous performance, the time was right to step down from his executive position at Southwest Airlines to launch a new airline. JetBlue took off on February 11, 2000, with an inaugural flight between New York City's John F. Kennedy International Airport and Fort Lauderdale, Florida. Today, the airline serves 20 cities around the country and intends to expand further. As you can see from the two graphs in Exhibit 1.5, JetBlue has obviously done something right. It is second only to Southwest Airlines in profitability and its market capitalization means that investors have high expectations for JetBlue's financial prospects.

To begin applying the strategy diamond to JetBlue, let's quickly review JetBlue's vision, which is to "bring humanity back to air travel" through product innovation and excellent service. It intends to be a low-fare, low-cost passenger airline that provides high-quality customer service. Using the strategy diamond, and public documents posted at www.jetblue.com, we can determine what strategy JetBlue has pursued in order to meet its stated objective.

- *In what* arenas *does JetBlue compete?* Management states that the

Exhibit 1.5 JetBlue and Its Industry

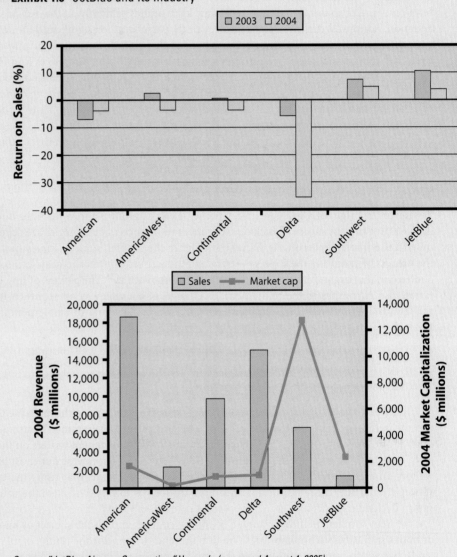

Source: "JetBlue Airways Corporation," Hoover's (accessed August 4, 2005).

company competes as a low-fare commercial air carrier, and caters to underserved but overpriced U.S. cities. Its main base of operations is John F. Kennedy airport in New York City, which serves the largest travel market in the country.

⟫

- *What* vehicles *does JetBlue use to enter the arenas in which it competes?* JetBlue started from scratch and has achieved all of its growth in flights per day through internal growth. The firm could have grown by purchasing regional airlines, but chose not to.

- *What are its* differentiators? Price is a big part of JetBlue's strategy for winning new customers, but it also wants to develop the image that it is a low-fare airline with high-quality service. Although it offers only one class of service, the level of service is rather high for a low-fare airline. For instance, offering leather seating and individual in-seat live satellite TV.

- *How does JetBlue's staging—the speed of its expansion and the sequence of its growth initiatives—reflect its timetable for achieving its objectives?* JetBlue has grown from 1 route between 2 cities to routes serving 20 cities in just 3 years. At first, it limited itself to the East Coast (between its JFK home base and destinations in Florida and upstate New York), but it soon proceeded westward, establishing locations in Long Beach, California (to serve the Los Angeles area), Denver, Seattle, and most recently, San Diego. JetBlue has targeted more cities for future expansion.

- *What's the* economic logic *of JetBlue's strategy?* JetBlue's income statements show that its costs are significantly lower than

When former Southwest Airlines employee and JetBlue founder David Neeleman (shown vacuuming a plane) announced that he was launching a new airline company, people were aghast. Although the airline industry as a whole is undergoing dismal financial profits, JetBlue has found a way to prosper by effectively aligning the five elements of its strategy that is both internally consistent, and externally generates great market demand. The strategy includes low-fare but upscale service, complete with leather seats and satellite TV.

industry averages. These cost advantages appear to come from an *ability to perform key tasks in ways that are fundamentally less expensive* than those of competitors. By flying only one make of aircraft that is relatively fuel efficient, JetBlue also keeps maintenance and training costs down. By securing a home base at JFK at a time when the New York Port Authority was anxious to attract more air traffic, JetBlue secured lower airport fees. Locating in secondary locations (Long Beach instead of Los Angeles International Airport, Fort Lauderdale instead of Miami) also means lower-than-average airport fees. On the revenue side, although JetBlue offers very low fares, it wins customers from com-petitors and uses its low cost incentive as a means to convert non-fliers to JetBlue customers. It has also attracted customers by concentrating on underserved, high-priced routes. As a result, it now boasts the highest load factor of any major airline.

Walking through the JetBlue's strategy diamond helps illustrate its strategy. The plan looks sound, but what is required to implement such a plan? The next sections of this chapter provide an overview of this critical issue.

Sources: JetBlue Airways Corp., *2002 Annual Report on Form 10-K,* including on the "Investor Relations" link on JetBlue's Web page; JetBlue Airways Corp., *2003 Annual Report on Form 10-K,* JetBlue Airways Corp., *2004 Annual Report on Form 10-K.*

To implement strategies, organization leaders have numerous levers at their disposal. The framework summarizing these levers is shown in Exhibit 1.6. We categorize these levers into three broad categories: (1) *organization structure*, (2) *systems and processes*, and (3) *people and rewards*. The strategist uses these tools to test for alignment, which is the need for all of the firm's activities to complement each other and support the strategy.

In addition, strategic leadership engages in a few activities related to implementing the strategy that are unique to their positional authority. As the exhibit suggests, implementation includes the activities carried out by the organization that are aimed at executing a particular strategy. Often, the strategy that is realized through these implementation efforts is somewhat different from the original plan. These deviations from the original plan are a result of explicit alterations of the strategy that result from feedback during early implementation efforts as well as from the exploitation of serendipitous opportunities that were not anticipated when the strategy was formulated.

Organization Structure   *Structure* is the manner in which responsibilities, tasks, and people are organized. It includes the organization's authority, hierarchy, units, divisions, and coordinating mechanisms. At this point, we just need to remind ourselves of a few key questions that managers must consider when implementing a strategy:

■ Is the current structure appropriate for the intended strategy?

■ Are reporting relationships and the delegation of authority set up to execute the strategic plan?

■ Is the organization too centralized (or decentralized) for the strategy?

Systems and Processes   *Systems* are all the organizational processes and procedures used in daily operations. Obviously, these include control and incentive systems, resource-allocation procedures, information systems, budgeting, distribution, and so forth.

People and Rewards   The *people and rewards* lever of the model underscores the importance of using all of the organization's members to implement a strategy. Regardless of your strategy, at the end of the day, it's your people who will have implemented it. Competitive advantage is generally tied to your human resources.[19] Successful implementation depends on having the right people and then developing and training them in ways that

Exhibit 1.6 Implementation Framework

Source: Adapted from D. Hambrick and A. Cannella, "Strategy Implementation as Substance and Selling," Academy of Management Executive *3:4 (1989), 278–285.*

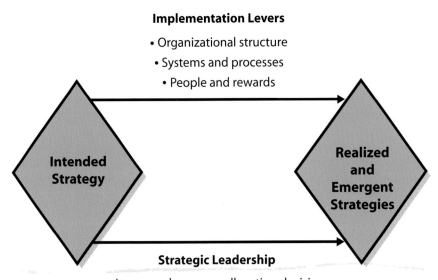

Implementation Levers

• Organizational structure
• Systems and processes
• People and rewards

Intended Strategy

Realized and Emergent Strategies

Strategic Leadership

• Lever- and resource-allocation decisions
• Develop support among stakeholders

support the firm's strategy. In addition, rewards—how you pay your people—can accelerate the implementation of your strategy or undermine it. We have all seen instances in which unintended consequences happen because a manager rewards "A" while hoping for "B."[20]

Strategic Leadership

Strategic leadership plays two critical roles in successful strategy implementation, and it is important to highlight them here so that you can incorporate them into your own assessment of a strategy's feasibility as well as ensure that you include these roles in your implementation plans. Specifically, as will be discussed in greater detail in Chapter 11, strategic leadership is responsible for (1) making substantive implementation lever and resource-allocation decisions and (2) developing support for the strategy from key stakeholders. Although a successful strategy is not generally formulated by a single person or a small group of leaders, successful strategy implementation requires active leadership to ensure that what emerges and what is realized are desirable.

WHAT IS COMPETITIVE ADVANTAGE?

Earlier we defined *strategy* as the central, integrated, externally oriented concept of how a firm will achieve its objectives. We noted that within a firm's business operations, its objectives will generally encompass some notion of being successful at selling products or services to customers. Because virtually all firms face competition when trying to serve these customers, to achieve its objectives, a firm will have to be perceived by at least some customers as superior to its competition. Thus, the concept of strategy suggests a relationship between strategy on the one hand and performance and competitive advantage on the other. Specifically, we explained that a strategy encompasses the pattern of actions taken by a firm to achieve its objectives. These premises lead us to a logical conclusion: The activities of strategic management are based on the assumption that *firms attempt to achieve a position of competitive advantage over their rivals when serving target customers.*[21] Or, to put it another way: Firms prefer to be winners in their respective industries rather than subpar or even average performers. This leads us to define **competitive advantage** as a firm's ability to create *value* in a way that its rivals cannot.

Performance itself, however, is not competitive advantage; it's merely a result of it. A firm may achieve relatively high short-term performance levels without gaining any substantial advantage over its rivals. Maybe the company just had an unusually good year or took drastic measures to cut costs (perhaps to unsustainably low levels). By the same token, a firm may enjoy significant competitive advantage in some lines of business but still perform more poorly than its competitors because of other underperforming business units.

The question that we now want to answer is: *Why are some firms able to achieve greater advantages over rivals than other firms?* All firms are not alike. Dell, for example, seems to have some capabilities that other computer manufactures, such as Hewlett-Packard and IBM, haven't been able to duplicate. Toyota enjoys a similar advantage in the automotive industry. In fact, many industries (including pharmaceuticals, soft drinks, and retailing) are *not* characterized by perfect competition, and many companies earn more than "normal" income for many years. In addition, some firms appear to outperform competitors consistently, which is likely an indication that they have some form of competitive advantage over their rivals. As we will see, however, it's become increasingly difficult for any one firm to sustain a competitive advantage over a long period of time.[22]

competitive advantage A firm's ability to create *value* in a way that its rivals cannot

Determinants of Competitive Advantage

The field of strategic management focuses on explanations of competitive advantage—on the reasons why companies experience above- and below-normal rates of returns and on the ways that firms can exploit the limits of perfect competition. Generally speaking, there are two primary perspectives on this issue (perspectives that, as we shall see, reflect contrasting but complementary points of view):

■ The *internal perspective* focuses on firms and potential internal sources of uniqueness.

■ The *external perspective* focuses on the structure of industries and the ways in which firms can position themselves within them for competitive advantage.

Bridging these two fundamental perspectives is a third view called *dynamic strategy*, which seeks to explain why competitive advantage does not typically last over long periods of time. Let's examine each of these perspectives, or theories, more closely.

The Internal Perspective   The internal perspective on competitive advantage is often called the *resource-based view of the firm*. It holds that firms are heterogeneous bundles of resources and capabilities. Proponents of this theory argue that firms are not "clones" of each other in terms of the resources that they own or to which they have access and that they have varying degrees of capability in performing different economic tasks. As a result, firms with superior resources and capabilities enjoy competitive advantage over other firms.[23] This advantage makes it relatively easier for these firms to achieve consistently higher levels of performance than competitors. Competitive advantage, therefore, arises when a company's resources allow its products, services, or businesses to compete successfully against rival firms in the same industries. The resource-based view also holds that a firm's bundle of resources may either hinder or help its entry into new businesses— an idea that we'll explore further in later chapters.[24]

The External Perspective   The external perspective on competitive advantage contends that variations in a firm's competitive advantage and performance are primarily a function of industry attractiveness. The external perspective suggests that competitive advantage comes from a firm's positioning within the competitive business environment.

The seminal work supporting this approach is Michael Porter's work on competitive strategy.[25] Porter's theory—sometimes called *industrial organization economics* (I/O economics)—suggests that firms should do one of two things: (1) position themselves to compete in attractive industries or (2) adopt strategies that will make their current industries more attractive. In some countries, for instance, carmakers lobby for import tariffs in order to make their domestic markets more attractive. When the strategy works, the access of foreign manufacturers to the market is limited, and the cost of participating in it is higher. (In later chapters, we'll explore in more detail the theoretical models and tools that help managers analyze, understand, and shape a firm's competitive environments.)

Fundamental Versus Dynamic Perspectives

Researchers have also realized that, in addition to internal and external determinants of competitive advantage, some industries or market segments are less stable than others. Not surprisingly, competitive advantage is more likely to endure in stable markets than in unstable ones. Conversely, the competitive advantage held by one firm over another tends to change very slowly in stable markets but more quickly in unstable ones.

The Fundamental Perspective   The global chocolate industry, for example, is relatively stable because a few firms—notably, M&M/Mars, Nestlé, and Hershey— dominate it in terms of both size and brands. In addition, demand for chocolate is relatively stable, growing with population growth. To stimulate growth, large companies try to formulate new candy bars. However, this type of growth is rather incremental and predictable. Smaller companies carve out niches in which to offer differentiated products, but this generally does not result in any significant upheaval of market dynamics. In such stable contexts, fundamental theories of competitive advantage usually explain most economic facts. The external (or positional) view of strategy tends to dominate questions of strategy formulation and implementation. Why? Because a firm's current market position, as gauged by market share or some other criterion, may be a good indicator of competitive advantage and provides a relatively accurate predictor of future performance. This view also tends to assume that industries are clearly defined, that competition is predictable, and that the future doesn't hold many surprises.

The Dynamic Perspective But what about industries—such as computer chips or laser printers or medical products—in which it seems that competitive advantage can shift in a matter of months or even days simply because of a new product release or some other technological breakthrough?[26] A so-called *dynamic perspective* on competitive advantage has become increasingly important in explaining the economic facts in such industries in which markets converge, technologies rapidly change competitive conditions, capital markets become increasingly impatient, firms compete in multiple markets and multiple industries against common rivals, and the costs of establishing a competitive position soar (and so increase dramatically the cost of failure). The dynamic perspective suggests that a firm's current market position is *not* an accurate predictor of future performance or sustainable competitive advantage. Why not? Because current market position itself is not a competitive advantage but rather an outcome of past competitive activities. From the dynamic perspective, we look to the past for clues about how the firm arrived at its current position and to the future in an effort to predict the look of the new competitive landscape.

The External Dimension of the Dynamic Perspective Of course, the dynamic strategy perspective has both external and internal dimensions as well. On the external side, it's useful in analyzing "high-velocity" markets—markets that are changing rapidly and unpredictably.[27] Often, such changes result from technology, but as we noted earlier, there are usually several contributing factors. The dynamic perspective is also a good tool for examining industries characterized by *multimarket competition*—those in which firms tend to encounter the same rivals in multiple markets.[28] Goodyear, Michelin, and Bridgestone, for instance, compete head-to-head in tire markets around the world. Another form of multimarket competition is illustrated by Nestlé and Mars; these companies battle it out in global industries ranging from pet foods to snack foods and will often use resources from one industry to bolster competitive position in another—say, by offering retailer discounts on pet food in exchange for shelf space for snack foods. For instance, Proctor & Gamble's entry into Vietnam appears to be less driven by the profit motive (P&G tends to lose money on Vietnamese soap sales) than by a determination to keep rival Unilever in check. If P&G had not entered the Vietnamese market, Unilever could have reaped monopoly-like profits and proceeded to use the windfall to pay for competitive efforts against P&G in other markets. By competing with Unilever in a market in which it has no competitive advantage (and may not even seek one), P&G's strategy reduces Unilever's ability to wage war on other fronts.

The Internal Dimension of the Dynamic Perspective The dynamic perspective can also help us to focus on a firm's resources and capabilities, particularly those that lead to a *continuous flow* of advantages in resources or market position and those that strengthen the firm's ability to embrace (and even foster) continuous and sometimes disruptive *change*. Risk taking, experimentation, improvisation, and continuous learning are—at least from the dynamic perspective—key features of successful firms. Later in the text, we will explore several relevant analytical tools for shaping strategy formulation and implementation, including capabilities assessment, strategic options, technology roadmaps, and game-theory modeling. You'll also learn how to combine your analysis of an industry's cumulative technological development with your assessment of whether a firm can exploit an innovative product or disruptive technology through its entire life cycle or whether it must instead leap from product to product at strategically defined crossover points.

Finally—and by way of bringing this chapter full-circle to our opening vignette on Sears and Wal-Mart—note that the dynamic perspective also provides valuable insight into the formulation and implementation of strategies at firms competing in ostensibly stable markets and industries. In its early years, for example, few observers would have predicted that Sears would eventually be vulnerable against a tiny rural upstart like Wal-Mart. Given its own constraints, however, Wal-Mart had to develop highly efficient inventory-management systems if it wanted to earn the same profits as Sears. In other words, Wal-Mart's strategy for competitive advantage differed from that of Sears: Instead of trying to fight Sears according to Sears' own rules of retail-industry competition, Wal-Mart executed a dynamic strategy that called for a radical change in the way that retail business was done (namely, competing in rural locations through the use of highly sophisticated and proprietary logistics capabilities). To keep costs low in serving its far-flung network of rural retail stores, Wal-Mart needed to develop a more efficient way to manage inventory and distribution. By the time Wal-Mart appeared on Sears' radar, it was too late for the once-dominant retailer to protect its market share. We would find the same theme in stories about Amazon.com versus Barnes & Noble and U.S. mini-mills versus major steel producers.[29]

SUMMARY

1. Understand what *strategy* is and identify the difference between business-level and corporate-level strategy. *Strategic management* is the process by which a firm manages the formulation and implementation of its strategy. A *strategy* is the central, integrated, externally oriented concept of how a firm will achieve its objectives. Strategies typically take one of two forms: business strategy or corporate strategy. The objective of a business strategy is to spell out how the firm plans to compete. This plan integrates choices regarding arenas (where the firm will be active), vehicles (how it will get there), differentiators (how it will win), staging (the speed and sequence of its moves), and economic logic (how it obtains its returns). The objective of corporate strategy is to spell out which businesses a firm will compete in, how ownership by the corporate parent adds value to the business, and how this particular diversification approach helps each business compete in its respective markets.

2. Understand why we study *strategic management*. It should be clear to you by now that strategic management is concerned with firm performance. Strategic management holds clues as to why firms survive when performance suffers. Strategy helps you to understand which activities are important and why and how a plan, absent good execution, is perhaps only as valuable as the paper it's printed on.

3. Understand the relationship between *strategy formulation* and *implementation*. *Strategy formulation* is the determination of what the firm is going to do; strategy implementation is how the firm goes about doing it.

These two facets of strategy are linked and interdependent. This interdependence is made strikingly clear by the strategy formulation model you are introduced to in this chapter, examples throughout the text, and the specific treatment of implementation levers in Chapter 11.

4. Describe the determinants of competitive advantage. Competitive advantage is realized when one firm creates value in ways that its competitors cannot, such that the firm clearly performs better than its competitors. Advantage is not simply higher relative performance; rather superior performance signals the ability of a firm to do things in ways its direct competitors cannot. The two primary views of competitive advantage—internal and external—are complementary and together are used to help formulate effective strategies. The internal view portrays competitive advantage to be a function of unique, firm-specific resources and capabilities. The external view holds that a firm's performance is largely a function of its position in a particular industry or industry segment given the overall structure of the industry. Profitable industries are considered attractive, and therefore, high firm performance is attributed to a firm's position in the industry relative to the characteristics of the industry or industry segment.

5. Recognize the difference between the *fundamental view* and the *dynamic view of competitive advantage*. Regardless of whether the firm takes an internal or external perspective toward competitive advantage, research shows that few firms persist in their dominance over competitors over prolonged periods of time. For most firms, therefore, competitive advantage is considered to be temporary.

The dynamic perspective assumes that a firm's current market position is not an accurate predictor of future performance because position itself is not a competitive advantage. Instead, the dynamic perspective looks at the past for clues about how the firm arrived at its present position and to the future to divine what the new competitive landscape might look like. It also holds that it's possible for the firm to influence the future state of the competitive landscape.

KEY TERMS

arena, 12	corporate strategy, 9	staging, 14	strategy formulation, 10
business strategy, 9	differentiators, 13	strategic management, 7	strategy implementation, 10
competitive advantage, 19	economic logic, 15	strategy, 8	vehicle, 12

REVIEW QUESTIONS

1. What is strategic management?

2. What are the key components of the strategic management process?

3. How does business strategy differ from corporate strategy?

4. What is the relationship between strategy formulation and strategy implementation?

5. What five elements comprise the strategy formulation diamond?

6. What are the internal and external perspectives of competitive advantage?

7. What are the fundamental and dynamic perspectives of competitive advantage?

8. Why should you study strategic management?

How Would you Do That?

1. Go to Warren Buffet's *Letter to Shareholder's* page at www.berkshirehathaway.com/letters/letters.html and read the most recent letter. How many of the strategy topics covered in this chapter can you find references to in the letter? Pick one of the businesses owned by Berkshire Hathaway and draft a strategy formulation diamond for it similar to the one outlined in the JetBlue example in the box entitled "How Would You Do That? 1.1."

2. Go back to the discussion of JetBlue in the box entitled "How Would You Do That? 1.1." Use the strategy implementation model in Exhibit 1.6 to identify what would be necessary to successfully implement JetBlue's strategy. How would the implementation levers be different for JetBlue than for some of the major airlines?

GROUP ACTIVITIES

1. Identify the characteristics of a firm that the members of your group would like to work for and try to identify an example of this type of firm. What's the difference between business and corporate strategy at this firm? How might that affect your experiences and opportunities in that organization? Use your knowledge of the firm's strategy to construct a high-impact job application cover letter to apply for a job with this firm.

2. How is international expansion related to business and corporate strategy? Identify a firm that may be thinking of expanding into new international markets. Apply the staging element of the strategy diamond to the firm's international expansion opportunities or plans. Which markets should it target first and why?

ENDNOTES

1. C. Hoge, *The First Hundred Years Are the Toughest: What We Can Learn from the Century of Competition Between Sears and Wards* (Berkeley, CA: Ten Speed Press, 1988); G. Weil, *Sears, Roebuck, U.S.A.: The Great American Catalog Store and How It Grew* (Briarcliff Manor, NY: Stein and Day, 1977); S. Walton with J. Huey, *Made in America: My Story* (New York: Bantam Books, 1992); A. Merrick and J. Hallinan, "Sears Pegs Its Revival on the Sale of Its Credit Card Unit," *Wall Street Journal* (Eastern edition), March 27, 2003, B4; K. R. Andrews, *The Concept of Corporate Strategy* 3rd ed. (Homewood, IL: Dow Jones/Irwin, 1987); C. W. Hofer and D. Schendel, *Strategy Formulation: Analytic Concepts* (St. Paul, MN: West, 1987); C. M. Christensen, "Making Strategy: Learning by Doing," *Harvard Business Review* 75:6 (1997), 141–156; V. Marsh, "Attributes: Strong Strategy Tops the List," *Financial Times*, November 30, 1998, p. 7; A. Grove, *Only the Paranoid Survive: How to Exploit the Crises Points That Challenge Every Company and Career* (New York: Currency Doubleday, 1999).

2. J. Pfeffer and R. I. Sutton, *The Knowing–Doing Gap: How Smart Companies Turn Knowledge into Action* (Boston: Harvard Business School Press, 2000).

3. *My Big Fat Greek Wedding* (HBO Video, 2003).

4. M. Porter, "What Is Strategy?" *Harvard Business Review* 74:6 (1996), 61–78.

5. D. C. Hambrick and J. W. Fredrickson, "Are You Sure You Have a Strategy?" *Academy of Management Executive,* 15:4 (2001), 48–59.

6. K. R. Andrews, *The Concept of Corporate Strategy* 3rd ed. (Homewood, IL: Irwin, 1987).

7. R. H. Waterman, T. J. Peters, and J. R. Phillips, "Structure Is Not Organization," *Business Horizons* 23:3 (1980), 14–26.

8. Andrews, *The Concept of Corporate Strategy* 3rd ed. (Homewood, IL: Irwin, 1987).

9. S. Brown and K. Eisenhardt, *Competing on the Edge* (Boston: Harvard Business School Press, 1998); R. A. Burgelman and L. Sayles, *Inside Corporate Innovation* (New York: Free Press, 1986).

10. R. A. Burgelman, "Fading Memories: A Process Theory of Strategic Business Exit in Dynamic Environments," *Administrative Science Quarterly* 39 (1993): 24–56.

11. Burgelman, "Fading Memories"; Grove, *Only the Paranoid Survive.*

12. This section draws extensively from Hambrick and Fredrickson, "Are You Sure You Have a Strategy?"

13. Personal interviews with company executives.

14. T. Carl, "After Growing on Small Towns, Wal-Mart Looks to World for More Expansion," Associated Press Newswires, March 26, 2003.

15. L. R. Roche, "IOC Praises Magic, Financial Success of S.L. Games," *Deseret News*, November 27, 2002, B6. Some of the details of this section come from personal interviews with Frasier Bullock, Chief Operating Officer and Chief Financial Officer of SLOC.

16. *The Strategy Execution Imperative: Leading Practices for Implementing Strategic Initiative* (Washington, D.C.: Corporate Executive Board, 2001); Christensen, "Making Strategy."

17. M. F. Porter, "Know Your Place: How to Assess the Attractiveness of Your Industry and Your Company's Position in It," *Inc.,* September 1991, 90.

18. P. F. Drucker, *The Practice of Management* (New York: HarperCollins, 1954), 352–353.

19. See J. B. Barney and P. M. Wright, "On Becoming a Strategic Partner: The Role of Human Resources in Gaining Competitive Advantage," *Human Resource Management* 37:1 (1998), 31–46; J. Pfeffer, *Competitive Advantage Through People* (Boston: HBS Press, 1994).

20. S. Kerr, "On the Folly of Rewarding A, While Hoping for B," *Academy of Management Journal* 18:4 (1975), 769–783.

21. J. B. Barney, "Firm Resources and Sustained Competitive Advantage," *Journal of Management* 17:1 (1991), 99–121; M. A. Peteraf, "The Cornerstones of Competitive Advantage: A Resource-Based View," *Strategic Management Journal* 14:3 (1993), 179–191.

22. R. R. Wiggins and T. W. Ruefli, "Sustained Competitive Advantage: Temporal Dynamics and the Incidence and Persistence of Superior Economic Performance," *Organization Science* 13:1 (2002), 82–105.

23. Barney, "Firm Resources and Sustained Competitive Advantage"; Peteraf, "The Cornerstones of Competitive Advantage"; B. Wernerfelt, "A Resource Based View of the Firm," *Strategic Management Journal* 5:2 (1984), 171–180.

24. Peteraf, "The Cornerstones of Competitive Advantage"; C. A. Montgomery and S. Hariharan, "Diversified Expansion by Large Established Firms," *Journal of Economic Behavior* 15:1 (1991), 71–99.

25. M. Porter, *Competitive Strategy* (New York: Free Press, 1980).

26. C. M. Christensen, *The Innovator's Dilemma: When New Technologies Cause Great Firms to Fail* (Boston: Harvard Business School Press, 1997).

27. Brown and Eisenhardt, *Competing on the Edge.*

28. J. Gimeno and C. Woo, "Multimarket Contact, Economies of Scope, and Firm Performance," *Academy of Management Journal* 42:3 (1999), 239–259.

29. Christensen, *The Innovator's Dilemma.*

After studying this chapter, you should be able to:

1. Explain how strategic leadership is essential to strategy formulation and implementation.

2. Understand the relationships among vision, mission, values, and strategy.

3. Understand the roles of vision and mission in determining strategic purpose and strategic coherence.

4. Identify a firm's stakeholders and explain why such identification is critical to effective strategy formulation and implementation.

5. Explain how ethics and biases may affect strategic decision making.

▶ David T. Kearns, 1982-1990
Diversify Xerox's businesses; improve quality and efficiency to ward off foreign competition.
Stock high: $13.29
Stock low: $5.88

▶ Paul A. Allaire, 1990-1999
Shed unprofitable, noncore businesses; add cutting-edge products to Xerox's product lineup.
Stock high: $59.81
Stock low: $3.75

*Our strategic intent is to help people find better ways to do great work—
by constantly leading in document technologies, products and services
that improve our customers' work processes and business results.*

HOW TO PULL A $15-BILLION COW OUT OF A DITCH

From an outsider's perspective, there was very little in Anne Mulcahy's background at Xerox to suggest that she'd be prepared for the kind of crisis management that awaited her.[1] Most recently, she'd been vice president for human resources and chief staff officer to former chief executive officer (CEO) Paul A. Allaire. The Xerox board promoted Mulcahy to president in May 2000, ousting G. Richard Thoman after a mere 13 months and reinstalling Chairman Allaire as CEO. When Allaire stepped down on August 1, 2001, Mulcahy became the first female CEO in Xerox history.

The Fall from the Nifty 50 The Xerox story is pretty well known. Introduced in 1959, the Xerox 914 copier transformed office work and installed Xerox as a charter member of the so-called "Nifty 50"—the 50 stocks most favored by institutional investors. Since the 1970s,

▶ **G. Richard Thoman,**
1999-2000
Reinvent and restructure Xerox to better compete in alternative markets; cut costs and bring in "new blood."
Stock high: $64.00
Stock low: $19.00

▶ **Paul A. Allaire,**
2000-2001
Restore profitability and investor confidence.
Stock high: $29.31
Stock low: $4.44

▶ **Anne M. Mulcahy,**
2001-present
Rescue Xerox from bankruptcy and reignite growth.
Stock high: $17.24
Stock low: $4.42

1995   2000

however, Xerox has been crippled by competition (mostly Japanese), repeated failures to capitalize on innovations coming out of its own Palo Alto Research Center (PARC), and tardiness in embracing digital imaging. After years of weak sales, the company was foundering, and employees were as disgruntled as customers. Then things went from bad to worse. In October 2001, Xerox reported its first quarterly loss in 16 years, and as debt piled up, the Securities and Exchange Commission began investigating the company's accounting practices.

Although the move from senior executive to CEO was a huge jump, Mulcahy was given the chance because she'd instilled confidence in the board. "She has the strategic mind and toughness to serve as CEO," said board member (and Johnson & Johnson CEO) Ralph Larsen.

Mulcahy was a popular manager with years of experience in dealing with customers. Granted, she'd never been involved in product development and didn't boast Allaire's financial expertise, but she'd demonstrated smart decision-making skills as head of the company's $6-billion division for small-office equipment. She'd also put together one of its biggest acquisitions—the $925-million purchase from Tektronix Inc. of a color-printing division that's now a source of fast-growing revenues (in large part because Mulcahy had preserved the division's autonomy and many of its business practices).

Running the Gamut from Enthusiasm to Pragmatism If there was ever any uncertainty about her qualifications as a CEO, they were soon dispelled. Mulcahy refined the Xerox vision and went out of her way to remind Xerox employees that the core values embedded in the company's mission statement had always been part of the firm's deep culture. More important, she moved decisively to align the firm's operations with its refined statement of mission and values.

Xerox Values
Since our inception, we have operated under the guidance of six core values:
- *We succeed through satisfied customers.*
- *We deliver quality and excellence in all we do.*
- *We require premium return on assets.*
- *We use technology to develop market leadership.*
- *We value our employees.*
- *We behave responsibly as a corporate citizen.*

On the less philosophical side, she sold Xerox's China and Hong Kong operations, and in March 2001 she raised $1.3 billion by selling half of its stake in a joint venture with Fuji. Mulcahy also proved willing to make other tough decisions. In June 2001, she closed down the unit that made desktop inkjet printers in Rochester, New York—a business that she'd once supported. Soon after taking the reins, she eliminated the company's stock dividend and announced that PARC would be spun off as a separate company.

Internally, she spread her message with a regular memo called "Turnaround Talk," which alternates between enthusiasm ("Together We Can Do It!") and pragmatism ("When we shut off the bottled water, it's not because we want to be mean-spirited. It's because all these little expenses . . . can spell the difference between losing money and turning a profit"). By 2002, stressing fidelity to the Xerox mission and long-term vision, she'd cut annual expenses by $1.7 billion, sold $2.3 billion worth of noncore assets, and reduced long-term debt to $9.2 billion, down from a high of $15.6 billion in 2000. Xerox returned to full-year profitability in 2002, generating $1.9 billion in operating-cash flow and $91 million in net income on $15.8 billion in sales.

The Next Chapter In July 2003, with Xerox gaining market share in important segments with new-product introductions, Mulcahy announced that the current chapter in the Xerox "turnaround story" had been closed. Her new challenge would be reigniting growth. Even during weak sales years, she'd invested $1 billion annually in research and development, and she's betting big on growth through such service businesses as document-management flow and computer networking.

The task of turning Xerox around has taken its toll on Mulcahy's personal life. Friends say that she laughs when asked about hobbies and executive-suite privileges like golf. Nowadays, reports *Business Week,* Mulcahy "only has time for work and her family, including her two teenage sons." But that, concludes the article, is "the kind of effort it takes to pull a $15-billion cow out of a ditch—and then try to make it run." ∎

STRATEGIC LEADERSHIP

Imagine starting a new job and then finding out that your job description includes the following items:

- You'll be personally responsible for the entire company's performance—success, or failure.
- You'll be relatively powerless to control most of what goes on in the organization.
- You'll have more authority than any other employee, but in using that authority, you'll make some people so unhappy that they'll harbor personal grudges against you.[2]

Congratulations: You're a CEO.

The basic responsibility of a CEO—*strategic leadership*—is so important that you'll find chapters on it in every management and organizational behavior book you pick up. Stories about leaders and leadership regularly command the covers and fill the pages of major business publications around the world. Some business leaders become celebrities.

What do these leaders do when they're on the job? *Leadership* is the task of exerting influence on other people's pursuit of goals in an organizational context. **Strategic leadership** is the task of managing an overall enterprise and influencing key organizational outcomes, such as company-wide performance, competitive superiority, innovation, strategic change, and survival. As the process of communicating the vision and mission that top executives espouse and model through their own actions, strategic leadership also sets the stage for strategy creation and implementation. Strategic leadership is often associated with individuals like Anne Mulcahy, but increasingly it's being exercised by teams of top executives. Given the complexity and speed of competitive change and uncertainty facing most firms today, this shift shouldn't be surprising.

strategic leadership Task of managing an overall enterprise and influencing key organizational outcomes

What This Chapter Is About

Most of this section explains why top executives, through their decisions and behavior, have both a symbolic and a substantive impact on the outcomes that concern a firm's key stakeholders. Thus we start by introducing the roles filled by top individual managers and management teams as they exercise strategic leadership. We'll discuss the functions of individuals and executive teams, as well as the conditions under which strategic-leadership efforts may flourish or founder. We will then discuss the ways in which vision, mission, values, and strategy relate to one another, and we'll show how vision and mission are reflected in the properties of strategy that we call *purpose* and *coherence*. Next, we'll introduce the principles of stakeholder analysis and explain why the best strategic leaders consider stakeholder interests when developing organizational vision and mission and strategies for realizing them. We conclude by showing how unethical and biased judgments can undermine even the best-laid strategic-leadership plans.

The Roles Leaders Fill

What do senior managers do? What occupies their days and nights and fills up their personal digital assistants (PDAs)? As our opening vignette suggests, their jobs are complex and multifaceted, and we can understand the CEO's job only by analyzing it in some detail.[3] Let's start by dividing executive activities into the three basic roles illustrated in Exhibit 2.1: *interpersonal, informational,* and *decisional.*

Interpersonal Roles Some executive tasks derive from the status and formal authority that come with the job. They're often interpersonal in nature and have a degree of symbolic value. Many of these roles may seem to have little to do with the practical exigencies of running a company, but they frequently occupy a great of deal of a CEO's time in all firms, from the smallest to the very largest.

Figurehead and Liaison As *figureheads,* top executives perform various ceremonial tasks, such as breaking ground at new facilities, hosting retirement dinners, and even fielding calls from irate stakeholders. As *liaisons,* they maintain relationships with external stakeholders, thus strengthening the company's links with its external environment. In this role,

Exhibit 2.1 The Roles That Leaders Play

Source: H. Mintzberg, The Nature of Managerial Work *(New York: Harper and Row, 1973).*

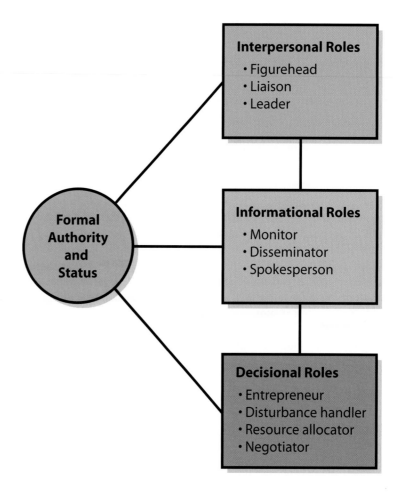

Formal Authority and Status

Interpersonal Roles
- Figurehead
- Liaison
- Leader

Informational Roles
- Monitor
- Disseminator
- Spokesperson

Decisional Roles
- Entrepreneur
- Disturbance handler
- Resource allocator
- Negotiator

they serve on the boards of other companies, meet with suppliers and customers, and participate in charities and civic organizations.

Leader Whereas the role of liaison is horizontal in nature, leadership is a vertical relationship: Top executives are *leaders* because employees and other stakeholders who don't possess their authority look to them for motivation and direction. In this chapter, we'll focus on senior-leadership responsibilities, such as providing vision, purpose, and direction.

Informational Roles Informational roles include those of monitor, disseminator, and spokesperson. As *monitor,* the executive taps into a larger network of contacts, colleagues, and employees to collect and collate the information needed to understand the organization and its environment. An effective monitor, says strategic-leadership expert Henry Mintzberg, "seeks information in order to detect changes, to identify problems and opportunities, to build up knowledge about his milieu, to be informed when information must be disseminated and decisions made."[4]

Sharing Information: Disseminator and Spokesperson Not surprisingly, information is never in short supply; in fact, information overload is a common condition of executive life. Top managers are bombarded with reports, analyses, and projections and information about both internal operations and external events. Obviously, the good monitor must know what to do with all of this information. Much of it, of course, is passed on to people both inside and outside the firm who can put it to use. In passing information to internal stakeholders, executives are *disseminators;* in passing it to external stakeholders, they're *spokespersons.*

As disseminators, CEOs communicate not only factual information, such as data received from bankers and consultants, but also what's often called *value-based information.* In leading Xerox through a period of change, for example, Anne Mulcahy spent much of her time communicating value statements to both internal and external stakeholders.

CEO Richard Notebaert (center) of Qwest Communications fields a question during an employee meeting. The firm's 40,000 employees are internal stakeholders. In communicating with them, Notebaert is playing the role of disseminator. CEOs often become the "face" people for their companies.

As spokespersons, CEOs perform such communications tasks as lobbying, public relations, and formal reporting. CEOs communicate with both boards of directors, to whom they report, and the general public. Needless to say, being an effective spokesperson means focusing on the most current, accurate, and relevant information.

Decisional Roles Perhaps the most obvious—some will say the most important—role of top managers is making key decisions about the company's strategy and future. In developing and implementing strategy, top executives may play any or all of four decisional roles: *entrepreneur, disturbance handler, resource allocator,* and *negotiator.*

The Entrepreneur As entrepreneur, the CEO designs the firm's strategy. Clearly, many people are involved in the process, but the CEO must ultimately authorize major strategic initiatives and supervise their implementation.

The Disturbance Handler Whereas the entrepreneurial role focuses on voluntary and proactive initiatives, disturbance handling deals with unforeseen situations or those in which the firm is involved involuntarily. Any number of "disturbances" can threaten the successful implementation of a strategy, including both internal and external conflicts. Internal conflicts, such as infighting by divisions or managers over responsibilities and authority, often require the CEO's arbitration. Likewise, the CEO will probably have to take action to smooth out conflicts in the distribution channel (a key's supplier's announcement, for example, that it will no longer deal with the company on an exclusive basis).

The Resource Allocator The role of resource allocator is crucial both to the task of formulating strategy and to the task of executing it successfully. If resources aren't effectively allocated, even a well-formulated strategy has little chance of success. With authority over the organization's financial, material, and human resources, the CEO is the only person who can manage the tradeoffs among competing strategic projects.

The Negotiator As a negotiator, the CEO is usually concerned with nonroutine transactions involving other organizations. Such decisions as whether to acquire or merge with another firm, to sell a major division, or to renegotiate a labor contract require significant participation from the CEO.

The Surprised CEO Obviously, then, being a CEO isn't easy.[5] What's astonishing, however, is the result of recent research showing that many new CEOs are quite surprised by many aspects of their jobs. Some report, for instance, that they're surprised at having to work with limited information and insufficient time to accomplish what they're expected to do.

Others are surprised that being a CEO means that they can no longer run day-to-day operations the way they once did. As heads of divisions or small companies, managers are much more deeply involved in nuts-and-bolts operations, but when they move into the executive suite of a large organization, they no longer have the time for hands-on management.

Yet other new CEOs learn the hard way that being the most powerful person in the organization doesn't mean that that you can use power as liberally as you please; power is a privilege best indulged in moderation. Conversely, many CEOs reach the top rung on the organizational ladder only to be reminded—sometimes rudely—that they still have to answer to a board of directors. Finally, new CEOs are often surprised at how hard they have to work to make their brilliant strategies understood and get them accepted by a broad range of stakeholders.

In addition, as demonstrated by Anne Mulcahy's situation, many who rise to senior leadership positions in large organizations often pay a price—sacrificing their personal and family lives in order to meet their managerial responsibilities. Roger Deromedi, the recently appointed CEO of Kraft Foods, notes that "I travel about 40 percent of the time, so life is a balancing act. People often don't make time with their spouse that's separate from time with their kids. I prioritize my wife and family, which means I don't have as much time for outside interests."[6]

The Skill Set of the Effective Strategic Leader: The Level 5 Hierarchy

Level 5 Hierarchy Model of leadership skills calling for a wide range of abilities, some of which are hierarchical in nature

What does it take to be an effective organizational leader? Obviously, neither all leaders nor leadership challenges are created equal. A diverse set of skills, therefore, can come in handy. In this section, we'll discuss the development of leadership skill sets in terms of a model called the **Level 5 Hierarchy**, which was popularized by management researcher Jim Collins in the book *From Good to Great*.[7] The key to this framework is the idea that leadership requires a wide range of abilities, some of which are hierarchical in nature—in other words, that before mastering certain higher-level abilities, one must first master certain lower-level skills.[8] Collins proposes the five levels of leadership skills summarized in Exhibit 2.2.

- *Level 1.* Before becoming an effective leader, you must prove highly competent in your work. On the first level of leadership, therefore, productive contributions of your talent, knowledge, hard work, and skills must be made.

- *Level 2.* Senior management is often a team endeavor, and CEOs must be able to delegate major responsibilities to teams of senior executives. At level 2, therefore, you must also show the ability to work effectively as a member of a team.

- *Level 3.* After teamwork abilities have been demonstrated, you need to show the ability to manage other people—the ability to organize people and marshal resources to achieve specific objectives.

- *Level 4.* Next, you must prove capable of leading a larger organization by generating broad commitment to a clear vision of the organization's future. At level 4, you need to show the ability to lead a group to superior levels of performance. Anne Mulcahy, for example, didn't reverse Xerox's fortunes by herself. She assembled a team with diverse backgrounds and capabilities and drew upon their collective abilities.

- *Level 5.* Level-5 leadership tends to feature an unusual, even paradoxical, combination of skills. Level-5 leaders not only express an unwavering resolve, or *professional will,* to achieve higher goals but demonstrate a surprising degree of *professional modesty.* Let's take a closer look at these two managerial attributes.

Professional Will Carrying out bold strategy moves requires commitment across the entire organization. A level-5 leader can translate strategic intent into the resolve needed to pursue a strategy—and usually to make hard choices—over a period of time.

Here's a good illustration. Walgreen Company was founded in 1901 by Chicago pharmacist Charles Walgreen. Eight years later, Walgreen began serving lunch at a new soda fountain, where, by the 1920s, he was doing his part to popularize the milk shake. Although food services remained a key part of Walgreen's business, the company realized during the 1960s that its classic soda-fountain operations were draining profits from the modern self-service retail operations that generated far greater sales per square foot. Now, to many people, soda fountains were a Walgreen hallmark, and because its history of food service

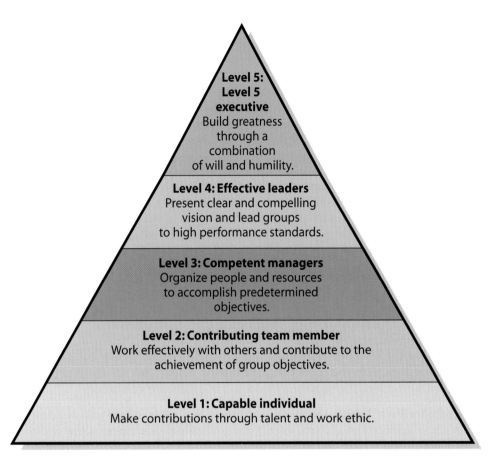

Exhibit 2.2 Level-5 Leaders: A Hierarchy of Capabilities

Source: Adapted from J. Collins, Good to Great: Why Some Companies Make the Leap . . . and Others Don't (New York: HarperBusiness, 2001).

was part of the firm's identity, there was considerable internal resistance to the idea of closing down the soda-fountain operations. In fact, CEO Charles Walgreen III found that phasing out food-service operations was more easily said than done; simply announcing his plan by no means ensured organization-wide cooperation. Ultimately, Walgreen set a deadline of five years, admonishing senior executives that "the clock is ticking." When reminded six months later that management had only five years to get out of the restaurant business, Walgreen reasserted his resolve to stick to the schedule: "Four and a half years," he replied.[9] In the final analysis, it was largely Walgreen's resolve that transformed the old model of the drugstore chain into a new (and more profitable) retail model.

Professional Modesty   Oddly, level-5 leaders also tend to be modest people—a fairly rare trait among people with upward career trajectories. Most research suggests that hubris is much more common than humility in the upper echelons of Corporate America, and given the drive that's needed to found or lead a successful firm, that fact shouldn't be surprising. And although examples abound of successful leaders who would not be described as modest, Collins' research suggests that companies that improve from average profitability and then beat the market over the long haul tend to be led by people who prefer to share credit rather than hog it. They tend to shun public attention, act with calm determination, and exercise their ambitions on the company's behalf rather than their own. They're also concerned about the future welfare of the company as well as its performance record during their own tenures.

What Does It Take to Be a CEO?

Having established the fact that senior executives influence the formation and implementation of strategy through both judgment and behavior, we know that it's worthwhile to understand what makes them think and act the way they do. We'll start by focusing on the characteristics of individual executives and the roles that they play in shaping strategic-leadership abilities.

Are you CEO material? Just what does it take? Charisma? Integrity? An Ivy League MBA? International management experience? Not surprisingly, there's no single answer to these seemingly simple questions. Although some answers involve such personality differences as charisma and emotional intelligence, others point to such demographic characteristics as gender, race, education, or work experience. There's little consensus on the issue of whether personality or background counts more, but understanding their actions is important if you want to understand successful leaders. With this fact in mind, let's take a closer look at all three perspectives on leadership characteristics: *personality differences, background and demographic differences,* and *differences in competence and actions.*

Personality Differences Largely because psychological traits can be measured through surveys and other quantitative approaches, a large amount of research has been done on the personality or psychological determinants of strategic leadership. Many of these studies focus on four personality characteristics: *locus of control, need for achievement, tolerance for risk or ambiguity,* and *charisma and emotional intelligence.*[10]

What's Your Tolerance for Ambiguity? Analyzing all of these characteristics goes beyond the purpose of this chapter, but you may find it instructive to investigate how you measure up on one key personality attribute—tolerance for ambiguity—compared to typical executives. *Tolerance for ambiguity* means that one tends to perceive situations as promising rather than threatening. If you are intolerant of ambiguity, then uncertainty or a lack of information, for example, would make you uncomfortable. Ambiguity arises from three main sources: novelty, complexity, and insolubility. You can use the ambiguity scale in Exhibit 2.3 to see how you measure up in terms of tolerance for ambiguity.

Personality Traits Versus Leadership Abilities If there is indeed a correspondence between certain personality characteristics and leadership abilities, then (at least in theory) boards of directors could sift through applicant pools and choose CEOs on psychological grounds. Unfortunately, the jury is still out on the question of whether "natural" leaders can be classified according to personality differences or identified through psychological test instruments. In fact, some researchers warn against placing undue importance on trendy personality screens. In short, personality characteristics may be important in some respects, but defining and isolating effective leadership abilities is a complex task.

Background and Demographic Differences *Background* differences typically refer to such factors as work experience and education, whereas *demographics* refers to such factors as gender, nationality, race, religion, network ties, and so forth.[11] Obviously, many factors of both kinds will figure prominently on your résumé.

Historically, the profile of the typical *Fortune*-500 top executive was a white male between the ages of 45 and 60 with a law, finance, or accounting degree from an Ivy League school.[12] Sociologists explain this pattern by pointing out that, for a long time, a large portion of the educated population—and thus of the managerial talent pool—consisted of white males. Moreover, white males were favored by certain structural features of the executive-employment market, including the usual prejudice of people to show favoritism toward people who are like them (in this case, white males).

Changes in demographics of business school students, as well as legal and social influence from lawsuits and legislation, have helped to diversify management ranks. Although there are significantly more female and minority managers at the start of the twenty-first century than there were just 20 years ago, few women and minorities have ascended to the level of CEO at the largest American companies. For instance, as of 2005 there were only 9 female CEOs among the 500 largest U.S. companies (1.8%), but this is double the number of just 9 years earlier. In addition, 16 percent of the corporate officers of these same companies are female, suggesting that change is happening, even if only gradually. It is interesting to note that the diversity of CEOs among privately owned smaller companies is much more reflective of the U.S. population. Although the diversity of large public companies has been slow to change, the diversity of leadership in smaller companies is much greater and growing.

Exhibit 2.3 Can You Tolerate Ambiguity?

You may have taken this survey earlier in the semester in preparation for this course. By definition, ambiguity characterizes strategic management and the study of strategy through cases. Your response to the case method itself is a function of your own attitude toward ambiguity. Take the following survey and tabulate your score to find out your tolerance for ambiguous situations.

Please respond to the following statements by indicating the extent to which you agree or disagree with them. Fill in the blanks with the number from the rating scale that best represents your evaluation of the item. There's a scoring key at the end of the survey.

1	Strongly disagree	5	Slightly agree
2	Moderately disagree	6	Moderately agree
3	Slightly disagree	7	Strongly agree
4	Neither agree or disagree		

1. An expert who doesn't come up with a definite answer probably doesn't know too much.
2. I would like to live in a foreign country for a while.
3. There is really no such thing as a problem that can't be solved.
4. People who fit their lives to a schedule probably miss most of the joy of living.
5. A good job is one where what is to be done and how it is to be done are always clear.
6. It is more fun to tackle a complicated problem than to solve a simple one.
7. In the long run it is possible to get more done by tackling small, simple problems rather than large and complicated ones.
8. Often the most interesting and stimulating people are those who don't mind being different and original.
9. What we are used to is always preferable to what is unfamiliar.
10. People who insist upon a yes or no answer just don't know how complicated things really are.
11. A person who leads an even, regular life in which few surprises or unexpected happenings arise really has a lot to be grateful for.
12. Many of our most important decisions are based on insufficient information.
13. I like parties where I know most of the people more than ones where all or most people are complete strangers.
14. Teachers or supervisors who hand out vague assignments give one a chance to show initiative and originality.
15. The sooner we all acquire similar values and ideals the better.
16. A good teacher is one who makes you wonder about your way of looking at things.

To score the instrument, **the even-numbered items must be reverse scored.** That is, the 7s become 1s, 6s become 2s, 5s become 3s, and 4s remain the same. After reversing the even-numbered items, sum the scores for all 16 items to get your total score. High scores indicate a greater *intolerance* for ambiguity. Use the comparison scores provided below to benchmark your own score, and read the following paragraphs to interpret the results.

Total Score

Subscores (follow same even/odd reverse scoring)

(N) Novelty score (sum 2, 9, 11, 13) _____

(C) Complexity score (sum 4, 5, 6, 7, 8, 10, 14, 15, 16) _____

(I) Insolubility score (sum 1, 3, 12) _____

Being intolerant of ambiguity (relatively high score) means that an individual tends to perceive situations as threatening rather than promising. Lack of information or uncertainty, for example, would make such a person uncomfortable. Ambiguity arises from three main sources: *novelty, complexity,* and *insolubility.* These three subscales exist within the instrument you just completed.
Comparison total scores: Senior executives 44–48, MBAs 55–60.

Source: S. Budner, "Intolerance of Ambiguity as a Personality Variable," Journal of Personality 30 (1982), 29–50.

Although there are still a lot of white males with Ivy League degrees in the upper echelons of American business, we're now finding much greater diversity among top-management teams. Again, however, we need to remember that boards don't rely on any single criterion when choosing a CEO. In fact, our opening vignette features a CEO who came up not by following the usual accounting or finance track but rather through strategic human resource management.

Beside the fact that it's unethical (and, in many countries, illegal) to discriminate in hiring and promotion, a number of practical explanations account for the increasing diversity in the ranks of top managers, both in the United States and elsewhere:

- Although an advanced degree remains a typical prerequisite for promotion, college education is now available to more people than ever before. All around the world, schools compete for the best and brightest regardless of race, gender, or religion, and employers reap the benefits of more diverse talent pools.

- Groups tend to make better decisions when they can draw on heterogeneous perspectives, especially when facing turbulent or uncertain environments. When uncertainty makes it difficult to predict the future, top-management teams make better strategic decisions when they get input from diverse sources.[13]

- Companies today need top managers with strong international skills gained through work experience abroad. Because these skills are still fairly rare, even among college graduates, firms must look harder and farther to find them.[14]

- Firms increasingly seek competitive advantage through the quality of their human capital—the people who work for them. Because human capabilities are color, gender, and ethnicity blind, people with greater background and demographic diversity are rising to the ranks of upper management. Indeed, any form of bias that prevents talented employees from being promoted will put a firm at a distinct competitive disadvantage, particularly in terms of its ability to attract and retain talented people.

Competence and Actions   Do actions speak louder than words (or perhaps even louder than personality, background, or demographic differences)? Among the main reasons that Anne Mulcahy rose to the top at Xerox was her experience as vice president and staff officer for customer operations in South and Central America, Europe, Asia, Africa, and China. Increasingly, the consensus on what it takes to make it to the top-executive ranks goes beyond skin color, gender, and even line items on a résumé. More companies are placing value on substantive work experience—looking as much for the knowledge gleaned from mistakes as for the successes accumulated along the way.

Mulcahy had already demonstrated courage and toughness when it came to making and sticking to decisions, and although such toughness may be a product of experience, many experts argue that superior executives are distinguished by a talent for strategic thinking. Mulcahy was promoted because of her proven strength as a business strategist as well as her decision-making toughness. What, exactly, does a "talent for strategic thinking" add to "toughness"? By *toughness,* we mean a willingness and ability to change an organization's strategic course even when that change represents a significant departure from its traditional way of doing business. Whereas the average manager emphasizes the efficient execution of a given plan, the strategic leader works not only to develop the plan in the first place, but to empower the organization to realize the vision behind it.

Strategists and nonstrategists differ in how they think about problems. Like personality differences, these differences are too broad to review in detail in this chapter. However, a few of these dimensions of strategic thinking are reviewed in the "Are You a Strategist?" exercise in Exhibit 2.4. Test yourself on a few dimensions of strategic leadership by taking the survey. As you can see, strategists are characterized by having a spirit of entrepreneurship and an eye to the future.

What Makes an Effective Executive Team?

In reality, of course, organizations need good managers as well as great leaders, just as armies need hard-working soldiers and inspirational generals. Ironically, one hallmark of

Answer each question with "Yes," "Mostly Yes," "Mostly No," or "No." Tally up the percentage of answers in each category.	Yes	Mostly Yes	Mostly No	No
1. Do you like to be entrepreneurial and come up with new ideas or plans but are also comfortable having others execute them? _____	☐	☐	☐	☐
2. Do you have clear guiding values for your actions (i.e., strategic intent and coherence)? _____	☐	☐	☐	☐
3. Do you think about your strengths and weaknesses before making major life choices? _____	☐	☐	☐	☐
4. Do you engage in activities that are in concert with your vision of the future and personal guiding values? _____	☐	☐	☐	☐
5. When you work with others, do you try to foster a climate where your colleagues can act freely in the interests of the objective you are seeking to achieve? _____	☐	☐	☐	☐
6. When you are working with others to achieve a certain objective, do you actively and regularly involve them in formulating the strategy to achieve that objective? _____	☐	☐	☐	☐
7. When working with others to achieve an objective do you seek harmony in matching your group's culture with your strategy? _____	☐	☐	☐	☐
8. Do you point out new directions and take novel approaches? _____	☐	☐	☐	☐
9. Have you been lucky so far (strategic leadership includes the ability to place oneself in positions that favor being lucky)? _____	☐	☐	☐	☐
10. Do you make a contribution to society and yourself (strategic leaders leave a legacy)? _____	☐	☐	☐	☐

If you answered "Yes" or "Mostly Yes" to these questions, congratulations—you have the makings of a strategic leader!

Exhibit 2.4 Are You a Strategist?

Source: Adapted from H. Hinterhuber and W. Popp, "Are You a Strategist or Just a Manager?" Harvard Business Review 70:1 (January–February 1992), 105–113.

great leadership is knowing when and how to follow the lead of others. In this section, we'll discuss the ways in which the interaction of members of a top-management team can influence—for better or for worse—the contributions of a strategic leader. (We'll also discuss the importance of top-management teams and teamwork in strategic leadership in later chapters as well. In Chapter 12, for instance, we'll show how the entrepreneurial process depends partly on collective effort and the marshaling of resources by the entrepreneur and the entrepreneurial team.) At the very least, the team has the advantage of a division of labor, and in any case, no single person, regardless of talent and ability, can single-handedly attend to all the details encountered at the top of today's complex organizations.

conceptlink

In Chapter 1, we define **arenas** as the element of strategy that specifies the areas in which a firm will be active.

Teamwork and Diversity   What does effective teamwork mean if the team consists of top-management personnel? Basically, effective teamwork requires three criteria:

1. The team responds to a complex and changing environment.

2. The team can manage the needs of interdependent but often diverse units, **arenas**, or functional areas.

3. The team is able to develop a coherent plan for executive succession.

There's a common key to satisfying the first two criteria: A team can accommodate diverse input while acting as an integrated unit. In other words, the team is composed of people who have diverse backgrounds in terms of demographics and experience but who can nevertheless work well together as a network and take advantage of the resources and knowledge they have access to by virtue of each team member's personal and professional networks. Large firms typically can afford, and often have, larger top-management teams than do smaller firms, which also means that executives in larger firms have access to broader personal and professional networks.

Succession Planning   The third area, succession planning, has received increased attention in recent years as turnover among upper-echelon executives has increased. This is the case even among small firms, although the process is often made more complex by the fact that potential successors may include family members, in addition to current executives and outsiders hired from other companies. As a practical matter, succession planning has become more important because the rate of CEO dismissals by relatively large public firms has increased by 170 percent from 1995 to 2003 (from 30 out of 2,500 to 75). Globally, CEO job security is declining, with average tenure decreasing by 23 percent between 1995 and 2003, to a low of 7.6 years. Twenty-eight percent of the 238 CEOs who departed in 2003 were outsiders—the highest proportion in any year since 1995.[15]

succession planning Process of managing a well-planned and well-executed transition from one CEO to the next with positive outcomes for all key stakeholders

Experts agree that a well-planned and executed succession process is essential for a successful transition. **Succession planning** is typically overseen by the board, often with an outside consulting firm, and usually involves the current CEO. In most cases, succession is typically considered final only when the new CEO is in place and the old one has departed. Why? Given the power that sitting CEOs may command, it's often better that a long-term CEO leave the company entirely. Boards, says Jeffrey Sonnenfeld, an expert on CEO succession, "should recognize that creators have a strong tendency to act like monarchs or generals, and both kinds have trouble giving things up."[16]

Even with CEO succession planning becoming more established and accepted in corporations around the world, its practice is a science tempered by a strong dose of art. The box entitled "How Would You Do That? 2.1" discusses the characteristics that a board might look for in new a CEO. The science part involves the development of a methodical approach to identifying desirable CEO characteristics and then drawing out a short-list of candidates from a broad field of wanna-be CEOs. As you can see, the art part comes into play when making the difficult judgments about who should make the short list and then ranking those candidates realistically in terms of their ability to meet the firm's strategic needs.

When the succession process founders, it can destroy the CEO's legacy—not to mention the company's health—by undermining investor confidence, depressing the stock price, creating dissension on the board, disrupting the continuity of ongoing initiatives, and even crippling the organization for years. Conversely, when the process goes well, a smooth transition fosters positive outcomes for the company and its stakeholders. General Electric, for example, conducted a meticulous search over several years before appointing Jeffrey Immelt, who ran the company's medical-systems division, to succeed CEO Jack Welch. By the time a final decision was made, according to insiders, Immelt had in effect been running the company for most of a year—planning acquisitions, attending employee reviews, and overseeing management team meetings. Similarly, when the founder and CEO of Boston auto-wash chain ScrubaDub sought to turn the leadership of the business over to his two sons, he did so only after they had thoroughly hashed out their respective roles and titles, the company's vision and mission, and their respective compensation and stock ownership packages. One brother now serves as CEO, responsible for R&D and operations, and the other serves as president, responsible for training, sales, and marketing.[17]

Sometimes, of course, the timing of a transition can't be predicted. In such cases, an even higher premium is placed on good managerial bench strength and prior planning. At McDonald's, for example, the promotion of Charlie Bell only hours after the sudden death of CEO Jim Cantalupo reassured employees and investors that the firm was under competent leadership. The smooth transition was possible only because the plan for Bell's succession was already in place, and a year later, when Bell himself resigned because of illness, the board already had Jim Skinner waiting in the wings. "The worst-case scenario planning of most companies," points out Jeffrey Sonnenfeld, "is only a Band-Aid transitional solution, not a strategic solution. McDonald's directors, by immediately naming a battle-tested insider, showed the wisdom of having a succession plan in place."[18]

THE IMPRINT OF STRATEGIC LEADERSHIP: VISION AND MISSION

Top executives provide the context for strategy formulation and implementation through the vision and mission that they not only espouse, but that they also model through their own actions. Sometimes, they're the originators of the vision and mission; at other times, they're caretakers or agents who work to sharpen employees' shared understanding of the vision and mission. In any case, the vision and mission remain central, and that's why the overarching model of strategy management that we introduced in Chapter 1 starts with vision and mission.

Defining *Vision* and *Mission*

We define **vision** as a simple statement or understanding of what the firm will be in the future. A statement of vision is forward looking and identifies the firm's desired long-term status. In contrast, a **mission** is a declaration of what a firm is and stands for—its fundamental values and purpose. Because it's difficult to execute a strategy if it can't be described or understood, firms with clearly and widely understood visions and missions find it easier to make strategic decisions entailing difficult tradeoffs.

Thus, as you can see in Exhibit 2.5, vision and mission influence strategy formulation and implementation. Sometimes this influence is exercised when leaders focus explicitly on defining or refining a firm's vision, as was the case with Mulcahy at Xerox. More often, however, an organization's vision and mission are well established and functional. In these cases, leaders work to formulate the firm's strategy in a manner that's consistent with the fundamental values and purpose expressed in its statements of core beliefs. A shared understanding of the firm's direction and values helps guide both executives and employees

vision Simple statement or understanding of what the firm will be in the future

mission Declaration of what a firm is and what it stands for—its fundamental values and purpose

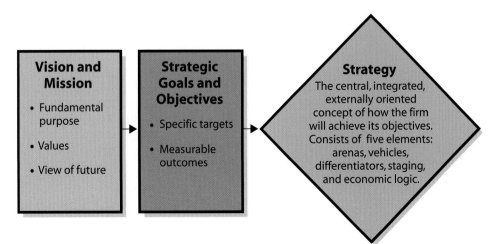

Exhibit 2.5 Vision, Mission, and Strategy

Source: D. C. Hambrick and J. W. Fredrickson, "Are You Sure You Have a Strategy?" Academy of Management Executive *15:4 (2001), 48–59.*

The Strategy for Finding the Right CEO

Well-run boards do not assume that CEOs are superhuman or have mystical powers to change a firm's fortunes overnight. However, as the opening vignette on Xerox highlights, the right CEO can make a huge difference in terms of substantive strategic decisions, symbolic actions, and figurehead activities. As a three-time CEO and a director on a number of boards, Betsy Atkins can attest that directors have learned a lot in recent years about hiring chief executives. From 1980 to 2000, the percentage of outside candidates selected for new CEO positions soared from 7 to 50 percent; however, firms found that outsiders were not the cure-all they had hoped for. As a result, boards are trying harder to promote from within rather than hiring charismatic, but untested, CEOs from the outside.

MAPPING STRATEGY: IDENTIFYING IMPLEMENTATION LEVERS AND VALUE-CREATING ACTIVITIES

Regardless of whether the search is internal or external, the board must build a consensus on what it is seeking in a CEO. Going into a search, the board must have a shared view of leadership, and directors must agree on the firm's strategic needs and how much strategic change they want; a search can be crippled from the start if some directors fear the new leader will change things too drastically or if they delude themselves into believing that the next CEO will be their corporate savior. Directors need to be able to assess internal or external candidates' passions and strength of convictions, as well as their ability to lead. One way to start the search and selection process is to simply map the firm's strategy onto specific tactical and longer-term operating needs. Good boards view succession planning as a way of systematically reflecting upon the specific levers that the CEO and other top managers can and should pull to effect organizational change. CEOs, although only one component in the organizational machinery, obviously affect the way in which value-creating activities are performed, monitored, and rewarded. Which value-creating activities a firm chooses to focus on and how they are implemented is, in turn, the cornerstone of competitive advantage. Yet because large companies perform literally hundreds of interrelated, value-creating activities, it can be difficult for even the most responsible boards—especially ones with several outside, "independent" directors—to understand clearly the way in which these many activities create value and, more to the point, how a new CEO can affect the success with which they are carried out.

To do this, board members must dig deep and ask tough questions. Boards must also develop better means for systematically obtaining relevant, specific information about how the company creates value. Recent comprehensive studies convincingly argue that a full 40 percent of directors do not have a sufficient understanding of their firms' value-creation process. This is the critical roadblock for good corporate governance, as companies adjust from legally mandated board compliance to strategically focused board empowerment. The lack of understanding is hardly surprising, given the way in which information generally flows from senior management to the board. In » many firms, for example, thick binders of market data and analysts' reports are compiled and distributed to directors by the chief financial officer (CFO) two weeks before the board convenes. How many directors have the time or inclination to comb through these binders? How do such masses of ill-digested information help them understand the value-creation process?

To remedy the gaps in board members' knowledge of their firms, many leading board-governance experts argue that boards should "map" the company's strategy at a high level so that they can visualize why and how performing certain activities helps to achieve objectives and goals along several critical dimensions—financial, customer, operational, and developmental. A strategy can illustrate the correlation—or set of cause-and-effect linkages and pathways—among employee retention, deeper understanding of customer needs, enhanced customer loyalty, bigger margins, and enhanced profitability.

BALANCING QUANTITATIVE AND QUALITATIVE FACTORS

Although numerous quantitative measurements are available, such as stock price history or background experience, the attributes that may have the greatest impact on a candidate's potential success are softer, qualitative ones. Atkins acknowledges that

directors need to be able to assess passion and strength of convictions as well as ability to lead. Atkins admits to her personal experience in this regard related to her brief tenure on the board of HealthSouth, a national chain of surgery and rehabilitation clinics. CEO Richard Scrushy, she recalls, was "impressive and forceful, [but] there was something about him that raised my antennae." She was right: Since 2003, 14 former HealthSouth employees, including all 5 of its former CFOs, have pleaded guilty to federal fraud charges. Scrushy is charged with 85 counts, including fraud, conspiracy, and money laundering. From that experience, Atkins learned that "the charismatic 'star' CEO leadership style is inconsistent with developing an open environment and an empowered management team."

Atkins did a better job at Lucent Technologies, where the board recruited CEO Pat Russo. Acknowledging that Lucent was going through significant upheaval and needed an inspiring, high-integrity team builder to stabilize and rebuild the company, the board set out to find someone with these qualitative attributes of leadership. That's how they settled on Russo.

Wiser for these experiences, Atkins is convinced that in evaluating candidates board members must assess their social interactions with the company's

directors. "It's a mistake," she says, to hire a CEO solely on the basis of formal presentations and discussions. Personal conversations often yield unexpected insight into a candidate's personality. An attentive interviewer, says Atkins, can detect the nuances in pregnant pauses that aren't always apparent in a preference write-up. After all, leadership is a collection of personal behaviors, political and people skills and judgment—and much of that is typically suppressed in formal settings. In social interactions, it's easier to ask open-ended questions, such as "What are you proudest of in your career?" or "What was the most difficult challenge you ever faced?" A director with a well-trained ear can then discover whether the candidate thinks in terms of building teams to accomplish objectives or is a lone ranger. "There's no way to analyze those qualities on a spreadsheet."

Atkins also thinks it's crucial for directors to do some background checking of their own rather than relying entirely on others. It's not that she doesn't trust executive-search firms. "It's just that they obviously have an incentive to close the transaction through a hiring decision, rather than prolong the debate."

Source: R. Fulmer & J. Conger, *Growing Your Company's Leaders* (New York: Amacom, 2004).

in their daily decisions and actions. Vision and mission, therefore, reinforce and support strategy; conversely, strategy provides a coherent plan for realizing vision and mission.

Once you've finished this and the next section, you should be able to identify a firm's vision and mission and understand their roles in more complex organizational activities. You'll understand how vision and mission are translated into strategic action, and you'll be able to make recommendations for improving organizational performance or competitive position. You'll see how vision and mission contribute to the organizational functions that we call *strategic purpose* and *strategic coherence.* Because strategy can be successful only to the extent that key stakeholders (customers, suppliers, government, and employees) facilitate its implementation, you'll also learn how to use the tool that we call *stakeholder analysis.*

What Should Vision and Mission Statements Encompass?

A study by the consulting firm Bain and Company reports that 90 percent of 500 firms surveyed issue some form of vision and mission statements.[19] Toward what end? Together, vision and mission statements not only express a firm's identity and describe its work but inform both managers and employees of the firm's direction. They're not strategies in and of themselves, but they convey organizational identity and purpose to critical stakeholders both inside and outside the firm.

Vision: The Uses of Ambition and Ambiguity   In the early 1950s, Sony stated its vision of "becoming the company that most changes the worldwide image of Japanese products as being of poor quality." Back in 1915, CitiBank (now CitiGroup) announced its grandiose vision of becoming "the most powerful, the most serviceable, the most far-reaching world financial institution the world has ever seen."[20] As these two examples suggest, vision statements generally express long-term action horizons, and they're ambitious by design, because ambition forces the firm to stretch both by challenging external competitors and by questioning the internal status quo. Because they're often ambiguous, they don't inhibit the firm from reaching for the stars (or at least aspiring to reach for the stars). Ambiguity also enables flexibility for changing strategy or implementation tactics when it looks as if business as usual isn't going to realize the expressed vision.

Mission: The Uses of Core Values   A firm will use its mission statement to identify certain core concepts, such as its purpose, or *raison d'être;* values and beliefs; standards of behavior; or corporate-level aims.[21] All employees are supposed to internalize core ideals and call upon them to guide their decisions and actions. At 3M, for example, a core value is the innovative solution of problems. Merck wants employees to preserve and improve human life, and Wal-Mart wants them to devote themselves to selling ordinary folks the same things that affluent people buy.[22]

Why Vision and Mission Statements Are Not Substitutes for Strategy

It should be obvious by now that clearly articulated, coherent, and widely understood vision and mission statements are not substitutes for strategy. Nevertheless, we need to spend a little time on this point.

In 1993, when outsider Lou Gerstner was hired as CEO and charged with the daunting task of saving IBM from potential ruin, he announced that "the last thing IBM needs (right now) is a vision." The statement was widely circulated (although press reports usually edited out the words "right now"),[23] as was Gerstner's charge that IBM's vision was nothing but a litany of platitudes, like those of firms who declare commitment to "total quality" or "customer service." Having discovered that some divisions at IBM were busier squabbling over the distribution of revenue than responding to customer needs, Gerstner was more interested in consistent and tangible managerial action.

Likewise, vision statements don't help much if managers view them as cure-alls for organization ailments or if they paint pictures of a future that's clearly unattainable.

Sometimes, a vision is so irrelevant to organizational reality that employees and customers simply reject it. Small firms, in particular, need a clear vision and mission to provide them with focus, but they also need a concrete strategy to translate concepts and resource constraints into profitable action. In the case of IBM, an enormous firm, Gerstner wanted to send a strong message to all employees that serious changes were needed if the company was to survive—changes that would extend far beyond any revamped statement of vision.

Vision and mission can be powerful tools, but because they're general and ambiguous by design, they must be realized through carefully crafted and executed strategy. Firms undergoing strategic change are especially susceptible to serious discrepancies between a new vision statement that's crafted on high and the organizational processes designed to realize it on the factory floor. As you can see from Exhibit 2.6, Gerstner did in fact have a clear vision for IBM (namely, to get it back to the top spot in its industry), but he first set out to anchor this vision in specific goals and objectives derived from a focused and clearly articulated strategy. IBM's prospects were gloomy back in 1993, but thanks to Gerstner's clear-headed understanding of the relationship between strategy and vision (and his talent for leadership), IBM is once again one of America's most admired companies.

Goals and Objectives

To be effective, then, visions and missions must be spelled out in terms of specific quantitative or qualitative **goals and objectives** for directing strategic actions. Often firms will also state a **superordinate goal** to serve as an overarching reference point for other goals and objectives. Wal-Mart's annual report, for example, states that the company will grow sales and profits by 20 percent per year; Ryanair says that it will be Europe's largest airline in seven years; Matsushita intends to become a "Super Manufacturing Company." Ultimately, the strength with which a firm's vision and mission are anchored in relevant goals and objectives will determine which ones walk the talk and which ones just talk the talk.

goals and objectives Combination of a broad indication of organizational intentions (*goals*) and specific, measurable steps (*objectives*) for reaching them

superordinate goal Overarching reference point for a host of hierarchical subgoals

If talk of visions and superordinate goals conjures up images of crystal balls and astrology, don't be too surprised. Some executives treat vision and mission statements as symbolic pronouncements, and in many organizations they exist on a different plane than actual strategy and strategic actions. Such discrepancies are symptomatic of various conditions. Perhaps the firm is floundering from a lack of clear or unique strategic direction; perhaps its strategy is too complex; maybe management has lost sight of the competitive realities facing the company.

- IBM will not be split up and its many parts will be even more closely coordinated.

- IBM will reassert its identity as customers' primary computing resource.

- The company will be the dominant supplier of technology in the industry.

- PowerPC, a new microprocessor design, will be IBM's centerpiece. Built into many future computers, it will run a wide range of standard industry software. And it will steeply cut manufacturing costs.

- Mainframes are no longer central to the strategy, but IBM will still make them, now with microprocessors.

- IBM is its own worst enemy. Employees must waste fewer opportunities, minimize bureaucracy, and put the good of the company before their division's.

Exhibit 2.6 Key Elements of Gerstner's 1993 Vision for IBM

Source: D. Kirkpatrick, "Gerstner's New Vision for IBM," Fortune, November 15, 1993, 119–124.

Research suggests that the best-performing firms boast clear visions and missions.[24] Effective strategic leaders craft these statements for a variety of reasons:

- To crystallize and disseminate the firm's strategy among employees
- To provide a shared logic for the firm's view of its internal and external environments and its treatment of stakeholders
- To galvanize concerted strategic action
- To link strategy formulation to implementation by tying vision and mission to specific and measurable goals and objectives

conceptlink

In Chapter 1, we describe the *balanced scorecard* as a strategic support system devised to help managers translate vision and strategy into business-level and operating-unit-level performance along several critical dimensions.

At many companies, managers are responsible for tracking strategic progress with a tool called a **balanced scorecard,** which is a system for translating vision and strategy into tangible performance measured by such criteria as return on sales, sales growth, and customer retention.

Finally, well-articulated and frequently shared vision and mission statements provide an impetus and rationale for ongoing strategic change, helping managers resolve the continuing tension between the static and dynamic facets of competitive situations.

STRATEGIC PURPOSE AND STRATEGIC COHERENCE

An overview of the examples presented in this chapter should tell you that it's relatively easy to compose a snappy vision statement. You should also have gathered by now that having vision and mission statements doesn't guarantee higher levels of performance. For one thing, some statements are more effective than others. How so? Research suggests the importance of the process used to develop and articulate statements. Performance, for example, is positively correlated with the integration of internal stakeholders—in other words, manager and employee satisfaction with the statement-development process.[25] This is yet one more reason why we'll focus on the stakeholder-analysis tool in the next section and why we stress the importance of considering stakeholders in the practice of strategic leadership. First, however, let's focus on the two most critical aspects of effective vision and mission statements: *strategic purpose* and *strategic coherence.*

Strategic Purpose

Vision and mission statements are actually statements of organizational identity and purpose that can guide executives in making corporate decisions. After all, one individual—even a group of individuals—can cope with only so much complexity in a problem. Vision and mission statements provide all employees with **strategic purpose**: a simplified, widely shared model of the organization and its future, including anticipated changes in its environment.

strategic purpose Simplified, widely shared mental model of the organization and its future, including anticipated changes in its environment

Tradeoffs, Options, and Other Decisions
Most major strategic decisions require tradeoffs—deciding on one course of action may necessarily eliminate other options. In addition, although some courses of action may satisfy the needs of some stakeholders, they may adversely affect others.

The consumer-products companies Mars Inc. and SC Johnson, for example, remain private corporations. When you visit either firm's Web site, you'll see that independence is a core value for both. Moreover, private ownership means greater flexibility in strategic choices: Because neither firm must cater to the stock market as a stakeholder, each can choose to make costly investments in the kinds of socially responsible programs that often draw fire from the shareholders of public companies. And the tradeoffs? The growth potential of each firm is limited, and it's more difficult to arrange for employee ownership, whether through direct share ownership or stock options.

Newman's Own, founded by actor Paul Newman and a partner in 1982, makes and sells salad dressing, lemonade, popcorn, salsa, steak sauce, and other food items through major grocery chains in the United States and abroad. In 2003, McDonald's announced that it would use Newman's Own dressings exclusively in its new Premium Salad line. Newman expects this alliance to increase profits by 25 percent. The firm's success derives from two policies anchored in its vision: (1) It insists on top-quality products with no artificial ingredients or preservatives. (2) It donates all after-tax profits to educational and charitable organizations, including UNICEF, Habitat for Humanity, and the Hole in the Wall Gang Camp for seriously ill children. The determination to combine commerce with philanthropy underlies a fairly unique vision, but it's guided the company's strategy for more than two decades. The tradeoff? Although adhering to a strongly held corporate philosophy helps managers choose certain courses of action over others, the decision to use more expensive natural ingredients means sacrificing higher short-term profitability.

Even a company with a more traditional profit orientation can be guided by a fairly simple vision. Michael Dell founded Dell Computers in 1984 on an investment of $1,000. His vision was to sell computer systems directly to customers. The company now has more than 55,000 employees and boasted revenues in excess of $49 billion in 2005.[26] Such rapid growth, however, means that the great majority of Dell employees are relative newcomers to the corporate family, which puts pressure on the company to preserve the values that guided it in its early years. Dell training, therefore, strives to imbue all employees with the "Soul of Dell"—the set of values that guides all of the firm's business practices.

As you can see in Exhibit 2.7, Matsushita Electric, the Japanese parent company of Panasonic, is preparing to stretch by comparing what the company does today with what it will have to do to become a "Super Manufacturing Company" in the future. Such a company, explains Matsushita CEO Kunio Nakamura, "must in essence be 'light and speedy.' Now when the nature of business is changing, emphasis will be placed on the maintenance, broadening and strengthening of IT, on R&D and marketing. Moreover, Matsushita at present is like a heavy lead ball loaded with assets. In the future we need to cast off superfluous assets and become a company that can move lightly like a soccer ball."[27]

The Challenge of Closing the Gap　The challenge posed by a strategic purpose is to close the gap between the firm's aspirations and its current capabilities and market positions. All strategies, for example, address the tradeoff between efficiency and effectiveness, and a firm can easily fall into the trap of adhering to its current strategy (say, becoming more efficient) even though customers no longer value its products (in other words, becoming less effective). Like long-term personal goals, the forward-looking aspect of strategic purpose means more than merely setting long-term goals that require stretch. Rather, an effective strategic purpose must be tied to a coherent set of activities, near-term goals, and objectives anchored in *measurable strategic outcomes*—that is, *strategic coherence*.

Strategic Coherence

An effective strategy is coherent. As we saw in Chapter 1, a firm's strategy entails an integrated set of choices regarding the five elements of the *strategy diamond*. **Strategic coherence**

strategic coherence Symmetric coalignment of the five elements of the firm's strategy, the congruence of functional-area policies with these elements, and the overarching fit of various businesses under the corporate umbrella

concept link

In Chapter 1, we identify the five elements of the *strategy diamond* as vehicles, differentiators, staging, arenas, and economic logic.

Matsushita's Goal: To Become a 21st-Century "Super Manufacturing Company"		
	Today: A Conventional Manufacturing Company	**Tomorrow: A 21st-Century Super Manufacturing Company**
Role	Providing goods	Providing solutions
Investment	Principally capital investment	Expansion of R&D, marketing, and IT investment
Information	From the company	Interactive/direct contact with customers
Organization	Pyramid	Flat and web

Exhibit 2.7 Creating Strategic Purpose at Matsushita

Source: "In the Pursuit of a Super Manufacturing Company," Panasonic *(accessed July 18, 2005), at matsushita.co.jp/corp/vision/president/interview2/en/index.html.*

(versus *incoherence*) is the symmetrical coalignment of the five elements of the firm's strategy, the congruence of policies in such functional areas as finance, production, and marketing with these elements, and the overarching fit of various businesses under the corporate umbrella. Successful firms depend on dozens of critical elements operating in concert and in balance. These elements are integrated so that everyone from design to manufacturing to marketing to accounting understands them in the same way.

In practice, some firms suffer from incoherent and fragmented strategies. For instance, a firm's decision to grow rapidly through acquisitions may be out of sync with its attempts to differentiate its products on the basis of strong brand equity. Some firms lack coherence because functional areas are treated like independent domains, as if they were silos of business activity that don't need orchestrated cooperation. Finally, some firms lack a coherent strategy because they move in and out of new businesses, as AT&T has done over the past two decades.

Applying the Strategy Diamond   How can firms achieve strategic coherence? The answer seems to be serious commitment to, and widespread communication of, well-understood and shared organizational vision and values. The strategy diamond framework is useful in testing the coherence of the elements of a strategy. We reintroduce it here because it's useful in testing for strategy coherence. From an internal perspective, a coherent strategy aligns all of the strategy's strategic, tactical, and design elements. From an external perspective, coherence is an alignment of the strategy with the industry environment and the vision of where and how the firm will be positioned in that environment in the future. Incoherence tends to plague firms that allocate resources primarily in response to competitors' strategies. As a result, it will appear as if their actions and functions are about average for the industry. In reality, of course, there's nothing distinctive about such a firm because it has in effect allowed its competitors to determine its strategy.

The Clear and Compelling Vision Statement   In many ways, strong vision statements function as guidelines for clear and compelling strategies that distinguish a firm from its competitors. What do we mean by "compelling"? Namely, that the underlying strategy is not only coherent but is accepted as truthful and useful by employees, customers, and other key stakeholders.[28] A clear vision of what the organization wants to achieve, coupled with an unambiguous understanding of its mission, helps managers make coherent strategic decisions.

STAKEHOLDERS AND STAKEHOLDER ANALYSIS

stakeholder Individual or group with an interest in an organization's ability to deliver intended results and maintain the viability of its products and services

Stakeholders are individuals or groups who have an interest in an organization's ability to deliver intended results and maintain the viability of its products and services. We've already stressed the importance of stakeholders to a firm's vision and mission. We've also explained that firms are usually accountable to a broad range of stakeholders, including shareholders, who can make it either more difficult or easier to execute a strategy. This is the main reason why strategy formulators must consider stakeholders' interests, needs, and preferences. Considering these factors in the development of a firm's vision and mission is a good place to start, but first, of course, you must identify critical stakeholders, get a handle on their short- and long-term interests, calculate their potential influence on your strategy, and take into consideration how the firm's strategy might impact stakeholders (beneficially or adversely).

As we've already seen, for instance, one key stakeholder group is composed of the CEO and the members of the top-management team. This group is important for at least three reasons:

1. Its influence as either originator or steward of the organization's vision and mission

2. Its responsibility for formulating a strategy that realizes the vision and mission

3. Its ultimate role in strategy implementation (a role that we'll discuss in more detail in Chapter 11)

Financial Performance Metrics	Nonfinancial Performance Metrics
▸ Return on sales	▸ Customer retention
▸ Return on assets	▸ Customer satisfaction
▸ Return on equity	▸ Customer complaints
▸ Sales per employee	▸ Employee turnover
▸ Sales growth	▸ Product returns
▸ Inventory turn	▸ Product quality
▸ Accounts receivable turn	▸ Patents
▸ Debt ratio	▸ New products released
▸ Current ratio	▸ Product development speed
▸ Cost reduction	▸ Reputation
	▸ Web traffic

Exhibit 2.8 Some Financial and Nonfinancial Performance Metrics

Typically, stakeholder evaluation of both quantitative and qualitative performance outcomes will determine whether or not strategic leadership is effective. We summarize some relevant performance outcomes in Exhibit 2.8. Different stakeholders may place more emphasis on some outcomes than other stakeholders who have other priorities.

Stakeholders and Strategy

Managers perform stakeholder analysis in order to gain a better understanding of the range and variety of groups and individuals who not only have a vested interest in the formulation and implementation of a firm's strategy but who also have some influence on firm performance. Strategists thus develop vision and mission statements not only to clarify the organization's larger purpose but to meet or exceed the needs of its key stakeholders.

Stakeholder analysis may also enable managers to identify other parties that might derail otherwise well-formulated strategies, such as local, state, national, or foreign governmental bodies. Finally, stakeholder analysis enables organizations to better formulate, implement, and monitor their strategies, and, as we'll see in Chapter 11, this is why stakeholder analysis is a critical factor in the ultimate implementation of a strategy.

Identifying Stakeholders

The first step in stakeholder analysis is identifying major stakeholder groups. As you can imagine, the groups of stakeholders who will be affected either directly or indirectly by or have an effect on a firm's strategy and its execution can run the gamut from employees to customers to competitors to governments.

Let's pause for a moment to consider the important constituencies charted on our stakeholder map. Before we start, however, we need to remind ourselves that stakeholders can be individuals or groups—communities, social or political organizations, and so forth. In addition, we can break groups down demographically, geographically, by level and branch of government, or according to other relevant criteria. In so doing, we're more likely to identify important groups that we might otherwise overlook.

With these facts in mind, you can see that, externally, a map of stakeholders will include such diverse groups as governmental bodies, community-based organizations, social and political action groups, trade unions and guilds, and even journalists. National and regional governments and international regulatory bodies will probably be key stakeholders for global firms or those whose strategy calls for greater international presence. Internally, key stakeholders include shareholders, business units, employees, and managers.

Steps in Identifying Stakeholders Identifying all of a firm's stakeholders can be a daunting task. In fact, as we will note again shortly, a list of stakeholders that is too long actually may reduce the effectiveness of this important tool by overwhelming decision makers with too much information. To simplify the process, we suggest that you start by identifying groups that fall into one of four categories: *organizational, capital market, product market,* and *social.* Let's take a closer look at this step.

Step 1: Determining Influences on Strategy Formulation   One way to analyze the importance and roles of the individuals who comprise a stakeholder group is to identify the people and teams who should be consulted as strategy is developed or who will play some part in its eventual implementation. These are *organizational stakeholders,* and they include both high-level managers and frontline workers. *Capital-market stakeholders* are groups that affect the availability or cost of capital—shareholders, venture capitalists, banks, and other financial intermediaries. *Product-market stakeholders* include parties with whom the firm shares its industry, including suppliers and customers. *Social stakeholders* consist broadly of external groups and organizations that may be affected by or exercise influence over firm strategy and performance, such as unions, governments, and activists groups. The next two steps are to determine how various stakeholders are impacted by the firm's strategic decisions and the degree of power that various stakeholders wield over the firm's ability to choose a course of action.

Step 2: Determining the Effects of Strategic Decisions on the Stakeholder   Step 2 in stakeholder analysis is to determine the nature of the effect of the firm's strategic decisions on the list of relevant stakeholders. Not all stakeholders are impacted equally by strategic decisions. Some effects may be rather mild, and any positive or negative effects may be secondary and of minimal impact. At the other end of the spectrum, some stakeholders bear the brunt of firm decisions, good or bad.

In performing step 1, companies often develop overly broad and unwieldy lists of stakeholders. At this stage, it's critical to determine the stakeholders who are most important based on how the firm's strategy impacts the stakeholders. You must determine which of the groups still on your list have direct or indirect material claims on firm performance or which are potentially adversely impacted. For instance, it is easy to see how shareholders are affected by firm strategies—their wealth either increases or decreases in correspondence with firm actions. Other parties have economic interests in the firm as well, such as parties the firm interacts with in the marketplace, such as suppliers and customers. The effects on other parties may be much more indirect. For instance, governments have an economic interest in firms doing well—they collect tax revenue from them. However, in cities that are well diversified with many employers, a single firm has minimal economic impact on what the government collects. Alternatively, in other areas individual firms represent a significant contribution to local employment and tax revenue. In those situations, the impact of firm actions on the government would be much greater.

Step 3: Determining Stakeholders' Power and Influence over Decisions   The third step of a stakeholder analysis is to determine the degree to which a stakeholder group can exercise power and influence over the decisions the firm makes. Does the group have direct control over what is decided, veto power over decisions, nuisance influence, or no influence? Recognize that although the degree to which stakeholders are affected by firm decisions (i.e., step 2) is sometimes highly correlated with their power and influence over the decision, this is often not the case. For instance, in some companies frontline employees may be directly affected by firm decisions but have no say in what those decisions are. Power can take the form of formal voting power (boards of directors and owners), economic power (suppliers, financial institutions, and unions), or political power (dissident stockholders, political action groups, and governmental bodies). Sometimes the parties that exercise significant power over firm decisions don't register as having a significant stake in the firm (step 2). In recent years, for example, Wal-Mart has encountered significant resistance in some communities by well-organized groups who oppose the entry of the megaretailer. Wal-Mart executives now have to anticipate whether a vocal and politically powerful community group will oppose its new stores or aim to reduce their size, which decreases Wal-Mart's per-store profitability. Indeed, in many markets, such groups have been effective at blocking new stores, reducing their size, or changing building specifications.

Once you've determined who has a stake in the outcomes of the firm's decisions as well as who has power over these decisions, you'll have a basis on which to allocate prominence

		Power of the Stakeholder over Strategic Decisions			
		Unknown	Little/no power	Moderate degree of power	Significant power
Effect of Strategy on the Stakeholder	Unknown				
	Little/no effect				
	Moderate effect				
	Significant effect				

Exhibit 2.9 Mapping Stakeholder Influence and Importance

Source: Adapted from R. E. Freeman, Strategic Management: A Stakeholder Approach (Boston, MA: Pitman, 1984).

in the strategy-formulation and strategy-implementation processes. The framework in Exhibit 2.9 will also help you categorize stakeholders according to their influence in determining strategy versus their importance to strategy execution. For one thing, this distinction may help you identify major omissions in strategy formulation and implementation.

Having identified stakeholder groups and differentiated them by how they are affected by firm decisions and the power they have to influence decisions, you'll want to ask yourself some additional questions:

- Have I identified any vulnerable points in either the strategy or its potential implementation?
- Which groups are mobilized and active in promoting their interests?
- Have I identified supporters and opponents of the strategy?
- Which groups will benefit from successful execution of the strategy and which may be adversely affected?
- Where are various groups located? Who belongs to them? Who represents them?

Although the stakeholder-analysis framework summarized in Exhibit 2.9 is a good starting point, you'll find that many of the strategic-analysis tools that we introduce in succeeding chapters will also help you determine which stakeholders may be most critical to the success of your chosen strategy (and why). Ultimately, because vision and mission are necessarily long-term in orientation, identifying important stakeholder groups will help you to understand which constituencies stand to gain or lose the most if they're realized. The effective application of stakeholder analysis for a newly appointed manager is described in the box entitled "How Would You Do That? 2.2". From this example, you can see why stakeholder analysis should be an important input into both strategy formulation and implementation and how the roles of certain stakeholders create important interdependencies between formulation and implementation.

ETHICS, BIASES, AND STRATEGIC DECISION MAKING

Because the stakes are so high when executives make strategic decisions, they must do everything they can to make sure that those decisions are sound. You should thus weigh two additional factors before committing yourself to a major strategic endeavor: (1) whether the decision is ethical and (2) whether any potential biases have clouded your strategic decision-making process.

Driving Stakeholder Analysis at Tritec Motors

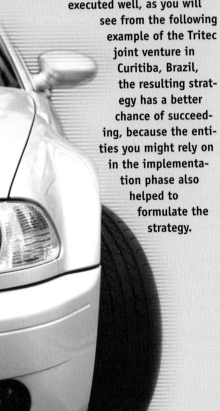

Two of the challenges of performing stakeholder analysis are determining how stakeholders are affected by a firm's decisions and how much influence they have over the implementation of the decisions that are made. Not all stakeholders are affected in the same way, and not all stakeholders have the same level of influence in determining what a firm does. When stakeholder analysis is executed well, as you will see from the following example of the Tritec joint venture in Curitiba, Brazil, the resulting strategy has a better chance of succeeding, because the entities you might rely on in the implementation phase also helped to formulate the strategy.

THE STALLED MOTOR MAKER

Formed in 2001, the Tritec joint venture between Daimler-Chrysler and BMW represented a $400-million state-of-the-art engine manufacturing facility in Curitiba, Brazil. From the start, however, production problems with the new motors were wreaking havoc with BMW's newly minted line of wildly successful Mini Coopers. On the Chrysler side, Daimler's acquisition of the U.S. firm resulted in the triage of the main line of vehicles that would receive engines from the Curitiba plant. In sum, the Curitiba plant was producing poor-quality engines for BMW, and Daimler was paying for half of a factory that it was not even using.

In stepped Bob Harbin, a 25-year employee of Chrysler. Bob was given 90 days to come up with a plan to fix Tritec's problems. This was a make-or-break assignment for Harbin. Fortunately, Harbin knew how to apply stakeholder analysis, and he knew that the key players he involved in designing the turnaround strategy would likely be instrumental in executing it as well. In some cases, even if they did not have a role in implementation, certain stakeholders, such as the Brazilian government, could actually hurt Tritec's turnaround chances.

THE DISCOVERY PROCESS

Harbin spent the first five days of his assignment meeting with top executives at Daimler and BMW, both to gain an understanding of their needs and expectations and to determine how

much discretion they would afford him if drastic changes were needed. After all, the corporate partners were essentially Tritec's financial backers and its only customers. Next, he spent two weeks in Curitiba meeting with everyone from the shop-floor employees to his future management team. He also spent time with key local parts suppliers as well as members of the newly installed Brazilian government. The government was particularly important because of the tax incentives and export credits that it had put into place to entice Tritec to Brazil; however, the change in government meant that those credits were in danger of being annulled. Throughout this discovery process, Harbin reiterated a common vision: "If we can't produce quality engines and get them to BMW on time, then the plant will likely be closed. No job, no tax revenues, no engines. Period." Not only did this quickly gain each stakeholder's attention, it also fostered cooperation and a sense of urgency among all the key players.

SENDING MESSAGES AND IMPLEMENTING A PLAN

After the first 30 days, Harbin assembled his leadership team based on impressions gained during his early interviews. Most of his team were Brazilians, which sent a strong message of confidence to the Brazilian workforce as well as to the Brazilian government. Together, Harbin and his team put together a rescue plan for the engine-manufacturing » process; he then took this plan back to Germany for endorsement by both BMW and Daimler. With the key pieces of the plan in place and the most important stakeholders squarely behind the plan—the alliance partners, the Brazilian government, Tritec's employees, and the new Tritec management team—Harbin began the steady process of turning around Tritec.

Although there were some minor setbacks along the way, within one year the factory was a world benchmark plant in many areas for both Daimler and BMW. By 2005, Tritec's production quality and efficiency were so high that even Toyota executives considered it one of the world's best-run auto-engine plants.

PLOTTING ROLES

Although every firm has multiple stakeholders, in this particular case the major stakeholders can be identified as BMW, Daimler-Chrysler, local employees, suppliers, the Brazilian government, and the leadership team. What roles did these stakeholders play in the tough decisions faced by Harbin? Let's take each stakeholder individually and plot them on the stakeholder-analysis grid (see Exhibit 2.A).

What role does BMW play in this situation? BMW is an owner/investor in the Tritec joint venture; thus on the power dimension BMW would be plotted in the far-right column, because it has voting and veto rights over all major decisions. However, BMW plays another role as well; it is the customer buying

| | | **Power of the Stakeholder over Strategic Decisions** | | | |
		Unknown	Little/no power	Moderate degree of power	Significant power
Effect of Strategy on the Stakeholder	Unknown				
	Little/no effect		Brazilian government		
	Moderate effect			BMW suppliers	Leadership team
	Significant effect		Employees		BMW Daimler-Chrysler

Exhibit 2.A   Stakeholder-Analysis Grid

the engines made in this factory. Thus, BMW simultaneously has an economic interest apart from its ownership stake. Consequently, BMW is located in two places on the stakeholder analysis grid.

Daimler's position is a bit more straightforward; it is an equity investor in the plant—thus it has an equity interest—and it has voting rights over all major decisions.

What position do the suppliers have? In terms of interests, they have a nonownership economic interest in the health of the plant. If the plant were to close, they would lose a major buyer. What influence/power do they have over decisions? They do not have major decisional power, but they do wield economic power.

What about employees? Employees do not directly influence factory decisions, but they do have an economic, nonequity stake in the factory. What about the Brazilian government? The government clearly has a stake in ensuring that local businesses are prosperous. However, that stake is not as direct or significant as an equity stake or employees' or suppliers' economic interest.

What does this analysis suggest? It suggests that if BMW does not get on board, all bets are off. Moreover, although the government is a critical stakeholder, at this stage of the game it is not as critical as making sure suppliers, employees, and management implement a plan that keeps BMW and Daimler-Chrysler satisfied.

It should be obvious by now that our conception of strategy is that it is a means to accomplish organizational goals. The fact that we see numerous examples in the media of corporate scandals suggests the unfortunate observation that some people justify any means to accomplish a desired goal. Although it would be unfair to suggest that most corporations engage in deliberate acts of malfeasance to accomplish their goals, and that all executives are crooks, it would likewise be unwise to ignore such potential problems and the safeguards that can help firms avoid unethical behavior. Although there's no reason why a sound strategy has to have any hint of unethical motives or tactics, managers must take precautions to ensure that their firms don't figure in the next headline trumpeting the ethical bankruptcy of Corporate America.

In addition to ethical lapses, strategic decision making can be subject to a number of common decision-making biases. When executives fail to recognize and account for them, they may unwittingly pursue a course of action that they'd otherwise avoid. In this section, we'll review some of the ethics- and bias-related issues that may arise in the course of strategic decision making.

Ethics and Strategy

A quick survey of business history and recent business news will give you a good idea of the disastrous effects that questionable strategies can have on shareholders, clients, and even decision makers themselves. Enron is the most notorious recent example, but it's certainly not the only—nor even the most egregious—case. In early 2004, for example, Royal Dutch/Shell Group announced that executives had knowingly overstated oil and gas reserves by 4.5 million barrels, or 23 percent. In October of that year, Shell announced that it would have to "restate" its reserves by another million barrels. Investors were naturally unhappy at being misled about the firm's key assets, and its management ranks soon underwent a major shakeup.[29] Executives at other companies—notably Adelphia, a telecommunications provider, and Tyco, a diversified manufacturer and services provider—have been indicted (and some convicted) for diverting firm resources to private use. In other instances, misbehavior has taken the form of fraud; at the hospital chain HealthSouth, for example, no fewer than five onetime CFOs have been convicted in a $2.5-billion case of accounting fraud.[30]

In February 2004, former Enron CEO Jeffrey Skilling (handcuffed) appeared in federal court in Houston, Texas, where he was charged with 35 counts of conspiracy, securities fraud, wire fraud, and insider trading. According to the government, Skilling presided over accounting schemes to inflate the energy-trading company's earnings, leading to its collapse (and the loss of thousands of jobs) in 2001. Some say Enron's flawed incentive system was to blame. Employees were lavishly rewarded for making the company look good, whether their actions were legal or not.

Why Organizations Are Vulnerable to Ethics Violations In some of these cases, a few key executives were responsible for the violations of legal and ethical standards. In others, the misdeeds required a larger cast of characters. So why shouldn't organizations just be careful to hire principled people? For one thing, companies are often vulnerable because of organization-level conditions. In this section, we'll review two of these conditions—*authority structures* and *incentive systems*—and show how avoiding certain pitfalls can reduce a firm's risk.

Authority Structures Whereas some organizational characteristics foster potential opportunities for exploiting the system, others discourage potential whistle-blowers from alerting the proper authorities.[31] For example, because responsibility is distributed throughout an organization and tasks are specialized, there's a tendency for people to assume that someone else will blow the whistle on suspicious activity. The phenomenon, of course, can also be observed in society at large, as in cases in which bystanders will ignore an accident or criminal activity on the assumption that someone else will intervene.

The authority structure of modern organizations also inhibits lower-level employees from disclosing questionable practices. People who are relatively obedient tend to follow the directions of legitimate authorities even when they know that what they're doing is dubious.[32] And, of course, whistle-blowing is not an attractive option when those who are engaged in the questionable behavior occupy positions of authority.

Incentive Systems The larger the potential reward, the more some people are willing to compromise their standards. Research shows, for instance, that business-unit managers are more likely to defer income to subsequent accounting periods when earnings targets in their bonus plans won't be met or when they've already reached maximum payouts.[33]

More recently, some analysts have questioned whether stock-option pay induces executives to make decisions designed to improve near-term stock prices rather than to enhance the firm's long-term competitive position. Because of the potential effect that financial incentives can have on managerial behavior, firms must take stronger measures to ensure that they're not "rewarding A, while hoping for B."[34]

The Role of Corporate Governance We'll discuss *corporate governance*—the roles of owners, directors, and managers in making corporate decisions—in more detail in Chapter 13. Here, we'll mention only that good corporate governance can reduce the risk of unethical and illegal activities. Because many unethical deeds are the work of individuals acting alone, quality governance can't guarantee ethical behavior. However, *poor* corporate governance provides a breeding ground for *un*ethical behavior. More and more firms are thus using governance mechanisms to discourage undesirable activities.

Threats to Rational Strategic Decision Making

When managers aren't fully aware of the biases influencing their judgment and strategic decision making, the quality of strategic decision making is bound to suffer. In this section, we'll sort potential biases into three sets of theories that we may hold about the conditions under which we make decisions: *theories about ourselves, theories about other people,* and *theories about our world.*[35]

Theories About Ourselves It shouldn't come as any surprise to hear that your self-perceptions influence your judgment and decisions. For instance, because strategic decision making is characterized by uncertainty and ambiguity, you'd expect that most senior executives are confident in their ability to make judgments under such conditions.

Some Common Illusions When self-confidence, however, borders on the belief in one's own superiority, rational decision making may be impaired. Confidence, for example, is sometimes associated with an **illusion of favorability**, under which people tend to give themselves more credit for their successes and take less responsibility for their failures. A

illusion of favorability Decision-making bias under which people tend to give themselves more credit for their successes and take less responsibility for their failures

illusion of optimism Decision-making bias that leads people to underestimate the prospect of negative future events while overestimating the prospect of positive outcomes

illusion of control Decision-making bias under which people believe that they're in greater control of a situation than rational analysis would support

escalation of commitment Decision-making bias under which people are willing to commit additional resources to a failing course of action

self-serving fairness bias Decision-making bias under which people believe that they're fair and want to act in ways that are perceived as fair and just

overconfidence bias Decision-making bias under which people tend to place erroneously high levels of confidence in their own knowledge or abilities

related bias, **illusion of optimism**, leads people to underestimate the prospect of negative future events while overestimating the prospect of positive outcomes.

Potentially compounding these biases is the **illusion of control**—a person's belief that he or she is in greater control of a situation than rational analysis would support. Research, for example, shows that when people are allowed to touch a playing card before it's been reshuffled into the deck, they're more likely to believe that they can find it again on a random draw than if they hadn't touched it. In reality, of course, their odds are the same under both circumstances.

Escalation of Commitment   These three illusions also contribute to a decision-making bias called **escalation of commitment**—the willingness to commit additional resources to a failing course of action. Obviously, this particular bias might well influence an executive's decision to change a strategy, to pursue an acquisition even though the bidding has reached astronomical levels, or to continue or discontinue a particular project related to current strategy.

Similarly, research shows that a manager who initiates a project is less likely to perceive that it's failing, more likely to remain committed to it, and more likely to continue funding it than the manager who comes on board after the project is underway. People also tend toward increased commitment to innovative products than to less innovative products. Such findings suggest that simply giving managers better information won't necessarily lead to better decisions. They also indicate that escalation of commitment is a more serious problem during new-product development than after a product has been rolled out.[36] In short, escalation of commitment seems to be a particularly dangerous decision-making bias, especially when we consider the ambiguity and uncertainty inherently involved in most strategic decisions.

Self-Serving Fairness Bias   According to some researchers, executives believe that they are fair people and want to act in ways that are perceived as fair and just. Like most people, however, they usually do a better job of tracking their own contributions to a project and thus tend to take more credit for good outcomes than they give. As a result of this tendency, which is called a **self-serving fairness bias**, executives may rationalize lavish pay and perks on the grounds that they earned them because they contributed more than others.

Overconfidence Bias   Finally, there's the pitfall of the **overconfidence bias**—people's tendency to place erroneously high levels of confidence in their own knowledge or abilities. This bias is compounded by the fact that people generally seek confirmatory evidence of their beliefs while discounting contradictory evidence. The combination of self-serving and overconfidence biases means that executives are quite likely to hold themselves and their organizations in high esteem. Research shows that executives who hold themselves in particularly high esteem are most likely to overpay seriously for acquisitions.[37]

The Consequences of Bias   So, what are the potential ethical consequences of strategic decision-making biases? The worst-case upshot of confidence-related biases is that some executives believe that they aren't subject to the same rules as everyone else. Top managers may delude themselves that they can get away with unethical or even felonious behavior because they believe either that they won't be caught or that, if they are, their status will protect them from the consequences.

If they succumb to self-serving fairness bias, the parties to an alliance or merger negotiation may proceed according to highly differing perspectives on what's fair and appropriate. Conceivably, such misperception can sabotage a deal that's good for the stakeholders whose assets have been entrusted to a company's negotiators. Overconfidence, then, can lead both to faulty judgments (and even ethical errors) based on misperception and to faulty judgments of fact.

Theories About Other People   In many ways, our theories about other people reflect our theories about ourselves:

- We give ourselves more credit than we deserve and others less.
- We expect more credit and reward and expect others to accept less.

- We view positive future outcomes as more likely than negative outcomes but believe that the outcomes achieved by others are more likely to fail.
- We think that we're better than others at judging uncertain futures and so give more credence to our plans than to those of others.
- We believe that although we're acting on the best knowledge of present and future conditions, others are acting on imperfect knowledge.

The combination of biases about ourselves and biases about others can be tied to such far-reaching negative outcomes as industry overexpansion, which often occurs because each industry incumbent assumes that the others won't take competitive action when in fact every firm almost certainly will. As a result, because each player acts on the assumption that it knows something that the others don't, an industry that can support only 10 production facilities becomes glutted with 20.[38]

Ethnocentrism and Stereotyping   In addition to these obvious biases, our theories about other people also encompass both *ethnocentrism* and *stereotyping*. **Ethnocentrism** is a belief in the superiority of one's own ethnic group, but it can be interpreted more broadly as the conviction that one's own national, group, or cultural characteristics are "normal" and ordinary. That belief, of course, renders everyone else foreign, strange, and perhaps dangerous.

In fact, we're all ethnocentric to some degree. Your ethnocentrism accounts for your opinion of foreigners' speech patterns and favored cuisines. Being ethnocentric, then, doesn't necessarily mean that you're hostile toward other groups, but it does mean that you probably regard your group as superior. Ethnocentrism is dangerous because it's automatic and often subtle.

In part, the illusion of superiority stems from the belief that one's own group has multiple dimensions, whereas other groups can be characterized according to one relatively homogeneous characteristic—say, nationality, gender, or ethnicity. When you've reached this stage, you're engaged in **stereotyping**—relying on a conventional or formulaic conception of another group based on some common characteristic. The fallacy of ethnocentrism, then, is the belief in your own group's superiority; the fallacy of stereotyping lies in ascribing limiting characteristics to an entire set of people.

> **ethnocentrism** Belief in the superiority of one's own ethnic group or, more broadly, the conviction that one's own national, group, or cultural characteristics are "normal"

> **stereotyping** Relying on a conventional or formulaic conception of another group based on some common characteristic

The Consequences of Ethnocentrism and Stereotyping   In terms of strategic and ethical decision making, ethnocentrism and stereotyping can have disastrous results. U.S. automakers, for example, ignored the Japanese competitive threat for decades because of a twofold mistaken belief: (1) that American car manufacturers were the best in the world and (2) that Japanese automakers could never produce high-quality vehicles. Thus ethnocentrism and stereotypes combined to blind U.S. (and European) carmakers to the emergence of extremely formidable rivals.

Stereotyping puts executives at risk of making unethical, unfair, and sometimes illegal decisions because it limits their evaluations of other people to group affiliation while ignoring individual qualities. Ethnocentrism exposes businesspeople to rationally and ethically unsound decisions because it exaggerates the differences between us and them.

Theories About the World   Today's top executives must be able to understand global events—or at least know where to get the information they need. Otherwise, it's too easy to misjudge the risks and consequences of an action with international ramifications. The trick, of course, is knowing what you don't know. Granted, it's often impossible to foresee all the possible consequences of a strategic choice, but a good starting point is the premise that "you can never do just one thing."[39] All actions, in other words, have multiple consequences, some intended, some unintended.

For example, the management of Levi Straus & Co. (LS&CO.) has a firm commitment to its corporate values. LS&CO. quickly stepped in to enforce a policy of not using contractors who employ child labor. Upon finding that a subcontractor in Bangladesh was employing children younger than 14, LS&CO. made the factory rectify the situation.

Levi's decision to demonstrate its commitment to ethical practices and global social responsibility by discouraging child labor had an unintended consequence: Because factory jobs were no longer available, poor families that depended on their daughters' incomes resorted to pushing them into prostitution. Where did Levi Straus go wrong? Arguably, a few fallacious theories about the world resulted in a faulty perception of certain stakeholders: Levi's looked initially only at the situation of the girls and inadvertently ignored the needs of their families. Once discovering the complication, LS&CO. decided to pay for the underage children to go to school and guarantee jobs in the factory once they were of age.

Similarly, imperfect theories about the world may lead executives to discount low-probability events or to underestimate the probability of certain activities becoming public. The effects of such poor judgment can snowball into strategic and ethical blunders. In the early 1970s, for example, internal safety tests on the Ford Pinto revealed that under rare rear-impact conditions the gas tank could explode. The defect could be remedied with a $10 part, but Ford opted for a less costly response and, what's worse, covered up its own test results when the fatal rear-end crash turned out to be more common and more deadly than the company had figured.[40] The more recent example of how Ford proactively responded to tire problems from its chief supplier Bridgestone/Firestone, which caused some SUVs to roll when experiencing a flat, suggests that Ford may have learned its lesson.

Related to these imperfections in strategic decision making is the fact that we tend to discount the future and to place lower values on collective outcomes. In other words, we often focus on today's problems because we believe them to be more important than those that may be encountered down the road. Similarly, because we're prone to underestimate the consequences of our actions on large groups, we tend to ignore collective outcomes. Ford's behavior in the Pinto case, for example, contributed to public perception that the auto industry couldn't, or wouldn't, police itself on the issue of safety—a reaction that, in turn, led to an unprecedented raft of auto-safety regulations.

Risk and Cause-and-Effect Assessment   As we've already suggested, uncertainty and risk are inescapable facets of executive life. A far-reaching decision may involve risks to jobs, worker or public safety, the environment, or corporate survival. Interestingly, research shows that we tend to perceive risks entailing potential losses differently than risks entailing potential gains: We tend to be *risk-seeking* when the outcome of an action is perceived as a gain but *risk-averse* when it's perceived as a loss—even when rational analysis would show that both outcomes are equally probable.[41]

What's more, even when we can rationally evaluate the probability of risks, we tend to overestimate our ability to control them by assessing cause-and-effect relationships. Many people know, for instance, that daily fluctuations in the stock market are random, but they still lend credence to theories about daily stock-price movements espoused by financial analysts. Moreover, we tend to overestimate the role of people in "causing" events. Why? Primarily because we find it easy to imagine people doing something different to prevent or correct an undesirable event. This tendency is unfortunate for CEOs and members of their executive teams because boards often replace them in order to demonstrate that they're dealing with the cause of failed strategies and recurring losses.

So, what do these decision-making biases mean for strategic and ethical decision making? The Ford Pinto example shows how both strategic and ethical decision making can be impaired by faulty theories about actions and events and the ways in which people respond to them. In many ways, it also shows how one set of risk perceptions could have led to different outcomes. Ford's behavior, for instance, may have been different if executives had framed the question facing them in some other way, such as "Would you pay $10 a Pinto to avoid passenger death and additional regulatory costs?"

A much broader issue, at least in terms of ethics, relates to our tendency to discount the future. Some analysts point to short-term thinking in order to explain decaying urban infrastructure, national budget deficits, the collapse of the world's lake and ocean fisheries, global warming, and environmental destruction.[42]

SUMMARY

1. Explain how strategic leadership is essential to strategy formulation and implementation. **Strategic leadership** is concerned with the management of an overall enterprise and the ways in which top executives influence key organizational outcomes, such as performance, competitive superiority, innovation, strategic change, and survival. Leaders typically play three critical roles—interpersonal, informational, and decisional—all of which support the firm's vision and mission and the implementation of its strategy. The **Level 5 Hierarchy** is a model of leadership skills that calls for a wide range of abilities, some of which are hierarchical in nature. Leaders can be distinguished by personality and demographic differences, and strategic leadership can be exercised either by individuals or groups.

2. Understand the relationships among vision, mission, values, and strategy. An organizational **vision** is a simple forward-looking statement or understanding of what the firm will be in the future. A **mission** is a declaration of what a firm is and what it stands for—its fundamental values and purpose. Together, mission and vision statements express the identity and describe the work of a firm. They also state the firm's direction. Vision and mission statements support strategy, which provides a coherent plan for realizing the firm's vision and mission.

3. Understand the roles of vision and mission in determining strategic purpose and strategic coherence. Guidance in making decisions is important because there's only so much complexity in a given problem with which any individual or group can reasonably cope. Vision and mission statements are thus useful because they inform all employees of the firm's **strategic purpose**—a simplified, widely shared model of the organization and its future, including anticipated changes in its environment. The challenge posed by a defined strategic purpose is closing the gap between aspirations on the one hand and current capabilities and market positions on the other. **Strategic coherence** refers to the symmetrical coalignment of the five elements of the firm's strategy, the congruence of functional-area policies with these elements, and the overarching fit of various businesses under the corporate umbrella.

4. Identify a firm's stakeholders and explain why such identification is critical to effective strategy formulation and implementation. Stakeholder analysis improves the understanding of the range and variety of parties who have a vested interest in the formulation and implementation of a firm's strategy or some influence on firm performance. The first step in stakeholder analysis is identifying stakeholder groups that are affected by or that may affect the firm's strategy. The second step calls for identifying those stakeholders who are important for strategy formulation and implementation, those for whom the strategy will be important, and those who are influential in determining the strategy. The third step involves categorizing stakeholders according to their influence in determining strategy versus their importance in its execution. Stakeholder analysis also helps expose any major omissions in strategy formulation and implementation.

5. Explain how ethics and biases may affect strategic decision making. Strategic leadership and strategic decision making have much in common. Indeed, strategic leadership can be characterized by strategic decision making and the actions in which it results. The effectiveness of strategic decision making is threatened when managers act unethically or without being fully aware of the biases influencing their judgment. Ethical lapses may reflect an individual shortcoming, but they can often be traced to a lack of clear organizational mechanisms for making individuals accountable for their actions. Decision-making biases, or threats to rational decision making in general, result from theories about oneself, theories about other people, and theories about one's world. They may impair both rational and ethical decision making and even an organization's ability to realize its vision and mission.

KEY TERMS

escalation of commitment, 54
ethnocentrism, 55
goals and objectives, 43
illusion of control, 54
illusion of favorability, 53

illusion of optimism, 54
Level 5 Hierarchy, 32
mission, 39
overconfidence bias, 54
self-serving fairness bias, 54

stakeholder, 46
stereotyping, 55
strategic coherence, 45
strategic leadership, 29
strategic purpose, 44

succession planning, 38
superordinate goal, 43
vision, 39

REVIEW QUESTIONS

1. Why is strategic leadership important for effective strategy formulation and implementation?

2. How do the characteristics of strategic leadership differ between individuals and teams?

3. What is a vision? A mission?

4. How are vision and mission related to strategy? What roles does strategic leadership play in realizing vision and mission?

5. How does strategy differ from vision and mission?

6. What is strategic purpose?

7. What is strategic coherence?

8. Who are a firm's stakeholders? Why are they important?

9. What tools can you use to identify the impact of various stakeholders on the firm and the impact of the firm on various stakeholders?

10. Why are ethics and biases relevant to strategic decision making and strategic leadership?

How Would you Do That?

1. Building on the CEO-successor selection process described in the box entitled "How Would You Do That? 2.1", devise a succession plan for the dean of your business school. Be sure to include the following in your succession-planning process: (a) Translate your school's strategy into actual operating needs and key activities; (b) identify the skills needed for these operating needs and activities; (c) outline an internal and external candidate search process; and (d) develop a list of goals and milestones and a compensation structure that ties actions to the strategic drivers of success at your school.

2. Based on the framework applied to Tritec Motors in the box entitled "How Would You Do That? 2.2", use the opening vignette on Anne Mulcahy at Xerox to map out the key stakeholders in her turnaround effort. Which stakeholders would you expect to be most resistant? Most supportive? Create a 90-day action plan for Mulcahy, following the example laid out by Bob Harbin in "How Would You Do That? 2.2".

GROUP ACTIVITIES

1. (a) Craft a vision and mission statement for your business school and then for your college or university as a whole. How are these statements related? How are they similar? How do they differ? How are they similar or different from those that you might draw up for a for-profit organization? (b) Using the vision and mission you crafted, develop a list of key stakeholders for your school and their relative power and stake in the school. Which of these stakeholder groups is accounted for in your vision and mission statement, and which ones are left out? Did you identify any stakeholder groups that could negatively affect your realization of this vision and mission?

2. What roles should strategic leadership play in the realization of the vision and mission statements that you articulated in the previous question? Whom have you identified as strategic leaders?

ENDNOTES

1. W. M. Bulkeley and J. S. Lublin, "Xerox Appoints Insider Mulcahy to Execute Turnaround as CEO," *Wall Street Journal* (Eastern edition), July 27, 2001, A3; P. Moore, "Anne Mulcahy: She's Here to Fix Xerox," *Business Week,* August 6, 2001, 47; A. Klein, "Xerox to Expand Color-Printing Business," *Wall Street Journal* (Eastern edition), September 23, 1999, B12; J. Bandler, "Xerox Profit Falls, but CEO Sees a 'Breakthrough,'" *Wall Street Journal* (Eastern edition), July 29, 2003, A3; J. Bandler, "Xerox Corp.: CEO Sees Improving Finances, Broadening Product Offering," *Wall Street Journal* (Eastern edition), May 16, 2003, B6; O. Kharif, "Anne Mulcahy Has Xerox by the Horns," *Business Week Online,* May 29, 2003 (accessed June 21, 2005), at www.businessweek.com/technology/content/may2003/tc20030529_1642_tc111.htm.

2. M. Porter, J. Lorsch, and N. Nohria, "Seven Surprises for New CEOs," *Harvard Business Review* 82:10 (2004), 62–72.

3. This discussion of the nature of CEO job responsibilities draws heavily from the seminal work of H. Mintzberg, *The Nature of Managerial Work* (New York: Harper and Row, 1973).

4. Mintzberg, *The Nature of Managerial Work,* 67.

5. Information in this paragraph is based on Porter, Lorsch, and Nohria, "Seven Surprises for New CEOs," 62–72.

6. Stanford Graduate School of Business Alumni Profiles (accessed July 12, 2005), at www.gsb.stanford.edu/news/profiles/deromedi.shtml.

7. J. Collins, *Good to Great: Why Some Companies Make the Leap . . . and Others Don't* (New York: HarperBusiness, 2001).

8. Collins, "Level 5 Leadership: The Triumph of Humility and Fierce Resolve," *Harvard Business Review* 79:1 (2001), 67–76.

9. Collins, "Level 5 Leadership," 73.

10. For a review of this material, see D. Whetten and K. Cameron, *Developing Management Skills,* 5th ed. (Upper Saddle River, NJ: Prentice Hall, 2002).

11. For a comprehensive review of this literature, see M. A. Carpenter, W. G. Sanders, and M. A. Geletkanycz, "The Upper Echelons Revisited: The Antecedents, Elements, and Consequences of TMT Composition," *Journal of Management* 30 (2004), 749–778.

12. M. Useem and J. Karabel, "Pathways to Corporate Management," *American Sociological Review* 51 (1986), 184–200.

13. S. L. Keck, "Top Management Team Structure: Differential Effects by Environmental Context," *Organization Science* 8 (1997), 143–156.

14. M. A. Carpenter, W. G. Sanders, and H. B. Gregersen, "International Experience at the Top Makes a Bottom-Line Difference," *Human Resource Management* 39:2/3 (2000), 277–285; Carpenter, Sanders, and Gregersen, "Bundling Human Capital with Organizational Context: The Impact of International Experience on Multinational Firm Performance and CEO Pay," *Academy of Management Journal* 44 (2001), 493–512.

15. C. Lucier, R. Schuyt, and J. Handa, "CEO Succession 2003: The Perils of 'Good' Governance" (accessed June 21, 2005), at www.boozallenhamilton.com.

16. S. Hamm, "Former CEOs Should Just Fade Away," *Business Week*, April 12, 2004 (Online Extra) (accessed July 12, 2005), at www.businessweek.com/magazine/content/04_15/b3878092_mz063.htm; J. Sonnenfeld, *The Hero's Farewell: What Happens when CEOs Retire* (New York: Oxford University Press, 1991).

17. P. Estess, "Twos Company," entrepreneur.com, May 1997 (accessed June 22, 2005), at www.entrepreneur.com/article/0,4621,227207,00.html.

18. C. Hymowitz and J. S. Lublin, "McDonald's CEO Tragedy Holds Lessons," *Wall Street Journal*, April 20, 2004, B1.

19. C. K. Bart and M. C. Baetz, "The Relationship Between Mission Statements and Firm Performance: An Exploratory Study," *Journal of Management Studies* 35 (1998), 823–853.

20. J. C. Collins and J. I. Porras, *Build to Last* (New York: Harper Business, 1997).

21. Bart and Baetz, "The Relationship Between Mission Statements and Firm Performance"; A. Campbell and S. Yeung, "Creating a Sense of Mission," *Long Range Planning* 24:4 (1991), 10–20; P. Drucker, *Management: Tasks, Responsibilities, and Practices* (New York: Harper and Row, 1974); R. D. Ireland and M. A. Hitt, "Mission Statements: Importance, Challenge and Recommendations for Development," *Business Horizons* 35:3 (1992), 34–42.

22. Collins and Porras, *Build to Last.*

23. D. Kirkpatrick, "Gerstner's New Vision for IBM," *Fortune*, November 15, 1993, 119–124.

24. J. Collins and J. Porras, "Building a Visionary Company," *California Management Review* 37 (1995), 80–100; W. Kim and R. Mauborgne, "Charting Your Company's Future," *Harvard Business Review* 80:6 (2002), 5–11.

25. Bart and Baetz, "The Relationship Between Mission Statements and Firm Performance."

26. "Company Background: The History and Overview of Dell" (accessed July 12, 2005), at www1.us.dell.com/content/topics/global.aspx/corp/background/en/index?c=us&l=en&s=corp.

27. About Panasonic: Vision (accessed January 11, 2005) at panasonic.co.jp/global/about/vision/index.html.

28. Kim and Mauborgne, "Charting Your Company's Future."

29. M. Curtin, "THE SKEPTIC: Thorough Shell Revamp, But Where's the Oil?" *Dow Jones International News*, October 28, 2004.

30. B. Berkrot, "First HealthSouth Sentencing Set for Wednesday," Reuters, November 11, 2003.

31. This discussion draws heavily on R. Gandossy and J. Sonnenfeld, "I See Nothing, I Hear Nothing: Culture, Corruption, and Apathy," in Gandossy and Sonnenfeld (eds.), *Leadership and Governance from the Inside Out* (Hoboken, NJ: Wiley, 2004), 3–26.

32. S. Milgram, *Obedience to Authority* (New York: Harper, 1974).

33. P. M. Healy and J. M. Wahlen, "A Review of the Earnings Management Literature and Its Implications for Standard Setting," *Accounting Horizons* 13 (1999), 365–383.

34. S. Kerr, "On the Folly of Rewarding A, While Hoping for B," *Academy of Management Journal* 18 (1975), 769–783.

35. This material draws from behavioral decision theory. Excellent references are D. Kahneman, P. Slovic, and A. Tversky, *Judgment Under Uncertainty* (Cambridge: Cambridge University Press, 1982); M. Bazerman, *Judgment in Managerial Decision Making* (New York: John Wiley, 1994); J. Janis, *Groupthink* (Boston: Houghton-Mifflin, 1982).

36. J. Schmidt and R. Calantone, "Escalation of Commitment During New Product Development," *Journal of the Academy of Marketing Science* 30:2 (2002), 103–118.

37. M. Hayward and D. C. Hambrick, "Explaining the Premiums Paid for Large Acquisitions: Evidence of CEO Hubris," *Administrative Science Quarterly* 42 (1997), 103–127.

38. E. Zajac and M. Bazerman, "Blindspots in Industry and Competitor Analysis: Implications of Interfirm (Mis)perceptions," *Strategic Management Journal* 16 (1991), 37–57.

39. G. Hardin, *Filters Against Folly* (New York: Penguin Books, 1985).

40. R. Nader, *Unsafe at Any Speed* (New York: Grossman, 1965).

41. This material draws from behavioral decision theory. Excellent references are D. Kahneman, P. Slovic, and A. Tversky, *Judgment Under Uncertainty* (Cambridge: Cambridge University Press, 1982); M. Bazerman, *Judgment in Managerial Decision Making* (New York: John Wiley, 1994); J. Janis, *Groupthink* (Boston: Houghton-Mifflin, 1982).

42. D. M. Messick and A. Tenbrunsel, *Behavioral Research and Business Ethics* (New York: Sage, 1996).

3

Examining the Internal Environment: Resources, Capabilities, and Activities

After studying this chapter, you should be able to:

1. Explain the *internal context of strategy*.

2. Identify a firm's resources and capabilities and explain their role in firm performance.

3. Define *dynamic capabilities* and explain their role in both strategic change and firm performance.

4. Explain how value-chain activities are related to firm performance and competitive advantage.

5. Explain the role of managers with respect to resources, capabilities, and value-chain activities.

▶ 1968
Driven by the desire to make better products in a better way, engineers Bob Noyce and Gordon Moore found the Silicon Valley startup Intel. Intel develops its first product, the 3101, a 68-bit memory chip (shown) the following year.

▶ 1971
Empowered by Noyce and Moore, Intel employees press for and develop the world's first commercial microprocessor, the 4004 (shown). IBM agrees to use a subsequent version of the microprocessor in 1981— a major sales victory for Intel.

STRATEGY INSIDE INTEL

In 1968, three engineers— Robert Noyce, Gordon Moore, and Andy Grove— left secure jobs at Fairchild Semiconductor to create a new company in Mountain View, California, called Intel.[1] Their goal: to build a company that would develop technology for silicon-based semiconductor chips.

Processing Competitive Threats   Initially, Intel (the name is a contraction of "*int*egrated *el*ectronics") made read-only memory chips for computers and experienced early success in the industry. Before long, however, Asian competitors stepped up their competitive practices, using low-cost capital financing, large advantages in economies of scale, and aggressive pricing to dominate global market share. In addition, technological improvements in new generations of memory chips continued at lightning speed. These forces

▶ **1986**
Intel develops its next chip design, the 286, and licenses it to other semiconductor manufacturers. The revenues are used to expand Intel's manufacturing capabilities and to build larger "fabs," or fabricators.

▶ **2005**
The "Intel Inside" campaign, initially launched in 1991, continues to make Intel the best-known semiconductor manufacturer across the globe.

1995   2000

memory-chip market, not the microprocessor market, based on Intel's senior executives' views that the firm's historic success in memory chips could be carried into the future. Rather, the company's production managers started shifting manufacturing capacity from memory chips to microprocessors because the yields per wafer square inch were higher. They followed a rather simple managerial rule—allocate production capacity based on a "margin-per-wafer-start." Margins on memory wafers were declining and margins for microprocessor wafers were increasing. In light of this change, Intel production managers shifted production capacity toward microprocessors, and they did so rapidly, because Intel's incentive and accountability systems rewarded plant managers based on wafer yields. Moreover, the chairman and CEO of Intel had successfully nurtured a strong internal culture that encouraged open debate about strategic initiatives and discouraged the use of hierarchy or position over the power of knowledge to make key decisions. The confluence of these factors—Intel's experiment with microprocessors, IBM's selection of the Intel chip, the excessive price competition in the memory market, and Intel's organizational processes that enabled plant managers to make these changes without explicit approval from senior management—enabled Intel to change rapidly from a memory-chip company to a microprocessor company.

Taking Strategic License   An important benefit of the change to microprocessors was the evolution of Intel's capabilities beyond narrow technical design to the implementation of complex design architectures in logic products, which gave Intel a much larger market domain. As the standard setter and chief supplier for the world's largest PC maker, Intel became a formidable player in the microprocessor industry. IBM, however, was reluctant to allow a small company be the sole supplier of such a key technology. Consequently, Intel chose to license the technology to other companies to satisfy IBM's concern. It licensed its next chip design, the 286, to other semiconductor firms, such as Advanced Micro Devices (AMD). Licensing reinforced Intel's status as an industry technology architecture leader, and it also enabled the company to supplement profits from its own sales with the healthy fees paid by licensees.

With a patent on the microprocessor design that had become the industry standard, Intel controlled a valuable intellectual property. The licensing fees paid by other firms were substantial; nevertheless, Intel moved to ease its dependence on outside manufacturers by adopting a three-pronged approach to improving its competitive position:

■ The company used revenues from licensing agreements and profits from chip sales to fund the expansion of its manufacturing capacity and manufacturing-processing capabilities. Intel realized that if it could improve the manufacturing process, it would not only control the technology that semiconductor firms used to make processors, but it might also be able to generate cost savings. With a superior manufacturing process in hand, Intel then increased manufacturing capacity by building larger fabrication plants (called "fabs"), which also resulted in superior economies of scale.

■ At the same time that Intel was building both innovation and manufacturing capability for microprocessors, the PC industry was expanding and credible threats to IBM were emerging. Compaq decided to adopt the 486 chip design after IBM decided to delay adoption of the chip, and other small PC companies soon followed Compaq's lead. The new chip proved to be a success with consumers. Because Intel had been investing in additional capacity in its fabs, it was able to exploit these new dynamics in the PC industry. Intel started revoking licensing agreements from other semiconductor companies for future generations of the Intel microprocessor. This move allowed Intel to capture a larger market share and boosted profits because canceling licenses eliminated competitors and the number of PC makers was increasing dramatically.

■ Intel set out to brand its product in order to make it the microprocessor of choice among end users, even if similar products entered the market. PC manufacturers, of course, preferred to source their technology from multiple suppliers. Thus, Intel still faced the threat that AMD or some other upstart would begin to compete aggressively and weaken its market share. Intel responded by advertising its product to end users—the individual consumers who purchase PCs from computer makers. The campaign was so successful that consumers turned out to be willing to pay higher prices for PCs with "Intel Inside." ■

INTERNAL DRIVERS OF STRATEGY AND COMPETITIVE ADVANTAGE

In this chapter, we'll introduce theories and models that explain why some firms outperform their rivals and others lag behind. You have probably been introduced to a very simple tool in other classes (such as marketing) called *SWOT analysis*. Recall that SWOT is an acronym for *s*trengths, *w*eaknesses, *o*pportunities, and *t*hreats. This chapter deals primarily with firms' strengths and weaknesses, or the resource-based inputs into the strategy process. These are internal characteristics of firms. Firms within an industry generally have different strengths and weaknesses, and those differences often have a strong bearing on which firms win competitive interactions. We will introduce you to more rigorous models that help managers diagnose their strengths and weaknesses and prescribe future actions to exploit their strengths or remedy their weaknesses. Of course, a complete understanding of a firm's strengths and weaknesses requires an understanding of competitors. Chapter 4 will introduce the basic tools for analyzing competitors, thereby enabling you to evaluate firms relative to their competitors.

concept**link**

In Chapter 1, we explain that the field of strategic management focuses on explanations of **competitive advantage,** which we define as a firm's ability to create value in a way that its rivals can't.

This chapter focuses on firms' resources and capabilities, the choices managers make when configuring the activities they chose to perform internally (versus outsourcing), and the role of managers in allocating, reconfiguring, and exploiting firm resources and capabilities. All firms, of course, must consider the external context when formulating and implementing strategy, but focusing on the internal perspective reminds us that firms differ in terms of resources and capabilities. We'll examine several models and analytical tools that will help you analyze and formulate competitive strategies.

Our opening vignette has already given us some insight into the internal sources of competitive advantage. Although the microprocessor industry is extremely competitive, Intel has been able to maintain its competitive advantage over most of its rivals for an extended period of time. This fact suggests that Intel has access to internal resources and capabilities that other firms do not. Many firms in the industry, for example, are capable of making innovations in chip design. Intel, however, has always been able to get new products to market faster than its competitors and get them there in the volume necessary to achieve significant cost advantages. This advantage in speed to market results, in part, from Intel's ability to convince computer makers to use its products and from its ability to move new products into production in a timely manner.

However, as we also noted in the opening vignette, at one point Intel was forced to license its technology to other manufacturers because its chief customer demanded multiple sourcing options. Being forced to license the technology to other firms meant that Intel didn't have the immediate in-house capacity to manufacture chips fast enough and in large enough quantities to satisfy market demand. The firm addressed this problem by investing heavily to improve its manufacturing processes. The related judgment and willingness of management to undertake such a risk—new semiconductor plants cost over $1 billion to build and take several years to complete—may be considered another of Intel's internal strengths. This combination of speed to market and manufacturing-process capability means that Intel can charge significant price premiums during the first months following a new-product release. Competitors who get to market later must settle for lower profits because prices have fallen.

As our description of Intel's history, strategy, and performance suggests, the firm's advantage is due, in part, to its use of engineering expertise to create valuable technologies, operational efficiencies to make its new products proprietary standards in the industry, and marketing skills to exploit its ability to speed products to market. Not surprisingly, its competitive advantage translates into higher levels of performance.

Firms in many other industries have also managed to do what Intel has done—namely, to outperform major competitors for extended periods of time. As you can see in Exhibit 3.1, such firms can be found in industries ranging from microprocessors to retail grocers to automobile makers. Notice that the average profitability (return on sales and return on assets) for firms within these very different industries varies significantly across firms over long periods of time. Intel's average return on assets (ROA) and return on sales (ROS), which are measures of financial performance that gauge profits as a percentage of total sales and total assets, respectively, dwarf those of its nearest competitor, Texas Instruments. In the exhibit, note that these figures are higher than competitors' in each year, as well as on average across all 10 years. Whether we look at high-tech industries, such as semiconductors, traditional heavy industry, such as automobile manufacturing, or a retail business, such as grocery stores, within industries some firms perform much better than others over time. For instance, Publix, Kroger, and Whole Foods appear to dominate the grocery business.

One of the primary purposes of this chapter is to help you understand how such differences in profitability materialize and what firms can do to improve their performance relative to firms in their industry.

Models of Competitive Advantage

This chapter presents the two dominant models that help to explain how and why some firms perform better than others. These two models both suggest that differences in long-term-performance outcomes across firms within the same industry are derived largely from different levels of competitive advantage. However, the source of competitive advantage differs between these perspectives. The first explanation as to why some firms perform better than others attributes this success to fundamental differences in what firms own and what they can do. The most basic part of this model deals with the roles played by a firm's *resources* and *capabilities*. A more advanced version of this model is necessary to understand how these differences evolve over time. The second model for why firms differ within industries focuses not on resources, but on *what activities firms choose to engage in.* This activity perspective, treated toward the end of this chapter, relies heavily on the value chain and the advantages firms might gain by configuring value-chain activities in ways to add more value to their products or services than competitors. We'll explain how these two models help to determine which firms are able to develop a competitive advantage and potentially perform above industry averages and which ones suffer from liabilities and struggle to keep up.

Management

Finally, whether we trace a firm's competitive advantage to its resources and capabilities or to the organization of its value-chain activities, we must always consider the role played by its managers. Senior and mid-level managers make key decisions about how to acquire, allocate, and discard resources, and they're also in charge of organizing a firm's value-chain activities. This is why we include managers' strategic decision-making capabilities as a potentially valuable internal input into strategy. Exhibit 3.2, on page 66, provides an overview of how resources, capabilities, and managerial decision making are interdependent; all are necessary to understand how and why firms perform differently within similar industry environments. As we'll explain in more detail later, notice how the role of management is both to use the resources and capabilities to devise strategies and to make decisions about reconfiguring resources and capabilities. Indeed, managers play the unique role of being both resources and capabilities and making choices about the stewardship and deployment of other resources and capabilities (our opening vignette on Intel is a case in point here).

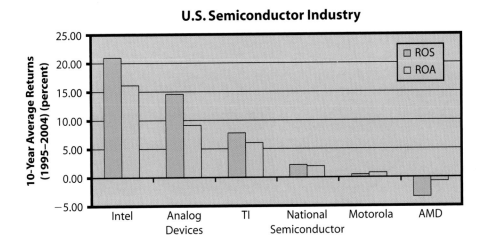

U.S. Semiconductor Industry

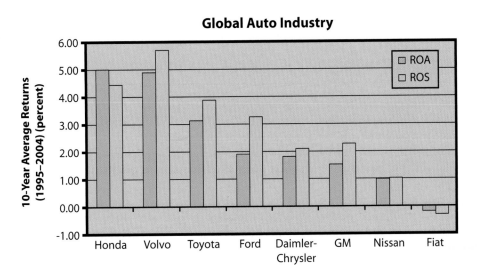

Global Auto Industry

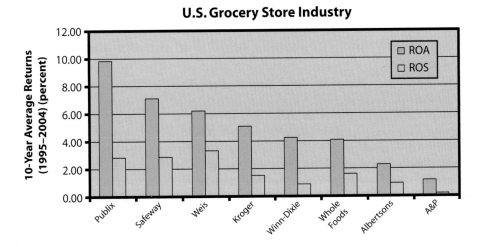

U.S. Grocery Store Industry

Exhibit 3.1 Comparative Performance in Selected Industries

Exhibit 3.2   Resources, Capabilities, and Managerial Decisions

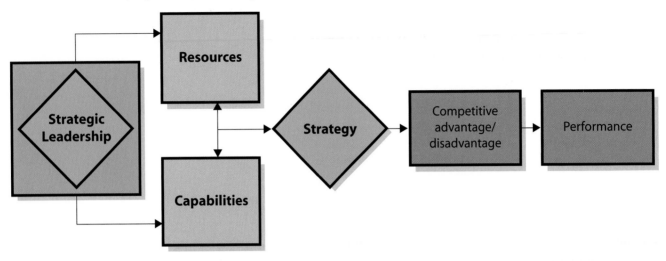

RESOURCES AND CAPABILITIES

concept link

In Chapter 1, we explain that the *internal perspective on competitive advantage* is often called the *resource-based view* of the firm because it holds that firms are heterogeneous bundles of resources and capabilities.

Resources and capabilities are the fundamental building blocks of a firm's strategy. The choices made by firms' managers relative to the five elements of a strategy, as organized by the strategy diamond, require resources and capabilities. For instance, if a firm wants to enter new arenas, it will need appropriate resources and capabilities in order to compete there. In addition, no matter how a firm plans to differentiate its products—whether on quality, image, or price—it needs the right resources and capabilities to make the differentiation real. Likewise, when a firm is deciding on the best way to enter a new market—whether by means of acquisition, alliance, or internal development—it has to consider its available resources and capabilities. Sometimes a firm uses a vehicle such as an acquisition or an alliance specifically for the purpose of acquiring resources or capabilities that it does not currently own.[2] Not surprisingly, successful strategies exploit the resources and capabilities that a firm enjoys and put the firm on a path to acquire missing resources and capabilities and upgrade existing ones, whereas unsuccessful strategies often reflect the fact that critical resources and capabilities are lacking.

Resources

resources Inputs used by firms to create products and services

What, exactly, do we mean by *resources*? **Resources** are the inputs that firms use to create goods or services. Some resources are rather undifferentiated inputs that any firm can acquire. For instance, land, unskilled labor, debt financing, and commodity-like inventory are inputs that are generally available to most firms. Other resources are more firm specific in nature.[3] They are difficult to purchase through normal supply chain channels. For instance, managerial judgment, intellectual property, trade secrets, and brand equity are resources that are not easily purchased or transferred. From this description, it is clear that some resources have physical attributes; these are referred to as *tangible* resources. Other resources, such as knowledge, organizational culture, location, patents, trademarks, and reputation are *intangible* in nature. Some resources have both tangible and intangible characteristics. Land, for instance, has physical properties and satisfies certain functional needs. At the same time, some properties may have value as a resource by virtue of their location, which is an intangible benefit arising from unique proximity to customers or suppliers due to preferences or relative location.

Because tangible resources are easier to identify and value, they may be less likely to be a source of competitive advantage than intangible resources. This is because their tangible nature gives competitors a head start on imitation or substitution. But some tangible resources are quite instrumental in helping firms achieve favorable competitive positions, partly because of their intangible benefits. Wal-Mart, for example, enjoys near-monopoly status in many rural locations. As the first large retailer in a rural market, Wal-Mart has locked out potential competitors who won't build facilities in locations that can't support two stores. Thus, one reason for Wal-Mart's formidable competitive position in rural markets is its tangible real estate. Similarly, Union Pacific Railroad's control of key rail property gives it a competitive advantage in the transportation of certain materials, such as hazardous chemicals.

Likewise, McDonald's controls much more than a valuable brand name (an intangible resource that does in fact convey a significant advantage). Like Wal-Mart, it also controls a great deal of valuable real estate by virtue of its location near high-traffic centers. Indeed, without its prime real-estate locations, McDonald's would have a less valuable brand name. Obviously, the pace at which McDonald's grew required a certain capability in finding the needed real estate.

Capabilities

Capabilities refer to a firm's skill in using its resources (both tangible and intangible) to create goods and services. A synonym that is often used to describe the same concept is *competences*. For simplicity, we use the term *capabilities*. Capabilities may be possessed by individuals or embedded in company-wide rules and routines.[4] In essence, they are the combination of procedures and expertise that the firm relies on to engage in distinct activities in the process of producing goods and services. Several examples of companies and their capabilities are listed in Exhibit 3.3. For instance, Wal-Mart is widely regarded as having excellent capabilities related to the management of logistics, which it uses to exploit resources such as large stores, store locations, its trucking fleet, and massive distribution centers.

Capabilities span from the rather simple tasks that firms must perform to accomplish their daily business, such as taking and fulfilling orders, to more complex tasks, such as designing sophisticated systems, creative marketing, and manufacturing processes. Collectively, these capabilities are the activities that constitute a firm's **value chain**. Not all capabilities are of equal value to the firm—a fact that has, in turn, given rise to the rapid growth of **outsourcing**. Outsourcing is contracting with external suppliers to perform certain parts of a company's normal value chain of activities. Later in the chapter, you will be introduced to a special class of capabilities known as *dynamic capabilities*.

Two other special classes of capabilities with which you should be familiar, if for no other reason than that they are part of the generally used business vocabulary, are *distinctive competences* and *core competences*. **Distinctive competences** (or *distinctive capabilities*) are

capabilities A firm's skill at using its resources to create goods and services; combination of procedures and expertise on which a firm relies to produce goods and services

value chain Total of primary and support value-adding activities by which a firm produces, distributes, and markets a product

outsourcing Activity performed for a company by people other than its full-time employees

distinctive competence Capability that sets a firm apart from other firms; something that a firm can do which competitors cannot

Exhibit 3.3 A Few Extraordinary Capabilities

Sources: G. Stalk, P. Evans, and L. E. Shulman, "Competing on Capabilities: The New Rules of Corporate Strategy," Harvard Business Review 70:2 (1992), 54–65; R. Makadok, "Doing the Right Thing and Knowing the Right Thing to Do: Why the Whole Is Greater Than the Sum of the Parts," Strategic Management Journal 24:10 (2003), 1043–1054.

Company	Capability	Result
Wal-Mart	Logistics—distributing vast amounts of goods quickly and efficiently to remote locations.	200,000-percent return to shareholders during first 30 years since IPO.
The Vanguard Group	Extraordinarily frugal system using both technological leadership and economies of scale for delivering the lowest cost structure in the mutual-fund industry.	25,000-percent return to shareholders during the 30-plus year tenure of CEO John Connelly. Shareholders in Vanguard equity funds pay, on average, $30 per $10,000 versus a $159 industry average. With bond funds, the bite is just $17 per $10,000.
3M	Generating new ideas and turning them into innovative and profitable products.	30 percent of revenue from products introduced within the past four years.

core competence Capability which is central to a firm's main business operations and which allow it to generate new products and services

the capabilities that set a firm apart from other firms. **Core competences** (or *core capabilities*) are those capabilities that are central to the main business operations of the firm; they are the capabilities that are common to the principle businesses of the firm and that enable the firm to generate new products and services in these businesses.

The relationship between resources and capabilities can be further illustrated by a few more examples. Intel's manufacturing capacity (i.e., its plants, equipment, and production engineers), its patented microprocessor designs, and its well-established brand name are among its key resources. Intel has also demonstrated the organizational capability to design new generations of leading-edge microprocessors and to do so rapidly. In addition, Intel has demonstrated marketing adroitness by creating the "Intel Inside" campaign, which stimulated greater demand and higher switching costs among end users—the customers of Intel's customers. This clearly suggests a marketing capability. The combination of Intel's resources and capabilities enables its managers to execute a value-creating strategy and achieve a formidable competitive advantage in the microprocessor industry.

In the oil industry, too, we can see that resources and capabilities aren't uniformly developed by all competitors. Some firms, for example, are highly integrated. These integrated firms are involved in every stage of the value chain, including risky and time-consuming oil exploration and extraction activities. BP, ChevronTexaco, ExxonMobil, and Royal Dutch/Shell all possess significant capabilities in exploration and extraction, refining, distribution, and marketing. As a result, they also own rights to significant petroleum deposits around the world, and these reserves are potentially valuable tangible resources. In contrast, other oil companies are involved primarily in "downstream activities." These companies gear their capabilities to refining, distribution, and marketing. Valero Energy and Sunoco, for instance, are the largest independent U.S. oil refiners and distributors. Neither, however, is active in exploration. Their resources include refineries, pipelines, distribution networks, and equipment, but both buy crude oil from other companies.

The important complementary relationship between one of McDonald's tangible resources (real estate) and one of its capabilities (its site-location skills) are highlighted in the following example. For instance, few people go out for the sole purpose of buying a hamburger or a taco. Most fast-food purchases are impulse buys, and this fact points to just one reason why site location is so important in the fast-food industry. Like magazines and candies strategically placed at supermarket checkout counters, fast-food outlets are situated by design. At one time, McDonald's used helicopters to assess the growth of residential areas: Basically, planners looked for cheap land alongside thoroughfares that would one day run through well-populated suburbs.

Today, the site-location process is even more high-tech. In the 1980s, McDonald's turned to satellite photography to predict urban sprawl. The company has developed a software package called *Quintillion*, which integrates information from satellite images, detailed maps, demographic information, CAD drawings, and sales data from existing stores. With all of this information at its disposal, McDonald's has taken the strategy of site location to new heights. Prime locations, of course, command prime dollars: The difference between the cost of a prime location and a mediocre site could be three times the price per square foot.[5]

The VRINE Model

VRINE model Analytical framework suggesting that a firm with resources and capabilities which are valuable, rare, inimitable, nonsubstitutable, and exploitable will gain a competitive advantage

In a given industry, then, all competitors do not have access to the same resources and capabilities—a fact that should have significant implications for the strategies that they develop. In addition, one firm's resources or capabilities aren't necessarily as effective as another's in helping it develop or sustain a competitive advantage. Why do some resources and capabilities enable some firms to develop a competitive advantage? Exhibit 3.4 summarizes five basic characteristics that determine whether a resource or capability can help a firm compete and, indeed, achieve superior performance: (1) value, (2) rarity, (3) inimitability, (4) nonsubstitutability, and (5) exploitability.

According to the **VRINE model** (for *v*alue, *r*arity, *i*nimitability, *n*onsubstitutability, and *e*xploitability), resources and capabilities contribute to competitive advantage to the

Exhibit 3.4 Applying the VRINE Model

	The Test	The Competitive Implication	The Performance Implication
Is it Valuable?	Does the resource or capability allow the firm to meet a market demand or protect the firm from market uncertainties?	If so, it satisfies the value requirement. Valuable resources are needed to compete in an industry, but value by itself does not convey an advantage.	Valuable resources and capabilities have the *potential* to contribute to *normal profits* (profits that cover the cost of all inputs, including capital).
Is it Rare?	Assuming that the resource or capability is valuable, is it scarce relative to demand or is it widely possessed by competitors?	Valuable resources that are also rare contribute to a *competitive advantage*, but that advantage may be only temporary.	A *temporary competitive advantage* can contribute to *above-normal profits*, at least until the advantage is nullified by other firms.
Is it Inimitable and/or Nonsubstitutable?	Assuming that the resource is both valuable and rare, how difficult is it for competitors either to imitate it or substitute other resources and capabilities that yield similar benefits?	Valuable and rare resources and capabilities that are difficult to imitate or substitute can contribute to *sustained competitive advantage*.	A sustained competitive advantage can contribute to *above-normal profits for extended periods of time* (until competitors find ways to imitate or substitute or environmental changes nullify the advantage).
Is it Exploitable?	If the resource or capability satisfied any or all of the preceding VRINE criteria, can the firm actually exploit it?	Resources and capabilities that satisfy the VRINE criteria but that cannot be exploited can still contribute to significant opportunity costs in the sense that competitors may have to invest large sums to match them. If they can be exploited, a firm may realize its potential competitive and performance implications.	Firms that control but don't exploit VRINE resources and capabilities generally suffer from lower levels of financial performance and depressed market valuations *relative to what they would enjoy if they could in fact exploit them* (although they won't be in as bad a shape as competitors who don't control any VRINE-certified resources and capabilities).

Source: Adapted from J. B. Barney, "Looking Inside for Competitive Advantage," Academy of Management Executive 9:4 (1995), 49–61.

extent that they satisfy the five components of the model. VRINE analysis helps managers systematically test the importance of particular resources and capabilities and the desirability of acquiring new resources and capabilities. In the following sections, we'll explain and provide examples of each VRINE characteristic.

Value A resource or capability is *valuable* if it enables a firm to take advantage of opportunities or to fend off threats in its environment.[6] Union Pacific (UP) Railroad, for example, maintains an extensive network of rail-line property and equipment on the U.S. Gulf Coast. It operates in the western two-thirds of the United States, serving 23 states, linking every major West Coast and Gulf Coast port and reaching east through major gateways in

Chicago, St. Louis, Memphis, and New Orleans. UP also operates in key north-south corridors (see Exhibit 3.5). It's the only U.S. railroad to serve all six gateways to Mexico, and it interchanges traffic with Canadian rail systems.

Its rail system is a tangible resource that enables UP to compete with other carriers in the long-haul transportation of a variety of goods. UP is, for example, the nation's largest hauler of chemicals, much of which traffic originates along the Gulf Coast near Houston, Texas. The company enjoys this advantage because it owns the physical resources necessary to compete in this market—the railway right of way through strategic areas—and because it has the specialized capability to transport chemicals safely and cost effectively. Government studies indicate that railroads are very efficient compared to alternative forms of transportation (such as truck and air) for the transportation of chemicals. Thus, railroad assets are valuable because they enable the company to provide a cost-effective means of transporting chemicals. In addition, because the Gulf Coast is the source for most chemical production in the United States, this network permits UP to take advantage of a market opportunity.

Alternatively, UP owns many right of way that are no longer active. These resources would appear to convey no value to UP unless it can find a new use for these properties although UP's ownership of them is a deterrent to new railroad industry events. Consequently, UP frequently sells these abandoned railway rights of way to communities for such things as bike trails, and not to competing railroad operators.

Finally, it is worthwhile to remember that some resources that can be sources of value can also be abused and consequently become sources of corporate overhead. For instance, consider a small fleet of business jets owned by a company. Occasionally, the company may need to be able to get top executives in and out of remote or congested locations quickly, which would make the jets a valuable resource. However, in other situations, the jets may be a costly convenience and an example of corporate excess that provide no real economic value.

If a firm cannot use a resource to minimize threats or take advantage of opportunities, then it probably doesn't enhance its competitive position. In fact, some experts suggest that owning resources that *don't* meet the VRINE criteria for value actually puts a firm at a competitive *disadvantage*. Why? Because the capital tied up in the resource could be put to better use,[7] the capital could be reinvested in other resources that do satisfy the value requirement of VRINE, or the capital could be redistributed to shareholders.

Exhibit 3.5 The Union Pacific Right-of-Way System

Source: Union Pacific, "System Map" (accessed August 4, 2005), at www.uprr.com/aboutup/maps/sysmap/index.shtml.

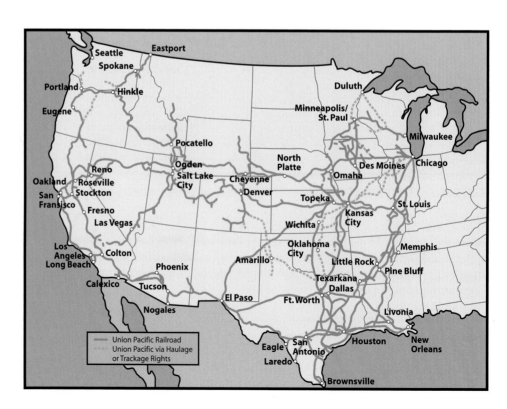

Rarity   *Rarity* is defined as scarcity relative to demand. An otherwise valuable resource that isn't rare won't necessarily contribute to competitive advantage: Valuable resources that are available to most competitors simply enable a firm to achieve parity with everyone else. Sometimes such resources may be called *table stakes,* as in poker, because they are required to compete in the first place. But when a firm controls a valuable resource that's also rare in its industry, it's in a position to gain a competitive advantage. Such resources, for example, may enable a company to exploit opportunities or fend off threats in ways that competitors cannot. When McDonald's signs an agreement to build a restaurant inside a Wal-Mart store, it has an intangible location advantage over Burger King and Wendy's that is not only valuable but also rare because it has an exclusive right to that geographic space.

How rare does a resource have to be in order to offer potential competitive advantage? It's a difficult question to answer with any certainty. At the two extremes, of course, *only one* firm has the resource or *every* firm has it, and the answer is fairly obvious. If only one firm possesses a given resource, it has a significant advantage. Monsanto, for instance, enjoyed an advantage for many years because it owned the patent to aspartame, the chemical compound in NutraSweet. As the only legal seller of aspartame, Monsanto dominated the artificial-sweetener market. Such is typically the case in the pharmaceutical industry for those who are first or second to patent and market a therapy for a particular disease.

Satisfying the rarity condition, however, doesn't necessarily require *exclusive* ownership. When a resource is controlled by a handful of firms, those firms will have an advantage over the rest of the field. Pfizer was first to the market for a drug to treat erectile dysfunction with its Viagra product, but it was later joined by two other products offered by competitors (Levitra® and Cialis®). Pfizer no longer has a monopoly in the market to treat this condition, but the three firms collectively control resources that are scarce relative to demand. Thus, Pfizer's resource, the patent for Viagra, would still seem to satisfy both the value and the rarity requirements of VRINE. Consider an example from another context. Both Toyota and Honda, for example, can build high-quality cars at relatively low cost, and the products of both firms regularly beat those of rivals in both short-term and long-term quality ratings. The criterion of rarity requires only that a resource be scarce *relative to demand.* It also follows, of course, that the more exclusive the access to a valuable resource, the greater the benefit of having it.

A firm that controls a valuable and scarce resource or capability may create a competitive advantage, but there is no assurance that the advantage will persist. We now turn to the two criteria that must be satisfied if the advantage is to be sustained.

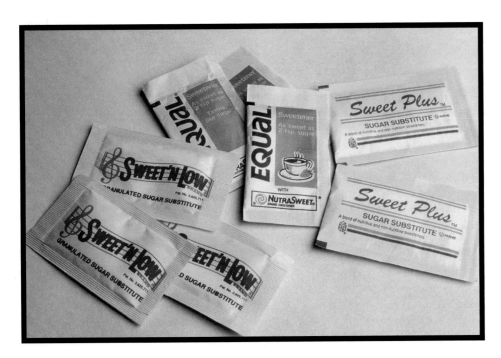

Monsanto enjoyed a competitive advantage for many years because it owned the patent to aspartame, the chemical compound in NutraSweet. The patent on aspartame ran out in 1992, and in 2000 Monsanto sold NutraSweet to private investors. NutraSweet now faces fierce competition from other aspartame-containing products, and newer and more popular nonaspartame-based sweeteners.

Inimitability and Nonsubstitutability   A valuable and rare resource or capability will grant an advantage only so long as competitors don't gain possession of it or find a close substitute. We review these two criteria jointly because they work in similar fashions. The criterion of *inimitability* is satisfied if competitors cannot acquire the valuable and rare resource quickly or if they face a cost disadvantage in doing so. The *nonsubstitutability* criterion is satisfied if a competitor cannot achieve the same benefit using different combinations of resources and capabilities. When a resource or capability is valuable and rare and contributes to a firm's advantage, one can assume that competitors will do all they can to get it. Of course, firms can acquire needed resources or capabilities in a number of different ways, including internal investment, acquisitions, and alliances. They can, for instance, form alliances in order to learn from and internalize a partner's capabilities.[8]

Some firms find alternative resources or capabilities that "mimic" the benefits of the original. For several years, for example, Barnes & Noble and Borders enjoyed formidable advantages in the retail-book industry. Their sheer size gave them an immense advantage over smaller players: Because they had access to more customers, they were able to take advantage of greater buying power. Eventually, however, Amazon.com's ability to substitute online for conventional retail marketing provided a feasible substitute for geographic accessibility to consumers. Generally speaking, then, valuable and rare resources can provide competitive advantage only as long as they're difficult to imitate or substitute.

The High Cost of Imitation and Substitution   Several factors can make resources and capabilities difficult to duplicate or substitute. A rival might, for instance, try to acquire a competitor or supplier that possesses the resource it needs.[9] But acquisitions of this kind often entail large premiums that result in a buyer's paying more for a resource than it cost competitors to develop the original.[10] In 1999, for example, when Cisco purchased Cerent in order to acquire fiber-optic data-transfer capabilities, it ended up paying $6.9 billion for a startup company with just $10 million in sales.[11] Cisco desperately wanted the capabilities of Cerent, but managers felt it would take too long to develop those capabilities internally. Absent Cisco's excellent capabilities in merger integration and new product distribution, therefore, the firm would be at a cost disadvantage relative to any competitor who could develop the same collective capabilities for less money.

Inimitability, Nonsubstitution, and Property Rights   Perhaps the most straightforward cause of resources and capabilities being difficult to imitate or substitute is property rights. Competitors can be prevented from copying resources if they are protected by ownership rights. For instance, patented items or processes cannot be directly copied during the term of the patent without the imitator's being subject to severe legal repercussions. Media companies own copyrights on titles in their libraries. Because of this, it is very difficult for competitors to substitute for Mickey Mouse. However, property rights alone do not protect all resources and capabilities from imitation or substitution.

Inimitability, Nonsubstitution, and Time   Another factor that can make resources and capabilities difficult to imitate or substitute is the unique historical conditions surrounding their development or the fact that their acquisition requires the passage of time.[12] Sometimes a firm's resources and capabilities are the result of unique historical events that converged to its benefit. For instance, in order to build troop moral during World War II, General Dwight D. Eisenhower requested that Coca-Cola be available to all American servicemen and servicewomen. To ensure that GIs could buy Coke for five cents a bottle, the government and Coca-Cola cooperated to build 64 bottling plants around the world. In the long term, Coke gained the competitive advantage of instant global presence, both in bottling capacity and brand recognition.[13] At war's end, Coke ramped up its overseas production and marketing and succeeded in penetrating new markets. In effect, Coke's market entry had been subsidized by the government, and rival Pepsi faced considerable cost disadvantages in competing with Coke's international presence. Coke's global advantage over Pepsi remains even today. Of Coke's $21.9 billion sales in 2004, fully 70 percent, were from outside North America, whereas just 54 percent of PepsiCo's $18.2 billion in beverage sales were from outside North America.[14]

The simple passage of time creates inimitability and nonsubstitutability as well, typically because the original owner may have built up the value of the resource or capability through a process of gradual learning and improvement that can't be matched through catch-up programs. For instance, firms that invest a given rate of R&D spending over an extended time period appear to produce larger gains in knowledge and intellectual property than firms that invest at twice the same level over half the time.[15] Thus, we can say that a resource is difficult to imitate if shorter development time results in inferior imitations.

Causal Ambiguity   Another factor that makes imitation difficult is **causal ambiguity**. For a number of reasons, it may be difficult to *identify* or *understand* the causal factors of a resource or capability—the complex combination of factors that make it valuable.[16] A firm, for example, may enjoy a resource that's resulted from a complex convergence of activities that the company itself doesn't fully understand.[17] For example, 3M enjoys an enviable capacity for innovation that, at least in part, is a function of company culture. A competitor may copy certain 3M policies—say, allowing employees to spend 10 percent of their time experimenting on potential new products—but it will be more difficult to imitate the complex culture of cooperation and rewards that facilitates innovation at 3M. The causal process, in other words, would be difficult to identify because it's *socially complex*. Products that are technologically complex are relatively easier to duplicate (say, by adopting such processes as reverse engineering) than are socially complex organizational phenomena.[18]

Exploitability   The fifth and final VRINE criterion reminds us that mere possession of or control over a resource or capability is necessary but not sufficient to gain a competitive advantage: A firm must have the organizational capability to *exploit* it; that is, the firm must be able to nurture and take advantage of the resources and capabilities that it possesses.

The question of exploitability is, of course, quite broad, but in this case, we're focusing on *a company's ability to get the value out of any resource or capability that it may generate.* Thus, the issue of an organization's exploitative capability incorporates all of the dimensions of a firm's value-adding processes. Although we may not deal directly with organizational processes until the final criterion in the VRINE model, bear in mind that, without this skill, a firm won't get much benefit from having met any of the first four VRINE criteria. A valuable resource or capability that is also possessed by many other competitors has the potential to give the firm competitive parity, but only if the firm also has the exploitative capabilities to implement a strategy that utilizes the resource or capability. Likewise, a

causal ambiguity Condition whereby the difficulty of identifying or understanding a resource or capability makes it valuable, rare, and inimitable

Causal ambiguity makes 3M's products hard to imitate. The company has a long history of innovation. Its culture makes it a socially complex organization that competitors can't quite duplicate.

firm that possesses a valuable and rare resource will not gain a competitive advantage unless it can actually put that resource to effective use.

In fact, many firms do have valuable and rare resources that they fail to exploit (in which case, by the way, their competitors aren't under much pressure to imitate them). For many years, for instance, Novell's core NetWare product gave it a significant advantage in the computer networking market. In high-tech industries, however, staying on top requires continuous innovation, and according to many observers, Novell's decline in the 1990s reflected an inability to innovate in order to meet the demands of changing markets and technology. But shortly after he was hired from Sun Microsystems to turn Novell around, new CEO Eric Schmidt arrived at a different conclusion: "I walk down Novell hallways," he reported, "and marvel at the incredible potential for innovation here. But Novell has had a difficult time in the past turning innovation into products in the marketplace."[19] The company, Schmidt confided to a few key executives, was suffering from "organizational constipation."[20] According to its new CEO, Novell had the resources and capabilities needed to innovate, but it lacked the exploitative capability (especially in its product-development and marketing processes) to get innovative products to market in a timely manner.

Xerox, too, went through a period when it was unable to exploit its resources to innovate products. At a dedicated facility in Palo Alto, California, Xerox had established a successful research team known as Xerox PARC. Scientists in this group invented an impressive list of innovative products, including laser printers, Ethernet, graphical-interface software, computers, and the computer mouse. All of these products were commercially successful, but, unfortunately for Xerox shareholders, they were commercial successes for other firms. Xerox couldn't get information about them to the right people in a timely fashion. Why? Largely because the company's bureaucracy tended to suffocate ideas before they had a chance to flow through the organization. Compensation policies ignored managers who fostered innovations and rewarded immediate profits over long-term success.[21]

The VRINE model can be used to assess any resource or capability in order to determine if it is a source or potential source of competitive advantage and, if so, whether that advantage is likely to be temporary or sustained. To illustrate how this is done, we use the VRINE model in the box entitled "How Would You Do That? 3.1" to analyze Pfizer's ownership of the patents for Zoloft as a possible source of competitive advantage.

Where Do Resources Come From? Our earlier definitions of *resources* and *capabilities* describe them as something the firm may own or possess. However, we have also suggested that many resources and capabilities cannot be easily purchased. Brand equity, for example, can't be readily purchased unless a company purchases an existing brand from another company. Otherwise, a brand will need to be developed, and that takes time. The brand equity of Coke, for example, has been developed through decades of marketing efforts with investments in the hundreds of millions per year. Toyota's reputation for quality automobiles has been developed through stringent quality-control methods; Intel's R&D capability is the result of years of investment. In other words, resources such as brand equity, reputation, and innovative capability result from policies and strategies that have been implemented over extended periods of time; they can't be acquired through one-time purchases.

DYNAMIC CAPABILITIES

Thus far, our discussion of resources and capabilities has portrayed a rather static view. However, the process of developing, accumulating, and losing resources and capabilities is inherently dynamic. We now introduce two concepts to demonstrate the dynamic aspects of resources and capabilities. The first deals with *stocks versus flows*; the second deals with a special class of capability referred to as a *dynamic capability*.

Resources as Stocks and Flows

Resources can be thought of as both stocks and flows. A firm's stock of resources and capabilities is what it possesses at any given point in time. However, that stock of resources and

How Do Drug Patents Stand Up to VRINE?

If you were studying Pfizer and the pharmaceutical industry using the VRINE model you would probably identify a number of resources and capabilities that may be the source of competitive advantage. You would probably identify patents, R&D capabilities, and marketing as key resources and capabilities. Let's walk through the VRINE model as applied to Pfizer's patents for Zoloft (sertraline HCl), an antidepressant known as a selective serotonin reuptake inhibitor (SSRI).

VALUE

Do Pfizer's two patents on Zoloft provide value? In any given year, about 7 percent of the U.S. population (approximately 20 million people) will express a depressive disorder. Approximately 16 percent of adults will experience depression at some point in their lives. Women are twice as likely as men to experience depression. Thus, it appears that having a patent for a treatment for depression would enable a pharmaceutical company to take advantage of a large market opportunity.

RARITY

Pfizer's patents on Zoloft give it the exclusive right to use the chemical compound sertraline HCl to treat depression (the patents are scheduled to expire in 2006). When the patents expire, generic drug makers will be able to sell copied versions of the drug. The patents for Zoloft are definitely rare during the term of the patents but will not be after they expire (assuming that several generic companies make the drug, its scarcity relative to demand will decline).

INIMITABILITY

Pfizer is certainly not the only large pharmaceutical company that desires to profit from therapies for depression. However, a patent makes direct imitation illegal until the patent expires.

NONSUBSTITUTABILITY

Competitors can and do attempt to find substitute compounds that have similar effects. Indeed, Zoloft itself was a Pfizer innovation in the face of Eli Lilly's patent for Prozac. Zoloft is not the only treatment for depression; other SSRIs include Prozac, Paxil, and others. The patents for Zoloft may convey temporary advantage, but Pfizer's value from them will probably erode over time as others invent substitute compounds and as the patents expires, resulting in direct imitation.

EXPLOITABILITY

To satisfy this VRINE criterion Pfizer needs to be able to move drugs from successful clinical trial to market distribution. Fortunately for Pfizer, distribution is one of its core competences. Indeed, Pfizer has more drug representatives than any other pharmaceutical company. Pfizer also has large cash reserves that can be used to bring sufficient quantities of the product quickly to market prior to the lapsing of the patents.

The verdict? As you may have guessed by now, Pfizer's patents on Zoloft stand up to the VRINE framework, suggesting that patents are a resource that can generate competitive advantage. Note, however, that Zoloft is such a resource because Pfizer also possesses the complementary resources and capabilities underlying its exploitability.

Sources: "Could Cymbalta Bring Cheer for Lilly?" *IMS Health.com*, August 23, 2004 (accessed August 4, 2005), at open.imshealth.com; C. Baysden, "Report: Blockbuster Drug Marketing Costs Average $239M," *Triangle Business Journal*, February 24, 2005 (accessed August 4, 2005), at triangle.bizjournals.com; "Medication for Depression: Antidepressant Medications," *Psychology Information Online* (accessed August 4, 2005), at www.psychologyinfo.com.

capabilities was created over time through a combination of initial endowment and accumulated investment. Consider the resource stock represented by a patent. To a large degree, the value of the patent depends on the level of innovation its original discovery represented, and that discovery was probably the result of years of investment and a process of trial and error. However, continual resource inflows may augment the value of the patent. For instance, additional R&D investments may lead to further discoveries that can be bundled with the original patent. Alternatively, investments in marketing efforts can spur demand, which leads to increased value. However, value also dissipates over time, as in the gradual expiration of the patent. The key point is that the value of resources and capabilities is a function of both the level (or stock) of resources and capabilities and the net effect of additional investment and depreciation.

This stock can be increased through development activities and sustained investment. It can be reduced through the divestiture of business units, loss of key personnel, and shifts in the competitive environment that alter the value of given resources. Remember, too, that strategic resources and capabilities are accumulated *over time*. Thus, the *process* of resource accumulation through dynamic capabilities is fundamentally different from the static possession of stocks of resources and capabilities.

Rebundling Resources and Capabilities

Beyond making investments to augment the accumulation of resources and capabilities, firms can make decisions about how resources and capabilities are utilized and configured, and thereby change their fundamental value. And although a firm can't easily change its stock of resources and capabilities, it can reconfigure or integrate them in new ways. **Dynamic capabilities** are processes by which a firm integrates, reconfigures, acquires, or divests resources in order to achieve new configurations of resources and capabilities.[22] In fact, the term *dynamic* is added to the description of these special kinds of capabilities because it refers to a firm's ability to modify and revise its resources and capabilities to match a shifting environment. The ability to reconfigure firm resources and capabilities is especially critical in markets that move quickly, and it is typically seen in complex areas of the firm, such as its culture, knowledge base, and ability to learn.

Dynamic capabilities are manifest in several ways. The ability to integrate different resources and capabilities to create new revenue-producing products and services is a dynamic capability.[23] Disney, for instance, recently launched its "Princess Line," which brings together merchandise based on famous female Disney characters. The effort required that Disney integrate development and marketing campaigns geared toward groups of characters that had before been developed and marketed separately.[24] Reconfiguring or transferring resources and capabilities from one division to another is another form of a dynamic capability. Mail Boxes Etc. (MBE), the postal center that was recently purchased by UPS, illustrates this fact. By encoding its knowledge of how to start up a master-area franchise, MBE created "templates" for future franchisees. New master-area franchisees are required to duplicate the template exactly prior to making any adjustments to meet local market needs. This is because their internal research shows that master-area franchisees who duplicate the template significantly outperform those who first customize the model.[25] The opening vignette about Intel also illustrates how resource-allocation rules can result in a dynamic capability to reallocate resources to new uses.

The rebundling of resources and capabilities is also accomplished through alliances and acquisitions. Resources and capabilities can both be acquired and lost through these vehicles. Cisco has been able to launch many new products by strategically acquiring bits and pieces of network architecture through acquisitions.[26]

The dynamic view of resources and capabilities differs somewhat from the traditional view. It emphasizes the need to renew resources and capabilities, either in order to keep pace with a changing environment or to reconfigure the organization proactively (i.e., to change the environment). One or both of these capabilities—the ability to adapt to change or to initiate it—is particularly important in industries in which time to market is critical, technological change is rapid, and future competition is difficult to forecast.[27] When incumbent firms, even strong companies, don't have such capabilities, they're likely to be

dynamic capabilities A firm's ability to modify, reconfigure, and upgrade resources and capabilities in order to strategically respond to or generate environmental changes

concept link

Among the three overarching themes of the book that we introduce in Chapter 1 is the principle that both firms and industries are *dynamic* in nature: Because their markets are dynamic, firms must develop dynamic capabilities to create value.

outmaneuvered by new competitors who are ready to introduce new industry standards.[28] Consequently, the value of a firm's portfolio of resources and capabilities is directly affected by its dynamic capability to reconfigure resources and capabilities to the evolving requirements of the competitive environment.

More complex forms of dynamic capabilities are typically associated with dynamic or turbulent environments. As we saw in our opening vignette, for example, Intel's internal organizational processes and organizational culture enabled it to make a dramatic change from one technological platform to another.[29] Specifically, the firm was able to shift scarce manufacturing resources from the memory-chip business to the emerging microprocessor business in a very brief period of time.

THE VALUE CHAIN

Earlier in the chapter, we demonstrated that firms in the same industry differ in their resources, capabilities, and dynamic capabilities and that these differences account for much of the variance in firm performance that we see within industries. Firms in the same industry may also differ in the scope and type of their value-chain activities. As we saw in our discussion of the *strategy diamond* model in Chapters 1 and 2, firms can make unique decisions about the value-chain *arenas* in which they'll participate within a given industry. Consider the oil industry, which we discussed earlier. Valero and Sunoco make very different choices about which value-chain activities to engage in (e.g., refining and distribution but not exploration) relative to the major integrated oil companies. Even if two firms possess similar resources and capabilities, it is still possible for one firm to gain the upper hand and achieve a competitive advantage. One way this can be done is by having a different configuration of value-adding activities.[30]

Firms make products or provide services by engaging in many different activities. The basic structure of these activities is embodied in the firm's value chain. Value-chain activities are of two types: primary activities and support activities. *Primary activities* include inbound logistics, operations, outbound logistics, marketing and sales, and service. *Support activities* include human resources, accounting and finance operations, technology, and procurement. The term *support activities* may seem to minimize the importance of these operations, but bear in mind that all activities—primary and support—are potential sources of competitive advantage (or disadvantage).

Exhibit 3.6 depicts the value chain for a hypothetical Internet startup. Notice that the primary activities are located along the horizontal axis and represent the value-added activities that are necessary to sell a product. For instance, an Internet retailer would need to access a product (either by purchasing it from a supplier or manufacturing it) and store merchandise that it plans to sell to customers. The operations of an Internet company are primarily electronic (e.g., server operations, billing, collections), but analogous operations are performed in all businesses. To fulfill orders, the outbound logistics steps of the value chain would include matching the merchandise with the order and organizing the shipping to the customer. Marketing and service functions differ a bit with an Internet company compared to a conventional retailer, but in reality the same functional marketing tasks are completed, just in different ways.

Support activities are represented on the top half of the vertical axis. Again, although these activities are generally portrayed as not being a part of the primary logistics involved in securing inputs, adding value, and fulfilling orders, when you see the types of activities performed by support functions, you begin to realize that any company would be hard-pressed to fulfill orders without these functions being performed.

Firms can use value-chain activities to create value by either finding *better* ways to perform the same activities or by finding *different* ways to perform them. However, any advantage obtained by doing the same activities but better than competitors may be short-lived. Best practices in activities are often rapidly diffused throughout industries. Eventually, rivals improve performance in activities that they once performed less efficiently than industry leaders. For instance, logistical tactics that prove efficient at one firm often show up at rival firms through consultants or as a result of outsourcing. Thus, performing the

conceptlink

In Chapter 1, we explain the *strategy diamond* as an integrated set of choices regarding arenas, vehicles, differentiators, staging, and economic logic. In Chapter 2, we define **strategic coherence** as the symmetrical co-alignment of these five elements of the firm's strategy and the congruence of functional-area policies with them.

conceptlink

In Chapter 1, we emphasize that the *strategic management process*, which outlines the means by which a firm intends to create value for customers, consists of activities designed to lead customers to prefer its products over those of its competitors.

Exhibit 3.6 The Value Chain for an Internet Startup

Support Activities

Firm infrastructure	• Financing, legal support, accounting				
Human resources	• Recruiting, training, incentive system, employee feedback				
Technology development	• Inventory system	• Site	• Pick & pack procedures	• Site look & feel • Customer research	• Return procedures
Procurement	• CDs • Shipping	• Computers • Telecom lines	• Shipping services	• Media	
	• Inbound shipment of top titles • Warehousing	• Server operations • Billing • Collections	• Picking and shipment of top titles from warehouse • Shipment of other titles from third-party distributors	• Pricing • Promotions • Advertising • Product information and reviews • Affiliations with other Web sites	• Returned items • Customer feedback
	Inbound logistics	Operations	Outbound logistics	Marketing & sales	After-sales service

Primary Activities

Source: The generic value chain model was developed by M. E. Porter, Competitive Advantage: Creating and Sustaining Superior Performance *(New York:* The Free Press, *1985), p. 47. The Internet firm example is the author's original application of the model.*

same activities better than rivals usually results in a temporary advantage. Alternatively, configuring value-chain activities in different ways than competitors makes it harder for rivals to imitate those activities. This is due to what is known as *tradeoff protection.*

Tradeoff Protection

conceptlink

In Chapter 2, we observe that most major strategic decisions involve *tradeoffs*—that deciding on one course of action generally eliminates other options.

By organizing their value-chain activities in unique and specific ways, firms may be able to make imitation quite difficult. Gaining advantage through value-chain configuration usually involves a rather complex system of activities. When a firm reconfigures the value chain, it exercises some tradeoffs. By adding or dropping certain activities, it may necessitate the elimination or addition of other activities. Rivals find it very difficult to imitate a system of interdependent activities because they have made some investments in their system of activities that may be irreversible. Generally, companies won't imitate activities if doing so would mean abandoning one or more activities that are essential to their own strategies.[31] In other words, they'll balk at the tradeoff.

To illustrate this point, let's consider some differences between the value-chain activities of Southwest Airlines and those of most other major U.S. airlines, which are summarized in Exhibits 3.7 and 3.8. Southwest has achieved unrivaled cost advantages among large airlines by radically pruning the number of activities that it performs and by undertaking others in nontraditional ways. As a result, the configuration of its value chain is fundamentally different from those of most other airlines. Southwest, for example, uses only one type of aircraft—a strategy that reduces maintenance and training costs. In addition, the chosen aircraft is efficient for the kind of shorter flights that comprise most of Southwest's schedule. Southwest has also cut many of the services normally provided by major carriers (such as baggage transfers, meals, and assigned seats).

As a result of its unique configuration of activities, Southwest operates at a significantly lower cost than its competitors. We can confirm this conclusion by taking a look at a

	Southwest	Major Airlines
Technology and Design	• Single aircraft	• Multiple types of aircraft
Operations	• Short-segment flights • No meals • No seat assignments • Single class of service • No baggage transfers to other airlines • Smaller markets and secondary airports in major markets	• Hub-and-spoke system • Meals • Seat assignments • Multiple classes of service • Baggage transfers to other airlines • Larger markets and major airports, some smaller markets served, largely through alliances with regional carriers
Marketing	• Limited use of travel agents • Word of mouth	• Extensive use of travel agents

Exhibit 3.7 Value-Chain Activities in the U.S. Airline Industry

Sources: Transportation Workers Union, TWU Airline Industry Review, *2004 (accessed February 18, 2005), at www.twuatd.org; Bureau of Transportation,* TransStats Reports, *2004 (accessed August 4, 2005), at www.transtats.bts.gov.*

Airline	2004 Revenue ($ millions [U.S.])	2004 Cost of Available Seat Miles (CASM)
AirTran	279	8.42
Alaska	656	10.03
American	4,541	9.72
AmericaWest	579	7.81
Continental	2,397	9.49
Delta	3,641	10.23
JetBlue	334	6.03
Northwest	2,753	10.31
Southwest	1,655	7.77
United	3,988	10.16
USAir	1,660	11.34

Exhibit 3.8 Comparative Costs for U.S. Airlines

Source: Comparative Airline Costs Fourth Quarter 2004 TWU Airline Industry Review, *a publication of the Transportation Workers Union, accessed February 18, 2005 (accessed at www.twuatd.org); Bureau of Transportation Statistics,* TransStats reports *(www.transtats.bts.gov).*

factor known as *CASM* (cost of available seat miles), which is a common measure of costs in the airline industry. As you can see in Exhibit 3.8, Southwest's CASM is significantly lower than that of every major competitor. Why don't other major airlines imitate Southwest's value chain? Primarily because doing so would mean ceasing certain activities that are fundamental to their operations. Although many airlines have stopped serving meals to save costs, they can't stop transferring luggage, abandon the hub-and-spoke system, or convert exclusively to Boeing 737s. So many tradeoffs would mean changing their business model completely. Thus, Southwest has protected its advantage by configuring its value-chain activities in such a way that imitating them is not attractive to competitors.

Further analysis of Exhibit 3.8 reveals another important insight. The airline with the lowest CASM is actually JetBlue. This recent startup has been able to imitate much of Southwest's value chain and then even make a few modifications that have further lowered costs (e.g., newer, more fuel-efficient planes, low-cost labor). This illustrates that although it may be very difficult for an established competitor to imitate the successful value-chain configuration of a leading company, a new entrant has much more flexibility to do so. A new firm that hasn't already made irreversible commitments to another value-chain configuration may be in a better position to imitate a successful value-chain configuration and even make improvements upon that model.

Innovation and Integration in the Value Chain   IKEA, a Swedish furniture company, has built a hugely successful business by almost completely reconfiguring the value-chain activities of the furniture industry by transferring delivery and assembly to the customer. IKEA's stores double as warehouses. The furniture is shipped in flat-packed boxes. Customers shop among display models, but then take the unassembled furniture off the shelves and assemble it at home. This significantly lowers the costs of production and distribution.

Similarly, Dell's success is based on an innovative reconfiguration of sales, distribution, and customer-service activities in the personal-computer industry that exploits the growing base of knowledgeable PC consumers around the world. Dell PCs use components manufactured entirely by suppliers. In addition, its distribution and marketing operations rest on a direct-sales model that avoids retailers. This combination of strategies—outsourcing component manufacturing and distributing finished products directly—was a radical departure from the business models that prevailed in the industry.

Many competitors have tried to imitate this model, but at Dell the model supports—and is integrally linked to—a *chain* of value-adding activities. Large established PC firms have never been able to duplicate Dell's cost structure because they haven't been willing or able to make all of the tradeoffs that would be necessary to imitate its value-chain activities.

The message in each of these examples is pretty much the same: The key to the value-chain approach to competitive advantage is not only developing value-chain activities that differ from those of rivals but also configuring them so that they're integrally related and can't be imitated without significant tradeoffs. *Value-chain fit* is important, Michael Porter reminds us, because it locks out imitators by "creating a chain of activities that is as strong as its strongest link."[32]

Outsourcing and the Value Chain

conceptlink

In Chapter 1, we show how the decision to *outsource* certain functions reflects a choice of **arenas**—of areas in which a firm will be active as opposed to those in which it won't be active.

Given that strategy is about making tradeoffs, one of the most fundamental tradeoffs managers make today is whether to outsource a historically integral value-chain activity. Indeed, the value chain forces managers to identify activities and capabilities the firm must possess itself and those that can be performed outside of the firm. Referring back to IKEA, one of IKEA's innovations was to outsource furniture assembly to the end consumer.

Outsourcing is not new; it is just that it has become so prevalent, and sometimes contentious, especially when it involves the loss of domestic jobs, that it may seem relatively new. Part of this prevalence is due to the broad number of choices managers have in terms of outsourcing; they are able to outsource nearly any activity that they please. Although outsourcing a value-chain activity may be feasible and lower a firm's direct costs and overhead, based on what you have learned about the resource and capability perspective, you should know that caution must be exercised. For instance, if a firm outsources its marketing or distribution function, it may lose access to the knowledge of customer preferences that inspired its early product breakthroughs in the first place. This perhaps explains why brand leaders such as Nike and Pacific Cycle (Schwinn brand) have outsourced functions such as manufacturing and have instead focused their efforts on activities surrounding product development, logistics, brand management, and customer retention and expansion.

STRATEGIC LEADERSHIP: LINKING RESOURCES AND CAPABILITIES TO STRATEGY

conceptlink

In Chapter 2, we define **strategic leadership** as the task of managing an overall enterprise and influencing key organizational outcomes.

The opening vignette in this chapter notes the central role of leaders in managing a firm's resources and capabilities. It is important to not lose sight of the fact that it is a firm's managers who scan its external and internal environments and consequently decide how to use resources and capabilities and how to configure value-chain activities based on their assessment of those sometimes rapidly changing environments. Indeed, the role of managers is so critical that some experts include managerial human capital among a firm's resources; others include management among a company's dynamic capabilities.[33] A recent McKinsey consulting report concluded that "companies that overlook the role of leadership in the early phases of strategic planning often find themselves scrambling when it's time to execute. No matter how thorough the plan, without the right leaders it is unlikely to succeed."[34] To incorporate these views, we regard managers as *decision agents*—the people who put into motion the processes that use the firm's resources and capabilities.

Senior Managers

In addition to deciding how to use resources and capabilities and configuring a firm's value-chain activities, senior managers also set the context that determines how frontline and middle managers can add value. Recall from the opening vignette that senior managers did not change Intel's strategy from memory chips to microprocessors—at least not until frontline managers made that change a *fait accompli*.

Strategy research has shown that senior managers in the most effective firms around the globe view their organizations as portfolios of processes—specifically, entrepreneurial, capability-building, and renewal processes—and key people, such as those who comprise the firm's middle and frontline managerial ranks.[35] Collectively, these processes may be seen as part of a firm's culture.

The *entrepreneurial process* encourages middle managers to be externally oriented—to seek out opportunities and run their part of the business as if they owned it. Senior managers who foster this process are stepping back from the notion that they are the sole visionaries and saviors of the company and instead seek to share this responsibility with the managers on the front lines. The *capability-building process* also looks to middle managers to identify, grow, and protect new ways to create value for the organization and its key stakeholders. In many ways, this process is the internal side of the externally oriented entrepreneurial process. Finally, the *renewal process* is senior managers' way of shaking up the firm and challenging its historic ways of operating; however, this process is based on information learned through current business activities performed elsewhere in the firm.

We can see all three of these processes taking place in the opening vignette about Intel. Senior management had put into place processes and a culture that encouraged entrepreneurial activities. Similarly, middle management helped the firm to develop new capabilities to capitalize on the microprocessor opportunity. Finally, senior management stepped in to validate this major change in strategy, based on upgraded organizational resources and capabilities related to logic-device architecture. The only piece missing from the opening case is the role played by senior management in the selection, retention, and promotion of middle and frontline managers.

Of course, not all senior managers are equipped equally to act effectively. Obviously, basic managerial talent isn't bestowed equally on all managers, even if they have risen to the highest levels in the organization. Moreover, specific experiences and backgrounds will make some managers better qualified to work with a specific bundle of resources. Researchers have discovered, for instance, that multinational firms (those with operations in several countries) achieve higher levels of performance when their CEOs have had some experience in foreign operations.[36] In addition, entrepreneurial operations must often rely on few or no valuable or rare resources. Managers of these enterprises generally start with ideas and goals and not much more. In such situations, the positive influence of managers is even more important.[37] Likewise, in firms facing financial or competitive turmoil, the galvanizing and enabling effects of superior senior management are also more pronounced.

Middle Managers

From the discussion on senior managers, you should be able to see that middle managers play a key role in what the firm is doing and what it may be adept at doing in the future.

Southwest Airlines founder and former CEO Herb Kelleher created a value chain for his company unlike that of any of his competitors. Using a low-fare, no-frills, no-reserved-seating approach, Southwest has managed to earn a profit for 30 years straight—an astonishing feat in the airlines industry.

The entrepreneurial, capability-building, and renewal processes all require the involvement, choices, and actions of middle and frontline managers. Executives must consider their leadership pool as they shape strategy and align their leadership-development programs with long-term aspirations. Particularly in large firms, the effect of senior executives on firm performance is a function of the choices they have made about the context in which frontline managers work and the appointment of particular managers themselves.

Strategic leadership researcher Quy Nguyen Huy has identified four areas where middle managers are better positioned to contribute to competitive advantage and corporate success than are senior executives:[38]

- **Entrepreneur.** Middle managers are close enough to the front lines to spot fires, yet far enough away to understand the bigger picture. Because middle management ranks are typically more diverse in terms of ethnicity, gender, experience, and geography, this group has the potential to contribute richer ideas than the senior-management team.

- **Communicator.** Middle managers are typically long tenured and have very broad social networks. This gives them great credibility with employees, and they are therefore better able to move change initiatives in nonthreatening ways. Their tenure also gives them deep knowledge about how to get things done in the organization.

- **Psychoanalyst.** Internal credibility also enables middle managers to be more effective in quelling alienation and chaos, as seen by high productivity among anxious employees during times of great change. Because they know their troops, frontline managers also know when and how to provide one-on-one support and problem solving.

- **Tightrope walker.** Particularly in the case of dynamic capabilities and dynamic environments, firms are faced with the need to balance continuity and radical change. Middle managers are well poised to accomplish this balancing act. With the right process in place courtesy of senior executives, middle managers can help the firm avoid inertia and too little change or slow change and also avoid the paralyzing chaos accompanying too much change too quickly.

In many ways, it's the central role of upper and middle management that distinguishes the internal perspective on strategy from the external perspective that we'll discuss in Chapter 4. After all, if competitive advantage results from the different characteristics of firms, then the key task in the role of management is to identify resources and capabilities, specify the resources that will create competitive advantage, locate an attractive industry in which to deploy them, and then select the strategy to get the most out of them. Finally, it's the job of managers to choose *when* to change a firm's mix of resources, capabilities, and targeted markets. As you learned in Chapter 2, the managements of smaller firms typically differ from those of larger firms in terms of their overall number, not the roles that they play. This means that in smaller firms senior leaders, often the owners or company founders, may wear many if not all of the middle and frontline manager hats described.

SUMMARY

1. Explain the *internal context of strategy*. Firms facing similar industry conditions achieve different levels of competitive advantage and performance based on their internal characteristics and managerial choices. Although firms must always take the external context into account when formulating and implementing strategy, the internal perspectives stress the differences among firm in terms of the unique resources and capabilities that they own or control. These perspectives offer important models and analytical tools that will help you to analyze and formulate competitive strategies.

2. Identify a firm's resources and capabilities and explain their role in its performance. Resources are either tangible or intangible. Resources and capabilities that help firms establish a competitive advantage and secure higher levels of performance are those that are valuable, rare, and costly to imitate. The VRINE model helps you analyze resources and capabilities. A resource or capability is said to be valuable if it enables the firm to exploit opportunities or negate threats in the environment. In addition, the firm must have complementary organizational capabilities to exploit resources and capabilities that meet these three conditions. Rare resources enable firms to exploit opportunities or negate threats in ways that those lacking the resource cannot. Competitors will try to find ways to imitate valuable and rare resources; a firm can generate an enduring competitive advantage if competitors face a *cost disadvantage* in acquiring or substituting the resource that is lacking. Unique historical conditions that have led to resource or capability development, time-compression diseconomies, and causal ambiguity all make imitation more difficult. Firms often use alliances, acquisitions, and substitution with less costly resources as mechanisms to gain access to difficult-to-imitate resources.

3. Define *dynamic capabilities* and explain their role in both strategic change and a firm's performance. The process of development, accumulation, and possible loss of resources and capabilities is inherently dynamic. The resource-accumulation process and dynamic capabilities are fundamentally different from the static possession of a stock of resources and capabilities. Dynamic capabilities are processes that integrate, reconfigure, acquire, or divest resources in order to use the firms' stocks of resources and capabilities in new ways. The ability to adapt to changing conditions or to proactively initiate a change in the competitive environment is particularly important in industries in which time-to-market is critical, technological change is rapid, and future competition is difficult to forecast.

4. Explain how value-chain activities are related to firm performance and competitive advantage. Firms produce products or offer services by engaging in many activities. The basic structure of firm activities is illustrated by the firm's value chain. The value chain is divided into primary and support activities. One way a company can outperform rivals is it can find ways to perform some value-chain activities better than its rivals or to find different ways to perform the activities altogether. Selective outsourcing of some value-chain activities is one way to perform activities differently. Competitive advantage through strategic configuration of value-chain activities only comes about if the firm can either deliver greater value than rivals or deliver comparable value at lower cost. The essence of the activity-based value-chain perspective of competitive advantage is to choose value-chain activities that are different from those of rivals and to configure these activities in a way that are internally consistent and that requires significant tradeoffs should a competitor want to imitate them.

5. Explain the role of managers with respect to resources, capabilities, and value-chain activities. Managers make decisions about how to employ resources in the formulation and implementation of strategy. Managers are the decision agents that put into motion the use of all other firm resources and capabilities; they are key to the success of a firm's strategy. Managers with specific experiences and backgrounds may be more qualified to work with a specific bundle of resources owned by a firm. The influence of managers is more pronounced in contexts such as entrepreneurial phases, turnarounds, and competitive turmoil.

KEY TERMS

capabilities, 67
causal ambiguity, 73
core competence, 68

distinctive competence, 67
dynamic capabilities, 76

outsourcing, 67
resources, 66

value chain, 67
VRINE model, 68

REVIEW QUESTIONS

1. What are resources? How do different types of resources differ?

2. What is a capability?

3. What are the five components of the VRINE model?

4. How do time and causal ambiguity relate to the value, rarity, and inimitability of a resource or capability?

5. What is the difference between a stock of resources and capabilities and a flow of resources and capabilities?

6. What are dynamic capabilities? How do they differ from general capabilities?

7. What is a firm's value chain? How does it figure into a firm's competitive advantage?

8. What is your role as a manager in linking resources and capabilities to strategy and competitive advantage?

How Would YOU Do That?

1. In the box entitled "How Would You Do That? 3.1," we walked through how to apply the VRINE model to evaluate the value of Pfizer's patents. Later in the chapter, we walked you through the concept of the value chain. Identify the value chain for another organization. Are there activities that this organization performs differently than its rivals? Start by looking at the firm's products, services, or target markets. Likewise, examine the programs of a few leading rivals. Do any of the rival firms' value-chain activities give them a competitive advantage? If so, why don't others imitate these activities?

2. What resources and capabilities does your focal organization possess? What are the resources and capabilities possessed by rivals? How do your focal organization's resources and capabilities fare relative to those of the rivals' when you apply the VRINE model to them?

GROUP ACTIVITIES

1. What is the role of luck in gaining possession of a particular resource or capability? Can a firm manage luck? Give an example of a resource or capability that a firm garnered through luck and determine whether it was subsequently well managed.

2. Some firms' products are so well known that the entire category of products offered in the industry (including rivals'

products) is often referred to by the leading firm's brand name (which is called an *eponym*). Identify one such product and discuss whether its brand recognition gives the leading firm a competitive advantage. Why or why not?

ENDNOTES

1. www.intel.com and Hoover's (accessed June 28, 2005); K. M. Eisenhardt and J. A. Martin, "Dynamic Capabilities: What Are They?" *Strategic Management Journal* 21 (2000), 1105–1121.

2. J. Haleblian and S. Finkelstein, "The Influence of Organizational Acquisition Experience on Acquisition Performance: A Behavioral Learning Perspective," *Administrative Science Quarterly* 44:1 (1999), 29–56; F. Vermeulen and H. Barkema, "Learning Through Acquisitions," *Academy of Management Journal* 44:3 (2001), 457–476.

3. D. J. Teece, G. Pisano, and A. Shuen, "Dynamic Capabilities and Strategic Management," *Strategic Management Journal* 18 (1997), 509–529.

4. R. R. Nelson and S. G. Winter, *An Evolutionary Theory of Economic Change* (Cambridge, MA: Belknap Press of Harvard University Press, 1982).

5. english.pravda.ru/usa/2001/11/03/20045.html and www.restaurantreport.com/qa/location.html (accessed June 28, 2005).

6. J. B. Barney, "Firm Resources and Sustained Competitive Advantage," *Journal of Management* 17:1 (1991), 99–120.

7. Barney, "Firm Resources and Sustained Competitive Advantage."

8. C. K. Prahalad and G. Hamel, "The Core Competence of the Corporation," *Harvard Business Review* 68:3 (1990), 79–92.

9. L. Capron and W. Mitchell, "The Role of Acquisitions in Reshaping Business Capabilities in the International Telecommunications Industry," *Industrial and Corporate Change* 7:4 (1998), 715–730.

10. P. R. Haunschild, "How Much Is That Company Worth? Interorganizational Relationships, Uncertainty, and Acquisition Premiums," *Administrative Science Quarterly* 39:3 (1994), 391–414.

11. B. Labaris, "Has Your Vendor Gone Buyout Crazy?" *Computerworld* 33:36 (1999), 34–35.

12. J. B. Barney, "Looking Inside for Competitive Advantage," *Academy of Management Executive* 9:4 (1995), 49–61; I. Dierickx and K. Cool, "Asset Stock Accumulation and Sustainability of Competitive Advantage," *Management Science* 35:12 (1989), 1504–1511.

13. M. Pendergrast, *For God, Country and Coca-Cola* (New York: Basic Books, 1993).

14. Coca-Cola, *2004 Annual Report*; PepsiCo, *2004 Annual Report.*

15. Dierickx and Cool, "Asset Stock Accumulation and Sustainability of Competitive Advantage."

16. Dierickx and Cool, "Asset Stock Accumulation and Sustainability of Competitive Advantage."

17. Nelson and Winter, *An Evolutionary Theory of Economic Change.*

18. Barney, "Looking Inside for Competitive Advantage"; Dierickx and Cool, "Asset Stock Accumulation and Sustainability of Competitive Advantage."

19. Author's personal communication with Margaret Haddox, Novell Corporate Librarian, October 2003.

20. Author's personal communication with former Novell executives, September 2003.

21. D. T. Kearns and D. A. Nadler, *Prophets in the Dark* (New York: HarperCollins, 1992); Barney, "Looking Inside for Competitive Advantage."

22. Eisenhardt and Martin, "Dynamic Capabilities."

23. Eisenhardt and Martin, "Dynamic Capabilities."

24. B. Orwall, "In Disney Row, an Aging Heir Who's Won Boardroom Bouts," *Wall Street Journal,* December 5, 2003, A1.

25. G. Szulanski and R. J. Jensen, "Overcoming Stickiness: An Empirical Investigation of the Role of the Template," *Managerial Decision Economics,* forthcoming.

26. Eisenhardt and Martin, "Dynamic Capabilities."

27. Teece, Pisano, and Shuen, "Dynamic Capabilities and Strategic Management."

28. C. Christensen, *The Innovator's Dilemma* (New York: Harper Business Press, 1997).

29. R. Burgelman, "Fading Memories: A Process Theory of Strategic Business Exit in Dynamic Environments," *Administrative Science Quarterly* 39:1 (1994), 24–56.

30. M. E. Porter, "What Is Strategy?" *Harvard Business Review* 74:6 (1996), 61–78.

31. Porter, "What Is Strategy?"

32. Porter, "What Is Strategy?"

33. Barney, "Firm Resources and Sustained Competitive Advantage."

34. T. Hseih and S. Yik, "Leadership as the Starting Point of Strategy," *McKinsey Quarterly* 1 (2005), 11–26.

35. S. Ghoshal and C. A. Bartlett, "Changing the Role of Top Management: Beyond Structure to Processes," *Harvard Business Review* 73:3 (1995), 86–96; C. A. Bartlett and S. Ghoshal, "Changing the Role of Top Management: Beyond Systems to People," *Harvard Business Review* 73:3 (1995), 132–134.

36. M. A. Carpenter, W. Sanders, and H. Gregersen, "Bundling Human Capital with Organizational Context: The Impact of International Assignment Experience on Multinational Firm Performance and CEO Pay," *Academy of Management Journal* 44:3 (2001), 493–512.

37. M. A. Carpenter, T. G. Pollock, and M. M. Leary, "Testing a Model of Reasoned Risk-Taking: Governance, the Experience of Principals and Agents, and Global Strategy in High-Technology IPO Firms," *Strategic Management Journal* 24:9 (2003), 803–820.

38. Q. Huy, "In Praise of Middle Managers," *Harvard Business Review* 79:8 (2001), 72–79.

After studying this chapter, you should be able to:

1. Explain the importance of the external context for strategy and firm performance.

2. Use PESTEL to identify the macro characteristics of the external context.

3. Identify the major features of an industry and the forces that affect industry profitability.

4. Understand the dynamic characteristics of the external context.

5. Show how industry dynamics may redefine industries.

6. Use scenario planning to predict the future structure of the external context.

▶ **Roberto C. Goizueta, 1981-1997**
Strategy: Seek out profitable new business lines and "kick Pepsi's can" by taking over Coke's distribution services via the launch of the Coca-Cola Bottling Company.
Stock high: $125.50
Stock low: $30.25

▶ **Wayne Callaway, 1986–1996**
Strategy: Foster the entrepreneurial spirit of Pepsi's people in order to compete more effectively in the global environment and in different industries, such as the fast-food market.
Stock High: $98.25
Stock Low: $21.62

▶ **Roger Enrico, 1996–2001**
Strategy: Jettison some of Pepsi's slow-growing businesses and take the bloat out of others. Win the Cola War by concentrating on emerging overseas markets not already dominated by Coke.
Stock High: $69.12
Stock Low: $27.56

1980   1985   1

A CHRONICLE OF THE COLA WAR

The Cola War is a defining feature of the history the soft-drink industry.[1] Its roots can be traced back to 1886, when a pharmacist in Atlanta, Georgia, concocted a headache tonic that he sold for five cents a glass. His bookkeeper named the remedy "Coca-Cola" and committed its secret formula to writing. About a decade later, and just a few hundred miles away in New Bern, North Carolina, another pharmacist created Pepsi Cola.

Over a century later, the stakes in the soft-drink industry are enormous. The average American consumes 53 gallons of carbonated beverages per year—about 29 percent of the total consumption of all liquids! Coke and Pepsi have battled for decades to conquer market share in what is regularly one of the most profitable mature industries in the world. Experts estimate that gross margins in soft-drink concentrate are approximately 83 percent and net margins about

▶ Douglas N. Daft, 2000-2004
Strategy: Repair Coke and restore a stock price deflated by saturated U.S. sales, failed acquisitions, and product contamination in Europe.
Stock high: $63.06
Stock low: $37.07

▶ Steve Reinemund, 2001-present
Strategy: Grow and diversify PepsiCo's businesses beyond the soft-drink market by motivating employees and providing superior leadership.
Stock high: $57.12
Stock low: $35.01

▶ E. Neville Isdell, 2004-present
Strategy: Promote Coke's 400 brands globally and diversify its product line to adapt to the changing beverage tastes of U.S. consumers.
Stock high: $51.16
Stock low: $38.41

1995   2000

35 percent. With such enormous profit potential at stake, it's no wonder that Coke and Pepsi go to great lengths to defend their turf.

Trading Punches Although Coke has long been dominant, Pepsi has worked hard to weaken its enemy's position. In 1950, for example, Pepsi recruited a former Coke marketing manager and proclaimed the battle cry "Beat Coke." In the 1960s, Pepsi launched its "Pepsi Generation" campaign to target younger buyers. In the mid-1970s, spurred by the success of blind taste tests in Texas, Pepsi launched a nationwide offensive called the "Pepsi Challenge." Coke, however, refused to retreat, countering with such tactics as retail-price cuts and aggressive advertising.

Coke's tactics intensified after Roberto Goizueta became CEO in 1981. Once in command, Goizueta more than doubled advertising, switched to lower-priced sweeteners, sold off noncarbonated-beverage businesses, and introduced new flavors and diet versions of existing brands. Coke's victories included Diet Coke, the most successful new product introduction of the 1980s. Then, however, Coke made a serious tactical error: It tried to reformulate the 100-year-old recipe for Coke. When consumers rebelled, Coke was forced to retreat to the original formula. Pepsi proclaimed the effort to reformulate Coke as an admission that Pepsi had a superior taste.

The value-chain activities that bring carbonated beverages to market are centered on four functions: production (producing concentrate), marketing (managing a portfolio of brands), packaging (bottling finished products), and distribution (distributing products for resale). Concentrate is the syrup that provides the distinctive flavor to soft drinks. Historically, the major beverage companies focused on the production of concentrate and marketing, and independent regional bottlers were tasked with packaging and distribution. Bottlers mixed the soft-drink concentrate with sweetener and carbonated water and then packaged and distributed the finished product in cans, bottles, or bulk (for restaurant and other on-premises sales). In the early years, both Coke and Pepsi expanded rapidly by granting franchises to independent bottlers around the country. This strategy avoided huge investments in capital-intensive bottling operations.

Bottling Operations However, as the industry matured, the economics of bottling operations changed. For one, older franchised bottling plants were proving to be inefficient. These plants were typically only large enough to serve the territory the bottler controlled through its franchise agreement. Although modern bottling technology made costs savings possible with larger plant sizes, local franchised bottlers had little incentive to invest in larger plants. Because franchise agreements typically limited bottlers to defined geographic markets, larger modern plants would often exceed their capacity requirements. Two trends resulted in a change in the bottling industry. First, a few bottling companies saw an opportunity to buy up local franchises in contiguous markets and restructure local operations by building large plants designed to serve multiple markets. As these bottling operations began to grow in size, they also grew in power relative to Coke and Pepsi, which posed a legitimate threat to Coke and Pepsi. This threat led to the second trend in the bottling industry. Even though bottling operations generated much less than half the operating margins of concentrate production, both Coke and Pepsi entered the bottling industry. They began buying up independent bottling operations, consolidating territories, and building newer, more efficient facilities.

Although entering the bottling industry could have diluted Coke's and Pepsi's earnings, they actually were able to use this move to improve their overall performance. They did this in two ways. First, by purchasing the bottling operations based on existing profitability, they were able to buy these strategic operations cheaply relative to their value once they restructured operations and made them more efficient. Second, both Coke and Pepsi later divested part of their holdings by spinning off bottling subsidiaries (based on higher profitability) but retaining significant holdings in these now partially owned subsidiaries. These ownership positions enabled them to counteract any power that these operations may have had in negotiations were they to be completely independently owned and operated.

A New Age In recent years, competition has taken on some new dimensions. Historically, the soft-drink industry has been distinct from the noncarbonated, nonalcoholic beverage industries. However, the success of bottled water and tea has attracted Coke and Pepsi to the noncarbonated, nonalcoholic beverage industries, blurring the traditional boundaries between the soft-drink and noncarbonated, nonalcoholic industries. In addition, soft-drink industry participants have been creating new products in existing segments as well as creating entirely new segments. Recently, firms have been launching new diet drinks aimed at attracting customers who would normally shun anything labeled as a diet product.

An outside observer might think that such a fierce battle for market share would gradually erode the combatants' profitability. Since the mid-1960s, however, both Coke and Pepsi have increased market share by about 11 percent, and both enjoy healthy profits. Entry barriers created by large market shares, tremendous brand equity, and ownership or control of regional bottlers explain much of this profitability. Of course, that increased market share had to be captured from weaker rivals, although competitors like Cadbury Schweppes and private label suppliers are making up ground as well. Perhaps the only thing that is certain at this point is that the global hostilities between the two cola superpowers are far from over. ■

THE EXTERNAL CONTEXT OF STRATEGY

To formulate an effective strategy—one that has a good chance of helping you achieve your objectives—it is crucial that you understand the external environment. It is the external environment that provides the business opportunities to the firm. However, the external environment is also a source of threats—forces that may impede the successful implementation of a strategy. The external environment in which firms compete exerts a strong influence on firms' profitability.

As we noted at the start of Chapter 3, where we discussed some tools for identifying the internal determinants of a firm's strengths and weaknesses, you should think of the chapters on the internal and external contexts of strategy as related sections of a single unit: Individually, each discussion provides you with only half of the information you need to analyze a firm's strategy.

In this chapter, you'll learn how to identify the external opportunities and threats that affect every firm's strategy. Taken together, these two chapters provide the tools that will enable you to perform a rigorous analysis of the firm's competitive environment and its capabilities to implement a strategy. In previous coursework, you probably approached these issues with *SWOT analysis*, which is a relatively simple tool. The tools provided in Chapters 3 and 4 will help you systematically analyze what you could only do intuitively with the SWOT tool.

The long-term profitability of both Coke and Pepsi has probably been influenced by the structure of the soft-drink industry. Many enterprising entrepreneurs have seen this long-term propensity to make lots of money in the soft-drink industry and have desired to share in that wealth. Many small, profitable companies have emerged, yet, none has succeeded in becoming a major player alongside Coke and Pepsi. In this chapter, you will begin to understand why some industries are more profitable than others, why some industries are easier to enter than others, and what firms can do to influence these environmental factors in their favor.

Industry- and Firm-Specific Factors

Knowing what industry- and firm-specific factors affect a firm is critical to understanding its competitive position and determining what strategies are viable. We can examine the complementary roles of industry- and firm-specific factors on firm performance in many different industries. For instance, consider the venerable position of Coca-Cola in the soft-drink industry. Clearly, Coca-Cola has some firm-level advantages over its competitors.

Exhibit 4.1   Comparative Industrywide Levels of Profitability, 1995–2004

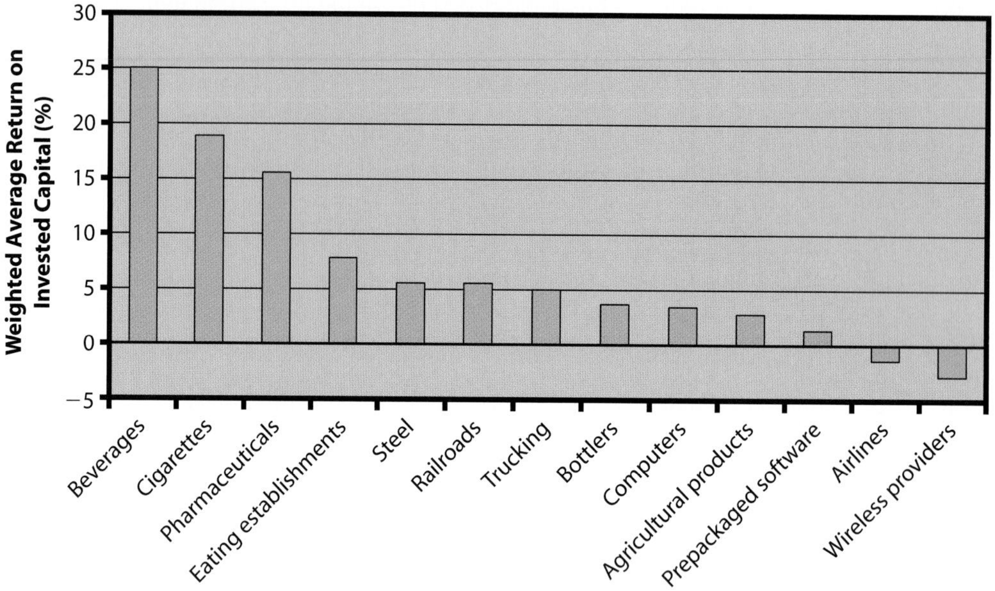

Source: Data from Standard & Poor's Compustat.

However, what happened when Coca-Cola entered the wine industry? The entry of Coca-Cola into the wine industry won't change at least two fundamental facts, namely, there is relatively little brand loyalty in wine, and the sale and distribution of the product is heavily regulated in most parts of the world. In 1977, Coke swallowed up industry giants Taylor Wine and Sterling Vineyard. As a beverage, wine is not entirely unrelated to Coke's core products, but unfortunately, Coke never mastered the complexities of a production and distribution process that's often as much an art as a science. After ringing up huge losses for a few years, Coke sold off its wine businesses—for much less than it initially paid for them. Evidently, some things don't go better with Coke.

As shown in Exhibit 4.1, profitability varies widely from industry to industry. Even without the analytical tools to which you'll be introduced in this chapter, you can see that there must be some things about the airline industry relative to the pharmaceutical industry that result in such drastic differences in profitability. Likewise, there are probably factors about the soft-drink industry that have helped Coke and Pepsi maintain such high profits over such an extended period of time. Why *are* some industries more profitable than others? For instance, why is the beverage industry (e.g., Coke, Pepsi, and their competitors) so much more profitable than the bottling industry?

What is needed to answer these questions are tools that allow you to systematically analyze a firm's external context. In the following sections you will be introduced to these tools. The proper use of these tools will help identify some of the major reasons industries differ so much in their long-term profitability.

We'll start this chapter by introducing methods for analyzing the macro environment and firms' industries. We then draw attention to the dynamic facets of the external environment.

Fundamental Characteristics of the External Context

conceptlink

In Chapter 2, we discuss the importance of *stakeholder analysis*, which we characterize as a series of steps for determining the nature and extent to which certain groups, both internal and external, have not only a vested interest in a firm's strategy, but also some influence on its decisions and performance.

Identifying the industry in which a firm competes is a logical starting point for analyzing its external context. By the fundamental characteristics of an industry, we mean those factors that are relevant to firm performance at a given point in time—the distinct features that you'd see if you could take an industry snapshot. Remember, too, that industry analysis will include many, but not all, of a firm's key external stakeholders. Thus, in order to avoid blind spots in an industry analysis, managers should always integrate their analysis of a firm's industry with a broader stakeholder analysis like that discussed in Chapter 2.

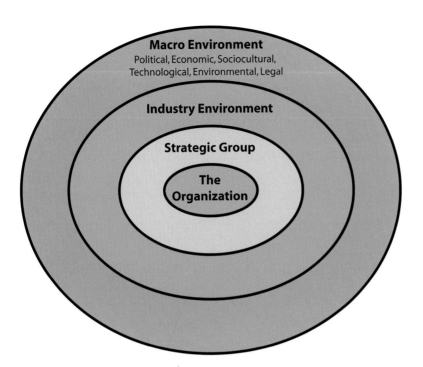

Exhibit 4.2 The External Environment of the Organization

Key Questions

Managers should ask the following questions when analyzing the firm's external context: "What macro environmental conditions will have a material effect on our ability to implement our strategy successfully?" "What is the firm's industry?" "What are the characteristics of the industry?" and "How stable are these characteristics?" By addressing such questions, managers can gain a better sense of a firm's strategic options and challenges. Managers must remain focused on the industry, not on a particular firm operating within it. Focusing on Coca-Cola alone will not provide much information on the general characteristics of the soft-drink industry, especially given the fact that Coke is far from average in terms of resources and capabilities. In addition, an industry analysis examines much more than simply the competitors in the industry. Our goal throughout this chapter is to present a deeper understanding of the external context in which *all* firms in an industry operate.

The external environment has two major components: the macro environment and the industry environment. The industry environment is composed of strategic groups—groupings of firms that seem to be more similar in certain ways than other members of the larger industry. The various levels of analysis necessary to examine a firm's external context are summarized in Exhibit 4.2. We will start with the macro environment most removed from the firm and work our way toward more micro analysis.

MACRO ENVIRONMENT

The macro environment refers to the larger political, economic, social, technical, environmental, and legal issues that confront the firm. To analyze the macro environment, we introduce the PESTEL model and present the determinants and consequences of globalization.

PESTEL Analysis

A simple but important and widely used tool that can be used to develop an understanding of the big picture of a firm's external environment is **PESTEL analysis**. PESTEL is an acronym for the *p*olitical, *e*conomic, *s*ociocultural, *t*echnological, *e*nvironmental, and *l*egal context(s) in which a firm operates. It provides a nonexhaustive list of potential influences of the environment on the organization. It helps managers gain a better understanding of the opportunities and threats they face and consequently aids them in building a better

PESTEL analysis Tool for assessing the political, economic, sociocultural, technological, environmental, and legal contexts in which a firm operates.

concept link

In Chapter 1, we define **arenas** as the areas, ranging from products and technologies to market segments and geographic locations, in which a firm will be active.

vision of the future business landscape and how the firm might compete profitably. PESTEL analysis is a useful tool for understanding market growth or decline. Its primary focus is on the future impact of macro environmental factors.

Firms need to understand the macro environment to ensure that their strategy is aligned with the powerful forces of change that are affecting their business landscape. When firms exploit changes in the environment, they are more likely to be successful than when they simply try to survive or oppose change. A good understanding of PESTEL also helps managers avoid strategies that may be doomed to failure for reasons beyond their control. Finally, understanding PESTEL is a good starting point for entering into a new country or region.

The fact that a strategy is congruent with PESTEL in the home environment gives no assurance that it will be so aligned in new geographic arenas. For example, when the online clothier Lands' End sought to expand its operations from the United States to Germany in 1996 it ran into local laws prohibiting Lands' End from offering unconditional guarantees on its products. In the United States, Lands' End had built its reputation for quality on its no-questions-asked money-back guarantee. However, this practice was considered illegal under Germany's regulations governing incentive offers and price discounts. The political skirmish between Lands' End and the German government finally came to an end in 2001, when the regulations were abolished. Although the regulations did not put Lands' End out of business in Germany, they did slow its growth there until the laws against advertising unconditional guarantees were abolished.

PESTEL analysis involves three steps. First, you should think through the relevance of each of the PESTEL factors to your particular context. Second, you identify and categorize the information that applies to these factors. Third, you analyze the data and draw conclusions. A mistake too many students make is to stop at the second step. A second common mistake is to assume that your initial analysis and conclusions are correct without testing your assumptions and investigating alternative scenarios.

The PESTEL analysis framework is presented in Exhibit 4.3. It has six sections, one for each of the PESTEL headings. The table includes sample questions or prompts, the answers to which will help you determine the nature of opportunities and threats in the macro environment. The questions are not meant to be exhaustive; rather, they are merely exemplars of the types of issues that you should be concerned about in the macro environment.

Political Factors   The political environment can have a significant influence on businesses as well as affect consumer confidence and consumer and business spending. Managers need to consider numerous types of political factors. For instance, the stability of the political environment is particularly important for companies entering new markets. In addition, government policies with respect to regulation and taxation vary from state to state and across national boundaries. Political considerations also encompass trade treaties, such as NAFTA, and regional trading blocks, such as ASEAN and the European Union (EU). Such treaties and trading blocks tend to favor trade among the member countries and to impose penalties or less favorable trade terms on nonmembers.

Economic Factors   Managers also need to consider the macroeconomic factors that will have near- and long-term effects on the success of their strategies. Factors such as inflation rates, interest rates, tariffs, the growth of the local and foreign national economies, and exchange rates are critical. Unemployment rates, the availability of critical labor, and the local labor costs also have a strong bearing on strategy, particularly as it relates to where to locate disparate business functions and facilities.

Sociocultural Factors   The social and cultural influences on business vary from country to country. Depending on the type of business the firm operates, factors such as the local languages, the dominant religions, leisure time, and age and lifespan demographics may be critical. Local sociocultural characteristics also vary on such things as attitudes toward consumerism, environmentalism, and the roles of men and women in local society. Making assumptions about local sociocultural norms derived from your experience in your home market is a common cause of early failure when entering new markets. However, even home-market norms can change over time, often caused by shifting demographics

Exhibit 4.3 The Dimensions of PESTEL Analysis

Political
- How stable is the political environment?
- What are local taxation policies and how do these affect your business?
- Is the government involved in trading agreements such as EU, NAFTA, ASEAN, or others?
- What are the foreign-trade regulations?
- What are the social-welfare policies?

Economic
- What are current and projected interest rates?
- What is the level of inflation, what is it projected to be, and how does this projection reflect the growth of your market?
- What are local employment levels per capita and how are they changing?
- What are the long-term prospects for gross domestic product (GDP) per capita and so on?
- What are exchange rates between critical markets and how will they affect production and distribution of your goods?

Sociocultural
- What are local lifestyle trends?
- What are the current demographics and how are they changing?
- What is the level and distribution of education and income?
- What are the dominant local religions and what influence do they have on consumer attitudes and opinions?
- What is the level of consumerism and what are popular attitudes toward it?
- What pending legislation affects corporate social policies (e.g., domestic-partner benefits, maternity/paternity leave)?
- What are the attitudes toward work and leisure?

Technological
- What is the level of research funding in government and industry and are those levels changing?
- What is the government and industry's level of interest and focus on technology?
- How mature is the technology?
- What is the status of intellectual-property issues in the local environment?
- Are potentially disruptive technologies in adjacent industries creeping in at the edges of the focal industry?

Environmental
- What are local environmental issues?
- Are there any pending ecological or environmental issues relevant to your industry?
- How do the activities of international pressure groups (e.g., Greenpeace, Earth First, PETA) affect your business?
- Are there environmental-protection laws?
- What are the regulations regarding waste disposal and energy consumption?

Legal
- What are the regulations regarding monopolies and private property?
- Does intellectual property have legal protections?
- Are there relevant consumer laws?
- What is the status of employment, health-and-safety, and product-safety laws?

due to immigration or aging populations. For example, Coca-Cola and Pepsi have grown in international markets due to increasing levels of consumerism outside of the United States.

Technological Factors The critical role of technology will be discussed in more detail later in the chapter. For now, suffice it to say that technological factors have a major bearing on the threats and opportunities firms encounter. Does technology enable products and services to be made more cheaply and to a better standard of quality? Do technologies provide the opportunity for more innovative products and services, such as online stock trading, reduction in communications costs, and increased remote working? How might distribution be affected by new technologies? All of these factors have the potential to change the face of the business landscape.

Environmental Factors   The environment has long been a factor in firm strategy, primarily from the standpoint of access to raw materials. Increasingly, however, this factor is best viewed as a direct- and indirect-operating cost for the firm, as well as from the lens of the footprint left by a firm on its respective environments in terms of waste, pollution, etc. For consumer-products companies such as Pepsi, for example, this can mean waste-management and organic-farming practices in the countries from which raw materials are obtained. Similarly, in consumer markets it may refer to the degree to which packaging is biodegradable or recyclable.

Legal Factors   Finally, legal factors reflect the laws and regulations relevant to the region and the organization. Legal factors may include whether the rule of law is well established and how easily or quickly laws and regulations may change. It may also include the costs of regulatory compliance. For instance, Coca-Cola's market share in Europe is greater than 50 percent, and as a result, regulators have asked that Coke give up shelf space to competitors' products in order to provide greater consumer choice.

As you can see, many of the PESTEL factors are interrelated. For instance, the legal environment is often related to the political environment in that laws and regulations will change only when politicians decide that such changes are needed.

Globalization

Over the past decade, as new markets have been opened to foreign competitors, whole industries have been deregulated; and state-run enterprises have been privatized; globalization has become a fact of life in almost every industry.[2] Because of this, the topic of globalization spans both the subjects of PESTEL analysis and industry analysis in both relatively stable and dynamic contexts. We define **globalization** as the evolution of distinct geographic product markets into a state of globally interdependent product markets.

globalization Evolution of distinct geograhic markets into a state of globally interdependent product markets

Globalization entails much more than a company simply exporting products to another country. Some industries that aren't normally considered global do in fact have strictly domestic players, but they're often competing alongside firms with operations in many countries, and in many cases, both sets of firms are doing equally well. In contrast, in a truly global industry, the core product is standardized, the marketing approach is relatively uniform, and competitive strategies are integrated in different international markets.[3] In these industries, competitive advantage clearly belongs to the firms that can compete globally.

A number of factors reveal whether an industry has globalized or is in the process of globalizing. In Exhibit 4.4, we've grouped them into four categories: *market, cost, government,* and *competition.*[4]

Markets   The more similar markets in different regions are, the greater the pressure for an industry to globalize. Coke and Pepsi, for example, are fairly uniform around the world because the demand for soft drinks is largely the same in every country. The airframe-manufacturing industry, dominated by Boeing and Airbus, also has a highly uniform market for its products because airlines all over the world have the same needs when it comes to large commercial jets.

Exhibit 4.4 Factors in Globalization

Sources: Adapted from M. E. Porter, Competition in Global Industries (Boston: Harvard Business School Press, 1986); G. Yip, "Global Strategy in a World of Nations," Sloan Management Review 31:1 (1989), 29–40.

Pressures Favoring Industry Globalization			
Markets	**Costs**	**Governments**	**Competition**
• Homogeneous customer needs • Global customer needs • Global channels • Transferable marketing approaches	• Large scale and scope economies • Learning and experience • Sourcing efficiencies • Favorable logistics • Arbitrage opportunities • High R&D costs	• Favorable trade policies • Common technological standards • Common manufacturing and marketing regulations	• Interdependent countries • Global competitors

Governments can have a huge impact on trade by setting industry-wide standards and regulations. In some parts of Western Europe, for example, people and freight can't travel easily from country to country without switching railroads. Because each country's rail standards and technology are different from its neighbors', rail lines are in some cases incompatible with one another.

Costs   In both the soft-drink and airframe-manufacturing industries, costs also favor globalization. Coke and Pepsi realize economies of scope and scale because they make such huge investments in marketing and promotion. Because they're promoting coherent images and brands, they can leverage their marketing dollars around the world. Similarly, Boeing and Airbus can invest millions in new-product R&D only because the global market for their products is so large.

Governments and Competition   Obviously, favorable trade policies encourage the globalization of markets and industries. Governments, however, can also play a critical role in globalization by determining and regulating technological standards. Railroad gauge—the distance between the two steel tracks—would seem to favor a simple technological standard. In Spain, however, the gauge is wider than in France. Why? Because back in the 1850s, when Spain and neighboring France were hostile to one another, the Spanish government decided that making Spanish railways incompatible with French railways would hinder a French invasion.

The cell-phone industry offers a more recent example. The EU has mobilized around one GSM standard, whereas most of the North American market adheres to another GSM standard or the CDMA standard that originally dominated most of the U.S. market. Although recent breakthroughs have made multistandard phones possible, these differences still create fragmented markets for cell-phone manufacturers, such as Motorola and Nokia. Moreover, the interdependence of the European and North American markets means that manufacturers must maintain a strong regional presence. Finally, recent entrants into the industry, including Samsung and NEC, already engage in other global operations. Thus, the problem of multiple standards and the entry of large global competitors both spur globalization in the industry.

Now that you understand how PESTEL analysis and an assessment of globalization can help you characterize the general conditions of the macro environment, you are prepared to delve deeply into industry analysis. The next section reviews critical information that will help you analyze the structure of an industry and better understand your competitors.

INDUSTRY ANALYSIS

In market economies where competition is encouraged and monopolies are not allowed, firms should be able to earn only "normal" profits—that is, enough return to cover the cost of production and the cost of capital. Why? Because of competition. When there is perfect competition, there are numerous sellers and buyers (no monopolies), perfect information, relatively homogenous products offered by different firms, and no barriers to entry or exit. What happens if firms earn greater-than-normal profits (as most managers and shareholders are trying hard to accomplish)? Competition will increase, usually through the entry of new firms into the industry, and profits will be driven back to normal levels. Conversely, if profits fall *below* normal levels, some firms will exit, easing competition and allowing profits to increase to normal levels. However, even a casual reexamination would suggest that many industries must not be held to the laws of perfect competition because we see some industries with long-run average profits far exceeding normal levels and others with profits way below such levels.

In this book, however, we have asserted more than once that the strategist's goal is to develop a *competitive advantage* over rivals. When one firm enjoys an inherent advantage over other firms in its industry, above-normal returns are possible (at least for the firm with the advantage) because competition under these conditions is not perfect. In contrast to the conditions of perfect competition, imperfect competition is characterized by relatively few competitors, numerous suppliers and buyers, asymmetric information, heterogeneous products, and barriers that make entry into an industry difficult. Industry analysis helps managers determine the nature of the competition, the possible sources of imperfect competition in the industry, and the possibility of the firm's earning above-normal returns.

I/O Economics and Key Success Factors

The insights that help managers analyze an industry originate in a discipline called *industrial organization (I/O) economics*. Fortunately, one does not need to be an economist to understand the basic tools of industry analysis. These tools enable managers to understand the business landscape in which the firm operates. These tools and the insights derived from their use should be used iteratively with the tools of internal analysis. However, for simplicity's sake we will hold constant the internal condition of the firm and focus on external conditions in this chapter.

One implication of industry analysis is that firms perform best when they select a strategy that fits the industry environment. Researchers often argue that the goal of managers should be to acquire the necessary skills and resources, often called the **key success factors (KSFs)**, to compete in their industry environment.[5] For example, KSFs in the soft-drink industry might include (1) the ability to meet competitive pricing; (2) extensive distribution capabilities, including ownership of vending machines and cold-storage cases; (3) marketing skills to raise consumer brand awareness in a highly crowded marketplace; (4) a broad mix of products, including diet and noncaffeinated beverages; (5) global presence; and (6) well-positioned bottlers and bottling capacity.

On the surface, this strategy-development process is similar to the process of strategy formulation and implementation that we discussed in Chapter 3, with one critical difference: According to the I/O approach, the appropriate strategy, key assets, and requisite skills are dictated by *industry* characteristics. Why do I/O researchers regard KSFs as a function of the industry? Simply because all firms in an industry must possess them in order to be viable. Thus, KSFs fit the definition of valuable resources as defined in Chapter 3 because they are like table stakes in a poker game: You need the money just to get a seat at the poker table. The soft-drink example shows that these stakes actually create barriers to entry because they are complex and costly to put in place. KSFs are resources and skills that would satisfy the *value* criteria from the VRINE model introduced in Chapter 3, though by definition they will not satisfy the *rareness* criterion. Thus, possessing KSFs will not grant a firm a competitive advantage over other key players in the industry, but it will permit it to compete against such firms.

I/O researchers also argue that the analyst should focus primarily on the industry as a whole, and not on a particular firm, because KSFs are easily transferred from one firm to another. Thanks to relatively efficient markets, firms can readily buy the KSFs they need. In summary, the I/O approach suggests that managers should study an industry in order to understand which strategies are rewarded most profitably and to acquire the industry-relevant KSFs required to implement them.

conceptlink

The tools for internal analysis that we discuss in Chapter 3 include the **VRINE model** for assessing a firm's resources and capabilities, **dynamic capabilities** as a measure of its ability to reconfigure its resources and capabilities, and the **value chain** as a measure of its ability to find better or different ways of performing its key activities.

key success factor (KSF) Key asset or requisite skill that all firms in an industry must possess in order to be a viable competitor

conceptlink

In Chapter 3, we describe the **VRINE model** as a five-pronged test for determining the extent to which a firm's **resources** and **capabilities** will contribute to competitive advantage: They're *valuable* if they allow a firm to take advantage of opportunities or fend off threats and *rare* if they're scarce relative to demand.

What Is an Industry?

Economists define an *industry* as a firm or group of firms that produce or sell the same or similar products to the same market. Is there such a thing as a one-firm industry? If a firm holds a *monopoly*—if it's the only seller in the market—then it's the only firm in the industry. Many utilities operate as monopolies (and are typically regulated or owned outright by government bodies).

Fragmentation and Concentration   In a *duopoly* or *oligopoly*, the market is dominated by only two or a few large firms, and the industry is characterized as concentrated. In our opening vignette on the Cola War, it is clear that the soft-drink industry is very concentrated. At the other end of the spectrum, industries in which there's no clear leader are characterized as fragmented.

How can we determine the extent to which an industry is concentrated or fragmented? One useful tool is the *concentration ratio,* which represents the combined revenues of the largest industry participants as a ratio of total industry sales. For manufacturing industries, the U.S. Department of Commerce calculates these ratios at different levels, according to the number of firms treated as the industry's largest—4, 8, 20, or 50. Thus, we refer to these ratios as C4, C8, C20, and C50, respectively. Industry concentration is one of several important factors in industry analysis, because concentration affects the intensity of competition in an industry. For instance, fragmented markets are believed to be more competitive than concentrated markets, whereas concentrated markets are more difficult to enter.

To determine what constitutes an industry, it is necessary to identify clear classifications of products or markets. In the case of Coke and Pepsi, for instance, the industry could be defined as the *beverage industry.* This industry would include every firm that manufactures beverages—Lipton (tea), Starbucks (coffee), Seagram's (liquor), Heineken (beer), Mondavi (wine), Ocean Spray (juice), Coke and Pepsi (soft drinks), and so on. However, such a broad definition makes analysis very difficult and probably obscures important micro-level structural features. Coke and Pepsi's industry could alternatively be defined as the *carbonated soft-drink* industry. There is no definitive rule as to where to draw the boundaries when analyzing an industry. The key is to not be so inclusive that important factors that differ across heterogeneous markets cannot be detected (e.g., Are there key differences between alcoholic-beverage markets and soft-drink markets?) nor so exclusive that important threats are missed (e.g., Does excluding bottled water from the carbonated soft-drink industry miss the main growth segments?).

Defining Industry Boundaries   Indeed, the answer to the question "What industry am I in?" is not as simple as it might seem, even if you're only thinking about something to drink. You'll probably be surprised by the implications of different answers that can be given to this deceptively simple question. This is because industries are typically composed of many segments with different structural characteristics. In the midst of the Cola War, both antagonists were looking for ways to grow. Hard-nosed head-to-head competition was one option, but a simpler strategy involved merely redefining what industry each company was in—say, *beverages* in general or, more particularly, *soft-drink beverages.* Toward this end, Coke bought Minute Maid in 1960, and since then Coke and Pepsi seem to have agreed that they're in the *nonalcoholic-beverage* industry, which includes not only soda but also juices and teas. Pepsi purchased Tropicana (juices) in 1999 and South Beach Beverage in 2000. Coke bought Odwalla (juices) in 2001.

Today, the hottest new-product area in the nonalcoholic-beverage business is water—bottled water, to be exact. Bottled water is a multibillion-dollar growth industry, and it's well on its way to becoming the most consumed beverage in America (except for soft drinks). With an active market consisting of nearly half of all Americans, bottled water is on track to surpass beer, milk, and coffee to become the second-best-selling beverage in the United States.

Exhibit 4.5 Concentration in Selected U.S. Industries

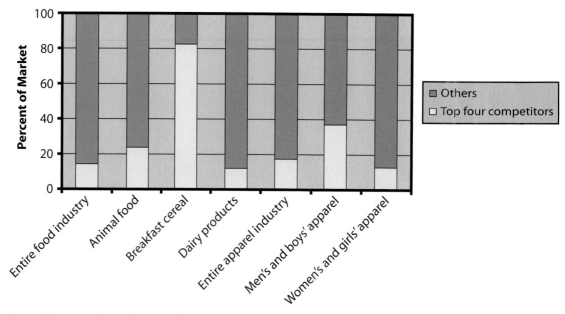

Source: U.S. Census Bureau, "Economic Census: Concentration Ratios," Economic Census 2002 (accessed July 15, 2005), www.census.gov/epcd/www/concentration.html.

Although Coke is big in soda, it comes in a distant third in the global bottled-water business.[6] With 70 brands in 160 countries, Nestlé, a Swiss company, controls nearly a third of the market, and its share is growing. In North America alone, Nestlé sells nine domestic brands, including Arrowhead, Poland Spring, and Deer Park, and five imported brands, including San Pellegrino and Perrier. Pepsi, with a nearly 10-percent share, comes in second with Aquafina, the top-selling single-serve bottled water in the United States. Coca-Cola is third (though not last) with Dasani, which has 8 percent of the market. Recently, however, Coke entered into a partnership with France's Groupe Danone that may vault it into second place once it begins producing, marketing, and distributing Danone's niche brands, which include Evian.

At least one thing should be clear by now: Before getting into an industry, the firm's managers must know the type of product and the geographic market that they're considering. Exhibit 4.5 underscores the importance of drawing industry boundaries in a way that enables managers to understand the dynamics of competition. As shown in Exhibit 4.5, concentration ratios vary dramatically among segments within the same broad industry group. In comparison to other industries, for example, the food industry is relatively fragmented: The four largest manufacturers account for only 14 percent of sales. Within this broad grouping, however, some areas are highly concentrated; the four largest competitors, for instance, account for a full 83 percent of breakfast-cereal sales. The apparel industry also consists of numerous segments. Concentration ratios in the men's and boys' segment are quite different from those in the women's and girls' segment: Sales are much more concentrated in the former. The differences in concentration ratios remind us that industry dynamics vary dramatically across various sectors of the same industry. As demonstrated by such differences in concentration ratios, the definition of an industry is critical to gaining an understanding of the competitive dynamics facing firms that operate in it and, ultimately, to the formulation of a strategy for competing in it.

A Model of Industry Structure

Once the boundaries of the industry to be analyzed have been identified, the next step is to examine the industry's fundamental characteristics and structure. The model shown in Exhibit 4.6 identifies five forces that determine the basic structure of an industry. These five forces were identified by Michael Porter as the industry **five-forces model**.[7] The horizontal axis is a stylized version of the industry value chain. An industry purchases inputs, or sup-

concept link

The **value chain** that we describe in Chapter 3 is the *organizational* value chain that consists of all the activities in which a firm engages in order to add more value than competitors and thus gain competitive advantage.

five-forces model Framework for evaluating industry structure according to the effects of rivalry, threat of entry, supplier power, buyer power, and the threat of substitutes

Exhibit 4.6 The Five Forces of Industry Structure

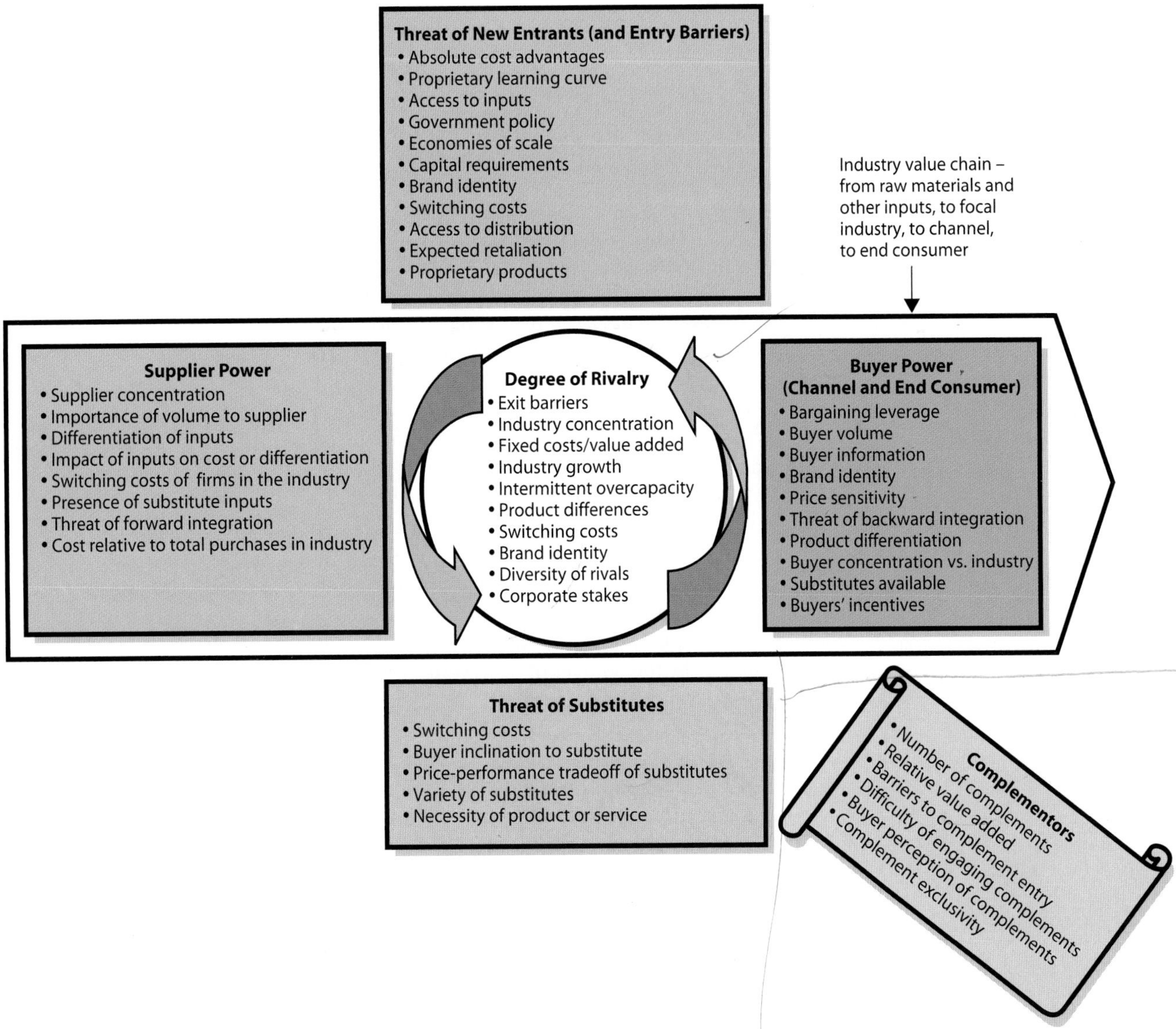

Source: Adapted from M. E. Porter, Competitive Strategy: Techniques for Analyzing Industries and Competitors *(New York: Free Press, 1980).*

plies, from other industries. Likewise, an industry sells its products or services to customers, which are often other businesses but may be retail consumers as well. In negotiations with suppliers and buyers, transactions are not always between parties of equal negotiating strength. The five-forces model draws attention to factors that systematically alter the negotiating strength in favor of suppliers, industry members, or buyers. Likewise, the model draws attention to threats posed by the possibility of new entrants (and conversely, the difficulty of exit) and possible substitute products from other industries or industry segments, either of which can pose threats to industry participants.

It's sometimes useful to think of these forces as countervailing sources of power all vying for a larger piece of the industry's total profits. Recall that when an industry is characterized by perfect competition, rivals in an industry will achieve normal levels of profitability—enough to pay for all factors of input, including the cost of capital. However, industries actually vary considerably in their average level of returns. A key reason for this variance in industry profitability is differences in the power of these five forces across different industries.

Rivalry Firms can compete in an industry in many ways. The intensity of competition is known as **rivalry**. The key questions to ask when analyzing the degree of rivalry in an

rivalry Intensity of competition within an industry

industry include: Who are the competitors? How do rival firms compete? Which firms will be identified as competitors? Because an understanding of the nature of rivalry is so important, we include a separate section on competitor analysis that details ways in which the future actions of competitors can be more accurately predicted.

At this stage of the analysis, it is important simply to come to a better sense of the overall nature of rivalry within an industry. The outcome associated with high degrees of rivalry is generally defined in terms of price competition. The most aggressive forms of competition include price wars. When firms are willing to sacrifice their margins through significantly lower prices, it can be assumed that the nature of the rivalry is very intense. This is not to say that competition isn't serious in industries in which price wars are not common. Rather, in those industries firms have found non-price-based forms of competition. From this definition of rivalry, it is easy to see that higher degrees of rivalry result in lower levels of average industry profitability: As price competition increases, average prices decline, resulting in lower levels of profitability.

What factors tend to increase rivalry? These factors can be categorized into attributes about firms within the industry and attributes about the products or markets themselves. First we will review the attributes of firms that make them likely to compete on prices. When there are numerous competitors, price competition is typically more intense than when there are only a few competitors. Consider the Cola War reviewed in the opening vignette. As intense as that rivalry has been, competition in most periods has focused on nonprice factors. Although advertising to build brand loyalty has been very expensive for Coke and Pepsi, it has been less harmful to profits than intense price wars. More generally, recall that the definition of perfect competition assumes that there are numerous buyers and sellers. In addition, price competition increases when competitors are of relatively equal size and power. Thus, rivalry is affected not only by the number of firms competing but also by how similar those firms are. For instance, the software industry includes many competitors, but Microsoft's size relative to most firms has the effect of marginalizing the threat of price competition.

Another firm-level factor that increases the threat of price competition is the degree to which the industry is strategically important to competitors. Recall that many firms are diversified and compete in multiple industries. Price competition tends to be fiercer when the industry is a key business for the major players in that industry.

Characteristics about the products and markets within an industry can also have a strong influence on the degree of price competition. Price competition tends to be fiercer in industries that are growing slowly. When a company's products are difficult to differentiate from those of competitors, they are forced to compete on price. Price competition is reduced when firms are able to create the impression that their products are different from those of competitors. Coke and Pepsi, for example, have spent billions of dollars to build brand equity and loyalty. Likewise, when there are very low costs for buyers to switch from one firm's offerings to another's, then competitors feel compelled to motivate buyer loyalty with aggressive pricing. Conversely, when customers face high switching costs, there is less pressure to keep prices low because a firm's buyers are somewhat locked in. Finally, industries characterized by high fixed costs, such as the airline industry, are more prone to price wars.

Threat of Entry and Exit Barriers   Not surprisingly, industries that boast relatively high average profitability attract the attention of firms operating elsewhere that are looking for promising new arenas in which to compete. Paradoxically, industries with consistently high average profitability also tend to be those that are the most difficult to enter. The degree to which new competitors may enter an industry and make rivalry more intense is known as the **threat of new entry**. Conditions that make it difficult to enter an industry are known as **barriers to entry**. Note that perfect competition is characterized by the absence of barriers to entry. Several industry characteristics contribute to such barriers, including strong brands, proprietary technologies, and other bases for product differentiation. Certain technologies, for instance, give their owners cost advantages that new entrants can't readily match or compensate for. In some industries, restricted access to investment capital or distribution channels constitutes barriers. Other industries, such as computerchip manufacturing, require large incremental capital investments in specialized manufac-

threat of new entry Degree to which new competitors can enter an industry and intensify rivalry

barrier to entry Condition under which it is more difficult to join or compete in an industry

turing facilities. In others, the need for location-based or preferential access to distribution networks can hinder or block entry by new players.

Consider the case of the soft-drink industry. With such perennially high levels of profit experienced by Coke and Pepsi, one would expect the industry to attract envious firms and entrepreneurs. And to be certain, there have been many new entrants at the margins and in newer segments not yet dominated by Coke and Pepsi. However, there has yet to be a successful entrant to the cola segment that has been able to capture a significant share of the market. A number of brave companies have tried. For instance, Sir Richard Bransen's Virgin Group has tried twice to enter the soft-drink market. In 1998, the British billionaire rode into New York's Times Square atop a tank, promising a battle with Coke and Pepsi. Virgin tried extensive hard-edge advertising to gain market awareness. However, it found it nearly impossible to secure premium shelf space in traditional retail outlets. In addition to facing a considerable brand-awareness chasm, Virgin discovered that the cost and time required to secure equal footing in retail establishments was prohibitive. After pulling out of the United States for a period, Virgin is giving it another try in America. The strategy this time is to be a niche player, having secured a deal for distribution through 7-Eleven stores.[8] Thus, entry barriers in the soft-drink industry include both extreme levels of brand loyalty and virtual control of prime distribution channels. The only competitive space available for new entrants in the near term appears to be on the periphery of the market. Thus, new entry is most often seen with local brands, private-label offerings, and specialty drinks.

The greater the degree of difficulty that potential entrants face in accumulating the resources necessary to compete in an industry, the higher the barriers to entry, and high barriers to entry have the effect of reducing potential competition by limiting supply and reducing rivalry. This results in higher prices and higher levels of average profitability than in industries in which there are fewer barriers to entry. Conversely, firms may face high **exit barriers** when it is very costly to leave an industry or market, particularly given the opportunity set possessed by any given incumbent. Firms with high exit barriers are typically forced to compete aggressively. For instance, the exit barriers in the airline industry are very high because air carriers have few opportunities outside of air travel, and those firms that exit the industry are likely to do so only by selling off their business and otherwise dissolving the firm.

Indeed, a firm may remain in an industry due to high exit barriers even when the business is not profitable. As an example, Litton Industries was very successful in building ships for the U.S. Navy the 1960s. However, when the Vietnam war ended and defense spending plummeted, Litton was so heavily invested in shipbuilding that it could not feasibly exit the industry, particularly given the high specialized investment in now-unattractive shipbuilding facilities. As a result, Litton was forced to stay in the shipbuilding market even though it was unattractive and declining.

Supplier Power In transactions between industry participants and firms in supply industries, the relative power of each party affects both the pricing of transactions and the profitability of each industry. The degree to which firms in the supply industry are able to dictate favorable contract terms and thereby extract some of the profit that would otherwise be available to competitors in the focal industry is referred to as **supplier power**. When focal-industry participants have negotiating strength, suppliers have limited bargaining power, and the focal industry acts to reduce supplier industry performance rather than the other way around. Suppliers are powerful when they control such factors as prices, delivery lead times, minimum orders, post-purchase service, and payment terms.

Supplier power arises when the suppliers are relatively concentrated, control a scarce input, or are simply bigger than their customers. In some cases, firms in a focal industry need a unique product or service and have only a few alternative suppliers to which to turn. In these instances, of course, suppliers can demand higher prices.

For instance, from the opening vignette it is easy to see that the soft-drink industry is very consolidated and the two major players are very large. They purchase most of their inputs in commodity markets (e.g., sweeteners, food coloring). As a result, suppliers have no leverage over soft-drink manufactures. In contrast, consider the situation from the

exit barriers Barriers that impose a high cost on the abandonment of a market or product

supplier power Degree to which firms in the supply industry are able to dictate terms to contracts and thereby extract some of the profit that would otherwise go to competitors in the focal industry

point of view of the bottlers, who buy soft-drink concentrate from manufacturers like Coke and Pepsi and cans and bottles from canning companies. The bottling industry faces significant supplier-power problems because their concentrate suppliers are heavily consolidated. When a firm has a franchise to bottle Coke (or Pepsi), the contract is exclusive, meaning that it has agreed to let Coke or Pepsi be its supplier in perpetuity. By contract, the bottler cannot buy cola products from any other concentrate maker. Thus, soft-drink bottlers face a condition of considerable supplier power.

Likewise, the jewelry business requires access to diamonds. Because South Africa's DeBeers controls over 50 percent of the world's diamond supply, it is in the position to force jewelry makers to pay high prices for its diamonds.

Even when an industry is sourcing products that may be considered commodities, such as textiles or wood, suppliers can impose payment terms that implicitly raise the cost of the resource for the focal industry. Such is the case when the supplier industry is more consolidated than the focal industry. Because the furniture industry, for example, is highly fragmented, no single manufacturer has very much power when bargaining with the larger wood and fabric suppliers who provide the industry's primary raw materials. Suppliers of wood have many possible firms to which to sell.

Supplier power is also high when firms in the supply industry present a threat of forward integration—that is, if it's possible for them to manufacture finished products rather than just sell components to manufacturers. Coke and Pepsi, for example, could easily integrate forward into bottling instead of just supplying bottlers with concentrate. They have demonstrated this by purchasing bottlers in the past. This potential gives them significant power in negotiating prices with their bottling networks.

Finally, suppliers are powerful when firms in the focal industry face significant switching costs when changing suppliers. For instance, companies purchasing enterprise resource planning (ERP) software have several supplier choices, including SAP, Oracle, and PeopleSoft. However, once a firm purchases from one supplier and incurs the significant implementation costs associated with ERP, it will be very reluctant to switch to another supplier because the costs of doing so are significant. Because of the high costs involved in switching ERP systems, firms switch suppliers less frequently than one would expect in a market with many sellers.

In summary, in transactions between industry participants and firms in supply industries, the relative power of each party affects both the pricing and profitability of each industry. When focal-industry participants have negotiating strength, suppliers have lim-

South Africa's DeBeers controls half of the world's diamonds. As such, it wields a great deal of buyer and supplier power and controls the prices that it both pays and charges for diamonds.

ited bargaining power, and the focal industry acts to reduce the supplier-industry performance rather than the other way around.

Buyer Power   The reciprocal of supplier power, **buyer power** is the degree to which firms in the buyers' industry are able to dictate favorable terms on purchase agreements that extract some of the profit that would otherwise be available to competitors in the focal industry. When firms in the focal industry sell to their customers (i.e., buyers), those transactions are subject to the same bargaining forces just reviewed for supplier power. Buyers, for example, whether in a business-to-business or business-to-consumer relationship, compete with sellers by trying to force prices down.

Several factors lead to buyers having high degrees of relative power over their suppliers. A buyer group has greater power in the exchange relationship with its suppliers when the buyers are prestigious and when their purchases represent a significant portion of the sellers' sales. By the same token, if a product has little value for the buyer group, buyers are more powerful negotiating with firms in the industry. A buyer group is also powerful when it has numerous choices, such as when the products and prices of multiple competitors are easy to compare. Tire makers, for instance, have little power over carmakers because their product is standardized and there are many competitors in the industry. If a tire maker tried to raise prices, large automobile manufacturers would turn to one of several other firms that could fill their needs. Conversely, when buyers have few alternatives, their power is minimal, and industry prices increase, resulting in higher than average industry profitability.

Consider the extreme case of the Green Bay Packers of the National Football League. The Packers have maintained a waiting list for season tickets for the past 43 years; the average wait is 30 years. Because there are few other entertainment alternatives in Green Bay, Wisconsin, there is essentially one seller and many buyers for the opportunity for professional sports entertainment. The team is certainly under no pressure to discount prices.[9]

Information also provides buyers with power, particularly when they have choices, when the products are relatively inexpensive, or when products are not heavily regulated. New-car buyers, for example, are relatively powerful not only because there are numerous makes and models in every category, but because they can now use the Internet to compare products and prices online. In contrast, dealers don't have a corresponding advantage when negotiating with carmakers because operating agreements require them to sell certain manufacturers' products.

Finally, buyers are powerful to the extent that they pose a threat of backward integration. Large brewers, for instance, could conceivably make their own beer cans (in fact, some do). The implicit threat that these buyers of aluminum cans could move backward into a supplier's industry naturally diminishes the supplier's price-setting power.

What About Retail Consumers?   Let's make a final—and critical—point about the role of buyer power in any definition of an industry. Note that the industry is the unit that we're analyzing: The focal point of our assessment of rivalry in an industry is the industry segment that we've chosen to analyze. Consequently, when we talk about buyers, we don't mean end retail consumers (unless, of course, we're analyzing a retail-market segment—grocery stores, new-car dealers, department stores, etc.). Japan's Matsushita Electric Industrial, for example, markets many well-known electronics brands, including Panasonic, Quasar, and JVC. When Matsushita markets Panasonic TVs, its targeted customers are not household consumers but, rather, large retail chains and electronics wholesalers. Certainly, retail consumers are important, but they don't negotiate directly with manufacturers, and they don't wield any direct power in nonretail segments. Consumers affect industry profits indirectly when they exercise power as the last link in an industry value chain. An analysis of Panasonic's industry segment would examine the relative power of Matsushita and its rivals in negotiating with retailers, such as Best Buy and Circuit City, who carry their products.

Threat of Substitutes   Sometimes products in other industries can satisfy the same demand as the products of the focal industry. The degree to which this is the case is known as the **threat of substitutes**. Recall, for example, our earlier discussion of bottled water and soft

buyer power Degree to which firms in the buying industry are able to dictate terms on purchase agreements which extract some of the profit that would otherwise go to competitors in the focal industry

threat of substitutes Degree to which products of one industry can satisfy the same demand as those of another

drinks. These two different types of products may be substituted for one another in satisfying the demand of some customers. If we defined Coke and Pepsi's industry as soft drinks, then bottled water would be a substitute to which we'd have to pay attention. Consider the case of the movie-rental business. Blockbuster faces direct competition from Hollywood Video, Movie Gallery, Netflix, and other regional and local chains. What are substitutes for DVD and video rental services? Customers' options seem to be increasing. Cable and satellite TV would seem to be a separate industry from movie rentals. However, movie channels available through these outlets would seem to be clear substitutes for movie rentals. And, more recently, the availability of on-demand movie streaming through cable and satellite providers seems to provide an even closer substitute product. Thus, the prices that Blockbuster and other movie-rental businesses can charge is to some extent limited by the availability of viable substitutes.

Even when market segments aren't as closely related as cable and satellite TV are to the movie-rental industry, products may still be potential substitutes. In the broadest sense, a *substitute* is any product that satisfies a common interest. The desire for leisure, for instance, can be satisfied with both books and travel. Narrowing the classification scheme, consider substitute products between segments in the travel industry. At Southwest Airlines, for example, the primary competition for many shorter flights comes not from other airlines but, rather, from competitors in the automobile- and bus-transportation segments. Thus, within certain geographic limitations, automobiles and bus service are substitutes for airline travel.

It should be clear by now that the prevalence of viable substitute products from other industries places pressures on the prices that can be charged in the focal industry. When there are no viable substitutes, there is less pressure on price. Consequently, average industry profits tend to be lower when clear substitutes are available.

The Impact of Complementors   As we noted at the beginning of this discussion, the five forces that we've just described comprise a model of industry structure proposed by Michael Porter. When these forces are strong, industry profitability tends to be reduced. More recently, some researchers have argued that the players outlined in the five-forces model do not always compete exclusively in zero-sum games. Sometimes these players work together to create value jointly rather than competing to divide the market. **Complementors** are players who provide complementary rather than competing products and services.[10]

> **complementor** Firm in one industry that provides products or services which tend to increase sales in another industry

The characteristics of complements are shown in Exhibit 4.6. Firms in the music and electronics industries, for example, sell products that must be used together. Each benefits from the other's presence. Likewise, when people buy hotdogs, an increase in sales of buns, condiments, and beverages is likely. These three products are marketed by complementary industry segments (which is why grocers can sell buns below cost to stimulate sales of higher-margin hot dogs). Sometimes firms in the same industry or suppliers and buyers simultaneously play the role of complementors. For instance, United and Delta compete fiercely in trying to attract customers to fill their seats. However, when upgrading their fleets to a newer plane, both airlines are probably better off when they jointly order a new model from Boeing or Airbus. Because both are in the market for new planes at the same time, aircraft manufacturers are able to achieve greater economies of scale with larger orders, thereby lowering the cost of new planes.

This example helps introduce a more formal definition of *complementor:* A complementor is any factor that makes it more attractive for suppliers to supply an industry on favorable terms or that makes it more attractive for buyers to purchase products or services from an industry at prices higher than it would pay absent the complementor. However, even though a firm or industry segment fulfills a complementor role, it may still compete with firms in the focal industry. A firm or industry segment may simultaneously play the roles of complementor and competitor (as in the Delta/United example). In addition, a complementor that results in increased focal-industry sales will not necessarily share equally in the increased bounty. These relationships still have elements of bargaining power akin to supplier and buyer relationships; one party to a complementor relationship may receive more of the benefit than the other even though both are better off.

Customers, then, are likely to put a higher value on the products of one industry segment when they already have or have access to complementary products from another segment.[11] The value of computer peripherals obviously increases as the number of personal computers increases. Likewise, the value of a commercial real-estate development is enhanced if there are neighboring amenities valued by business tenants, such as restaurants, entertainment venues, and transportation facilities. More new cars are sold when affordable financing is easier to get or dealers offer extended service warranties. Thus, financing and warranty arrangements can be regarded as complementors to the retail new-car market.

Finally, note one important difference between complementors and the other five forces in this model of industry analysis: Whereas the five forces typically work to *decrease* industry profitability, the presence of strong complementors may *increase* profits by increasing demand for an industry's products.

Using the Industry-Structure Model An understanding of the five industry forces and complementors can help managers evaluate the general attractiveness of an industry as well as the specific opportunities and threats facing firms in their focal segment. An industry is most attractive—that is, has the highest profit potential—when attractive complementors furnish positive externalities and when the effects of the other five forces are minimal. The pressure on operating margins will be significantly lower than in industries in which suppliers or buyers exercise high levels of power, in which entry barriers are low, and in which abundant substitute products are available.

How does industry analysis affect strategy formulation? A good industry analysis will enable an executive to answer a few basic questions with much greater certainty than could be done before the analysis. Some of these questions include the following: Does the firm's current strategy fit with current industry conditions? What changes in the industry may result in misalignment? Which elements of the firm's strategy will need to be altered to exploit future industry conditions?

When using the five-forces model to formulate strategy, remember that these forces are not static. The actions of various industry players keep industry conditions in an almost constant state of flux. Consequently, unattractive industry structure isn't necessarily an omen that profitability is destined to be marginal. Wise strategists use information gleaned from the study of industry structure to formulate strategies for dealing with threats highlighted by industry analysis.

Remember, too, that this type of analysis views industry forces from an overall industry perspective and not from that of any particular firm. The industry-wide effect of these forces will determine whether an industry is attractive or not. We walk through the use of Porter's five-forces analysis in the box entitled "How Would *You* Do That? 4.1."

Strategic Group and Competitor Analysis

One of the purposes of industry analysis is to develop a clear understanding of who the firm's competitors are and what their behaviors are likely to be in the future. Consequently, after completing a five-forces analysis, it is often helpful to investigate more deeply the strategies and behaviors of the firm's competitors. We briefly review two frameworks that managers find useful in gaining an understanding of their competitors: *strategic-group analysis* and *competitor analysis*.

Strategic Groups By the time you've finished your industry analysis, you will probably have realized that rival firms, though often similar, are rarely identical. The U.S. airline industry, for instance, has several full-service carriers, such as United, American, and Delta, but there are also a number of discount airlines (Southwest and JetBlue) and regional carriers (Skywest and Midwest Express). The European airline industry has a similar structure. In the department-store industry, Wal-Mart and Nordstrom obviously take different approaches to strategy and rarely compete directly for the same customers. In the beer industry, Anheuser-Busch, SABMiller, and MolsonCoors have more in common with each other than any of them has in common with Sam Adams or Heineken.

A distinguishable cluster of competitors within an industry is called a strategic group. A **strategic group** is a subset of firms that, because they have similar strategies, resources, and capabilities, compete against each other more intensely than with other firms in the industry.[12] When groups of firms share strategies, resources, and capabilities that differ from those of

In Chapter 3, we define a firm's **resources** as the inputs that it uses to create goods or services and its **capabilities** as its skill in using its resources.

strategic group Subset of firms which, because of similar strategies, resources, and capabilities, compete against each other more intensely than with other firms in an industry

A Five-Forces—Plus Complementors—Analysis of the U.S. Airline Industry

Let's apply the five-forces model to the U.S. airline industry to illustrate how it is used in practice. The first step is to identify the industry—where to draw the boundaries to start the analysis. Examination of data maintained by the U.S. Department of Transportation reveals that the Department categorizes the airline industry into four groups: international, national, regional, and cargo. International carriers are characterized by firms with large planes that fly just about anywhere in the world. Companies in this segment typically have revenues in excess of $1 billion. National airlines have revenues between $100 million and $1 billion and fly domestically only. Regional airlines are smaller airlines with revenues below $100 million. Cargo airlines do not fly commercial passengers; they specialize in the transportation of goods. We could analyze all airlines, but cargo lines serve very different customers. In practice, we may iterate through a few boundary definitions, but for simplicity let's focus on national airlines (sales of at least $1 billion). Note that this will include all U.S. international airlines as well because they are also large national airlines.

RIVALRY

The next step would be to identify the key players in the national passenger-airline market. Who are the rivals? You could turn to numerous available data sources to identify the key players. Using hoovers.com, we identify the top-three competitors as United, American, and Delta; other competitors include AirTran, Alaska Air, America West, Continental Airlines, Hawaiian Air, JetBlue, Northwest Airlines, Southwest Airlines, and US Airways. These competitors are not all competing the same way, and you may want to sketch out how different groups compete (e.g., low cost, hub-and-spoke networks), but we leave that for another exercise. How competitive is this industry? Is competition based on price or nonprice competition? It would not take a lot of research to discover that this is a highly competitive industry. Most airlines make extremely low returns; indeed, many are currently losing money. The annals of airline history document many price wars, and airlines also compete with nonprice competitive tactics such as frequent-flier programs.

POWER OF SUPPLIERS

Who are the suppliers to national airlines? Most, such as caterers, airports, airplane manufacturers, and security firms, are oligopolies, meaning that the airlines are in a less advantageous position. Key suppliers include makers of aircraft, and two companies, Boeing and Airbus, dominate that market and are able to garner significant profits at the airlines' expense by virtue of their specialized positions and government subsidies. The other key supply for airlines is fuel. Due to macro environmental issues (e.g., oil shortages), the price of fuel is currently proving a very problematic issue for airlines. However, this is not a »

function of supplier power but, rather, conditions in the oil market.

POWER OF BUYERS

To whom do national airlines sell their services? Buyers can be categorized into three primary groups: business travelers, leisure travelers, and buyers of large blocks of seats known as consolidators, who buy excess seat inventory at large discounts. What bargaining power do these customers have? Switching costs are very low, though airlines have increased them somewhat through frequent-flier programs. Buyers are price sensitive, but they have very little individual buyer power.

THREAT OF SUBSTITUTES

What is the likelihood that airline customers will use alternative means of transportation? When it comes to business travelers, this would seem minimal. However, communication technology has proven to be a viable substitute for some forms of business travel. For leisure travelers, the threat of substitutes is mainly for shorter flights. Thus, alternatives such as auto and bus transportation are more viable substitutes for regional airlines

and national airlines that specialize in shorter flights (e.g., Southwest).

THREAT OF NEW ENTRANTS

The capital intensity of the airline industry would appear to pose a formidable entry barrier. However, JetBlue, AirTran, and other entrants have proven that financing is available when there is a convincing business plan and when economic conditions are conducive to the business model proposed. Brand name and frequent-flier plans would also seem to be deterrents to entry. However, JetBlue's success demonstrates that customers are willing to switch airlines if the price is right.

THE ROLE OF COMPLEMENTORS

The primary complementors in the airline industry are vacation-industry participants, credit card companies, and rental-car agencies. Credit card companies have teamed up with airlines to augment frequent-flier programs. Vacation-industry firms team up with airlines to bundle services and stimulate demand in both industries. Rental-car companies team up with airlines to offer promotions and customer loyalty programs. Because

such loyalty marketing programs decrease price competition, they tend to be good for incumbent profitability.

In summary, it would appear that supplier power, buyer power, substitutes, and complementors do not pose ominous threats to the airline industry. The only two forces within the industry that could account for the poor performance of the industry would seem to be relatively low entry barriers and competitive rivalry.

The implications of this analysis vary depending on which competitor we are interested in. What Delta should do to better align itself with industry conditions is not at all what Southwest should consider. A quality industry analysis would be the same regardless of the company of interest, but the implications would vary.

Sources: J. E. Ellis, "The Law of Gravity Doesn't Apply: Inefficiency, Overcapacity, Huge Debt . . . What Keeps U.S. Carriers Up in the Air?" *BusinessWeek,* September 26, 2005, p. 49; H. Tully, "Airlines: Why the Big Boys Won't Come Back," *Fortune,* June 14, 2004, p. 101.

other groups, they face different opportunities and threats, even though they operate within the same industry.[13] One way to recognize differences in opportunities and threats is to examine the different effects of the five forces on different strategic groups. Barriers to entry in the beer industry, for example, may vary significantly in the way they affect different strategic groups. Which is more likely to emerge, a local premium brand or a global midmarket brand? Obviously, it's the former. Why? Because barriers to entry, including the required capital investment, the power of established brands, and such incumbent advantages as retail slotting allowances, are too strong among the makers of widely distributed midmarket brands.

Mapping Strategic Groups Mapping the strategic groups in an industry is a good exercise. Start by identifying the dimensions that most clearly differentiate firms. In Exhibit 4.7, for example, we differentiate groups in the bicycle industry according to pricing and distribution channel. In other cases, we may use firm size or geographic scope—any key factor that distinguishes the members of one strategic group from those of another. The best criteria are usually the same ones that would be used to segment a market.

Remember, however, that the objective is to identify *direct competitors*. Thus, the segmentation dimensions should reveal strategic groups characterized by the most intense *internal competition*. The circles on the map in Exhibit 4.7 are placed in the space that best depicts the center spot of that particular strategic group. The size of the circles represents the relative size of the group. Notice that the size of the low-end mass-merchandizing segment is roughly equivalent to the size of the segment that focuses on higher-quality bikes sold through independent bike shops (e.g., Trek, Specialized). In this industry, some competitors attempt to sell through both major distribution channels, but in aggregate these make up a smaller portion of the market.

The fact that we can segment market competitors into their central locations in the business landscape doesn't mean, of course, that strategic groups don't also compete with other strategic groups. Relatively similar groups are more likely to be mutual threats than are groups with significantly different characteristics. For instance, Trek faces more competition from Cannondale brands than it does from Huffy. However, for its lower-end models, Trek does experience some competition with Schwinn. Similarly, luxury-hotel chains face a greater threat from high-quality business hotels than from the economy-hotel market. In addition, when firms first expand they often have less difficulty moving into strategic groups that have similar bases of operations than into more distantly related groups. Marriott, for example, moved into budget hotels (with its Fairfield Inn chain) only after it had successfully expanded into a midmarket space served by its Courtyard by Marriott chain.

Exhibit 4.7 A Strategic Map of the U.S. Bicycle Industry

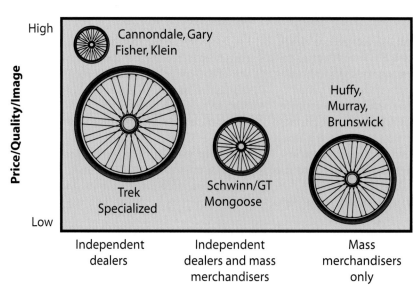

We analyze strategic groups to get a more detailed look at the competitive environment in which firms operate. Through such an analysis, we can more readily identify a firm's closest competitors (something that most decision makers can usually do intuitively). More importantly, however, we can also better identify any probable *future competition* that we might otherwise ignore or underestimate. Likewise, analyzing strategic groups helps us identify growth opportunities because it makes us focus on potential competitive positions that are compatible with a firm's unique set of resources and capabilities.

Predicting Competitors' Behaviors   After identifying the firm's closest rivals, it is important to gain a better understanding of what their future behaviors are likely to be. The specific rivals that are most pertinent to the analysis are those in the firm's same strategic group, those likely to move into the group, and those operating in groups that the firm may enter in the future. In the opening vignette on the Cola War, it is clear that Coke and Pepsi care deeply about what the other is doing. Neither wants to be caught off guard by a move the other may make in the future. Likewise, as new strategic groups have emerged in the beverage industry, such as in the flavored ice teas or premium sodas, they have had to pay more attention to these upstarts.

Several goals can be achieved by closely analyzing the firm's closest competitors. For instance, you may gain a better understanding of what competitors' future strategies will be. Similarly, you may gain a better appreciation for how competitors will respond to your strategic initiatives. Finally, you may also conclude that your firm's actions may influence competitors' behaviors, and some of these reactions may be to your benefit (or detriment). Although the firm's strategy should not be *determined* by competitors' behaviors, it should be *influenced* by what you think your competitors' behaviors are likely to be.

Porter suggests a four-step approach for making predictions about competitors. The first step in predicting the behaviors of competitors is to understand their objectives. These objectives are often surprisingly easy to determine if the companies are publicly held firms, because they are usually communicated with regularity to shareholders through disclosure documents. The second step is to determine the competitors' current strategies. If you have already completed a strategic-group map, you probably have a good idea of what those strategies are. Further insight can be gained by using the strategy diamond and using public documents to see what competitors are doing in terms of arenas, vehicles, differentiators, staging, and economic logic. The third step is a bit more difficult, but it is critical to understanding the competitors' future behaviors: What assumptions does each competitor hold about the industry and about itself? People's behaviors are strongly influenced by the assumptions they make about themselves and the world. Again, communications between top executives and shareholders often hold insights into what these assumptions may be. Finally, the competitors' future behaviors will likely be related to the resources and capabilities they possess. What are the competitors' key strengths and weaknesses?

After addressing these four primary questions, you are in a position to make reasonable predictions about what your competitors are likely to do in the future. For instance, are they about to change their strategy? You may also gain insights into their likely reaction to any initiatives you are pondering.

conceptlink

In Chapter 1, we characterize the *strategy diamond* as the integrated set of choices that a firm makes about these five elements.

DYNAMIC CHARACTERISTICS OF THE EXTERNAL CONTEXT

The various models and analytical tools that we've discussed so far can provide an excellent snapshot of a firm's external context. In some industries, such a snapshot view gives a fairly accurate portrayal of what the business landscape will be like for the foreseeable future. In other cases, however, a snapshot captures little more than a first impression: The essential features of many industries are often undergoing gradual or rapid change. What's worse, snapshot views may give an overblown picture of a firm's competitive advantage: All we see may be a firm that's staked out a nice position in an attractive market, reaps enormous profits, and regularly makes large deposits in the bank. But if you'll recall our story about Sears and Wal-Mart at the beginning of Chapter 1, you know that competitive advantage doesn't always stand the test of time and that overconfidence in the strength of one's competitive position is often a prelude to organizational decline.

Research increasingly shows that the durability of competitive advantages varies by industry or market.[14] For instance, the structural characteristics of some industries, such as utilities and transportation, will shift very little in the absence of significant regulatory changes. Other industries or markets may be undergoing gradual changes that may evolve into the kind of dramatic changes that we described in our story about Sears and Wal-Mart, where the change in market structure was dramatic but evolved over a long period of time. This is typically the case in the consumer-products industry. As a rule, the relatively static analysis afforded by the five-forces model, plus the complementors dimension, applies best to industries such as these.

Industries in a third category, however, may be undergoing substantial change, whether because of the scale and scope of environmental changes, because of the rapid pace of such changes, or because of a combination of both. Dramatic change, for instance, can result from deregulation, which may bring about significant changes in key success factors and completely redesign the competitive playing field. Deregulation in the airline industry gave rise to discount carriers such as Southwest Airlines and JetBlue. Once a segment of niche players, the discount segment now poses a serious threat to the traditional hub-and-spoke segment dominated by American and United.

Dramatic changes in technology can dramatically change the business landscape and alter the nature of competitive advantage within an industry. In such cases, a relatively stable industry can be thrown into disarray until a new equilibrium is reached. Up until the mid-1980s, for example, the pineapple industry was relatively sleepy and fragmented. Then, Fresh Del Monte (a Cayman Island company separate from the U.S. Del Monte) introduced a new variety developed by scientists at the Pineapple Research Institute. This "Extra Sweet Gold" pineapple has a bright gold color, rather than the pale yellow of the traditional pineapple; it is sweeter, less acidic, and highly resistant to parasites and rotting. Early introductions into the U.S. market were limited to a few cities on the East Coast. The pineapple was so well received that Fresh Del Monte quickly raised prices and exported the pineapple to all major U.S. markets. Despite higher prices, the Extra Sweet Gold captured 70 percent of the market.

What propelled Fresh Del Monte to the top of the market and allowed it to maintain the lion's share of what one would normally consider to be a commodity market? Fresh Del Monte successfully exploited a technological development that other firms ignored. Once it proved successful, Fresh Del Monte claimed proprietary rights to this particular strain of pineapple and was able to forestall other producers from planting the same variety. Eventually, the courts ruled that Fresh Del Monte did not have exclusive legal rights to this strain of pineapple, and companies such as Chiquita and Dole are now converting much of their production to this particular strain. Once again, dominance in the pineapple industry is up for grabs.

In this part of the chapter, we'll describe some tools for analyzing industries and formulating strategy in a dynamic context. We start by reviewing the most fundamental reason why some industries are more dynamic than others—the fact that the five forces or essential complementors are changing, not static. We then discuss two macro-level drivers of industry change: the *industry life cycle* and *discontinuities*. Although globalization itself is a profoundly important driver of change, as you read earlier in the chapter, it often goes hand in hand with the changes that accompany industry evolution and technological discontinuities.

Drivers of Change: Making the Five-Forces Model Dynamic

While learning to apply the various facets of industry analysis, you probably observed that some of your conclusions about industry structure would have to be modified if a given factor, such as the competitive behavior of one or more firms, altered any one of the five forces. One way to focus on the dynamic nature of the external context is to stop thinking of your analysis in terms of an industry snapshot and start thinking of it in terms of a "storybook" that shows how an industry structure is changing or may change. Any of the five forces that we have described so far can change significantly, and when that happens, the industry's structure and balance of power will probably be upset. Again, remember that some industries are dynamic simply because of the *rapid pace* of change. Think about the almost daily releases of new products in such markets as cell-phone handsets, laser-jet printers, and digital cameras.

Exhibit 4.8 lists a few potential sources of change and their effects on industry structure and profitability. Entry barriers, for instance, may be weakened, perhaps because of changes in technology. The industry may be in its early stages, with many firms jockeying for position, many of whom will probably go out of business or be acquired as the industry matures. As the industry becomes more dynamic, such factors as substitutes and complementors may become more important. Finally, as an industry matures, buyers become more knowledgeable about product features and costs. We'll start our discussion of industry-change drivers by examining the effects of changing industry life cycles.

Industry Life Cycle   Exhibit 4.9 illustrates the **industry life cycle**. An industry's life cycle is the pattern of evolution it follows from inception through to its current state and

industry life cycle Pattern of evolution followed by an industry from inception to current and potential future states

Exhibit 4.8 Dynamics of Industry Structure

Industry Rivalry
- *Increase in industry growth* ➔ Reduced rivalry and less pressure on prices
- *Globalization of industry* ➔ Increased rivalry as new foreign players enter the market, pressure for scale economies leading to consolidation, and market domination by fewer but larger competitors
- *Change in mix between fixed and variable costs* ➔ Shift to greater fixed costs creating more pressure to maintain sales levels and leading to greater propensity to compete on price

Threat of New Entrants
- *Decline in scale necessary to compete effectively* ➔ Increased rivalry because it's easier for start-ups to enter and effectively compete
- *Increases in customer heterogeneity* ➔ Easier entry because some customer segments are likely to be underserved plus increased ability to protect those segments that the firm serves well
- *Increased customer concentration* ➔ Reduces threat of new entry, leading to less pressure to compete on price

Bargaining Power of Suppliers
- *Increasing concentration of firms in supply industries* ➔ Greater supplier power and likelihood of reduced profitability in focal industry
- *Forward-integration by some key suppliers* ➔ Loss of power in focal industry because of reduction in number of viable suppliers
- *Emergence of substitute inputs that are good enough to satisfy basic needs* ➔ Reduction of supplier power and increased profits for focal industry

Bargaining Power of Buyers
- *Increased fragmentation of buyers' industry* ➔ Reduction in buyer power as the number of potential buyers increases and size of buyer industry declines relative to size of focal industry
- *Improvement in buyer information* ➔ Increased buyer power because of ability to compare
- *Emergence of new distribution channels* ➔ Reduction in buyer power because focal industry has more options

Threat of Substitutes
- *Emergence of a new substitute* ➔ Reduced ability to maintain high prices due to more buyer alternatives
- *Decline in the relative price performance of a substitute* ➔ Reduction in the threat of substitutes and pressure to maintain lower prices

Role of Complementors
- *Emergence of new complementors* ➔ Increased demand and less pressure on prices in focal industry
- *Higher barriers to entry in complementor industry* ➔ Greater complementor leverage and ability to profit from complementary relationship
- *Lower barriers to entry in complementor industry* ➔ Reduction in leverage of individual complementors leading to net increase of possible firms who can serve as complementors and increased demand

---

Source: Adapted from M. E. Porter, Competitive Strategy: Techniques for Analyzing Industries and Competitors *(New York: Free Press, 1980).*

Exhibit 4.9 Industry Life Cycle Curve

Sources: Adapted from K. Rangan and G. Bowman, "Beating the Commodity Magnet," Industrial Marketing Management *21 (1992), 215–224; P. Kotler, "Managing Products Through Their Product Life Cycle," in* Marketing Management: Planning, Implementation, and Control, *7th ed. (Upper Saddle River, NJ: Prentice Hall, 1991).*

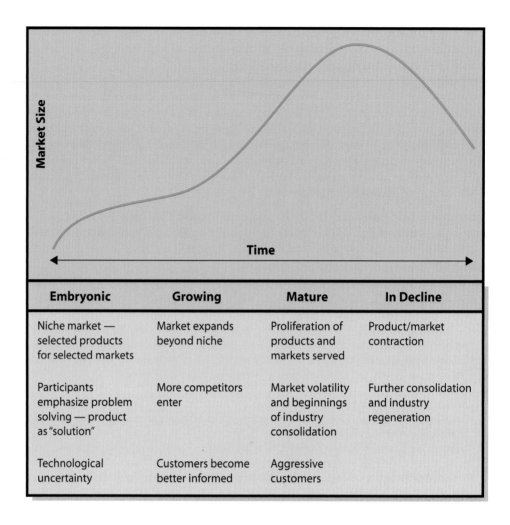

Embryonic	Growing	Mature	In Decline
Niche market — selected products for selected markets	Market expands beyond niche	Proliferation of products and markets served	Product/market contraction
Participants emphasize problem solving — product as "solution"	More competitors enter	Market volatility and beginnings of industry consolidation	Further consolidation and industry regeneration
Technological uncertainty	Customers become better informed	Aggressive customers	

commoditization Process during industry evolution by which sales eventually come to depend less on unique product features and more on price

possible future states. You have probably learned of a similar concept in your studies of marketing relating to the product life cycle. It so happens that competitive dynamics often follow a similar evolution at the industry level—from the point at which an industry emerges to the point at which it matures or perhaps even stagnates. The industry life cycle is a powerful driver of industry dynamics because it's a phenomenon characterized by change.

Evolution and Commoditization One common result of this evolution is that an industry tends to become characterized by price competition, partly because many or most of its incumbents acquire similar resources and capabilities and so offer fairly similar products. This trend is called **commoditization**—the process by which sales eventually come to depend less on unique product features and more on price.[15] Commoditization even affects technologically sophisticated products. Take the cell-phone industry for example. Although handset sales are booming thanks to the addition of cameras, music players, and fancy software, cell-phone voice services are fast becoming a basic commodity distinguished primarily by price. It is a pattern that other industries, from airlines to personal computers, have followed in recent decades as onetime technological breakthroughs became widely available.

Some cell-phone service providers are introducing new services, such as picture messaging and video downloads, but the revenue they generate is minuscule alongside the vast sums spent on voice calls, and their growth is expected to be slow. In Europe, there has been an influx of so-called no-frills service providers that basically use a model similar to that of low-cost airlines. Even the U.S. market, although still growing, has already become more commoditized, with prices plunging and companies locked in fierce competition for new customers. A marked slowdown in revenue growth could exacerbate the long-running price war in the United States, where competition has pushed the average per-minute cost of a call down more than 65 percent in the past four years, according to Yankee Group, a consulting firm.[16] One effect of the slowdown is increasing globalization and consolidation in the cell-phone industry, as some of Europe's big service providers look for revenue growth by expanding outside their home markets. Demand for cell-phone services is growing much faster than analysts had expected in Southeast Asia, Africa, Latin America, and other emerging markets, which tend to be dominated by a couple of local players.

Evolution and Reinvigoration   As some industries mature, however, certain segments may emerge to reinvigorate them, sometimes even restoring their status as growth industries (as a matter of fact, it's hard to imagine any industry that doesn't have at least one growth segment). The bicycle industry, for example, has existed for more than 200 years, and during that time, technological advances have periodically increased the product's popularity and given rise to growth segments in an otherwise stagnant industry. In the 1960s, for instance, the emergence of children's bike designs and the 10-speed accelerated sales. More recently, the mountain bike has not only spurred sales growth but has spawned many new specialized bike-manufacturing companies.

Evolution and Information   Although most of the factors involved in the evolution of an industry are fairly obvious, the role of information and customer learning has only recently begun to attract the attention of researchers.[17] We're beginning to see, for example, that the effects of learning, information, and competition can conspire to enable newer entrants to replace industry leaders, especially in the later stages of industry-wide change. The emergence of computer retailer Dell is an excellent example. Originally, because Dell targeted sophisticated buyers—buyers who were technologically savvy and who needed little education on the uses of a personal computer—it was able to invest less money in pre- and post-sales activities. Dell could sell leading-edge PCs at a relatively low price and still make a profit, and as the market matured and price competition became more intense, Dell was able to leapfrog IBM and other larger companies.

Evolution and Tactics   The effect of customer learning and information often isn't apparent until later in the life cycle. In the early stages, because there's usually a lack of knowledge and information about new products, customers tend to look to industry incumbents not only as a source of education but as a form of insurance in the way of more extensive product support. During the transition from introduction to growth, as once-new products establish themselves and become accepted, incumbents often add extra services, such as shipping, training, or extended warrantees at little or no cost in order to retain sales momentum through the growth phase. Taken together, these factors usually mean higher *average* margins in the early stages of growth because high and increasing operating costs are usually offset by relatively high prices. Again, such was the case in the early years of the PC market, when it was dominated by such players as IBM and Compaq. Discounters like Dell were considered fringe players back when they occupied a small, specialized market niche.

Technological Discontinuities   The link between technological discontinuities and industry change should be readily apparent from our discussion of industry evolution as a driver of change.[18] Moreover, technology is one of the key factors in the PESTAL framework you learned about earlier in the chapter: Discontinuities are a special, intensive case of technological change in action. Get in the habit of thinking broadly about the nature of the changes that create technological discontinuities. Technological discontinuities are much more extreme than mere incremental technological change.

To examine these extreme forms of change, it is important to understand first that technological discontinuities include both changes in science-based technologies (such as innovations) and business-process technologies (such as new business models). The two major forms of technology are *process technology* and *product technology*. Process technology refers to the devices, tools, and knowledge used to transform inputs into outputs. Product technology creates new products.[19] Needless to say, technological changes can have traumatic effects on industries and firms.[20] Indeed, major technological changes often alter firm environments and industry structures significantly. Of course, not all technological changes affect competitors and industries equally. Some, for example, work to the advantage of incumbents, others to that of new entrants.

Disruptive Product-Related Change   Patterns of technological change often reflect gradual *incremental* evolutionary change. However, other forms of episodic change are also prone to punctuate industry evolution; we characterize these forms of change as *discontinuous* change.[21] Discontinuous technological change occurs when breakthrough technologies appear, sometimes sustaining the competencies of incumbent firms and sometimes destroying them. Competency-sustaining technologies are typically introduced by incumbents. Those that destroy incumbents' competencies are called **disruptive technologies**. In many instances, these disruptions have been introduced by new firms.[22]

For instance, of 116 major innovations introduced in the minicomputer industry (the precursor to the personal computer), 111 were incremental sustaining technological improvements and only 5 were disruptive. All 111 sustaining technologies were introduced by incumbents, whereas all 5 disruptive technologies were introduced by outsiders—firms specializing in new personal computers. In the disk-drive industry, virtually every new generation of technology has led to the demise of the market leader. The arrival of the personal computer, for example, heralded the downfall of every major competitor in the minicomputer industry.[23]

Disruptive Process-Related Change   It's important to remember that disruptive technologies can be process related as well as product related. The development of total quality manufacturing (TQM) methods, for instance, eventually elevated the Japanese auto industry to world-class status. TQM programs such as six sigma are process innovations. No automaker in the world can now ignore the competitive threat posed by such firms as Toyota and Honda, and, in fact, many who once did are now struggling to emulate the TQM methods pioneered by these one-time fringe players.

More recently, when Southwest Airlines radically changed the business model that had long dominated the industry, established full-service airlines originally took little notice. Why? Because Southwest's new process couldn't help them meet the needs of their most profitable customers. In time, however, the number and length of Southwest's flights reached the point at which the services provided by its model could satisfy the demands of customers who normally used larger airlines.

Likewise, Wal-Mart's business model was originally of little threat to Sears because it focused on rural areas that Sears was happy to ignore. Eventually, Wal-Mart's model was transferable to larger markets, but it was too late for Sears to respond. A similar pattern unfolded in the U.S. steel industry. At first, large firms such as U.S. Steel ignored the emergence of so-called "mini-mills" because their unsophisticated technology was efficient only in turning out the least profitable products. But as the capabilities of mini-mill technology improved, so did the ability of the new firms to enter more profitable segments of the industry.

When Industries Divide

The industry life cycle model is too simplistic to describe the evolution of many industries. In some cases, one industry becomes two or more distinct but related industries. One cause of such a split is the decision by a firm to divest a once-core business that has been separated from the firm's original core because of industry changes. As a rule, the divestiture is prompted by the emergence of a new market.

Such was the case with 3Com Corporation and its Palm division. 3Com originally specialized in modems, which have both hardware and software components. In developing this interface, 3Com innovated a new product that linked the two components. It was called the Palm Pilot, and it soon defined the new personal data assistant (PDA) industry. Once convinced that the PDA industry was distinct from its core business in the modem industry, 3Com sold off its Palm division in a public stock offering. New entrants into the PDA industry began to specialize in either the software or hardware side of the business, with Sony, Compaq, and Dell making hardware and Palm and Microsoft selling software. Now Palm is weighing the idea of breaking up into two smaller firms—one that specializes in software and one that develops hardware. Remember: Before 3Com's original innovation, there was no such thing as a PDA industry—let alone any subindustries.

Finally, industries may divide when the market for a particular product becomes large enough that firms can economically justify dedicating a distribution channel to it.

---

disruptive technology
Breakthrough product- or process-related technology that destroys the competencies of incumbent firms in an industry

This type of division typically results in new industry *segments* or *subindustries* rather than in new industries. A good example is the emergence of so-called *category killers* in various retail industries—industry segments composed of large, highly specialized retail chains, such as PETsMART or Home Depot and Lowe's. They're called "category killers" because they aim to dominate whatever category they participate in by offering the broadest possible assortment of goods at the lowest possible prices. The Internet has spawned a number of such segments and some well-known firms, including Amazon.com and BarnesandNoble.com in books and Travelocity.com and Expedia.com in travel.

When Industries Collide

Although some changes lead to industry division, others result in new industry definitions that consolidate two or more separate industries into one. As you read this section of the chapter, note the distinction between industry *consolidation* and industry *concentration*. Whereas *concentration* results in an industry with fewer players, *consolidation* results in fewer industries. Ironically, changes in concentration can lead to either consolidation or division.[24]

Today, for example, both the global media and entertainment industries seem to be agglomerations of many once-distinct industries. The definition of the media industry now includes firms with a significant presence in both program distribution (they own or control television networks) and program content (they own or develop new shows). The largest incumbents are often called media and entertainment *conglomerates* (which suggests organizations composed of unrelated divisions), but in reality the dominant players, including Fox, Disney, Viacom, and VivendiUniversal, have consolidated a broad range of functions that were once performed by suppliers, substitutes, complementors, or even customers.

Industry division and convergence happens over time. Opportunities to create significant value tend to be greatest for firms that lead the charge in convergence and division of industries. However, when firms define their industries very broadly, performing external analysis becomes much more complicated. For instance, framing a printing company like Kinko's as a simple printer versus a marketing-communications firm connotes a broadly different set of industry conditions.

Now that you're familiar with a few key drivers of industry change, it is important that you understand the particular implications of technological and business-model breakthroughs for both the pace and extent of industry change. The *rate* of change may vary significantly from one industry to the next. The rate of change in the computing industry, for example, has been much faster than in the steel industry. nevertheless, changes in both industries has prompted complete reconfigurations of industry structure and the competitive positions of various players. The idea that all industries change over time and that business environments are in a state of constant state of flux is relatively intuitive. As a strategic decision maker, therefore, the question you need to keep asking yourself is, how accurately does current structure (which is relatively easy to identify) predict future industry conditions?

USING SCENARIOS TO PREDICT THE FUTURE

Strategic leaders use the information revealed by the application of industry analysis to uncover what the traditional SWOT framework calls *opportunities* and *threats*. You can use SWOT analysis to assess the implications of your industry analysis, both for your focal firm and for an industry in general. However, SWOT analysis works best with one situation or scenario and provides little direction when you're uncertain about potential changes to critical features of the scenario. Scenario planning can help in these cases.

Scenario Planning

Scenario planning helps leaders develop detailed, internally consistent pictures of a range of plausible outcomes as an industry evolves over time. The results of scenario planning can also be incorporated into strategy formulation and implementation, particularly

conceptlink

In Chapter 1, we define **staging** as the timing and pace of strategic moves and indicate that, as a process of matching opportunities with available resources, it entails the assessment of possible outcomes.

through the staging component of the strategy diamond. An understanding of the PESTEL conditions; the level, pace, and drivers of industry globalization; and the dynamic five-forces model will also provide insight into the outcomes of certain scenarios.

The purpose of scenario planning, however, is to provide a bigger picture—one that displays specific trends and uncertainties. Developed in the 1950s at the global petroleum giant Royal Dutch/Shell, the technique is now regarded as a valuable tool for integrating changes and uncertainties in the external context into overall strategy.[25] Unlike forecasts, scenarios are not straight-line, one-factor projections from present to future. Think of them as complex, dynamic, interactive stories told from a future perspective. To develop useful scenarios, executives need a rich understanding of their industry along with broad knowledge of the diverse PESTEL and global conditions that are most likely to affect them. Exhibit 4.10 details the six basic steps in scenario planning.

The process of developing scenarios and then conducting business according to the information that they reveal makes it easier to identify and challenge questionable assumptions. It also exposes areas of vulnerability (in a country, an industry, or a company), underscores the interplay of environmental factors and the impact of change, allows for

Exhibit 4.10 Six Steps in Scenario Planning

Step 1: Define target issue, time frame, and scope for scenarios. The scope will depend on your level of analysis (i.e., industry, subindustry, or strategic group), the stage of planning, the nature and degree of uncertainty, and the rate of change. Generally, four scenarios are developed—summarized in a grid—to reflect extremes of possible worlds. To fully capture critical possibilities and contingencies, it may be desirable to develop a series of scenario sets.

Step 2: Brainstorm a set of key drivers, decision factors, and possible scenario departure or divergence points. These could include social unrest, shifts in power, regulatory change, market or competitive change, and technology or infrastructure change. Other significant changes in external contexts, such as natural disasters, might also be considered.

Step 3: Develop the framework by defining two specific axes. These axes should represent two dimensions which provide the greatest uncertainty for the industry. In the box titled "How Would You Do That 4.2," for instance, the example on the credit-union industry identifies changes in the playing field and technology as the two greatest areas of uncertainty up through the year 2005.

Step 4: Flesh out the pictures. Show in detail how the four worlds would look in each scenario. It's often useful to develop a catchy name for each world as a way to further develop its distinctive character. One of the worlds will probably represent a slightly future version of the status quo, whereas the others will be significant departures from it. In our credit-union scenarios, *Chameleon* describes a world in which both the competitive playing field and technology undergo radical change, whereas *Wallet Wars* describes an environment of intense competition but milder technological change; in *Technocracy*, the radical changes are in technology, whereas in *Credit-Union Power*, credit unions encounter only minor change on both fronts.

Step 5: Specify indicators that can signal which scenario is unfolding. These can be either trigger points that signal that the change is taking place or milestones that mean that the change is more likely (e.g., if a particular but little known technological standard is adopted by a large industry supplier, such as Microsoft, or customer, such as CitiGroup).

Step 6: Assess the strategic implications of each scenario. Micro-scenarios may be developed to highlight and address business-unit- or industry-segment-specific issues. Consider needed variations in strategy, key success factors, and the development of a flexible, robust strategy that might work across several scenarios.

Sources: Adapted from P. J. H. Schoemaker, "When and How to Use Scenario Planning," Journal of Forecasting 10 (1991), 549–564; Schoemaker and C. A. J. M. van der Heijden, "Integrating Scenarios into Strategic Planning at Royal Dutch/Shell," Planning Review 20:3 (1992), 41–46; P. J. H. Schoemaker, "Multiple Scenario Development: Its Conceptual and Behavioral Foundation," Strategic Management Journal 14 (1993), 193–213.

robust planning and contingency preparation, and makes it possible to test and compare strategic options. Scenarios also help businesses manage information overload by focusing attention on trends and uncertainties with the greatest potential impact.

Once you've determined your target issue, scope, and time frame, you'll draw up a list of driving forces that's as complete as possible and organized into relevant categories (say, science/technology, political/economic, regulatory, consumer/social, industry/ market). As you proceed, be sure to identify *key* driving forces—the ones with the greatest potential to affect the industry, subindustry, or strategic group of interest.

Trends and Uncertainties   When analyzing the driving forces for change, be sure to distinguish between *trends* and *uncertainties*. Trends are forces for change whose direction—and sometimes timing—can be predicted. We can be reasonably confident, for example, in projecting the number of consumers in North America, Europe, and Japan who will be over age 65 in the year 2010. If businesses in your target industry serve these consumers, then the impact of this population growth will be significant; you may view it as a key trend. For other trends, you may know the direction but not the pace. China, for example, is experiencing a trend of economic growth, and a spate of foreign investments depends on the course of infrastructure development and consumer spending power in this enormous market. Unfortunately, the future pace of these changes is uncertain.

In contrast, uncertainties—forces for change whose direction and pace are largely unknown—are more important for your scenario. European consumers, for example, tend to distrust the biotechnology industry, and given the welter of competing forces at work—industry, academia, consumer groups, regulators—we can't predict whether they will be more or less receptive to biotechnology products in the future. Labeling regulations, for instance, may be either strengthened or relaxed in response to changing consumer opinion.

In some cases, you might want to consider the possibility of significant disruptions—steep changes that have an important and unalterable impact on the business environment. A major disaster—such as the attack on the World Trade Center—can spur regulatory and other legal reforms with major and lasting impact on certain technologies and competitive practices. The box entitled "How Would *You* Do That? 4.2" provides sample scenarios created for the credit-union industry and gives you an idea how scenario analysis could be applied to another industry setting. As you can see, the scenario analysis in this box identifies the entry of new competitors and the impact of technology as the two primary sources of uncertainty about the future.

Develop Scenarios for Credit Unions

Based on a PESTAL analysis, experts in the credit-union industry would identify two significant macroeconomic factors: (1) regulatory—affecting both the types of businesses that credit unions can compete in and the entry of new players and consolidation of existing ones; and (2) technological—the speed with which new technologies related to banking are both developed and adopted by consumers. These two dimensions define the major areas of uncertainty facing credit-union executives in the next decade. Based on these dimensions and following the steps outlined in Exhibit 4.10, four scenarios illustrated in Exhibit 4.11 can be developed.

Exhibit 4.11 Scenarios for the Credit-Union Industry

		Changes in the Playing Field	
		Minor	Major
Technological Change	Gradual	**Credit-Union Power 2005:** Both technology and the playing field have changed at a moderate pace, making this the most stable scenario. Even with moderate change in these areas, however, the changing basis of competition, new business models, human resource challenges, and industry dynamics are different enough to pose significant challenges for many financial-services companies.	**Wallet Wars 2005:** Prompted by free-market economics, the playing field is changing radically, enabling credit unions and other financial-services institutions to compete more intensely. At the same time, technical innovations have not developed as quickly as many observers and analysts had predicted.
	Radical	**Technocracy 2005:** The wide-scale adoption of the Internet by U.S. consumers has led to massive technological innovation for financial-services companies, increasing their range of distribution channels as well as their products, services, and geographic scope. Regulations and other changes in the playing field, however, have been slow to follow.	**Chameleon 2005:** Radical changes occurring in the playing field and in technology make this a highly tumultuous scenario for all credit unions. The nature of competition has evolved so much that banks and credit unions compete directly—under the same rules of the game. This situation has caused a wide-scale convergence of cultures among various financial-services providers, testing the boundaries of the traditional credit-union mission.

Source: Adapted from Credit Union Executives Society, 2005: Scenarios for Credit Unions, an Executive Report (Madison, WI: Credit Union Executives Society, 1999).

SUMMARY

1. Explain the importance of the external context for strategy and firm performance. In order to understand the threats and opportunities facing an organization, you need a thorough understanding of its external context, including not only its industry, but the larger environment in which it operates. The proper analysis of the external context, together with the firm-level analysis you learned in Chapter 3 (e.g., VRINE, value chain), allow you to complete a rigorous analysis of a firm and its options. You could say that with these tools you can now perform a thorough and systematic (rather than intuitive) *SWOT analysis*; that is, an assessment of a firm's *strengths*, *weaknesses*, *opportunities*, and *threats*.

2. Use PESTEL to identify the macro characteristics of the external context. PESTEL analysis and an understanding of the drivers of globalization can be used to characterize the macro characteristics of the firm's external environment. PESTEL is an acronym for the *political*, *economic*, *sociocultural*, *technological*, *environmental*, and *legal* contexts in which a firm operates. Managers can use PESTEL analysis to gain a better understanding of the opportunities and threats faced by the firm. By knowing the firm's opportunities and threats, managers can build a better vision of the future business landscape and identify how the firm may compete profitably. By examining the drivers of globalization, managers can identify how market, cost, governments, and competition work to favor the globalization of an industry.

3. Identify the major features of an industry and the forces that affect industry profitability. The major factors to be analyzed when examining an industry are rivalry, the power of suppliers, the power of buyers, the threat of substitutes, and the threat of new entrants. When suppliers and buyers have significant power, they tend to be able to negotiate away some of the profit that would otherwise be available to industry rivals. Thus, profits tend to be lower than average in industries that face high levels of supplier and buyer power. Likewise, as the threat of new entrants and the availability of substitutes increases, the ability of rivals in the industry to keep prices high is reduced. Rivalry within an industry decreases profitability. High levels of rivalry result in heavy emphasis on price-based competition. Rivalry is reduced when products are differentiated. Strategic-group analysis is used to gain a better understanding of the nature of rivalry. Whereas industry profits tend to be reduced when any of the five forces are strong, the presence of complementors results in the opposite; they increase the ability of firms to generate profits. Finally, an analysis of competitors' objectives, current strategies, assumptions, and resources and capabilities can help managers predict the future behaviors of their competitors.

4. Understand the dynamic characteristics of the external context. The various models and analytical tools presented can provide an excellent snapshot of a firm's external context. In some industries, such a snapshot view gives an accurate portrayal of what the business landscape will look like for the foreseeable future. Not only do the five forces of industry structure change, and very rapidly in some industries; other drivers of change in which managers must be attuned to include the stage and pace of transition in the industry life cycle and technological discontinuities.

5. Show how industry dynamics may redefine industries. In some cases, one industry becomes two or more distinct, but often related, industries. Industries may also divide when the market for a particular product becomes large enough that firms can economically justify dedicating a distribution channel to it. Whereas some changes lead to industry division, others result in new industry definitions that consolidate two or more separate industries into one. Industry convergence and division happen over time, and firms that identify such changes and initiate early changes have a better opportunity to create value.

6. Use scenario planning to predict the future structure of the external context. Scenario planning helps firms develop detailed and internally consistent pictures of a range of plausible outcomes as an industry evolves over time. It can be used to help formulate effective strategies. Scenarios are complex, dynamic, interactive stories told from a future perspective, making it easier to identify and challenge questionable assumptions. Scenario planning also exposes areas of vulnerability, underscores the interplay of environmental factors and the impact of change, allows for robust planning and contingency preparation, and makes it possible to test and compare strategic options.

KEY TERMS

barrier to entry, 100
buyer power, 103
commoditization, 112
complementors, 104

disruptive technology, 114
exit barriers, 101
five-forces model, 98
globalization, 94

industry life cycle, 111
key success factor (KSF), 96
PESTEL analysis, 91
rivalry, 99

strategic group, 105
supplier power, 101
threat of new entry, 100
threat of substitutes, 103

REVIEW QUESTIONS

1. What constitutes the external context of strategy?
2. What are the five forces affecting industry structure?
3. What are complementors?
4. What is a key success factor (KSF)?
5. What are strategic groups?
6. What factors increase industry dynamics?
7. What is the industry life cycle?
8. What is a technological discontinuity?
9. How does globalization affect the external context of strategy?
10. What is industry redefinition?
11. What is scenario planning? When would you use it?

How Would *you* Do That?

1. The box entitled "How Would *You* Do That? 4.1" illustrates the five-forces model for the airline industry. Use the analysis there as an example and perform a five–forces analysis for one of the following industries: soft drinks, cable television, or cell-phone service providers. What are the one or two most important issues that arise in your analysis that managers in that industry must take into account when they revisit their strategies?

2. Using the scenario-planning example in the box entitled "How Would *You* Do That? 4.2" as a model, create a scenario that predicts the future of the airline industry. What are reasonable best-case scenarios? What does a pessimistic view look like? Are some competitors better prepared for the range of outcomes than others?

GROUP ACTIVITIES

1. Pick two of the industries listed in Exhibit 4.1, one on the high end of profitability and one on the low end. What are the boundaries of these industries? What are their market and geographic segments? Who are the key players? Draw up a five-forces model of each industry and compare and contrast their industry structure. Now shift your analysis to the dynamic five-forces model. What dimensions of the five-forces model are most likely to change in the near future? Which are most likely to stay relatively stable? Answer these questions for both 5- and 10-year windows.

2. Develop a simple scenario for one of the industries you selected for Group Activity 1. What were the key dimensions of uncertainty (pick only two)? Did your findings in this exercise influence your responses to the questions in Group Activity 1? If so, in what ways? If you examined more than one segment within your focal industry, how did your scenarios differ from segment to segment?

ENDNOTES

1. J. C. Maxwell, *Beverage Digest Fact Book 2001* (Bedford Hills, NY: Beverage Digest Company, 2001); D. B. Yoffie, *Cola Wars Continue: Coke and Pepsi in the Twenty-First Century* (Cambridge, MA: Harvard Business School Press, 2002); J. C. Louis and H. Yazijian, *The Cola Wars* (New York: Everest House, 1980).

2. G. Yip, "Global Strategy in a World of Nations," *Sloan Management Review* 31:1 (1989), 29–40.

3. M. Porter, *Competition in Global Industries* (Boston: Harvard Business School Press, 1986); Yip, "Global Strategy in a World of Nations."

4. Porter, *Competition in Global Industries;* Yip, "Global Strategy in a World of Nations."

5. R. Amit and P. J. H. Schoemaker, "Strategic Assets and Organizational Rent," *Strategic Management Journal* 14 (1993), 33–46; J. A. Vasconcellos and D. C. Hambrick, "Key Success Factors: Test of a General Framework in the Mature Industrial-Product Sector," *Strategic Management Journal* 10 (1989), 367–382.

6. "A Fruit Revolution," *Convenience Store News* 41:4 (2005), 20; J. Cioletti, "Flavoring the Market," *Beverage World* 124:3 (2005), 6; B. Bobala, "Water Wars," March 10, 2003 (accessed July 15, 2005), www.fool.com/news/commentary/2003/commentary030310bb.htm.

7. M. Porter, *Competitive Strategy: Techniques for Analyzing Industries and Competitors* (New York: Free Press, 1980).

8. S. Leith, "Virgin Cola Returns—but More Quietly," *Atlanta Journal Constitution,* July 1, 2004, E1.

9. www.packersnews.com/archives/news/pack_10906648.shtml (accessed July 15, 2005).

10. A. Brandenburger and B. Nalebuff, *Co-Opetition* (New York: Currency Doubleday, 1996).

11. Much of this section is adapted from important studies in the field of game theory, and we'll return to the topic when we discuss strategic alliances and other cooperative strategies. At this point, we offer merely an overview. See A. Dixit and B. Nalebuff, *Thinking Strategically: The Competitive Edge in Business and Politics and Everyday Life* (New York: W. W. Norton, 1992); and A. Brandenburger and B. Nalebuff, *Co-Opetition.*

12. R. E. Caves and M. E. Porter, "From Entry Barriers to Mobility Barriers: Conjectural Decisions and Contrived Deterrence to New Competition," *Quarterly Journal of Economics* 91 (1977), 241–262; H. Daems and H. Thomas (eds.), *Strategic Groups, Strategic Moves and Performance* (New York: Pergamon, 1994); M. E. Gordon and G. R. Milne, "Selecting the Dimensions that Define Strategic Groups: A Novel Market-Driven Approach," *Journal of Managerial Issues* 11:2 (1999), 213–233; A. Nair and S. Kotha, "Does Group Membership Matter? Evidence from the Japanese Steel Industry," *Strategic Management Journal* 22:3 (2001), 221–235.

13. R. E. Caves and M. E. Porter, "From Entry Barriers to Mobility Barriers"; J. McGee and H. Thomas, "Strategic Groups: Theory, Research and Taxonomy," *Strategic Management Journal* 7 (1986), 141–160.

14. R. Wiggins and T. Ruefli, "Competitive Advantage: Temporal Dynamics and the Incidence and Persistence of Superior Economic Performance," *Organization Science* 13 (2002), 82–105.

15. L. Argote, *Organizational Learning: Creating, Retaining, and Transferring Knowledge* (Boston: Kluwer Academic Publishers, 1999); A. S. Miner and P. Haunschild, "Population Level Learning," *Research in Organizational Behavior* 17 (1995), 115–166.

16. D. Pringle, "Slower Growth Hits Cellphone Services Overseas in EU, Japan, Saturation Leads to Some Contraction; Looking Beyond Voice," *Wall Street Journal,* May 23, 2005, A1.

17. See G. Moore, *Crossing the Chasm* (New York: Harper Business Essentials, 2002); C. Shapiro and H. R. Varian, *Information Rules: A Strategic Guide to the Network Economy* (Boston: Harvard Business School Press, 1998).

18. N. Rosenberg, *Technology and American Economic Growth* (New York, Harper & Row, 1986); M. L. Tushman and P. Anderson, "Technological Discontinuities and Organizational Environments," *Administrative Science Quarterly* 31 (1986), 439–465.

19. W. P. Barnett, "The Organizational Ecology of a Technological System," *Administrative Science Quarterly* 35 (1990), 31–60; R. M. Henderson and K. B. Clark, "Architectural Innovation: The Reconfiguration of Existing Product Technologies and the Failure of Established Firms," *Administrative Science Quarterly* 35 (1990), 9–30.

20. Tushman and Anderson, "Technological Discontinuities and Organizational Environments."

21. Tushman and Anderson, "Technological Discontinuities and Organizational Environments."

22. C. M. Christensen, *The Innovator's Dilemma* (Cambridge, MA: Harvard Business Press, 1997).

23. Christensen, *The Innovator's Dilemma.*

24. Consolidation may result from increased concentration when bigger players in an industry absorb the functions of suppliers, substitutes, complements, or customers (a process under way in the global media and entertainment industries). By getting bigger, these firms broaden the definition of their operations, but successfully managing all the components of a broader operation is a separate matter. Concentration often results in division when players that have grown too big can no longer give adequate attention to some segment of their market or some facet of their operations. Division also occurs when, because of increased concentration, a new market emerges to attract large firms.

25. P. J. H. Schoemaker, "When and How to Use Scenario Planning," *Journal of Forecasting* 10 (1991), 549–564; P. J. H. Schoemaker and C. A. J. M. van der Heijden, "Integrating Scenarios into Strategic Planning at Royal Dutch/Shell," *Planning Review* 20:3 (1992), 41–46; P. J. H. Schoemaker, "Multiple Scenario Development: Its Conceptual and Behavioral Foundation," *Strategic Management Journal* 14 (1993), 193–213.

Creating Business Strategies

After studying this chapter, you should be able to:

1. Define *generic strategies* and explain how they relate to a firm's strategic position.

2. Describe the drivers of low-cost, differentiation, and focused strategic positions.

3. Identify and explain the risks associated with each generic strategic position.

4. Show how different strategic positions fit with various stages of the industry life cycle.

5. Evaluate the quality of a firm's strategy.

► **1976**
With a staff of five, Trek
begins making steel bikes in a
barn in Waterloo, Wisconsin.
It positions itself as a high-quality,
high-priced manufacturer,
distributing through independent
dealers only.

► **1982**
The first Trek mountain bike
hits the trail. Trek sponsors
its first bike race and further
diversifies its product line
by offering accessories
and clothing.

A TALE OF THREE WHEELS IN THE BICYCLE INDUSTRY

In 2004, over 18.3 million bicycles were sold in the United States.[1] According to industry trade reports, the total retail value of bikes, parts, and accessories was more than $5.7 billion. Who sold all of these bicycles and bike-related products? There are literally hundreds of bicycle manufacturers in the United States, but most are small, specialized firms. Pacific Cycle, which designs, markets, and imports a full range of bikes and recreation products under such familiar brand names as Schwinn, GT, Mongoose, Mongoose Pro, Pacific, InSTEP, Roadmaster, Flexible Flyer, Powerlite, Murray, and Dyno, sells more bicycles than any other company in North America. Its powerful brand portfolio serves virtually all consumer demographics, price categories, and product categories (e.g., children's, mountain, and racing bikes).

▶ **2002**
Trek diversifies further, launching Trek Travel for booking worldwide bike vacations.

▶ **2005**
Sponsored by Trek, Lance Armstrong wins his seventh straight Tour de France on a Trek Madone SSLX.

1995   2000

In fact, Pacific is one of the fastest-growing branded consumer-product companies in the United States. It has achieved its success by combining its aggressive acquisition of power brands with low-cost outsourcing, efficient supply-chain management, and multichannel retail distribution. Channels include leading mass-market retailers such as Wal-Mart, Target, and Toys "R" Us; sporting goods chains such as Dick's, The Sports Authority, and Gart Sports; and independent dealers serving local markets. The company's brands appeal to the full spectrum of demographics, price preferences, and image and usage criteria that are critical to targeting the key consumer segments served by each channel. This broad-based marketing strategy enables Pacific to provide retailers with one-stop shopping and to respond efficiently to changes in the marketplace. Pacific Cycle was recently acquired by Doral Inc., and now operates as an independent strategic business unit (SBU).

Another successful bike maker, Trek Bicycle, has revenues similar to those of Pacific Cycle. It was founded by partners Richard Burke and Bevill Hogg in 1976. With $25,000 in seed money, Burke and Hogg started building bikes by hand in a Wisconsin barn. From the beginning, they targeted upper-end users, and success came quickly. Today, customers pay top dollar for smooth suspensions, custom paint jobs, and innovations in racing geometry. With annual sales of about $400 million, Trek is now the country's number-one maker of high-quality bikes and was perhaps the first U.S. bike maker to overcome European resistance to American-made cycles by focusing on quality and innovation, which have long been company hallmarks. Trek introduced its first mountain bike line in 1983, the first bonded-aluminum road bike in 1985, and a carbon-fiber road bike in 1986.

Although most of the firm's growth has been fueled by internally developed products, Trek has also made a few strategic acquisitions, including Gary Fisher Mountain Bike and two mountain bike competitors (Bontrager and Klein) in 1995. Trek now makes various types of bicycles, including mountain, road, children's, recumbent, police, and BMX bikes. Internationally, Trek bikes are sold through wholly owned subsidiaries in 7 countries and through distributors in 65 others. Trek designs all of its bikes at its Wisconsin headquarters and manufactures a quarter of them in this country. Finally, sponsoring seven-time Tour de France winner Lance Armstrong has given the company tremendous exposure and the centerpiece for a marketing plan that, as one Trek executive puts it, can be summed up as "Lance, Lance, Lance."

Whereas Pacific Cycle and Trek represent the larger players in the U.S. market, Montague fits the profile of a boutique-style bike firm. Frustration prompted Harry Montague, a Washington, D.C., architect and inventor, to develop the Montague line of high-performance, travel-friendly bicycles: He was unable to find anything but small-wheeled folding bikes, and they were both uncomfortable and inefficient for serious cyclists who wanted to take their bikes in the car or on public transportation. After much trial and error, Montague succeeded in developing a full-size high-performance folding bicycle that he then custom-built and sold out of his garage for D.C.-area riders.

The business moved out of the garage when Harry's son David was required to draw up an extensive business plan for a course in entrepreneurship at the MIT Sloan School of Business. David designed a formal business plan around his father's bicycle, and as soon as David had passed the course, he and his father formed the Montague Corp. to design and produce full-size bicycles that sacrifice little in performance while providing convenience for a targeted market of customers. Today, Montague is the world's leading manufacturer of folding bikes. All Montague bikes fold into a compact size in less than 30 seconds without the use of tools. They have been sold to the military for tactical use and to several car manufactures for promotional packaging with SUVs.

Pacific Cycle, Trek, and Montague are all in the same industry, but each pursues a very different strategy in an attempt to meet the needs of customers. In this chapter, you will be introduced to the basics of business strategy—the tools and models that will help you formulate coherent strategies for competing within an industry context. ■

AN INTRODUCTION TO BUSINESS STRATEGIES

In this chapter, we build on Chapters 3 and 4 by discussing ways in which firms formulate business strategies that capitalize on their resources and capabilities to exploit opportunities in their competitive environments. At the same time, we set the stage for Chapter 6, which explores strategy in dynamic contexts. As we saw in Chapter 1, *business strategy* refers to the choices that a firm makes about its competitive posture. These choices can be summarized by the *strategy diamond* and its *five elements of strategy*. For the diversified firm, business strategy is typically applied at the level of the strategic business unit (SBU). An SBU is an organizational subunit within a diversified corporation that is responsible for a specific business or group of related businesses. For instance, in the opening vignette you learned about Pacific Cycle, which is an SBU of Doral Inc. SBU strategy is similar to business strategy—but with one important exception: Because an SBU is an organizational unit within a larger firm, the SBU environment includes not only elements external to the firm but also elements of the parent firm. (We'll have more to say about SBUs in the chapters on corporate and global strategy because the choice of what value-chain operations and geographic and/or product markets to include in an SBU should flow from the overarching corporate strategy).

As we saw in our opening vignette about three bicycle companies, there's more than one way to compete in an industry. Pacific Cycle, for example, markets a product for virtually every segment, offers a range of quality in its product mix, and keeps costs down by outsourcing all of its production to China and Taiwan. Trek, meanwhile, though also a large company with a broad product mix, focuses on specialized and innovative product attributes to target specific customer segments and one channel—independent bike distributors. Montague is an entirely different company, marketing a highly specialized product targeted at a narrow range of potential customers.

As a rule, competitive positions can be established in many different ways, and the task of finding the best configuration of positions is the subject of this chapter. We'll start by introducing a well-established framework for strategic positioning developed by Michael Porter and then describe the conditions under which particular strategic positions are viable. We'll also examine ways in which alternative strategic positions are compatible with

conceptlink

In Chapter 1, we explain that **business strategy** refers to the ways in which a firm will compete against present and future rivals *within a particular business*; the *five elements of strategy* refer to the choices that it makes in determining *how* to compete against its rivals.

To avoid head-to-head competition, Pacific Cycle positions itself differently than Trek. Pacific makes many different brands, selling them at various prices in numerous retail outlets. To keep costs down, it manufactures its bikes exclusively in countries where labor costs are low.

different stages of the industry life cycle. Finally, because a successful strategy must be consistent with both a firm's resources and the competitive environment, we'll conclude by describing a process for testing the quality of a strategy according to this criterion.

TYPES OF STRATEGIES—FINDING A POSITION THAT WORKS

concept link

In Chapter 4, we identify **rivalry** as one of Porter's five forces of industry structure, define it as the intensity of competition in an industry, and explain that high degrees of rivalry are usually reflected in price competition.

Strategic positioning refers to the ways managers situate a firm relative to its rivals along important competitive dimensions. The strategic-positioning model that we present in this chapter is a classic framework in the field of strategic management—Michael Porter's *generic strategy model.* Recall that under the industry-structure model that we introduced in Chapter 4, the key force in an industry—indeed, the force around which all others revolve—is rivalry among the firms in the industry. The purpose of strategic positioning is to reduce the effects of rivalry and thereby improve profitability, and the generic strategies that derive from the strategic-positioning model are related to the industry-structure model: They help managers stake out a position for their firm relative to its rivals *in ways that reduce the effects of intense rivalry on profitability.* In this section, we'll introduce Porter's generic strategies.

Strategic Positioning and the Generic Strategy Model

The concept of strategic positioning is a useful starting point in dealing with issues deriving from the strategy diamond model that we explored in Chapter 1—namely, issues related to *arenas, differentiators,* and *economic logic.* Strategic position helps to answer basic questions about the arenas in which a firm will compete (specifically, questions about the breadth of geographic and product scope). An automobile manufacturer, for example, must decide whether to compete in all geographic markets and all product lines (say, everything from high-performance to economy-priced cars—as you might see when contrasting Porsche with Daimler-Chrysler).

This model also helps decision makers deal with questions about a firm's tactics for motivating customers to choose its products over those of competitors. Will customers buy from a firm because it offers the lowest-priced luxury sedan (such as the Buick Park Avenue), because it's known for its quality (say, Lexus), or because it offers the most valuable brand image (perhaps Mercedes Benz)? Likewise, the choice between these two criteria— low cost and differentiation—is critical to the issue of economic logic: The success of either choice depends on complementary decisions about how best to generate profit. For instance, Trek attempts to position its brands as possessing superior quality, and therefore warranting higher prices, through endorsements by industry superstars such as Lance Armstrong and exclusive distribution through independent bike dealers.

A firm's choice of position depends on two important factors: (1) firm resources and capabilities and (2) industry structure. Formulating a strategy means using tools such as those that we introduced in Chapters 3 and 4 to make critical decisions about how and where to compete—that is, how to position a company relative to its rivals. In addition, if a firm hopes to exploit opportunities while withstanding competitive threats from within its industry, its strategy should be built on its unique resources and capabilities.

Generic Strategies

In this section, we'll discuss one of the most durable concepts in the field strategic management—Michael Porter's concept of the generic strategies by which firms develop defensible strategic positions. In particular, we'll explain the logic of four positions— *low-cost, differentiation, focused cost leadership,* and *focused differentiation*—and show how each can reduce the negative effects of industry rivalry.

Cost and Differentiation In 1980, Michael Porter introduced an integrated theory of strategy based on principles of industrial organization (I/O) economics. Porter's model revised the concept of how firms achieve competitive advantage by going beyond the basic (and often wrong) notion that market share is the key to profitability. In part, Porter's theory considered the structure of an industry and its effect on the performance of firms within it (an idea that we introduced in Chapter 4). Porter also demonstrated the economic logic behind some prescriptions for choosing among viable means of gaining competitive advantage.[2] Porter's strategy model hinges on two dimensions: the potential source of strategic advantage and the breadth of the target market.

According to Porter, two key factors affect the economic logic (or the source) of competitive advantage. These alternative sources of advantage are having a lower cost structure than industry competitors and having a product or service that customers perceive as differentiated from other products in the industry—to the point that they will pay higher prices than what is charged for other products in the industry. In other words, a firm can gain a significant advantage over rivals in one of two ways:

■ It can produce an essentially equivalent product at a lower cost than its rivals.

■ It can produce a differentiated product and charge sufficiently higher prices to more than offset the added costs of differentiation.

We can use Porter's two dimensions—cost and differentiation—to develop a simple two-by-two matrix for visualizing alternative competitive positions; the alternative positions suggested by this model are what we mean by **generic strategies**. Exhibit 5.1 illustrates this model. Bear in mind that in order to be consistent with the overall model of strategy that we presented in Chapter 1 and avoid confusing Porter's categories with the more general concept of strategy, we'll refer to Porter's generic strategies as *strategic positions*. These strategic positions are not *strategies* in the way we define them using the strategy diamond. Rather, they are configurations of several elements of a firm's strategy.

Along the horizontal dimension of Exhibit 5.1, firms choose the underlying economic logic by which they intend to establish a competitive advantage—that is, whether to compete on differentiation or cost. *Differentiation* refers to a general condition of perceived product "uniqueness" that causes customers to be willing to pay premium prices. When are customers willing to pay more for a product? Generally, premium prices are paid when a firm is able to uniquely satisfy a customer's needs. This satisfaction could be along the dimensions of quality, image, speed, access, or other identifiable dimensions of perceived need. However, firms can gain advantage in other ways as well. As shown on Exhibit 5.1, firms may decide to seek higher returns and a competitive advantage by keeping costs lower than those of competitors.

Scope of Involvement Firms also make choices about the arenas in which they'll compete when they decide how broadly they'll compete for customers—a decision known

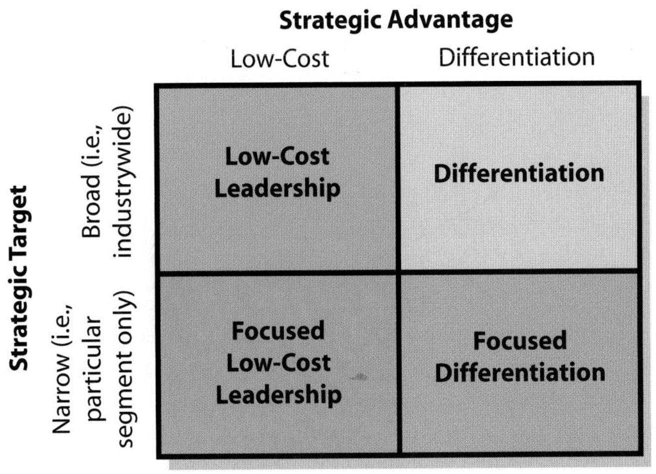

conceptlink

In Chapter 4, we characterize *industrial/organization (IO) economics* as the discipline developed to analyze the nature of competition, identify the **key success factors**, and assess the possibility of making above-normal profits in an industry.

generic strategy Strategic position designed to reduce the negative effects of rivalry, including *low-cost, differentiation, focused cost leadership, focused differentiation,* and *integrated positions*

Exhibit 5.1 The Strategic Positioning Model

Source: Adapted from M. E. Porter, Competitive Strategy *(New York: The Free Press, 1980).*

as *scope of involvement*. In other words, firms make choices about which customers to pursue. Some firms compete broadly by trying to offer something for virtually everyone; others focus their efforts on narrower segments of the market. The vertical dimension in Exhibit 5.1 measures the scope of the market arenas in which a firm chooses to compete.

Four generic strategic positions result from the decisions measured by the model in Exhibit 5.1: *low-cost leadership, broad differentiation, focused (or niche) cost leadership,* and *focused (or niche) differentiation.* Let's look more closely at each of these positions.

Low-Cost Leadership   A strategic position that enables a firm to produce a good or offer a service while maintaining total costs that are lower than what it takes competitors to offer the same product or service is known as **low-cost leadership**. Not surprisingly, a firm that can produce substantially similar products at a lower cost has a significant competitive advantage. With a cost advantage, a firm can sell products for lower prices while still maintaining the same margins as rivals. In the process, of course, it will also gain market share. However, the same firm could keep its prices at market level and reap higher margins than competitors. In this case, it will accumulate surplus resources that it can either distribute to shareholders or use to finance future strategic initiatives. As a rule, however, because taking a low-cost position means sacrificing features or services, firms that stake out this position try to satisfy basic rather than highly specialized customer needs.

> **low-cost leadership** Strategic position based on producing a good or offering a service while maintaining total costs that are lower than what it takes competitors to offer the same product or service

The low-cost position works in many industries. In the bicycle industry, for instance, Pacific Cycle keeps manufacturing costs down by standardizing design and outsourcing production to low-cost labor markets. Unlike some low-cost leaders, Pacific also offers a wide array of products, many of which have strong brand equity, such as Schwinn and Mongoose—a strategic decision more often associated with a strategy of differentiation. Remember, however, that most of these brands came into Pacific's portfolio through acquisitions, and the company retained the brand names because they enjoy greater brand awareness than "Pacific Cycle." In the wine industry, Gallo Wines has achieved a low-cost leadership position by innovating cost-effective blending techniques, having lower costs due to scale of operations, developing efficiencies in the grape-procurement function, and generating scale economies in marketing and distribution.

In summary, with the low-cost position, firms attempt to deliver an acceptable product that satisfies basic needs at the lowest possible cost. In doing so, the firm attempts to create a sustainable cost gap over other firms. Successfully following this path results in above-industry-average profits. However, cost leaders must maintain parity or proximity in satisfying the basic needs of buyers. Doing so is a challenge, because it generally requires tradeoffs—eliminating some features or services in order to drive costs down.

Some well-known companies, including Wal-Mart, Southwest Airlines, and Home Depot, are successful low-cost leaders. Interestingly, each of these companies started out as a focused low-cost competitor but took up a more broad-based position as it grew.

Differentiation   If a firm markets products whose quality, reliability, or prestige is discernibly higher than its competitors', and if its customers are willing to pay for this uniqueness, the firm has a competitive advantage based on **differentiation**. Successful differentiation enables firms to do one of two things:

> **differentiation** Strategic position based on products or offers services with quality, reliability, or prestige that is discernibly higher than that of competitors and for which customers are willing to pay

- Set prices at the industry average (and gain market share because consumers will choose higher quality at the same price).
- Raise prices over those of competitors (and reap the benefits of higher margins).

Trek Bicycles, for example, is a broad-based differentiator: Although it offers products in numerous segments, its products boast high quality and demand price premiums over products from Pacific Cycle.

Coca-Cola and Pepsi—which spend billions to develop brand equity, sell in most markets, and strive to win customers through brand image—are also well-known differentiators. Or consider Mercedes Benz, perhaps the world's leading manufacturer of premium passenger cars. What differentiates Mercedes' products? A reputation for innovative engineering, safety, and comfort, along with product design aimed at buyers who will pay premium prices for the image that goes along with a Mercedes.[3] Interestingly, although most Americans regard Mercedes as a focused differentiator because only affluent customers can afford its products, Europeans have a different view. In Europe, Mercedes markets a wide line of products, ranging from the tiny SmartCar to more familiar luxury sedans.

In the motorcycle market, Honda, Yamaha, and Suzuki all have something for virtually every enthusiast. Honda's lineup, for instance, starts with the entry-level XR50R, which comes with semiautomatic gears to help youngsters learn off-road riding. Honda then proceeds to appeal to almost every other segment of the market with products ranging upward to the Gold Wing ST1300, a six-cylinder touring bike equipped with sophisticated sport-type suspension, antilock brakes, and luxury touring features.

A successful differentiation position requires that a firm satisfy a few basic criteria. First, it must uniquely satisfy one or more needs that are valued by buyers and do so in a manner superior to that available from most competitors. However, doing so will result in higher costs in some value-chain activities. Thus, the second requirement that must be satisfied is that customers must be willing to pay higher prices for the added points of differentiation. Consequently, companies successful at a differentiation position pick cost-effective forms of differentiation. The results are above-industry-above profits.

An example of a successful broad differentiator is Stouffers, the frozen-food company. Stouffers spends more on high-quality inputs than its competitors, it has developed a technology to make a superior sauce, and it offers innovative menus. Stouffers combines these features with high-quality packaging, the use of food brokers to get broad distribution, and advertising that creates the perception of quality. The price premium that Stouffers is able to generate exceeds the cost to improve frozen-food entrees above industry norms.

Focused Low-Cost Leadership   A strategic position that enables a firm to be a low-cost leader in a narrow segment of the market is known as **focused cost leadership**. JetBlue, a recent entry into the commercial-airline market, is a focused low-cost competitor that serves a small subset of commercial travelers who are price sensitive. Using a variation on Southwest Airline's early business model, JetBlue managed during its first few years of operation to keep its operating costs per airline seat mile lower than even Southwest's. It was the most profitable commercial U.S. airline in 2002 and 2003 and second behind only Southwest in 2004.

focused cost leadership Strategic position based on being a low-cost leader in a narrow market segment

Focused Differentiation   When unique products are targeted to relatively small segments, the positioning strategy is called **focused differentiation**. The greater the differentiation, the smaller the market segment to which a product will appeal: As quality is continually improved or luxury features added, fewer customers can afford the higher prices. In the bicycle industry, for example, Montague focuses on a small, specialized segment of the market that demands unique product features. You also may be familiar with Cannondale, another focused differentiator that produces high-end mountain bikes. Unfortunately for Cannondale, however, the firm sought to leverage its reputation for quality mountain bikes in the motocross motorcycle market and went bankrupt as a result. It found that the resources and capabilities required to compete in mountain bikes, such as sturdy, high-performance frames, were very different than those required for gas-engined bikes—namely high-performance engines and drive trains. Moreover, motorcycles are not typically sold by the same dealers that sell bikes.

focused differentiation Strategic position based on targeting products to relatively small segments

Likewise, Mercedes Benz imports into the United States only its most expensive top-of-the-line models in each product category. In the United States, therefore, Mercedes is a focused differentiator that markets only to the most affluent customers. Even more focused are such companies as Rolls-Royce and Ferrari. In the motorcycle industry, Harley-Davidson, which makes only larger models targeted at very specific segments of the market, is a more focused differentiator than Honda. Harley's lowest-priced motorcycle begins at about $6,500. Recently, other firms have entered this market space and have tried to out-focus Harley-Davidson. For instance, Orange County Choppers, which was made famous by the *American Chopper* TV series (see photo on page 130), sells only made-to-order

Harley-Davidson has successfully focused its business strategy on the large high-priced end of the motorcycle market. Other manufacturers, such as Orange County Choppers, have tried to muscle into Harley's well-defined market space with bikes such as the Fire Bike shown here.

integrated position Strategic position in which elements of one position support strong standing in another

motorcycles. Therefore, Orange County Choppers focuses on a very small segment of the overall motorcycle market.

Integrated Positions   In reality, few firms are faced with such stark alternatives as being either a low-cost leader or a differentiator. Some firms are able to achieve an **integrated position**—one in which elements of one position support a strong standing in the other. Elements of a differentiating position can in fact be adopted by low-cost competitors. Many low-cost companies, for instance, develop strong brand images even though branding typically supports a differentiation strategy. Heavy reliance on branding enables McDonald's to position itself as a reliable, high-quality provider of low-cost fast food. Conversely, firms usually associated with differentiated products have succeeded in managing costs. Toyota, for example, keeps its costs below those of major competitors while maintaining extremely high levels of quality. (In particular, quality-improvement programs have proved valuable for both differentiation and cost-cutting efforts.)

Another example is IKEA Svenska AB, which manages to remain the world's largest home-furnishings retailer while specializing in stylish but inexpensive furniture. IKEA's success can be traced to its vast experience in the retail market, where it practices both product differentiation and cost leadership. IKEA outlets are essentially warehouses stacked with boxes of unassembled furniture. The company operates under a fairly unique premise: namely, that value-conscious buyers will perform some of the tasks that other retailers normally perform for them, such as transporting and assembling their own furniture. By transferring these functions to the customer, IKEA can drive costs down and, therefore, offer prices low enough to fit most budgets. Thus, IKEA targets a rather large segment of the market, ranging from young low- to middle-income families. At the same time, the company has established a highly differentiated image with its enormous selection of self-assembly home furnishings and fun in-store experiences.

Firms that have integrated low-cost and differentiation positions can be found in most industries. So can firms whose products don't seem to fall into either category. As Exhibit 5.2 shows, integrated—and enviable—positions have in fact been forged in the auto industry. Note, for instance, that both Honda and Hyundai generate better profit margins than Chevrolet. Chevrolet seems to be stuck in the middle. The hazards of this type of

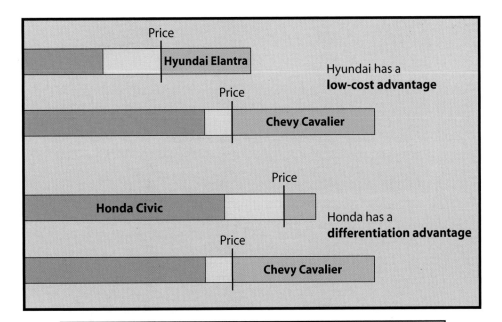

Exhibit 5.2 Integrated Positions: Low-Cost, Differentiation, Stuck-in-the-Middle

straddling position between low cost and differentiation are reviewed later in the chapter. Honda enjoys better margins because it commands higher prices by delivering more consumer value, much of which derives from such intangibles as resale value, lower maintenance costs, and overall quality. Consequently, even though the initial price of the Chevy Cavalier is significantly lower, the Honda Civic is actually less expensive to own in the long run. So is the Hyundai Elantra, which boasts both lower total ownership costs and lower manufacturing costs. Although this example only compares one model from each of these three automakers for purposes of simplicity, the implications for strategic positions apply at the level of the firm's entire portfolio.

Generic Strategy and Firm Resources As we've seen, the appropriate generic strategy for any firm depends on two factors: (1) its resources and capabilities and (2) the condition of its industry environment. A firm with innovative capabilities, for example, will generally favor differentiation strategies. Why? Because the ability to make product improvements, whether incremental and radical, enables a firm to offer newer and more unique products directed at specific customer needs. Intel favors heavy investment in product innovation so that it can remain on the leading edge of new-product introductions in the microprocessor industry. This strategy enables the company to charge higher prices during the early stages of the product life cycle, generating increased cash flows that it can, in turn, invest in building its brand and further differentiating its products.

Alternatively, capabilities in large-scale manufacturing and distribution generally favor low-cost strategies. Cooper Industries, for example, has developed skills in consolidating companies in mature tool, hardware, or electrical-product industries, infusing them with modern manufacturing technology and increasing supplier power over critical customer segments. In particular, the ability to modernize manufacturing processes (the company calls it Cooperizing) gives the firm a cost advantage over many competitors.

The results of successful low-cost, differentiation, and integrated positions are illustrated in Exhibit 5.3. It is critical to remember that these successful positions are predicated on the effective implementation of the drivers of cost or differentiation advantage, or both. In the next section, we explore these drivers in detail.

concept link

In Chapter 3, we define a firm's **resources** as the inputs that it uses to create goods or services and its **capabilities** as its skill in using its resources.

Exhibit 5.3 The Interplay
Between Cost and
Differentiation

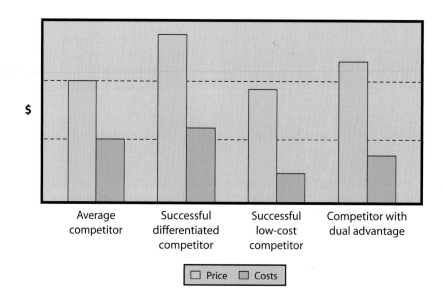

ECONOMIC DRIVERS OF
STRATEGIC POSITIONING

Choices in strategic positioning are also influenced by economic logic. Thus in order to
fully understand the logic behind different strategic positions, we need to identify the different economic drivers that encourage strategic positions and foster their success. In this
section, we'll describe some of the key economic drivers of both low-cost and differentiation strategies. (Remember that because *focus* strategies are special variations on these two
basic types of strategy, the same economic drivers apply to them.) In order to understand
how firms manage to implement the strategies that produce the advantages that they enjoy,
we need to understand economic drivers and how they function.

Drivers of Low-Cost Advantage

Firms have different production costs for several reasons. Some of the more common (and
important) include economies of scale, learning, production technology, product design,
and location advantages for sourcing inputs. In this section, we'll review some of the more
important sources of potential cost advantage. A successful low-cost strategy means that a
firm is proficient at exploiting some of these drivers. Conversely, of course, firms that are
unable to leverage these cost drivers either need to acquire the capabilities and resources to
do so or to reevaluate their prospects as low-cost leaders.

economy of scale Condition under
which average total cost for a unit of
production is lower at higher levels
of output

Economies of Scale

Economies of scale exist during a given period of time *if the
average total cost for a unit of production is lower at higher levels of output.* To better understand the nature and importance of economies of scale, we need to review the various types
of production costs:

- *Fixed costs* (such as rent and equipment) remain the same for different levels of
production.
- *Variable costs* are the costs of variable inputs (such as raw materials and labor); they
vary directly with output.
- *Marginal cost* is the cost of the last unit of production.
- *Total cost* is the sum of all production costs; it increases as output goes up.
- *Average cost* is the *mean* cost of total production during a given period (say, a year).

Economies of scale exist if *average costs* are lower at higher levels of production. Under
what circumstances might it cost less to manufacture more products during one given time
period than during another?

Economies of scale result from a variety of efficiencies, all related to higher volumes of production relative to a given asset base: spreading fixed costs over greater volume, specializing in a specific production process, practicing superior inventory management, exercising purchasing power, spending more effectively on advertising or R&D.

Economies of scale result primarily from the first reason—spreading fixed costs over greater levels of output. It stands to reason that within the feasible range of production at a given facility, increasing output will enable the firm to spread its fixed costs over greater levels of production. If, for example, R&D costs account for a significant portion of the firm's total cost, larger scale enables the firm to cut average cost by spreading R&D costs over more units of production.

In addition, greater scale often encourages the use of more sophisticated inventory-management systems. Some of these systems, though not cost-effective at lower volumes, bring significant rewards at sufficiently large scales of production. Audi, for instance, persuaded suppliers to locate operations in facilities adjacent to its newly centralized facilities in Ingoldstadt, Germany. In turn, the carmaker was able to implement just-in-time inventory techniques that didn't work when smaller-scale manufacturing operations were more widely dispersed.[4] Similarly, when numerous inputs are involved, the price depends, in part, on the volume purchased. That's why large buyers often have more leverage in negotiating price. Wal-Mart, for example, is renowned (even notorious) for exercising its buying power to hold down input costs.

If branding plays a key role in the firm's strategy, larger scale often provides a significant advertising advantage. In order to influence consumer decisions, advertising must first reach a certain "threshold" at which it creates awareness. If two firms of significantly different size allocate the same *proportion* of revenues to advertising, they'll achieve significantly different levels of awareness. Thus, large firms allocate more total dollars for advertising and reap the benefit of greater awareness. In addition, large firms can bargain for price discounts in various media that aren't extended to smaller accounts.

Diseconomies of Scale   Do not, however, make the mistake of assuming that size automatically ensures economies of scale. In reality, almost all operations processes are subject to the **diseconomies of scale** that occur when average total cost *increases* at higher levels of output.

Diseconomies of scale can result from bureaucracy, high labor costs, and inefficient operations. Moreover, a firm may have economies of scale in some value-chain activities that result in diseconomies of scale on other dimensions. For instance, consider the world of institutional fund management. The 20 largest fund managers control over 40 percent of professionally managed money in the world. According to research by Mercer Oliver Wyman, a large consulting practice specializing in financial services, fund management is a very scale-sensitive business. A fund manager with a $10,000,000 portfolio incurs the same costs as a manager with a $100,000,000 portfolio. However, Mercer notes that although some expenses are lower in the large funds (due to scale economies), others must be larger, because the highest-performing firms in every segment of the industry are smaller boutique firms.[5]

Large-scale operations can also lead to inflexibility—and increased costs—in the face of changing needs.[6] This is what happened to General Motors in the early 1990s. After spending billions to complement its massive scale with an appropriate level of automation, GM discovered that its technological upgrade didn't allow it to switch platforms fast enough to respond to shifts in the market. Inflexibility in the face of changing consumer preferences and new-model introductions by competitors actually caused costs at GM's newly automated plants to go up, not down.

Minimum Efficient Scale   How, then, can a firm achieve optimal performance? Ultimately, the objective is to find the scale necessary to achieve the lowest possible average cost. Let's examine this concept in a little more detail.

As we've just seen, costs may decline at some ranges of production but increase at others. This fact suggests that *total average cost* can be represented by a *U*-shaped curve that has a minimum point. The output level that delivers the lowest possible costs is the **minimum**

diseconomy of scale Condition under which average total costs per unit of production increases at higher levels of input

Exhibit 5.4 Scale and Cost

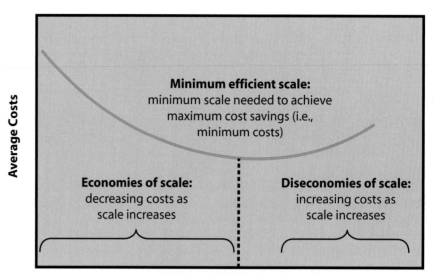

Minimum efficient scale:
minimum scale needed to achieve
maximum cost savings (i.e.,
minimum costs)

Average Costs

Economies of scale:
decreasing costs as
scale increases

Diseconomies of scale:
increasing costs as
scale increases

Scale of Current Operations
(e.g., Current Volume of Production)

minimum efficient scale (MES)
The output level that delivers the lowest
total average cost

efficient scale (MES). Often, firms operating below or above MES suffer from a cost disadvantage. Generally, there is a range of scale—or of output levels—at which costs will be minimized. MES is the smallest scale necessary to achieve maximum economies of scale. It's critical to decisions about a firm's scale of operations because it targets the level of production needed to enjoy all the benefits made possible by large scale. It also establishes the size that a new entrant must achieve in order to match the scale advantages enjoyed by incumbents. Exhibit 5.4 illustrates some possible relationships between economies of scale, diseconomies of scale, and minimum efficient scale. Although MES understandably varies by industry and market segment, the exhibit generally conveys the idea that managers must take into account economy-of-scale tradeoffs when making investments in service or production capacity.

MES and Technology   Not surprisingly, MES is also a function of technology. Obviously, an industry may employ more than one type of technology. In the steel industry, for example, some plants—so-called minimills—use electric-arc furnaces, whereas old-line integrated steel companies continue to use blast-arc furnaces. Minimills are designed to make steel in a simple three-stage process that starts with scrap metal, whereas integrated steel manufacturing requires investments in equipment that start earlier in the value chain with iron ore and coal. Consequently, the scale requirements of the two technologies are quite different, and minimills can achieve MES at roughly one-tenth the scale required for efficient operation at an integrated mill.

With some technologies, MES is reached only at relatively low levels of production, and although there's no scale advantage at higher levels, neither is there any disadvantage. Some technologies result quite quickly in a disadvantage at a scale larger than MES, whereas still others support wide ranges of scale without generating any real cost differences.

The Learning Curve   In addition to scale economies, other factors can contribute to lower operating costs. Two firms of the same size, for example, may have significantly different operating costs because one has progressed farther down the **learning curve**—in other words, it has excelled at the process of learning by doing. The basic principle holds that *incremental production costs decline at a constant rate as production experience is gained*; the steeper the learning curve, the more rapidly costs decline. This idea is attributed to T. P. Wright, who proposed a theory for basing cost estimates on the repetitive operations of airplane-assembly processes in 1936.[7] (In the 1970s, the Defense Department commissioned research to refine learning-curve mathematics so that it could make more precise cost estimates.) See the box entitled "How Would *You* Do That? 5.1" for more on the learning curve.

learning curve Incremental
production costs decline at a constant
rate as production experience is gained;
the steeper the learning curve, the more
rapidly costs decline

Before reading any farther, be sure that you understand the difference between economies of scale and the learning curve. Although both are related to the quantity produced, the underlying mechanisms are quite different. Economies of scale reflect the scale of the operation *during any given period of time*—the volume of current production. Cost decreases attributable to the learning curve reflect *the cumulative level of production since the production of the first unit*.

Putting the Learning Curve to Use   It is important to understand the relationship between experience and costs in a firm's use of technology for several reasons. For one, managers can make more accurate total-cost forecasts when they're preparing bids for large projects. In addition, taking the learning curve into consideration may enable managers to make more aggressive pricing decisions. Japanese motorcycle and automobile manufacturers, for example, considered the expected future costs savings associated with the learning curve when setting entry prices for the U.S. market. Although initial prices may actually have been below *current* production costs, they were set to reflect *future* cost estimates. The low prices also enabled the Japanese to make rapid gains in market share. Resulting higher volumes not only contributed to economies of scale, but also reduced costs due to learning. Later, Asian computer-chip manufacturers adopted the same strategy for entering the U.S. market.[8]

Multiunit Organizations and the Learning Curve   A related effect of the learning curve occurs when a multiunit organization transfers learning from one unit to another.[9] Franchise systems, for instance, can to codify their knowledge about the most effective way to operate a store. Technically, therefore, each new franchise doesn't have to start from scratch. Rather, every unit benefits from corporate training programs that give new franchisees a head start at tackling the learning curve. Because units can share new knowledge about effective practices, multiunit firms can make faster progress in mastering learning curves than single-unit operations.

Other Sources of Cost Advantage   Other potential sources of cost advantage include *economies of scope, production technology*, and *product design*.

Economies of Scope   As the term suggests, *economies of scope* are similar to economies of scale. They refer, however, to potential cost savings associated with *multiproduct* production. When a firm produces two or more products, it has greater scope of operations than a firm that produces only one. If such a firm can share a resource among one or more of its products—thereby lowering the costs of each product—it benefits from **economies of scope**.[10] We discuss this concept more fully in Chapter 7 because it's fundamental to diversification as a corporate strategy. Economies of scope, however, are available not only to large diversified firms but also to small privately held enterprises that are just beginning to expand their product offerings.

economy of scope Condition under which lower total average costs result from sharing resources to produce more than one product or service

Here we offer a simple example to help you understand economies of scope.[11] The multipurpose table and furniture industry is made up of a fragmented group of about 60 major manufacturers who share a $1-billion market. One of these companies, Mity-Lite, was formed in 1987 by Gregory Wilson when he was in the church-furniture business. The company's original product line consisted of folding tables targeted at such institutional users as schools, churches, civic organizations, and hospitals. From the outset, Mity-Lite used a heat- and vacuum-thermoforming process to mold engineering-grade plastics, combining this process with durable folding-metal frames to build tables that are both much lighter and more durable than competing particle-board or plywood tables. As the company grew, it learned to implement a number of changes in both its manufacturing process and product designs—changes that have increased production volumes, improved quality, and lowered costs.

After a decade of successful market penetration, Mity-Lite had developed a reputation as a leading designer, manufacturer, and marketer of folding-leg tables. With excess capacity in his Orem, Utah, plant, Wilson began to study possible growth options. Because customers of folding-leg tables often buy folding or stacking chairs at the same time, Wilson saw at least one opportunity to expand into complementary products. He soon discovered that the same technology he used to form durable tables could be used to manufacture

How to Take the Learning Curve on Two Wheels

How can the learning curve actually help a company? To consider this question, let's review a problem faced by East Side Bikes, a hypothetical maker of custom cruiser bicycles. East Side's latest hit product is a bike with an amazing resemblance to a motorcycle. The marketing manager for a high-end sporting goods retailer recently saw the bike at a trade show, fell in love with it, assured East Side that she can sell them in her company's stores, and initiated negotiations for an initial order of 100 bikes. Of course, for such a large order she expects a good price. How can East Side take the principle of the learning curve into consideration in forecasting its cost and offering the most attractive price?

Because East Side has already made four prototypes, the firm knows that it took 30 hours to make the first bike, 27 hours for the second, and 24.30 hours for the last (fourth) bike made. (Fortunately, there were four prototypes; it's never wise to estimate trends with only two data points.) Using the concept of the learning curve, East Side can systematically use historical data to estimate future costs. East Side can do this in several ways. (Bear in mind, by the way, that we could measure either in terms of costs or hours; for the sake of simplicity, we'll use hours throughout this exercise.)

One way to estimate future costs is simply to calculate projected values

Exhibit 5.5 The Time Value of Learning at East Side Bikes

Number of Bikes Produced	Hours per Bike
1st	30.00 actual
2nd	27.00 actual
4th	24.30 actual
8th	21.87 est.
16th	19.68 est.
32nd	17.71 est.
64th	15.92 est.
128th	14.34 est.

using some basic math. To do this, we need to know a fundamental rule for quantifying the learning curve: For every doubling of *cumulative* production levels, costs decline at a constant rate. In our example, cumulative production has reached four bikes. In other words, it's doubled twice—once from one to two and again from two to four. If we calculate the percentages for each doubling, we see that (conveniently enough) we have a 90-percent learning curve: The hours to make the second bike were 90 percent of the first, and the fourth was 90 percent of the second. Now we just repeat the process to estimate future costs: In other words, we take 90 percent of current production as our estimate for costs *once cumulative production doubles again*, repeating the process until we've reached our target level of production (100

bikes). Using this quick and dirty method, we see that the time we'll need per bike falls to approximately 15 hours by the time we've reached 100 bikes. Our findings are summarized in Exhibit 5.5.

This procedure works fine for small batches, but it could become quite cumbersome for large production runs. In more complicated situations, we need the actual *learning-curve formula*. With this formula and a good calculator or spreadsheet, we can project costs for a specific estimated number of units rather than having to interpolate from a table of values that increase at doubling rates.

Here's the formula for estimating learning curves:

$$y = ax^{-b}$$

where *y* is the cost per unit for the *xth* unit produced; *a* is the

Chapter 5   Creating Business Strategies   137

cost of the first unit produced; x is the cumulative number of products produced (or desired level if the rate of learning, b, is already determined); and b is the *rate* at which costs are reduced every time cumulative production doubles (always a negative number calculated from other known quantities). Using this formula and a spreadsheet, we can project future costs for any level of production and thus make a more informed decision about our costs. Our new findings are summarized in Exhibit 5.6.

If you're math averse, you may prefer to resort to one of several aids. First, we could draw up a table in which we plug in the *rates* for several common learning curves (i.e., the figures needed to plug b into the previous formula). Then we can find our solutions by combining these rates with our spreadsheet capabilities, as shown in Exhibit 5.7.

If you want things even simpler, you could visit a NASA Web site that contains a "learning-curve calculator" at www.jsc.nasa.gov/bu2/learn.html. Using this handy device, you can plug in a few basic data and wait for it to solve the problem for you. (*Hint:* Use the Crawford version of the calculator, which corresponds to the current formulation used in business.)

Exhibit 5.6 The Learning Curve at East Side Bikes

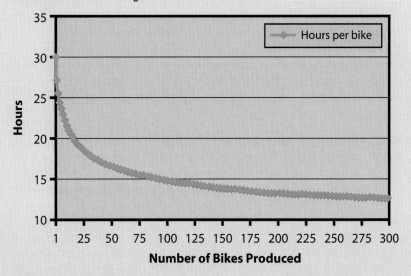

Exhibit 5.7 Spreadsheet for East Side Bikes

Learning Curve	80%	85%	90%	95%
Rate of Learning	−.322	−.234	−.152	−.074

chairs. Moreover, because expansion into chair production didn't require a new plant, the cost of the manufacturing facility could be shared in the production of both tables and chairs. These cost savings reflect economies of scope. From its small beginnings as a supplier of church furniture, Mity-Lite has grown an average of 35 percent per year and has become an international player in the institutional furniture industry.

Production Technology   Naturally, different production technologies entail different costs. Often, a new entrant who wants to compete against industry incumbents with significant scale and experience advantages tries to match or beat incumbents' costs by introducing a production technology that's subject to different economics. JetBlue, for instance, has the lowest operating costs of all major U.S. airlines, and the source of its successful strategy—its production technology—compares quite favorably with the technologies used by other airlines.

Similarly, Nucor Steel originally entered an industry that wasn't particularly attractive from a traditional point of view. Profits were low, capital intensity was high, and the bargaining power of buyers was strong (i.e., steel is a commodity, which means that buyers make purchase decisions primarily on price if all other factors are equal). In addition, most incumbents had the advantage of a century's worth of experience. Nucor, however, didn't use the same technology as its incumbent competitors. Rather than building an integrated mill with blast-arc furnaces, Nucor opted for the lower-cost electric-arc technology favored by minimills.[12]

Product Design   Similarly, product design can sometimes be altered to lower a firm's production costs.[13] When Canon, for example, decided to enter the photocopier industry, incumbents such as Xerox had formidable advantages in scale and experience. Canon, however, redesigned the photocopier so that it required fewer parts and allowed for simpler assembly. The new design dropped Canon's costs below those of Xerox and enabled the new entrant to gain significant market share at Xerox's expense.

Finally, different sourcing practices result in different cost structures. Some firms try to attain lower production costs by locating their operations in cheaper labor markets. Others outsource manufacturing altogether. Pacific Cycle, for instance, makes bikes for less than Trek, whose operations are in the United States, by outsourcing much of its production to China and Taiwan.

In Chapter 3, we define **outsourcing** as any *value-chain activity* performed for a company by people other than its full-time employees.

Drivers of Differentiation Advantages   In order to sell products at premium prices, firms must make their uniqueness and value apparent to customers. In this section, we'll review the economic logic and some of the common drivers of a successful differentiation strategy. As a rule, differentiation involves one or more of the following product offerings: *premium brand image, customization, unique styling, speed, more convenient access,* and *unusually high quality.*

When Toyota introduced its premium Lexus line in 1989, its strategy was based on extensive market analysis and product-development efforts. Relying on its ability to manufacture high-quality automobiles, Toyota was confident that it could penetrate the highly profitable luxury-car segment. In fact, managers regarded the whole idea as quite logical, given the brand image already enjoyed by Toyota. Consequently, the company launched and developed an entirely new brand with a separate dealer network. High quality was a Lexus trademark from the beginning, with the new luxury car winning its first J.D. Power and Associates number-one ranking in the 1990 Initial Quality Study. Being named one of *Car & Driver*'s 10 best and the Motoring Press Association's Best Imported Car of the Year also bolstered the Lexus image.

Bear in mind, however, that although quality earned a slew of technical awards for Lexus, targeted marketing created something even more important—customer awareness. In practice, a differentiation strategy means that marketers understand how to *segment* the market in which they intend to compete—a process known as *market segmentation*. They must identify specific subgroups of buyers who have distinguishable needs, select one or more of these unique buyer needs, and satisfy them in ways that competitors don't or can't.

Curves International, for instance, saw a unique opportunity to segment the fitness-club industry by targeting women who desired a nonintimidating environment. Curves' equipment is different from that of competitors, not only because it's designed for women but because it uses hydraulic-resistance equipment that eliminates the need to worry about weight stacks. In addition, the Curves program features a convenient 30-minute exercise routine. Since its founding in 1992, Curves has opened more than 9,500 locations, and the company's success suggests that the segment it targeted was indeed overlooked or underserved by industry incumbents.

Creating Value and Promoting Willingness to Pay The goal of differentiation is to be able to demand a price sufficient to do two things: (1) recoup the added costs of delivering the value-added feature and (2) generate enough profit to make the strategy worthwhile. The point of differentiation is to drive up the customer's **willingness to pay**—that is, to induce customers to pay more for the firm's products or services than a competitors'. The producer wants to drive a wedge between what customers are willing to pay and the costs of acquiring the resources needed to add value to the product. (Conversely, a low-cost strategy entails keeping costs down to compensate for customers' paying lower prices for undifferentiated products or services.)

willingness to pay Principle of differentation strategy by which customers are willing to pay more for certain product features

THREATS TO SUCCESSFUL COMPETITIVE POSITIONING

For a firm using any of the generic strategies that we've discussed in this chapter, success hinges on a number of factors. Does the firm have the right resources, such as those that may accrue from scale or learning, for implementing a low-cost strategy? Will the marketplace reward a differentiator? In some markets (those which, like steel, are more commodity-like), customers' purchase decisions are driven much more strongly by price than by product features, and in these cases there's not much that firms can do to justify higher prices. A summary of the common drivers of differentiation and low-cost advantage, along with the threats to those positions, is listed in Exhibit 5.8. Under most circumstances, a successful strategic position must satisfy two requirements: (1) It must be based on the firm's resources and capabilities, and (2) it must achieve some level of consistency with the conditions that prevail in the industry.

Threats to Low-Cost Positions

In terms of these two critical requirements, let's look first at the numerous threats facing firms aiming for a low-cost competitive position. First, the firm may face threats on the technological front. In particular, the resource that makes it possible for a firm to compete on the basis of cost—often a certain technology—can be imitated. Efficient production

	Drivers	**Threats**
Low Cost	• Economies of scale • Learning • Economies of scope • Superior technology • Superior product design	• New technology • Inferior quality • Social, political, and economic risk of outsourcing
Differentiation	• Premium brand image • Customization • Unique styling • Speed • Convenient access • Unusually high quality	• Failing to increase buyers' willingness to pay higher prices • Underestimating costs of differentiation • Overfulfilling buyers' needs • Lower-cost imitation

Exhibit 5.8 Low Cost and Differentiation: Drivers and Threats

and process technologies can move from firm to firm by any number of means, such as consultants with clients throughout the industry and the movement of key personnel from company to company.

Granted, even though an imitator may acquire comparable technology, the original firm may still enjoy the benefits of greater experience and the learning curve. A more serious threat to low-cost competitors is the possibility that another firm may introduce a new technology—one which, like mini-mill technology in the steel industry, supports a different scale and a more efficient learning process. In such cases, even small latecomers can establish cost positions significantly lower than those of larger, more experienced low-cost leaders.

Second, low-cost leadership means offering an acceptable combination of price and quality. A real threat to an intended low-cost position is the failure to offer sufficient quality to satisfy buyers' basic needs. Over the past decade, for example, Kmart's experiments in low-cost positioning have been thwarted not only by Wal-Mart's ability to stake out an even lower-cost position, but by Kmart's own inability to offer a retail experience of comparable quality (customers complain of empty shelves, uninviting environments, and less helpful staff).

Recently, another serious threat has arisen to low-cost competitors in labor-intensive industries: increased public awareness of questionable labor practices in developing countries. Struggling to keep wage costs as low as possible, many companies (some unwittingly) have entered into agreements with suppliers who enforce excessive work hours, deny basic employee services, employ children, and violate what, at least in the United States, are considered acceptable working conditions. Watchdog groups regularly publicize such cases, and reforms push up costs.[14] Many multinational companies have established codes of ethical conduct for suppliers, but enforcing these standards—inspecting and auditing overseas suppliers—also increases costs. Managers must be certain that their foreign sourcing arrangements are in compliance with their corporate values.

Threats to Differentiation Positions

Needless to say, the intent to provide a differentiated product doesn't necessarily result in competitive advantage and enhanced profitability. A number of factors can sabotage a differentiation strategy. Obviously, a differentiating feature that buyers don't care about merely increases costs without increasing willingness to pay, which cuts into profit margins. Until recently, for example, Audi suffered from the fact that although its manufacturing costs were comparable to those of BMW and Mercedes, it couldn't get customers to pay comparable prices. In effect, Audi was either overfulfilling the needs of buyers who were in the market for well-made but more modestly priced cars or underfulfilling the needs of customers in the market for high-image, high-quality cars.

In addition, failing to understand the total costs entailed by differentiation can derail a differentiation position. The cost of differentiation has no direct effect on customers' willingness to pay, and in most industries, cost-plus pricing is not an option. Jaguar, for example, found itself in an apparently enviable position in the early 1980s: It had a highly differentiated product with good brand recognition and strong customer appeal, and unlike Audi's targeted customers, car buyers were willing to pay premium prices for Jaguars. Unfortunately, antiquated manufacturing processes had driven costs so high that, even with products selling in the top price range, the company lost money. Many of its operations weren't even automated, but ironically, Jaguar took pride in its traditional hands-on methods—in part because managers believed that brand recognition and customer loyalty were tied to an appreciation of the individualized manufacturing process. Ford purchased Jaguar in 1990 and, after studying the company's operations, revamped assembly plants in an effort to combine the best aspects of both traditional and modern methods. Ford, for instance, retained the practice of installing hand-sewn leather interiors and natural-wood inlays but significantly modernized the processes for assembling bodies and power trains.[15]

Two additional reasons differentiation can fail are overfulfillment and ease of imitation. When product features exceed buyer needs, the added costs to provide these unwanted features, coupled with customers' lack of willingness to pay for this differentiation, results in significantly lower margins. Finally, creating differentiation that competitors can emulate quickly or cheaply undermines any advantage that it might afford. Naturally, once competitors have matched a product's unique feature, it's no longer unique and will probably lose its ability to command premium prices. In some industries, patents provide short-term protection for innovative products. In others, companies must seek alternative means of protection. In the soft-drink industry, where products are easily imitated (they are, after all, simple combinations of water, sugar, color, and flavoring), Coke and Pepsi discourage imitation by exercising power of scale over suppliers and buyers and conducting aggressive marketing campaigns to sustain brand image.

Threats to Focus Positions

Although focused low-cost or focused differentiation positions are specialized cases of low-cost leadership and broad differentiation and thus subject to all the same threats as those just reviewed, they face one additional threat that deserves mention. Firms that implement focus positions face the threat of being out-focused by competitors. A firm relying on a focus strategy may lose its advantage by attempting to grow and consequently attempt to meet the needs of too many customers. If that happens, a competitor or new entrant may then more successfully target the needs of the original focused group of customers. As existing or new competitors identify new or previously unexploited needs of the segment, they may be in a better position to uniquely satisfy the needs of that segment. For instance, Harley-Davidson faces the threat that custom chopper shops will pull away customers because they can more uniquely satisfy the needs of a segment of Harley's market.

Threats to Integrated Positions

In his original analysis of generic strategic positions, Porter, arguing that they were mutually exclusive, warned against the temptation to straddle positions: Firms that try both to differentiate and to achieve a low-cost position will end up **straddling** two inconsistent positions.

All firms, Porter suggested, must make decisions about positioning their products and will consequently choose one strategy over the other. Developing a low-cost strategy means that a firm must forgo subsequent opportunities to enhance product uniqueness or quality (that is, to develop a position based on differentiation). In this respect, selected strategies and forgone opportunities must be regarded as tradeoffs. H&R Block, for example, can't enter the field of high-level estate and tax planning because such services require the kind of high-cost specialists that a low-cost competitor can't afford. Thus, Block trades off the advantages of high-margin services for the advantages of a low-cost tax-preparation business. By the same token, a "pure" differentiator trades off the cost-saving advantages of producing standardized products for the advantages of satisfying a demand for customized products.

Although many firms have succeeded in pursuing integrated strategies, it's still critical for managers to understand the tradeoffs they make when they opt for one position over the other. Virtually no firm can succeed in being all things to all customers. For one, firms need to know exactly what opportunities they're forgoing.

Second, knowing what tradeoffs can be made in an industry helps managers recognize what competitors can and can't do in attempts to juggle strategies. Why, for instance, can't United, American, and Delta lower their costs to match those of Southwest Airlines? Many of the specific practices by which Southwest maintains its lower-cost position entail tradeoffs that the other carriers can't make. United, Delta, and American don't have the option of flying just one type of aircraft, even if it would save on training and maintenance costs. Nor can they abandon their expensive hub facilities, which are integral to the logistics of their flight systems, even though the hub system and its accompanying gate fees are much more costly than Southwest's reliance on secondary airports and smaller destination cities.

STRATEGY AND FIT WITH INDUSTRY CONDITIONS

In Chapter 1, we introduced the strategy-diamond model of strategy formulation. Recall that an important input into this model is a firm's objectives. Earlier in the chapter we detailed generic strategies *by type*, but in order to show how the strategy-diamond and

straddling Unsuccessful attempt to integrate both low-cost and differentiation positions

concept**link**

In Chapter 2, we observe that most strategic positions involve *tradeoffs*—that deciding on one course of action generally eliminates other options.

generic-strategy models are compatible, we need to remind ourselves that when managers decide on generic competitive positions, they aren't deciding on strategies themselves: Rather, they're stating *objectives* with respect to several elements of their overall strategy—indicating precisely how they intend the firm to deal with differentiators, economic logic, and certain aspects of arenas.

We know, too, that industry conditions have an important effect on strategy formulation. One way to illustrate this effect is to examine the threats and opportunities presented to a company during different phases of the industry life cycle. In this section, we'll treat each phase of the life cycle as if conditions are not likely to change in the short term. In other words, in order to show how alternative strategies function under different life-cycle conditions, we'll take advantage of the fact that industry analysis gives us a "snapshot" view of an industry at a particular point in its life cycle. In reality, of course, many industries are changing rapidly, and in Chapter 6, we'll turn our attention to strategies that take advantage of changes, such as the rapid and sometimes managed evolution of an industry from one stage in its life cycle to the next.

Strategies for Different Industry Conditions

Industry conditions should inform strategic leaders and have an influence on the strategies their firms formulate. Of course, not all firms will respond similarly to different industry conditions, but conditions at different phases of an industry life cycle provide differential opportunities and constraints. Consequently, firms' strategies tend to vary across these different phases. Exhibit 5.9 summarizes some of the more common effects of the industry life cycle on the elements of firms' strategies.

Embryonic Stage   During an industry's *embryonic* phase, when business models are unproven, no standardized technology has been established, capital needs generally outstrip the resources and capabilities of startups, and uncertainty is high. Early movers—those who succeed in establishing solid competitive positions during this stage—can set themselves up to be in a strong position during later phases of the industry life cycle.[16] Because primary demand is just being established and customers lack good information on the relative quality of products, successful differentiation tactics during this phase include getting a strong foothold and building capacity to meet growing demand.

Growth Stage   As industries enter periods of rapid growth, incumbent firms increase market share by taking advantage of footholds established earlier. Rapid growth increases speed down the learning curve and presents leaders with an opportunity to establish low-cost positions that are difficult to imitate, at least in the short term. During this phase, however, technologies can change as new entrants learn from and improve on the work of early movers.

After introducing the Pilot, for example, Palm enjoyed an apparently formidable advantage in the PDA industry. The Palm Pilot was hailed as the most successful consumer-product launch in history, reaching sales of 2 million units within three years and surpassing the adoption rates of camcorders, color TVs, VCRs, and cell phones.[17] Although it considered itself primarily a hardware-device company, Palm developed its own operating system because it was dissatisfied with Microsoft's system for handheld devices. But as the PDA industry grew in size, it caught Microsoft's attention. Before long, Microsoft had renewed interest in its own operating system, and other new competitors, some of whom already had complementary relationships with Microsoft, entered the PDA-software industry.[18] There's obviously an advantage in moving early, gaining a foothold that supports quick growth, and reaping cost advantages by moving quickly along the learning curve, but it doesn't necessarily constitute an impenetrable competitive barrier. New technologies and changing industry competitive structure remain threats.[19]

During the growth phase of an industry, firms make important decisions about how they intend to grow: They determine the strategic vehicles that they'll use to implement their preferred strategies. High-tech companies, for example, may seek alliances with estab-

conceptlink

We introduce the **industry life cycle** in Chapter 4, where we emphasize that the *evolution* of industries from emergence to maturity and even stagnation drives the strategies of the companies that compete in them.

Exhibit 5.9 Life-Cycle Strategies

Phase of Industry Life Cycle	Arenas	Vehicles	Differentiators	Staging	Economic Logic
Embryonic	Staying local	Internal development Alliances to secure missing inputs or distribution access	Target basic needs, minimal differentiation	Tactics to gain early footholds	Prices tend to be high Costs are high; focus is on securing additional capital to fund growth phase
Growth	Penetrating adjacent markets	Alliances for cooperation Acquisitions in targeted markets	Increase efforts toward differentiation Low-cost leaders emerge through experience and scale advantages	Integrated positions require choice of focusing first on cost or differentiation	Margins can improve rapidly because of experience and scale Price premiums accrue to successful differentiators
Mature	Globalizing Diversifying	Mergers and acquisitions for consolidation	More stable positions emerge across competitors	Choices of international markets and new industry diversification need rational sequencing	Consolidation results in fewer competitors (favoring higher margins), but declining growth demands cost containment and rationalization of operations
Decline	Abandoning some arenas if decline is severe Focusing on segments that provide the most profitability	Acquisitions for diversifying Divestitures enable some competitors to exit and others to consolidate larger shares of the market	Fewer competitors result in less pressure for differentiation, but declining sales results in greater pressure for cost savings	Timing of exit from selected segments or businesses	Rationalizing cost

lished firms in adjacent industries, similar to the embryonic stage, in order to fill in gaps in their own range of competencies. Such is the case in the biotechnology industry; virtually all of the pure biotech companies have established alliances with large pharmaceutical companies in order to access clinical-trial expertise and marketing capabilities.[20] During the growth stage, too, firms with desirable resources become attractive acquisition targets, both for incumbents wanting to grow rapidly and for firms in related industries seeking to enter the market.

Maturity Stage As industries mature and growth slows, products become more familiar to the vast majority of potential customers. Product information is more widely available, and quality becomes a more important factor in consumer choice. A mature market, therefore, increases the ability of firms to reap premium prices from differentiation strategies.

Mature industries often undergo *consolidation*—the combination of competitors through merger or acquisition. Consolidation is often motivated by the twofold objective of exploiting economies of scale and increasing market power. The U.S. bicycle industry profiled through the examples of Pacific Cycle, Trek, and Montague, for instance, has experienced a virtual cascade of mergers and acquisitions for the better part of a decade. Although each new combination promises cost saving through greater economies of scale, evidence of significant savings remains inconclusive at best. Market power is a factor because many bicycle companies want to stay large enough to serve the needs of high-volume distribution channels such as Wal-Mart.

Decline Stage In declining industries, products can take on the attributes of quasi commodities. Because price competition can be intense, containing costs is critical, and firms with low-cost positions have an advantage. Although customers don't entirely ignore differentiated products, declining sales discourage firms from investing in significant innovations.

During this stage, many firms consider the strategy of exiting the industry. Generally, the decision to exit means selling the company or certain divisions to competing firms. Because demand is declining, the industry probably suffers from overcapacity. Thus, reducing the number of competitors can enhance the profitability of those firms that remain. But this fact doesn't mean that exit signifies failure. In many cases, exit can be the best use of shareholders' resources.

A short case study about General Dynamics (GD) drawn from the defense industry demonstrates the potential benefits of exiting an industry during its decline stage.[21] GD was founded in 1899 as the Electric Boat Co. and a year later produced the first workable submarine, which it sold to the U.S. Navy. By the 1950s, GD was a full-fledged defense contractor, producing missiles, rockets, nuclear-powered submarines, and military aircraft. In the mid-1950s, due to the wide range of its defense-industry operations, the company changed its name to General Dynamics Corp. During the 1970s and 1980s, GD emerged as the only defense contractor to supply major systems to all branches of the U.S. military.

Despite many successful weapons programs, however, GD's profitability dropped during the late 1980s, largely because of changes in government procurement processes. In addition, the Cold War thawed rapidly in 1989 and 1990, with the Soviet withdrawal from Afghanistan, the fall of the Berlin Wall, and the collapse of Communist governments across Eastern Europe. Needless to say, the proliferation of arms treaties dampened the demand for weapons systems. GD was particularly hard hit because it was the least diversified of all defense contractors, with a full 87 percent of its revenue tied to defense-system sales.

In 1989, GD hired William Anders as chairman and CEO. His specific charge was to turn the floundering company around. Motivated by lucrative contracts that included generous incentives tied to stock-price performance, Anders and his top-management team set about implementing a radical new strategy. Anders' team made immediate changes, cutting capital spending to 20 percent of the level just two years earlier (saving $337 million). They lost over $1 billion in sales and slashed R&D spending targets by 50 percent. Spending cuts were followed by massive layoffs. Anders was quite public in his pronouncements that the defense industry suffered from overcapacity, too many competitors, and dwindling demand. He publicly urged the industry to consolidate.

Over a two-year period beginning in late 1991, GD sold seven defense businesses for more than $3 billion, emerging as a much smaller and more focused company. Revenues for the new GD were a mere 34 percent of levels of two years earlier, but exiting from so many markets enabled GD to eliminate 94 percent of its outstanding debt, repurchase over 13 million shares of stock, increase dividends by 140 percent, and issue special dividends totaling $50 per share. At the end of this massive downsizing and business-exit campaign, GD had returned $3.4 billion to shareholders and debt holders. Moreover, despite the massive reduction in size, GD's market capitalization increased from about $1 billion in January 1991 to almost $2.9 billion by the end of 1993. Shareholders who held their stock during the three-year restructuring campaign realized a return of over 550 percent.

General Dynamics was once the only defense contractor able to supply products to all branches of the military. After the Cold War ended, however, the company found many of the markets for its products in decline and exited a host of them.

TESTING THE QUALITY OF A STRATEGY

Now that you have command of an adequate repertory of strategy-formulation tools—namely, the strategy-diamond, VRINE, industry-structure, and the strategic-positioning models—you should be able to use them to test the quality of a firm's strategy. Clearly, developing a successful business strategy is a complex task. Although we've focused in this chapter on decisions regarding competitive position and strategic interactions, we must also stress that evaluating the effectiveness of a strategy requires that you apply all the tools and models that we've discussed in the first four chapters of this book. In this section, we'll lay out a simple five-step process that makes use of all of these tools and models to evaluate the quality of a firm's strategy.[22] These steps are summarized in Exhibit 5.10.

Does Your Strategy Exploit Your Firm's Resources and Capabilities?

Your first step is determining whether your strategy and competitive position exploit your firm's resources and capabilities. Low-cost strategic positions require manufacturing resources and capabilities that are likely to contribute to a cost advantage. For instance, Pacific Cycle is the lowest-cost bike distributor in the United States by virtue of its lean operations and the complete outsourcing of bike manufacturing to Taiwan and China. Likewise, a differentiation position depends on your ability to produce quality products and to project the necessary image of quality. In Trek's case, it has been careful to cultivate its high-performance image by sponsoring bike luminaries such Lance Armstrong and selling only through the exclusive independent-dealer channel. When two firms follow similar strategies, you must determine whether you can use your resources to implement your strategy more economically than your competitors can. Finally, you need to be sure that you have the capital resources—both financial and human—necessary to pull off your strategy.

Does Your Strategy Fit with Current Industry Conditions?

Next, you must ask whether your strategy fits with the current conditions in your competitive environment. You need to know whether that environment is hostile, benign, or somewhere

Exhibit 5.10   Testing the Quality of Your Strategy

Key Evaluation Criteria	
1. Does your strategy exploit your key resources?	With your particular mix of resources, does this strategy give you an advantageous position relative to your competitors?
	Can you pursue this strategy more economically than your competitors?
	Do you have the capital and managerial talent to do all you plan to do?
	Are you spread too thin?
2. Does your strategy fit with current industry conditions?	Is there healthy profit potential where you're headed?
	Are you aligned with the key success factors of your industry?
3. Will your differentiators be sustainable?	Will competitors have difficulty imitating you?
	If imitation can't be foreclosed, does your strategy include a ceaseless regimen of innovation and opportunity creation to keep distance between you and the competition?
4. Are the elements of your strategy consistent and aligned with your strategic position?	Have you made choices of arenas, vehicles, differentiators, staging, and economic logic?
	Do they all fit and mutually reinforce each other?
5. Can your strategy be implemented?	Will your stakeholders allow you to pursue this strategy?
	Do you have the proper complement of implementation levers in place?
	Is the management team able and willing to lead the required changes?

Source: Adapted from D. C. Hambrick and J. W. Fredrickson, "Are You Sure You Have a Strategy?" Academy of Management Executive *15:4 (2001), 48–59.*

in between. Essentially, you want to be sure that you understand the profit *potential* of both your current position and the position toward which your strategy is taking you. Pacific Cycle viewed the big-box retailers and consolidation of the bike industry as opportunities for profitable growth. Ironically, Trek viewed the same environment with an eye toward shoring up relationships with independent bike dealers as a way to combat the influx of sales through low-cost, big-box retail channels. Thus, you need to determine whether your strategy aligns with the key success factors favored by your competitive environment.

Are Your Differentiators Sustainable?

If competitors can imitate your differentiators, can you protect your current relationship with your customers? Imitation can erode competitive advantage, but some forms of imitation can reinforce brand loyalty to individual firms. Frequent-flier programs, for example, are very easy to imitate, but customers who have accumulated many miles with one carrier are harder to steal than those who don't have very many miles. Ironically, then, imitation in this case actually serves to increase existing brand loyalty and, potentially, to benefit both firms. Frequent-flier programs put up barriers to customer mobility, and without some kind of barrier that increases the cost of switching brands, a firm with easily imitated differentiators will have to rely on a continual stream of innovative offerings in order to sustain revenues.

Are the Elements of Your Strategy Consistent and Aligned with Your Strategic Position?

Your next step is determining whether all of the elements of your strategy diamond are not only internally consistent but that they are also aligned with your strategic position, whether the one you occupy currently or the one toward which your strategy may direct you in the future. The challenge is to ensure that your choices of arenas, vehicles, differentiators, staging, and economic logic are mutually reinforcing and consistent with your objective, whether it's to be a low-cost leader, a differentiator, or a focused firm. For instance, to be poised for the growth phase, your strategy will need to accommodate rapid growth through the use of acquisitions or significant internal development of additional products and services. If you do not do so, your firm will be marginalized. This may be an acceptable outcome if the intended strategic position is one of focus. Alternatively, if your industry is approaching the end of the growth phase, have you implemented appropriate cost-containment measures that will be required when additional price competition increases? The key is to make clear and explicit links between the vision of the firm, your strategy, and industry conditions. When these factors are aligned, the likelihood of achieving your objectives is maximized. When one of these features is not in alignment with the others, lack of coherence almost always causes the firm to slip behind competitors.

Can Your Strategy Be Implemented?

It does no good to concoct a brilliant strategy within the safe confines of your office at headquarters if your firm can't implement it. To test whether your strategy can be implemented, you need to make sure that it's aligned with the appropriate implementation levers. For instance, do you have the appropriate people, the necessary systems and processes, and incentives that are congruent with your objectives? If not, can you make these modifications within the organization in time to execute the strategy? Do you have the sufficient managerial talent and interest to pursue the strategy? One of the biggest obstacles to firm growth is insufficient managerial resources (e.g., time, people, interests) to focus on the details of execution. As a startup, for instance, JetBlue has set aggressive objectives for financial returns, growth, and a focused low-cost leadership position. Among other things, executing this strategy will mean continually hiring new employees who fit the company culture—people who share the core values of the firm. Otherwise, it will be vulnerable to the sort of labor problems that have beset other low-cost airlines. The most successful firms routinely discuss the integration of strategy and leadership. For instance, all discussions of new strategic initiatives will include answers to the question of "who exactly will get this done?" If there is no clear answer to this question, or if those individuals are likely to be spread too thin as a consequence, even attractive plans should not be given a green light.

SUMMARY

1. Define *generic strategies* and explain how they relate to a firm's strategic position. Strategic positioning is the concept of how executives situate or locate their firm relative to rivals along important competitive dimensions. The strategic-positioning model—Porter's generic strategy model—is an enduring classic in the field of strategic management. Porter's strategy model uses two dimensions: the potential source of strategic advantage and the breadth of the strategic target market. The four generic strategies are low-cost leader, differentiation, focused low-cost, and focused differentiation.

2. Describe the drivers of low-cost, differentiation, and focused strategic positions. Low-cost leaders must have resources or capabilities that enable them to produce a product at a significantly lower cost than rivals. Successful low-cost leaders generally have superior economies of scale, are farther down the learning curve, or have superior production or process technologies than their rivals. However, to substantially reduce costs over rivals, low-cost leaders generally have to be willing to make tradeoffs—they cannot offer all the features, attributes, and quality that a successful differentiator can. Likewise, successful differentiators will normally have to accept higher costs than low-cost leaders. To make a differentiation strategy pay off, firms must segment the market so that customer needs are well understood, products are designed to uniquely satisfy those needs, and the products offered drive up a customers' willingness to pay. Firms that attempt to straddle both positions generally do not perform well along either dimension. However, some firms have been successful at integrating basic features of both low-cost and differentiation. Those that do, typically perfect one set of economic drivers before trying to complement those with the seemingly inconsistent drivers associated with the other economic logic. A focused strategy is generally the application of a low-cost or differentiation approach to a narrowly defined arena.

3. Identify and explain the risks associated with each generic strategic position. Successful strategic positions are still vulnerable. Threats to low-cost leadership include not having the resources necessary to implement the position, having low-cost drivers imitated by firms with better products, and not having sufficient quality to attract buyers. Threats to a differentiation strategy include increasing costs significantly to differentiate a product only to misperceive customer preferences, excessive cost to provide the targeted differentiation, and differentiating in ways that are easily imitated. A firm relying on a focus strategy risks growing too large, trying to meet too many needs, and then being out-focused by a more specialized company. An integrated position runs the risk of unsuccessfully straddling the logic of seemingly inconsistent economic drivers, resulting in neither a low cost position nor a differentiated one.

4. Show how different strategic positions fit with various stages of the industry life cycle. During embryonic stages, primary demand is just beginning, and customers lack good information on the relative quality of products. Thus, building a strong foothold and the capacity to meet growing demand are more important than aggressively differentiating products. During growth stages, building on early footholds provides incumbents with an opportunity to gain market share and move down the learning curve and establish low-cost positions. Maturity stages bring lower levels of growth, and information is widely available to customers. Differentiation can reduce competitive threats and result in higher prices. During industry decline, price competition intensifies and cost containment becomes more important.

5. Evaluate the quality of the firm's strategy. The quality of a firm's strategy can be assessed by answering a few questions that can be answered by the basic tools of strategy, including the strategy diamond, the VRINE model, the industry structure model, and the strategic-positioning model. First, you must determine whether the strategy and competitive position exploit the firm's resources and capabilities. Strategic positions such as low-cost leadership and differentiation have economic assumptions that cannot be satisfied in the absence of complementary resources and capabilities. Second, a quality strategy will also fit with the external environment—the current environment and the anticipated environment in dynamic contexts. Third, a firm's differentiators must be sustainable. Fourth, all of the elements of the strategy diamond must be internally consistent and aligned with the current or desired strategic position. Finally, a quality strategy is one that can be implemented by the firm. Brilliant plans are of little value if the firm is unable to execute them.

KEY TERMS

differentiation, 128
diseconomies of scale, 133
economies of scale, 132
economies of scope, 135

focused cost leadership, 129
focused differentiation, 129
generic strategies, 127
integrated position, 130

learning curve, 134
low-cost leadership, 128
minimum efficient scale (MES), 134

straddling, 141
strategic positioning, 126
willingness to pay, 139

REVIEW QUESTIONS

1. What do we mean by *generic strategies*?

2. What criteria must be met in order for differentiators and low-cost leaders to be successful?

3. What is the relationship between economies of scale and minimum efficient scale?

4. What are economies of scope?

5. How does the learning curve work?

6. What is market segmentation? What role does it play in strategic positioning?

7. What is willingness to pay? How does it relate to strategic positioning?

8. How does the industry life cycle affect business strategy?

9. What are the steps in testing the quality of a strategy?

How Would you Do That?

1. Let's revisit the learning curve and change some of the assumptions made in the box entitled "How Would *You* Do That? 5.1." Assume that the first bike took 100 hours, the second 85, and the fourth 72.25. What would the incremental "cost" in hours be for the 16th bike? For the 124th? For the 1,000th? Try to find these numbers using both the formula presented in the feature and the learning curve calculator located at www.jsc.nasa.gov/bu2/learn.html.

2. Based on the information in the box entitled "How Would *You* Do That? 5.1," assume that you have determined that established leaders have such an experience advantage that you'll never catch their cost position. Devise a realistic strategy for entering and competing against an established player that has a significant low-cost leadership position.

GROUP ACTIVITIES

1. Review the opening vignette about the three bicycle manufacturers. Use the strategy diamond and the generic strategy model to describe the positioning strategy of each firm. Based on what you know about the bicycle industry, can you identify any underserved (or overserved) segments?

2. Go back to Exhibit 4.1 in Chapter 4. Identify low-cost leaders from two of these industries. What seem to be the drivers of their cost-leadership positioning strategies? Are they the same? If not, why?

ENDNOTES

1. Personal interview with Trek executives, fall 2004; "Trek Bicycle Corporation Hoover's Company In-Depth Records," *Hoover's*, www.hoovers.com (accessed September 28, 2005); S. Silcoff, "Dorel Buys Biggest U.S. Cycle Maker: Gains 27% of U.S. Market Share with US$310M Purchase of Schwinn, GT Brands," *Financial Post*, January 14, 2004, p.1; www.montagueco.com/aboutusourhistory.html (accessed October 20, 2005).

2. M. E. Porter, *Competitive Strategy* (New York: Free Press, 1980).

3. http://www.autointell.net (accessed July 15, 2005).

4. Personal interview with Audi senior management, May 2003.

5. S. Targett, "U.S. Companies Win at the Scale Game," *Financial Times*, February 16, 2004, p. 9.

6. R. Sanchez, "Strategic Flexibility in Product Competition," *Strategic Management Journal* 16 (1995), 135–149.

7. See S. S. Liao, "The Learning Curve: Wright's Model vs. Crawford's Model," *Issues in Accounting Education* 3 (1988), 302–315.

8. A. S. Grove, *Only the Paranoid Survey: How to Exploit the Crisis Points That Challenge Every Company* (New York: Currency, 1996).

9. E. D. Darr, L. Argote, and D. Epple, "The Acquisition, Transfer, and Depreciation of Knowledge in Service Organizations: Productivity in Franchises," *Management Science* 41 (1995), 1750–1762.

10. D. Teece, "Economies of Scope and the Scope of the Enterprise," *Journal of Economic Behavior and Organization* 1 (1980), 223–247.

11. Interview with Mity-Lite corporate officers, November 2004. See also www.mity-lite.com.

12. C. Christensen, *The Innovator's Dilemma* (New York: Harper Business Press, 2000).

13. C. K. Prahalad and G. Hamel, "The Core Competence of the Corporation," *Harvard Business Review* 68:3 (1990), 79–91.

14. See www.sweatshops.org/; www.uniteunion.org/sweatshops/sweatshop.html; and www.business-humanrights.org/Home.

15. Personal interview with Jaguar executives, June 2003.

16. D. C. Hambrick, I. A. MacMillan, and D. L. Day, "Strategic Attributes and Performance in the BCG Matrix: A PIMS-Based Analysis of Industrial Product Businesses," *Academy of Management Journal* 25 (1982), 510–531.

17. D. B. Yoffie and M. Kwak, "Mastering Strategic Movement at Palm," *Sloan Management Review* 43:1 (2001), 55–63.

18. Yoffie and Kwak, "Mastering Strategic Movement at Palm."

19. Hambrick, MacMillan, and Day, "Strategic Attributes and Performance in the BCG Matrix."

20. F. T. Rothaermel and D. L. Deeds, "Exploration and Exploitation Alliances in Biotechnology: A System of New Product Development," *Strategic Management Journal* 25:3 (2004), 201–221.

21. J. Dial and K. B. Murphy, "Incentives, Downsizing, and Value Creation at General Dynamics," *Journal of Financial Economics* 37 (1990), 261–314; company annual reports, hoovers.com (accessed September 28, 2005).

22. This section draws heavily on D. C. Hambrick and J. W. Fredrickson, "Are You Sure You Have a Strategy?" *Academy of Management Executive* 15:4 (2001), 48–59.

6

Crafting Business Strategy
for Dynamic Contexts

After studying this chapter, you should be able to:

1. Identify the challenges to sustainable competitive advantage in dynamic contexts.

2. Understand the fundamental dynamics of competition.

3. Evaluate the advantages and disadvantages of choosing a first-mover strategy.

4. Analyze and develop strategies for managing industry evolution.

5. Analyze and develop strategies for technological discontinuities.

6. Analyze and develop strategies for high-speed environmental change.

7. Explain the implications of a dynamic strategy for the strategy diamond and strategy implementation.

▶ **2000**
College student Shawn Fanning taps out code for a digital file-sharing program that changes the music industry forever. Napster is born.

▶ **2002**
Napster underestimates the competitive and regulatory barriers it faces and goes bankrupt after being sued by the music industry. Software developer Roxio Inc. buys Napster a year later.

▶ **2003**
Apple Computer begins selling 99-cent songs over the Internet to enhance the sales of its popular iPod. A host of competitors emerge.

ROXIO AND THE RESURRECTION OF NAPSTER

When someone draws up a conclusive list of the software that made the Internet what it is, somewhere among e-mail and Web browsers there will be a spot for Napster.[1] Napster was really two pieces of software: freely available "client" software that ran on home computers, enabling individuals to copy music to their PCs and play it for free, and a central Napster-run server that dispensed information about music. When it arrived in late 1999, Napster showed how easily music could be distributed without a costly infrastructure (namely, recording-artist royalties and record stores). The timing was also right; as consumer preferences were shifting to entertainment-on-demand, big players such as Sony and Samsung were providing stylish, miniaturized portable music systems, and there was little in terms of clear legal precedent against music sharing. By facilitating music sharing, Napster sent ripples of

▶ **2004**
Digital music generates more than $300 million in sales annually, drastically altering the competitive landscape for brick-and-mortar music retailers everywhere. Roxio resurrects the "Napster" name for its digital site.

▶ **2005**
Fanning launches Snocap.com, a new service for the music industry that can identify songs illegally swapped online.

1995   2000

panic through the music industry, which depended on the traditional music-industry infrastructure to generate a considerable amount of revenue. In June 2002, after four years of legal battles with the Recording Industry Association of America (RIAA), which represents every major U.S. music label, Napster filed for bankruptcy. At the time, Napster had listed assets of $7.9 million and liabilities of more than $101 million.

Because of the crash in the value of most Internet stocks and the bankruptcy of firms like Napster, times were tough for pure-play Internet businesses. Only a few hardy rarities, such as Yahoo!, Google, and eBay, managed to stay alive and prosperous. In the same year, however, the online-music industry came roaring back. At the beginning of 2003, Apple Computer started selling songs over the Internet for 99 cents each, and within a year, players as diverse as Roxio, RealNetworks, Wal-Mart, Microsoft, Sony, Viacom, Yahoo!, BestBuy, and Amazon.com had entered the industry. In one week alone, five of these large companies entered or announced their intent to enter the music-download business. Rarely has technology had such a rapid, radical effect on an industry's existing business practices and distribution channels.

Among these new, remodeled, and reborn companies was Napster itself, which had been purchased by Roxio Inc. in 2003. Roxio itself had gone public in 2000 as a software-only firm specializing in the development and sale of CD-recording products to both original-equipment manufacturers (OEMs) of PCs and CD-recordable-drive manufacturers, integrators, and distributors. In preparation for the Napster launch, Roxio courted two tech-industry players once spurned by Napster—Microsoft and music producers. Why Microsoft? Roxio supplies the CD-burning software bundled with all new PCs operated by Microsoft XP. As for music producers, Roxio, unlike the original Napster, intended to keep them happy by abandoning the idea of free music sharing.

The question for Roxio was whether it would still be around in five years, after the online-music business had shaken out. It faced competition not only in its original software business, but in its new online-music business as well. Approaches to providing online music included the following:

- The *à la carte approach* (employed by Roxio and Apple's iTunes). For 79 cents to $1.20, customers can buy any number of individual tracks (or albums for $9.99 and up). After downloading music onto their hard drives, they can burn it onto CDs, copy it to portable music players, or stream it through home-entertainment centers.
- The *subscription model* (used by emusic). Customers pay a monthly fee to download a specified number of songs. For $9.99 a month, emusic lets customers download 40 songs (65 for $14.99) and use them any way they want.
- The *streaming model* (favored by RealNetwork's Rhapsody). Music lovers pay a monthly fee to listen to as many songs as they can stand and, for a little extra (usually under a dollar a track), download their favorites.

The uncertainty created by the availability of competing technological standards was heightened by the fact that the idea of online-music consumption had only just begun to catch on.

Going forward, Roxio aimed to compete by keeping its hand in the turbulent online-music business while keeping a firm grip on its position as the number-one seller of CD- and DVD-burning software. This strategy meant that the company had to maintain strong ties with Microsoft as well as with other tech-industry heavyweights, such as RealNetworks, and the music industry—an array of stakeholders who view Roxio as everything from a partner to competitor. Moreover, Roxio would also need to keep close tabs on firms that manufacture CD and DVD burner/players. Why? Because they may enter the software business as a means of differentiating increasingly commoditized hardware products.

Perhaps the most telling factor in this story of dynamic strategy in dynamic contexts is the sale of Roxio's software business to competitor Sonic Solutions in January 2004 and the subsequent renaming of the surviving online-music company to Napster. In May 2005, Yahoo! entered the online-music fray with a service priced at half that of Napster's—now that's a dynamic context! Today, Napster has adapted its distribution model to include a Napster Light, where you can download songs for 99 cents, and Napster To Go, which gives you unlimited downloads for $9.95 per month. Perhaps the greatest testimony to the competitiveness and dynamism of this market space is Napster's profitability: From the date of its spinoff from Adaptec through 2005, Napster has never shown a profit. ■

STRATEGY AND DYNAMIC CONTEXTS

In this chapter, we build on Chapter 5 by showing you how firms can develop resource-based competitive advantages in the face of dynamic competition. Although the notion of the industry life cycle you studied in Chapter 5 suggests that strategy should always be dynamic, because it must be externally oriented to be effective, the dynamic competition we refer to here requires dynamic strategies by virtue of the rapid and sometimes unpredictable changes taking place in the firm's external environment. For most industries, certain features of the industry are dynamic. In some industries, these features are central to success in the largest and most lucrative parts of the industry. As you can see from our opening vignette about the online-music business, dynamic strategies still require firms to make coherent tradeoffs between the economic logic of low cost and differentiation as the primary factors in any strategy for getting customers to buy their products. Dynamic competition, however, challenges a firm to improve its game continuously, and maybe even figure out how to rewrite the rules of competition.

This challenge is what differentiates the relatively stable context of strategy explored in Chapter 5—even for strategies that address one stage of the industry life cycle—from the *dynamic* context of strategy. Moreover, successful dynamic strategies increasingly require the nearly seamless integration of formulation and implementation and tend to reward an appetite for experimentation and risk taking. This is why, after understanding what constitutes a dynamic context, you will also learn how to use dynamic-strategy tools such as the value curve and real-options analysis.

We start by identifying the specific ways in which dynamic contexts can undermine competitive advantage. Then we'll discuss the development of strategies designed to address competitive interactions and two other primary drivers of dynamism we identified in Chapter 4: industry evolution and technological discontinuities (Chapter 8 is devoted to global strategy and, as such, addresses globalization, the other driver of change identified in Chapter 4). An important theme in this section is the effect of *change drivers*—the conditions that make contexts dynamic. Remember, however, that because change is often rapid rather than gradual, we must focus on strategy under conditions of *high-speed change*. Finally, we conclude by applying the five-elements of the strategy diamond to strategies in dynamic contexts. When you're finished with this chapter, you should be able to formulate a strategy for managing the dynamic context and prepare a plan for implementing it.

THE CHALLENGES TO SUSTAINABLE COMPETITIVE ADVANTAGE

It's important to understand why dynamic conditions can undermine competitive advantage, whether with blinding speed or over an extended period of time. Indeed, as we saw in the opening vignette, even though it may seem that an industry has changed overnight, many of the seeds of that apparently dramatic change may have been sown and nourished over a fairly long period. For instance, changes in consumer preferences and portable music technologies evolved over an extended period of time. In addition, change often results from a combination of drivers, several of which you learned about in earlier chapters and which are reviewed further in this chapter.

Recall from earlier chapters that competitive advantage is developed when a firm can create value in ways that rivals cannot. And the likelihood of developing a competitive advantage is facilitated by possessing resources and capabilities that fulfill the VRINE criteria. Firms with VRINE resources and capabilities are much more likely to be able to create strategic positions of low cost and differentiation than firms that lack such resources and capabilities. Challenges to sustained competitive advantage include anything that threatens VRINE resources and capabilities. Consequently, we need to examine the types of change that make valuable resources and capabilities lose their value; that make valuable and rare resources and capabilities become common; that make valuable and rare resources and capabilities easy to imitate or substitute; and that weaken a firm's ability to exploit resources and capabilities that satisfy the value, rarity, inimitability, and nonsubstitutability criteria of the VRINE model.

In addition, formulating strategies either to protect against threats from or to exploit the opportunities associated with dynamic environments generally encompass special cases of finding new ways to generate a low-cost or differentiation advantage. Because dynamic markets move at a much faster pace than stable markets, strategies for dealing with dynamic markets involve special attention to the *arenas* and *staging* elements of the strategy diamond.

The three dimensions that cause dynamic contexts that we focus on are *competitive interactions, industry evolution,* and *technological disruptions.* These categories are inter-related and are intended to help you think about the different facets of a changing competitive landscape. The relative speed of changes in these categories further complicates strategy in dynamic contexts.

Competitive Interaction

Competitive interactions are composed of two related factors: the interactions between incumbents and the interactions of new entrants and incumbents. The interactions caused by new entrants are a particular source of dynamism when they use a new business model—that is, a strategy that varies significantly from those used by incumbents.

Industry Evolution

Rivalry and the nature of competition, as we pointed out in Chapter 4, often change as a function of industry evolution—from differentiation to cost, or vice versa. Because a successful low-cost strategy requires different resources and capabilities than a differentiation strategy, a change in the basis of competitive advantage will cause advantage to shift over time from firms with the obsolete resources and capabilities to those favored by industry conditions.

Technological Change

Technological change may foster similar shifts, especially when change is discontinuous, so that it does not sustain existing leaders' advantage. Additionally, technological change is particularly risky when it primarily affects business *processes*. The Progressive Direct online-insurance market is an example of this. Progressive bypasses traditional and costly insurance agents and relies instead on direct sales through the Internet. In doing so, Progressive is able to offer some of the lowest-priced insurance products on the market. And to ensure that customers shop with Progressive first, the company provides quotes for competitors' policies, and will even sell them instead if a consumer prefers that. Progressive makes money both ways, through the sale of its own polices and through the commissions it receives from the sale of competitors' policies. Discontinuities that affect *product* technology often favor differentiation strategies. In the moderate to high-end segment of the photo industry, for instance, the current technological shift from chemical film to digital photography gives firms like Sony an opportunity to establish a competitive stronghold based on their electronic-miniaturization capabilities in an industry that it might never have entered prior to the digital age. Similarly, Apple's pricey iPod portable music device takes advantage of the technological shift reviewed in the opening vignette on Napster.

Speed of Change

Over and above any particular change driver, the speed of change is a critical factor in keeping up with the basis of competition in an industry. Speed tends to compound the effects of every

Product-technology changes make for a dynamic marketplace. New digital technology quickly adopted by Sony gave it an advantage over Kodak, which was slow to react.

change driver, whether industry evolution, technological discontinuities, or other causes. As the pace of change increases, so, too, must a firm's ability to react swiftly to (and even anticipate) changes in the basis of competitive advantage. In extreme cases, a firm needs the ability to *lead* industry change.[2] *Reacting to change* means detecting and responding quickly to unexpected customer demands, new government regulations, or competitor's actions. *Anticipating change* means foreseeing the appearance of global markets, the development of new market segments, and emergence of the complementary or conflicting technologies.

Familiarity with the scenario-planning tool that we introduced in Chapter 4 should give you some insight into the factors that are critical in the strategic ability to anticipate change. Change leaders are consistently able to develop new technologies, products, and markets; raise industry standards and customer expectations; and increase the pace and frequency of product cycles. Because of these stiff requirements, few firms are able to maintain sustained competitive advantage in dynamic markets.

BUSINESS STRATEGY AND COMPETITIVE INTERACTION

Major actions taken by one firm are typically noticed by rivals. In fact, because some actions generate strong *re*actions, wise strategists try not only to anticipate them but to formulate strategies that will result in an optimal outcome from the process of action and reaction. In this section, we'll review some basic principles of competitive interaction and its implications for strategy formulation.

Strategy and Strategic Positioning in the Face of Competition

How do these principles complement the principles of strategic decision making that we've already discussed in prior chapters? We know that managers can use tools such as the strategy diamond, the VRINE model, and industry-structure analysis to formulate a strategy and hammer out a strategic position. We know, too, that the firm's strategy and strategic position should be consistent with its strengths and its ability to seize opportunities presented by its

concept**link**

In Chapter 5, we emphasize that **strategic positioning** involves the ways in which a firm situates itself relative to its rivals, especially with regard to three factors of the *strategy-diamond model—arenas, differentiators,* and *economic logic.*

competitive environment. Finally, we know that strategic-positioning decisions are supported by a wealth of tactical decisions made to implement and reinforce the firm's strategy.

Now consider the possible effects of all this decision making in a context of interactive competition. Four underlying phases of competitive interaction are summarized in Exhibit 6.1. Let's say that a regional title-insurance company has developed a strategy designed to help it grow into a premier national company. That strategy will involve a sequence of activities: entry into adjacent regional markets, followed by increased focus on differentiators designed to build brand awareness, followed by more rapid expansion through acquisitions funded by an increasingly valuable stock price.[3] In its first phase, such an aggressive series of tactical moves may go unnoticed or ignored by competitors. Eventually, however, if customer reactions in phase 2 appear or are anticipated to be positive, then other firms will formulate responses to the first firm's competitive behavior, as shown in phase 3. In phase 4, competitors evaluate the results of their interactions, and the cycle may then recommence.

Competitive actions can generate a wide range of competitive responses.[4] *Competitive interaction theory* suggests that because competitive actions will generate reactions, a firm's managers should predict reactions to its actions and use that information to determine what would be the best course of action given competitors' likely reactions.[5] Competitive action can be initiated in phase 1 in essentially four ways: aggressiveness, complexity of the competitive-action repertoire, unpredictability, and tactics that delay the leaders' competitive reaction. The responses to those various actions have been shown to play out differently in terms of the competitive advantage of the challenger and the challenged.

With regard to competitive aggressiveness, strategy research has shown that a challenger can erode the leadership position of another firm by rapidly launching many assaults on the leader in a short period of time. Such interaction explains how Nike overtook Reebok's dominant sports-shoe position in the late 1980s and how, in 2005, SABMiller regained market-share-growth leadership from Anheuser Busch in the light beer segment. SABMiller did so through a combination of aggressive advertising that suggested that Anheuser Busch's beers lacked flavor and backed it up with consumer surveys saying that the SABMiller's beers had more and better taste.

Similarly, the more complexity and unpredictability inherent in these aggressive moves, the more likely the attacker will succeed in improving its market position. Complexity and unpredictability play to the attacker's advantage by confusing the industry leader and putting it on the defensive. As a result, the leader may also lose focus on the coherent execution of its strategy, as seen by the fragmentation of scarce resources to defending multiple competitive fronts. For example, Anheuser Busch was so thrown off by SABMiller's aggressive tactics that it responded by launching a new beer, Budweiser Select, and advertising it as a flavorful, high-quality beer. SABMiller turned around and pointed to the new product as further evidence that Anheuser Busch's products did not have taste.

Exhibit 6.1 Phases of Competitive Interaction

Source: Adapted from K. G. Smith, W. J. Ferrier, and C. M. Grimm, "King of the Hill: Dethroning the Industry Leader," Academy of Management Executive 15:2 (2001), 59–70.

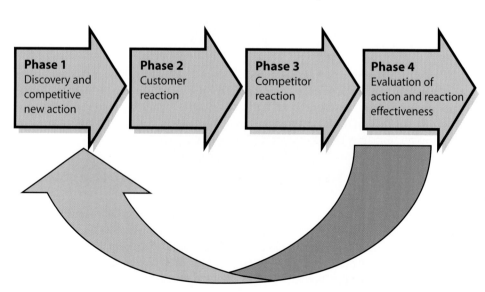

Phase 1 Discovery and competitive new action

Phase 2 Customer reaction

Phase 3 Competitor reaction

Phase 4 Evaluation of action and reaction effectiveness

Finally, to the extent that the challenger can engage in competitive moves that are difficult to respond to quickly or simply catch the leader unaware, the attacker can gain competitive market position. Strategy research has shown, for instance, that Nike's competitive success can be partially attributed to the fact that Nike initiated new competitive moves (e.g., promotions, new-product launches, endorsements) and responded to Reebok's actions much faster than Reebok responded to Nike's.[6] This same research has shown such tactics to hold true in industries ranging from telecommunications and personal computers to airlines and brewing.

When leading companies face new competitors who utilize new business models that are disruptive—strategies that are both different from and in conflict with those of incumbents—they face vexing dilemmas. Should they respond to these new entrants with disruptive strategies and, if so, how? These types of innovations essentially result in a possible change in the rules of competition within the industry. Such disruptions have several common characteristics. First, compared to incumbents, these firms typically emphasize different product attributes. Second, they generally start out as rather low-margin businesses. Third, they can grow into significant companies that take away market share. However, because of tradeoffs with value-chain activities that are essential to the incumbents, these new firms' business models cannot be imitated in short order by incumbents. Examples of these types of disruptive entrants are found in many industries, such as rental cars (Enterprise), retailing (Amazon.com), retail brokerage (E*Trade and Charles Schwab), steel (Nucor), and airlines (Southwest, JetBlue, and RyanAir). Devising appropriate strategies to deal with these types of competitive interactions is particularly difficult.

conceptlink

In Chapter 3, we define its **value chain** as a firm's collective capabilities, ranging from the conduct of simple tasks to the performance of complex processes, stressing that the ability to reconfigure value-chain activities in ways that are hard to duplicate can give a firm *tradeoff protection*.

Competitive Dynamics and the Positioning of Incumbents

Incumbents, such as Anheuser Busch, deserve special attention because they are increasingly viewed as Goliaths in the many David-and-Goliath competitive interactions unfolding around the world. In the mid-1990s, the front pages of the business press were littered with stories decrying the demise of the brick-and-mortar business and the rise of e-commerce and the dot-com. Inasmuch as most firms currently occupied real estate rather than cyberspace, the trend—or at least warnings about its repercussions—threatened most of them with extinction. Some, of course, did disappear, but most did not. As a matter of fact, the Internet phenomenon—and especially the breakneck speed with which it became a regular feature of the cultural landscape—underscored a number of strategies that incumbents can adopt to respond to rapid changes in the environment of an industry. As usual, the success of these strategies depends on a given firm's strengths and weaknesses. They are, however, particularly attractive to incumbent firms because they depend on—and can even reinforce—a firm's basic strengths. Each seeks a resource-based competitive advantage—that is, a position in which the exploitation of a resource makes that resource stronger and more resilient. Hopefully, the firm is organized per the VRINE framework to realize value from the stronger and more resilient resource.

Competitor-response strategies can be thought about in a number of different ways. Incumbent firms can respond to sources of industry dynamism through any of the following strategies: (1) containment, (2) neutralization, (3) shaping, (4) absorption, or (5) annulment. As shown in Exhibit 6.2, these responses typically vary in terms of the ease with which the external threat can be controlled and the corresponding level of action taken in response. We'll discuss and provide examples of each strategy in the following sections.

conceptlink

As we describe it in Chapter 3, the **VRINE model** holds that a firm with resources and capabilities that are valuable, rare, inimitable, non-substitutable, and exploitable will gain a competitive advantage.

Containment The containment strategy works well when the firm has identified the threat at an early stage. (You may detect facets of this strategy in the bundling or process-innovation strategies that we described in the context of industry evolution in Chapter 5.) Although firms sometimes select one of these strategies, they typically resort to a combination that aligns well with their particular resources and capabilities. American Airlines, for instance, can compete with Southwest not only by increasing the benefits of its frequent-flier program but by using its bargaining power to secure more exclusive airport gates (thus

Exhibit 6.2 The Spectrum of Competitive-Responses Strategies

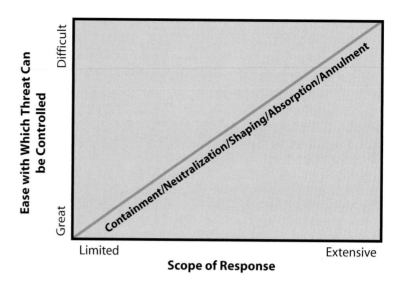

effectively raising Southwest's distribution costs at airports where it used to share gates with American).

Similarly, a large consumer-products company can release a copy-cat product that both leverages the new market created by a competitor and can be sold through its own existing channels. Consider, for example, the fact that retailers in industries from clothing to groceries typically charge *slotting fees*—fees that suppliers pay for access to retailers' shelf space. Because of this practice, any new product may bump an existing product from retail shelves, and if the one that gets bumped is a new entrant's only product, the containment strategy will have been highly effective.

Neutralization   If containment does not work, then leaders will try to neutralize the threat. Incumbents who pursue a neutralization strategy aggressively often succeed in short-circuiting the moves of innovators or new entrants even *before* they make them—or at least in forcing them to seek out the incumbent as a partner or acquirer. Microsoft, for example, is so aggressive at adding free software features to its popular Windows platform that new software firms routinely include partnership with Microsoft as part of their entry strategies.

A more common neutralization tactic, however, is the threat or use of legal action. (Because such action is often taken in concert with partners, we'll revisit it as an aspect of cooperative strategy in Chapter 8.) Recall from our opening case that one reason for Napster's initial downfall was legal action taken by the recording industry. In fact, the Recording Industry Association of America (RIAA) launched such a fierce legal attack on Napster that it forced even smaller Napster-like firms to stay out of the fray.[7] The German media giant Bertelsmann AG later acquired the Napster name when it realized that the Internet upstart was trying to engage in a legitimate music-sharing business. (When Bertelsmann couldn't turn a profit in the music-sharing business, Roxio was later able to acquire Napster and its assets for only $5 million.) Meanwhile, the RIAA also attempted to neutralize the Napster model by setting up an industrywide sharing standard, but this initiative collapsed when the major record labels squabbled about intellectual property rights, technology, and pricing.

Shaping   Sometimes, of course, it's simply not possible to contain or neutralize the growth of a new product, often due to antitrust laws. Moreover, in some cases, the new product may be attractive to the incumbent even if the incumbent can't gain full control of it. Today, for example, a state of peaceful coexistence prevails between the American Medical Association (AMA) and chiropractic medicine. For decades, however, the AMA had characterized chiropractors as quacks. Eventually, the AMA used regulators and educators as part of a strategy to *shape* the evolution of chiropractic practice until chiropractics transformed itself into a complement to conventional healthcare, as defined by the AMA.

Large firms can also use funding to pursue shaping strategies. Intel, for example, maintains its Intel Capital unit as one of the world's largest corporate venture programs for investing in the technology segment. The concept is fairly simple: Each investment is aimed at helping businesses that, if successful, will need Intel products to grow. In many ways, then, Intel is not only creating future markets for its own products but discouraging demand for competing products and technology and co-opting potential future competitors at the same time.

Absorption The purpose of this strategy is to minimize the risks entailed by being either a first mover or an imitator. Sometimes, the approach is direct: The incumbent identifies and acquires the new entrant or establishes an alliance. In the late 1980s, for instance, Microsoft identified money-management software as a potentially attractive, high-growth market. It therefore entered into an agreement to acquire Intuit, the market leader, which offers such products as Quicken, QuickBooks, and TurboTax. Unfortunately, antitrust action forced Microsoft to abandon the purchase, and it resorted to a containment strategy—namely, by developing its own product, Microsoft Money (although Intuit's Quicken still has an 80-percent market share). If it's difficult to acquire the new entrant, the incumbent may also try to leverage a buyout by taking control over industry suppliers or distribution channels.

Annulment Incumbents can annul the threat of new entrants by improving their own products. In many ways, for example, Kodak has so successfully improved the quality of film-based prints that they're superior to many digital-based alternatives. The annulment strategy, however, is less about quashing the competition than about making it irrelevant. Indeed, to excel at an annulment strategy a firm must often assume the role of first mover—a position that entails considerable risk. Kodak forestalled the advance of digital photography, but Kodak executives knew that in order to stay in the photo business, the company eventually had to shift to digital.[8] For this reason, firms usually resort to annulment only when the competition is otherwise unstoppable.

IBM provides another excellent example of a firm that annulled a competitive threat by sidestepping it.[9] In the early 1990s, IBM was faced with a flagging core business in PCs and minicomputers. Its first strategic shift catapulted IBM into second place behind Microsoft as a PC- and networking-software powerhouse. Its next move entrenched the company in the IT and Internet consulting markets, where it emerged as the largest firm among such competitors as Accenture. Next, IBM took on such companies as EDS to become the market leader in outsourcing IT and service solutions. Throughout this transition process, IBM leveraged its resources, capabilities, and dynamic capabilities in services and software. In many ways, IBM, though ostensibly on the defensive, was also wielding the tools of offensive strategy, effectively combining improvisation and experimentation with deft staging and pacing. As a result of this complex strategy, IBM not only emerged as a leader in information technology but, at the same time, avoided the commoditization pressures that affected PC firms such as HP-Compaq. Most recently, it has completely exited its core PC manufacturing business by spinning off this part of its operations to China-based Lenovo.

The Pitfalls of the Retaliatory Mindset

A word of warning about the five strategies covered in this section—and a good reason why you need to pay close attention to the sections that follow. Although they are certainly viable strategies for dynamic markets, many of the strategies are nonetheless purely defensive. If you rely on them exclusively, you'll soon stumble over an important pitfall of purely defensive strategizing: *Any firm that invests in resources and capabilities that support retaliation to the exclusion of innovation and change may only be prolonging its inevitable demise.*

Here's a good example. Ralston Purina was long considered one of the most efficient and competitively aggressive pet-food companies in the world. Every time a competitor made a move or a new entrant set foot in the market, Ralston responded with a twofold defensive strategy: undermining prices in the competitor's stronghold markets while simultaneously attacking its weaker markets. Although its defensive posture secured Ralston's market leadership for over 20 years, it also ensured that the company lagged behind the

For more than 20 years, Ralston Purina fiercely—and successfully—defended its position as top dog in the pet-food industry. Unfortunately, the company put so much energy into its defensive strategy that it had little left for innovation. Ralston sold out to Nestlé in 2003.

industry in terms of innovation. In 2003, Ralston sold out to Nestlé, whose constant attention to innovative products had positioned it to take over Ralston's slot as industry leader.

First Movers, Second Movers, and Fast Followers

Before further analyzing particular strategies, we must first understand the idea of *first-mover* and *second-mover firms*. Although the first- versus second-mover categories are related to the principles of competitive interaction that we discussed in Chapter 5, in this chapter, we focus on the relative magnitude of the firm's actions. Specifically, here we are talking about the introduction of a new product or service that defines or redefines a new market segment, whereas in Chapter 5, competitive interaction involved actions taken within a preexisting market segment. In particular, we need to know how each approach to technological discontinuities depends on a firm's resources and capabilities. The principle of dynamic strategies holds that firms consider their relative strengths when they determine whether to lead or to respond to change.

first mover Firm choosing to initiate a strategic action, whether the introduction of a new product or service or the development of a new process

second mover (often *fast follower*) Second significant company to move into a market, quickly following the first mover

First movers are firms that choose to initiate a strategic action. This action may be the introduction of a new product or service or the development of a new process that improves quality, lowers price, or both. Consequently, you may see firms pursuing either differentiation or low-cost strategies here. **Second movers** are simply firms that aren't first movers, but their actions are important nonetheless.[10] A second mover, for instance, may simply imitate a first mover—that is, those aspects of its new product, service, or strategy that meet its needs—or it may introduce its own innovation.[11]

takeoff period Period during which a new product generates rapid growth and huge sales increases

First-Mover Strategy and the Industry Life Cycle Being a second mover doesn't necessarily mean that a firm is a *late* mover; in fact, many effective second movers can legitimately be characterized as *fast followers*—even if the elapsed time between first and second moves is several years. Why isn't the lag necessarily detrimental? For one, new products don't always catch on right away. They may eventually generate rapid growth and huge sales increases, but this period—widely known as the **takeoff period**—starts, *on average*, at some point within six years of the new-product introduction.[12] Although the industry life cycle suggests that the drivers of industry demand evolve over time, it doesn't predict how *quickly* they'll evolve. Indeed, it may take some new products a decade or more to reach the growth stage, and only then will they attract competitors.

By the same token, of course, *habitually* late movers will eventually fall by the wayside. Typically, survivors are either first movers or relatively fast followers. Late movers usually survive only if they're protected by government regulation, monopolistic or oligopolistic industry positions, or extensive cash reserves. Increasingly, however, competitive advantage results from the ability to manage change and harness the resources and capabilities consistent with first- or second-mover strategies.

The Pros and Cons of First-Mover Positioning   Intuitively, we tend to think of first movers as having a distinct advantage: After all, many races are won by the first contestant out of the starting blocks. The history of the Internet offers a wealth of first-mover success stories. The market dominance of Amazon.com, for instance, reflects a first-mover advantage—namely, the firm's ability to charge higher prices for books. According to a recent study, a 1-percent price increase reduced Amazon.com sales by 0.5 percent; at BarnesandNoble.com, however, the same price hike cut sales by a relatively whopping 4 percent.[13]

However, if you take a close look at Exhibit 6.3, you'll see that first-movers don't always attain dominant positions. For instance, you are probably familiar with the Microsoft XBox, the Palm Pilot PDA, and the Boeing 747, but did you know that the first electronic games, PDA, and commercial jets were released by Atari, Apple (the Newton in 1993), and deHaviland, respectively? In some cases, a first-mover strategy can even be a liability, and in many others, the first mover isn't necessarily in a position to exploit the advantages of being first.

A first-mover advantage is valuable only under certain conditions:

- A firm achieves an absolute cost advantage in terms of scale or scope.
- A firm's image and reputation advantages are hard to imitate at a later date.
- First-time customers are locked into a firm's products or services because of preferences or design characteristics.
- The scale of a firm's first move makes imitation unlikely.[14]

First movers also bear significant risks, including the costs not only of designing, producing, and distributing new products, but of educating customers about them. Let's say, for example, that you're a midsized consumer-products company with a promising new product. When you stop to consider the immense power wielded by a certain member of your distribution channel—say, Wal-Mart—you'll recall how dependent you are on one giant retailer to help you attract a market large enough to make your product profitable. Meanwhile, certain second movers (say, Unilever or Procter & Gamble) may take the time to evaluate your new product and decide to compete with it only when it's developed some traction in the market (at some point during the takeoff period). Sometimes, a patient (and sufficiently powerful) second mover simply acquires the first mover; sometimes, a second mover introduces a similar product, perhaps of higher quality or with added features.

In short, first-mover advantages diminish—and fast-follower advantages increase—under a variety of conditions, including the following:

- Rapid technological advances enable a second mover to leapfrog a first mover's new product or service.
- The first mover's product or service strikes a positive chord but is flawed.
- The first mover lacks a key complement, such as channel access, that a fast follower possesses.
- The first mover's costs outweigh the benefits of its first-mover position. (Fast followers, for example, can often enter markets more cheaply because they don't face the initial costs incurred by the first mover.)

First Movers and Industry Complements   An additional framework for assessing whether a firm should pursue a first-mover or fast-follower strategy incorporates the factor of *industry complements* (see Chapter 4). Exhibit 6.4, for example, provides a framework that explains why a number of notable first movers fared poorly despite apparently advantageous positions one would expect them to extract by virtue of being a first mover. What's the moral of the lessons collected in Exhibit 6.4? Basically, they remind us that any firm contemplating a first-mover strategy should consider the inimitability of its new product, the switching costs holding together current customer relationships, and the

concept link

We define **complementors** in Chapter 4 as players who provide complementary rather than competing products, but we also emphasize a broader definition of *complementor* as any factor (such as an efficient distribution channel) that makes it more attractive for a firm to participate in an industry or segment. Here, the definition expands to include any asset that makes it more feasible to exploit an innovation or other opportunity.

Exhibit 6.3   A Gallery of First Movers and Fast Followers

Product	Pioneer(s)	Imitators/Fast Followers	Comments
Automated teller machines (ATMs)	DeLaRue (1967) Docutel (1969)	Diebold (1971) IBM (1973) NCR (1974)	The first movers were small entrepreneurial upstarts that faced two types of competitors: (1) larger firms with experience selling to banks and (2) the computer giants. The first movers did not survive.
Ballpoint pens	Reynolds (1945) Eversharp (1946)	Parker (1954) Bic (1960)	The pioneers disappeared when the fad first ended in the late 1940s. Parker entered 8 years later. Bic entered last and sold pens as cheap disposables.
Commercial jets	deHaviland (1952)	Boeing (1958) Douglas (1958)	The pioneer rushed to market with a jet that crashed frequently. Boeing and Douglas (later known as McDonnel-Douglas) followed with safer, larger, and more powerful jets unsullied by tragic crashes.
Credit cards	Diners Club (1950)	Visa/Mastercard (1966) American Express (1968)	The first mover was undercapitalized in a business in which money is the key resource. American Express entered last with funds and name recognition from its traveler's check business.
Diet soda	Kirsch's No-Cal (1952) Royal Crown's Diet Rite Cola (1962)	Pepsi's Patio Cola (1963) Coke's Tab (1964) Diet Pepsi (1964) Diet Coke (1982)	The first mover could not match the distribution advantages of Coke and Pepsi. Nor did it have the money or marketing expertise needed for massive promotional campaigns.
Light beer	Rheingold's & Gablinger's (1968) Meister Brau Lite (1967)	Miller Lite (1975) Natural Light (1977) Coors Light (1978) Bud Light (1982)	The first movers entered 9 years before Miller and 16 years before Budweiser, but financial problems drove both out of business. Marketing and distribution determined the outcome. Costly legal battles, again requiring access to capital, were commonplace.
PC operating systems	CP/M (1974)	Microsoft DOS (1981) Microsoft Windows (1985)	The first mover set the early industry standard but did not upgrade for the IBM PC. Microsoft bought an imitative upgrade and became the new standard. Windows entered later and borrowed heavily from predecessors (and competitor Apple), then emerged as the leading interface.
Video games	Magnavox's Odyssey (1972) Atari's Pong (1972)	Nintendo (1985) Sega (1989) Microsoft (1998)	The market went from boom to bust to boom. The bust occurred when home computers seemed likely to make video games obsolete. Kids lost interest when games lacked challenge. Price competition ruled. Nintendo rekindled interest with better games and restored market order with managed competition. Microsoft entered with its Xbox when perceived gaming to be a possible component of its wired world.

Source: Adapted from S. Schnaars, Managing Imitation Strategies *(New York Free Press, 1994), 37–43.*

strength of its complementary assets.[15] It should, for example, consider its distribution channels as important complementary assets. Industry key success factors are also complementary assets, as is access to capital.

Let's say, for instance, that a firm makes a critical breakthrough in cancer therapy. Before putting any product on the market, it will need to conduct a decade's worth of animal and clinical trials, and if it doesn't have hundreds of millions of dollars in the bank, it won't be able to pay for such extensive preliminary testing. New PC-software applications often depend on Microsoft because its operating system and bundled software constitute a whole set of complements—a product, a channel, and a potential competitor. As you can see from the illustrations in Exhibit 6.3, in the context of the framework summarized in Exhibit 6.4, first-movers

Status of Complementary Assets

	Freely available or unimportant	Tightly held and important
Weak protection from imitation	It is difficult for anyone to make money: Industry incumbents may simply give new product or service away as part of its larger bundle of offerings	Value-creation opportunities favor the holder of complementary assets, who will probably pursue a fast-follower strategy
Strong protection from imitation	First mover can do well depending on the execution of its strategy	Value will go either to first mover or to party with the most bargaining power

Bases of First Mover Advantages

Exhibit 6.4 Evaluating a Firm's First-Mover Dependencies on Industry Complements

tend to succeed if their initial advantages are unique and defensible *and* if they're in a position to exploit the complementary assets needed to bring a new product to market.

STRATEGIES FOR MANAGING INDUSTRY EVOLUTION

Underlying competitive interaction, changes in rivalry, and first- versus second-mover strategies cause fundamental changes in an industry. Here we discuss strategies for industry evolution, followed by strategies for technological change. Because all industries evolve and mature, a firm's strategy must always anticipate the repercussions of change. As we saw in Chapter 5, for example, strategies may differ from one stage of the industry life cycle to another. The strategic management of industry evolution involves not only dealing with the industry life cycle but also strategies for changing arenas and strategies for responding to changes in a firm's environment. We saw in Chapter 4, for instance, that scenario planning can reveal the "trigger points" at which an industry is likely to undergo dramatic change. Moreover, a thorough understanding of industry evolution and its implications for strategy will help you better understand the three characteristics of the dynamic context that we introduced in the previous section—technological discontinuities, and speed of change. As noted in Chapter 4, globalization is a further complicating factor. Each of these facets also characterizes the larger evolutionary framework of an industry. One particular challenge associated with industry evolution that goes beyond the industry life cycle challenges outlined in Chapter 5 is the pressures of commoditization.

The Pressures of Commoditization

Managers must consider the pressure for change exerted by *commoditization*, which we defined in Chapter 4 as the process by which industrywide sales come to depend less on unique product features and more on price. As industry products become perceived as undifferentiated, the ability of firms to generate premium pricing diminishes. Consequently, differentiation strategies are vulnerable to the pressures of commoditization.

Research suggests that firms can choose from among four alternatives to deal with the pressures of commoditization.[16] The manager, however, must make difficult choices in

conceptlink

In introducing the industry life cycle in Chapter 4, we emphasize the *evolution* of the industries in which companies compete. In Chapter 5, we explain the different evolutionary conditions of the **industry life cycle**—*embryonic, growth, maturity, decline*—that influence the dynamics of strategic opportunities and threats.

conceptlink

In Chapter 4, we explain that *scenario planning* is designed to provide an overview of specific trends and uncertainties and to outline a range of plausible strategic outcomes as an industry evolves over time.

conceptlink

In Chapter 4, we explain that **commoditization** is a common trend in the evolution of an **industry life cycle**.

terms of timing—for instance, if the firm changes its strategy too soon, it risks losing extra profits, but if it moves too late, it may never be able to regain the market lost to newcomers or incumbents who moved sooner. As you will see, two of these tactics anticipate commoditization, whereas the other two are typically more useful once it's clear that commoditization has set in. All four tactics have clear implications for four of the five elements in the strategy diamond—namely, arenas, differentiators, pacing, and economic logic.

Anticipating Commoditization   Firms can take one of two approaches to deal with commoditization before it sets in. The first approach is a special case of differentiation. It is designed to protect an incumbent's ability to charge premium prices. The second approach is designed to reinforce a low-cost position. These two approaches are outlined in the following sections.

Value-in-Use Approach   The first approach is a value-added, or "bundling," approach by which the firm increases service benefits while simultaneously either raising or holding prices. The value-in-use approach is a special case of differentiation. Note that if the increase in service, as a value-added feature, isn't valuable to customers, it simply raises the firm's cost base in the face of declining prices. Timken, a century-old bearing maker headquartered in North Carolina, provides a stellar example of this approach. Timken has actually increased profits on machined parts that most people would view as commodities because they're also available from numerous foreign competitors. Many of these competitors, however, market only a few simple products on the basis of price. In contrast, Timken bundles commodity-like roller bearings with additional key components in order to provide customers with products that exactly match their needs.[17]

Here's another example. Badger Meter Inc., a maker of water-flow meters, faced a flood of foreign competition and heavy domestic price competition in 2004. But instead of cutting prices in order to accommodate the global market, Badger chose to increase product quality, bundling the meters with state-of-the-art electronic radio-meter-reading technologies and targeting only markets willing to pay more for the significantly lower cost-of-use provided by bundled products.[18]

This strategy requires heavy investment in R&D—namely, the know-how necessary for combining parts that must otherwise be assembled by buyers. Critical to this innovative value proposition is a basic understanding of customers' product-acquisition, possession, and usage costs. It's an approach that firms such as Timken and GE use to pass on higher quality, improved reliability, and lower costs to customers.

Process-Innovation Approach   The second approach to anticipating commoditization is *process innovation*. With this approach, the firm tries to lower its cost position so that it can further cut prices. These lower costs are generally found in process innovation, which enables the firm to reduce its own operating and service costs. One way firms do this is by eliminating services that others provide and finding alternative ways to substitute for those services.

Dell is perhaps the best example of a firm that uses this strategy. From the very start, Dell was able to offer the lowest-priced computers by buying and quickly assembling components for direct sale to knowledgeable customers. Dell carries little parts inventory and avoids obsolescent inventory by bypassing traditional distribution channels. It also has few returns because customers have designed their own end products. Perhaps more important, in pursuing this strategy, Dell also developed proprietary direct-sales processes that are now benchmarked by firms in industries ranging from automobiles to airline tickets.

Responding to Commoditization   More often than not, firms find themselves in the position of having to respond to pricing and other competitive pressures instead of driving them.

Market Focus   One approach to this situation is so-called *market focus*. This is a special case of a *focused-differentiation strategy*, which we described in Chapter 5. In this case, however, the firm transitions from serving a broad market to focusing on a selected subset of

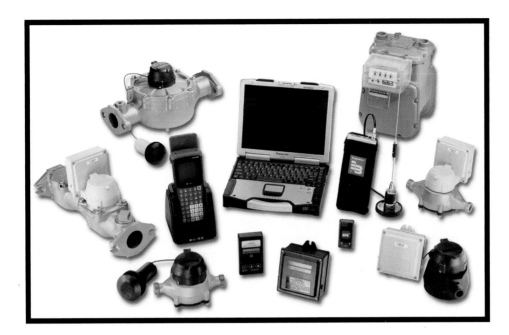

Badger Meter, Inc., a Milwaukee-based, water-meter manufacturer, faced a torrent of low-priced competitors in 2004. Instead of cutting its prices, Badger lowered the floodgates by successfully bundling its meters with state-of-the-art meter-reading products.

the market. It requires that the firm narrow, or focus, its customer base. It typically entails all of the following tactics:

■ Maintaining or increasing service level (as in value-added strategy)
■ Initially reducing the number of customers served
■ Increasing prices (or at least avoiding further reductions)

Because this strategy usually emphasizes profits over sales growth, it generally results in a drop in market share. What is the value proposition? It permits the firm to target a small segment of the overall market that's willing to pay more for increased service. As with value-adding or bundling, however, the increased service must deliver value to the customer in the form of greater revenues (i.e., helping the customer sell more) or lower costs (i.e., lowering the total cost of use or ownership).

Although market-focus tactics work for firms in a variety of industries and situations, variations are most often pursued by companies that are in financial distress or in the process of restructuring. Thus, when retail chains Kmart and KB Toys laid out restructuring plans, they started by reducing the number of customers they served; in other words, they closed less-profitable stores. The message in both instances was the same: Given the firm's geographic location and customer relationships, some market segments or customer groupings were more attractive than were others.

Service Innovation *Service innovation* is a tactic for achieving a cost advantage. It is especially challenging because it requires a firm to seek price competitiveness by eliminating services that were once bundled with its product. An intermediate move is often seen in commercial banking: The bank seeks to be price competitive in core products, such as bank loans, while tacking on fees for services that were once bundled with loans because they could be subsidized by higher interest rates and cash on hand. In other industries facing commoditization pressures, companies resort to similar incremental changes. Airlines, for example, may charge for food and extra baggage, hotels for cable TV and computer hookups. In an extreme case, a firm might remake itself from a high-price, high-service competitor into a low-cost, no-frills competitor. The fact that this strategy is rarely successful indicates how risky it is.

At the same time, however, we saw in Chapter 5 that it's quite difficult for a firm to be effective in multiple segments whose competitive requirements are diametrically opposed. Very rarely does a firm compete successfully in one segment as a focused differentiator and in another as a focused low-cost player. Strategies are most effective when firms leverage *unique, firm-specific resources and capabilities.* That's why the best response to industry commoditization is usually one of the following:

- Improve services and raise prices to serve a more narrowly defined market.
- Serve a larger market but lower costs and prices through process improvements.

Trying to do both doesn't generally work because it carries penalties similar to the stuck-in-the-middle situation described in Chapter 5.

STRATEGIES FOR TECHNOLOGICAL CHANGES

Chapter 4 introduced you to the concept of *technological disruptions*, which can cause leading firms to fall by the wayside. A stylized version of how this process unfolds is depicted in Exhibit 6.5. The exhibit illustrates a truncated industry life cycle—sometimes called a double-S curve due to its interlocking industry life cycles. Industries do not have to fall into decline. Decline is often forestalled by the introduction of a new technology that propels the industry into another growth phase. A *technological discontinuity* is an innovation that dramatically advances an industry's price-versus-performance frontier; it generally triggers a period of ferment that is closed by the emergence of a dominant design. A period of incremental technical change then follows, which is, in turn, broken by the next technological discontinuity.[19] What is most striking about the diagram, however, is that different firms often operate on different curves. This means that a firm that excelled in the bottom left-hand curve of Exhibit 6.5 may be displaced by a new entrant that introduces the new curve in the upper right-hand corner of the diagram.

Keep in mind that *technology* is a very broad term. We tend to think of technology rather myopically, focusing only on pure technological innovations. However, the types of disruptions illustrated in Exhibit 6.5 may also be *process innovations* (such as Charles Schwab's migration to online trading), *application innovations* (such as GM's integration of Global Positioning Systems into vehicles through the OnStar system), and *business model innovations* (such as Amazon.com's move from online bookselling to becoming a logistics provider for countless retailers).[20]

If the new technology is introduced by an incumbent firm, it stands a good chance to continue its dominance. For instance, in the aircraft-manufacture business Boeing has long been an innovator in the development of new airframes and has persisted as a leading firm, though

concept link

In Chapter 4, we identify *technological discontinuities* as one of the key drivers of change in a firm's external context; we also observe that, as technologies which typically destroy incumbent technologies, **disruptive technologies** are usually introduced by new firms and should be distinguished from competency-sustaining technologies, which are often introduced by incumbents.

Exhibit 6.5 The Effect of Technological Disruption

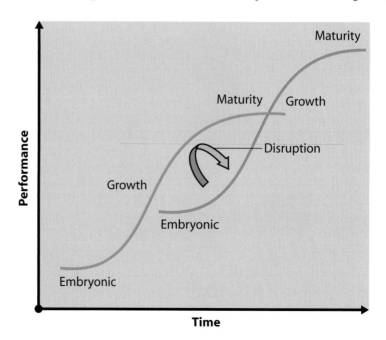

the technology of the most efficient design has changed numerous times. Some discontinuous technologies are introduced by new entrants, and because they change the face of the business landscape by altering who the leaders are, they are often referred to as *disruptive technologies*. When the new technology is developed by new entrants, incumbent firms face the very real possibility that they will be marginalized or eliminated. For instance, every leading firm in the minicomputer business was wiped out by firms that innovated and marketed the PC.

What can firms do to avoid or withstand a technological discontinuity? Research suggests that to withstand such technological changes, firms must either proactively create new opportunities for themselves or react defensively in ways to counteract the powerful forces of change. We reviewed these defensive strategies in the prior section. Here we review a few ways in which incumbents have been successful by creating new opportunities in response to dynamic markets or in anticipation of a changing market.

Creating New Markets

A strategy for dealing with and sometimes anticipating industry evolution or creating the technological discontinuities described in Exhibit 6.5 involves the creation of a new market segment. In this section, we will review the basic dimensions of new-market creation: high-end and low-end disruptions.

The Dimensions of New-Market Creation
Most companies have no trouble focusing on their existing rivals and actively trying to match or beat what their rivals have to offer customers. However, as a result of this focus on rivals' behaviors, strategies often converge. This convergence grows stronger the more conventional wisdom exists in the industry about how to compete. This type of convergence is often associated with incremental innovation. It will rarely result in breakthroughs that create new markets.

Creating new-market space, essentially the creation of a new value curve, requires a different approach and a different way of thinking about innovation. Instead of looking for the next incremental improvement, new markets are often created when managers create innovations that build on the best of the existing industry, import ideas from other industries, and eliminate some features that industry incumbents take for granted but which are not critical to key customers. This style of new-market creation has been shown to work in both faced-paced industries and those that are seemingly stagnant—both conditions that are ripe for significant changes. Faced-paced industries are dynamic by definition. Stagnant industries are often ripe for change—through new technologies that will send the industry on a new growth trajectory or through shakeout, which is a dynamic process but usually in a very negative sense for many incumbents.

The key to discovering a new-market space lies in asking four basic questions. These questions are illustrated in the Four Actions Framework shown in Exhibit 6.6. By answering these questions, you will be able to define a new value curve for an industry or at least, a segment of an industry. First, what product or service attributes that rivals take for granted should be *reduced* well below the industry standard? Second, what factors should be *eliminated* that the industry has taken for granted? Third, what product or service attributes should be *raised* well above the industry standard? And fourth, are there any factors that the industry has never offered that should be *created*? By finding answers to these questions, managers could modify a firm's strategy either so that its products are further differentiated from competitors', so that its cost structure is driven significantly below that of competitors or, conceivably, both. In addition, by following this path, firms often generate net new customers; they grow the business by means other than stealing customers from competitors.

As a result of using the value-curve tool, firms can develop strategies that challenge and change the rules of competition. Research suggests that new value curves tend to fall into one of three categories: high-end disruptions, low-end disruptions, or hybrid.

High-End Disruption
A new-market disruption which significantly changes the industry value curve by disrupting the expectations of customers by vastly improving product performance is referred to as **high-end disruption**. High-end disruption often results in huge new markets in which new players unseat the largest incumbents. Incumbents can also use

high-end disruption Strategy that may result in huge new markets in which new players redefine industry rules to unseat the largest incumbents

Exhibit 6.6 The Four-Actions Framework: The Key to the Value Curve

Source: Adapted from W. C. Kim and R. Mauborgne, "Blue Ocean Strategy," California Management Review 47:3 (2005), 105–121.

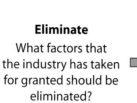

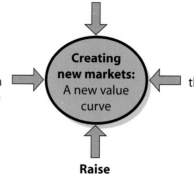

The key to discovering a new value curve lies in answering four basic questions.

Reduce
What factors should be reduced *well below* the industry standard?

Eliminate
What factors that the industry has taken for granted should be eliminated?

Creating new markets:
A new value curve

Create/Add
What factors that the industry has never offered should be created or added?

Raise
What factors should be raised *well above* the industry standard?

new-market disruption strategies. To do so, they need to shift competitive focus from head-to-head competition to the task of redefining the business model for at least a part of the existing market. A new-market-creation strategy, for example, may enable a firm to avoid the pitfalls of commoditization and evolution, but pursuing it doesn't necessarily mean that the same firm will become or even intends to become the industry leader. Cirque du Soleil significantly disrupted the circus industry by incorporating many features more common in Broadway theater than in traditional circuses, generating significant new growth and higher profits than any other traditional circus.

Low-End Disruption   Recall the concept of *disruptive technologies*. Some disruptive technologies appear at the low end of industry offerings and are referred to as **low-end disruptions**. Incumbents tend to ignore such new entrants because they target the incumbents' least valuable customers. These low-end disruptions rarely offer features that satisfy the best customers in the industry. However, these low-end entrants often use such footholds as platforms to migrate into the more attractive space once their products or services improve. Indeed, by the time they do improve, these low-end disruptions often satisfy the needs of the center of the market better than incumbents' products do because incumbents have been busily making incremental improvements to satisfy their best clients' demands even while these improvements cause the firms to outshoot the needs of the center of the market. Southwest Airlines has been a very successful low-end disrupter, satisfying only the most basic travel needs and eliminating many services that had been taken for granted by established airlines.

Hybrid Disruption Strategies   As you might expect, most newcomers adopt some combination of new-market and low-end disruption strategies. Today, it may look as if it Amazon.com has pursued a single-minded low-end disruption strategy, but along the way, it also has created some new markets, mainly by bringing more buyers into the market for books. Many Amazon customers buy in the quantities they do because of the information that the Amazon site makes available. The strategies of such companies as JetBlue, Charles Schwab, and the University of Phoenix are also hybrids of new-market and low-cost disruption strategies.[21] JetBlue's focused low-cost strategy, for instance, has been able to achieve the lowest-cost position in the industry by eliminating many services (a business model it borrowed from Southwest) but also adding services which increased customer loyalty. In addition, they targeted overpriced but underserved markets, thereby stimulating net new demand—both taking a portion of the existing market and creating a new market by attracting consumers who couldn't ordinarily afford air travel. Schwab pioneered discount brokerage as a new market but has since enticed legions of clients from full-service

low-end disruption Strategy that appears at the low end of industry offerings, targeting the least desirable of incumbents' customers

brokers such as Merrill-Lynch. The University of Phoenix is taking a strategic path much like the one blazed by Schwab.

The Value Curve

Now that we have described how firms create new-market space by being high-end, low-end, or hybrid disruptors, we'll describe the **value curve**, a convenient tool to help managers visualize how new disruptions might be targeted. The box entitled "How Would *You* Do That? 6.1" illustrates the application of this tool to the wine industry using [yellow tail]®.[22] The tool's purpose is to visually plot how major groups of firms are competing. This tends to reveal the underlying assumptions firms are making about the market and customers. The first step is to determine the existing key success factors as perceived by incumbents. List these factors along the horizontal axis. The vertical axis is used to rate the level of delivery of the major groups of firms. For instance, if room comfort were one of the key success factors that you had identified when evaluating the hotel industry, then you would rate establishments like Hyatt and Marriott much higher than hotels like Motel 6 and Best Western. The scale you use is not as important as the judgment you use in segregating different levels of products and services along the key success factors. Generally, you can plot firms by the central tendency of the major strategic groups, rather than each firm individually.

As you will recall from the earlier definition of strategic groups in Chapter 4, a strategic group is a cluster of firms that pursue similar strategies within an industry. For instance, even without plotting them you would assume that most of the major airlines would have very similar value curves and, therefore, constitute one strategic group. Plotting Southwest Airlines, as well as Southwest's imitators, such as JetBlue, or Ryanair in Europe, would probably reveal a strikingly different value curve. The next step is to plot the performance of each group on the key success factors identified. For each strategic group, you then draw the line that connects the points plotted on the graph—this is that group's value curve. It visually represents how those firms present their products to customers along key buying criteria. It conceptually represents the underlying logic incumbents use in positioning their products. Being able to visualize how competitors perform along these differentiators helps reveal the assumptions being made by the industry. It also helps you to determine which assumptions might be tested. Along these dimensions, question whether some levels of delivery on the key success factors can be reduced or eliminated; likewise, question whether some can be increased or whether new points of differentiation can be added.

A Shift in the Focus of Strategic Thinking Shifting focus from conventional head-to-head rivalry to creating new market space requires a different strategic mind-set. Some of the fundamental differences in assumptions between viewing strategy as head-to-head competition and thinking instead about creating new markets are summarized in Exhibit 6.8 on page 172. Whereas the traditional view emphasizes actions and capabilities that are determined by competitors' moves, new-market creation emphasizes *actions and capabilities that eclipse the competition rather than meet it head on.* [yellow tail], this company discussed in the box entitled "How Would *You* Do That? 6.1," provides a nice example of such a strategy in dynamic contexts.

STRATEGIES FOR TURBULENT AND HYPERCOMPETITIVE MARKETS

You may already be wondering if anything could further complicate the job of drawing up a strategy that must deal—sequentially or simultaneously—with such factors as the industry life cycle and discontinuities. There is the dimension of *time*. Imagine, for example, that one or more of the change drivers that you have to deal with is moving extremely fast—so fast that you find yourself describing market conditions as turbulent or hypercompetitive. Such markets do exist: They're characterized by frequent, often bold, and typically dynamic moves on the part of

value curve A graphical depiction of how a firm and major groups of its competitors are competing across its industry's factors of completion

concept link

In Chapter 4, we define **key success factors (KSFs)** as key assets or requisite skills that every firm must possess in order to be a viable competitor. We also explain how to "map" *strategic groups.*

[yellow tail]® Creates a New Value Curve in the Wine Industry

Let's uncork an example of the value curve in action. With over $20 billion in annual revenues, the U.S. market is the largest contiguous wine market in the world. As a result, [yellow tail] eyed the U.S. wine market with great anticipation. However, the market is intensely competitive, and California wines command two-thirds of all U.S. wine sales. This intense competition is further fueled by the fact that wines are produced and imported from almost every continent on the planet, and new entrants increasingly sell their wines at very low prices.

The threat of new entrants to the wine industry is very high; suppliers (wine-grape growers) are powerful; wineries are concentrated (C8 is 75 percent); sales channels are powerful because of consolidation; consumers are powerful because of the breadth of choices; and substitutes (any beverage) are many. Moreover, complements, such as the *Wine Spectator* and wine experts such as Robert Parker, are also powerful, because they rank wines based on taste and price, potentially swaying channel and consumer purchases. These factors suggest that the industry is not very attractive to new entrants. In fact, an old saying in the wine industry is that if you want to make $5 million, you need to start with $40 million!

So what does this mean with regard to the value curve and dynamic strategy? If we map the wine industry based on the characteristics of the dominant players and those factors considered essential to success, we would produce a map similar to the one in Exhibit 6.7. Notice that Exhibit 6.7 captures the dominant strategic groups—wineries competing in the budget or high-price segments; while the third line portrays the unique position carved out by [yellow tail]. A new entrant could fight it out in the already hypercompetitive and overcapacity high-price or budget wine segments, or it could try to have a presence in both segments and use the resulting scale to its advantage. However, as you learned in Chapter 5, a straddling strategy is often a recipe for failure.

[yellow tail] arrived at this new value curve through a process of strategic steps taken over many years. It all began way back in the 1820s, when the first Casellas began crafting wine in Italy, moving to Australia in 1951 to pursue their hopes and dreams of a better life. After years of growing and selling grapes to local wineries in 1969, when the Casella's decided it was time to put their own winemaking skills to use, the Casella winery was born. A new generation of Casellas entered the family business in 1994 and embarked on an ambitious expansion to build a new winery with a vision of blending Old World heritage with New World technology. Today, Casella Wines is run by fifth and sixth generation Casella family members. In 2000, Casella Wines joined forces with another family-run company, W. J. Deutsch & Sons, to bring Casella wines and [yellow tail] to the United States.

You can use the value curve to see how [yellow tail] reconfigured the way it defined being a winery; offering wines at a moderate price; avoiding wine lingo;

»

encouraging impulse purchases with its catchy labels; and targeting only two high-demand wines, chardonnay and Shiraz. It also added new features that incumbents did not offer—easy drinking, ease of selection (again, only two varieties), and a spirit of fun and adventure. [yellow tail] used the four-actions framework to create a new value curve. It created alternatives instead of competing head-on with the major players. It converted noncustomers to customers by luring traditional beer and cocktail drinkers with its catchy labels and easy-drinking wines. Sold around $7 a bottle, the [yellow tail] Shiraz is the top-selling imported red wine in the U.S., while the [yellow tail] Merlot and Chardonnay are both number two in their respective categories. This year, the Australian brand could sell 8 million cases in the U.S.

Ultimately, the choice between new-market and low-end disruption strategies depends on a firm's resources and capabilities, and ability to then execute the chosen strategy. [yellow tail] conceived of a new way to approach the wine industry, but it did so with the knowledge that it possessed the resources and capabilities to do so.

Exhibit 6.7   A Value Curve for the U.S. Wine Industry

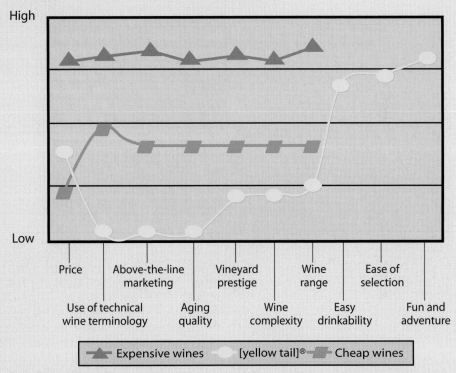

Source: Adapted from W. C. Kim and R. Mauborgne, "Blue Ocean Strategy," California Management Review 47:3 (2005), 105–121.

Sources: W. C. Kim and R. Mauborgne, "Blue Ocean Strategy," *California Management Review* 47:3 (2005), 105–121; Wine Institute, "Strong Sales Growth in 2004 for California Wine as Shipments Reached New High," April 5, 2005 (accessed July 12, 2005), www.wineinstitute.org; www.elitewine.com/site/index.php?lang=en&cat=news&art=159 (accessed July 12, 2005).

Dimensions of Competition	Head-to-Head Competition	New-Market Creation
Industry	Emphasizes rivalry	Emphasizes substitutes across industries
Strategic group and industry segments	Emphasizes competitive position within group and segments	Looks across groups and segments
Buyers	Emphasizes better buyer service	Emphasizes redefinition of the buyer and buyer's preferences
Product and service offerings	Emphasizes product or service value and offerings within industry definition	Emphasizes complementary products and services within and across industries and segments
Business model	Emphasizes efficient operation of the model	Emphasizes rethinking of the industry business model
Time	Emphasizes adaptation and capabilities that support competitive retaliation	Emphasizes strategic intent— seeking to shape the external environment over time

competitors, and they seem to be beset by constant change and conditions of disequilibrium. What causes turbulence? It may be caused by short product life cycles, short product design cycles, new technologies, frequent unanticipated entry by outsiders, incumbent repositioning, and redefinitions of market boundaries as industries divide or merge.

It helps here to recount some recent examples of what might be considered turbulence, or at least hectic change. Bear in mind that, in reality, none of the usual disruptions is likely to cause overnight change in an industry. Often, however, firms perceive disruptions to be more traumatic than they are because they're finally surfacing after root causes have festered unheeded for years, maybe even decades. For instance, it took Microsoft 15 years to grow from a boutique software firm to the global operating-system monopolist with over $30 billion of cash on its balance sheet. Atari doubled its home-game business every year, growing from $50 million in sales in 1977 to $1.6 billion in sales in 1982. Similarly, Compaq Computer, prior to its merger with Hewlett-Packard, grew from zero revenues in 1985 to $1 billion in revenues in less than five years, overtaking IBM as the leader of the Intel-based PC market. Finally, Sony shipped 10 million CD-ROM players prior to 1992, shipped 10 million in the next 11 months, and then 10 million after that in the following five months.

In this section, we'll discuss strategies that may create rapid change, capitalize on it, or both. Any strategy that depends on rapid change requires that a firm's resources and capabilities support flexibility and responsiveness. In some cases, such strategies may prove extremely efficient, even though their outcomes aren't always positive. This situation may sound contradictory, but consider this fact: Firms that are leaders in turbulent and hypercompetitive markets are often like laboratories constantly conducting basic R&D activities. (We'll say more in Chapter 12 about new ventures and corporate *intrapreneuring*.) Although many of their experiments fail, the firms themselves succeed, either because their successes simply outnumber their failures or because the benefits of a few successes heavily outweigh the costs of numerous failures.

A Model for Competing in the Face of Hypercompetition

Competing in turbulent environments requires finesse in addressing the staging element of the strategy diamond. In many ways, strategies in this context require the regular deployment and testing of options—options with new growth initiatives, new businesses, and

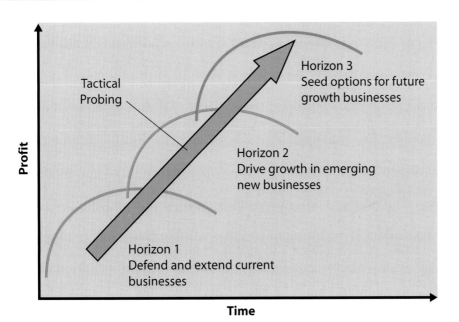

Exhibit 6.9 Creating Options for Future Competitive Advantage and Profitability

new ways of doing business. In this section, we review the findings of recent research on how firms manage the staging of strategy in order to succeed in turbulent or hypercompetitive environments. Research on strategy in this particularly dynamic context is typically anchored in so-called *systems, chaos,* or *complexity theories.* They're peppered with such biological terms as *self-organizing systems* and *co-adaptation,* and they're concerned with the same phenomenon—adaptation to a changing external environment in which change may be rapid and its direction uncertain.[23] By and large, they all share a basic premise: Firms need some degree of ability to thrive in chaotic environments in order to survive. In one study of several firms competing on the edge of chaos, researchers encountered the following three levels of activity, summarized by the curves in Exhibit 6.9:[24]

- Activities designed to test today's competitive strategy (defending today's business)
- Activities designed to lead to tomorrow's competitive strategy (drive growth in emerging businesses)
- Activities designed to influence the pacing and timing of change (seeding options for future new businesses and growth initiatives)

Improvisation and Simple Rules   The lower left-hand curve depicted in Exhibit 6.9 is the defense of existing businesses. Strategy in hypercompetitive contexts differs from that in more stable contexts in that the former is typically accomplished through managerial **improvisation**: managerial practices that contribute to a culture of frequent change dictated by a few **simple rules**. This view holds that when the business landscape was simple and relatively stable, companies could manage complex strategies. However, given the complexities that businesses in turbulent environments face, they need to simplify their strategies into a select set of cast-iron rules that define direction without confining it. The idea is borrowed from the practice of jazz musicians, who are, of course, masters of improvisation. Much of their music is spontaneous yet at the same time carefully organized around identifiable themes—simple rules—determined by the capacities and constraints of the instruments and musicians involved.

The range and diversity of musical outcomes is infinite, even though the practice of jazz improvisation acknowledges a few simple rules. Each player, for example, must know who the soloist is going to be, and the soloist must build off the work of other band members; players must expect occasional mishaps, and even learn to incorporate them into the performance. The simple rules typically involve autonomy, passion, risk tolerance, innovation, and listening. As with all good strategies, however, regardless of context, simple rules are not broad or vague (they require conscious tradeoffs). As we'll soon discuss, business strategies designed to accommodate experiments with processes, arenas, priorities, timing, and exit must also acknowledge a few simple rules.[25]

improvisation Managerial practices that contribute to a culture of frequent change, especially in turbulent or hypercompetitive contexts

simple rules Basic rules for guiding improvisation by defining strategy without confining it

Sequencing Past and Future   The middle and upper right-hand curves of Exhibit 6.9 represent activities focused on the future—the conditions toward which the change-oriented activities at the foundation of the strategy are aimed. At the same time, however, future products will embody indelible links to the past. In this model of business strategy, the bridge between past activities and future conditions is built on a substructure of experimentation and learning. For instance, S. C. Johnson found that one of its innovative home pesticide products in Europe could not pass U.S. regulatory hurdles, preventing its introduction in that country. However, through experimentation with its fragrances division, a key technology in the product was thought to be valuable and gave rise to the introduction of Glade PlugIns in 1993. S. C. Johnson effectively joined knowledge embedded in previously disconnected and geographically removed operating units (pesticides and fragrances divisions) to create an entirely new product category in the home air-freshener industry.

Successful new-business conditions are a reflection of those strategies that have been most successful. Ineffective strategies are jettisoned or marginalized as customers migrate toward firms with strategies that best meet their needs. Thus, managers use their understanding of the competitive environment to guide their selection and reconfiguration of portions of yesterday's business practices. Dell, for example, developed its direct-sales model for the consumer and small-business PC market, and when it entered the large-business computer-server market, it adapted its direct-sales model by providing onsite customer service. The model, however, had evolved: In this sector, while maintaining a very modest level of onsite staff for its largest corporate clients, most of Dell's consumer service is provided by a Web-based platform. With virtually a single stroke, Dell had changed the industry business model in a way that favored and further strengthened the model that had long been its fundamental source of competitive advantage. In other words, Dell's dynamic move forward into the server market was anchored in its past strengths in the PC market, and it has had a profound effect on the strategies of other firms as they've attempted to adapt to signals from the environment.

Tactical Probing   A striking feature of this model of dynamic strategy is the close relationship between tactical moves and strategy evolution. Simple rules enable the firm to excel in a given business, but they also give rise to experimentation that leads to options on future businesses—horizons 2 and 3 in Exhibit 6.9. Often, we don't think of the operating decisions that we call tactics as *strategic* activities because, in and of themselves, they're fairly inconsequential in affecting cost or competitive impact. In dynamic markets, however, many tactical moves can be used as low-cost "probes" for experimentation—testing the current strategy and suggesting future changes.

Tactics, in other words, can be both tools for competing today and experiments in new ways of competing tomorrow. Consider the case of discount broker Charles Schwab. When the company found itself being squeezed on one side by deep-discount Internet startups such as E*Trade and discount initiatives by full-service brokers such as Merrill Lynch on the other, it experimented with new ways of reinforcing customer relationships and identifying new markets. In particular, Schwab developed futures-trading programs, simplified its mutual-fund offerings, and launched Internet-based products and services. Some of these probes, of course, went nowhere (Schwab aborted a line of credit cards and a foray into online mortgages). But those that did succeed enabled Schwab both to further differentiate itself from bare-bones discounters and to gain ground in markets dominated by full-service brokers.

conceptlink

In Chapter 1, we observe **staging**, as the *timing and pace* of strategic moves, entails the assessment of possible outcomes. In Chapter 4, emphasizing that industry analysis must reflect the evolution of industries *over time*, we underscore the importance of staging as a response to transitions in the **industry life cycle** and to **technological discontinuities**.

Setting Pace and Rhythm   Finally, as managers move from one horizon to another they must concern themselves with the speed and pace of change. You're already familiar with this aspect of strategy because you're familiar with the staging diamond of the five-elements strategy model. Many managers, however, fail to appreciate fully the role played by time and timing in formulating and executing strategy. Consider, for example, the various approaches to staging and pacing described in Exhibit 6.10. Obviously, attention to pacing and staging can prompt a company to think more seriously about the need for constant experimentation and probing. The concluding example of 3M may partially explain why that firm is consistently able to generate new and innovative products.

British Airways	"Five years is the maximum that you can go without refreshing the brand... We did it [relaunched Club Europe Service] because we wanted to stay ahead so that we could continue to win customers."
Emerson Electric	"In each of the last three years we've introduced more than 100 major new products, which is about 70 percent above our pace of the early 1990s. We plan to maintain this rate and, overall, have targeted increasing new products to [equal] 35 percent of total sales."
Intel	The inventor of Moore's Law stated that the power of the computer chip would double every 18 months. IBM builds a new manufacturing facility every nine months. "We build factories two years in advance of needing them, before we have the products to run in them, and before we know the industry is going to grow."
Gillette	Forty percent of Gillette's sales every five years must come from entirely new products (prior to its acquisition by P&G). Gillette raises prices at a pace set to match price increases in a basket of market goods (which includes items such as a newspaper, a candy bar, and a can of soda). Gillette prices are never raised faster than the price of the market basket.
3M	Thirty percent of sales must come from products that are fewer than four years old.

Exhibit 6.10 Staging and Pacing in the Real World

Source: S. Brown and K. Eisenhardt, Competing on the Edge: Strategy as Structured Chaos (Boston: Harvard Business School Press, 1998).

Putting a Value on Staging and Pacing

Just as strategy in dynamic contexts is understandably complex, so has the need to analyze the options that such complexity creates grown in importance. Although some of the analytical tools that can be used to analyze options are rather complex, it is valuable to have a general understanding of how they work. For instance, more firms are relying on such tools as **real-options analysis** to evaluate the substantive financial aspects of their dynamic strategies. Beyond the complex financial models that characterize real-options analysis, you should also see that a real-options mind-set provides managers with greater strategic flexibility in how they approach projects. Interestingly, firms that manage the timing aspect of their strategy well will also gain a better understanding of the internal rhythm by which they introduce new products. They realize that this rhythm must be synchronized not only with their own resources and capabilities but also with the needs and characteristics of key suppliers and customers.

real-options analysis Process of maximizing the upside or limiting the downside of an investment opportunity by uncovering and quantifying the options and discussion points embedded within it

The idea behind real options is to preserve flexibility so that the firm has an ability to be well positioned in the future when the competitive environment shifts. A perfectly positioned firm can become ill-positioned as the industry evolves, as new competitors emerge, and as technology makes current core competencies obsolete. By making small investments that preserve the option of taking a new course of action in the future, a firm can maintain its advantage. As an example, Intel invests heavily in internal R&D; however, it determined that it was unlikely to be the source of most innovations that could change how processing technology is used. Consequently, Intel made a conscience decision to invest in startups. By being a partial owner of the startups, Intel would have inside information on many new technologies being developed elsewhere. Intel has no obligation to increase its investment in these operations or to buy the products or internalize these innovations. However, by making these small investments, it has the option of doing so in the future.

Real-options analysis is based on the idea that strategic flexibility and adaptation are functions of experimentation and probing and, as such, should have implications for the way managers evaluate alternatives. Real options is a particularly useful tool for financially evaluating strategic alternatives because it recognizes not only that managers get valuable information after a new strategic initiative is launched, but that informed responses can make a big difference in the success of the new strategy. So, what are real options? Quite simply, a real option is *the opportunity (though by no means the obligation) to take action that will either maximize the upside or limit the downside of a capital investment.* The purpose of real-options analysis is to uncover and quantify an initiative's *embedded options* or critical decision points. Ironically, of course, the greater the uncertainty and flexibility in the project, the greater the potential value of having options in managing it. The traditional method of evaluating project performance involves the use of discounted cash flow (DCF) analysis; the most common is what is referred to as *net present value (NPV)*. NPV calculates the present value of a project by forecasting future cash flows and subtracting the initial investment. Some researchers now argue that NPV and DCF calculations should be viewed as a narrow subset of real options—one that's useful only in evaluating projects with little or no uncertainty and flexibility.

Increasingly, managers in industries characterized by large capital investments and high degrees of uncertainty and flexibility (such as oil and gas, mining, pharmaceuticals, and biotechnology) are beginning to think in terms of real options. These companies typically have plenty of the market and R&D data needed to make confident assumptions about uncertain outcomes. They also have the sort of engineering-oriented corporate culture that isn't averse to complex mathematical tools.

Although real-options analysis is not a cure-all for strategic uncertainty, the technique is getting much more attention not only in the fields of finance and strategic management but among other companies and industries as well. In addition to those industries cited earlier, the automotive, aerospace, consumer-goods, industrial-products, and high-tech industries are also interested in real-options analysis. Intel, for example, now trains finance employees in real-options valuation and has used the technique to analyze a number of capital projects. As a starting point, we suggest that you introduce yourself to real options by considering the following five categories:[26]

- *Waiting-to-invest options.* The value of waiting to build a factory until better market information comes along may exceed the value of immediate expansion.
- *Growth options.* An entry investment may create opportunities to pursue valuable follow-up projects.
- *Flexibility options.* Serving markets on two continents by building two plants instead of one gives a firm the option of switching production from one plant to the other as conditions dictate.
- *Exit (or abandonment) options.* The option to walk away from a project in response to new information increases its value.
- *Learning options.* An initial investment may generate further information about a market opportunity and may help to determine whether the firm should add more capacity.

An Example of Real Options at Work   Here is an example of how a strategist might evaluate the investment in a potential new drug.[27] This example has aspects of all five of the real-options categories just mentioned—from *waiting to invest* to *learning*. One of the most dynamic industry contexts is in the biomedical sciences and the discovery of new drugs. When a pharmaceutical company starts to develop a new compound, it does not know if a new marketable drug will come out at the end of the project. However, opportunities and risks are tightly linked with each other, and this is specifically true for innovation investments. The higher the risk, the higher the possible return. We know this from most introductory financial-investments courses. The value of an investment can be exponentially increased if inherent risk can be limited. This is where so-called real options come into play. For the pharmaceutical firm, the "real" option generated through its innovation activities is the option to sell a "real" new product or service to the market in the future, after the development process has been successfully finished.

Let's get started. A pharmaceutical company developed a new drug that it wanted to take to market. The drug had to pass three clinical trials to test its efficacy before being reviewed by the FDA for final approval. Based on scientific evidence and academic research, the probabilities of passing each of the three phases were 75, 50, and 65 percent, respectively. The FDA approval probability, assuming the drug passed the trials, was 85 percent. The company estimated the costs of the entire trial-and-approval process to be $23 million.

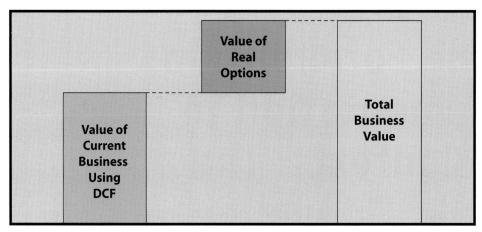

Exhibit 6.11 The Value of Real Options

Source: L.E.K. Consulting LLC, Shareholder Value Added: Making Real Decisions with Real Options (accessed September 12, 2005), www.lek.com/ideas/publications/sva 16.pdf.

Current business value + Real-options value = Total business value

Given all of this information about risks and costs, how can we use real-options valuation to determine if the company should proceed with the clinical trials? The equation, according to one possible application of real-options analysis, goes as follows: First, you create a decision tree incorporating all possible outcomes of future trials and all of management's decisions in each event. The NPV of each possible "end state" is calculated using the DCF model. Then, starting with the final year of the evaluation phase and working backward, assume that management chooses the highest NPV alternative at each decision point. This process clarifies whether it makes sense to abandon, repeat, or proceed should any of the trials fail.

Assuming you did the calculation correctly, it turned out to be optimal to reformulate if the first trial failed, repeat the second trial if it failed, and abandon the drug if the third trial failed. To calculate the NPV for the first trial, you eliminate the lower (unchosen) NPV scenarios to arrive at an adjusted NPV of $9.3 million (75% × 13.2 + 25% × −2.5).

If you were to evaluate this decision using the most common investment-analysis tool, DCF analysis, you would end up with an NPV of −$1.8 million. That calculation would have gone like this: First you would have calculated the overall probability of success (75% × 50% × 80% × 83% = 25%) and of failure (100% − 25% = 75%) and then the DCF value itself (25% × $62 million + 75% × −$23.1 million = −$1.8 million). The value of the decision-tree valuation, and of the real-options approach, is significantly higher because it recognizes the value of the real options present in the flexibility of management to choose at each decision point (in the event of failure in each respective phase) the remaining option that has the highest NPV.

In many cases, it is through a real-options mind-set, summarized in Exhibit 6.11, that firms also come to understand how this rhythm (i.e., timing and pacing of investments) determines the pace of transitions from old to new markets, including the speed with which they exit the old ones. It's an important element of strategy to understand because firms often find it harder to drop old products than to launch new ones. Cisco Systems, for instance, has been successful in dynamic markets (especially telecommunications equipment) largely because of its ability to assess product life cycles, identify products that have no future, and then manage the exit strategy. Cisco continues to make money on products that it no longer produces by outsourcing both production and sales while retaining commissions on future sales.

FORMULATING AND IMPLEMENTING DYNAMIC STRATEGIES

In this final section we focus on the ways in which dynamic strategies should be reflected in your application of both the strategy diamond and the strategy-implementation models. The formulation and implementation facets of crafting strategy in dynamic contexts are brought together in the box entitled "How Would *You* Do That? 6.2," which focuses on the printing company R. R. Donnelley. (Because we devote Chapter 11 to a more detailed dis-

Integrating Formulation and Implementation in Dynamic Contexts: The Case of R.R. Donnelley

R. R. Donnelley is one of the largest commercial printers in the world, reporting 2004 revenues of over $7 billion. Based on an analysis of the commercial print industry's five forces and its complements, you would conclude it is an unattractive industry, principally because it's characterized by extremely high fixed costs (large, expensive printing presses that need to run 24/7 to be profitable, excess industry production capacity, intensive rivalry, powerful customers). With the explosion of the Internet and digital and ink-jet print-on-demand technologies, multiple sophisticated substitutes

and complements for traditional printed products and means of conveying information are available. So, in 2004 Donnelley's top-management team sought to redefine itself and its industry, embarking on a strategy to move beyond being a simple commercial printer to become an information-management company and a leader in marketing communications.

Recognizing that Donnelley faces a dynamic market and uncertain future, the following text describes how you might draw on what you have learned up to this point to propose a strategy for Donnelley that acts on its new company vision.

FORMULATION

Recall that our basic framework to formulate a strategy, or to analyze a firm's strategy, is the strategy diamond. Let's walk through the five elements of Donnelley's strategy.

- *Arenas.* Retain leadership position in providing information-management services to the burgeoning financial-services industry; focus new resource allocation on investments in proprietary-software development and

marketing-communications service offerings; use direct sales channels and leverage existing customer base; roll out marketing capabilities first in the United States, followed by Canada, Europe, Asia, and Latin America. We will focus on developing and leveraging core technologies based on proprietary-software and marketing-communications workflow. We will be the one-stop shopping source for our customers marketing-communications needs.

- *Vehicles.* We will focus on acquisitions to quickly gain the software development and marketing-communications skills, use internal development to push these skills through the organization, and build alliances with advertising agencies for sales and marketing of this marketing-communications solution.

- *Staging.* In the next 12 months, we will add a new corporate-level division responsible for the marketing-communications initiative, acquire the software and marketing companies for their expertise, and create a dialogue about the vision with our traditional print division managers so that we ≫

have a solid understanding of the new cross-divisional rules of engagement and opportunities. Within three years we will build market credibility, invest in more software and marketing-communications talent, and begin rolling out the vision and related marketing-communications offerings in non–U.S. geographic markets. We will also look at organic and acquisition growth opportunities to provide this solution beyond the financial-services industry (such as pharmaceutical firms and other heavily regulated industries). Alliances with advertising agencies and other creative firms will be sought out during this period. Within five years we will further push the global roll out of the vision and services and evaluate the potential divestiture of our traditional capital-intensive print assets.

- *Differentiators.* We will provide a single vendor solution focused in the area of marketing communications supported by world-class work-flow technologies and outsourcing capabilities. These differentiators will be offered in narrowly defined markets to ensure

customer intimacy, which allows us to show them how our services make our customers more efficient and more competitive.

- *Economic logic.* We will garner premium prices due to our comprehensive, unique, and industry-focused service offerings, proprietary-technologies and service capabilities, value-added consulting services, and customer intimacy.

IMPLEMENTATION

Our management team will allocate financial resources to the growth of the new division and the organizational changes required to align what we do in the firm with the new vision. Our team will invest its time in getting all divisions on board with the vision, see how their business fits the vision, and adjust the strategy so that division needs and capabilities are fully reflected. We also recognize that we will need to spend time building up a portfolio of acquisition targets and alliance partners and building relationships with those important future stakeholders in our vision and success.

To achieve this strategy we will reorganize, adapt systems and processes,

and change the incentive structure. As indicated in staging, we will establish a new corporate-level division that will be responsible for coordinating this strategy. The separate division will also make acquisition integration more effective and focus the objectives of future alliances. New systems and processes will emphasize working protocols across divisions to sell this Donnelley marketing-communications solution, provide seamless price quoting from a customer's perspective, and offer product development and consultative selling. Incentives will be redesigned to emphasize selling the full marketing-communications solution instead of individual pieces, such as printing. We will also reward, recruit, and promote individuals who move the one-firm concept forward.

Sources: Adapted from analysis of company's annual and 10-K reports, information provided throughout the company Web site at www.rrdonnelley.com, and "For Digital Printers, the Profit Clock Just Ticks Away," *Printing News East*, July 22, 1996 (no author cited).

cussion of implementation levers and organizational structure, our remarks in this section will provide just a basic introduction.)

Focusing on Arenas and Staging

Let's look first at our model of strategy formulation, which is critical because it establishes a set of simple rules for describing the business and showing how it creates value. Of course, all five elements of strategy are important and must be managed in concert, but the *arenas* and *staging* diamonds are especially important. In addition to recognizing the need for dynamic capabilities, focusing on these facets of strategy is what differentiates a dynamic strategy from a strategy developed for more stable contexts.

The Role of Arenas   Arenas designate your choice of customers to be served and the products to be provided. In each section of this chapter on dynamic strategy—sections dealing with industry and product evolution, technological discontinuity, and turbulence—we've tried to emphasize that the strategist is always making important and reasoned choices about the firm's mix of customers, noncustomers, products, and services. The remaining four diamonds of strategy—vehicles, differentiators, staging, and economic logic, will tell the strategist whether the mix of arenas is consistent with what we called a *coherent* strategy in Chapter 2.

Moreover, the role of arenas in the firm's strategy will vary according to the factor of the dynamic environment being considered. In the context of *industry evolution*, for example, arenas must fit with a firm's resources, capabilities, and dynamic capabilities. With regard to *technological discontinuities*, the role of arenas, though overlapping with its role in low-end disruption strategies, was broadened to include noncustomers, particularly when the strategy is designed to create new markets. *Globalization*, introduced in Chapter 4, adds yet another dimension to the role of arenas: If a firm is going global, managers need to apply what they have learned about competing in one geographic arena to the task of competing in others. Finally, in dealing with *turbulent and hypercompetitive markets*, managers need to think of arenas as laboratories—sites in which to conduct experiments or launch probes into the possible future of the firm and its strategy.

The Role of Implementation Levers   In terms of strategy implementation, the previous discussion provides you with some perspective on the type of strategy that needs to be implemented. In applying any implementation framework, such as the five elements of strategy, the elements of the model must be balanced—in this case, a dynamic strategy should be reflected in organizational structures, systems, and processes that accommodate the strategic needs of firms in turbulent and hypercompetitive environments. One element of strategy formulation—staging—can also serve to bridge formulation and implementation because the staging component can specify how certain levers will be employed along the way.

Because accurate forecasting is quite difficult in dynamic contexts, scenario planning may be incorporated into the initial stage of the strategy. Scenario planning can be used to identify tipping points in the external environment that may signal when market demand or competitor characteristics are on the verge of significant change. Increasingly, real-options analysis (or at least some set of analytical tools to examine how time and experience may change the supply and demand characteristics of the target markets) should be included as well.

Finally, both the strategic leadership of senior management and the culture of the organization that they foster should reflect a commitment to reasoned risk taking, learning, and responding to change. Indeed, it's hard to promote core values that support the strategy implementation in dynamic contexts if top management doesn't practice and champion them. That's just one reason why we studied strategic leadership in such detail in Chapter 2.

SUMMARY

1. Identify the challenges to sustainable competitive advantage in dynamic contexts. Dynamism can undermine competitive advantage—sometimes with blinding speed, but more typically over some extended period of time. Indeed, as noted in the opening vignette, although it may seem that the music industry has changed overnight, many of the seeds for that dramatic change were sown and nourished over an extended period of time. Technological discontinuities can alter the basis of competition and the requisite resources and capabilities for competitive advantage. The speed of change in an industry itself is a significant factor; it can either complement or compound the effects of industry evolution, technological discontinuities, and globalization.

2. Understand the fundamental dynamics of competition. Firms do not generate and implement strategies in a vacuum. Competitive interaction can be characterized by four phases, starting with the discovery by the focal firm of a new competitive action. The following two phases involve some combination of customer and competitor reaction. The final phase involves competitor interaction evaluation. Competitive interaction theory has shown that the way a competitor initiates these actions can determine its effectiveness. Actions that are aggressive, complex, unpredictable, and can delay a competitor's response usually result in the greatest competitive gains for the attacker. Specific tactics for hypercompetitive markets include containment, shaping, absorption, neutralization, and annulment.

3. Evaluate the advantages and disadvantages of choosing a first-mover strategy. First movers are firms that initiate a strategic action before rivals, such as the introduction of a new product or service or a new process that provides a traditional product or service of dramatically higher quality or at a lower price, or both. Second movers are relatively early movers (because they are still not last-movers), but delayed enough to learn from first movers. Effective second movers are sometimes referred to as *fast followers.* They are distinguished from late movers, whose tardiness penalizes them when the market grows. First movers do not always have an advantage because there are significant risks associated with being the first to introduce new products, services, and business models.

4. Analyze and develop strategies for managing industry evolution. Strategies may differ from one stage of the industry product life cycle to another. The strategic management of industry evolution involves these strategies, as well as the ability to *change* arenas and strategies along with changes in the environment. Using legal protections (e.g., patents, copyrights) is one way to protect a firm during industry evolution. Other value-added means of protecting a firm from commoditization include bundling strategies, process innovation, focused differentiation, and service innovation. A bundling strategy bundles increased service benefits with existing products (those valued by customers) while raising or maintaining firm prices. With process innovation, the firm seeks to lower prices through reductions in operating costs. A focused differentiation strategy in response to commoditization recognizes that to be able to extract premium prices, the firm must serve a narrower segment of the market. A service innovation approach attempts to increase margins by stripping away services that were formerly included with basic products.

5. Analyze and develop strategies for technological discontinuities. An approach for dealing with, and sometimes leading, technological discontinuities involves the creation of a high-end or low-end disruption. High-end disruptions generally result in the creation of a new market and require the introduction of new product or service features (and may even result in the elimination of some features) that are considered necessary by incumbent firms. Low-end disrupters offer products and services that lack many of the features taken for granted by incumbents, but the product still satisfies the basic needs of many customers. Being a disrupter is tricky, because new sales and customers come from niches that are not already being served or that are being served poorly by the largest firms. Over time, however, the "fringe" firms begin attracting the mainstream customers based on their combination of pricing and customer value added. Ultimately the choice of a new-market or low-end disruption strategy rests on where the firm believes its resources and capabilities lie. In the box entitled "How Would *You* Do That? 6.1" provides an example of value-curve mapping for [yellow tail] wines. Essentially, the firm must map the key differentiators in the industry (i.e., those items that drive willingness to pay) and then develop a strategy that makes the focal firm clearly distinct from its competitors and at the same time do so in a way that essentially creates a new market.

6. Analyze and develop strategies for high-speed environmental change. When one or more sets of industry change drivers are moving extremely fast, the market is often referred to as *turbulent* or *hypercompetitive.* Turbulent and hypercompetitive markets are in constant disequilibrium because of frequent, bold, and dynamic moves by competitors. Turbulence is a result of short product life cycles, short product design cycles, new product and business process technologies, frequent unanticipated entry by outsiders, incumbent repositioning, and redefinitions of market boundaries due to mergers and divestitures. Strategies for these environments require flexibility and rapid response capability.

7. Explain the implications of a dynamic strategy for the strategy diamond and strategy implementation. Vision is critical in that it serves as a set of simple rules that describe the business and how it creates value. The example from R. R. Donnelley in the box entitled "How Would *You* Do That? 6.2" shows how formulation and implementation can be woven together in a sophisticated manner to achieve Donnelley's new simple-rules vision. Although all five elements of strategy are important and must be managed in concert, the arenas and staging diamonds are perhaps most important in dynamic markets. And, like the five elements of strategy, a balance among the implementation levers is critical. These levers must accommodate environmental turbulence and hypercompetitive environments. The strategic flexibility demanded of these environments requires that organization structure and systems can be easily decoupled and recombined as circumstances change. Rigid bureaucracy is generally incompatible with turbulent environments. Strategic leadership must further support the firm's ability to identify the need for and undertake strategic change.

KEY TERMS

first mover, 160
high-end disruption, 168
improvisation, 173

low-end disruption, 168
real-options analysis, 175

second mover, 160
simple rules, 173

takeoff period, 161
value curve, 169

REVIEW QUESTIONS

1. What are four sets of challenges to sustained competitive advantage outlined in this chapter?

2. What is the relationship between first and second movers?

3. What is industry commoditization? What are two strategies a firm may undertake to combat industry commoditization?

4. What is a new-market-creation strategy?

5. What is a low-end disruption strategy?

6. What are the three layers of activity that underlie strategies for turbulent and hypercompetitive markets?

7. What is the role of timing and pacing in strategies for turbulent and hypercompetitive markets?

8. How might you apply real-options analysis, financially and conceptually, in the context of strategies for turbulent and hypercompetitive markets?

9. What five defensive strategies might industry incumbents pursue in turbulent and hypercompetitive markets?

10. What are the implications of dynamic strategies for strategy formulation and implementation?

How Would you Do That?

1. Pick an industry and use the box entitled "How Would *You* Do That? 6.1" as a template to map its value curve. What are the key success factors that define industry participation? Does there appear to be more than one strategic group in this industry operating with different value curves? Can you come up with a new value curve that would change the industry?

2. Identify an industry that you believe is very dynamic and identify the drivers of that dynamism. Now pick a firm in that industry and formulate a strategy and basic implementation scheme to exploit its dynamic context. Use the R. R. Donnelley example presented in the box entitled "How Would *You* Do That? 6.2" as a template for your recommendations.

GROUP ACTIVITIES

1. If you were the CEO of Napster (which started out as Roxio in the opening vignette), what material from this chapter would be most relevant to you? How would this material help you to formulate a strategy? What might key components of that strategy be? Now put yourself in Microsoft's shoes; would you see either Sonic Solutions or Napster as a threat? If so, what strategy would you formulate in response?

2. Review the list of first- and second-mover firms in Exhibit 6.3. What specific resources and capabilities do you think successful first movers must possess? What specific resources and capabilities do you think successful second movers and fast followers must possess? Do you think that a firm could be both a first mover and fast follower if it wanted to be?

ENDNOTES

1. N. Wingfield and E. Smith, "With the Web Shaking Up Music, a Free-for-All in Online Songs," *Wall Street Journal*, November 19, 2003, A1; N. Wingfield and E. Smith, "Microsoft Plans to Sell Music over the Web," *Wall Street Journal*, November 17, 2003, A1; www.roxio.com (accessed June 28, 2005). "Napster Lives Again as Legal Distributor of Music on the Web," *The Wall Street Journal*, 25 February 2003, A10; N. Wingfield, "Roxio Agrees to Acquire Napster Assets," *The Wall Street Journal*, November 18, 2002, B4.

2. S. Brown and K. Eisenhardt, *Competing on the Edge* (Boston: Harvard Business School Press, 1998).

3. D. C. Hambrick and J. W. Fredrickson, "Are You Sure You Have a Strategy?" *Academy of Management Executive* 15:4 (2001), 48–59.

4. M. Chen, "Competitor Analysis and Interfirm Rivalry: Toward a Theoretical Integration," *Academy of Management Review* 21 (1996), 100–134; M. Chen and D. C. Hambrick, "Speed, Stealth, and Selective Attack: How Small Firms Differ from Large Firms in Competitive Behavior," *Academy of Management Journal* 38 (1995), 453–482.

5. A. M. Brandenburger and B. J. Nalebuff, *Co-Opetition* (New York: Currency Doubleday, 1996).

6. K. G. Smith, W. J. Ferrier, and C. M. Grimm, "King of the Hill: Dethroning the Industry Leader," *Academy of Management Executive* 15:2 (2001), 59–70.

7. www.riaa.org (accessed July 28, 2005).

8. www.kodak.com (accessed July 15, 2005).

9. R. D'Aveni, "The Empire Strikes Back: Counterrevolutionary Strategies for Industry Leaders," *Harvard Business Review* 80:11 (November 2002), 5–12.

10. M. E. Porter, *Competitive Strategy* (New York: Free Press, 1979), 232–233.

11. For a particularly rich discussion of these differences, see S. Schnaars, *Managing Imitation Strategies* (New York: Free Press, 1994), 12–14.

12. G. Tellis, S. Stremersch, and E. Yin, "The International Takeoff of New Products: Economics, Culture, and Country Innovativeness," *Marketing Science* 22:2 (2003), 161–187.

13. A. Goolsbee and J. Chevalier, "Price Competition Online: Amazon versus Barnes and Noble," *Quantitative Marketing and Economics* 1:2 (June, 2003), 203–222.

14. Schnaars, *Managing Imitation Strategies,* 37–43; J. Covin, D. Slevin, and M. Heeley, "Pioneers and Followers: Competitive Tactics, Environment, and Growth," *Journal of Business Venturing* 15:2 (1999), 175–210.

15. This framework is adapted from A. Afuah, *Innovation Management: Strategies, Implementation, and Profits,* 2nd ed.

(New York: Oxford University Press, 2003). An earlier version appears in Schnaars, *Managing Imitation Strategies,* 12–14.

16. K. Rangan and G. Bowman, "Beating the Commodity Magnet," *Industrial Marketing Management* 21 (1992), 215–224; P. Kotler, "Managing Products through Their Product Life Cycle," in *Marketing Management: Planning, Implementation, and Control,* 7th ed. (Upper Saddle River, NJ: Prentice Hall, 1991), P. Kotler, "Product Life-Cycle Marketing Strategies," in *Marketing Management,* 11th ed. (Upper Saddle River, NJ: Prentice Hall, 2003), 328–339.

17. C. Tejada, "The Allure of 'Bundling,'" *Wall Street Journal*, October 7, 2003, B1.

18. www.badgermeter.com (accessed July 15, 2005).

19. P. Anderson and M. L. Tushman, "Technological Discontinuities and Dominant Designs: A Cyclical Model of Technological Change," *Administrative Science Quarterly* 35 (1990), 604–633.

20. G. A. Moore, "Darwin and the Demon: Innovating within Established Enterprises" *Harvard Business Review* 82:7/8 (2004), 86–92.

21. These examples are drawn from an extensive and detailed list provided by C. Christensen and M. Raynor, The Innovator's Solution. Boston, MA: Harvard Business School Press (2003).

22. W. C. Kim and R. Mauborgne, "Value Innovation: The Strategic Logic of High Growth," *Harvard Business Review* 75:1 (1997), 102–113; Kim and Mauborgne, "Charting Your Company's Future," *Harvard Business Review* 80:6 (2002), 76–82.

23. See, for example, S. Kauffman, *At Home in the Universe: The Search for the Laws of Self-Organization and Complexity* (New York: Oxford University Press, 1995); M. Gell-Mann, *The Quark and the Jaguar* (New York: W. H. Freeman, 1994); J. Casti, *Complexification: Explaining a Paradoxical World through the Science of Surprise* (New York: HarperCollins, 1994); R. Lewin, *Complexity: Life at the Edge of Chaos* (New York: Macmillan, 1992).

24. Brown and Eisenhardt, *Competing on the Edge.*

25. K. Eisenhardt and D. Sull, "Strategy as Simple Rules," *Harvard Business Review* 79:1 (2001), 106–116.

26. M. Amram and N. Kulatilaka, *Real Options: Managing Strategic Investment in an Uncertain World* (New York: Oxford University Press, 1998); E. Teach, "Will Real Options Take Root? Why Companies Have Been Slow to Adopt the Valuation Technique," *CFO Magazine,* July 1, 2003, 73.

27. Example adapted from J. Daum, *The New New Economy Analyst Report,* December 28, 2001.

After studying this chapter, you should be able to:

1. Define *corporate strategy.*

2. Understand the roles of economies of scope and revenue-enhancement synergy in corporate strategy.

3. Explain the different forms of diversification.

4. Understand when it makes sense for a firm to own a particular business.

5. Describe the relationship between corporate strategy and competitive advantage.

6. Explain the role of corporate strategy in both stable and dynamic contexts.

▶ **Reginald H. Jones,**
CEO, General Electric, 1972–1981
Strategy: Continue to diversify GE's holdings primarily via internal research and development. Move into international markets.
Stock high: $75.87
Stock low: $30.12
Market cap 1981: $14 billion

▶ **John "Jack" F. Welch,**
CEO, General Electric, 1981–2001
Strategy: Focus on cost cutting, efficiency, and deal making to achieve consistent earnings. Divest some of GE's businesses and decentralize operations to eliminate corporate bureaucracy.
Stock high: $166.00
Stock low: $37.70
Market cap 2001: $490 billion

1980   1985   19

DIVERSIFICATION AT GE, 3M, AND MITY ENTERPRISES

General Electric General Electric (GE) was established in 1892 in New York, the product of a merger between two manufacturers of electrical equipment, Thomson-Houston Electric Co. and Edison General Electric Co. (Thomas Edison was one of the directors).[1] GE's early products included such Edison inventions as light bulbs, elevators, motors, and toasters. In 1896, GE was among the 12 original companies to be included in the newly created Dow Jones Industrial Average, and it's the only one that's still on the list.

By 1980, although GE was earning $25 billion in revenues from such diverse businesses as plastics, consumer electronics, nuclear reactors, and jet engines, it had become as lethargic as it was large. The following year, John F. (Jack) Welch was named chairman and CEO and charged with reinvigorating the bureaucratically top-heavy

▶ **Jeffrey R. Immelt,**
CEO, General Electric, 2001–present
Strategy: Focus on creativity and risk taking versus cost cutting and deal making to develop new products and services in new markets. Divest less-profitable businesses and enter hot new growth markets.
Stock high: $41.55
Stock low: $22.00
Market cap 2005: $358 billion

1995   2000

company. Welch decentralized operations and announced a vision that called for GE to participate only in high-performing businesses in which it could be the number-one or number-two competitor. Although GE divested itself of many of its businesses, including air conditioning, housewares, and semiconductors, it remains one of the most diversified companies in the United States, if not the world. Today, the company's products and services include aircraft engines, locomotives and other transportation equipment, appliances (kitchen and laundry equipment), lighting, electric-distribution and electric-control equipment, generators and turbines, nuclear reactors, medical-imaging equipment, network television (NBC), and plastics.

How did GE evolve from an electronics company to an enormous conglomeration of many businesses? Over the years, GE developed some of the businesses through its own R&D efforts. However, many of its current operations are the result of acquisitions. Indeed, GE is one of the most frequent acquirers of other businesses in the world. Between January 2000 and December 2004, GE acquired more than 250 different companies and spent more than $78 billion to do so. Its financial-services arm, which includes commercial finance, consumer finance, equipment management, and insurance, accounts for nearly half of the company's $150 billion in sales. In terms of stock-market capitalization, GE ranks behind only ExxonMobil.

3M Minnesota Mining and Manufacturing (3M) was founded in 1902 to sell corundum (an extremely hard mineral comprised largely of aluminum oxide that is used as an abrasive) to grinding-wheel manufacturers. Within a couple of years, the fledgling company was specializing in sandpaper, but it wasn't until the 1920s, when it began focusing on technological innovation, that 3M finally hit its stride. Eventually, two products—Scotch-brand masking tape (introduced in 1925) and Scotch-brand cellophane tape (1930)—became so successful that they virtually guaranteed the company a long and prosperous future. Today, 3M has seven operating units—transportation; display and graphics; health care; safety, security, and protection; electrical and communications products; industrial adhesives; and consumer and office products. They make thousands of products, ranging from masking tape to asthma inhalers, boasting such household names as Scotchgard, Post-it Notes, Scotch-Brite, and Scotch tape. Sales outside of the United States account for more than half of the company's $20 billion in yearly revenues.

Coupled with enormous R&D spending (over $1 billion per year), 3M's policy of allowing scientists to dedicate 10 percent of their working time to experimentation has yielded a number of highly profitable innovations. Of course, not all divisions and innovations have been equally successful, and the company has spun off some divisions, including low-profit imaging and data-storage ventures. 3M closed its audiotape and videotape businesses and got out of billboard advertising.

3M has entered most of its businesses through internal innovation. In contrast to GE, 3M completed only 10 acquisitions between January 2000 and December 2004 and spent only a little more than $500 million on these deals in total.

MITY Enterprises MITY Enterprises designs, manufactures, and markets innovative furniture for use by institutional clients, such as schools, churches, hospitals, and government agencies. Founded in 1987, the company's first product was an innovative lightweight, yet durable, folding-leg table that could be used in situations that required affordable multiuse furniture. Over the years, the company added tables of multiple sizes. The company noticed that most customers ordering tables also needed chairs as well. In its early years, customers were referred to other manufacturers for these purchases. Eventually, the company diversified into chair manufacturing as its first venture away from tables. The company developed a process for making stacking chairs that utilized the same heat-and-vacuum thermoforming process for molding engineering-grade plastics that was used to make tables. After the development of this new product line, MITY's sales increased significantly because the stacking chairs could be sold in tandem with its tables. Later, through an acquisition, the company entered the market for specialty furniture used by long-term healthcare institutions.

The company focuses on meeting the needs for efficient, low-cost furniture for institutional use, not outfitting corporate boardrooms and executive offices. The company's line of multipurpose room furniture now includes such offerings as lightweight, durable, folding-leg tables (its original product), stacking chairs, folding chairs, lecterns, and other products used in multipurpose rooms. Through its subsidiary Broda Enterprises, the company designs, manufactures, and markets healthcare seating and accessories, which are used primarily by long-term healthcare facilities located in the United States and Canada.

As can be seen from these brief descriptions, firms are often involved in more than one business. Some firms, like GE, participate in an incredible number of seemingly unrelated business operations. Others, like 3M, have grown into many businesses but seem to be clustered in a few related industries. Other firms, like MITY Enterprises, are smaller companies, but they, too, seem to grow to a point where they venture out of their original businesses to experiment in other product lines. In this chapter, we will introduce you to the basic concepts necessary to understand and manage corporate strategy, including the diversification of firms. ■

CORPORATE STRATEGY

Why would a firm that makes light bulbs also make elevators? If you're in the table business, does it make sense to be in the chair business, too? If your core business activities result in innovative new products, should you retain ownership of these products and the units responsible for them, or does it make more sense to sell them? Questions such as these are fundamental to corporate strategy.

As we pointed out in Chapter 1 and have emphasized throughout this book, *corporate strategy* must address issues related to decisions about entering or exiting an industry. Specifically, effective corporate strategies must answer three interrelated questions:

- In which business *arenas* should a company compete?
- Which *vehicles* should it use to enter or exit a business?
- What underlying *economic logic* makes it sensible to compete in multiple businesses?

At the same time, however, corporate strategy also deals with issues affecting the overall management of a multibusiness enterprise, such as top-level efforts to orchestrate cross-business-unit synergies. **Synergy** is the case when the combined benefits of a firm's activities in two or more arenas are more than the simple sum of those benefits alone. After all, corporate-level strategy must maintain strategic coherence across business units and facilitate cooperation (or competition) among units in order to create value for shareholders. Thus, although fundamentally related to each other through the common goal of achieving competitive advantage, business strategy and corporate strategy have different objectives.

synergy Condition under which the combined benefits of activities in two or more arenas are greater than the simple sum of those benefits

Most large and publicly traded firms are amalgamations of business units operating in multiple product, service, and geographic markets (often globally); they are rarely single-business operations. Obviously, companies approach corporate strategy in different ways, and as you can see from Exhibit 7.1, corporate portfolios can be built in a number of different ways. Although MITY Enterprises has diversified into new products, they're all related to the institutional-furniture market niche. At the other end of the spectrum, GE not only makes everything from light bulbs to locomotives, but offers financial services for virtually any business or consumer need. In between, we find 3M, whose business units, though highly diversified, reflect common core competencies—the unique resources and knowledge that a company's management must consider when developing strategy—in innovation and adhesive technology.[2]

Exhibit 7.1 Diversification Profiles

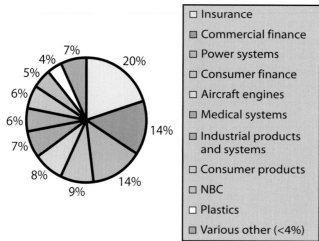

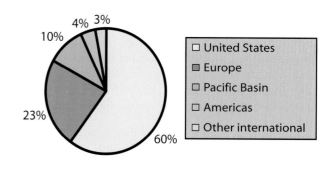

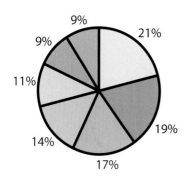

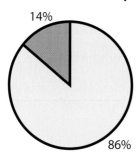

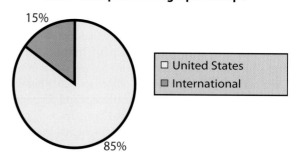

Recall that we introduced the important fact that most firms are multiproduct organizations in our earlier discussions of industry analysis, value chains, and market segmentation. That's why we're now going to discuss in some detail the ways in which managers can create (and squander) value through **diversification**. In this chapter, we'll focus on six key aspects of corporate strategy as it affects diversification decisions:

diversification Degree to which a firm conducts business in more than one arena

1. We'll review our understanding of corporate strategy and define *diversification* and show how both concepts have changed over time.

2. We'll identify the potential sources of economic gain that make diversification attractive.

3. We'll describe alternative forms of diversification.

4. We'll present a rationale, or logic, for guiding corporate decisions about adding businesses.

5. We'll revisit the relationship between corporate strategy and competitive advantage.

6. We'll amplify our discussion of the roles of corporate strategy in dynamic contexts.

We will build our discussion around many of the elements of the strategy diamond. This framework is useful because it allows you to choose those elements of strategy formulation and implementation that are essential to developing a firm's corporate strategy under specific conditions. As was made apparent in the Chapter's opening vignette, a firm's corporate strategy usually evolves over time. All three of our firms in the vignette have entered and/or exited business arenas. They have used the various major vehicles of strategy to facilitate these changes. The economic logic of diversification often incorporates such levers to achieve synergy and transfer knowledge between business units. The timing and pacing of such moves must be orchestrated in ways that do not negate the possible benefits of diversification.

The Evolution of Diversification in the United States

In the United States, the first form of organizational diversification was probably **vertical integration**. In order to secure needed resources, large firms often moved "upstream" in the industry value chain—that is, closer to the source of the raw materials they needed.[3] Early on, for example, General Motors began operating its own steel plants in order to supply its auto-frame and body factories. During the early phases of the industrialization of the United States, many large firms also began investing in businesses that, though related to their operations, were not part of their original industry value chains. DuPont, for instance, started out making gunpowder and eventually applied the scientific discoveries generated by that business to enter new businesses, such as dynamite and nitroglycerine (1880), guncotton (1892), and smokeless powder (1894). Ultimately, DuPont controlled most of the U.S. explosives market. The company then diversified into paints, plastics, and dyes until antitrust action forced it to divest some of its explosive powder business.

conceptlink

In Chapter 5, we underscore the importance of the **staging** element of the **strategy diamond** in competing in turbulent environments; in particular, we stress the need to manage the speed and pace of strategically planned changes.

vertical integration Diversification into upstream and/or downstream industries

John D. Rockefeller conglomerated hundreds of oil companies in the 1800s into a "trust" called Standard Oil. Although the companies were supposed to operate independently from one another, they worked like a monopoly, controlling the price and flow of oil in the industry. The U.S. government broke up Standard Oil in 1881, but not before Rockefeller had become the richest man in the world.

In the late nineteenth century, the booming U.S. economy fostered a period of rapid consolidation. The Sherman Act of 1890 introduced federal antitrust law and led to the eventual breakup of many large monopolistic companies. In 1891, for instance, the courts ordered Rockefeller's Standard Oil to split into six separate companies. Similar rulings broke up other companies deemed to be anticompetitive.

By the 1960s, many large firms began expanding into areas unrelated to their core businesses, because this type of growth was generally exempt from antitrust restrictions. Unrelated diversification became a corporate strategy of choice, and soon a breed of corporations emerged that was characterized by curious mixes of operations. ITT's portfolio managed to accommodate telephones, donuts, hotels, and insurance. For a brief history of the diversification of ITT over time, see Exhibit 7.2.

Although it addressed certain problems entailed by antitrust constraints, the **conglomerate** model raised new issues of its own. How could a company manage a portfolio of far-flung enterprises? The need to address such questions fostered experiments in new management tools and models. One of the most popular of these tools was **portfolio planning**. Without knowing it, you are probably already familiar with the conglomerate version of portfolio planning. With this tool, a company identified all of its businesses that were "dogs"—those businesses in which it didn't have a strong competitive position and that were located in bad industries. Such businesses were sold. Businesses that had very strong competitive positions but were in slow-growth industries were referred to as "cash cows." Portfolio planning dictated that cash cows should be maintained because the cash flow could be channeled into promising high-growth businesses ("stars"). This simplistic portfolio-planning approach has been debunked. The most basic reason is that it provides

conglomerate Corporation consisting of many companies in different businesses or industries

portfolio planning Practice of mapping diversified businesses or products based on their relative strengths and market attractiveness

Exhibit 7.2   A Brief History and Genealogy of a Conglomerate

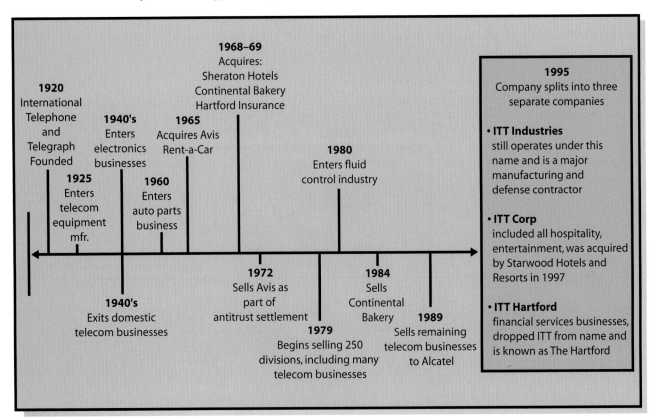

no fundamental competitive logic for which businesses should be entered and which should be maintained. Such overly simplistic tools led to such questionable diversification moves as telecommunications companies entering the hotel industry simply because the growth opportunities were attractive.

Shareholder dissatisfaction, especially on the part of institutional investors, coupled with the threat of hostile takeover opportunities, put pressure on conglomerates to reorganize in more manageable forms. Unwieldy portfolios of unrelated business units began to give way to more focused portfolios of related operations.[4] This move toward a more focused corporation can be seen in the more recent years of ITT, as illustrated in Exhibit 7.2.

Business history is littered with stories of failed growth and diversification strategies. The lesson taught by such cases is pretty clear: In and of itself, diversification not only doesn't necessarily create shareholder value but may in fact dissipate it. However, as we'll see later in the chapter, the logic behind *certain types* of diversification remains compelling. Indeed, substantial empirical evidence indicates that some forms of diversification can create significant shareholder wealth. Which types or forms of diversification are these? In the next part of the chapter, we'll identify and discuss the conditions necessary for value creation and the tools that can be used to increase its likelihood.

concept link

Recall that among the "three overarching themes" which we introduced in Chapter 1 was the following dictum: "Strategic leadership is essential if a firm is to both formulate and implement *strategies that create value.*" A few pages later, we proposed three fundamental questions of **corporate strategy**, including: "How can we, as a corporate parent, *add value* to our various lines of business?"

ECONOMIC LOGIC OF DIVERSIFICATION: SYNERGY

Expanding the firm's scope—whether the addition of new vertical, horizontal, complementary, or geographic arenas—doesn't necessarily create value for shareholders. Strategists need to understand the sources of potential value creation from diversification, and they need to know how to determine whether a firm can leverage those sources. That's why we're going to turn to two concepts that are critical in evaluating opportunities for diversification and value creation: *economies of scope* and *revenue-enhancement opportunities*. Collectively, these are often referred to as *synergy*.

Economies of Scope

We introduced the concept of economy of scope in Chapter 5, where we simply associated it with a firm's success in sharing a resource among one or more of its products. In this chapter, we'll provide a more complete definition and explain why economies of scope are one of the two key factors in determining whether a corporate strategy is adding value through the diversification of its business portfolio.

As you learned in Chapter 5, economies of scope are reductions in average costs that result from producing two or more products jointly instead of producing them separately. Economies of scope are possible when the company can leverage a resource or value chain activity across more than one product, service, or geographic arena. Although we focus on productive resources for the sake of presentation, you should recognize that economies of scope are possible in all value-chain activities, not simply production. For instance, comarketing of two products may provide cost savings (it may also help increase revenue-enhancement synergies).

Sources of Economies of Scope
What tactics result in economies of scope? Economy-of-scope savings generally result when a firm uses common resources across business units. Or to put it another way: Whenever a common resource can be used across more than one business unit, the company has the *potential* to generate economies of scope. If, for instance, the cost of material that's common to two or more products is lower when purchased in greater quantity, then jointly producing two products may increase purchase volume and, therefore, cut costs. The ability to join the procurement function in this case and buy materials jointly creates an economy of scope.

Likewise, a manufacturing facility that achieves minimum efficient scale for one product may have excess capacity that it can put to use in producing other products. In this case, the total cost for both products will be lower because the cost of the common facility can be spread across two businesses. Sometimes the common resource is located farther down the firm's value chain. For instance, if a firm distributes products through a system with access to a large customer base, it may be able to add products to that system more cheaply than competitors launching similar new products that may need to create dedicated distribution networks from scratch. Coke and Pepsi enjoy such economies of scope in the markets for soft drinks, noncarbonated beverages, and bottled water.

Revenue-Enhancement Synergies

Another manifestation of synergy and a measure of whether a portfolio of businesses jointly held under single corporate ownership creates more value than independent ownership is revenue enhancement through joint ownership. Revenue-enhancement synergy exists when the whole is greater than the sum of the parts. Simply put, if two business units are able to generate more revenue because they're collectively owned by a single corporate parent, the strategy of common ownership is synergistic. Revenue-enhancement synergy may result from a variety of tactics, such as bundling products that were previously sold separately, sharing complementary knowledge in the interest of new-product innovation, or increasing shared distribution opportunities.

Consider how Disney leverages its various resources to create revenue-enhancement synergies. The result of its web of collaborative activities is a consistent stream of new revenue sources that demonstrate a direct line between creativity in product design and financial acumen.[5] At the same time, Disney's collaborative context doesn't specify the forms that synergies must take; it merely reflects the principle that they should be profitable for all of the units involved. Two movies, for example, *The Little Mermaid* and *The Lion King*, became television shows. Another, *Toy Story*, was rolled out as a video game. Both *The Lion King* and another movie, *Beauty and the Beast*, became smash-hit Broadway musicals. The managers of Disney Tokyo share best practices with managers at Disney World in Orlando and Euro Disney outside Paris. Big Red Boat, a cruise line that specializes in Caribbean vacations, and Disney World, which offers vacation packages in Orlando on Florida's east coast, collaborate to build traffic in both venues. Characters from one animated series make cameos in others, and all shows are circulated through Disney's line up of cable- and network-television channels, which include all or part of ABC, ESPN, A&E, E! Entertainment, and The History Channel. The voices of both live-action and animated characters circulate through Radio Disney.

Sources of Revenue-Enhancement Synergies   Revenue-enhancement synergies generally arise from bundling and joint-selling opportunities. In recent years, for example, firms in the financial-services industry have been actively acquiring or merging with firms in adjacent sectors in order to bundle products for current customers in different sectors.

A more specific example is found in the opening vignette. Founded in Orem, Utah, in 1987, MITY Enterprises originally made folding tables targeted at such institutional users as schools and churches. A decade later, when the company found itself with excess capacity in its Orem plant, managers began thinking about growth options. Because MITY's technology could be used to manufacture chairs and other types of furniture as well as tables, the company decided to expand into complementary products. MITY thus achieved synergy in two ways:

- Because expansion didn't require a new plant, the cost of the existing facility was spread across the various operations needed for different products.
- Because its manufacturing and distribution operations were geared toward multiple products, MITY's customers were more likely to buy more than one of its products, thus generating incremental sales that the firm could not otherwise have gained.

Similarly, firms in various sectors of the financial-services industry have been actively acquiring and merging with firms in adjacent sectors in order to be able to bundle related products and cross sell to existing customers.

Economic Benefits of Diversification

Because mutual gains may be derived from either cost savings or revenue-enhancement synergies, a corporation that maintains ownership over multiple business units may have an advantage over competing businesses that are owned and managed separately. A company achieves this so-called "parenting advantage" when the joint cash flows of two or more collectively owned business units exceed the sum of the cash flows that they would generate independently.

When their collective market value exceeds the independent market values of a portfolio of business units, the financial markets will typically recognize the existence of a parenting advantage. Of course, the market doesn't compare business units by assigning both collective and independent value. Investors, however, can make reasonable estimates of a business unit's potential independent value. How? By using the market multiples (e.g., price earnings ratios or other similar multiples) of independent competitors in the industry within which its business units compete to compare the parent corporation's market value with the combined hypothetical values of its business units.

How and When to Seek Synergy   Two processes can generate synergy: sharing resources and transferring capabilities. We've discussed resource sharing extensively in our discussion of economies of scope. Transferring capabilities is actually a special case of resource sharing that can create both cost savings and revenue-enhancement. Yum! Brands, for instance, can transfer knowledge about site location, franchise development, and internationalization from one restaurant brand to another. Black & Decker can share knowledge about small electric motors across its power-tool and kitchen-appliance units. Honda transfers knowledge gained about high-performance engines from its Formula-1 racing activities not only to its automobile division, but also to units that produce motorcycles and lawn-care and recreational equipment.

Limits of Diversification Benefits

Remember, however, that neither economies of scope nor revenue enhancement materialize simply because firms expand into new lines of business. In other words, it's not *necessarily* cheaper to produce two products jointly in a single firm than separately in distinct firms. Indeed, in many cases, diversification creates **diseconomies of scope**—average cost increases resulting from the joint output of two or more products within a single firm.

diseconomies of scope Condition under which the joint output of two or more products within a single firm results in increased average costs

The critical question is *when economies of scope are likely to materialize*. Often, firms that can't demonstrate that diversification has generated economies of scope or revenue-enhancement synergies are forced to divest themselves of some units. During the 1990s, AT&T attempted to reap synergies across such businesses as long-distance telephone services, wireless cell-phone service, and cable TV. However, it was never able to generate the cross-selling and synergistic outcomes it projected. Thus, in 2002 the company made the decision to split the company apart; some divisions were split off as separate companies, others were sold to competitors. The restructuring at AT&T reflects a failed diversification strategy; the sale of the surviving long-distance company to SBC Communications further testifies that AT&T's forays into new industries did not create the value and shareholder enthusiasm its leaders had hoped for. Ironically, SBC Communications changed their name to AT&T after acquiring the company. But, names can be deceiving; it is the shareholders and managers of SBC Communications that now own and manage the assets of the original AT&T long distance company. Of course, such divestitures are not always the result of failed diversification. Sometimes, a firm is quite successful but because of a change in strategy decides to divest itself of some successful businesses.

As the AT&T example illustrates, it often turns out that the collective value of a firm's portfolio is less than the total hypothetical value of the same businesses operated independently. In this case, the strategy of common ownership dissipates potential shareholder value. When investors—and corporate raiders, in particular—suspect the prospect of a significant diversification discount—the profits to be gained from buying the parent firm and selling off its portfolio piecemeal—a firm becomes a prime candidate for takeover and forced restructuring. Many investors have made huge profits by gaining control of an overly diversified company and selling various parts to firms in related areas—firms that are often willing to pay premium prices for operations related to their own.

Two things increase a firm's level of diversification: the number of separate businesses it operates and the degree of relatedness of those businesses. Relatedness is typically assessed by how similar the underlying industries are. The most diversified firms are those that own lots of businesses in very disparate industries; this is known as **unrelated diversification**. Firms that own many businesses clustered in a few industries are pursuing what is known as **related diversification**. Both forms of diversification can create management problems.

The harmful side effects of too much diversification include increased transaction and bureaucratic costs and burgeoning complexity. As firms become larger and multidivisional, corporate office functions tend to grow rapidly. If not held in check, these bureaucratic costs may exceed the benefits of diversification. Likewise, diverse firms may fall victim to doing too much internally and underutilize outside suppliers. Often the transaction costs of sourcing externally are sufficiently lower than the costs of organizing this activity internally. Finally, diversification increases firm complexity. For instance, the organization of a firm with 10 businesses that span 5 industries is inherently more complex than a firm of the same size that operates only in one or a few industries. Complex firms are more difficult to manage than simple, focused firms. Research shows, for example, that diversified firms pay significantly higher compensation to attract and retain top management personnel than more focused firms of similar size.[6] Why? Because there are fewer top executives who are capable of managing complex firms. Bureaucratic costs, transaction costs, and complexity can all impede management's designs to create synergies.

If diversified firms are more difficult to manage—that is, if it's demonstrably harder to realize the benefits of diversification—then it stands to reason that there are real limits to those benefits. Indeed, research indicates that there's a point at which both the benefits of diversification and firm performance begin to decline. Exhibit 7.3 illustrates the relationship between diversification and two measures of firm performance—*return on assets* (ROA) and *total shareholder returns* (TSR). In analyzing the data for the S&P 500 and S&P midcap firms over an eight-year period, we find that the relationship between diversification and performance takes the form of an inverted U (∩). At the median level of diversification, performance is much higher than at low levels of diversification (25th percentile) or

unrelated diversification Form of diversification in which the business units that a firm operates are highly dissimilar

related diversification Form of diversification in which the business units operated by a firm are highly related

Exhibit 7.3 Diversification and Performance in S&P 500 and S&P Midcap Firms (1992–2000)

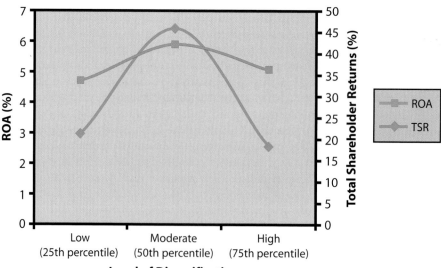

high levels of diversification (75th percentile). These findings tell us that, on average, although diversification seems to benefit shareholders up to a point, it begins to dissipate value at high levels of diversification. Moderate values are typically achieved by firms which, like 3M, are active in several businesses that are somewhat related to each other.

When examining the relationship between diversification and performance reviewed in Exhibit 7.3, it is important to understand that there are exceptions to these averages. Some highly diversified firms perform quite well. For instance, GE is very diversified and over the long-term has performed very well, much better than most firms diversified at that level (and even single business firms). High levels of diversification, such as the conglomerate firm, can be very effective strategies in countries with developing capital markets. When capital markets are not as efficient as they are in developed countries, diversified firms can internally generate lower costs of capital than they can obtain in capital markets. Consequently, it can be efficient for firms to diversify and own more businesses than would be efficient in countries such as the United States, the United Kingdom, or Germany.

Resource Relatedness and Competitive Similarity

To create economies of scope and revenue-enhancement synergies, a firm's resources should match its business activities. For this reason, whether they're thinking about entering a new business arena or evaluating the suitability of a firm's portfolio for a proposed diversification move, strategists must assess the extent to which a firm's resources and capabilities match the needs of potential subsidiaries. One way to assess this match is in terms of how related the businesses are. When unrelated diversification is taken to the extreme—when there are many businesses and they are largely unrelated—firms are referred to as *conglomerates*. When there's a good match between the resource needs of parent and subsidiary—when diversification is related—it's more likely to create value. It's not critical, however, that both parent and subsidiary possess the *same* set of resources and capabilities. Indeed, in seeking to diversify, many firms are trying to acquire and bundle complementary resources and capabilities. The key issue is whether the match or fit between resources will help the parties compete more effectively.

Dominant Logic   Parent firms and their subsidiaries need to assess their fit on more than just the resources it takes to compete. In determining fit, we want to know if the combined firm can better compete both in its own industries and in that of the subsidiary. In turn, the key issue is the consistency of each firm's *dominant logic* with that of the other. **Dominant logic** refers to the way in which managers view the firm's competitive activities and make critical resource-allocation decisions. A multibusiness firm is a collection of dominant logics, and effective management depends on the similarity of these various logics. In general, it is easier to manage a firm that does not require dissimilar dominant logics across business units. For instance, the jobs of the top executives at 3M and GE are significantly more complex than at MITY Enterprises—and this would be the case even if MITY were as large as these other firms.

If the dominant logics of its businesses are similar, a firm's managers can respond more quickly and effectively to strategic issues. Conversely, when dominant logics differ significantly, managers will generally be slower and less decisive. Decision-making delays can be hazardous, especially in high-speed industries such as cell phones and computer peripherals; perhaps more important, dissimilarity in dominant logic increases the likelihood that when managers finally do make decisions they'll make bad ones.

Not surprisingly, the strategic characteristics of businesses in a diversified portfolio may vary widely. Two businesses, for instance, may depend on very different technologies, industry competitive structures, and customer-buying routines. Strategic variability, therefore, can make it much more difficult to manage the portfolio. The more similar the contexts across which its businesses compete, the easier it is to manage a firm's portfolio and to create value through economies of scope and revenue-enhancement synergy.

conceptlink

We introduced the criterion of fit in a slightly different context in Chapter 5, where we discussed the need for a **business strategy** to *fit* the conditions currently prevailing in an industry.

dominant logic Way in which managers view a firm's competitive activities and make corporate resource-allocation decisions

The maximum opportunities to exploit potential economies of scope and revenue enhancement synergies lie at the intersection of two dimensions: (1) the fit among parent–subsidiary resources and (2) the fit of parent–subsidiary dominant logics. Conversely, the least promising opportunity for creating value through common ownership occurs when there's a misfit on both of the same dimensions. When there's a misfit, managers need to make organizational adjustments. Later in this chapter, we'll present two models that can help determine these adjustments.

Ulterior Motives for Diversification

In addition to reducing costs and increasing revenue-enhancement opportunities, managers may have self-serving motives for diversification—motives that aren't necessarily in shareholders' best interests. Among these, we'll mention three: *risk reduction*, *empire building*, and *compensation*.

At first glance, risk reduction would seem to be a natural reason for diversifying. In fact, it's probably the reason cited most often by students who haven't yet been formally introduced to the pros and cons of corporate diversification. Why isn't the strategy of reducing risk by diversifying generally in shareholders' best interests? Because it's much cheaper for the shareholders themselves to diversify in other ways. They can, for example, diversify equity risk by building a diversified stock portfolio—a strategy that, compared to the cost of diversifying a corporate portfolio, is fairly inexpensive.

When executives embark on growth and diversification because they desire to manage a larger company, they are said to be engaging in empire building. Rarely will empire building result in shareholder value or higher margins. However, empire building almost always results in greater notoriety and prestige for top executives. Although some executives may pursue empire building simply because of hubris, there are opportunistic reasons why they would do so as well. This simple reason is that executives of larger companies are paid more than executives of smaller companies. The main determinant of how much CEOs are paid is company size. Therefore, growing and diversifying the company generally results in executives being paid more.

FORMS OF SCOPE AND DIVERSIFICATION

A firm that wants to expand the scope of its operations has several options. In this section, we'll show how a company can expand its arenas, the three dimensions of *vertical*, *horizontal*, and *geographic*.

Vertical Scope

vertical scope The extent to which a firm is vertically integrated

concept link

In Chapter 4, where we introduced the **five-forces model** of industry structure, we explained that **buyer power** sometimes poses the threat of *backward (vertical) integration*, whereby a powerful buyer could take over the function of a supplier.

Sometimes a firm expands its **vertical scope** out of economic necessity. Perhaps it must protect its supply of a critical input, or perhaps firms in the industry that supply certain inputs are reluctant to invest sufficiently to satisfy the unique or heavy needs of a single buyer. Beyond such reasons as these—which are defensive—firms expand vertically to take advantage of growth opportunities. Vertical expansion in scope is often a logical growth option because a company is familiar with the arena that it's entering.

In some cases, a firm can create value by moving into suppliers' or buyers' value chains if it can bundle complementary products. If, for instance, you were to buy a new home, you'd go through a series of steps in making your purchase decision. Now, most homebuilders concentrate on a fairly narrow aspect of the homebuilding value chain. Some, however, have found it profitable to expand vertically into the home-financing business by offering mortgage-brokerage services. Pulte Homes Inc., one of the largest homebuilders in the country, set up a wholly owned subsidiary, Pulte Mortgage LLC, to help buyers get financing for new homes. This service not only simplifies the home-buying process for many of Pulte's customers, but it also allows Pulte to reap profits in the home-financing industry. Automakers and dealers have expanded into financing for similar reasons.

Homebuilders like Pulte and D.R. Horton have found a way to create value by moving down the home-buyer's value chain. Both companies now offer mortgage services, a complementor to the home building industry, making it easier for customers to buy their homes. Pulte and D.R. Horton benefit as well because they earn the revenues associated with mortgage financing.

The Pitfalls of Increased Vertical Scope Although a firm's business segments lie adjacent along an industry's value chain, the structural features of the industries of these business segments (e.g., the industry five forces and complementors) may be fundamentally different. Thus, even though an adjacent segment is profitable, it doesn't follow that it's a good area for a firm to enter. Perhaps, for example, the firm doesn't have the resources needed to compete against established firms. Similarly, incumbents may enjoy significant cost advantages in performing the activities of their segment. Finally, the unwritten rules of competition in a segment, as well as the nature of strategic interactions, may be fundamentally different from those in a firm's base industry. A company should conduct thorough internal, industry, and competitor analyses before moving vertically into an adjacent segment of its industry value chain.

Horizontal Scope

A firm increases its **horizontal scope** in one of two ways:

- By moving from an industry market segment into another, related segment
- By moving from one industry into another (unlike vertical-scope expansion, the movement here is into other industries not in the firm's existing value chain of activities)

The degree to which horizontal expansion is desirable depends on the degree to which the new industry is related to a firm's home industry. Industries can be related in a number of different ways. They may, for example, rely on similar types of human capital, engage in similar value-chain activities, or share customers with similar needs. Obviously, the more such factors that are present, the greater the degree of relatedness. When, for example, Coke and Pepsi expanded into the bottled-water business, they were able to take advantage of the skill sets that they'd already developed in bottling and distribution. Moreover, because bottled water and soft drinks are substitutes for one another, both appeal to customers with similar demands.

However, when Pepsi expanded into snack foods, it was clearly moving into a business with a lesser degree of relatedness. Although the distribution channels for both businesses are similar (both sell products through grocery stores, convenience stores, delis, and so forth), the technology for producing their products are fundamentally different. In addition, although the two industries sell complementary products—they're often sold at the same time to the same customers—they aren't substitutes.

concept**link**

As we explained in Chapter 4, Porter's **five forces model** of industry structure includes **rivalry**, **supplier power**, **buyer power**, **threat of substitutes**, and *threat of new entrants*. Recall that we added a sixth force—threat of **complementors**.

concept**link**

We discuss *competitive interaction theory* in Chapter 6, where we describe the nature of competitive actions and reactions among firms in an industry or segment.

horizontal scope Extent to which a firm participates in related market segments or industries outside its existing value-chain activities

Cost Savings and Revenue Enhancement Opportunities   Why is increased horizontal scope attractive? Primarily because it offers opportunities in two areas:

- The firm can reduce costs by exploiting possible economies of scope.
- The firm can increase revenues through synergies.

Because segments in closely related industries often use similar assets and resources, a firm can frequently achieve cost savings by sharing them among businesses in different segments. The fast-food industry, for instance, has many segments—burgers, fried chicken, tacos, pizza, and so on. YUM! Brands Inc., which operates KFC, Pizza Hut, Taco Bell, A&W Restaurants, and Long John Silvers, has embarked on what the company calls a "multi-brand" store strategy. Rather than house all of its fast-food restaurants in separate outlets, YUM! achieves economies of scope across its portfolio by bundling two outlets in a single facility. The strategy works, in part, because customer purchase decisions in horizontally related industries are often made simultaneously: In other words, two people walking into a bundled fast-food outlet may desire different things to eat, but both want fast food, and both are going to eat at the same time. In addition, some of these combinations allow two food services that cater to purchases with different peak hours to share physical resources that would otherwise be largely unused during off-peak hours.

Profit Pools   One tool managers can use to evaluate adjacent market opportunities (whether vertical, horizontal, or complementary) is the **profit pool**. Beginning with a modified version of the firm and industry value chain, the profit pool incorporates key complementary businesses near the point at which a firm is directly involved in customer transactions. The profit pool helps managers identify the size of value-chain segments (according to total sales) and the attractiveness of each segment (according to segment-by-segment profitability). As a map of the industry value chain, it reveals the breadth and depth of its alternative profit pools—each of the points along an industry's value chain at which total profits can be calculated.[7] Exhibit 7.4 illustrates the application of this tool to the U.S. auto industry.

Some profit pools, of course, will be deeper (i.e., more profitable) than others. Moreover, depth may vary within a given value-chain segment. In the manufacturing segment of the PC industry, for instance, Dell enjoys much higher profit margins than Gateway.

profit pool Analytical tool that enables managers to calculate profits at various points along an industry value chain

Exhibit 7.4   The U.S. Auto Industry's Profit Pool

Source: Adapted from O. Gadiesh and J. L. Gilbert, "Profit Pools: A Fresh Look at Strategy". Harvard Business Review, *(76:3) 1998, 139-147.*

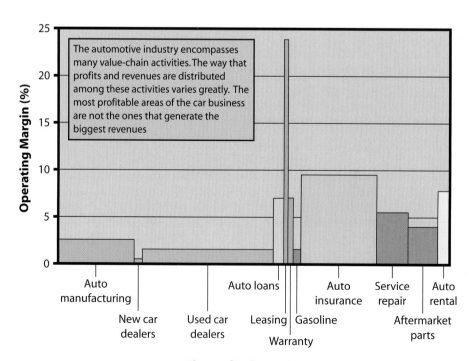

Segment profitability may also vary widely by product and customer group. Note that profit pools aren't stagnant; like industries in general, they change over time. Finally, and perhaps most importantly, the profit pool reminds us that *profit* concentration in an industry rarely occurs in the same place as *revenue* concentration.

Thinking in terms of profit pools also highlights a basic managerial mistake that's often made when developing corporate strategy. Firms often pursue strategies that focus on growth and market share on the assumption that profits automatically follow growth and size. *Profitable* growth, however, requires a clear understanding of an industry's profit pool. A profit-pool map, for example, will reveal the segments in which money is actually being made in an industry. More importantly, it may show where profits *could* be made. Consider, for instance, the consumer truck-rental business, in which U-Haul, Ryder, Hertz-Penske, and Budget are fierce competitors.[8] U-Haul, though the first entrant and largest player, faced significant disadvantages in the 1990s. Because its fleet was older, its maintenance expenses were considerably higher than those of competitors with newer fleets. U-Haul also charged lower prices than competitors. Lower revenues, coupled with higher expenses, generally result in lower margins. Indeed, U-Haul was barely breaking even on truck rentals. At the same time, however, U-Haul actually outperformed all of its competitors. Why? U-Haul beat its competitors because it went beyond its core business of truck rentals. It seized opportunities in complementary businesses that were relatively untapped, such as moving and storage accessories. By selling boxes, trailers, temporary storage space, tape, and other packing materials that truck renters would need, U-Haul squeezed out 10-percent operating margins in an industry in which the average was less than 3 percent.

Geographic Scope

A firm typically increases **geographic scope** by moving into new geographic arenas without altering its business model. In its early growth period, for instance, a company may simply move into new locations in the same country. More often, however, increased geographic scope has come to mean *internationalization*—entering new markets in other parts of the world.

geographic scope Breadth and diversity of geographic arenas in which a firm operates

For a domestic firm whose operations are confined to its home country, the whole globe consists of potential arenas for expansion. Remember, however, that just as different industries can exhibit different degrees of relatedness, so, too, can different geographic markets, even those within the same industry. We can assess relatedness among different national markets by examining a number of factors, including laws, customs, cultures, consumer preferences, distances from home markets, common boarders, language, socio-economic development, and many others. We do so in Chapter 8.

Economies of Scale and Scope Geographic expansion can be motivated by economies of scale or economies of scope. R&D, for example, represents a significant, relatively fixed cost for firms in many industries, and when they move into new regions of a country or global arenas, they often find that they can spread their R&D costs over a larger market. For instance, the marginal cost for a pharmaceutical firm to enter a new geographic market is lower compared to the R&D and clinical-trial costs entailed in bringing a new drug into the U.S. market. Once the costs of development and entry are covered, entering new geographic markets not only brings in new revenues, but because fixed costs have been spread over the new, larger market, the average cost for all the firm's customers goes down. It should come as no surprise, then, that industries with relatively high R&D expenditures, such as pharmaceuticals and hi-tech products, are among the most globalized.

Strategy and the Local Environment Sometimes, firms expanding into new geographic markets find that they must adapt certain components of their strategies to accommodate local environments. In this country, for instance, Dell is famous for the business model that allows it to skip middlemen and go directly to suppliers and customers. In its early years, Dell experimented with a retail-distribution strategy but quickly retrenched. As it has expanded into some international markets such as India and China, however, Dell has found that it must, at least temporarily, delay the implementation of its direct model, at least for the consumer and small business markets, even though it worked well for

In the United States, Dell has traditionally sold its computers straight to consumers without going through intervening middlemen or retail stores. In Asia, however, this strategy works only with institutional buyers, such as governments, schools, and businesses. As a result, Dell had to change its distribution strategy there.

government and large business buyers. Why? Basically because it needs local intermediaries to help develop both a base of business and acceptable levels of awareness among those particular buyers. Once the market has been penetrated to a sufficient degree, the direct model is implemented and used to reach consumers and small businesses.

Although Dell provides a nice example of adaptation, most global firms tend to approach the subject of corporate strategy from the perspective of their domestic market—can be problematic. Microsoft is a case in point here. The respective regulatory authorities of the United States and the countries of the EU employ very different traditions and models of competition, which in turn means that strategies must vary across these important markets. Had you not been aware of these differences, you might think that Microsoft implemented an ideal resource-based corporate strategy in its diversification into Europe. It bundled its Windows operating system with the Explorer browser and other software to increase customers' perceptions of value and, therefore, willingness to pay. It also used its extensive experience with PC software and operating systems and applications to better penetrate the market for software and operating systems in the server market, where customers are primarily businesses. Finally, Microsoft also tried to lock out competitors by including its Media Player as a standard feature in both its server and home PC operating systems.

The EU took exception to this strategy.[9] The European Commission recently signaled it would keep up the pressure on Microsoft, saying the company's "illegal behavior is still ongoing." It also warned that it remains concerned about Microsoft's "general business model," saying that it "deters innovation and reduces consumer choice in any technologies which Microsoft could conceivably take an interest in and tie with Windows in the future." In addition to a fine of over $600 million, the EU gave Microsoft 90 days to release versions of its Windows operating systems for home PCs and servers without the Windows Media Player and begin providing rivals access to the details of the code underlying its proprietary server systems. This is not the first time such differences in regulatory environments have been ignored or underestimated by global firms. Just a few years earlier, the European Commission's ruling dealt a fatal blow to the all-but-done merger between Honeywell and GE.[10]

WHO SHOULD OWN THE BUSINESS?

Should a company own a subsidiary or buy a new business just because it appears that value can be created by owning the business? Perhaps not. Such a decision should be based on answers to two questions, both dealing with the process of creating shareholder value:

- Does the business unit add value to the corporation?
- Does the corporation owning the business unit add more value than alternative ways of linking a business to the corporation?

Determining Comparative Value

A good litmus test for determining whether a firm should own a particular business is whether owning it creates shareholder value. It's not always easy to apply, but there are ways by which managers and investors can put it to use. A firm with a diversified portfolio, for instance, can see how its own market and financial performance stands up to the performance of more focused competitors in the same industries in which it operates individual units. Although the statistical and econometric procedures for making such comparisons are beyond the scope of this text, most experienced managers can intuitively answer the question by simplifying it. Basically, they ask themselves whether the corporation would be worth more as is (i.e., owning its business units) than if the business units were owned by shareholders as separate entities. Or, in the case of considering expansion into new businesses, they ask not only whether their company will be worth more jointly with the new business (controlling for the increased investment needed), but also if the business would be worth more if it accessed the resources of the target business in an alternative way. For instance, rather than buying the business, the company could strike an alliance to gain access to what is needed. The alternatives need to be compared in juxtaposition to each other. The decision should not focus simply on whether value is created but whether the most value is created.

Common ownership may be less valuable than separate ownership for a number of reasons. One is simply the cost of overhead. Any value created by owning a new business should exceed the overhead costs incurred by owning the additional business. Second, if a firm is so diversified that corporate complexity diminishes the effectiveness of management, then separate ownership may very well create more value than the company owning the new business.

How to Create Value

How do we know if ownership of two or more businesses adds value for shareholders? We ask ourselves whether the firm's financial or market performance is better because its businesses are bundled instead of separately owned. If the answer is yes, we can move on to two other issues pertaining to the value created by different forms of ownership: (1) the issue of *ownership versus alliance* and (2) the issue of *mode of entry*.

Alternatives to Direct Ownership Even if analysis suggests that common ownership makes a portfolio more valuable than separate ownership, managers must still pose further questions. In particular, they need to ask themselves if there are other ways to achieve the same value without the financial disadvantages entailed by direct ownership.

Instead of owning a new business outright, for example, a firm may be able to create value by entering an alliance or joint venture with another firm in the industry. As usual, there are both pluses and minuses. An alliance is typically less costly to manage than direct ownership, but it doesn't give the firm the advantages of ownership; the firm merely enjoys certain rights to share in the returns of a joint activity, but also incurs other risks. (We'll discuss alliances more fully in Chapter 9. At this point, you simply need to realize that an alliance is a viable alterative to direct ownership.)

Alternative Modes of Entry   What about alternative modes of entry? The two common modes of entry are (1) *internal development* and (2) *acquisition* of new businesses. Like level of ownership, mode of entry may affect shareholder value. Acquisitions, for instance, enable quick entry but entail significant upfront capital costs. Internal development may boast lower upfront costs, but the risks are high, and it generally takes a long time to build a business from scratch.

(We'll review the pros and cons of acquisitions in greater detail in Chapter 10. For now, simply remember that acquisitions—as well as divestitures—make it possible for a firm to change rapidly an arena in which it competes. Needless to say, the costs of acquiring and divesting business units will affect shareholder value.)

COMPETITIVE ADVANTAGE AND CORPORATE STRATEGY

At the business level, competitive advantage reflects the relative position of a firm compared to positions of industry rivals. At the corporate level, it reflects management's success in creating more value from the firm's business units than those units could create as stand-alone enterprises or subsidiaries. Our goal is to identify the conditions under which the strategy of owning a corporate portfolio of businesses creates value for shareholders.

You are already familiar with the element of arenas in business strategy. Sometimes a firm chooses a corporate strategy of competing in only one arena. However, the corporate strategy of many firms involves operating in more than one arena. Corporate strategy becomes more complicated if the competitive or operational characteristics of those arenas differ in some way, whether subtly or substantially. Ultimately, it is the combination of arenas, resources (i.e. VRINE), and implementation that determines whether the corporate strategy leads to competitive advantage.

Arenas

Theoretically, a firm can compete in any combination of discrete business arenas. In practice, of course, firms rarely enter arenas randomly but rather select those that are logically connected to the arenas in which they already participate. The key to logical connection is *relatedness*. Businesses can be related along several different dimensions, including similarity in markets, use of identical resources, and reliance on comparable dominant logic.

Resources provide the basis for corporate competitive advantage. The nature of corporate resources varies along a continuum, and whether the resources are specialized or general dictates the limits of a firm's scope and the manner of organizational control and coordination and the effectiveness of corporate headquarters. Although most firms maintain some degree of relatedness among the various businesses in which they participate, some combinations require greater relatedness than others. Finally, it's not always easy to determine the dimensions along which corporate businesses are related.

Some conglomerates are actually portfolios of strategic business units within which several related businesses are combined for management purposes. GE, for instance, participates in such far-flung enterprises as jet engines, elevators, light bulbs, appliances, and financial services. Each of these businesses, however, is located in a business unit with conceptually similar units.

Resources

As we saw in Chapter 3, resources and capabilities are tangible or intangible, and their usefulness in creating a competitive advantage depends on five factors: (1) how valuable they are, (2) whether they're rare in the industry, (3) whether they're costly to imitate, (4) the availability of substitutes, and (5) whether the firm has complementary capabilities to exploit them.

At this point, we need to remember that these factors apply to the usefulness of resources in creating competitive advantage at the *business* level. At the corporate level in the VRINE framework (e.g., valuable, rare, inimitable, nonsubstitutable, exploitable), they must be supplemented by an additional factor: namely, how *specialized* or *general* a firm's resources are.

Specialized Resources **Specialized resources** have a narrow range of applicability. Knowledge about fiber-optics, for example, is fairly specialized, whereas managerial know-how and skill are more general in nature. Granted, fiber-optics has many uses in multiple contexts (such as telecommunications, electronics, routing and switching equipment), but its utility is more limited than that of a general resource such as general managerial skill.

specialized resources Resource with a narrow range of applicability

General Resources **General resources** can be exploited across a wide range of activities. For instance, expertise in efficient manufacturing and mass-marketing techniques can be exploited in any number of contexts. In fact, many companies have created significant shareholder value by leveraging these general resources across different businesses engaged in a variety of industries. General resources aren't confined to narrow applications, and the extent of resource specialization affects both a firm's scope and its organizational structure.

general resources Resource that can be exploited across a wide range of activities

Implementation

As explained in Chapters 1 and 2 and will reaffirm in 11, *implementation levers* include organizational structure, systems and processes, and people and rewards. Strategic leaders use these levers to implement strategies. The success with which diversified firms are managed in accord with key organizational features has a significant effect on the level of value that can be created through their portfolios. Implementation levers that are critical for corporate strategy vary from firm to firm, but some of the more important levers to achieve successful diversification include knowledge-transfer mechanisms, coordination mechanisms, rewards, and corporate oversight.

concept**link**

In Chapter 1, we organized *implementation levers*—tools for executing a strategy—into three categories: (1) organization structure; (2) systems and processes; (3) people and rewards.

Knowledge transfer enables a diversified firm to apply superior performance results observed in one organizational business unit to other units that are not performing as well. In practice, knowledge transfer is difficult because it may not be entirely clear what is causing the superior performance in the high-performing unit. Three mechanisms facilitate knowledge transfer. First, just the knowledge that superior results are being achieved in another business unit can be used to reset performance expectations for future performance in other units. In this case, no real knowledge of actual practices is transferred, but the superior performance is used to create stretch goals that motivate learning in other units. Second, underperforming units can study the operational practices of high-performing business units to determine the source of superior performance. Finally, knowledge transfer is perhaps best facilitated when members of lower-performing business units simply seek advice from the higher-performing units. It is often the case that high-performing business units have explicit routines and practices that can be detailed by key employees in those units.[11]

Coordination mechanisms are the management systems and processes that facilitate intrafirm activity. Coordination depends on a variety of structural mechanisms, including reporting relationships, informal meetings and exchanges, and detailed policies and procedures for such activities as intrafirm transfer pricing. Greater relatedness of businesses within a firm requires more intense coordination across business units. Why? Because resources in highly related diversified firms are often shared across business units. Illustratively, more cross-business coordination is needed at 3M than at GE. For instance, adhesive technology is used in multiple divisions in 3M, and this knowledge sharing requires coordination. Alternatively, knowledge transfer or resource sharing (other than cash) does not occur between GE's jet-engine and consumer-finance divisions. Consequently, 3M can generate more revenue-enhancement synergy between related units than GE can generate between unrelated businesses, but to reap these possible benefits requires that energy and resources be devoted to coordination efforts.

Successful diversification may require adjustments in how managers are compensated and rewarded. Generally speaking, a firm with a broad (highly diversified) portfolio should reward managers differently than a focused or related diversified firm.[12] Why? In a firm with a broad scope, division-level managers do not share resources and cooperate to implement their strategies. Consequently, it is more effective to reward managers for the performance of their divisions than to reward (and punish) them for the performance of divisions that they have no control of or influence over. Conversely, in a related diversified firm, managers of different divisions are generally required to share resources and cooperate to implement their strategies. As a result, it is more effective to reward managers for the firm's collective performance than to focus all rewards on division-level performance. For instance, when division-level profits drive bonuses, managers have little incentive to help other divisions.

When corporate-level management grows unwieldy, it can be a drag on corporate earnings. What factors should determine the size and organization of corporate-level management? Basically, two factors govern this decision: the firm's resources and the scope of its involvement in disparate arenas. When a firm's portfolio contains numerous unrelated units that aren't significantly interdependent, it doesn't need heavy corporate-level oversight; there's not much that corporate-level management can do to add value on a day-to-day basis (a good example is Warren Buffet's Berkshire Hathaway Inc.). By contrast, when a firm's portfolio consists of highly interdependent businesses, more corporate-level control is needed to facilitate the sharing of resources and to oversee interbusiness transactions (e.g., S. C. Johnson, whose businesses include insect-control, home-cleaning, and plastic products).

Now that we've identified the ingredients of a good corporate strategy, we need to remind ourselves that it's the alignment of these ingredients in support of a firm's mission and vision that makes it possible for its managers to implement the firm's corporate strategy and create competitive advantage at the corporate level. Indeed, the configuration of these elements will determine whether a firm achieves corporate-level competitive advantage.

CORPORATE STRATEGY IN STABLE AND DYNAMIC CONTEXTS

By this point, you probably have a strong suspicion that corporate strategy is developed according to the relative dynamism of the context in which an organization operates. You are, of course, correct, and in this section we'll see how corporate strategy is designed to take dynamic context into account. Moreover, because alliances and acquisitions are vehicles for both business and corporate strategy, we'll elaborate on this theme in subsequent chapters as well. We'll see, for example, that, depending on whether a firm's context is stable or dynamic, different strategy vehicles are likely to play different roles. In particular, alliances and acquisitions have different implications for the allocation of a firm's resources and capabilities. We'll show that because certain issues arise in both stable and dynamic contexts, differences are often matters of emphasis. At the same time, however, we'll stress the point that even if the *content* of strategy is similar in both stable and dynamic contexts context will still have an effect on its *implementation*.

Corporate Strategy in Stable Contexts

Many of the traditional notions of the relationship between diversification and corporate strategy are based on analyses of companies operating in relatively stable contexts. As we've seen, historically a firm may have diversified into a high-growth industry because growth prospects in its current industry were unattractive. That's why Kansas City Southern (KCS), a railroad, got into financial services in the late 1960s and soon owned almost 90 percent of the Janus Group of mutual funds. But recall, too, our observation that this form of unrelated diversification often fails. Indeed, due to an obvious lack of synergy between the rail industry and mutual funds—plus an increasing level of management conflict between its railroad and mutual-fund divisions—KCS divested Janus in 1999 (a move widely approved by the market).[13]

Stable Arenas and Formal Structures   As we've seen, creating synergies among its businesses is an important part of a corporation's strategy. Synergies can come from shared know-how, coordination of business-unit strategies, shared tangible resources, vertical integration, and pooled negotiating power.[14] In relatively stable environments, such synergies are typically conceived as functions of static business-unit arenas and the formal structural links among them. Corporate-strategy objectives focus primarily on synergies as means of achieving economies of scope and scale. In fact, corporate strategy explicitly defines the form and extent of the coordination and collaboration among business units. Thus, the managers of individual units are often compensated according to a combination of division- and corporate-level performance. Generally speaking, the overarching objective of corporate strategy in a stable environment is ensuring that the firm operates as a tightly interwoven whole.

The best example of such strategy in action is probably the related diversified firm. Masco Corporation, a multibillion-dollar manufacturer and distributor of plumbing fixtures and other home-building and home-repair supplies, is just such a firm. Starting with Delta Faucets in the early 1960s, Masco built up a diversified portfolio of manufacturing businesses by acquiring well-run firms in a variety of industries. Today, Masco is one of the leading makers of home-improvement and home-building products and a powerhouse in the do-it-yourself industry dominated by such retail chains as Home Depot and Lowe's. We've summarized the breadth of Masco's holdings in Exhibit 7.5. Operating a tightly knit set of businesses is an effective corporate strategy for Masco. Why? Primarily because each business alone is unattractive, and by combining them under one corporate roof, Masco gives them greater selling and merchandising power in dealing with aggressive customers such as Home Depot. In addition, because its businesses are sufficiently related, Masco can leverage manufacturing, design, marketing, distribution, and merchandising expertise across them.

Corporate Strategy in Dynamic Contexts

Masco's strategy would be problematic for firms competing in more dynamic contexts. Adaptec Inc., for instance, was once an integrated maker of both computer hardware and software. The strategy was logical because the firm could extract synergies from operations in such complementary businesses. Adaptec soon discovered, however, that rapid changes in technologies and advances by competitors were weakening its ability to maneuver well in both areas. In 1999, therefore, Adaptec spun off its software side as Roxio through an IPO.

Even a seemingly focused business like Palm, which makes PDAs, can find it difficult to perform well in both hardware (Palm Pilot PDAs) and software (the Palm operating system), and as of this writing, Palm is contemplating a split into two separate companies. Ironically, as late as 2000, 3Com, then a supplier of computer, communications, and compatibility (network-interfacing) products, spun off Palm as a separate business for similar reasons.[15] In turn, Palm used the proceeds from its own IPO to strengthen its position in the market for handheld devices and operating systems. 3Com now concentrates on its core networking business, along with research and development in emerging technologies.

Diversification in Dynamic Contexts   Despite the examples of Adaptec and 3Com, both of which have used divestitures to increase corporate focus, diversification can be a viable strategy in dynamic contexts. Bear in mind, however, that firms seeking to diversify in dynamic contexts usually need strong resources and capabilities in the areas of learning, knowledge transfer, and rapid responsiveness. If corporate ownership hinders nimbleness and response time in a dynamic environment, it's more likely to be an encumbrance than an advantage. It's hard enough to manage competitively in dynamic contexts without having to struggle under excess layers of corporate hierarchy.

Coevolution   The ebbs and flows of firms' corporate strategies in dynamic contexts are best described as a web of shifting linkages among evolving businesses—a process that some researchers call **coevolution**.[16] Borrowed from biology, the term *coevolution* describes successive changes among two or more ecologically interdependent species that adapt not only

coevolution Process by which diversification causes two or more interdependent businesses to adapt not only to their environment, but to each other

Exhibit 7.5 Masco: A Holding Company at a Glance

Domestic	International
Cabinet and Related Products	
d-Scan Inc.	AlmaKüchen, Germany
Diversified Cabinet Distributors	Alvic, Spain
KraftMaid	Aran Group, Italy
Merillat	Berglen Group, UK
Mill's Pride	Grumal, Spain
Texwood Industries	Moores Group Ltd., UK
Zenith	Tvilum-Scanbirk, Denmark
	Xey, Spain
Plumbing Products	
Aqua Glass	A & J Gummers, UK
Brass Craft	Breuer, Germany
Brasstech	Bristan Ltd., UK
Delta Faucet	Damixa, Denmark
H&H Tube	Glass Indromassaggio SpA, Italy
Mirolin	Hansgrohe AG, Germany
Peerless Faucet	Heritage, UK
Plumb Shop	Hüppe, Germany
Watkins Manufacturing	NewTeam Limited, UK
	Rubinetterie Mariani, Italy
	S.T.S.R., Italy
Decorative Architectural Products	
Behr	Avocet, UK
Franklin Brass (Bath Unlimited)	SKS Group, Germany
GAMCO (Bath Unlimited)	
Ginger	
Liberty Hardware	
Masterchem	
Melard (Bath Unlimited)	
Vapor Technologies	
Specialty Products	
Arrow Fastener	Alfred Reinecke, Germany
Cobra	Brugman, Holland
Computerized Security Systems (CSS)	Cambrian Windows Ltd., UK
Faucet Queens	Duraflex Ltd., UK
Gamco/Morgantown Products	Gebhardt, Germany
MediaLab	Griffin Windows, UK
Milgard Manufacturing	Jung Pumpen, Germany
PowerShot Tool Company	Missel, Germany
	Premier Manufacturing Ltd., UK
	Superia Radiatoren, Belgium
	Vasco, Belgium

to their environment but also to each other. Business units coevolve when senior managers do not target specific synergies across business units but rather allow business-unit managers to determine which linkages do and don't work. As business-unit managers search for fresh opportunities for synergies and abandon deteriorating linkages, internal relationships tend to shift. As in the organic world, coevolution can result in competitive interdependence, with one unit eventually absorbing another or rendering it unnecessary. Coevolution means that cross-business synergies are usually temporary, and managers must learn to deal with the fundamental tension that results from the agility afforded by fewer linkages and the efficiency afforded by more. Finally, research suggests that in successful coevolving companies, managers, rather than trying to control, or even predict, cross-business-unit synergies, simply let them emerge in the "natural" course of corporate operations.[17]

Ironically, of course, coevolution means that units owned by the same corporation are potentially both collaborators and competitors. This paradoxical relationship is perhaps easiest to detect when a firm operates both traditional and e-business units. It's less obvious when it arises because new technologies have emerged to threaten established processes, but the costs of allowing a competitor—even one with which you share a corporate umbrella—to gain a technological advantage are often steep. In dynamic contexts, corporate strategy usually takes the form of temporary networks among businesses, and if strategic alliances are added into the mix, the network may include companies that the corporation doesn't own as well as those it does.

Divestitures and corporate spin-offs can be effective strategic vehicles for dealing with the sort of disruptive innovations that we discussed in Chapters 4 and 6, and they also figure frequently in stories of corporate coevolution.[18] Because disruptive technologies compete with established technologies, it may not be enough to simply reorganize them as new units under the same corporate umbrella. The resulting problems from retaining ownership of the disruptive part of the business range from the creation of messy internal politics to simply starving the new business of resources so that it eventually fails. We've summarized the key differences between corporate strategies in stable and dynamic contexts in Exhibit 7.6. The box entitled "How Would You Do That 7.1," demonstrates dynamic corporate strategy at Disney.

conceptlink

In Chapter 6, we describe a *disruptive strategy* as one which—such as the introduction of a new business model—differs from and conflicts with the strategies used by industry incumbents. We also explain that if a new technological innovation dramatically advances an industry's price-versus-performance frontier, the industry has experienced *technological discontinuity*.

Stable Contexts	Dynamic Contexts
Top-management team emphasizes collaboration among the businesses and the form of that collaboration.	Top-management team emphasizes the creation of a collaborative context that is rich in terms of content and linkages.
Collaboration is solidified through stable structural arrangement among wholly-owned businesses.	Collaboration is fluid, with networks being created, changed, and disassembled between combinations of owned and alliance businesses.
Key objectives are the pursuit of economies of scale and scope.	Key objectives are growth, maneuverability, and economies of scope.
The business units' roles are to execute their given strategies.	The business units' roles are to execute their strategies and seek new collaborative opportunities.
Business units' incentives combine business with corporate-level rewards to promote cooperation.	Business units' incentives emphasize business-level rewards to promote aggressive execution and collaborative-search objectives.
Balanced-scorecard objectives emphasize performance against budget and in comparison to within-firm peer unit.	Balanced-scorecard objectives gauge performance relative to competitors in terms of growth, market share, and profitability.

Exhibit 7.6 Comparison of Corporate Strategies in Stable and Dynamic Contexts

Diversification in a Dynamic Context at Disney

What did Disney do when it wanted to enter a business opportunity that seemed to be at odds with the historical core values and image of Disney? For instance, Disney's studio business felt it needed to produce edgier film products in order to exploit opportunities in that market. How did Disney add this arena and implement its corporate strategy effectively?

To answer this, let's first examine Disney's corporate strategy. Its vision is to be the industry leader in providing creative entertainment experiences. The arenas in which Disney participates in are focused on family entertainment and include media networks (38%), studio entertainment (28%), theme parks and resorts (26%), and consumer products (8%). A few of the fundamental resources that Disney shares across these arenas are the Disney name and legacy, the library of films and Disney's cast of animated and real-life characters, capabilities in the creation and management of world-class entertainment, and service-management expertise (this is obviously an abbreviated list of resources and capabilities).

Implementation is the glue holding these arenas and resources together. Although the company appears to be diversified into related arenas, each business is treated as a profit center, and managers are compensated according to business-unit performance. To overcome the lack of cross-division cooperation that this might motivate, Disney has historically relied on special "synergy-management" positions. Imagine the powerful scope economies that are created when Disney launches a hit character and then leverages the fictional personality through every channel, from toy licensing to Disney Radio. Just as important, however, is the skill with which Disney pulls the right implementation levers to make this synergistic dynamo work.

We want to see which leadership and implementation levers were necessary to modify Disney's corporate strategy so that it could enter the arena of mature film entertainment, an arena that is highly competitive and dynamic. For instance, consider the challenges when Disney wanted to produce such movies as *Kill Bill I* and *Kill Bill II*. These edgy features are hardly consistent with the public image of Mickey Mouse. Yet, they do allow Disney to leverage its corporate resources in the broader area of entertainment to create value.

To attempt to solve this inconsistency, Disney has created specialized divisions, such as Buena Vista and Touchstone, which develop movies that might otherwise taint the image of core Disney assets. Thus, Disney's implementation lever that was most critical in this corporate strategy decision was structure. However, adding new arenas and changing one lever, such as structure, often requires adjustments in other areas of strategy and implementation, including resources and capabilities. For example, live-action films require producers and directors with different skill sets and relationships than those possessed by animated designers.

Apparently, this is not an easy corporate strategy to duplicate. Sony, for example, developed no synergies between its Walkman radio products and its powerhouse music business, nor did its hit movie *Men in Black* have anywhere near the collective financial impact of Disney's *The Lion King*. The question is whether Disney can take advantage of its synergy powerhouse for its edgy films in the same way it exploits it with cartoons. Can you imagine a McDonald's kid meal with a *Kill Bill* toy? The jury is currently out on this Disney corporate strategy.

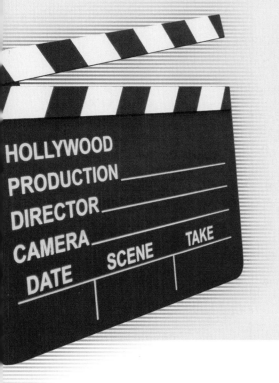

SUMMARY

1. Define *corporate strategy.* Corporate strategy encompasses issues related to decisions about entering and exiting businesses. A fundamental part of corporate strategy is the decision about what business *arenas* to enter and exit. However, corporate strategy also encompasses the overall management of the multibusiness enterprise, such as corporate headquarters' efforts to orchestrate the cross-business-unit synergies. Corporate strategy deals with the logic for owning more than one business within a firm.

2. Understand the roles of economies of scope and revenue-enhancement synergy in corporate strategy. Expanding the scope of the firm, whether vertically, horizontally, or geographically, does not necessarily create value. Value is created by either lowering costs or increasing revenues through diversification. This can take place when economies of scope result from diversification, such as when two businesses are able to share the same resources. Revenue-enhancement synergies can also create value. For synergies to be present because of joint ownership, the combined revenues of two distinct businesses must be greater when owned jointly than when operated independently. These economic gains are more likely when there is resource similarity between businesses and when the dominant logics necessary to manage the businesses are similar.

3. Explain the different forms of diversification. Firms have several options when expanding the scope of their operations beyond the original business definition. In this chapter, we discussed the concept of diversification along three trajectories of new business arenas: vertical, horizontal, and geographic (global). Vertical scope is ownership of business activities along the firm's vertical value chain. Horizontal scope, typically called diversification, is increased by owning businesses in different industry segments or different industries entirely. Geographic scope entails moving into new geographic areas, typically new countries.

4. Understand when it makes sense for a firm to own a particular business. A firm's ownership of a particular business should be driven by two related questions: (1) Does the business unit add value to the corporation (or vice versa)? (2) Does ownership add more value than

alternative ways to link the business to the corporation? A firm should acquire multiple businesses if it would gain superior market and financial performance than if a similar collection of businesses were owned independently. There are alternative methods to participate in additional businesses (e.g., alliances), and executives should be certain that owning additional enterprises adds more value than linking up with them through these less costly alternatives.

5. Describe the relationship between corporate strategy and competitive advantage. Competitive advantage at the corporate level is a function of the fit among arenas, resources, and organizational systems, structures, and processes. When these are connected in a coherent fashion, the corporation is more likely to achieve its long-term objectives. When resources are specialized, the firm will likely find greater value creation opportunities in a narrow scope of business arenas. Conversely, general resources can be applied across a greater spectrum of businesses. Firms with a broad scope of business activities have different demands for organization structure, systems, and processes than firms that are narrowly focused on a specific set of business arenas.

6. Explain the role of corporate strategy in both stable and dynamic contexts. In relatively stable environments, synergies are typically achieved through static definitions of the business-unit arenas and formal structural links among them. Corporate strategy objectives are aimed primarily at using synergies to achieve economies of scope and scale and, in fact, the strategy explicitly defines the form and extent of business units' coordination and collaboration. Firms in dynamic contexts must usually have strong resources and capabilities in the areas of learning, knowledge transfer, and rapid responsiveness for diversification to yield benefits. Otherwise, the nimbleness and responsiveness required of business units in dynamic contexts is dampened as a consequence of corporate ownerships being more of an encumbrance than an advantage. In dynamic environments, allowing managers of business units to pursue a pattern of synergistic relationships that mimics biological coevolution is generally more advantageous than corporate-forced synergistic relationships.

KEY TERMS

coevolution, 205
conglomerate, 190
diseconomies of scope, 193
diversification, 188

dominant logic, 195
general resources, 203
geographic scope, 199
horizontal scope, 197

portfolio planning, 190
profit pool, 198
related diversification, 194
specialized resources, 203

synergy, 187
unrelated diversification, 194
vertical integration, 189
vertical scope, 196

REVIEW QUESTIONS

1. How does corporate strategy differ from business strategy?

2. How has the practice of corporate strategy evolved over time?

3. What is a conglomerate?

4. How can managers decide whether they should diversify into a new business?

5. What are the types of diversification and how is value created by each type?

6. What is the difference between economies of scope and synergies?

7. What is the relationship between diversification and firm performance?

8. What factors tend to limit the attractiveness of diversification?

9. How does a dynamic industry context affect the possible benefits of diversification?

How Would YOU Do That?

1. The box entitled "How Would *You* Do That? 7.1" examines Disney's entry into the live-action film market. What specific resources and capabilities might Disney share across its traditional family oriented businesses and this new one? Internally, Disney executives view one of their dynamic capabilities as that of being the best at creating world-class entertainment within financial constraints. What are your thoughts on this view? As you think about Disney and what you view as its resources and capabilities, what arenas should it consider for future diversification or divestiture moves?

GROUP ACTIVITIES

1. Chose two firms that are well known to your group members—perhaps firms that you've done case analyses on in the past. For each of these firms, identify their vertical, horizontal, and geographic scope. Having done that, evaluate the resources that are necessary for each business arena for the firms. How similar are the resource requirements? Identify the dominant logic in each of their main lines of business (if you picked a very diversified firm, just choose the largest two or three business segments). How similar are they across the business divisions?

2. Try to apply the profit pool tool to another industry. Where would you turn for data to do this? How "friendly" is that data for the purposes of using this tool? If you are having trouble being precise, make informed estimations for what you are missing. You will likely find some profit pools that are deeper than others. Why are there big differences between segments? Which firms in the value chain are best able to enter these attractive segments?

ENDNOTES

1. Corporate descriptions were compiled based on corporate histories on corporate Web sites (www.ge.com, www.3m.com, www.mityinc.com); business descriptions were compiled based on information available at www.hoovers.com (accessed July 15, 2005).

2. See especially C. K. Prahalad and Gary Hamel, "The Core Competence of the Corporation," *Harvard Business Review* May–June (1990), 79–91; K. P. Coyne, S. Hall, J. D. Clifford, and P. Gorman, "Do You Really Have a Core Competency," *McKinsey Quarterly* 1 (1997), 40–54.

3. A. Chandler, *Strategy and Structure: Chapters in the History of the American Industrial Enterprise* (Boston: MIT Press, 1962).

4. G. F. Davis and S. K. Stout, "Organization Theory and the Market for Corporate Control: A Dynamic Analysis of Characteristics of Large Takeover Targets: 1980–1990," *Administrative Science Quarterly* 37 (1992), 605–633; G. F. Davis, K. A. Diekman, and C. H. Tinsley, "The Decline and Fall of the Conglomerate Firm in the 1980s: A Study in the Deinstitutionalization of an Organization Form," *American Sociological Review* 59 (1994), 547–570.

5. S. Wetlaufer, "Common Sense and Conflict: An Interview with Disney's Michael Eisner," *Harvard Business Review* 78:1 (2000), 44–48. See also K. Eisenhardt and C. Galunic, "Co-evolving: At Last a Way to Make Synergies Work," *Harvard Business Review* (2000), 91–101.

6. A. D. Henderson and J. W. Fredrickson, "Information Processing Demands as a Determinant of CEO Compensation," *Academy of Management Journal* 39 (1996), 575–590; W. G. Sanders and M. A. Carpenter, "Internationalization and Firm Governance: The Roles of CEO Compensation, Top-Team Composition, and Board Structure," *Academy of Management Journal* 41 (1998), 158–178.

7. O. Gadiesh and J. L. Gilbert, "Profit Pools: A Fresh Look at Strategy," *Harvard Business Review* 76:3 (1998), 139–148.

8. For more details on this example and other examples, see Gadiesh and Gilbert, "Profit Pools."

9. J. Kanter, D. Clark, and J. R. Wilke, "EU Imposes Sanctions on Microsoft—Fine, Disclosure Penalties Aim to Undercut Dominance; Continued Pressure Signaled," *Wall Street Journal,* March 25, 2004, A2; M. Wingfield, "DOJ Calls EC's Record Fine of Microsoft 'Unfortunate,'" Dow Jones Newswires, March 25, 2004; B. Mitchener and J. Kanter, "Monti's Initiatives on Commerce Leave an Enduring Mark," *Wall Street Journal,* March 25, 2004, A2.

10. Y. Akbar, "Grabbing Victory from the Jaws of Defeat: Can the GE-Honeywell Merger Force International Competition Policy Cooperation?" *World Competition* 25:4 (2002), 26–31.

11. G. Szulanski, R. Cappetta, and R. J. Jensen, "When and How Trustworthiness Matters: Knowledge Transfer and the Moderating Effect of Causal Ambiguity," *Organization Science* 15 (2004), 600–613.

12. C. W. L. Hill, M. A. Hitt, and R. E. Hoskisson, "Cooperative versus Competitive Structures in Related and Unrelated Diversified Firms," *Organization Science* 3 (1992), 501–521.

13. A. Stone, "Can Kansas City Southern Keep Its Janus Spin-Off on Track?" *Business Week,* August 31, 1999, 27.

14. M. Goold and A. Campbell, "Desperately Seeking Synergy," *Harvard Business Review* 76:5 (1998), 131–143.

15. L. Bransten and S. Thurm, "For Palm Computers, an IPO and Flashy Rival," *Wall Street Journal*, September 14, 1999, B1.

16. Eisenhardt and Galunic, "Coevolving"; S. Brown and K. Eisenhardt, *Competing on the Edge* (Boston: Harvard Business School Press, 1998).

17. Eisenhardt and Galunic, "Coevolving"; Brown and Eisenhardt, *Competing on the Edge.*

18. C. Christensen, *The Innovator's Dilemma* (New York: Harper Collins, 1997).

Looking at International Strategies

After studying this chapter, you should be able to:

1. Define *international strategy* and identify its implications for the strategy diamond.

2. Understand why a firm would want to expand internationally and explain the relationship between international strategy and competitive advantage.

3. Describe different vehicles for international expansion.

4. Apply different international strategy configurations.

5. Outline the international strategy implications of the static and dynamic perspectives.

▶ **Dell in the United States**
Michael Dell founds Dell in 1985, based on a strategy of selling PCs directly to individual U.S. consumers. By 2001, Dell ranks number one in global market share.

▶ **Dell in India**
To sell computers to individual consumers in India, Dell changes its strategy and begins distributing its products through Indian distributors.

1980   1985

DELL GOES TO CHINA

In 1999, Dell was the second-largest player in both the U.S. and worldwide PC markets.[1] However, Dell had a negligible presence in many regions of the world, most notably China, where it ranked a distant seventh in PC sales. Dell executives considered this lagging position to be problematic, given that computer-industry analysts were predicting that by 2002, China would become the second-largest PC market behind the United States. Consequently, Dell set ambitious China sales-growth targets in 1999, with a goal of achieving 10 percent of its global PC sales from China by 2002, which would amount to nearly 50 percent of PC sales for the entire Asian region.

For many U.S. companies, China is attractive simply due to its size, but it is also a competitive environment fraught with many hazards—and it can turn potential profits into a cash-flow black hole. Although

▶ **Dell in China**
To make headway in China, Dell first tapped a network of Chinese distributors, then sales through Chinese retailers, to sell PCs to individual consumers. In five years' time, Dell transforms itself from a market laggard to a market leader in China, and today uses product kiosks in China, just as it does in the United States, to let consumers look at the systems. If they decide to buy, they place their order online at the kiosk or call and order by phone later.

1995   2000

sourcing components and products from China has proven successful for many global firms, tapping the Chinese consumer market appears to be an entirely different matter. By 1999, for example, Motorola and Kodak had already sunk many millions of dollars into China hoping for large domestic market share and commensurate profits but instead were reeling from enormous and continuing losses. Dell's management was not ignorant of these warning signals but viewed the situation as "if we're not in what will soon be the second-biggest PC market in the world, then how can Dell possibly be a global player?"

The Dell-in-China situation showcases all five elements of strategy in action. It also shows how a firm must engage these elements flexibly and entrepreneurially to do business in markets different from their home markets. That is, internationalizing firms face challenges as to how to be global yet local at the same time and to what extent they should be global or local. China is a relatively new geographic arena for Dell. Within this country arena, Dell is targeting certain market segments, or sub-arenas; it is also using different channels as part of its market-segmentation strategy.

In terms of vehicles, and regardless of global location, Dell typically goes it alone in terms of assembly and distribution, entering into alliances only for its inputs and raw materials. A key facet of Dell's competitive advantage is distribution via its Dell Direct model—an online PC assembly and sales-on-demand powerhouse. In China, however, Dell initially formed alliances with independent distributors for the consumer market, a channel it had learned to exploit in its earlier entry into India. This was a risky move for Dell but also one that showed that management recognized that it had to be flexible and act in a locally sensitive fashion in approaching new geographic markets. Dell initially planned to use Chinese distributors, as it had in India, and then migrate sales over a five-year period to the typical kiosk-sales model it employs in other parts of the world, further allowing it to leverage its Dell Direct model. Dell was able to draw immediately on the model for the large multinational-firm market, with which it already had established customer relationships. It could also use the Dell Direct model for the government-users market. As in all of its other markets, Dell continued to exploit a performance-for-value differentiation strategy and leverage its unique Dell Direct service model to maintain its solid relationship with its corporate and government clients.

In terms of staging, Dell flipped its distribution model on its head. This is a third example of how the company flexibly adapted its historic strategic approach to enter into China. In the United States, Dell built up its Dell Direct model through the direct-to-consumer market; it entered the corporate-customer market once only after it had established a strong, profitable foothold with consumers. In China, however, the Dell Direct market was more commercially viable with corporate customers, who have both the cash and access to infrastructure to make the Dell Direct model work effectively. Although Dell initially worked through distributors in China for the consumer market, its staging plan was to migrate these consumers eventually to its Dell Direct model over a period of five years, which it did successfully.

Finally, Dell's economic logic is one of both scale and scope economies. It can leverage its size to gain the best terms and prices for the best technologies for the products it sells. It can use this cost advantage to compete in China and at the same time further enhance the Dell Direct model's footprint on the global computer market.

By the end of 2004, Dell reported that in just five years, it had become China's third-largest provider of computer systems and services. In 2004 alone, Dell's shipment growth in China was nearly 60 percent, four times that of the rest of the industry, and its revenues grew nearly 40 percent. China had become Dells' fourth-largest national market, and combined Asia Pacific–Japan operating income amounted to $313 million, 10 percent of its global income. Perhaps the icing on the cake came when IBM announced on December 9, 2004, the sale of its entire PC division to Lenovo, a Chinese multinational firm. This leaves Dell, Hewlett-Packard, and Lenovo as the world's top three PC makers. Industry analysts are placing their bets on wildly efficient Dell to broaden its lead, both globally and in China. Exhibit 8.1 presents some of the reasons why Motorola, Kodak, and IBM experienced difficulties in the China market, but it paints a rosier picture for astute firms such as Dell. So far, it appears that Dell's global strategy, and its flexible approach to entering countries like China, is paying off. ■

Exhibit 8.1 China: A Black Hole or a Diamond Mine?

Sources: Adapted from annual reports provided at www.walmart.com, www.ge.com, and Economist Unit White Paper, Coming of Age: Multinationals in China, June 2004.

If you read front-page stories from *Business Week*, the *Economist*, the *Financial Times*, *Forbes*, *Fortune*, or the *Wall Street Journal*, it almost seems to be accepted wisdom in the business world that the China accounts of almost all foreign firms are unprofitable. That is, it is difficult, if not impossible, to make a profit selling products to the business and consumer markets in China. Executives in multinational companies (MNCs) are easily dazzled by the prospect of selling to one billion consumers. For instance, think of how many pairs of shoes a 10-percent share of the Chinese market would represent to Nike!

However, many early entrants failed to give sufficient attention to the fact that only a small segment of the Chinese market was ready for expensive Western products. In addition, some firms encountered unexpected costs caused by corruption among local officials. Historically, this perception has not been far from the truth. It is not difficult to uncover a number of horror stories detailing the misadventures of foreign firms that have overestimated the size of the domestic Chinese market, underestimated the difficulties of accessing it, and ended up losing lots of money.

But beware of such urban legends. China has not been nearly the unmitigated disaster for foreign firms that such stories suggest. Many large Western companies have found the going tough, but the China operations of numerous companies have been hugely profitable. Although many MNCs have lost money trying to sell to the domestic market, they have made a great deal by using China as a sourcing and export base.

This aspect of foreign firms' business in China is often overlooked because it is difficult to record. The financial gains generated by cheap sourcing in China are impossible to document because they show up not as accounting items in their own right but rather in the profits MNCs make in their traditional markets in the United States and Europe. Similarly, that the export operations of foreign firms often show little or no profit is less a reflection of reality than of transfer pricing as foreign firms attempt to avoid capital controls and taxes in China.

It works like this. Imagine that a parent company in the United States receives an order from a European customer for 1,000 notebook computers at $700 each. Assume also that the computers cost $600 a unit. Typically, the parent company would subcontract its factory in China to produce this order and pay it $610 for each unit (foreign firms know that a factory operating at a loss would be suspicious and thus attract the unwanted attention of officials). This is the value of the export from China, although a change of invoice en route means it enters the United States at $700, which is the price the European customer pays directly to the parent company in the United States. In this way, the U.S. firm keeps most of the money offshore. So although official records may show that the China factory is making a profit of $10,000, in reality it has generated net earnings of 10 times that amount.

The money MNCs make from using China as a sourcing and exporting base may be difficult to trace, but it is far from negligible. Wal-Mart buys more than $12 billion in goods from China every year; Motorola's sourcing in the country totaled $2.8 billion in 2003; and GE plans to increase sourcing in China to $5 billion by 2005. Moreover, more than 50 percent of China's total exports—equivalent to $240 billion in 2003—are produced in foreign-invested factories. When trying to assess an MNC's overall performance in China, it makes less sense to ask how much money foreign firms have made *in* the country than how much they have made *from* it.

INTERNATIONAL STRATEGY

What is *international strategy*? When should managers consider such a strategy? In the narrowest sense, a firm's managers need only think about international strategy when they conduct some aspect of their business across national borders. Some international activities are designed to augment a firm's business strategy, such as sourcing key factors of production to cheaper labor markets (i.e., attempts to become more competitive within a core business). Other international activities represent key elements of the firm's corporate strategy (i.e., entering new businesses or new markets). Whether expanding internationally to reinforce a particular business's strategy or as part of a corporate strategy, international expansion is a form of diversification because the firm has chosen to operate in a different market.

Throughout this text, you have been exposed to many organizations, both those focused on one primary geographic region and others that are very global in their operating scope. For some organizations, a global mind-set pervades managerial thinking and is explicit in the firm's vision, mission, goals, objectives, and strategy. With other firms, international strategy may be very new. If this is the case, an international strategy must be carefully prepared for through staging and the other dimensions of the strategy diamond.

As shown in Exhibit 8.2, as of 2005, firms varied significantly in terms of their international presence. Papa John's, for instance, has a relatively miniscule dependence on non–U.S. markets for its revenues. However, even firms that are purely domestic must be attuned to international opportunities and threats. Competitors may emerge from parts of the globe where the firm does not conduct activities, and domestic competitors can radically change the home-market status quo through their international activities. For instance, Domino's Pizza derives 28 percent of its $4.2 billion in annual sales from non–U.S. markets, and these sales are spread over 50 countries.[2] By the end of this chapter, you will learn that keeping an eye on other firms' international activities is essential to avoid being blindsided by a new competitor or industry change.

The preventative cure for such myopia is a broad awareness of international strategy. We encourage you to internalize a broad perspective of international strategy as well. In the broadest sense, a firm needs to consider its international strategy when any single or potential competitor is not domestic or otherwise conducts business across borders. Increasingly, it is this latter context that makes it imperative that almost all firms think about the international dimensions of their business, even if they have no international operations whatsoever. Thus, a firm's **international strategy** is how it approaches the cross-border business

concept link

In Chapter 1, we define **staging** as the *timing and pace* of strategic moves; in Chapter 4, where we stress that analyzing an industry means charting its evolution *over time*, we underscore the importance of staging in the strategic response to transitions in an industry.

international strategy Process by which a firm approaches its cross-border activities and those of competitors and plans to approach them in the future

Exhibit 8.2 The International Presence of Selected MNCs

Company	Domestic Market	Products	Total Sales ($ millions)	Sales in Domestic Market %	Sales in Foreign Markets %
Nokia	Finland	Cell phones	37,031	1	99
Audi	Germany	Automobiles	29,378	32	68
Clarion	Japan	Audio equipment	1,540	52	48
Apple	U.S.	Computers, electronics	8,279	59	41
eBay	U.S.	Online auctions	2,165	65	35
Papa John's	U.S.	Pizza	917	96	4

Exhibit 8.3 International Strategy and the Five Elements of the Strategy Diamond

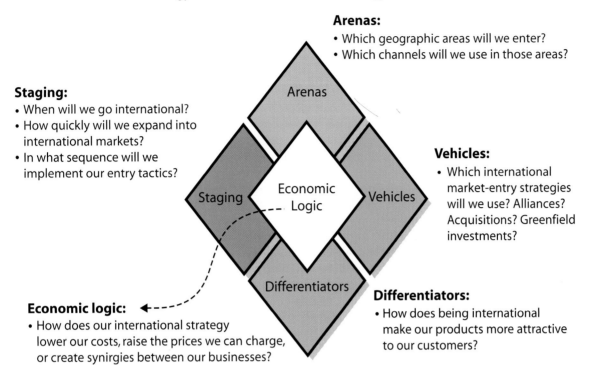

Arenas:
• Which geographic areas will we enter?
• Which channels will we use in those areas?

Staging:
• When will we go international?
• How quickly will we expand into international markets?
• In what sequence will we implement our entry tactics?

Vehicles:
• Which international market-entry strategies will we use? Alliances? Acquisitions? Greenfield investments?

Differentiators:
• How does being international make our products more attractive to our customers?

Economic logic:
• How does our international strategy lower our costs, raise the prices we can charge, or create synirgies between our businesses?

activities of its own firm and competitors and how it contemplates doing so in the future. International strategy essentially reflects the choices a firm's executives make with respect to sourcing and selling its goods in foreign markets.

It probably comes as no surprise to you that all of the world's largest corporations are global as well. A simple review of the top-10 firms among *Fortune's* Global 500 provides you with a snapshot of these global behemoths each year, in terms of who is largest and who has the best global reputation. What may be surprising, however, is the increasing presence of arguably tiny firms that are global very early in their lives, such as Skype (which started in Sweden and went global in a year) and Logitech (which started in Switzerland and California and was global from inception).

As you work through this chapter, you will see how international strategy must be reflected in all facets of the strategy diamond. Exhibit 8.3 summarizes some of the key strategic questions that firms must answer, such as Dell did in the opening vignette, as they expand into international markets.

INTERNATIONAL STRATEGY AND COMPETITIVE ADVANTAGE

Why expand internationally? Given the complexities and risks of managing business activities across borders, it is imperative to understand why any firm would take on the often significant costs of doing so in terms of time, dollars, and managerial attention. One reason is simply necessity. Increasingly, many experts in the field of strategic management view global expansion as necessary for just about every medium and large corporation. This opinion is based on a few basic observations: (1) that capital markets and employees favor fast-growing firms, and many domestic markets in developed countries are becoming saturated; (2) that efficiencies in all value-chain activities are linked across borders, and the linkages and pressures for efficiency continue to escalate; (3) that knowledge is not uniformly distributed around the world, and new ideas increasingly are

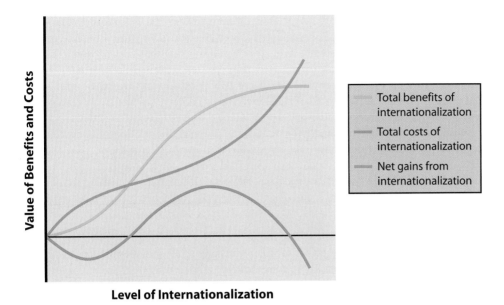

Level of Internationalization

Exhibit 8.4 The Benefits and Costs of Internationalization

Source: Lu, J. W. & P. W. Beamish, "International Diversification and Firm Performance: The S-Curve Hypothesis," Academy of Management Journal, *47 (2004), 598–609.*

ment, the more country environments a firm must deal with, the greater the difficulty in coordination operations across these diverse environments.

Offsetting Costs and Benefits Thus, as shown in Exhibit 8.4, the costs associated with internationalization can offset the possible benefits of operating in multiple markets. The potential economic benefits of internationalization are modest at first, and then become quite significant before leveling off. These potential increases in revenue must of course be balanced with the costs of internationalization. Costs are significant in early efforts to internationalize. After a presence is established, economies of scale and scope kick in, and the incremental costs of further expansion are minimal. However, bureaucratic and management costs can spike at extreme levels of internationalization. This increase in costs is similar to the notion of diseconomies of scale introduced in earlier chapters. Consequently, research suggests that performance gains from internationalization, come not at the early stages but at moderate to high levels; however, at very high levels of internationalization, firms tend to suffer performance declines.[7] The key for managers is to find a way to exploit the possible advantages of economies of scale and scope, location, and learning without having them offset by the excessive costs of internationalization. This dynamic tension between the costs and benefits of internationalization is summarized in Exhibit 8.4. The tradeoff between costs and benefits of internationalization results in an S-curve relationship between internationalization and firm performance.

Key Factors in International Expansion

International strategy, particularly in the form of international expansion, can contribute to a firm's competitive advantage in a number of interrelated ways. The four most important aspects are *economies of scale and scope, location, multipoint competition,* and *learning.* Firms must understand the specific benefits in one or more of these areas if they are to say yes to international expansion plans.

Global Economies of Scale and Scope Referring back to the strategy diamond, international strategy affects a firm's economic logic through its implications for economies of scale and scope. Larger firms are not necessarily more efficient or more profitable, but in some industries, such as pharmaceuticals and aircraft manufacturing, the enormous costs of new-product development require that the firm be able to generate commensurate sales, and this increasingly requires firms to have a global presence.

concept link

Recall our definition of a **diseconomies of scale** in Chapter 5 as the condition under which average total costs per unit of production increases at higher levels of output.

concept link

In Chapter 1, we explain the role of **economic logic** in the **strategy diamond** by describing it as the means by which a firm intends to generate positive returns over and above the cost of its capital. In Chapter 5, we show that the economic logic of an **economy of scope** revolves around cost savings associated with multiproduct production. In this chapter, we stress the strategy of lowering average costs by sharing resources on a global scale.

For instance, R&D costs are skyrocketing in many industries. This requires that firms in those industries seek a larger revenue base, typically outside of their home countries. This relationship is demonstrated by strategy research showing that the performance benefits from R&D increase with a firm's degree of internationalization: Firms generate more profits out of their R&D investments if they are also highly global.[8] One reason for this is that there is a minimum threshold of R&D investment necessary to launch a new product. When the firm can amortize those costs across many markets, it can in effect lower its average cost per sale. It is interesting to note that, when graphed, the relationship between performance, R&D investment, and internationalization further demonstrates the S-curve relationship between internationalization and firm performance discussed earlier in this chapter. Such economies of scale can also be realized for intangibles, such as a firm's brand, much as CitiGroup, McDonald's, and Coca-Cola leverage their brands in practically every country in the world.

Scale and Operating Efficiency   The larger scale that accompanies global expansion only creates competitive advantage if the firm translates scale into operating efficiency. As you learned in Chapter 5, cost savings are not axiomatic with larger scale. Larger scale must be managed to avoid diseconomies of scale. As with economies of scale in general, the potential scale economies from global expansion include spreading fixed costs and increasing purchasing power.[9] Attempts to gain scale advantages must be focused on resources and activities that are scale sensitive, and it means that these resources and activities must be concentrated in just a few locations.[10] However, if these resources and activities are concentrated in a few locations, they can become isolated from key markets, which may lead to delayed responses to market changes.

Economies of Global Scope   A specialized form of scope economies is available to firms as they expand globally. Recall that scope economies were defined as the ability to lower average costs by sharing a resource across different products. The example of MITY Enterprises reviewed in an earlier chapter was that of a firm that manufactures heavy-duty plastic and metal tables for institutional users (e.g., schools, churches). MITY Enterprises is able to use excess capacity in its manufacturing facility to produce chairs. By sharing this resource, MITY's average cost for tables and chairs is reduced. Numerous scope economies are similarly available to firms that expand globally. For example, CitiGroup, McDonald's, and Coca-Cola profit from scope economies to the extent that the different country markets share the benefits of brand equity that these firms have built up over time. The opening vignette on Dell, too, provides several examples of scope as well as scale economies across different geographic and customer markets, starting with its ability to take advantage of its brand; its capability to leverage its Dell Direct sales model and related Internet sales and support technologies; its experience and relationships with distributors in India and then China; and its different geographic units' ability to pool their purchasing power for key components, such as CPUs, from powerful suppliers like Intel.

Consider how a supplier to McDonald's could exploit economies of global scope, which in turn provide it with economies of scale in production and other related value-chain activities. McDonald's needs the same ketchup products in Europe and South America as it does in the United States. A vendor with sufficient global scope to satisfy McDonald's worldwide demand for ketchup would be an attractive sourcing alternative to McDonald's compared with sourcing this supply from numerous local suppliers.[11] In this case, global scope gives a supplier an opportunity to generate revenue that it would be unable to generate in the absence of global scope. Of course, McDonald's global scope also gives it access to more suppliers from around the globe, including local suppliers in many markets. Local suppliers may also have some advantages over global players in terms of being able to provide more immediate service and greater knowledge of local business practices. Thus, firms like McDonald's are in the enviable position of being able to source the lowest cost inputs and use lower local prices and service levels to force global suppliers to keep prices down and service levels high.

Huge international chains, such as McDonald's, are able to achieve economies of scope, thereby lowering the costs of inputs they purchase both globally and in local markets.

Attempts to gain economies of scope also face numerous hazards as well. Although economies of scope are possible as resources are shared across markets, strategy must still be executed at the national level.[12] In cases such as China, the United States, and Europe, where the "nation" is actually composed of distinctly different subgeographic markets (cantons in China, states in the U.S., and countries in Europe), successful execution at the local level is further complicated. This can easily lead to tension between the need to identify and satisfy the local client contact and the aim of lowering costs by sharing resources and having actions coordinated across markets.

Location National and regional geographic location has an impact on competitive advantage as well, because of its implications for input costs, competitors, demand conditions, and complements. A basic five-forces industry analysis can be used to determine the importance of a given location. The analysis of industry structure should include such features as barriers to entry, new entrants, substitutes, and existing competitors, both domestic and international. Related and supporting industries that are forward and backward in the value chain, as well as true complements, also need to be identified.

With such an analysis in hand, the value chain and five-forces analysis can be geographically segmented to consider how and why rivalry may play out differently in different locales. In terms of customer, for instance, an analysis of consumption trends among the top 25 countries in the global soft-drink industry shows that India and China exhibit fairly steady growth. A firm's managers can thus assess the desirability of investing in one market versus another, the competitive consequences of such an investment, and the value-chain activities needed to locate in which regions. For instance, India and China may be prime locations to launch new growth initiatives for large players like Coca-Cola and Pepsi. Such an analysis should show how the firm's strategy has connected the dots, so to speak, in terms of linking resources, capabilities, and locations.

Arbitrage Opportunities Beyond the five-forces and value-chain assessment, location differences also present an opportunity for arbitrage. Arbitrage represents the age-old practice of buying something in one market and selling it another market where it garners a higher price. Historically, the value added in such arbitrage was simply tracking down a desirable commodity, such as spice, tea, or silk, from a faraway land, and transporting it to a market that would pay a premium for it. Companies can improve performance and potentially build competitive advantage by optimizing the location of their value-chain activities. Significant cost differences for different types of value-chain activities exist around the globe. A firm that can optimize the intercountry cost differences better than its rivals will have a cost advantage. The caveat here is that arbitrage opportunities may be fleeting in that once identified and lacking entry barriers, competitors can quickly realize them as well. Therefore, a firm that relies on arbitrage as a core part of its competitive strategy must possess greater capabilities in continually identifying new arbitrage opportunities as well as in increasing entry barriers for competitors trying to follow it.

The CAGE Framework Generally, the greater the distance covered and the greater the value differences between the disconnected markets, the greater the profit potential arising from arbitrage. However, greater distance also tends to be accompanied by greater entry costs and risks. Although most people tend to think of distance in geographic terms, in the area of international strategy distance can also be viewed in terms of culture, administrative heritage, and economics. As summarized in Exhibit 8.5, this broader **CAGE framework**—Culture, Administrative, Geographic, and Economic—provides you with another way of thinking about location and the opportunities and concomitant risks associated with global arbitrage.[13] CAGE-related risks would be most relevant in industries in which

CAGE framework Tool that considers the dimensions of culture, administration, geography, and economics to assess the distance created by global expansion

Exhibit 8.5 The Cage Distance Framework: Opportunities for Global Arbitrage

Cultural Distance	Administrative Distance	Geographic Distance	Economic Distance
Attributes Creating Distance			
Different languages; Different ethnicities; lack of connective ethnic or social networks; Different religions; Different social norms	Absence of colonial ties; Absence of shared monetary or political association; Political hostility; Government policies; Institutional weakness	Physical remoteness; Lack of a common border; Lack of sea or river access; Size of country; Weak transportation or communication links; Differences in climates	Differences in consumer incomes; Differences in costs and quality of: • natural resources • financial resources • human resources • infrastructure • intermediate inputs • information or knowledge
Industries or Products Affected by Distance			
Products have high linguistic content (TV); Products affect cultural or national identity of consumers (foods); Product features vary in terms of size (cars), standards (electrical appliances), or packaging; Products carry country-specific quality associations (wines)	Government involvement is high in industries that are: • producers of staple goods (electricity) • producers of other "entitlements" (drugs) • large employers (farming) • large suppliers to government (mass transportation) • national champions (aerospace) • vital to national security (telecom) • exploiters of natural resources (oil, mining) • subject to high sunk costs (infrastructure)	Products have a low value-of-weight or bulk ratio (cement); Products are fragile or perishable (glass, fruit); Communications and connectivity are important (financial services); Local supervision and operational requirements are high (many services)	Nature of demand varies with income level (cars); Economies of standardization or scale are important (mobile phones); Labor and other factor cost differences are salient (garments); Distribution or business systems are different (insurance); Companies need to be responsive and agile (home appliances)

Source: Recreated from www.business-standard.com/general/pdf/113004_01.pdf.

language or cultural identity are important factors, the government views the products as staples or as essential to national security, or income or input costs are key determinants of product demand or cost.

Application of the CAGE framework requires managers to identify attractive locations based on raw material costs, access to markets or consumers, or other key decision criteria. For instance, a firm may be most interested in markets with high consumer buying power, so it uses per capita income as the first sorting cue. This would result in some type of ranking. For example, one researcher examined the fast-food industry and found that based on per capita income, countries such as Germany and Japan would be the most attractive markets for the expansion of a North American-based fast-food company. However, when the analysis was adjusted for distance using the CAGE framework, the revised results showed that Mexico ranked as the second-most-attractive market for international expansion, far ahead of Germany and Japan.[14]

Any international expansion strategy would still need to be backed up by the specific resources and capabilities possessed by the firm, regardless of how rosy the picture painted by the CAGE analysis. Think of international expansion as a movement along a continuum from known markets to less-known markets; a firm can move to more CAGE-proximate neighbors before venturing into markets that are portrayed as very different from a CAGE-framework perspective.

The opening vignette on Dell further demonstrates the usefulness of the CAGE framework. As you saw in the case of Dell, the vehicles it used to enter China were just as important in its China strategy as the choice of geographic arena it entered. For Dell's corporate clients in China, a CAGE framework would reveal relatively little distance on all four dimensions, even geographic, given the fact that many PC components are sourced from China. However, for the consumer segment, the distance is rather great, particularly on the dimensions of culture, administration, and economics. One outcome here could have been Dell's avoidance of the consumer market altogether. However, Dell opted to choose an alliance with distributors whose knowledge base and capabilities enabled it to better bridge the CAGE-framework distances until it was in a position to engage its Dell Direct model with consumers (staging and pacing).

So what have we learned by using CAGE in the context of Dell, and international expansion more generally? You should now see that the CAGE framework can be used to address the questions of where to expand internationally (which arena) and how to expand (by which vehicle). It can also help you map out the staging and pacing of your strategic international expansion moves so as to maximize the strategy's anchoring in the firm's VRINE-based resources and capabilities.

Multipoint Competition Chapter 6 introduced the advantages firms can develop through multimarket competition. When the firm competes in multiple international markets, as a special kind of multimarket tactic, the stronghold assault becomes available. *Stronghold assault* refers to the competitive actions a firm takes in another firm's key markets, particularly when the attacking firm has little presence in that market. In the case of international strategy, stronghold assault refers to attacks on the geographic markets that are most important to a competitor's profitability and cash flow. A classic example of international stronghold assault is provided by the actions of French tire manufacturer Michelin and the U.S. tire company Goodyear in the 1970s.[15] Early on, both firms had negligible market presence in each other's respective domestic markets (Europe and the United States). Michelin became aware of Goodyear's intent to expand its presence in Europe, so it started selling its tires in the United States at or below its actual cost. Although these sales were a miniscule part of Michelin's overall sales, Michelin's sales tactic forced Goodyear to drop its prices in the United States, and hence lower the profitability of its largest market.

As discussed in Chapter 6, such multimarket competitive tactics often initially benefit customers at the expense of competitors until a new market equilibrium is reached. Moreover, Michelin's low-price ploy earned it a larger share of the U.S. market, such that

concept link

We introduce the **VRINE model** in Chapter 3 as a five-pronged test for determining the extent to which a firm's **resources** and **capabilities** will contribute to competitive advantage: value, rarity, inimitability, nonsubstitutability, and exploitability.

the lost profits in the United States began to take a toll on Michelin's overall profitability. In addition, nothing prevented Goodyear from doing the same thing in Michelin's home markets, further eroding both firms' profitability. Eventually, both firms ended up in the international courts charging each other with "dumping"—selling goods below cost in a foreign country.

Even today, stronghold assault is a motivation for global investment, but as the Michelin case highlights, it must be used with care and is typically not sustainable. Therefore, firms that employ this tactic should also have strategies in the staging component that take into account when and how the firm will shift from price competition to more sustainable bases of competition. For this reason, stronghold assault is used not only to underprice a competitor's products in its home market but also to simply eliminate the competitor's home market monopoly. Just as with the Cola Wars, the Michelin–Goodyear war left the industry landscape forever changed, and both firms had to adjust their strategies to survive in the new industry structure that resulted.

Learning and Knowledge Sharing   Learning is very important to the success of a firm's international strategy for a variety of reasons. At the very least, a firm with operations that cross borders must learn how to cope with different institutional, legal, and cultural environments. For the most successful firms, international expansion is used as a vehicle for innovation, improving existing products in existing markets, or coming up with new ideas for new markets. It is one thing to use such tools as the five-forces, value-chain, and CAGE frameworks to identify profit or arbitrage opportunities, for instance, but it is quite another thing to exploit them successfully and profitably. For instance, Michelin initially shipped products to the United States and didn't care whether it made money on them because it viewed any losses as insignificant. But eventually that tactic caused the U.S. market to grow in importance as part of the French tire maker's overall global sales, and it had to reckon with making this part of its business profitable or admit defeat and abandon the U.S. market—one of the auto industry's largest and most profitable markets.

Similarly, Dell first used Chinese distributors in serving the consumer segment in China, but this is a much less profitable vehicle and differentiator than its core distribution and sales engine—the Dell Direct model. Dell's goal was to migrate from its Chinese distributors and eventually learn enough about the Chinese marketplace to use its direct-sales vehicle, which can be accessed through kiosks placed in busy foot-traffic locations.

Like the product-diversified firm, the geographic-diversified firm must somehow learn how to ensure that the benefits of being international outweigh the added costs of the infrastructure necessary to support its nondomestic operations.

Learning and local adaptation appear to be particularly difficult for U.S. firms, even when they are very big firms that already have an international presence. For instance, with nearly a half-billion dollars in annual sales, Lincoln Electric completed its largest acquisition ever in 1991—the $70-million purchase of Germany's Messer Gresheim, a manufacturer of welding equipment, which was Lincoln's core business.[16] Although Lincoln maintained the bulk of its business in the United States, it had over 40 years of marketing and manufacturing experience in Canada, Australia, and France. Moreover, the company was in the process of aggressively ramping up manufacturing and sales operations in Japan, Venezuela, Brazil, the Netherlands, Norway, and the U.K. With the acquisition of Gresheim, as with the other newly established international operations, Lincoln's management simply assumed that it could transplant its manufacturing approach, aggressive compensation and incentive systems (Lincoln pays employees only for what they produce), and culture—the three key success factors in the U.S. business—to the newly obtained German and other foreign operations. Within a year, the European operations were in disarray; losses were mounting in Japan and Latin America; and Lincoln reported a quarterly consolidated loss of $12 million—the first quarterly consolidated loss in the company's 97-year history.

Although Lincoln eventually recovered from the brink of disaster and ruin, it only did so after top management recognized and took steps to remedy the harsh reality that it had insufficient international experience, a dearth of experience in and knowledge about running a globally dispersed organization, and no understanding of how to manage foreign operations and foreign cultures. Part of its salvation involved scaling back many of the foreign operations it had acquired, giving the firm breathing room to develop its international operating and managerial capabilities. As a consequence of its learning from its failures abroad, Lincoln is now a global success story, as summarized in excerpts from its 2003 annual report shown in Exhibit 8.6.

Learning, Knowledge, Transfer, and Innovation Beyond the rather obvious aspects of learning shown in the Lincoln Electric case, a firm that has operations in different countries has the opportunity to increase innovation and transfer knowledge from one geographic market to another. For example, SC Johnson's European operations learned about a product that involved the combination of household pesticides and a simple plug-in device. In Europe, this product was sold in stores to consumers who needed a cheap and efficient deterrent for mosquitoes and other annoying insects. SC Johnson demonstrated its ability to learn from its European operation by transferring the technology to its fragrance division in the United States, thus giving rise to a whole new category of air-fresheners called Glade Plug-ins.[17]

A second facet of this form of learning is to locate a firm or a particular aspect of its operations in a part of the world where competition is the fiercest. So, for example, a U.S.

Exhibit 8.6 How Lincoln Electric (Eventually) Achieved Global Success

Source: Annual Report, 2003.

To Our Shareholders: Our carefully planned, ongoing strategy to expand Lincoln Electric's global footprint while growing market share, improving profitability, maximizing cash flow, and enhancing shareholder value continued on course in 2003. As the clear worldwide leader in the arc welding industry, our Company is truly in the strongest position of its long and successful history. Despite overcapacity in our industry and tough competition as companies fought for a shrinking volume of orders, we were able to persevere in 2003 and take advantage of opportunities in the global markets.

Net income for 2003 was $54.5 million, or $1.31 per diluted share. Net sales were $1.04 billion. Cash flow from operations in 2003 was a very strong $95.7 million and was significantly affected by voluntary funding of $40 million to the Company's U.S. pension plans. This was $20 million more funding than in 2002. Without the incremental pension funding, cash flow was $115.7 million. Both our sales and our profitability in 2003 were approximately split between our U.S. and non-U.S. businesses, excluding our nonconsolidated joint ventures in Turkey and China.

Today: Lincoln Electric is the world's largest designer and manufacturer of arc welding and cutting products. Growing global demand from the energy and construction sectors is fueling growth in pipeline and other infrastructure projects that require welding products. The Company's major end markets include metal forming and fabrication; pipeline, building, bridge, and power facility construction; transportation and defense industries; equipment manufacturers in construction, farming, and mining; retail resellers; and the rental market.

At Lincoln Electric, our corporate vision is to continue to be the undisputed world leader in sales, technology, profitability and enhanced shareholder value in the arc welding industry.

automaker might locate a product facility in Japan. Ironically, although one goal of such a move is to actually to compete on Japan's own turf against incumbents Toyota and Honda, the learning objective would be to try to emulate and learn from Japan's auto manufacturers' leading-edge production practices and transfer that advanced knowledge to the U.S. company's plants in other parts of the world, such as the United States, Canada, and Mexico. Similarly, because France and Italy are leaders in the high-fashion industry, companies such as DuPont and W. L. Gore & Associates, which aim to compete with leading-edge fabrics such as Lycra and Gore-Tex, place high value on those countries as production and marketing locations because of the learning opportunities about future customer preferences (e.g., touch, feel, color, etc.). In this view, the strategically most important markets will be those which feature not only intrinsic market attractiveness but an opportunity to learn and innovate in ways that can improve the organization's operations, products, and services around the globe.[18]

Sharing Knowledge Across Business Units Finally, large multinationals can exploit opportunities for inter-business-unit collaboration, which results in valuable knowledge sharing.[19] Sharing knowledge across business units has several tangible benefits. First, it enables firms to transfer best practices across national and business-unit boundaries. Because these best practices are proprietary—and probably tailored to the idiosyncrasies of the firm—they are more likely to result in competitive advantage than borrowing best practices from other firms. Why? Because all competitors have access to that information as well.

An example of this type of knowledge sharing is illustrated by a case study of BP PLC. A U.S. business unit that operates service stations was looking for novel ways to reduce costs in BP convenience stores. A manager borrowed ideas from colleagues in the Netherlands and the U.K. about how to reduce working-capital requirements. Copying these practices and implementing them in the United States resulted in a 20-percent reduction in working capital.

Sharing knowledge across business units can also uncover revenue-enhancement opportunities. The country manager of GlaxoSmithKline in the Philippines found a new drug therapy for tuberculosis in the company's R&D lab in India. Although this therapy was not widely known within the company because it represented a very small slice of the multinational firm's business, it represented a huge market opportunity in the Philippines and other developing countries, where tuberculosis is more widespread than it is in Europe and the United States.

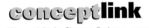

We explain in Chapter 7 that a *revenue-enhancement synergy* exists when two firms can generate more revenue because they're jointly owned by a corporate parent.

ENTRY VEHICLES INTO FOREIGN COUNTRIES

The strategy diamond says that a critical element of a firm's strategy is how it enters new markets. With international strategy, these new markets just happen to be in different countries, with different laws, infrastructure, cultures, and consumer preferences. The various entry mechanisms are referred to as *vehicles of strategy*. Consequently, a critical element of international expansion is determining which vehicles to use to enter new global markets. The first choice that managers must make is whether they will enter a foreign country with a vehicle that requires the firm to put some, or even considerable, capital at risk. As shown in Exhibit 8.7, firms can choose among a variety of nonequity and equity vehicles for entering a foreign country.

The second choice that managers must make is the form of the vehicle. Typically, each form offers differing levels of ownership control and local presence. Although firms can expand internationally in a number of different ways, we present them to you under three overarching foreign-country entry vehicles: *exporting*, *contractual agreements* and *alliances*, and *foreign direct investment (FDI)*, either through the acquisition of a company or simply starting one from scratch. At the end of this section, we will briefly discuss the use of importing as a foreign-country entry vehicle; it is somewhat of a stealth form of internationalization.

Exhibit 8.7 Choice of Entry Modes

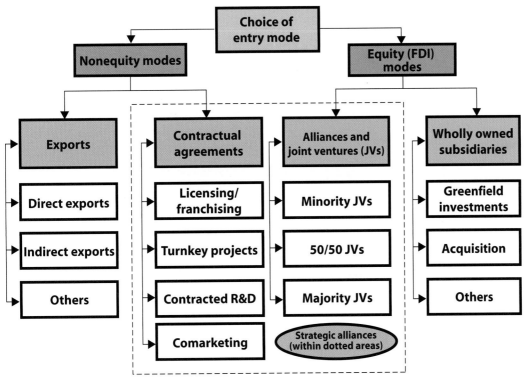

Source: Adapted from Pan, Y. and D. Tse, "The Hierarchical Model of Market Entry Modes," Journal of International Business Studies, 31 (2000), 535–554.

Foreign-country entry has been viewed historically as a staged process. Like the industry life cycle, the internationalization life cycle starts with a firm importing some of its raw materials or finished product for resale at home, followed perhaps by exporting products or raw materials abroad, and lastly ending in some type of partial or full ownership of plant, equipment, or other more extensive physical presence in a foreign country. These stages could be accomplished using vehicles ranging from simple contracts for purchases or sales on a transaction basis, through alliances, and perhaps even via mergers or wholesale acquisitions. Lincoln Electric, which was discussed in the previous section, offers an example of international growth through acquisition.

Over time, research has suggested that although some firms do follow such stages, they are better viewed as being more descriptive than predictive. Specifically, some firms follow the stages, starting with importing through foreign direct investment, whereas others jump right to the direct investment stage as their first internationalization effort.[20] It is also helpful to note that the different entry vehicles have differing degrees of risk and control. For instance, a company that is only exporting its products abroad is typically risking only payment for the product and, perhaps its reputation if the product is not serviced well in the foreign locale. This also shows how little control the exporter has over the downstream activities once it has shipped the product. Although the exporter may have some legal or distribution agreement with local firms, this is very little control compared to ownership of local factories or distribution or partial ownership through some form of alliance. In this section, we will walk you through these alternative entry vehicles. Examples of firms following them and the basic tradeoffs among them are summarized in Exhibit 8.8.

Exporting

Exporting is exactly the opposite of importing; it can take the form of selling production or service inputs or actual products and services abroad. With the advent of the Internet

exporting Foreign-country entry vehicle in which a firm uses an intermediary to perform most foreign marketing functions

Exhibit 8.8 Vehicles for Entering Foreign Markets

Source: Examples drawn from in A. Gupta, and V. Govindarajan, "Managing Global Expansion: A Conceptual Framework," Business Horizons, March/April 2002, 45–54.

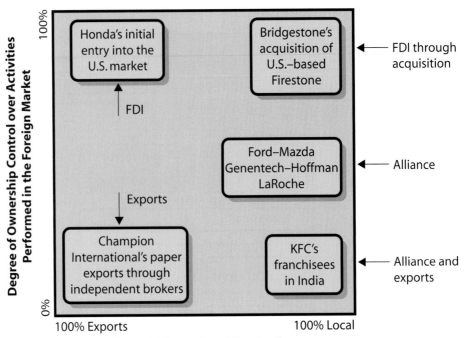

and electronic banking, the physical entry barriers to becoming an exporter are lower than ever before. Although the importer is ultimately responsible for the issues relating to customs, packaging, and other trade requirements, the exporting firm will generally only be successful to the extent that it can deliver a product or service that meets customers' needs.

Costs of Exporting Exporting is a popular internationalization vehicle with small firms because the costs of entering new markets are relatively minimal with this vehicle. Exporters generally use local representatives or distributors to sell their products in new international markets. The main costs associated with exporting are transportation and meeting the packaging and ingredient requirements of the target country. Consequently, exporting is most common to international markets that are relatively close to the domestic market or to markets in which competitors and substitutes for the firm's products are not readily available. A large percentage of the born-global firms discussed later in the chapter used exporting as a vehicle to go global quickly.[21]

Licensing and Franchising Exporting can take the form of shipping a product overseas and leaving marketing and distribution up to a foreign customer. It can also take the form of licensing or franchising, turnkey projects, R&D contracts, and comarketing. Due to some of the characteristics of these latter vehicles, as shown in Exhibit 8.7, such contractual arrangements are often considered a form of strategic alliance. Licensing and franchising provide a case in point. When a firm licenses its products or technologies in another country, it transfers the risk of actually implementing market entry to another firm, which pays the licensor a fee for the right to use its name in the local country. Franchising in a foreign country works similarly to franchising in a domestic market. A firm receives a sign-up fee and ongoing franchise royalties in exchange for teaching the franchisee how to open and operate the franchisor's business in the local market.

The risk, of course, to the licensor or franchisor is that the licensee or franchisee will violate the terms of the agreement, either to the detriment of the product or service itself, by refusing to pay agreed-upon fees or royalties or simply selling a copy of the product or service under another name (that is essentially stealing the intellectual property entirely). The primary risks to the franchisee or licensee are that the product or service will not perform as promised or that the licensor or franchisor will do something that diminishes the market attractiveness of the product or service.

Turnkey Projects, R&D Contracts, and Comarketing The latter three forms, turnkey projects, R&D contracts, and comarketing, are specialized contractual agreements whereby a firm agrees to build a factory, conduct a specific R&D project, or comarket or cobrand a product such that the contracting firm has used it as a foreign-market entry vehicle. For example, the Norwegian firm Kvaerner A/S contracts to build paper mills and deep-sea oil rigs for Brazilian paper and petroleum companies; the German firm Bayer AG contracts a large R&D project to the U.S. firm Millennium pharmaceuticals with the work undertaken in both firm's respective countries; McDonald's in Japan packages its kids meals with characters that are familiar to Japanese children based on characters like Pokémon or Hello Kitty that are popular at the time.

Alliances

Alliances are another common foreign-market entry vehicle. Because we devote an entire chapter to alliances later in the text, here we simply explain why alliances are so commonly used for international expansion. Often, alliances are chosen because of government regulations. For example, only recently did the Chinese government allow non-Chinese ownership of companies in China. As a result, firms could only enter China through various partnerships. Alliances may also be used as an international-strategy vehicle due to management's lack of familiarity with the local culture or institutions or because the complexity of operating internationally requires the firm to focus on the activities it does best and to outsource the rest. Some combination of these three factors—regulations, market familiarity, or operational complexity—typically explain why alliances are so often used by firms competing internationally. The box entitled "How Would *You* Do That? 8.1" provides an example of how the British retailer Laura Ashley responded to one of these motivations for an international alliance—the simplification of global operating complexity—and how it chose its ultimate alliance partner.

Foreign Direct Investment

Foreign direct investment (FDI), as the term implies, is an international entry strategy whereby a firm makes a financial investment in a foreign market to facilitate the startup of a new venture. FDI tends to be the most expensive international entry tactic because it requires the greatest commitment of a firm's time and resources. FDI can be implemented in several ways, such as through acquisitions or through a so-called greenfield alliance—the startup of a foreign entity from scratch. This latter form of FDI is called **greenfield investment**. In the previous section, we reviewed how alliances can be a vehicle to foreign market entry. As you will learn in Chapter 9, alliances do not require any equity investment. However, many alliances do involve equity investment, and when they do in the context of foreign market entry, it is a special case of greenfield investment. For instance, Daimler-Chrysler and BMW each invested $250 million to start a new engine factory in Curitiba, Brazil.

foreign direct investment (FDI) Foreign-country entry vehicle by which a firm commits to the direct ownership of a foreign subsidiary or division

greenfield investment Form of FDI in which a firm starts a new foreign business from the ground up

Acquisitions and Equity Alliances Because greenfield investment usually involves the greatest risk, expense, and time, many firms pursue FDI through acquisitions or alliances (you will learn more about these particular strategy vehicles in Chapters 9 and 10). Acquisitions provide the firm with rapid entry because the firm purchases existing businesses that are already staffed and successfully operating. For instance, when the battery-maker Rayovac entered Brazil in 2005, it did so by purchasing Microlite, the dominant battery maker in Brazil. Similarly, South African Breweries purchased Miller Brewing in 2002 to gain an instant presence and production capacity in one of the largest beer markets in the world, the United States.

Finding a Global Partner to Deliver the Goods

In the early 1990s, U.S. executive Jim Maxmin was brought in as CEO to turn around Laura Ashley, Ltd., the flagging and bloated British fashion retailer. At the time, Laura Ashley was vertically integrated, with operations spanning design, manufacturing, distribution, and retail sales. It had 481 retail shops located around the world, primarily in North America (185 shops), the United Kingdom (184 shops), and Europe (65 shops). Revenues in 1992 were $261 million,

and the firm had experienced three year's of declining sales and cumulative annual losses totaling nearly $30 million.

Maxmin's objective was to focus Laura Ashley's strategy on what the firm did best—namely, design and retail functions. Product quality had steadily declined, leaving production as a question mark, and Ashley's distribution system, as measured by its in-stock performance, was in shambles. This meant that the firm would need to fix or outsource production and distribution in some way that allowed the firm to maintain its quality in these areas and ultimately return the venerable firm to its historic profitability. Making the issues all the more complex was the fact that Laura Ashley's retail presence was international, so that any solution would need to coordinate products not only among the firm's distribution warehouses in the United Kingdom, Holland, New Jersey, California, Canada, Paris, and Australia but among its retail stores in those same parts of the world.

Maxmin viewed an alliance with a strong international distribution company as one solution because it would allow Laura Ashley to focus on the product and the customer (design, production, and retail) and free it from owning and managing the distribution infrastructure. To develop a strategic alliance, Maxmin would need to find a partner who would agree to collaborate to achieve mutually

agreed-upon goals and with whom Laura Ashley could pool key value-chain resources and capabilities. To ensure that an alliance would have some chance of succeeding, Maxmin identified three fundamental criteria that would need to be satisfied by its future partner:

1. *Complementary needs and competencies:* Laura Ashley would target partners who were dedicated to the distribution business, who had international expertise and capabilities, and who needed international partners like Laura Ashley to help them grow.

2. *Similar management styles and operating systems:* Under Maxmin, Laura Ashley had adopted the simple strategic vision of "simplify, focus, act" as a way to guide turnaround efforts. Maxmin was looking for a partner with a similar orientation. In addition, Laura Ashley had a very poor information-technology infrastructure, and it would need this to be first class for it to survive. Thus, Maxmin was also looking for a distribution partner that would allow Ashley to upgrade its operating systems to a world-class standard.

3. *Divergent strategic objectives:* Maxmin did not want a partner who wanted to be, or might evolve into, a potential competitor. This ruled out using the distribution capabilities of one »

of its suppliers or partnering with another retailer that had strong distribution capabilities and infrastructure, such as Wal-Mart.

So with whom did Maxmin ally with? FedEx ("when you absolutely positively have to get it there overnight"). Even though FedEx was large at the time, with nearly $8 billion in revenues, the Laura Ashley relationship was still relatively substantial and gave FedEx further dedicated business worldwide. At the same time, FedEx offered Ashley both immediate world-class distribution capability and a longer-term opportunity to learn about global logistics from one of the best logistics firms on the planet. In Maxmin's terms, "The alliance is not about trucks and sheds. Logistics gives the organization an opportunity to achieve competitive advantage by focusing on its core competencies."

As you will learn in the next chapter, however, an alliance is not a panacea for a firm's ills nor is it a substitute for strategy. What this means for Laura Ashley in practical terms is that the firm must now identify what competencies are truly "core," in the sense that they differentiate Laura Ashley's business operations and offerings from those of competitors. It's one thing for Maxmin to say "we are going to focus on our core competencies"; it's another thing to execute this somewhat ambiguous statement profitably. By aligning the remaining

facets of the strategy diamond with this new strategy vehicle, Laura Ashley stands a chance of delivering the good to shareholders and other key stakeholders.

At the same time, relationships between alliance partners evolve over time, such that one partner may increase its relative power in the relationship and begin to exploit its partner, in the form of passing on higher costs. Though it is unlikely that Laura Ashley will be able to diversify profitably into a logistics company like FedEx, Laura Ashley may become so dependent upon FedEx that it can leave the relationship only by doing irreparable damage to its strategy, a future viability. A related risk is that Laura Ashley may lose touch with some of its customers as a result of this new outsourced distribution arrangement. If this diluted touch somehow also dilutes the firm's unique ability to link insights into customer taste and preferences with the design capabilities that differentiate it, then the FedEx arrangement may simply prolong and then contribute to the eventual demise of Laura Ashley. You would want to accommodate both these risks through the staging facet of the strategy diamond, along with a regular review of the fit among the other four facets.

Sources: K. Rankine, "Getting Lost, and Found, in the Translation: Former Laura Ashley Boss Jim Maxmin Has a New Book,

a New Theory and His Own Language," *The Daily Telegraph* (London), September 20, 2003, 34; F. Schwadel, "Laura Ashley Taps Newcomer to Bring Profit Back in Vogue," *Wall Street Journal* (Europe), July 18, 1991, 3; R. Hobson, "Eliminate Unnecessary Cost and Structure: Logistics Focus," *The Times* (London), November 8, 1993, 11.

South African Breweries, the maker of Castle Lager, successfully entered one of the largest beer markets in the world—the United States—by acquiring Miller Brewing Company in 2002. The combined corporation is known as SABMiller.

After its horrendous experiences with rapid international expansion, Lincoln Electric amended its corporate policy on FDI: It now engages only in FDI through alliances with local players in order to maximize the knowledge needed about local market conditions, both in terms of production and market demand. Sometimes alliances are dictated by the necessity to have a certain proportion of local content in a product, such as a car or motorcycle, in order to sell the product into a nonlocal market. Brazil and China are two examples of countries that have stringent local-content laws. Minimum efficient scale is another explanation for the use of alliances as an FDI foreign-entry tactic.

For example, the Daimler-Chrysler and BMW alliance mentioned earlier was necessary because neither company could justify the volume of production needed by the new plant to justify it economically. Therefore, the two firms joined forces to form Tritec, a state-of-the art automotive engine factory that supplies parts for BMW's Mini Cooper assembly plant in the United Kingdom and DaimlerChyrsler's PT Cruiser assembly plants in Mexico, the United States, and South Africa.[22]

Importing and International Strategy

importing Internationalization strategy by which a firm brings a good, service, or capital into the home country from abroad

In many ways, **importing** is a stealth form of internationalization because firms will often claim they have no international operations and yet directly or indirectly base their production or services on inputs obtained from outside their home country. Firms that engage in importing must be knowledgeable about customs requirements and informed about compliance with customs regulations, entry of goods, invoices, classification and value, determination and assessment of duty, special requirements, fraud, marketing, trade finance and insurance, and foreign trade zones. Importing can take many forms, from the sourcing of components, machinery, and raw materials to the purchase of finished goods for domestic resale to outsourcing production or services to nondomestic providers.

Outsourcing and Offshoring   This latter activity, international outsourcing, has taken on the most visible role in business and corporate strategy in recent years. International outsourcing is not a new phenomenon. For instance, Nike has been designing shoes and other apparel for decades and manufacturing them abroad. Similarly, Pacific Cycle does not make a single Schwinn or Mongoose bicycle in the United States but instead imports them from Taiwanese and Chinese manufacturers. It just seems that international outsourcing is new because of the increasingly rapid pace with which businesses are sourcing services, components, and raw materials from developing countries such as China, Brazil, and India.

Information technologies (IT), such as telecommunications and the widespread diffusion of the Internet, have provided the impetus for the international outsourcing of services as well as factors of production. Such *business process outsourcing (BPO)* is the delegation of one or more IT-intensive business processes to an external nondomestic provider which, in turn, owns, administers, and manages the selected process based on defined and measurable performance criteria. Sometimes this is referred to as *offshoring* because the business processes (including production/manufacturing) are outsourced to a lower-cost location, usually overseas. Offshoring refers to taking advantage of lower-cost labor in another country. Although outsourced processes are handed off to third-party vendors, offshored processes may be handed off to third-party vendors or remain in-house. This definition of offshoring includes organizations that build dedicated captive centers of their own in remote, lower-cost locations. The many U.S. firms that have established *maquiladoras* (assembly plants) in Mexico are examples of offshoring without outsourcing.

Firms in such service and IT-intensive industries as insurance, banking, pharmaceuticals, telecommunications, automobiles, and airlines seem to be the early adopters of BPO. Of the industries just mentioned, insurance and banking are able to generate savings purely because of the large proportion of processes they can outsource, such as claim processing, loan processing, and client servicing through call centers. Among those countries housing BPO operations, India appears to be experiencing the most dramatic growth for services that require English-language skills and education. BPO operations have been growing 70 percent a year and are now a $1.6 billion industry, employing approximately 100,000 people. In India alone, BPO has to grow only 27 percent annually until 2008 to deliver $17 billion in revenues and employ a million people.[23]

More generally, foreign outsourcing and offshoring locations tend to be defined by how automated a production process or service can be made, the relative labor costs, and the transportation costs involved. When transportation costs and automation are both high, then the knowledge-worker component of the location calculation becomes less important. You can see how you might employ the CAGE framework to evaluate potential outsourcing locations. However, in some cases firms invest in both plant and equipment and the training and development of the local workforce. Brazil is but one case in point, with examples from Ford, BMW, Daimler-Benz, and Cargill. Each of these multinational organizations is making significant investments in the educational infrastructure of this significant emerging economy.[24]

INTERNATIONAL STRATEGY CONFIGURATIONS

How a firm becomes involved in international markets, which appears to be increasingly important, if not obligatory, for many if not all firms, differs from how it configures the interactions between headquarters and country operations. It is important to note that international-strategy configuration is as much about strategy formulation as it is about implementation, because management is making choices about which value-chain components to centralize, where to centralize those operations geographically, and the degree to which those decentralized and centralized value-chain activities will be managed and coordinated. Remember, too, that strategy helps a firm manage important tradeoffs that differentiate it and its products from competitors.

Resolving the Tension Between Local Preferences and Global Standards   In this section, we discuss the underlying tensions created between a firm's attempts to be responsive to the local needs of diverse sets of customers and yet remain globally efficient. Meeting the ideal tradeoff between customizing for local needs and achieving cost efficiencies requires further tradeoffs with respect to the firm's value chain regarding which activities will be standardized and which will be locally tailored. These are the central tradeoffs a firm must wrestle with in designing and managing its international strategy.

Globalizing firms must reconcile the natural tension that exists between local preferences and global standards. The domination of local preferences over the search for global efficiencies, left unchecked, often leads to what strategy researchers describe as *national fragmentation*.[25] In addition, local adaptation of products and services is significantly more expensive than relying on global standards. Consequently, attempting to achieve high levels of local responsiveness will almost always lead to higher cost structure.[26] A product that is uniform across markets is highly efficient to produce because the firm can simply design a factory of the most efficient size in a location that most efficiently balances the costs of inputs with the transportation costs of getting outputs to the desired markets. If this product has the same brand around the world, then marketing and promotion efforts are similarly focused on that single brand. However, even products like Coca-Cola, which appear to be ubiquitous, have different flavorings, packaging, and promotion constraints in each market. Some of these constraints are a function of local regulatory pressures; others reflect underlying differences in consumers' tastes. Just as important, other constraints are a function of the competitive norms that have prevailed in the industry, either globally or locally. The variations of international strategy configuration that we cover in this section are summarized in Exhibit 8.9.

We will also speak briefly about born-global firms in this section because more and more organizations appear to have operations that span national borders early in their existence. As you will see, born-global firms employ an amalgam of exporting and FDI, but do so much more rapidly than firms have in the past. In the strategy diamond, exporting and FDI would be considered vehicles, and the timing and sequencing of the usage would be viewed in the context of staging. Each of these vehicles provides a firm and its management with experience and knowledge about cross-border business practices.

Multinational Configuration

Each of the configurations identified in Exhibit 8.9 presents tradeoffs between global efficiency and local responsiveness. Recognize that these configurations are "pure forms" and that, in reality, most firms' international configurations vary slightly or significantly from those shown in Exhibit 8.9. By definition, strategy must be internally consistent and externally oriented. However, management must make judgments as to what an external orientation means in terms of how the strategy takes competitive pressures and consumer preferences into account. At the same time, management must also make judgments about the firm's internal resources and capabilities to support a particular international-strategy configuration. This explains why firms with seemingly very different international-strategy configurations can coexist in the same industry.

When Lincoln Electric first embarked on becoming a global firm, it had relatively independent operations in many markets around the world. It used its strongest national positions to **cross-subsidize** market-share battles or growth initiatives in other countries. Such an approach is typically referred to as a **multinational configuration** because the firm is essentially a portfolio of geographically removed business units that have devoted most of their resources and capabilities to maximizing local responsiveness and uniqueness. Firms which, like Lincoln Electric, employ a multinational configuration have the objective to develop a global presence but may or may not use the same brand names in each market or consolidate their buying power or distribution capabilities.

International Configuration

Another configuration, sometimes simply referred to as an **international configuration,** centralizes some resources, such as global brand and distribution capabilities, in order to

cross-subsidizing Practice by which a firm uses profits from one aspect of a product, service, or region to support other aspects of competitive activity

multinational configuration Strategy by which a firm is essentially a portfolio of geographically removed business units that have devoted most of their resources and capabilities to maximizing local responsiveness and uniqueness

international configuration The firm leverages key resources and capabilities by centralizing them to achieve economies of scale, but it decentralizes others, such as marketing, so that some activities can be somewhat localized

Exhibit 8.9 International Strategy Configurations, Global Efficiency, and Resource Requirements

	Relatively Few Opportunities to Gain Global Efficiencies	**Many Opportunities to Gain Global Efficiencies**
Relatively High Local Responsiveness	**Multinational Configuration** Build flexibility to respond to national differences through strong, resourceful, entrepreneurial, and somewhat independent national or regional operations. Requires decentralized and relatively self-sufficient units. **Example:** MTV initially adopted an international configuration (using only American programming in foreign markets) but then changed its strategy to a multinational one. It now tailors its Western European programming to each market, offering eight channels, each in a different language.	**Transnational Configuration** Develop global efficiency, flexibility, and worldwide learning. Requires dispersed, interdependent, and specialized capabilities simultaneously. **Example:** Nestlé has taken steps to move in this direction, starting first with what might be described as a multinational configuration. Today, Nestlé aims to evolve from a decentralized, profit-center configuration to one that operates as a single, global company. Firms like Nestlé have taken lessons from leading consulting firms such as McKinsey and Company, which are globally dispersed but have a hard-driving, one-firm culture at their core.
Relatively Low Local Responsiveness	**International Configuration** Exploit parent-company knowledge and capabilities through worldwide diffusion, local marketing, and adaptation. The most valuable resources and capabilities are centralized; others, such as local marketing and distribution, are decentralized. **Example:** When Wal-Mart initially set up its operations in Brazil, it used its U.S. stores as a model for international expansion.	**Global Configuration** Build cost advantages through centralized, global-scale operations. Requires centralized and globally scaled resources and capabilities. **Example:** Companies such as Merck and Hewlett-Packard give particular subsidiaries a worldwide mandate to leverage and disseminate their unique capabilities and specialized knowledge worldwide.

Source: C. Bartlett, S. Ghoshal, and J. Birkenshaw, Transnational Management *(New York: Irwin, 2004).*

achieve costs savings, but decentralizes others, such as marketing in order to achieve some level of localization. This strategy is common among firms that have created something in their home market that they wish to replicate in foreign markets, allowing them the economies of scale and scope necessary to create and exploit innovations on a worldwide basis. Heavy R&D companies such as Intel and Pfizer fit this mold: Even though the products that they produce are relatively standardized around the world, local marketing and distribution channels differ.

Global Configuration

A pure **global configuration** focuses only on global efficiency. A global configuration is one that makes a tradeoff between local responsiveness and the lower costs associated with global efficiency. With this configuration, production and sourcing decisions are designed to achieve the greatest economies of scale. Firms following this configuration potentially sacrifice the higher prices that follow customization, but they are counting on the likelihood that their products or services will meet enough needs to be demanded without finely tuned customization. Firms in commodity industries such as steel and copper, such as BHP-Billeton, fall into this category. Because end-customers make purchase decisions based on price alone, the firm is organized to realize the lowest possible production costs.

Transnational Configuration

The final international-strategy configuration that we discuss, the **transnational configuration,** is one that attempts to capitalize on both local responsiveness and global efficiency. When successfully implemented, this approach enables firms to achieve global economies of scale, cross-subsidization across markets, and the ability to engage in retaliatory and responsive competition across markets. This configuration is available to companies with high degrees of internationalization. However, as with any other strategic tradeoff, it is extremely difficult to find the balance between cost efficiencies and the ability to customize to local tastes and standards. McDonald's is often used as an example of a firm that fits this configuration because it uses its purchasing power to get the best prices on the global commodities it uses for inputs yet tries to tailor its menu offerings to fit local tastes and cultural preferences.

Born-Global Firms

One reason that global strategy—and the four international strategy configurations—will become an increasingly important topic is the fact that more and more firms, even very small ones, have operations that bridge national borders very soon after their founding. Perhaps appropriate for the Internet age, this new breed of firms that emerged in the 1990s is being dubbed "born global" because their operations often span the globe early in their existence. A common characteristic of such firms is that their offerings complement the products or capabilities of other global players, take advantage of global IT infrastructure, or otherwise tap into a demand for a product or service that at its core is somewhat uniform across national geographic markets. Although many firms may fall into this category by virtue of their products, the operations and customers of born-global firms do actually span the globe. Born-global firms position themselves globally, exploiting a combination of exporting and FDI.

Logitech, the computer-mouse and peripherals company, is perhaps one of the best early examples of a successful born-global firm.[27] It was founded by two Italians and a Swiss, with operations and R&D initially split between California and Switzerland. Logitech's primary focus was on the PC mouse, and it rapidly expanded production to Ireland and Taiwan. With its stylish and ergonomic products, Logitech had captured 30 percent of the global mouse business by 1989, garnering the startup a healthy $140 million in revenues. Today, Logitech is an industry leader in the design and manufacture of computer-peripheral devices. It has manufacturing facilities in Asia and offices in major cities in North America, Europe, and Asia Pacific and employs more than 6,000 people worldwide.[28]

Skype is one of the most recent born-global firms, and you may already have it on your laptop or home computer, taking advantage of its free Internet phone technology (*voice-over-IP,* or *VOIP*).[29] At any point in time, millions of users are logged in to Skype, and the program and service have made such a strong impression that the phrase "skype me" has replaced "give me a call" in some circles. Initially founded in Sweden as Tele2, Skype is now headquartered in Luxembourg, with offices in London and Tallinn, Estonia. It received significant venture-capital funding from some of the largest venture-capital firms in the world, and was recently acquired by eBay. Skype was founded by the inventors of Kazaa, one of the most popular Internet file-sharing software programs in the world. Both Logitech and Skype exhibit a number of characteristics required for successful global startups.

How to Succeed as a Global Startup Successful global startups must complete two phases. In the first phase, managers ask, "Should my firm be a global startup?" If they can answer yes to all or most of the follow-up questions entailed by phase 1, then they need to be sure that they can quickly build the resources and capabilities identified in phase 2. Research has shown that those firms unable to connect the dots in phase 2 were forced to cease operations after short, albeit sometimes lively, adventures.[30]

During phase 1—*and before moving on to phase 2*—managers should consider questions that will help them determine whether the firm should be a global startup:

- Does the firm need human resources from other countries in order to succeed?
- Does the firm need financial capital from other countries in order to succeed?
- If the firm goes global, will target customers prefer its services over those of competitors?
- Can the firm put an international system in place more quickly than domestic competitors?
- Does the firm need global scale and scope to justify the financial and human capital investment in the venture?
- Will a purely domestic focus now make it harder for the firm to go global in the future?

If the answer to all or most of these questions is yes, managers can commit to moving the firm into phase 2 and put together the tools they will need to move the firm into the global market:

- Strong management team with international experience
- Broad and deep international network among suppliers, customers, and complements
- Preemptive marketing or technology that will provide first-mover advantage with customers and lock out competitors out from key suppliers and complements
- Strong intangible assets (both Logitech and Skype have style, hipness, and mindshare via their brands)
- Ability to keep customers locked in by linking new products and services to the core business, while constantly innovating the core product or service
- Close worldwide coordination and communication among business units, suppliers, complements, and customers

So why do we introduce the concept of global startups at this point in the text? One reason is because of their increasing prevalence, which is driven, in part, by globalizing consumer preferences, mobile consumers, large global firms, and the pervasiveness of the Internet and its effects. The second reason, which should become clear after reading the next section, is that dynamic contexts typically give rise to the need for firms to strive for a global presence and to understand global markets early in their evolution.

INTERNATIONAL STRATEGY IN STABLE AND DYNAMIC CONTEXTS

A recent McKinsey study suggests that the creativity which some companies have located in emerging economies, and which have resulted in inexpensive but high-quality products, will now compel incumbents to go down the same road.[31] This assertion gets at the heart—the question of urgency and timing—of how international strategy is approached in relatively stable versus dynamic contexts. Moreover, it also suggests that industries that might have been considered relatively stable will increasingly take on dynamic characteristics as a result of global competition. In many ways, what you have learned so far about business and corporate strategies in dynamic contexts is equally applicable in purely domestic and already globalizing organizations. The key difference, however—a difference that we hope is apparent after reading this chapter—is that cross-border business adds another level of complexity to both strategy formulation and execution and, that unfortunately, such complexity may be unavoidable for firms in dynamic contexts.

Global Context and Industry Life Cycle

Recall from earlier chapters that we differentiated between external- and internal-based views of strategy. The internal view emphasizes resources, capabilities, and activities as the source of competitive advantage, whereas the external view draws attention to how firms need to adapt or modify their competitive positions and strategies to the external environment to position themselves in a manner conducive to superior returns. These views have implications for the dynamic nature of international strategic action as well. Taking the external perspective, for instance, typically draws managerial attention to the dynamic nature of the industry life cycle and how that drives decisions to internationalize. Specifically, as an industry matures, the international implications of industry structure—and therefore strategic choices and firm behavior—should change in fundamental ways.[32]

First-Mover Advantage In the introductory stage of an industry's life cycle, the external perspective would expect firms to engage in few exports, largely because the market for the industry's products is still highly uncertain and there are few accepted quality, service, or technological standards. As you will see, the length of this stage may vary significantly by country. Firms should begin to export during the growth stage of industry life cycle because new entrants enter the market and compete for existing customers. Early movers in the domestic market then have an opportunity to be early movers in foreign markets as well and to continue growth even as domestic competition heats up. As the industry matures, exports gain even more steam in the face of domestic market saturation, and firms start producing products abroad to satisfy foreign demand and to search for global efficiencies. Industry shakeout and consolidation also tend to follow industry maturity, and consolidation through acquisitions leads to a few large global companies.

Staging and Geographic Markets Similarly, when discussing international strategy from an external perspective, the fact that geographic markets differ in many legal, cultural, and institutional ways—differences which, in turn, are likely to have implications for product demand—must also be taken into account. Indeed, demand characteristics of geographic markets have been shown to evolve at different rates. For example, the time from new-product introduction to the growth stage (sometimes called market takeoff) in Portugal may occur after a longer period of time than the same transition in Denmark. Indeed, although the average period of time between a new-product or -service introduction and market takeoff is 6 years, a new product takes only about 4 years to take off in Denmark, Norway, and Sweden, compared to 9 years in Greece and Portugal (the U.S. averages 5.3 years).[33]

Role of Arenas in Global Strategies Identification of arenas ensures that the most critical national markets are identified and brought into the plan. Similarly, even with thoughtful treatment of staging and arenas, structures, systems, and processes must be in complete alignment with the firm's vision and global intent. A firm that strives to execute the most complex global strategy—the transnational strategy—must have enormous investments in its ability to coordinate and integrate activities around the globe, complemented by customer characteristics that enable such a global strategy to create true value.

Resources and Global Strategy The resource-based perspective has important implications for international strategy in dynamic contexts as well. It is here, too, that the questions of staging and geographic arenas from the strategy diamond model are critically important to effective international strategies. From the resource-based perspective, staging is important because the firm's global resources and capabilities do not materialize overnight. Lincoln Electric's experience is a case in point here. Lincoln's pace of international expansion exceeded its organizational capabilities to integrate foreign acquisitions, let alone manage them once they were integrated. Lincoln also attempted to internationalize

conceptlink

In Chapter 6, we defined **first movers** as firms that choose to initiate a strategic action. We also pointed out that the benefits of first-mover strategy are subject to conditions in the **industry life cycle**. In Chapter 1, we noted that the need for early wins was one factor in driving **staging**—i.e., timing—decisions.

almost exclusively through acquisitions. However, research on foreign expansion reveals that the firms most successful at internationalizing combine greenfield investments with acquisitions and alliances.[34] Simply expanding through greenfield investment can lead to inertia and lack of learning. Acquisitions help broaden a firm's knowledge base. However, exclusive reliance on acquisitions is not only costly but makes knowledge transfer and learning more difficult. Firms that balance greenfield investments and acquisitions seem to transfer more knowledge and create more value than firms that rely on either process exclusively.

Capabilities and Global Strategy One of the fundamental ideas of having a dynamic view of strategy is to continuously build and renew firm capabilities. Many born-global firms fall into this dynamic-context category nearly from inception. By continuously evolving its stock of resources and capabilities, a firm maximizes its chances of adapting to changing environmental conditions. Thus, when a firm decides to enter a particular new foreign market, it must also embark on developing the resources necessary to make that market-entry decision a success. At the same time, what it learns in those new geographic markets should be evaluated for application or adaptation to existing market positions.

In addition, as a firm internationalizes and becomes more dependent on a particular foreign location, the need for high-level capabilities to perform the local activities increases commensurately.[35] For instance, as Ikea expands around the globe, its ability to understand local furniture markets increases. However, these needs are greatest in markets where it faces the most exposure; Ikea's early missteps in the United States have been attributed to lack of market intelligence.[36] This leads us to our closing section on global strategy in dynamic contexts.

Developing a Mind-Set for Global Dynamic Competitiveness

Given the emphasis on the importance of leadership skills throughout this text, it should come as no surprise that what may make or break the effectiveness of a firm's international strategy is the internationally related capabilities and global mind-set of the firm's executives, particularly in dynamic markets. Moreover, such capabilities and mind-set may enable one firm to change a once relatively stable competitive context into a dynamic and vibrant one. In the box entitled "How Would *You* Do That? 8.2," international strategy researchers have identified four particularly effective tactics that organizations can use to develop global leaders.

Global Perspective The global mind-set has two distinct but related dimensions. The first dimension is something that strategy researchers simply refer to as global perspective.[37] Executives with a global perspective require a combination of specific knowledge and skills. In terms of knowledge, executives with a global mind-set have an appreciation for the fact that countries and their peoples differ culturally, socioeconomically, and sociopolitically, view those differences as potential opportunities as opposed to threats, and can link such differences to necessary adaptations in business operations. In addition, they also recognize that the management processes guiding those business operations must also be adapted to cultural, socioeconomic, and sociopolitical differences.

It is this latter aspect of knowledge that leads to the international-skills aspect of global perspective. In this instance, skills are the experience gained from *acculturation*— living in other cultures for extended periods of time as an expatriate. It also refers to the leadership skills necessary for managing a culturally diverse managerial team and worldwide workforce. The end result of this combination of knowledge and skills is that the firm is able to build strong relationships within the organization across geographies and with customers in different geographic locations.

Learning on a Worldwide Scale In many ways, the second dimension of a global mind-set requires the first dimension as a foundation. The second dimension is the capacity to learn from participation in one geographic market and transfer that knowledge to other operations elsewhere in the world. This means that the firm not only has globally

Tactics for Developing Globally Minded Executives

A study of top-management teams across Asian, European, and North American firms identified four particularly effective tactics for developing global leaders. Although these tactics may seem obvious, they are not universally utilized, evidenced by the striking fact that even in multinationals, fewer than 15 percent of executives have substantive international experience. The researchers identified the following four tactics:

- *Travel*. This tactic aims to put managers in the middle of foreign cultures so that they can learn first-hand about people, schools, economy, political system, markets, and so on. It is important that such travel be unfettered as much as possible by the filters created by private drivers and fancy hotels. The executives who gain the most experience from international travel actually spend time with end consumers and local suppliers so that they see with their own eyes what opportunities and challenges may lie ahead. More firms are beginning to use "inpatriates"—foreign-country nationals who are integrated into the host company's corporate headquarters as a means to further knowledge transfer.

- *Teams*. This tactic involves the formation of teams composed of members from different cultures. Although part of the objective of such teams is to tailor solutions for particular country environments, an important by-product of this tactic is that the team members gain experience working with people from countries other than their own. The firms that have been most effective at exploiting this type of global acculturation have done so by taking three steps: (1) making sure a manager has been a member of a multicultural team before assuming a leadership position; (2) ensuring that the first multicultural-team experience is within one function, such as finance or marketing, before that member is introduced to a cross-functional, multicultural team; and (3) seeing to it that all members are provided prior and ongoing training in cross-cultural communication, team dynamics, and conflict resolution.

- *Training*. Although training was mentioned as an important component of the team-development tactic, it can also, if properly orchestrated, be a tactic in and of itself to gain a global mind-set and to build a within-firm global network. First, program participants should be drawn from geographically diverse units. Second, the training can foster intercultural understanding and cooperation by focusing on broad topics such as vision, strategy, change management, and interunit cooperative business initiatives, as well as specifically addressing cross-cultural communication, multicultural-team dynamics, and conflict resolution.

- *Transfers*. The most effective—though most expensive—tactic for developing global leaders is the actual transfer of individuals to foreign assignments. Such expatriate assignments tend to be the most effective because they typically force individuals to become immersed in the local culture. Expatriate assignments are the most expensive because the compensation packages often include doubling of the base salary, buying or paying for rent on the local housing, and providing for the feeding and education of the expatriate's family members. In practice, it is also expensive because many expatriates return sooner than expected, **»** often because their family members have trouble adjusting to the new country setting or because they leave the company altogether perhaps due to some aspect of the expatriate assignment, perhaps due to their being hired away by a local competitor. Firms that exploit this tactic most effectively take the following steps: (1) explicitly considering how the person and firm will use that person's experience in the future; (2) factoring in the person's family and how he or she will handle the move; (3) providing the training identified in the team and training tactics mentioned earlier; (4) furnishing a high-level home country mentor so the expatriate always has ties to headquarters; and (5) clearly spelling out the repatriation timeframe and possible career paths once the assignment is complete. These last two steps are key, because even 25 percent of the expatriates who have *successfully completed* an overseas assignment leave the firm after one year!

So if travel, teams, training, and transfers are the appropriate tactics for developing globally minded executives, where would you introduce this into the formulation and implementation aspects of your strategy? Well, if your firm is in a competitive field where it must grow or acquire global executive competencies quickly, then it

would need to quickly recruit or promote individuals with the requisite global skills into the top management team. As you saw with Lincoln Electric, if a firm does not involve key decision makers with international management experience and skills in the formulation process, its international strategy may lead it into rocky waters. Depending on how critical these skills are for the firm's strategy and future success, you would need to integrate them in some way into the staging facet of the strategy diamond, and then leverage one or more of the tactics that were identified in this feature.

As we have demonstrated throughout this chapter, and have summarized in Exhibit 8.3, you also would need a clear vision about how an expansive global strategic posture is reflected in all five facets of the strategy diamond. From a personal standpoint, you may be interested in the two following related data points. First, large-sample strategic management studies have shown that firms perform better when their CEO and top executives have the global skills that complement their international strategy. Second, those studies also show that the executives themselves receive higher pay in those firms that can leverage their global experience. So not only is interna-

tional experience fun to obtain, it also appears you can take it to the bank.

Sources: Adapted from H. Gregersen, A. Morrison, and J. Black, "Developing Leaders for the Global Frontier," *Sloan Management Review* 40:1 (1998), 21–32; J. Black, H. Gregersen, M. Mendenhall, and L. Stroh, *Globalizing People Through International Assignments* (Boston: Addison-Wesley, 1998); M. Harvey and M. Novicevic, "The Influences of Inpatriation Practices on the Strategic Orientation of a Global Organization," *International Journal of Management* 17:3 (2000), 362–372. M. A. Carpenter and W.G. Sanders, "The Effects of Top Management Team Pay and Firm Internationalization on MNC Performance," Journal of Management 30:4 (2004), 509–528; M. A. Carpenter, W. G. Sanders, and H. Gregersen, "Bundling Human Capital with Organizational Context: The Impact of International Assignment Experience on Multinational Firm Performance and CEO Pay," Academy of Management Journal 44:3 (2001), 493–512.

Research has found that firms which internationalize via a mixture of strategies, acquisitions, alliances, and greenfield investments tend to be more successful. Lincoln Electric, based in Cleveland, Ohio, discovered this firsthand. After initially relying primarily on acquisitions to grow overseas, Lincoln Electric determined that, to be successful, individual acquisitions had to be part of an integrated global strategy that also used joint ventures and greenfield startups. The result was the global industry leader we see today with 26 manufacturing locations in 18 countries.

savvy executives, but that these executives form an effective network of communication throughout the organization on a worldwide scale. You can tell that a firm and its managers possess this second dimension when the firm is routinely able to take knowledge gained in one market and apply it elsewhere, as was demonstrated in the case of SC Johnson's transfer of a plug-in household insect repellent product from Europe to the development of a new category of air-freshener products in the United States—Glade PlugIns.

Such learning also means that executives recognize how failure in one market can help the firm overcome failure in another. Lincoln Electric's failure with its unique incentive scheme in Germany taught it to introduce and experiment with an incentive structure in its Mexican operation on a gradual, bottom-up basis. As a result, the entire Mexican production operation has been transformed: The firm's executives recognized that failure in Germany could be used to develop a staging strategy for growth—and, ultimately, dramatic success—in its Mexican operation. Ironically, the more quickly a firm is able to cycle such knowledge throughout the firm, the less likely it is to stretch its managerial capabilities too thin over its expanding global empire.[38]

Obviously, the development of a global mind-set is more easily said than done. Our hope is that, given the fact there are very few industries or markets untouched by global competition (just look around your classroom for instance and you will likely see at least one person from another country), you will take it upon yourself to start investing in your own global mind-set.

SUMMARY

1. Define *international strategy* and identify its implications for the strategy diamond. A firm's international strategy is how it approaches the cross-border business activities of its own firm and competitors and how it contemplates doing so in the future. International strategy essentially reflects the choices a firm's executives make with respect to sourcing and selling its goods in foreign markets. A firm's international activities affect both its business strategy and its corporate strategy. Each component of the strategy diamond may be affected by international activities.

2. Understand why a firm would want to expand internationally and explain the relationship between international strategy and competitive advantage. Firms often expand internationally to fuel growth; however, international expansion does not guarantee profitable growth and should be pursued to help a firm build or exploit a competitive advantage. International expansion can exploit four principle drivers of competitive advantage: economies of scale and scope, location, multipoint competition, and learning. However, these benefits can be offset by the costs of international expansion, such as the liabilities of newness and foreignness and governance and coordination costs.

3. Describe different vehicles for international expansion. Foreign-country entry vehicles include exporting, alliances, and foreign direct investment (FDI). Exporters generally use local representatives or distributors to sell their products in new international markets. Two specialized forms of exporting are licensing and franchising. Alliances involve partnering with another firm to enter a foreign market or undertake an aspect of the value chain in that market. FDI can facilitate entry into a new foreign market and can be accomplished by greenfield investment or acquisition. Although importing is not technically a form of international expansion, it does provide firms with knowledge, experience, and relationships on which future international expansion choices and activities can be based.

4. Apply different international strategy configurations. The different forms that international strategies may take are driven by tradeoffs in attempts to customize for local needs and to pursue global cost efficiencies. The multinational configuration seeks to achieve high levels of local responsiveness while downplaying the search for global efficiencies. The international configuration seeks relatively few global efficiencies and markets relatively standard products across different markets. The global configuration seeks to exploit global economies and efficiencies and accepts less local customer responsiveness (i.e., more standardized products). The transnational configuration attempts to simultaneously achieve global efficiencies and a high degree of local product specialization.

5. Outline the international strategy implications of the stable and dynamic perspectives. Cross-border business adds another level of complexity to both strategy formulation and execution, and unfortunately such complexity may be unavoidable for firms in dynamic contexts. As products mature, firms' international strategies evolve, often moving from little global involvement during the introductory phase to high degrees of internationalization in mature markets. Resources need to be renewed more rapidly in dynamic markets. Thus, when a firm enters a new foreign market, it must also embark on developing the resources necessary to make that market-entry decision a success. In addition, what is learned in new markets can be leveraged for application in existing markets. Obviously, these objectives can be best achieved when managers with an international mind-set are in place.

KEY TERMS

CAGE framework, 222
cross-subsidize, 234
exporting, 227
foreign direct investment (FDI), 229

global configuration, 236
greenfield investment, 229
importing, 232
international configuration, 234

international strategy, 216
multinational configuration, 234

transnational configuration, 236

REVIEW QUESTIONS

1. What is meant by *international strategy*?

2. Which aspects of the strategy diamond are related to international strategy?

3. What are the four most important ways a firm's international strategy can be related to its competitive advantage?

4. What three foreign-country entry vehicles are emphasized in this chapter?

5. What is typically the most cost- and time-intensive entry vehicle?

6. What are the four international strategy configurations discussed in this chapter?

7. On what two dimensions do the four international strategy configurations differ?

8. What does the external perspective tell you about international strategy in dynamic contexts?

9. What does the resource-and-capabilities-based perspective tell you about international strategy in dynamic contexts?

10. What role do managers play in effective international strategies, particularly in dynamic contexts?

How Would YOU Do That?

1. Refer to the box entitled "How Would *You* Do That? 8.1." What sources of information can management draw upon to identify the ideal international alliance partner? What risks is Laura Ashley taking when it becomes so dependent on one firm, such as FedEx? What can Laura Ashley do to reduce its dependence on FedEx?

2. The box entitled "How Would *You* Do That? 8.2" maps out what an organization can do to develop managers with a global mind-set. Many experts argue that a business student must have a global mind-set to be competitive in the human-capital marketplace. Your assignment is to design a learning program for yourself that would advance your global mind-set through an internship. What is the learning purpose of your internship? What are your specific global learning objectives? What experiences would contribute to meeting those objectives? What firms would you target for this mission, and what resources would you engage to approach them? Now, approach a firm and take action on your global mind-set agenda!

GROUP ACTIVITIES

1. Why have firms typically followed an international strategy path that started with importing or exporting, followed by alliances, and then FDI? What risks do born-global firms face in trying to do all of these at once? What resources and capabilities must they possess to do all of these effectively at once?

2. Are all Internet firms global by definition? What opportunities and barriers does the Internet present to firm internationalization?

ENDNOTES

1. P. Ng, "Dell: Selling Directly, Globally" (Hong Kong: Centre for Asian Business Cases, 2000); N. Chowdury, "Dell Cracks China," *Fortune,* June 21, 1999, 120; D. Chi, L. Manlu, D. Downing, and A Tung, "Kodak in China" (France-China: INSEAD/CEIBS, 2000); "Telecom Tremors," *Business Week,* October 16, 2000, p. 68; Dell Annual Report, 2004, www.dell.com; W. M. Bulkeley, E. Ramstad and K. Linebaugh, " IBM, Lenovo Plan Joint PC Venture," *Wall Street Journal,* December 7, 2004, A3.

2. www.dominos.com.

3. The imperatives are summarized in A. Gupta and V. Govindarajan, "Managing Global Expansion: A Conceptual Framework," *Business Horizons* 43:2 (2000), 45–54.

4. R. Tomkins, "Battered PepsiCo Licks Its Wounds," *The Financial Times,* May 30, 1997, 26.

5. A. K. Gupta and V. Govindarajan, "Converting Global Presence into Global Competitive Advantage," *Academy of Management Executive* 15 (2001), 45–56.

6. J. W. Lu and P. W. Beamish, "International Diversification and Firm Performance: The S-Curve Hypothesis," *Academy of Management Journal* 47 (2004), 598–609.

7. Lu and Beamish, "International Diversification and Firm Performance."

8. Lu and Beamish, "International Diversification and Firm Performance."

9. A. D. Chandler, *Scale and Scope: The Dynamics of Industrial Capitalism* (Cambridge, MA: Harvard University Press, 1990).

10. Gupta and Govindarajan, "Converting Global Presence into Global Competitive Advantage."

11. Gupta and Govindarajan, "Converting Global Presence into Global Competitive Advantage."

12. Gupta and Govindarajan, "Converting Global Presence into Global Competitive Advantage."

13. P. Ghemawat, "The Forgotten Strategy," *Harvard Business Review* 81:11 (2003), 76–84.

14. P. Ghemawat, "Distance Still Matters," *Harvard Business Review* 79:8 (2001), 1–11.

15. K. Ito and E. L. Rose, "Foreign Direct Investment Location Strategies in the Tire Industry," *Journal of International Business Studies* 33:3 (2002), 593–602.

16. This anecdote is based on an interview with Lincoln Electric's chairman emeritus in D. Hastings, "Lincoln Electric's Harsh Lessons from International Expansion," *Harvard Business Review* 77:3 (1999), 163–174.

17. Based on information from a personal interview with Sam Johnson.

18. Adapted from A. Gupta and V. Govindarajan, "Managing Global Expansion: A Conceptual Framework," *Business Horizons* 43:2 (2000), 45–54.

19. The points in this paragraph draw heavily on the work of M. T. Hansen and N. Nohria, "See How to Build a Collaborative Advantage," *Sloan Management Review* Fall (2004), 22–30.

20. J. Johanson and J. Vahlne, "The Internationalization Process of the Firm," *Journal of International Business Studies* 8 (1977), 23–32; F. Weidershiem-Paul, H. Olson, and L. Welch, "Pre-Export Activity: The First Step in Internationalization," *Journal of International Business Studies* 9 (1978), 47–58; A. Millington and B. Bayliss, "The Process of Internationalization: UK Companies in the EC," *Management International Review* 30 (1990), 151–161; B. Oviatt and P. McDougall, "Toward a Theory of International New Ventures," *Journal of International Business Studies* 25 (1994), 45–64.

21. O. Moen, "The Born Globals: A New Generation of Small European Exporters," *International Marketing Review* 19 (2002), 156–175.

22. www.tritecmotors.com.br.

23. Gupta and Govindarajan, "Managing Global Expansion."

24. www.fordfound.org, www.tritecmotors.com.br, and www.cargill.com.br.

25. G. Hamel and C. K. Prahalad, "Do You Really Have a Global Strategy?" *Harvard Business Review* 63:4 (1985), 139–148.

26. Gupta and Govindarajan, "Converting Global Presence into Global Competitive Advantage."

27. B. Oviatt and P. McDougall, "Global Start-Ups: Entrepreneurs on a Worldwide Stage," *Academy of Management Executive* 9:2 (1995), 30–44.

28. www.logitech.com.

29. www.skype.com.

30. Summarized from Oviatt and McDougall, "Global Start-Ups."

31. J. S. Brown and J. Hagel, "Innovation Blowback: Disruptive Management Practices from Asia," *McKinsey Quarterly* January (2005).

32. M. Porter, *Competitive Advantage* (New York: Free Press, 1998).

33. G. Tellis, S. Stremersch, and E. Yin. 2003. "The International Takeoff of New Products: Economics, Culture and Country Innovativeness," *Marketing Science* 22:2 (2003), 161–187.

34. F. Vermeulen and H. Barkema, "Learning Through Acquisitions," *Academy of Management Journal* 44 (2001), 457–476; M. A. Hitt, M. T. Dacin, E. Levitas, and J. Arregle, "Partner Selection in Emerging and Developed Market Contexts: Resource-Based and Organizational Learning Perspectives," *Academy of Management Journal* 43 (2000), 449–467.

35. Gupta and Govindarajan, "Converting Global Presence into Global Competitive Advantage."

36. "Furnishing the World," *The Economist,* November 19, 1994, 79–80.

37. B. Kedia and A. Mukherji, "Global Managers: Developing a Mindset for Global Competitiveness," *Journal of World Business* 34:3 (1999), 230–251.

38. Gupta and Govindarajan, "Managing Global Expansion."

After studying this chapter, you should be able to:

1. Explain why strategic alliances are important strategy vehicles.

2. Explain the various forms and structures of strategic alliances.

3. Describe the motivations behind alliances and show how they've changed over time.

4. Explain alliances as both business- and corporate-level strategy vehicles.

5. Understand the characteristics of alliances in stable and dynamic competitive contexts.

6. Summarize the criteria for successful alliances.

▶ **1996**
White Wave launches "Silk" soy milk, which is sold in regular, refrigerated milk cartons. Sales of Silk following its first week on the market approach White Wave's total first-year sales in 1977.

▶ **1998**
White Wave creates a better tasting soy milk in new flavors and eventually adds products such as soy-based coffee creamer, yogurt, and smoothies to its lineup. Distribution remains limited to health-food stores.

1980   1985   19

THE ALLIANCE LIFE CYCLE AT WHITE WAVE

It's not hard to imagine how a weaker firm might enter into an alliance with a stronger partner in hopes of partaking of some of its strengths, only to be stripped of its precious few valuable resources or capabilities in the process.[1] It happens, of course, but it's also possible for a weaker company—if it's clearly focused on its strategy and has a realistic understanding of alliance dynamics—to come out on top in a partnership deal or for partners to experience a win-win relationship.

White Wave, which launched Silk soy milk in 1996, is a case in point. The company's marketing strategy is highly innovative; it packages soy milk in conventional milk cartons and sells it alongside dairy milk in the refrigerated section of the grocery store. Previously, soy milk had always been sold in small, unrefrigerated boxes through the niche channel of health- and natural-food stores. After all, people

▶ **1999**
Silk gets better distribution along with shelf space in major supermarket chains after entering into an alliance with Texas-based Dean Foods, now the largest dairy milk processor in the United States.

▶ **2002**
Dean Foods purchases White Wave. Silk commands an 80-percent share of the soy milk market, due in large part to White Wave's integration into Dean.

1995   2000

who drank it reported that that they tolerated the unpleasant taste and texture because it was good for them.

Although Colorado-based White Wave had been in the soy-based-foods business since the mid-1960s, it did not own any of its own soy-milk production facilities. Initially, production was contracted to a California producer. That early alliance, however, was less than optimal because White Wave not only ended up paying most of its profit margins to the producer, but had little control over product quality. The latter problem was a real sticking point because existing production standards for soy milk resulted in a concoction that typically tasted like a milkshake made with warm water and blackboard chalk.

To deal with these limitations and to gain more control over both profits and quality, White Wave purchased a used ice-cream plant and began experimenting with soy formulations that simulated the taste and texture of dairy milk. The company also added new varieties and flavors, such as soy-based coffee creamer and chocolate- and strawberry-flavored soy milk. Distribution, however, remained largely limited to traditional health-food stores. Another growing distribution channel, Whole Foods, a 170-store chain of natural- and organic-food retail outlets, had begun to carry the product as well.

In 1999, White Wave entered into an alliance with Dean Foods, now the country's largest milk processor. (Ironically, this commercial step forward was considered a philosophical setback for White Wave's founder, whose vision—perhaps a little too ambitious—called for replacing dairy-milk consumption in the United States with the consumption of soy milk.) Dean invested $15 million in White Wave in exchange for a 35-percent ownership stake. What was the value of the arrangement for White Wave? For one, it made it possible for the smaller firm to pay the *slotting fees*—the allowances required by retailers to provide vendors with shelf space—necessary to put its Silk soy milk in just about every grocery store in the United States. In most stores, White Wave also gained exclusive access to the dairy section (recall that most soy milk was sold in unrefrigerated cartons in the health-food section). Before long, sales of soy milk skyrocketed, and national and international retailers, including Safeway and Ahold, began encouraging dairy-milk producers to add Silk to their product lineups. As a result, demand for the company's products increased its power relative to grocers, thus enabling White Wave to save on costly slotting fees and further solidify its advantage over other soy-milk suppliers.

In 2001, however, the Dean–White Wave alliance hit a bump when Dean merged with another milk processor and Dean's new top-management team chose to exercise an option to purchase White Wave at a prearranged price. White Wave's management had hoped to keep the company separate from Dean for several more years even though the alliance agreement gave Dean the option to purchase White Wave. Initially, White Wave balked at the price, and eventually, the two firms agreed on a price far in excess of the original. Why would Dean pay a price in excess of what the alliance contract stipulated? Part of the deal was that White Wave management, including White Wave founder Steve Demos, agreed to run Silk operations at Dean for 10 years. Dean knew that its own management team did not understand the soy market well, and a big part of the Silk brand was tied to the goodwill that Demos had created for the upstart firm. Today, despite competition from such powerhouse food processors as Heinz and General Mills, Silk commands an 80-percent share of the soy-milk market, in large part because its integration into Dean gives it access to 119 plants from which it can respond fluidly to demand fluctuations. As a result of the Dean buyout, Silk much more fully satisfies its original mission: "To creatively lead the full integration of natural soy foods into the average American diet through socially responsible and environmentally sustainable business practices." ■

STRATEGIC ALLIANCES

Why do firms enter alliances? Was the agreement between White Wave and Dean Foods typical? Are most alliances successful? Do they eventually lead to buyouts? By the end of this chapter, you should be able to answer these and many other questions about the formation, implementation, and termination of strategic alliances. Like most relationships, alliances have a beginning and an end. As you work through the chapter, you'll see that the opening vignette on White Wave and Dean Foods features many of the characteristics of strategic alliances. Alliances often enable participants to share in investments and rewards while reducing the risk and uncertainty that each firm would otherwise face on its own. In addition, shared activities enable each organization to focus its resources on what it does best. Finally, alliances foster economies of scale and scope—both within the partner firms and between partners and the alliance vehicle—that companies wouldn't otherwise be able to achieve, at least not in the same cost-effective manner.

Studies have shown that companies that participate most actively in alliances outperform the least-active firms by 5 to 7 percent.[2] Some might argue that this performance premium results from the fact that better-run firms are also simply better at initiating and managing alliances. In the early 1990s, for instance, BMW and DaimlerChrysler determined jointly that the minimum efficient economic scale of a small auto-engine facility would be a plant capable of producing 400,000 engines annually. Separately, however, each firm had internal demand for only 200,000 engines per year. The solution? An alliance through which they shared the cost of building a new plant large enough to turn out 400,000 engines. BMW uses the motors in its line of Mini Coopers, and DaimlerChrysler uses them in both its Neon and PT Cruiser lines.

Remember, however, that alliances are not strategies in and of themselves. Rather, as shown in Exhibit 9.1, which reprises the five elements of the strategy diamond, an alliance is simply one *vehicle* for realizing a strategy. In addition, an effective alliance must be consistent with the economic logic of the strategy. In this chapter, we'll review the critical features that firms must master if they're going to use alliances effectively and in a manner that's consistent with the economic logic underpinning their overall strategies.

A **strategic alliance** is a partnership in which two or more firms combine resources and capabilities with the goal of creating mutual competitive advantage. An alliance may involve sharing resources related to only one key activity in the partners' value chain, such as R&D. As shown in Exhibit 9.2, however, it may involve many activities. For example, the partners may

strategic alliance Relationship in which two or more firms combine resources and capabilities in order to enhance the competitive advantage of all parties

conceptlink

In defining **economies of scale** and **economies of scope** in Chapter 5, we focused on the value of a firm's sharing resources in its production function. In Chapter 7, we stress that economies of scale and scope are possible in all **value-chain** activities.

Exhibit 9.1 The Place of Alliances in the Five Elements Model

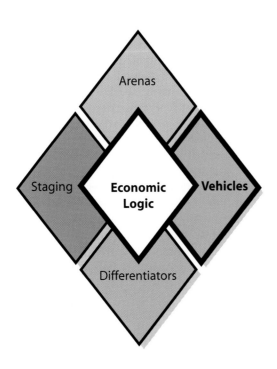

Exhibit 9.2 Possible Alliance Linkages

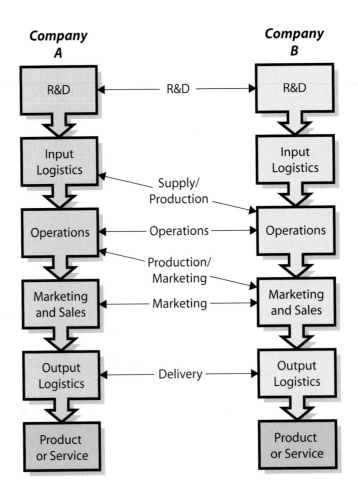

conceptlink

IIn Chapter 8, we note that global expansion creates **competitive advantage** only when the firm turns larger scale into greater operating efficiency. We also stress the importance of R&D as a **value-chain** activity in enhancing not only cost-effectiveness and new-product development, but the sharing of knowledge.

work together to develop new products via shared R&D and also cooperate on the production and marketing of the new products. Indeed, the number and combinations of linkages is practically endless. Note, too, that an alliance may be strategic to one firm and only tactical or operational to the other. Wal-Mart, for example, has long sought to reduce the number of its suppliers through a variety of so-called *sole-sourcing* and *just-in-time supply agreements*. Both types of agreements mean that a buyer has chosen only one or a few suppliers for its raw materials, and with the just-in-time arrangement, it expects that the supplier will provide the buyer with those materials at the exact point in time that they are needed in the production process. In terms of investment in distribution infrastructure, sales volume, and concentration of sales to one buyer, such agreements may be strategic for the supplier but not necessarily to Wal-Mart, which is rarely dependent on any one supplier. In 1994, for instance, when Rubbermaid sought to raise its prices to Wal-Mart, its single largest customer, the giant retailer responded by dropping Rubbermaid products from every one of its stores.[3] Only after Rubbermaid was acquired by Newell in 1999 was it restored to Wal-Mart's good graces.

Growth of Alliances Given its attractive features—as well as increasing competitive intensity in most industries—it shouldn't be surprising that the use of alliances as a strategy vehicle has grown dramatically in the last few decades. As a percentage of revenues, alliances ballooned from 2 to nearly 16 percent between 1980 through 1995. In particular, as of 2005, large multinational corporations have over 20 percent of their total assets tied up in alliances.[4] For U.S. firms, alliance partners are largely, and not surprisingly, concentrated in Asia and Europe.

Failure Rates Note, however, that despite their apparent popular use, the failure rate for alliances is about 50 percent (and nearly 70 percent in some cases). An alliance can be deemed a failure when one or more of the partners did not achieve its objectives and, in more dismal cases, when one partner benefited but the other partner was left worse off competitively. Clearly, alliances can be high-risk as well as high-return vehicles for realizing a firm's strategy.[5]

Interestingly, however, such a high failure rate doesn't surprise economists and many other experts. Why? Most economic theories assume that, left to their own devices, individual entities will behave in their own *self-interest*. The success of an alliance, of course, depends on the willingness of partners to subordinate their own interests to those of the alliance, but even when partners start out by suspending self-interest, circumstances can change dramatically over time, compromising even the best of intentions.

In the remaining sections of this chapter, we'll examine the various forms that alliances can take, and we'll show how the objectives underlying them have evolved over time. We'll discuss alliances as strategy vehicles and explain the risks to which they're prone. We'll also focus on the ways in which both the objectives and structures of alliances vary in stable versus dynamic contexts. Finally, because so many alliance failures are due to faulty implementation, we'll conclude by discussing four specific ways to improve the probability of alliance success.

FORM AND STRUCTURE OF ALLIANCES

Note that we've been using the term *strategic alliances* as a catchall term. In reality, cooperative arrangements can take a number of forms. Exhibit 9.3 summarizes the vast continuum of forms that cooperative arrangements, including strategic alliances, may take. As you can see, the two primary dimensions on which alliances can be categorized are the nature of the *commitment* (e.g., timeframe and resources) and respective *ownership* of the alliance and inputs into the alliance (ranging from cash to people to technology). The shaded regions represent those areas where the cooperative arrangements are most likely to be described as strategic. In this section, we'll explain a few of these arrangements.

Exhibit 9.3 Examples of Cooperative Arrangements in the Continuum of Organizational Forms

Level of Commitment	No Linkages Beyond Transaction	Information Sharing	Asset, Resource, and Capability Sharing	Cross-Equity (partners take ownership in one party or each other)	Shared Equity
Permanent				*Keiretsu* in Japan or *chaebols* in South Korea	Caltrex, which was jointly owned by Chevron and Texaco prior to their merger
Long-Term	Outsourcing	Many technology standards consortia	Technology collaborations such as the PowerPC chip between Motorola, IBM, and Apple	Anheuser-Busch's cross-ownership with Kirin in Japan and Modelo in Mexico	Stand-alone joint ventures such as Dow-Corning
Transactional	Purchase agreements that are renewable annually or every several years	Agreements to distribute products or services	Cross-licensing such as that between Disney and Pixar or R&D partnerships as between Millennium Pharmaceuticals and some of its smaller partners		
	Simple purchase order for commodities, sometimes called a spot transaction	Short-term agreements on functions such as advertising or manufacturing to achieve efficiencies—for example, contract brewing of Miller Beer by Anheuser Busch			
	Nonequity Alliances			**Equity Alliances**	

Source: Adapted from J. Harbison and P. Pekar, Smart Alliances: A Practical Guide to Repeatable Success (San Francisco: Jossey-Bass, 1998).

Dow Corning Corporation, the Michigan-based silicon-products maker, is a joint venture between Dow and Corning, as its name suggests. In joint ventures, partners often invest on an equal basis and split corporate ownership and control down the middle.

Joint Ventures and Other Equity Alliances

The form of an alliance depends on such factors as legal structure and the number and objectives of participants. In a **joint venture**, for instance, two companies make equity investments in the creation of a third, which exists as an independent legal entity. This is the case with Dow-Corning, which, as the name suggests, is a joint venture between Dow and Corning; it falls under the shared-equity category in Exhibit 9.3. Many joint ventures are 50/50 splits in ownership and control, but they need not be equal partnerships.

It isn't necessary, however, for an alliance to create a separate legal entity or share equal ownership. In many cases, **equity alliances** involve unequal partners. This may be the case when one partner owns a greater percentage of the alliance's equity than another partner; when a separate legal entity is not established, and one partner instead takes partial ownership of the other partner; or when contracts are used to govern the sharing and respective rights regarding contributed assets, resources, or capabilities. Millennium Pharmaceuticals, for example, prefers arrangements in which larger partners take a percentage ownership not only in Millennium itself, but also a minority-percentage interest in any alliance with a separate legal structure. (It also manages several strategic alliances with traditional 50/50 splits.[6])

Nonequity Alliances

The most common form of strategic alliance involves neither equity interest nor separate organizations. Arrangements such as *sole-sourcing, just-in-time supply agreements, licensing, cobranding,* and *franchising* often fall under the heading of *nonequity alliances.*

Nonequity alliances are typically contracts that call for one firm to supply, produce, market, or distribute another's goods or services over an extended period of time. Starbucks, for instance, has extended the presence of its brand into a number of customer-contact locations through alliances with such companies as Barnes & Noble (bookstore cafés), United Airlines (in-flight coffee service), Dryer's (coffee ice cream), Pepsi (Frappacino ready-to-drink coffee), and Kraft (ground and whole coffee beans distributed through grocery stores). The various strategic roles that these nonequity alliances play for Starbucks are shown in Exhibit 9.4.

Multiparty Alliances

Thus far, we've described alliances involving two partners. Other types of alliances, such as **consortia**, usually involve many participants, perhaps even governments. As shown in Exhibit 9.3, the primary contribution to these cooperative arrangements is information,

joint venture Alliance in which two firms make equity investments in a third legal entity

equity alliance Alliance in which one or more partners assumes a greater ownership interest in either the alliance or another partner

nonequity alliance Alliance that involves neither the assumption of equity interest nor the creation of separate organizations

consortia Association of several companies and/or governments for some definite strategic purpose

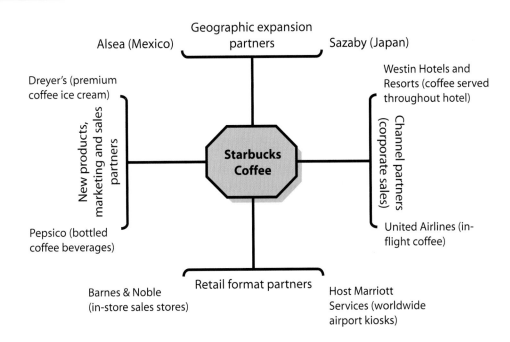

Exhibit 9.4 Starbucks Coffee: Creating Value Through a Set of Alliances

Source: Adapted from J.D. Bamford, B. Gomes-Casseres, and M. S. Robinson, Mastering Alliance Strategy: A Comprehensive Guide to Design, Management, and Organization (San Francisco, CA: John Wiley & Sons, 2003), p. 22.

though there may be some cost sharing as well. Perhaps the most complex multifirm alliances are those in the technology arena. SEMATECH, for example, is a consortium of semiconductor manufacturers established in the mid-1980s to prop up the U.S. semiconductor industry, which at the time was considered to be of strategic importance to national defense. To some extent, SEMATECH's cooperative structure was modeled after joint projects by which Japanese semiconductor producers which were responsible for advancing their collective technological competencies in the late 1970s.[7] The consortium has since evolved to include both U.S. and non–U.S. firms, and a related venture called SEMI/SEMATECH (or SEMI) is an alliance of suppliers to the semiconductor industry.[8]

concept link

Recall that, in Chapter 3, we divide *competences* into two categories: While **core competences** are central to a firm's main operations, **distinctive competences** set it apart from other firms. Competences, we note, are **capabilities**, and transferring capabilities, as we observe in Chapter 7, is one of two ways of generating **synergy** (the other being sharing **resources**).

WHY ALLIANCES?

Not surprisingly, firms participating in effective alliances can improve their competitive position and gain competitive advantage. Remember that one alternative to an alliance is a purchase contract. However, there are significant limits as to what can and cannot be contracted, particularly in dynamic contexts. Put bluntly, contracts alone are not always sufficient to coordinate and control partners' behaviors. In this section, we review how the use of alliances is related to competitive advantage and how the motivation for using alliances has evolved over time.

Alliances and Competitive Advantage

Alliances can help firms achieve their objectives in several ways. Alliances not only spread the risk of business ventures by sharing that risk with other firms; they also give firms access to knowledge, resources, and capabilities that the firm might otherwise lack. Alliances achieve these potential building blocks of competitive advantage in four ways: *joint investment, knowledge sharing, complementary resources,* and *effective management.*[9]

Joint Investment Alliances can help to increase returns by motivating firms to make investments that they'd be unwilling to make outside a formal alliance relationship. This advantage is particularly important in light of the fact that productivity gains are possible when activities linked in the value chain are supported with transaction-specific investments. For instance, White Wave's Silk brand and the knowledge and factories that enable it to produce soy products were investments that were specific to Dean's early alliance with White Wave.

In many situations, a supplier won't make an investment pertaining specifically to an exchange with one buyer. Why? Because the investment would tie the supplier too closely to one buyer and expose it to too much risk, the greatest risk being that the buyer reneges on its commitment to buy the supplier's products or services or grinds the supplier down on price due to its dependence on the single buyer.[10] For instance, if you invested $10 million in a piece of equipment that made products that could be sold only by Wal-Mart, you would be very dependent on Wal-Mart because of the asset specificity of such an investment. A buyer, therefore, often integrates backward vertically in the value chain, making the necessary investment to internalize the supply. The supplier's hesitancy, however, can be overcome if the buyer is willing to enter a formal arrangement that reduces the supplier's risk. Both supplier and buyer can benefit not only from gains in efficiency but also from savings in the bureaucratic costs entailed by vertical integration.

Knowledge Sharing   One common reason of entering into alliances is to learn from partners. Learning, however, requires partners to cooperate in transferring knowledge. Although partners may not be equally capable of absorbing knowledge, two factors can help to facilitate the transfer of knowledge: (1) mutual trust and familiarity between partners and (2) consistent information-sharing routines, such as that obtained through higher-level executive contact, integrated information systems, and employee swapping and cross-company career paths. As an example of the latter, John Deere regularly exchanges key employees with alliance partner Hitachi in certain product segments.

Complementary Resources   In Chapter 3, we saw that a firm's resources and capabilities are the primary sources of competitive advantage. When partners combine resources and capabilities, they may be able to create a stock of resources that's unavailable to other competitors in the industry. If that stock combines complementary resources and capabilities, then the alliance may be able to generate a shared advantage. Finally, if the combination of resources and capabilities is valuable and rare, the alliance may be able to generate greater profits than the sum of the partners' individual profits. Thus, when Nestlé and Coke combined resources to offer canned tea and coffee products, the alliance offered a vehicle that was more attractive than going it alone due to complementarities between the parties.[11]

Effective Management   One way to judge the appropriateness and effectiveness of an alliance is through comparing its costs with the alternatives of an arm's-length transaction or formal internal integration (providing the activity internally or buying a company that can provide the activity). The second way to judge whether an alliance is effective is if it helps build a competitive advantage. This evaluation process is sometimes referred to the *buy or make* decision, with alliances lying somewhere in between the two extremes.

Look at the principle from the following perspective: A potential problem in any alliance is that one partner may take advantage of another. To minimize this risk, many alliances call for formal protection mechanisms, such as equity investments (which should align incentives) or formal contracts (which should outline expected behavior and remedies for violations). Although such mechanisms are costly, they may still be cheaper than formal integration of activities within one firm. However, some experts argue that the true cost savings of alliances comes to those firms that can rely on less formal managerial control over their partners' behavior and instead depend on self-enforcement and informal agreements. Informal arrangements, of course, require a great deal of trust, which is likely to develop only after multiple dealings between partners.[12] We'll address the subjects of learning and trust more fully in the concluding section of this chapter.

Recall from the VRINE framework that resources and capabilities are the basis of competitive advantage only when they satisfy certain criteria: They must be valuable, rare, difficult to imitate, and supported by organizational arrangements. The same holds true for an alliance. Six conditions under which an alliance may satisfy the criteria of the VRINE

---

conceptlink

In Chapter 7, we explain **vertical integration** as moving "upstream"—closer to needed sources of inputs—in the industry value chain or "downstream"—closer to the ultimate customer. The **value chain**, of course—which we defined in Chapter 3 as the total of the value-adding activities by which a firm produces, markets, and distributes products—runs both upstream and downstream.

conceptlink

We emphasize in Chapter 5 that incremental production costs decline as production experience—*learning* in the production function—is gained. Here, we observe that the same principle holds in every function in which the transfer of *information* is important.

conceptlink

In Chapter 7, where we show that companies can expand *vertically*, *horizontally*, or *geographically*, we explain that **horizontal scope** can be achieved in one of two ways: (1) by moving from one industry segment to another or (2) by moving from one industry to another.

framework are outlined in the following list. Alliances may serve to build a competitive advantage if:

- Rivals cannot ascertain what generates the returns because of causal ambiguity surrounding the alliance.
- Rivals can determine what generates the returns but cannot quickly replicate the resources due to time-compression diseconomies.
- Rivals cannot imitate practices or investments because they are missing complementary resources (i.e., they have not made the previous investments that make subsequent investments economically viable) and because the current costs associated with prior investments are now prohibitive.
- Rivals cannot find a partner with the necessary complementary strategic resources.
- Rivals cannot access potential partners' resources and capabilities because they are indivisible.
- Rivals cannot replicate a distinctive and socially complex institutional environment that has the necessary formal and informal controls that make managing alliances possible.

If an alliance (or network of alliances) satisfies these criteria, it has probably developed a collaborative advantage that helps each member firm achieve a competitive advantage over rivals outside the alliance.

concept link

In discussing the **VRINE model** of **resources**, **capabilities**, and **competitive advantage** in Chapter 3, we explain **causal ambiguity** as the difficulty in identifying the *complex combination of factors* that make a resource or capability valuable.

Alliance Motivation over Time

Although the overarching motivation behind alliances—the pursuit of competitive advantage—hasn't changed, the ways in which alliances contribute to such advantage have. This is one reason why it is so critical for you to understand strategic management from a dynamic perspective. In the late 1980s, in an effort to better understand why alliances were becoming increasingly common, the consulting firm Booz-Allen began studying the alliance practices of 1,000 U.S. firms. Among other things, the study revealed dramatic changes in the motivations that impelled firms to enter alliances over the course of several decades.[13] Critical to any understanding of this change is recognizing the factor that we've been emphasizing: A firm is motivated to enter an alliance because it eventually expects its resources and capabilities to yield competitive advantage.

Product Performance As shown in Exhibit 9.5, alliances formed during the 1970s emphasized product and service performance. The alliance strategy of Corning Glass Works (now called Corning) exemplifies this focus. Its alliance with Dow (Dow-Corning) allowed Corning to leverage its advanced glass-making capabilities in new products and new markets, both at home and abroad.

Market Position In the 1980s, firms tended to stress the building and reinforcing of market position. Microsoft and Intel, for example, joined to form Wintel. The motivation behind this informal alliance was pretty basic: Microsoft's Windows family of operating systems functioned best on PCs with Intel's chips, and as long as Microsoft kept increasing processing-speed requirements, Intel could count on consistent product demand. The Wintel alliance played a major role in the two firm's eventual dominance. Over the course of the alliance, each provided value to the other and its customers through its area of specialization, and both profited by spurring the growth of the whole desktop industry and providing continual improvements to product users.

Resources and Capabilities More recently, corporations have begun to emphasize more complex benefits, such as organizational learning and the development and accumulation of valuable resources and capabilities. Note that these drivers represent *cumulative* needs. In other words, the drivers behind many of today's alliances assume that a firm possesses the ability to manage the benefits of product performance and market position. They also reflect the fact that both products and markets are likely to change and that the only defensible or sustainable sources of competitive advantages are the ability to foresee and perhaps create significant changes. In that view, alliances are viewed as effective vehicles for creating new capabilities, products, markets, and capabilities.

Exhibit 9.5 Changing Motivation for Alliances

1970s	1980s	Post 2000
Product-Performance Focus	**Position Focus**	**Learning and Capabilities Focus**
Produce with latest technology	Build industry stature	Ensure constant stream of new prospects with advancing technology
Market beyond national borders	Consolidate position	Proactively maximize delivered value
Sell product, stressing performance	Gain economies of scale and scope	Optimize total cost by product/consumer segment
		Gain advantage in response to changing conditions and opportunities

Source: Adapted from J. Harbison and P. Pekar, Smart Alliances: A Practical Guide to Repeatable Success (San Francisco: Jossey-Bass, 1998).

Consider the case of Wal-Mart. The seeds of Wal-Mart's success outside the United States were sown in a capabilities-focused alliance it formed with the Mexican firm Cifra in the mid-1990s.[14] The objective of the alliance was to marry Cifra's unique resources and capabilities, such as brand name, site selection, currency-inflation management, captive manufacturing, and government connections, with Wal-Mart's strong information-technology-based retail business model and financial resources to broaden Cifra's lead over competitors and launch 145 new super Cifras in Mexico.[15] At the time, Cifra was the second-largest public firm in Mexico and its largest retailer. Wal-Mart was attracted to this partner because it wanted to learn about doing business in Mexico; ultimately, it hoped to use this knowledge to help it enter and compete in Brazil, Argentina, and other parts of Latin America. As for Cifra, it both co-opted a potential competitor and learned how to adapt Wal-Mart's proven retailing systems to its Mexican operations. Although the two firms worked well together, they occasionally disagreed about management of jointly operated stores. In 1997, Wal-Mart put an end to the friction by acquiring 51 percent of Cifra for $1.2 billion.[16] Following a restructuring that eliminated redundancies and married the firms' respective strengths in distribution (Cifra) and systems (Wal-Mart), things have been running smoothly. The alliance has proven to be one of Wal-Mart's most successful; it's now leveraging the knowledge gleaned from it to fuel an aggressive acquisition-based growth strategy in Brazil.[17] Having partnered with Seiyu Co. Ltd., one of Japan's top retailers, it's also using the model of its Cifra alliance to enter the Japanese market.[18]

ALLIANCES AS STRATEGY VEHICLES

Almost any organization is a potential alliance partner, and deciding with whom to partner is a matter of a firm's business and corporate strategies.

Alliances and Business Strategy

Let's start by considering factors related to business strategy—strategy that determines how a firm competes in a chosen industry. A quick review of the five-forces model and related complementors of industry structure that we introduced in Chapter 4 reinforces the number and variety of a firm's potential partners. Who might these allies be?

- **Rivals.** Although there are certainly legal prohibitions against cooperative arrangements among competitors that harm consumers, rivals will often engage in strategic alliances. The various airline alliances, such as One World and Star, are a case in point.
- **New entrants.** Industry incumbents can ally with new entrants to diversify or to co-opt a future potential rival. Wal-Mart's alliance with Cifra is a good example of this.
- **Suppliers.** Increasingly, firms are developing alliances with key suppliers. These can take on the form of sole-sourcing and just-in-time arrangements or include more complex forms, such as Tritec, in which the supplier is formed by two rivals.
- **Customers.** The customer-incumbent relationship is the flip side of the incumbent-supplier relationship.
- **Substitutes.** These products and services pose a threat to the incumbent. Through an alliance, this threat can actually be exploited. For instance, soy milk is a clear substitute for dairy milk. Instead of actively competing against the growing market for soy milk, Dean Foods established a joint venture with, and then acquired, industry leader Silk.
- **Complementors.** Recall that complements are those products or services that, when bundled together, create greater value than when acquired separately. An alliance between an industry incumbent and a complement can lock out competitors. As a case in point, most major fast-food chains provide Coke or Pepsi products, not both.

The Value-Net Model and Co-Opetition One way to think about all of the players identified in the industry-structure model in a manner that highlight possible alliance possibilities is to rearrange the players into the **value-net model**. This model is illustrated in Exhibit 9.6. Notice that in this model we place the firm of interest in the center and link it to all possible exchange partners. In allowing them to identify opportunities for cooperative relationships among all possible exchange partners and even competitors, the value-net model helps managers find alternatives to conventional win-lose business scenarios.

> **value-net model** Map of a firm's existing and potential exchange relationships

How might a firm establish a cooperative relationship with a competitor? Consider a firm like Motorola, which may in some business situations be a competitor to Intel, such as in the sale of microprocessors. In other situations, it may be in a partnership with Intel, such as in the development of a new technology. Still in other situations, Motorola might be a customer of Intel, sourcing key components for a particular product.

Co-opetition The term **co-opetition** refers to a situation in which firms are both competitors and cooperative partners. The purpose of co-opetition is to find ways of increasing the

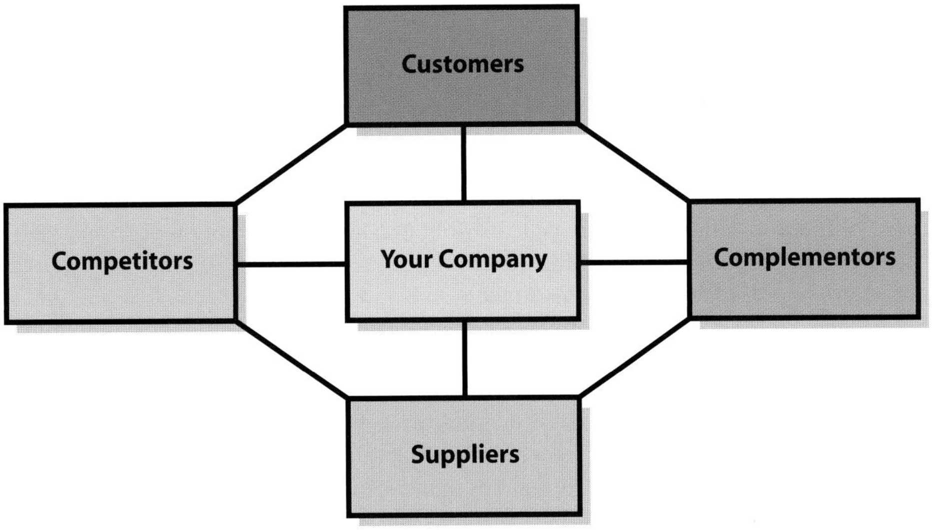

> **Co-opetition** Situation in which firms are simultaneously competitors in one market and collaborators in another

Exhibit 9.6 The Value Net

Source: Adapted from A. Brandendburger and B. Nalebuff, Co-Opetition (New York: Doubleday 1996).

total value created by parties in the value net, not just determining how to compete for industry profits. The value net helps managers find potential partners; in other words, it helps them to identify those parties that are possible complementors rather than just competitors. In the following two sections we illustrate how the value net can be applied to various types of alliances.

Alliances can figure into most aspects of business strategy, but they generally provide means of managing competitive pressures, uncertainty, or both. Business-strategy alliances tend to fall into two major categories: *vertical alliances* or *horizontal alliances.*

Vertical Alliances

A **vertical alliance** is formed when a firm partners with one or more of its suppliers or customers (typically, the latter only occurs in business-to-business relationships). The purpose of a vertical alliance is to leverage partners' resources and capabilities in order to meet two goals: (1) to create more value for the end customer and (2) to lower total production costs along the value chain. In a sense, the vertical alliance is an alternative for vertical integration, the *corporate* strategy whereby a firm takes ownership of downstream supply or upstream distribution or other marketing functions.

J. H. Dyer, a prominent strategy professor who specializes in the study of strategic alliances, has found that vertical alliances can create lean value chains by reducing total supply-chain costs in four areas: transaction, quality, product-development, and logistics costs:[19]

- *Transaction costs* are often lower among alliance partners than among firms in third-party arm's-length transactions.
- Because quality is often improved, *quality-related costs*—those associated with defects, returns, and warranty work—go down.
- When partners share knowledge and human capital and focus their efforts on improving product design and quality, vertical alliances can control *product-development costs.*
- Reduced warehousing and transportation costs not only reduce inbound *logistics costs* but result in lower inventory costs as well.

Vertical alliances also improve value to the customer by making it possible for alliance partners to increase speed to market, improve quality, introduce newer technologies and features, and respond more quickly to market changes. Exhibit 9.7 shows how Timken applies the net value to vertical integration alliances by bundling its product offerings.

Horizontal Alliances

Horizontal alliances are partnerships between firms in the same industry. These types of alliances enable competitors, or potential competitors, to gain a presence in multiple segments of an industry. As a component of a firm's value net, a horizontal alliance, which gives a company access to multiple segments of an industry, can create value in a number of ways. First, it can reduce risk. For instance, when two oil-exploration firms enter into a joint venture, they spread the risk entailed by the costs of drilling. Likewise, Kraft's alliance with Starbucks gives it a super-premium coffee brand that it can distribute through the grocery channel to complement not only its Maxwell House and Yuban brands in the same channel but also its Gevalia brand in the direct-marketing and business-to-business channels. Mondavi's various alliances with top wine-producers in Chile, Italy, Argentina, and France give it access to a broader range of high-quality wines than it could support if it had to rely solely on its own resources.

Horizontal alliances can also help partners achieve greater efficiency. Thus, when McDonald's and Disney cooperate in promotions, each leverages its advertising expenditures. In addition, although Disney benefits from McDonald's promotion of Disney characters and programming, McDonald's benefits from the popular appeal of Disney characters, which appear as toys in products aimed at kids.

Finally, horizontal alliances foster learning in the development and innovation of new products. SEMATECH and the Automotive and Composites Consortium (launched by GM, Ford, and Chrysler) are good examples of learning alliances. In the case of SEMATECH, for instance, all U.S.–based semiconductor manufacturers pooled their knowledge of the production process to improve it and were collectively able to turn the competitive tide against the rising dominance of Japanese firms. The Apple–Sony partnership that developed the PowerBook is a good example of firms using horizontal alliances to access complementary

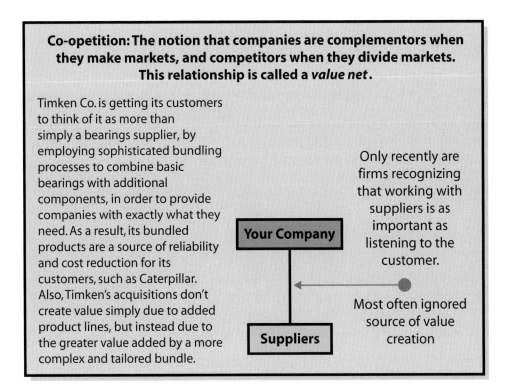

Co-opetition: The notion that companies are complementors when they make markets, and competitors when they divide markets. This relationship is called a *value net*.

Timken Co. is getting its customers to think of it as more than simply a bearings supplier, by employing sophisticated bundling processes to combine basic bearings with additional components, in order to provide companies with exactly what they need. As a result, its bundled products are a source of reliability and cost reduction for its customers, such as Caterpillar. Also, Timken's acquisitions don't create value simply due to added product lines, but instead due to the greater value added by a more complex and tailored bundle.

Your Company

Suppliers

Only recently are firms recognizing that working with suppliers is as important as listening to the customer.

Most often ignored source of value creation

Exhibit 9.7 The Co-Opetition Value Chain at Timken

skills. Finally, horizontal alliances can help firms overcome political obstacles. In China, for example, the Otis Elevator–Tianjin joint venture enabled Otis to enter an attractive and growing market that at the time was inaccessible without a local partner.

Let's return for a moment to the concept of co-opetition, which is based on the principle that firms must often cooperate and compete simultaneously. Because horizontal alliances make allies of competitors, it's crucial that all parties understand the conditions that favor success in such ventures. First, they're potentially beneficial when partners' strategic goals converge and competitive goals diverge. When, for instance, Philips and DuPont collaborated to make compact discs (CDs), neither firm was invading the other's markets for other products. In addition, horizontal alliances are more likely to succeed when the partners are chasing industry leaders, as when Asian semiconductor-chip makers collaborated in making memory chips in an effort to cut into Intel's market share. Finally, in successful horizontal alliances, all partners acknowledge the fact that, though each must be willing to share knowledge, each can and must protect proprietary skills. For example, the Fuji Photo–Xerox alliance, established in 1962, allows the two makers of copiers and printers to collaborate in the Japanese and Pacific Rim markets. In return for access to these markets, Fuji is entitled to a 75-percent share in the joint profits. Fuji agreed to the arrangement because it believed that it could protect its film business in these markets; Xerox, meanwhile, believed that the venture would not endanger its copier business elsewhere in the world.

Corporate and International Strategic Alliances

Although alliances are typical business-strategy vehicles, they can also be vehicles for corporate strategy. As we saw in Chapter 7, corporate strategy is largely concerned with two activities:

■ Determining the right mix of businesses in the corporate portfolio
■ Ensuring that this mix creates shareholder value

Let's consider each of these activities in terms of decisions about alliances. As for portfolio mix, alliances are vehicles for exploring and implementing diversification options. Through its office-copier business, for instance, a company like Xerox may have developed a set of technologies that may provide access into the intensely competitive desktop-copier and computer-printer businesses. In an alliance with a strong partner like Fuji Photo of Japan, it can share the risk and development costs related to an uncertain diversification move.

Corporations can also use alliances to create value across a portfolio of individual businesses. At first glance, for example, you might think of venture capitalists (VCs) and their various investments as independent entities. They do, however, represent strategic alliances. How so? Whereas the VC provides capital and managerial expertise, the entrepreneurial firm provides an opportunity for new products. From a corporate-strategy perspective, the VC firm can create more value for its investments by identifying key individuals in one firm who could help create value for its other units. The VC firm Softbank, for example, leverages its investments in broadband-application and broadband-provider companies by circulating its best and brightest managers and technologists among its wholly owned companies as well as those in which it has investments.[20] Likewise, a diversified firm can also broker relationships among its portfolio businesses.

Alliances and International Strategy   Finally, as shown in the example of the international partnership between Laura Ashley and FedEx presented in Chapter 8, a firm's international strategy should issue from its business- and corporate-strategy objectives. Many of the alliances that we've described in this chapter are international in nature: Either they involve partners from different countries or the alliance itself is headquartered in a country different from those of the partners. Cross-border alliances differ from domestic alliances in that governments, public policies, and national cultures often play significant roles. Also important, of course, are differences in workplace regulations and socioeconomic conditions.

Not surprisingly, in international contexts, decisions about internal and external vehicles through which to execute a firm's strategy are much more complex than in domestic contexts. Multinational corporations, for instance, may be better than alliances in facilitating the flow of knowledge across borders. Analysis of patent citations by semiconductor companies suggests that multinationals are better than both alliances and market forces in fostering cross-border knowledge transfer, primarily because they can use multiple mechanisms for transferring knowledge and are more flexible in moving, integrating, and developing technical knowledge.[21]

Alliance Networks

Related to the study of the strategic functions of alliances is the concept that alliances are taking on characteristics of networks. Network theory has two implications for organizational practice. First, as alliances become a larger component of a firm's strategy, the strategy discussion will shift from particular alliances as a vehicle to networks of alliances as a vehicle. In this sense, the firm is operating as a hub, or node, in a complex array of owned, partially owned, and nonowned businesses. Looking back at the value net portrayed in Exhibit 9.6, you can imagine how multiple alliances among complementors, competitors, suppliers, and customers might easily come to resemble a web of complex network relationships.

Second, as networks themselves take on the characteristics of organizations, competition among networks should arise both within and across industries. Exhibit 9.8 lists several alliance networks formed in the past, some of which have been dissolved or restructured as the nature of the partners' relationships or the competitive environment has evolved. The clearest current example of network competition can probably be found in the airline industry, where three alliances—Star, One World, and Sky Team—are battling for air passengers.

Risks Arising from Alliances

As we mentioned in the introduction to this chapter, one of the potential benefits of an alliance is the reduction of risk or uncertainty borne by any one party. With that said, however, we must point out that cooperative ventures can be risky. There are six potential alliance risks:

Business or Industry	Selective Rival Constellations
Hardware and Software for Interactive TV	▶ Motorola, Scientific Atlanta, Kaleida ▶ Time Warner, Silicon Graphics ▶ Intel, Microsoft, General Instruments ▶ H.P., TV Answer
Video CDs	▶ Sony and Philips ▶ Toshiba, Time Warner, Matsushita, others
Global Telecommunications	▶ AT&T Worldpartners (includes 12 partners) ▶ British Telecom and MCI ▶ Sprint, Deutsche Telekom, France Telecom
Automobiles and Trucks	▶ G.M., Toyota, Isuzu, Suzuki, Volvo ▶ Ford, Mazda, Kia, Nissan, Fiat, VW ▶ Chrysler, Mitsubishi, Daimler-Benz
Biotechnology Research	▶ Genentech network ▶ Centocor network
Pharmaceutical Marketing (United States)	▶ Merck and Medco (merger) ▶ SmithKline and DPS (merger) ▶ Eli Lilly and PCS (merger) ▶ Pfizer and Value Health ▶ Pfizer, Rhône-Poulenc, Caremark, others
Global Airline Services	▶ Delta, Swissair, Singapore Airlines, SAS ▶ KLM and Northwest ▶ British Airways and USAir
Global Comercial Real Estate Services	▶ Colliers International (44 companies) ▶ International Commercial (23 companies) ▶ Oncore International (36 companies) ▶ New America Network (150 companies) ▶ Cushman & Wakefield (52 alliances) ▶ CB Commercial (70 affiliates) ▶ Grubb & Ellis (six affiliates)

Exhibit 9.8 Networks of Alliances

Sources: For interactive television, see "The Living Room War," *Business Week*, June 7, 1993, p. 100. For video CDs, see Jeffrey Trachtenberg, "Sony Alliance with Philips Faces Threat," *Wall Street Journal*, January 23, 1995, pp. A3, A5. For global telecommunications, see "Alliance Networks, Untangled," *Alliance Analyst*, February 3, 1995, pp. 1–5. For automobiles and trucks, see Nitin Nohria and Carlos Garcia-Pont, "Global Strategic Linkages and Industry Structure," *Strategic Management Review* (Summer 1991): 105–124. For biotechnology, see John Freeman and Stephen R. Barley, "The Strategic Analysis of Interorganizational Relations in Biotechnology," in *The Strategic Management of Technological Innovation*, ed. R. Loveridge and M. Pitt (New York: John Wiley, 1990), chap. 6. Pharmaceuticals data based on various press reports; for example, "Eli Lilly Agrees to Restrictions on Buying PCS," *Wall Street Journal*, October 26, 1994, p. A3. For airlines, see John Goodman, "Battle for the Skies: British Airways' Bid for USAir," Harvard Business School Case no. 9-793-059 (rev. 8/93) and "Swissair's Alliances," in David B. Yoffie and Benjamin Gomes-Casseres, *International Trade and Competition: Cases and Notes in Strategy and Management* (New York: McGraw-Hill, 1994). For commercial real estate, see Richard Kindleberger, "Global Reach," *Boston Sunday Globe*, December 4, 1994, pp. A1, A4.

■ **Poor Contract Development** This problem is relatively self-explanatory. Typically, the hardest part of drawing up good alliance contracts is negotiating rights, particularly those pertaining to termination prior to the intended maturity date.

■ **Misrepresentation of Resources and Capabilities** This issue arises when a partner *misrepresents*, intentionally or unintentionally, the quality or quantity of a resource or capability—say, a crucial technology or the availability of staff with particular skill sets—that its partners deem critical to the success of the venture.

■ **Misappropriation of Resources and Capabilities** *Misappropriation* occurs when one partner takes something of value, whether to the partner itself, to the alliance, or to both. Sometimes misappropriation is so endemic that would-be partners garner reputations for misappropriation. China, for example, has a notoriously poor reputation when it comes to protecting intellectual and trademark property rights.

■ **Failure to Make Complementary Resources Available** Related to the risk of misappropriation is the risk that a partner may fail to make available a promised complementary resource, such as a valuable technology or the people with the skills needed to implement or design new products or processes.

■ **Being Held Hostage Through Specific Investments**   Sometimes, even when such resources are made available, the firm that needs them may become so dependent on the alliance that it's virtually held hostage. Resources can range from a proprietary technology that the partnership controls or simply a production capability controlled by one of the partners. Trek Bicycles, for example, outsources much of its production to an Asian manufacturer called Giant. The alliance allows Trek to focus on the design, marketing, and distribution of high-quality bikes. In turn, Giant enjoys economies of scale in production. Giant, however, is also a competitor of Trek and, given Trek's dependence on Giant's production capabilities, Giant could conceivably raise its prices to Trek in order to gain price advantage over Trek in the latter's primary markets. Or consider the arrangement by which Rayovac (Spectrum) licenses its core battery technology from Matsushita, on whom it was dependent for a key technology.

■ **Misunderstanding a Partner's Strategic Intent**   The Trek and Rayovac examples provide a jumping off point for exploring another alliance risk. Both Trek and Rayovac are not only dependent on their partners for a critical resource, but they're much smaller than their partners and much weaker financially. It would be relatively easy for Giant to exploit and weaken Trek—perhaps eventually buy it out for relatively little investment. Likewise, Matsushita could raise licensing fees for its battery technology or even suspend Rayovac's access to it altogether. In addition, although Matsushita sells consumer-electronics products (under the Panasonic label), its share of the U.S. battery market is quite small. Conceivably, one way of increasing it would be to weaken Rayovac, undermining its U.S. competitor to the point at which it would become an easy acquisition target. In each case, then, it's crucial for the vulnerable partner to have a strong sense of whether its larger partner is interested in a co-opetition strategy or a winner-take-all strategy.

ALLIANCES IN STABLE AND DYNAMIC CONTEXTS

Another factor in determining whether an alliance is a suitable strategic vehicle is the level of stability or dynamism of a firm's competitive context. Relative dynamism of an industry context may affect an alliance decision in two ways:

■ From a practical standpoint, relatively stable environments are much more forgiving of mistakes, such as poor choices in partners or alliance structures.

■ Because they make maintenance and management easier, stable environments allow firms to participate in more alliances. Likewise, although wasted time, effort, and resources are undesirable in any situation, relatively stable contexts provide firms with the luxury of learning from their mistakes and regrouping.

Consider, for example, an alliance between Nestlé and Mars that allows Nestlé to put Mars-brand M&Ms in its ice creams. The success or failure of this alliance is not going to make or break either company. As we'll soon see, however, in dynamic contexts, competitive stakes are typically much higher, and any distraction of a firm's resources or managerial time and attention can have serious consequences. If, for instance, Millennium Pharmaceuticals chooses an unsuitable partner, it will not only lose time and money, but it also risks the possibility that while it's busy trying to manage the alliance, a competitor will make some advance in product or technology that gives it a significant advantage. Such risks place tremendous pressure on firms not only to choose the right partners (and the right number of partners), but to structure alliances so that they contribute to the development and enhanced value of its resources and capabilities.

Relative Stability and Alliance Motivation

The relative stability of context also affects the objectives that partners set for an alliance. In many ways, relative stability has played a role in the evolution of alliance motivation that we discussed previously. In relatively stable environments, for example, partners are typically seeking access to production technologies or markets. Their objective is essentially to consolidate market positions and generate economies of scope and scale.[22] These objectives also motivate firms in dynamic contexts, but under such conditions, firms are also motivated to use alliances as means of identifying new market threats and opportunities and of

Nestlé and Mars share an alliance whereby Nestlé is allowed to put Mars M&Ms in its ice creams. Because the companies compete in a relatively stable competitive environment, however, the success or failure of the alliance isn't likely to make or break either firm.

providing dynamic capabilities with which to respond to changes (and perhaps even to drive changes) in the competitive landscape.

Relative Stability and the Coevolution Model of Corporate Strategy

Focusing on relative stability will also help us to better understand the coevolution model of corporate strategy that we outlined in Chapter 7. Recall that *coevolution* means orchestrating a web of shifting linkages among evolving businesses. In making alliances, a firm opts to develop vertical, horizontal, or complementary linkages with other firms instead of seeking them solely among wholly owned businesses. The use of alliances in such a web enables a firm to develop its specific dynamic capabilities in concert with the best resources and capabilities available. Just as important, alliances sustain a specific focused strategy. Periodically, for instance, certain alliances can be abandoned and others added. Thus, if a firm is pursuing, say, a growth strategy, the coevolution approach suggests that it drop alliances developed around commoditized products and add those with partners who are active on the technology frontier or in other forward-looking strategies for enhancing competitive advantage.[23]

WHAT MAKES AN ALLIANCE SUCCESSFUL?

In the final section of this chapter, we'll focus on five areas in which organizations can increase the probability of alliance success:

- Understanding the determinants of trust
- Being able to manage knowledge and learning
- Understanding alliance evolution
- Knowing how to measure alliance performance
- Creating a dedicated alliance function

The first four apply readily to firms of all sizes, both domestic and international. The last usually pertains to larger firms and those that otherwise use alliances as a key vehicle for strategy execution. Understanding what's involved in all five areas puts managers in a better position to design alliances that will contribute to a firm's competitive advantage.

Understanding the Determinants of Trust

It may be stating the obvious to say that alliances perform better when partners trust each other. Research suggests that a network of trustworthy partners can itself be a competitive advantage, as can be a reputation for trustworthiness.[24] Unfortunately, because not all partners are equally trustworthy, parties in alliances often must rely on a variety of mechanisms to safeguard their interests. Formal mechanisms, such as long-term contracts, stock ownership, and collateral bonds, can signal credible long-term commitments to alliance partners. They do not, however, ensure information sharing, which is critical to alliance success. Partners foster interorganizational trust by using understandable and predictable processes. Informal mechanisms, such as firm reputation and personal trust among managers and officers, are also keys to creating long-term value.

Mutual trust generates several benefits. It results in conditions that increase the value of the alliance and, therefore, the probability that it will contribute to competitive advantage.[25] As you can see in Exhibit 9.9, for instance, trust leads to a greater willingness to make investments in assets customized to the alliance. When such partnership-specific investments raise the potential for hold-up, they're also more likely to yield the economies of scope and scale that make such partnerships pay off economically. The investment in Tritec by BMW and DaimlerChrysler is a good example, because both firms invested considerable time and dollars in the plant and it is delivering some of the most dependable and efficiently produced four-cylinder car engines in the industry.

Besides increasing learning by encouraging investment in mechanisms that promote greater information sharing, trust reduces the costs of monitoring and maintaining an alliance.

Exhibit 9.9 Benefits of Trust

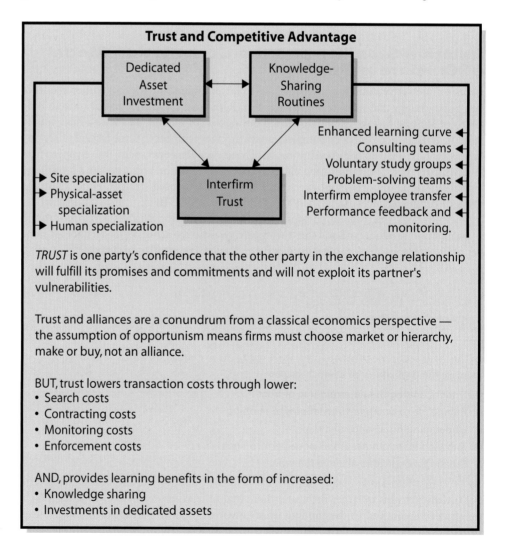

Trust and Competitive Advantage

Dedicated Asset Investment ⟷ Knowledge-Sharing Routines

Interfirm Trust

- Site specialization
- Physical-asset specialization
- Human specialization

- Enhanced learning curve
- Consulting teams
- Voluntary study groups
- Problem-solving teams
- Interfirm employee transfer
- Performance feedback and monitoring.

TRUST is one party's confidence that the other party in the exchange relationship will fulfill its promises and commitments and will not exploit its partner's vulnerabilities.

Trust and alliances are a conundrum from a classical economics perspective — the assumption of opportunism means firms must choose market or hierarchy, make or buy, not an alliance.

BUT, trust lowers transaction costs through lower:
- Search costs
- Contracting costs
- Monitoring costs
- Enforcement costs

AND, provides learning benefits in the form of increased:
- Knowledge sharing
- Investments in dedicated assets

Savings can result from such simple gestures as foregoing new legal agreements for small changes in the arrangement or from such critical decisions as an agreement to rely on a simple management structure rather than a more complicated structure requiring a board of directors.

Relational Quality   Because trust is so important to alliance performance, firms need to focus on the areas that affect it most. One approach to identifying these areas is called **relational quality**, which identifies four key elements in establishing and maintaining interorganizational trust.[26] You'll probably find one or more of these elements to be intuitively obvious, but research suggests that organizations don't do a good or consistent job of paying attention to them.

relational quality Principle identifying four key elements (initial conditions, negotiation process, reciprocal experiences, outside behavior) in establishing and maintaining interorganizational trust

Initial Conditions   The first element refers to the mutual attitudes of the parties before negotiations begin. Attitudes may be based on prior experiences or on reputation. Sometimes they reflect a larger set of political and economic circumstances. As we noted earlier, for example, China's reputation for condoning property-rights abuses would probably make a prospective partner wary of allying with a Chinese firm.

The Negotiation Process   Prior experience with the process can influence the attitudes that any party brings to the negotiating table. Initial conditions provide a foundation for the development and upgrading of resources and capabilities, but the social interactions that characterize the negotiations process will determine whether any promise in the negotiations is eventually realized. Your own relationships provide a relevant example here. When you meet someone, for instance, you may feel positive about that person due to his or her behaviors or prior reputation. However, your interaction with that person after the initial meeting will determine whether a friendship and otherwise productive relationship develops.

Reciprocal Experiences   Once some level of interorganizational trust is established, stock and flow reflect the partners' reciprocal experiences. Do they, for instance, share information openly, disclose potential problems, or behave in other ways that add to the stock of existing interorganizational trust?

Outside Behavior   Trust is also a function of the reputation the organization develops as a consequence of its interactions with other organizations outside of the alliance. When Wal-Mart dropped Rubbermaid as a supplier, other suppliers undoubtedly became concerned about the degree to which the retailer could be trusted as a partner.

Managing Knowledge and Learning

For many firms, learning from alliance partners is one of the primary objectives of entering an alliance. In addition to reflecting trust, the ability of a partner to learn increases the collective benefits derived by every partner in the alliance. However, wanting to learn, though obviously important, isn't enough to make learning take place.[27] Learning is enhanced if a firm develops specific processes for managing knowledge exchange. Some explicit activities enable firms to learn from alliances.

Learning and Supplier Support at Toyota   Toyota is one of the most successful firms at managing learning through alliance networks and provides a helpful example of knowledge-management best practices. Research by J. H. Dyer highlights Toyota's success in managing its alliances so that knowledge and productivity gains accrue to all alliance members.[28] In studying Toyota's U.S. alliance networks, Dyer found that Toyota's U.S. suppliers were able to achieve efficiency gains in manufacturing that suppliers for GM and Ford couldn't match. In fact, Toyota's suppliers outperformed the other automakers' suppliers despite the disadvantage of being newer and at an earlier stage of the learning curve. Performance *improvements* far outpaced those of other suppliers, and *absolute* performance rapidly surpassed that of suppliers to American firms. Dyer suggests that these efficiency gains resulted from concentrated efforts to ensure not only that learning flowed both ways but that suppliers learned from each other, not just from Toyota. The strategy depends on the carmaker's Toyota Supplier Support Center (TSSC), which has 20 consultants working with U.S. suppliers.

Let's look at the process a little more closely. Toyota divides its suppliers into groups of 6 to 12, with direct competitors assigned to separate groups. To keep interactions fresh, group composition changes every three years. Each group meets with Toyota consultants to decide on a theme for the year, such as styling, demographic fit, supplier relations, and so on. Representatives from each group visit each supplier's plant over a four-month period, examining operations and offering suggestions for improvement. Finally, Toyota hosts an annual meeting at which each group reports on the results of the year's learning activities.

The results have been impressive—an average improvement of 124 percent in labor productivity and inventory reductions of 75 percent. The lesson is quite clear: Alliances result in significant productivity gains when learning is facilitated by coordinated efforts to exchange knowledge and disseminate best practices within the network. Note, too, that such a high level of learning is made possible by an overarching commitment to mutual trust.

Understanding Alliance Evolution

At the outset of this chapter, we asked whether you thought the outcome of White Wave's alliance with Dean Foods was a common one. In this case, we encountered an interesting turn in the course of certain alliances, particularly equity joint ventures: namely, that what starts out as an alliance may eventually become an acquisition.[29] In fact, one study found that nearly 80 percent of equity joint ventures end in the sale of one partner to another.[30] The researchers suggested that managers who don't look out for this twist in the road may run head-on into an unplanned divestiture or acquisition. Although some alliances are actually structured to terminate in the eventual transfer of ownership, most are not, and unplanned sales may erode shareholder value.

Of course, a sale that's well managed and planned in advance can be to a firm's advantage. The same study indicated that alliances can advance a firm's long-term strategy by providing companies with a low-cost, low-risk means of previewing possible acquisitions.

At the same time, it should come as no surprise that relationships between partners may change over time. Indeed, if one partner is aggressively pursuing a coevolution strategy that involves alliances, these changes should be monitored closely and included in the ongoing strategy of both the alliance and its partners. As the box entitled "How Would *You* Do That? 9.1" shows, the history of Fuji Xerox is a good illustration of well-managed coevolution.

Measuring Alliance Performance

Ironically, one reason for the high failure rate of alliances is the fact that few firms have effective systems for monitoring alliance performance.[31] In the short term, a lack of monitoring systems means that managers who are responsible for the alliance must rely more on intuition than on good information. The long-term consequences are even more serious: When problems do surface, it's much more expensive to fix them. Moreover, performance may have declined so drastically that one or more of the partners starts looking for ways to exit the alliance—an event that often starts a downward spiral toward more performance problems and eventual termination.

Although it may, therefore, seem eminently logical for firms to put monitoring systems in place, there are at least three barriers to getting it done:

- Partner firms often have different information and reporting systems. DaimlerChrysler and BMW, for instance, have quite different quality, production, and financial-reporting systems. The systems at their alliance firm, Tritec, differ from those of both partners. The two carmakers have recently decided that, despite the expense in time and money, Tritec will "translate" its performance data into information that can be accessed through both DaimlerChrysler's and BMW's systems.

- Even when firms go to great lengths to gauge performance, the inputs that the alliance receives from its corporate parents can be difficult to track and account for. For example, say a manager from DaimlerChrysler joins a Tritec team and that team develops a novel new manufacturing approach. Very often it is difficult to determine whether it was the specific team member or the larger team that came up with the new idea.

- Similarly, it's also difficult to put a precise value on alliance outputs. What price or value, for example, would you attach to the alliance-based knowledge that a partner uses to improve operations in other parts of the organization?

Managing Coevolution at Fuji Xerox

Some of the best examples of coevolution reinforce the important roles played by time and investments. Take the case of Fuji Xerox, which provides some insight into the resources and capabilities acquired through alliances. This alliance between Fuji Photo and Xerox also provided fertile ground for the successful turnaround of Xerox itself by Anne Mulcahy, which you read about in the opening vignette to Chapter 2.

The Fuji Xerox alliance had been in place for several years, but it was not until early 1970 that it began to bear fruit as a source of competitive capabilities and knowledge for both the alliance and the partners. Xerox was in dire financial straights at the time, having positioned its products against then high-powered rivals such as Eastman Kodak and IBM but being undermined at the same time by low-cost Japanese manufacturers. The first transition was the transfer of Fuji Photo's manufacturing plants in 1970 to the Fuji Xerox alliance and the resulting development of low-cost manufacturing capabilities by the venture. Following the development of these capabilities, from 1976 to 1978, Xerox initiated R&D and technology-reimbursement agreements between itself and Fuji Xerox. This transfer agreement fostered the design and fabrication of copy machines for distribution in Europe and the United States.

Over the next decade, Fuji Xerox continued to upgrade its resources and capabilities in low-end copiers and printers, and Xerox aggressively absorbed these advantages as they grew in importance in the global marketplace. For instance, following an agreement to allow Fuji Xerox control over its own R&D, Fuji Xerox began to internalize Japanese total-quality-control manufacturing processes. Xerox, in turn, adopted these processes, and at the same time used the Fuji Xerox alliance as a platform to expand it own products' presence in Japan.

Ironically, the success and rapid growth for the Fuji Xerox alliance was a function of the autonomy granted to it by its parents. By 1991, those parents established a new alliance, Xerox International Partners, to market the Fuji Xerox printer mechanism outside of Japan to companies such as Hewlett-Packard, which were largely captive to the industry leader, Canon. At the same time, this same mechanism satisfied the majority of Xerox and Rank Xerox (another alliance) low-end copier sales. Although the alliances were largely autonomous, top executives at Xerox and Fuji Xerox were careful to set up top-executive "summits" twice a year, exchange key personnel, and fund joint research programs to avoid redundant and wasteful R&D efforts.

It was on this platform of global success that Anne Mulcahy made a case for the acquisition of the color-printer division of Tektronix by Xerox in 2000. These color-printer capabilities, were shared, not surprisingly, with Fuji Xerox, which flourishes to this day, with Xerox owning 25 percent and Fuji Photo owning 75 percent. As for Xerox? Well, you know much of the rest of that story from the vignette in Chapter 2.

Sources: Adapted from B. Gomes-Casseres, "Competing in Constellations: The Case of Fuji Xerox," *Strategy and Business* First Quarter (1997), 4–16; www.fujixerox.co.jp/eng/company/history (accessed July 15, 2005) and the Xerox Fact Book (2005–2006), at www.xerox.com (accessed November 8, 2005).

Dedicated Alliance Function

Recent research indicates that cooperative strategies are more likely to succeed when a firm has a dedicated alliance function.[32] A dedicated alliance function may simply be one manager who is responsible for setting up, tracking, and dissolving the firm's alliances; however, typically this function is managed by a group of individuals working together as a team. In many ways, such a function is a structural solution to the need to manage trust, learning, evolution, and performance in a systematic fashion. Although some firms can't afford this added management function, the benefits make it worth looking for a way to fill this role. A firm might, for example, assign a chief alliance officer, whose responsibilities are outlined in Exhibit 9.10.

The first two steps in the components of a dedicated-alliance-function process are often the most critical. Regardless of the levels of trust, learning, and capabilities that an alliance boasts, it won't be productive under either of the two following situations:

- When alliances are not clearly delineated as a vehicle for the firms' strategies
- When there simply isn't a good fit between partners

Good intentions alone do not make alliances work. Nothing can replace a good strategy that spells out the role of alliances in a firm's strategy and partner fit.

When Do Partners Fit?

The issue of fit isn't easy to resolve, and to do so, firms must be able to answer yes to the following questions:

- *Strategic fit:* Are the partners' objectives compatible? For how long?
- *Resource and financial fit:* Are the partners willing and able to contribute the resources and competencies?
- *Cultural fit:* Can the partners understand each other? Do they share the same business logic and commitment?
- *Structure, systems, and processes fit:* Can the decision-making and control mechanisms be aligned?
- *Additional fit criteria:* What other key questions should be on the table, such as timing, other alliances, alliance alternatives, environmental context, and competitive pressures?

Because we're interested in alliances as a strategy vehicle, the first question pertains to *strategic fit.* Researchers at the consulting firm of McKinsey and Company have identified lack of strategic fit as a common starting point for those alliances that eventually failed.[33] In many ways, the opening vignette on White Wave provides an example of an alliance where strategic fit was good because White Wave needed better access to the grocery-store channel and capital than it could attain on its own. Sometimes, alliances between weaker

Exhibit 9.10 Components of a Dedicated Alliance Function

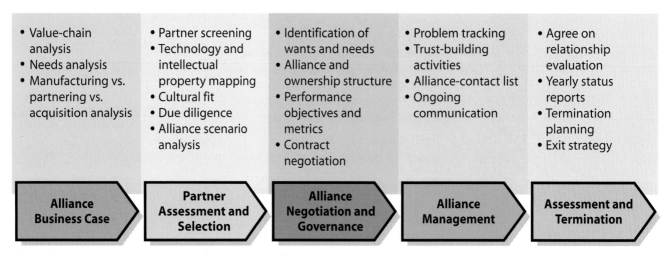

Source: *Adapted from J.P. Dyer, P. Kale, and H. Singh, "How to Make Strategic Alliances Work," Sloan Management Review, 42:4 (2001), 121–136.*

and stronger firms even lead the weaker firm to a position of strength, in which case the alliance is usually dissolved, or in other cases, such as White Wave, in which the stronger partner acquires the weaker one. Partnerships among complementary equals tend to be the strongest and longest lasting. In some cases, competitive tensions and industry conditions may lead one partner to acquire the other, usually after about seven years. In other cases, the partners remain strong and independent. Some alliances, such as Fuji Xerox, exemplify true coevolution and are most likely to survive for much longer than seven years. In the case of Fuji Xerox, the alliance has lasted several decades and has spawned additional complementary alliances.

The second question concerns *resource and financial fit.* This question deals with either the availability of a resource or the willingness and ability of a partner to make that resource available. Questions of *cultural fit* typically relate to the cultural characteristics of the organizations themselves. In the early years of SEMATECH, for instance, Intel's participation was problematic because Intel's highly competitive culture clashed with the cooperative culture being fostered by the consortium.[34] Though *structural fit* can be a simple matter of making financial-reporting systems compatible, conflicts may arise over arrangements of authority and decision making.

Finally, in determining fit, a company should take situation-specific factors into consideration. Is the firm, for example, already involved in too many alliances? Is the timing right? Do competitive conditions currently favor alliances as a strategy vehicle? The box entitled "How Would *You* Do That? 9.2" shows what happened when Millennium Pharmaceuticals applied a checklist for assessing partner fit in determining whether to enter into an alliance with a potential partner. The answer, as you can see, was no.

Dyer's research shows that it's difficult to develop the rich alliance capabilities that will satisfy a checklist like Millennium's. At the same time, however, Dyer notes that firms that succeed in developing the requisite capabilities may be better competitors as a result. Not only may such capabilities contribute to near-term performance and competitive position, but they may also enhance the reputation of a company as a preferred partner. Wal-Mart, for example, though known as a very aggressive competitor, has established a solid reputation in Latin America as a dependable partner. As noted earlier, Wal-Mart is now leveraging these alliance skills and the reputation built through local partnerships to fuel its growth in China and Japan.

General Motors President Rick Wagoner (left in photo) and Japan's Suzuki Motors President Osamu Suzuki give the thumbs-up as they unveil Suzuki's new concept sports car during a press conference in Tokyo, October 19, 1999, one day before the Tokyo Motor Show. GM, Suzuki, and Isuzu Motors announced that they were forming an alliance on the global market.

Assessing Alliance Fit at
Millennium Pharmaceuticals

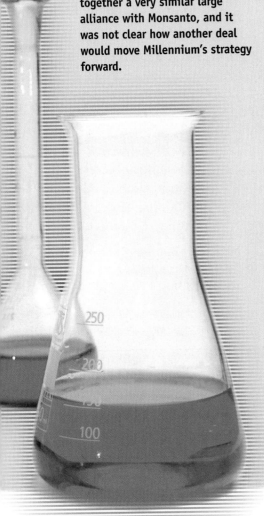

Millennium Pharmaceuticals was faced with a huge alliance opportunity—it involved lots of cash and a savvy global partner with a great deal of experience. Why, then, would Millennium turn such a deal down? Using the following alliance-fit framework, Millennium decided that it was best to pass on this alliance:

- *Strategic fit?* In general, the strategic fit was good. However, Millennium had recently put together a very similar large alliance with Monsanto, and it was not clear how another deal would move Millennium's strategy forward.

- *Resource fit?* Other than money, the global partner did not bring much to the table in terms of new resources and capabilities. In fact, Millennium would be putting most of its unique capabilities to work, which in turn could stretch its technical and research staff with no benefit other than additional cash in the bank. At the time, Millennium was strong financially.

- *Cultural fit?* The potential partner was a large, private agribusiness firm, whereas Millennium was a relatively small, public biotech firm. In initial meetings, there was some indication with the potential partner that top management was keen on an alliance but that lower-level managers were out of the loop. Cultural misfit often arises when line managers are not involved in the alliance-building process from the very start.

- *Structural fit?* This, too, was a big question mark. Millennium's management had the impression that the partner would not grant it the autonomy or flexibility that it desired in its alliances. Thus, the structure appeared too rigid from Millennium's perspective.

- *Other questions?* Because Millennium was still contemplating other options and partnerships, it was not as if this was the only opportunity in the market. Finally, the top-management team determined that it was not really excited about the alliance beyond the fact that the partner had a

great reputation and brought lots of cash to the relationship.

So, you are probably asking what happened to Millennium after it passed up such a lucrative deal. Shortly thereafter, Millennium and Abbott formed a five-year alliance primarily for collaborative research and development in the area of metabolic diseases. The companies agreed to share equally the cost of developing, manufacturing, and marketing products on a worldwide basis. The arrangement with Abbott also includes an equity investment by Abbott in Millennium, amounting in total to $250 million over several years, and a technology exchange and development agreement. Moreover, Millennium and Aventis expanded their joint development pipeline to include an aggregate of 11 additional discovery projects that were previously pursued outside the joint collaboration by Millennium or Aventis. These new assets included chemokine receptors, kinases, and integrins, which are important as potential drug-development target classes in inflammatory disease research. As a result of this expansion, that alliance yielded approximately 50 jointly funded discovery projects. Soon, Millennium had created more than 20 alliances with leading pharmaceutical and biotechnology companies—close to $2 billion of committed funding. You can learn more about why Millennium sees such a network of alliances as a central vehicle in its strategy—to eventually become a full-fledged pharmaceutical firm—through its R&D page at www.millennium.com.

SUMMARY

1. Explain why strategic alliances are important strategy vehicles. Alliances enable participants to share in investments and rewards, while reducing the risk and uncertainty that each firm must bear on its own. Such sharing also enables firms to focus their efforts on what they do best, while benefiting from the similarly focused efforts of their partner firms. In economic terms, alliances may lead to higher firm performance by enabling firms to realize economies of scope and scale that would otherwise not be realized if they had to operate on their own.

2. Explain the various forms and structures of strategic alliances. Alliances can take many forms. A joint venture is the most complex form because it results in the establishment of a third, independent entity. Joint ventures, in which partners contribute cash and other resources to the partnership, fall into the broader category of equity alliances. Nonequity alliances are the most common form of alliance. These typically take the form of contracts to supply, produce, market, or distribute a firm's goods or services. Sole-sourcing, just-in-time supply agreements, licensing, and cobranding are examples of nonequity alliances. Equity and nonequity alliances may involve many participants. Such alliances are sometimes called *industry associations, cartels, cooperatives,* or *consortia.*

3. Describe the motivations behind alliances and show how they've changed over time. Although firms seek economies of scope and scale from alliances, their ultimate objective is that the alliance contribute to their competitive advantage. The VRINE framework can be applied to alliances. If the alliance creates something of value, has benefits that are both rare and difficult to imitate (including less costly imitation by a simple market purchase agreement or wholly owned business), and the partners are able to extract value from the alliance (i.e., the resources and capabilities in the alliance are supported by features of the organization), then a firm can reap competitive advantages. Over time, the basis for alliance advantage has shifted from simple efficiencies and economies of scope and scale to a vehicle for organizational learning and innovation.

4. Explain alliances as business- and corporate-level strategy vehicles. The five-forces model and value net are good tools for both identifying potential partners and reaffirming that just about any firm related to the business can be considered a potential partner. Business strategy alliances fall into two categories: vertical and horizontal. Vertical alliances link a focal firm to downstream raw materials and other critical inputs; upstream they link that same firm to marketing, arenas, and other channels of distribution. Horizontal alliances enable firms in one segment of the industry to partner with firms in other segments. Strategic alliances are also a useful vehicle for a firm's corporate and international strategies. Cross-border alliances differ from domestic-only alliances in that government, public policies, and national culture often play a more visible role. Alliances can also take on the characteristic of a network when clusters of companies compete against each other for customers or new technology standards. Finally, cutting across all these alliances are six risks that contribute to their failure or lackluster performance. These risks range from poor contract development to the misinterpretation of a partner's strategic intent.

5. Understand the characteristics of alliances in stable and dynamic competitive contexts. Just as strategies may vary according to context, so, too, should the expectations and design features of alliances as a strategy vehicle. Stable contexts afford firms the luxury of managing many alliances. Although the choice of alliance partners is always important, any one alliance failure is unlikely to break the company. However, in dynamic contexts the stakes are much higher. Such heightened stakes can take the simple form of greater dollar investments in new technological platforms but typically are manifest in a rapidly evolving environment where being in the wrong partnership today could mean the ultimate demise of the firm later. The use and design of alliances in dynamic contexts fits well with the co-evolution model introduced in Chapter 7. That is, alliances are included in the firm's orchestration of a web of shifting linkages among evolving businesses.

6. Summarize the criteria for successful alliances. Five interrelated criteria for effective alliance implementation were emphasized in this chapter. First, firms must understand the determinants and benefits of trust. Alliances that are based on trust benefit from lower transactions costs, greater economies of scope and scale, and greater learning and knowledge management. Second, firms must be good at managing knowledge and knowledge flows. This means that they should establish learning objectives for each alliance and mechanisms for realizing them. The third criterion is the need to understand alliance evolution. Alliances may follow different pathways depending on their initial conditions and partner relations, and an understanding of both the role of initial conditions and the potential pathways will inform the establishment of an alliance and its management once it is in place. Linking the alliance to a performance management system is the fourth criterion. Such tracking will help to ensure both near-term benefits and the avoidance of problems that may fester for lack of attention. Finally, firms should consider the establishment of some systematic and coherent structural response to the unique and complex management challenges that alliances give rise to. This structure can take the form of an individual with the title of chief alliance officer or, where appropriate and financially feasible, the establishment of a dedicated alliance function.

KEY TERMS

consortia, 252

co-opetition, 257

equity alliance, 252

horizontal alliance, 258

joint venture, 252

nonequity alliance, 252

relational quality, 265

strategic alliance, 249

value-net model, 257

vertical alliance, 258

REVIEW QUESTIONS

1. What is a strategic alliance?

2. Do most strategic alliances succeed?

3. What forms can strategic alliances take?

4. What is the difference between an equity and a nonequity strategic alliance?

5. Provide an example of a nonequity strategic alliance.

6. Why do firms enter into alliances?

7. What are the three forms of strategic alliance that support business strategy?

8. What do the value-net and industry-structure models tell you about potential alliance partners?

9. How do alliances serve as a vehicle for corporate strategy?

10. What risks do alliances pose to partner firms?

11. How do alliances differ in stable and dynamic contexts?

12. What are the five criteria for successful alliances?

How Would **YOU** Do That?

1. The box entitled "How Would *You* Do That? 9.1" presents the example of Fuji Xerox and the evolution of Xerox's competitive capabilities as a result of that alliance. Use the VRINE framework to map the resources and capabilities that you believe evolved at Xerox as a result of the Fuji Xerox alliance. Why might these resources and capabilities be valuable in a dynamic competitive environment?

2. The box entitled "How Would *You* Do That? 9.2" shows how Millennium Pharmaceuticals evaluated a potential alliance partner. Apply the Millennium fit framework to the alliances of another firm you are familiar with. Do these appear to be good alliances? Do any of the alliances suggest that your focal firm is on a pathway to acquire its partner or be acquired by it?

GROUP ACTIVITIES

1. Increasingly, firms such as Corning (www.corning.com) and Millennium Pharmaceuticals (www.millennium.com) claim to have a core competency and competitive advantage based on their ability to manage alliances. Develop statements that both defend and critique this proposition. Identify risks that firms run when their strategy is essentially a network of alliances.

2. Identify a firm and document its alliance activity over the past 5 to 10 years (visit the Web site of a public firm, particu-

larly the "history" page). Examine the list of officers at the company (these are always detailed in the annual report and often on the firm's Web site). Do they appear to have a dedicated alliance function? What kinds of changes would they have to make if they were to follow the recommendations on implementation levers necessary to achieve an effective dedicated alliance function? What would be the costs and benefits of such a change?

ENDNOTES

1. P. Zachary, "Why the Soy Milk Still Reigns," *Business 2.0,* April 2004, 73–74; White Wave, "Mission Statement," About Us (accessed June 1, 2005), at www.silkissoy.com/index.php?id = 1.

2. J. Harbison and P. Pekar, *Smart Alliances: A Practical Guide to Repeatable Success* (San Francisco: Jossey-Bass, 1998).

3. C. Wolf, "Rubbermaid Struggles to Put Lid on Problems: Company's Earnings Tumble after Price Increase Backfires," *Cincinnati Enquirer,* April 8, 1996, D1.

4. J. Cook, T. Halevy, and B. Hastie, "Alliances in Consumer Packaged Goods," *McKinsey on Finance,* Autumn 2003, 16–20.

5. J. Bleeke and D. Ernst, *Collaborating to Compete* (New York: Wiley, 1993); D. Ernst and T. Halevy, "When to Think Alliance," *McKinsey Quarterly* 4 (2000), 46–55.

6. www.mlnm.com/media/strategy/index.asp (accessed July 15, 2005).

7. For detailed discussions of the Japanese projects, see K. Flamm, *Mismanaged Trade? Strategic Policy and the Semiconductor Industry* (Washington, D.C.: Brookings Institution, 1996), 39–126; J. Sigurdson, *Industry and State Partnership in Japan: The Very Large Scale Integrated Circuits (VLSI) Project* (Lund, Sweden: Research Policy Institute, 1986). For a dissenting assessment, see M. Fransman, *The Market and Beyond: Cooperation and Competition in Information Technology Development in the Japanese System* (Cambridge: Cambridge University Press, 1992).

8. Semiconductor Equipment and Materials International, About Us (accessed June 6, 2005), at http://wps2a.semi.org/wps/portal/_pagr/103/_pa.103/259.

9. J. H. Dyer and H. Singh, "The Relational View: Cooperative Strategies and Sources of Interorganizational Competitive Advantage," *Academy of Management Review* 23 (1998), 660–679.

10. O. E. Williamson, *The Economic Institutions of Capitalism* (New York: Free Press, 1985).

11. G. Hamel and C. K. Prahalad, *Competing for the Future* (Boston: Harvard Business School Press, 1994).

12. J. B. Barney and M. H. Hansen, "Trustworthiness as a Source of Competitive Advantage," *Strategic Management Journal* 15 (1995), 175–190; Dyer and Singh, "The Relational View."

13. Harbison and Pekar, *Smart Alliances.*

14. Ortega, "Wal-Mart to Expand Mexican Business by Greatly Enlarging Cifra Venture," *Wall Street Journal*, June 1, 1992, B5.

15. A chart that nicely summarizes this marriage of resources and capabilities can be found at www.smartalliancepartners.com/chartofweek093.html (accessed August 15, 2005).

16. C. Torres, "Sudden Targets: Foreigners Snap Up Mexican Companies," *Wall Street Journal*, September 30, 1997, A1.

17. A. Welsh and A. Zimmerman, "Wal-Mart Snaps Up Brazilian Chain," *Wall Street Journal*, March 2, 2004, B3.

18. Y. Ono and A. Zimmerman, "Wal-Mart Enters Japan with Seiyu Stake," *Wall Street Journal*, March 15, 2002, B5.

19. J. H. Dyer, *Collaborative Advantage: Winning through Extended Enterprise Supplier Networks* (New York: Oxford University Press, 2000).

20. www.softbank.co.jp (accessed August 12, 2005).

21. P. Almeida, J. Song, and R. M. Grant, "Are Firms Superior to Alliances and Markets? An Empirical Test of Cross-Border Knowledge Building," *Organization Science* 14 (2002), 157–171.

22. Harbison and Pekar, *Smart Alliances*; E. Bailey and W. Shan, "Sustainable Competitive Advantage Through Alliances," in E. Bowman and B. Kogut, eds., *Redesigning the Firm* (New York: Oxford University Press, 1995).

23. S. Brown and K. Eisenhardt, *Competing on the Edge* (Boston: Harvard Business School Press, 1997).

24. Barney and Hansen, "Trustworthiness as a Source of Competitive Advantage."

25. Dyer, *Collaborative Advantage.*

26. A. Arino, J. de la Torre, P. S. Ring, "Relational Quality: Managing Trust in Corporate Alliances," *California Management Review* 44:1 (2001), 109–134.

27. G. Probst, "Practical Knowledge Management: A Model That Works," *Prism* (Arthur D. Little Consultants), Second Quarter (1998), 17–29.

28. Information in this section is drawn from J. H. Dyer, *Collaborative Advantage.*

29. J. Bleeke and D. Ernst, *Collaborating to Compete* (New York: Wiley, 1993).

30. Bleeke and Ernst, *Collaborating to Compete.*

31. J. P. Dyer, P. Kale, and H. Singh, "How to Make Strategic Alliances Work," *Sloan Management Review* 42 (2001), 121–136. According to the authors, 51 percent of the alliances surveyed had no performance-monitoring systems, and only 11 percent believed that they had good systems in place.

32. Dyer, Kale, and Singh, "How to Make Strategic Alliances Work."

33. J. Bleeke and D. Ernst, "Is Your Strategic Alliance Really a Sale?" *Harvard Business Review* 73:1 (1995), 97–102.

34. L. D. Browning, J. M. Beyer, J. C. Shetler, "Building Cooperation in a Competitive Industry: SEMATECH," *Academy of Management Journal* 38:1 (1995), 113–151.

After studying this chapter, you should be able to:

1. Explain the motivations behind acquisitions and show how they've changed over time.

2. Explain why mergers and acquisitions are important strategy vehicles.

3. Identify the various types of acquisitions.

4. Understand how the pricing of acquisitions affects the realization of synergies.

5. Outline the alternative ways to integrate acquisitions and explain the implementation process.

6. Discuss the characteristics of acquisitions in different industry contexts.

▶ Lagging badly behind Yahoo! Japan, in 2002, eBay shuts down eBay Japan, which was launched in 2000 as a joint venture with a Japanese firm. eBay's stock falls from $52 to $49 per share following the news but rebounds the next day—a testament to CEO Meg Whitman's adroit leadership of the firm. Market capitalization following failed venture: $14 billion

▶ eBay acquires Billpoint in 1999, hoping to develop "a company that will set the industry standard for person-to-person payment on the Internet." However, Billpoint fails to catch on. Whitman announces eBay will acquire rival PayPal and pull the plug on Billpoint. eBay's stock price falls from $60 to $56 per share on the news. Market capitalization following failed merger: $16 billion

EBAY + PAYPAL: HOW TO ACQUIRE CUSTOMERS

eBay, as most people know, is an Internet-auction site on which some 135 million registered customers buy and sell tens of thousands of products ranging from Beanie Babies to used cars.[1] The company generates revenues through advertising and by charging listing and selling fees. eBay is growing fast, and it's an amazing success story: Revenues have increased at an average rate of more than 80 percent annually for the past five years and earnings at an even faster clip—109 percent in earnings per share. The company has grown through a combination of internal development (offering new services and expanding into new product and geographic arenas) and external activities, including alliances, joint ventures, and acquisitions.

eBay typically relies on acquisitions and partnerships to enter new international markets. In Japan, eBay partnered with computer firm

► Whitman continues to turn eBay into a broader marketplace for personal and commercial goods by acquiring Butterfields, an upscale San Francisco auction house, in 1999. But the strategy to sell high-end products via the Internet fails, and in 2002 eBay sells Butterfields to Bonhams, a brick-and-mortar auction house, for significantly less than it paid. eBay's stock drops modestly from $57 to $55. Market capitalization following failed merger: $16 billion

► In 2005, eBay agrees to acquire VoIP provider Skype Technologies—the creator of Kazaa, the free music-sharing program that riled the music business. Financial analysts question the high price and the companies' compatibility, but not Whitman's ability to put eBay's stock price on a long-term upward trajectory. The price holds roughly steady at $38 per share following the announcement. Market capitalization following merger announcement: $52 billion

NEC. This partnership failed, however, and the company shut down its Japanese operations, leaving Yahoo! in control of the Japanese online-auction market. Likewise, not all of eBay's acquisitions have been successful. In 1999, for example, eBay made a bid to enhance its presence in the market for prestige products by purchasing Butterfields, an established auctioneer of high-end merchandise. When the marriage failed (in 2002), eBay sold Butterfields. In 1999, eBay attempted to capture a significant share of the online-payment-services sector by acquiring Billpoint, a small person-to-person credit card transaction company, and investing in its technology in order to imitate the popular PayPal. eBay Payments by Billpoint never caught on with eBay customers as they continued to prefer PayPal. eBay abandoned Billpoint in 2002 and purchased PayPal.

PayPal's network builds on the existing financial infrastructure of bank accounts and credit cards to create a global payment system. Its revenue comes from float in the personal accounts and fees charged for Premier and Business Accounts. eBay management viewed PayPal's strategy as complementary to its own. Both business models, shown in Exhibit 10.1, for example, relied on transaction-based revenue sources. Neither required inventory or warehousing of merchandise, and neither maintained any sales force to speak of. Finally, both strategies called for high operating leverage and low capital requirements. Under eBay, PayPal gets approximately two-thirds of its revenue from online-auction participants. It serves more

Exhibit 10.1 eBay and PayPal Business Models

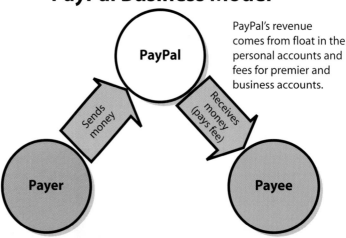

eBay Business Model

eBay's revenue comes from auction—posting fees paid by sellers.

eBay

Posts auction, pays fee

Wins auction

Seller

Contract and payment occur between buyer and seller

Buyer

PayPal Business Model

PayPal's revenue comes from float in the personal accounts and fees for premier and business accounts.

PayPal

Sends money

Receives money (pays fee)

Payer

Payee

than 64 million users, about 85 percent of whom are individuals. The average transaction size is about $55.

PayPal didn't come cheap. The sale entailed a 100-percent stock transaction, and the price—about $1.5 billion—represented a 20-percent premium over PayPal's stock value prior to the announced acquisition. Thus, eBay paid a premium of about $250 million, and on the day that the sale was announced the market discounted eBay's stock price by 7 percent. After successfully negotiating and closing this transaction, eBay CEO Meg Whitman was left with the reality of trying to make it work. She either had to identify significant cost savings or find new revenue-enhancement opportunities (i.e., synergies) in order to recoup the capital that was necessary to snag PayPal. ∎

MOTIVES FOR MERGERS AND ACQUISITIONS

Why do firms acquire companies rather than entering new businesses on their own or through alliances? Was eBay's acquisition of PayPal a typical acquisition? Are most acquisitions successful? Why do companies often pay huge costs, such as the 20-percent premium that eBay paid for PayPal, to acquire another firm? By the end of this chapter, you should be able to answer these and other questions about mergers and acquisitions (M&As). Indeed, as you work through the chapter, you'll see that our opening vignette on eBay and PayPal introduces many of the features common to acquisitions.

Differences Between Acquisitions and Mergers

Although it is regular practice to use the terms *mergers* and *acquisitions* together, and sometimes interchangeably, they aren't the same thing. The differences can be subtle, and depending on who's using the terms and in what country, each term tends to have different meanings. Disputes over differences in legal definitions can end up in court. For instance, Chrysler investor Kirk Kerkorian sued DaimlerChrysler in 2001 for billions based on the argument that the marriage of Daimler with Chrysler in 1997 was actually an acquisition by Daimler and not a merger. What was Kerkorian's interest in the transaction being labeled an acquisition? An acquisition would result in much more money being paid to Chrysler shareholders, including Kerkorian.[2]

Technically, the term **acquisition** means that a transfer of ownership has taken place— that one firm has bought another. A **merger** is the consolidation or combination of one firm with another.[3] When the term *merger* is used, it often refers to a class of mergers known as *mergers of equals*. These mergers are typically between firms of relatively equal size and influence that fuse together to form one new larger firm. Although there are many technical, legal, and detailed differences between mergers and acquisitions, for our purposes in understanding how they serve as vehicles of strategy, they are more similar than dissimilar. Consequently, we will focus on how firms use M&As to pursue their objectives.

We will emphasize the motives for M&As and the strategic implications of those motives. The motives behind M&As fall into three basic categories: *managerial self-interest*, *hubris*, and *synergy*. In this section, we'll review these three types of motives and assess the effects of M&As undertaken in pursuit of each of them. Because the first two motives usually don't reflect shareholders' best interests, the rest of the chapter will focus on M&As undertaken in pursuit of synergy.

Managerial Self-Interest

Sometimes senior managers make decisions based on personal self-interest rather than the best interests of shareholders. We call this behavior **managerialism**. Conceivably, managers can make acquisitions—and even willingly overpay in M&As—in order to maximize their own interests at the expense of shareholder wealth. Executive compensation, for instance,

acquisition Strategy by which one firm acquires another through stock purchase or exchange

merger Consolidation or combination of two or more firms

managerialism Tendency of managers to make decisions based on personal self-interest rather than the best interests of shareholders tends to be linked to firm size. Managers might, therefore, enhance their paychecks by making acquisitions that accomplish nothing more than enlarging the firm.[4] As you have learned, getting bigger, in and of itself, does not create shareholder wealth.

Likewise, because year-end bonuses (and job security) are often tied to the firm's earnings, some managers might pursue diversification in order to stabilize annual earnings. Managers could, therefore, make acquisitions in order to boost earnings by diversifying the firm's revenue stream.[5] Certainly, organic growth could achieve the same goal but not as quickly. In any case, diversification of a firm's revenue stream creates little value for shareholders. Why? Because, as we've seen, they can diversify their personal securities portfolios much more cheaply.

Hubris

In the mid-1980s, economist Richard Roll posed what he called the *hubris hypothesis* to explain, at least in part, why acquisition premiums are so large and yet acquisitions remain so common.[6]

As we've already pointed out, when a publicly traded firm is acquired by another firm, the purchase price almost always exceeds the target firm's market value. The average premium—the amount received by the target firm's shareholders in excess of the value of their stock—was between 30 and 45 percent during the 15-year period between 1989 and 2004. Why would anyone pay such a generous premium? After all, the targets market value prior to the acquisition bid was the market's best estimate of the target firm's future cash flows.

According to Roll, managers not only make mistaken valuations but often have unwarranted confidence both in their valuations and in their ability to create value. This attitude, says Roll, reflects **hubris**—a Greek term denoting excessive pride, overconfidence, or arrogance. Hubristic managers may overestimate their own abilities to implement potential synergies.

A final word: Although we're going to focus on synergy as a motivation for acquisitions, you shouldn't ignore the other two motivations—managerialism and managerial hubris—when you're evaluating M&As. When managerialism and hubris are kept in check, acquiring firms are more likely to realize synergies and positive performance benefits.

Synergy

When M&As are undertaken in pursuit of synergy, managers are guided by the belief that the value of two firms combined can be greater than the sum value of the two firms independently. This category includes all forms of M&As that are motivated by value creation. Synergy may derive from a number of sources, including reduced threats from suppliers, increased market power, potential cost savings, superior financial strength, economies of scope and scale, and the sharing and leveraging of capabilities.

Reducing Threats   As was noted in Chapter 7, sometimes a supplier cannot or will not make an investment that's specific to an exchange with one buyer. Why might this situation arise? Perhaps the investment would tie the company too closely to one buyer, expose it to too much risk, or overtax its financial means. In any case, the buyer may need to integrate vertically, backward into the supply chain.[7] The quickest way to do this is through an acquisition. Some of Cisco Systems acquisitions of Network Switch technology companies are examples of this type of backward integration.

Increasing Market Power and Access   If a company improves its competitive position by means of a merger or acquisition, it may be possible to derive potential market power from the deal. Firms have market power when they can influence prices, and price competition is reduced significantly when rivalry is reduced. In the banking industry, for example, some mergers—especially those involving two moderate-sized banks—seem to have been motivated by a desire to improve market power. Thus, when First Union purchased Wachovia, the combined company vaulted into the number-four slot among U.S. banks. When Daimler merged with Chrysler in an effort to exploit potential synergies, its share in

In 1992, PepsiCo purchased Carts of Colorado, a small manufacturer of mobile merchandising carts and kiosks. The carts and kiosks help businesses sell their products in hard-to-reach and temporary places. One of PepsiCo's first successful cart locations was in the Moscow subway system.

the global automotive market increased significantly. And the merger was designed to improve market access for both companies in geographic arenas where they were weak but their merger partner was strong. Another example of improved access is provided by PepsiCo. In 1992, for example, when PepsiCo still owned Pizza Hut, Taco Bell, and Kentucky Fried Chicken, it purchased Carts of Colorado (CC), a small food-cart (e.g., kiosk) manufacturer, for $7 million, seeing it as the ideal means of installing new restaurants quickly and cheaply. Not only did the purchase give PepsiCo access to new cart technology, but it also provided it with an inexpensive means for quickly establishing fast-food outlets in high-traffic locations. One of PepsiCo's first successful cart locations was in the Moscow metro system.

Realizing Cost Savings   Cost savings are the most common synergy and the easiest to estimate. Financial markets tend to understand and accept cost savings as a rationale and are more likely to reward savings-motivated M&As with higher stock prices than other forms of synergy. Revenue-enhancement opportunities, such as increasing total sales through cross-selling and enhanced distribution, also represent a significant upside in many M&As. It's more difficult, however, to calculate and implement revenue-enhancement synergies (sometimes called *soft synergies*) than cost-savings synergies.

conceptlink

We explain in Chapter 7 that a *revenue-enhancement synergy* exists when the whole—whether resulting from an **alliance** or some form of M&A—generates more revenue than the sum of its parts.

Increasing Financial Strength   Other synergies can be created by various forms of financial engineering. An acquisition, for instance, can lower the financing costs of the target firm when the two firms' respective credit ratings are markedly different and significant debt is involved. Such would be the case if a company with AAA-rated debt were to buy a B-rated company. Various tax benefits also provide unique financial synergies. If, for example, the target company has operating loss carry-forwards (i.e., financial losses that the IRS allows firms to apply to future years' earnings) that can't be fully utilized, the acquiring company can use them to reduce the tax bill of the combined firm.

Sharing and Leveraging Capabilities   Transferring best practices and core competencies can create value. This form of synergy is important in the resource-based view of competitive advantage. According to this view, one reason for acquiring another firm would be to absorb and assimilate the target's resource, knowledge, and capabilities—all of which, as we saw in Chapter 3, may be primary sources of competitive advantage. When firms combine resources and capabilities through M&As, they may be able to create a bundle of resources that is unavailable to competitors. If the combined resources and capabilities are complementary, the competitive advantage may be long term. If the combination is valuable and rare, the acquiring firm may be able to generate profits greater than the sum of the two firms' individual profits. Bear in mind, however, that transferring resources, knowledge, or capabilities can create long-term competitive advantage only if the cost of the acquisition doesn't exceed the cost to other firms of accumulating comparable resource stocks.

MERGERS, ACQUISITIONS, AND STRATEGY

Three points need to be kept in mind when considering acquisitions as a part of a corporate firm's strategy. First, as with other elements of strategy, managers need to be clear about the economic logic: How does the acquisition help the firm earn profits? Second, managers need to consider alternatives to the acquisition, such as developing the new business internally rather than buying it. Third, acquisitions are fraught with hazards that can end up ruining the projected returns, and managers need to know what these hazards are and how to navigate around them.

The Vehicle and Its Economic Logic

Acquisitions enable firms to enter new businesses quickly, reduce the time and risks entailed by the process of starting new businesses internally, and rapidly reach minimum efficient scale. Research shows, however, that M&As come with significant risks and uncertainties of their own. Although some acquisitions succeed, such as eBay's acquisition of PayPal, others fail to produce anticipated synergies, resulting in small losses, and some fail miserably, resulting in huge losses. eBay, for instance, was forced to sell Butterfields at a significant loss in terms of both dollars and managerial time and attention. In this chapter, we'll discuss some of the keys to making acquisitions serve as an effective vehicle for growth and, at the same time, avoiding common potential pitfalls.

What we said of alliances in Chapter 9 also holds true for mergers and acquisitions: They are not strategies in and of themselves; rather, as we're reminded in Exhibit 10.2, which reprises the five-element model of strategy, alliances simply constitute one *vehicle* for realizing a strategy—that is, for entering or exiting a business. However, acquisitions have significant implications for other elements of strategy. Acquisitions take firms into new are-

Exhibit 10.2 The Place of Acquisitions in the Five Elements Model

Source: Adapted from Hambrick and Fredrickson, "Are You Sure You Have a Strategy?" Academy of Management Executive 15:4 (2001), 48–59.

M&A and the Strategy Diamond. While mergers and acquisitions are explicitly vehicles of strategy, they have major implications for arenas, staging, and economic logic as well.

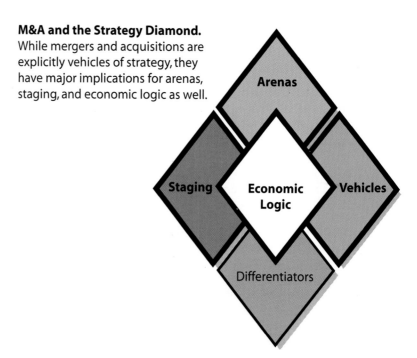

nas. Acquisitions that result in diversification are used in the staging of corporate strategies. And finally, acquisitions have implications for the financial success of strategies—for the realization of the anticipated economic logic of the strategy.

Perhaps because they enable companies to accelerate their strategies, acquisitions are quite popular. The number of acquisitions over the past few decades suggests that they constitute a fundamental element of many firms' strategies. Research suggests that firms average about one acquisition per year, but of course, there's tremendous variance in firms' propensity for using acquisitions as a growth vehicle.[8] Not surprisingly, the financial success of any given acquisition depends on a number of factors and has a significant effect on the overall economic logic of a firm's strategy. As you can see in Exhibit 10.3, which summarizes acquisition activity involving U.S. firms between 1995 and 2004, the value of acquisitions involving U.S. firms demonstrates that acquisitions represent a major economic activity. As you can also see, acquisition activity peaked near the turn of the century. That wave coincided with the tremendous bull market when firms used their inflated stock prices as currency to purchase other firms.

Despite—and because of—their economic consequences, M&As get a lot of bad press and do come in for criticism from scholars and consultants as well. We can attribute this criticism—at least in part—to the high visibility of many spectacular acquisition mistakes. Notable acquisition "mistakes" include AT&T's acquisition of NCR, Quaker's acquisition of Snapple, and AOL's acquisition of Time Warner. As is the case of so many acquisitions, the managers who made these deals seemed to be unable to make them work.

Quaker, for instance, purchased Snapple thinking that it could create profitable synergies between Snapple and its own Gatorade.[9] Apparently, however, Quaker failed to do its preacquisition homework, particularly when it came to the differences in the distribution networks of the two products. There were troublesome delays in implementing key aspects of the acquisition, and Snapple's market position in relation to newer brands was seriously eroded. The pressure from analysts and shareholders grew so intense that just two years after acquiring Snapple, Quaker pulled the plug on the acquisition and sold it for $300 million—a hefty $1.5 billion less than it paid for it. After just three years of repositioning Snapple, the new owner, Triarc, sold the brand for $1.45 billion to Cadbury Schweppes PLC, where it's now successfully positioned in a portfolio of brands run by a company with the capabilities necessary to build the Snapple brand. Snapple's financial-market roller-coaster ride, which is illustrated in Exhibit 10.4, provides a good lesson in the combination of risks and opportunities that often accompany acquisitions as a strategy vehicle.

From what we've seen so far, it's clear that **divestiture**—the selling off of a business and the flip side of acquisition—is also a key strategic vehicle. eBay, AT&T, and Quaker all

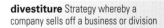
divestiture Strategy whereby a company sells off a business or division

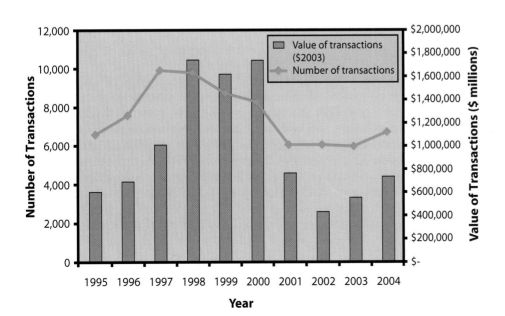

Exhibit 10.3 U.S. Acquisition Activity, 1995–2004

Source: Data compiled from SDC Platinum, a product of Thompson Financial.

Exhibit 10.4   Ups and Downs at Snapple

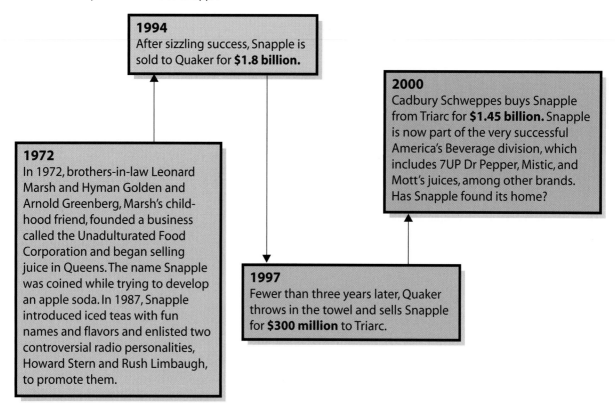

1994
After sizzling success, Snapple is sold to Quaker for **$1.8 billion.**

2000
Cadbury Schweppes buys Snapple from Triarc for **$1.45 billion.** Snapple is now part of the very successful America's Beverage division, which includes 7UP Dr Pepper, Mistic, and Mott's juices, among other brands. Has Snapple found its home?

1972
In 1972, brothers-in-law Leonard Marsh and Hyman Golden and Arnold Greenberg, Marsh's childhood friend, founded a business called the Unadulterated Food Corporation and began selling juice in Queens. The name Snapple was coined while trying to develop an apple soda. In 1987, Snapple introduced iced teas with fun names and flavors and enlisted two controversial radio personalities, Howard Stern and Rush Limbaugh, to promote them.

1997
Fewer than three years later, Quaker throws in the towel and sells Snapple for **$300 million** to Triarc.

exited businesses by selling business units to competitors. In this chapter, we focus primarily on acquisitions as vehicles for entering or expanding businesses, but remember that closely related types of transactions enable firms to exit businesses as well.

When deciding to enter a new business, companies have alternative vehicles from which to choose, including *internal development*, *alliances*, and *acquisition*. We reviewed the motivations behind alliances in Chapter 8. Here, we'll explain why the tradeoffs between internal development and acquisition—make or buy decisions—are important considerations when deciding whether to enter a new business through acquisition.

Benefits of Acquisition over Internal Development

One of the primary advantages of acquisition over internal development is *speed*. Although an acquisition quickly establishes a foothold in a new business, internal development can take years. A corollary benefit is critical mass. An acquisition ensures that a firm enters a new business with sufficient size and viable competitive strength. The acquiring firm, for example, can be assured of entering at minimum efficient scale for cost purposes. As another advantage, acquisitions provide access to complementary assets and resources. In developing a new business, a firm invests its existing stock of resources and capabilities, and although it may develop new resources and capabilities in the process, there's always the chance that it may simply expend existing resources. With an acquisition, new resources and capabilities can be integrated with those of the buyer, who may actually improve its competitive position in other businesses as well. Finally, entry by acquisition may foster a less competitive environment. By acquiring an existing firm in a new business, the buyer eliminates a competitor that would otherwise remain in the market.

Drawbacks of Acquisition over Internal Development

Conversely, firms may find it preferable for several reasons to enter new businesses by means of internal development. First, acquisitions are often more expensive than internal development. Buyers often pay steep premiums for existing companies. In many cases, these premiums outweigh any potential benefits of the acquisition, and in some cases, they make it economically more viable either to enter through internal development or to avoid entry altogether. In short, firms must often decide against entering new businesses because they aren't likely to generate sufficient return on capital to justify the premium cost. In addition, the acquiring firm will often inherit several unnecessary adjunct businesses. As an acquirer, you must either be willing to run these unwanted businesses or go through the administrative hassle of spinning them off.

Second, although acquisitions represent a major one-time commitment of resources, internal development entails incremental investment over time. The internal-development process, therefore, allows for many points at which the project can be assessed and reevaluated before further investment is made. If, for example, economic circumstances change, a firm can pull the plug. Acquisitions, on the other hand, are typically all-or-nothing propositions.

Finally, organizational conflict may emerge as a potential problem; the eruption of *cultural clashes* can impede the integration of two firms. The process of integration requires significant effort, and firms may encounter setbacks or even failure. Because integration is such a major factor in making M&As work, we'll discuss it in greater detail later in the chapter.

As you can see, many potential roadblocks can make it difficult for firms to realize economic gains from acquisitions. Taken together, the greater the cost in capital and time, the more synergies managers will have to squeeze out of the deal.

TYPES OF MERGERS AND ACQUISITIONS

There are many types of M&As, and each has a particular purpose—a specific rationale for creating synergies. In this section, we'll survey the different forms of M&As and link the economic logic of each form to firm strategy.[10] Because the logic behind each form varies, so, too, do the criteria for their success.

Types of Acquisitions

Acquisitions can figure into most aspects of business strategy, but they're generally regarded as a means of managing competitive pressures, uncertainty, or both. Thus, business-strategy acquisitions, like business-strategy alliances, tend to be fundamentally related to the firm's core business through *vertical, horizontal,* or *complementary relationships.*

A vertical acquisition has three purposes:

- To secure a reliable supply
- To leverage the resources and capabilities of upstream activities in order to create more value for the end customer
- To reduce total production costs across the value chain

Coca-Cola and Pepsi each have engaged in several vertical acquisitions over the years as they have purchased independent bottling operations. These acquisitions are downstream vertical acquisitions—they buy some of their customers. Recall from the opening vignette in Chapter 4 that Coke and Pepsi sell most of their core product (concentrate) to bottlers who then mix the concentrate with other ingredients, bottle the product, and distribute it to retail outlets. Coke and Pepsi were able to reduce some threats that were beginning to emerge from large bottlers, as well as infuse more efficiency into these downstream activities, by consolidating bottling operations into more efficient regional operations.

conceptlink

"Downstream" acquisitions are a response to **buyer power**, which we define in Chapter 4 as the degree buyers in an industry can dictate favorable terms to supplier firms. The converse, of course, is **supplier power**, and in Chapter 4, we characterize both forms of power as implicit threats. In Chapter 9, we characterize such **vertical-integration** strategies as **alliances** in terms of a firm's **value-chain** activities.

Best Buy's 2002 acquisition of the Geek Squad, a Twin Cities computer-support service, was a product-market extension.

In contrast, horizontal acquisitions help fill out the company's product offerings. The Cadbury Schweppes purchase of Snapple was a horizontal acquisition that helped fill out the buyer's beverage portfolio, particularly in the growing juice and tea segment.

A complementary acquisition involves a complementary business—one that increases the sale of another product. Best Buy's recent acquisition of the Geek Squad, a computer-support service, is a complementary acquisition: When computer-service capability is bundled with retail computer sales, each business potentially increases sales of the other's product.

A More Complex Classification   Because this simple breakdown of acquisitions into vertical, horizontal, and complementary relationships is a little oversimplified, let's take a look at the typology proposed by Harvard professor Joseph Bower, illustrated in Exhibit 10.5, which will give us a better understanding of the strategic logic behind more complex forms of acquisition.[11] Though developed through a study of extremely large acquisitions (over $500 million), this schema provides a useful way of thinking generally about M&As.

Product and Market Extension   In a *product-extension acquisition*, the acquiring company expands its product line by purchasing another company. Basically, the buyer has decided that it can reap higher rewards by buying a company with an existing product than by developing a competitive product internally. In a *market-extension acquisition*, one company buys another that offers essentially the same products as the buyer but that has a platform in a geographic market in which the buyer has no presence.

The journey of Snapple that we described earlier in this chapter is an interesting example of two different companies using the same acquired firm for the purpose of product extension. Conceivably, Quaker Oats could have developed its own line of fruit juices, lemonades, and teas. At the time, however, Quaker management believed that an internally developed line would lag too far behind those of incumbent firms in the market segment. Likewise, Cadbury Schweppes certainly has the capability to develop new drinks internally but has chosen to cultivate expertise in extending product offerings through the acquisition of established brands.

geographic roll-up Strategy whereby a firm acquires many other firms in the same industry segment but in different geographic arenas in an attempt to create significant scale and scope advantages

Geographic Roll-Ups   A **geographic roll-up** occurs when a firm acquires firms that are in the same *industry* segment but in many different *geographic* arenas. It's not the same strategy as market extension. With a roll-up, the acquiring company is trying to change the

Exhibit 10.5 Bower's Classification of Acquisitions

	Product/Market Extension	Geographic Roll-up M&A	Overcapacity M&A	Industry Convergence	M&A as R&D
Example	Pepsi's acquisition of Gatorade	Service Corporation International's more than 100 acquisitions of funeral homes	DaimlerChrysler merger	AOL's acquisition of TimeWarner	Intel's dozens of acquisitions of small high-tech companies
Objectives	Synergy of similar but expanded product lines or geographic markets	Efficiency of larger operations (e.g., economies of scale, superior management)	Eliminating capacity, gaining market share, and increasing efficiency	Anticipation of new industry emerging; culling resources from firms in multiple industries whose boundaries are eroding	Short cut innovation by buying it from small companies
Percent of All M&A Deals	36%	9%	37%	4%	1%

Source: J. L. Bower, "Not All M&As Are Alike—and That Matters," Harvard Business Review 79:3 (2001), 92–101.

nature of industry competition in a fundamental way; it seeks to become a large regional, national, or international player in what's probably been a fragmented industry. The purpose of a roll-up is achieving economies of scale and scope. Prior to its merger with First Chicago, for example, Banc One had grown from a small regional bank in Ohio to a large national bank by buying smaller local and regional banks around the country. (The merged company is called Bank One.) In a roll-up, the acquiring company usually retains the resources and management of acquired companies but imposes its processes on them.

Entrepreneur Bradley Jacobs made a fortune deploying the roll-up strategy to build two extremely successful companies in two different industries. In the waste-management business, Jacobs used United Waste Systems as a roll-up company to buy small trash-hauling firms in a fragmented industry. He later sold the company to USA Waste Services (now Waste Management) and used the proceeds to launch another start-up—one that would use the same roll-up strategy to consolidate the equipment-rental industry. He launched United Rentals by purchasing six heavy-equipment leasing firms and then proceeded to buy equipment-rental companies all across the country. Through a series of more than 60 acquisitions in 7 years, it has become the largest equipment-rental company in the United States.

What's the rationale behind a roll-up strategy? Basically it's that a large regional or national player can achieve economies of scale that smaller local firms can't. Centralized management, for example, may improve overall operational effectiveness, and a national firm may have the resources to win customer accounts that smaller local firms don't have. United Rentals, for instance, may be able to win equipment-rental contracts with large customers who want a single national provider for all of their heavy-equipment needs.

M&As as R&D Some firms use acquisitions in lieu of or in addition to internal R&D. Usually, the acquiring firm buys another company in order to gain ownership of its technology. The strategy is common in industries in which technology advances rapidly and in which no single company can do all the innovating that it needs to continue competing effectively.

Exhibit 10.6 M&As as R&D

Source: Public records (10-K and annual reports).

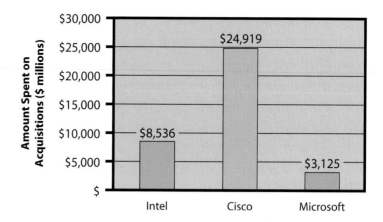

In the computer industry, this strategy has been used to good effect by such firms as Cisco, Microsoft, and Intel. Exhibit 10.6 indicates how important acquisitions are to these companies as R&D vehicles. First of all, bear in mind that the average U.S. company engages in approximately one acquisition per year. In the 5-year period between 1999 and 2003, each of these three companies averaged more than 10 acquisitions per year. All three, of course, allocate money for internal R&D, but each also spends considerable sums to acquire new technologies by buying startups that have made promising innovations. The strategy, of course, represents a tradeoff.

To get a better idea of what this tradeoff entails, consider the acquisition expenses of Intel and AMD. Both firms devote significant capital to traditional internal R&D projects. However, Intel made dozens of acquisitions during the past several years, whereas AMD has made only three. This suggests that these two firms in the same industry have very different approaches to R&D. Intel apparently uses acquisitions as an opportunity to acquire potential future innovations from small startup companies with promising technologies.

Overcapacity M&As   The purpose of an *overcapacity acquisition* is to reduce the number of competitors in a mature industry in which capacity exceeds decreasing demand. In essence, parties to an overcapacity acquisition are trying to consolidate the industry. Such is the case, for instance, when two companies in the same industry merge (or one acquires another) in order to rationalize the industry and reduce overcapacity. Overcapacity mergers are often explained as attempts to create economies of scale, but in many cases both companies are already large enough to be operating at a minimum efficient scale. Improved efficiencies come from reducing redundant operations and trimming the size of combined units. This was the rationale behind Daimler's merger with Chrysler (which, as we've seen, now looks more like an acquisition). The banking industry, in which firms are jockeying for market position and trying to create greater economies of scale, has experienced extensive overcapacity-M&A volume in the past decade.

Industry Convergence M&As   When two industries start to overlap and become highly complementary, they begin to *converge*. When this happens, we see an increase in the level of M&As involving firms in the converging industries. In the media and entertainment industries, for example, Time Inc. had an extensive print-media business and some cable operations (as well as HBO). Warner Brothers Inc. had a bigger presence in cable operations and a huge library of movies. In 1990, the two companies combined through Time's acquisition of Warner to form Time Warner (which acquired Turner Broadcasting in 1996 and which was later acquired by AOL in 2001) in order to consolidate media content and distribution. In response to the AOL–Time Warner combination, Viacom, whose core business was cable-TV production and distribution, bought Paramount, a movie and TV producer (1993); Blockbuster, a chain of video outlets (1994); and the TV network CBS (2000). In 1996, Disney, already a media conglomerate, bought ABC, including cable broadcaster ESPN (1996). The entertainment-industry's landscape continues to shift as firms try to find the right mix of businesses to compete effectively in converging industries.

The logic behind M&As in converging industries holds that such calculated investments will put firms in a better competitive position if and when industry boundaries erode. One can also view acquisitions in this environment as attempts by companies to acquire resources that, although less valuable in the present competitive environment, will be critical in projected new industry contexts.

Investor/Holding Company M&As   Although we won't discuss this category in much detail, Bower points out that it represents a significant portion of total acquisition activity. In investor/holding company transactions, independent investors or holding companies purchase existing firms. Such might be the case when an investment fund engages in a leveraged buyout of a company. Rather than merge the purchased company with other firms in its portfolio, the buyer tries to bring some management, operating, and financial discipline to the company, intending to sell it later at a profit. In other cases, investors (such as Warren Buffett's Berkshire Hathaway) purchase companies for long-term ownership and management.

International Acquisitions   Bower's classification doesn't provide a specific category for international M&As. However, the issues confronting firms during international acquisitions are significant and you may need to examine the issues of differing cultures, laws, and competitors very closely before executing an international acquisition. An international acquisition can be of any of the types reviewed (e.g., R&D, product/market extension, rollup, convergence, overcapacity, holding company). Our analysis of data compiled by Thompson Financial Services reveals that since 1990, cross-border M&As have accounted for 20 percent of all M&A activity. Obviously, the use of acquisitions as a strategy vehicle by any firm wanting to enter a new international arena should flow from its business- and corporate-strategy objectives, but firms must be aware that the international context introduces significant complexity into M&A transactions.

PRICING AND PREMIUMS

In this section, we'll review some of the basic M&A issues relating to their potential success. These issues include pricing, premiums, and establishing a walk-away price.

Pricing

There's no single correct price for an acquisition or merger. Why? Simply because the value of a target depends on how well it fits with the acquiring company. Price will ultimately depend on a number of more specific factors, including the target's intrinsic value, its current market value, and the value to be gained from any potential synergies between the target and buyer. Estimates of intrinsic value and the value of potential synergies are determined by managers of the acquiring firm, investment bankers, and outside analysts.

Intrinsic and Market Value   **Intrinsic value** is the present value of a company's future cash flows from existing assets and businesses. As the term suggests, **market value** is the current market capitalization of a firm, which is typically calculated by multiplying the number of shares outstanding by their market price. It can be higher or lower than a company's intrinsic value, with the difference reflecting a number of factors. Markets make important adjustments in the valuation of a firm, evaluating future growth opportunities that will result in products and generate additional cash flows, assessing discounts for bad management or excessive diversification, or awarding premiums to firms that are likely become the targets of bidding wars.

intrinsic value Present value of a company's future cash flows from existing assets and businesses

market value Current market capitalization of a firm

purchase price Final price actually paid to the target firm's shareholders of an acquired company

synergy value Difference between the combined values of the target and the acquiring firm after the transaction and the sum of the values of the two firms taken independently

conceptlink

In discussing criteria for successful **alliances**—*partnerships* of two or more firms—in Chapter 9, we note that the question of *strategic fit* is twofold: "Are the partners' objectives compatible? For how long?"

acquisition premium Difference between current market value of a target firm and purchase price paid to induce its shareholders to turn its control over to new owners

The **purchase price** is the value actually paid to the target firm's shareholders. Like market price, it may be either higher or lower than intrinsic value, but it's almost always greater than current market value. The only exception to this rule involves target firms that are in dire financial condition.

Synergy Value   The **synergy value** of an acquisition is the difference between the combined values of the target and the acquiring firm after the transaction and the sum of the values of the two firms taken independently. Interestingly, synergy value can be computed both on an intrinsic basis and on a market basis. *Intrinsic synergy value* is the sum of cost savings, revenue enhancements, financial-engineering activities, and tax benefits generated by the transaction. It may take several years to realize these values. *Market-based synergy* value is the financial market's expectation of management's ability to extract intrinsic value.

Because synergy value is a function of the *strategic fit* of the acquiring and the target firms, each bidding firm may value the target differently. In addition, the market may react differently in evaluating different bidding firms. When, for instance, Vodafone and Bell Atlantic both made bids for AirTouch, Bell Atlantic's stock price dropped while Vodafone's price went up—even though Vodafone entered the bidding with a higher offer. Why? The market believed that Vodafone and AirTouch could achieve greater synergies than Bell Atlantic and AirTouch.

Premiums

The difference between current market value and the purchase price is called the **acquisition premium**. It's what induces shareholders of the target to turn control of the firm over to new owners. Analysis of the transactions tracked by Thompson Financial Services suggests that in the United States average acquisition premiums have ranged between 30 and 45 percent during each of the past 15 years. Paying premiums for acquisitions, however, presents a basic problem for managers of would-be buyers. When the managers of an acquiring firm agree to pay a premium for a target firm, they must expect that they will be able to generate better returns by combining the firms than the firms would achieve independently. Where is this increase in return supposed to come from? Apparently from the synergies achieved by the combined firms.

The Synergy Trap   In a study of acquisition premiums, Mark Sirower of the Boston Consulting Group (BCG) explained what he called the "synergy trap."[12] He argued that premiums present two problems for managers:

- Premiums increase the level of returns that must be extracted from the combined businesses.
- Because of the time value of money, delays in implementing and extracting synergies increase the ante on required performance improvements. In other words, the longer it takes to implement performance improvements, the lower the likelihood that the acquisition will be successful.

Not surprisingly, paying too much for an acquisition can not only jeopardize the success of an acquisition, but it can also cause irreparable damage to the acquiring firm. Regularly in his letters to shareholders, Warren Buffett has reminded shareholders of Hathaway that paying too much for a company can lead to disastrous effects. The box entitled "How Would *You* Do That? 10.1" goes into more depth on the issue of premiums and their effects on acquisition success.

Reaching a Walk-Away Price   Given what you now know about the synergy trap (and perhaps about Warren Buffett's shrewdness as a strategic investor), it shouldn't surprise you to learn that in 2000, when Coke CEO Douglas Daft tried to buy Quaker Oats in order to add Gatorade to the company's product line, board member Buffett opposed the idea. Buffett argued that the bidding by Coke and Pepsi had driven the premium too high and Coke should walk away from the negotiations. (The board rejected Daft's plan.) Similarly, in 2004, cable operator Comcast made a tender offer for Disney of 0.78 share of

The Impact of Premiums on Required Synergies

How would you translate the premium paid in an acquisition into actionable division budgets for the coming year? Every time an acquisition is completed, it affects how division managers operate. Indeed, it often affects the targets that the CEO imposes upon them in terms of revenue targets and expense containment. To illustrate how this happens, let's go back to eBay's acquisition of PayPal. The opening vignette noted that eBay paid a premium of $250 million (a 20-percent premium over PayPal's market value prior to the acquisition).

Sirower's "synergy trap" is a useful managerial tool here. Let's start with our objective: We need to know the synergy required to make the deal a success. Let's call this SR for short. The SR to justify a premium paid can be calculated with various degrees of sophistication, including the use of discounted uneven cash flows and probability statistics. But that level of sophistication isn't necessary to get in the ballpark. We have simplified the various formulas and created a simple table of factors that will help you understand the concept. The three factors that you'll need to know are (1) the premium expected to be paid, (2) the number of years before you expect synergies to be implemented, and (3) the cost of capital of the firm.

Exhibit 10.7 provides a table of factors that can be used to determine the annual synergies required to make the acquisition a success.

Exhibit 10.7 Synergy Required to Justify $10-Million Premium

Years Until Synergies Are Implemented	Cost of Capital		
	10%	15%	20%
0	0.100	0.150	0.200
1	0.110	0.173	0.240
2	0.121	0.198	0.288
3	0.133	0.228	0.346
4	0.146	0.262	0.415
5	0.161	0.302	0.498

Locate the intersection of the years assumed to make the synergies materialize and the cost of capital. Then multiply that factor by the premium paid to determine just how much synergy must be generated through the combination of annual cost savings and new revenue improvements. If we assume that synergies will materialize immediately after the acquisition, then the amount of synergy that must be achieved is determined by simply multiplying the cost of capital by the premium. However, as you can see, as the years increase before synergies are implemented, or as the cost of capital increases, the amount of synergy that must be generated increases very quickly (the amount of synergy required is reflected in the yellow area of the exhibit).

In the case of eBay's acquisition of PayPal, the premium was approximately $250,000,000. So if the company thought that it would take two years to implement the synergies and it knew that their cost of capital was 15 percent, then the operational synergies required could be estimated by multiplying the premium by the factor as follows: $250,000,000 × 0.198 = $49,500,000. What does this number represent? It is the amount of additional net income that is needed from the acquisition of PayPal over and above the existing net income of both companies combined. So in addition to the net income for both companies that existed prior to the merger, eBay would have to find almost an additional $50 million in synergies just to pay for the premium.

In 1982, CEO Warren Buffett reminded Berkshire Hathaway shareholders that "the market, like the Lord, helps those who help themselves. But, unlike the Lord, the market does not forgive those who know not what they do. . . . [A] too-high purchase price for the stock of an excellent company can undo the effects of a subsequent decade of favorable business development."

Comcast Class A stock for each Disney share. It was forced to withdraw the offer, however, because the value of its stock subsequently dropped too far: There came a point at which Comcast would have to pay out too many shares to reach the offered value. In effect, that point was Comcast's "walk-away price."

Escalation of Commitment and the Winner's Curse   Establishing a walk-away price is relatively easy; sticking to it is not. One reason for this is that executives escalate the commitment to their initiative as they proceed through a transaction. This—coupled with excessive fear of failure—means that bidders are sometimes seduced into making questionable decisions. Bidders who allow their prices to get carried away (or allow themselves to get carried away with their bidding) often suffer from the so-called **winner's curse**. Although the bidders win the "prize," they're saddled with the consequences of having paid too much.

winner's curse Situation in which a winning M&A bidder must live with the consequences of paying too much for the target

THE ACQUISITION PROCESS

So far we've focused mostly on the technical side of M&As: what they are and how they're used as strategy vehicles, along with the roles of pricing and premiums. The success of M&As as a strategy vehicle, however, depends on much more than the choice of a good target and paying the right price. The process by which M&As are completed and targeted firms are integrated into acquiring firms can have a significant bearing on success or failure. Indeed, some experts say that it's the single largest factor.[13]

Stages of the Acquisition Process

Exhibit 10.8 presents a model that proposes four major stages in an acquisition: *idea generation*, *justification* (including due diligence and negotiation), *integration*, and *result*. Problems at any stage can sow the seeds of failure.[14] This model identifies two types of problems: *decision-making problems* and *implementation* or *integration problems*. Whereas integration problems occur during the integration stage, decision-making problems can arise during the idea-generation, justification, and integration stages.

Idea   The *idea* is the impetus for the acquisition. Some firms have well-articulated strategies that state the conditions under which acquisitions will be the vehicle of choice for

A Process Perspective

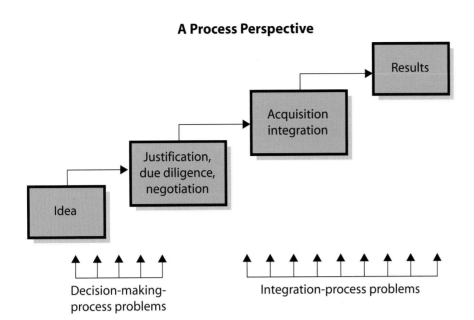

Decision-making-
process problems

Integration-process problems

Exhibit 10.8 Acquisition
Process Stages

*Source: Adapted from P. C.
Haspeslagh and D. B. Jemison,
Managing Acquisitions: Creating
Value Through Corporate Renewal
(New York: Free Press, 1991), 42.*

implementing strategic plans. Recall, for instance, the case of United Rentals' roll-up strategy: Acquisitions were a key vehicle in the firm's strategy. Conversely, Quaker Oats' purchase of Snapple was an opportunistic (and ill-considered) move. Whereas some firms have well-defined strategies, others don't. Such firms may be more opportunistic in the use of acquisitions. They may make a deal primarily because it looks like a good opportunity at the time, not because acquisition is an integral part of well-developed strategies. Most firms probably fall somewhere between these two poles.[15]

Justification, Due Diligence, and Negotiation The major analytical stage of an acquisition includes the processes that a firm goes through to develop the internal and external logic for the acquisition. Researchers Philippe Haspeslagh and David Jemison contend that several critical decisions must be made at this stage: strategic assessment, developing a widely shared view, a degree of specificity, organizational conditions, implementation timing, and a walk-away price.

- *Strategic assessment* is the process of determining how an acquisition will contribute to overall strategy and competitive position. It should do more than analyze the target: It should address the issue of how the acquisition will affect the acquiring firm's pursuit of its core objectives. Managers should also make sure that their assessment isn't too static: It should consider the firm's future needs as its industry evolves.

- Because many people will be involved in implementing an acquisition and integrating the target firm into the parent, it's important that the purpose and strategic logic of the acquisition be widely understood by members of the organization. The following is a list of questions that managers should ask at this stage of an acquisition:[16]

  1. What is the strategic logic behind this acquisition? Does it correspond with the firm's strategy? Why this company?
  2. Is the target industry attractive? What are the key segments? What is the prognosis about industry evolution?
  3. If this is an international acquisition, what are the key differences between this country and our experience? Do these differences have performance implications?
  4. Does an analysis of the target company (products and services, market position, customers, suppliers, distribution channels, costs, etc.) suggest that it is healthy and viable in the long term?
  5. How well does this company fit with ours? What are the expected benefits, and what might impinge on the realization of those benefits?
  6. What integration approach will be necessary (e.g., absorption, preservation, symbiosis, holding company)? Who will lead this process? How will we be organized?

conceptlink

Recall our discussion of *scenario planning* in Chapter 4, where we emphasize the need of managers to develop not only a broad picture of plausible outcomes as an industry evolves, but a coherent picture of specific trends and uncertainties.

7. Have alternative *scenarios* been considered? What is the outcome given reasonable optimistic, baseline, and pessimistic assumptions?

8. Is the valuation reasonable? What do alternative valuation methods conclude (accounting based, market based, NPV, option)?

■ Managers should be as specific as possible in identifying the possible benefits and problems of an acquisition throughout the organization. This step is important for two reasons:

1. If operational managers aren't aware of the potential sources of synergies identified by upper management and the acquisition team, they'll have a hard time determining what's expected of them. Moreover, if they understand that synergies are needed but have little idea about how to gain them, the task is just as daunting. Let's go back to Quaker Oats' purchase of Snapple. Perhaps some acquisition managers understood Snapple's operations but no one seemed to understand fully the differences between the two industries' distribution systems. Operating-level managers were thus left to discover and deal with them through trial and error. A good deal of time and effort was wasted in trying to implement the acquisition in ways that simply didn't jibe with Quaker Oats' business model.

2. Although identifying possible problems is also important, some acquisition teams tend to understate them, usually because they're afraid of causing key decision makers to shy away from the deal.[17] All in all, it's much better for all parties to know what the potential roadblocks are; they can be dealt with more effectively if the acquisition team provides some suggested solutions.

Understand the Conditions Required for Creating Synergies   Managers must understand the organizational factors on which key synergies hinge and the organizational conditions necessary to implement desired synergies. Synergies in a cross-border acquisition, for example, may depend on the transfer of a functional skill from one company to another. If so, executives at the acquiring firm must identify the managers and key employees who are critical to the transfer. Even when the numbers look good, more and more firms are scuttling acquisitions because of a lack of organizational fit—which can undermine possible synergies. Screening criteria and means of achieving these criteria that are utilized by Cisco Systems, one of the most successful high-technology acquirers, are summarized in Exhibit 10.9. Cisco regularly uses acquisitions to supplement internal R&D. However, Cisco discovered that the ability to realize synergies was to manage the entire process actively, from screening possible acquisitions to diligently managing the integration process.

Exhibit 10.9 Organizational-Fit Acquisition Screening by Cisco Systems

Screening Criteria	Means of Achieving Criteria
Offer both short- and long-term win-wins for Cisco and acquired company	• Have complementary technology that fills a need in Cisco's core product space • Have a technology that can be delivered through Cisco's existing distribution channels • Have a technology and products that can be supported by Cisco's support organization • Is able to leverage Cisco's existing infrastructure and resource base to increase its overall value
Share a common vision and chemistry with Cisco	• Have a similar understanding and vision of the market • Have a similar culture • Have a similar risk-taking style
Be located (preferably) in Silicon Valley or near one of Cisco's remote sites	• Have a company headquarters and most manufacturing facilities close to one of Cisco's main sites

Control the Timing of Implementation and Integration Timing is critical in most acquisitions. It's important because of the time value of money. In addition, stock markets can be volatile, which is important when a firm is paying for an acquisition with its own stock. Moreover, timing is critical because acquisitions cause major disruptions in both the target and acquiring firms. Many organizational problems arise from disruption in the lives of affected employees who may be impacted by the acquisition; such problems can be lessened if implementation and integration are achieved quickly.

Establish a Walk-Away Price Finally, managers should settle on the maximum price that they're willing to pay for the target firm. As we've already seen, it's wise to set a walk-away price early in the process, before rival bidders get caught up in *escalation of commitment* and overestimate the value that they believe will be derived from the acquisition. Potential synergies are often uncertain and ambiguous, and they'll vary from one prospective buyer to the next. Problems arise when managers mistake a rival's higher bid as a signal that they've overlooked some attractive feature of the deal; in responding with a more competitive offer, they're often overpaying.

In Chapter 2, we characterize **escalation of commitment**—the willingness to commit further resources to a failing course of action—as the product of an "illusion" and, as such, a threat to rational strategic decision making.

Integration Many acquisitions fail during the integration stage. The best means of integrating an acquisition varies from case to case, and failure to identify it can cancel any potential synergies that may have been derived from the deal. Determining the best process for implementing and integrating an acquisition means understanding potential interactions between the target and the acquiring firm. Because this stage is so important, we'll devote the next section to presenting a model for dealing with integration problems.

INTEGRATING AND IMPLEMENTING AN ACQUISITION

In this section, we'll see how the potentially conflicting needs of *strategic interdependence* and *organizational autonomy* can affect optimal organizational structure following a merger or acquisition.

Strategic Interdependence

Let's go back to one of the basic principles laid down in this chapter: The primary purpose of M&As is to create synergies—value that can be created by combining two firms that isn't available to them as stand-alone firms. To what extent should the target firm and acquiring firm remain strategically interdependent? It depends on the types of resource sharing and skill transfers anticipated by the two firms. When the logic of the acquisition requires that they share tangible and intangible resources, the success of the deal usually requires a relatively high level of interdependence. Likewise, when the logic of the deal calls for transferring people with different functional skills in order to share knowledge, it entails more interdependence between the two organizational units than if it called simply for a transfer of general management skills. However, when the resources being transferred are primarily financial (say, borrowing power or excess cash), very little interdependence is required.

Need for Autonomy

The value of some acquisitions lies largely in the retention of key people and transfers of capabilities. Key people, however, often leave once their firm has been acquired—especially when the acquisition disrupts their operating procedures and their autonomy in conducting them. Just how much autonomy should be granted an acquired firm? There's no single answer, of course, but the following is good rule of thumb: The amount of autonomy depends on whether it is necessary to create value. Granted, even this response is a little too simple. Perhaps, for example, autonomy is necessary only in certain facets of the acquired firm's operations, whereas others can be easily assimilated.

In 1988, when Nestlé set out to purchase British candy maker Rowntree York (makers of such candies as Kit Kat and Rolo) in order to extend its reach in chocolates and confectionary markets, it found that it could not, in accord with its usual policy, fully integrate its latest acquisition. Rather, to get the deal approved by Rowntree, Nestlé had to allow Rowntree executives to remain in the U.K. and run the strategic office in charge of all confectionary businesses. Similarly, when Dean Foods purchased soy-foods producer White Wave (the subject of our opening vignette in Chapter 9), it depended so heavily on the leadership and reputation of White Wave CEO Steve Demos that it set up White Wave as a separate subsidiary and retained Demos on a 10-year contract.

Types of Integration

Using the two factors of interdependence and autonomy, we can divide M&A transactions into four basic types, which are identified in Exhibit 10.10 as *absorption*, *preservation*, *holding*, and *symbiosis*.

Absorption   When the logic underlying the acquisition requires extensive interdependence and little autonomy, the integration can take the form of *absorption*—complete consolidation of the target firm with the acquiring company. Naturally, the larger the target firm, the longer it will take to fully absorb it, and sometimes certain facets of the consolidation take longer than others. When, for instance, Franklin Quest, a workload-management and workload-consulting firm, purchased the Covey Leadership Center, a leadership-development specialist, to form Franklin Covey in 1997, the strategy called for absorption. Franklin managers, however, were surprised at how long it took to consolidate some aspects of the merged companies, including information systems and company culture. Other examples include eBay's acquisition of PayPal, Cadbury Schweppes' acquisition of Snapple, and Pepsi's acquisition of South Beach, a maker of exotic teas and juices.

Preservation   When there's a high need for autonomy and a low need for interdependence, a strategy of *preservation*—the transfer of financial and general management expertise only—may be advisable. Haspeslagh and Jemison argue that preservation creates value through nurturing and learning. Learning, for example, may take place when a company makes an initial acquisition designed to be a platform for later growth through additional acquisitions. In this case, the acquiring company may make very few changes in the target and simply strive to learn the business before initiating further moves. Some of Wal-Mart's early international acquisitions followed the preservation model as the U.S. retailer gleaned knowledge about local markets before shifting to the absorption model. The acquisition of White Wave by Dean Foods took a similar approach.

Holding   This type of acquisition, which calls for low degrees of both autonomy and interdependence, is relatively rare. Holding companies that own businesses in the same industry fit this profile. For most of its history, for instance, Bank One grew by buying local

Exhibit 10.10 Types of Acquisition Integration

Source: Adapted from P. C. Haspeslagh and D. B. Jemison, Managing Acquisitions: Creating Value Through Corporate Renewal (New York: Free Press, 1991), 145.

	Need for Strategic Interdependence	
	Low	**High**
High	Preservation	Symbiosis
Low	Holding	Absorption

Need for Organizational Autonomy

banks in new geographic areas. Little autonomy was granted because Bank One would implement its own set of financial and operational controls and enforce strict oversight and monitoring. At the same time, little interdependence was forced because acquired banks had relatively little need to interact with one another.

Symbiosis Symbiosis—which calls for both high levels of autonomy and interdependence—is probably the most difficult to implement. Autonomy is needed to preserve the capabilities possessed by the target firm. Because Cisco Systems, for example, generally targets firms that are developing new technologies, it often finds it necessary to grant extreme levels of autonomy or risk losing key employees. Indeed, key employees are such a key factor in the value of acquired firms that Cisco spends an average of $1 million per acquired employee. At the same time, of course, if Cisco couldn't develop interdependence between itself and an acquired company, the anticipated synergies wouldn't materialize. Consequently, Cisco has achieved some level of expertise at finding quick ways to integrate the existing products of target firms into its own product line while allowing target firms the necessary autonomy to exercise their creativity.

The Implementation Process

No matter what approach managers take, integrating an acquisition is a difficult process and not a one-time event. We can, however, learn some lessons from so-called **serial acquirers**—companies that engage in frequent acquisitions—that will be useful in understanding how the process can be handled smoothly.

> **serial acquirer** Company that engages in frequent acquisitions

It's a Continual Process, Not an Event The best serial acquirers start the integration process during initial screening interviews and negotiations, well before closing the deal. During this process, called **due diligence**, executives and lower-level managers at both companies begin to plan for the postdeal structure of the combined firm. Although some pretransaction discussions can be awkward, they're essential in identifying both potential obstacles and additional opportunities. Once the deal is closed, specific decisions must be executed and prearranged organizational structures implemented. The lesson, in short, is that it's better to make tough decisions early rather than delaying them. Firms such as GE Capital and Cisco, which have successfully integrated many acquisitions (and some not so successfully), have found that initiating and pursuing a comprehensive integration and communications process is the lynchpin for success.

> **due diligence** Initial pre-closing screening, analysis, and negotiations for an acquisition

Integration Management Is a Full-Time Job Many firms make the mistake of assuming that people at all levels in both organizations will work together to make the acquisition as seamless as possible. Unfortunately, so many organizational issues are involved in integrating an acquired company that line managers often can't oversee operations *and* manage the integration process. Many successful acquirers, therefore, appoint an *integration manager*. Ideally, this person will be someone from the due-diligence team who understands both companies. Having met many line managers in both organizations, the integration manager spearheads integration efforts, guiding newly acquired managers through the maze of the new organizational hierarchy.

At GE Capital, for instance, integration managers introduce both executives and employees of the acquired firm to the business requirements and organizational standards of the new parent company. They also deal with a number of seemingly mundane issues that have been found to hamper integration efforts, such as communicating information about benefits and human resources policies. They educate new employees about such idiosyncratic features of the firm as culture, business customs, and even acronyms. Finally, in order to prevent unnecessary overload and redundant activities, they channel information requests from the parent company to both new managers and those who are veterans of the original organization.

GE Capital has found that individuals with strong personal and technical skills make the best integration managers and typically draws candidates from one of two pools. First, the company recruits "high-potential individuals"—people with strong functional-area management credentials and leadership potential. These people function best as integration managers when the integration is highly structured and relatively uncomplicated. For more complex integrations, GE Capital relies on seasoned veterans who know the company well. Experience has shown that these individuals can be drawn from every functional area.

Key Decisions Should Be Made Swiftly   As we've already seen, speed is of the essence in the acquisition process simply because of the cost and the time value of money. Certain organizational factors also dictate swift integration. For one, employees—both those of the target firm and those of the acquiring firm—are naturally concerned about the impact of the acquisition on their jobs. As much as executives and managers would like everyone to feel like a team player with a secure place in the organizational lineup, when they're worried about their jobs, people succumb to distractions. Successful acquirers have found that it's best not to prolong the suspense: Decisions about management structure, key roles, reporting relationships, layoffs, restructuring, cost cutting, and other career-affecting aspects of the acquisition should be announced as soon as possible—even within days of the acquisition announcement. Telling employees that everything will be "business as usual" is almost never being honest and will probably hamper the integration process. In addition, swift implementation of the integration process allows the firm to get on with its primary task—creating value. Because sluggish integration makes it more difficult to focus on this task, it weakens the value-creation process.

Integration Should Address Technical and Cultural Issues   When integrating acquisitions, most managers tend to focus on technical issues. At Cisco, for example, a key technical issue is the rapid integration of the target's products into the Cisco system so that sales representatives can begin selling the new product line. Successful integration means identifying and addressing such issues as early as possible.

Issues related to corporate culture should also be addressed immediately. Some of these issues are as simple as meeting and greeting new employees. The cultures of any two firms are bound to be different, and the faster managers and employees can meld the two organizations, the more smoothly the integration will proceed. Even when two organizations seem to have a lot in common, profound cultural differences may exist that could threaten successful integration. When, for instance, Franklin Quest merged with Covey, many observers expected cultural integration to be smooth. After all, the two businesses were highly complementary, and because both firms were located in Utah, they had similar employee bases. In addition, the two CEOs were well acquainted with one another. Surprisingly, however, the two cultures were highly dissimilar. For instance, Franklin Quest was built on a culture of efficiency, whereas Covey eschewed efficiency for effectiveness. Everything from products to company vision statements were tied to these critical underlying philosophies. During the acquisition process, executives dismissed these differences as semantics, but discovered during the integration phase that these were rather incongruent philosophies. In addition, more functional things, such as incompatible accounting systems, also impeded quick integration. Successful acquirers identify cultural clashes early; in fact, they may walk away from deals when the potential clashes are too severe.

ACQUISITIONS IN DIFFERENT INDUSTRY CONTEXTS

Not surprisingly, M&A activity varies across industries. It is determined largely by the development phase in which a given industry finds itself and by the extent of industry dynamism. In addition, competitive conditions will determine whether acquisition is a suitable strategy vehicle for a firm in a given industry and what the most viable type of acquisition may be. In this section, we'll discuss the role of M&As and industry context in terms of the industry life cycle and the level of industry-wide turbulence.

M&As and Industry Life Cycle

Recall the model of industry life cycle and industry dynamics that we presented in Chapter 4. In this section, we'll use this model to illustrate how different types of acquisitions play different roles in each stage.

Introduction   During the introduction stage, acquisitions tend to involve the purchase of startup firms by well-established firms in related but more mature industry segments. Many partial acquisitions may occur, with established companies making equity investments in startups but not acquiring them outright. Thus, at this stage M&As tend to be R&D and product- and market-extension acquisitions.

Growth   During this phase, we see several types of acquisitions. Established companies from one industry segment may start entering other segments with greater frequency, looking mostly for proven and growing targets. Although some M&A activity may be for R&D, most of it is likely to be for the purpose of acquiring products that are proven and gaining customer acceptance. The geographic roll-up also becomes more common, especially at the end of the growth stage and through the maturity stage. In high-velocity industries, industry-convergence acquisitions appear and continue into the maturity stage.

Maturity   At this point, we begin to see overcapacity acquisitions. Why? During the growth stage, the industry witnessed the entry of new firms and aggressive expansion, with numerous competitors jockeying for competitive position. Capacity built during this period often exceeds the long-term needs of the segment, and as demand starts to flatten, companies see consolidation as a way to rationalize the industry. Overcapacity M&A activity continues throughout the decline stage of the cycle.

M&As in Dynamic Contexts

Dynamic contexts are often home to firms that engage in acquisitions at a frantic pace. What is it about dynamic contexts that makes acquisitions such popular strategy vehicles? In Chapter 4, we discussed factors that can alter an industry landscape, particularly discontinuities and globalization. These factors tend to accelerate acquisitions. Note that within these two broad categories, many factors can affect the attractiveness of acquisitions as strategy vehicles. We'll focus on *technological change, demographic change, geopolitical change, trade liberalization*, and *deregulation*.[18]

conceptlink

In Chapter 4, we emphasize *discontinuous change* as disruptions in industry evolution that are often introduced by new entrants into the industry. We also observe in the same chapter that in the form of *technological discontinuities* or **disruptive technologies**, such changes can be subject to *PESTEL analysis*—a model for understanding a firm's **external environment** and, as such, for analyzing changes in the technological aspect of that environment wrought by *globalization*.

Technological Change   In high-velocity industries, technological change and innovation can transpire at lightning speed, and some firms respond with aggressive acquisition campaigns. Both Cisco and Microsoft, for example, use acquisitions to ensure that innovation and technological change among competitors don't contribute to the erosion of their strong competitive positions.

Demographic Change   Demographic changes, such as the aging of the population and mass emigration, may alter customer profiles significantly. Spanish-language speakers, for instance, are an increasingly important market segment for U.S. media companies. Thus, when the Tribune Company merged with Times-Mirror in 2000, it acquired *Hoy*, the leading Spanish-language daily in New York and one of the fastest-growing publications of its kind. The Tribune Company has recently launched editions in Chicago and Los Angeles.

Geopolitical Change   Such events as the fall of the Iron Curtain, the emergence of the European Union, the opening of China, and conflict in the Middle East all have significant effects on the operations of global companies. In some cases, changes enhance opportunities for acquiring established companies in new locations. In others, they foster divestiture. For example, IBM was able to divest its personal computer division to the Chinese firm Lenova in 2005 largely because of the rapid growth and commercialization of the domestic Chinese marketplace, which was fostered by the loosening of some government interventions.

Trade Liberalization   Trade liberalization also opens new opportunities for doing business. In the wake of the European Union and the North American Free Trade Agreement

(NAFTA), for example, cross-border acquisition activity increased in industries conducting business in those regions. Wal-Mart's acquisition of the successful Mexican retailing giant, Cifra, is a case in point. Geographic proximity and NAFTA make it cost-effective for Wal-Mart to stock its shelves in the United States with goods assembled in Mexico as well as provide otherwise more expensive U.S.–made goods to Mexican consumers through Cifra's outlets. Wal-Mart gains improved economies of scope and scale as a result of NAFTA.

Deregulation   Finally, deregulation has had a major impact on the volume of M&A activity in a number of industries. Prior to deregulation, for instance, the wave of M&As that swept the banking industry would not have been possible. Regulation and deregulation have also affected acquisitions and divestitures in the telecommunications industry. AT&T, for example, was allowed to exist as a virtual monopoly until 1984, when antitrust action forced its breakup. The seven so-called Baby Bells divided up local service, leaving the parent company, AT&T, with long-distance and telecom-equipment businesses. Following subsequent deregulation, M&A activity has put the industry in a state of almost constant change.

M&As and Coevolution

As with alliances, the use of acquisitions in dynamic contexts fits into the coevolution model of corporate strategy. Recall our definition of coevolution as the orchestration of a web of shifting linkages among evolving businesses. In the case of acquisitions, the firm chooses to develop more formal, hierarchical linkages among businesses, whether along vertical, horizontal, or complementary lines, instead of seeking such linkages only among partner businesses. Acquisitions in this web enable firms to absorb the capabilities of their targets in order to develop specific dynamic capabilities in concert with the best resources and capabilities available on the market. Just as important, acquisitions (at least well-conceived ones) support a specific, focused strategy. Consequently, in keeping with this strategy, certain businesses are periodically pared off and others added. If, for instance, the firm is pursuing a growth strategy, the coevolution perspective would suggest that it divest slow-growth businesses and products and acquire firms that are operating on the technology frontier or that offer some other basis for future competitive advantage.[19]

SUMMARY

1. Explain the motivations behind acquisitions and show how they've changed over time. The three basic motivations for acquisitions are synergy, manager self-interest, and hubris. Synergy is the primary motivation for acquisitions, and it can be generated in many different ways. Synergies can come from cost savings, revenue enhancements, improved competitive position, financial engineering, and the transfer of resources, best practices, and core competencies between targets and acquiring firms. Manager self-interest can motivate some acquisitions because many managers find it attractive to lead larger organizations, size and diversification can help smooth earnings, and compensation is higher for managers of large firms. This motive is known as *managerialism*. Hubris is exaggerated self-confidence, and it can result in managers' overestimating the value of a potential acquisition, having unrealistic assumptions about the ability of an acquisition to create synergies, and being too willing to pay too much for a transaction. Thus, hubris results in more acquisitions than would be the case if it were kept in check.

2. Explain why mergers and acquisitions are important strategy vehicles. Acquisitions enable firms to enter new businesses quickly. One of the key benefits of an acquisition over internal development of a new business is that the time and risks associated with business startup are reduced significantly. For instance, if the acquisition is of a firm of sufficient size, minimum efficient scale is achieved immediately. In addition, proven products are already in distribution. Acquisitions can also put firms in a position to achieve significant synergies—they can create value when the two firms combined are more valuable than when owned separately.

3. Identify the various types of acquisitions. Several types of acquisitions are possible, and each has a specific purpose. A product- or market-extension acquisition has the aim of expanding the products offered or markets served. A geographic roll-up is a series of acquisitions of firms in the same industry segment but in different geographic segments. A R&D acquisition is the purchase of another company for the purpose of acquiring its technology. An overcapacity, or consolidation, acquisition is the combination of two large firms in a mature industry that has excess capacity for slowing demand. An industry-convergence acquisition occurs when the boundaries between two industries start to fade and firms need to participate increasingly in both industries to be competitive; firms often use acquisitions to enter the converging industry. Finally, a significant portion of acquisitions are transactions by investors or holding companies (not an existing operating company) that are purchasing a company as an investment.

4. Understand how the pricing of acquisitions affects the realization of synergies. The pricing of an acquisition is critical to its success. The price of an acquisition normally exceeds its current market value by a significant premium. And although there is no one correct price for an acquisition target, managers of each potential acquiring firm can estimate the potential synergies between their company and the target. The price a firm is willing to pay for a target should be based on these synergies. Using Sirower's formula for acquisition premiums, managers can calculate the maximum premium they should be willing to pay. Likewise, if the price that is needed to make the acquisition is known first (such as in bidding situations), managers

can easily estimate the required performance improvements that would be necessary. The greater the premium paid, the more synergies that must be extracted from the deal to make it economical. Likewise, the greater the premium, the more important it is to realize the synergies quickly.

5. Outline the alternative ways to integrate an acquisition and explain the implementation process. How an acquisition is integrated should be a function of the target firm's need for autonomy and the strategic interdependence between the target and the acquired company. The four alternative modes of integration include absorption (extensive interdependence, low need for autonomy), preservation (low interdependence, high need for autonomy), holding (low interdependence, low need for autonomy), and symbiosis (high need for autonomy and high interdependence). Successful implementation requires recognition that acquisition integration is a continual process, that dedicated managers are required to oversee the process, that the process is enhanced by swift decisions, and that it focuses on both technical and cultural issues.

6. Discuss the characteristics of acquisitions in different industry contexts. Different types of acquisitions are seen with greater frequency at different stages of the industry life cycle. During the introduction stage, acquisitions tend to by firms in related segments acquiring technology (R&D acquisitions) or products of startups (product extensions). During the growth phase of the industry life cycle, several types of acquisitions are common. Some R&D acquisitions by later-moving established companies from related industry segments acquiring a now-proven technology still take place. But given that in the growth phase products have achieved more accepted status, many more product-extension acquisitions are seen. The geographic roll-up tends to appear at the waning stages of the growth phase. In high-velocity industries, industry-convergence acquisitions also start to appear. During the maturity stage, overcapacity acquisitions start to emerge, and roll-ups and product-extension acquisitions continue. Overcapacity acquisitions continue throughout industry decline. Industry turbulence, such as technological change, demographic change, geopolitical change, trade liberalization, and deregulation are all forms of industry shock that tend to increase acquisition activity because they change the competitive landscape.

KEY TERMS

REVIEW QUESTIONS

1. What is an acquisition?

2. Why would firms use acquisitions rather than create a new business internally?

3. What are the possible motives for acquisitions?

4. What are the ways in which synergies can be created in acquisitions?

5. How easy or difficult is it to achieve the alternative types of synergies?

6. What are the various types of acquisitions?

7. How do market-extension acquisitions and geographic roll-ups differ?

8. Give examples of product extension, overcapacity, and R&D acquisitions.

9. What is an acquisition premium?

10. How can you calculate the synergies that must be extracted from an acquisition with a given premium?

11. How do acquisitions tend to be used in different stages of the industry life cycle?

12. What are the alternative ways in which acquisitions can be integrated into the purchasing firm? How do managers determine which method to use?

How Would you Do That?

1. Identify a company that has recently announced an acquisition. Study the terms of the deal and identify to the extent possible the intrinsic value of the target, its market value, and the acquisition price. What was the acquisition premium? Using the synergy formula presented in the box entitled "How Would *You* Do That? 10.1," determine the performance improvements required to justify this acquisition premium. Calculate the required performance improvements with different assumptions as to how long it will take to implement them, say one, three, and five years. What is the difference in these required performance improvements if the acquisition premium is 50 percent lower that what was paid? What if it is 50 percent higher?

GROUP ACTIVITIES

1. Pick a firm of interest to your group. Identify potential acquisition candidates. Explain why these companies would make sense as an acquisition target. Evaluate and describe possible implementation barriers to this acquisition.

2. Pick a firm of interest and peruse its annual reports over a 5- to 10-year period. Assess the information presented on

M&As in the annual reports. Do you see any explicit mention of the link between strategy formulation and implementation with respect to the acquisition mentioned in the annual reports? (See the chairman's letter to the shareholders as a starting place.) What are the before and after scenarios that you find regarding the M&As?

ENDNOTES

1. N. Wingfield and J. Sapsford, "eBay to Buy PayPal for $1.4 Billion," *Wall Street Journal*, July 9, 2002, A6; N. Wingfield, "eBay Completes PayPal Deal, Gaining Web-Payments Heft," *Wall Street Journal*, October 4, 2002, B8; N. Wingfield, "eBay's Profit More Than Triples as Transaction Revenue Surges," *Wall Street Journal*, October 18, 2002, B4.

2. "Kerkorian Files Briefs in Lawsuit Alleging Deception by Daimler," *Wall Street Journal*, June 19, 2001, A4.

3. See R. F. Bruner, *Applied Mergers and Acquisitions* (Hoboken, NJ: John Wiley & Sons, 2004).

4. P. Wright, M. Kroll, and D. Elenkov, "Acquisition Returns, Increase in Firm Size, and Chief Executive Officer Compensation: The Moderating Role of Monitoring," *Academy of Management Journal* 45 (2002), 599–608.

5. Y. Amihud and B. Lev, "Risk Reduction as a Managerial Motive for Conglomerate Acquisitions," *The Bell Journal of Economics* 12 (1983), 605–617.

6. R. Roll, "The Hubris Hypothesis of Corporate Takeovers," *Journal of Business* 59 (1986), 197–216.

7. O. E. Williamson, *The Economic Institutions of Capitalism* (New York: Free Press, 1985).

8. P. Haunschild, "How Much Is That Company Worth?: Interorganizational Relationships, Uncertainty, and Acquisition Premiums," *Administrative Science Quarterly* 39 (1994), 391–411; W. G. Sanders, "Behavioral Responses of CEOs to Stock Ownership and Stock Option Pay," *Academy of Management Journal* 44 (2001), 477–492.

9. R. F. Bruner, *Deals from Hell: M&A Deals That Rise Above the Ashes* (New York: Wiley, 2005).

10. This typology was developed by J. T. Bower, "Not All M&As Are Alike—and That Matters," *Harvard Business Review* 79:3 (2001), 92–101.

11. Bower, "Not All M&As Are Alike."

12. M. L. Sirower, *The Synergy Trap: How Companies Lose at the Acquisition Game* (New York: Free Press, 1997).

13. Haspeslagh and Jemison, *Managing Acquisitions*; D. B. Jemison and S. B. Sitkin, "Corporate Acquisitions: A Process Perspective," *Academy of Management Review* 11:1 (1986), 145–163.

14. Brunner, *Applied Mergers and Acquisitions*; Haspeslagh and Jemison, *Managing Acquisitions*.

15. Haspeslagh and Jemison, *Managing Acquisitions*, 42.

16. Haspeslagh and Jemison, *Managing Acquisitions*.

17. Haspeslagh and Jemison, *Managing Acquisitions*.

18. Brunner, *Applied Mergers and Acquisitions*, 88.

19. S. L. Brown and K. M. Eisenhardt, *Competing on the Edge: Strategy as Structured Chaos* (Boston: Harvard Business School Press, 1998).

11

Part Five
Implementation,
New Ventures,
and Governance
in Dynamic
Contexts

Employing Strategy
Implementation Levers

After studying this chapter, you should be able to:

1. Understand the interdependence between strategy formulation and implementation.

2. Demonstrate how to use organizational structure as a strategy implementation lever.

3. Understand the use of systems and processes as strategy implementation levers.

4. Identify the roles of people and rewards as implementation levers.

5. Explain the dual roles that strategic leadership plays in strategy implementation.

6. Understand how global and dynamic contexts affect the use of implementation levers.

▶ **1957**
Bill Gore, a scientist for DuPont, suggests using polytetrafluoroethylene (commonly known as Teflon) to insulate wires and cable. However, DuPont isn't interested. In 1958, Gore and his wife, Vieve, begin the New Year by starting their own business based on Bill's idea in the basement of their Delaware home.

▶ **1969**
Bob Gore discovers a way to stretch Teflon into a rainproof, insulated fabric, which becomes known as GORE-TEX®. Cable produced by Gore goes to the moon with astronauts Edwin Aldrin, Jr. and Neil Armstrong.

1980   1985   19

W. L. GORE & ASSOCIATES: WEAVING THE FABRIC OF ORGANIZATIONAL CULTURE

Perhaps best known for its GORE-TEX® fabrics, W. L. Gore & Associates makes fabrics, as well as electronic, industrial, and medical products.[1] Founded in 1958 by Wilbert (Bill) L. Gore, the company has been around for 48 years, thanks to a fortuitous early discovery, tireless entrepreneurship, and dedicated employees who continue to pursue the creation of value through innovation.

In 1941, Bill Gore, then a scientist at DuPont, began researching and developing plastics, polymers, and resins, helping to develop, among other products, a synthetic substance known as Teflon®. Gore left DuPont in 1958 to start a business for Teflon-type products, and the company's original product line consisted of Teflon-insulated

▶ 1970s and 1980s
W. L. Gore & Associates develops the GORE-TEX® material into a wide array of products, including filters, fabrics for outerwear, and fiber for space suits.

▶ 2004
Fast Company magazine names W. L. Gore & Associates the most innovative company in America. W. L. Gore & Associates, which produces a wide array of products ranging from guitar strings to medical supplies, employs approximately 7,400 people in 45 locations around the world—not bad for a company that began in a home basement.

1995   2000

electronic wires and cables. Today, the privately held company boasts 7,400 employees around the world and $1.84 billion in annual sales. The majority of its stock is owned by the Gore family, with the remainder held by employees.

But back to Teflon, an extremely versatile polymer known as PTFE (polytetrafluoroethylene, or CF_2CF_2). Bill Gore had set out to develop applications for PTFE that didn't interest DuPont, but it was his son Bob, who had a doctorate in chemistry, who hit the product-development jackpot. In 1969, he discovered a way to stretch Teflon at the microscopic level, creating a membrane with holes large enough to release body heat and moisture but small enough to deflect raindrops. In 1976, Gore received a patent for the GORE-TEX material, which proved to have applications in such diverse products as space suits, outerwear, filters, and artificial arteries, and the company soon experienced explosive growth.

By the 1980s, GORE-TEX fabric had become the company's core product. Eventually, of course, Gore's patent expired, opening the door to a host of competitors. Although the company retains patents on several subsequent products and processes, in some cases it's eschewed the patent route, suspecting that patents often supply competitors with blueprints on how to innovate around unique technologies. Instead, in some cases it protects proprietary knowledge within the company. Gore thus relies on highly secretive manufacturing processes to which employees have access only on a strict need-to-know basis. Outsiders are barred from certain sections of Gore facilities, and many internal personnel have never witnessed key processes in operation.

In 1975, Gore entered the medical-products industry with a GORE-TEX-based graft designed to replace human arteries. In the late 1990s, the company developed a filter system that converts carcinogenic by-products of industrial combustion into water and harmless chemicals. Today, Gore's diverse product line includes ELIXIR® guitar strings, fiber for GLIDE® dental floss, GORE-TEX and WINDSTOPPER® fabrics, and numerous highly specialized medical products.

Gore is guided by four core values:

- Employees should be treated fairly, and they should extend the same fairness to everyone with whom they come in contact.
- Employees are free to encourage and help colleagues grow in knowledge, skill, and scope of responsibilities.
- Employees can choose the projects to which they commit themselves.
- Employees should consult with each other before committing to any action that could affect the reputation of the company.

From the outset, Bill Gore wanted a unique company culture that fostered innovation, and in this respect, Gore is in fact much different from most companies. For instance, there are no official bosses and very few job titles. Employees are called "associates," and when they're hired, new associates are assigned to "sponsors" within their functional areas. Sponsors mentor new associates and instill a healthy attitude toward commitment, and as associates' commitments change, they may choose new sponsors. Gore's philosophy revolves around the principle that growth is fueled by innovation and that innovation is fostered by a culture based on commitment and experimentation.

Because of the desire to maintain a distinct and deeply shared culture, hiring new associates is a critical process that includes multiple interviews with other employees as well as with HR specialists. Because there are no official bosses, the company lacks a formal hierarchy and does not have rigid channels of communication. Without titles, associates aren't locked into specific tasks. They're encouraged to take on new project commitments and to communicate freely with anyone who can help them develop those commitments. Gore refers to its organizational structure as "the lattice."

Depending on the requirements of the task or project at hand, every associate is potentially connected with every other associate, and leaders are associates who are followed by other associates. Salary is based on peer feedback on the contributions made by teammates, and committees composed of leaders from each functional area determine salary structure. Salaries ultimately depend on an associate's contributions to the success of a given business rather than technical expertise alone.

Most companies of Gore's size and success have gone through IPOs so that the founders can cash out their equity and raise capital to fuel growth. Gore, however, has resisted the lure of the IPO, not because the Gore family isn't interested in earnings, but because they don't want to sacrifice innovation and long-term prosperity to the pressure of capital markets to demonstrate short-term earnings performance. ■

INTERDEPENDENCE OF STRATEGY FORMULATION AND IMPLEMENTATION

By now, you should have a very good idea of what makes a good strategy: Good strategies enable an organization to achieve its objectives. You've also learned how to describe and evaluate business and corporate strategy formulation according to the strategy diamond. You know that *strategy formulation* is *deciding what to do* and that *strategy implementation* is the process of *executing what you've planned to do.*[2] You understand that neither formulation nor implementation can succeed without the other, and you're aware that the most successful firms often adjust strategies and execution according to feedback from the implementation process itself. That's why the processes of formulation and implementation are iterative and interdependent, with the objective being a consistent and coherent set of strategy elements and implementation levers. As Exhibit 11.1 reminds us, the overarching model of strategy hinges on the integral relationship among *formulation* (the process of aligning the five elements of the strategy diamond), *implementation levers*, and *strategic leadership*. In this chapter, we'll focus on issues concerning strategy implementation—specifically, implementation levers and the aspects of strategic leadership that facilitate successful implementation.

When a firm is experiencing difficulties, it's always good to ask three questions:

- Is the strategy flawed?
- Is the implementation of the strategy flawed?
- Are both the strategy and implementation flawed?

It shouldn't come as any surprise that, more often than not, implementation problems are the source of performance problems.[3] Obviously, no strategy can be effective if its implementation isn't. By the same token, although we tend to attribute success to effective strategies, some of the most stellar performers achieve competitive advantage because of *how* they execute their strategies.

conceptlink

In Chapter 2, we define **strategic leadership** as the task of managing an overall enterprise and influencing organizational outcomes. We explain that strategic leaders are equally responsible for **strategy formulation** and **implementation**, and in Chapter 1, we stressed the two critical roles played by leaders in implementation: (1) deciding on **resource allocations** and (2) developing **stakeholder** support.

Exhibit 11.1 Formulation and Implementation

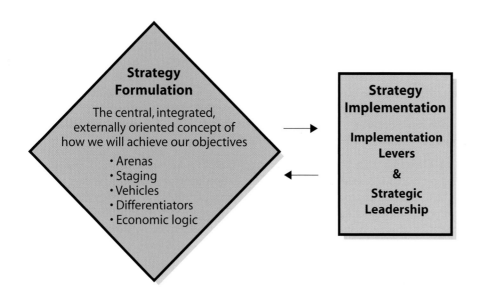

Strategy Formulation

The central, integrated, externally oriented concept of how we will achieve our objectives

- Arenas
- Staging
- Vehicles
- Differentiators
- Economic logic

Strategy Implementation

Implementation Levers

&

Strategic Leadership

A Model Company

The opening vignette on Gore describes a company whose strategy implementation integrates all of the key elements of the overarching implementation model outlined in Exhibit 11.1 (and indeed, it hits on all the points of the more detailed implementation framework we will review later in the chapter):

■ Gore's implementation levers function in unison to support a focused strategy of growth through innovative new products.

■ The lack of formal titles, hierarchy, and bureaucracy reflect a flat organizational structure that facilitates both the flow of information and quick decision making (though this presents a challenge to coordination and rapid change at an organizational level).

■ Systems are in place to identify new-product opportunities, to ensure that they have product champions, and to reward employees for their contributions to both product lines and the company's overall profitability.

■ Because the selection and retention of people, in terms of both necessary skills and personal fit with the organization, are a critical factor in Gore's success, these functions are rigorously managed. Attention to human resources also reinforces a deep culture that values leading-edge innovation, and top management reiterates the importance of the firm's "core values."

■ Gore operates in both international and dynamic contexts. It competes in areas of leading-edge technology in different markets around the globe. Because of this, it limits the size of its facilities to about 200 people or fewer, reinforcing operating flexibility and responsiveness to local conditions.

■ Finally, Gore's product-line strategy provides an excellent example of the iterative nature of implementation and formulation. For example, its strategy to enter the dental-floss market under the Glide brand reflects the confluence of the firm's valuable resources and its unique array of implementation levers. A new manager was able to assume accountability for this previously unknown product based on Gore's Teflon technology, launch the product in a small town using word-of-mouth advertising, and grow the product's share of market from 0 to 22 percent in just 8 years.[4] Just as important were the allocation of strategic resources and the effective communication of the strategy itself to key stakeholders.

By the end of this chapter, you should be able to identify the implementation levers and strategic-leadership functions that drive successful strategies. You should be able to identify levers that are in need of repair and propose a plan for using certain levers to implement a strategy more effectively.

The Knowing-Doing Gap

Let's go back to a couple of admonitions that we cited in Chapter 1:

■ "A strategy . . . is only as good as its execution."[5]

■ "The important decisions, the decisions that really matter, are strategic. . . . [But] more important and more difficult is to make effective the course of action decided upon."[6]

These principles apply to our focus in this chapter as well: By and large, firms find it much more difficult to implement good ideas than to generate new ideas and knowledge. A recent study, for instance, found that 46 percent of large companies surveyed regarded themselves as good or excellent at generating new knowledge; only 14 percent of the same firms reported having launched new products based on the application of new knowledge.[7] This difference between what firms *know* and what they *do* has been dubbed the **knowing-doing gap**.[8] Let's look a little more closely at this phenomenon.

knowing-doing gap Phenomenon whereby firms tend to be better at generating new knowledge than at creating new products based on that knowledge

What Causes the Knowing-Doing Gap?   One explanation of the knowing-doing gap is the fact that the strategy-formulation process itself isn't shared with those stakeholders, including lower-level managers, who will be integral in rolling out the strategy. Other observers argue that, even if all the right stakeholders are included in the strategy-formulation process, management often fails either to determine whether the proper implementation levers are in place or to take appropriate strategic-leadership actions.

Obstacles, External and Internal   Some experts believe that strategy-implementation failures result from management's inability to assess potential implementation obstacles.

Some obstacles reside in the external environment. Prior to its merger with Hewlett-Packard, for example, Compaq's attempts to mimic Dell's direct-sales model met with stiff resistance from its existing retail base, including such outlets as CompUSA and Best Buy. Of course, obstacles also exist inside the firm—a fact that we've already touched on by emphasizing the importance of assessing existing resources, implementation levers, and management-action plans. In diversified firms, the parent company itself may be an internal obstacle, particularly if one business unit is proposing a strategy that puts it in direct competition with another.

The Impact of Culture   One of the most critical, and yet most overlooked, internal implementation obstacles is a firm's *culture*. Culture sometimes presents management with a persistent challenge: It's both difficult and time consuming to change, and it can be a source of competitive advantage.[9] **Culture** consists of the core organizational values that are widely held and shared by organizational members (including employees, managers, and owners). Recent studies have found evidence confirming the theory that firms with strong shared values are better at implementing strategies and achieving higher levels of performance than firms with weaker values. Across industries, for example, firms with strong cultures generally achieve higher average levels of return on investment, net income growth, and change in share price.[10] In addition, firms with strong cultures seem to be less variable in their performance outcomes.[11] Finally, these positive effects of shared values on performance appear to be even stronger in highly competitive markets.[12] Why? Perhaps because effective strategy implementation is even more important in highly competitive industries, where there's less room for error.

> **culture** Core organizational values widely held and shared by an organization's members

Sometimes, company culture reflects the values of the CEO and other top managers, whereas at others leaders steward and protect existing values. Shared values are typically few in number, deeply embedded in the organization, give meaning and identity to the firm's members, and state the purpose of the firm's work. The shared values of Gore may be one of the reasons why it thrives despite having a structure that seems too chaotic for a firm of its size. Gore's values can be summed up as fairness, freedom, commitment, and consultation. Associates, for instance, are expected to treat one another fairly. They're given the freedom to grow in knowledge, skill, and scope of responsibility. Gore expects associates to spend 10 percent of their time tinkering with new ideas and to demonstrate commitment to their chosen projects. Finally, although everyone is empowered to make decisions, any management decision that may affect the firm's image or performance must be run past other associates.

In short, a firm's strategy must be consistent with its shared values if it's to be implemented successfully. Thus, it's crucial that strategists understand what's really important to members of the organization. First, of course, they need to ask whether employees have any shared values. If the answer is no, top management may have to spend some time developing and communicating a core set of values and getting organizational members to buy into them.

Mismatches   Not surprisingly, mismatches between strategy and implementation levers or between strategy and strategic-leadership actions are easy to recognize in hindsight. Of course, they're much more difficult to catch in real time. Executives who are responsible for formulating strategy are often prone to making overly optimistic projections and downplaying the obstacles to execution. Consider, for instance, the number of hardware and software firms that have attempted to become IT-solution providers by adding a consulting arm to their existing business. Most have failed, usually because they lacked the organization to execute the strategy.[13] SAP provides a good example of this.

As a provider of ERP software, SAP grew quickly at first because of demand for its unique product. In its zeal for growth, however, the firm neglected to focus on structure, employee retention, and balance between rewards for sales and rewards for profitability. SAP eventually recovered (as you will see in the box entitled "How Would *You* Do That? 11.1"), but only after a new CEO dramatically revamped the firm's infrastructure, cost controls, and human resource policies.[14]

As the SAP example in the "How Would *You* Do That?" box shows, implementation levers tend to be interrelated, which means that a change in one will probably require a

conceptlink

In discussing threats to rational decision making in Chapter 2, we explain some of the biases that can lead to such flawed judgments. In Chapter 10, we detailed the threat of **managerialism**—the tendency of managers to make decisions based on personal rather than stakeholder interests—to the process of implementing mergers and acquisitions.

Picking Up the Pieces at SAP

The enterprise software company SAP dodged a bullet, but just barely. It did so not by overhauling its strategy but rather by dramatically changing its leadership and implementation approach. We will focus on SAP America, one of the largest subsidiaries of the German firm SAP, because it characterizes much of what took place globally in this firm. From 1992 through most of 1996, SAP America's revenues grew at an astounding triple-digit annual rate, from $49 million to an annualized $818 million. The number of employees over that same period grew from 284 to 1,621. This rapid growth was spurred by two things. First, SAP had what many U.S. multinationals perceived to be the best ERP product on the market. The product was highly profitable due to its relatively standardized design and high market demand. Second, SAP was a fairly decentralized organization, with functional emphasis primarily in sales and on an incentive system that rewarded sales and sales growth. Career paths were unclear and focused on regions, but because the compensation was so lucrative, employees could earn huge salaries based on sales and then jump ship to a firm where their career and mobility might be more clearly laid out. As a result, SAP America was built for speed (though not efficiency), and its rocket-like sales growth reflected the levers and leadership that were in place.

Coming into late 1995, however, the rocket seemed to be running out of fuel. The combination of growing competition from the likes of Oracle and Siebel systems, market saturation, and a lack of organizational accountability that was a by-product of the growth focus was beginning to undermine SAP's profitability, customer service, and reputation. SAP Germany's kick in the pants to SAP America started with the promotion of then-CFO Kevin McKay to the position of CEO (and the departure of the old CEO, Paul Wahl, to competitor Siebel Systems). McKay moved quickly to increase cultural sensitivity to costs and cost management, implement an administrative structure to bolster the organization's overall professionalism, and formalize human resource policies.

This latter step took the form of hiring an HR director (no one had held that role at SAP America before, despite all of the hiring that had gone on) who put a formal HR system in place. These decisions were complemented by increased R&D funding to explore the Internet applications of SAP software, a platform that the software giant had ignored up to that point. At the same time, McKay subtly shifted SAP's strategy from one of pure growth through new accounts to account "farming"—an increased focus on garnering a greater share of each existing customer's IS business needs, coupled with the modification of the firm's reward system to reward such behaviors.

While these changes caused many people to leave SAP, this loss was more than offset by the hiring of new executives and workers who bought into the new organizational arrangements and SAP's vision. By 2000, the firm had successfully launched a Web-based version of its software, called MySAP, and regained its position of industry leadership.

Sources: SAP Annual General Shareholders' Meeting, Mannheim, Germany, May 3, 1997; SAP 1997–2003 Financial Reports (accessed on July 15, 2005), www.sap.com/company/investor/reports/pastfinancials/index.epx; Harvard Business School Case 9-397-067, SAP America, December 3, 1996; N. Boudette, "How a German Software Titan Missed the Internet Revolution," *Wall Street Journal,* January 18, 2000, A1.

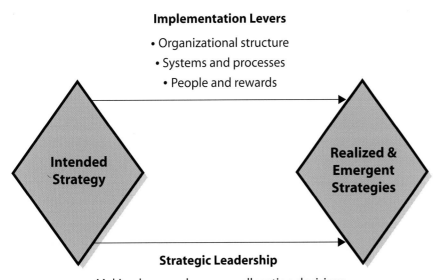

Exhibit 11.2 Key Facets of Strategy Implementation

change in all or some of the others. We'll deal with further examples of these interrelationships in the following sections, but at this point, we suggest that you use the following statement to guide you in your study of the material in this chapter:

> [T]he strategist will not be able to nail down every action step when the strategy is first crafted, nor should this even be attempted. However, he or she must have the ability to look ahead at the major implementation obstacles and ask, "Is this strategy workable? Can I make it happen?"[15]

By the end of this chapter, you'll be able not only to answer questions such as these, but offer recommendations for employing implementation levers and taking strategic-leadership actions. These two facets of strategy implementation—levers and leadership—are summarized in Exhibit 11.2.

IMPLEMENTATION LEVERS

We have been using the term *implementation lever* without providing a precise definition. Before we explore the concept in detail, therefore, it may be useful to make clear that **implementation levers** are mechanisms that a strategic leaders has at his or her disposal to help execute a strategy. Although anything that enables an executive to get leverage to execute change can be considered an implementation lever, we categorize the major levers as *structure, systems and processes,* and *people and rewards*. In this section, we will go into some depth on each of these.

implementation lever
Mechanisms used by strategic leaders to help execute a firm's strategy

Recall that we introduced and described the three main categories into which **implementation levers** could be divided back in Chapter 1: (1) organizational structure; (2) systems and processes; and (3) people and rewards.

Structure

Because structure is the implementation lever that usually gets the most attention in an organization, we'll start with it. Alfred Chandler's classic research on the interdependence of strategy and structure based on studies of General Motors, DuPont, and Sears raised the topic to prominence in the 1960s.[16] Today, practically every issue of the *Wall Street Journal* announces that some firm is busy "restructuring" or reporting decreased earnings due to "restructuring charges." Most firms develop *organizational charts,* which are static representations of their structure. But what is *structure* itself? We'll define **organizational structure** as the relatively stable arrangement and division of responsibilities, tasks, and people within an organization. Organizations are composed of people who are assigned to certain

organizational structure
Relatively stable arrangement of responsibilities, tasks, and people within an organization

divisions and who perform certain delegated and specialized tasks. The *structure* of an *organization*, therefore, is the framework that management has devised to divide tasks, deploy resources, and coordinate departments.[17] Structure provides a way for information to flow efficiently from the people and departments who generate it to those who need it. Structure also spells out *decision rights*—policies that tell individuals who's responsible for generating particular information and who's authorized to act on it.

Control and Coordination   Briefly, structure includes a firm's authority hierarchy, its organizational units and divisions, and its mechanisms for coordinating internal activities. Organizational structure performs two essential functions:

- It ensures control.
- It coordinates information, decisions, and the activities of employees at all levels.

As both functions become more complex, firms generally modify their structure accordingly. Structure should be consistent with the firm's strategy. The more diversified the firm, the more the structure that will have to be designed to accommodate coordination. After all, if a firm is participating in related businesses, it is probably trying to exploit synergies—a task that, as we saw in our chapters on corporate and international strategy, often requires sharing information and resources across product or geographic divisions. Conversely, the more focused the firm is on a single business (or even on each of multiple unrelated businesses), the more its structure should be designed to emphasize control. As we'll see, the popular means of organizing firm structure include the *functional, multidivisional, matrix,* and *network* forms.[18]

Traditionally, both scholars and managers have thought of structure as being determined by a firm's strategy,[19] and in most cases, this assumption is valid. We'll soon see, however, that structure can result in new or modified strategies. In fact, the way in which tasks are delegated and resources deployed can produce rather dramatic changes in a firm's strategy.

With respect to structure, a key question is whether the firm's current structure facilitates the implementation of its strategy and provides the information it needs to revise its existing strategy. At all times, a firm's structure should seek a balance between the control needed to achieve efficiency and unity of direction and the delegation of authority required to make timely decisions in a competitive environment. Let's examine two cases in which new structure resulted directly in changes in strategy.

How Structure Influences Strategy (I)   After developing an innovative process for economically producing industrial gas onsite at customers' factories, the French firm Air Liquide (translated as *liquid air*) began locating personnel at client sites. This restructuring gave employees at customer sites more decision-making autonomy. Before long, on-site employees discovered a host of new services that Air Liquide could offer its clients, such as handling hazardous materials, troubleshooting quality-control systems, and managing inventory. The result, of course, was a wealth of new business opportunities—most of which offered higher margins than the company's core gas production and distribution business. Such services now account for 25 percent of Air Liquide's revenues, as opposed to just 7 percent before the restructuring.[20]

How Structure Influences Strategy (II)   Part of this next story was presented in the opening vignette to Chapter 6 on dynamic strategies. In the early 1980s, Intel derived more than 90 percent of its revenue from the manufacture of memory chips. A feature of its organizational structure is credited with being the key to its transformation into a maker of PC microprocessors in a span of less than two years. Although they appear similar, the capabilities underlying effective competition in memory versus microprocessors differ. Originally, Intel's structure permitted production managers to make production decisions based on a set of established rules. Among other things, these rules stipulated that managers allocate production capacity based on margins per square inch of silicon wafer. In response to this requirement, production managers started shifting manufacturing capacity from memory chips to microprocessors (previously just a small side business), because the margins were much greater. Interestingly, this shift wasn't dictated or orchestrated by senior management. In fact, Intel's senior management didn't ratify the decision to become a microprocessor manufacturer until well after microprocessors had come to account for about 90 percent of company-wide output.[21]

Forms of Organizational Structure

In this section, we'll review four basic forms of organizational structure: *functional, multidivisional, matrix,* and *network.* We also briefly describe partnerships and franchises. Consider these structures to be "pure" forms. In reality, they're just basic models on which many variations have been played. Later in the chapter, we'll show how they've been modified to accommodate global and dynamic contexts.

Functional Structure A **functional structure** organizes its activities according to the specific functions that a company performs. As shown in Exhibit 11.3, common units include finance, sales and marketing, production, and R&D. From a practical standpoint, any of the functions in a firm's value chain can be organized as a unit in a functional structure.

> **functional structure** Form of organization revolving around specific value-chain functions

Functional structures tend to work best in smaller firms and those with few products or services. Platypus Technologies, for instance, is a small nanotechnology firm with 30 employees,[22] most of whom are R&D scientists working in the lab. Obviously, however, Platypus also has small departments dedicated to finance, marketing, and human resources.

Functional organization helps managers of smaller firms improve efficiency and quality by fostering professionalism in the performance of specialized tasks. Bear in mind, however, that as firms grow and become more complex (perhaps by venturing into multiple lines), a functional form can become downright dysfunctional. Often, problems arise if each functional unit begins to focus too narrowly on its own goals and operations, thus losing sight not only of other functional activities but of customer needs and corporate objectives. This phenomenon has given rise to the term *functional silos.*

The functional organizational model may also exacerbate problems in multiproduct, multimarket firms. Expansion, whether into product or geographic markets, can become problematic if the strategy that's appropriate in one market doesn't work very well in another. The types of products, for example, that enjoy dominant domestic share may not meet the needs of foreign consumers. Similarly, a firm involved in two different product markets may find that the same competitive methods don't work equally well in both or that different markets call for different sales channels. When a functional structure is used in contexts characterized by varying market demands and sales characteristics, functionally structured organizations may be sluggish in responding to changing customer demands and in accessing potential new customers.

Multidivisional Structure One solution to the problems of managing activities in multiple markets is the **multidivisional structure**, illustrated in Exhibit 11.4. Divisions can be organized around geographic markets, products, or groups of related businesses, with division heads being responsible for the strategy of a coherent group of businesses or

> **multidivisional structure** Form of organization in which divisions are organized around product or geographic markets and are often self-sufficient in terms of functional expertise

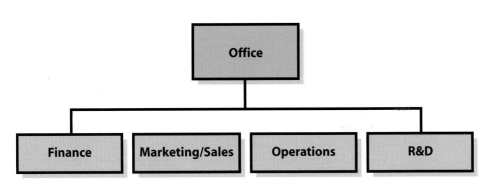

Exhibit 11.3 The Functional Structure

Functional structures tend to work best in smaller firms, such as Platypus Technologies, LLC, a Wisconsin nanotechnology firm, which employs about 30 people.

conceptlink

In Chapter 5, we defined a *strategic business unit (SBU)* as an organizational subunit within a diversified corporation that's responsible for a specific business or group of related businesses; we emphasized that the SBU environment includes both elements *external to* the firm and elements of the parent firm.

markets. Such strategic specialization means that strategic decisions are more likely to be appropriate and timely. It also enables firms to design compensation systems that reward performance at the business-unit, versus functional, level.

One of the first companies to adopt a multidivisional structure, GM is mostly organized according to product divisions (GM Trucks, Chevrolet, Buick, Cadillac, Saturn, and so forth). Each division maintains a finance function, a marketing function, and so on. Multidivisional structure makes it possible to implement division-specific incentives and performance-accountability standards, and because each division has ready access to key resources, multidivisional structure also fosters speedier reactions to opportunities and challenges.

Multidivisional structure is also effective in coordinating diverse economic activities. Headquarters, for example, plans, coordinates, and evaluates all operating divisions, allocating the personnel, facilities, funds, and other resources needed to execute divisional strategies. Divisional managers, meanwhile, are in charge of most of the functions revolving around major product lines and, as such, are typically responsible for divisional financial performance.

Exhibit 11.4 Typical Multidivisional Organization

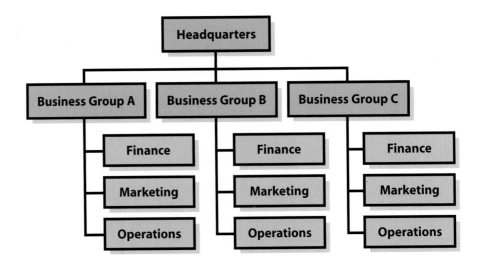

For instance, Emageon, a 225-employee provider of advanced visualization tools to hospitals and other medical organizations, has two divisions.[23] One offers electronic hardware, and its sales force works with executives who are responsible for IT decisions at target customers. The second division specializes in software for x-rays and CAT scans, and because physicians usually make the software-purchase recommendations, Emageon's software sales force focuses on them. Together, the two divisions provide a complete solution for firms in Emageon's target industry, and as it so happens, each can cross-sell the other's products.

Of course, multidivisional structure is not without drawbacks. It can, for instance, foster undesirable competition between divisions. Emageon doesn't have this problem, but it's not hard to see how GM's higher-end Buicks bump up against its lower-priced Cadillacs.

In addition, when each division is functionally self-contained, there may be costly duplications of staff functions that could be handled more efficiently under some other form of organization. Finally, coordination across divisions can be difficult if cooperation is in the best interests of one division but not those of another.

Matrix Structure   The matrix structure, which is represented in Exhibit 11.5, is a hybrid between the functional and multidivisional structures. A **matrix structure** is designed to take advantage of the benefits of both basic forms—namely, functional specialization and divisional autonomy. As you can see in Exhibit 11.5, two reporting channels exist simultaneously. In our hypothetical company, for instance, there are functional divisions for finance and marketing, but personnel from both divisions are assigned to specific product or geographic divisions. A finance specialist, therefore, reports simultaneously to a finance executive and an executive in one or another of the product or geographic divisions.

matrix structure Form of organization in which specialists from functional departments are assigned to work for one or more product or geographic units

Exhibit 11.5   Hypothetical Matrix Structure

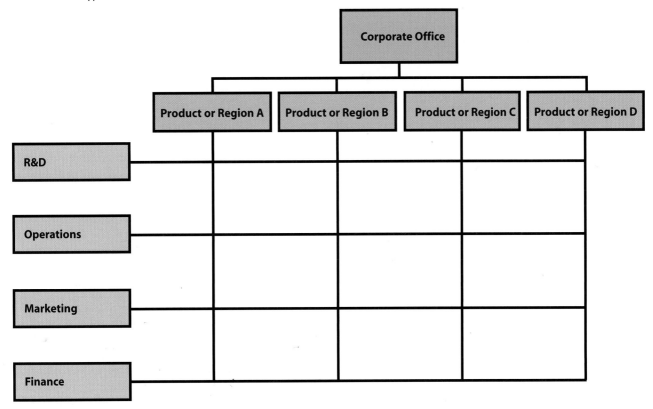

Source: E. Prewitt, "GM's Matrix Reloads," CIO, September 1, 2003.

The Swiss–Swedish technology giant Asea Brown Boveri (ABB) furnishes perhaps the most dramatic example of the matrix structure in action. In the early 1990s, the firm was composed of more than 900 matrix units. Any structure that sets up so many dual loci of authority is going to have problems with conflicts over authority and accountability. At ABB, however, managers in one matrix unit rarely exercise direct authority over their counterparts in other units. (Dealings between units, therefore, often depend on managers' skills in the arts of negotiation and persuasion.) Moreover, the matrix provides flexibility by making it possible to organize teams around specific projects, products, or markets.

The utility of a matrix structure increases when the pressures facing a firm are unpredictable and require both high degrees of control and extensive coordination of resources. Many firms find it difficult to implement the matrix structure because it calls for high levels of resource sharing across divisions; in fact, it's generally feasible only when strong culture and shared values support cross-division collaboration. As it turns out, even though ABB enjoyed a strong culture, the company eventually realized that coordinating 900 matrix units was far too complex. Massive restructuring began in early 2000, and today, though still operating under a matrix structure, ABB has reduced the number of its operating units by about half.

Network Structure   A more recent development in organization design, the **network structure** consists of small, semi-autonomous, and potentially temporary groups that are brought together for specific purposes—a team, for example, that's been assembled to work on a new-product idea. A network structure also includes external linkages with such groups as suppliers and customers. Sometimes these external linkages take the form of strategic alliances, which you learned about in Chapter 9. Authority is based on the control of resources, knowledge, and expertise, rather than on hierarchical rank, and because it's highly flexible, a firm can reconfigure staff and resources rapidly enough to exploit rich but fleeting bubbles of opportunity. Drawbacks include the potential for confusion and ambiguity.

Gore's "lattice" organization is a special (and extreme) version of a network structure. Although difficult to diagram here, imagine what an organizational structure would look like for Gore, with its approximately 7,400 associates working in more than 45 plants and sales locations worldwide. Sales and customer-service sites are located in Argentina, Australia, Austria, Brazil, China, Finland, France, Germany, Greece, Hong Kong, India, Italy, Japan, Korea, Malaysia, the Netherlands, New Zealand, Poland, Russia, Scotland, Singapore, Spain, Sweden, Taiwan, and the United States. Manufacturing operations are clustered in the United States, Germany, Scotland, Japan, and China. Gore separates its products into 10 categories: aerospace, automotive, chemical processing, computers/telecommunications/electronics, energy, environment, industrial/manufacturing, medical/healthcare, military, and textiles. As is the typical network organization, Gore employees work in small teams and are encouraged to participate in direct one-on-one communication with other Gore associates, customers, and suppliers.

Partnerships and Franchises   Before leaving this section, we should mention two additional forms of organization structure—the professional partnership and the franchise system. Although both are as much forms of legal ownership as they are organizational structures, they offer a few unique structural characteristics that can be brought to bear on persistent organizational problems. In addition, because both are common fixtures on the business landscape, it's important that you understand their role in the national economy.

Professional Partnerships   In several industries, the professional partnership is the structural form of choice. In a professional partnership, the company is organized as a group of partners who own shares or units in the company. Generally, the partners vote on a managing partner who will act as a supervisor, but this person serves at their pleasure. Consequently, a senior partner has significant authority and prestige but perhaps not nearly the power that a CEO of a large firm has over subordinates. Partnerships are pyramid-shaped structures, with each partner having a number of associates (of various levels). Industries in which the partnership form is common include the legal offices, accounting firms, consulting firms, adver-

network structure Form of organization in which small, semiautonomous, and potentially temporary groups are brought together for specific purposes

tising agencies, and real estate companies. Until recently, investment-banking firms were structured as partnerships, but most have converted to publicly held corporations. The management structure of investment-banking firms has remained relatively the same, but the change to a corporate form has enabled firms to increase their capitalization.

Franchise Structure The franchise system not only transfers ownership of local facilities to a franchisee, it likewise shifts all local management responsibility to the franchisee. One purpose of using a franchise model is that it enables a firm to grow rapidly because much of the capital costs are picked up by the franchisees. However, the franchise model fundamentally changes the organizational structure of the firm. A franchisee assumes all management responsibility for individual business locations. For the right to the franchisor's business model and brand name, the franchisee pays a royalty percentage and other fees to the franchisor.

Systems and Processes

When asked to think about the systems and processes needed to manage an organization, people usually mention information systems (IS). In reality, an IS is just one type of vital system. Systems and processes make it possible to manage budgeting, quality control, planning, distribution, and resource allocation in complex contemporary organizations.

In Chapter 2, we pointed out that ambitious vision and mission statements don't automatically translate into higher levels of financial performance.[24] Conversely, of course, a myopic focus on financial-accounting results, such as return on equity or return on sales, may cause managers to lose sight of long-term strategic initiatives and divert their attention from other key stakeholders.[25] For this reason, many firms are developing performance-measurement and management systems that enable them to balance the need to report short-term financial returns with the need to pursue longer-term (and often intangible) objectives. Various approaches can be used to gauge the success with which implementation levers are aligned with strategic objectives; the most common term for these performance-management systems is the *balanced scorecard.*

The Balanced Scorecard
The **balanced scorecard** has evolved into what might just as well be called a *strategy scorecard*. It's a strategic management support system devised to help managers measure vision and strategy against business- and operating-unit-level performance along several critical dimensions.[26]

The balanced-scorecard approach teaches three fundamental lessons:

■ Translate strategy into tangible and intangible performance metrics (recall the summary of financial and nonfinancial performance measures summarized in Exhibit 2.8 of Chapter 2).
■ Use a *strategy map* to align metrics with strategy.
■ Make strategy a continuous and dynamic process.[27]

Let's look a little more closely at each of these principles.

Relying on a Range of Metrics Managers should pay attention to a variety of performance metrics, not just to short-term financial-performance indicators. Granted, financial performance is the easiest metric to apply, but other indicators are just as critical in diagnosing and maintaining the long-term health of an organization. The balanced scorecard prevents managers from relying solely on short-term financial or other outcome measures and forces them to focus instead on those measures, both tangible and intangible, that are relevant to the elements of value being delivered to key stakeholders.

Leading proponents of this approach advise managers to consider four perspectives on performance: *financial, customer, internal business process,* and *learning and growth:*

■ The *financial perspective* involves strategy for growth, profitability, and risk when viewed from the shareholder's or owner's perspective.
■ The *external-relations perspective* pertains to strategy for creating value and differentiation from the perspective of the customer.

balanced scorecard Strategic management support system for measuring vision and strategy against business- and operating-unit-level performance

Exhibit 11.6   Translating Vision and Strategy in Action Through the Balanced Scorecard System

Financial			
Objectives	Measures	Targets	Initiatives

"To succeed financially, how should we appear to our shareholders?"

External			
Objectives	Measures	Targets	Initiatives

"To achieve our vision, how should we appear to our customers?"

Vision and Strategy

Internal Business Process			
Objectives	Measures	Targets	Initiatives

"To satisfy our shareholders and customers, what business processes must we excel at?"

Learning and Growth			
Objectives	Measures	Targets	Initiatives

"To achieve our vision, how will we sustain our ability to change and improve?"

- The *internal-business-process perspective* reflects strategic priorities among processes according to their contributions to customer and shareholder satisfaction.
- The *learning-and-growth perspective* focuses on the organization's priorities for fostering change, innovation, and growth.

Exhibit 11.6 illustrates the links among these four perspectives and a firm's vision and strategy. It can also serve as a worksheet for identifying a performance metric, its target level, and the specific initiatives aimed at achieving the target. Recall that the overarching strategic management process introduced in Chapter 1 flows from vision to goals and objectives and then to the strategy diamond, which sets out how those goals and objectives are to be achieved. You can think of the balanced scorecard as an elaborate summary of the goals and objectives in the strategic management process. Essentially, management must distill tangible and intangible strategic objectives for each area down into specific measures that will be used to gauge those objectives. Targets are then set for those measures and initiatives that are launched to reach the desired targets. Ideally, these measures will have leading, pacing, and lagging characteristics such that management can tell if they are moving forward, how well and quickly they are doing so, and when initiatives are drawing to a successful conclusion.

Developing a Strategy Map   Exhibit 11.6 shows how managers can begin the strategy-mapping process. The next, and most critical, step of the process is to develop a *strategy map* wherein managers link all performance metrics to the firm's strategy. Many managers begin mapping systems and processes by diagramming activities across the four perspectives that we've already developed: (1) financial, (2), external relations (3) internal business processes, and (4) learning and growth.

An example of this cause-and-effect approach to strategy mapping is shown in Exhibit 11.7. The strategy map states objectives—in terms of business processes, cycle time, productivity, and other important internal processes—to guide key activities. When map-

Exhibit 11.7 The Balanced Scorecard in the Context of a Strategy Map

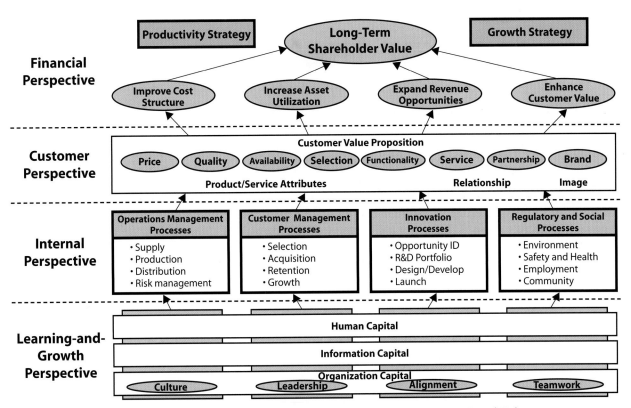

Sources: Adapted from R. Kaplan and D. Norton. The Strategy-Focused Organization, Boston: Harvard Business Press (2001); www.valuebasedmanagement.net/methods_strategy_maps_strategic_communication.html.

ping learning-and-growth objectives, managers should indicate what must be done—in terms of people and product and process development—if learning-and-growth processes are to be developed and sustained.

The two remaining perspectives—external relations and financial—state objectives that reflect the desired outcomes. How, for instance, does the firm want customers, partners, and other external stakeholders to perceive it? How will planned activities ultimately translate into financial results and economic value? As the box entitled "How Would *You* Do That? 11.2" demonstrates, a balance scorecard can smooth the process of strategy implementation. Linking objectives in this way helps managers articulate causality between objectives—a key factor in linking strategy to relevant performance measures.[28]

Making Strategy a Continuous and Dynamic Process To ensure that a strategy remains continuous and dynamic, managers must succeed at two tasks:

■ Disseminating the key features of a strategy and stipulating responsibilities for executing it throughout the organization

■ Linking the strategy with the financial budget

In one important sense, the balanced scorecard can serve as a tool for communicating vision, mission, and strategy throughout an organization—a theme to which we'll return later in the chapter when we discuss the roles of strategic leadership in strategy implementation. Employees who've participated in developing and revising a balanced scorecard should have a fairly in-depth understanding of a firm's strategy and of the ways in which underlying maps come together to support it. During the process, they should also develop

Developing a Balanced Scorecard for the NUWC

Exhibit 11.8 shows the first steps in the mapping process at the U.S. Naval Undersea Warfare Center (NUWC), the Navy's full-spectrum research, testing, and engineering center for submarines, autonomous underwater systems, and weapons systems associated with undersea warfare. As a result of the strategic-mapping process, which involved communication among managers in all parts and levels of the organization in addition to external stakeholders, three organizational themes emerged—innovation, affordability, and putting the customer first.

In turn, these themes led to the development of a system of performance metrics that is aligned with the clearly articulated strategic direction of NUWC. (This example, by the way, shows that the concept of the balanced scorecard can be applied to both nonprofit and for-profit organizations.)

The next step (for NUWC or any other organization) is to develop objectives, measures, targets, and initiatives for each of the key perspectives. These perspectives should then be used to develop the overarching strat-

egy map. If there are inconsistencies between pieces in the map, then the relevant stakeholders can use this information as an opportunity to refine the implementation of the strategy, including revision of the objectives, measures, targets, and initiatives. Because the perspectives and their underlying objectives are related to strategic priorities, the system goes well beyond a mere listing of things to do or key performance indicators. By means of the mapping process, all metrics are related to strategic objectives.

Exhibit 11.8 Balanced Scorecard Development at the Naval Undersea Warfare Center (NUWC)

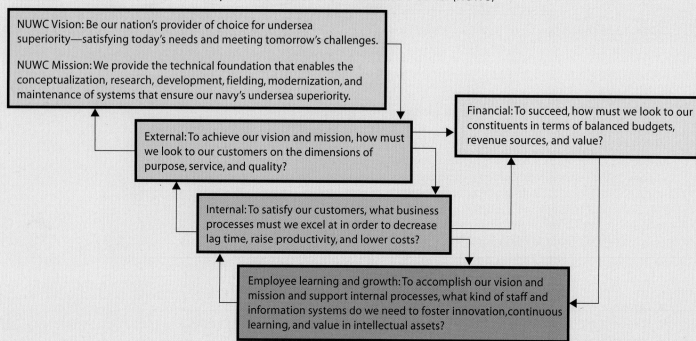

Source: Adapted from G. Harrigan and R. Miller, "Managing Change Through an Aligned and Cascading Balanced Scorecard," Perform 2:2 (2003), 20–26.

a good sense of whether the organization's culture will support the strategy. Finally, beyond simple communication, the dissemination process can foster broader support for the strategy among stakeholders, improve understanding of how the balanced scorecard works to ensure that the strategy is effectively implemented, and furnish a mechanism for receiving feedback.

To be sure, in the form of operational budgets, the process of financial budgeting not only provides a feedback tool, but also helps to determine resource allocation. However, operational budgets impose a form of outcome control that, by its very nature, tends to constrain managers and hamper investment in new capabilities and products.

In contrast, a *strategic* budget focuses on identifying and acquiring new customers, new capabilities, new operations, and new products. The balanced scorecard is important in determining the mix and amount of spending in the strategic budget, and the relationship between strategic priorities and the scorecard is further reinforced when compensation is tied to financial and nonfinancial measures. Microsoft, for instance, now ties the compensation of its top 600 officers to customer-satisfaction scores, a critical nonfinancial performance measure in the company's balanced scorecard.[29]

People and Rewards

This subset of implementation levers draws attention to the importance of people and the rewards that can be used to align their energies and actions with the organization's objectives. We'll treat people and rewards together because inappropriate incentives and controls can frustrate the efforts of even the best people. Let's go back to our earlier example of the impact of inadequate compensation policies on SAP's strategy. One problem was that the company's compensation system rewarded people for generating new sales regardless of whether SAP product packages were priced to yield a profit for the firm. In terms of sales, the firm grew quickly, but SAP eventually realized that, over time, many of its customer relationships were costing it more money than it was making.

People Employees are sometimes called a firm's *human capital* in order to distinguish them from fixed assets and financial capital. Individually, people are a critical component in strategy formulation and implementation. Collectively, people comprise the firm's culture, and such culture contributes strongly to a firm's dynamic capabilities and competitive advantage. Barclay's Global Investors (BGI) provides a good case in point of how a firm's culture of action orientation and self-reliance can and must be aggressively nurtured and protected:

> One of the things we discovered was that there are certain basic things—values, vision, the culture of the firm—that are not up for discussion. You can discuss it in the sense of explaining it and understanding it, but it's not something that is going to be changed. It's important for people to understand that. When you become part of BGI, this is what you are signing up for. And quite frankly, we've still got a small hard-core group of our managing directors that still are questioning it. So we are at the point of saying to them, "Well, maybe it's best that you go someplace else, because these things aren't up for discussion."[30]

As we've indicated on several occasions, a strategy will succeed only if a firm has the right people with the right experience and competencies. As the BGI example demonstrates, this also includes people who share and steward the corporate culture. Thus, recruitment, selection, and training with an eye to competencies and values are critical to strategy implementation. In a recent study, management researcher Jim Collins examined 11 firms that went from good to excellent performance and sustained it over a 15-year period. He then compared these firms with peer companies that had similar prestudy performance but never reached the level of great performance. In all 11 cases of good-to-great companies, making sure they had the right people working was a major priority for CEOs early in their tenures. Collins reports that many executives believe the people lever to be the most crucial to the successful implementation of strategy. Successful CEOs, according to Collins, "attended to people first [and] strategy second. They got the right people on the bus, moved the wrong people off, ushered the right people to the right seats—and then

concept link

We introduce the **VRINE model** of **resources**, **capabilities**, and **competitive advantage** in Chapter 3, where we suggest that human capital can be a source of advantage, especially when it contributes to **causal ambiguity**— complex conditions within an organization that competitors find it hard to imitate. In Chapter 6, we characterize threats to sustained competitive advantage anything that threatens VRINE resources and capabilities.

they figured out where to drive it."[31] In BGI's case, for example, management's clarity on the requisite values and principles each employee should hold enabled managers to identify quickly those individuals who fit the desired BGI culture.

So how do people influence firm performance? In many organizations, of course, the skills of their people make it possible for them to do what they do best.[32] That's why the VRINE framework regards such expertise as an important part of a firm's bundle of strategic capabilities. Some consultants and scholars think that these bundles of skills, all the way down to the level of those possessed by teams and even specific individuals, are the key factor in a firm's long-term viability and its ability to innovate new products.[33] People decisions are critical to performance because decisions about which and how many people to employ hinge on the desire either to improve efficiency or generate new revenues.[34]

Because human resources are generally a firm's largest operating cost, many managers focus on reducing this cost. Moreover, the stock market tends to react positively to downsizing.[35] Ironically, however, research shows that although downsizing results in a short-term stock-price improvement, it's often followed by productivity declines that can take several years to correct.[36] These results are consistent with research showing that when a firm's HR policies focus on enhancing its human capital, there are positive effects on several dimensions of operational performance (such as employee productivity, machine efficiency, and the alignment of product and service capabilities with customers' needs).[37]

The continued success of highly profitable growth companies results largely from skill in recruiting people who fit the organization, adhere to its values, and work toward common goals. Both JetBlue and Southwest Airlines, for example, expend considerable effort making sure that new hires will fit the firm. When hiring new sales and marketing talent, W. L. Gore not only puts prospects through a series of rigorous, behavior-oriented interviews, but usually hires associates from outside the industry. The reason? Gore worries that people from within the industry have picked up habits that aren't consistent with Gore's ways of doing things. John Spencer, who designed an innovative marketing plan for Gore's Glide dental floss, was a former U.S. Navy midshipman and nuclear-submarine engineer— hardly qualifications for getting dental floss to market.

Regardless of the specifics of the strategy, at the end of the day, success depends on hiring the right people and developing and training them in ways that support a firm's strategy. Competitive advantage, therefore, is inextricably bound up in a firm's human capital.[38] Unfortunately, many firms don't seem to appreciate fully the role of people in developing and sustaining a competitive advantage. One study found that only 50 percent

Many companies focus on staffing cuts because employees represent their largest expense. Although Wall Street usually reacts positively to such moves, firms that downsize often experience long-term performance declines.

of managers in firms today believe that human capital matters; only about half of those actually launch human-resource initiatives, and only about half of those stick to those initiatives.[39] Not surprisingly, the remaining one-eighth includes such world-class companies as Southwest Airlines, General Electric, and Microsoft. According to the authors of another recent study, few leaders seem to understand that their "most important asset walks out the door every night."[40]

The importance of having the right people is accentuated in human-capital-intensive industries. If, for instance, a key resource in a firm's industry is access to oil fields, it doesn't have the same concern about resources as a firm whose key resource is access to scientific knowledge. Oil fields can't quit and jump to a competitor, demand higher wages, reject authority, lose motivation, or become dissatisfied with management and coworkers.[41] Consequently, firms in human-capital-intensive industries must develop strategies to reduce the risk of losing the human capital. Besides fostering job satisfaction, companies can develop firm-specific knowledge that's less transferable to other firms. Profit-sharing initiatives encourage valuable people to stay with an employer because they have a stake in any value that they help to create. Adjusting organization structure to eliminate authoritative and mechanistic processes and to accommodate more egalitarian and participative models reduces turnover.[42]

Rewards Although rewards are technically the function of a system, we discuss them in this section because of their obvious relationship to people. An old management adage is *you get what you measure.* In reality, however, this proposition may need to be altered slightly: In the real workplace, it seems that what gets done is that which is rewarded.[43] Some experts grant that although organizational culture may be difficult to change, **reward systems**, which determine the compensation and promotion of an organization's employees, express and reinforce the values and expectations embedded in its culture.[44] Thus, any strategist who wants to get things done must think and act flexibly with regard to compensation and align rewards not only with strategy, but also with other implementation levers.

> **reward system** Bases on which employees are compensated and promoted

The Components of the Reward System Reward systems have two components:

- Performance evaluation and feedback
- Compensation, which can consist of salary, bonuses, stock, stock options, promotions, and even such perquisites as cars and coveted office spaces

Single-business firms usually have one reward system, although the compensation component will probably vary by functional area. Salespeople, for instance, will have incentives based on sales growth, particularly profitable sales growth, whereas employees in production and procurement will have incentives based on quality, cost control, and customer service. Again, rewards are designed to encourage achievement of the organization's strategic objectives, and neither rewards nor penalties apply to performance that's unrelated to those objectives.

Rewards as a Form of Control Like structure, systems, and processes, rewards also serve as a form of control. Rewards necessarily require that performance and behavior targets be stipulated, but their control function can take one of two forms: outcome controls or behavioral controls.

Outcome Controls **Outcome controls** monitor and reward individuals and groups based on whether a measurable goal has been achieved. Such controls are generally preferable when just one or two performance measures (say, return on investment or return on assets) are good gauges of a business's health. Outcome controls are effective when there's little external interference between managerial decision making and business performance. It also helps if little or no coordination with other business units is required, because each unit's people will be seeking to maximize their performance on the targeted measure. Because of this, outcome controls often provide a disincentive for cross-unit collaboration.

> **outcome controls** Practice of tying rewards to narrowly defined financial criteria

Behavioral Controls **Behavioral controls** involve the direct evaluation of managerial decision making, not of the results of managerial decisions. Behavioral controls tie rewards to a broader range of criteria, such as those identified in the balanced scorecard. Behavioral

> **behavioral controls** Practice of tying rewards to criteria other than simply financial performance, such as those broadly identified in the balanced scorecard

controls and commensurate rewards are typically more appropriate when many external and internal factors can affect the relationship between a manager's decisions and organizational performance. They're also appropriate when managers must coordinate resources and capabilities across different business units.

Compensation in the Diversified Firm   Although diversified firms may rely on a single reward system for all business units, reward systems usually vary in order to reflect both overall corporate strategy and the competitive environment and strategy of each business unit. A diversified company like GE, which owns several unrelated businesses, achieves the best results by linking the pay of division managers to the performance of the units that they manage. On the business-unit level, therefore, outcome-based controls and reward systems are aligned with both corporate strategy and organization structure.

However, in a diversified firm that expects divisions to share resources and otherwise cross-subsidize each other, the same sort of compensation would provide *disincentives* for resource sharing. Division managers who are paid solely on the basis of business-unit performance, for instance, might reasonably conclude that it's not in their best interest to subsidize other divisions because doing so may jeopardize their own units' performance and, therefore, their pay.

Conversely, a diversified firm that's trying to generate synergies across business units can increase the likelihood of desired outcomes by linking unit managers' rewards to actual decisions and other balanced-scorecard criteria rather than to individual unit performance.[45] To encourage managers to recognize their own stakes in organizational prospects, rewards often include stock-based incentives or bonuses based on firmwide performance.

To further illustrate how reward systems can affect strategy implementation, let's consider the ways in which incentive systems can impact the realization of postmerger synergies. Many mergers are driven by the belief that two companies can generate net new revenue if they're combined in one firm. But what if compensation systems don't reward employees for sharing knowledge and resources? Obviously, synergies probably won't materialize. Mergers between commercial and investment banks, for instance, are often hampered by incongruent incentive systems.[46] Key employees of commercial banks are typically rewarded for managing relationships, whereas investment bankers are rewarded for doing deals. Paying bankers to do deals is generally at odds with the need for commercial banks to minimize risk and retain customers. Alternatively, investment bankers generally earn bigger bonuses on larger and higher-risk deals.

conceptlink

Recall from Chapter 7 the principle that **synergy** is generated by two processes: (1) sharing **resources** and (2) transferring **capabilities**.

STRATEGIC LEADERSHIP AND STRATEGY IMPLEMENTATION

Strategic leadership plays two critical roles in successful strategy implementation. We're going to highlight them here so that you can incorporate them into your assessment of a strategy's feasibility and include them in your implementation plans. Specifically, strategic leadership is responsible for:

- Making substantive implementation lever and resource-allocation decisions
- Communicating the strategy to key stakeholders

Let's take a closer look at both of these roles.

Decisions About Levers

We hope that it is obvious to you that the choices about which levers to employ and when to employ them do not appear out of thin air as a result of executive action (and sometimes inaction or neglect). The examples you have seen in this chapter, and in other parts of the text, have emphasized the importance of aligning strategy with the appropriate implementation levers. For instance, the executives at Gore are very careful to preserve the organization's deep culture of innovation and the unique levers that reinforce this culture and, ultimately, the firm's strategy and competitive advantage. New ventures by Gore, such as the successful Glide dental floss product, are also launched with all of these key supporting implementation levers in place.

Like strategy-formulation decisions, decisions about levers involve important trade-offs regarding what the firm will and will not do. Misalignment between the levers and the strategy can arise because management has made poor choices about which levers to employ, is employing too simple or too complex a repertoire of levers for the given situation, or the organization or its competitive environment has changed such that the levers need to be changed but have not been. For example, a firm that is small, experiencing the growth stage of its respective arena, and facing little direct competition may be well served by a functional structure, relatively little bureaucracy, and an incentive system that empha-sizes growth and innovation. However, as the firm grows, its operations typically become more complex, including diversification into new product and geographic markets. Similarly, it is likely that it will face growing competition and cost pressures. Top manage-ment should probably be in the process of changing the implementation levers to favor some form of multibusiness or matrix structure and a compensation system that rewards financial accountability and not just growth. Absent such important management choices about which levers to employ, the firm may lose its once-strong competitive foothold.

Decisions About Resource Allocation

A good strategy guides managers in making decisions about the allocation of resources. Again, a good strategy tells managers what the firm should and shouldn't be doing, and thus helps them decide on important tradeoffs—an extremely important function because an organization that tries to be all things to all people by investing equally in every value-chain activity is doomed to mediocrity at best. Top managers must allocate resources in ways that are consistent with the firm's strategy and make the tradeoffs that this entails. Unfortunately, internal interests—whether political, self-serving, or misguided—can sabo-tage effective resource-allocation decisions and undermine even well-crafted strategies.

Both the misallocation of resources and the failure to make hard investment choices often result from a firm basing its resource allocation on that of its competitors. As a result, not only does the firm become less distinctive from a competitive standpoint, but many of the key players in an industry start to look like clones of one another.

Let's look at the ways in which different carriers in the airline industry manage—and don't manage—certain tradeoffs.[47] Exhibit 11.9 summarizes the key areas in which com-mercial airlines make strategic resource-allocation decisions (if you look back at the example of [yellow tail] wine in Chapter 6, you will see a similar picture of the importance

concept link

We point out in Chapter 2 that strategic leaders must master the art of the *tradeoff*. The decision to take one course of action usually eliminates other options. In Chapter 3, we discuss the concept of *tradeoff protection*. Because every tradeoff contributes to a system of interdependent value-chain activities, competitors—who have already invested in their own **value-chain** tradeoffs—may find it hard to imitate those of their rivals.

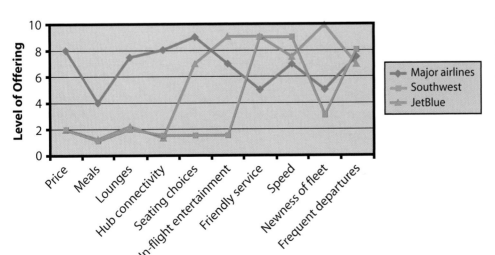

Factors of Competition

Exhibit 11.9 Resource Allocation Decisions in the Airline Industry

Source: Adapted from W. C. Kim and R. Mauborgne, "Charting Your Company's Future," Harvard Business Review 80:6 (2002), 76–82.

of resource-allocation tradeoff choices in the wine industry). As you can see, in the airline industry, the key resource-allocation choices are numerous and range from price for tickets to frequent departure times. Recall that these lines are not meant to depict trends but rather the different patterns of resource-allocation choices made by the respective parties. What's striking is the fact that most major airlines seem to be mimicking each other's resource-allocation decisions. Two exceptions are Southwest and JetBlue, which, as you can tell from their resource-allocation decisions, are following decidedly different strategies. Some have even suggested that for Southwest, with its extensive network of short routes and frequent departures, the greatest competition actually comes from customers' automobiles! JetBlue's management committed itself to allocation decisions that would support the airline's overarching strategy, even when tempted with less expensive options. As a low-cost airline, for instance, JetBlue decided that it needed a modern fleet of new, fuel-efficient aircraft. Used aircraft would have been significantly cheaper (but only in the short run), and management could have rationalized the savings of precious startup capital. Such a shortcut, however, would have been inconsistent with the specific low-cost economic logic of the firm's strategy.

The point to be made here—and which we've made throughout this book—is that competitive advantage goes to those firms who develop unique advantages. Most of the time, such firms develop unique advantages because they make independent resource-allocation decisions instead of mimicking those of everybody else in the industry. Remember, too, that resources and capabilities—especially those that are likely to distinguish a firm from its competitors—are usually scarce. Scarcity takes many forms; a firm, for example, may have a team of brilliant researchers who can only work on so many projects for so many hours in a week. Managers, therefore, must revisit their strategy diamond and make at least two difficult decisions when allocating the firm's resources and capabilities: (1) what to direct at each arena and (2) what to direct to each differentiator.

Communicating with Key Stakeholders About Strategy

concept link

In Chapter 2, we explain in detail the role of *stakeholder analysis* as a **strategic-leadership** function.

From the outset, we've emphasized the interdependence of strategy formulation and implementation. In many ways, because suppliers, customers, and an organization's own managers will ultimately contribute to the strategy's success or failure, the process of communicating with stakeholders about strategy begins in the strategy formulation process itself. It is, therefore, a strategic-leadership function.

In performing this strategic-leadership role, managers must evaluate both the need and the necessary tactics for persuasively communicating a strategy in four different directions: *upward*, *downward*, *across*, and *outward*.[48]

Communicating Upward   Increasingly, firms rely on bottom-up innovation processes that encourage and empower middle-level and division managers to take ownership of strategy formulation and propose new strategies. Such is particularly the case at highly diversified firms, but even fairly focused firms such as W. L. Gore endorse bottom-up processes. Communicating upward means that someone or some group has championed the strategy internally and has succeeded in convincing top management of its merits and feasibility.

Communicating Downward   Communicating downward means enlisting the support of the people who'll be needed to implement the strategy. Too often, managers undertake this task only after a strategy has been set in stone, thereby running the risk of undermining both the strategy and any culture of trust and cooperation that may have existed previously. Starting on the communication process early is the best way to identify and surmount obstacles, and it usually ensures that a management team is working with a common purpose and intensity that will be important when it's time to implement the strategy.

Communicating Across and Outward   The need to communicate across and outward reflects the fact that implementation of a strategy will probably require cooperation from other units of the firm (*across*) and from key external stakeholders, such as material and capital providers, complementors, and customers (*outward*). Internally, for example, the strategy may call for raw materials or services to be provided by another subsidiary; perhaps it depends on sales leads from other units. Recall, for instance, our earlier example of Emageon. Emageon couldn't get hospitals to adopt the leading-edge visualization software that was produced and sold by one subsidiary until its hardware division started cross-selling the software as well. This internal coordination required a champion from the software side to convince managers on the hardware side of the need and benefits of working together.

External constituencies play a comparable role, and a strategy must similarly be communicated to them. Managers can use stakeholder analysis to identify these key players and determine whether suppliers, customers, complementors, and relevant regulatory agencies support the firm's strategy. In the early 1990s, for instance, when IBM first launched its ThinkPad, the product was an unexpected hit with customers. The launch, however, was so successful that IBM's key component suppliers couldn't keep up with IBM's demand, thus costing the company sales on what should have been an even more profitable rollout.

The Three C's of Strategy Communication Just as communicating the strategy to stakeholders is a key factor in successful strategy implementation, so, too, is having the right people in place to communicate it. As one researcher puts it, "The strategy champion must have three C's—contacts, cultural understanding, and credibility."[49]

Contacts Contacts are key because implementing a strategy—particularly one that's dynamic and innovative—often entails some back-channel maneuvering. 3M's Post-it notes, for instance, made it to market only because an enterprising manager convinced internal people to supply clerical and other support staff with experimental versions of the product as a means of demonstrating that there was actually a market. Within Gore, its lattice structure fosters contacts among thousands employees around the globe. Externally, Gore's introduction of Glide through word-of-mouth advertising directed at a small, local drug-store chain and dentists' offices is another example of successful back-channel tactics.

Cultural Understanding Cultural understanding refers to the fact that the people communicating the strategy need to have a rich familiarity with the organization's culture, policies, and procedures. In an earlier example on BGI, you saw how culture provides a screen

IBM's ThinkPad, launched in the early 1990s, was an unexpected hit. However, IBM couldn't produce ThinkPads fast enough to keep up with demand, so potential sales suffered.

for recruitment, retention, and promotion. It may also provide strategy communicators with insights into internal and external network dependencies that may not be obvious but that nonetheless will be essential to the effort to sell across and outward.

Credibility   Needless to say, it helps if strategy communicators are respected by management, peers, and staff, all of whom expect them to present ideas with a good chance of success. Credibility is based on perceptions of trustworthiness, reliability, and integrity. Yet studies indicate that many employees just don't believe or trust their organizational leaders. According to Bruce Katcher, president of Discovery Surveys, a Massachusetts–based firm specializing in employee-opinion and customer-satisfaction surveys and focus groups, just 53 percent "of employees believe the information they receive from senior management."[50] He bases the figure on a review of the company's database of 30,000 respondents from 44 international companies. Closing the credibility gap can be helped by developing regular—at least annual—processes to gauge real employee perceptions about their managers' level of leadership as well as other issues, including morale, obstacles to higher performance, pet peeves, or key irritants. Managers must then pay attention to the findings and demonstrate real commitment to act on them. When actions speak louder than words, employees will have more reason to trust those above them.

IMPLEMENTATION LEVERS IN GLOBAL FIRMS AND DYNAMIC CONTEXTS

As we've observed throughout this text, firms are increasingly facing challenges that are both global and dynamic in nature. In this section, we'll show how implementation levers can be adapted to these particularly important contingencies. We'll also link strategy implementation explicitly to strategy formulation through the staging component of the strategy diamond model.

Implementation Solutions for Global Firms

As you learned in Chapter 8, two critical needs confront firms in implementing global strategies: the need for *efficiency* and the need for *local responsiveness*.[51] In this section, we want to stress their role in terms of implementation levers and their function in executing globalization strategies. Paralleling the strategy research on global strategy, research has found that firms deeply involved in international business adopt one of four structural forms in the effort to manage the tension between the need for efficiency and the need for local responsiveness.[52] As we'll see, most of these forms place more emphasis on one or the other of these two competing forces and build on the general understanding of structure you have amassed thus far from this chapter. These four structural solutions accommodate the four international-strategy configurations discussed in Chapter 8: multinational, international, global, and transnational. Each configuration is characterized by different structures, systems, and processes.

Structure for Multinational Configurations
This structural solution resembles a decentralized federation, much like the relationship between the U.S. federal government and the 50 state governments. Assets and resources are decentralized, and foreign offices are given the authority to respond to local needs when they differ from those of the home market. Control and coordination are managed primarily through the interactions of home-office corporate executives and overseas executives, who are usually home-country managers who've been dispatched to run foreign offices.

From the perspective of top management, the corporation is a portfolio of relatively independent businesses located around the globe. SAP, for example, adhered to this model for much of the 1990s, until it determined that it fostered costly duplications of effort across markets and inadequate coordination among units across borders. Indeed, because SAP's customers were global firms with better coordination and integration than SAP itself, many of them managed to get SAP to compete against itself for new system sales.

Nestlé, for instance, would get bids from SAP U.S. and SAP U.K. without informing either party that they were actually bidding against one another.

Structure for International Configurations The structure supporting an international strategy reveals an organization that is a coordinated group of federations over which more administrative control is exerted by home-country headquarters. For reasons of both efficiency and strategy, firms like SAP typically evolve into this structure. SAP itself, for example, adopted it at the end of the 1990s when it realized that its customers were taking advantage of its multinational structure.

Under this model, although resources, assets, and responsibilities are delegated to foreign offices, additional control—usually in the form of more formal management systems, such as centralized planning and budgeting—is exercised centrally. This control facilitates global account management, so that services provided to global clients can be made uniform in terms of quality and price. As a rule, top management regards overseas operations as appendages to the domestic firm. Local units, therefore, are highly dependent on home-office coordination of resource allocation, knowledge sharing, and decision approval.

Structure for Global Configurations Ideally, firms adopting a global configuration have a structure that is based on the centralization of assets, resources, and responsibilities. Foreign offices are used to access customers, but demand is filled by centralized production. This form of organization was pioneered by firms such as Ford, which exported standardized products around the globe, and was popular among Japanese companies undertaking globalization in the 1970s and 1980s. The global configuration affords much less autonomy to foreign offices or subsidiaries than either the multinational or international models. Operational control is tight and most decisions centralized. Top management views foreign operations as pipelines for distributing products to a global, but homogeneous, marketplace.

Structure for Transnational Configurations Each of the three preceding organizational models responds in a different strategic fashion to the challenge of balancing the two fundamental demands of managing across borders. The global configuration, for example, is clearly designed to achieve maximum efficiencies, largely through scale economies derived from centralized production. Because decisions and resources are controlled locally, the multinational form is well suited to respond to local needs. The international model attempts to meet local needs while retaining central control. The transnational model is designed to accommodate both demands.

The structure for transnational configurations (or *transnationals*, for short) was designed to achieve not only efficiency and local responsiveness but innovation as well. Its structural characteristics enable firms—at least those that are able to manage it—to achieve multidimensional strategic objectives. The key functions in this multidimensional strategy are *dispersion*, *specialization*, and *interdependence*. Resources and capabilities are dispersed to local units, and a networked control system is designed to achieve both coordination and cooperation. Because geographically dispersed organizational units are strategically interdependent, large flows of products, resources, and personnel, as well as value-chain activities, are channeled through the structure. To some extent, McDonald's, which features both standard and locally tailored menu items at outlets around the globe, depends on this structure. The structure fits with McDonald's transnational strategy and affords the global food company greater flexibility in adapting to local tastes while enabling it at the same time to exploit the global economies of scale that it enjoys by virtue of its size and geographic breadth.

People and Rewards Solutions in Global Firms As firms expand globally, they face the critical issue of how to find and reward managers. On the one hand, using local managers can enhance a firm's understanding of local markets. On the other hand, using home-country managers strengthens the relationship between the foreign subsidiary and the parent company.

Naturally, operating subsidiaries in culturally distant locations gives rise to a great deal of uncertainty. Research suggests that a company's policy for finding and rewarding foreign managerial staff can have a significant bearing on its performance. For instance, multinationals that use overseas management positions as a training ground for future executives of the parent significantly outperform those that allow senior managers to ascend to the top ranks without spending time in overseas posts.[53]

The performance of foreign subsidiaries may be affected when parent-country nationals, or expatriates, are sent to manage them. When multinationals have subsidiaries in culturally distant locations (as opposed to those that are just geographically distant), costs and risks increase because of a so-called *information-asymmetry* problem: Onsite overseas information may not be readily available to the parent company.[54] When a multinational relies more on parent-country nationals than local managers, the information-asymmetry problem gradually diminishes: As subsidiaries gain experience in conducting transactions with home-country nationals, there's less need for deploying expatriates. Indeed, research shows that when a multinational firm staffs a culturally distant foreign subsidiary with parent-country managers, it improves subsidiary performance, largely because it's easier to exercise cultural control and enhances the transfer of firm-specific resources from the parent to the subsidiary.[55]

Apparently, however, this positive effect decreases over time because host-country nationals not only acquire knowledge and skills from expatriate managers, but also adopt the shared values of the parent company. Not surprisingly, given the high cost of managing an expatriate workforce (not to mention the high percentage of expatriate failure), reliance on expatriates is declining.

Implementation Levers in Dynamic Contexts

We observed early in this text that, because competitive pressures are compounded in dynamic, "high-velocity" industries, companies' strategies necessarily grow more complex. Moreover, the difficulties in *implementing* strategies in such industries are an order of magnitude more challenging than those of implementing strategies in relatively stable industries. As we've also seen, the task is becoming even more complex and difficult because dynamic markets are increasingly becoming global markets as well. Consider, for instance, the threat to a firm in a global industry that needs to develop or adopt a radically new technology in order to survive industry evolution. In Chapter 6 we described a special problem known as the innovator's dilemma—a situation where new entrants innovate in low-end, unattractive segments of the market that leaders tend to overlook because margins are apparently lower there, only to have those new entrants migrate into the more profitable segments with lower cost structures and increasingly popular products.[56] Firms have developed several structural adaptations to deal with the problems of implementing strategies in dynamic contexts, and in this section, we'll examine two of the most effective adaptations: the *ambidextrous organization* and the use of *patching* among diversified firms.

The Ambidextrous Organization

Even a firm that's successful at executing a strategy can face a problem as its industry becomes well established: In particular, it's difficult to retain market leadership when a new disruptive technology (product or process) is pioneered and introduced by another firm. The incumbent also faces a disadvantage because it invests in order to sustain an advantage, not (like the new entrant) to destroy one.

Incremental Change Versus Radical Innovation: Revisiting the Innovator's Dilemma
This is the essence of the innovator's dilemma, and despite leaders who are perfectly capable of recognizing the problem, it often persists because of structural deficiencies among many organizations. When, for example, one division of a leading incumbent tries to pioneer its own version of disruptive technology, the rest of the organization may resist. Why? Perhaps because the status quo is perceived to be in the best interests of managers and employees. Or perhaps submerged but strong facets of the organizational culture favor the continued influence of large established divisions.

concept link

Such a situation, as we observe in Chapter 6, reflects a "turbulent" or "hypercompetitive" market—one characterized by frequent, bold, dynamic moves on the part of competitors, especially new entrants. We also explain the importance of understanding **implementation levers** in such *dynamic contexts*. Recall, too, from Chapter 4 the distinction between *discontinuous* and incremental changes and the discussion of why *new entrants* in a market often initiate the former.

Granted, many firms are skilled at introducing refinements into their current product lines. Usually such organizations don't resist moderate innovation because it's perceived as a means of sustaining or improving current competitive positions. At the same time, however, the same firms may face monumental obstacles when they try to introduce *radical* changes or offer products that require disruptive technologies. In that case, of course, they're faced with a paradoxical problem: To flourish in the long run, they must exploit existing advantages and explore innovations that will probably alter the industry significantly in the future. In other words, if a firm wants to sustain long-term competitiveness in a dynamic context (and most, of course, do), it must learn to integrate both incremental changes and radical innovations.

The **ambidextrous structure** is one response to this problem.[57] In fact, the idea evolved from studies of how firms dealt with the problem of simultaneously integrating two types of innovations:

ambidextrous structure
Organizational structure for dynamic contexts in which project teams are organized as structurally independent units and encouraged to develop their own structures, systems, and processes

- *Incremental innovations* are those that make small improvements in existing products and operations and that are aimed at existing customers.

- *Discontinuous innovations* are those that make radical advances that may alter the basis of competition in an industry and that are aimed at new customers.[58]

Four Structures for Handling Innovation   Researchers identified four basic forms of organization among the companies studied:

- A functional form in which innovation efforts are completely integrated into an existing organization structure.

- A cross-functional or matrix-style form in which groups of people from established organizational divisions are formed to work outside the functional hierarchy.

- A form in which teams or units, though nominally independent and working outside the established hierarchy, are limited in their independence and relatively unsupported by the organizational hierarchy.

- An "ambidextrous" form in which project teams focusing on radical improvements are organized as structurally independent units and encouraged to develop their own structures, systems, and processes. As you can see in Exhibit 11.10 on page 330, these semiautonomous units may be integrated into the organizational hierarchy only at the senior-management level.

Researchers found that the ambidextrous structure was quite effective in facilitating the integration of radical innovations; 93 percent of radical innovations were launched by firms characterized as ambidextrous. Firms that pursued radical innovation through autonomous units bound to the organizational hierarchy only through senior management had very high success rates for launching new products or operations. Conversely, firms trying to achieve radical innovation within the existing corporate hierarchy found that their efforts were often stymied. Finally, the ambidextrous form also fostered innovations that were initiated under some other organizational form and only later moved into an ambidextrous structure.

Among other things, these findings reveal just how difficult it is for firms to compete in dynamic industry environments that require not only constant incremental innovations, but periodic radical innovations as well. The "ambidextrous" allows for the simultaneous maintenance of the status quo (incremental business improvements made through conventional organizational units) and proactive preparation for future industry-wide alterations (radical innovation made through units that are unencumbered by existing organizational practices and allowed to implement strategies consistent with the requirements of competitive conditions).

Diversified Firms in Dynamic Markets: Patching   A multidivisional firm operating in diverse product markets can create new synergies by actively managing the structure of its corporate portfolio through a process known as *patching*. **Patching** is the process of regularly remapping businesses in accordance with changing market conditions and restitching them into new internal business structures.[59] It can mean combining, splitting, or transferring units or exiting businesses or adding new ones. Patching is particularly effective in dynamic markets because it enables managers to exploit the best business

patching Process of remapping businesses in accordance with changing market conditions and restitching them into new internal business structures

Exhibit 11.10   The Ambidextrous Organization

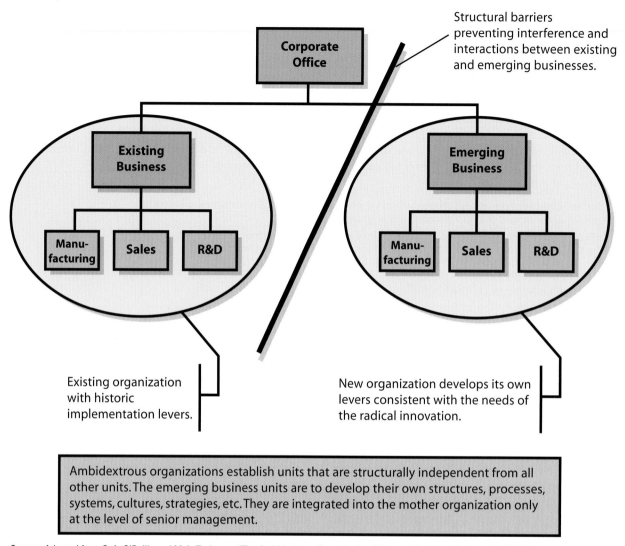

Structural barriers preventing interference and interactions between existing and emerging businesses.

Existing organization with historic implementation levers.

New organization develops its own levers consistent with the needs of the radical innovation.

Ambidextrous organizations establish units that are structurally independent from all other units. The emerging business units are to develop their own structures, processes, systems, cultures, strategies, etc. They are integrated into the mother organization only at the level of senior management.

Source: Adapted from C. A. O'Reilly and M. L. Tushman, "The Ambidextrous Organization," Harvard Business Review *82:4 (2004), 74–81.*

opportunities while bypassing less promising ones. However, as you can imagine, patching is very complex to manage and requires a culture and workforce that is action oriented and flexible, such as the one described at BGI.

Here's an example of patching at work. Originally, Hewlett-Packard's laser-printing business was a small startup operation with only modest growth expectations. Shortly after launch, however, sales climbed to 10 times the expected level (100,000 units per month instead of the forecasted 10,000). As new applications for related technologies, such as the ink-jet printer, emerged, management stripped them away from the laser-printer business and patched them onto other business units. This technique of patching units not only allowed managers in the laser-printer unit to focus on their core growth business but ensconced the ink-jet business in a unit where it could get the support it needed to get off the ground, develop into a growth business, and become a major source of cash flow. In this case, patching required the transfer not only of a businesses but of related resources and personnel as well.

With patching, therefore, structure is intentionally altered so that managers can better maintain focus on core and growth businesses while seeding and protecting new opportunities. Because it requires managers to view organizational structure as flexible and contingent, they tend not to fret about getting a new structure exactly right. In addition, although patching is a proactive tool, it usually involves relatively small and incremental changes. Change, however, is ongoing, as managers constantly search for new combinations. To make patching work, firms need to adjust internal systems so that when a business is detached from one division and restitched elsewhere, company-wide systems don't require extensive modification. Compensation systems, for instance, need to be fairly consistent across organizational borders.

Finally, we should note some key differences between patching and the ambidextrous organizational structure. Patching is a tool that helps diversified firms operate in multiple product or geographic markets. It doesn't involve radical technologies, but rather leverages either existing businesses or new but related businesses. It works when systems are consistent across the organization. In contrast, the ambidextrous organization is designed to enable radically new businesses to develop unencumbered by existing structures and processes.

Linking Strategy Implementation to Staging

Before wrapping up this chapter, we'd like to underscore the relationship between implementation levers and a specific facet of strategy formulation. Recall that the staging element of the strategy diamond refers to the timing and pacing of strategic moves. Staging decisions typically depend on available resources—resources that include structures, systems and processes, and people and rewards. From the opening vignette on Gore, you gained some insight into how the firm coupled a unique resource base—its knowledge and intellectual property relating to Teflon—with the implementation levers necessary to launch new and highly innovative ventures. Thus, management of the implementation process should anticipate the staging objectives of the strategy.

More generally, it would be a rare case in which a change in strategy did not have implications for implementation. Consider, for instance, a firm that's considering expansion into foreign markets. It can achieve this strategic goal through a variety of vehicles, including exporting, alliances or acquisitions, and the establishment of foreign offices from which to conduct value-chain activities. If international staging is an explicit component of the firm's strategy, then managers must start modifying other implementation levers. In other words, they must determine whether the firm has the appropriate structure, systems, human capital, expertise, and culture to support its evolution into a global competitor. If, for example, the vehicle of choice calls for alliances or acquisitions, then the related skills and capabilities must be acquired as well. If the vehicle is exporting, the firm will need to acquire people who understand customer demands and distribution channels in foreign markets.

SUMMARY

1. Understand the interdependence between strategy formulation and implementation. Strategy formulation and implementation are interrelated. The introductory section of the chapter showed you the various ways in which formulation and implementation are interrelated and provided you with an overarching model for thinking about how to translate an abstract strategy into concrete action. You also learned that the relationship between formulation and implementation is not necessarily a linear one. In some cases, the itera-

tive evolution of strategy is advantageous and desirable. The section closed with a discussion of why implementation efforts can and often do fail. Organizational culture can be one barrier to (or facilitator of) to effective strategy execution and strategic change.

2. Demonstrate how to use organizational structure as a strategy implementation lever. Organizational structure exists to perform two essential functions within the organization: ensuring control and coordinating the efforts of managers and employees. As control and coordination become more difficult, firms generally modify their structure to improve control and coordination. Popular forms of organizing firm structure include the functional, divisional, matrix, and network forms. The structure chosen should be consistent with the firm's strategy. For instance, the more diversified the firm, the more the structure will need to accommodate coordination. The more focused the firm is in a single business, or in several unrelated businesses, the more the structure should emphasize control.

3. Design systems and processes as strategy implementation levers.
Formal processes and procedures used by a firm should support the execution of strategy. Information systems are the most common systems, but all systems should be considered for their alignment with strategy (and other implementation levers). For instance, management control, performance and rewards, budgeting, quality, planning, distribution, client management, and resource allocation are all managed by systems. Systems can affect what people pay attention to and what information they have access to.

4. Understand the roles of people and rewards as implementation levers.
For a strategy to succeed, a firm needs the right people with the right experiences and competencies. As a result, recruitment, selection, and training are critical to strategy implementation. Because human resources, or staffing issues, are often large sources of operating costs, too much focus may be placed on reducing the staffing costs. Investments in human resource systems have positive effects on multiple dimensions of firm performance. The importance of people is even more important in high-human-capital industries. Rewards are an important implementation lever. They reflect the degree to which a firm employs outcome versus behavioral controls. Rewards are composed of both performance evaluation and feedback and incentives, such as compensation and promotion. Ultimately, rewards enable the firm to get the right people to do the right things for the firm, such that it can achieve its goals and objectives.

5. Explain the dual roles that strategic leadership plays in strategy implementation.
This section showed you that strategy implementation is much more than simply putting the right levers into place. The levers are important, but they must also be complemented by strategic-leadership actions. The two actions we emphasized were decisions about resource allocation and levers and communicating the strategy to stakeholders. The resources and capabilities that differentiate a firm from its competitors are by definition scarce. Strategic leadership shows its mettle by making difficult tradeoffs in terms of the levers chosen and where and where not to deploy scarce resources. Communicating the strategy to stakeholders requires that managers promote and get strategic buy-in from top management, lower-level workers, other key organizational units, and external stakeholders, such as suppliers, customers, and complementors.

6. Understand how global and dynamic contexts affect the use of implementation levers.
As a firm becomes more global, it faces contradictory needs for efficiency and local responsiveness. Depending on the primacy of these two demands, four structural solutions are available: multinational, international, global, and transnational. The solution for transnationals is the most complex; transnationals attempt to simultaneously achieve global efficiency and maximum local responsiveness. As in global contexts, coordination and control are made more difficult in dynamic contexts. In addition, being able to protect potentially radical innovations can be accommodated through the ambidextrous structure. Diversified firms in high-velocity environments can increase the likelihood of synergies by using patching techniques, which essentially assumes that the organizational structure is flexible and allows for the constant reconfiguration of business units. This enables managers to remain focused on high-volume businesses by placing high-potential-growth businesses in units that can better exploit these opportunities. This section closed by showing you how to link formulation and implementation through the staging component of the strategy diamond.

KEY TERMS

ambidextrous structure, 329	functional structure, 311	multidivisional structure, 311	patching, 329
balanced scorecard, 315	implementation levers, 309	network structure, 314	reward system, 321
behavioral controls, 321	knowing-doing gap, 306	organizational structure, 309	
culture, 307	matrix structure, 313	outcome controls, 321	

REVIEW QUESTIONS

1. What is strategy implementation?

2. How are formulation and implementation related?

3. What are the basic forms of organizational structure? When is each appropriate?

4. What are some common systems and processes that are relevant to strategy implementation?

5. How are people relevant to strategy formulation and implementation?

6. How can rewards affect strategy?

7. What are the roles of strategic leadership in successful strategy implementation?

8. How does globalization affect organization structure?

9. What are organizational solutions to the problems caused by dynamic environments?

10. What component of the strategy diamond maps most closely to issues related to strategy implementation?

How Would you Do That?

1. In the box entitled "How Would *You* Do That? 11.1," you learned how SAP America responded to performance problems primarily through changes in strategy implementation. Find one or two firms that were once high flyers but that have recently fallen on hard times. Are these hard times primarily a function of a flawed strategy, flawed strategy implementation, or both? Using SAP as an example, what changes would you suggest in terms of implementation?

2. The example of the NUWC in the box entitled "How Would *You* Do That? 11.2" demonstrated the strategy-mapping process and how to develop a balanced scorecard. Review Exhibits 11.7 and 11.8 and generate suggestions for specific objectives, measures, targets, and initiatives that would complete NUWC's use of the scorecard. If you prefer using the scorecard with a for-profit firm then apply the framework from scratch to a firm of your choosing.

GROUP ACTIVITIES

1. Apply the concepts of strategy formulation and implementation to your college experience. What was your objective in going to college? When did your strategy for achieving this objective emerge? Has it ever changed? How would you adapt the implementation levers and strategic leadership roles to evaluate how well you have implemented your strategy? What is your overall personal evaluation?

2. Refer to the opening case on Gore. Assume that, for reasons of estate planning, the Gore family (75 percent owners of the company) decided to take the company public through an IPO. What would be the effect on the firm's strategy and implementation practices if this were to happen? What, if anything, would need to change?

ENDNOTES

1. www.gore.com/en_xx/aboutus/timeline/index.html (accessed November 16, 2005); D. Anfuso, "Gore Values Shape W. L. Gore's Innovative Culture," *Workforce* 78:3 (1999), 48–53; www.hoovers.com.

2. K. R. Andrews, *The Concept of Corporate Strategy* (Homewood, IL: Irwin, 1987); *The Strategy Execution Imperative: Leading Practices for Implementing Strategic Initiatives* (Corporate Executive Board, 2001); C. M. Christensen, "Making Strategy: Learning by Doing," *Harvard Business Review* 75:6 (1997), 141–156.

3. D. Hambrick and A. Cannella, "Strategy Implementation as Substance and Selling," *Academy of Management Executive* 3:4 (1989), 278–285.

4. P. C. Judge, "How Will Your Company Adapt?" *Fast Company* 128 (2001); S. Ellison, "P&G Is to Buy Glide Dental Floss, A Popular Brand," *Wall Street Journal*, September 17, 2003, A19.

5. M. Porter, "Know Your Place: How to Assess the Attractiveness of Your Industry and Your Company's Position in It," *Inc.*, September 1991, 90.

6. P. F. Drucker, *The Practice of Management* (New York: HarperCollins, 1954), 352–353.

7. R. Ruggles, "The State of the Notion: Knowledge Management in Practice," *California Management Review* 40 (1998), 82–83.

8. J. Pfeffer and R. I. Sutton, *The Knowing-Doing Gap* (Boston: Harvard Business School Press, 2000).

9. J. R. Kotter and J. L. Heskett, *Corporate Culture and Performance* (New York: Free Press, 1992); C. A. O'Reilly and J. A. Chatman, "Culture as Social Control: Corporations, Culture and Commitment," in B. M. Staw and L. L. Cummings, eds., *Research in Organizational Behavior* 18 (Greenwich, CT: JAI Press, 1996), 157–200; J. B. Sønrensen, "The Strength of Corporate Culture and the Reliability of Firm Performance," *Administrative Science Quarterly* 47 (2002), 70–91.

10. Kotter and Heskett, *Corporate Culture and Performance.*

11. Sønrensen, "The Strength of Corporate Culture and the Reliability of Firm Performance."

12. R. S. Burt, S. M. Gabbay, G. Holt, and P. Moran, "Contingent Organization as a Network Theory: The Culture Performance Contingency Function," *Acta Sociologica* 37 (1994), 345–370; Sønrensen, "The Strength of Corporate Culture and the Reliability of Firm Performance."

13. A. Slywotzky and D. Nadler, "The Strategy Is the Structure," *Harvard Business Review* 82:2 (2004), 16.

14. SAP Harvard Business School Case, SAP America 9-397-067, December 3, 1996.

15. Hambrick and Cannella, "Strategy Implementation as Substance and Selling," 278.

16. A. Chandler, *Strategy and Structure* (Cambridge, MA: MIT Press, 1962).

17. R. L. Daft, *Management*, 6th ed. (New York: Southwestern, 2003).

18. L. G. Hrebiniak and W. Joyce, *Implementing Strategy* (New York: MacMillan, 1984).

19. Chandler, *Strategy and Structure.*

20. Slywotzky and Nadler, "The Strategy Is the Structure," 16.

21. R. A. Burgelman, "Fading Memories: A Process Theory of Strategic Business Exit in Dynamic Environments," *Administrative Science Quarterly* 39 (1994), 24–56.

22. www.platypustech.com (accessed July 15, 2005).

23. www.emageon.com (accessed July 15, 2005).

24. C. K. Bart and M. C. Baetz, "The Relationship Between Mission Statements and Firm Performance: An Exploratory Study," *Journal of Management Studies* 35:6 (1998), 823–853.

25. W. G. Sanders and M. A. Carpenter, "Strategic Satisficing? A Behavioral-Agency Perspective on Stock Repurchase Announcements," *Academy of Management Journal* 46 (2003), 160–178.

26. G. Reilly and R. Reilly, "Using a Measure Network to Understand and Deliver Value," *Journal of Cost Management* 14:6 (2000), 5–14; R. Kaplan and D. Norton, *The Strategy-Focused Organization* (Watertown, MA: Harvard Business School Press, 2001).

27. "The Balanced Scorecard's Lessons for Managers," *Harvard Management Update*, October 2000, 4–5.

28. R. Simons, *Levers of Control: How Managers Use Innovative Control Systems* (Boston: Harvard Business School Press, 1995); M. J. Epstein and J. F. Manzoni, "The Balanced Scorecard & Tableau de Bord: A Global Perspective on Translating Strategy into Action," INSEAD Working Paper 97/63/AC/SM (1997).

29. E. Schonfeld, "Baby Bills," *Business 2.0* 4:9 (2003), 76–84.

30. Quote from BGI's head of human resources, Garret Bouton, in J. Pfeffer and R. I. Sutton, *The Knowing-Doing Gap*, 227.

31. J. Collins, "Level 5 Leadership," *Harvard Business Review* July–August (2001), 66–76.

32. J. Bradach, *Organizational Alignment: The 7-S Model* (Boston: Harvard Business School Publishing, 1996).

33. C. K. Prahalad and G. Hamel, "The Core Competence of the Corporation," *Harvard Business Review* 79:1 (1990), 1–14; R. Nelson and S. Winter, *An Evolutionary Theory of Economic Change* (Cambridge, MA: Harvard University Press, 1982); D. J. Teece, G. Pisano, and A. Shuen, "Dynamic Capabilities and Strategic Management," *Strategic Management Journal* 18 (1997), 509–534; K. M. Eisenhardt and J. A. Martin, "Dynamic Capabilities: What Are They?" *Strategic Management Journal* 21 (2000), 1105–1121.

34. B. Becker and B. Gerhart, "The Impact of Human Resource Management on Organizational Performance: Progress and Prospects," *Academy of Management Journal* 39 (1996), 779–802.

35. W. N. Davidson III, D. L. Worrell, and J. B. Fox, "Early Retirement Programs and Firm Performance," *Academy of Management Journal* 39 (1996), 970–985.

36. C. Chadwick, L. W. Hunter, and S. M. Walston, "The Effects of Downsizing Practices on Hospital Performance," *Strategic Management Journal* 25:5 (2004), 405–428.

37. M. A. Youndt, S. A. Snell, J. W. Dean Jr., and D. P. Lepak, "Human Resource Management, Manufacturing Strategy, and Firm Performance," *Academy of Management Journal* 39 (1996), 836–866.

38. See J. B. Barney and P. M. Wright, "On Becoming a Strategic Partner: The Role of Human Resources in Gaining Competitive Advantage," *Human Resource Management* 37 (1998), 31–46; J. Pfeffer, *Competitive Advantage Through People* (Boston: Harvard Business School Press, 1994).

39. J. Pfeffer, *The Human Equation* (Boston: Harvard Business School Press, 1998).

40. F. Luthans and C. M. Yousseff, "Human, Social, and Now Positive Psychological Capital Management: Investing in People for Competitive Advantage," *Organization Dynamics* 33:2 (2004), 143–160.

41. R. W. Coff, "Human Assets and Management Dilemmas: Coping with Hazards on the Road to Resource-Based Theory," *Academy of Management Review* 22 (1997), 374–402.

42. See Coff, "Human Assets and Management Dilemmas."

43. B. Gerhart and S. Rynes, *Compensation* (Beverly Hills, CA: Sage Publications, 2003).

44. J. Kerr and J. Slocum, "Managing Corporate Culture Through Reward Systems," *Academy of Management Executive* 1:2 (1987), 99–108.

45. C. W. L. Hill, M. A. Hitt, and R. E. Hoskisson, "Cooperative Versus Competitive Structures in Related and Unrelated Diversified Firms," *Organization Science* 3 (1992), 501–521.

46. CIBC Corporate and Investment Banking (A). Harvard Business School Publishing, 1999.

47. Adapted from W. C. Kim and R. Mauborgne, "Charting Your Company's Future," *Harvard Business Review* 80:6 (2002), 76–82.

48. Hambrick and Cannella, "Strategy Implementation as Substance and Selling," 278–285.

49. N. Wreden, "Executive Champions: The Vital Link Between Strategy Formulation and Implementation," *Harvard Management Update* 7:9 (2002), 3–5.

50. www.clemmer.net/excerpts/pf_credibility.html (accessed October 25, 2005).

51. The information in this section draws heavily upon the work of Christopher Bartlett and Sumantra Ghoshal, *Managing Across Borders: The Transnational Solution* (Boston: Harvard Business School Press, 1989).

52. Bartlett and Ghoshal, *Managing Across Borders.*

53. M. A. Carpenter, W. G. Sanders, and H. B. Gregersen, "Bundling Human Capital with Organizational Context: The Impact of International Assignment Experience on Multinational Firm Performance and CEO Pay," *Academy of Management Journal* 44 (2001), 493–511.

54. Y. Gong, "Subsidiary Staffing in Multinational Enterprises: Agency, Resources, and Performance," *Academy of Management Journal* 46 (2003), 728–739.

55. Gong, "Subsidiary Staffing in Multinational Enterprises."

56. C. Christensen, *The Innovator's Dilemma* (Boston: Harvard Business School Press, 1997).

57. C. A. O'Reilly and M. L. Tushman, "The Ambidextrous Organization," *Harvard Business Review* 82:4 (May–June 2004), 74–81.

58. For details of this study, see O'Reilly and Tushman, "The Ambidextrous Organization."

59. This section draws heavily on K. M. Eisenhardt and S. L. Brown, "Patching: Restitching Business Portfolios in Dynamic Markets," *Harvard Business Review* 77:3 (1999), 72–82.

After studying this chapter, you should be able to:

1. Define *new ventures*, *initial public offerings (IPOs)*, and *corporate renewal* and explain how they are related to strategic management.

2. Understand entrepreneurship and the entrepreneurial process.

3. Describe the steps involved in new-venture creation and corporate new venturing.

4. Map out the stages leading up to an IPO.

5. Understand the external and internal causes of organizational failure.

6. Outline an action plan for strategic change and corporate renewal.

► 1987
Urban Juice & Soda Co. is born in Vancouver, Canada, after founder Peter van Stolk, a former ski instructor, sees a market opportunity for "alternative" soft drinks.

► 2000
Rechristened "Jones Soda," the company sets up shop in Seattle and embarks on an "alternative" distribution strategy to sell its offbeat beverages.

ENTREPRENEURSHIP AT JONES SODA COMPANY

Building a company around a product like turkey-and-gravy-flavored soda sounds like a sure-fire route to failure—particularly in an industry known for the hypercompetitive behavior of heavyweights, like Pepsi and Coke.[1] Often, however, counterintuitive leadoff products are the stuff that successful new ventures are made of, and the Thanksgiving-themed soda is just one of many unique products offered by innovative (and profitable) Seattle-based Jones Soda Co. According to *Beverage Digest*, although Jones currently enjoys less than a 1-percent market share, sales are growing rapidly in the United States, Canada, and Western Europe.

Founded in Vancouver, Canada, by Peter van Stolk, Jones Soda started out in the early 1990s as Urban Juice & Soda Co. Originally the western Canadian distributor of such successful lines as Just Pik't

▶ 2004
Jones Soda products get picked up by Starbucks and continue to find their way into major restaurant, convenience store, and grocery chains.

▶ 2005 and Beyond
Jones Soda introduces a new line of organic teas. Founder Peter van Stolk continues to think creatively and think big.

1995   2000

Juices, Arizona Iced Tea, and Thomas Kemper sodas, by 1994 Urban was firmly established as a full-line beverage distributor with a reputation for picking winners. Armed with a strategy for producing and selling its own line of sodas, the company rechristened itself Jones Soda and moved to Seattle in 2000.

Jones Soda's initial distribution strategy was as unconventional as its product line. Jones Soda placed coolers emblazoned with its signature flame logo in such unique venues as skate, surf, and snowboarding shops; tattoo and piercing parlors; fashion and national retail clothing outlets; and music stores. The next step in its distribution strategy called for an up-and-down-the-street assault on the marketplace by placing products in convenience and food stores. As sales volume increased, Jones moved up to larger chain stores such as Starbucks, Panera Bread, Barnes & Noble, Safeway, Albertson's, and 7-Eleven.

Beyond its bootstrap-distribution strategy, Jones has relied on a number of other unique marketing tactics, all of which reflect the firm's concept of soda as a fashion statement. To this end, Jones invites customers to submit suggestions for new flavors, photos to go on labels, and pithy messages to be printed inside bottle caps. The objective is to make customers feel that the brand belongs to them. The most recent innovation consists of 12 packs with customized labels.

The premise underlying Jones's business strategy is that the commercial success of any alternative brand will, in large part, be determined by its brand image. And because beverages in the alternative category have limited life cycles, Jones believes that it must engage in an ongoing process of creating new brands, products, and product extensions for its long-term success.

Since 1997, Jones has operated exclusively as a beverage manufacturer and marketer of its own brands. In August 1999, it created a new brand, Jones WhoopAss, an energy drink. In April 2001, the company introduced Jones Juice, a product extension of Jones Soda, which was subsequently renamed Jones Naturals. In November 2001, it created Jones Energy, another energy drink. In February 2005, it announced the upcoming launch of Jones Organic Teas, which will have 60 calories per serving and will be sweetened with organic cane sugar. Jones Organics will come in 14-ounce proprietary clear glass bottles with a fruit design on the front label.

Jones uses a lean organizational structure. It focuses on developing and marketing new products and outsources other critical value-chain activities. Jones uses contract packers to prepare, bottle, and package its products. In addition, it uses independent trucking companies to ship product from the contract packers to independent warehouses. From these independent warehouses, Jones's products are delivered by independent trucking companies to distributors. Distributors sell and deliver products either to subdistributors or directly to retail outlets, and distributors and subdistributors are responsible for stocking retailers' shelves with Jones's products.

In 2001 and 2002, Jones experienced a significant blow that required it to reevaluate its strategy, restructure the firm, and refocus on core markets. First, a couple of key distributors went bankrupt, disrupting the availability of Jones's product. As a result, Jones evaluated its prospects in each geographic territory in North America and determined that margins could be improved by abandoning the northeastern and southeastern U.S markets. As a result, and as shown in Exhibit 12.1, Jones's sales dipped in 2002. However, this restructuring was instrumental in pushing the company back into profitability.

Although still a relatively small company, with only $27 million in sales, industry observers give van Stolk's company a good shot at further rapid growth. If they're right, Jones may be ripe for either a secondary offering of equity (the company's shares are traded over the counter [OTC] under the symbol JSDA) or an acquisition by a larger consumer-products company (a position similar to that of Snapple when it was acquired by Quaker Oats in 1994). Large firms often look to small innovative companies as a source of innovation and potential corporate renewal. When asked about the future of Jones Soda, van Stolk, ever the entrepreneur, quips, "I think it will be a big company like Microsoft or Starbucks someday, but not necessarily in soda." ∎

	2004	2003	2002	2001
Sales ($ millions)	$27.5	$20.1	$18.6	$23.3
Net income ($ millions)	1.3	0.3	(1.2)	(1.7)
Employees	51			
Headquarters	Seattle, Washington			
Top management team	Peter van Stolk, CEO Jennifer Cue, COO & CFO			

Exhibit 12.1 Jones Soda at a Glance

Sources: www.jonessoda.com (accessed November 17, 2005); www.hoovers.com (accessed November 17, 2005).

FROM NEW-VENTURE CREATION TO CORPORATE RENEWAL

Why are we going to discuss entrepreneurship and turnaround management (otherwise known as *corporate renewal*) in the same chapter? Throughout this text, we've described companies of various ages, sizes, and competitive positions. In this chapter, we want to focus on three particularly important phases or stages that can punctuate the life cycle of a firm:

- The birth of new ventures
- The transition from new venture to a more established firm, either as a public company via an initial public offering (IPO) or the incorporation of more professional management
- The rescue of established ventures

Not surprisingly, strategic management is critical to firms in all of three of these phases. At first glance, it may seem that these three stages are far removed from one another, but by the end of this chapter, we will show that the entrepreneurial process is an important common thread that runs through all of them. Managers of startups, for example, must learn firsthand what it takes to develop and grow a business, whereas managers of distressed firms must recover the entrepreneurial orientation from which the firm originally emerged. This approach will demonstrate why what you've learned about strategy is equally applicable to both small and large firms as well as new and old ones.

If we've underscored any one concept in this book, it's that *strategies provide solutions to problems*. It just so happens that today new ventures face problems whose solutions involve not only the identification of a new opportunities but the development of organizational resources and capabilities to operate profitably in that domain. The IPO, meanwhile, enables a firm not only to capitalize (literally as well as figuratively) on its initial success but to gain access to the financial resources needed to fuel future growth. Some firms do not need to resort to an IPO to support their growth, but they do at least make a transition from a visionary leadership style to one that increasingly incorporates aspects of professional management practices. In established firms, such entrepreneurial behavior faces the same growth-management problems as those faced by startup firms. (An established firm, of course, must also deal with problems arising from its history and prior activities.) Finally, the five elements of a strategy are critical to any firm—established or new—that is engaged in entrepreneurial activity. Indeed, all of the tools of strategic management can be applied to problems arising from both new-venture creation and corporate renewal.

New-Venture Creation Versus Corporate Renewal

Note that in emphasizing new ventures, IPOs, and turnarounds, we're presenting a slightly simplified view of the organizational life cycle. **New-venture creation** refers to entrepreneurship and the creation of a new business from scratch, whereas **corporate renewal**

new-venture creation Entrepreneurship and the creation of a new business from scratch

corporate renewal Outcome of successful strategic change in the context of an established business

refers to successful strategic change. **Initial public offerings** (IPOs) and/or the institutionalization of professional management often occur in the relatively early stages in a firm's life cycle. All firms start somewhere, and some firms go public. In addition, nearly all firms experience distress at some point, and corporate renewal prevents established firms—and sometimes even new and newly public ones as well—from vanishing from the face of the competitive landscape. As we already noted, because all three involve the creation of something new, all three stages in the organizational life cycle can engage in the entrepreneurial process. Indeed, as our opening vignette on Jones Soda indicates, a firm's success gives it a lot of options: It may remain independent, go public (as Jones did several years ago), or merge with an established firm seeking to enhance its future prospects.

In the sections that follow, you'll get a better idea of what entrepreneurship is and how the entrepreneurial process works. You'll also see how the same process may either lead to an IPO and professional management or provide an impetus for corporate renewal. By the end of the chapter, you'll understand the range of strategic ventures from startup to turnaround and see how strategic management is relevant to new enterprises. You'll also be able to identify the warning signs of organizational trouble and outline a resource-based turnaround plan for a struggling organization.

ENTREPRENEURSHIP AND THE ENTREPRENEURIAL PROCESS

Because of stories like the one in our opening vignette, you probably think of lone, self-reliant individuals like Peter van Stolk when you think about entrepreneurship and the creation of new ventures. Research shows, however, that, no matter how important one individual is to an organization, its ultimate success depends as much on the entrepreneurial team as on the lead entrepreneur.[2] Dell, for instance, would have gone bankrupt in the early 1990s had it not recruited talented executives from IBM and Apple.

What Is Entrepreneurship?

Beyond the common misconception of entrepreneurship as an individual enterprise, people tend to associate it with a variety of images, from garage inventors to rogue executives who leave established employers to form their own companies. Such images have some validity, and throughout this chapter, you'll encounter certain behaviors that tend to characterize successful entrepreneurs. With this fact in mind, let's define **entrepreneurship** as the consequence of actions based on the identification and exploration of opportunity in the absence of obviously available resources. The **entrepreneurial process**, then, is the set of activities leading up to and driving the entrepreneurial venture.

Successful entrepreneurs, whether those who start new firms or who work within companies, are often those who challenge orthodoxy. *Orthodoxies* are the deeply held and broadly shared beliefs about what drives success within "the industry." Orthodoxies are not necessarily incorrect conceptualizations of the current market. Indeed, orthodoxies achieve their status because they do represent the status quo. However, orthodoxies also create blind spots to the recognition of new opportunities. Most industries have orthodoxies along several dimensions:

- Who the customer or end user is
- The type of interface and interaction with the customer or end user
- How benefit is defined and value is delivered
- How product/service functionality is defined
- What form the product/service should take
- How processes are structured and managed
- The "ideal" cost and pricing structure

Consider the examples reviewed in Exhibit 12.2 of a few notable business ideas and the orthodoxies they had to surmount to see the light of day. Consider how the fortunes of

- "This 'telephone' has too many shortcomings to be seriously considered as a means of communication. The device is inherently of no value to us."
  — Western Union internal memo, 1876
- "The wireless music box has no imaginable commercial value. Who would pay for a message sent to nobody in particular?" — David Sarnhoff's associates in response to his urgings for investment in the radio in the 1920's
- "There is no reason anyone would want a computer in their home." — Ken Olson, President, Chairman and Founder of Digital Equipment Corp., 1977
- "The concept is interesting and well-formed, but in order to earn better than a 'C,' the idea must be feasible." — A Yale University management professor in response to Fred Smith's paper proposing reliable overnight delivery service. Smith went on to found Federal Express Corp.
- "A cookie store is a bad idea. Besides, the market research reports say America likes crispy cookies, not soft and chewy cookies like you make." — Response to Debbi Fields' idea of starting Mrs. Fields' Cookies
- "There will never be a market in selling stock over the Internet." — David Komansky, Merrill Lynch Chairman & CEO, 1999

Exhibit 12.2 Orthodoxies That Have Created Entrepreneurial Blind Spots

Source: G. Hamel and C. K. Prahalad, Competing for the Future *(Boston: Harvard Business School Press, 1994).*

some companies may have been different had they been able to overcome the orthodoxy internally and capitalize on the ideas and opportunities these innovations represent.

The Entrepreneurial Process

In this section, we'll elaborate on the entrepreneurial process, which, as you can see in Exhibit 12.3, integrates and coordinates three elements:

- Opportunity
- Key resources and capabilities
- The entrepreneur and the entrepreneurial team

Because it emphasizes a need for balance and symmetry among its elements, this process model fits well with most of the theories that we've discussed throughout this

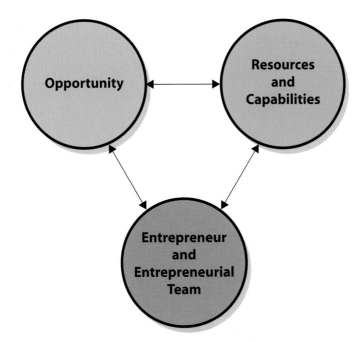

Exhibit 12.3 The Entrepreneurial Process

Source: J. Timmons, New Venture Creation *(New York: Irwin-McGraw-Hill, 1999).*

book. It's also consistent with emerging research that considers entrepreneurship a function in most firms, regardless of their age or size.[3] For that reason alone, you'll see strong affinities with the resource- and dynamic-capabilities-based perspectives that we've described throughout the book.

The Starting Point: Opportunity

Perhaps the biggest difference between strategy in existing firms and new ventures is the starting point. Most researchers agree that the starting point for new ventures is opportunity, whereas the strategy for existing firms typically begins with an assessment of the firm's underlying resources and capabilities.[4] You might be surprised to learn that you already possess some of the tools that may help you unearth a valuable business opportunity. Recall our discussion of new-market-creation, low-end-disruption, and new-market-disruption strategies in Chapter 6: All three of these strategies provide a solid basis for identifying market opportunities. New-market-creation strategies are designed to eliminate, reduce, create, or raise some previously assumed dimension of product/market supply and demand. New-market-disruption strategies are an entrepreneur's dream because they're designed to enable a firm that's created a new market to grow into a dominant player in a new but huge industry. Google is a good example of this. Just a scant six years before it went public in 2004, a firm that now has more than $1 billion in revenue was bringing in less than $100,000 in a virtually nonexistent industry.[5] Low-end-disruption strategies involve identifying a business that will let a firm shift customers from a high-cost-to-serve to a low-cost-to-serve business model.

An entrepreneur identifies an opportunity and then seeks to cobble together the resources and capabilities to exploit it. Opportunities also can be identified by individuals who have close contact with scientific breakthroughs. In fact, scientific, technological, or process discoveries often inspire people to seek market opportunities. This is one reason why universities are increasing investments to support research faculty in the protection of intellectual property and identification of commercial opportunities. The University of Wisconsin-Madison, for instance, maintains an Office of Corporate Relations that, among other services, assists individual researchers in the creation of new ventures. After all, faculty and staff members who create an early stage technology are often in the best position to develop it. Not only do they possess unsurpassed technical knowledge about their discoveries, but they're often in a position to appreciate the promise that they hold.

So far, we've focused on the element of opportunity in the entrepreneurial process. Our context, however—the intersection of technology and entrepreneurship—already suggests ways in which other elements—namely, resources and capabilities and people (the

Six years before going in public in 2004, Google, founded by Sergey Brin and Larry Page, was bringing in less than $100,000 a year. Today, Google Inc.'s annual revenues exceed $3 billion.

entrepreneur and entrepreneurial team)—are involved in the process. We discussed resources and capabilities in Chapter 3, and the VRINE framework that we presented there is as relevant in an entrepreneurial setting as it is in that of an established firm. Within the entrepreneurial firm, however, there's likely to be significant overlap between the people element and the resource-and-capabilities element. Why? Sometimes, the new opportunity is based in a technology whose benefits are recognizable only when it's complemented by the specific technical knowledge and experience of the people who created it. Similarly, if the opportunity is revealed by a "good idea," the entrepreneur and entrepreneurial team must often rely on their own personal resources, experience, and persuasiveness to acquire the needed resources and capabilities, including financial capital.

Although there is no litmus test for determining the characteristics of successful entrepreneurs and the people who make the best members of an entrepreneurial team, it's clear that without them, a new venture will never get off the ground. Sometimes, as we've already seen, key people are among the intangible resources and capabilities that distinguish the potential new venture as an opportunity rather than just another good idea. As a practical matter, it's the entrepreneur who drives the entrepreneurial process and assures that all three elements—opportunity, resources and capabilities, and people—are in place and balanced. Because individuals have limits, team members are often selected because they bring skills that complement those of the lead entrepreneur and will ensure that the firm has the necessary human capital to achieve the objectives that it's set.

NEW-VENTURE CREATION AND CORPORATE NEW VENTURING

Entrepreneurship, which is the outcome of the entrepreneurial process, is embodied in the launch of a new venture. As we've already explained, the first step in new-venture creation is identifying an opportunity. Unfortunately, there's no rule of thumb for deciding on the next step. All we can say is that, typically, entrepreneurs begin a process of experimentation involving the confluence of several activities over time.

New-Venture Scenarios

Exhibit 12.4 summarizes these activities. As you can imagine, the traditional view of new-venture creation calls for the entrepreneur to exploit an opportunity by drawing up a business plan, obtaining external financing, and then launching the new product. A more realistic view allows for an alternative sequence of events that begins when the entrepreneur uses his or her own resources to launch a product and then seeks financing to stay in the

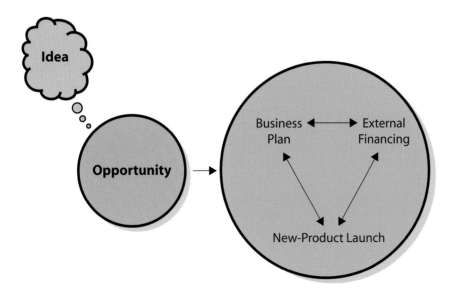

Exhibit 12.4 Activities in New-Venture Creation

game. The business plan often comes after the launch because its purpose is to obtain financing or to generate market interest (in the form of additional financing or purchase of the business) by explaining the venture's history and prospects.

Financing the New Venture   Commercializing a new venture requires capital for startup needs. The financing activity of the new venture can take many forms, with sources ranging from credit cards to venture capitalists to banks. You might expect most successful ventures to have access to adequate capital, but you'd be surprised. In fact, many successful entrepreneurs (and their investors) suspect that too much money, too early, produces more damage than good.[6] How, you're probably asking yourself, can excess cash possibly be a problem? Remember, first of all, that financing rarely comes without strings attached. Thus, entrepreneurs who depend on significant cash flow from loans or investor capital often find their flexibility considerably reduced. Second, ample funding can obscure potential problems until their consequences become irreversible. Finally, deep financial pockets shelter the new firm from the need to innovate in all aspects of its business. Nevertheless, without adequate startup financing, a new venture has difficulty getting off the ground.

bootstrapping Process of finding creative ways to support a startup business financially until it turns profitable

  Bootstrapping means exploiting a new business opportunity with limited funds. Many new ventures are bootstrapped: A study of about 100 of *Inc.* magazine's list of the 500 fastest-growing small companies in the United States found median startup capital to be around $20,000 in real terms.[7] Ironically, the fastest-growing firms typically require the most money because they have to support increases in inventories, accounts receivable, staffing, and production and service facilities.

The Business Plan   Once the new product has been launched and startup financing secured, many entrepreneurs draw up a formal business plan that brings all the elements of the new venture together for a specific purpose: namely, to ensure key stakeholders that the firm has a well-considered strategy and managerial acumen. Even if such a plan isn't necessary for communicating with external stakeholders, preparing one is still a good idea. At the very least, it will help the entrepreneur to reexamine the five elements of strategy and look for ways of bringing them together to create a viable and profitable firm.

  In addition, a business plan provides the entrepreneur with a vehicle for sharing goals and objectives—and plans for implementing them—with members of the entrepreneurial team. Focusing on the staging component of the five elements of strategy, for example, is a good way to set milestones and time lines and otherwise manage the scale and pace of a new company's growth. Finally, when it does come time to seek external funding to support the firm's growth, the plan provides a coherent basis for engaging professionals who can not only help the entrepreneur obtain financing, but also offer advice on strengthening customer relationships and finding strategic suppliers.

  Familiarity with the five elements of the strategy diamond, implementation levers, and frameworks for analyzing external organizational context is helpful with drawing up a business plan. Although there are variations in form, the content of most plans covers the same topics. A multitude of examples—as well as software packages for creating a detailed and professional-looking document—are available on the Web.[8] Exhibit 12.5 provides a summary of what is normally contained in a comprehensive business plan. It is important to keep in mind that the process of systematically thinking through the nine steps in the exhibit is probably more important than the business-plan document itself.

  Finally, a word of warning. All too often, would-be entrepreneurs tend to equate a good business plan with the probability of success in running a business. Needless to say, however, a well-crafted plan does not ensure a successful business. At this point in the process, the probability of success depends more heavily on the strength of the three elements that were present at the start of the process—a good opportunity (including the right timing), the right entrepreneurial team, and the necessary resources and capabilities. A business plan is no more a substitute for strategy and strong execution than a clear vision and mission or even such strategic vehicles as alliances and acquisitions. That's why consultants often suggest that entrepreneurs think of the business plan not only as a helpful and necessary starting point but as a continuous work in progress.[9]

Exhibit 12.5 Table of Contents of a Typical Business Plan

1. **Executive summary.** One to three pages highlighting all key points in a way that captures the interest of the reader. Stress the business concept here, not the numbers. It is the unique value proposition and business model that really matter.

2. **Company description.** Provide a brief description of the company's business, organization, structure and strategy. Provide a summary of how the company's patents or licenses to patents are connected with the development and introduction of products.

3. **Products and services.** Include a layman's overview of how the company's technology and patents relate to its products and services. Describe the products or services the company will sell, including a discussion of why people will want them, what problems they solve, and how much customers are likely to pay for them (i.e., the willingness to pay criteria).

4. **Market analysis.** Identify the need for the product, the extent of that need, who the customers will be, and why they will buy your product. This section should also include a discussion of competitors or potential competitors and why the product will have a competitive advantage over their offerings. Include considerations of barriers to entry in this market.

5. **Proprietary position.** If the new venture's market position will rely on patents or licenses to patents, discuss how these patents will contribute to the company's competitive position and whether other patents (competitors or otherwise) might limit the company's ability to market its products. If similar products do not already exist, discuss the alternative means by which customers are likely to meet the needs the product addresses.

6. **Marketing and sales plan.** Show how the company plans to attract and maintain customers. Discuss product pricing, promotion, and positioning strategy.

7. **Management team.** Describe the management team with special emphasis on its track record at accomplishing tasks similar to those it will face in making the company successful. Investors place major emphasis on the management team, viewing it as the critical ingredient in catalyzing the growth of the company and responding to the unexpected.

8. **Operations plan.** Describe how the day-to-day operations of the company will be organized and carried out to produce the products and services described above.

9. **Finances.** Identify the capital that will be required to build the business and how it will be used. Include projections of revenues and expenses that show investors how they will get their money back and what return they can expect on their investment.

Corporate New Venturing

The previous section discussed new venturing as a process engaged in by entrepreneurs. However, many successful innovations and new ventures are sponsored by existing organizations. What you have learned about entrepreneurial new venturing applies equally well to the process of **corporate new venturing**—the creation of new businesses by established firms. In addition, your knowledge of co-opetition and coevolution should give you a pretty good idea of some of the challenges and opportunities encountered during the process of corporate new venturing. However, the resources and capabilities of established firms and the corporate environment in which they do business differ. These factors often kill corporate new ventures before they get off the ground (or at least keep performance below levels that firms might have achieved through other investments or even by simply

corporate new venturing
New-venture creation by established firms

conceptlink

In Chapter 9, we define **co-opetition** as a situation in which competitors collaborate with each other. We characterize **coevolution** in Chapter 7 as a strategy for seeking fresh opportunities for **synergies** in multiple businesses or arenas. Both, in other words, are methods for seeking and identifying **new opportunities**.

buying a portfolio of market stocks).[10] The stellar innovation track records of firms such as Merck, 3M, Motorola, Rubbermaid, Johnson & Johnson, Corning, General Electric, Raychem, Hewlett-Packard, Wal-Mart, and many others demonstrate that bigness is not in itself antithetical to new venturing. At the same time, however, these are but a few of the thousands of large firms around the world.[11] Understanding the obstacles to entrepreneurship in large established firms will put you on firmer ground when it comes time to translate what you know about entrepreneurship into the process of corporate new venturing. Corporate new venturing can take on one or a combination of two forms: establishing a new business or creating a new ventures division.

Establishing a New Business   A firm may seek to develop a new business around some valuable process or technological breakthrough. Typically, an executive or group of executives will champion the innovation, and the process will proceed when the business concept has been tentatively validated and many of the major uncertainties resolved or reduced.[12] Attention then shifts from opportunity validation to the process of bringing the new business to life. Efforts are directed at assembling resources and capabilities, meeting production and sales goals, and solidifying organization. Interestingly, researchers note that creating a business climate supportive of entrepreneurial activity is the most difficult task faced by a large company trying to integrate an innovative new business.[13]

As a general rule, new-venture activities are less predictable and are, therefore, riskier than those in which a firm traditionally engages. In particular, such activities face three obstacles:

- Although false starts and failures can sometimes be important learning mechanisms, most large firms naturally try to mitigate them by improving efficiency.
- Moreover, new ventures often meet resistance because they challenge long-established assumptions, work practices, and employee skills. After all, by definition *new* means *different*.
- Ironically—and most importantly—large organizations often lavish *too many resources*, including cash, on new ventures. How can this practice be a problem? To be successful at corporate new venturing, large firms must learn to be simultaneously patient and tolerant of risk on the one hand and stingy on the other. The need for stinginess comes from the observation by strategy researchers that corporate new ventures tend to thrive when their managers must face new markets on the same realistic terms that startups typically do outside the corporate bureaucracy.

New-Venture Division   The second form of corporate new venturing, in which the firm sets up an internal new-venture division, is actually a structural solution to these obstacles. In many ways, this division acts like a venture capitalist or business incubator, working to provide expertise and resources and impart structure to the process of developing the new opportunity.

In this case, too, the opportunity may revolve around some proprietary process, product, or technological breakthrough. This approach is designed to achieve one of two possible objectives:

- The creation of a high-growth new venture that the firm can sell off through an IPO at a significant profit
- The creation and retention of a new business that will fuel growth and perhaps foster corporate renewal

The advantage of the structural approach is that it provides a system for investing in a team that's assigned specifically to new-venture creation. If the system is managed properly, new-venture divisions can function like the best venture-capital operations—that is, they can be cost conscious while still encouraging risk taking, experimentation, and novel, market-oriented solutions. A new-venture division—for that matter, new venturing in any form—is a form of diversification, with the firm betting that it has the resources and capabilities to do something new.

The structural approach first became popular in the late 1960s, when 25 percent of the *Fortune* 500 maintained internal venture divisions.[14] The next wave came in the late 1970s and early 1980s, when large players such as Gillette, IBM, Levi Strauss, and Xerox launched internal new-venture groups.[15] Next came the Internet boom, when many firms set up divisions to run e-commerce operations that mirrored their traditional brick-and-mortar operations.

The success of new venture divisions can be measured in several ways. Using an internal rate of return metric, many of these divisions perform quite well. However, the performances of these divisions are generally not up to the levels of those achieved by private equity venture capital firms.[16] Why? Although a firm may have proprietary access to a valuable technology, it probably doesn't possess the necessary venture-capitalist managerial skills and experience. In addition, when it's in the hands of a new-venture division, the new business is isolated from the rest of the organization. This separation is often necessary to protect the new venture, as you saw with the discussion of the ambidextrous organizational structure in Chapter 11. However, if the loose linkages with the parent company, which are necessary to secure resources and transfer information, are severe or dysfunctional, then the parent firm is insulated from the new business and thus less likely to learn from its successes and failures. In addition, the new venture risks being starved for resources and capabilities possessed by the parent firm.

concept link

Recall our discussion of the **ambidextrous organization** in Chapter 11, where we characterize it as a solution to the so-called *innovator's dilemma*: the need of a firm simultaneously to manage *incremental* and *discontinuous innovations*.

Is corporate new venturing, then, doomed to failure? Of course not. Firms must, however, be careful to balance the requirements of entrepreneurial ventures—such as a supportive entrepreneurial climate—with the benefits of sustained linkage to the parent firm. The natural tension and potential dysfunction created by the need for separateness yet connectedness must be carefully managed. Entrepreneurship Professor David Garvin of the Harvard Business School recently reviewed the history of corporate new venturing. He suggested that corporate new ventures are more likely to succeed when they:[17]

■ Are developed and validated in firms with supportive, entrepreneurial climates
■ Have senior executive sponsorship
■ Are based on related rather than radically different products and services
■ Appeal to an emerging subset or current set of customers
■ Employ market-experienced personnel
■ Test concepts and business models directly with potential users
■ Experiment, probe, and prototype repeatedly during early development
■ Balance demands for early profitability with realistic time lines
■ Introduce required systems and processes in time, but not earlier than the new venture's evolution required
■ Combine disciplined oversight and stinginess with entrepreneurial autonomy

Professor Garvin's guidelines for successful corporate venturing suggest that there are other inherent tensions in the decision-making process as well. Many of the guidelines in this list call for incorporating a resource-based approach into the new-venturing process. Even when a firm succeeds in creating a climate that's supportive of entrepreneurship, the evolving characteristics of the new venture may result in a unit that's more distinctive from than complementary to the core businesses. In that case, it might be wise for the parent firm to allow the new business to function independently—physically and legally. In part, the increase in new-venture public offerings can be attributed to the willingness of firms to take this advice. With this fact in mind, we turn in the next section to a discussion of IPOs.

INITIAL PUBLIC OFFERINGS AND MANAGERIAL PROFESSIONALISM

As firms grow, they face the need to transition to a more complex organizational form. Sometimes this form is dictated by the need for access to additional capital and professional management or managerial professionalism alone. Increasingly, experts are starting to view the IPO as a pivotal point in a firm's transition from small and entrepreneurial to large and established. An IPO takes place when a firm offers ownership shares through a public stock market.[18] In 2000, for instance, Krispy Kreme was a highly successful private company that decided to facilitate expansion by issuing an IPO. Typically, investment bankers (underwriters) and stockbrokers value the firm and place the stock with investors. Of course, a number of different transition vehicles are possible—alliances, mergers, sales, outright failure (the most common exit route). Given their recent visibility and rise to virtual holy-grail status among entrepreneurs, it's important to understand the workings of IPOs in greater detail.

How Does an IPO Work?

How does an organization orchestrate an IPO? Once it's decided to make a securities offering, the company establishes a market value in the private sector. This value is estimated by an investment-banking institution, which will also sell the firm's shares to public investors. During this process, the company files an **S-1 statement**, which states its value proposition and financial prospects, with the Securities and Exchange Commission (SEC) and various state securities commissions. Finally, the company and its brokerage firm "time" the offering to get maximum value from the sale of its stock.

> **S-1 statement** Legal document outlining a firm's financial position in preparation for an initial public stock offering

One thing that companies are required to discuss at length are the challenges they face that could adversely affect shareholders. Jones Soda, for example, discloses in its S-1 prospectus that "We rely heavily on our independent distributors, and this could affect our ability to efficiently and profitably distribute and market our product, and maintain our existing markets and expand our business into other geographic markets."

Usually, the *prospectus* describes the perceived business opportunity, outlines the firm's strategy for exploiting it, and details its current products and activities, generally in the context of the company's overall expansion strategy. The firm must clearly define its vision and describe its mission, business initiatives, and objectives. As we observed earlier in this chapter, the business plan should also spell out the firm's approach to the five elements of strategy and the implementation levers necessary for executing its strategy, and it should do so in a way that's clear and compelling for potential investors. Because investors will want to know what goals the firm has set for itself, treatment of staging is especially important.

Cost of an IPO

When preparing a securities offering, consider the old saying that you need money to make money. The IPO process could easily require $400,000 in professional fees alone. Investment bankers exact a heavy toll for shepherding a firm through an IPO. A normal 6.5-percent commission would skim $1,625,000 off the top of a $25-million offering! As an illustration, Exhibit 12.6 estimates the IPO costs for a $25-million offering.

Financial and Legal Requirements   The firm will have to pass certain financial tests. An independent SEC-approved CPA firm, for example, must audit the firm's financial statements for the previous three years. If the firm hasn't been audited over that period, the process may take months. If the company has been around for more than five years, it will have to include financial information from previous years in the (S-1) registration and prospectus statement.[19]

An SEC-approved CPA will require that all legal work be done and be done properly. If the firm doesn't pass the CPA's audit tests, it won't be issued an *unqualified opinion* on its financial statements. Instead, it will receive a *qualified opinion*—a statement of the auditor's opinion that the audit reflects certain limitations, such as financial irregularities, lack of controls, and so forth. That's not good: In the securities world, an unqualified opinion is sometimes called the "blue screen of death," and it's particularly grave for the IPO.

The "Road Show"   Once the firm has met the financial and legal requirements, it enters the pre-IPO period and launches a **road show**, which is a series of presentations in which members of the top-management team, particularly the CEO, promote the company to interested investors and analysts. Depending on the quality of the road show, the firm may even get commitments from investors to buy shares of its stock. However, bear in mind that there are restrictions on the people to whom managers can talk and what they can talk about, and what's more, these rules change frequently. Obviously, top executives need to know the rules before they hit the road.

> **road show** Series of presentations in which top management promotes an IPO to interested investors and analysts

Pre-IPO costs over two years,	
1. Upgrading accounting and MIS	$150,000
2. New personnel and board members	150,000
3. Management/administrative time	100,000
Minimum Pre-IPO Costs	**$400,000**

IPO-Process costs 90 days,		
6.5% underwriter commission		
$25 million IPO		$1,625,000
IPO professional fees		
1. Legal fees	$ 150,000	
2. Preliminary/final prospectus printing	100,000	
3. Translation	30,000	
4. Investors relations	40,000	
5. Accounting	50,000	
6. Road show and preparations	50,000	
7. Initial stock exchange listing fee	10,000	
Minimum IPO professional fees		430,000
Minimum IPO-Process Costs		**$2,055,000**

Post-IPO costs every year thereafter,		
1. Investor relations and Web site	100,000	
2. Directors' fees, travel costs, etc.	100,000	
3. Directors' liability insurance	50,000	
4. Corporate image, public relations	50,000	
5. Annual stock exchange fee	5,000	
6. Management/administration costs	100,000	
Minimum Annual Post IPO-Costs		**$405,000**

Total Minimum Cost of a $25 million IPO	**$2,860,000**

Exhibit 12.6 Minimum Costs of Going Public to Raise $25 Million

Source: P. Downing, "IPO Launch Fraught with Perils," The Ottawa Citizen, High-Tech Report, October 12, 1998.

As pressure for financial transparency increases, the SEC may eventually require companies to open road-show presentations, which are now restricted to analysts and institutional investors, to individual investors, not only to expand the audience for promotional activities but to level the playing field in terms of access to information. The SEC hasn't yet worked out the logistics, but one way to give individuals access to road shows would be to broadcast them on the Internet. Road-show meetings with stock analysts, which must be open to the public, are often broadcast over the Web.

Once the road show is over, the firm's brokers will want to time the offering so that shares become available under the most favorable market conditions.[20] For example, a high-tech company wouldn't want its stock brought to market during a sell-off in technology stocks. The firm's brokers may prefer things to be uneventful so that the IPO can make news. They might try to time the firm's offering to coincide with other attractive IPOs, taking advantage of a window during which investors feel eager to get in the game.

An IPO or a More Formal Organization?

Given the complexities and costs of an IPO, it is no surprise that not all growing firms go public. Recall that an IPO is part of the growth path of a firm because it provides access to additional capital as well as the opportunity and motivation to put more professional management in place. Professional management may take the form of executives experienced with running larger firms, rapidly growing firms, or those that require management of significant organizational change. The need to shift from purely entrepreneurial management to more formal or professional management was initially discovered by Professor Daryl Wyckoff in his study of the trucking industry.[21] Wyckoff coined the term the *Bermuda Triangle of Management* to describe the region where firms are faced with the need to cross over from entrepreneurial to formal management. The Bermuda Triangle is an infamous area in the Atlantic Ocean where legend has it that ships and planes enter but never escape; Wyckoff argued that firms face a similar scenario and that those trucking firms that never completed the shift from informal to formal, professional management apt to fail and disappear from the scene.

Part of the explanation for the Bermuda Triangle effect is economic. Wyckoff found that the operating ratio (expenses as a percentage of revenues) in the trucking industry varied by firm size; large and small companies were generally more profitable than midsized companies (those ostensibly stuck in or trying to get through the Bermuda Triangle). Part of the effect was managerial. Wyckoff noted that small firms were informally managed and large firms were professionally managed.

What does formal, professional management entail? Based on his work with the trucking industry, Wyckoff concluded that formal management includes delegation of authority; detailed and frequent measurement systems; formalized, performance-based reward systems; formal ground rules, procedures, and resource-allocation systems; and separation of ownership and management. Although Wyckoff's work dates from the 1970s, more recent examples are easy to find. Recall the saga of SAP in the late 1990s, which struggled as it grew but ultimately succeeded by successfully transitioning from an informal to a formal management system.

WHY DO ORGANIZATIONS FAIL?

The new-venture process, whether undertaken by a new firm or within an existing firm, represents the beginning of a new organization. However, successful new ventures do not ensure long-term prosperity. Firms often must make major changes in order to survive, and the Bermuda Triangle phenomenon aptly demonstrates this. Before considering how firms can change to return to prosperity, it may be useful to review the broader set of explanations as to why organizations fail. Knowing the causes of failure will help us better understand what is needed to guide a firm through a strategic change to correct problems and avoid complete failure.[22]

Both public and private firms may experience distress at any point in their life cycle, and research indicates that a set of common factors underlies business failure. To be fair, it's usually much easier to determine the cause of organizational failure after the failure rather than before, but understanding and learning from the mistakes of other management teams is the responsibility of everyone charged with leading a business.

In the United States, publicly traded firms are required to disclose known risks that could lead to business failure. These risks are disclosed in the firm's annual 10-K filings and in S-1 filings when the firm first goes public. For instance, Jones Soda lists a number of risks that could affect the viability of its business. Some of these risks are summarized in Exhibit 12.7.

As you can see from reviewing the risks that have been identified by the managers of Jones Soda, most of the risks identified as sources of potential business failure fall into two broad categories: *external* and *internal*. In the next section, we look at both categories in some detail.

External Causes of Organizational Failure

You will recall that there are two major contexts facing firms that determine the success of their strategies: in Chapter 3 you were introduced to the internal context of strategy and in Chapter 4 you learned about the external context. Just as these factor affect the success of strategies, it should not be surprising that causes of failure can also be categorized similarly. External causes of organizational failure reflect trends and events that strike at the core of a

Exhibit 12.7 Business Risks of Jones Soda

- We rely heavily on our independent distributors, and this could affect our ability to efficiently and profitably distribute and market our product, and maintain ourexisting markets and expand our business into other geographic markets.

- Our ability to maintain our distribution network and attract additional distributors will depend on a number of factors, many of which are outside our control. Some of these factors include: the level of demand for our brands and products in a particular distribution area, our ability to price our products at levels competitive with those offered by competing products, and our ability to deliver products in the quantity and at the time ordered by distributors.

- Opposition from traditional non-alcoholic beverage manufacturers may adversely affect our distribution relationships and may hinder development of our existing markets, as well as prevent us from expanding our markets.

- We have limited working capital and may need to raise additional capital in the future.

- We rely on third-party packers of our products, and this dependence could makemanagement of our marketing and distribution efforts inefficient or unprofitable.

- We generally do not have long-term agreements with our distributors, and we incur significant time and expense in attracting and maintaining key distributors.

- We compete in an industry that is brand-conscious, so brand name recognition and acceptance of our products are critical to our success.

- We compete in an industry characterized by rapid changes in consumer preferences, so our ability to continue developing new products to satisfy our consumers' changing preferences will determine our long-term success.

- Our business and financial results depend on maintaining a consistent and cost-effective supply of raw materials.

- Our sales are affected by seasonality.

- The loss of key personnel would directly affect our efficiency and profitability.

- We could be exposed to product liability claims for personal injury or possibly death.

- Our inability to protect our trademarks, patent and trade secrets may prevent us from successfully marketing our products and competing effectively.

- Our business is subject to many regulations and noncompliance is costly.

- The current U.S. economic uncertainty and international conflict with Iraq may have an adverse impact on our sales and earnings, and our shipping costs have increased.

- The market and liquidity for our shares is limited.

Source: Jones Soda 2004 10-K filing.

company's business. Some of these changes, such as population trends in peacetime, occur slowly and predictably. Others, such as natural disasters and wars, occur suddenly and with a severity that may change the shape of much more than the business world. Failure to foresee the possibility of such events and to consider their implications is an invitation to trouble. Remarkably enough, a recent study of 51 failed organizations found that not one of the failures was the result of unforeseeable events.[23] In each case, managers observed, discussed, and then disregarded the relevant change in the external environment.

External change may take one of four forms: *economic, competitive, social,* and *technological.*

Economic Change

A boom can cover many sins, and good economic times often mask organizational problems. A bust, however, can turn many small glitches into big problems. A list of economic problems includes (but is certainly not limited to) slackening overall demand, currency devaluation, international monetary crises, interest-rate hikes, and credit squeezes. Common sense would suggest that when economic activity levels off or declines, the number of failures will increase and vice versa. As a matter of fact, that's exactly how it works out.

At the same time, however, although economic change does indeed contribute to decline and failure, we should keep its role in proper perspective. According to one study, only 9 percent of all failures are caused chiefly by economic factors. The same study also found that during any economic cycle, good performers outperformed laggards by astonishing rates: While good performers' earnings per share grew at 33 percent annually, those of poor performers declined by 23 percent.[24] Can we draw any conclusions from these findings? Perhaps that good management can offset poor economic conditions.

conceptlink

In discussing Porter's **five-forces model** of industry structure in Chapter 4, we define **rivalry** as the intensity of competition within an industry; we also observe that degrees of rivalry can generally be measured in terms of intensity of *price competition*. Here, we stress the role of new-product introduction as a form of economic pressure that can intensify price competition.

Competitive Change

Because so many events can drastically change the competitive landscape—the emergence of low-cost foreign competitors, the entry of new companies in an industry, the merger of two competitors—most companies operate in a world of constantly shifting competition. Thirty-five percent of all business failures are related to competitive change (i.e., the emergence of competition plus loss of market).[25] Usually, competitive change takes the form of price competition, as competitors lower prices in order to introduce products into new markets (a trend that's particularly common during economic downturns). In response, incumbents often try to keep factories at near-capacity production despite decreased demand.

A more sudden and less predictable type of competition comes from foreign countries or the appearance of a new technology. Foreign competition has been a fact of life for many years now, and in the United States, it's had a particularly devastating impact on clothing (shoes and textiles), consumer electronics, and steel. Failures in these industries highlight the importance of monitoring the external competitive environment.

Social Change

Because it generally takes a fairly long time for a society to accommodate significant changes, social change is usually less abrupt and less obvious than other forms of external change. The first signs of changes in Americans' attitudes toward work, such as the balance of men and women professionals and an aging workforce, have been evident for decades, but many companies still don't fully understand how the shift affects them.

Although such trends are hard to quantify, companies must realize that failure to recognize and respond to social changes can be extremely costly. Numerous companies have lost touch with markets or customers because they failed to observe or react to such social trends as changes in lifestyles, in the composition of given populations, or in attitudes toward such issues as pollution and personal health. Krispy Kreme, for example, the acclaimed purveyor of fried donuts, blamed a slowdown in business on the changing dietary habits of carbohydrate-conscious consumers. Apparently taken by surprise, the company issued its first profit warning since going public, thereby adding fuel to investor worries about its growth prospects.[26] Companies can even lose touch with their own employees, and the consequences may range from declining productivity to work stoppages.

Again, however, we should repeat that changes such as these tend to occur slowly, over long periods of time, and in one recent survey, CEOs agreed that in most industries reasonably astute management should be able to keep up with them.[27]

Technological Change

It's not overstating the case to say that global markets are what they are today because today's technologies make it possible to move information, products, and people quite easily. Technological change is a result of advances in information-transportation technology.

Information Technology The absolute amount of knowledge in the world has been growing at an increasing rate. Between 1965 and 1980, for example, the number of scientific articles published per day rose from 3,000 to 8,000, and because knowledge feeds on itself, this pattern isn't likely to change. In any case, even if the rate of increase were to diminish, the existing knowledge base would still be so large that the absolute increase in units of knowledge per unit of time would remain large throughout at least the first half of the next century.

Just as important, the growing number of advanced communications technologies will greatly increase the availability of all knowledge that is produced. Combined with the rate at which new knowledge is being generated, technology has also increased the *availability* of information substantially.

Transportation Technology Transportation technology has increased the number of markets to which a business has access and the speed with which they can be accessed. Moreover, we now know a lot more about markets to which we've long had access, and not surprisingly, the effects of changes in information and transportation technology are closely related. The decline in U.S. manufacturing employment, for example, in is a direct consequence of automation (information technology) and importation (manufacturing and transportation technologies).

The increasing availability and complexity of information make the task of focusing on relevant information more daunting than ever. This fact is especially important. As we said at the beginning of this section, organizational failure is rarely a consequence of unforeseen events. Rather, it very often results from management's failure to make the best use of relevant information.

Internal Causes of Organizational Failure

It's nearly impossible to say exactly what percentage of business failures result from internal causes, but most experts agree that internal causes of failure are more common than external ones. Failure is generally the result of a bad strategy, poor executive judgment, or financial mismanagement.

Strategy Failure By now it should be clear that a good strategy is preferable to a poor one and that expert implementation will always outperform poor implementation. Also, recall that a quality strategy exploits opportunities in the marketplace. It also enables the firm to fit with the current competitive environment and adapt to changes so that it will be well positioned when the competitive environment changes. When a firm's strategy is poorly adapted to the current environment or a change in the environment results in a major misalignment, quick decline may result.

Management Failure Why does poor management lead to failure? A recent study addressed the common assumption that failures are due to inept or incompetent CEOs or senior executives. After interviewing executives from over 50 failed firms, the researcher concluded that people who become CEOs of large corporations are almost always remarkably intelligent.[28] That's not surprising: They reach the top because they are regarded as the most capable, and are repeatedly chosen for positions over their fellow managers. So, how do smart managers lead organizations to failure? Some of these concepts were reviewed in Chapter 2, but we revisit a few of them here.

Dictatorial management styles, for instance, can be problematic. In a dictatorship, leaders ignore input from others, who soon stop offering it. Dictatorial managers tend to become either averse to change or unable to implement it effectively because they lack information they need.

A related problem is *lack of managerial depth*, which is often a by-product of dictatorial leadership. It arises when a strong leader refuses to be surrounded by equally strong people. When this problem sets in, it tends to compound itself. Lack of managerial depth has been cited as a contributing factor to the failure of several organizations. CEO Roger Smith of GM was notorious for getting rid of fellow executives who regularly disagreed with him, either firing them or exiling them to relatively desolate corners of the organization. As a result, the organization lost touch with a changing marketplace and saw its market share decline precipitously.

Economic changes such as rising crude oil and gasoline prices, can certainly contribute to business failures, but research shows they aren't the main cause. If anything, downturns "magnify" a company's shortcomings and put managers and their strategies to the test.

conceptlink

In Chapter 2, we cite *authority structures* as a key condition underlying a firm's vulnerability to ethics violations: Responsibility is usually distributed—and diluted—throughout a large organization. We also discuss **incentive systems** as a potential source of ethical problems.

Another effect of flawed leadership is the tendency of top management to become unbalanced. A management team is unbalanced when experience in one product or functional area dominates the team, the board of directors, or both. Let's say, for example, that the CEO and the board of directors are executives with financial backgrounds. Once they reach a financial decision, it's not likely to be questioned, even by other top managers with financial experience.

Finally, although individual dishonesty and fraud are not as common as we might be led to believe by such cases as Enron, WorldCom, and Tyco, they can and do cause severe damage to organizations. They're especially dangerous when they involve systemic failures in a company's accounting and auditing functions. WorldCom, for example, admitted that in order to meet Wall Street expectations, it had inflated its profits by $3.8 billion between January 2001 and March 2002. Only *systemic* financial failure could lead to such a mammoth collapse.

A weak finance function can have a devastating impact on an organization, in part because it's ultimately a reflection of larger management problems. It may present itself in the form of an unbalanced executive team with little financial knowledge or experience or as a more general organizational defect that fosters inadequate financial controls, a weak auditing function, or both. One of the greatest dangers of a weak financial function—*creative accounting*—emerges during economic downturns. Fudging earnings or sales is a great temptation during a downturn, but it's a less attractive option in a firm with a strong financial function.

Warning Signals of Organizational Decline   At this point, you undoubtedly realize that organizations are complex and that a lot can go wrong with them. You may also be wondering if there are any early warning signals that would prompt someone to start questioning a firm's strategy or its execution or simply the reliability or competency of its leaders. You can rely on certain indicators that reflect a variety of factors. The tools presented in Chapter 4—PESTEL, industry-structure, and scenario-analysis tools—can be good *qualitative* indicators. Regular evaluation of the quality of a firm's strategy is another qualitative indicator. A strategy that does not fit with current external environmental conditions or the near-term environment will lead to organizational decline.

Not surprisingly, financial indicators are a common signal of the potential for decline. For instance, unexpected declines in earnings or revenues are always a red flag. So are declining customer-satisfaction scores. MCI's rapid demise was foreshadowed by several quarters of record-breaking numbers of customer complaints about service quality. Sometimes incipient problems can be discovered by assessing financial ratios (profitability, operating, liquidity, and debt ratios are a good start) in terms of historical or industry data. In addition to the signals provided by operating leverage and sustainable-growth rate, discussed later in the chapter, you can also use a combination of ratios to predict financial problems. Several of these tools are showcased in the box entitled "How Would *You* Do That? 12.1."

STRATEGIC CHANGE AND ORGANIZATIONAL RENEWAL

Not surprisingly, strategic management—particularly in dynamic contexts—is a process for dealing with strategic change and organizational renewal. As was discussed in Chapter 11, implementing a change in strategy involves transforming the firm from its current state to a different one through the use of implementation levers and strategic leadership. In many ways, therefore, you already have a good foundation for understanding the processes of change and renewal in certain situations—namely, in firms that aren't yet facing crises.

A key premise is that all business environments are in a state of change. To remain successful, firms must take one of two actions: stay aligned with changes in their environments by responding quickly or actively anticipate changes in customer demographics, future technologies, and potential new products/services, and thereby recreate their industries.

Strategic change can be defined as significant changes in resource-allocation choices or business activities that align the firm's strategy with its vision. Strategic change could also encompass changes that are undertaken to inform the firm what its new vision should be. Strategic change is difficult. Consider the problem of orthodoxies reviewed earlier in the chapter. When a firm explicitly or tacitly adheres to orthodoxies to the point that it creates rigidities in the way management thinks about the firm and its environment or rigidities in internal practices, the difficulty of strategic change is compounded.

conceptlink

We formally define **implementation levers** in Chapter 11 as the mechanisms by which a strategic leader can help to execute a firm's strategy. We had, however, introduced the three categories of levers—as (1) organization structure, (2) systems and processes, and (3) people and rewards—back in Chapter 1. In Chapter 7, where we underscore the importance of implementation in using corporate strategy to create **competitive advantage**, we focus on the category of levers which includes structure, systems, and processes.

strategic change Significant changes in resource-allocation choices, in the business and implementation activities that align the firm's strategy with its vision, or in its vision

The Change Process

Although change is rarely a linear process, it can be helpful to think of the elements of change in such a fashion in order to appreciate the magnitude of the effort. Using the principles you've already learned about the strategic-management process, let's consider all that must happen in order to implement a strategic change successfully. Exhibit 12.8 illustrates

Exhibit 12.8 A Pathway for Strategic Change

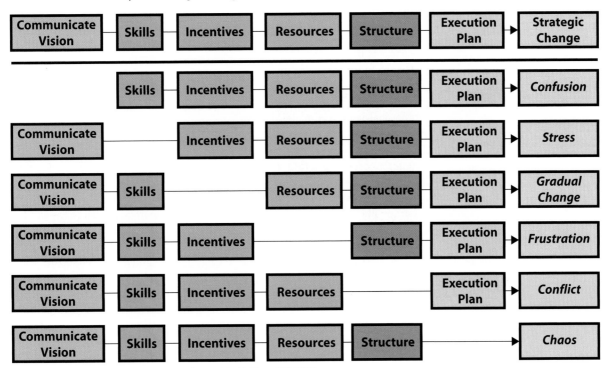

Source: A. Marcus, Management Strategy *(New York: McGraw-Hill, 2004).*

Are Jones Soda's Numbers Fizzy or Flat?

Here we will use the 2004 annual results from Jones Soda to walk you through a handful of financial-analysis tools that you can use quickly to get a sense of a firm's financial strength. These tools are most often used to gauge the financial health and prospects of large firms, but they can be used to assess any new venture. These types of analyses can be used to determine whether the economic logic underlying the firm's strategy is actually paying off and to suggest implementation levers that may need to be pulled in the case that problems are discovered or predicted.

Z-SCORE MODEL

Let's start with the Z-Score model, the brainchild of Edward I. Altman, who is considered to be the dean of insolvency predictors. Altman was the first person to develop a highly accurate prediction model. A recent test of Altman's Z-Score found that it was 95-percent accurate in classifying companies. Altman's model takes the following form:

$$Z = 1.2A + 1.4B + 3.3C + 0.6D + .99E$$

where

A = Working capital/total assets

B = Retained earnings/total assets

C = Earnings before interest and taxes/total assets

D = Market value of equity/book value of total debt

E = Sales/total assets

If Z is less than 1.8, then the firm is classified as "high likelihood of failure."

Although the model was developed to analyze manufacturing companies, it can also be applied to nonmanufacturing organizations by modifying the formula. The formula is modified by omitting the fifth component (E). The adjusted formula seems to provide equally valid predictive results. Applying the model to Jones Soda's 2004 annual report, you would find:

$$Z = 1.2(.48) + 1.4(.55) + 3.3(.16) + .6(1.0) + .99(.34) = 2.8$$

Because Z is greater than 1.8, it suggests that Jones is not failing.

GAMBLER'S RUIN MODEL

Another mathematical model that we will consider is the gambler's ruin prediction of bankruptcy. The formula is designed to predict the failure of manufacturing and retailing companies up to five years in advance. The model was originally developed by Jarrod Wilcox of the Boston Consulting Group. Under this approach, bankruptcy is probable when a company's net liquidation value (NLV) becomes negative. NLV is defined as the total asset-liquidation value minus total liabilities. From one period to the next, a company's NLV is increased by cash inflow and decreased by cash outflow. Wilcox combined the cash inflow and outflow and defined the new number as "adjusted cash flow." All other things being equal, the probability of a company's failure increases the smaller the company's beginning NLV, the smaller the company's adjusted (net) cash flow, and the larger the variation of the company's adjusted cash flow over time. Wilcox uses the gambler's ruin formula to show that a company's risk of failure depends on (1) the above factors (e.g., company size) plus (2) the size of the company's adjusted cash flow "at risk" each period—i.e., the size of the company's "bet." For instance, over a 2-year period Jones Soda's liquidation value increased from $2.4 million to $4.3 million while net cash flow (operations minus investments plus or minus financing) decreased from $266,000 to $18,000, mostly due to increases in capital expenditures. Although the company's liquidation value was positive, it had placed a bigger "bet," which puts it at risk.

SUSTAINABLE GROWTH

Another useful model for evaluating a firm's financial health is the sustainable-growth rate. The value obtained from this analysis is the rate of growth the company can sustain with its current

»

capital structure. Inasmuch as many firms get into trouble because they simply "grow broke," the sustainable-growth rate is a useful tool.

To calculate the sustainable-growth rate for a company, you need to know how profitable the company is as determined by its return on equity (ROE). You also need to know what percentage of a company's earnings per share is paid out in dividends, which is called the dividend-payout ratio. From there, multiply the company's ROE by its plowback ratio, which is equal to 1 minus the dividend-payout ratio.

Sustainable-growth rate = ROE × (1 − dividend-payout ratio)

Let's go through another example using Jones. Jones' ROE is 30 percent and no dividends are paid out of its earnings. Based on the formula and a net profit in 2004 of $1.3 million divided by an equity of $4.3 million, Jones has a sustainable-growth rate of 30 percent [0.30 × (1 − 0%)]. Now that we know Jones' sustainable-growth rate is 30 percent, we should be concerned if the company promises that it can sustain a growth rate of well above that from now until eternity. From 2003 to 2004, Jones's sales grew 37 percent, from $20 million to over $27 million. If you had calculated Jones's sustainable growth rate in 2003, you would have come up with 12.5 percent. This means that Jones is continually growing faster

than the growth it can support using the existing debt and equity (Jones raised an additional $1.9 million in equity between 2003 and 2004). To maintain this or a higher growth rate, Jones would have to become more profitable (which would boost its ROE), pay out fewer dividends as a percentage of earnings (which would reduce the dividend-payout ratio, but that is already at zero), or obtain more money through borrowing or the equity markets (as it did with the additional equity acquired in 2003).

OPERATING LEVERAGE

Finally, operating leverage can give you an idea how sensitive a firm's profits are to small increases or decreases in revenues. If scenario planning shows that many able competitors are liable to jump into the fray or that the firm's revenues will likely go down in the future for other reasons, this metric can be used to determine if fixed costs need to be cut immediately, before profitability suffers.

Operating leverage can be calculated simply by dividing *gross margin* (sometimes called *gross profit*) by *net profit margin*. The beauty of this indicator is that it shows very quickly the extent to which a percentage-profit decrease will be reflected in a percentage decrease in profitability. In 2004, for instance, Jones had a gross margin of 34.8 percent and a net profit margin of 4.8 percent. If you

do the math, you'll find that Jones had an operating leverage of about 7.25. What does this number mean? It means that a 1-percent decrease in revenues would result in a 7-percent decrease in profits (unless some element of the firm's fixed-cost structure was dramatically reduced). From this exercise, you should conclude that Jones is reasonably healthy, at least in financial terms. However, given that most of its competitors, such as Coke and Pepsi, are huge, many financial changes would need to be made for it to grow to their size on its own.

this process and the possible outcomes if any of the elements of the change effort are missing. The model should also reinforce your understanding of the interdependence of strategy formulation and implementation.

First, in order to change, the firm must have a new vision of the desired end state. This new vision must be communicated to those who will effect the change. As we have noted numerous times, because a vision is not a strategy, the new vision will require an executive plan—a strategy—that will serve as a map of the strategic-change process.

Executing strategy is a task of all managers, indeed all employees, not just the work of those who dream up new strategies. Consequently, the change effort requires skills embodied in the people of the organization. However, what tasks people spend their time on is heavily influenced by incentives. To get people to change their behaviors, as is often needed when an organization is trying to change its strategy, the firm will have to provide incentives. Next, it is critical to recognize that talented people with proper incentives will find it much easier to work toward the new vision if the organization allocates the resources necessary to accommodate the desired changes. These resources can be evaluated using the VRINE framework to gain a richer understanding of the unique opportunities or challenges faced by a particular change effort.

An effective strategy, and in this case a strategic change, often requires modification, or at least clarification, of organizational structure. Finally, a plan that connects the dots in the change process must be put into place and widely communicated.

When all of these pieces of the change process are in place, a firm is likely to manage successfully the shift from one strategy to another—and the outcome is likely to be successful strategic change. Yet if any single step is missing, it undermines the entire change effort. Note that each missing step has different potential consequences for the change effort. Consider a few possible outcomes should we remove any one of the steps of strategic change. First, if there is no guiding vision, organization members are likely to be extremely confused about why all these efforts are to be undertaken. If there is no execution plan, a chaotic state is likely to emerge, with various managers pursuing different pathways to the desired end state. If the organization does not have the right people who possess the skills necessary to carry out the efforts, extreme levels of stress will probably result among those who are left to shoulder the burden they are ill-equipped to carry.

Should the wrong incentives be in place, the organization is likely to change much slower than it could, or worse, actually pursue an unintended pathway because that is what is actually rewarded. If resources are not allocated, extreme levels of frustration are likely to emerge because managers and employees feel that they have been given a difficult goal without any institutional support. Finally, if the organizational structure does not accommodate the intended change, then there will be confusion and conflict over reporting and cooperative relationships.

Turnaround Management

The strategic-change process as just described is difficult work. However, all change is not created equal. Sometimes, there comes a point when a firm's future prospects seem hopeless, and this section is about strategy from that point forward. When an organization is going downhill fast, what can be done to turn it around? When the word *turnaround* comes into play, managers typically do not have the luxury of time, and the strategic-change framework presented in the previous section, though relevant, is also time consuming. Remembering that causes of failure are rooted in strategy, management, and financial mismanagement, we will now walk through five stages of the turnaround-management process summarized in Exhibit 12.9.[29] We identify five distinct stages, but before we proceed, here are five caveats that you should bear in mind in thinking about these stages:

- Because every turnaround is unique, each stage is not necessarily distinguishable in every turnaround.
- The number of stages involved in each turnaround stage will depend on the seriousness of the financial crisis facing a given company: The more dire the trouble, the more stages the turnaround process is likely to involve.

Exhibit 12.9 Stages in the Turnaround Process

Stages	Management Change	Evaluation	Emergency	Stabilization	Return-to-Normal
Objectives and Action Items	1. Select new top-management team. 2. Weed out impediments. 3. Select a turnaround manager.	1. Can it survive? 2. Identify strategy. 3. Develop plan. 4. Determine nature of turnaround.	1. Survival. 2. Positive cash flow. 3. Raise cash. 4. Take charge. 5. Get control of cash.	1. Enhance profitability. 2. Restructure business to increase ROI.	1. Seek profitable growth. 2. Build competitive strengths.

Source: Adapted from Thomas D. Hays, III, CTP, Certified Turnaround Professional, Nachman Hays Brownstein.

- The importance of each stage will vary from case to case. Sometimes, for instance, analysis will be more important than action, whereas the opposite will be true in other cases.
- A company can find itself involved in more than one stage at a time. Stages can overlap, and some tasks may affect more than one stage.
- The length of time required to address each stage is not only fluid but can vary greatly. The major factors in determining the amount of time entailed by each stage include the size of the company and the severity of its financial straits. Addressing every stage in the process may take 12 to 36 months.

The following stage-by-stage description of the turnaround process can be used as a template for designing a change-management program for a company in financial trouble. To illustrate how a successful turnaround can be accomplished, review the turnaround experience at ISH summarized in the box entitled "How Would *You* Do That? 12.2."

Stage 1: Changing Management Changing management means one of two things: either changing the way management approaches organizational problems or changing the personnel at the top of the organization, which is more often the case. Most CEOs and other officers will not relinquish power easily. Often egos make it difficult for them to admit that a downturn is really happening or that they're incapable of pulling the company out of its nosedive. The first step, therefore, is setting up a top-management team to lead the turnaround effort. In some cases, the board of directors may recruit turnaround specialists; bankers and corporate attorneys are also usually involved. As outsiders, turnaround specialists come aboard unfettered by obligations to the incumbent management team or the firm's current strategy. During this stage, the turnaround team will weed out and replace any top officials who may impede the turnaround effort. In general, it is believed that the benefits of the leadership capabilities that outsiders bring far outweigh their lack of organizational or industry experience.[30]

Stage 2: Analyzing the Situation Before making any major changes, turnaround leaders must determine the chances of the firm's survival, identify appropriate strategies for turning it around, and develop a preliminary action plan. The first days, therefore, are devoted to fact finding and diagnosing the scope and severity of the problems at hand.

In the meantime, the team must deal with various stakeholder groups. The first group often consists of angry creditors who may have been kept in the dark about the company's financial status. Employees are confused and nervous. Customers, vendors, and suppliers are wary about the firm's future. It's essential that the turnaround team be open and frank with all of these groups.

Once the major problems have been identified, the team develops a strategic plan with specific goals and detailed functional actions. To keep the process moving and to make sure

A Successful Turnaround at ISH

How exactly would you implement the turnaround steps in Exhibit 12.9? Here we illustrate the turnaround process for ISH GmbH, one of Europe's largest and most successful cable companies. Formerly part of Deutsche Telekom, in April 2002 this supplier of cable services to approximately 4 million homes in the German state of North Rhine Westphalia (NRW) was in a state of total business failure—bleeding cash, losing money, and in default on nearly €2.7 billion (€ is the symbol for euros) in debt. This is the story of ISH's resurrection from the organizational graveyard.

STAGE 1: CHANGING MANAGEMENT

In April 2002, ISH's management brought in the strategy-consulting and turnaround firm AlixPartners to help it analyze its books and cash flow. AlixPartners is a professional turnaround firm recently credited with profit improvement at beleaguered Kmart. Nearly 120 days later, ISH shareholders appointed Jim Bonsall to fill the role of CEO. Bonsall is a principal with AlixPartners and has 25 years experience working with European and multinational public and private companies.

STAGE 2: SITUATION ANALYSIS

Ironically, when AlixPartners was brought in, ISH management was completely unaware of the depth of the firm's problems. Although this may sound surprising, a management team may lose track of the need for change when its members are too heavily invested in the status quo. Initial analyses revealed that, although the firm had recorded current liabilities of €7 million, the actual number was €500 million! Management was also unaware that ISH was in default on many of its secured-debt facilities. These amounted to nearly €2.5 billion; thus, its total liabilities were approximately €3 billion.

STAGE 3: EMERGENCY ACTION

The complexities of Germany's insolvency code nearly always result in the total liquidation of a firm's assets. Once difficulties are discovered, a troubled firm has 21 days to resolve relationships with creditors prior to being declared insolvent. To take advantage of this three-week window of opportunity, AlixPartners worked quickly to gain 120 days of additional short-term bank financing and assigned teams of AlixPartners professionals to ISH's 17 largest vendors. Teams met weekly, and the objective was to educate bankers and vendors on the balance sheet and operating strengths of ISH while preventing a premature declaration of insolvency. By the end of the 120-day period, not only had insolvency been avoided, but the firm had reached agreement among the major creditors on an operating plan for going forward.

STAGE 4: RESTRUCTURING ISH

Shareholders officially appointed Bonsall as CEO of ISH in late 2002. However, restructuring had actually started in the emergency-action stage in April of that year. Bonsall's early agenda for his tenure as CEO included establishing core organizational values, improving the company's image, solving problems using a team approach, and achieving profitability and industry leadership. He sought to do this by institutionalizing a balanced-scorecard system and tying a reward system to it that supported his objective of transforming the firm into a customer- and data-driven organization. Bonsall achieved these objectives the hard way: by achieving results and restoring trust and confidence in the company's goals.

One of the biggest early restructuring tasks was to reorient ISH » away from the Internet and back to its cable-television business. The company had put the vast majority of its time, money, and effort on building up its Internet subscriber base and had only 5,000 Internet subscribers to show for these efforts (versus its core, but neglected, resource of 4 million cable subscribers).

STAGE 5: NORMALCY AND ISH'S RETURN TO INDUSTRY LEADERSHIP

Bonsall's management team agreed that the best way to grow the cable business would be to offer more selection and technical innovation through a digital-program offering in the key cities of Cologne, Düsseldorf, Bochum, and Neuss. All this would have to be achieved in the first year following the restructuring, starting in December 2003. ISH overcame numerous institutional and technical complications to achieve the digitalization objectives.

Signs that the ISH turnaround was succeeding was the fact that by January 2004, cable outages had become a thing of the past and customer satisfaction was increasing. ISH saw itself as a company that provided its 4 million customers with entertainment. Soon, the company would launch a showcase with up to 50 additional channels and Near Video on Demand. Bonsall expected a standard offering for the whole of Germany to be marketed jointly by all

cable regions. ISH continued to offer high-speed Internet—with download speeds of 2 MB and upload speeds of 512 KB, leaving the competition behind in the residential customer segment.

ISH was the first cable company in Germany to offer its customers digital cable. The company was again achieving its earnings targets and generating significant value for its stakeholders. It continued to invest heavily in cable media technology and in rolling out its digital platform across the other major parts of NRW through 2004. This successful turnaround earned AlixPartners the 2003 International Turnaround of the Year award from the Turnaround Management Association.

In early 2005, Bonsall engineered the merger of ISH into another strong German cable operator, IESY. In fact, some would gauge the effectiveness of a turnaround manager by the speed with which they eliminate the company's need for them, as Bonsall had done at ISH. By July of 2005, he had already taken the reins back in the United States of another organization in need of restructuring—the Engine and Power Train Group of Tecumseh Products Company (Nasdaq: TECUA and TECUB). Tecumseh cited the need for a turnaround executive like Bonsall who had a strong and diverse multinational operating background and a proven track record of improv-

ing organization's customer service, operations, and profitability.

This turnaround summary was compiled from information available from www.turnaround.org, www.ish.com, www.alixpartners.com, and a summary of the turnaround in J. Bonsall, "Inside a German Turnaround," *Turnaround Management* Spring (2004). For information on Kmart, see K. Dybis, "Kmart Rings Up $200 Million Profit: Stock Soars as Embattled Retailer Reports Upswing for Nov., Dec., Its First Since 2000," *The Detroit News,* January 6, 2004, A1. Tecumseh Announce Performance Improvement Program, www.alixpartners.com/EN/pr_tecumseh.html, accessed December 16, 2005.

that priorities are adhered to, goals should be sequenced to correspond directly with the staging facet of the strategy diamond. Then the team must sell its plan to the key members of the organization, including the board of directors, the management team, and employees. Presenting the plan to key external parties—bankers, major creditors, and vendors—goes a long way toward regaining their confidence and financial support.

Stage 3: Implementing an Emergency Action Plan   When the firm's condition is critical, the team's plan is usually both drastic and simple. Emergency surgery is performed to stop the bleeding and improve the organization's chances of pulling through. At this time, as employees are laid off or entire departments eliminated, emotions tend to run high. Such cuts should be made thoughtfully and objectively, but swiftly.

The turnaround team must also turn its attention to cash, which is the lifeblood of the business. It must establish a positive operating cash flow as quickly as possible, and it must make sure that there's enough cash to implement its turnaround strategies. Unprofitable divisions or units are often unloaded, sometimes after some quick, corrective surgery.

Stage 4: Restructuring the Business   Once the bleeding has stopped, losing divisions sold off, and administrative costs cut, the turnaround team directs its efforts toward making current operations effective and efficient. Increasing profits and return on assets and equity usually means restructuring. In many ways, this stage is the most difficult: Cutting losses is one thing, but achieving an acceptable return on investment is another. In the new, leaner company, some facilities may be closed; the company may even withdraw from certain markets or target its products toward different markets.

Finally, as the company restructures for competitive effectiveness, the right mix of people becomes quite important. Reward and compensation systems, another implementation lever, are changed to reinforce the turnaround effort and to get people thinking "profits" and "return on investment." Everyone who still has a job must remember that survival, not tradition, is the number-one priority in reshaping the business.

Stage 5: Returning to Normal   In the final stage of the turnaround process, the company slowly returns to profitability. At earlier stages, the turnaround team focused on correcting problems. Now, however, it focuses on institutionalizing an emphasis on profitability, return on equity, and enhancing economic value. At this point, for example, the company may initiate new marketing programs to broaden its business base and increase market penetration. Financially, the firm shifts its emphasis from generating cash flow to maintaining a strong balance sheet, finding long-term financing, and setting up strategic

When sales and new franchise openings declined, Krispy Kreme's emergency plan included closing six factory stores and six smaller outlets as well as outlets of a Montana bakery it had acquired just a year earlier.

accounting and control systems. Return to normalcy also entails a psychological shift: Rebuilding momentum and morale is almost as important as restoring ROI. Corporate culture must be renewed and reshaped, and negative attitudes must be transformed into positive attitudes.

SUMMARY

1. Define *new ventures, initial public offerings (IPOs),* and *corporate renewal* and explain how they are related to strategic management. New-venture creation is the creation of a new business from scratch. Young entrepreneurial firms often use initial public offerings (IPOs) to access the world's stock markets for capital. Corporate renewal is the outcome of actions and processes that return a failing or potentially failing firm to firm financial footing and resumption of profitable growth. All three activities require good strategies and solid execution.

2. Understand entrepreneurship and the entrepreneurial process. Entrepreneurship is the consequence of actions taken based on the perception and exploration of opportunity in the absence of obviously available resources. The entrepreneurial process leads to entrepreneurship and consists of the coordination of opportunity, key resources and capabilities, and the entrepreneur and entrepreneurial team.

3. Describe the steps involved in new-venture creation and corporate new venturing. Entrepreneurial firms and established large firms follow the same steps in the new-venture creation process. The biggest difference between entrepreneurial new venturing and corporate new venturing is that the new venture in the latter context must overcome the fact that most large organizations are driven by the need to protect and optimize the use of existing resources and capabilities and discourage entrepreneurship and the pursuit of opportunity. New-venture creation starts with the identification of an opportunity. Opportunities can be distinguished from ideas in that they pass tests relating to market demand, market structure and size, and potential profitability. The remaining steps in new-venture creation are the drafting of a business plan, obtaining financing, and launching the new product or service. The order of these final three steps will vary significantly.

4. Map out the stages leading up to an IPO. Once a firm has validated a good opportunity and has some amount of prior success, its owners may seek to access capital

through an IPO. First, the firm undergoes the legal and accounting preparation for a securities offering. Second, the firm contracts with an investment banker to establish a value for the firm and eventually sell its shares. During this process, the firm files a registration document called an S-1 statement with the appropriate legal authorities. Finally, the firm and its investment bankers time the offering to coincide with a market that will likely provide the highest initial bids for the company's stock. An IPO typically provides access to capital and motivation to install more formal and professional management processes. If the firm does not have the capital needs, it may bypass the IPO and install professional management directly.

5. Understand the external and internal causes of organizational failure. The four main sources of external change that may lead to organizational failure are economic change, competitive change, social change, and technological change. Although there are many possible internal causes of organizational failure, most can be traced back to either management problems or an ineffective finance function. However, an ineffective finance function is essentially a reflection of larger management problems.

6. Outline a plan of action for strategic change and corporate renewal. Successful strategic-change efforts require communicating a new vision, defining an executive plan, having the right people and skills, getting incentives right, allocating needed resources, and altering the organizational structure if necessary. However, if the firm's financial condition has deteriorated to the point of near failure, a turnaround plan is necessary. The first stage of a turnaround plan is a change of management. It may also mean that the existing team must be replaced with executives who are able to assess the situation quickly and develop a plan to remedy the firm's woes. During the second stage, the management team determines the business' chances of survival, identifies appropriate strategies, and develops a preliminary action plan. The third stage is not required in all firms. The third stage is the implementation of an emergency-action plan when an assessment in the previous stage has determined that the firm is in critical condition. Oftentimes, assets are sold and parts of the business shuttered to avoid further crisis. The fourth stage is the actual restructuring of the business to align the organizational structure with the five elements of the strategy diamond. If all has gone as planned, the firm enters the fifth stage, during which it returns to normalcy and profitable growth.

KEY TERMS

bootstrapping, 344
corporate new venturing, 345
corporate renewal, 339
entrepreneurial process, 340

entrepreneurship, 340
initial public offering, (IPO) 340

new-venture creation, 339
road show, 348

S-1 statement, 348
strategic change, 355

REVIEW QUESTIONS

1. What is entrepreneurship?

2. What is the entrepreneurial process?

3. How is the entrepreneurial process related to strategy?

4. What steps are involved in new venture creation?

5. What is a business plan?

6. How do entrepreneurial new-venture creation and corporate new-venture creation differ?

7. What must organizations do to prepare for an IPO?

8. What are some of the external causes of organizational failure?

9. What are some of the internal causes of organizational failure?

10. What are the stages of a turnaround plan?

11. How do you know that a turnaround has been successful?

How Would you Do That?

1. The box entitled "How Would *You* Do That? 12.1" introduced a number of financial tools for predicting a firm's financial troubles. Pick a public company that has recently announced financial woes and run these analyses on its financial results for the past three years. Do any of the indicators seem to detect looming problems? What might be the limits of these financial tools?

2. The box entitled "How Would *You* Do That? 12.2" presented the successful turnaround of ISH GmbH. Identify another company in the business press that you believe to be in the turnaround process. Based on Exhibit 12.9, which stages has it entered and what have managers chosen to do in those stages? What stages remain? What do you think are the key challenges facing management in returning this firm to normalcy?

GROUP ACTIVITIES

1. Entrepreneurship starts with an idea. Without being critical or judgmental, brainstorm a set of 10 ideas that could lead to the startup of a new business. Screen your ideas and select those that would enjoy the greatest market demand, the most attractive market structure and size, and the best profit margins. Which of these screens caused most of the ideas to be discarded? What additional information would you need to seek out to answer all the screening questions?

2. For the opportunities that your team generated in the previous question, which ones would be better pursued in an entrepreneurial setting and which ones in a corporate new-ventures setting? What was the basis for this distinction? Would the entrepreneurial or corporate setting have influenced your assessment of the opportunity? Why or why not?

ENDNOTES

1. *Beverage Digest,* November 8, 2002; www.jonessoda.com (November 17, 2005); www.hoovers.com (November 17, 2005); G. Prince, "Come Together," *Beverage World,* December 1995, 50–54; J. Blake, "A Pioneer of Pop Culture," *Wisconsin State Journal,* March 18, 2004: I1.

2. W. Bygrave and J. Timmons, *Venture Capital at the Crossroads* (Boston: Harvard Business School Press, 1992).

3. For a comprehensive discussion, see J. Timmons, *New Venture Creation* (New York: Irwin-McGraw-Hill, 1999).

4. J. Eckhardt and S. Shane, "Opportunities and Entrepreneurship," *Journal of Management* 29:3 (2003), 333–349; J. Eckhardt and S. Shane, "The Individual-Opportunity Nexus: A New Perspective on Entrepreneurship," in Z. Acs and D. Audretsch, eds., *The Handbook of Entrepreneurship Research* (Boston: Kluwer, 2003), 161–191.

5. From Google, S-1 statement, 2004.

6. Timmons, *New Venture Creation;* A. Bhide, "Bootstrap Finance," *Harvard Business Review* 70:6 (1992), 109–117.

7. Bhide, "Bootstrap Finance."

8. Among other sites, try www.bplans.com, www.sba.gov/starting/businessplan.html, www.morebusiness.com, and www.businessplans.org.

9. Timmons, *New Venture Creation.*

10. H. Chesbrough, "Designing Corporate Ventures in the Shadow of Private Venture Capital," *California Management Review* 42:3 (2000), 31–49.

11. Z. Block and I. MacMillan, *Corporate Venturing* (Boston: Harvard Business School Press, 1995).

12. D. Day, "Raising Radicals: Different Processes for Championing Innovative Corporate Ventures," *Organization Science* 9 (1994), 148–172.

13. D. Garvin, *A Note on Corporate Venturing and New Business Creation* (Boston: Harvard Business School, 1997).

14. N. Fast, *The Rise and Fall of Corporate New Venture Divisions* (Ann Arbor: UMI, 1978).

15. R. Gee, "Finding and Commercializing New Business," *Research-Technology Management* 37:1 (1994), 49–56.

16. Chesbrough, "Designing Corporate Ventures."

17. D. A. Garvin, "What Every CEO Should Know About Creating New Businesses," *Harvard Business Review* 82:7–8 (July–August 2004).

18. M. Pagano, F. Panetta, and L. Zingales, "Why Do Companies Go Public? An Empirical Analysis," *Journal of Finance* 53:1 (1998), 27–64.

19. Because the regulations on IPOs are constantly changing; you may find it interesting to consult the source of these changes at www.sec.gov/index.htm.

20. R. Rajan and H. Servaes, "Analyst Following of Initial Public Offerings," *Journal of Finance* 52:2 (1997), 507–529; J. Ritter and I. Welch, "A Review of IPO Activity, Pricing, and Allocation," *Journal of Finance* 57:4 (2002), 1795–1828.

21. D. Wyckoff, *Organizational Formality and Performance in the Motor Carrier Industry* (Lexington, MA: Lexington Books, 1973).

22. Much of this material is drawn from M. A. Carpenter, *A Primer on Turnarounds* (Chicago: Association of Certified Turnaround Professionals, 2004).

23. S. Finkelstein, *Why Smart Executives Fail* (New York: Portfolio Press, 2003).

24. D. B. Bibeault, *Corporate Turnaround: How Managers Turn Losers Into Winners!* (New York: Beard Books, 2001).

25. Bibeault, *Corporate Turnaround.*

26. C. Terhune, "Krispy Kreme Issues Profit Warning—After 1st Forecast Reduction Since IPO, Stock Falls 29%; Low-Carb Fervor Is Blamed," *Wall Street Journal,* May 10, 2004, A8.

27. Finkelstein, *Why Smart Executives Fail.*

28. Finkelstein, *Why Smart Executives Fail.*

29. Thomas D. Hays, III, CTP, Certified Turnaround Professional, Nachman Hays Brownstein, Chicago, IL.

30. P. Tourtellot, "Turnarounds: How Outsiders Find the Inside Track," *Turnaround Management,* Spring (2004).

After studying this chapter you should be able to:

1. Explain what *corporate governance* means.

2. Explain how corporate governance relates to competitive advantage and understand its basic principles and practices.

3. Identify the roles of owners and different types of ownership profiles in corporate governance.

4. Show how boards of directors are structured and explain the roles they play in corporate governance.

5. Explain and design executive incentives as a corporate governance device.

6. Explain how the market for corporate control is related to corporate governance.

7. Compare and contrast corporate governance practices around the world.

▶ 1996
Al "Chainsaw" Dunlap (shown here touting a copy of his book, *Mean Business*) becomes Sunbeam's CEO. He restructures the company's board, slashes half of the firm's employees, and closes dozens of plants. Sunbeam's stock climbs from $12 to $44 in barely a year's time. Market cap (pre-Dunlap): $1.1 billion

▶ 1997–1998
Sunbeam's stock price hits a record high of $50 a share. But with R&D budgets slashed, new-product development slows, and Sunbeam misses its sales targets. Dunlap then embarks on an alternative growth strategy of acquiring other companies (and downsizing them). Market cap (all-time high): $5 billion

CORPORATE GOVERNANCE IN ACTION AT SUNBEAM

Sunbeam Products was founded in 1910 when it introduced its first product, an electric iron. Today, it makes a variety of products, such as coffeemakers, can openers, blenders, wafflemakers, toasters, mixers, and irons. In 1996, Sunbeam was struggling to turn itself into a profitable enterprise.[1] Six years earlier, Paul Kazarian, with the financial backing of Michael Price and his Mutual Series mutual funds, had purchased Sunbeam from the creditors of bankrupt Allegheny. Kazarian became the CEO and chairman but was fired by the board in 1993. After his successor also failed to turn the company around, the board turned to the famous (or infamous) Al Dunlap.

Dunlap's management philosophy includes several tenets: (1) shareholders are the most important corporate constituents—indeed they

▶ April 1998
Sunbeam is accused of "channel stuffing," faulty revenue projections, and accounting improprieties. Dunlap tries to reassure shareholders by announcing another round of massive layoffs. Sunbeam's stock price falls nearly 25 percent in a single day (to under $35). Market capitalization (following April 1998 drop): $3.3 billion

▶ June 1998
Dunlap gets "axed" by Sunbeam's board of directors (many whom were handpicked by Dunlap). Sunbeam's stock price tumbles to pennies on the dollar and then plateaus, for a time, to about $6. The stock is delisted in 2001 by the NYSE due to a lack of capitalization. Dunlap is later charged with defrauding shareholders and pays $15 million to settle their legal claims. Market cap (post Dunlap): $566 million

1995   2000

are the only constituents that should matter to CEOs; (2) most corporations have bloated bureaucracies; (3) drastic layoffs are usually needed to save failing companies; (4) these layoffs should be quick, one-time events so that employees are not constantly looking over their shoulders wondering if they are the next to be fired; (5) CEOs should be paid mostly through stock options and stock grants and rewarded like stars when they perform well and fired when they do not; (6) the board of directors should be composed of members who have a significant personal investment in the firm's stock. A few notable quips from Dunlap follow:

- "Scott was a microcosm of [bad management]. Its shareholders would have been better off captured by terrorists. They'd have been treated better" (*Financial Times,* 1994).

- "If you see an annual report with the term 'stakeholders,' put it down and *run,* don't walk, away from the company. It means the company has its priorities upside down" (*Mean Business,* p. 197).

- "When I become 'Rambo in Pinstripes' or 'Chainsaw Al,' who sells assets and fires people, I have empathy for those let go. But what I keep uppermost in my mind is not that I cut away 35 percent, but that I saved 65 percent" (*Mean Business,* p. 23).

- "You can't overpay a great executive. I'm in the business of creating shareholder value. I intend to create a lot of value for me and for everyone else. Don't you think I'm a bargain?" (*Sun-Sentinel,* 1998).

When Dunlap took control of Sunbeam on July 19, 1996, his contract was heavily weighted with performance incentives. His base salary was just over $1 million. He demanded that he not be paid an annual bonus. Rather, he negotiated for 2,500,000 shares in Sunbeam stock options and 1,000,000 shares in restricted stock grants. In addition, Dunlap used his own money to purchase $3,000,000 in Sunbeam stock. Dunlap also negotiated to restructure the board of directors and require all members to buy a significant stake of stock in the company. One new outside director recruited by Dunlap was Charles Elson, a law professor at Stetson College of Law in Gulfport, Florida. Dunlap was attracted to Elson because he was an academic advocate of board accountability and the need for board members to own stock. One idea of Elson's that attracted Dunlap was his research, which showed boards were more likely to fire CEOs if board members were required to invest in the company.

Based on his reputation for turning around stagnant companies similar to Sunbeam, Wall Street again anticipated another successful turnaround and pumped up Sunbeam's stock price in the months after Dunlap's hire. The stock jumped from $12.25 per share to over $25 per share in the first months of Dunlap's tenure. True to his philosophy, Dunlap acted quickly. He slashed the workforce in half, closed some factories, moved others to Mexico, and sold some businesses. Although downsizing was an essential element of his strategy, he also promoted a plan to grow revenues significantly. He promised to double sales in three years!

Growth proved to be a bit problematic. Dunlap planned for growth to come from internal development, but he had slashed R&D support significantly, so research into new products was hampered. In addition, it was discovered that in Dunlap's revenue projections, he had estimated a six-month lead time for new-product development. However, competitors in the same industry needed approximately two years to develop new products and get them to market, causing some to say that Dunlap's proforma income estimates were largely fictitious. Consequently, new revenue from internally developed new products trailed early projections by a significant margin. This caused Dunlap to turn to alternative growth initiatives; in early 1998, Sunbeam completed three acquisitions—Coleman, Signature Brands (e.g., Mr. Coffee), and First Alert—totaling $2.5 billion.

In April 1998, Sunbeam finally disclosed that projections were overly optimistic and that the company might suffer a loss for the quarter. This resulted in an immediate 25-percent tumble in the stock price. Dunlap tried to reassure shareholders by announcing another 40-percent workforce reduction (violating his previously stated tenet that layoffs should be one-time events during turnarounds).

Pressure from Sunbeam's shareholders, Wall Street analysts, and media critics mounted as hints of trouble began to filter out of headquarters. At a special board

meeting that Dunlap hastily called to answer media allegations of accounting improprieties, Dunlap lost his cool with board members who asked about the next quarter's
earnings. At one point during the meeting, he demanded that the board leave his
management team alone to run the company as he saw fit or that they buy him out of
his contract immediately. The board called a recess to the proceedings and met privately without Dunlap to discuss this odd turn of events. At that point, no one on the
board had any inclination to fire Dunlap. Yet Dunlap's ultimatum led them to wonder
if they had the full story. After a short but intense fact-finding investigation, the board
determined that the company's current financial condition was much worse than
Dunlap had led them to believe. At a meeting the next day, the outside members of
the board voted unanimously to terminate Dunlap, stating in a press release that they
had "lost confidence in Dunlap's leadership."

Ironically, the leader of the board revolt against Dunlap was none other than Charles
Elson, the law professor advocate for shareholders' rights whom Dunlap had personally recruited to the board. Indeed, Elson would later reminisce that his tenure on
Sunbeam's board was an experiment of his own theory; he mortgaged his home to
raise over $100,000 to buy 5,000 shares of Sunbeam stock, putting his own money on
the line. Elson suspected that his willingness to take an adversarial lead against the
man who recruited him was due to his personal investment in the company.

What consequences did Al Dunlap face for failing to turn around Sunbeam to the
board's satisfaction? First, he lost his job. Second, all those stock options that he was
given when he was hired (and the additional options he loaded up with when his contract was renewed in early 1998) lost their value when the firm's stock price tumbled.
In addition, as a result of being fired, he forfeited his options. So, even if the stock
price were to recover later under different leadership, he would not benefit. Third, the
stock he purchased when hired lost much of its value. ■

WHAT IS CORPORATE GOVERNANCE?

This chapter brings the strategy dialogue full circle. As the opening vignette illustrates,
shareholders, employees, and other stakeholders run the risk that managers will engage in
practices detrimental to the value, health, and vitality of the firm. As you learned in
Chapters 1 and 2, the CEO and members of the top-management team set and guide the
vision for the firm and its stakeholders and are responsible for formulating and implementing the strategy that realizes that vision. Al Dunlap was one of the best-known corporate turnaround artists of the 1990s. He was hired as Sunbeam's new CEO to implement a
restructuring but was fired almost two years later when the company's financial performance and stock price began to decline. Many of the controversies that had surrounded
him at his previous jobs followed him to Sunbeam: his rejection of the multiple stakeholder
view of corporate governance, his aggressive managerial style, his shaky relations with the
media, and his high level of pay.

Once shareholders invest in a firm, they have relatively little direct control over what
happens within the firm. This separation of the ownership of the capital necessary to fund
a business enterprise from the day-to-day operational management of business affairs is
the crux of what is known as the **agency problem**. From shareholders' perspectives, the
solution to the agency problem is to find ways to ensure that corporate resources and profits are not squandered, that executives will not make choices that benefit themselves at
shareholders' expense, and that shareholders will receive a positive return on their investment.[2] The means and mechanisms used to ensure that managers act in accordance with
investors' best interests are the topic of this chapter.

It should also be noted that whether a company resides in a country with a strong orientation toward shareholders' rights, such as the United States or the United Kingdom, or is
located in a country with relatively weak shareholders' rights and stronger protection for

agency problem Separation of its
ownership from managerial control of
a firm

other stakeholders, such as Germany or France, all companies have a corporate governance system. The differences across these national contexts are discussed later in the chapter.

Corporate governance is the system by which organizations, particularly business corporations, are directed and controlled by their owners. However, all organizations—public, private, and nonprofit—have some form of governance in place. Corporate governance addresses the distribution of rights and responsibilities among different participants in the organization, such as the board, managers, shareholders, and other stakeholders, and spells out the rules and procedures for making decisions on corporate affairs. By doing this, governance also provides the structure through which the company's objectives are set and the means of attaining those objectives and monitoring performance.[3] Dunlap's disdain for the stakeholder view of governance is a bit deceiving; he simply believes that shareholders are the only stakeholders worthy of consideration. A broader stakeholder view of governance is that the firm, as a function of its governance, seeks to benefit other stakeholders beyond shareholders. This is sometimes called the "triple bottom line" in the corporate world, because a firm's strategy and related investments have financial performance objectives and social and environmental objectives as well. In this chapter, we introduce you to the language and principles of corporate governance.

CORPORATE GOVERNANCE AND COMPETITIVE ADVANTAGE

Before considering specific governance mechanisms that can protect shareholders, consider the following overarching question: *What effect does corporate governance have on firm survival, performance, and competitive advantage?* Although the answer to this question is actually very complex and the governance mechanisms themselves required by regulators and peer pressure are very costly to implement and maintain, strong evidence suggests that shareholders favor good governance and that it can help firms outperform those with poor governance.

Evidence That Governance Works

Germany provides a case in point with respect to an important governance mechanism—stock-based incentive plans. Prior to 1998, German law did not permit firms to issue U.S.– and U.K.–styled stock-option pay to executives. A few firms found creative ways around this legal roadblock and implemented pay schemes that mimicked stock options. This led the German legislature to reconsider the prohibition. By 1998, the law had been rewritten to allow limited forms of stock-based compensation. Once the legal obstacle was removed, about half of Germany's largest firms quickly adopted stock-based incentive plans. Early adopters of such plans were rewarded by the stock market with higher share prices; however, these incentives also seemed to lead to new strategies in these firms; many started to restructure by divesting non-core business operations.[4]

Similar effects for governance mechanisms have been illustrated among Italian firms. In Italy, large investors have traditionally shied away from small and midsize companies because of concerns about liquidity and poor standards of corporate governance. To alleviate these concerns and help attract capital to this important economic segment, the Italian stock exchange, the Mercato Italiano di Borsa, started a new exchange called STAR. It was designed to be a separate market for small and midsize companies that follow strict governance prescriptions. Some of these prescriptions include provisions that the board must include a minimum number of independent directors and use performance-based compensation to reward both management and members of the board. Comparing the results of this index of well-governed firms with the general index of other small and midsized firms that do not adhere to these governance profiles illustrates the potential value of good governance. Even taking into consideration the possibility that better-managed firms are more likely to join the new STAR exchange, the companies on the STAR exchange have

Small- and midsized Italian firms typically have been poorly governed. To encourage investment in these companies, the Italian Stock Exchange, called the Mercato Italiano di Borsa, started a new exchange for them called STAR. Companies listed on STAR adhere to strict corporate governance rules. As a group, these companies consistently outperform those listed on the Borsa.

consistently outperformed their counterparts on the Borsa; during 2004, STAR firms achieved 24.5-percent greater returns than their counterparts.[5]

Consider the effect of governance mechanisms on the survival and market capitalization of Internet-based companies launched in the United States. These companies were risky for investors because they used new business models and lacked objective operating data that investors could analyze. This created significant uncertainty in the valuation of these new firms. Because of the lack of traditional indicators of quality that would enable analysts to value the firms objectively, the markets seemed to turn to secondary information sources as indicators of the underlying quality of these risky firms. Market valuations of these firms have been tightly linked to the firms' corporate governance characteristics (e.g., executive and director stock-based incentives, institutional and large-block stock ownership, board structure, and venture capital participation). Indeed, these governance factors were much stronger predictors of firm valuation and survival than things such as firm sales and profits.[6] The market seems to put more faith in risky new firms with good governance characteristics than in their counterparts with loose oversight by rewarding firms perceived to have good governance with significantly higher valuations.

Finally, consider the recent cases of corporate fraud and malfeasance in the United States. Corporate scandals have shaken the foundations of American business. In a short period, investors watched billions of dollars of wealth evaporate and dozens of individual managers and employees suddenly found themselves on the street or, worse, incarcerated. As it turns out, firms that engaged in the most egregious scandals exhibited several warning signs, as evidenced in the nature of how the corporate governance was structured. Sometimes effective governance may not prevent executive fraud, but it enables the firm to recover from its consequences. In summary, corporate governance has a strong bearing on the ability of firms to create a competitive advantage and exploit that advantage for the benefit of shareholders.

The Case of Krispy Kreme   Some of these warning signals, as shown in the case of Krispy Kreme in Exhibit 13.1, were actually detected by organizations such as Governance Metrics International (GMI), which rates the quality of a firm's governance practices. Could careful attention to corporate governance issues have saved Krispy Kreme investors lots of money? In other words, is corporate governance some kind of expensive window dressing, or does it actually impact the bottom line? Analysis of Krispy Kreme's stock price

Exhibit 13.1 Early Warning Signals of Problems with Krispy Kreme from GMI

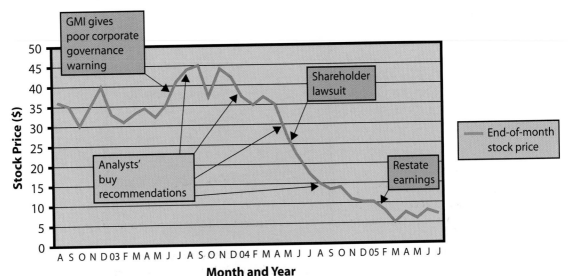

This exhibit summarizes a press release from Governance Metrics International (GMI), a New York City organization that provides governance ratings on public companies around the world.

Source: M. Maremont and R. Brooks, "Fresh Woes Batter Krispy Kreme; Doughnut Firm to Restate Results, Delay SEC Filing; Shares Take a 15% Tumble," Wall Street Journal (Eastern edition), January 5, 2005, A3.

performance, analysts' recommendations, and the warnings of a GMI suggest that good governance has a positive impact on firm performance.

On January 4, 2005, Krispy Kreme Doughnuts Inc. announced that it was filing a financial restatement; its stock had fallen 73 percent over the previous 12 months. How did Krispy Kreme lose so much of its value in such a short period of time? GMI, which had begun evaluating firms in 2002, first rated Krispy Kreme in June 2003, and compared to all other U.S. companies, Krispy Kreme scored a below-average 4.0 for its corporate governance practices. (On GMI 10-point scale, an average company earns about 6 points.) Among other things, GMI cited a relatively large number of nonindependent directors and related-party transactions and a lack of disclosure about ethical codes of conduct. In short, GMI concluded that the company did not have a strong overall governance record. Seven months later, in January 2004, GMI rerated the company, and its score had dropped to 2.5. At this stage, none of Krispy Kreme's financial woes had been discovered or announced, but the declining GMI scores clearly pointed to risk. Five months later, in May 2004, a shareholder suit was initiated, and in July, an SEC investigation was announced.

However, over this same period, several Wall Street firms were recommending the stock. On August 22, 2003, one had an outperform rating on the stock (even though it was a downgrade from a top pick), and as of January 2005, Krispy Kreme still had an outperform rating. On December 17, 2003, another Wall Street firm initiated coverage with a buy recommendation, as did another on March 30, 2004. Another initiated coverage on September 13, 2004, with a hold recommendation, and yet another issued a strong buy on September 28, 2004.

GMI is the first to admit that governance should not be the only screen in stock selection, but with this kind of downward move in ratings, one would think that financial analysts would have tempered their enthusiasm. Some analysts now believe that corporate governance attributes can have a strong influence on the quality of earnings. Further evidence of this belief is the recent action of Morningstar, one of the most respected investment advisory firms, to grade firms on an A-through-F scale based on the degree to which companies align their corporate governance practices with shareholders' interests.[7]

Corporate Governance and Strategy

Corporate governance is related to strategy formulation and implementation in several ways. The most visible roles are in establishing controls and incentives. Boards should ensure that the firm's vision and mission are reflected in its strategy, monitor the way that strategy is executed, and insure the top executives' reap appropriate career and financial consequences in cases of failure or success.

The risk that managers will deviate from an organization's stated purpose and its guiding documents increases when managers are not the owners of the firm.[8] For instance, when the founders of a company raise capital through an IPO, they generally exchange a significant portion of the firm's stock for the financial capital needed to fund the operations and growth of the firm. After going public, the founders of an IPO firm dilute their ownership, often become minority owners of the firm, and instantly accept accountability for their actions to independent outside shareholders. Likewise, executives of older or large publicly held firms are generally owners of very small percentages of the firm.[9] For instance, research shows that the median level of executive ownership is 0.06 percent of outstanding shares.[10]

How do shareholders hold executives accountable for their actions and ensure that the firm is operated in a manner consistent with the firm's mission? What recourse do shareholders have if they find executives formulating strategies that lack coherence or fail to create value or, worse, engaging in unethical or illegal practices? A number of corporate governance mechanisms help shareholders avoid losing control of the corporation to unscrupulous or incompetent management.

The Major Parties in Corporate Governance

An agency relationship exists when one party, the **agent**, acts on behalf of another party, the **principal**. In corporations like Sunbeam, shareholders are viewed as principals, and key executives like Dunlap are viewed as agents.[11] Generally, a few assumptions can be made about principals and agents that highlight the potential problems in an agency relationship.

> **agent** Party, such as a manager, who acts on behalf of another party
>
> **principal** Party, such as a shareholder, who hires an agent to act on his or her behalf

First, let's consider the interests of agents and principals in a corporation. What is it that each party wants from the relationship? Most theoretical treatments of the agency relationship in a modern corporation assume that both shareholders and executives are self-interested decision makers. This does not mean that they have no interest in the well-being of the other party; it simply means that they will generally make decisions that are in their own best interests. When the interests of shareholders and executives are virtually identical—when their goals are in alignment—then the agency problem is small. In this situation, executives will do what shareholders want them to do because it serves their own interests as well as those of the firm's shareholders.

However, in most situations, the interests of principals and agents do not naturally overlap completely; some things that would be in shareholders' best interests may be detrimental to those of executives and vice versa. For example, high executive salaries logically reduce corporate profits, which may be reflected in lower relative earnings per share if the higher pay has not led to higher firm performance in the first place. Similarly, executives may choose to diversify the firm to smooth earnings and reduce their own employment (or unemployment) risk without actually improving the competitive position of the firm. Thus, the key for shareholders is either to find a way to align the interests of executives with their own or to closely monitor and control what executives do so that shareholders' interests are protected.

Codes of Governance

Many markets and investor groups around the globe have formulated **codes of governance**—ideal governance standards to which firms should adhere. Some of these are followed voluntarily; others are formalized by law. Codes of governance are aimed at four main issues: shareholder equality—upholding shareholder rights; accountability by the board and management; disclosure and transparency through accurate and timely financial and nonfinancial reporting; and independence (audits and oversight; directors).

> **codes of governance** Ideal governance standards formulated by regulatory, market, and government institutions

Sir Adrian Cadbury, who retired as the Chairman of Cadbury Schweppes in 1989, was instrumental in creating the "Cadbury Code," published in 1992. The Cadbury Code, which advocates improved corporate governance practices, became the model for corporate reform in Europe and around the world.

The Cadbury Code   Following a series of corporate scandals in the United Kingdom and the United States, Sir Adrian Cadbury, former chairman of Cadbury Schweppes, raised the public's awareness and stimulated debate on corporate governance. His most celebrated achievement is the Cadbury Code, his namesake and a code of best practices that has served as a model for reform around the world.

What is the Cadbury Code's history? In 1991, the Cadbury Commission was established in the United Kingdom to help raise corporate governance standards and increase the level of confidence in financial reporting and auditing by clarifying the respective responsibilities and obligations of relevant entities. In 1992, the Cadbury Committee issued a report with suggestions for corporate governance reform among U.K. companies. Known as the Cadbury Code of Best Practice, the report made 19 recommendations for better firm governance. Since that time, similar codes have been crafted in many countries around the world, including Brazil, the Netherlands, Oman, the Philippines, Russia, Switzerland, Canada, France, Germany, Italy, and the United States. In all, more than over 50 countries have adopted their own codes (see Exhibit 13.2 for examples of several of these codes). The burden placed on firms by these codes varies across the globe. However, all of these new codes significantly increased the stringency recommended governance standards within their respective countries.

Some codes impose a comply-or-explain burden on firms. For instance, the SEC now requires companies to disclose whether they have financial experts on their audit committees and, if not, to explain why not. As indicated in Exhibit 13.2, although all of the codes do not impose the same requirements, their aims and recommendations overlap considerably.

The Sarbanes-Oxley Act   Perhaps the most far-reaching governance reforms in the United States—at least from the standpoint that they are legal requirements—are seen in the Sarbanes-Oxley Act of 2002. What was the motivation for these new requirements? Just a few household names: Adelphia, Enron, Arthur Andersen, WorldCom, and Tyco. When corporate names like these synonymous with scandal and greed, public confidence in stock as a secure investment wavers. The Sarbanes-Oxley Act was signed into law on July 30, 2002, in response to these corporate scandals. Now, all companies are required to file periodic reports with the SEC. Noncompliance comes with significant penalties. The essential components of Sarbanes-Oxley deal with accounting oversight, auditor independence, disclosure, analysts' conflicts of interests, accountability for fraud, and attorney's responsibilities.[12]

Exhibit 13.2 Examples of Codes of Governance

Country	What is the recommendation on director independence?	Can the same executive be both CEO and chairperson?	Is auditor rotation required?	Is disclosure required if the company does not comply with the recommendations?
Brazil CVM Code (2002)	As many as possible	Split recommended	Not addressed	No
Russia CG Code (2002)	At least one-quarter	Split required by law	Not addressed	No
Singapore CG Committee (2001)	At least one-third	Split recommended	Not addressed	Yes
United Kingdom Cadbury Code[1] (1992)	Majority	Split recommended	Periodic rotation of lead auditor	Yes
United States Conference Board and CalPers (2003)[2]	Substantial majority	Separation is one of three acceptable alternatives	Recommended[3]	No

[1]In 2003, a combined code made further additions to the code, but these basic principles remain.
[2]Just one of several codes in existence in the United States.
[3]The Sarbanes-Oxley Act requires that the lead audit partner be rotated every 5 years and that audit firms be changed either after 10 years of continual relationship or if former audit partner is employed by the company.

Public Company Accounting Oversight Board   Sarbanes-Oxley resulted in the creation of the Public Company Accounting Oversight Board to oversee the audits of public companies. This board sets standards and rules for audit reports. All accounting firms that audit public companies must register with the oversight board. This board also inspects, investigates, and enforces compliance by these registered firms. A few of the new governance compliance rules that resulted from Sarbanes-Oxley include:

- Auditors must list the nonaudit services they are unable to perform during an audit.
- Audit-firm employees who leave an accounting firm must wait one year to become an executive for a former client.
- Transactions and relationships that are off the balance sheet but that may affect financial status must now be disclosed.
- Personal loans from a corporation to its executives are now largely prohibited.
- Research analysts for securities firms must now file conflict-of-interest disclosures. For instance, analysts must report whether they hold any securities in a company or have received corporate compensation.
- Brokers and dealers must disclose if the public company is a client.
- Altering, destroying, concealing, or falsifying records or documents with the intent to influence a federal investigation or bankruptcy case is subject to fines and up to 20 years of imprisonment.

Securities laws like Sarbanes-Oxley are complicated and confusing. But failing to follow the Act's new restrictions and procedures can result in severe penalties.

Whether legal or voluntary, all governance guidelines appear to have four agency control mechanisms in common. These relate to (1) ownership concentration and power, (2) boards of directors, (3) incentive compensation, and (4) the market for corporate control. Each of these mechanisms, reviewed in the following sections, can work to decrease the likelihood that managers will act in ways detrimental to shareholders.

OWNERSHIP AND THE ROLES OF OWNERS

The ownership of for-profit firms can be subdivided into different ownership types, such as public and private firms (although the definition of public versus private varies from the U.S. definition in different parts of the world). A private firm is one in which the owner(s) has not listed shares of the firm on a public exchange; shares are typically owned largely by the founding families or by an investment group, such as a leveraged-buy-out firm or venture capitalist. A public firm has sold shares to the general investing public, but how those publicly traded shares are dispersed or concentrated varies significantly and leads to another way to categorize public firms.

Dispersion of Ownership   Some firms have a few select owners who control significant stakes in the firm. Consequently, these parties have so much voting power that they can have significant influence and control over the firm's strategy and governance. Sometimes they use that influence to determine who stays in power as CEO or chair of the board. An example of an owner-controlled firm is Nike; founder Philip Knight resigned as CEO, but he still owns 92 percent of the firm's class A stock and remains chair of the board of directors. Other firms have highly dispersed ownership, and managers also own small percentages of the firm's stock.

The dispersion of stock ownership affects the type and magnitude of agency problems investors face. However, the presence of a powerful owner does not remove all forms of agency problems. One specific type of problem arises when a single powerful owner uses that power to extract private benefits from the company at the expense of other, less powerful owners. The fraud case against Adelphia alleges just such behavior. Members of the Rigas family were convicted of using their ownership power and board control to enable them to use corporate assets as collateral for personal and family loans, ultimately squandering the company's fortunes.[13]

Even when ownership is dispersed and no shareholder's ownership approaches a majority interest, some shareholders are in a position to influence corporate policies. In the United States, the SEC considers an ownership position of 5 percent sufficient to wield significant influence. Owners who control 5 percent or more of a firm's shares are referred to as *blockholders,* and this level of ownership or control must be publicly disclosed. Blockholders are considered powerful because voting blocks that large can sway boards of directors on important votes.

Exhibit 13.3 demonstrates a few different ownership profiles. The nature of executive/shareholder relationships varies across the firms in the exhibit. At Coca-Cola for instance, managers are very cognizant that over 13 percent of the company's stock is controlled by two individuals: Warren Buffet and James Williams. Both of these investors are members of the board of directors as a result of their sizeable investments. Contrast that profile with that of Dell, where the only major individual investor is founder Michael Dell.

institutional investors Pension or mutual fund that manages large sums of money for third-party investors

Institutional Behaviors   FedEx has another type of powerful owner to deal with. Vanguard, Barclays, and Capital Research and Management Company each owned more than 5 percent of the company in 2004. Investors such as Vanguard are known as **institutional investors**; the money they control is capital invested in mutual funds and pension funds controlled by the company. Sometimes these institutional investors own large blocks of individual companies. Most institutional investors are relatively passive investors: They essentially vote with their feet by purchasing or selling a stock based on their outlook for the firm's performance, and therefore the potential performance of the firm's stock. But they can also become quite active should the need arise, and some institutional investors, such as CalPers (the California Public Employees' Retirement System) and SWIB (State of Wisconsin Investment Board), are by their charter activist investors.[14]

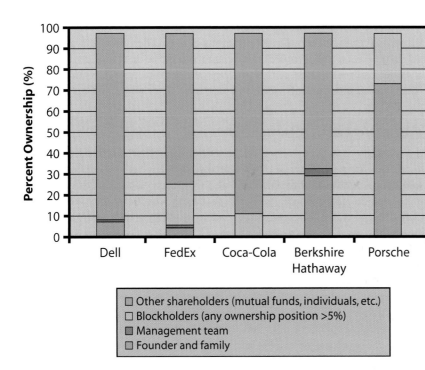

Exhibit 13.3 Ownership Structure Comparison

Source: Company annual reports.

Different types of institutional investors seem to have preferences for firms with different strategies. For instance, recent research has found that the managers of public pension funds prefer to invest in firms that follow strategies that attempt to exploit internal innovation, whereas investments made by managers of professional investment funds revealed preferences for firms that attempt to acquire innovations externally through acquisitions.[15] For sure, managers of these two types of institutional funds do not limit their investments to these types of firms, but their portfolios demonstrate nonrandom preferences.

Perhaps the most important lesson in this observation for managers of firms is the idea that owners do not have a unified voice. Economic theories make assumptions about shareholders and their preferences, but in reality different types of shareholders have different preferences. For instance, examine the types of owners that control Porsche, the German sports-car manufacturer. It is unlikely that the family who owns most of Porsche would vote the same way on many corporate issues that independent mutual-fund managers would because the issues that are important to each are not always the same. Indeed, as you examine the marketing material for different mutual funds, you will notice that many of them have different objectives. The implication for managers is that they must understand who owns the company and what their interests are.

THE BOARD OF DIRECTORS

One of the chief monitoring devices available to shareholders is the board of directors. All publicly held companies are required to have a **board of directors**. A board of directors—a group of individuals who formally represents the firm's shareholders—is charged with overseeing the work of top executives. The legal roles of the board include hiring and firing top executives, monitoring management, ensuring that shareholders' interests are protected, establishing executive compensation, and reviewing and approving the firm's strategy. Informal roles played by boards include acting as conduits of information from external sources, providing leads for acquisition and alliance-partner candidates, influencing important external parties such as industry regulators and foreign government policy makers, and providing advice and counsel for the CEO and other top executives.

Although corporate laws vary around the globe, resulting in some differences in board practices, the general responsibility of the board of directors is to ensure that executives are

board of directors Group of individuals that formally represents the firm's shareholders and oversees the work of top executives

acting in shareholders' best interests. In the United States, shareholders elect members of the board of directors. In the wake of numerous high-profile financial scandals in recent years, boards have been under increasing pressure to exercise their monitoring responsibility with greater vigilance.[16] Part of this pressure comes from the U.S. Congress, which has created laws that require public firms to put particular governance reforms into place.[17]

Insiders Versus Outsiders

A board of directors is typically composed of several very experienced individuals. Most of these individuals are generally not officers of the company but, rather, are employed by other companies. Executives of the firm who also serve on the board are often referred to as *insiders;* those on the board who are not employed by the firm otherwise are known as *outsiders.* Outsiders can typically be more independent in fulfilling their board responsibilities, but being an outsider does not necessarily make a director independent. For instance, the independent judgement of a director who has another business relationship with the company may be compromised.

Most institutional investors and watchdog groups prefer a large majority of independent directors. This helps to avoid conflicts of interests in carrying out fundamental responsibilities. As a result, there is a strong movement to increase the percentage of board members who are independent outsiders. However, insiders, although not independent, have access to more critical knowledge of the business and its environment and have the potential to add critical insight to board deliberations.[18]

Boards in the United States are typically made up of a majority of outside directors, along with one or more senior executives of the firm. Although there is the presumption that outside directors make for a more vigilant board, this is not always the case. First, outside directors may not be independent; they may have business dealings with the firm or friendship ties to the CEO. Similarly, by virtue of their position, CEOs have considerable control over outside directors, which may make it difficult for them to be truly independent. These relationships can affect how they monitor and advise management. Although watchdog groups seem to clamor for more independent outsiders on boards, research reveals that in some circumstances, increasing the number of insiders (i.e., executives) on the board can increase the board's effectiveness. For instance, when the firm operates in highly technical areas, insiders can provide better information than can many independent outsiders.[19]

What To Do About the CEO Chair   In approximately 70 percent of U.S. public firms, the CEO also serves as the chair of the board of directors. Debate continues as to the wisdom of an "independent chair" structure in American corporate culture. As evidenced by the prevalence of dual CEO/chairs in the United States, corporations are generally resistant to the idea of separating the two positions. Although separating the roles of CEO and board chair is more common in European corporations[20] (and is one of the Cadbury guidelines in the United Kingdom), it remains the exception in the United States. However, the two roles are actually quite distinct, and there is a movement to separate the two jobs. In other countries, norms and laws lead to other configurations. In Germany, because such duality is prohibited, the CEO and the board chair are always different people. When the roles are split, it is critical that the board chair not take operational roles, just as the CEO shouldn't attempt to run the board.

The logic for combining the posts includes the need for specialized information that an outsider could not have and a lack of qualified candidates. The logic for splitting is monitoring: One cannot effectively serve as referee and player at the same time. Many critics of U.S. corporate governance practices believe, however, that true board independence may ultimately—within the next decade—require a serious reexamination of this historic combination of powers.[21] Consequently, pressure is increasing to separate these two positions so that the board can more effectively monitor top executives. Some large U.S. companies that have recently transitioned from a combined chair/CEO to a split model include Boeing, Dell, Walt Disney, and Oracle.

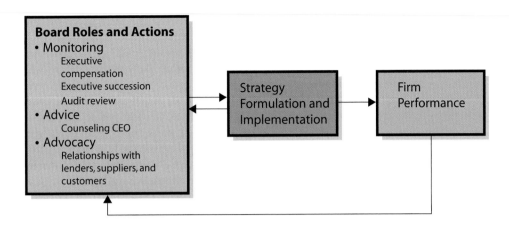

Exhibit 13.4 Board Roles and Actions

The Board's Activities and the Company's Strategy

Boards generally are organized into several committees, with key board responsibilities being assigned to different committees. For instance, all companies listed on the New York Stock Exchange (NYSE) must have an audit committee, which is responsible for selecting the independent auditor and reviewing the reports provided by that outside auditor. Because independent audits of books and records is critical to effective monitoring, the NYSE requires that the audit committee be composed only of outsiders; insiders may not be responsible for ensuring the independence of the audit. In addition, boards have compensation committees that are charged with setting the level of executive compensation.

The relationship between the board and firm strategy and performance is illustrated in Exhibit 13.4. Let's review each of these mechanisms and discuss how managers can utilize the board to further the purposes of the firm.

Monitoring   One of the key roles of the board of directors is to monitor the performance of top executives and potentially replace management when necessary. **Monitoring** is the process of the board acting in its legal and fiduciary responsibility to oversee executives' behaviors and performance and to take action when necessary to replace management. The opening vignette on Sunbeam provides an example of this role. Some of the most important decisions made by the board are hiring and firing the CEO and other senior executives. Effective boards make sure that they have an executive succession plan that keeps the firm prepared in the event that a new CEO is needed. Some forms of succession, such as retirement, are easier to plan for than others. Orderly succession seems to have better results than sudden termination and turning to a new outsider to fix the firm's problems. A recent study of CEO successions in U.S. companies illustrates this point (see Exhibit 13.5).

monitoring Functioning of the board in exercising its legal and fiduciary responsibility to oversee executives' behavior and performance and to take action when it's necessary to replace management

conceptlink

In Chapter 2, we emphasize that, along with *teamwork and diversity*, **succession planning**—the process of managing the transition from one CEO to another with the best outcomes for all key **stakeholders**—is among the most important functions of an effective *executive team*.

Exhibit 13.5 CEO Firing

Source: M. Wiersema, "Holes at the Top: Why CEO Firings Backfire," Harvard Business Review *80:12 (2002), 70–77.*

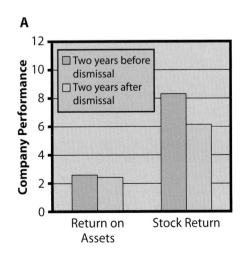

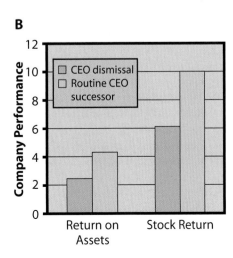

Firing is a drastic monitoring device that should be used judiciously. More routine monitoring mechanisms include meeting regularly as a board, hiring competent external auditors, and diligently reviewing financial and operating results. Evidence suggests that when a CEO is fired for firm-performance reasons, it is more likely that the board will recruit an outsider as a replacement. Although outsiders do bring a fresh perspective, research shows that they are more likely than not to deploy strategies that lead their firms to underperform, not outperform, their competition. Indeed, the best-performing firms, following the forced replacement of the CEO, appear to be those run by executives who already have experience at the company they are leading.[22] Perhaps the best case-in-point here is the placement of Jack Welch, a GE manager, into the CEO role. Welch dramatically changed the firm's strategy and created the diversified powerhouse we know today.

Advising Managers   Although increasing emphasis is being placed on the monitoring roles of boards, recent research has shown that just as much, if not more, value is to be had by tapping into the expertise and contacts of the board and using board members as confidants and information sources. On the other hand, many critics of corporate governance argue that CEOs who have social ties and friendships with board members could put shareholders at risk because these relationships may make the board less likely to monitor the CEO effectively.

As the introductory vignette on Sunbeam points out, this is not always the case—in the end, Dunlap's ouster was championed by the outside board member (Charles Elson) who Dunlap had appointed. Research indicates that social ties typically fail to reduce the level of board-monitoring activity and that, in fact, such social ties improve the ability of the CEO to tap board members for advice and counsel on strategic issues. This suggests that social ties between CEOs and board members may increase board involvement rather than decrease it.[23] The same research found that CEOs were more willing to turn to board members for advice when they had social ties to these members—when they considered the relationship to be friendship based, not solely monitoring based. This suggests that when CEOs perceive they have a loyal board, they will involve the board more in strategic decision making.

Finally, the research also demonstrated that firms in which CEOs collaborate with board members on strategic issues outside of board meetings perform significantly better than firms that limit CEO/board interactions to purely monitoring roles. The trend is to encourage board members to be more actively involved, as opposed to passively involved (i.e., simply a rubber stamp on the executive team's recommendations). For instance, General Electric now requires that its board members spend time at its various facilities around the world in addition to the regular boardroom meetings.

Because more advice and counsel interactions between board members and executives leads to improved firm performance, managers and board members alike are interested in how these interactions can be exploited for shareholders' benefit. How can the board be structured to maximize the positive strategic counsel that can take place between the board and the CEO? Simply adding more directors to the board is not an effective method for increasing these interactions; increasing the number of board members who can provide CEOs with appropriate strategic knowledge does increase board–CEO involvement.[24] Research shows that positive CEO–board interactions are maximized when the selection of outside board members matches the competitive environment facing the firm. When firms are in relatively stable competitive environments, the advice and monitoring of board members is enhanced when outside board members are drawn from other firms that are strategically related to the firm. In these stable environments, the knowledge and experience that board members gain in their own firm translates well to the firm they monitor.

However, when the firm is located in a very unstable competitive environment, board involvement is most effective when outside board members are drawn from strategically dissimilar firms. This is probably due to the fact that in unstable environments, boards need to tap into multiple experiential backgrounds to help make sense of the firm's competitive environment. Given the increasingly active role that directors play in strategy and the greater demands of the job, it should come as no surprise that the complexion of the boardroom is changing. Boards today are typically larger and more diverse, and members are more highly paid, than in years past.[25]

Using the Board as a Lever of Power and Influence   Finally, boards also provide access to external resources, and it is not uncommon for a director to sit on multiple boards (a characteristic called a *board interlock*). These resources can range from access to capital, to new knowledge, to the ability to influence other external stakeholders, such as investors, banks, and regulators. CEOs often sit on the boards of other firms, though, given their time constraints, they often sit on only one or two others at the most. When asked why they would invest the required time and effort in another firm's success, they often respond that it is the learning component that drives their choice. They report that they learn from the CEO and executives of the other firm and benefit from the knowledge and contacts possessed by their peer directors.[26]

Beyond the straightforward fact that a board position may provide access to resources and be a lever of power or influence over other important stakeholders, some believe that such influence and power can get out of hand. One aspect of this perspective is CEO-centric from the standpoint that CEOs may be tempted to seek out other CEOs to sit on their boards if those potential board members are highly paid at their home firms. Landing highly paid CEOs as directors will probably lead to a board that will be supportive of paying high wages for CEOs. For instance, critics of corporate excess, such as the Conference Board or Institutional Shareholders Services, point to research showing that the CEOs of the boards of companies on which Home Depot's CEO Bob Nardelli sits are overpaid relative to their peers and that Nardelli himself is overpaid.[27]

As you learned in the opening paragraph of this section, it is not unusual for directors to sit on multiple boards or for companies to be interconnected via their directors. For instance, PepsiCo director Robert E. Allen also sits on the board of Bristol-Myers Squibb. Ironically, Coca-Cola director James D. Robinson III, also sits on the board of Bristol-Myers Squibb, leaving you to wonder how the Cola Wars play out in the Bristol-Myers' boardroom. Debate continues as to whether such board interlocks help firms perform better by virtue of their access to better information or simply allow corporations to collude at the expense of the public at large. Although there is no evidence that consumers are generally

CEOs such as Home Depot's Robert Nardelli often sit on the boards of other firms as a so-called learning experience. But some people believe the practice leads to inflated salaries for CEOs and other corporate governance problems.

harmed by such interrelationships at the board level, strategy research has shown that directors themselves may be more effective as monitors if they are linked to certain firms given the competitive standing and environmental turbulence facing the focal firms.[28] It has also been shown that common board ties can influence many other important factors, ranging from the choice of CEO to a firm's strategy in the face of failing performance.[29]

EXECUTIVE COMPENSATION

Recall our discussion, in Chapter 10, of **managerialism**—the tendency of managers to make decisions based on personal self-interest rather than on the best interests of shareholders. Because executive compensation is often tied to firm size, for example, managers may decide to make acquisitions that do nothing but make firms bigger.

incentive alignment Use of incentives to align managerial self-interest with shareholders'

One of the fundamental conditions that leads to a potential agency problem in publicly held companies is the separation of firm ownership from company management. When professional managers, rather than the owners themselves, run the operations of a firm, situations can arise in which there may be conflicts of interests—where what is best for shareholders is not necessarily what is best for management. For instance, consider a situation in which the company could receive an attractive buyout proposal from a competitor. Shareholders might be interested in pursuing this buyout if the premium they are being offered for their shares is attractive. However, management may not be as interested in the buyout if their employment is threatened. Incentives are sometimes used to alleviate this potential conflict. Of course, it is also true that sometimes incentives can unwittingly exacerbate conflicts of interest. This is why it is important to understand how incentives work, including how people tend to respond to different types of incentives.

One possible solution to these potential conflicts of interest is to structure incentive arrangements so that managers are rewarded for doing what is in shareholders' best interests. **Incentive alignment** can be used to solve the agency problem. For instance, to avoid managers' hesitancy to examine acquisition-buyout options, boards can include "golden parachute" provisions in managers' compensation packages, which offer significant bonuses when loss of employment is a consequence of an acquisition.

In practice, structuring executive compensation to completely overcome all possible conflicts of interests is impossible. A number of mechanisms are frequently used to increase the incentive alignment between shareholders and executives. We review some of these common mechanisms in this section, but we also point out how each mechanism has its limitations.

Executive Ownership

Perhaps the most direct way to align incentives is to require that executives own stock in the firm. The theory here is rather obvious: If you are an owner of the company you should behave more like an owner and less like a hired hand. In recent years, many firms have established ownership guidelines for senior executives. Consider the case of Dendrite International, which is discussed in the box entitled "How Would *You* Do That? 13.1." However, the ownership requirement may backfire. Executives cannot diversify their risk exposure as well as large shareholders. Shareholders can spread their risks across many firms, but an individual executive who is required to invest heavily in the company is likely to have a very unbalanced investment portfolio.

In addition, executives risk their human capital—that is, their reputation and future job opportunities—through the employment relationship. For U.S. firms in particular, the Sarbanes-Oxley governance reforms now require that the CEO and CFO certify that the firm's financial statements are accurate, and they can be jailed if the statements are proven to be fraudulent or misrepresentative of the facts. This increases the pressures of top executives' jobs, one indication of which is the fact that CFO turnover has increased by about 23 percent over the last three years.[30] Consequently, executives suffer heavy exposure to firm-specific risk. This type of risk exposure could lead some executives to become very risk averse. Consequently, boards need to be very careful in structuring executive compensation so that they understand just what types of behaviors they are encouraging through the economic incentives they provide.

Establishing Executive-Ownership Requirements at Dendrite International

As an illustration of a recent adopter of an executive stock-ownership plan, consider Dendrite. Dendrite (DRTE), a leading supplier of specialized software to the global pharmaceutical industry that was founded in Australia in 1986 and is now headquartered in Bedmaster, New Jersey, implemented a formal stock-ownership plan for its 20 senior-most executives and all of its nonemployee directors. The new program mandates ownership of Dendrite stock, ranging from 15,000 to 100,000 shares, depending on the executive's position.

The ownership requirements set by Dendrite are based on owned common stock, not stock options. Ownership of the predetermined number of shares must be achieved within five years, with an initial number attained in three years. Restrictions have been placed on the receipt of additional equity-based compensation and sale of Dendrite shares until ownership commitments are attained. The executive participants may obtain shares through purchase on the open market, receiving incentive compensation in shares or exercising options and holding shares.

In addition to instituting share-ownership requirements, Dendrite also made changes to its executive compensation program. Executives may now elect to receive incentive compensation in stock instead of cash. If the executive elects to receive stock, these shares are restricted from sale for one year, and the executive will receive a number of options equal to the number of restricted shares. Replacement options will be granted for shares used to exercise vested options.

By the start of 2005, Dendrite's executive stock ownership plan was fully in place. In addition, all of Dendrite's directors—executive and independent—owned at least some Dendrite stock, further aligning the board, top manager, and shareholder interests. While Dendrite is in a highly competitive and dynamic industry, it is notable that since beginning the implementation of the executive stock ownership plan in 2000, the firm has managed to garner shareholders a strong return. For instance, as of the end of 2005 shareholders had earned a three-year average return of 28 percent, versus the S&P 1500 return of 12 percent. Standard and Poors also ranked the firm among the top tier of its peers, in terms of overall performance and outlook.

Is an executive stock ownership plan an easy pathway to competitive advantage? Probably not, but at least it is an important lever in a firm's corporate governance repertoire to provide executives and directors an incentive to see that the right strategy is being executed well.

Sources: "Dendrite International Board Mandates New Executive Share Ownership Policy; Program Reflects Positive Expectations," *BusinessWire,* February 8, 2000; Standard and Poors Quantitative Stock Report; DRTE (Dendrite International), December 17, 2005.

Exhibit 13.6 Executive Stock Ownership in 2004

Source: Adapted from Fredrick W. Cook & Co., Inc., "Stock Ownership Policies: Prevalence and Design of Executive and Director Ownership Policies Among the Top 250 Companies," www.fwcook.com/ surveys.html (accessed November 29, 2005), September 2004.

	Largest 250 Companies with Stock Ownership Guidelines		
	Number of Companies	**Percent of Companies**	**Percent Increase from 2001 to 2004**
Executives	142	57	58
Directors	123	49	127

Stock-Ownership Policies   In an attempt to make sure that senior management acts in the best interest of shareholders, many firms have established executive stock-ownership policies. How prevalent are these programs, how are they put into place, and what do they require of executives? Based on research by F.W. Cook, a large executive compensation consulting firm, the prevalence of executive and director stock-ownership guidelines has increased and is expected to continue to increase over the next several years because of the perception that it is one of the best forms of governance (see Exhibit 13.6).

Ownership guidelines are generally grouped into two types: traditional and retention programs. Traditional stock-ownership guidelines establish ownership levels through a multiple-of-salary approach. Retention programs express ownership as a percentage of the gains resulting from the exercise of stock options and other equity-based incentives, such as restricted stock. These two types of stock ownership are sometimes used together. For example, some firms may require that executives retain their shares (or some percentage of their shares) acquired through stock options until they own five times their salary in company stock.

Stock-ownership requirements vary among firms that have such plans. For instance, among firms that have multiple-of-salary plans, the median value of stock ownership required is about $5 million, but it ranges from a mere $100,000 to over $20 million. The median multiple is five times the executive's salary; the highest requirement is at Mellon Financial Corporation, where the CEO is required to have 25 times the executive's salary.

Implementing a stock-ownership plan requires time. Most CEOs do not have sufficient liquid assets to immediately buy the needed shares when a plan is implemented. Consequently, most firms allow CEOs several years to acquire the required shares (most companies allow five years). Alternatively, if companies use the retention method, no time requirement is necessary because they are only concerned with what is retained from granted options.

As noted in Exhibit 13.6, firms are increasingly requiring that their members of the board also own stock. The level of required ownership is much lower than for CEOs. The median level of required ownership among firms that have such requirements is either five times their annual director retainer or 5,000 shares. These levels equate to approximately $200,000.

Incentive Compensation

Firms use various forms of incentive compensation to reward executives and align the interests of their top-management team with those of shareholders. The two most common incentives are annual bonus plans and stock options. In recent years, firms have been increasing their reliance on newer forms of pay, such as restricted stock grants and long-term accounting-based incentive plans. Exhibit 13.7 illustrates how different firms in the food industry emphasize various incentive mechanisms when paying their CEOs.

Annual Bonus Plans   Perhaps the oldest form of incentive pay is the annual bonus plan. The idea behind bonus plans is that the board can subjectively evaluate executives'

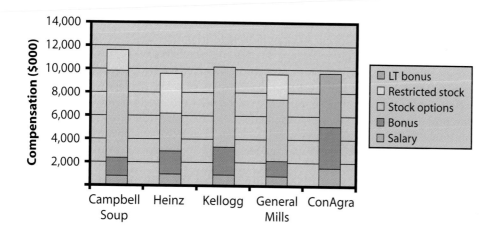

Exhibit 13.7 CEO Pay Comparison

Source: Company annual reports.

performance on multiple dimensions and allocate a year-end cash award as appropriate. In theory, bonus plans should be linked to firm performance indicators. The bonus-plan incentive has two principle drawbacks. First, when bonuses are tied to accounting indicators of performance, executives may be motivated to make accounting decisions that maximize their possible bonus payout. For instance, research has found that firms are more likely to increase income deferrals when senior executives have reached the maximum payout under terms of their bonus plan.[31] Second, linking pay to annual bonus performance can have the unintended consequence of short-term bias and inattention to long-term strategic needs. For instance, some research shows that bonus plans can lead to the underfunding of R&D initiatives.[32]

However, bonuses do have some appealing characteristics. For instance, the board can tie them to multiple desired outcomes, including both financial performance and other important outcomes such as customer satisfaction and quality. In addition, the board can more easily revoke or withhold bonuses than it can other long-term incentives that it loses control of once they are granted. The effectiveness of annual bonus programs really comes down to how well the board links them to the achievement of desired objectives.

Stock Options   One of the most popular incentive devices of the past 20 years has been the executive stock-option plan. The idea behind stock options is to align incentives by simulating the effects of executive stock ownership in situations where executives lacked the capital to become owners. An employee stock option is similar to a call option available in financial markets, with important differences.

A **stock option** gives an employee the right to buy a share of company stock at a later date for a predetermined price. That predetermined price is called the *strike price*. In practice, most companies grant stock options with a strike price equal to the firm's share price on the date the option was granted. The option will specify the period of time for which the employee has the right to exercise the option, and most option packages have a 10-year option period. The rationale for the use of stock options is that they motivate executives to act like owners and take reasonable risks. Advocates of stock options like their supposed win–win attributes: If executives do not create shareholder value in the form of higher stock prices, the options will be worthless. Recall the opening vignette about Sunbeam; Al Dunlap received stock options, but he was unable to realize any value from them.

Like most incentive plans, options do have their downside. Although used to simulate stock ownership, in reality they do not generally achieve this objective. This is because options and stock ownership have asymmetric risk properties. When executives own stock, they win if the stock price increases and they lose actual wealth if the stock price declines. With stock options, only the upside potential is conveyed. The only cost to executives is an opportunity cost.

Decision makers, such as executives, behave quite differently when they have something to lose. Indeed, upside potential and downside risks seem to motivate different behaviors. Research shows that stock options may increase excessive risk taking beyond the

stock options Incentive device giving an employee the right to buy a share of company stock at a later date for a predetermined price

level of risk desired by shareholders.[33] For instance, executives with large proportions of their pay package derived from stock options tend to pursue aggressive acquisition and divestiture strategies; buying and selling divisions frequently is a key part of their corporate strategy. For instance, GE has historically used stock options heavily, and it may be no coincidence that it is one of the most prolific acquirers of other companies in the world. Likewise, in the opening vignette, Al Dunlap was quick to use acquisitions to solve his revenue problems rather than exercising patience with internal development programs. Conversely, firms run by executives with high levels of stock ownership are much less likely to pursue acquisitions and divestitures and focus more on internally developed strategies.[34]

Other Long-Term Incentives   Restricted stock and long-term incentive plans are more recent compensation initiatives that are designed to help avoid the potential problems associated with annual bonus plans and stock options. To tie executives' financial rewards to shareholder value while avoiding the lack of downside risk associated with stock options, some firms have begun granting a special kind of common stock—a *restricted stock grant*—as part of the executive compensation package. These grants have restrictions built in to ensure that managers do not sell the stock to convert it to cash (and thus lose the incentive power of stock ownership). The restrictions usually entail vesting over a period of three to five years and prohibitions on the sale of the stock for some extended period of time. The popularity of restricted stock has grown significantly in the past several years because of the wave of bad press associated with stock-option abuses.

Long-term incentive plans are long-term bonuses that tie payouts to accounting returns over a three- to five-year period. The idea is that it is more difficult to manipulate profits over an extended period of time. In addition, using longer-term accounting profits as the performance metric may help executives avoid short-term myopia and help them to remain focused on the future.

After reviewing the variety of performance pay options available to top executives, it should come as no surprise that a CEO's compensation is more dependent on firm profitability than that of other managers and salaried workers. Unions, shareholder watchdog groups, and other interested stakeholders often criticize the level of pay that CEOs are able to make, claiming that their rewards for good performance may be excessive and that they sometimes achieve these high levels of pay without achieving stellar performance. How do some CEOs achieve high levels of pay without high levels of performance? Usually because they were given lots of stock options. Executives can make a great deal of money from options because any increase in the firm's stock price results in money for the CEO even if the firm's stock price gains are far outpaced by competitors. Exhibit 13.8 illustrates that star

concept**link**

We devote considerable space in Chapter 10 to discussing the relative benefits—in terms of **economic logic**—of *acquisition* versus *internal development*.

long-term incentive plans
Incentive plan tying future bonus payouts to defined accounting-return targets over a three- to five-year period

Exhibit 13.8 Highest Paid CEOs

Sources: Company annual reports and ExecuComp Service of Thomson Financial.

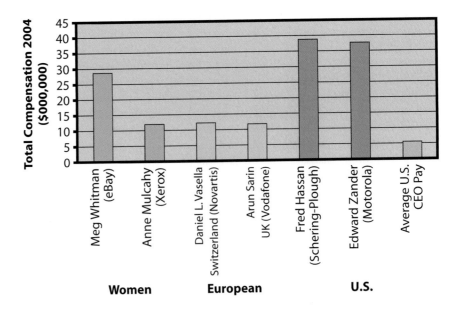

compensation can attract attention because it is so counter normative. You can see from the Exhibit that the average level of CEO pay among large U.S. companies and the two highest-paid executives in the United States and Europe, as well as the two highest-paid female CEOs in the world. Extreme performers such as these are the cases that create the headlines every year. However, although CEO pay is very high relative to that of almost everyone else (except perhaps movie stars and star athletes!), their compensation levels are also highly variable. As illustrated in Exhibit 13.9, CEO pay tends to track corporate profits to a greater degree than the pay of salaried workers.

The Well-Designed Incentive Plan Notwithstanding recent abuses, if firms are careful about how they use incentives, monetary rewards are powerful tools that can be used to increase the likelihood that executives act in shareholders' interests. Proper use of incentives tied to long-term performance metrics (as opposed to the current stock price) increases the likelihood that executives will make necessary capital investments.[35] For instance, facing intense competition, cutbacks in military spending, and years of underperformance, in 1991 the board of directors of General Dynamics hired a new management team and charged it with formulating a strategy to create shareholder wealth. The company established strong links between shareholder wealth and managerial compensation through a combination of bonuses, options, and restricted stock. This pay-for-performance plan is largely credited with providing the incentive to devise a strategy that was politically unpopular but economically successful. The new management team downsized, restructured, and exited some of its businesses by selling divisions to competitors but in the process, it created gains for shareholders of approximately $4.5 billion. Scholars documenting this case suggest that such a dramatic and successful strategy would have been unlikely without these financial incentives.[36] The key to using incentives is to find the appropriate performance metrics (i.e., those identified in the balanced scorecard) and to link executive pay to these outcomes.

Options can be a part of a well-designed incentive package, but evidence suggests that option pay should be balanced with other types of incentives, such as annual bonus plans and stock ownership. In addition, research suggests that too much focus has been placed on keeping the CEO's pay level in line with market forces and not enough has been placed on the incentives of other key executives. For instance, the best-performing firms tend to compensate their second-level managers (i.e., CFO, COO, etc.) at levels more closely related to the pay of the CEO rather than have a star system where the CEO's pay significantly outpaces that of other top managers. This is probably due to the fact that strategic management is inherently a team function, and huge gaps in pay between the CEO and other officers creates an unhealthy social context in which to operate as an effective team.[37]

concept link

In Chapter 11, we define the **balanced scorecard** as a strategic management support system for measuring vision and strategy against business- and operating-unit level performance. We stress that, as a tool for evaluating *systems and processes*, it's a tool for monitoring the outcomes of **implementation levers**.

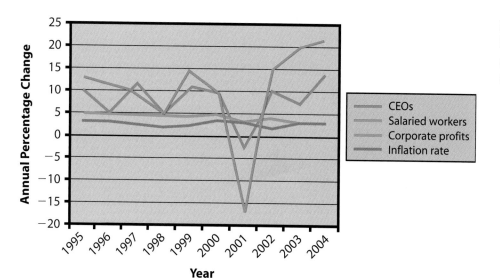

Exhibit 13.9 U.S. Executive Pay Trends

Source: U.S. Bureau of Labor Statistics.

Firms that have large gaps in pay across top managerial ranks suffer negative effects. For instance, firms with large pay gaps seem to undermine their ability to develop managerial talent because manager turnover increases significantly when pay gaps are large.[38] Thus, to maximize performance, firms need to adjust both absolute and relative pay levels to achieve the proper fit with their strategic context.

The box entitled "How Would *You* Do That? 13.2" examines some of the factors that firms should consider when structuring CEO compensation. When establishing CEO pay and aligning it with a firm's intended strategy, recognize that boards of directors are often criticized but rarely praised for how they structure CEO incentives.

THE MARKET FOR CORPORATE CONTROL

market for corporate control
Phenomenon by which the possibility that corporate control can be shifted to competitors or other buyers encourages management to operate a firm effectively and ethically

Several types of battles for the control of large corporations can take place. For instance, the problems Sunbeam faced during the Al Dunlap period eventually landed the company in bankruptcy in February 2001. In December 2002, the company emerged from Chapter 11 and changed its name to American Household, which experienced its own share of financial trouble. Eventually, Sunbeam was bought by Jarden in early 2005, becoming part of that company's consumer-solutions division. The acquisition and integration of Sunbeam's assets and product lines into Jarden Corporation was the outcome of an active market for corporate control. Collectively, this phenomenon is referred to as the **market for corporate control**. *Corporate control* is the right to choose the members of the board of directors of a company and to control all major decisions made by a company.[39] One of the principle ways of gaining corporate control is through mergers and acquisitions. Corporate raiders, competitors, and leveraged-buyout firms are investors who buy underperforming firms, restructure them, and then sell them for a profit. Because misbehavior or underperformance may lead to shareholders replacing the board and the CEO or other firms or investors attempting to buy out a firm and replace its management, the market for corporate control helps to keep managers in line.

The Trend Toward Takeovers and Buyouts   In the United States, the market for corporate control was spurred by hostile takeover activity and leveraged buyouts in the 1980s. Corporate raiders such as T. Boone Pickens, Carl Icahn, Saul Steinberg, Ted Turner, and Michael Milliken discovered great financial opportunities in seizing control of someone else's business, often at bargain prices. With millions of dollars at stake, these raiders aroused massive public attention and, depending on one's point of view, were either the villains or the saviors of American business.[40] The hostile takeover threat is alive and well today. Beginning in 2003 and eventually culminating in a successful acquisition in 2005, Oracle engaged in an 18-month battle to gain control of PeopleSoft.

Overall, researchers have concluded that corporate takeovers generate positive gains, that the target firm's shareholders benefit, and that the bidding firm's shareholders do not lose out. However, the success of a hostile takeover depends on the takeover premium paid. This work ties in well with the notion of resources and competitive advantage because the market for corporate control can be viewed as an arena in which managerial teams compete for the rights to manage corporate resources.[41]

conceptlink

In Chapter 10 we define an **acquisition premium** as the difference between the current *market value* of a target firm and the *purchase price* paid to induce its shareholders to turn its control over to new owners.

Although the market for corporate control may indeed be the last line in the sand, in terms of corporate governance, it should also be evident that it is one of the most costly and emotion-wrenched governance remedies beyond the replacement of the CEO by a firm's board. When a firm is the target of a raider or a fight for control of a board, it is a potential signal that the firm's board and its management has been ineffective or, at the very least, that the board and management see no way to combat the competition without merging with or being acquired by another entity. In Chapter 10 on mergers and acquisitions, you learned that many of the gains associated with acquisitions go to the seller, not the buyer. Therefore, although the market for corporate control may serve to discipline management, it is a very costly and time-consuming remedy to implement, and its benefits to the buyer will always be of concern. Moreover, as you will learn in the following section, the market for corporate control can only be an effective governance mechanism to the extent that the capital markets and governance mechanisms in place in a country allow hostile acquisitions to occur in the first place.

THE FACES OF CORPORATE GOVERNANCE AROUND THE WORLD

Although conflicts between managers and owners occur around the globe, the specific nature of the problems and the norms for guarding against them vary markedly. Governance problems are not unique to the United States, even though they may seem most visible to you; for instance, the Netherlands' Ahold Group (grocery stores), Italy's Parmalat (dairy and food products), France's Vivendi (entertainment), and the French-Belgian firm Elf (petroleum) are all very recent examples of scandal-ridden non–U.S. multinationals.

Most of these firms' problems can be traced to faulty governance and, in the end, fraudulent accounting and executive excess much like that which eventually brought down Enron, MCI, and Tyco. Some of these differences are illustrated by recent cross-national comparisons of corporate governance practices, which differ considerably around the globe. For instance, ownership is heavily dispersed in the United States but much more concentrated in Canada, Germany, Japan, and China. In the last three countries, national and state governments also often own major stakes of public companies. In countries where ownership is highly concentrated, owners typically have a corresponding high level of influence over corporate affairs. Finally, board composition differs greatly from country to country: Owners and workers typically sit on the board in France, Germany, Japan, and China, whereas outsiders and managers occupy those seats in U.S., U.K., and Canadian companies.[42]

Differing National Governance Practices

As implied by these differences in governance practices across the globe, the effects of particular governance mechanisms are somewhat dependent on the national context in question. For instance, a recent comparison of the relationship between ownership structure and R&D investment revealed that in the United States, the owner–manager relationship tends to be more adversarial, whereas in Japan it is more cooperative. Managers and shareholders in Japan are often members of the same *keiretsu*, which is a set of companies with interlocking business relationships and shareholdings. This often creates ties between potential adversaries.

On the basis of these differences, ownership concentration in the United States serves as a control mechanism and affects how resources are allocated in the firm; in Japan, because the relationship is not adversarial and monitoring in nature, it does not tend to have an effect on investment behaviors.[43] This difference is dramatized by T. Boone Pickens' hostile-takeover attempt of Japanese firm Koito Manufacturing in 1989. At the time, Pickens' firm Mesa Petroleum owned a 20-percent stake in Koito, which in the United States would guarantee him a position on the board and a large say in corporate matters. In Japan, Pickens was snubbed by the Japanese directors because of his hostile approach. As a result, he was unable to negotiate a board seat, ultimately foiling his takeover attempt. Although it appears that the governance environment is changing in Japan, as evidenced by the more recent successful hostile takeover of Yushiro Chemicals by American-led Steel Partners in 2004, these changes are taking effect very slowly.[44]

French and German firms have different types of owners than those found in the United States and the United Kingdom. In France, nonfinancial corporations and state governments are the largest shareholders, particularly with regard to some of the country's largest employers. The same holds true for Germany, but banks are also major owners there. It is not unusual for German banks to own both debt and equity in the same corporation. In

How to Hire and Compensate the Big Banana

Hiring and compensating the CEO is one of the chief responsibilities of the board of directors. After all, the CEO is expected to foster the formulation of a leading-edge strategy and champion it. Ultimately, the CEO is held accountable for the strategy's successful execution. When Chiquita was looking for a new CEO during late 2003, the board decided that the best candidate would come from outside the firm. By deciding to hire an outsider, the Chiquita board added some complexity to its search because it would need to entice a candidate to leave his or her current employer. In addition, the board wanted to offer a compensation package that would result in incentives consistent with Chiquita's objectives—incentives that would motivate the CEO to formulate a strategy

that achieved its vision and mission. The Chiquita board had identified the firm's objectives as the delivery of quality products to consumers and quality returns to its shareholders. In addition, the board wanted to transform Chiquita into a global leader in premium-branded foods.

In its search for a new CEO, Chiquita solicited the assistance of an executive-recruiting firm (a "headhunter"). The search eventually targeted Fernando Aguirre, an executive at Procter & Gamble. Aguirre had 23 years' experience in brand management, consumer marketing, and turnarounds at P&G. In 1992, Aguirre became president and general manager of P&G Brazil, and in 1996 he was named president of P&G Mexico. In 1999, Aguirre became vice president of P&G's global and U.S. snacks and food products. In July 2002, Aguirre was named president for special projects, reporting directly to P&G's chairman and CEO.

Chiquita's philosophy is that executives should own significant stakes in the company and that their pay, on average, should approximate the 50th percentile of the pay and pay-component ranges, as indicated by market data. Especially high-performing executives should be paid

at a higher percentile (up to approximately the 75th percentile); lower-performing executives should be paid at a lower percentile. In recent years, however, the board has shifted its emphasis away from stock options in the belief that restricted stock is generally a more efficient and less costly form of equity compensation. In order to determine whether executives are paid enough but not too much, the board of directors regularly engages independent compensation-consulting firms to gather market data and make recommendations.

The company examined the performance and executive compensation practices of a peer group of 32 companies; its two closest competitors are Dole and Del Monte. Comparative data for these two companies are provided in Exhibit 13.10.

Chiquita's objectives were twofold: offer a compensation package that would attract Aguirre away from P&G and structure it in a way that was consistent with its corporate philosophy. With this in mind, Chiquita offered a three-year contract to Mr. Aguirre with the following terms:

- *Annual salary:* $700,000.
- *Annual bonus:* A target bonus of 130 percent of annual

Exhibit 13.10 Executive Compensation Among Competitors

	Chiquita	**Dole**	**Del Monte**
Sales 2004 ($ millions)	$2,613	$4,773	$2,171
Net income ($ millions)	96	84	134
CEO salary ($ thousands)	What is appropriate?	950	810
CEO bonus ($ thousands)	What is appropriate?	1,368	870
CEO total compensation ($ thousands)	What is appropriate?	4,387	7,394

Source: Company annual reports.

salary; actual bonus can range from 9 to 140 percent of salary. The determination of the actual bonus level is up to the discretion of the board but is based on specific objectives outlined at the beginning of the fiscal year.

- *Restricted stock awards:* Two grants were issued. The first grant of 110,000 shares would vest in 2008 but only if Aguirre was still employed by the company. The second grant of 150,000 would vest

in 30,000 increments based on the firm's stock prices reaching $26, $28, $30, $32, or $34 over any 40-day trading period. Any of these shares not vested by 2008 would be forfeited.

- *Stock options:* Although the board has moved away from stock options generally, it was necessary to include options in Aguirre's package to attract him to Chiquita. Therefore, the board used them to help Aguirre reach the stock-

ownership threshold faster. Aguirre was granted an option to purchase 325,000 shares of common stock at $23.16 (the price of the stock on the day of his hire). These options would vest in 25-percent increments in January of 2005, 2006, 2007, and 2008. To make sure that options had the desired incentive effect, the board put restrictions on these options: Any shares owned as a result of exercising options could not be sold until Aguirre reached and maintained ownership of Chiquita stock valued at five times his annual base salary, or $3,500,000 of stock at his 2004 salary level (5 × $700,000).

Chiquita did not offer Aguirre a long-term incentive plan, but these incentives are used with other senior managers who don't participate in the restricted stock program. For the position of CEO, Chiquita's board believes that the annual cash bonus and generous use of restricted stock grants offer the right mix of both short- and long-term incentives to motivate the type of strategy it would like to have formulated and implemented.

Source: Chiquita proxy statement filing (form DEF 14A), April 20, 2004.

addition to the direct voting power that banks have due to their ownership position, banks also control a significant number of proxy voting positions from depositors who use the bank as a trustee for ownership purposes.

The Case of Germany

Because of the varying ownership structures, boards of directors are very different across countries. For instance, Germany has a two-board system (sometimes called a *two-tiered board*): the management board and the supervisory board. The management board is responsible for managing the enterprise. Its members are jointly accountable for the firm's management. The chair of the management board coordinates its work. The supervisory board appoints, supervises, and advises the members of the management board and is directly involved in decisions of fundamental importance to the enterprise. The chair of the supervisory board coordinates its work. The supervisory board is similar to the board of directors of U.S. firms, with two major exceptions. First, one-half of the board's seats are allocated to representatives of shareholders and one-half to representatives of labor. To break potential tie votes, the board chair (who is always a representative of owners) is given two votes. Second, executives are not permitted to serve on the supervisory board.

Contrast the situation in Germany with U.S. firms, where about 75 percent of the board's seats are occupied by outsiders and 25 percent by insiders. Much more often than not, the chair of the board in a U.S. firm is also the CEO of the firm. Also note that members of the board in U.S. firms are elected by shareholders; no seats are allocated to any other stakeholder by right. That would seem to give shareholders considerable power. However, potential board members nominated by people other than the current board are rarely elected to the board in the United States. Consequently, CEOs have considerable power over the board in many U.S. companies. Conversely, in France and Germany it is relatively easy for owners to nominate and elect members of the board. The board-election processes in Canada and the United Kingdom resemble those in the United States more so than in the continental European countries.

The Case of China

China is perhaps the newest market to face corporate governance issues. With its flagship stock exchanges set up in Shanghai and Shenzhen, the China securities market started in 1990. At that time, only 10 companies were listed on the stock exchanges. After 15 years of exponential growth, the Chinese securities market has reached a considerable size, and Chinese as well as non-Chinese individuals and firms are allowed to own stock. At the end of 2005, well over 1,000 firms were listed on Chinese exchanges, with shares owned by Chinese citizens (these types of shares being referred to as A-class shares). The number of companies listed in the local market with shares owned by foreign investors (B-class shares) was 108; among them, 26 companies issued B shares only, while the rest issued both A and B shares. Forty-six companies have overseas listings (H-class shares).[45]

Given China's history of operating as a closed economy, it is probably not surprising that the majority of companies listed on the Chinese exchanges started off as state-owned enterprises. This heritage is also evident in the ownership structure of public firms, where the percentage of state ownership remains relatively high across all industries. As a result, in virtually all cases, Chinese public firms are controlled by state-owned or state-controlled shareholders. The remaining trading shares are typically owned by a combination of individual and institutional investors.[46] Such government control of public corporations is most often seen in countries where, historically, the government owned the largest companies and gradually privatized them. In Brazil, for instance, the government still has veto power over the operations of Embraer and Petrobras, two of the world's largest airplane and oil companies, respectively. French and Russian residual ownership of many large organizations reflects this heritage as well.

SUMMARY

1. Explain what *corporate governance* means. Corporate governance is the means and mechanisms used to ensure that managers act in accordance with investors' best interests. It encompasses the system by which organizations are directed and controlled by their owners. Corporate governance is related to strategy formulation and implementation in several ways. Corporate governance ensures that the firm's vision and mission are reflected in its strategy and the way that strategy is executed. Governance mechanisms include monitoring and incentive devices, such as pay and promotion, that can bring managements' actions in line with shareholders' interests.

2. Explain how corporate governance relates to competitive advantage and understand its basic principles and practices. Evidence suggests that shareholders favor good governance and that it can help firms outperform those with poor governance characteristics. To the extent that governance helps firms maximize returns and minimize agency problems, firms with good governance may have a competitive advantage over those lacking appropriate oversight and incentives. Young firms with good governance outperform their counterparts with loose oversight and poor incentives. Corporate scandals, such as those at Enron, Tyco, and WorldCom, are more likely to affect firms with inappropriate incentives and lax boards.

3. Identify the roles of owners and different types of ownership profiles in corporate governance. A public firm is one that has sold shares to the general investing public. How those publicly traded shares are dispersed and traded in the stock market varies significantly. Some firms have a few select owners who control significant stakes in the firm. Consequently, these parties have so much voting power that they can have significant influence and control over the firm's strategy and governance. Generally, the presence of strong owners minimizes agency problems. However, the presence of a powerful owner does not remove all agency problems. One specific type of problem arises when a single powerful owner uses that power to extract private benefits from the company at the expense of other, less powerful owners.

4. Show how boards of directors are structured and explain the roles they play in corporate governance. One of the chief monitoring devices available to shareholders is the board of directors. The general responsibility of the board of directors is to ensure that executives act in shareholders' best interests. All publicly held companies are required to have a board of directors. The legal roles of the board include hiring and firing top executives, monitoring management, ensuring that shareholders' interests are pro-

tected, establishing executive compensation, and reviewing and approving the firm's strategy. There is the presumption that independent outsiders make for a more vigilant board; however, insiders on the board can improve governance when the firm operates in highly technical areas and technical expertise is needed on the board to help board members better understand the firms' environment and internal resources. The three key roles played by boards include (1) monitoring the activities of senior executives, thereby protecting shareholders' interests; (2) providing advice to managers; and (3) using their power, influence, and networks in the business community and political circles to aid the company.

5. Explain and design executive incentives as a corporate governance device. Incentives can be used to lessen potential conflicts of interests between executives and shareholders. Compensation can be structured so that managers are rewarded for doing what is in shareholders' best interests. Stock ownership is the strongest way to link shareholders' and executives' incentives. Bonus pay is a subjective incentive that can link pay to performance. Its potential drawbacks are short-term bias and that it provides executives with incentives to manipulate earnings. Stock options have been the most heavily used incentive. Although they provide upside financial benefits, such as stock ownership, they do not convey a downside financial risk beyond opportunity cost. Recently, restricted stock grants and long term incentive plans have become popular because they seem to overcome the limitations of bonuses and options.

6. Explain how the market for corporate control is related to corporate governance. The threat that a firm may become the target of a battle for corporate control and takeover is an external governance mechanism that helps to limit the consequences of bad management. When management performs poorly, the firm may become the target of a hostile takeover, either by disgruntled investors who want to replace the management and the board or by opportunistic investors looking to buy a company on the cheap and reap profits through dramatic restructuring. In either case, the existing management team will typically be terminated. Thus, this mechanism is a draconian backstop to the other internal mechanisms.

7. Compare and contrast corporate governance practices around the world. Governance practices differ around the globe in accordance with local laws and societal norms. Governance in the United States and the United Kingdom is shareholder-centric; in other countries, other stakeholders have much greater formal standing. For instance, in Germany labor has the right to appoint one-half of the board members. Ownership structure in Europe and Asia differs dramatically from the ownership of U.S. companies, and these differences have profound consequences for strategy formulation and implementation. Large corporate and government ownership blocks are common in Europe and Asia, whereas in the United States the majority of stock ownership is through pension plans and mutual funds. These funds tend to own relatively small percentages of any given company.

KEY TERMS

agency problem, 369
agent, 373
board of directors, 377
codes of governance, 373

corporate governance, 370
incentive alignment, 382
institutional investors, 376

long-term incentive plans, 386
market for corporate control, 388

monitoring, 379
principal, 373
stock options, 385

REVIEW QUESTIONS

1. Explain what is meant by corporate governance.

2. Who are the principals and agents in the modern corporation? How do their interests differ?

3. How does governance affect firm performance and competitive advantage?

4. How can large, powerful owners reduce the agency problem? How can they exacerbate the problem?

5. When are inside directors beneficial to the functioning of the board of directors?

6. What are the three primary roles played by boards? How do boards carry out these roles?

7. What is the difference between stock options and restricted stock? What are the advantages and disadvantages of each?

8. What is the market for corporate control? What role does it play in solving or exacerbating the agency problem?

9. What are some primary differences and similarities in governance practices between the United States and other countries?

How Would YOU Do That?

1. Refer back to the box entitled "How Would *You* Do That? 13.1," which discussed the establishment of executive stock ownership requirements at Dendrite International. Many business press outlets, such as *Business Week* and *Fortune*, publish articles that are critical of the corporate governance practices, particularly executive compensation, of one firm or another. Using these outlets, identify a recent example of a company that has been criticized for its governance practices and determine whether executive or director stock ownership was a factor in this criticism. What action plan for remedying this situation would you propose?

2. Identify a firm that is looking for a new CEO (or pick one whose CEO you think should be replaced!). Using the box entitled "How Would *You* Do That? 13.2" as a model, imagine that a firm is turning toward a compensation model that requires the CEO to own stock. What, specifically, do you think the compensation package should look like? How different will your company be from the competition in terms of the compensation package offered to the new CEO? (Hint: Pull up competitors' 10-K statements on the Web.) What are the implications of these differences?

GROUP ACTIVITIES

1. Prior to class, visit the Web site theyrule.net. This Web site enables you to conveniently map out the interlocking boards of directors of U.S. firms. Develop or pick from the various interlock arrangements, print out your example, and bring it to class for discussion. What are the implications of the interlocks you identified for strategy formulation and implementation? What is provocative about your network structure? How might it affect the formulation and implementation of strategy?

2. Identify a company that is currently subject to an attempted hostile takeover (the *Wall Street Journal* or various online sources can help you do this quickly). What are the dynamics that are involved in this potential takeover? Who are the key stakeholders in this battle? Who do you see benefiting and losing if this takeover is successful? Does it appear that this hostile takeover would create value?

ENDNOTES

1. This vignette is based on published accounts of Dunlap's career and a personal interview with Charles Elson, who was a featured speaker at the 2003 Directors Summit, University of Wisconsin, Madison, accompanied by snippets from the business press provided by Elson. A. J. Dunlap, *Mean Business: How I Save Bad Companies and Make Good Companies Great* (New York: Simon & Schuster, 1996); T. Jackson, "Scott's Clean Sheet: Tony Jackson Speaks to Al Dunlap," *Financial Times,* October 27, 1994, p. 18; J. A. Byrne, "How Al Dunlap Self-Destructed: The Inside Story of What Drove Sunbeam's Board to Act," *BusinessWeek,* July 6, 1998, p. 58.

2. A. Shleifer and R. W. Vishny, "A Survey of Corporate Governance," *The Journal of Finance* 52:2 (1997), 737–783.

3. E. F. Fama and M. C. Jensen, "Separation of Ownership and Control," *Journal of Law and Economics* 26 (1983), 301–325; A. Shleifer and R. W. Vishny, "A Survey of Corporate Governance," *The Journal of Finance* 52:2 (1997), 737–783.

4. A. Tuschke and W. G. Sanders, "Antecedents and Consequences of Corporate Governance Reform: The Case of Germany," *Strategic Management Journal* 24 (2003), 631–649.

5. Exchange News: Statements from Angelo Tantazzi, Chairman of Borsa Italiana and Massimo Capuano, CEO of Borsa Italiana, www.exchange-handbook.co.uk/news_story.cfm?id=50739 (accessed November 29, 2005); T. C. Hoschka, "A Market for the Well Governed," *The McKinsey Quarterly* 3 (2002), 26–27.

6. W. G. Sanders and S. Boivie, "Sorting Things Out: Valuation of New Firms in Uncertain Markets," *Strategic Management Journal* 25 (2004), 167–186.

7. For more, see www.gmiratings.com and www.morningstar.com (accessed July 15, 2005).

8. E. F. Fama and M. C. Jensen, "Separation of Ownership and Control," *Journal of Law and Economics* 26 (1983), 301–325; M. C. Jensen and W. H. Meckling, "Theory of the Firm: Managerial Behavior, Agency Costs and Ownership Structure," *Journal of Financial Economics* 3 (1976), 305–360; Shleifer and Vishny, "A Survey of Corporate Governance"; J. P. Walsh and J. K. Seward, "On the Efficiency of Internal and External Corporate Control Mechanisms," *Academy of Management Review* 15 (1990), 421–458.

9. A. A. Berle, Jr. and G. C. Means, *The Modern Corporation and Private Property* (New York: McMillan, 1932).

10. E. Ofek and D. Yermack, "Taking Stock: Equity-Based Compensation and the Evolution of Managerial Ownership," *Journal of Finance* 55:3 (2000), 1367–1384.

11. P. Milgrom and J. Roberts, *Economics, Organization, and Management* (Upper Saddle River, NJ: Prentice Hall, 1992).

12. www.sec.gov (accessed July 15, 2005).

13. "Prosecutors Say Rigases Owe $2.5 Billion," *New York Times,* December 15, 2004, C2. Jack Hitt, "American Kabuki: The Ritual of Scandal." *New York Times,* July 18, 2004, 1.

14. www.calpers.org and www.swib.state.wi.us (accessed July 15, 2005).

15. R. E. Hoskisson, M. A. Hitt, R. A. Johnson, and W. Grossman, "Conflicting Voices: The Effects of Institutional Ownership Heterogeneity and Internal Governance on Corporate Strategies," *Academy of Management Journal* 45 (2002), 697–716.

16. M. Peers, J. Carreyrou, and B. Orwall, "Vivendi CEO Loses Key Board Support, Endangering His Job," *Wall Street Journal,* (2002) July 1: A1; L. Panetta, "It's Not Just What You Do, It's the Way You Do It," *Directors & Boards* 27 (2003), 17–21.

17. www.aicpa.org/info/sarbanes_oxley_summary.htm (accessed November 29, 2005).

18. B. Baysinger and R. E. Hoskisson, "The Composition of Boards of Directors and Strategic Control: Effects on Corporate Strategy," *Academy of Management Review* 15 (1990), 72–87.

19. Baysinger and Hoskisson, "The Composition of Boards of Directors and Strategic Control."

20. J. Dahya, A. Lonie, D. Power, "The Case for Separating the Roles of Chairman and CEO: An Analysis of Stock Market and Accounting Data," *Corporate Governance* 4 (1996), 71, 76. This study examined the impact of separating or combining the roles of CEO and chair in the United Kingdom. The authors found that a "significant positive market reaction . . . followed the separation of the responsibilities of chairman and CEO." Also, companies that announced a separation subsequently performed better than their counterparts based on several accounting measures. Conversely, companies that announced combination of the positions resulted in "the largest negative market response the day after the announcement."

21. "The function of the chairman is to run board meetings and oversee the process of hiring, firing, evaluating, and compensating the CEO . . . Without the direction of an independent leader, it is much more difficult for the board to perform its critical function," M. C. Jensen, "Presidential Address: The Modern Revolution, Exit and the Failure of Internal Control Systems," *Journal of Finance* 48 (1993), 831, 866; "Wearing both hats is like grading your own paper," A. Hansen, deputy director of the Council of Institutional Investors, as quoted in "A Walk on the Corporate Side," *Trustee* 49:10 (1996), 9, 10. See also, C. E. Bagley and Richard H. Koppes, "Leader of the Pack: A Proposal for Disclosure of Board Leadership Structure," *San Diego Law Review* 34:1 (1997), 149, 157–158.

22. C. Lucier, R. Schuyt, and J. Handa, "The Perils of Good Governance," *Strategy+Business* 35 (2004), 1–17.

23. J. D. Westphal, "Collaboration in the Boardroom: Behavioral and Performance Consequences of CEO–Board Social Ties," *Academy of Management Journal* 42 (1999), 7–24.

24. M. A. Carpenter and J. D. Westphal, "The Strategic Context of External Network Ties: Examining the Impact of Director Appointments on Board Involvement in Strategic Decision Making," *Academy of Management Journal* 44 (2001), 639–651.

25. G. Strauss, "Board Pay Gets Fatter as Job Gets Hairier," *USA TODAY,* March 7, 2005, B1; T. Johnson-Elie, "Boards Slowly Opening up to Women, Minorities—Time Is Right, Seasoned Executive Jackson Says," *Milwaukee Journal Sentinel,* June 1, 2005, 1.

26. B. Lechem, *Chairman of the Board* (London: Wiley, 2002).

27. www.thecorproratelibrary.com and www.issproxy.com (accessed July 15, 2005).

28. M. A. Carpenter and J. D. Westphal, "The Strategic Context of External Network Ties."

29. M. McDonald and J. D. Westphal, "Getting by with the Advice of Their Friends: CEOs' Advice Networks and Firms' Strategic Responses to Poor Performance," *Administrative Science Quarterly* 48 (2003), 1–32; J. D. Westphal and J. W. Fredrickson, "Who Directs Strategic Change? Director Experience, the Selection of New CEOs, and Change in Corporate Strategy," *Strategic Management Journal* 22 (2001), 1113–1138; J. D. Westphal, M. D. Seidel, and K. S. Stewart, "Second-Order Imitation: Uncovering Latent Effects of Board Network Ties," *Administrative Science Quarterly* 46 (2001), 717–747.

30. E. White, "Call It Sarbanes-Oxley Burnout: Finance-Chief Turnover Is Rising," *Wall Street Journal,* April 5, 2005, A1.

31. P. M. Healy and J. M. Wahlen, "A Review of the Earnings Management Literature and Its Implications for Standard Setting," *Accounting Horizons* 13 (1999), 365–383.

32. R. E. Hoskisson, M. A. Hitt, and C. W. L. Hill, "Managerial Incentives and Investment in R&D in Large Multiproduct Firms," *Organization Science* 4 (1993), 325–341.

33. W. G. Sanders, "Behavioral Responses of CEOs to Stock Ownership and Stock Option Pay," *Academy of Management Journal* 44 (2001), 477–492; W. G. Sanders, "Incentive Alignment, CEO Pay Level, and Firm Performance: A Case of 'Heads I Win, Tails You Lose'?" *Human Resource Management* 40 (2001), 159–170.

34. W. G. Sanders, "Behavioral Responses of CEOs to Stock Ownership and Stock Option Pay," *Academy of Management Journal* 44 (2001), 477–492.

35. D. F. Larcker, "The Association Between Performance Plan Adoption and Corporate Capital Investment," *Journal of Accounting and Economics* 5 (1983), 3–30.

36. J. Dial and K. J. Murphy, "Incentives, Downsizing, and Value Creation at General Dynamics," *Journal of Financial Economics* 37 (1995), 261–314.

37. M. A. Carpenter and W. G. Sanders, "Top Management Team Compensation: The Missing Link Between CEO Pay and Firm Performance," *Strategic Management Journal* 23 (2002), 367–374.

38. M. Bloom and J. G. Michel, "The Relationships Among Organizational Context, Pay Dispersion, and Managerial Turnover," *Academy of Management Journal* 45 (2002), 33–42.

39. Berle and Means, *The Modern Corporation and Private Property.*

40. R. Slater, *The Titans of Takeover* (New York: Beard Books, 1999).

41. M. C. Jensen and R. S. Ruback, "The Market for Corporate Control: The Scientific Evidence," *Journal of Financial Economics* 11 (1983), 5–50.

42. E. R. Gedajlovic and D. M. Shapiro, "Management and Ownership Effects: Evidence from Five Countries," *Strategic Management Journal* 19 (1998), 533–553; R. Tricker, *Pocket Director* (London: The Economist Books, 1999).

43. P. M. Lee and H. M. O'Neill, "Ownership Structures and R&D Investments of U.S. and Japanese Firms: Agency and Stewardship Perspectives," *Academy of Management Journal* 46 (2003), 212–225.

44. B. Bremner and M. der Hovanesian, "So 'Takeover' Does Translate: Foreigners Are After Japanese Companies—With Better Governance as One Result," *BusinessWeek,* February 9, 2004, 51.

45. www.oecd.org (accessed July 15, 2005).

46. www.oecd.org (accessed July 15, 2005).

Part 6 **Case Studies** **Pulling It All Together**

Preparing for Case Discussions

The case method is one of the most effective means of management education. It is widely used in schools of business throughout the world, and this use is predicated upon the belief that tackling real business problems is the best way to develop practitioners. Real problems are messy, complex, and very interesting.

Unlike other pedagogical techniques, many of which make you the recipient of large amounts of information but do not require its use, the case method requires you to be an active participant in the closest thing to the real situation. It is a way of gaining experience without spending a lot of time. It is also a way to learn a great deal about how certain industries and businesses operate, and how managers manage in them. There are few programmable, textbook solutions to the kinds of problems faced by real general managers and other leaders. When a problem becomes programmable, the leader gives it to someone else to solve on a repeated basis using the guidelines he or she has set down. Thus the case situations that you will face will require the use of analytical tools and the application of your personal judgment.

SOURCES OF CASES

Most of the cases in this course are about real companies. You will recognize many of the names of the companies, although some of them may be new to you. These cases were developed in several different ways. In some instances, a company came to a business-school professor and requested that a case be written on that company. In other situations, a professor sought out a company because he or she knew that the company was in an interesting or difficult situation. Often, the company agreed to allow a case to be written. Sometimes, cases were written solely from public sources. In these instances, there may be less "inside" information about the company incorporated in the case, but generally there is still enough rich information to motivate a rigorous analysis and discussion of the situation at hand. In rare instances a true company was disguised because the case content is rich for learning but the company desires anonymity or is a private firm.

OVERVIEW OF CASE PREPARATION

There is only one secret to good case-based learning, and that is good preparation on the part of the participants. Because this course has been designed to "build" as it progresses, class attendance is also very important. But, what you learn from case discussion will be a function of how well you prepare.

When you prepare for class, we recommend that you plan on reading the case *at least* three times. The first reading should be a quick run-through of the text in the case. It should give you a feeling for what the case is about, who the major players are, and the types of data that are contained in the case. For example, you will want to differentiate between facts and opinions that may be expressed. In every industry, there is a certain amount of "conventional wisdom" that may or may not reflect the truth.

On your second reading you should read in more depth. Many people like to underline or otherwise mark up their cases to pick out important points that they know will be needed later. Your major effort on a second reading should be to understand the business and the situation. You should ask yourself questions like: (1) Why has this company survived? (2) How does this business work? (3) What are the basic economics of this business? It is important that you clearly spell out the five elements of the strategy diamond here. During this reading, you should also carefully examine the exhibits in the case. It is generally true that the case writer has put the exhibit there for a purpose. It contains some information that will be useful to you in analyzing the situation. Ask yourself what that information is when you study each exhibit. You often will find that you will need to apply some analytical technique (e.g., ratio analysis or growth rate analysis) to the exhibit in order to benefit from the information in the raw data. More often than not, data from more than one exhibit will need to be combined to develop innovative and meaningful insights about the case.

By the time you read the case the third time, you should already have a good idea of the fundamentals of the case. Now you will be searching to understand the specific situation. Your objective will be to get at the root causes of problems and gather data from the case that will enable you to make specific action recommendations. Before the third reading, you may want to review the assignment questions in the course description. It is during and after the third reading that you should be able to outline your answers to the assignment questions. Just as important, you should be able to determine whether these are the most relevant and important questions facing the organization and its management.

CLASS DISCUSSIONS

Often an instructor will ask a few class members several leadoff questions. If you have prepared the case, and are capable of answering the assignment question, you should have no difficulty with these leadoff questions. An effective leadoff assignment can do a great deal to enhance a class discussion. It sets a tone that enables the class to probe more deeply into the issues of the case. Although instructors may differ in their preferences, it is often desirable to take a particular stand, even take on the role of devil's advocate, regarding case questions. One benefit of the case method is that it offers a better context in which to experience missteps and miscalculations than does your first job assignment. In this regard, cases give you an opportunity to exercise reasoned risk taking and make specific recommendations under conditions of uncertainty, just as real leaders would. If you are asked to make recommendations, they will be more compelling if they are specific, grounded in analysis of case data and information, and demonstrate a solution that the firm may be uniquely able to exploit.

The instructor's role in the class discussion is to help, through intensive questioning, to develop your ideas. This use of the Socratic method has proved to be an effective way to develop thinking capability in individuals. The instructor's primary role is to manage the class process and to ensure that the class achieves an understanding of the case situation. There is no single correct solution to any of these problems. There are, however, a lot of wrong solutions. Therefore, you will try to come up with a solution that will enable you to deal effectively with the problems presented in the case.

THE USE OF EXTRA- OR POST-CASE DATA

Unless otherwise instructed, you are encouraged to deal with the case as it is presented. You should put yourself in the position of the general manager involved in the situation and look at the situation through his or her eyes. Part of the unique job of being a general manager is that many of the problems they face are dilemmas. There is no way to come out a winner on all counts. Although additional data might be interesting or useful, being a "Monday morning quarterback" is *not* an effective way to learn about strategic management. Therefore, you are strongly discouraged from acquiring or using extra- or post-case data.

Some case method purists argue that a class should never be told what actually happened in a situation. Each person should leave the classroom situation with his or her plan for solving the problem, and none should be falsely legitimized. The outcome of a situation may not reflect what is, or is not, a good solution. You must remember that because a company did something different from your recommendations and was successful or unsuccessful, this is not an indication of the value of your approach. It is, however, interesting and occasionally useful to know what actually occurred. Therefore, your professor may decide to tell you what happened to a company since the time of the case, but you should draw your own conclusions from that.

CASE PREPARATION DETAILS

We just reviewed our logic for case preparation. In this section, we outline in a worksheet format the type of analysis that you might complete before coming to class. Note that in this worksheet, we do not segment the three readings reviewed above. During your three readings you should simply fill in the relevant information, and at the conclusion of your third pass you should have collected enough information, analyzed the material, and come to a personal view as to what should be done.

Case Title: _____

Case Assignment Questions:

Who are the main players (name and position)?

_____

_____

_____

What business(es) and industry or industries is the company in?

_____

_____

_____

What are the issues and problems facing the company? (Sort them by *importance* and *urgency.*)

_____

_____

_____

Why did this problem emerge? (Identify causal chain.)

_____

_____

_____

Are the apparent problems the real problems or only symptoms of the real problems?

_____

_____

_____

What are the characteristics of the environment in which the company operates?

_____

_____

_____

What are the characteristics of the industry that the company is in and how is the industry changing over time?

_____

_____

_____

What is the firm's strategy, in terms of the five strategy elements, for competing in this context?

_____

_____

_____

What are possible solutions to the identified problems?

_____

_____

_____

Are there any possible problems with your suggested recommendations? What contingencies need to be accommodated?

_____

_____

_____

Try to model the problem and solution by drawing a diagram. Identify the problem, what is causing it, what is making the problem worse (or potentially hiding the problem), and what can be done to mitigate or eliminate it. Use the strategy models to help you think through the steps that must be taken to intervene and solve this problem.

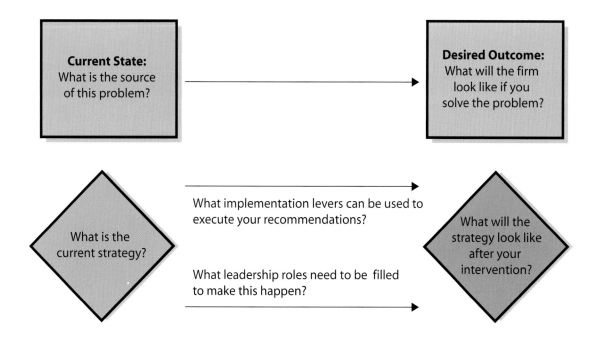

"Think of Kmart as a sick uncle. He has been coughing and wheezing for years. Now he has to have major surgery. We hope he survives the knife. But he will never be what he once was."

–Tom Walsh, *Free Press* **Columnist, January 2002**

"We will emerge as a vital enterprise, focusing on providing value to our customers and our stakeholders."

–Julian Day, Kmart CEO, in April 2003

Kmart—Fall of a Retailing Giant

BSTR – 56

KMART GOES BUST

In January 2002, leading US-based retailer Kmart filed for bankruptcy protection under Chapter 11[1] after it was unable to meet its payment obligations to suppliers due to severe financial problems. The company's (the second-largest discount retailer and the third-largest general merchandise retailer in the US) losses amounted to $2.45 billion in 2001 (Refer [to] Exhibit 1 for key financials). Since Kmart was the largest retailer in US history to declare bankruptcy (2,114 stores at the time of the declaration), the announcement came as a major shock to industry observers, customers and employees alike.

ICFAI UNIVERSITY This case was written by **A. Mukund,** ICFAI Center for Management Research (ICMR). It is intended to be used as a basis for class discussion rather than to illustrate either effective or ineffective handling of a management situation. The case was compiled from published sources. © 2003, ICFAI Center for Management Research. All rights reserved. No part of this publication may be reproduced, stored in a retrieval system, used in a spreadsheet, or transmitted in any form or by any means—electronic or mechanical, without permission. To order copies, call 0091-40-2343-0462/63 or write to ICFAI Center for Management Research, Plot # 49, Nagarjuna Hills, Hyderabad 500 082, India or email icmr@icfai.org. Website: www.icmrindia.org.

[1] Organizations/individuals can file for Chapter 11 bankruptcy under US bankruptcy law to deal with financial problems of a huge magnitude. Those who file for Chapter 11 can propose a payment plan and seek approval of the same from their creditors. Chapter 11 essentially rewrites many of the contracts the debtor has with the creditors, and thereafter both parties act according to the new agreement.

In March 2002, Kmart decided to close 284 stores throughout the US and lay off 9% of its employees (22,000) as part of its reorganization plan. The then Chairman, Chuck Conaway (Conaway) said, "The decision to close these under-performing stores, which do not meet our financial requirements, is an integral part of the company's reorganization effort." In that year, closures were carried out in 44 US states and Puerto Rico.

Over the next year, the total number of stores closed went up from 284 to 600, while the total number of employees laid off increased from 22,000 to 67,000. Many senior executives were also laid off—reportedly, around 25%–35% of senior level positions were eliminated. Thousands of vendors dependent on Kmart for selling their merchandise were affected badly.

Kmart's share prices reflected the company's uncertain future: while the stock traded at $13 in August 2001, it had reached an abysmal low of 11 cents in February 2003—a loss of $6.7 billion in market capitalization in less than two years. In December 2002, the stock was even delisted from the New York Stock Exchange (Refer [to] Exhibit 2 for Kmart's stock chart). The downfall of the once mighty company soon came to be seen as the result of problems on a number of fronts: strategic, operational, marketing, human resources and business ethics.

BACKGROUND NOTE

Kmart's story dates back to 1899, when Sebastian S. Kresge (Sebastian) set up the S.S. Kresge Company (Kresge) in Detroit, US. The company established a network of retail stores that sold everything for 5 and 10 cents. The low pricing strategy worked well, and by 1912 the company

Exhibit 1   Kmart—Key Financials

Consolidated Selected Financial Data	2001	2000	1999	1998	1997
Summary of Operations					
Total Sales	$36151	$37028	$35925	$33674	$32183
Comparable Sales %	(0.1%)	1.1%	4.8%	4.8%	4.8%
Total Sales %	(2.4%)	3.1%	6.6%	4.6%	2.4%
US Kmart Total Sales %	(2.4%)	3.1%	6.6%	5.6%	5.0%
Cost of sales, buying and occupancy	29,936	29658	28111	26319	25152
Selling, general and administrative expenses	7588	7402	6558	6283	6178
Restructuring, impairment and other charges	1099	—	—	19	114
Interest expense, net	344	287	280	293	363
Continuing income (loss) before income taxes, preferred dividend, and reorganization items	(2816)	(332)	1020	798	418
Chapter 11 reorganization items	184	—	—	—	—
Net income (loss) from continuing operations	(2587)	(244)	633	518	249
Discontinued operations	169	—	(230)	—	—
Net income (loss)	**(2418)**	**(244)**	**403**	**518**	**249**
Per Common Share					
Basic:					
Continuing income (loss)	$(5.23)	$(0.48)	$1.29	$1.05	$0.51
Discontinued operations	$0.34	$—	$(0.47)	$—	$—
Net income (loss)	$(4.89)	$(0.48)	$0.82	$1.05	$0.51
Diluted:					
Continuing income (loss)	$(5.23)	$(0.48)	$1.22	$1.01	$0.51
Discontinued operations	$0.34	$—	$(0.41)	$—	$—
Net income (loss)	$(4.89)	$(0.48)	$0.81	$1.01	$0.51
Book Value	$6.87	$12.50	$13.10	$12.12	$11.15
Financial Data					
Working capital	$7620	$3751	$4083	$4174	$4237
Total assets	14298	14832	15208	14255	13625
Liabilities subject to compromise	8060	—	—	—	—
Long-term debt	330	2084	1759	1538	1725
Long-term capital lease obligations	857	943	1014	1091	1179
Trust convertible preferred securities	889	887	986	984	981
Capital expenditures	1456	1089	1277	981	678
Depreciation and amortization	824	777	770	671	660
Current ratio	12.6	1.9	2.0	2.1	2.3
Basic weighted average shares outstanding (millions)	494	483	492	492	487
Diluted weighted average shares outstanding (millions)	494	483	562	565	492
Number of stores	2114	2105	2171	2161	2136
US Kmart store sales per comparable selling square footage	$235	$236	$233	$222	$211
US Kmart total selling square footage (millions)	154	153	155	154	151

(Dollars in millions, except for share data)

Source: www.kmart.com.

Exhibit 2   Kmart—Stock Price Movements

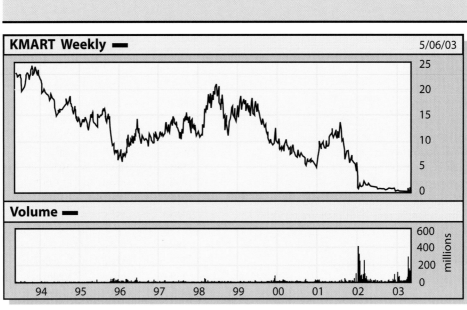

Source: www.bigcharts.com.

expanded to 85 stores, worth $10 million. In 1918, Kresge was listed on the New York Stock Exchange. During the First World War and the Great Economic Depression, the company's low prices model kept it running. By the mid-1920s, Sebastian opened the forerunner of today's discount stores in the form of stores that sold items for $1 or less.

In 1929, the company's Canadian subsidiary, S.S. Kresge Company, Ltd. was founded. By the end of the year, it ran 19 stores in Canada. In 1937, Kresge opened a store in the first suburban shopping center in the US, the Country Club Plaza in Kansas City, Missouri. As more companies entered the retailing arena and competition intensified, Kresge launched a newspaper advertising program that became highly popular and successful. The campaign was extended to radio in due time. Over the next few decades, the company established many retail outlets across the country and became a name worth reckoning with in the US retailing industry.

In 1959, Harry B. Cunningham (Cunningham), a seasoned retailing expert, became the President of Kresge. Cunningham decided to launch a discount department store to help the company's stores stand apart from the rest of the players. Thus, the first Kmart store was opened in Garden City, Michigan, in 1962. In that same year, 17 more Kmart stores were opened. These stores contributed a major chunk of the company's sales of $483 million for that year.

In 1966, Kmart recorded $1 billion in revenues for the first time through its 915 stores, of which 162 were Kmart stores. In 1968, Kmart (Australia) Ltd. was set up in association with G. J. Coles & Coy Ltd. of Australia, with Kresge holding 51% of the venture's equity. Kmart started advertising on TV in 1968. The company's biggest promotional effort, however, was in the form of printed circulars distributed to

millions of households each week (continued even into the 21st century). In 1972, Kmart's headquarters was shifted to Troy, Michigan, and Robert E. Dewar replaced Cunningham as Chairman of the Board and CEO. In 1976, Kresge became the first company in the US to launch 271 stores (retail space of 17 million square feet) in just one year.

By 1977, over 95% of Kresge's sales were being generated through Kmart stores. As a result, the company decided to change its name to Kmart. In 1978, Kmart exchanged its 51% interest in Kmart (Australia) for a 20% stake in G. J. Coles & Coy Ltd. In 1980, Vice Chairman Bernard M. Fauber became the Chairman and CEO.

During the 1980s, Kmart's growth started slowing down as competitors such as Wal-Mart raised customer expectations regarding service and quality. Kmart's merchandise began to be seen as poorly made, cheap and 'tacky.' Wal-Mart's 'everyday low prices' model and good customer service led to Kmart's performance deteriorating alarmingly.

Kmart responded to the threat posed by Wal-Mart by diversifying its product offerings. This was achieved by acquiring well-known retail chains (specialty stores) in different categories. Unlike earlier, Kmart could now offer a much wider variety of products to its customers. As a part of this plan, Kmart purchased book retailer Walden Book Co. and home improvement solutions seller Home Centers of America (renamed Builders Square) in 1984. In 1985, the company increased its stake in Coles Myer Ltd. (the erstwhile G. J. Coles & Coy) to over 21%. In 1987, Kmart sold off its Kresge stores (most of them to McCrory Corporation) to fully concentrate on Kmart.

In 1987, after Bernard M. Fauber stepped down, Joseph E. Antonini was made the Chairman, President and CEO. In the same year, Kmart began its association with Martha Stewart[2] (Martha), a move that proved to be extremely beneficial in the long run. Martha offered her merchandise exclusively through Kmart stores and her 'Martha Stewart Everyday' label was easily Kmart's most recognizable brand. Other private labels offered at Kmart (Sesame Street, Jaclyn Smith, Route 66, Kathy Ireland, Thom McAn, White Westinghouse, Benchtop and BestYet) were also quite popular.

Kmart had very strong ties with many of the above suppliers. According to a source at Reach Marketing (a consulting firm), the fact that as many as 600 of Kmart's stores were in urban markets motivated these suppliers to offer their brands through Kmart. The source commented, "Kmart is in the best position to reach the cross-cultural constituency, especially Latinos and African Americans who are the most loyal to Kmart. The urban areas are where retailers will continue to grow. Kmart also gives an entry-level price for everything from consumer electronics to casual apparel."

The next step taken by Kmart to meet the Wal-Mart onslaught came in 1990 in the form of a $3.5 billion, five-year plan. This initiative involved the opening of new stores and the enlargement and modernization of existing ones. As part of this plan, the company opened the first Kmart Super-Center in Medina, Ohio. SuperCenters were designed to offer customers the benefits of a 'one-stop-shop' grocery store along with a discount store. They offered services such as a bakery, video rental, deli[3] and groceries in addition to merchandise offered in the discount store format.

As part of the plan, Kmart also acquired other established retail chains. It bought the sporting goods retailing chain The Sports Authority (TSA) in 1990, acquired 90% of the office supplies company OfficeMax in 1991 and bought book retailer Borders Inc. in 1992. As a result of the above moves, Kmart had as many as 2,350 stores in the early 1990s—a period regarded as the 'peak' in the company's history.

In 1992, Kmart entered the European market by purchasing 13 stores in the Czech Republic and Slovakia. This move aimed at making the company's presence felt globally. By now, Wal-Mart had become the undisputed leader in the U.S. discount retailing industry, forcing Kmart to rethink many of its earlier strategic moves.

In 1993, the company undertook a restructuring plan involving its US and Canadian operations. The plan involved the closure of 400 underperforming stores during 1994–96; divestiture of various non-core businesses to raise $5 billion;

reduction of sales, general and administrative expenditure by $1.3 billion; and an overhaul of the management team. In 1994, Kmart entered Mexico and Singapore through joint ventures with El Puerto de Liverpool, and Metro (Private) Ltd. respectively.

As part of its restructuring initiatives, Kmart diluted and divested its holdings in many of its businesses during the mid-1990s. In 1994, it divested its complete stake in Coles Myers Ltd. In the same year, Kmart completed the initial public offering of TSA (70% stake) and OfficeMax (75% stake). The following year, it sold off Borders Group Inc. and the remaining stake in TSA and OfficeMax (despite the stake disposal, Kmart continued to honor the lease agreements of these three companies, amounting to $350 million by the beginning of the 21st century).

According to a *BusinessWeek* article, Kmart's expansion into specialty stores during the 1990s was a big mistake that resulted in severe financial problems for the company. Director James B. Adamson (Adamson) said, "We were on the precipice of death." To set things right, Floyd Hall (Floyd), an experienced retailer was brought in. He replaced Joseph E. Antonini in 1995.

In 1996, Floyd carried out a strategic overhaul of Kmart stores to make them cleaner, brighter and easier to shop at. As a part of this initiative, some of the stores were renamed 'Big Kmart.' The pantry department (which sold frequently purchased consumable goods) in these stores was shifted to the front, and it was decided to focus more on the Children's and Home Fashion departments. By the end of the year, around 62% of the stores had been thus converted.

Since many of its stores outside the US were not profitable enough, Kmart decided to discontinue them. In 1996, the company sold its stores in the Czech Republic and Slovakia. According to reports, the move aimed at allowing the company to focus fully on its troubled US operations. The Singapore and Mexico ventures were also discontinued in 1996 and 1997 respectively. Kmart Canada and the Builders Square chain were also sold off in 1997.

By the end of the 1990s, the company had 2,114 stores in all the 50 states of the US, Puerto Rico, the US Virgin Islands and Guam. Around 85% of the population of the US stayed within 15 miles of a Kmart store. The company owned 120 of these stores, while the rest were leased properties. Most of these stores were one-floor, free-standing units, with sizes ranging from 40,000 to 190,000 square feet.

In December 1999, Kmart started an e-commerce company, BlueLight.com as a 59% subsidiary. The company was set up to offer Kmart's products online and also to provide various Internet services to customers. Other investors in the venture were SOFTBANK Venture Capital (18.5%), BlueLight.com management and employees (15%), Martha Stewart Living Omnimedia, and Yahoo! When BlueLight failed to generate the expected profits, Kmart bought out the other minority investors, making it a wholly-owned subsidiary.

---

[2] Martha Stewart is a media personality and businesswoman who has a huge fan following in the US, especially among the female population. She has to her credit many bestselling books, an Emmy award–winning television show, a website, syndicated newspaper columns, a national radio show, a mail-order catalog and various popular products for the household. Bedding, bath, outdoor living, garden, baby, organizing, cleaning and household products were offered under the Martha Stewart Everyday label.

[3] A short form of the world 'delicatessen.' It refers to any shop selling cooked/prepared foods.

KMART UNDER CONAWAY

In May 2000, Conaway replaced Floyd as the CEO of Kmart—and things were never the same again. In addition to Wal-Mart, the company was struggling hard to compete with another discount retailer, Target. Competition from these two companies led to a fall in Kmart's market share (Refer [to] Table 1) and financial performance (for 2000, Kmart posted a loss of $244 million).

Kmart had become infamous for not keeping its stores clean and for not stocking enough goods. Customers had to wait in long queues for shopping at its stores. Even Martha complained of distribution problems and the difficulty customers had locating her products. For such customers, she said, "If you are frustrated, keep looking."

Conaway identified the following as Kmart's major problems: poor inventory management (resulting in empty store shelves); lack of customer focus; and a poor, undifferentiated marketing strategy. His turnaround plan involved bringing in new executives, closing underperforming stores, improving inventory management and customer service standards, and developing a new marketing and advertising plan. The plan gave priority to correcting anomalies in Kmart's supply chain. This was because problems with the supply chain were seen as a major reason for Kmart's poor performance vis-à-vis Wal-Mart (refer to Table 2).

Conaway earmarked $2 billion to fix the above problems by overhauling the entire supply chain and bringing in new technology (web-enabled registers and scanners) to improve the inventory tracking and checkout times.[4] Other initiatives to eliminate 'bad' practices were also made. One such initiative was the setting up of a team that worked towards simplifying work in the stores. Employees who gave good waste elimination ideas were rewarded with stock in the company.

Investors and the media were unanimous in their appreciation of Conaway's plans for turning Kmart around. A retailing analyst quoted in *BusinessWeek* said, "He is nothing but open, honest, and straightforward about Kmart's problems. It is a shocker." Martha echoed this view, "It is so very pleasing to have someone at the helm who is more analytical and proactive." Commenting on Kmart's plans to set up a new distribution network and focus on IT, an analyst said, "Conaway was trying to make up for a lack of spending for technology, infrastructure and warehousing that was not done in many years." After deciding to invest heavily in IT, Kmart even hired former Deloitte Consulting retail expert Randy Allen as CIO in September 2000.

After the above initiatives were implemented, the employees were expected to have more time on their hand[s] to pay attention to customer[s] and improve customer service levels. To further improve customer service, a new customer feedback system using automated voice response technology was introduced to help customers rate their shopping experience or lodge complaints. Conaway even planned to link employee bonuses with their customer service records. Finally, to shake the 'dull' image of Kmart as compared to Wal-Mart and Target, Conaway decided to limit sales promotion to special deals on items that were unique to Kmart and change the merchandise mix to focus more on women and children.

Table 1   US Retailing Industry—Market Share

Company	Wal-Mart	Kmart	Target	Others	Total
1990	30	30	10	30	100
2000	55	17	13	15	100

Source: www.forbes.com.

Table 2   Wal-Mart vs. Kmart—the Supply Chain Issue

Wal-Mart had begun investing in information technology (IT) way back in the 1960s and had pioneered the use of electronic cash registers and automated inventory management systems. By the 1980s, Wal-Mart was making extensive use of electronic data interchange (EDI) and had also implemented an Internet-linked supply chain management system. Its IT infrastructure acted as the backbone of its excellent logistics framework. The company added to its IT staff and investment as required to 'squeeze more value' out of its stores and systems. Kmart, however, had not made any substantial investments in IT even by the 1990s and lagged way behind Wal-Mart. A January 2002 *Computerworld* article stated, "Kmart went from being the IT leader in retail to an embarrassment. Kmart was not just an also-ran—it was not even in the race."

Kmart's lack of focus on implementing IT solutions and the absence of modern logistics and supply chain management tools did it a lot of harm. The company changed three Chief Information Officers (CIOs) within a span of five years in the 1990s. Its supply chain management practices reportedly left a lot to be desired and its inventory problems were well-known. According to an article in *Forbes,* around 1,600 trailers had to be parked at the back of the company's 2,100 stores to stock excess inventory. As a result, Kmart's inventory loss due to damage/theft was 4.5%, twice the industry average. By the late 1990s, while Wal-Mart had an inventory turnover of 7.3 times per year, Kmart had a turnover of just 3.6 times per year.

While Wal-Mart's single, integrated and company-wide distribution network worked quite efficiently, Kmart frequently struggled with its split distribution network. Also, Kmart lost out on the advantages of the just-in-time inventory management style that Wal-Mart followed. Kmart's antiquated systems led to severe bottlenecks and made merchandise planners unclear about sales trends. As a result, the stores were stocked with items that customers did not want. Store clerks had too much paperwork on their hands to be able to pay the required amount of attention to customers.

Compiled from various articles.

---

[4] This was reportedly the first 'big' expenditure on IT at Kmart; company sources revealed that this amount was more than what the company had spent on IT in the past decade!

Though Conaway made efforts to spruce up the distribution system and for better upkeep of the stores, he failed to make the customers aware of these changes. Kurt Barnard (Barnard), President of Barnard's Retail Trend Report, said, "He failed to let 270 million shoppers know that Kmart is a new store for the American family. Meanwhile, 270 million American shoppers kept nursing the image that Kmart was a dirty place and had too much out-of-stock." To add to Kmart's problems, before its renewed focus on IT investments could yield any results, the retailing industry plunged into a recession.

TOWARDS BANKRUPTCY

Under the above circumstances, Conaway's and Schwartz's (who joined in September 2002) 'obsession' to beat Wal-Mart and Target was untimely. Conaway and Schwartz wanted to leave no stone unturned in their quest to beat the competition. In 2001, while Kmart posted a loss of $1.3 billion on sales of $36 billion, Wal-Mart posted a profit of $6.7 billion on sales of $217 billion (Refer [to] Exhibit 3 for a brief note on the industry environment for these companies).

In fiscal 2001–02, Kmart reduced its prices significantly, hoping to beat Wal-Mart and Target. Under this initiative, named the BlueLight Always campaign, the company planned to sell over 50,000 items at everyday low prices. Reportedly, the directors of the company, including Adamson, expressed their displeasure with regard to the BlueLight Always program. In fact, Adamson recommended a trial-run of the program. However, Conaway went ahead with a full-fledged implementation of the program. Adamson later commented, "They (Conaway and Schwartz) carried it too far without the board's knowledge."

As expected, the two competitors fought back and Kmart's move backfired. According to a Strategy Development Group newsletter, by trying to blindly follow the leader Wal-Mart (offering everyday low prices), Kmart lost its own identity of being a promotional shopping destination. Customers used to Kmart's promotional offers did not like the consistent value proposition and refused to patronize its stores. Barnard said, "Customers simply did not respond to the low prices. Competing on price with Wal-Mart does not work. Hopefully they will never do it again. It was a bloody experience for them." Moreover, Kmart did not have the buying power and operational efficiency of Wal-Mart to sustain the everyday low prices model.

In August 2001, Kmart posted a loss of $95 million for the second quarter of the financial year. Kmart now decided to reduce its advertising expenditure substantially to reduce costs; the number of pages in its advertising circulars was reduced by 20%. As a result, sales did not pick up even during the Halloween shopping season. Meanwhile, Wal-Mart and Target expanded their promotional efforts to attract more customers. Not surprisingly, the company posted a loss of $224 million for the third quarter of 2001.

Conaway accepted his mistake, stating, "There is no doubt we made a mistake by cutting too much advertising too fast. It also did not help that we decreased our promotion while our competition actually increased theirs." Due to a decline in customers and reduction in prices, the company recorded a $2.4 billion loss in 2001.

On January 2, 2002, Wayne Hood, an analyst with Prudential Securities, downgraded Kmart's stock from 'hold' to the seldom used 'sell' rating, and said that filing for bankruptcy would be the best option for Kmart. The same day, Kmart's stock declined by 17%. Soon after, Standard & Poor's (S&P), a credit rating agency, lowered its Kmart credit rating and removed it from its benchmark index of 500 leading stocks. Another leading credit rating agency, Moody's, too lowered Kmart's debt to 'junk.' Over the next two weeks, Kmart shares fell by 70% and its market capitalization came down to $900 million from $2.7 billion on December 31, 2001.

At this juncture, Fleming Inc. (Fleming[5]), Kmart's food and pantry products supplier, decided to stop shipments to the company's stores. Fleming sources revealed that Kmart owed it $78 million and that it had suspended supplies till it was assured of Kmart's financial position. Soon after, Scotts Co., a supplier of lawn and garden care products, also decided to suspend shipments till details about Kmart's financial position were available. On January 22, 2002, a day after Fleming stopped shipments, Kmart filed for bankruptcy. S&P further downgraded Kmart's debt from 'CCC' (low junk) to 'D.'

Not only was Kmart the largest retailer in the US to go bankrupt, it was also on the list of the biggest bankruptcies ever, along with companies like Enron. This 'distinction' was not the only thing it had in common with Enron. Soon, various illegal and unethical business practices at Kmart started becoming public knowledge. Many top company executives, including Conaway and Schwartz, were accused of misappropriating company funds and manipulating financial statements. While the company was embroiled in numerous legal battles, it began working on its reorganization plans to emerge from bankruptcy by April 2003.

THE REORGANIZATION INITIATIVES

After almost a year of arranging funds, streamlining operations, organizing store closures and laying off employees, Kmart filed its plan of reorganization with the bankruptcy court in January 2003. As per the plan, ESL Investments (ESL) and Third Avenue Value Fund were to be the two main investors. ESL converted claims worth $2 billion into stock

---

[5] The association between Kmart and Fleming started in February 2001 with Fleming being given the rights for most of Kmart's food and pantry product supplies. The agreement was to last till February 2011.

Exhibit 3   A Brief Note on the Industry Environment for Kmart

The US retailing industry, worth $2.2 trillion in the mid-1990s, generated over 21% of the total private sector employment in the country. In 2000, the industry reported a growth of 7%. Many companies did not experience the expected growth due to intense competition, a stagnating market base and heavy investments. In addition, margins were very low in this industry, approximately 3% of sales. Acquisitions and broader product offerings had become the 'survival tools' in the industry during the early 2000s.

Discount stores formed an integral part of the industry. Although growth in this segment had declined from 11.5% in the late 1980s to 10% in the 1990s, the segment continued to witness a lot of action. The three leading players in this segment in the country were Wal-Mart, Target and Kmart. Wal-Mart was not only the market leader in the US, Canada and Mexico; it had emerged as the number one retailing company in the world by 2003. It had over 4,700 stores and led the industry thanks to its legendary everyday low prices formula. For the year ended January 2003, it recorded revenues of $246.53 billion and a net income of $8.04 billion.

Target was a 1,100 discount store chain that had rapidly built its presence in the country due to its upscale, 'fashion-forward' merchandise. For the year ended January 2003, it recorded revenues of $43.92 billion and net income of $1.65 billion (Refer [to] Table 3 for market shares from 1996–98 and Table 4 for a comparison between the key players).

Table 3   US Discount Store Industry—Market Shares

Company	1996	1997	1998
Wal-Mart	22	23	22
Kmart	9	9	8
Target	5	6	5
Regional Discounters	12	10	12
Specialty Discounters	23	25	23
Warehouse Clubs	13	13	12
Off-Price Apparel/Other	7	5	6
Other Discount Mass Merchants	9	9	12

Table 4   US Discount Store Industry—Comparing the Key Players (1998 Figures)

Company	Kmart	Wal-Mart (2)	Target	JC Penney	Sears (4)	Discount Store Average
Sales per Selling Square Feet	$222	$459	$316	$210	$317	$327
Comp Sales Growth	4.8%	9.0%	6.1%	(1.9)% (3)	1.1%	6.3%
EBIT Margin	3.3% (1)	6.6%	6.8%	5.2%	8.6%	5.2%
Total Selling Square Footage (million)	154	258	73	92	96	N/A
Total Stores	2161	2884	851	3904	3043	N/A

(1) Percentage includes income before Voluntary Early Retirement Program.
(2) All information, except Earnings Per Common Share, presented for Wal-Mart domestic Discount Stores, Super Centers and Sam's Clubs only.
(3) Comp Sales Growth and EBIT Margin is for JC Penney Department Stores and Catalog only.
(4) All information, except Earnings Per Common Share, presented for Sears domestic operations only.

Source: biz.yahoo.com and www.kmartcorp.com.

and put up $109 million in cash for running the business. These two were to invest around $140 million in exchange for shares in the reorganized Kmart (with a combined stake of 54%). And subject to certain conditions, ESL was to provide [an] additional $60 million of convertible unsecured note financing.

ESL also agreed to use the cash received by it (as a holder of Kmart's bank debt of approximately $152 million) to purchase more equity. Other holders of Kmart's debt were to be given 40 cents for each dollar of debt held. Holders of Kmart notes and debentures, trade creditors, service providers and landlords were to receive stock in the reorganized company.

Kmart's five-year business plan forecasted profit earning by 2004 and sales of $30.2 billion by 2007. The new President, Julian Day[6] (Day), said, "Our business plan is based on our expectation that we will continue to implement several key operational initiatives, including our focus on being 'the store of the neighborhood' and further testing

---

[6] Day had significant experience in the retail business, having worked with Sears, Roebuck & Co. (Sears) as the Chief Financial Officer and Chief Operating Officer. After leaving Sears in 1999, he had become a retail adviser. His appointment at Kmart broke his semi-retirement.

of the 'store of the future' prototype, with the goal of achieving significant improvements in the customer experience. We intend to continue to eliminate underperforming stock-keeping units and reallocate shelf space to more profitable items. Our marketing activities will continue to emphasize our roots as a high/low retailer and the popular exclusive brands like Joe Boxer, Martha Stewart Everyday, and Thalia."

In the same month, Kmart received the bankruptcy court's approval for $2 billion in exit financing from GE Commercial Finance, Fleet Retail Finance Inc., and Bank of America. This credit facility (secured by inventory) replaced the existing $2 billion debtor-in-possession (DIP) facility. The credit facility aimed at helping the company meet its working capital needs and borrowings for seasonal inventory increases. Day concluded, "We are confident that with the continued support of vendor partners through, among other things, the vendor lien proposed in our plan of reorganization and the $2 billion exit financing facility we have arranged, we will be able to continue to improve the shopping experience, win back customers we have disappointed in the past and return to profitability."

As a result of the costs incurred due to store closures and employee lay-offs, Kmart posted a loss of $3.22 billion for 2002. Apart from the company's inherent problems, the general decline in customer confidence and the dull post-Christmas season too contributed to a 10% decline in like-for-like sales.[7] Since the delivery of goods by suppliers was erratic, Kmart had inadequately stocked shelves, which discouraged many shoppers from buying at its stores. However, Day said that the situation was improving and that efforts to control costs and enhance margins were showing results. Kmart's gross margin of 21% was considered rather healthy by analysts.

However, Kmart's losses in 2002 prompted analysts to declare that its future was bleak and that it would find it very difficult to become successful again. James McTevia, Chairman of financial and management consulting firm McTevia & Associates, said, "It is inconceivable to me how a company in the retail industry in this environment can come out of Chapter 11 with these kinds of losses. If they do not stop the losses, they will eventually go out of business."

REORGANIZATION ROADBLOCKS

In February 2003, Kmart reported a $54 million net loss on revenues of $2.7 billion. In the same month, the bankruptcy court approved Kmart's plan of reorganization with minor modifications. The confirmation hearing for the plan was scheduled to be finished on April 14 and 15, 2003. The company revealed that as per preliminary projections, it foresaw earnings before interest, taxes, depreciation and amortization of $51 million for the three months ending March 26, 2003. From the beginning of 2003, sales were $4.06 billion, a little higher than the $4.01 billion mentioned in the plan submitted to the court.

The first obstacle to the reorganization came in the form of a dispute with a company called Capital Factors (CF). Kmart owed $20 million to CF, a company which bought Kmart's accounts receivables at a discount and assumed the risk of collecting the money. CF had appealed against a court decision (in 2002) which approved Kmart's plans to make payments to critical vendors. As this issue remained unsettled, CF filed an emergency motion to block the approval of the plan by the court before the reorganization hearing started.

Another major obstacle to Kmart's reorganization plan was its dispute with Fleming. After Kmart filed for bankruptcy, its orders to Fleming became very small and the latter's business was severely affected. Thereafter, the two parties jointly announced that their contract was being terminated. While initially Fleming claimed that Kmart owed it $27 million, by March 2003, it increased this figure to $1.47 billion. Kmart contested the claim, stating that it was artificially inflated. In March 2003, the two companies entered into an agreement to settle the dispute. Kmart agreed to pay Fleming $37 million and also to arrange for ESL's purchase of Fleming's claims, worth $385 million. The dispute with CF also ended in April 2003, after Kmart entered into an agreement with the former. Kmart agreed to make certain concessions to CF and ESL agreed to buy an unspecified portion of CF's debt.

When the hearing for Kmart's reorganization plan started in April 2003, over 170 objections were raised by local taxation authorities, landlords, banks and suppliers. Since these parties tried to ensure that the company paid its debts, the hearing went on for four days. The plan was approved on April 22, 2003 even though it hit another roadblock in the form of a patent dispute with Wal-Mart. Kmart said that it would come out of the bankruptcy by May 5, 2003, instead of April last week as planned earlier. Expressing his joy at these developments, Day said, "Let me say how jubilant I am, how jubilant everybody at Kmart is."

LIFE GOES ON—KMART'S FUTURE PLANS

Liquidation sales had begun at 317 Kmart stores across the US in January 2003. Heavy discounts were offered and sales off take was quite impressive. To lure back customers to the stores that continued to remain in business, Kmart launched the 'Savings Are Here To Stay' promotion in February 2003.

---

[7] Like-for-like or same-store sales refer to the sales generated by an organization given the resources (the number of stores) that were operational in the same period in the previous year. Thus, it would exclude any new stores established/acquired during the current year or period under consideration. The idea is to judge how the company has performed in absolute terms when compared to the previous year.

The campaign included in-store events, lucky draws and money saving offers in the form of coupon books (worth over $150 in savings on major brands and exclusive Kmart merchandise). The coupon books were distributed free of cost through newspapers and were also made available at all Kmart stores.

Kmart also planned to renovate its stores by making wider aisles, installing brighter lighting, and ensuring faster check-outs. In addition, it planned to rectify the damage done to its relationship with various suppliers. To improve its operational efficiencies, Kmart developed the 'Top-Sellers Program.' Under this program, Kmart store managers were given more authority to select the high-volume products to be ordered and determine the quantity required. This program was implemented after the company realized that managers who exercised such authority usually recorded the best sales.

Kmart also worked towards developing a new business plan and marketing strategy that would increase sales to $30.2 billion and profit to $181 million by 2004 and $644 million by 2007. Day revealed that instead of relying on an everyday low-price strategy, Kmart would bank on weekly specials, focus on exclusive brands (Martha Stewart Everyday linens and cookware, and clothes designed by Mexican singer Thalia) [and] offer a wider brand portfolio and a demographically designed product range to lure back customers.

Kmart was hoping that its 'neighborhood-oriented' approach would help it find a niche 'between' Wal-Mart and Target. Kmart even planned to begin adding stores (around 70) from 2004 onwards, the year it expected to become profitable again. Since Kmart's turnaround depended on the level of improvement in the US economy and retailing industry, the company's plans were being regarded as very ambitious. Arun Jain (Jain), a Marketing Professor at the University of Buffalo in New York, said, "Their forecasts and goals are very, very ambitious. What this shows, though, is they have honed in on a strategy to succeed, which is their only chance to survive."

Regaining its earlier market position was not going to be easy for Kmart. Competitors had made the most of Kmart's problems by expanding their retail networks and luring away its customers. In April 2003, commenting on Wal-Mart's increasing dominance, Richard Hastings, chief economist at Bernard Sands (a New York–based retail consulting firm), said, "Everybody today lives under the shadow of Wal-Mart."

In the first week of May 2003, Kmart finally emerged from bankruptcy. While the court cases against former Kmart personnel continued, the SEC declared that it would not penalize the company by imposing fines for the follies of its former employees. ESL's Edward Lampert was made the Chairman of Kmart Holding Corp.'s board. The company's stock began trading again on the New York Stock Exchange.

The company's losses for fiscal 2002 amounted [to] $3.22 billion. Many problems still persisted, especially with respect to the employees. Since it had laid off a huge number of employees, it faced an acute shortage of workers in many stores. According to a website posting made by anonymous Kmart employees, many floor associates were operating cash registers because the company could not afford to hire any more people. Store shelves were empty not because of lack of merchandise, but because employees did not find enough time to stock the shelves—they were busy performing duties related to customer service, operating cash registers and carrying out other mandatory tasks.

Though the company had emerged from bankruptcy, it was still too early to determine whether it would be able to meet its revenue and profitability targets. However, what was certain was the fact that Kmart's emergence from bankruptcy would provide no solace to the thousands who lost their jobs and those who suffered directly or indirectly due to the closure of its stores.

Questions for Discussion

1. What problems did Kmart suffer from when Conaway entered the picture? Critically comment on the restructuring efforts undertaken by Conaway to set things right. Why do you think his plans did not meet with success?

2. On January 22, 2002, Kmart filed for bankruptcy. Analyze the incidents prior to this and describe how each one of them played a part in the collapse of the company. Would you agree that Conaway was the only villain here? Give reasons to support your stand.

3. Examine the reorganization plan and the strategic game plan drafted by the 'new' Kmart. In light of the above, what is the likely future of the company? What other measures do you think the company should take to cope with competition from Wal-Mart and Target?

Additional Readings & References

1. Muller, Joann & Brady, Diane, **A Kmart Special: Better Service,** www.businessweek.com, September 4, 2000.
2. **Kmart Files Chapter 11,** www.money.cnn.com, January 22, 2002.
3. Yue, Lorene & Angel, Cecil, **Shipment of Food Grinding to a Halt,** www.freep.com, January 22, 2002.
4. Russell, Nancy, **Retailing Giant Kmart Files for Bankruptcy,** www.wsws.org, January 26, 2002.
5. Hayes, Frank, **Lessons From Kmart,** *Computerworld,* January 28, 2002.
6. Patsuris, Penelope, **For Kmart, Bankruptcy May Be Best,** www.forbes.com, March 01, 2002.
7. Isaacs, Jerry, **US Retailer Kmart Cuts 22,000 Jobs,** www.wsws.org, March 09, 2002.
8. **Insights on Strategy,** www.ratoffconsulting.com, April 2002.
9. Ferraro, Cathleen, **Kmart to Fire 35,000,** www.sacbee.com, January 15, 2003.
10. Walsh, David, **Mass Job Destruction at US Retailer Kmart,** www.wsws.org, January 18, 2003.
11. Dybis, Karen, **Kmart Gets New CEO,** *The Detroit News,* January 20, 2003.

12. Dybis, Karen, **Will Kmart Battle Plan Work?,** *The Detroit News,* January 24, 2003.

13. Hudson, Mike, **Kmart Pins Comeback on "Neighborhood" Plan,** *The Detroit News,* January 26, 2003.

14. Dixon, Jennifer, **Judge OKs Closing 318 More Kmarts,** www.freep.com, January 29, 2003.

15. Bott, Jennifer, **Bankruptcy Blues: Kmart Workers Face Job Loss, Tough Search,** www.freep.com, March 17, 2003.

16. Bosak, Pete, **Deep Discounts Lure Shoppers to Kmart,** www.tribune-democrat.com, March 18, 2003.

17. Coons, Ken, **Kmart Fights $1.4 Billion Claim by Fleming,** www.seafood.com, March 18, 2003.

18. Dybis, Karen, **Kmart Settles Claim for $ 400 Million,** *The Detroit News,* March 21, 2003.

19. Runk, David, **Kmart: Strategy Working,** www.lenconnect.com, March 25, 2003.

20. Ahlberg, Erik, **Judge Approves Claim Settlement Between Kmart & Fleming,** http://biz.yahoo.com, March 25, 2003.

21. Kaiser, Emily, **Kmart Braces for Reorganization Hearing,** www.reuters.com, April 14, 2003.

22. Kaiser, Emily, **Kmart Vows to Become a Leaner Operation,** www.reuters.com, April 15, 2003.

23. **Objections Jeopardize Kmart Plan,** www.usatoday.com, April 16, 2003.

24. Robinson, Mike, **Kmart Officials "Jubilant" as Bankruptcy Court OKs Reorganization Plan,** www.nola.com, April 23, 2003.

25. Walsh, Tom, **Kmart a Little Wobbly from Its Experience,** www.freep.com, April 24, 2003.

26. Krotz, L. Joanna, **Kmart's 5 Big Blunders,** www.bcentral.com.

27. *The Detroit Press.*

28. www.freep.com.

29. www.bankrupt.com.

30. www.bigcharts.com.

31. www.kmartcorp.com.

32. Company Annual Reports.

Charlotte Beers at Ogilvy & Mather Worldwide (A)

9-495-031

It was December 1993, and during the past year and a half, Charlotte Beers had found little time for reflection. Since taking over as CEO and chairman of Ogilvy & Mather Worldwide in 1992, Beers had focused all her efforts on charting a new course for the world's sixth-largest advertising agency. The process of crafting a vision with her senior management team had been—by all accounts—painful, messy, and chaotic. Beers, however, was pleased with the results. Ogilvy & Mather was now committed to becoming "the agency most valued by those who most value brands."

During the past year, the agency had regained, expanded, or won several major accounts. Confidence and energy appeared to be returning to a company the press had labeled "beleaguered" only two years earlier. Yet, Beers sensed that the change effort was still fragile. "Brand Stewardship," the agency's philosophy for building brands, was not well understood below the top tier of executives who had worked with Beers to develop the concept. Internal communication efforts to 272 worldwide offices were under way, as were plans to adjust O&M's structures and systems to a new set of priorities. Not the least of the challenges before her was ensuring collaboration between offices on multinational brand campaigns. The words of Kelly O'Dea, her Worldwide Client Service president, still rang in her ears. "We can't lose momentum. Most change efforts fail after the initial success. This could be the prologue, Charlotte . . . or it could be the whole book."

OGILVY & MATHER

In 1948, David Ogilvy, a 38-year-old Englishman, sold his small tobacco farm in Pennsylvania and invested his entire savings to start his own advertising agency. The agency, based in New York, had financial backing from two London agencies, Mather & Crowther and S. H. Benson. "I had no clients, no credentials, and only $6,000 in the bank," Ogilvy would later write in his autobiography, "[but] I managed to create a series of campaigns which, almost overnight, made Ogilvy & Mather famous."[1]

Ogilvy's initial ads—for Rolls-Royce, Schweppes, and Hathaway Shirts—were based on a marketing philosophy that Ogilvy had begun developing as a door-to-door salesman in the 1930s, and later, as a pollster for George Gallup. Ogilvy believed that effective advertising created an indelible image of the product in consumers' minds and, furthermore, that campaigns should always be intelligent, stylish, and "first class." Most of all, however, David Ogilvy believed that advertising must sell. "We sell–or else" became his credo for the agency. In 1950, Ogilvy's campaign for Hathaway featured a distinguished man with a black eye patch, an idea that increased sales by 160% and ran for 25 years. Other famous campaigns included Maxwell House's "Good to the Last Drop" launched in 1958 and American Express's "Don't Leave Home Without It," which debuted in 1962.

Research Associate Nicole Sackley prepared this case under the supervision of Professor Herminia Ibarra as the basis for class discussion rather than to illustrate either effective or ineffective handling of an administrative situation.

---

[1] David Ogilvy, *Blood, Beer, and Advertising* (London: Hamish Hamilton, 1977).

Gentlemen with Brains

David Ogilvy imbued his agency's culture with the same "first class" focus that he demanded of creative work. Employees were "gentlemen with brains," treating clients, consumers, and one another with respect. "The consumer is not a moron," admonished Ogilvy. In a distinctly British way, collegiality and politeness were highly valued: "We abhor ruthlessness. We like people with gentle manners and see no conflict between adherence to high professional standards in our work and human kindness in our dealings with others."[2]

At Ogilvy's agency, gentility did not mean blandness. Ogilvy took pride in his agency's "streak of unorthodoxy." He smoked a pipe, refused to fly, and peppered his speeches with literary references and acerbic wit. He once advised a young account executive, "Develop your eccentricities early, and no one will think you're going senile later in life." In a constant stream of letters, he made his dislikes clear: "I despise toadies who suck up to their bosses. . . . I am revolted by pseudoacademic jargon like *attitudinal, paradigms,* and *sub-optimal.*" He also exhorted his staff to achieve brilliance through "obsessive curiosity, guts under pressure, inspiring enthusiasm, and resilience in adversity." No one at Ogilvy & Mather ever forgot the full-page announcement he placed in the *New York Times:* "Wanted: Trumpeter Swans who combine personal genius with inspiring leadership. If you are one of these rare birds, write to me in inviolable secrecy."

---

[2] David Ogilvy, *Confessions of an Advertising Man* (New York: Atheneum, 1963).

In 1965, Ogilvy & Mather merged with its partner agencies in Britain to form Ogilvy & Mather International.[3] "Our aim," wrote David Ogilvy, "is to be One Agency Indivisible; the same advertising disciplines, the same principles of management, the same striving for excellence." Each office was carpeted in the same regal Ogilvy red. Individual offices, however, were run independently by local presidents who exercised a great deal of autonomy.

David Ogilvy retired in 1975. Succeeding the legendary founder proved daunting. "The next four chairmen," commented one longtime executive, "did not have his presence. David is quirky; they were straightforward, middle-of-the-road, New York." Ogilvy's successors focused on extending the network offices internationally and building direct response, marketing research, and sales promotion capabilities. Revenues soared in the 1970s, culminating in record double-digit gains in the mid-1980s (see **Exhibit 1**). The advertising industry boomed, and Ogilvy & Mather led the pack. Nowhere was the agency's reputation greater than at its New York office, heralded in 1986 by the press as "the class act of Madison Avenue."

Advertising Industry Changes

The booming economy of the 1980s shielded the advertising industry from the intensifying pressures of global competition. Companies fought for consumer attention through

---

[3] Dictionary of Company Histories, 1986.

Exhibit 1   Selected Financial and Organization Data

1984–1988

	1984	1985	1986	1987	1988
Revenues (in thousands)	$428,604	$490,486	$560,132	$738,508	$838,090
Net income (in thousands)	25,838	30,247	26,995	29,757	32,950
Operating profit (in thousands)	49,191	45,355	47,764	57,933	65,922

Source: The Ogilvy Group Annual Report, 1988.

1989–1993[a]

	1989	1990	1991	1992	1993
Total annual billings (in thousands)[b]	$4,089,000	$4,563,700	$5,271,000	$5,205,700	$5,814,100
Revenues (in thousands)	592,600	653,700	757,600	754,800	740,000
Percent change in net income[c]	NA	4.7	−2.8	1.9	5.3
Operating margin	NA	6.4	4.1	4.9	7.6

Source: Advertising Age.
[a]Financial information for 1989–1993 is not comparable to 1984–1988 due to the restructuring of the company following sale to WPP Group, plc. It is the policy of WPP Group, plc not to release revenue and net income information about its subsidiaries.
[b]Represents an estimate by *Advertising Age* of the total value of all advertising and direct marketing campaigns run in a given year.
[c]The percent increase or decrease is given from an undisclosed sum at base year 1989.

marketing, and advertising billings grew—on average, between 10% and 15% per annum. Brand manufacturers—challenged by the growth of quality generic products and the diverse tastes of a fragmented mass market—created multiple line extensions and relied on agencies' creative powers to differentiate them. As business globalized, so did agencies. Responding to clients' demands for global communications and a range of integrated services, agencies expanded rapidly, many merging to achieve economies of scale as "mega-agencies" with millions in revenues worldwide.

After the stock market crash of 1987, companies reconsidered the value added by large advertising budgets. Increasingly, many chose to shift resources from expensive mass media and print campaigns towards direct mail, cable, telemarketing, and sales promotion. Fixed fees began to replace the agencies' historical 15% commission on billings. Long-standing client-agency relations were severed as companies sought the best bargains. Viewed by some as ad factories selling a commodity product, the mega-agencies were challenged by new, "boutique" creative shops. The globalization of media and pressures for cost efficiencies encouraged companies to consolidate product lines and to sell them in more markets worldwide. They, in turn, directed agencies to transport their brands around the world. The advertising agency of the 1990s—often a loose federation of hundreds of independent firms—was asked to launch simultaneous brand campaigns in North America, Europe, and the emerging markets of Asia, Latin America, and Africa.

Organizational Structure

By 1991, Ogilvy's 270 offices comprised four regions. The North American offices were the most autonomous, with office presidents reporting directly to the Worldwide CEO. Outside North America, presidents of local offices—sometimes majority stakeholders (see **Exhibit 2**)—reported to country presidents, who in turn reported to regional chairmen. Europe was coordinated centrally, but—with significant European multinational clients and a tradition of high creativity—the region maintained its autonomy from New York. To establish a presence in Latin America, Ogilvy obtained minority ownership in locally owned agencies and formed partnerships with local firms. The last region to be fully formed was Asia/Pacific, with the addition of Australia, India, and Southeast Asia in 1991 (see **Exhibit 3** for organization chart).

Between and across regions, "worldwide management supervisors" coordinated the requirements of multinational clients such as American Express and Unilever. WMSs served as the point of contact among multiple parties: client headquarters, clients' local subsidiaries, and the appropriate Ogilvy local offices. They were also responsible for forming and managing the core multi-disciplinary account team. More important, they facilitated the exchange of information throughout the network, attempting to ensure strategic unity and avoid operating at cross-purposes.

Exhibit 2   **Percent of Regional Offices Owned by O&M Worldwide**

	# of Offices	100%	>50%	<50%	0%
North America	40	80	20	0	0
Europe	97	63	24	8	5
Asia/Pacific	66	57	36	7	0
Latin America	48	25	6	21	48

Over time, Ogilvy & Mather came to pride itself as "the most local of the internationals, the most international of the locals." Local delivery channels and the need for consumer acceptance of multinational products required specialized local knowledge and relationships. Local and global clients also served as magnets for each other: without local accounts, country offices were unable to build sufficient critical mass to service multinational clients well; without multinational accounts to draw top talent, the agency was less attractive to local clients.

With a "light center and strong regions," most creative and operating decisions were made locally. The role of Worldwide Headquarters in New York, staffed by 100 employees, was limited largely to ensuring consistency in financial reporting and corporate communications. Key capital allocation and executive staffing decisions were made by the O&M Worldwide board of directors, which included regional chairmen and presidents of the most powerful countries and offices such as France, Germany, the United Kingdom, New York, and Los Angeles.

The Ogilvy offices represented four core disciplines: sales promotion, public relations, advertising, and direct marketing.[4] Sales promotion developed point-of-purchase materials such as in-store displays and flyers. Public relations offices worked to promote clients' corporate reputation and product visibility. Advertising focused on mass marketing, establishing the core of a client's brand image through the development and production of television commercials, print campaigns, and billboards. Direct Marketing created and delivered targeted advertising—from mail order catalogues to coupons and television infomercials—designed to solicit a direct response from consumers. While the latter three resided within the regional structure, O&M Direct was an independent subsidiary. In the late 1980s, the Ogilvy board of directors decided to focus on advertising and direct marketing, the firm's chief competitive strengths. Unlike advertising, Direct's business in the 1980s remained chiefly local, but expanded explosively. By 1991, O&M Direct had received numerous industry accolades and was ranked the largest direct marketing company in the world.

---

[4] The number of Ogilvy offices by discipline in 1994 were as follows: 83 Advertising, 60 Direct Response, 12 Promotional, 23 Public Relations, and 92 in other areas, including highly specialized market research firms.

Exhibit 3   Ogilvy & Mather Worldwide Organization Chart, 1991

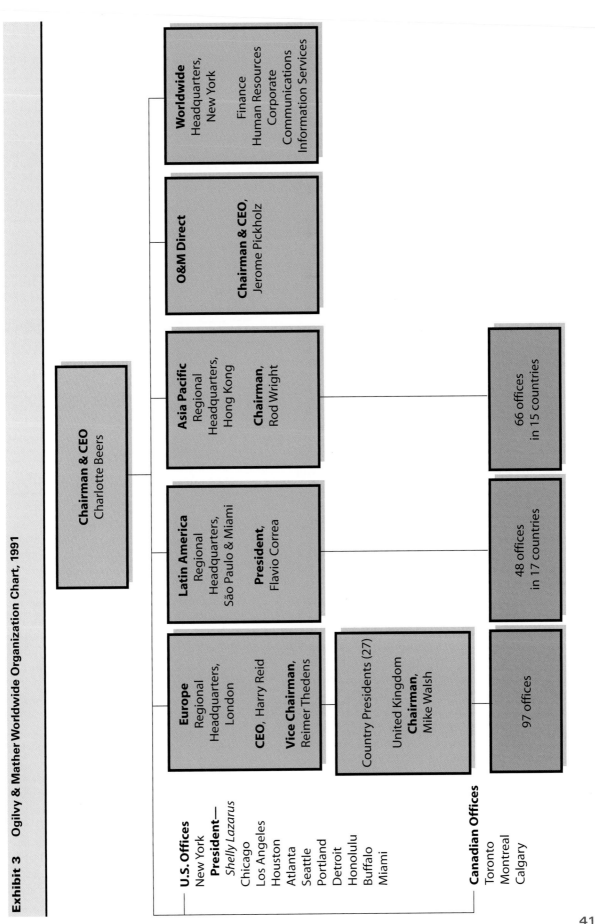

Chairman & CEO
Charlotte Beers

U.S. Offices
New York
President—
Shelly Lazarus
Chicago
Los Angeles
Houston
Atlanta
Seattle
Portland
Detroit
Honolulu
Buffalo
Miami

Europe
Regional
Headquarters,
London

CEO, Harry Reid

Vice Chairman,
Reimer Thedens

Country Presidents (27)

United Kingdom
Chairman,
Mike Walsh

97 offices

Canadian Offices
Toronto
Montreal
Calgary

Latin America
Regional
Headquarters,
São Paulo & Miami

President,
Flavio Correa

48 offices
in 17 countries

Asia Pacific
Regional
Headquarters,
Hong Kong

Chairman,
Rod Wright

66 offices
in 15 countries

O&M Direct

Chairman & CEO,
Jerome Pickholz

Worldwide
Headquarters,
New York

Finance
Human Resources
Corporate
Communications
Information Services

"Beleaguered" Ogilvy & Mather

As clients demanded lower costs and greater service, Ogilvy & Mather—like many large agencies at the time—was slow to make adjustments. In 1988, Ogilvy was ranked the sixth-largest advertising firm in the world. As one executive remembered:

> Everything was going well. All we had to do was wake up in the morning and we were plus 15%. So why did we need to change? Our vision was "just keep doing the same thing, better." We failed either to recognize or acknowledge what were the first real indications that life around here was about to change fundamentally.

In May 1989, WPP Group Plc, a leading marketing services company, acquired Ogilvy & Mather for $864 million.[5] WPP, led by Harvard Business School–trained Martin Sorrell, had already purchased the J. Walter Thompson agency for $550 million two years earlier.[6] The takeover was hostile, with agency executives—including CEO Kenneth Roman—opposed. "It was a shock," explained one long-time executive. "We were a proud company with a constant stock market growth, the masters of our destiny. Suddenly, we were raided." Within months of the takeover, CEO Roman resigned. "Ken had absolutely nothing in common with WPP. There was a lack of trust, an air of conflict, adversaries, and invasion," remembered another. A number of top creative and account executives followed Roman, leaving Ogilvy & Mather for other agencies.[7]

Graham Phillips, a 24-year Ogilvy veteran, was appointed Roman's successor. One executive who worked with Philips described him as "a brilliant account guy and a very good manager who identified our need to become a total communications company. But few would describe him as an inspirational leader."

In 1989, the agency lost major advertising assignments from Unilever and Shell. In 1990, Seagram's Coolers and Nutrasweet withdrew their multinational accounts.[8] Account losses in 1991 proved particularly damaging to the New York office, the agency's center and standard-bearer. "If New York thrives, the world thrives. If New York fails, the world fails" went a familiar company adage. New York's client defections were explained by one executive as a failure in leadership: "The office was run by czars with big accounts. People got used to a highly political way of working and work deteriorated." In 1991, Campbell Soup withdrew $25 million in business, Roy Rogers $15 million, and American Express—the account for which Ogilvy had won "Print Campaign of the Decade"—pulled out $60 million.[9] "Losing American Express had symbolism far beyond what the actual business losses were," recalled one Ogilvy executive. "People who were loyal Ogilvy employees, believers for years,

disengaged. They threw up their hands and said, 'This place is falling apart.'"

Despite declines in revenue, the agency found itself unable to adapt to clients' changing demands. Budgets were not reduced at local offices, even as large clients pushed Ogilvy to streamline and centralize their accounts. "We were a high-cost operation in a low-cost world. There was a lack of financial discipline, a lack of focus on cost, and a lack of structured decision making on business issues," noted one executive. Another faulted the firm's tradition of local autonomy and failure to institute systems for managing collaboration: "We were spending a lot of money at the creative center without cutting back locally—building costs at both ends."

Recalling the atmosphere at the time, another executive concluded, "A shaken confidence permeated the whole company. We talked about change and what we needed to do ad nauseam, but nothing was happening. We tried to work within the old framework when the old ways of working were irrelevant."

At the end of 1991, Phillips stepped down as CEO, telling the press: "I have taken Ogilvy through a very difficult period in the industry. I had to let go people whom I had worked with for 27 years, and that wears you down." In April, Charlotte Beers was appointed CEO and chairman of Ogilvy & Mather Worldwide, the first outsider ever to lead the company.

CHARLOTTE BEERS

The daughter of a cowboy, Beers grew up in Texas, where she began her career as a research analyst for the Mars Company. In 1969, she moved to Chicago as an account executive with J. Walter Thompson. Once there, she cultivated success with clients Sears, Kraft, and Gillette, combining a Southern Texan charm with sharp business acumen. Beers rose quickly to senior vice president for Client Services.

At Thompson, Beers was known for her passionate interest—unusual in account executives—in the philosophy of marketing. Commented Beers, "I try never to discuss with clients only the stuff of business. I focus on advertising as well—on the ideas." Once described on a performance evaluation as "completely fearless," Beers earned a reputation for her ability to win over clients. Colleagues retold the story of how Beers impressed a roomful of Sears executives in the early 1970s by taking apart, then reassembling, a Sears power drill without skipping a beat in her pitch for a new advertising campaign.

In 1979, Beers became COO of the Chicago agency Tatham-Laird & Kudner. Her success in winning the mid-sized agency several new brands with Proctor & Gamble helped turn the firm around. Accounts with Ralston-Purina and Stouffer Foods followed. Beers was elected CEO in 1982 and chairman of the board in 1986. In 1987, she became the first woman ever named chairman of the American Association of Advertising Agencies. One year later, she led TLK through a merger with the international agency Eurocome-

[5] Christie Dugas, "The Death of Ogilvy and an Era," *Newsday*, May 17, 1989.

[6] Ibid.

[7] "Change Comes to Fabled Ogilvy," *New York Times*, April 12, 1992.

[8] "Beers Succeeds Phillips at O&M Worldwide," *Adweek*, April 13, 1992.

[9] "Operation Winback," *Advertising Age*, February 1993.

RSCG. Tatham's billings had tripled during Beers's tenure, to $325 million.

Beers Takes Over

Beers's appointment, recalled O&M veterans, created initial apprehension. Commented one executive, "She was from a smaller agency in Chicago and had not managed multiple offices. O&M is a worldwide company, and she had never worked outside the United States. And, she was not from Ogilvy." Added another, "This is an organization that rejects outsiders."

Her approach quickly made an impression with Ogilvy insiders. "It was clear from day one, that Charlotte would be a different kind of leader. Full of life. Eyes open and clearly proud of the brand she was now to lead. Here was somebody who could look around and see the risks, but wasn't afraid to turn the corner even though it was dark out," said one executive. "We had leaders before, who said all the right things, were terribly nice, did a good job, but they didn't inspire. Charlotte has an ability to inspire—Charlotte has presence." Commented another executive, "She is delightfully informal, but you always know that she means business." Within two months of her appointment, Beers dismissed a top-level executive who had failed to instigate necessary changes.

Activate the Assets

"When I took over," recalled Beers, "all the press reports talked about 'beleaguered' Ogilvy. My job was to remove, 'beleaguered' from our name." In her first six weeks, Beers sent a "Hello" video to all 7,000 of Ogilvy's employees. It began:

> Everybody wants to know my nine-point plan for success and I can't tell you that I know yet what it is. I'm building my own expectations and dreams for the agency—but I need a core of people who have lived in this company and who have similar dreams to help me. That's going to happen fast, because we are rudderless without it. David [Ogilvy] gave us a great deal to build on, but I don't think it's there for us to go backwards. It's there to go forward.

Beers concluded that people had lost sight of Ogilvy's still impressive assets—its vast network of offices worldwide, its creative talent, and its distinguished list of multinational clients. "We must," she told senior executives, "activate the assets we already have." In her second month at Ogilvy, Beers observed a major client presentation by the heads of five O&M offices:

> It was a fabulous piece of thinking. We had committed enormous resources. But in the end, they didn't tell the clients why it would work. When the client said, "We'll get back to you," they didn't demand an immediate response, so I intervened. "You saw a remarkable presentation, and I think you need to comment." Ogilvy had gotten so far from its base, that talented people lacked the confidence to speak up.

For Beers, her early interactions with a key client symbolized the state of the company. "He kept retelling the tale of New York's downfall: how we blew a major account in Europe and how our groups fought among one another. The fourth time I heard this story," remembered Beers, "I interrupted. 'That's never going to happen again, so let's not talk about it anymore. Let's talk about what we can accomplish together.'"

Beers spent much of her first months at Ogilvy talking to investors and clients. For Wall Street, she focused on the quality of Ogilvy's advertising. "I refused to do a typical analyst report," she said. "When the Wall Street analysts asked me why I showed them our ads, I told them it was to give them reason to believe the numbers would happen again and again." Clients voiced other concerns. "I met with 50 clients in six months," recalled Beers, "and found there was a lot of affection for Ogilvy. Yet, they were also very candid. Clients stunned me by rating us below other agencies in our insight into the consumer." Beers shared these perceptions with senior managers: "Clients view our people as uninvolved, distant, and reserved. We have organized ourselves into fiefdoms, and that has taken its toll. Each department—Creative, Account, Media, and Research—are often working as separate entities. It's been a long time since we've had some famous advertising."

To restore confidence both internally and externally, Beers maintained that the agency needed a clear direction. "I think it's fair to say Ogilvy had no clear sense of what it stood for. I wanted to give people something that would release their passion, that would knit them together. I wanted the extraneous discarded. I wanted a rallying point on what really matters."

For Beers, what mattered was brands. "She is intensely client- and brand-focused," explained one executive. "You can't go into her office with financial minutia. You get about two seconds of attention." Beers believed that clients wanted an agency that understood the complexity of managing the emotional as well as the logical relationship between a consumer and a product. "I became confident that I knew what clients wanted and what Ogilvy's strengths were. It was my job to be the bridge." Beers, however, was as yet unsure what form that bridge would take or how it would get built. One of her early challenges was to decide whom to ask for help in charting this new course:

> I knew I needed their involvement, and that I would be asking people to do much more than they had been, without the benefits of titles and status. I avoided calling on people on the basis of their titles. I watched the way they conducted business. I looked to see what they found valuable. I wanted people who felt the way I did about brands. I was looking for kindred spirits.

The "Thirsty for Change" Group

Over the next few months, Beers solicited ideas for change from her senior managers, asking them to give candid evaluations of disciplines and regions, as well as of one another. In a style that managers would describe as "quintessential Charlotte," Beers chose to meet with executives one-on-one and assigned them tasks without regard to their disciplinary backgrounds. She commented, "I was slow to pull an executive committee together. I didn't know who could do it. It was a clumsy period, and I was account executive on everything—everything came to me." At first, some found the lack of structure unnerving. Noted one executive, "People weren't quite sure what their roles were. It caused discomfort. We began to wonder, 'Where do I fit? Who is whose boss?'" Another added, "She was purposely vague in hopes that people would stretch themselves to new configurations." Several executives, though cautious, found Beers's talk of change inspiring and responded with their ideas.

By May 1992, Beers had identified a group whom she described as "thirsty for change." Some were top executives heading regions or key offices; others were creative and account directors who caught her eye as potential allies. Her selection criterion was "people who got it"—those who agreed on the importance of change. All had been vocal about their desire to move Ogilvy forward. She sent a memo inviting them to a meeting in Vienna, Austria, that month:

Date: May 19, 1992   **HIGHLY CONFIDENTIAL**
From: Charlotte Beers

To: LUIS BASSAT, President, Bassat, Ogilvy & Mather—Spain

BILL HAMILTON, Creative Director—O&M New York

SHELLY LAZARUS, President—O&M New York

KELLY O'DEA, Worldwide Client Service Director, Ford and AT&T—London

ROBYN PUTTER, President and Creative Director—O&M South Africa

HARRY REID, CEO—O&M Europe, London

REIMER THEDENS, Vice Chairman—O&M Europe, Frankfurt

MIKE WALSH, President—O&M, United Kingdom, London

ROD WRIGHT, Chairman—O&M Asia/Pacific, Hong Kong

Will you please join me . . . in re-inventing our beloved agency? I choose you because you seem to be truth-tellers, impatient with the state we're in and capable of leading this revised, refreshed agency. We want to end up with a vision for the agency we can state . . . and excite throughout the company. Bring some basics to Vienna, like where we are today and where we'd like to be in terms of our clients and competition. But beyond the basics, bring your dreams for this great brand.

BRAND STEWARDSHIP

The Vienna meeting, recalled Beers, "put a diversity of talents in a climate of disruption." Having never met before for such a purpose, members were both tentative with each other and elated to share their perspectives. Two common values provided an initial glue: "We agreed to take no more baby steps. And it seemed clear that brands were what we were going to be about."

Beers asked Rod Wright, who had led the Asia/Pacific region through a vision formulation process, to organize and facilitate the meeting. Wright proposed a conceptual framework, based on the McKinsey "7-S" model,[10] to guide discussion of the firm's strengths and weaknesses. He also hoped to generate debate. "We don't have passionate arguments in this company. We avoid conflict, and debates go off line. When you use a framework, it's easier to depersonalize the discussion."

Reactions to the discussion ranged from confusion to disinterest. "It was theoretical mumbo-jumbo," commented one participant, "I tend to be far more pragmatic and tactical." Added another, "I don't have much patience for the theoretical bent. I wanted to get on with it." Wright admitted, "They rolled their eyes and said, 'You mean we've got to do all that?'" Beers agreed: "The B-school approach had to be translated." As the discussion unfolded, the group discovered that their personalities, priorities, and views on specific action implications diverged widely.

One debate concerned priorities for change. Shelly Lazarus diagnosed a firm-wide morale problem. She argued for restoring confidence with a pragmatic focus on bottom-line client results and counseled against spending much energy on structural changes. Mike Walsh agreed but insisted that the group take time to articulate clearly its vision and values. But Kelly O'Dea had become frustrated with Ogilvy's geographical fragmentation and argued that anything short of major structural changes would be insufficient.

Participants were also divided on whether the emerging brand focus was an end or a starting point. The "Creatives" in the group[11]—Luis Bassat, Bill Hamilton, and Robyn Putter—flanked by Beers, Lazarus and Walsh were interested primarily in finding an effective vehicle for communicating O&M's distinctive competency. An eloquent statement, they felt, would sell clients and inspire employees. The others—O'Dea, Wright, Harry Reid, and Reimer Thedens—wanted a vision that provided guidelines for an internal transformation. Summarized Wright, "One school of thought was looking for a line which encapsulates what we do: our creative credo. The other was looking for a strategy, a business mission to guide how we run the company."

---

[10] Wright's model included 10 issue categories: shared values, structures, stakeholders, staff, skills, strategy, suggestions, solutions, service systems, and a shared vision.

[11] Within advertising and direct marketing, "creatives" develop the art and copy for each media outlet of a brand campaign.

Yet another discussion concerned the route to competitive advantage. Bassat, Putter and Hamilton, commented one participant, felt that Ogilvy had lost sight of the creative product in its rush to worry about finances—"we'd become too commercial." A recommitment to better, more imaginative advertising, they believed, would differentiate the firm from its competitors. Reid and Thedens, architects of a massive re-engineering effort in Europe, insisted on financial discipline and tighter operations throughout the company as the only means of survival in the lean operating environment of the 1990s. Wright and Thedens added the O&M Direct perspective. Convinced that media advertising by itself was becoming a commodity product, each pressed for a commitment to brand building through a broader, more integrated range of communication services.

At the close of the meeting, remembered one attender, "There was a great deal of cynicism. 'Was this just another chat session?' we asked ourselves. But, we also had a sense that Charlotte felt right. She fit."

In August 1992, the group reassembled at the English resort Chewton Glen. Members presented Beers with their respective lists of priorities requiring immediate attention. Taken together, there were 22 "to do" items ranging from "examine the process by which we develop and present creative ideas" to "improve our delivery of services across geographical divisions." Beers recalled, "No one can focus on 22 things! I was so depressed, I stayed up all night and wrote a new list." She delivered her thoughts the next day:

> I think we have hit bottom and are poised for recovery. Poised but not assured. Our job is to give direction for change. So here is where I start. For 1993, we have three—and only three—strategies. They are:

1. *Client Security.* Let's focus our energy, resources and passion on our present clients. It takes three years to replace the revenue from a lost client. Under strategy one, there's a very important corollary: We must focus particularly on multinational clients. This is where we have our greatest opportunity for growth and where our attitudes, structure, and lack of focus have been obstacles.

2. *Better Work, More Often.* Without it, you can forget the rest. Our work is not good enough. Maybe it will never be, but that's O.K.—better to be so relentless about our work that we are never satisfied. You tell me there's nothing wrong with our credo, "We Sell, or Else," but you also say we need some fresh thinking on how to get there. We must have creative strategies that make the brand the central focus.

3. *Financial Discipline.* This has been a subject of high concentration but not very productively so. We simply have not managed our own resources very well, and that must change.

These 1993 strategies were linked to the emerging vision by a declaration: "The purpose of our business is to build our clients' brands." One participant recalled, "The idea of brand stewardship was still embryonic. Charlotte clearly understood it in her own mind but was just learning how to communicate it. She used us as guinea pigs to refine her thinking." But some expressed concern: "There was no disagreement that the 1993 strategy was correct. It was fine for the short-term but we needed a long-term strategy."

Through the fall of 1992, group members worked to communicate the strategy—dubbed the "Chewton Glen Declaration"—to the next level of managers. Beers directed her energy toward clients, working vigorously to win new and lost accounts. She spoke about the emotional power of brands, warning them of the abuse inflicted by agencies and brand managers who failed to understand the consumers' relationship with their products. Ogilvy & Mather, Beers told clients, was uniquely positioned to steward their brands' growth and development. Clients were intrigued. By October, O&M boasted two major successes: Jaguar Motor cars' entire U.S. account and the return of American Express's $60 million worldwide account.[12] The press hailed, "Ogilvy & Mather is back on track."

Worldwide Client Service

The Chewton Glen mandate to focus on multinationals heightened the need for better global coordination. Although Ogilvy had pioneered multinational account service in the 1970s, the firm in the 1990s remained "segregated into geographic and discipline fiefdoms" that hampered the development and delivery of brand campaigns worldwide. Noted O'Dea, "What most clients began to seek was the best combination of global efficiencies and local sensitivity, but we were not set up to facilitate that. We had the local strength, but international people were commandos with passports and begging bowls, totally dependant on the goodwill of local agencies and their own personal charisma."

In the fall of 1992, Beers asked O'Dea to head a new organization, Worldwide Client Service, that would "tap the best brains from anywhere in the world for each account." O'Dea envisioned dozens of virtual organizations, each focused on a multinational client, with multiple "centers" located wherever their respective clients maintained international headquarters. Under WCS, members of multinational account teams became "dual citizens," reporting both to their local office presidents and WCS supervisors. One WCS director noted, "International people coordinating multinational accounts used to be regarded by the local offices as staff. We thought we were line; the clients treated us like line; but internally, we had no real authority. What WCS did was give us teeth by giving us line responsibility for our accounts—tenure, profits, growth, and evaluation of local offices."

WCS brand teams were structured to mirror their clients' organizations. Some WCS directors served largely as consultants, while others ran highly centralized operations,

---

[12] "Operation Winback," *Advertising Age*, February 1993.

with a core team responsible for the entire creative and client development process. "We had to reinvent ourselves in the client's footprint," remarked the WCS account director for Kimberly-Clark. His counterpart at Unilever agreed but noted that current trends favored centralization. "Speed, cost-efficiency, and centralization are our clients' priorities. What matters is not just having good ideas, but getting those ideas to as many markets as possible, as **fast** as possible."

By 1993, O'Dea began to travel the world presenting the possibilities of transnational teams without borders. "Good sell-ins had to be done. Office heads had to understand that there were no choices—global accounts had to be managed horizontally. We'd be dead if we didn't do it," said Reid.

Tools for Brand Stewardship

"The first six months were high excitement, high energy, and a steep learning curve," said Beers. "That was followed by 12 months of disappointment and frustration. It didn't look as if we were getting anywhere." In December 1992, Beers asked Robyn Putter and Luis Bassat, two of the firm's top creative talents, for help in developing the emerging notion of "Brand Stewardship." They answered: "If we are to be successful, we must 'audit' our brands. We must ask the kinds of questions that will systematically uncover the emotional subtleties and nuances by which brands live." Beers took their insight directly to existing and prospective clients. One manager remembered:

> Clients immediately bought into Brand Stewardship. That created pressure to go public with it before we had every "i" dotted and "t" crossed. We didn't have a codified process, but Charlotte would talk to clients and we'd have to do it. Clients came to O&M offices saying, "I want a brand audit." And, our offices responded with, "What's a brand audit?" One client asked us for permission to use the term. We had to move quickly, or risk losing ownership of the idea.

Beers responded by asking a group of executives to elaborate the notion of a brand audit. Led by Walsh, they produced a series of questions designed to unveil the emotional as well as the logical significance of a product in the users' lives: "What memories or associations does the brand bring to mind? What specific feelings and emotions do you experience in connection with using this brand? What does this brand do for you in your life that other brands cannot?" The insights gathered from these questions—which became the brand audit—would, in Beer's words, "guide each brand team to the rock-bottom truth of the brand." Focusing on two of Ogilvy's global brands—Jaguar and Dove—Beer's working group struggled to articulate in a few words and images each brand's unique "genetic fingerprint." The result was O&M's first BrandPrints

- A Jaguar is a copy of absolutely nothing—just like its owners.

- Dove stands for attainable miracles.

Crafting a Vision

As the "technology" of brand stewardship developed, the senior team continued to wrestle with the formulation of a vision statement. Some argued, "We have the vision— it's Brand Stewardship." Others maintained that Brand Stewardship was but a tool to be used in attaining a yet undefined, future state. Further, as O'Dea explained, "Nearly everyone had had some contact with Brand Stewardship and WCS but they viewed them as separate and isolated actions without a strategic context."

The solution to the impasse, for some, was to include a larger group in the vision formulation. "We needed to decide collectively what we were going to be. If you have 30 people deciding and 30 people who have bought into the vision, then they have no reason not to go out and do it," reasoned Wright. Walsh agreed: "You get the 30 most influential people in the company to open their veins together—which hasn't happened in a very long time." Others, including Beers, worried about losing control of the end result. Advocates for a larger group prevailed, and the entire O&M Worldwide board of directors along with eight other local presidents attended the next meeting in July 1993 at the Doral Arrowwood, a conference center in Westchester, New York.

The purpose of the meeting, explained one of the organizers, was to get final agreement on the vision and where brand stewardship fit in. Feedback from clients on brand stewardship and WCS was used to guide the initial discussion. Participants' recollections of the three-day event ranged from "ghastly" to "painful" and "dreadful." Noted Lazarus, "It seemed an endless stream of theoretical models. Everyone was frustrated and grumpy."

The turning point, Beers recalled, took place at the end of a grueling first day, when one person voiced what many were thinking: "He said, 'There's nothing new here. I don't see how Brand Stewardship can be unique to Ogilvy.' This was very helpful. One of the negatives at Ogilvy is all the real debates unfold outside the meeting room." The next morning, Beers addressed the group: "Certainly, the individual pieces of this thinking are not new. But to practice it would be remarkable. I have heard that in any change effort, one-third are supporters, one-third are resisters, and one-third are apathetic. I'm in the first group. Where are you?"

With Beers's challenge precipitating consensus, attenders split into groups to tackle four categories of action implications. One group, which included Beers, was charged with crafting the specific wording of the vision. A second began to develop a statement of shared values that would integrate traditional Ogilvy principles with the emerging values of the new philosophy. "That was hard to agree on," recalled Wright. "At issue was how much of the past do we want to take forward." The third group worked on a strategy for communicating the vision to all levels and offices throughout the company. Plans for a Brand Stewardship handbook, regional conferences, and a training program were launched. A fourth group was asked to begin thinking about how to realign titles, structures, systems, and incentives to support the new vision.

After heated brainstorming and drawing freely from the other three groups to test and refine their thinking, Walsh remembered that, finally, "there it was: '**To be the agency most valued by those who most value brands.**'" Summing up the meeting, one attender said, "There had been an amazing amount of distraction, irrelevance, and digression. I didn't think we could pull it together, but we did." (See **Exhibit 4** for the final version of the Vision and Values statement.)

MOVING FORWARD

Through the fall of 1993, Beers and her senior team worked relentlessly to spread the message of Brand Stewardship throughout the agency. It was a slow, sometimes arduous, process. By the end of the year, they had identified several issues that they felt required immediate attention.

Spreading the Gospel

Compared to clients' enthusiasm, reactions to Brand Stewardship within the agency were initially tepid. Across disciplines, employees below the most senior level lacked experience with, and knowledge of how to use, the principles of Brand Stewardship. O'Dea remarked, "Brand Stewardship has not seeped into everyday practice. Only a minority of the O&M population truly understands and embraces it. Others are aware of Brand Stewardship, but not deeply proficient. Many are still not true believers."

Account executives who misunderstood the concept were at a loss when their clients demanded it. Planners expressed confusion about how to use Brand Stewardship to develop a creative strategy.[13] Recalled one executive, "People didn't understand such basic things as the difference between a BrandPrint and an advertising strategy."

Greater familiarity with the process did not always mitigate opposition. Admitted Beers, "We didn't always have much internal support. It did not sound like anything new." Another problem was that a brand audit might suggest a change of advertising strategy. "Doing an audit on existing business can be seen as an indictment of what we have been doing," noted one executive. Lazarus concluded:

It will only be internalized throughout the organization with experience. I did a Brand Stewardship presentation recently with some of our account people. The client was mesmerized. They wanted the chairman of the company to see the presen-

tation. Now, that had an effect on the people who were with me. I can bet you that when they make the next presentation, Brand Stewardship will be their focal point.

Perhaps the greatest resistance came from the creative side. "We've got to get greater buy-in from the creative people," noted Walsh. Their initial reactions ranged from viewing the BrandPrint as an infringement on their artistic license—"I didn't believe in recipe approaches. They can lead to formulaic solutions," said one early convert—to the tolerant skepticism reported by another: "The creatives tell me, 'If it helps you get new business, that's great, but why are you in my office talking about this? I have a deadline and don't see what this has to do with creating advertising.' But you can't develop a good BrandPrint without cross-functional involvement."

Others questioned the relevance of Brand Stewardship for O&M Direct. While clear to Beers that Brand Stewardship clarified the rewards to clients from integrating advertising and direct marketing, some were slow to see this potential. Dispelling the popular notion that direct encourages short-term sales while advertising builds brands over the long-term, Thedens argued, "You can't send a message by mail that contradicts what you show on television. Both disciplines sell and both build the brand."

One executive concluded that the biggest problem was insufficient communication: "Anyone who heard it firsthand from Charlotte bought in. From the moment she opens her mouth to talk about brands, you know she has a depth of understanding that few people have. The problem is that, until recently, she has been the only missionary." Although the senior team had started "taking the show on the road," Walsh felt they were too few for the magnitude of the task: "The same six or seven people keep getting reshuffled. The result is that follow-through is not good." O'Dea, however, pointed out that the new missionaries had different tribes to convert. He emphasized the importance of translating the vision into a new role for each employee:

We need to move beyond a vision that is useful to the top five percent of account and creative people, to one that has meaning for everyone at Ogilvy. The Information Systems staff should see themselves as brand stewards, because without information technology, we can't respond with appropriate speed. I want the Media people to say, "I will not buy airtime on these T.V. shows because they don't fit the BrandPrint." Creatives at O&M Direct developing coupon designs must be as true to the BrandPrint as creatives in advertising. Everyone must see themselves as costewards of the vision.

Local/Global Tensions

Success in 1993 winning several large multinational accounts created further challenges for the embryonic WCS. Their goal of helping clients to develop a consistent brand image globally created tension in the firm's traditional balance of power.

---

[13] Account executives managed the agency's contact with clients, bringing in new accounts and coordinating information flow between other functions and the client. Planners worked with account executives to establish creative marketing strategies.

Exhibit 4   Statement of Vision and Values, 1993

To our people, our clients, and our friends—

The winds of change are blowing through Ogilvy & Mather. We are raising the sights of everybody in the company to a sweeping new vision:

TO BE THE AGENCY MOST VALUED
BY THOSE WHO MOST VALUE BRANDS

Not that we have ever been unmindful of the importance of brands. Quite the contrary. Our new thrust gets a big boost from ingrained Ogilvy & Mather strengths. Its roots lie in the teachings of David Ogilvy that reverberate through our halls. We have always aimed to create great campaigns with the spark to ignite sales and the staying power to build enduring brands.

> *What's new is a restructuring of resources, an arsenal of modern techniques, and an intensity of focus that add up to a major advance in the way we do business. We call it BRAND STEWARDSHIP—the art of creating, building, and energizing profitable brands.*

The new techniques and procedures of Brand Stewardship have already proved their value for many important brands. As I write they are being put to work for others. In March we will launch them formally—in print, on tape, and throughout the Ogilvy & Mather network.

This will affect the working habits of every professional in the agency, to the benefit, I am convinced, of every brand we work for. I predict that it will bring out the best in all of you—creatively and in every other aspect of your work—and add a lot to the pleasure and satisfaction you get out of your jobs.

As a first formal step the Board of Directors is putting forward the new statement of Shared Values on the facing page. You may notice that several of the points are taken from principles that have guided the company since its start—principles that were most recently set on paper in 1990 when David Ogilvy brought our Corporate Culture up to date.

Thus the Shared Values perform two functions: they *expand* our culture to reflect inexorable change, and in the same breath they *reinforce* its timeless standards.

All vital cultures—national, artistic, corporate—tend to evolve as conditions change, preserving valuable old characteristics as new ones come into the spotlight. In just that way these Shared Values now take their place at the forefront of the dynamic culture of Ogilvy & Mather.

Charlotte

Charlotte Beers
Chairman, Ogilvy & Mather Worldwide

Exhibit 4   (continued)

The market in which we compete is not a static one. To progress toward our new Vision will demand restless challenge and frequent change. The values we share, however, the way we do things day-to-day, will remain constant.

We work not for ourselves, not for the company,
not even for a client. We work for Brands.

———————

We work with the client, as Brand Teams. These Teams represent
the collective skills of our clients and ourselves. On their performance,
our client will judge the whole agency.

———————

We encourage individuals, entrepreneurs, inventive mavericks: with such
members, teams thrive. We have no time for prima donnas and politicians.

———————

We value candor, curiosity, originality, intellectual rigor, perseverance, brains—
and civility. We see no conflict between a commitment to the highest professional
standards in our work and to human kindness in our dealings with each other.

———————

We prefer the discipline of knowledge to the anarchy of ignorance. We pursue
knowledge the way a pig pursues truffles.

———————

We prize both analytical and creative skills. Without the first, you can't know
where to go; without the second, you won't be able to get there.

———————

The line between confidence and arrogance is a fine one.
We watch it obsessively.

———————

We respect the intelligence of our audiences:
"The consumer is not a moron."

*We expect our clients to hold us accountable for our Stewardship of their Brands.
Only if we have built, nourished, and developed prosperous Brands, only if we
have made them more valuable both to their users and to their owners,
may we judge ourselves successful.*

WCS pressed local agencies to give priority to brands with high global development potential over local accounts. For local agencies, however, local accounts often provided the most stable revenue stream and greatest profit. Further, in their zeal to exercise their newfound "line" responsibility, WCS supervisors were viewed at times as overstepping the bounds of their authority.

While tension had always existed between the centers and local markets, the increasingly centralized brand campaigns exacerbated conflicts. "Local agencies were used to always giving the client what they wanted," explained one WCS supervisor, "I had to start telling them to stop over-servicing the client." Some balked. Local expertise had always been one of Ogilvy's greatest competitive strengths. As one senior executive explained, "Certain local offices have not responded well to some of the advertising created centrally. One downside of global work is that it can end up being middle-of-the-road. When this happens, it's bad for an office's creative image locally."

But with costs escalating both centrally and locally, many felt that "the local barons" had to be reigned in. "How do we help our clients globalize," asked Walsh, "when our local management will conspire to keep them geographically oriented?"

For smaller agencies, issues of creative pride and autonomy were especially salient. Under the new system, the central WCS team developed the BrandPrint and advertising campaign with input from local offices. Local offices then tailored execution to regional markets. But while large offices usually served as the center for at least one global account, smaller offices, explained one WCS director, "are more often on the receiving end now. They begin to feel like post boxes. How do you attract good people to smaller offices if they never get to run big accounts?"

Beers felt that maintaining flexibility was key. "Some of our competitors—McCann Erickson is a good example—are excellent at running highly centralized campaigns. For us to view WCS that way would be a mistake. WCS should build upon, not diminish, our local strength." Creative and execution roles, she explained further, should shift according to the locus of the best ideas or relevant resources:

I want to continue to cultivate the tension between local and center. The easiest thing would be to have far more dominance centrally. It is more efficient, and the clients like it, because they invariably wish they had more control at the center. The reality is that nothing substitutes for full-blown, local agencies where the people are talented enough to articulate the heart of the brand, to interpret it in a sophisticated way, and—if necessary—to change it. If you have messengers or outlets, you will never execute well. The best ideas have unique, local modifications. One brand campaign we tested, for example, was an absolute win around the world, except in Asia, where the humor did not translate well. Our creative director in Asia worked with the idea, and it became the print campaign we use globally.

Also on her mind was the brewing controversy about how to split fees and allocate costs between WCS and local offices. Agency compensation on large accounts consisted frequently of fixed fees that were negotiated up front. With new clients, it could be difficult to estimate the range of Ogilvy services needed and the extent of local adaptation that would be required. Agencies in more distant markets were asked to contribute—sometimes without compensation—when the need for additional local work was discovered. Local presidents complained that, although WCS accounts pulled their people away from local accounts with clear-cut billable time, their portion of multinational fees was small. WCS, on the other hand, maintained that they were being forced to absorb more than their fair share of local costs.

Beers recounted one specific incident that unfolded in December. "Kelly told me that one of our offices had refused to do any more work for a client, because they did not have any fees. I said to him, 'I think you ought to talk to them about our new way of working and how much promise there is in it. Give them more information. If they still can't see their way, have them come to me.' You ask for collaboration," she concluded, "but occasionally you act autocratically."

As conflicts continued to erupt, senior management was divided on the solution. "We have highly individual personalities running our offices. With 272 worldwide," one account director observed, "it's been like herding cats." Debate swirled around the degree of management structure required. Lazarus advocated [commonsense] resolutions between the global account director and local agency presidents: "In our business, the quality of the work that gets done all comes down to the people who are doing it, not to bureaucratic structures. If you create the right environment and you have the right people, you don't need a whole structure." Others, O'Dea and his WCS corps included, insisted that organizational changes were necessary to make Brand Stewardship a reality agencywide. Walsh agreed: "What we don't have is a structure, working practices, remuneration, praise of people—all based on Brand Stewardship." Referring to the trademark Ogilvy color, Beers offered her perspective:

We have to make Ogilvy "redder." The finances should follow our goal of killing geography as a barrier to serving the brand. . . . Let's get the emotional content high and the structure will follow. We have people in the company who would prefer it the other way, but I want to get it done in my lifetime. So much of what happens at Ogilvy is cerebral, thoughtful and slow. We can't afford to move at a "grey" pace.

At the end of 1993, yet another issue had come to the fore. With large multinational accounts, some WCS heads controlled billings that easily surpassed those of many countries in the network. The agency, however, had always accorded the greatest prestige and biggest bonuses to presidents of local offices, countries, and regional chairmen. Brand Stewardship now required top-notch brand stewards and organizations centered around products and processes rather than Ogilvy office locations. "I ask people to collaborate, but I don't pay them for it. This company has never asked its feudal chiefs to consider the sum," observed Beers. She pondered how to attract the best and the brightest to WCS posts, knowing she would be asking them to leave the safety of turf to head brand-focused, virtual organizations.

The "thirsty for change" veterans believed another hurdle would be learning to work better as a team. Said Lazarus, "I don't think we make a lot of group decisions. We talk about it, but decisions tend to get made by Charlotte and by the specific individuals who are [affected]." But implementation revived many of the debates of the first Vienna

meeting. "I think we are all still very guarded," explained Walsh. "As each meeting goes by, it's a bit like a lump of ice slowly melting—our edges getting smoother all the time." Lazarus hoped that team members would grow "comfortable enough to disagree openly with one another." Battling a culture she had once described as "grotesquely polite" was still on Beers's list of priorities as she considered the group she had assembled to help carry the change forward.

By December 1993, Charlotte Beers assessed the year's progress: "Clients love Brand Stewardship. Competitors are trying to copy it. And internally, we lack consensus." She wondered what course of action in 1994 would provide the best stewardship of the Ogilvy brand.

Trilogy Farm (A)

Diana J. Wong-MingJi, Eastern Michigan University

Michelle Lane, Bowling Green State University

CASE OBJECTIVES AND USE

Trilogy Farm illustrated the entrepreneurial struggles of a three-year-old business in the hunter jumper barn business. Michelle Heine, the new business owner, had assumptions and expectations that were confronted by numerous unexpected challenges from inside and outside the organization. The central strategic issue focused on aligning internal resources and capabilities with trends in a competitive environment that was generally based upon "gentlemanly agreement." Multiple conflicts among employees concerning the strategic direction, such as the tension between providing costly high quality service versus keeping tight control over costs, required management attention. The success of the hunter jumper business was closely tied to the customers' ability to win equestrian competitions.

A clear vision was established for the strategic direction of the business. But significant challenges confronted the implementation of what appeared to be contradictory features such as being fun and serious.

CASE SYNOPSIS

Michelle Heine bought a hunter jumper barn business as an investment to fulfill her love of horses and riding. By the third year, she was reconsidering whether the venture was worth all the unexpected difficulties that included splitting up with the partner she had entered into the business with, constant conflicts between her employees, tensions between customers, and unexpected costs that left her with increasing debt every month. Both the competitive environment and

Contact Person: Diana J. Wong-MingJi, Eastern Michigan University, Department of Management, College of Business, 300 W. Michigan Avenue, Ypsilanti, MI 48197, dwong@emich.edu.

business cycle fluctuations had little impact on the business because of the upper socioeconomic income levels of the customer base.

As a small business owner, Michelle also began to engage in a related diversification activity to supplement her cash flow. She imported German horses to train and sell in the U.S. market. As a result, her business moved quickly from a local focus to a global one. There were indications that the international angle would provide worthwhile opportunities. The problem centered on how importing and selling German horses aligned with her existing strategy and where firm resources should be allocated.

Michelle Heine, the owner and general manager of Trilogy Farm, was out riding on her favorite horse, Zeus, when her cell phone rang. Terry, the property manager, was calling to complain about the new saddles that Jessica had purchased. He expressed exasperation with the expensive purchase and wanted to return the saddles for more economically affordable ones or else delay the purchase until the winter season. As Terry vented his frustration about Jessica's extravagance, Michelle could feel her own stress level rising. Was her cherished 31-acre horse farm, a hunter jumper barn operation, worth all the trouble? The constant bickering between Terry and Jessica, the head trainer, was just one of many difficulties that Michelle had been dealing with over the past three years.

BACKGROUND OF TRILOGY FARM

Trilogy Farm is in southeast Michigan, across the state line from Toledo, Ohio. It is a hunter jumper barn with three different types of horses—thoroughbreds, quarter horses, and warm bloods. With no significant prior business experience or horse farming capabilities, Michelle bought the hunter jumper barn in 2000 as an investment to fulfill her, as well as her daughter's, love for riding. Trilogy Farm provides boarding for horses, training for riders at the beginning and intermediate competition levels, training horses for sale, as well as opportunities for equestrian competitions at home and in the Midwest region.

The previous owners were gradually exiting from the horse farm business when Michelle bought the farm from them. At one time, they had 20 race horses in the barn, but the number had dropped to 13 by the time Michelle purchased the farm. After the sale to Michelle, the owners kept six acres for the remaining horses. Michelle leased space in the barn back to them, as they continued to live on the property. The previous owners were very knowledgeable about horses and provided a convenient resource of information. However, Michelle eventually discovered that the owners continued to feel and behave as if they still owned the place. This became a challenge in the process of developing and managing the business.

Before purchasing the farm, Michelle loved horses and her 12-year-old daughter started to compete in equestrian events, which required regular training to develop the necessary skills for advancement in competitions. Hence, Michelle bought Trilogy Farm with an initial loan of $300,000. The purchase involved a like-kind exchange of farm ground for Trilogy Farm's 36 acres, horse barns, and a few horses. When Michelle bought the farm, she expected to invest some sweat equity to do some necessary repairs and renovations to some of the mess and dilapidated conditions of the physical infrastructure. Michelle stated, "When you start a business, it needs to be something you love just because of the hours you have to spend dealing with it."

The farm was in serious disrepair—broken-down fencing, rusted buildings, and an old horse therapy swimming pool that was full of garbage. At one time, the property had four working barns. But only two were useable when Michelle entered the business. The other two barns had suffered fires and had turned into piles of burnt debris. One of the two useable barns had 46 stalls for boarding. The other barn had 32 stalls that were in poorer condition. The farm also had an indoor riding arena to hold lessons and host riding competitions during poor weather. Michelle described the start of the business as follows:

> We cleaned up the property, but the expenses were much higher than we budgeted. We accrued more expenses that required a second loan for $40,000. When we started the business, we were heavily in debt. After putting up the fencing, we started with 13 customers, which provided some cash flow. The actual work to repair the place took 3 months.

In addition to the physical facilities, four horses came with the purchase of the property, and Michelle bought four more horses for the riding lesson program as well as an additional one for her daughter. Michelle intended to sell the four horses that were included in the purchase of the farm. But Michelle only managed to sell two of them because one had to be put down and a buyer could not be found for the other one. Maintaining a horse cost approximately $200 a month for feed and care.

A NEW CLUBHOUSE

The vision for Trilogy Farm was to create a riding facility that had a professional approach to training and horse care in a casual, relaxed, and fun atmosphere. This reflected Michelle's general philosophy, values, and attitude toward life. She built a new clubhouse as a way to fulfill her vision of the business.

Michelle not only cleaned and repaired the farm facilities but also added a brand new heated and air-conditioned 2,000-square-foot clubhouse. The clubhouse was added to the end of the indoor riding arena, which provided for views of both indoor and outdoor activities. It provided a space for the customers to socialize, relax, watch television, or play piano. It included a kitchen, play area for small children, lounge space, and a large meeting room with large windows for lesson viewing. Parents used the facility to watch their children ride without having to be outside in the elements. Michelle wanted the clubhouse to be a distinctive feature to attract customers because most farms don't have family areas in which to relax. At those farms, people would ride and go home.

At Trilogy Farm, customers used the clubhouse extensively. But having the customers hanging around too much created an unexpected set of problems. More gossiping occurred. Some people picked on others they didn't like. When some girls criticized other girls and barn staff, a whole new set of problems arose. Also, the clubhouse was always messy because people left their food and related trash around. This became a frustration when Michelle ended up having to constantly clean up the mess.

THE PARTNERS

Michelle formed a partnership with her daughter's trainer, Pamela Wallace, to enter into the hunter jumper barn business. Although Michelle did not have experience in running a horse farm, she had the ability to leverage the necessary capital resources. Pamela's role and responsibilities revolved around being the head trainer and running the barn. Although she did not invest any capital in Trilogy Farm, Pamela brought 10–12 years of experience in the horse farm industry that included working as a trainer, running a barn, and engaging in a partnership. She also brought customers from a nearby stable barn to help get the business started. Prior to her move to Trilogy Farm, Pamela had a conflict with the owner of Classicala and left to go to Toledo Horse Sports Barn before entering into the partnership with Michelle. When their partnership formed, Michelle had known Pamela for 15 months.

Michelle described the partnership formation as follows:

> My business partner felt that rather than putting money into the business, her expertise was sufficient. I found out over time that if you don't have your personal cash in the business, you don't look at spending in the same way. I did not pursue or check references. Also, we could not agree on the operating agreement terms. So we never signed an operating agreement between us. She wanted half ownership of the operating company, but it had no net value. I owned the land under a separate company. But the problem was that she had no assets for the bank as collateral. So I ended up having to take all the risks.

The two women worked together on the business plan and developed three scenarios. The worst case scenario showed keeping the starting customer base and a small lesson program to create cash flow. The moderate case scenario was based on a 25 percent growth in the customer base and the generation of a 10 percent return on investment (ROI). The best case scenario saw filling the barn, tripling the number of boarders, and having a full lesson program with three full-time trainers. This generated a 25 percent ROI. However, most of the numbers provided by Pamela concerning the cost of running the operations were significantly underestimated, and the business quickly accrued a high debt load. Also, the projections for business growth did not come to fruition. Although Trilogy Farm attracted many customers, because of their dissatisfaction with the training, they did not stay. Subsequently, Michelle found out that Pamela did not have the capability to train beyond the beginner level.

"Our girls beyond beginners were not doing well at horse shows because they were making the same mistakes," said Michelle. "It became obvious that I needed to make a decision to end the partnership because Pamela's qualifications were exaggerated."

After two years into the business, Michelle dissolved the partnership with Pamela. Pamela moved out of town because her husband was transferred. Her new location was too far for most customers to follow. At that point, Michelle became the sole owner of Trilogy Farm. She managed to regain all the customers who had left, with the exception of two. The business grew to a level that was much closer to the forecasted projections. But cash flow was still a problem. After paying for variable costs, the income was insufficient to cover the fixed costs due to the high debt load accrued by the company during the first two years of operation. Michelle could not continue to operate with a cash deficit for much longer.

SUPPLIERS

Trilogy Farm dealt with three major suppliers for grain, hay, and bedding. The grain suppliers varied because grains can be sourced from a wide range of suppliers. Hay was the largest variable expense at $2 per day per horse. The additional feeding of hay at lunchtime, which was started by the new head trainer, Jessica Hogan, increased monthly expenses by $400. The hay supplier was one of the best. Michelle said, "He can always get me hay when no one else can get hay. When there is a drought or bad weather, he is always reliable. We may pay a little more, but he allows me flexibility when the cash flow is tight. At the worst, I was five months behind in paying."

Bedding suppliers were usually furniture manufacturers who provided wood shavings. When the economy experienced a downturn, wood shaving production declined because furniture purchases decreased, which in turn affected production. As a result, the supply of wood shavings fluctuated with the business cycle. Although Michelle always had access to shavings, she wanted consistently better quality bedding for her horses. Good quality bedding was not always available from her supplier as sometimes the shavings were too fine and dusty. But switching bedding suppliers could be risky because a long-term relationship with a supplier is important to accessing a consistent supply, regardless of the quality.

In the meantime, Michelle also researched different alternatives to shavings such as compressed wood pellets that were dust free and become spongy when wet. Some horses had allergies to dust and required medication as well as a hair net to filter the dust. The new bedding was easier to clean, with no dust and less waste. So even though the bedding was more expensive to purchase, it offered significant savings in terms of labor costs, dust generation, and the amount of waste removed from stalls that required disposal. However, the stall floor needed to be in better condition and perfectly flat to prevent a horse's weight from redistributing the wood pellets and thus forcing him to end up sleeping on the hard flooring.

EMPLOYEES AND CONFLICTS

As the owner/manager, Michelle managed the overall business and operations. She had a property manager, Terry Towner, who supervised seven part-time employees, maintained the property, and sustained relationships with suppliers. Terry was conscientious about keeping costs down and knew how to cut costs. He worked hard and had more than 10 years of extensive experience in the horse barn business that included running a barn and management and care of stables. Terry's capabilities also included being a talented custom car builder. His mechanical skills were important to the functioning of Trilogy Farms because they saved Michelle from having to find and pay outside tradespeople to do various incidental repairs to the farming equipment. In addition to his job at Trilogy Farm, Terry had a landscaping and lawn care business during the summer months.

Michelle hired Jessica Hogan as the head trainer after Pamela left. Jessica was much younger and had less experience than Pamela as far as giving riding lessons. But, as opposed to Pamela, Jessica was more enthusiastic and extremely talented. She rode and trained horses extensively and competed successfully at all levels. Jessica's responsibilities included handling all the horse care, supervising two other part-time trainers, creating the lesson programs, dealing with horse shows, selling horses, and training horses. But she primarily focused on the well-being of the horses. Jessica wanted the best for the horses and her customers, which meant feeding the horses extra hay and grain and buying more expensive supplies such as bridles, saddles, and riding equipment. This resulted in constant conflicts with cost-conscious Terry.

The difficulties between Jessica and Terry also spilled over to the other employees. Jessica influenced other employees to dislike Terry. Tensions ebbed and flowed. Both Jessica and Terry often complained to Michelle about each other. Michelle felt like she was refereeing squabbles between her two daughters when they were children.

Michelle also hired a bookkeeper, Mandy Jones. After Mandy helped organize the financial information, Michelle gained a better understanding of the financial situation. In the first year of operation, Trilogy Farm losses amounted to $68,000 (in 2000). The second year losses totaled $38,000 (in 2001).

LESSON PROGRAMS AND RIDERS

Trilogy Farm's riding lesson program differed from those offered at other hunter jumper barns. Michelle limited the size of lessons to a maximum of six riders at one time, while other barns allowed as many as 20 riders in one lesson. Given the limitations of the indoor riding arena, the maximum capacity of the lesson program was about 75 riders per week. Michelle's original calculations showed that she needed 20 boarders and 25 lessons per week to break even. The boarders provided low margins after the variable costs were covered. The pasture space had a capacity for 35 horses. However, higher costs meant that Michelle needed to increase the size of the lesson program. Trilogy Farm's lesson prices were competitive with nearby farms. The cost of a private lesson for half an hour was $35, and a one-hour lesson was $45. A one-hour group lesson was $25 per rider. Hence, the group lessons provided the best revenue source.

Michelle described the riding lesson program. She said, "We limit the size of the lesson to no more than six riders at a time, while other barns allow as many as 20 in one lesson. At one barn, there are no limits to the number of riders in a group lesson. People who come to our barn normally stay because we have small lesson groups and a nice facility."

The riding program focused on beginners and intermediates. After advancing beyond the intermediate skill level, riders tended to leave because they competed at much higher levels than the other riders at Trilogy Farm. Trilogy Farm did not have enough high-caliber riders to support a horse show schedule for the high-level shows in the A circuit

(considered the highest level of horse training and jumper competition).

Most of the riders came from middle- to high-income households. Ninety percent of the customers were children between the ages of 7 to 18, mainly girls. Most of the customers who were serious riders lived within a convenient distance from the barn. They rode four to five times per week with about two group lessons per week. Serious riders competed in horse shows and accumulated points to move up through the increasingly competitive and more professional circuits, from schooling shows to the national level. Consequently, the hunter jumper barn business was insulated from economic fluctuations because a large percentage of the customers were very committed to advancing through the levels of competition and had the necessary socio-economic resources to support their interests.

HORSE INDUSTRY

The hunter jumper barn business is part of the U.S. horse industry, which includes a number of related but separate segments such as racetrack operations; horse shows; and breeding, training, maintaining, and riding horses. During the early 2000s, the U.S. horse industry included approximately 6.9 million horses for both commercial and recreational purposes. Hunter jumper barns focused on the recreational and horse showing segments. Table 1 identifies the number of horses and participants for each business segment of the horse industry.

In 1999, the median horse-owning household income was $60,000. Fourteen percent of horse-owning households had incomes under $25,000; 38 percent were under $50,000; and 64 percent were under $75,000. Approximately 1.9 million people owned horses, but 3.6 million participated in showing and 4.3 million participated in recreation, with some overlap between the two activities. The participants identified in Table 1 did not include the millions of spectators and supporters of the industry.

Table 1 Different Types of Horse Businesses in the United States, 1999

Activity	Number of Horses	Number of Participants
Recreation	2,970,000	4,346,100
Showing	1,974,000	3,607,900
Racing	725,000	941,400
Other—farming, rodeo, polo, police	1,262,800	1,607,900
TOTAL	6,931,800	7,062,500*

*The sum of participants by activity does not equal the total number of participants because individuals were counted in more than one activity.

Source: The American Horse Council, *The Economic Impact of the Horse Industry in the United States,* 1999.

HORSE SHOWING

Horse shows were an integral dimension of the hunter jumper barn business. A barn's status and reputation were closely tied to training successful riders who moved up through the different circuits by advancing their riding skills. A particular hunter jumper barn focused on training riders for one or the whole range of competition levels. The skill level of riding was divided into four riding levels or circuits—A, B, C, and schooling shows. (See Appendix 1, Horse Show Circuits for more details.)

The A circuit was the highest level of competition. The USA Equestrian organization monitored and regulated the competitions in the A circuit with a professional approach. For example, random drug tests were conducted. The A circuit had national competitions in different locations around the country all year long. At the competitions, riders earned points that accumulated throughout the calendar year. Once riders achieved a certain number of points, they advanced to the finals. An A circuit horse show generally lasted between 1 and 2 weeks, and costs amounted to approximately $2,000 per show per competitor. The number of shows a rider entered depended on their ambitions—how motivated they were to select the shows, accumulate points, and travel in the national circuit. The final national competitions took place in locations such as Madison Square Garden in New York City.

The B and C circuits were state level competitions. The rules and policies differed from state to state. But the general competition structure still applied, with riders competing to accumulate points to advance through the ranks. The difference between B and C was that C level riders were novices and beginners who jumped at heights of up to 2 feet 9 inches. If a rider earned too many points or got too many blue ribbons in the C circuit, he or she had to move to the A or B circuit for the next show season. Costs for participating in a C circuit horse show amounted to approximately $150–200 for 2 days, not including the cost of trainer or trailering—the transportation of the horse. Trilogy Farm charged a flat rate of $50 for trailering horses to local horse shows. Charges for trailering to B circuit competitions were based on mileage. Many of the B and C circuit competitions were as far as 200 miles away. A horse show on the B circuit lasted for 3 days, and the costs reached about $500 per rider, including food and lodging. Trilogy Farm earned a net margin of about 15 percent plus the trailering fees for doing horse shows. Usually the trainer or groom did the hauling.

The lowest level of competition was schooling shows, which were novice competitions held at individual hunter jumper barns. Sometimes a few barns collaborated to put on a competition. The competitions were for early beginners to give them an opportunity to experience a horse show competition, and the horses had an opportunity to stay in a different location. Trilogy Farm participated in horse showing in the B and C circuit competition levels, and conducted three of its own schooling shows each year. The attending barns that had riders competing were responsible for providing their own decorations, material, and food for the horses, trainer, groom, and transportation of the horses to the competition site. Trilogy Farm had an opportunity to show off its facilities by hosting competitions.

HUNTER JUMPER BARN COMPETITORS

At the southeast Michigan–Ohio state line and within the greater metropolitan area of Toledo, there were about 12 hunter jumper barns in 2002 and numerous other horse stables of different sizes. Four hunter jumper barns were located within 6 miles of Trilogy Farm. But Trilogy Farm had the closest proximity to Toledo, which has the major market and two of the highest household income school districts in the area. The Detroit metropolitan area was more than an hour away, and customers did not travel that far for riding lessons on a regular basis. Trilogy Farm, along with four other hunter jumper barns, focused primarily on the Toledo market.

Stonehaven Farm, located a mile away, was Trilogy Farm's closest geographical competitor. The facility was very nice with the capacity to handle forty boarders. Stonehaven had a large lesson program with many lesson times throughout the week. They focused on beginner and intermediate levels. But they did not do external horse showing very often.

Fox Meadow Farm was 3 miles away. It was by far the most prestigious hunter jumper barn in the area, with a beautiful barn and riding arena. The facility had 60 stalls. The horses were expensive and meticulously cared for with a significant amount of attention. The riders came from wealthy backgrounds. Riders from Fox Meadow competed at the highest level, the A circuit, and achieved a national reputation with substantial media attention. Fox Meadow also was well-known due to its community involvement. In the winter, the riders traveled to Florida for competitions. The lesson program was large, with 10–15 riders per group; group lessons for beginners had no limits. Fox Meadow had 15 acres, which limited the amount of time the horses could spend outdoors.

Hunters Run Farm, located next to Fox Meadow, had a 15–20 year history in the business. Hunters Run was spun off from Fox Meadow as a result of a divorce, so the ex-spouses ran each respective operation. Hunters Run was Trilogy Farm's closest competitor, with a similar lesson program, horse training and care, and horse showing schedule. Hunters Run riders attended many of the same horse shows as Trilogy Farm's riders in the B and C circuits. But Hunters Run had a larger operation, with the capacity to manage 80 horses. They had two large barns and two smaller ones. Their lesson programs drew riders from the Scouts and the Sylvania Community Center, which led to community involvement similar to that at Fox Meadow.

Riverdale Farm had been in operation for approximately 10 years when Michelle came to the market to buy a farm in 2000. She considered Riverdale, which was 6 miles away from Trilogy Farm, as a possible purchase because its owners had it up for sale. But Riverdale Farm's barn had only 20 stalls. The barn was beautiful, with automatic water fill dispensers and individual fans for the horses so they did not become overheated. The 30 acres had lovely hilly pastures for grazing and riding. Riders and their families had a beautiful clubroom to use. Riverdale provided a lesson program and boarding. The facility catered to adults who enjoyed riding and wanted to socialize in the facility but did not want to compete in the Michigan Hunter-Jumper Association horse shows or A level shows. But Riverdale competed in the quarter horse circuit and had western as well as English riding. Michelle did not consider the purchase to be financially feasible, because the number of stalls for boarders would not provide a sufficient cash flow. Also, the location was more than 8 miles away from Toledo, which significantly deterred potential customers. Recently, the owner had withdrawn the barn from the market and decided not to sell, so they remained a competitor.

COMPETITION BETWEEN HUNTER JUMPER BARNS

Michelle explained the competitive relationships between the hunter jumper barns as follows:

> Competition in the hunter jumper business is based on a gentlemanly agreement, which means that we don't actively seek out customers from barns in the area. If people want to switch barns, we normally talk to the other barn owner before the switch is made. When customers switch, we need to go to the competitor's barn to pick up the horse and all the equipment. The exchange needs to be done with respect for the other business. Also, owners tend to see each other almost every weekend at horse shows. Moving from one barn to another is like switching from one team to another. It seems like there is enough business to go around so it doesn't have to be cutthroat.

Customers often made the switch when a trainer was absent. For example, when Trilogy Farm's first trainer was away for a couple of weeks, she brought in unqualified substitute trainers to teach in the lesson program. One substitute was a customer and another was a girl who cleaned the stalls. During this time, two customers left Trilogy Farm.

When customers began making an exodus from Trilogy Farm, they expressed unhappiness about the training. In addition to the two customers who left during the trainer's absence, four others approached Michelle about leaving. During a horse show, a barn owner approached Michelle to inform her that Trilogy Farm customers were approaching her barn (Hunters Run), to inquire about making a switch. The barn owner advised Michelle that she should find out what the issue was. The owner of Hunters Run had the impression that customers were unhappy with the training. Michelle immediately met with all the customers face to face to discuss the matter. She said later, "I discovered that they were unhappy with the quality and inconsistency of the training. They would give me another chance if I could fix the problem. I was even unhappy with my own daughter's training."

As a result, Michelle made some important changes, such as dissolving her business partnership and hiring a new head trainer. Then she managed to retain almost all her customers.

CONCLUSION

Toward the end of her third year in the hunter jumper barn business, Michelle attempted to improve her cash flow. She approached local schools and the YMCA to set up lesson programs to generate an additional market base. However, she also embarked in a different direction and began to import German horses to train and sell because the market conditions were good for German horses and the margins are much more lucrative on German horses than for others. German horses have a reputation for more pleasant dispositions that were valued in the U.S. market. A buyer helped to identify potential horses from Germany and made the necessary arrangements for Michelle's purchase. Michelle marketed the German horses on a Web site and received inquiries from across the country. A couple flew in from California to inspect one of the German horses as a purchase for their young son. They expressed a high level of interest and wanted to make purchase arrangements. For Michelle, this new business endeavor has different challenges that involve doing business in the international economy. The imported horses need quarantining and must meet regulatory requirements. In addition, they present a different set of transportation logistics.

The dilemmas and challenges continued to weigh heavily on Michelle's mind as to whether her love of horses and riding were worth the stress of being in a business that had constant cash flow difficulties and management problems with employees. She was not sure how the importing and training of horses fit into the business, even though it was a possible source of cash flow. Consequently, Michelle needed to decide whether to continue with the business, sell Trilogy Farm as an ongoing operation, close and sell Trilogy Farm, or explore other business models that would eliminate her management problems and create a positive net profit.

APPENDIX 1   HORSE SHOW CIRCUITS

As of 2000, there were four major categories of horse shows in the hunter jumper competitions. At the highest level of competition, shows were conducted nationally, referred to as the A circuits, and managed by the USA Equestrian organization. These shows took place all over the United States and culminated at the end of the calendar year with indoor shows at Harrisburg, Virginia; Devon, Pennsylvania; and Madison Square Garden, New York City, for competitors who earned enough points to qualify. A circuit show often ran for 1 to 2 weeks and cost each participant $2,000 or more. See Table 2 for more information.

Within the state of Michigan, there were B and C circuit shows sanctioned by the Michigan Hunter-Jumper Association (MHJA) that ran from October to September. Finals happened in September, with special classes for the top riders in each area to prepare to compete for the championships. Heights of the jumps were up to 3 feet 3 inches at B shows and up to 2 feet 9 inches at C shows. C-level riders who won more than six blue ribbons in a calendar year could not continue showing at the C level and had to move up to

Table 2	Horse Show Circuits		
Show Type	Average Jump Heights	Average Cost per Show	Average Number of Participants per Class
National A	3'3" and up	$2,000	30 and up
Michigan B	3'0" to 3'6"	$450	12 to 30
Michigan C	2'3" to 2'9"	$250	6 to 20
Schooling Show	1'9" to 2'9"	$150	2 to 12

Source: horsesdaily.com/news/index.html.

the B level. Also, C-level riders who jumped their horses higher than 2 feet 9 inches at any MHJA show could no longer compete at the C level.

Local barns provided additional opportunities for horse shows. The schooling shows were for riders who were new to horse showing. Sometimes points were awarded and sometimes they were not. Year-end awards depended on the level of sophistication of the barns and their show management. Often, two or three barns formed a minicircuit to attend each others' shows with their beginners.

4

The Formula One Constructors

by Mark Jenkins

Combined Case
Case study
Reference no 301-056-1

This case describes four examples of the creation of sustained competitive advantage in a highly competitive technological context. F1 motorsport is the pinnacle of automotive technology and involves highly specialized constructors designing and building single seat racecars which compete for annual championships which bring huge financial and reputational rewards. These four cases explore the stories of three contrasting companies: Ferrari, McLaren and Williams in terms of how they both created and lost the basis for sustained competitive advantage.

"Between two and four on a Sunday afternoon this is a sport.
All the rest of the time it's commerce."

Frank Williams, Managing Director, Williams F1

In 1945 the Fédération Internationale de l'Automobile (FIA) established Formula A as the premier level of motorsport. In the years that followed Formula A became referred to as Formula One and a drivers' world championship was introduced in 1950. The first world champion was Giuseppe Farina of Italy driving an Alfa Romeo. At that time Alfa dominated the racing along with the other Italian marques of Ferrari and Maserati. Drivers such as Juan Fangio, Alberto

Ascari, Jack Brabham, Jim Clark and Graham Hill were to take the championship during the '50s and '60s driving cars built by Alfa Romeo, Ferrari, Mercedes-Benz, Lancia, Cooper and Lotus. By the mid sixties Formula One had moved from being a basis for car manufacturers to promote and test their products, to a highly [specialized] business where purpose built cars were developed through leading edge technology to win a TV sporting event enjoying the third highest TV audience in the world, surpassed only by the Olympics and World Cup Soccer.

There have been between 10 [and] 14 race car manufacturers or constructors competing in Formula One at any one time. The constructors themselves can be grouped into a number of different categories. In 2002 the top three teams were Ferrari, Williams and McLaren, all medium sized businesses turning over between $250 and $350 million per annum. Today it is estimated that it takes between $30 and $50 million capital investment in research facilities to set up the minimum basis for being competitive. For the first three years of their entry into F1 in 2002 Toyota [is] estimated to have committed $1 billion [of] capital and running costs, of which only one fifth come from sponsorship. The top teams would typically have their own testing and development equipment which would including wind-tunnels and other facilities. The larger teams employed between 450 and 650 people in their Formula One operations, a quarter of whom travel around the world attending Grand Prix every two to three weeks throughout the F1 season (March to November). Labour costs account for around 25% of the budget. All the teams would have highly qualified technical staff which would include race engineers (who work with the driver to set up the car), designers, aerodynamicists, composite experts (to work with specialised carbon-composite materials) and systems specialists.

The revenues to run these operations come from a number of sources: commercial sponsorship from non-automotive companies such as cigarettes, insurance and drinks (e.g., Marlboro, BAT, Reemtsma, Allianz, Beck's and Red Bull); support through the provision of free products and services such as [tires], fuel and lubricants (e.g., Bridgestone, Michelin, Petronas, Shell & Elf) and systems/communications support (e.g., Hewlett Packard, Vodaphone, Computer Associates & Sun Microsystems). In order to secure these inflows of capital and services the top teams have sophisticated marketing departments to establish and manage the relationships with these sponsors. More recently the automotive manufacturers have become major sources of finance with Ford, DaimlerChrysler, BMW, Honda and Toyota all becoming major partners, and in some cases owners or shareholders of the F1 teams.

Revenue is also provided by prize money generated by winning championship points allocated on a sliding scale for the first eight places. The prize money is a way of dividing up the royalties earned from media coverage and other revenues which is negotiated, on behalf of all the teams, by the constructors association (FOA). For 2003 Ferrari estimated that $30 million (9.7%) of their revenues would come from prize money.

Most of the constructors are located in what has been referred to as 'motorsport valley,' an area of the UK covered by a broad arc centred around Oxford, stretching into East Anglia and down into Surrey. Whilst there are other teams located in other countries such as Ferrari (Maranello, Italy); Toyota (Cologne, Germany) and Sauber (Hinwil, Switzerland), the remaining seven teams for 2003 all have bases in motorsport valley. The focus on the UK has been attributed to the network of specialist engineering talent which is fundamental to success in F1, as summarised by the MD of the Renault team, Flavio Briartore: *If you like proscuitto you come to Italy. If you like champagne you come to France. For Formula One you come to England. I don't like the English weather, but the best engineering is here.*

The Formula One Constructors provide a unique context to consider the competitive advantage of different multi-million pound [organizations] over time. The pace of change and the basis of advantage is constantly changing, shown by the fact that since the start of the world championships, only two constructors have won the championship consecutively more than four times (McLaren 1988–91; Ferrari 1999–2002) and only Ferrari (1975–1977) and Williams (1992–1994) have won for three consecutive years. The remainder of the case considers each of these periods of competitive dominance in chronological order.

FERRARI 1975–1977

The period 1975–77 saw a renaissance of the Ferrari team. Their last Formula One World Championship had been won in 1964, one of the few reminders of the glorious '50s and early sixties when the bright red cars of Ferrari dominated

motor racing. In the mid seventies they won 15 of the 45 races during 1975, 1976 and 1977.

Ferrari are the oldest of all the Grand Prix teams who are still racing. Their heritage gives them a special place in the hearts of all motor racing enthusiasts. Founded by Enzo Ferrari, an ex-driver and manager of the Alfa Romeo racing team in 1950, they and other Italian marques such as Maserati and Alfa dominated the sport during the 1950s. Ferraris have taken part in more than 550 grand prix (the next highest is McLaren with 440) and, despite the variable nature of the team's performance, drivers continue to view a contract with Ferrari as something very special. Perhaps this is why world champions such as Alain Prost, Nigel Mansell and Michael Schumacher have been attracted to the team at times when their cars have been far from the fastest or most reliable.

In an era when the majority of constructors are British specialists who buy in central components such as engines and gearboxes, Ferrari are distinctive in that they have always done everything themselves: engine, gearbox, suspension, chassis are all made at their Maranello factory, which enjoys the most up-to-date facilities in terms of designing, developing and building all the necessary components of a race-car. Whilst other constructors such as McLaren and Williams will paint their cars whatever colour required by their flagship sponsor, Ferraris always have been and, one assumes, always will be, bright red, the national colour of Italy, a throwback from the time when F1 cars were colour coded by country of origin. The cars have, until recently, very little evidence of sponsorship, it has always been the Ferrari emblem—a black prancing horse—which has the most prominent position. The Italian public see Ferrari as a national icon as observed by Niki Lauda in an interview in 1996:

> The Italians love you when you win and hate you when you lose and whatever you do, win, lose or simply break wind everyone in Italy wants to know about it!

The influence of Enzo Ferrari or *Il Commendatore* as he was frequently known, was total and the myths and stories surrounding him still permeate the team, despite his death in 1988. It was legendary that Ferrari himself hardly ever attended a race and very rarely left the Maranello factory where his beloved cars were made; he relied on the media and his advisors for information, which often created a highly political atmosphere in the team. Ferrari's first love was motor racing, this was despite having created a very successful range of road going cars which he saw primarily as the source of funding for his racing. The merger between Fiat and Ferrari in 1969 provided Ferrari with a huge cash injection. Ferrari had sold 40% of the company to Fiat and allowed Fiat to build the road cars; however Enzo, who was then 71, would retain control of the racing operation to concentrate on his first love, motor racing at the highest level: Formula One.

The resources which Ferrari have at their disposal [have] always been the envy of every other team; they had always built their own engines and have a large technical team dedicated to the task of engine design and development. In 1971 they opened their own test track at Fiorano, literally a few hundred yards from the Maranello factory. At the time it was the most advanced and sophisticated test circuit in the world, enabling the cars to be constantly tested and developed between the track and the factory. This effectively gave Ferrari their own grand prix circuit; all their competitors were obliged to hire a circuit such as Silverstone in the UK and transport their cars and equipment for a two or three day test. Ferrari himself attended most of the tests and would make sure he was kept informed as to exactly what was being tested and why. Enzo himself had always declared his love for the distinctive sound and power of a Ferrari engine, as indicated by former Ferrari driver, Nigel Mansell:

> Enzo Ferrari believed that the engine was the most important part of the race car. Colin [Chapman, head of Lotus] believed it was the chassis.

The early seventies began shakily for Ferrari; the new ownership and influence from Fiat meant increased resources, but also increased pressure for results. In 1971 the cars were very fast, but not reliable. It got worse in 1972 and 1973 with cars only finishing every other race and rarely in the points. Enzo himself had been suffering poor health and the team seemed unable to turn around despite having the huge resources of Fiat at its disposal. However, through 1974 things began to change. A few years earlier Ferrari engineers had commissioned a small firm in the UK, TC prototypes, to build three chassis for the 1974 car using the monocoque structure, derived from aircraft [design], [favored] by the English constructors. Mauro Forghieri had also been recalled to Ferrari in 1973 as technical director; Forghieri had been responsible for some of the more successful Ferraris of the 1960s, but had fallen from grace and spent the later part of the 1960s working on 'special projects.'

In addition to the arrival of Forghieri, a new team boss was also appointed to try and turn Ferrari fortunes around. At 25 years old, a qualified lawyer with connections to the Agnelli family who owned Fiat, Luca di Montezemolo, was an unlikely right-hand man for *Il Commendatore*. However, he was given a relatively free hand by Ferrari and brought much needed management discipline to the team. Whilst there had always been a huge supply of talent at Ferrari, particularly in the design and development of engines, gearboxes and suspension systems, it had not always reached its collective potential. Enzo's autocratic style of 'divide and rule' had created much confusion and rivalry within the team. Montezemolo defined strict areas of responsibility in order to reduce the amount of interference and internal politics. This created a situation where the various technical teams (chassis and suspension; engine; gearbox) concentrated on and were fully accountable for their own area. Montezemolo was also instrumental in the recruitment of driver Niki Lauda. Lauda was of Austrian aristocratic descent, but was totally committed to his racing. He had been very successful in Formula Two but was having a torrid time

with the ailing BRM team in Formula One. In 1973 Enzo Ferrari told Lauda he wanted him to drive for Ferrari, an offer which very few drivers have ever refused.

In 1974 Ferrari was in the ascendance. Lauda and the design team had embarked upon an exhaustive testing and development [program] at the Fiorano test track. The new car, the 312B, was very much the fastest car on the track. However, there were still reliability problems and although Lauda was leading the championship at the British Grand Prix, the lead was lost through technical problems which resulted in Emerson Fittipaldi in a McLaren taking the eventual honors.

In 1975 the fruits of Forghieri's creative ideas and the intensive testing at Fiorano were exemplified in the new 312T, which featured a wide, low body with a powerful 'flat 12' 12 cylinder engine and a revolutionary transverse (sideways mounted) gearbox, which improved the balance of the car, making it handle extremely well. Whilst the new car was not ready until the season had already started, Lauda, with the support of [teammate] Regazzoni, was able to easily secure both the drivers' and constructors' world championships. The Ferraris dominated the 1975 season; with their elegant handling and the power advantage of the engine, they were in a class of their own. Because the majority of the competition all had the same engine gearbox combination (Ford V8 and Hewland gearbox), they were unable to respond to a chassis/gearbox/engine combination which was unique to Ferrari.

1976 continued in much the same vein with Lauda and Regazzoni winning the early races. The intensive testing did not let up and new ideas and innovations, such as a revised rear suspension system, were constantly being tried out. On the management front, Montezemolo had been promoted to head up Fiat motorsport, which included the Lancia rally programme as well as Ferrari, and Daniele Audetto was moved from managing the rally team to Sporting Director at Ferrari. However, things were not to go as smoothly as in 1975. At the German Grand Prix Lauda lost control of the car in the wet and crashed in flames. He was rescued by four other drivers, but not before suffering severe burns and inhaling toxic fumes. His life was in the balance for some weeks whilst the grand prix series continued with James Hunt (McLaren) reducing Lauda's lead in the championship. Miraculously Lauda recovered from his injuries and although still badly scarred, he returned to race for Ferrari. He and Hunt went into the last grand prix of 1976 (Japan) with Lauda leading by three points. There was heavy rain and Lauda pulled out of the race, leaving the drivers' championship to Hunt, although Ferrari still collected the constructors' championship. Whilst, on paper, it was a good year, by rights Ferrari should have dominated 1976 as they had 1975. Audetto who, perhaps not surprisingly, had been unable to live up to the role created by Montezemolo and had failed to develop a strong relationship with Lauda, returned back to the world of rallying. Ferrari went into 1977 in a state of disarray.

In 1977 Ferrari were still the team to beat, although the testing and development lost through Lauda's six week convalescence seemed to have reduced the crushing dominance which the team had earlier shown. The competition [was] also beginning to find ways of catching up. The Brabham team moved away from the Ford V8 and used an Alfa Romeo 'flat 12' similar to the Ferrari engine. Tyrrell launched the revolutionary P34 six wheeled car, which seemed to be the only car able to stay with the Ferrari. Ferrari themselves were not standing still and launched the 312T2 in 1976, which was a significant development of the original 312T. Ferrari won the 1977 drivers' and constructors' championship, but this was the end of the partnership with Niki Lauda; the relationship had never been the same since the Nurburgring accident. Lauda left to join Brabham but did not regain the world championship until he drove for McLaren in 1984. Whilst Lauda was not perhaps the fastest racer on the track he was always able to develop a car and build relationships with the design team, which enabled Ferrari to translate the driver's senses into reliable technical solutions.

The unprecedented run of Ferrari success continued in 1978, with the 312T3 car driven by two highly talented drivers. Argentinean Carlos Reutemann was joined by the flamboyant Gilles Villeneuve and whilst they were not able to win the constructors championship they achieved a very strong second place. In 1979 Reutemann was replaced by South African Jody Scheckter whose consistency contrasted with Villeneuve's erratic speed. Scheckter won the drivers' championship, with Ferrari taking the constructors' championship. Their greatest moment was when Scheckter and Villeneuve finished first and second at the Italian grand prix at Monza.

However, 1979 was the last time that Ferrari were to win a Drivers' World Championship for 21 years. 1980 was something of a disaster for Ferrari. Scheckter and Villeneuve were totally uncompetitive in the 312T5 car, which, whilst a significant development from the 312T4, was outclassed by the competition. New innovations in aerodynamics brought the 'ground effect' revolution, pioneered by Lotus and quickly adopted by Williams and Brabham. Here the underside of the car featured two 'venturi,' or channels [on] either side of the driver. These were aerodynamically designed to create a vacuum, which stuck the car to the track, allowing faster cornering. Sliding strips of material or 'skirts' were used to create a seal for the air flowing under the car. Whilst the Ferrari's engine was one of the most powerful it was a 'flat 12', meaning that the cylinders were horizontal to the ground, creating a low and wide barrier which gave no opportunity to create the ground effect achieved with the slimmer V8 engines. In 1978 Alfa Romeo had launched a V12 engine to replace their flat 12 for this very reason. No such initiative had been taken at Ferrari, who were concentrating on a longer term project to develop a V6 turbocharged engine. Autosport correspondent Nigel Roebuck provided a succinct overview of Ferrari's 1980 season: "Maranello's flat-12, still a magnificent racing engine, is incompatible with modern chassis. Villeneuve and Scheckter were competing in yesterday's cars." The lowest point came in the Canadian Grand Prix when the reigning world champion, Jody Scheckter, failed to qualify his Ferrari for the race, a bit like Italy failing to qualify for the soccer World Cup. Once again the full wrath of the Italian press descended on the team.

MCLAREN 1988–1991

The period from 1988 to 1991 was highly unusual in the hyper-competitive world of Formula One where the pace of change is rarely matched in any other competitive environment. This period was notable because of the dominance of one constructor. In one year the McLaren team won 15 of the 16 races; such dominance had not been seen before and will almost certainly never be seen again.

Founded by the New Zealand F1 driver Bruce McLaren in 1966, the McLaren team had their first victory in the Belgian Grand Prix of 1968. Tragically McLaren himself was killed two years later while testing a sports car for the American Can-Am series at Goodwood. Lawyer and family friend Teddy Mayer took over as Team Principal and the team continued to develop and in 1974 secured a long-term sponsorship from Philip Morris to promote the Marlboro brand of cigarettes. This was a partnership that was to last until 1996, probably the most enduring relationship between a constructor and a 'flagship' sponsor. In September 1980 Ron Dennis became joint Team Principle with Mayer, a position which he took over solely in 1982, when Mayer was 'encouraged' by Philip Morris to take a less active role in the management of McLaren. In the previous year McLaren moved from their modest site in Colnbrook to a modern facility at Woking in Surrey, South of London.

Dennis had been a mechanic for the highly successful Cooper team in 1966, but left to set up his own Formula Two (a smaller, less expensive formula) team in 1971. By the end of the '70s he had built up a reputation for professionalism and immaculate presentation. His Project Four company brought in designer John Barnard, who had some radical ideas about using carbon [fiber], rather than metal, as the basis for a race car chassis. These ideas were to provide the basis for the radical MP4 car. Both Dennis and Barnard were perfectionists, with Dennis's obsession with immaculate presentation and attention to detail complemented by Barnard's uncompromising quest for technical excellence. As John Barnard observed in an interview the entire nature of the organization shifted: *We changed from being mechanic [led] to a team which was totally controlled by the drawing office. Ron used to tell everyone time and time again, 'I don't care if we're the last two cars on the grid, we'll be the smartest and the best presented', and that attitude built into the company once it was launched.*

In 1986 John Barnard left to join the struggling Ferrari team. Barnard was considered by many to be the reason for McLaren's developing dominance. The partnership between

Dennis and Barnard had been stormy, but a huge amount had been achieved through the energy of these two individuals. Dennis [provided] the managerial and commercial acumen and Barnard highly innovative design skills (by the end of the '90s Barnard was still regarded by many as the best designer in F1, and many budding engineers [. . .] sought to work with him). To replace Barnard Brabham, designer Gordon Murray was brought into the team, perhaps best known for developing the innovative 'fan car' for Brabham in 1978. Murray, like Barnard, was at the leading edge of F1 car design.

Halfway through 1987 McLaren announced that they had recruited two of the top drivers in F1 to their team—Alain Prost and Ayrton Senna—for the 1988 season. This was unusual as most teams tended to have a clear hierarchy with a lead driver being supported by a 'number two' who was [. . .] regarded as less skilful and/or less experienced than the lead driver. However, McLaren appeared to feel that they would be able to deal with the potential problems which such a structure could cause, as reported in [*Motorsport*]:

> Ayrton Senna is being moved from Lotus to McLaren to join Prost in one of the most professional and well balanced teams of all time. Prost and Senna have been announced as joint number one drivers, and McLaren International has shown in the past that it is well capable of handling two top drivers, which few other teams have managed.

Ayrton Senna, the young Brazilian, had made a name for himself as being extremely talented and totally committed, but very difficult to manage. In his previous team, Lotus, he is alleged to have blocked the recruitment of second driver Derek Warwick, as he regarded him too great a threat and persuaded the team to bring in the less experienced and younger Johnny Dumfries instead. Prost and Senna were real contrasts: Senna was fast and had unparalleled commitment to winning races; Prost was fast too, but a great tactician and adept at team politics, making sure that the whole team was behind him. However, it was ultimately Senna who was able to change the balance of power within the team.

In 1988 the Honda powered MP4 car was without question the fastest and most reliable car on the circuit. This meant that effectively the only real competition for Prost and Senna was each other. In a remarkable year McLaren won 15 out of the 16 grand prix. This competition between two highly committed and talented drivers resulted in one of the most enduring and bitter feuds the sport has ever known. In 1988 Senna swerved at Prost as they raced wheel to wheel at 190 mph. Prost told him, "If you want the world championship badly enough to die for it, you are welcome." In 1990 the acrimony with Senna culminated in Prost moving to Ferrari. Senna now had the team to himself. But the battle between them continued, reaching a dramatic climax at the Japanese Grand Prix when Senna forced Prost's Ferrari off the road, and as a consequence became world champion. Despite these darker moments, Senna's brilliance was undis-

puted. The accolades from the industry following his tragic death in 1994 were sincere and he is widely regarded as one of the greatest drivers of all time.

The other element in the success of the McLaren in 1988 was the fact that Ron Dennis had negotiated exclusive use of Honda V10 engines. The engines were supported by a significant commitment from Honda in both people and resources, Honda using this as [an] opportunity to develop some of their most talent[ed] engineers. In 1988 Honda engines were [some] of the most powerful and certainly the most reliable. Honda had been engine supplier to the Williams team since 1983. Sadly Team Principal Frank Williams was seriously injured in a car accident in 1986, which left him tetraplegic. This caused concern in Honda over the future of the Williams team.

The combination of Prost and Senna made McLaren an attractive alternative to Williams for Honda, as identified by a journalist at the time:

> Honda, said our source, want to dominate F1 and it knows it can never do that if it does not have Prost.

Honda switched allegiance from Williams exclusively to McLaren for 1988 after also supplying the Lotus team (and driver Ayrton Senna) in 1987. This meant that Honda powered cars had won six consecutive world championships from 1986 to 1991 (Williams: 86 & 87; McLaren 88, 89, 90 & 91).

Ron Dennis and his professional management style has been synonymous with the success of McLaren, indicating that the era of the 'one man band' Formula One constructor was past. His record since taking over in 1982 has been unsurpassed. Eddie Jordan, principal of the Jordan team, made the following statement when planning to enter F1 in 1990:

> I know it sounds far fetched, but I want to emulate Ron Dennis. He's won that many Grand Prix, he's won that many championships, he's been on pole that many times and he's got the best drivers. Everyone hates him; but they only hate him because he's the best. I believe I'm as good as he is: I believe I'm in the same league, but only time will tell.

Dennis's negotiating and marketing abilities were legendary throughout Formula One. McLaren also created their own marketing consultancy operation where the smaller teams engaged them to find sponsors. In 1991 *Management Week* had Ron Dennis on the front cover with the question: "Is Ron Dennis Britain's best manager?" Dennis likens the management of McLaren to that of a game of chess: " . . . you've got to get all the elements right, the overall package, the budget, the designer, the engine, the drivers, the organisation." John Barnard once likened working with Dennis as "being in a room with a hand grenade rolling about without its pin, about to go off and make a horrible mess." Dennis is renowned for being hyper-competitive and once chastised a driver who was delighted with finishing second with the comment—"Remember, second is the first of the losers." Dennis's ambitions went beyond F1 and in 1988 [he] began a project to build a road going car, the McLaren F1. In many ways this mirrored the development of Ferrari, who had made the progression from producing dedicated race cars to also develop road going cars. The McLaren F1 was launched in 1994 and with a price tag of £634,000 with a top speed of 231 mph became the most expensive and fastest road going car in the world.

However in 1992 the Renault powered Williams was developing into the fastest and most reliable car on the circuit. In September, following widespread speculation, Honda confirmed that that they were pulling out of F1 racing. Honda's reasons were simple—they had been hugely successful and achieved all of their objectives; it was now time to stand back from F1 and find some new challenges. Whilst Dennis had been told about Honda's thinking in late 1991, it appeared that he hadn't taken it seriously enough and the team had no real engine alternatives. This meant they lost valuable winter development time as they tried to find a new engine supplier. In 1993 they competed with 'off the shelf' customer Ford engines available to any team who had the cash to buy them. Senna's skills still gave McLaren five victories, despite having a less than competitive car. However, at the end of 1993 Senna left the McLaren team to move to Williams, whom he saw as having the superior car and engine combination. Former world champion and adviser to Ferrari Niki Lauda saw this as the terminal blow: "Senna was a leader. He told them exactly what was wrong with the car. Hakkinen (Senna's replacement) is not in a position to do that, so the reaction time is much longer. Senna motivated the designers." John Hogan, VP of European marketing for Philip Morris and holder of the McLaren purse strings, saw the problem as design leadership and was advocating that Barnard be brought back to McLaren.

The mid-nineties were a particularly difficult period for McLaren. Having tried Peugeot engines in 1994 they moved to Mercedes in 1995. However, 1995 was perhaps best remembered for the debacle at the start when neither Nigel Mansell or Mika Hakinnen could fit into the new £50 million MP4/10 and then Mansell's alleged £4.5 million contract to race for the year fell apart when neither he nor the car came up to expectations. On a more positive note 1995 was significant in that it heralded a new partnership between McLaren and Mercedes. Mercedes had been considering a major commitment to F1 and in 1995 they concluded a deal which involved their taking equity stakes in McLaren (40%) and also in specialist engine builder Ilmor engineering based near Northampton (25%, increased in 2002 to 55%) who were to build the Mercedes engines used in F1. This relationship was not just about F1 and would ultimately involve the design and manufacturer of the new Mercedes SLR sportscar using F1 technology and materials due to be launched in 2003.

In 1996 the relationship between McLaren and Philip Morris came to an end, Philip Morris moving support of their Marlboro brand to Ferrari driver Michael Schumacher, whilst McLaren entered into a substantial agreement with German based tobacco firm Reemtsma to support their West brand. In 1997 McLaren acquired the services of Williams' designer Adrian Newey for a reputed £2 million contract. Newey's design talents coupled with a more powerful and reliable Mercedes engine [. . .] meant that McLaren again became one of the top F1 teams. Another interesting aspect of the McLaren approach is that, with the exception of John Barnard, their technology leaders have tended to be retained within the McLaren Group. Gordon Murray moved from F1 to lead the design of road going cars, first the McLaren F1 and now the Mercedes SLR; in 2002 Jaguar Racing almost poached Adrian Newey from McLaren, but Newey responded to an offer from Ron Dennis to reduce his F1 involvement and to allow him time and space to work on some new projects involving the design of hulls for racing yachts.

WILLIAMS 1992–1994

If the McLaren MP4 was the [dominant] car in the late eighties, the Williams F1 FW15 & 16 powered by a Renault V10 was the car to beat in the early 1990s. During the period 1992–94 Williams cars won 27 out of 48 races, they secured the F1 constructors' title[s] for all three years and the world championship for drivers was won in a Williams in 1992 (Nigel Mansell) and 1993 (Alain Prost).

Like most of the founders of the Formula One constructors, Frank Williams began as a driver, perhaps not of the same standing as Bruce McLaren or Jack Brabham, but nonetheless someone who lived, breathed and loved motor racing. His desire to remain in the sport led him to develop a business buying and selling racing cars and spare parts and in 1968 Frank Williams (Racing Cars) Ltd was formed. A series of triumphs, tragedies and near bankruptcies led up to the establishment of Williams Grand Prix Engineering in 1977 when Frank Williams teamed up with technical director Patrick Head. Frank Williams' approach and style owes a lot to the difficult years in the seventies when he survived on his wits and very little else, including at one time operating from a telephone box near the workshop when [his] phones were disconnected, as he hadn't been able to pay the bill. His style could be described as autocratic, entrepreneurial and certainly frugal, despite the multi-million pound funding he managed to extract from the likes of Canon, R. J. Reynolds and Rothmans. Williams saw his role as providing the resources for the best car to be built and [hiring] the best driver to sit in it. His long-standing relationship with Head was pivotal to the team and brought together a blend of entrepreneurial energy and technical excellence needed to succeed in F1.

The first car from this new alliance was the FW06, designed by Patrick Head [. . .] with support from Saudi Airlines. The team enjoyed some success in 1980/81 by winning the constructors' championship both years and with Alan Jones winning the drivers' title in 1980. Jones was a forthright Australian who knew what he wanted and was not afraid to voice his opinions. His approach to working with the team was very influential and coloured Frank Williams' view of drivers:

> *I took a very masculine attitude towards drivers and assumed that they should behave—or should be treated—like Alan.*

A further success occurred in 1986/87 with Nelson Piquet winning the drivers' title in 1987 and Williams the constructors' title in both years. This was despite the road accident in 1986 which left Frank Williams tetraplegic and confined to a wheelchair. However, the most dominant period in the history of Williams, so far, has been the period from 1992–1994 when they were able to win the constructor championship for three consecutive years.

Williams' 1986/87 success had been in part due to the use of powerful and reliable Honda engines. However, Frank Williams' accident in 1986 caused concern at Honda over the future of Williams and in 1987 they made their engines available to Lotus and withdrew from Williams (a year before the end of the contract) to supply McLaren in the 1988 season. 1988 was Williams' worst season, as they were forced to suddenly switch to 'off the shelf' Judd V10 engines, which were available to anyone who wanted one. Williams didn't win a single race, whilst McLaren won 15 out of the 16 Grand Prix of 1988 and a disillusioned Nigel Mansell left and went to Ferrari. Frank Williams had to search frantically for a new engine deal, which he found in 1990 with Renault. At the end of 1985 Renault had withdrawn from Formula One as a constructor, having failed to win a world championship over the previous eight seasons. However, they continued their engine development activities with the aim of building a new F1 engine to meet the new non-turbo standards due to be introduced in 1989. Frank Williams was able to form an agreement for Renault to supply him with the new V10 engine. This relationship became a far reaching and durable one, with Renault putting human and financial resources into the project with Williams. [Williams] also sought to develop the relationship further and extended their activities with Renault by running their team of saloon cars for the British Touring Car Championship, and also [providing] engineering input and the Williams name for a special edition of the Renault Clio.

In 1990 a lack of driver talent meant that the team [was] only able to win two races. In 1991 Nigel Mansell was persuaded to return from retirement by Frank Williams and narrowly missed taking the 1991 title, but in 1992 the team dominated the circuits, effectively winning the championship by the middle of the season. Nigel Mansell went into the record books by winning the first five consecutive races of the season. This was a phenomenal achievement as it emphatically demonstrated that McLaren were no longer at the top; Williams most certainly were. However, deterioration in the relationship between Williams and Mansell led to the driver's retirement from F1 at the end of the year.

The Williams approach to design and development of a car was always the highest priority. Patrick Head had always been one of the more conspicuous of the technical directors in Formula One, a role which is often put into the shade by the head of the team and driver. In a sport where personnel change teams frequently, the stable relationship between Williams and Head (and up to 96, Adrian Newey, who was a brilliant aerodynamicist and design assistant) provided enviable continuity compared with the rest of the field. Whilst Head's designs had often been functional rather than innovative, he had always been able to take a good idea and develop it further. These have included ground effect (originally developed by Lotus), carbon-composite monocoque (McLaren), semi-automatic gearbox (Ferrari), and active suspension (Lotus). The car development process was always a top priority at Williams and Head was supported by many junior designers who then went on to be highly influential in Formula One, such as Neil Oatley and Adrian Newey (both now with McLaren), Frank Dernie (Ligier, Lotus and Arrows) and Ross Brawn (Benetton and now Ferrari).

This focus on developing the car and engine combination has sometimes meant that the driver took second place in the Williams philosophy, despite the fact that a good test driver, who could tell the technicians what needed to be done to the car to improve its performance, was essential to the development process. There had been a number of high profile disputes between drivers and Williams which had, in part, been attributable to Frank Williams' "masculine" approach to dealing with drivers. Controversy broke out when the relationship between Williams and two top British drivers broke down. In 1992 Nigel Mansell left when he felt his 'number one' driver position was threatened by the recruitment of Alain Prost for 1993 (although Prost himself left the following year for the same reason regarding the hiring of Ayrton Senna). A similar situation arose when the 1996 world champion, Damon Hill, was not retained for the 1997 season and was replaced with Heinz-Harald Frentzen. In an interview with the *Sunday Times*, Patrick Head set out the reasons for the decision not to hold on to Hill:

> *We are an engineering company and that is what we focus on. Ferrari are probably the only team where you can say the driver is of paramount importance and that is because [Michael] Schumacher is three-quarters of a second a lap quicker than anyone else.*

This emphasis on the driver being only part of the equation was not lost on Paul Stewart, who was concentrating on developing the Stewart Grand Prix entry to F1:

> *If you haven't got the money none of it is possible, so money is one key to success—but what makes a difference is how the money is used. It's not down to any one thing like a driver or a engine, but the interaction that matters. If you look at the Williams team, they rely on a solid framework, their organisation, their engine, their car design is all amalgamated into something that gives a platform for everyone*

to work on. They don't believe putting millions into a driver is going to make all the difference.

Williams' emphatic dominance in the 1992 season was due to a number of factors: the development of the powerful and reliable Renault engine was perfectly complemented by the FW15 chassis, which incorporated Patrick Head's development of some of the innovations of the early nineties, namely semi-automatic gearboxes, drive-by-wire technology and their own active suspension system. As summarised by a senior manager at Williams F1:

I think we actually were better able to exploit the technology that was available and led that technology revolution. We were better able to exploit it to the full, before the others caught up . . . it wasn't just one thing but a combination of ten things, each one giving you another 200/300th of a second, if you add them up you a get a couple of seconds of advantage.

However, other teams were also able to use these innovations and in 1993 the Benetton team made a great deal of progress with both the gearbox and suspension innovations largely attributed to the development skills of their new driver, Michael Schumacher. Williams' technical lead coupled with the tactical race skills of Alain Prost, supported by promoted test driver Damon Hill (due to Mansell's sudden exit) secured the 1993 world championship and constructors' championship for Williams F1.

1994 was a disastrous year, but not for reasons of performance, as Williams won the constructors' championship for the third successive year (this was always their declared primary objective, with the drivers' championship very much a secondary aim). Frank Williams had, for some time, regarded Brazilian Ayrton Senna as the best driver around and, now with the obvious performance advantage of the FW15 chassis and the Renault V10 engine, Senna was keen to move to Williams. The problem was that a bitter and prolonged feud between Senna and Prost, originating from their time together at McLaren, meant that if Senna arrived Prost would leave. This was exactly what happened. Prost decided to retire (though he returned to run his own team) and Ayrton Senna was partnered [with] Damon Hill for the 1994 season. However, tragedy struck in the San Marino Grand Prix at Imola on 1 May 1994 when Senna was killed in an accident, an event which not only devastated the Williams team but the sport as a whole. Also due to the accident having occurred in Italy key members of the Williams team along with the organizers of the race were charged with manslaughter, a case which was only recently dropped by the Italian authorities.

For the remainder [of] the season Hill found himself as lead driver supported by the new test driver, David Coulthard, and a couple of 'comebacks' from Nigel Mansell. Whilst Williams lost the drivers' title to the rising star of German driver Michael Schumacher, amazingly despite these huge setbacks Williams retained the constructors' title for 1994.

In 1995 the Benetton team was eclipsing the Williams domination. Benetton had developed a car using many of the technological innovations used by [. . .] Williams (with the help of ex-Williams designer Ross Brawn). In addition, Renault's ambitions to match Honda's previous domination of the sport as an engine supplier from 1986 [to] 1991, lead them to supply Benetton with their engines as well as Williams, a decision which incensed Head and Williams. 1995 was the year of Benetton and Michael Schumacher, breaking the three year domination of the Williams team. However, in 1996 Schumacher moved to the then uncompetitive Ferrari team for £27 million, putting him in 3rd place in the *Forbes* chart of sports top earners. This left the way clear for Williams to dominate the season, with Benetton failing to fill the gap left by Schumacher.

FERRARI 1999–2002

Following on from their dominance in the mid-seventies, Ferrari's strategy of focusing on the development of a V6 turbo charged engine paid off in 1982 and 1983 when they were able to secure the constructors' championship. In the mid-eighties more and more investment was poured into the Italian facilities but to no effect on performance. A key problem was that new developments in aerodynamics and the use of composite materials had emerged from the UK's motorsport valley. Ferrari had traditionally focused on the engine as their key competitive advantage, which made perfect sense given that unlike most of the competition [they] outsourced their engines from suppliers such as Cosworth. However, it appeared that these new technologies were effectively substituting superior engine power with enhanced grip due to aerodynamic downforce and improved chassis rigidity.

In an effort to introduce a greater understanding of aerodynamics in [race car] design British designer Harvey Postlethwaite became the first non-Italian Technical Director of Ferrari in 1984, and in 1986 British designer John Barnard was recruited to the top technical role. However, Barnard was not prepared to move to Italy as he felt that his technical team and network of contacts in the UK would be essential to the success of his position. Surprisingly, Enzo Ferrari allowed him to establish a design and manufacturing facility near Guildford in Surrey that became known as the Ferrari 'GTO' or Guildford Technical Office. It seemed that rather than being a unique and distinctively Italian F1 team Ferrari were now prepared to imitate the British constructors who Enzo had once, rather contemptuously, referred to as the '*Garagistes*.' The concept of the GTO is that it would concentrate on the development of the following year's car, whereas in Maranello, under Postlethwaite, they would focus on building and racing the current car. However, the fact that Barnard was defining the technical direction of Ferrari meant that he became increasingly involved in activities at both sites.

Enzo Ferrari's death in 1988 created a vacuum which was filled by executives from the Fiat organization for a number of years. Ferrari's death meant that Fiat's original stake in Ferrari had been increased to 90%, and this greater investment led to growing attempts to run Ferrari as a formal subsidiary of the Fiat group. Barnard became frustrated with the interference and politics of the situation and left to join Benetton in 1989. However in 1992 Fiat appointed Luca di Montezemolo as CEO with a mandate to do whatever was needed to take Ferrari back to the top. Montezemolo had been team manager for Ferrari during its last successful period in the mid-seventies; subsequently he had taken on a range of high-profile management roles including running Italy's hosting of the Soccer World Cup in 1990. One of Montezemolo's first actions was to re-appoint John Barnard as technical director and re-establish GTO. He was quoted in *The Times* as follows: *In Italy we are cut away from the Silicon Valley of Formula One that has sprung up in England.* With an Englishman heading up design he followed this up with the appointment of a Frenchman, Jean Todt, to handle the overall management of the team. Both appointments were clear signals to all involved in Ferrari that things were going to change. Todt had no experience in F1 but had been in motorsport management for many years and had recently led a successful rally and sportscar programme at Peugeot.

However, the physical separation between design and development in Guildford and the racing operation in Maranello led to increased problems and eventually Barnard and Ferrari parted company in 1996, this time for good. This opened the way for Ferrari to recruit driver Michael Schumacher and a number of the key individuals in the Benetton technical team which had helped him to his world titles in 1994 and 1995. Todt and di Montezemolo also chose not to make a direct replacement for the role of technical supremo who would both lead the design of the car and the management of the technical activity, but they split the role between a chief designer, Rory Byrne who had overall responsibility for designing the car, and Ross Brawn who managed the entire technical operation; these were roles which both had undertaken in working with Schumacher at Benetton. However, the contractual arrangement with John Barnard had been one where the GTO designers were paid through his private company; when he left they all went with him and Byrne and Brawn faced the task of building up a new design department—around 50 people, based in Italy, from scratch.

As part of their recruitment of Michael Schumacher in 1996 Ferrari entered into a commercial partnership with tobacco giant Phillip Morris to use their Marlboro brand on the Ferrari cars. In a novel arrangement Phillip Morris, rather than Ferrari, paid Schumacher's salary, and would also make a significant contribution to Ferrari's annual operating budget. In addition to Marlboro Ferrari also entered into a long-term partnership with Shell to provide both financial and technical support to the team; this was a departure for Ferrari who had previously always worked with Italian petroleum giant Agip. In these kinds of arrangements Ferrari led a trend away from selling space on cars to long-term commercial arrangements, with coordinated marketing strategies for commercial partners to maximize the benefits of their investments.

This rejuvenated team provided the basis for Michael Schumacher's current dominance of F1. In 1997 they raced the Barnard-developed Ferrari and finished second in the constructors' championship. Their competitiveness continued to improve and in 2000 they won their first constructors' championship [in] 21 years—although the drivers' championship went to Mika Hakkinen in a McLaren-Mercedes. However, in 2001 Ferrari secured both championships and it was at this point that they felt they had truly returned to the glory of the mid-seventies. In 2002 Schumacher and Ferrari were so dominant that a series of regulation changes were introduced to try and make the racing more competitive. This was made all the more evident due to Ferrari's tradition of having a lead driver, which meant that often the second driver [was] asked to move over in order for the lead driver to maximize his world-championship points. This happened in a particularly blatant manner at the 2002 Austrian Grand Prix when Ferrari number 2, Rubens Barrichello, moved over just before the finish line to allow Michael Schumacher to win. This produced an angry reaction from fans worldwide and made both the governing body—the FIA—and Ferrari reflect on the wisdom of such a blatant use of team orders.

Whilst Schumacher's talent as a driver and a motivator of the team (he learnt Japanese to converse with an engine technician recruited from Honda) was clearly critical, another key aspect in Ferrari's advantage for 2002 had been their relationship with Bridgestone [tires]. In 2000 Bridgestone had been the sole supplier to all F1 teams and therefore [tires] were no longer a potential source of advantage; however, in 2001 Michelin entered F1 and Ferrari's main rivals—Williams, McLaren and Renault—eventually switched to Michelin. At the time the regulations stipulated that each manufacturer could create only two specific [tire] compounds. For Bridgestone, who now only supplied Ferrari and a number of less competitive teams, the choice was clear—they had to design and develop their compounds specifically for Michael Schumacher and Ferrari; everyone else would have to make do with this specification. For Michelin the problem was more complex with many top teams and drivers [. . .] vying for a compound that specifically suited their car and driving style. Inevitably the Michelin solution was a compromise across many drivers and teams; however, for 2003 the regulations have been relaxed and the [tire] companies can develop specific compounds for each team/driver, although Michelin still [has] the problem [of spreading] their development resources over a number of leading teams.

For 2003 it appears that the competition of the three other leading teams, McLaren, Williams and Renault, all running on Michelin [tires], is much stronger; however, it is still anyone's guess as to whether Ferrari will be the first constructor ever to secure a record breaking five consecutive constructors' titles.

APPENDIX 1   SUMMARY OF WORLD CHAMPIONS

Year	Driver	Car/Engine	Constructor's Cup
1950	Giuseppe Farina	Alfa Romeo	
1951	Juan Manuel Fangio	Alfa Romeo	
1952	Alberto Ascari	Ferrari	
1953	Alberto Ascari	Ferrari	
1954	Juan Manuel Fangio	Maserati	
1955	Juan Manuel Fangio	Mercedes-Benz	
1956	Juan Manuel Fangio	Lancia-Ferrari	
1957	Juan Manuel Fangio	Maserati	
1958	Mike Hawthorn	Ferrari	Vanwall
1959	Jack Brabham	Cooper/Climax	Cooper/Climax
1960	Jack Brabham	Cooper/Climax	Cooper/Climax
1961	Phil Hill	Ferrari	Ferrari
1962	Graham Hill	BRM	BRM
1963	Jim Clark	Lotus/Climax	Lotus/Climax
1964	John Surtees	Ferrari	Ferrari
1965	Jim Clark	Lotus/Climax	Lotus/Climax
1966	Jack Brabham	Brabham/Repco	Brabham/Repco
1967	Denny Hulme	Brabham/Repco	Brabham/Repco
1968	Graham Hill	Lotus/Ford	Lotus/Ford
1969	Jackie Stewart	Matra/Ford	Matra/Ford
1970	Jochen Rindt	Lotus/Ford	Lotus/Ford
1971	Jackie Stewart	Tyrrell/Ford	Tyrrell/Ford
1972	Emerson Fittipaldi	Lotus/Ford	Lotus/Ford
1973	Jackie Stewart	Tyrrell/Ford	Lotus/Ford
1974	Emerson Fittipaldi	McLaren/Ford	McLaren/Ford
1975	Niki Lauda	Ferrari	Ferrari
1976	James Hunt	McLaren/Ford	Ferrari
1977	Niki Lauda	Ferrari	Ferrari
1978	Mario Andretti	Lotus/Ford	Lotus/Ford
1979	Jody Scheckter	Ferrari	Ferrari
1980	Alan Jones	Williams/Ford	Williams/Ford
1981	Nelson Piquet	Brabham/Ford	Williams/Ford
1982	Keke Rosberg	Williams/Ford	Ferrari
1983	Nelson Piquet	Brabham/BMW	Ferrari
1984	Niki Lauda	McLaren/Porsche	McLaren/Porsche
1985	Alain Prost	McLaren/Porsche	McLaren/Porsche
1986	Alain Prost	McLaren/Porsche	Williams/Honda
1987	Nelson Piquet	Williams/Honda	Williams/Honda
1988	Ayrton Senna	McLaren/Honda	McLaren/Honda
1989	Alain Prost	McLaren/Honda	McLaren/Honda
1990	Ayrton Senna	McLaren/Honda	McLaren/Honda
1991	Ayrton Senna	McLaren/Honda	McLaren/Honda
1992	Nigel Mansell	Williams/Renault	Williams/Renault
1993	Alain Prost	Williams/Renault	Williams/Renault
1994	Michael Schumacher	Benetton/Ford	Williams/Renault
1995	Michael Schumacher	Benetton/Renault	Benetton/Renault
1996	Damon Hill	Williams/Renault	Williams/Renault
1997	Jacques Villeneuve	Williams/Renault	Williams/Renault
1998	Mika Hakkinen	McLaren/Mercedes	McLaren/Mercedes
1999	Mika Hakkinen	McLaren/Mercedes	Ferrari
2000	Michael Schumacher	Ferrari	Ferrari
2001	Michael Schumacher	Ferrari	Ferrari
2002	Michael Schumacher	Ferrari	Ferrari

Note: Constructors' championship is based on the cumulative points gained by a team during the season. Currently each team is limited to entering two cars and drivers per race.

Prince Edward Island Preserve Co.

9A91G005

In August 1991, Bruce MacNaughton, president of Prince Edward Island Preserve Co. Ltd. (P.E.I. Preserves), was contemplating future expansion. Two cities were of particular interest: Toronto and Tokyo. At issue was whether consumers in either or both markets should be pursued, and if so, how. The choices available for achieving further growth included mail order, distributors, and company controlled stores.

BACKGROUND

Prince Edward Island Preserve Co. was a manufacturing company located in New Glasgow, P.E.I. which produced and marketed specialty food products. The company founder and majority shareholder, Bruce MacNaughton, had realized that an opportunity existed to present P.E.I. strawberries as a world-class food product and to introduce the finished product to an "up-scale" specialty market. With total sales in the coming year expected to exceed $1 million for the first time, MacNaughton had made good on the opportunity he had perceived years earlier. It had not been easy, however.

MacNaughton arrived in P.E.I. from Moncton, New Brunswick in 1978. Without a job, he slept on the beach

IVEY Professor Paul W. Beamish prepared this case solely to provide material for class discussion. The author does not intend to illustrate either effective or ineffective handling of a managerial situation. The author may have disguised certain names and other identifying information to protect confidentiality.

Richard Ivey School of Business
The University of Western Ontario

for much of that first summer. Over the next few years he worked in commission sales, waited tables in restaurants, and then moved to Toronto. There he studied to become a chef at George Brown Community College. After working in the restaurant trade for several years, he found a job with "Preserves by Amelia" in Toronto. After six months, he returned to P.E.I. where he opened a restaurant. The restaurant was not successful and MacNaughton lost the $25,000 stake he had accumulated. With nothing left but 100 kilograms of strawberries, Bruce decided to make these into preserves in order to have gifts for Christmas 1984. Early the following year, P.E.I. Preserves was founded.

The products produced by the company were priced and packaged for the gift/gourmet and specialty food markets. The primary purchasers of these products were conscious of quality and were seeking a product which they considered tasteful and natural. P.E.I. Preserves felt their product met this standard of quality at a price that made it attractive to all segments of the marketplace.

Over the next few years as the business grew, improvements were made to the building in New Glasgow. The sense of style which was characteristic of the company was evident from the beginning in its attractive layout and design.

In 1989 the company diversified and opened "The Perfect Cup," a small restaurant in P.E.I.'s capital city of Charlottetown. This restaurant continued the theme of quality, specializing in wholesome, home-made food featuring the products manufactured by the company. The success of this operation led to the opening in 1990 of a small tea room at the New Glasgow location. Both of these locations showcased the products manufactured by the P.E.I. Preserve Co.

In August 1991, the company opened a small (22 square metre) retail branch in the CP Prince Edward Hotel. MacNaughton hoped this locale would expand visibility in the local and national marketplace, and serve as an off-season sales office. P.E.I. Preserves had been given very favourable lease arrangements (well below the normal $275 per month for space this size) and the location would require minimal financial investment. As Table 1 suggests, the company had experienced steady growth in its scope of operations.

MARKETPLACE

Prince Edward Island was Canada's smallest province, both in size and population. Located in the Gulf of St. Lawrence, it was separated from Nova Scotia and New Brunswick by the Northumberland Strait. The major employer in P.E.I. was the various levels of government. Many people in P.E.I. worked seasonally, in either farming (especially potato), fishing, or tourism. During the peak tourist months of July and August, the island population would swell dramatically from its base of 125,000. P.E.I.'s half million annual visitors came "home" to enjoy the long sandy beaches, picturesque scenery, lobster dinners, arguably the best tasting strawberries in the world, and slower pace of life. P.E.I. was best known in Canada and elsewhere for the books, movies and (current) television series about Lucy Maud Montgomery's turn-of-the-century literary creation, Anne of Green Gables.

P.E.I. Preserves felt they were competing in a worldwide market. Their visitors were from all over the world and in 1991 they expected the numbers to exceed 100,000 in the New Glasgow location alone. New Glasgow (population 200) was located in a rural setting equidistant (15 kilometres) from Charlottetown and P.E.I.'s best-known North Shore beaches. In their mailings they planned to continue to promote Prince Edward Island as "Canada's Garden Province" and the "little jewel it was in everyone's heart!" They had benefitted, and would continue to benefit, from that image.

MARKETING

Products

The company had developed numerous products since its inception. These included many original varieties of preserves as well as honey, vinegar, mustard, and tea (repackaged). (Exhibit 1 contains a 1990 price list, ordering instruc-

tions, and a product picture used for mail order purposes.) The company had also added to the appeal of these products by offering gift packs composed of different products and packaging. With over 80 items, it felt that it had achieved a diverse product line and efforts in developing new product lines were expected to decrease in the future. Approximately three-quarters of total retail sales (including wholesale and mail order) came from the products the company made itself. Of these, three quarters were jam preserves.

With the success of P.E.I. Preserves, imitation was inevitable. In recent years, several other small firms in P.E.I. had begun to retail specialty preserves. Another company which produced preserves in Ontario emphasized the Green Gables tie-in on its labels.

Price

P.E.I. Preserves were not competing with "low-end" products, and felt their price reinforced their customers' perception of quality. The 11 types of jam preserves retailed for $5.89 for a 250-millilitre jar, significantly more than any grocery store product. However, grocery stores did not offer jam products made with such a high fruit content and with champagne, liqueur or whisky.

In mid-1991, the company introduced a 10 per cent increase in price (to $5.89) and, to date, had not received any negative reaction from customers. The food products were not subject to the seven per cent National Goods and Services Tax or P.E.I.'s 10 per cent Provincial Sales Tax, an advantage over other gift products which the company would be stressing.

Promotion

Product promotion had been focused in two areas—personal contact with the consumer and catalogue distribution. Visitors to the New Glasgow location (approximately 80,000 in 1990) were enthusiastic upon meeting Bruce, "resplendent in the family kilt," reciting history and generally providing live entertainment. Bruce and the other staff members realized the value of this "Island Touch" and strove to ensure that all

Table 1

Operation	Year Opened				
	1985	1989	1990	1991	Projected 1992
New Glasgow—Manufacturing and Retail	X	X	X	X	X
Charlottetown—Restaurant (Perfect Cup)		X	X	X	X
New Glasgow—Restaurant (Tea Room)			X	X	X
Charlottetown—Retail (CP Hotel)				X	X
Toronto or Tokyo?					X

Exhibit 1   P.E.I. Preserves Mail Order Catalogue

Mail Order

Canada

Prince Edward Island Preserve Co.
RR# 2 Hunter River
Prince Edward Island
Canada
C0A 1N0

Tel. (902) 964-2524
Fax. (902) 566-5565

PRODUCTS

Preserves

1. Strawberry & Grand Marnier	250ml	5.69
2. Raspberry & Champagne	250ml	5.69
3. Wild Blueberry & Raspberry in Champagne	250ml	5.69
4. Strawberry, Orange & Rhubarb	250ml	5.69
5. Raspberry & Peach	250ml	5.69
6. Blueberry, Lemon & Fresh Mint	250ml	5.69
7. Black Currant	250ml	5.69
8. Gooseberry & Red Currant	250ml	5.69
9. Sour Cherry Marmalade	250ml	5.69
10. Orange Marmalade with Chivas Regal	250ml	5.69
11. Lemon & Ginger Marmalade with Amaretto	250ml	5.69
12. Strawberry & Grand Marnier	125ml	3.60
13. Raspberry & Champagne	125ml	3.60
14. Wild Blueberry & Raspberry in Champagne	125ml	3.60
15. Raspberry & Peach	125ml	3.60
16. Black Currant	125ml	3.60
17. Orange Marmalade with Chivas Regal	125ml	3.60

Honeys

18. Summer Honey with Grand Marnier	250ml	5.95
19. Summer Honey with Amaretto	250ml	5.95
20. Summer Honey with Grand Marnier	125ml	3.50
21. Summer Honey with Amaretto	125ml	3.50

Mustards

22. Hot & Spicy Mustard	250ml	3.95
23. Champagne & Dill Mustard	250ml	3.95
24. Honey & Thyme Mustard	250ml	3.95
25. Hot & Spicy Mustard	125ml	2.75
26. Champagne & Dill Mustard	125ml	2.75
27. Honey & Thyme Mustard	125ml	2.75

Vinegars

28. Raspberry Vinegar	350ml	5.95
29. Black Currant Vinegar	350ml	5.95
30. Peach Vinegar	350ml	5.95
31. Raspberry Vinegar	150ml	3.50
32. Black Currant Vinegar	150ml	3.50
33. Peach Vinegar	150ml	3.50

Specials

34A. Catharines Hors d'oeuvre & Pasta Sauce	250 ml	6.49
35. Catharines Hot Antipasto	250 ml	5.69
36. Catharines Antipasto	250 ml	5.69

Spices (recipes included)

37A. Bloody Mary, Bloody Caesar Mix	3.95
38A. Apple Spices - for pies, butters, chutneys	3.95
39A. Mulling Spices - for wine, cider, or ale	4.95
40A. Hot Chocolate - rich & tasty, just add hot water	4.95

Tea - No tea is fresher than ours

41. a) Monks Blend b) Strawberry c) Raspberry
41. d) Earl Grey e) English Breakfast f) Blackcurrant

42. Sachets	50 g	2.95
43. Tea by the Pound, all blends	1 lb	14.95

order tea by # and letter, i.e. 43c is 1 lb. of raspberry tea.

Maple Products

44A. Pure Maple Syrup	100 ml	3.95
45A. Pure Maple Syrup	250 ml	5.95
46A. Pure Maple Syrup	500 ml	10.95
47A. Maple Syrup with Light Rum	250 ml	5.95
48A. Maple Butter, excellent on pancakes, toast or baking	250ml	5.95

Coffees - We think this is the best coffee available

First Colony - ground coffee, available 8 oz. and 2 oz.

49A. Columbian Supremo	8 oz.	6.49
50A. Irish Cream 50B. Swiss Chocolate Almond	8 oz.	6.49
50C. Chocolate Raspberry Truffle	8 oz.	6.49
51A. Special House Blend	2 oz.	2.25

52. All flavours available in 2 oz. packs
(order coffee by # and letter, i.e. 52C is a 2 oz Chocolate Raspberry Truffle)

Teapots - If you've had tea with us, these are the ones!

56. Executive Tea set	Black with Sterling Silver		49.95
57.		Sky Blue with Sterling Silver	49.95
58.	1-2 cup teapot 1 cup & saucer	Fern Green with Gold Inlay	49.95
59.		Rust with Gold Inlay	49.95
60. Romance Tea set	Black with Sterling Silver		59.95
61.		Sky Blue with Sterling Silver	59.95
62.	1-2 cup teapot 2 cups & saucers	Fern Green with Gold Inlay	59.95
63.		Rust with Gold Inlay	59.95

64. Gift Packages - We pack all for long journeys!

A. P.E.I. Summer House		24.99
B. Taster's Choice Duo	2-125 ml Preserves Crated	8.25
C. Taster's Choice Trio	2-125 ml Preserves, 1-125 ml Honey Crated	11.95
D. Crated vinegars	2-150ml Fruit Vinegars Crated	7.49
E. Crated Preserves (2 jars)	250 ml size	12.49
F. Crated Preserves (3 jars)	250 ml size	17.95
G. Tea-for-Two	1-125 ml Preserves, Tea, 1-125 ml Honey	11.95

75. 8" Brass Planter - filled with Swiss Chocolate, Hot Chocolate, Chocolate Coffee and more 23.99
76. 6" Brass Planter - 1-125 ml Preserve, 1-125 ml Honey with Liqueur, Honey Dipper and Chocolate 16.50
77. 4" Brass Planter - 125 ml Honey with Liqueur and Honey Dipper 10.95
78. Wicker House - 2-250 ml Preserves with Liqueur, 1-250 ml Honey with Liqueur, 100 ml Maple Syrup, Irish Cream Coffee, Strawberry Tea 39.95
79. 14" Wicker Hamper - 1-125 ml Preserve, 1-125 ml Honey with Liqueur, 1 Raspberry Tea, 1 Irish Cream Coffee, Honey Dipper 32.95
80. Hunter Green S M L XL Sweatshirt 29.95
87% Cotton, 13% Poly, Preshrunk
81. Deep Lavender S M L XL Sweatshirt 29.95
87% Cotton, 13% Poly, Preshrunk

(continued)

visitors to New Glasgow left with both a positive feeling and purchased products.

Visitors were also encouraged to visit the New Glasgow location through a cooperative scheme whereby other specialty retailers provided a coupon for a free cup of coffee or tea at P.E.I. Preserves. In 1991, roughly 2,000 of these coupons were redeemed.

Approximately 5,000 people received their mail order catalogue annually. They had experienced an order rate of 7.5 per cent with the average order being $66. They hoped to devote more time and effort to their mail order business in an effort to extend their marketing and production period. For 1991 to 1992, the order rate was expected to increase by as much as 15 per cent because the catalogue was to be mailed two weeks earlier than in the previous year. The catalogues cost $1 each to print and mail.

In addition to mail order, the company operated with an ad hoc group of wholesale distributors. These wholesalers were divided between Nova Scotia, Ontario, and other locations. For orders as small as $150, buyers could purchase from the wholesalers' price list. Wholesale prices were on average 60 per cent of the retail/mail order price. Total wholesale trade for the coming year was projected at $150,000, but had been higher in the past.

Danamar Imports was a Toronto-based specialty food store supplier which had previously provided P.E.I. Preserves to hundreds of specialty food stores in Ontario. Danamar had annually ordered $80,000 worth of P.E.I. Preserves at 30 per cent below the wholesale price. This arrangement was amicably discontinued in 1990 by MacNaughton due to uncertainty about whether he was profiting from this contract. P.E.I. Preserves had a list of the specialty stores which

Gift Packaging
Friends, we have many packaging ideas, too many for our catalogue. If you wish us to do up a basket in a certain price range, or any special order for that matter just give us a call, fax or mail in your request. We are here for you!

Exhibit 1   **(continued)**

shortages. From Bruce's perspective, the company's banker (Bank of Nova Scotia) had not been as supportive as it might have been. (The bank manager in Charlottetown had last visited the facility three years ago.) Bruce felt the solution to the problem of cash shortages was the issuance of preferred shares. "An infusion of 'long term' working capital, at a relatively low rate of interest, will provide a stable financial base for the future," he said.

At this time, MacNaughton was attempting to provide a sound financial base for the continued operation of the company. He had decided to offer a preferred share issue in the amount of $100,000. These shares would bear interest at the rate of eight per cent cumulative and would be non-voting, non-participating. He anticipated that the sale of these shares would be complete by December 31, 1991. In the interim he required a line of credit in the amount of $100,000 which he requested to be guaranteed by the Prince Edward Island Development Agency.

Projected Sales for the Year Ended January 31, 1992 were:

New Glasgow Restaurant	$ 110,000
Charlottetown Restaurant	265,000
Retail (New Glasgow)	360,000
Wholesale (New Glasgow)	150,000
Mail Order (New Glasgow)	50,000
Retail (Charlottetown)	75,000
Total	$1,010,000

OPERATIONS

Preserve production took place on site, in an area visible through glass windows from the retail floor. Many visitors, in fact, would videotape operations during their visit to the New Glasgow store, or would watch the process while tasting the broad selection of sample products freely available.

Exhibit 2   P.E.I. Preserve Co. Ltd. (Manufacturing and Retail) Statement of Earnings and Retained Earnings year ended January 31, 1991 (Unaudited)

	1991	1990
Sales	$478,406	$425,588
Cost of sales	217,550	186,890
Gross margin	260,856	238,698
Expenses		
Advertising and promotional items	20,632	6,324
Automobile	7,832	3,540
Doubtful accounts	1,261	—
Depreciation and amortization	11,589	12,818
Dues and fees	1,246	2,025
Electricity	7,937	4,951
Heat	4,096	4,433
Insurance	2,426	1,780
Interest and bank charges	5,667	17,482
Interest on long-term debt	23,562	9,219
Management salary	29,515	32,600
Office and supplies	12,176	10,412
Professional fees	19,672	10,816
Property tax	879	621
Rent	—	975
Repairs and maintenance	6,876	9,168
Salaries and wages	70,132	96,386
Telephone and facsimile	5,284	5,549
Trade shows	18,588	12,946
	249,370	242,045
Earnings (loss) from manufacturing operation	11,486	(3,347)
Management fees	—	7,250
Loss from restaurant operations— Schedule 2	3,368	—
Earnings before income taxes	8,118	3,903
Income taxes	181	1,273
Net earnings	7,937	2,630
Retained earnings, beginning of year	9,290	6,660
Retained earnings, end of year	$ 17,227	$ 9,290

Exhibit 3   P.E.I. Preserve Co. Ltd. Schedule of Restaurant Operations (Charlottetown and New Glasgow) year ended January 31, 1991 (Unaudited)

	SCHEDULE 2 1991
Sales	$306,427
Cost of Sales	
Purchases and freight	122,719
Inventory, end of year	11,864
	110,855
Salaries and wages for food preparation	42,883
	153,738
Gross Margin	152,689
Expenses	
Advertising	2,927
Depreciation	6,219
Electricity	4,897
Equipment lease	857
Insurance	389
Interest and bank charges	1,584
Interest on long-term debt	2,190
Office and supplies	2,864
Propane	2,717
Rent	22,431
Repairs and maintenance	3,930
Salaries and wages for service	90,590
Supplies	12,765
Telephone	1,697
	156,057
Loss from Restaurant Operations	$ 3,368

Production took place on a batch basis. Ample production capacity existed for the $30,000 main kettle used to cook the preserves. Preserves were made five months a year, on a single shift, five day per week basis. Even then, the main kettle was in use only 50 per cent of the time.

Only top quality fruit was purchased. As much as possible, P.E.I. raw materials were used. For a short period the fruit could be frozen until time for processing.

The production process was labour intensive. Bruce was considering the feasibility of moving to an incentive-based salary system to increase productivity and control costs. Because a decorative cloth fringe was tied over the lid of each bottle, bottling could not be completely automated. A detailed production cost analysis had recently been completed. While there were some minor differences due to ingredients, the variable costs averaged $1.25 per 250-millilitre bottle. This was made up of ingredients ($0.56), labour ($0.28) and packaging ($0.20 per bottle, $0.11 per lid, $0.03 per label and $0.07 per fabric and ribbon).

Restaurant operations were the source of many of Bruce's headaches. The New Glasgow Restaurant had evolved over time from offering "dessert and coffee/tea" to its present status where it was also open for meals all day.

Management

During the peak summer period, P.E.I. Preserves employed 45 people among the restaurants, manufacturing area and retail locations. Of these, five were managerial positions (see Exhibit 5). The company was considered a good place to work, with high morale and limited turnover. Nonetheless, most employees (including some management) were with the com-

Exhibit 4 P.E.I. Preserve Co. Ltd. Balance Sheet as at January 31, 1991 (Unaudited)

	1991	1990
Current Assets		
Cash	$ 5,942	$ 592
Accounts Receivable		
Trade	12,573	6,511
Investment tax credit	1,645	2,856
Other	13,349	35,816
Inventory	96,062	85,974
Prepaid expenses	2,664	6,990
	132,235	138,739
Grant Receivable	2,800	1,374
Property, Plant and Equipment	280,809	162,143
Recipes and Trade Name, at Cost	10,000	10,000
	$425,844	$312,256
Current Liabilities		
Bank indebtedness	$ 2,031	$ 9,483
Operating and other loans	54,478	79,000
Accounts Payable and accrued liabilities	64,143	32,113
Current portion of long-term debt	23,657	14,704
	144,309	135,300
Long-term Debt	97,825	99,679
Deferred Government Assistance	54,810	—
Payable to Shareholder, non-interest bearing, no set terms of repayment	43,373	49,687
	340,317	284,666
Shareholders' Equity		
Share capital	55,000	5,000
Contributed surplus	13,300	13,300
Retained earnings	17,227	9,290
	85,527	27,590
	$425,844	$312,256

pany on a seasonal basis. This was a concern to MacNaughton who felt that if he could provide year round employment, he would be able to attract and keep the best quality staff.

Carol Rombough was an effective assistant general manager and bookkeeper. Maureen Dickieson handled production with little input required from Bruce. Kathy MacPherson was in the process of providing, for the first time, accurate cost information. Natalie Leblanc was managing the new retail outlet in Charlottetown, and assisting on some of the more proactive marketing initiatives Bruce was considering.

Bruce felt that the company had survived on the basis of word-of-mouth. Few follow-up calls on mail order had ever been done. Bruce did not enjoy participating in trade shows—even though he received regular solicitations for them from across North America. In 1992, he planned to participate in four *retail* shows, all of them in or close to P.E.I. Bruce hoped to be able eventually to hire a sales/marketing manager, but could not yet afford $30,000 for the necessary salary.

The key manager continued to be MacNaughton. He described himself as "a fair person to deal with, but shrewd when it comes to purchasing. However, I like to spend enough money to ensure that what we do—we do right." Financial and managerial constraints meant that Bruce felt stretched ("I haven't had a vacation in years") and unable to pursue all of the ideas he had for developing the business.

THE JAPANESE CONSUMER

MacNaughton's interest in the possibility of reaching the Tokyo consumer had been formed from two factors: the large number of Japanese visitors to P.E.I. Preserves, and the fact that the largest export shipment the company had ever made had been to Japan. MacNaughton had never visited Japan, although he had been encouraged by Canadian federal government trade representatives to participate in food and gift shows in Japan. He was debating whether he should visit Japan during the coming year. Most of the information he had on Japan had been collected for him by a friend.

Japan was Canada's second most important source of foreign tourists. In 1990, there were 474,000 Japanese visitors to Canada, a figure which was expected to rise to one million by 1995. Most Japanese visitors entered through the Vancouver or Toronto airports. Within Canada, the most popular destination was the Rocky Mountains (in Banff, Alberta numerous stores catered specifically to Japanese consumers). Nearly 15,000 Japanese visited P.E.I. each year. Excluding airfare, these visitors to Canada spent an estimated $314 million, the highest per-capita amount from any country.

The Japanese fascination with Prince Edward Island could be traced to the popularity of Anne of Green Gables. The Japanese translation of this and other books in the same series had been available for many years. However, the adoption of the book as required reading in the Japanese school system since the 1950s had resulted in widespread awareness and affection for "Anne with red hair" *and* P.E.I.

The high level of spending by Japanese tourists was due to a multitude of factors: the amount of disposable income available to them, one of the world's highest per person duty-free allowances (¥200,000), and gift-giving traditions in the country. Gift giving and entertainment expenses at the corporate level are enormous in Japan. In 1990, corporate entertainment expenses were almost ¥5 trillion, more than triple the U.S. level of ¥1.4 trillion. Corporate gift giving, while focused at both year end (seibo) and the summer (chugen), in fact, occurred throughout the year.

Gift giving at the personal level was also widespread. The amount spent would vary depending on one's relationship with the recipient; however, one of the most common price points used by Japanese retailers for gift giving was offering choices for under ¥2,000.

Exhibit 5   Key Executives

President and General Manager—Bruce MacNaughton, Age 35

Experience:
Seventeen years of "front line" involvement with the public in various capacities;
Seven years of managing and promoting Prince Edward Island Preserve Co. Ltd;
Past director of the Canadian Specialty Food Association.

Responsibilities:
To develop and oversee the short-, mid-, and long-term goals of the company;
To develop and maintain quality products for the marketplace;
To oversee the management of personnel;
To develop and maintain customer relations at both the wholesale and retail level;
To develop and maintain harmonious relations with government and the banking community.

Assistant General Manager—Carol Rombough, Age 44

Experience:
Twenty years as owner/operator of a manufacturing business;
Product marketing at both the wholesale and retail level;
Personnel management;
Bookkeeping in a manufacturing environment;
Three years with the Prince Edward Island Preserve Co. Ltd.

Responsibilities:
All bookkeeping functions (i.e. Accounts Receivable, Accounts Payable, Payroll);
Staff management—scheduling and hiring;
Customer relations.

Production Manager—Maureen Dickieson, Age 29

Experience:
Seven years of production experience in the dairy industry;
Three years with the Prince Edward Island Preserve Co. Ltd.

Responsibilities:
Oversee and participate in all production;
Planning and scheduling production;
Requisition of supplies.

Consultant—Kathy MacPherson, Certified General Accountant, Age 37

Experience:
Eight years as a small business owner/manager;
Eight years in financial planning and management.

Responsibilities:
To implement an improved system of product costing;
To assist in the development of internal controls;
To compile monthly internal financial statements;
To provide assistance and/or advice as required by management.

Store Manager—Natalie Leblanc, Age 33

Experience:
Fifteen years in retail.

Responsibilities:
To manage the retail store in the CP Hotel;
Assist with mail order business;
Marketing duties as assigned.

The Japanese Jam Market

Japanese annual consumption of jam was approximately 80,000 tons. Imports made up six to nine per cent of consumption, with higher-grade products (¥470 or more per kilo wholesale CIF) making up a third of this total. Several dozen firms imported jam, and utilized a mix of distribution channels (see Exhibit 6). Prices varied, in part, according to the type of channel structure used. Exhibit 7 provides a common structure. Import duties for jams were high—averaging

Exhibit 6   Jam Distribution Channel in Japan

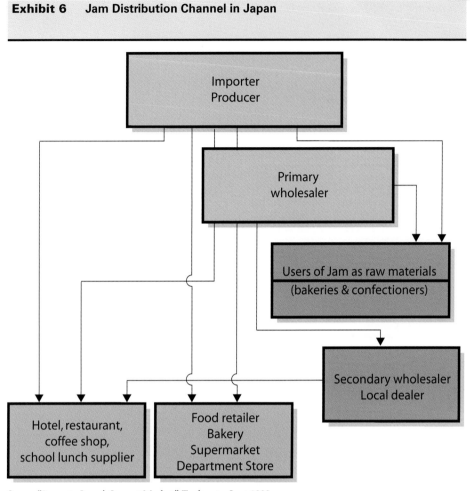

Source: "Access to Japan's Import Market," *Tradescope*, June 1989.

about 28 per cent. Despite such a high tariff barrier, some firms had been successful in exporting to Japan. Excerpts from a report on how to access Japan's jam market successfully are contained in Exhibit 8.

CANADIAN WORLD

In spring 1990, P.E.I. Preserves received its biggest ever export order; $50,000 worth of product was ordered (FOB New Glasgow) for ultimate shipment to Ashibetsu, on the northern Japanese island of Hokkaido. These products were to be offered for sale at Canadian World, a new theme park scheduled to open in July 1990.

In 1981, Japan's first theme park was built outside Tokyo. Called Tokyo Disneyland, in 1989 it had an annual revenue of $815 million, 14.7 million visitors, and profits of $119 million. Not surprisingly, this success has spawned a theme park industry in Japan. Over the past decade, 20 parks with wide-ranging themes have opened. Another 16 were expected to open in 1991–1992.

The idea to construct a theme park about Canada was conceived by a Japanese advertising agency hired by the Ashibetsu city council to stop the city's declining economy. The city's population had decreased from 75,000 in 1958 to 26,000 in 1984 due principally to mine closures.

With capital investment of ¥750 million, construction started in mid 1989 on 48 of the 156 available hectares. The finished site included six restaurants, 18 souvenir stores, 16 exhibit event halls, an outdoor stage with 12,000 seats, and 20 hectares planted in herbs and lavender.

The theme of Canadian World was less a mosaic of Canada than it was a park devoted to the world of Anne of Green Gables. The entrance to the Canadian World was a replica of Kensingston Station in P.E.I. The north gateway was Brightriver Station, where Anne first met with Matthew. There was a full-scale copy of the Green Gables house, Orwell School where you could actually learn English like Anne did, and so forth. Canadian World employed 55 full-time and 330 part-time staff. This included a high school girl from P.E.I. who played Anne—complete with (dyed) red hair—dressed in Victorian period costume.

In late August 1991, Canadian World still had a lot of P.E.I. Preserves' products for sale. Lower than expected sales could be traced to a variety of problems. First, overall

Exhibit 7   Example of Price Markups in Japan

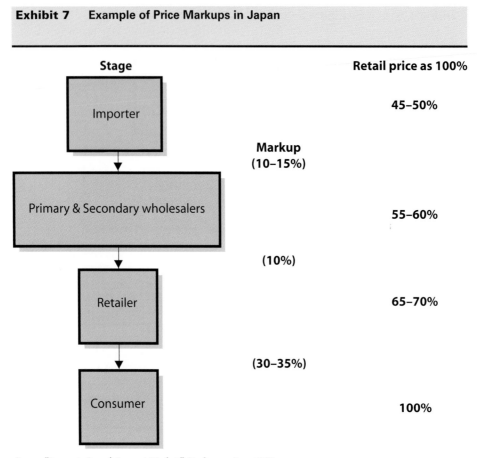

Stage		Retail price as 100%
Importer		45–50%
	Markup (10–15%)	
Primary & Secondary wholesalers		55–60%
	(10%)	
Retailer		65–70%
	(30–35%)	
Consumer		100%

Source: "Access to Japan's Import Market," *Tradescope*, June 1989.

attendance at Canadian World had been 205,000 in the first year, significantly lower than the expected 300,000. Second, the product was priced higher than many competitive offerings. For reasons unknown to Canadian World staff, the product sold for 10 per cent more than expected (¥1,200 versus ¥1,086).

Wholesale price in P.E.I.	$3.50
Freight ($4.20/kilo, P.E.I. to Hokkaido)	0.80
Duty (28% of wholesale price + freight)	1.20
Landed cost in Japan	5.50
Importer's Margin (15%)	0.83
Price to Primary Wholesaler	6.33
Wholesaler Margin (10%)	0.63
Price to Retailer	6.96
Canadian World mark up (30%)	2.09
Expected retail price	$9.05
Exchange (Cdn$1.00 = 120 yen)	¥1,086

Third, the product mix chosen by the Japanese buyers appeared to be inappropriate. While it was difficult to locate any of the company's remaining strawberry preserves in the various Canadian World outlets which carried it, other products had not moved at all. Canadian World personnel did not have a tracking system for product-by-product sales. Fourth, the company's gift packs were not always appropriately sized

or priced. One suggestion had been to package the preserves in cardboard gift boxes of three large (250-millilitre) or five small (125-millilitre) bottles for eventual sale for under ¥2,000.

An increasing portion of all of the gifts being sold at Canadian World were, in fact, being made in Japan. Japanese sourcing was common due to the high Japanese duties on imports, the transportation costs from Canada, and the unfamiliarity of Canadian companies with Japanese consumer preferences.

THE TOKYO MARKET

With 10 million residents, Tokyo was the largest city in Japan and one of the most crowded cities anywhere. Thirty million people lived within 50 kilometres of Tokyo's Imperial Palace. As the economic centre of the nation, Tokyo also had the most expensive land in the world—US$150,000 per square metre in the city centre. Retail space in one of Tokyo's major shopping districts would cost $75 to $160 per square metre or $1,600 to $3,400 per month for a shop equivalent in size to that in the CP Prince Edward Hotel. Prices in the Ginza were even higher. In addition to basic rent, all locations required a deposit (guarantee money which would be repaid when the tenant gave up the lease) of at least $25,000. Half of the locations available in a recent

To expand sales of imported jam or to enter the Japanese market for the first time, it is necessary to develop products after precise study of the market's needs. Importers who are making efforts to tailor their products to the Japanese market have been successfully expanding their sales by 10 per cent each year. Based on the analysis of successful cases of imported jam, the following factors may be considered very important.

Diversification of consumer preferences: Strawberry jam occupies about 50 per cent of the total demand for jam and its share is continuing to rise. Simultaneously, more and more varieties of jam are being introduced.

Low sugar content: European exporters have successfully exported low sugar jam that meets the needs of the Japanese market. Jam with a sugar content of less than 65 per cent occupies a share of 65 to 70 per cent of the market on a volume basis.

Smaller containers: Foreign manufacturers who stick to packaging products in large-sized containers (650 grams, 440 grams, 250 grams), even though their products are designed for household use, have been failing to expand their sales. On the other hand, foreign manufacturers who have developed products in smaller containers (14 grams, 30 grams, 42 grams) specifically for the Japanese market have achieved successful results.

Fashionable items: Contents and quantity are not the only important aspects of jam. The shape and material quality of the containers and their caps, label design and product name can also influence sales. It is also important that the label not be damaged in any way.

Development of gift items: Sets of various types of imported jams are popular as gift items. For example, there are sets of 10 kinds of jam in 40-gram mini-jars (retail price ¥2,000) sold as gift sets.

Selection of distribution channel: Since general trading companies, specialty importers and jam manufacturers each have their own established distribution channels, the selection of the most appropriate channel is of the utmost importance.

Source: "Access to Japan's Import Market," *Tradescope,* June 1989.

survey also charged administrative/maintenance fees (five to 12 per cent of rent), while in about one-third of the locations a "reward" (gift) was paid by tenants to the owner at the time the contract was signed. For a small site it might amount to $10,000 to $15,000.

THE TORONTO MARKET

With three million people, Toronto was Canada's largest city and economic centre. It contained the country's busiest airport (15 million people used it each year) and was a popular destination for tourists. Each year, roughly 20 million people visited Toronto for business or vacation.

MacNaughton's interest in Toronto was due to its size, the local awareness of P.E.I., and the high perceived potential volume of sales. The company did not have a sales agent in Toronto.

The Toronto market was well served by mass market and specialty jam producers at all price points. Numerous domestic and imported products were available. Prices started as low as $1.00 (or less) for a 250-millilitre bottle of high sugar/low fruit product. Prices increased to $2.00 to $2.50 for higher fruit, natural brands and increased again to $3.00 to $3.50 for many of the popular branded imports. The highest priced products, such as P.E.I. Preserves, were characterized by even higher fruit content, highest quality ingredients, and a broader selection of product offerings.

The specialty domestic producers were from various provinces and tended to have limited distribution areas. The specialty imports were frequently from France or England. The Canadian tariff on imports was 15 per cent for most countries. From the United States, it was 10.5 per cent and declining.

The cost of retail space in Toronto varied according to location but was slightly lower than that in Tokyo. The cost of renting 22 square metres would be $100 per square metre per month (plus common area charges and taxes of $15 per square metre per month) in a major suburban shopping mall, and somewhat higher in the downtown core. Retail staff salaries were similar in Toronto and Tokyo, both of which were higher than those paid in P.E.I.

Future Directions

MacNaughton was the first to acknowledge that, while the business had been "built on gut and emotion, rather than analysis," this was insufficient for the future. The challenge was to determine the direction and timing of the desired change.

Carrefour vs. Wal-Mart: The Battle for Global Retail Dominance

"La Commission Européenne autorise la fusion CARREFOUR-PROMODES qui donne naissance au 2éme distributeur mondial."[1] The words virtually screamed across the screen of Carrefour's webpage on January 25, 2000 as the European Commission finally ruled on Carrefour's friendly US$16.6 billion takeover bid for its rival Promodes.

Only one year after winning the Soccer World Cup, France was offering Europe another champion. With around 9,000 stores in 21 countries and combined net sales of US$49.2 billion, the new Carrefour was Europe's top retailer, vaulting over Germany's Metro AG, the continent's former number one (Exhibit 1 provides a list of the top European retailers). The bid took analysts by surprise as Carrefour and Promodes, the fifth and seventh largest European retailers respectively, were better known for their long history of vigorous rivalry.

The deal was seen by many as a defensive move by the French retailing establishment after the world's largest retailer, Wal-Mart, boosted its presence in Europe with a US$10 billion [takeover] of Britain's ASDA in June 1999 (Exhibit 2 provides a brief description of [the] world's top grocery retailers). The marriage was clearly an externally driven affair. "I am convinced that if we had not moved, somebody else would have it done for us," declared Luc Vandevelde, Promodes' CEO.

Wal-Mart discretely entered the European market in 1997 through the acquisition of 21 warehouses from the German chain Wertkauf GmbH. In 1998 it acquired a further 74 warehouses from Spar Handels AG. But it was only after the acquisition of ASDA that French retailers took the American threat seriously. When Wal-Mart started approaching top French retailers looking about for potential acquisition opportunities, including, interestingly, both Carrefour and Promodes, French retailers soon began to recognize that their world had changed dramatically and they needed to adjust their strategies accordingly and quickly.

Faced with the potential threat of a hostile [takeover] from Wal-Mart, the two rival French chains decided that a joint effort was their best defense. Apart from reinforcing their defensive position in Europe, the merger widened Carrefour's impressive lead in several Latin American and Asian countries as well. Together, the two companies generally held first or second position in all the markets where they were present. Some of these markets, like South America, were already facing direct competition from Wal-Mart (Exhibit 3 provides a summary of Carrefour's and Wal-Mart's geographic distribution of stores). Also, the skill mix of the two firms was complementary. Promodes brought to the union a reputation for solid inventory and distribution systems, an area where Carrefour had long lagged behind Wal-Mart. Carrefour was looked upon as a customer-retailing innovator, an area where Promodes was generally weaker and Wal-Mart had near legendary status.

Carrefour was set to challenge Wal-Mart around the globe. "We're creating a world-wide retail leader," said Carrefour's CEO Daniel Bernard. In its approach to the European market Wal-Mart knew it faced fierce competition from local players. However, it could never predict that because of its own actions it set about creating its most feared competitor ever and had done so on a global scale. A war of titans was about to take place.

THE DISCOUNT RETAILING INDUSTRY

The discount retail industry emerged in the United States in the mid-1950s. Americans, accustomed to the supermarket

[1] "European Commission clears the merger of CARREFOUR and PRO-MODES to create the world's second largest retailer."

Exhibit 1   Top European Food Retailers (US$ Millions)

	Country	Control Structure	Estimated European Sales (US$ m)	Market Share (%)
1 Metro	Germany	Listed	34,594	4.7
2 Tesco	UK	Listed	30,548	4.1
3 Intermarche	France	Coop	30,408	4.1
4 Rewe	Germany	NA	26,450	3.6
5 Carrefour	France	Listed	23,799	3.2
6 Aldi	Germany	Family	22,800	3.1
7 Promodes	France	Listed/Family	22,017	3.0
8 Lederc	France	Coop	22,000	3.0
9 Auchan	France	Family	21,870	3.0
10 J. Sainsbury	UK	Listed	21,438	2.9
11 Edeka/AVA	Germany	Coop	19,500	2.6
12 Casino	France	Listed/Rallye	14,810	2.0
13 Asda	UK	Listed	13,836	1.9
14 Safeway	UK	Listed	12,303	1.7
15 Tengelmann	Germany	Family	11,950	1.6
16 Migros	Switzerland	NA	11,280	1.5
17 Lidl & Schwarz	Germany	Family	10,639	1.4
18 Ahold	Netherlands	Listed	10,529	1.4
19 Somerfield	UK	Listed	10,000	1.4
20 SchweizCoop	Switzerland	NA	7,900	1.1

Source: Warburg Dillon Read (Europe), estimate as of 11 November 1998.

concept and better informed, as manufacturers intensified TV advertising after World War II, took the concept of self-service to heart. The basic discount concept relied on charging gross margins that were 10 to 15 percent lower than those found in department stores for general merchandise. To ensure profitability with the lower margins, operational selling costs were kept to a minimum: fixtures were distinctly unluxurious; in-store selling was limited; and ancillary services, such as credit and delivery, were scarce.

The growth of the industry was nothing short of spectacular. In the United States, the growth into the 1970s cranked ahead at compound annual rates averaging around 25 percent. Such opportunity attracted many players at the local, regional and national level. Throughout the 1970s the industry continued to grow but at the much slower rate of 9 percent per annum. By the 1980s this had slowed further to around 7 percent per year. As the competitive landscape filled up, the industry players were under intensifying pressure to push costs down, increase store-selling areas and widen their market coverage. This led to a flurry of mergers and acquisitions aimed at increasing profit from the scale economies resulting from aggregated purchase power and the spreading of operational fixed costs. Between 1986 and 1993 concentration increased substantially, with the top 5 retailers accounting for 62 percent of the sales in 1986 and 72 percent in 1993.

In Europe the discount industry concept lagged American developments. Carrefour invented the "hypermarket"[2] concept in the early 1960s, with many players following in its footsteps by increasing the surface area of their existing supermarket chains and diversifying into non-food items. Due to the fragmentation of the European market and the lower liquidity of its capital markets, the concentration of European retailers was much lower than in the U.S. As late as 1998, the top 5 retailers accounted for only 20 percent of the total of the market with the top 20 holding only 51 percent of the market.

The smaller size of the individual European markets drove discount players to move abroad as early as the beginning of the 1970s. To succeed and grow in this environment, European players had to adapt their operations to different cultures, and this naturally led to a more decentralized approach to the business. Furthermore, although Europe, in total, was the biggest retail market in the world, the lower levels of concentrations and the decentralization of

---

[2] According to the *Libre Service Actualites*, a hypermarket could be physically distinguished by a sales area of at least 27,000 sq. ft., a large variety of food and general merchandise, self-service and payment at central checkouts, and a car park with a minimum capacity of 1,000 vehicles. Furthermore, hypermarkets operate on lower unit margins, are built on cheaper land and have lower operating expenses per unit sold than a traditional supermarket.

Exhibit 2   Top Global Grocery Retailers

Retailers (Country of Origin)	Revenues 1997 (US$ Millions)	CAGR (%)	Store Formats	Geographic Presence 1998
Wal-Mart Stores (U.S.)	117,960	12.7% (3 year to FY98)	Discount Superstore (1,869 stores—Wal-Mart), Discount Department Stores (564 stores—Wal-Mart Supercenters); Warehouse Club (451 stores—SAM's Club); International (701 stores)	*North America:* U.S. (2,433 stores), Canada (153 stores); *Europe:* Germany (95 stores); *Central and South America:* Mexico (416 stores), Argentina (13 stores), Puerto Rico (15 stores), Brazil (14 stores); *Asia:* Indonesia, China (3 stores)
Metro Holding AG (Germany)	43,000	6% (4 year to FY98)	*Total stores:* 2,085; Cash & Carry, Department Stores, Hypermarkets, Food Stores, Consumer Electronics, Home Improvement, Apparel	*Europe:* Germany (1,723 stores), Austria, France, Switzerland, the Netherlands, Italy, Belgium, Spain, Poland, Hungary, Luxembourg, Greece, Turkey, Romania, Denmark, Great Britain; *Asia:* China
Ito-Yokado (Japan)	40,100	3% (5 year to FY97)	Retail Stores (400 stores); Restaurants (800 restaurants); Convenience Stores (17,000+ stores including 10,000+ Seven-Eleven)	Global
Albertson's Inc. (U.S.)	33,400	8.3% (3 year to FY98)	*Total Stores:* 983; Combination Food-Drug Stores, Supermarkets, Warehouse Clubs (40 stores—Max Food and Drug)	*North America:* U.S. (985 stores)
Auchan SA (France)	33,300	27% (3 year, 94–97)	Hypermarkets, Electronics Superstores, Garden Products Stores	*Europe:* France, Portugal, Spain, Italy, Poland, Hungary, Luxembourg; *Central America:* Mexico
Rewe Zentrale AG (Germany)	32,000	7% (3 year, 94–97)	Supermarkets and Hypermarkets (60 stores—Otto Mess, Jumbo and Globus); Travel Agencies (284 agencies—Atlas); Consumer Electronics Stores (68 stores—Uni-Markt, Electroland, Diehl); Supermarket (5,977 stores); Discount Stores (2,045 stores—Penny)	*Europe:* Germany (5,500 stores); 11,230 stores in Czech Republic, Austria and Poland
Royal Ahold (The Netherlands)	25,300	17.6% (5 year to FY97)	*Total stores:* 3,600+; Supermarkets, Hypermarkets, Convenience Stores, Specialty Stores, Wholesaling Operations, Food Manufacturers	*Europe:* [the] Netherlands (1,500+ stores), Belgium, Czech Republic, Poland, Portugal, Spain; *North America:* U.S. (536 stores); *Asia:* Singapore, China, Indonesia, Malaysia, Thailand; *South America:* Argentina, Brazil, Chile, Ecuador, Paraguay, Peru
Carrefour SA (France)	28,933	6% (3 year to FY98)	*Total Stores:* 1,640; Hypermarkets (325 stores), Deep Discount stores (370 stores—Ed l'Epicier and Ed le Marche), Supermarkets (800 stores—Comptoirs Moderne), Convenience Stores and Frozen/Prepared Food Outlets	*Europe:* France, Spain (Pryca), Italy, Portugal, Turkey; *South and Central America:* Argentina, Brazil, Chile, Colombia, Mexico; *Asia:* China, Korea, Hong Kong, Malaysia, Taiwan, Thailand

Exhibit 2   (continued)

Retailers (Country of Origin)	Revenues 1997 (US$ Millions)	CAGR (%)	Store Formats	Geographic Presence 1998
J Sainsbury plc (UK)	28,600	8% (5 year to FY97)	*Total Stores:* 800; Retail Chains; Bank (Sainsbury Bank) Supermarket (400 stores—Sainsbury's) Supermarkets (127 stores—Shaw's); Hypermarkets (13 stores—Savacentres); Garden & DIY (298 stores—Homebase)	*Europe:* UK; *North America:* U.S.
Aldi (Germany)	28,500	4% (3 year, 94–97)	*Total Stores:* 4,000+	*Europe:* Germany (3125 stores), Austria (200 stores), Belgium (280 stores), Denmark (180 stores), France (325 stores), U.K. (200 stores), Italy (100 stores), the Netherlands (330 stores), Poland (1 store); *North America:* U.S. (500 stores)
Intermarché (France)	28,200	9% (3 year, 94–97)	Supermarkets independently owned (1,558 stores—Intermarché, Ecomarché, Supermarché and CDM); Hypermarkets (78 stores); DIY stores (335 stores—Bricomarché); Clothing stores (100 stores—Vétimarché); Restaurants (53 restaurants—Restaumarché)	*Europe:* France, Belgium, Italy, Poland, Portugal, Germany, Spain
Promodés SA (France)	27,300	6% (5 year to FY97)	*Total Stores:* 4,800+; Hypermarkets (Continent); Supermarkets (Champion and Mega Fresco); Convenience Stores (Shopi, 8 a Huit, Codec, Di per Di, Superettes); Discount Stores (Dia); Specialist Distribution (Promocash, Prodirest, Negoce, the Puntocash, Docks Market)	*Europe:* France (614 Hypermarkets & Supermarkets and 987 Convenience Stores), Belgium, Spain, Germany, Italy, Portugal, Greece; *South America:* Argentina; *Asia:* Indonesia, South Korea
Kroger (U.S.)	26,567	5.6% (3 year FY98)	Food Stores (1,410 stores); Convenience Stores (797 stores); Manufacturing Sites (34 sites)	*North America:* U.S.

Source: MVI, Euromonitor, OneSource, Wright Investors Service, Annual Reports, Press.

European players made it difficult for them to achieve the same level of benefit from economies of scale as their American counterparts.

As the discount retail industry developed, the formats found operating became more structured. Nowadays, the market has coalesced into five formats worldwide: hypermarkets, discount department stores, hard discounts, category killers and warehouse clubs and cash & carry.

Hypermarkets are identified by their size and product mix. They range in sales area from 5,000 sq. mt. (55,000 sq. ft.) to 15,000 sq. mt. (165,000 sq. ft.) and possess a 50/50 split between food and non-food products. In both general categories the assortment is large—in terms of the number of product categories one can find—and deep—in terms of the number of the brands within any specific category. Hypermarkets are fresh product oriented and this is considered to be [a source] of differentiation that generates client loyalty. The atmosphere is one of cleanliness with sophisticated presentation and customer oriented merchandise. The service is considered the best amongst the four formats and the promotional effort is very high, with promotions focused, in the majority, on food segment products.

Exhibit 3   Carrefour SA and Wal-Mart Stores Inc.—Store Count by Format, 1999 (Carrefour values only include outlets within the consolidation)

Carrefour SA	Hypermarkets	Supermarkets	Hard Discount
Europe			
France	179	526	418
Spain	112	180	1,532
Portugal	5	—	273
Italy	6	—	—
Turkey	5	—	—
Poland	7	6	—
Czech Republic	3	—	—
Greece	4	—	142
Total	321	712	2,374
Americas			
Argentina	22	—	106
Brazil	69	83	—
Mexico	17	—	—
Chile	2	—	—
Colombia	2	—	—
Total	112	83	106
Asia			
Taiwan	23	—	—
Malaysia	6	—	—
China	21	—	—
Korea	12	—	—
Indonesia	5	—	—
Singapore	1	—	—
Hong Kong	4	—	—
Thailand	9	—	—
Total	81	—	—
Total	514	795	2,480

Wal-Mart Stores Inc.	Discount Store[s]	Supercenters	SAM's Club
Americas			
United States	1,801	721	463
Canada	166	—	—
Mexico	397	27	34
Argentina	—	10	3
Brazil	—	9	5
Puerto Rico	9	—	6
Total	2,373	767	511
Europe			
Germany	—	95	—
United Kingdom	—	232	—
Total	0	327	0
Asia			
Korea	—	5	—
China	—	5	1
Total	0	10	1
Total	2,373	1,104	512

Source: Carrefour and Wal-Mart Annual Reports.

The discount department store format is similar to the hypermarket. It can be distinguished by a 30 percent space allocation to the food products (with a consequential lower depth in each food category assortment); a no-frills atmosphere; lower service levels (identical to that of a category killer but superior to that found in warehouses clubs and cash & carries); and an [everyday]-low-price policy. Promotions rarely number more than one a month equally split between food and non-food categories.

Hard discounting is a concept initiated in Germany in the early 1960s, aimed at achieving the lowest possible costs. Hard discount stores are characterized by a sales area ranging from 500 sq. mt. (5,500 sq. ft.) to 1,000 sq. mt. (11,000 sq. ft.). They sell a limited food assortment offering only one size of one product per category of product. Private labels represent 85 percent of the assortment and, for each category, clients will find either the private label product or the national brand product, but not both. As a result of assortment simplification, hard discount operations have between 500 to 1,000 SKUs (compared to an average of 30,000 SKUs in a hypermarket). Contrary to other formats goods are served from palettes. Not a cent is wasted on service with shoppers having to pay for shopping bags and payments are only accepted in cash. The resulting concept allows hard discounters to sell goods at 30 percent below nationally branded products.

Category killers are operationally very similar to discount department stores but focus [on] a single category (e.g., Toys 'R' Us in the toys category). Category killers offer the widest and deepest range of products within the category. Normally they do not offer a significant price advantage, but do offer enough so as not to lose clients to other discounters. Their broad product offerings at competitive prices are possible through logistical and operational specialization and by favorable terms with suppliers.

Warehouse clubs and cash & carries are very similar concepts but they do possess slight differences. Cash & carries allocate more space to food departments and, consequently, the depth of the food assortment is superior. About 70 percent of their promotional efforts focus on food items. Both formats are business oriented (normally through membership cards) and can be differentiated from the other formats through their lower level of service and lower prices.

THE COMPANIES

Carrefour

The second largest retailer in the world after Wal-Mart, Carrefour had humble beginnings. The first store, a 650 sq. mt. (7,000 sq. ft.) basement operation in a Fournier department store in Annecy, France, was opened by Marcel Fournier and Louis Defforey in the summer of 1960. This was followed quite quickly by the first Carrefour "hypermarket," which was established at the intersection of five roads (Carrefour means "crossroads") in Sainte-Genevieve-des-Bois outside Paris. The store was a first of its kind; it covered 2,500 sq. mt. (27,000 sq. ft.) and provided parking for 450 cars. It was an initial test of the one-stop shop formula where consumers could get almost all of their shopping needs satisfied at one location. The store provided self-service grocery shopping at discount prices and stocked items such as clothing, sporting equipment, auto accessories, and consumer electronics.

French consumers were enthusiastic in their acceptance of the Carrefour hypermarket concept and the company grew rapidly. Between 1965 and 1971, sales growth exceeded 50 percent per annum with non-food items accounting for about 40 percent of the total volume. Starting in 1970, Carrefour opened the first of its "commercial centers," colossal operations with piling areas as large as 25,000 sq. mt. (270,000 sq. ft.). By the end of 1971, the company was operating 16 wholly owned stores, had an equity interest in 5 stores operated as joint ventures, and had franchise agreements with 7 additional stores.

With a move into Belgium in 1969, Carrefour began its internationalization and by 1999, after the merger with Promodes, it had 681 hypermarkets, 2,259 supermarkets, 3,124 hard discount stores, and 1,921 convenience stores and other formats selling under its banner. The stores were located mostly in France but also throughout Europe, Asia, and Latin America.

The Hypermarket Concept and Strategy   The hypermarket concept was invented by Carrefour. Carrefour's hypermarkets averaged 10,034 sq. mt. (108,000 sq. ft.) and were usually located within a commercial center. The firm's location strategy was to place stores outside towns in areas where highways provided easy access and land could be acquired inexpensively. The company also favored simple facility construction. This gave it a total investment per square meter of selling space in a fully equipped store equal to about one-third that of traditional supermarkets and department stores.

The high degree of consumer acceptance that fuelled Carrefour's growth stemmed, in large part, from factors such as convenience and price. Almost any product a consumer could think of purchasing more than once a year could be bought at a Carrefour store. The company even operated discount gasoline outlets at many stores. Indeed, Carrefour operated 5 of the 10 largest volume gasoline stations in France.

Although convenience was undoubtedly a strong factor in Carrefour's growth, so too was price. Carrefour's prices averaged 5 to 10 percentage points under those of retailers in traditional outlets. Gross margins on food and non-food products differed somewhat, but Carrefour operated on an average gross margin of about 15 percent, which, in 1988, translated into a 4.5 percent operating margin after SG&A (Exhibit 4 provides a financial summary of Carrefour).

Exhibit 4   Carrefour SA, Financial Summary 1992–1999 (€ Millions)

	1992	1993	1994	1995	1996	1997	1998	1999*
Operating Results								
Net Sales	17,857	18,782	20,779	22,046	23,615	25,805	27,409	51,948
License Fees and Other Income	202	199	178	194	179	214	274	583
Cost of Goods Sold	14,850	15,632	17,116	17,969	19,067	20,601	21,629	40,824
Operating, SG&A Expenses	2,853	2,926	3,334	3,671	3,995	4,533	5,024	9,909
Interest Cost	−7	−278	−45	−241	−98	−91	48	272
Taxes	92	133	148	211	250	320	351	599
Net Income	271	568	404	630	580	656	632	927
Financial Position								
Current Assets	3,434	3,412	3,786	4,228	4,702	4,820	5,235	12,343
Net Property P&E	3,024	3,152	3,550	4,113	5,133	6,452	7,141	12,113
Current Liabilities	4,966	4,793	5,475	5,701	6,803	6,741	9,633	17,911
Long-term Borrowings	802	673	636	686	576	1,331	2,211	6,733
Shareholder's Equity	1,923	2,207	2,394	2,983	3,711	4,516	4,857	7,905
Share Information								
Market Capitalization	4,514	8,160	8,419	11,339	19,795	18,418	24,984	51,285
Shares (Million)	451	448	449	451	462	462	466	698
Price/Book Value (€)	3.00	4.57	4.67	4.82	6.82	5.28	6.67	11.39
Price/Earnings (€)	22.69	16.87	26.70	21.54	41.58	33.72	40.25	69.79
Dividend Yld (%)	2.06	1.22	1.42	1.31	0.95	1.24	1.07	0.67
Financial Ratios (%)								
Return on Assets	4.5	8.8	6.2	8.6	6.9	6.7	5.6	3.1
Return on Shareholders' Equity	17.1	29.5	18.3	26.3	19.4	17.7	14.0	10.1
Operational Data								
Number Domestic Stores (H/O)**	118/367	114/432	114/481	117/465	117/356	117/367	117/782	179/944
Number International Stores	83/2	90/11	108/39	128/48	158/0	191/0	234/0	335/2331
Number Employees (000)	76	82	90	101	104	113	133	194

*Carrefour and Promodes Consolidated Proforma accounts over the whole 1999 year; ** H – Hypermarket; O – Other Formats (does not include Picard Surgeles – Frozen Food Chain in France with 457 stores in 1999).

Source: Bloomberg 2000, Annual Reports.

As competitors picked up the concept, Carrefour felt the need to differentiate itself and to better respond to client needs. Differentiation for Carrefour meant developing a local products purchasing base and selling private labels. Purchasing locally was one of [. . .] Carrefour's key strategies, both in France and internationally. This was seen as a way to please local authorities and to meet local customers needs. Buying locally supported Carrefour's specialization strategy, which aimed to position it as the leader in every fresh product department (butchery, bakery, delicatessen, etc.).

Private labels provided customers with a value-for-money offer over national brand products. The private label program was started in 1976, and by 1993 Carrefour offered almost 4,300 lines of its own branded products. This line was so extensive that in some countries there were only Carrefour products in certain categories. The proposition was a good one for consumers since technical quality was equivalent to national brand products and the prices normally ranged between 15 to 35 percent lower than that of national brands. Although Carrefour's overall pricing was heavily promotional, with frequent sales and special discounts supported by weekly circulars, its private label offering had a fixed price all year round.

To further increase its responsiveness to local needs, Carrefour decentralized management. Each store manager operated a store with almost complete freedom in decision making. One Carrefour store manager (who incidentally was paid FF12,000 per month versus FF2,500 two years earlier when he was a store manager in a smaller competing supermarket chain) made the following comment: "My previous job was demoralizing. It took a month to get authorization to buy something for the store that cost FF14. Now I am free to make all of my own decisions. I can hire 10 people, buy a new refrigeration unit, or hire a band for a parking lot festival."

The decentralized operations were later recognized as a key success factor underlying Carrefour's national and international achievements. The ability to react to local conditions had enabled the stores to thrive in such diverse locations as Taiwan and Argentina, and in erratic economic circumstances, like the hyperinflationary period in Brazil.

Headquarters and Control   Initially, Carrefour was divided into two levels, headquarters and stores. The head office in Paris contained the "Direction Général," which dealt with long-term strategy and policy [and] financial and technical matters, and provided advice when requested. It also acted as a source of "intellectual capital" in terms of information and experience. One of [the] major responsibilities of the headquarters was the selection of new store locations.

As the complexity of controlling the stores' marketing efforts and integrating the company image and operations as a whole, while keeping a decentralized structure, increased more levels of control were added over the years. For example, for a country like Spain or France, each store would report to a regional headquarters, which would then report to the national headquarters and this national headquarters would then report to the European officer. The European officer jointly with other world region officers and the CEO would constitute the Executive Committee in charge of managing Carrefour's operations globally. Initially this committee was physically located in Paris at Carrefour's global headquarters, but after 1998 each world region officer was deployed to live in the region s/he was managing. (Exhibit 5 provides a structure of Carrefour officers and Exhibit 6 provides operational indicators by division.)

The financial control function was held at the regional headquarter[s] level, although a great degree of freedom was given to store managers in terms of formulating forecasts. Forecasts were prepared at the department level in each store and would include both sales and margins. These were then negotiated with the store manager and, when an agreement was reached, the forecast was sent to the headquarters' controller (normally before mid-December). The controller, jointly with the store managers in the region, would then vet the forecasts for consistency with previous performance, company strategy and the expectations developed from similar forecasts from other stores. The store manager had the final word on the forecast.

Store managers were judged on whether they met their forecasts and on profit performance. Individual stores' monthly performance figures were often used for benchmarking and were then sent to all store managers and department heads so they could compare their performance with other stores. Store managers in the same region met regularly to discuss budgets and share information and experiences. Store managers were not paid based on reaching precise results but "good" performance was rewarded with pay increases and promotions. Due to the subjectivity of these performance measures, a store manager in a good region sometimes had faster career development [than] a store manager in a bad region, but a store manager unwilling to manage a store in a bad region would be seen as not "sharing the Carrefour spirit."

Store Operations   Store managers and department heads were the key people in the stores. The store manager and his/her department heads had nearly total responsibility and control over their store. The store manager allocated the area for each department within the store and was in charge of general advertising and decoration policies for the store. Jointly with department heads, s/he would decide on the product mix and make sure that all departments presented coherent positioning. Each department was a profit center, with its own targets and income statements. The department head had full responsibility over purchasing, promotion, pricing and motivating and training his/her assistants.

Department heads decided what they wanted to buy and from where. They would buy centrally through Carrefour's central purchasing only when the advantages of mass purchasing outweighed the advantages of local buying. This meant that the range of products varied from store to store and that a supplier would (at least initially) have to negotiate with all the stores in order to guarantee the presence of its products in a certain region or at a national level. In order to leverage its purchasing power, Carrefour had, over the years, centralized negotiations with some suppliers at the headquarters level. With aggregate agreements covering all stores, these suppliers could be confident of their products' presence in most all stores, both regionally and nationally (depending on the arrangement). Nevertheless, for many products local buying was essential. This was especially the case in areas where regional specialties and highly perishable products were seen as sources of differentiation. Generally, product mix varied from store to store and local products could represent up to 30 percent of an individual store's food sales.

Pricing was the complete responsibility of department heads, both for the products purchased locally and centrally.[3] In order to ensure the veracity of its aggressive pricing policy Carrefour conducted extensive price scannings of all competitors within 5 minutes driving time of any store. These scannings were done 3 to 4 times a week for the top 20 percent of products, which accounted for 80 percent of sales, and once a week for the remaining products. Prices

---

[3] Centralized purchased products were "sold" to all the stores at a transfer [price] set by the headquarters. This transfer price was used as "their" cost by department heads when their department's margins were calculated.

Exhibit 5   Carrefour SA Officers, 1999

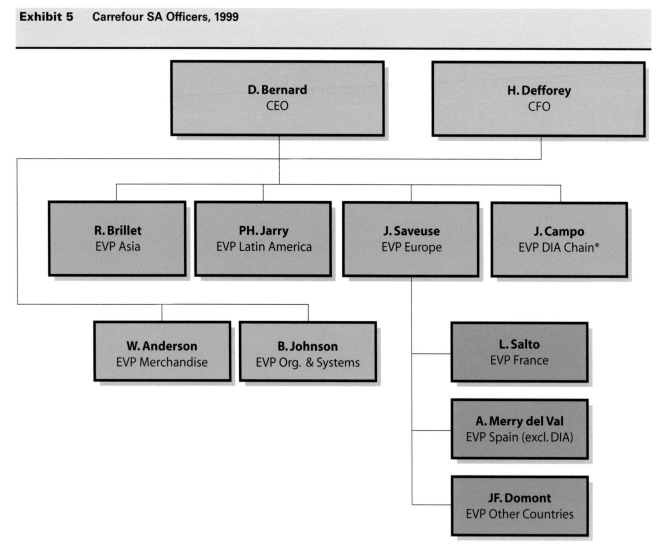

*DIA is a hard discount chain formerly developed and owned by Promodes.

were then set either equal to or below the competitor's level. Invariably because of its decentralized pricing system, customers at four Carrefour stores in a large city could find the same product being offered at four different prices.

Due to Carrefour's extreme level of store decentralization support areas that were not directly under store responsibility, such as IT and logistics, were normally treated as vendors. Over time this led to under-investment and the company's support services generally lagged behind the market leaders in terms of efficiency. For example, department heads would order products centrally without caring about economic order quantity or any other logistic matter. When it came to IT, managers [were] fairly parochial. For their needs only cashier operations and basic information on sales and margins were of interest. Communications were distinctly low-tech; any transmission of information with external partners, including with headquarters, was done through fax sheets. For example, in the budget process, the

same figure could be introduced into a spreadsheet up to four times at the four different organizational levels (store, regional, national and international headquarters). As a result, operating and SG&A expenses amounted to 18 percent of sales when compared with the 16 percent experienced by Promodes or Wal-Mart.

Any person, despite his/her formal education, could potentially become the president of Carrefour. A typical "Carrefour-man" would start from the bottom of the store level and work his/her way up through dedication and performance. Although this path has changed in recent years, Carrefour promoted managers internally, hiring from the outside only when the skills needed could not be found in-house. On-the-job-training was applied to all the levels in the store. All managers and department heads were trained in existing stores for at least a year. A prospective store manager would move through all the departments of the store, and if they were appointed to a new store, they would be on-site at

Exhibit 6   Carrefour SA, Net Sales, Operational Income, and Total Assets, by Division, 1997–1999

(€ Millions)	1997	1998	1999*
Net Sales			
France	14,685	15,524	32,347
Europe	3,809	3,920	11,272
America	5,739	6,222	5,580
Asia	1,572	1,742	2,749
Total	25,805	27,409	51,948
Operational Income			
France	472	595	1,298
Europe	174	173	288
America	197	232	173
Asia	42	31	39
Total	885	1,031	1,798
Total Assets			
France	5,426	8,577	NA
Europe	3,648	4,349	NA
America	3,478	3,467	NA
Asia	701	990	NA
Total	13,253	17,383	NA

*Carrefour and Promodes consolidated pro forma accounts.

Source: Carrefour Annual Reports.

the beginning of the construction. Each level in Carrefour was responsible for training and developing the level below.

Model of Expansion: Joint Ventures and Franchises

Throughout the late 1960s and early 1970s, Carrefour's rapid growth was made possible by the fact that the firm had been able to get two new construction permits per year. As more firms entered the discount retail market, the competition for permits became more fierce as many firms and individuals fought for authorization to build in attractive locations.

In the late 1960s, in order to achieve a more rapid pace of expansion than the firm could achieve if it were limited to two new stores per year, Carrefour offered to share its retailing know-how, trademark, and consumer goodwill with potential partners both in France and elsewhere in Europe; either in exchange for an ownership interest in stores under construction or franchise fees. Carrefour's ownership interests in joint ventures ranged from 10 percent to 80 percent. Under a typical franchise arrangement, Carrefour received 0.2 percent of total store sales and its central buying office for non-food products (SAMOD, an 89 percent owned subsidiary of Carrefour) received 1 percent of a store's sales of non-food items. Franchisees were required to use a control system similar to Carrefour's and to submit their forecasts and results to Carrefour's controller.

Because of increasing competition between Carrefour's wholly owned stores and its franchised stores and the failure of some franchisees to operate according to the strict company policies, all franchise agreements were discontinued in January 1973. These agreements were either turned into joint ventures or dissolved completely. From that moment on, joint ventures were the only shared ownership model of expansion used by Carrefour. As participation in some joint ventures was lower than the legal accounting consolidation requirement—and hence some of the activity did not appear in the financial statements—the true expanse of Carrefour's operations tended to be underestimated. For example, the firm's 1999 Annual Report presented sales of €58,548 (including taxes) from 4,246 outlets worldwide while, in reality, the total sales realized under the Carrefour brand was actually €77,533 from over 8,000 stores worldwide. (Exhibit 7 provides segmentation by region and concept of sales under Carrefour's banners.)

Limitations to Growth in Europe

The growth of the hypermarket was not without its political and social consequences. The hypermarket forced an economic rationalization of the traditional retail sector that was especially severe for many small shopkeepers. Almost 80,000 of the 203,600 small retail shops in operation in France in 1961 had disappeared by 1971. These small shopkeepers represented a significant political force in France and slowing down the growth of hypermarkets was seen as the way [to address] their concerns. The French government—and later on nearly every country in Europe—made it difficult to obtain construction permits to build large new retail stores. This prompted some discount retailers to offer plans for large commercial centers where space could be leased to as many as 40 independent shopkeepers. This type of plan allowed small merchants to set up specialty stores and boutiques and it usually generated some measure of local merchant support for the issuance of permits.

However, in an attempt to attack the problem in broader terms, the French National Assembly passed legislation in 1972 to tax retail stores in order to provide pensions for small shopkeepers who were unable to continue in business. The tax was to be paid by all retail merchants; the heaviest burden was to be borne by operators of large stores built after 1962. Carrefour's tax amounted to roughly 0.15 percent of sales.

International Expansion

The success of Carrefour's hypermarket concept in France soon drew international attention as other retailers in other countries sought to learn and duplicate the process. Carrefour's international expansion was begun initially through joint venturing with local partners. These partnerships were seen as the best way of merging the company's format and systems with the local knowledge of merchandise preferences, vendor relationships and human resources possessed by their local partner.

Exhibit 7   Carrefour SA, Sales Under Banners Incl. VAT, 1999*

	Hypermarkets	Supermarkets	Hard Discount	Other
France				
3,966 outlets	227 outlets	1,078 outlets	418 outlets	2,243 outlets
42,288 €m	Sales = 23,761 €m	Sales = 11,986 €m	Sales = 1,387 €m	Sales = 5,154 €m
54.5% of total sales	Space = 1,760,890 sq. mt.	Space = 1,523,679 sq. mt.	Space = 259,165 sq. mt.	
Europe				
4,636 outlets	260 outlets	1,098 outlets	2,600 outlets	678 outlets
25,536 €m	Sales = 14,365 €m	Sales = 5,717 €m	Sales = 2,839 €m	Sales = 2,615 €m
32.9% of total sales	Space = 2,201,524 sq. mt.	Space = 1,307,438 sq. mt.	Space = 613,450 sq. mt.	
Americas				
301 outlets	112 outlets	83 outlets	106 outlets	
6,712 €m	Sales = 6,235 €m	Sales = 383 €m	Sales = 94 €m	
8.7% of total sales	Space = 918,731 sq. mt.	Space = 135,498 sq. mt.	Space = 35,377 sq. mt.	
Asia				
82 outlets	82 outlets			
3,017 €m	Sales = 3,017 €m			
3.9% of total sales	Space = 663,045 sq. mt.			
Total				
8,985 outlets	681 outlets	2,259 outlets	3,124 outlets	2,921 outlets
77,553 €m	47,377 €m	18,087 €m	4,320 €m	7,769 €m
	61.0% of total sales	23.3% of total sales	5.6% of total sales	10.1% of total sales

*Stores under banners gather all integrated stores, and franchised stores or stores of partners (including GB in Belgium, GS in Italy, Modelo Continente in Portugal and Marinopoulos in Greece).

Source: Carrefour Annual Report.

With the French legislation limiting its growth within the country, Carrefour decided to internationalize its concept and entered Belgium in 1969. As the legislation and competitiveness became tighter, Carrefour stepped up its international expansion during the mid-1970s, developing its first operation outside Europe with the opening of its first hypermarket in Brazil in 1975. By 1985, Carrefour had stores in 10 countries.

Three years later Carrefour decided to export its hypermarkets to the U.S. by opening a 31,000 sq. mt. (330,000 sq. ft.) store in suburban Philadelphia. One year later, Asia [was] the target, with Taiwan being its first choice. In the U.S. wide aisles, clerks on roller skates and sixty checkout lanes greeted American customers, but few came because of scant advertising and limited selection. Competitors cut prices and a local labor union picketed over wages, benefits, and work rules, eventually reaching a settlement several lawsuits later. In 1993, a year after opening a second store in New Jersey, Carrefour closed both U.S. hypermarkets and exited the market.

Regardless of the bad experience in the U.S. amongst Carrefour managers, the Taiwanese experience was considered the most challenging in terms of adaptability to local needs. The ability to react to local conditions was long seen as the key success factor in Carrefour's international accom-

plishments to date. Appendix A describes the major issues the management faced in developing the Taiwanese operation.

By 1995 Carrefour had more stores internationally than it did in France, and by the end of 1999 it was the most international retailer in the world with operations in 21 countries around the globe.

Wal-Mart

Wal-Mart was founded by Sam Walton and his brother, James "Bud" Walton, in 1962. The Walton boys revolutionized discount retailing, with the result that by 1989 Wal-Mart was the world's largest retailer. The Walton's proposition was simple, deliver a wide array of merchandise at discount prices topped up by [. . .] friendly service. By 1998, it was servicing more than 100 million customers weekly and had a sales volume of US$138 billion with an overall operating margin of 5.8 percent (Exhibit 8 provides a financial summary of Wal-Mart Stores, Inc.).

The Walton brothers opened their first Wal-Mart Discount City store in Rogers, Arkansas, after Ben Franklin management—the Walton's operated a number of franchised stores from the chain—rejected a suggestion to open discount stores in small towns. The Discount City store concept consisted of servicing small and middle-sized towns at

Exhibit 8 Wal-Mart Stores, Inc., Financial Summary 1992–1999 (US$ Millions)

	1992	1993	1994	1995	1996	1997	1998	1999
Operating Results								
Net Sales	55,484	67,345	82,494	93,627	104,859	117,958	137,634	165,013
License Fees and Other Income	497	645	914	1,146	1,319	1,341	1,574	1,796
Cost of Goods Sold	44,175	53,444	65,586	74,564	83,663	93,438	108,725	129,664
Operating, SG&A Expenses	8,321	10,333	12,858	14,951	16,788	19,358	22,363	27,040
Interest Cost	323	517	706	888	845	784	797	1,022
Taxes	1,172	1,358	1,581	1,606	1,794	2,115	2,740	3,338
Net Income	1,991	2,337	2,677	2,764	3,088	3,604	4,583	5,745
Financial Position								
Current Assets	10,198	12,115	15,338	17,331	17,993	19,352	21,132	24,356
Net Property P&E	9,793	13,175	15,874	17,098	20,324	23,606	25,973	35,969
Current Liabilities	6,754	7,406	9,973	11,454	10,957	14,460	16,762	25,803
Long-term Borrowings	4,845	7,960	9,709	10,600	10,016	9,674	9,607	16,674
Shareholders' Equity	8,759	10,752	12,726	14,756	18,168	20,441	22,911	27,113
Share Information								
Market Capitalization	73,538	57,491	48,849	51,108	52,166	90,115	182,501	307,468
Shares (Million)	4,596	4,599	4,598	4,594	4,586	4,570	4,482	4,448
Price/Book Value ($)	9.13	5.78	4.01	3.62	3.19	5.05	9.18	12.68
Price/Earnings ($)	39.88	25.71	19.14	17.94	17.91	27.58	44.02	57.60
Dividend Yld (%)	0.33	0.52	0.80	0.90	0.92	0.68	0.38	0.29
Financial Ratios (%)								
Return on Assets	NA	11.7	10.6	8.9	9.0	9.4	10.7	12.2
Return on Shareholders' Equity	NA	26.7	24.9	21.7	20.9	19.8	22.4	25.1
Operational Data								
Number Domestic Stores	2,138	2,439	2,558	2,667	2,740	2,805	2,884	2,985
Number International Stores	10	24	226	276	314	601	715	1,004
Number Employees (000)	434	528	622	675	728	825	910	1,140

Source: Bloomberg 2000, Annual Reports.

prices equal to or lower than prices in nearby cities. In 1972 Sam Walton took the 30 existing stores public using the proceeds of the offering to build a warehouse that allowed him to buy large volumes of merchandise at lower prices. Due to the strategy of covering small towns, virtually ignored by other competitors, the expansion progressed rapidly without any substantive direct competition until the mid-1980s. However, by 1993, Wal-Mart was in 47 states and its expansion led to competition with Kmart, Target, Sears and J.C. Penney, for which the established players were ill prepared.

In the 1990s the company moved beyond its rural expansion strategy and began diversifying into grocery operations (Wal-Mart Supercenters), membership warehouse clubs (SAM's Clubs) and deep discount warehouse outlets (Bud's Discount City). By this time the company also felt it was now prepared for forays outside the United States.

Sam Walton led the company until 1988, being a powerful CEO whose philosophy drove every aspect of the business. He believed in empowering yet controlling employees,

maintaining Wal-Mart's costs and prices below everybody else's, and [he] aimed at logistics excellence by maintaining technological superiority.

Empowering Employees By 1998 Wal-Mart was the largest private employer in the U.S. employing 910,000 associates (*employees* in Wal-Mart terminology). Associates were given responsibility, recognition and a share of the profits and were expected to be totally committed to the company and its success. "As Wal-Mart associates we know it is not good enough to simply be grateful to our customers for shopping in our stores—we want to demonstrate our gratitude in every way we can! We believe that doing so is what keeps our customers coming back to Wal-Mart again and again." Wal-Mart associates strove to provide exceptional customer service and everything possible was done to make shopping at Wal-Mart a friendly experience.

Associates were well rewarded for their commitment and dedication. Sam Walton believed that taking care of his associates—in terms of moral and motivational boosts in addition to financial rewards—was the first and most fundamental step to taking care of his customers. Wal-Mart was the living embodiment of Sam Walton—it operated in a fun, unpredictable and interesting sort of way. Financially, managers, supervisors and store personnel with over one year of employment had incentive compensations or bonuses based on store profits and were offered stock ownership.

To give associates at all levels a perspective of the total business, training was extensive and located away from the home office. New associates shared in the experience and culture of Wal-Mart by being trained by assistant managers from other stores, and store managers received training in the distribution centers to get an understanding of the internal workings of the distribution network. Suggestion programs were taken seriously and were not only a good way to involve associates in the business but were also estimated to be responsible for an annual savings of up to 2 percent of net sales. The typical management team member was a middle-aged executive who [had] worked in Wal-Mart since high school or college.

In 1988, David Glass was named CEO and President. Glass started as executive VP of finance in 1976 and was known to be as frugal as Sam Walton himself. Like all the regional VPs, buyers and corporate officers, he spent two to three days a week visiting stores. Wal-Mart did not operate regional offices; instead it owned a fleet of aircraft and [held] centralized regional VP weekly meetings in the main headquarters. Every Friday morning, at the weekly merchandise meeting, store and individual product sales were discussed and, on Saturday morning, management, associates, friends and relatives participated in an informal information-sharing motivation session. By Monday decisions taken over the weekend were implemented throughout the stores.

"Everyday Low Prices" Sam Walton's obsession with keeping prices below competitors led him to check his and the competition's stores thoroughly, counting the number of cars in the car park and going so far as to [take] a tape measure and [evaluate] shelf space. He looked out for good ideas and was not afraid to copy them. This attitude assured that "Everyday low prices" was a genuine strategy and not just a slogan. Wal-Mart offered brand name products at prices consistently lower—approximately 2–4 percent—than those found at department or specialty stores.

The everyday-low-price strategy implied that there were few promotions. Although other major competitors, including Carrefour, typically ran 50 to 100 advertised circulars per year—spending 2.1 percent of discount store sales on advertising—Wal-Mart produced only 12–13 major circulars per year—spending 1.5 percent of sales.

Because retail competition was mainly local, the everyday-low-price guarantee required that each store manager set his/her own prices. They also were responsible for product offerings and shelf space allocation decisions, all of which were based on market specific inventory and sales data supplied by advanced information systems. A study done in the mid-1980s showed that Wal-Mart's prices were 1 percent lower than Kmart's when the two stores were located next to each other and were 6 percent higher when Wal-Mart operated with no Kmart nearby.

Technological Superiority Technological superiority was seen as a competitive advantage by Wal-Mart. Technology was used not only in setting price and product offerings, but also in areas such as communication, distribution and the control of supplier relations. Wal-Mart's information systems expense was estimated to be 1.5 percent of sales compared with 1.3 percent for its direct U.S. competitors.

Wal-Mart operated a satellite system that enabled communication and electronic scanning throughout the store [and] supplier and distributor networks. The satellite system allowed requests for merchandise at the point of sale to be transmitted to the headquarters or to a supplier's distribution centers instantly. For the most part, distribution was centralized in Wal-Mart's distribution centers and a system known as cross-docking[4] was used to reduce handling and inventory costs. A study in 1993 estimated Wal-Mart's inbound logistic costs at 3.7 percent of store sales compared with 4.8 percent for its direct U.S. competitors. Wal-Mart's truck fleet delivered to stores 24 hours a day and picked up merchandise from suppliers on return trips, running at a sixty percent capacity on backhaul.

To even better manage the supply chain, Wal-Mart's [relationship] with its 3,600 suppliers was enhanced by an Electronic Data Interchange (EDI) system. By the late 1980s key suppliers were already directly managing Wal-Mart's merchandise inventory. All Wal-Mart's suppliers received a planning packet with information about the specific department with which the vendor was dealing as well as Wal-Mart's expectations from the relationship. Vendor negotiations were centralized and were done in undecorated standard interviewing rooms. Wal-Mart restricted its suppliers to companies who limited the workweek to sixty hours, provided safe working conditions and did not employ child labor. No single supplier was expected to account for more than three percent of the company's purchases.

---

[4] Cross-docking is a method of order replenishment. The supplier picks and palletises for each store and delivers to the cross-dock facility. The cross-dock facility receives and unloads shipments and sorts and stages pallets for each store, shipping them when the cut-off point (e.g., one full truck) is reached. An overview of the Wal-Mart system can be found in "Competing on Capabilities: The New Rules of Corporate Strategy," by George Stalk, Philip Evans, Lawrence E. Shulman, *Harvard Business Review*, March/April 1992, 57–69.

Wal-Mart was organized into three operating divisions: Wal-Mart store division, SAM's Club (membership warehouse club), and the international division. The Wal-Mart store division included discount stores (the initial Wal-Mart format selling general merchandise) and supercenters (a combination discount store and supermarket). (Exhibit 9 provides a structure of Wal-Mart officers and Exhibit 10 provides operational indicators by division for Wal-Mart.)

Discount Stores The discount store phenomenon emerged in the 1950s as the low price alternative to supermarkets. In order to survive on gross margins that were 10–15 percent below standard retailers,' discount stores cut all possible costs. Frills were non-existent, ancillary services were unknown and in-store selling was limited. Wal-Mart's discount stores were no exception in this area. To assure customer satisfaction Wal-Mart relied on the human touch in caring for the customer, like having "people greeters" welcome customers into the shop.

Wal-Mart stores offered shopping in several departments including family apparel, health and beauty aids, household needs, electronics, toys, fabrics and crafts, lawn and garden, jewelry and shoes. Although Wal-Mart bet on offering brand name products it also sold private labels in apparel (25 percent of the product offerings were private labeled), health and beauty care, dog food, [and] others. The company also offered a premium quality private label line under the "Sam's Choice" brand with a 26 percent price advantage over comparable branded products. Inventory in stores was kept at a minimum, representing ten percent of store space; the traditional U.S. retailers used 25 percent of their space for inventory. A typical facility covered 100,000 sq. ft. of floor space and, from the 1980s, stores were constructed only in areas where they could be expanded (after 1992 nearly 90 percent of the expanded discount stores were transformed into supercenters).

Supercenters In 1987, the first Wal-Mart Supercenter was opened. Interestingly, Wal-Mart, watching the entry of French companies into the U.S. also tested its own variant of the hypermarket concept. Later, as the French threat waned and they exited the market, this was abandoned in favor of smaller supercenters. A Wal-Mart Supercenter provided one-stop family shopping convenience. The store combined a full

Exhibit 9   Wal-Mart Stores Inc., Officers, 1999

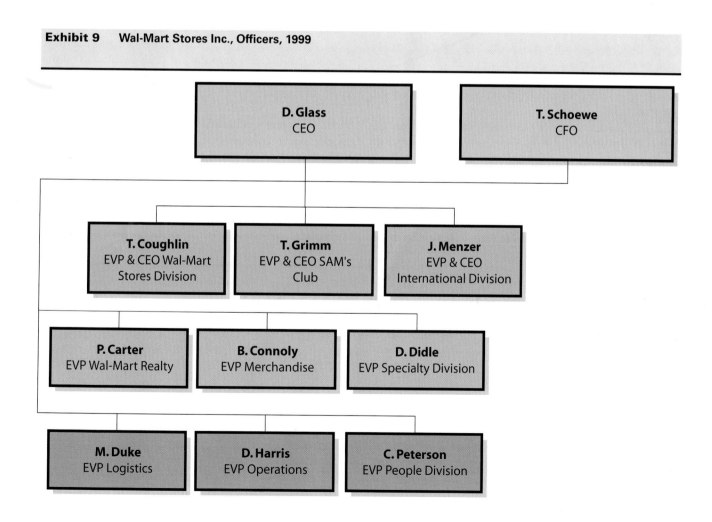

Exhibit 10   Wal-Mart, Net Sales, Operational Income, and Total Assets, by Division, 1997–1999

(US$ Millions)	1997	1998	1999
Net Sales			
Wal-Mart Stores	83,820	95,395	108,721
SAM's Club	20,668	22,881	24,801
International	7,517	12,247	22,728
Other	5,953	7,111	8,763
Total	117,958	137,634	165,013
Operational Income			
Wal-Mart Stores	5,833	7,075	8,419
SAM's Club	616	707	759
International	262	551	817
Other	−208	−213	110
Total	6,503	8,120	10,105
Total Assets			
Wal-Mart Stores	16,229	16,950	18,213
SAM's Club	2,933	2,834	3,586
International	7,390	9,537	25,330
Other	18,832	20,675	23,220
Total	45,384	49,996	70,349

Source: Wal-Mart Annual Reports.

line of groceries and a general merchandise department store under one roof.

Supercenters were designed to save customers time and money by joining grocery shopping with specialty services like bakeries, delis, photo labs and hair salons—everything a shopper could dream of in 120,000 to 130,000 sq. ft. These specialty and convenience shops had two great advantages: they attracted customers and offered margins of 35 to 45 percent—quite a benefit when basic food retailing was known to give very low margins (the industry average in 1992 was two percent). Kmart bought into the concept in the early 1990s and Target in 1995.

SAM's Clubs   In 1983, Wal-Mart opened three Sam's Warehouse Clubs. Warehouse clubs supplied members with brand name merchandise at warehouse prices for personal use or resale. Being dependent on high volume to compensate for the narrow profit margins, they limited the number of SKUs sold and offered institutional or multi-pack sizes. SAM's Clubs were not felt to be competing with Wal-Mart's discount stores directly and were run by a completely different management group.

In the early 1990s, as SAM's Club's competitors chose to grow by filling in the gaps in their existing markets rather [than] by entering new ones, its management chose a bold defensive move. Rather than giving competitors any openings into the concept space, SAM's Club's management purposely chose to cannibalize their own sales by opening addi-

tional SAM's Clubs in many markets. This situation created over capacity in the market, triggering consolidation and a decrease of comparable stores sales for the first time. But the strategy appeared to have the desired effect. In 1993 SAM's Club acquired The Wholesale Club and Kmart's Pace Clubs, managing to keep its dominant position in the warehouse segment of the industry.

International Expansion   Although the early 1990s saw Wal-Mart operating more than 2,000 stores worth more than US$73 billion, the stagnant American economy was making it difficult to sustain the company's historic double-digit comparable store sales growth. With limited domestic options, Wal-Mart, for the first time, began to consider expansion outside the U.S. seriously.

Wal-Mart's first external foray was into Mexico where, in 1991, it formed a partnership with CIFRA, Mexico's most successful retailer (CIFRA's 1997 sales were US$5,267 million). The success of Wal-Mart's Mexican expansion was seen by several analysts as the result of an improved economic landscape; the promise associated with the North American Free Trade Agreement (NAFTA); and familiarity and demand for U.S. products, as many of the middle class population had relatives living in the U.S. or were under the influence of the "American-way-of-life."

Wal-Mart's external efforts in Mexico and the move into Puerto Rico and Argentina in 1992 did little to bolster the company's fortunes. Sales growth was down again in 1993 and the firm's stock plummeted 22 percent, destroying nearly US$17 billion of value. For the first time, the giant's performance was being doubted. However, the company continued moving offshore. In 1994 it purchased 122 Woolco stores in Canada and quickly converted their operations to the Wal-Mart format. However, to assuage local fears, the company moved carefully, giving Canadian vendors equal opportunity to supply [its] stores.

In 1995, Wal-Mart acquired Lojas Americanas in Brazil. Although success in Canada was expected and predictable, South America was the biggest challenge to date for Wal-Mart. It was the first region where cultural habits were different from those of the U.S. and where it faced highly competitive and well established competitors, such as Carrefour. In Argentina, for instance, sales stumbled at first, as Wal-Mart was selling cuts of meat and cosmetics preferred in the U.S. In Brazil it was selling golf clubs in a country [where] golf is an elite game and few consumers have money to care for and purchase the equipment. However, four years after entering Argentina, Wal-Mart seemed to have learned its lesson as Donald C. Bland, president and CEO of Wal-Mart Argentina suggested, "following our blueprint too closely wasn't a good idea." Wal-Mart caught up with local competitors, not only by catering to the demand for locally preferred items, but also by changing its store layout to integrate French touches, such as wide aisles.

Wal-Mart also discovered that Carrefour was a nimble competitor. "They're just relentless, the toughest competitor

I've ever seen anywhere," said a retail executive who watched Carrefour ward off Wal-Mart in Brazil and Argentina in the mid-1990s. To counter Wal-Mart, Carrefour slashed prices, remodeled, and even relocated stores. When a planned Wal-Mart store opening in one Argentine city was delayed by construction problems for four months, Carrefour seized the opportunity to renovate its closest store. Wal-Mart was aware that a Carrefour shopper who stopped to buy groceries or a pair of tennis shoes could also get a watch repaired, order mobile telephone service, rent a car, or book plane tickets and hotel rooms for a vacation. Wal-Mart offered few such services. Carrefour had been an innovator in store design, softening the look of its warehouse-size buildings by installing wood floors and non-fluorescent lights in some departments and putting service counters in the food department, where shoppers can get meat, cheese, and bread sliced to order.

In 1996, Wal-Mart made its first attempt at selling in Asia by entering China with a subsequent entry into Korea in 1998. It entered the European market by acquiring the German retailer Werkauft in 1997 and followed this up two years later as it went on to acquire another German chain, InterSpar, and ASDA, a British retailer.

By the end of 1998, with three continents covered and 3,599 stores (715 of them outside the U.S.) generating sales of US$138,000 million, Wal-Mart was closer than ever to achieving Sam Walton's dream of "lower[ing] the cost of living for everyone, not just in America. . . . [W]e'll give the world an opportunity to see what it's like to save and have a better lifestyle, a better life for all."

Nevertheless, when compared with Carrefour, Wal-Mart took a cautious approach to foreign expansion, with foreign sales in 1998 accounting for only nine percent of Wal-Mart revenues, against [. . .] 44 percent for Carrefour.

Promodes

Promodes was founded by Paul-Auguste Halley and Leonor Duval Lemonnier in Normandy, France, in 1961. From the very beginning the company diversified into different concepts within France. The first supermarket opened in Mantes-la-Ville in 1962 and the first cash & carry outlet opened in 1964. Following in the footsteps of Carrefour's hypermarket success, Promodes opened its first hypermarket in 1970 in Mondeville, the present location of its headquarters. As the competitiveness and construction restriction laws in France tightened, Promodes further diversified into convenience stores in 1972 and into hard discount in 1979.[5]

The 1970s also saw Promodes expanding into new geographic markets. The firm developed in European operations by entering Germany and Spain in 1976, Portugal in

1985, Italy in 1987, Greece in 1990, Turkey in 1996 and the Belgian market in 1998. The first transcontinental move happened when it purchased Southeastern U.S.–based Red Food Stores chain in 1980. Through its "Dia" hard discount chain, Promodes entered Argentina in 1997. The first venture in Asia was in Taiwan in 1996, but in 1998, Promodes decided to sell its position in the Taiwanese joint venture to invest in a store in Indonesia instead.

Although the bulk of its international investments were successful, Promodes faced major setbacks in the U.S. and Germany. In the U.S. Promodes' attempt to sell both food and non-food products at its Red Food Stores was unsuccessful and the chain was sold to Dutch retailer Royal Ahold in 1994. After several years of accumulated losses, Promodes decided to sell its German hypermarket subsidiary in 1996.

At the time of the merger with Carrefour, Promodes had 62 percent of its sales in France, 29 percent in Spain and the rest in other countries. Globally it operated about 175 hypermarkets, 535 supermarkets, 2,185 hard discounters and 1,763 convenience stores. It also supplied institutions and restaurants through its 201 cash & carries. Hypermarkets accounted for 42 percent of the sales, supermarkets accounted for ten percent, hard discounters for twelve percent, cash & carries for eight percent and convenience stores and others for 28 percent.

To manage this diversified portfolio of business, Promodes' management structure was organized differently from Carrefour or Wal-Mart (which are organized by geographic areas and store concepts respectively). Instead, Promodes' management structure was organized by a symbiosis of both. Under CEO Paul-Louis [Halley] (Paul-Auguste's son that took over as CEO in 1971) there were four operational divisions: France, hypermarket Spain, discount international, and Hard discount international.

Until the marriage, Promodes was considered Carrefour's major retail rival but its performance was nowhere near as good. Its diversification into different concepts translated into lower operational margins—3.5 percent against Carrefour's 4.5 percent—and lower return on the assets in place (Exhibit 11 provides a financial summary of Promodes).

THE DEAL

Wal-Mart Takes Europe by Storm

With the purchase of 21 warehouse-sized stores from the German chain Wertkauf GmbH in 1997, Wal-Mart's entry into the European retail scene was anything but quiet. German consumers, the most price sensitive in Europe, quickly warmed to the [Everyday]-low-[p]rice slogan as well as the customer service often lacking at domestic retailers' stores, much to the consternation of the staid and established

---

[5] The "hard discount" store is different from the former concepts. Hard discounting started in Spain, not France, and nowadays Promodes' hard discount operations are number one in [. . .] Spain.

Exhibit 11   Promodes, Financial Summary 1992–1998 (€ Millions)

	1992	1993	1994	1995	1996	1997	1998	1999
Operating Results								
Net Sales	12,836	13,751	14,434	15,333	15,784	16,871	19,619	—
License Fees and Other Income	126	114	88	138	145	166	223	—
Cost of Goods Sold	10,609	11,287	11,847	12,534	12,852	13,687	15,842	—
Operating, SG&A Expenses	2,000	2,193	2,248	2,483	2,584	2,772	3,307	—
Interest Cost	191	196	191	187	171	175	240	—
Taxes	51	42	66	80	98	127	131	—
Net Income	111	147	170	187	224	276	322	—
Financial Position								
Current Assets	2,911	2,982	3,462	3,847	3,726	3,975	4,878	—
Net Property P&E	1,401	1,469	1,470	1,660	1,948	2,066	2,488	—
Current Liabilities	3,422	3,339	3,592	4,368	4,427	4,771	5,994	—
Long-term Borrowings	844	1,033	778	826	671	537	1,998	—
Shareholders' Equity	653	861	1,298	1,133	1,508	1,722	1,953	—
Share Information								
Market Capitalization	1,396	2,947	2,700	3,140	4,196	7,119	11,615	—
Shares (Million)	17	18	18	18	19	19	19	—
Price/Book Value (€)	2.41	4.00	2.38	3.32	3.27	4.73	6.79	—
Price/Earnings (€)	21.95	26.98	19.68	20.09	21.76	28.91	39.63	—
Dividend Yld (%)	1.58	0.94	1.28	1.37	1.23	0.84	0.63	—
Financial Ratios (%)								
Return on Assets	3.0	3.4	3.8	3.8	4.1	4.9	5.3	—
Return on Shareholders' Equity	19.0	22.5	19.7	14.4	19.8	18.3	18.7	—
Operational Data								
Number Domestic Stores	—	—	—	—	—	—	—	—
Number International Stores	—	—	—	—	—	—	—	—
Number Employees (000)	43	47	44	47	48	58	74	—

Source: Bloomberg 2000.

German retail sector. In 1998, Wal-Mart acquired a further 74 warehouses from Hamburg-based Spar Handels AG, a company that posted a pre-tax loss on ordinary activities in 1998 and predicted no real recovery in 1999 because of increased price competition. As Wal-Mart's presence in Germany increased, Metro AG—Germany and Europe's largest retailer at the time—sped up the takeover of control of its franchised wholesaling businesses, liquidating businesses totaling one-third of its sales to fund [. . .] the reorganization.

Although Wal-Mart's initial moves were restricted to Germany, the continent's largest economy, two acquisitions in slightly over a year caught the attention of other European retailers as they speculated about Wal-Mart's future moves. "If Wal-Mart was to buy a large competitor, it would create a snowball effect and lead to a more rapid concentration than what is economically justified . . . [However,] we see the future with serenity despite the arrival of big monsters like

Wal-Mart," said Luc Vandevelde, Promodes' CEO, at a breakfast meeting of Belgian company executives.

[On] June 14, 1999, Wal-Mart announced the acquisition of English retailer Asda Group for £6.7 billion. "It's going to be a shock to the system," said a retail analyst. "But it also suggests that Wal-Mart is very serious about Europe. They will go for well established major players that they can turn to their way of operating while preserving the best of their successes." European retailers had long feared the arrival of the world's largest retailer, whose name was synonymous with low prices. With margins averaging double those of continental European food chains, they had a lot to lose. With the purchase of Asda, Wal-Mart's biggest to date, the company doubled its international sales to more [than] US$25 billion.

Even though Asda's acquisition was a colossal investment and dwarfed earlier moves in Germany, analysts believed Wal-Mart would further build its presence in Europe within the year. As an analyst at Hypo Vereinsbank AG in Munich put it, "Wal-Mart is a latent danger, it will continue to seek [takeover] candidates in the next few months and could weaken the position of current market leaders." A number of British retailers' share prices fell in the days following the Asda acquisition announcement as analysts' predicted that Wal-Mart could offer retail prices as much as 5 percent below those being offered by its competitors. Kingfisher, whose plan to acquire Asda was ruined by the Wal-Mart acquisition, saw its share price fall 2.5 percent. Sainsbury's shares fell 2.2 percent. Boots, the UK's largest drug retailer, experienced a 1.6 percent decline in market value. Safeway, whose share price shrunk 32 percent in 1998, was seen as particularly vulnerable to predators and the countries' two largest supermarket chains, Tesco and Sainsbury, were expected to seek a merger.

Meanwhile, France's Carrefour, the world's eighth-biggest grocery retailer and [the] Netherlands' Ahold, [. . .] number seven worldwide, were expected to accelerate their global expansion plans. According to Ahold's CEO Cees van der Hoeven, "things are happening fast and we want to be part of that consolidation . . . I am reviewing ten potential [takeover] candidates." Carrefour declined to comment directly on the latest moves by Wal-Mart but spokesman Christian d'Oleon seemed to be throwing down the gauntlet with his statement that "Carrefour has the means, the people and the projects to continue alone."

On June 20, 1999, the edition of the *Financial Mail on Sunday* noted that if Wal-Mart were serious about entering Europe's second largest market, it could no doubt do so by bidding for Carrefour, then valued at £16 billion, Promodes or Auchan. When contacted about such speculation Carrefour reiterated its previous declarations. According to Daniel Bernard, "Carrefour has the means to remain independent and to develop itself." Promodes' CEO Paul-[Louis] Halley, whose family controls the Promodes Group, said his company was not interested in selling to anyone. Auchan, also family-controlled, said it did not want to be acquired by Wal-Mart, which had initiated [takeover] talks with the company approximately two years before.

On August 30, 1999, Carrefour launched a friendly €15.9 billion bid for rival Promodes, thereby potentially creating Europe's largest retailer with a market value of US$48 billion. The deal, which would have to be subject to regulatory approval, would create a company with annual sales of €52 billion, vaulting it above Germany's Metro, the European number one before the bid. The Promodes move was seen as the first shot in a battle for consolidation of the European retail sector. "Carrefour would probably prefer to buy Promodes than have it snatched up by Wal-Mart, giving the U.S. group a big chunk of its market," noted an analyst at Paris-based CCR Actions. Furthermore, the marriage would give the joint company a chance to dominate France's retail

market, where laws limiting the building [of] new large stores had long given favor to small shopkeepers.

Promodes' operations were expected to strengthen Carrefour's position in many ways. Firstly, as Europe would account for over 85 percent of the joint group's revenues it would lessen the volatility of Carrefour's extensive and growing investments in emerging markets, providing more long-term stability in operating performance. Secondly, a wider presence in the low growth but stable European markets would provide a stronger cash-flow base on which Carrefour could continue its international expansion. Thirdly, food would account for over 75 percent of the new group's revenues, up from 60 percent before, smoothing the cyclicality of Carrefour's non-food business.

Analysts believed that the operating strengths of the proposed merger would be offset by significant risks, particularly on Carrefour's financial structure. Coming just one year after the debt funded acquisition of Comptoirs Modernes, the taking on of Promodes with its weaker financial structure would stretch Carrefour's financial structure further, even if the transaction was going to be entirely financed with new equity. Additionally, much of Promodes' international expansion was built up through a series of joint venture agreements that gave it options on control (e.g., in Italy, Argentina, Belgium and Greece), which, if Carrefour sought to exercise them, would mean a further large cash outlay with consequences for the group's financial position.

However, overall the market seemed to approve of the Carrefour-Promodes merger as Carrefour's shares jumped 9.7 percent to a record close of €154 and Promodes' shares gained 7.7 percent to €893, also a record close. "While there may be initial concerns on earnings dilution in the short term, the strategy of the deal is compelling, creating a clear leader in Europe for retail and a strong base for further global expansion," said an analyst at Goldman Sachs & Co, which upgraded Carrefour to "market outperformer" from "market performer." Analysts believed in the strong market position of the new Carrefour. With stores on three continents it had the potential to manage its global supply chain and negate Wal-Mart's near legendary cost advantage. In one swoop, Carrefour not only became Europe's largest retailer but surpassed Wal-Mart in two critical South American markets that [were] the key to Wal-Mart's global expansion, Brazil and Argentina.

As [a] consequence of this string of moves and countermoves, retail stocks were on edge across the continent. Analysts and investors clearly expected the latest merger to precipitate a rash of other deals. Metro shares traded up 2.3 percent at €52.6 as the company said it was watching the Carrefour-Promodes deal's developments closely. However, even with its €54 billion valuation, there was no indication that Carrefour was safe. As one analyst remarked "Wal-Mart [given its US$242 billion market value] could still easily come in and buy the enlarged group if it wanted to." However, a hostile bid for either Carrefour or Promodes was looked on as difficult as both had family shareholders that controlled a significant amount of the stock.

The Regulatory Approval Process

By mid October, most analysts viewed the Carrefour-Promodes [merger] as a done deal. The Halley family and their allies had already offered more than 50 percent of their shares and no news of any counter offer had emerged by 6 October, the final due date of counter offer submittance under the terms of the deal. Nevertheless, the need for European Union (EU) approval for the merger to be effective was an ongoing issue. Analysts were confident of the approval; as one analyst said, "[f]or me there is a one percent chance that Brussels stops the deal, while Paris, zero percent. They would prefer to have a group called Carrefour that is second in the world rather than see Carrefour taken over by Wal-Mart and Promodes by Ahold."

Under EU merger and acquisition rules companies had to make a regulatory [filing] with all the necessary information within seven days of announcing their plan to merge. Although it is rare for companies to respect the seven-day deadline and the Commission seldom bothers to call them to order, the Carrefour-Promodes deal filing took an exceptionally long time. They announced their marriage at the end of August and the merger notification was filed with the EU's competition watchdog on 5 October, but was declared incomplete twice on grounds of insufficient information. The companies' failure to meet EU information requirements was seen as a signal of disagreement with regulators about how the purchase should be reviewed. The European Commission stated that it would not start its formal investigation of the acquisition until it considered the application complete. A probe could then take between one and five months, depending on the seriousness of the antitrust concerns.

Further, following the [merger] announcement several unexpected problems arose within the Carrefour-Promodes universe. Both France and the Catalan regional governments expressed concerns that the merged company would have a virtual food market monopoly. In France, the combined company would control more than half the supermarket and hypermarket shopping space in Bourges, Calais, Chateauroux and Caen; and, in Spain, the regional government of Catalonia stated that the new group would have a 30 percent market share in the region when compared to the 20 percent average in the rest of Spain, and within some towns that figure would be as high as 70 percent.

Internally, the merger created some collateral casualties. In Spain, George Plassat, Pryca's CEO,[6] announced his resignation after learning he was not expected to lead the merged company. In Portugal, Belmiro de Azevedo announced he was

looking out for a partner to acquire Promodes' 22 percent stake in Modelo-Continente[7] after no agreement was reached on the price Carrefour would pay for Belmiro's 70 percent stake. As Belmiro kept control of the joint venture, the entrance of a new partner was critical because, as he noted, "[the merger between Carrefour and Promodes] could create a strange partner/ competition situation" because Carrefour was Modelo-Continente's main competitor in Portugal.

On 29 November, with EU Competition Commissioner Mario Monti voicing antitrust concerns, Carrefour shares fell 5.5 percent to €176.7, the biggest one-day drop in ten months, and Promodes fell 2.8 percent to €1,025. Monti pointed out that the combined company's potential dominance of retail and supply networks in some markets as well as its extensive buying power were issues needing investigation. An analyst at SG Securities said, "[t]here are no worries about the Commission giving its approval to the merger, but it is annoying because it wastes time and maintains an atmosphere of uncertainty."

In the beginning of January 2000, just after the millennium parties, the European Commission announced the deadline for ruling on the merger between the two companies was extended by two weeks to 25 January because France and Spain had sought referral of parts of the case. The two-week extension was mandatory when national authorities ask to rule on a merger themselves. Aware that these issues could delay the Commission's decision, Carrefour, early on in the Commission's one-month routine investigation of the merger, made concessions to satisfy EU worries about "upstream activities." It offered to sell four supermarkets in France and four in Spain to win approval. Some analysts believed the retailer might have to sell as many as 30 properties worldwide, as the Commission could block or force changes to mergers between companies with combined global sales of €5 billion and EU sales of €250 [million] each, even if companies were from outside the 15-nation EU. On 25 January the Commission was supposed to rule on whether the concessions went far enough or [. . .] whether to open a full four-month investigation, thereby perhaps fatally delaying the deal.

On 24 January Carrefour named Leon Salto to succeed Luc Vandevelde as Chief Executive of Promodes after Vandevelde left to join Marks & Spencer. Vandevelde's expected role following the consummation of the merger was as second in command at the new Carrefour, under Chairman Daniel Bernard. The post would no longer be filled, said a spokesman. "Vandevelde had global ambitions," said an analyst at Williams de Broe in London. "I'm not sure it was ever expected he'd be around for long." Salto, previously a Managing Director for Promodes' French opera-

---

[6] Pryca is Carrefour's banner for Spain.

[7] Modelo-Continente was a joint venture between Belmiro de Azevedo's group (SONAE) and Promodes to operate hypermarkets in Portugal. SONAE owned 70 percent, Promodes 22 percent, and the remaining 8 percent was floated on the Lisbon Stock Exchange.

tions, would head Carrefour France once the acquisition took effect.

On 25 January at 16:00 GMT the European Commission issued a press release conditionally clearing Carrefour's purchase of Promodes, referring the rest of the deal to the French and Spanish authorities. However, neither of those reviews would have the power to stop the merger going ahead. An adapted version of that press release is reproduced in Appendix B. "The Brussels decision is good news for the group, for our collaborators, for our partners and suppliers and for our shareholders," stated Daniel Bernard, the new group CEO after the EU announcement.

THE NEW CHALLENGE: A GLOBAL MARKET MEANS GLOBAL COMPETITION

At the time the deal between Carrefour and Promodes was cleared by the EU, analysts recognized that Wal-Mart was under the threat of being left without the critical mass of stores in key markets to become a major European player. Its biggest European holding, Britain's Asda, was only one-fifth the size of the bulked up Carrefour. Equally, the merger highlighted Wal-Mart's need to counter Carrefour's expansion in emerging markets. Only hours after unveiling the Promodes deal, Carrefour announced the acquisition of three Brazilian chains, boosting its market share in the country to over 20 percent, against only 1.4 percent for Wal-Mart. The new Carrefour was now the number one retailer in Brazil, Argentina, and Taiwan, as well in France, Spain, Portugal, Greece, and Belgium.

Although Carrefour and Wal-Mart had clashed head on in Mexico, Brazil, Argentina and Korea, they had respectfully stayed out of each other's key markets. Carrefour withdrew from the United States after a first unsuccessful attempt in the 1980s and had stayed out of Britain and Germany, the two European countries Wal-Mart had recently entered. Likewise, Wal-Mart had stayed away from Carrefour's strongholds in France and Southern Europe. However that situation was expected to change as European governments moved to protect small merchants through the control of large new store openings. The only way to grow in Europe seemed to be through acquisition and, after Germany and [the] UK, Wal-Mart was clearly expected to target France. On the other hand, Carrefour lacked a presence in three key mature markets: the UK, Germany, and the United States, which would balance the risk of its investments in emerging markets.

In fact, Daniel Bernard announced to a New York meeting of the National Retail Federation in January 2000 that "when one is the number two in the world, one cannot exclude a presence in the United States, nor remain indifferent to the changes in such a dynamic market that has grown 10 percent in volume. [. . .] Great Britain and Germany are also markets we are looking at." He added that circumstances had changed and Carrefour was watching the progress of Wal-Mart's Supercenters closely, suggesting that the United States may be ready for French hypermarkets. "But you cannot start from zero. You have to get there via an acquisition," Bernard coyly concluded.

As the two chains were quickly moving toward a frontal clash, questions arose in observers' minds regarding which chain was better prepared to win in an [increasingly] global marketplace.

APPENDIX A   FIRST MOVE IN ASIA: THE TAIWAN EXPERIENCE

With the increasing competitiveness of the European and American markets and with the increasing growth of the Asian economies, Carrefour looked to Asia as a potential market for its future development. The first move was into Taiwan in 1989.

Due to specificities of the Taiwanese culture, Carrefour was aware it could not just transfer concepts that had proven successful in France or any other country for that matter. The decision was made to adapt the Carrefour concept to the particularities of the local environment—at the store level, in the product offerings and the management culture.

Because of the distinction in Taiwan between land for industrial use and land for commercial use, Carrefour had to operate in urban areas where stores could not be located on flat open land, but had to be situated in buildings, basements or ground floors in high-density areas. Following traditional Taiwanese store concepts, decoration and layout were kept simple. Another new and completely unexpected challenge was the protection that had to be negotiated with local Triads—the Chinese mafia.

The product offering was limited in order to deal in greater volumes and obtain competitive prices from suppliers. In order to catch up with the changing shopping habits of the Taiwanese people, Carrefour introduced pilot departments in all the stores to test new ranges of products (e.g., in 1991 the top selling flavors in food products were peanut and lemon, but in 1994 they were vanilla, chocolate and strawberry). The conclusions of these studies were later to spread to all the stores at a national level. As the top selling articles changed every six months, a major challenge for Carrefour was following the market very closely.

In order to adapt to these highly changing conditions, Carrefour had to adapt its human resources and vendor relationship management. Department heads were much more autonomous [than] their French counterparts. They had the responsibilities of a business-within-the-business for their department—handling everything from supplier relationships to hiring, promoting and firing staff and from price definition to full product selection. All the pressures of sales and margin were on their shoulders. To incentivize performance, department heads and store managers had a bonus linked to store results and a base salary, which, in the case of store managers, was between NT$120,000 to NT$200,000 (US$4,400 to US$7,400).

Initially, department heads were French expatriates but, because of internal staff stress, by 1996 three out of eight heads were Taiwanese. As expatriate managers had difficulties in learning the language and understanding the local culture the promotion of local workers was seen as a way to mingle both cultures and avoid internal conflict. As Philippe Ravelli, a local French store manager put it, "the key difference between the French and the Chinese culture lies in the priority given to three basic elements in the daily life. For the Chinese, emotion (qing) comes first, followed by reason (li) and law. For us French, the law comes first, reason comes second, and emotion last."

Vendor relationships were also particularly complex. Local suppliers were totally lacking in information regarding basic data, such as sales and inventory levels. Delivery was also a problem as there were no standards for things like pallet sizes. Salespersons visiting Carrefour to present their products often had samples but no catalogues, product reference numbers or order forms. Suppliers believed they sold products and not service. Many times, in comparison to Western countries where manufacturers constantly assail retailers, local suppliers had to be called in to show their products.

Despite the difficulties, Carrefour made it work and today the company is considered a success in Taiwan, not only because of having reached roughly FF25 million of profit in the third year of operation, but also because of the way it has shaped itself to local habits and been able to shape them. A visit to the "French" hypermarket is, for many families in Taiwan, the equivalent of a Sunday daytrip.

APPENDIX B   ADAPTED VERSION OF EUROPEAN COMMISSION'S PRESS RELEASE

Brussels, 25 January 2000

The Commission has decided to refer the analysis concerning the acquisition of Promodes by Carrefour to the national Competition authorities in France and Spain. The referral requests concern a number of local retail markets. "We have made sure that our referral decisions cover all the local areas where the operation is susceptible to create competitive problems affecting the choice of the end-consumer," Mr. Mario Monti, EU Commissioner for Competition, has explained. The European Commission has also authorised the other aspects of the planned acquisition, subject of a certain number of undertakings. Carrefour has committed itself to remedy certain problems identified on the supply markets.

The concentration between Carrefour and Promodes will mainly affect the French and the Spanish market. In France, the new group with 27 percent will be market leader on the retail market with a 10 percent distance to the next players, Leclerc (around 17 percent) and Intermarche (around 15 percent). Casino and Auchan both have around 13 percent, System U around 6 percent and Cora 5 percent. In Spain, Carrefour/Promodes will have combined market shares of approximately 26 percent; that means [it will be] three times larger than the next competitors Eroski, Auchan and Hipercor (each around 8 percent). In addition, the new group will be particularly strong in large surfaces, that is, hypermarkets, which are the most profitable form of distribution in Spain.

According to the information of the Commission Carrefour/Promodes could obtain particularly strong market positions in certain local retail markets. Following its practice in previous cases the Commission has referred the analysis of these local areas to the competent authorities of France and Spain, following their request. It is the understanding of the Commission that in those areas, where the new group's market position will not be sufficiently counterbalanced by the presence of other players, the respective overlaps creating competitive concerns will be removed by the divestiture of sales outlets.

Concerning the supply markets, the Commission has concluded that, although Carrefour/Promodes will become market leader in France and Spain, the market position obtained by the new group will not lead to the creation of dominance.

Finally, the parties committed themselves to put in place a certain number of initiatives in order to address concerns raised by several suppliers with regard to the short- and long-term consequences of the concentration. With regard to small and medium-sized enterprises (SMEs), Carrefour has committed itself to abstain from modifying any supply-contracts, which are in force on the day of the Commission's decision, for the time of their duration.

Carrefour has also undertaken not to unilaterally break [any] of its commercial relationships with certain producers supplying both Carrefour and Promodes, for a period of three years from the date of the Commission'[s] decision. The Commission has taken note of these commitments, the implementation of which will be subject to regular reports by Carrefour.

The procedures before the national competition authorities: In France, the procedure will take at maximum six months. The Minister of Economic Affairs will have to decide within two months whether or not to consult the Conseil de la Concurrence, who will then have to issue an opinion within four months. Afterwards, the Minister of Economic Affairs will have a couple of days to take his final decision.

In Spain, the Spanish Department of Competition has one month to decide whether or not to seize the Tribunal for Competition affairs. The later will have to give its opinion within three months. The Spanish Government, on the basis of a proposal of the Minister for Economic Affairs, will have to take its final decision after three months at the latest. In any event, both the French and the Spanish Competition authorities, according to the European Community Merger Regulation (ECMR), will have to publish their report or issue the conclusions of their examination at the latest four months after the date of the Commission's referral decision.

The Chinese Fireworks Industry

9A99M031

In February 1999, Jerry Yu was spending the Chinese New Year holidays in Liuyang (lee-ou-yang), a city known as "the home of firecrackers and fireworks," located in Hunan Province in China. Jerry was an ABC (America-Born-Chinese). With an MBA, he was running a small family-owned chain of gift stores in Brooklyn, New York. Liuyang was his mother's hometown. During his visit, his relatives invited him to invest in a fireworks factory that was owned by a village. Mr. Yu had been impressed by the extravagant fireworks shows he had seen during the festival; however, he wanted to assess how attractive the Chinese fireworks industry was before he even looked at the financial details of the factory.

HISTORY OF FIREWORKS AND FIRECRACKERS

Fireworks referred to any devices designed to produce visual or audible effects through combustion or explosion. The art

of making fireworks was formally known as pyrotechnics. Firecrackers were a specific kind of fireworks, usually in the form of a noisemaking cylinder. Firecrackers were often strung together and fused consecutively, a staple of Chinese New Year celebrations, weddings, grand openings, births, deaths and other ceremonial occasions.

The main ingredients of fireworks had remained almost the same over the past thousand years: 75 parts-by-weight potassium nitrate, 15 parts charcoal and 10 parts sulfur. It burned briskly when lighted, but did not erupt or make any noise. When it was found that a projectile could be thrust out of a barrel by keeping the powder at one end and igniting it, black powder became known as gunpowder. Today, smokeless powder has replaced black powder as the propellant in modern weaponry, but black powder remains a main ingredient in fireworks, both as a propellant and as a bursting charge.

It was generally believed that the Chinese were the first makers of fireworks. The Chinese made war rockets and explosives as early as the sixth century. One legend said that a Chinese cook, while toiling in a field kitchen, happened to mix together sulfur, charcoal and saltpetre, and noticed that the pile burned with a combustible force when ignited. He further discovered that when these ingredients were enclosed in a length of bamboo sealed at both ends, it would explode rather than burn, producing a loud crack. This was the origin of firecrackers. In fact, the Chinese word for firecrackers—bao-zhu—literally means "exploded bamboo."

The loud reports and burning fires of firecrackers and fireworks were found to be perfect for frightening off evil spirits and celebrating good news at various occasions. For more than a thousand years, the Chinese had been seeing off past years and welcoming in new ones by firing firecrackers.

Fireworks made their way first to Arabia in the seventh century, then to Europe sometime in the middle of the 13th century. By the 15th century, fireworks were widely used for religious festivals and public entertainment. Most of the early pyrotechnicians in Europe were Italians. Even today, the best-known names in the European and American fireworks industry [are] Italian in origin. From the 16th to the 18th century, Italy and Germany were the two best known areas in the European continent for fireworks displays.

In 1777, the United States used fireworks in its first Independence Day celebration, and fireworks have become closely associated with July Fourth celebrations ever since.

Up until the 1830s, the colors of the early fireworks were limited, but by 1999, there were six basic colors used in fireworks.

LIUYANG—THE HOMETOWN OF FIRECRACKERS AND FIREWORKS

According to historical records in China, firecrackers and fireworks "emerged during the Tang dynasty (618–907 AD), flourished during the Song Dynasty (960–1279 AD), and originated in Liuyang." For more than a thousand years, Liuyang had been known as the "hometown of firecrackers and fireworks of China," a title that was officially conferred to Liuyang by the State Council of China in 1995. As early as 1723, Liuyang fireworks were chosen as official tributes to the imperial family and were sold all over the country. Exports started early: by 1875, firecrackers and fireworks were being shipped to Japan, Korea, India, Iran, Russia, Australia, England, [the] U.S., and other countries. In China, the name Liuyang had become almost synonymous with firecrackers and fireworks. Liuyang-made firecrackers and fireworks won numerous awards over its long history of fireworks making.

The long history and tradition had made fireworks more than just a livelihood for the Liuyang people. Almost every native person in the area knew something about fireworks making, or had actually made firecrackers or fireworks in their lifetime. As a result, Liuyang claimed an impressive pool of skilled labor. Firecrackers and fireworks had become the pillar industry of Liuyang, employing more than 400,000 people in peak seasons, or about one-third of the total population in the Liuyang District (including Liuyang City and the surrounding counties). Liuyang claimed more than 500 fireworks manufacturers. Among them, only one was a state-owned-enterprise (SOE) with more than 1,000 workers. The rest were owned either by villages or families. Among them, about a dozen or so were medium to large factories with employment between 100 to 500 workers. The rest were small workshops employing anywhere from 10 to 50 people, depending on market demand.

Liuyang was the top fireworks exporter in the world, making up 80 per cent of fireworks export sales of Hunan Province, and 60 per cent of that of China (see Exhibit 1 for information on revenue and export sales of Liuyang fire-

Exhibit 1 Liuyang Firecrackers and Fireworks: Total Revenue and Export Sales (US$000)

	1992	1993	1994	1995	1996
Total Revenue	49,639	55,542	86,747	126,506	134,940
Tax Revenue	5,099	7,010	11,829	15,422	18,434
Export Sales	15,100	30,200	51,240	84,030	85,560

Source: Liuyang Firecrackers and Fireworks Exhibition, 1998.

works). The trademarked brand "Red Lantern" had become well known to fireworks-lovers around the world.

The Product

Fireworks could be classified into two categories: display fireworks and consumer fireworks. The display fireworks, such as aerial shells, maroons, and large Roman candles, were meant for professional (usually licensed) pyrotechnicians to fire during large public display shows. They were devices that were designed to produce certain visual or audio effect at a greater height above the ground than the consumer fireworks, which the general public could purchase in convenience stores and enjoy in their own backyards. Display fireworks were known as Explosives 1.3 (Class B prior to 1991) in the U.S. The consumer fireworks belonged to Explosives 1.4 (Class C prior to 1991). The difference lay mainly in the amount of explosive components contained in the product. Canada had a similar classification system. In the U.K., it was more carefully divided into four categories: indoor fireworks; garden fireworks; display fireworks; and display fireworks for professionals only.

There were many varieties of fireworks. Liuyang made 13 different types with more than 3,000 varieties. The major types included fountains, rockets, hand-held novelties, nail and hanging wheels, ground-spinning novelties, jumping novelties, floral shells, parachutes and firecrackers.

Historically, firecrackers made up 90 per cent of the total production and sales. Over the past 50 years or so, however, there had been a shift away from firecrackers to fireworks. In 1999, firecrackers made up only about 20 per cent of the total sales. The skill levels of fireworks-making had been greatly improved. For instance, the old-day fireworks could reach no more than 20 metres into the sky, while the new ones could go as high as 400 metres.

Not much had changed in fireworks-making. Over the last few decades, numerous novelties were added to the fireworks family. However, innovation had never reached beyond product variations. The ingredients had remained more or less the same. The process technology had not changed much either, although some manual processes, such as cutting the paper, rolling the cylinders, mixing powder, and stringing the cylinders could now be done by machines.

Safety Issues

The fact that fireworks were made with gunpowder and listed under explosives brought about the issue of safety. Numerous accidents related [to] fireworks had resulted in tragic human injuries and considerable property damages. As a result, fireworks had become heavily regulated in most countries.

According to the manufacturers, fireworks were the most dangerous during the production process. Powder mixing and powder filling, in turn, were the two most dangerous procedures. The workers had to abide by strict safety measures. Even a tiny spark caused by the dropping of a tool on the floor or the dragging of a chair could start a major explosion. The quality of the ingredients was also of significant importance. Impure ingredients could greatly increase the possibility of accidents. In Liuyang, almost every year, there would be one or more accidents that resulted in deaths and damages.

Once the fireworks were made, they were relatively safe to transport and store. Even in firing, good quality fireworks rarely caused any problems if everything was done properly. Most of the fireworks-related accidents occurred during private parties or street displays, and quite often involved children playing with fireworks that needed to be handled by adults, or adults firing shells that required professional expertise. Most accidents were linked to consumer backyard events rather than to public displays.

According to the United States Consumer Products Safety Commission's (CPSC) data, injuries related to fireworks had declined by 44 per cent, even though their use had increased (see Exhibit 2). For 1997, there were an estimated 8,300 fireworks-related injuries, 32 per cent of which were caused by firecrackers. Of all the injuries related to firecrackers, 42 per cent involved illegal firecrackers.

Children from ages five to 14 were the most frequently involved in fireworks-related injuries. However, fireworks were not the only consumer product that might cause injuries to this age group. According to a 1997 CPSC Injury Surveillance Report, fireworks were actually safer than some much more benign-looking products, like baseballs, pens and pencils. However, fireworks-related injuries were usually the most dramatic and the most widely publicized accidents, which partly explained the fact that fireworks was the only category among the products listed in Exhibit 3, for which prohibition, instead of education and adult supervision, was often urged.

In the United States, multiple government agencies were involved in regulating fireworks. The Bureau of Alcohol, Tobacco and Firearms (BATF) controlled the manufacture, storage, sales and distribution of explosives, i.e., Class B fireworks. The CPSC regulated Class C consumer fireworks, and the Department of Transportation dealt with the transportation of fireworks. Although at the federal level, fireworks and firecrackers were allowed as long as the safety features were up to the standard, local governments would have their own different regulations regarding fireworks consumption. Out of the 50 states, 10 would not allow any fireworks, five would allow novelty fireworks, 18 would allow "safe and sane" fireworks, while the remaining 17 would allow essentially all consumer fireworks. For display fireworks, permits would have to be obtained from federal and local authorities and fire departments.

All legal consumer fireworks offered for sale in the United States had been tested for stability by the Bureau of Explosives and approved for transportation by the U.S. Department of Transportation. Because of the limited amount of pyrotechnic composition permitted in each individual unit, consumer fireworks would not ignite spontaneously during storage, nor would they mass-explode during a fire. Therefore, no special storage was required.

In most of Europe, similar regulations were in place for safety considerations, only the requirements were regarded as less stringent. In Canada, however, regulations were extremely restrictive. On the list of fireworks companies that were allowed to sell fireworks to Canada, no Chinese companies were found.

Exhibit 2	Total Fireworks Consumption and Estimated Fireworks-Related Injuries in [the] U.S.: 1994 to 1998		
Year	Fireworks Consumption, Millions of Pounds	Estimated Fireworks-Related Injuries	Injuries per 100,000 Pounds
1994	117.0	12,500	10.7
1995	115.0	10,900	9.4
1996	118.0	7,800	6.2
1997	132.8	8,300	6.2
1998	112.6	7,000	6.2

Source: American Pyrotechnics Association.

THE FIRECRACKERS AND FIREWORKS INDUSTRY IN CHINA

The firecrackers and fireworks industry in China was dominated by small family-owned-and-operated workshops. It was essentially a low-tech, highly labor-intensive industry. After 1949, government-run factories replaced the family-owned workshops. The increased scale and government funds made possible the automation of some processes. However, the key processes like installing powder, mixing color ingredients [and] putting in fuses, were still manually done by skilled workers.

The factories themselves were made up of small workshops that stood away from each other, so that in case of an

Exhibit 3   Estimated Emergency Room Treatment per 100,000 Youths (Ages 5 to 14)

Activity	Value
Bicycle	806
Baseball	321
Ice & Rollerskating	308
Stairs, Steps	271
Fences	106
ATVs, Mopeds, Minibikes	64
Skateboards	63
Fishing	48
Nonpowder Guns, BBs, Pellets	25
Pens & Pencils	12
Fireworks	8

Source: American Pyrotechnics Association.

accident the whole factory would not explode. For the same safety consideration, the workshops were usually located near a water source and in sparsely populated rural areas, to reduce the noise and explosion hazard.

After the reform towards market economy started in 1979, most of the factories were broken up and became family-run units of production again. It was hoped that this privatization might help to motivate people better, to increase their productivity and consequently raise the output. However, this move also served to restrict further technological innovations. There were hardly any research and development (R & D) facilities, nor [were] human and capital resources allocated to R & D in most fireworks companies. The few resources that were available were all spent on product varieties. Even in Liuyang, out of the 400,000 or so people working in the industry, only four were engineers with advanced professional training and titles. The 40 some research facilities scattered in Liuyang area were poorly funded and equipped.

In fact, the majority of the workers were regular farmers who had learned how to make fireworks just by watching and following their elders. They would come to work in fireworks workshops when there were jobs to be done, and return to till their fields if there were none. In Liuyang, for instance, only four to five factories were operating year-round. The rest of the 500-plus workshops would operate as orders came in. Since the fireworks-making communities were very concentrated geographically and had lasted for generations, only a few places (like Liuyang) came to claim a large pool of skilled fireworks-makers.

Although Liuyang was by far the most well-known place for making fireworks in China, it faced increasing

competition within the country. Also located in Hunan Province, Liling was another major manufacturing community of fireworks. Liling fireworks might not enjoy the same reputation and variety as Liuyang products, but they were fierce in price competition. In the neighboring Jiangxi Province, Pingxiang and Wanzai fireworks had become strong competitors both in price and quality, especially on the low- and medium-priced market. In the high-end product market, especially in large-type display fireworks and [the] export market, Dongguan in Guangdong Province, had taken advantage of its closeness to Hong Kong and more sophisticated management and marketing practices, and snatched market share from Liuyang.

The initial capital requirement for starting a fireworks-manufacturing facility was relatively low. To set up a factory with the necessary equipment for making large display shells would require RMB1,000,000.[1] However, setting up a small family workshop making consumer firecrackers and fireworks would require less than RMB100,000. Consequently, the number of small manufacturers mushroomed after the government started to encourage private business ventures.

The labor cost was low in the area. Skilled workers engaged in major processes would earn an average of RMB800 to RMB1,000 per month. A non-skilled worker would be paid only RMB300 to RMB400 every month. Therefore, the labor cost took no more than 20 per cent of the total cost. For the small private workshops, the percentage would be around 10 per cent.

---

[1] In 1999, the exchange rate was around 8.30 yuan per US$1.00.

The main raw materials for fireworks were gunpowder, color ingredients, paper, fuse and clay soil. None would be difficult to procure. The prices and supply were both quite stable. The one possible problem in supply was quality. Major manufacturers would usually establish long-term relationships with their suppliers to guarantee the quality of the materials. The small workshops would often go with the lowest prices, sometimes at the cost of quality, which could lead to fatal results.

The emergence of the small companies intensified competition. The private workshops were flexible and quick in responding to market demand. They did not entail much administrative cost. Compared to government-owned or some collectively-owned factories, they did not have the social responsibilities of health care, retirement benefits and housing. They usually did not do any product research or design. Oblivious to intellectual property protection, they would copy any popular product design and sell it for much less. The resulting price drop had become a serious problem for the whole industry. As the profit margin kept shrinking, some workshops would hire cheap unskilled workers, use cheap equipment and raw materials to cut down on cost. The results could be disastrous. Fireworks-related damages and injuries and factory accidents were reported every year, pushing the authorities to impose stricter regulations.

THE DOMESTIC MARKET

Firecrackers and fireworks had long been an integral part of any ceremonies held in China. Until recently, demand had been stable, but had risen in the past two decades because of increased economic development and living standards. Economically, market reform and unprecedented growth had given rise to the daily appearance of multitudes of new companies and new stores. As people's income level and living standards kept rising, fancier and pricier fireworks and firecrackers were desired over the cheap simple firecrackers, thereby creating more profit opportunities for fireworks manufacturers. Almost every household would spend at least a couple of hundred yuan on firecrackers and fireworks during the Spring Festival.

However, since the beginning of the 1990s, increased concerns over environmental pollution and safety of human life and property led more and more cities to regulate the consumption of fireworks and firecrackers. Every year, high profile fireworks-related accidents were reported and emphasized on mass media before and after the traditional Spring Festival. Some articles even condemned firecrackers and fireworks as an old, uncivilized convention that created only noise, pollution and accidents. In a wave of regulations, city after city passed administrative laws regarding the use of fireworks. By 1998, one-third of the cities in China had completely banned the use of firecrackers and fireworks. Another one-third only allowed fireworks in designated places. This led to a decline in domestic market demand.

In the meantime, domestic competition grew intensely. The reform towards a market economy made it possible for numerous family-run workshops to appear. They competed mainly on price. Almost every province had some fireworks-making workshops or factories, many set up and run with the help of skilled workers who had migrated from Liuyang. These small establishments usually were located in rural, underdeveloped areas where labor cost was minimal. The manufacturing was done manually, sometimes without safety measures, using cheap raw materials and simplified techniques. The products were sold locally at low prices, making it difficult for Liuyang fireworks to sell in those areas. To make things worse, these products would often copy any new or popular product designs coming out of Liuyang or other traditional fireworks communities, even using their very brand names.

In the past, fireworks were sold through the government-run general merchandise companies. Eventually, private dealers took over a large part of the business. Overall, the distribution system was rather fragmented. The old government-run channels were not very effective, especially for general merchandise. In the new distribution channels, wholesale dealers would get shipments directly from the manufacturers, and then resell to street peddlers and convenience stores.

In the countryside, wholesale markets would appear in focal townships, with wholesale dealers and agents of the manufacturers setting up booths promoting their products. Small peddlers in the surrounding areas would get supplies from the market and then sell them in small towns or villages. The wholesale markets in China were important outlets for distributing general merchandise like fireworks.

In the display fireworks market, the buyers were often central and local governments, who would purchase the product for public shows on national holidays or special celebrations. Obviously, a local company would have advantages in supplying to [the] local government in its area. Large fireworks shows usually would use invited bidding to decide on suppliers. The amount of fireworks used could range from RMB100,000 to several million yuan, depending on the scale of a fireworks show.

Account receivables and bad debt control was a problem not just for fireworks manufacturers, but for all businesses in China. Bad debts and lack of respect for business contracts had created a credit crisis in China. The bad debt problem greatly increased transaction costs, slowed down the cash turnover, and had become a headache for fireworks manufacturers. Some had chosen to withdraw from selling in the domestic market, although the profit margin was higher than in the export market.

Legal restrictions, local protectionism, cutthroat price competition, hard-to-penetrate distribution channels and bad debt were impacting negatively on the domestic sales of Liuyang fireworks. In 1997, seeing the decline of its fireworks sales, Liuyang Firecrackers and Fireworks Industry Department, the government agency in charge of the overall development of the pillar industry, decided to start an offensive strategy. First, it opened local offices in most of the 29 provinces, major cities and regions to promote Liuyang fireworks. Second, it regulated the prices that Liuyang fireworks companies could quote and sell in export sales. Third, it resorted to a government-to-government relationship in order to secure contracts for large public fireworks displays in each province. One year after introducing the offensive strategy, Liuyang fireworks sales had increased.

THE EXPORT MARKET

Since the opening of the Chinese economy in 1979, exporting had become a major market for the Chinese fireworks industry. As one of the most celebrated products out of China, export sales of fireworks had risen between 1978 and 1998. According to government statistics, the recorded export sales of firecrackers and fireworks reached US$143 million and US$172 million in 1994 and 1995 respectively. The estimate for 1998 was about US$200 million.

The general belief was that China-made fireworks actually made up about 80 per cent to 90 per cent of the world's fireworks market. The products from China were rich in variety and low in price, but also had a lower reputation in quality control, packaging and timing control, compared to the products made in Japan and Korea. China-made fireworks also would wholesale for much lower prices, usually 80 per cent lower than similar products made in Japan or Korea.

There was little overall co-ordination of export sales. As more and more companies were allowed to export directly, competition kept intensifying and the profit margins on export sales kept slipping. Some manufacturers would even sell at or below cost, just to get the tax refund that the government set aside to encourage export, which could sometimes reach 20 per cent. As a result, underpricing each other became a common practice. Therefore, despite its dominant share of the world market, the Chinese fireworks export industry enjoyed limited profitability. Exhibit 4 provides a comparison of the free on board (FOB) prices quoted by the Chinese companies to U.S. markets versus the prices quoted by the U.S. importers and wholesalers to the retailers and end users on some consumer and display fireworks items. The importers enjoyed a high markup even after paying the 12.5 per cent U.S. import duty. Of course, the importers had to absorb the cost of getting permits, shipping, storing and carrying the inventory for three to four months before making the sales.

Besides suffering from low profit margin, the Chinese fireworks makers were also risking losing their brand identities. Given the low cost and reasonably good quality of the Chinese fireworks, many large fireworks manufacturers and dealers in the West started to outsource the making of their brand-name fireworks. Failing to see the importance of brand equity, the Chinese fireworks manufacturers were sometimes reduced to mere manufacturing outfits for for-

Exhibit 4   Comparison of FOB Import Prices from China and Wholesale Prices of Chinese Fireworks in [the] U.S.

Product Type	Packing	FOB China[1] US$	Wholesale in [the] U.S.[2] US$
Thunderbombs	12/80/16	12.40	42.00
Tri-Rotating Wheel	24/12	15.50	48.50
Changing Color Wheel	72/1	20.70	57.60
Jumping Jack	20/48/12	16.70	60.00
Cuckoo	24/6	14.50	50.40
Ground Bloom Flower	20/12/6	16.40	62.40
Color Sparkler	24/12/8	16.60	66.74
Moon Traveller	25/12/12	9.20	40.00
Crackling Whips	72/12	16.99	50.40
Aerial Display	4/1	19.40	68.00
Evening Party	12/1	12.60	60.00
Assorted Fountain	18/4	10.30	64.20
Assorted Rockets	36/12	24.20	68.00
4" Display Shell w/ Tail	36/1	52.65	165.00
6" display	10/1	41.82	160.00
8" display	6/1	54.53	190.00
12" display	2/1	60.95	190.00

Sources: China Sunsong Fireworks Corp. and Web sites of various fireworks wholesalers in [the] U.S.
[1]FOB major ports in South China. Cost, Insurance, Freight to major ports in [the] U.S. would be $3.00 to $4.00 more per carton.
[2]U.S. import duty rate for fireworks from China was 12.5 per cent.

eign companies, gradually losing their own brands. There were also fireworks merchants in Korea, Japan or Spain, who would buy the products from China, and then repackage them, or replace the fuses with better quality ones, then resell them for much higher prices.

The export market was usually divided into five blocks: Southeast Asia, North America, Europe, South America and the rest of the world. The most popular market had been Europe, where the regulations on fireworks were less stringent, and orders were of larger quantities and better prices. The United States was considered a tough market because of complex regulations and high competition, nevertheless a necessary one if a company wanted to remain a viable world-player. The Canadian market was virtually closed to the Chinese fireworks due to its regulations, although most of the fireworks consumed in Canada were imported, and had probably originated in China before being repackaged in other countries. The result of the stricter regulations in Canada was higher prices for consumers. It was estimated that a fireworks display that cost less than $3,500 in the U.S. would cost Canadians $8,000.

The foreign importers were powerful buyers for several reasons. First, they were very well informed, both through past dealings with China and the Internet. Second, they were able to hire agents who were very familiar with the industry in China. Third, they could deal directly with the factories that were willing to take lower prices. Fourth, there were basically no switching costs, so they could play the suppliers against each other.

The diversity of the cultures in the destination countries greatly reduced the seasonality of the fireworks production and sales. As a result, orders evened out throughout the year. However, the peak season was still towards the end of the year. For the U.S., it was before July 4. Usually, the importers would receive the shipment two or three months beforehand.

The Internet was gradually becoming a marketing outlet for Chinese fireworks. According to a fireworks company's office in Shenzhen, 20 per cent to 30 per cent of the business inquiries they got were through the Internet. However, export sales were still made mainly through foreign trade companies or agents.

In recent years, foreign investments were also funneled into the fireworks industry. In Liuyang, four of the large fireworks factories had foreign investments, made mainly by the fireworks trading companies in Hong Kong.

In 1999, about four-fifths of the 5,000 or so containers of fireworks exported from China annually, were consumer fireworks. However, demand for display fireworks was growing at a faster pace. It was predicted that the demand for display fireworks would increase as organized public shows grew more popular; at the same time, demand for consumer fireworks was expected to decline as regulations were getting stricter. Fireworks shows were increasingly being used in promotional campaigns, and were finding customers among amusement parks, sports teams and retailers for store openings, anniversaries and holiday celebrations.

The Future of the Fireworks Industry in China

The managers of the Chinese fireworks companies that Jerry talked to expressed mixed feelings towards the future outlook of their industry. One pessimistic view was that this was a sunset industry and held that regulations were killing the industry. Moreover, as people became more environmentally-conscious and more distracted by the endless diversities of modern entertainment, traditional celebrations using firecrackers and fireworks would die a gradual death. As to the function of attracting public attention for promotional purposes, fireworks also faced challenges from new technologies, such as laser beams combined with sound effects.

In fact, "make-believe firecrackers" already appeared as substitutes in China. These were made of red plastic tubes strung together like firecrackers with electric bulbs installed inside the tubes. When the power was turned on, the lights would emit sparks, accompanied by crackling reports that sounded like firecrackers. These were being used at weddings and grand openings in cities where firecrackers and fireworks were banned. More interesting substitutes were spotted at some weddings in Beijing, where people paved the road with little red balloons, and made the limousine carrying the bride and groom run over the balloons to make explosive cracking sounds as well as leave behind red bits and pieces of debris. Also, more and more young couples were getting married in western styles, in a church or a scenic green meadow outdoors, where serene and quiet happiness prevailed over the traditional noisy way of celebrating. Therefore, some managers believed that firecrackers and fireworks were doomed to fade off into history.

The more optimistic view, however, was that the industry would not die at all. If the right moves were made by the industry, it could even grow. Some said that tradition would not die so easily. It was in their national character for the Chinese to celebrate with an atmosphere of noisy happiness. Moreover, even in the West, the popularity of fireworks was not suffering from all the regulations. No real substitutes could replace fireworks, which combined the sensual pleasures of visual, audio and emotional stimuli. For instance, the U.S. Congressional resolution in 1963 to use bells to replace fireworks in celebrating Independence Day never really caught on.

Fireworks were also being combined with modern technologies like laser beams, computerized firing and musical accompaniment to make the appeal of fireworks more irresistible. The safety problem was not really as serious as people were made to believe, and would only improve with new technological innovations like smokeless fireworks.

However, both sides agreed that the Chinese fireworks industry would have to change its strategy, especially in international competition, to stay a viable and profitable player.

THE DECISION

Meanwhile, Jerry had to decide whether it was worthwhile to invest in the fireworks industry. He wondered whether he could apply the industry analysis framework he had studied in his MBA program.

The Richard Ivey School of Business gratefully acknowledges the generous support of The Richard and Jean Ivey Fund in the development of this case as part of the RICHARD AND JEAN IVEY FUND ASIAN CASE SERIES.

"What I'm known for is transferring best practices. That's particularly important in this economic environment, when you have to maximize revenues through existing assets."

–Bob Nardelli, CEO of Home Depot, in 2001[1]

Home Depot's Strategy Under Bob Nardelli

BSTR141

FIRST MANHATTAN STORE

In September 2004, The Home Depot Inc. (Home Depot), the biggest home improvement retailer in the world, opened a new store in New York's up-market Manhattan region. The store, spread over 105,000 square feet, employed over 300 'associates'[2] and featured a range of home improvement products, specially geared to the needs of Manhattan's residents.

Based on the findings of extensive consumer research, Home Depot incorporated a number of features in the new store that would appeal to an urban customer base. For instance, the store had a door attendant to hail cabs, and a help desk to offer information and schedule appointments with in-house designers. The products in the store were also more upscale than in the company's traditional stores, which

stocked mainly cheap and functional items. "We've got nails. We've got electrical sockets. But we've also got $7,000 rugs," said Tom Taylor, the company's Eastern Division president, on the products on offer at the new store.[3]

The company also planned to offer special "how-to" clinics on themes like "how to create a garden on a fire escape", "how to make 500 square feet seem like 5000", etc. "Our new Manhattan location is a retail marvel and proof positive that The Home Depot continues to break the mold in how we approach new formats, new markets and new customers," said Bob Nardelli (Nardelli), the company's CEO.[4] The company also planned to open a second store in Manhattan by the end of 2004.

Over the years, Home Depot had grown chiefly by opening stores in new locations. However, the Manhattan store was a departure from the norm in that it was the first store to be opened in a large metropolitan area as against the company's earlier strategy of concentrating on suburban areas and small towns. Analysts said that the reason for the changed approach was a saturation of markets in suburban localities, which was limiting Home Depot's growth and revenue. By targeting metropolitan locations, Home Depot aimed to offset the saturation setting in its traditional suburban outlets. Nardelli said that if the format worked in Manhattan, it would give the company access to other large metropolitan areas.

BACKGROUND NOTE

Home Depot traces its roots to 1978, when Bernie Marcus (Marcus) and Arthur Blank (Blank) developed the concept

---

[1] Patricia Sellers, "Exit the Builder, Enter the Repairman," *Fortune,* 2001.

[2] Home Depot called its employees 'associates.'

[3] Elizabeth Lazarowitz, "Home Depot Goes Urban, Opens First Manhattan Store," news.yahoo.com, September 9, 2004.

[4] ir.homedepot.com.

of large, warehouse-like stores, which stocked large varieties of home-related products, and sold them at the lowest possible prices. The stores targeted mainly "do-it-yourselfers,"[5] and adopted a "no-frills" approach to selling [merchandise]. On June 22, 1979, the first three Home Depot stores were opened in Atlanta. By the end of 1979, Home Depot had 200 associates, and had crossed $7 million dollars in sales.

In 1981, Home Depot made a public issue, raising over $4 million. Most of the money was ploughed into opening new stores. In 1984, Home Depot's shares were listed on the New York Stock Exchange. In the early 1980s, Home Depot grew very rapidly, and by 1985, the company had 50 stores and $700 million in revenues. In 1986, the stores' sales touched the $1 billion mark.

In 1991, Home Depot established its first Expo Design Center in San Diego. The Expo Design Centers carried higher-end products compared to Home Depot and sold complete solutions to household needs, such as modular kitchens, assembled bathrooms, etc. In the same year, the company's sales crossed five billion dollars. In the mid 1990s, Home Depot collaborated with the Discovery Channel and Lynette Jennings (a popular television personality and authority on home decorating and design in the U.S.) on a home improvement program, called *HouseSmart,* which was televised daily. By 1996, there were over 500 Home Depot outlets. Most of the outlets were in suburban areas and near small towns.

In 1997, Marcus stepped down and Blank became the CEO of Home Depot. In the same year, the company entered into a joint agreement with S.A.C.I. Falabella, the top departmental store in Chile and Peru, to open home improvement stores in Chile. By 1998, the company had entered South America, opening stores first in Chile and later in Puerto Rico. In 1998, Home Depot initiated its Tool Rental program, which allowed customers to rent tools for their home improvement projects. Another important event that year was the introduction of a computerized job application process, which made the recruitment process simpler and more efficient. In 1999, the company announced its environment-friendly wood policy, through which it vowed to stop selling goods that were made from wood cut in ancient and ecologically important forests. In his announcement of the policy, Blank affirmed that Home Depot would eliminate wood products from endangered sources like the rain forests, and some types of wood like cedar, redwood and lauan, giving preference instead to certified wood.

In 2000, Nardelli became the CEO of the company. The company opened stores in Canada and Argentina and expanded its international operations. However, the Argentinean and Chilean operations were not successful and the company withdrew from South America in 2001. In 2002, Marcus retired and Nardelli was appointed chairman in his

place. The company expanded into Mexico, mainly through the acquisition of Mexican home improvement chains like Total Home, and Del Norte. It also opened sourcing offices in China to enable the purchase of cheap products from China and other labor-intensive Asian countries.

In 2003, Home Depot had sales of $64.8 billion and $4.3 billion in earnings (Refer [to] Exhibit 1 for annual financials of Home Depot). By the end of 2003, it had 1635 stores and employed over 300,000 associates. The stores stocked over 40,000 products related to home building, improvement and repair. (Refer [to] Exhibit 2.) In addition to Home Depot stores, the company also operated several specialized subsidiaries (Refer [to] Exhibit 3 for a profile of Home Depot's subsidiaries). In 2004, Home Depot was the largest home improvement store in the world, and the second largest retailer in the U.S. (behind Wal-Mart) and the third largest retailer globally.

Exhibit 1   Home Depot—Annual Financials (2002–04)

Income Statement (all amounts in millions of USD except share data)	January 04	January 03	January 02
Revenue	64,816.0	58,247.0	53,553.0
Cost of Goods Sold	43,160.0	39,236.0	36,642.0
Gross Profit	21,656.0	19,011.0	16,911.0
Gross Profit Margin	33.4%	32.6%	31.6%
SG&A Expense	13,734.0	12,278.0	11,215.0
Depreciation & Amortization	1,076.0	903.0	764.0
Operating Income	6,846.0	5,830.0	4,932.0
Operating Margin	10.6%	10.0%	9.2%
Nonoperating Income	59.0	79.0	53.0
Nonoperating Expenses	62.0	37.0	28.0
Income Before Taxes	6,843.0	5,872.0	4,957.0
Income Taxes	2,539.0	2,208.0	1,913.0
Net Income After Taxes	4,304.0	3,664.0	3,044.0
Continuing Operations	4,304.0	3,664.0	3,044.0
Discontinued Operations	0.0	0.0	0.0
Total Operations	4,304.0	3,664.0	3,044.0
Total Net Income	4,304.0	3,664.0	3,044.0
Net Profit Margin	6.6%	6.3%	5.7%

Source: www.hoovers.com.

Exhibit 2   Home Depot's Product Categories

- Building and Remodeling
- Home Décor and Organizing
- Outdoor Living
- Tools and Hardware

Source: www.homedepot.com.

[5] Customers who preferred to purchase products and do their home improvements themselves instead of contracting them out.

Exhibit 3   Home Depot's Specialized Ventures

Expo Design Centers

Expo Design Centers were showrooms, which put customers in complete and finished settings. For instance, a completely set-up kitchen or bathroom was displayed and customers were allowed to make modifications in the setting. They featured more lifestyle and designer products than general Home Depot Stores, which emphasized functionality. Most of the products at Expo Centers had to be special ordered and they stocked very few items in the stores.

The Home Depot Supply

The Home Depot Supply was part of Home Depot's growth strategy to expand into emerging markets and professional customer channels. The division served professional customers' needs by offering products and services that complemented Home Depot's core retail business. Home Depot Supply served the diverse needs of business-to-business customers, with a national focus on production homebuilders, facility maintenance professionals, construction contractors and government customers.

The Home Depot Landscape Supply

Home Depot Landscape Supply was a store selling a complete range of landscape products and services, including delivery, tool rental, etc. The stores stocked products like saplings, shrubs, indoor plants and gardening tools, and catered to professional landscapers as well as amateur gardeners.

The Home Depot Floor Store

This was a specialized division selling flooring materials and accessories like rugs and carpets, targeting professional flooring contractors as well as do-it-yourself customers. The company even provided installation to customers. These stores also stocked minimum [merchandise] and most of the sales were through special order.

Georgia Lighting

Georgia Lighting sold an extensive collection of fine decorative and antique lighting, accent furniture, antiques, and a complete line of unique accessories. This division boasted the largest lighting showroom in the U.S.

Adapted from www.homedepot.com.

Changes Under Nardelli

When Nardelli became the CEO of Home Depot in late 2000, there was widespread interest in industrial circles. Home Depot had thus far been managed only by its founders (Marcus until 1997 and then Blank till 2000). Marcus had an iconic status at Home Depot, and analysts often compared his position in the company to that of Wal-Mart's Sam Walton.

Although Blank's personality was distinct from that of Marcus, there were no significant changes in the company's operations or its culture under him. "If you like the package of the last 19 years, you can count on more of the same," Blank said when he succeeded Marcus.[6] Analysts expected that when Blank retired, the board would choose someone from within the company to succeed him, even though there was no heir apparent in the company. Nardelli's appointment came as a surprise to many analysts and company insiders because he was a complete outsider, and one with no retail experience.

Nardelli had a detail-oriented style of management. He had worked at General Electric (GE) for 27 years, and was one of the three contenders to succeed Jack Welch in 2000. Like many of the top executives at GE, Nardelli had a deep belief in "processes" and believed that better processes led to better products, and consequently, better profits. Many analysts felt that Nardelli, with his experience [with] GE and its focus on processes and systems, was the right person for Home Depot at that juncture, when it was passing through a difficult phase.

The rapid growth in Home Depot in its first two decades came largely from its setting up of new stores. In the late 1990s, the company's growth rate began to slow. The company said that the lower rate of growth was a reflection of the slowing economy (which resulted in a slump in home building), expensive labor and falling lumber prices (which resulted in a lower level of total sales). However, analysts believed that the main reason for the slowdown was market saturation.

In the first quarter of 2001, Home Depot's profits rose only 16 percent, which was considerably lower than the company's five-year annual average of 25 percent. Soon after the announcement of the first quarter 2001 results, David Buchsbaum (Buchsbaum), an analyst at Wachovia Securities, said, "They're certainly at or near their store-saturation point. From now on, they have to garner growth through more efficient operation of the existing store base."[7] Analysts agreed that major changes were imperative in Home Depot's culture and strategic direction to put the company on a high growth trajectory again, and many of them were confident that Nardelli was well qualified to bring about these changes. Over the early 2000s, Nardelli made several changes in Home Depot's operations and business strategy, which helped the company streamline its activities and grow in a balanced manner.

Rationalizing Store Openings

One of the biggest threats for retail businesses is unplanned and excessive growth, which can result in stores being set up too close to each other, eventually cannibalizing each other's customer base. Traditionally, Home Depot increased its

---

[6] Nicole Harris, "Home Depot: Beyond Do It Yourselfers," *BusinessWeek*, June 30, 1997.

[7] Sam Jaffe, "New Tricks in Home Depot's Toolbox?" *BusinessWeek*, June 5, 2001.

number of stores by 20 percent every year. While this rate of expansion worked well in the initial years, by the late 1990s analysts felt that the number of stores was growing too fast. By the late 1990s, the company had set up more stores than it could conveniently manage, while failing to invest in the systems that would help in their management. "Same store" or "comparable store" sales[8] had been declining since the mid-1990s, and while new stores were successful in increasing their revenues, the older stores were not performing well. In 2000, comparable store sales increased only four percent, as compared to around ten percent in the 1990s. "Store growth will need to slow at some point. Investors are starting to see that we're very close to the saturation point," said Buchsbaum.[9]

Nardelli decided to stop the proliferation of stores and to ensure that expansion was balanced. The first thing that Nardelli did on being appointed CEO was to lower the target for store openings in 2001 by nine percent. Home Depot eventually opened 204 stores in 2001, which was the same number as in 2000. Nardelli reasoned that growth should come from internal changes in existing stores, rather than new store openings, so that the overall performance of the company would be positive and strong. The company also began to choose locations for new stores more carefully to ensure that they were not set up too close to other Home Depots.

Improving the Supply Chain

Until 2000, Home Depot did not have any formal system for inventory management or purchasing. While many of its competitors were switching to automated inventory management systems, Home Depot was still logging in each shipment manually. In the stores, employees spent more time restocking shelves and taking inventory counts than in assisting customers. One survey conducted in the late 1990s revealed that Home Depot's sales associates spent 70 percent of their time restocking and 30 percent helping customers.

Soon after Nardelli became CEO, he introduced a new service program for all the stores, which required employees to restock at night and spend maximum time with customers during service hours. He also mandated that the new program be adopted in all the stores by the end of 2001. A survey conducted after the new program was adopted showed that the time associates spent with customers and the time they took to restock shelves had been reversed. This improved the service at the stores considerably and Nardelli estimated that the change would bring in additional revenues of $2.8 billion in 2001.

To cut down on excess inventories, Nardelli decided to adopt a leaner approach. Storekeepers were trained to take a scientific approach to ordering new stocks and avoid excessive inventory. He also told managers to increase "inventory velocity," or the speed at which products flowed through the store. This would ensure that stores did not purchase more goods than they needed, keeping inventory costs as low as possible.

Purchasing at Home Depot was also ridden with inefficiencies. Home Depot had nine operating regions, and purchasing was fully decentralized in all the regions. Individual buyers from the nine regions dealt separately with suppliers for their regional purchases. This created a number of inefficiencies in the overall system.

To correct this situation, Nardelli centralized Home Depot's purchasing function, locating it at Atlanta. He believed that centralization would eliminate inefficiencies, as well as increase negotiating power with sellers. The number of suppliers was also cut down to facilitate standardization. The company estimated that centralization of purchasing and standardization of suppliers increased the company's gross margins by one percentage point—a major achievement in the retailing industry.

Betting on IT

Home Depot was a laggard in the adoption of Information Technology (IT). Most of the systems—inventory, purchasing, recruitment, performance appraisal—were not up to date. In fact, when Nardelli joined the firm, there wasn't even a system for the different stores to be connected through e-mail. This increased the cost of coordination between stores.

Nardelli moved to apply IT constructively throughout the company. Systems like inventory, appraisal, etc., were taken up for automation. "There's an enormous amount of room to improve margins just by advancing its information technology," said Robert Morse, manager of the Wall Street Fund.[10]

In the early 2000s, Home Depot began introducing self-checkout kiosks at some of its stores. This reduced the time spent by customers on their check-outs and cut the queues at cashiers. In 2004, the company started deploying a massive software program that would automate quotes, scheduling and order tracking. Nardelli said that the company was spending 12 times more on IT in 2004 than in 2000. By 2004, the company had self-checkout [facilities] at more than 800 of its stores, and it was estimated that 32 percent of the customers used them.

In-Store Improvements

Home Depot stores had always been laid out like warehouses, with a large number of products displayed [on] huge shelves from the ceiling to the floor. The idea was to create a

---

[8] A retail industry metric used to measure the growth from stores that have been open a year or more.

[9] Sam Jaffe, "What's Hammering Home Depot?" *BusinessWeek*, October 18, 2000.

[10] Sam Jaffe, "New Tricks in Home Depot's Toolbox?" *BusinessWeek*, June 5, 2001

warehouse-like atmosphere where people could purchase all that they needed for home improvement at discount prices. However, surveys in the early 2000s revealed that this layout had lost its appeal for most people. Improvements in the retailing industry in the early 2000s led shoppers to favor stores that were bright, clean and open and contributed to the enjoyment of the shopping experience.

In the early 2000s, Home Depot began making changes to its store layouts on these lines. For instance, lighting displays were moved to the front in many stores, so as to make them brighter and more inviting. The stores also did away with floor to ceiling displays and began displaying many of the products at eye level for customers to look at easily. "You'll see a lot more of our sets come down. It makes for a better shopping experience," said Carol Tomé, the company's CFO.[11] This also made the stores more customer-friendly as products were easier to access. In-store innovations also helped improve customer service. For instance, instead of stacking up paint cans on shelves, most Home Depots set up color solution centers, where customers could consult with experts in the field to choose colors or order special colors for their homes. Better store displays helped Home Depot keep up with competitor Lowe's Companies Inc. (Lowe['s]), a company that had a good reputation for its customer-friendly store layout.

Emphasizing the Service Angle

Nardelli also shifted the focus in Home Depot from its traditional customer base of "do-it-yourselfers" to people who preferred a full basket of services. Nardelli reasoned that, while some people liked to purchase products and do their home improvements themselves, a far greater number of them preferred to hire someone to do it for them. He believed that Home Depot could increase its margins considerably by offering installation and other services to people who purchased merchandise from the stores.

Prior to 2000, Home Depot offered installation services in some of its stores, but the service was not standardized or uniform across stores. Besides, it was restricted to the surrounding locality and even within those areas, not all the customers were aware that such services were available.

The company moved to increase awareness about these services in the early 2000s, by putting up toll-free installation numbers on all the company's signboards and advertisements. It also set up service desks in front of all its stores, where customers could register for home consultations regarding their home improvement projects. Customers could also register over the Internet.

Home Depot entered into tie-ups with contractors, who did the installations on behalf of the company. Before selection, a contractor had to go through a comprehensive screening process, which included a detailed criminal and immigration background check. The contractors were also required to wear an identity card issued by Home Depot. In early 2004, the company had tie-ups with over 6000 contractors all over the U.S. It also acquired a few small installation companies to expand the business. In 2003, Home Depot spent $248 million on the acquisition of several small installation companies, including Installed Products USA, which installed roofing and fences, and RMA Home Services, which provided siding and window installation.

Nardelli believed that many customers would find it more convenient to get their installations done by someone from Home Depot, rather than appointing a contractor themselves. It would also endear Home Depot to contractors, who took up 30 percent of the company's sales. After tying up with Home Depot, many contractors increased their purchases and stocks of Home Depot [merchandise] to use in installations that did not originate at Home Depot.

In 2004, the installation unit was the fastest-growing unit of the company, expanding at 40 percent per year. The company had 25 national installation programs, covering roofing, siding, fencing, windows, decking and sheds. The company ensured that high standards were maintained in the installation business through its careful screening of the contractors with whom it tied up. In addition to this, customers were required to call in and rate the installation job before the contractors were paid. The company said that most of the callers rated the jobs eight or higher on a scale of ten.

Home Depot also began targeting professionals like plumbers, carpenters and builders, who, according to the company's research, spent three times more than amateur customers. The company set up Home Depot Pro in 2001 to cater specifically to professionals. The Pro stores were laid out differently from the regular Home Depot outlets and were staffed by experienced store assistants. Products were also sold in larger packs or in bulk. Some of the regular Home Depot stores also introduced hours catering specially to professionals, and many of them took up the Pro initiative program, where there was a special desk to serve professionals. Targeting professionals pitted Home Depot against smaller companies that specialized in specific areas of home-building supply, but analysts felt that Home Depot's huge size gave it a competitive advantage in the home improvement market.

Exploring New Markets

In the early 2000s, as the market in the U.S. was getting saturated and competition from other stores was increasing, Home Depot began exploring options overseas. In the late 1990s, the company had made a foray into Chile and Argentina. However, the ventures were not very successful and it had to withdraw from the markets.

But [the] next time around, Home Depot was more successful and by 2004, it had stores in Canada, Mexico, Puerto Rico and the District of Columbia. Analysts also

---

[11] Dean Foust, "Home Depot's Remodeling Project," *BusinessWeek,* January 9, 2004.

believed that, given its good cash position (around $5.2 billion in cash reserves in 2003) and strong balance sheet, the company was likely to try for some acquisitions in Europe. They said that Home Depot had the potential to become a strong player in Europe.

Home Depot was also looking at China as a market with great potential. In 2002, the company opened offices in Shanghai and Shenzhen to obtain customer data as a preliminary to setting up shop in the country. "We have studied China for some time. It's got a great capability in terms of a growing economy," said Bill Patterson, who was appointed to the newly created position of Home Depot president of Asia.[12]

In addition to overseas expansion, the company also began to focus on setting up more stores in urban areas in the U.S. during the 2000s. The urban stores were smaller than regular Home Depot stores and carried products that city people were interested in. The company opened its first urban format store in Brooklyn, New York, in 2001. The company maintained that the store was getting a mixed response, and it was clear that the higher overhead costs in urban areas would not justify the setting up of too many urban stores.

THE CHALLENGES

It was not easy for Nardelli to initiate changes at Home Depot. While most people acknowledged that significant changes in Home Depot's strategy of the 1990s were required, Nardelli faced a large amount of criticism from various quarters for the changes he made at Home Depot.

Firstly, critics said that Nardelli was moving too fast and that the changes that he was making were too drastic. Analysts said that this rate of transformation could upset old timers at Home Depot, who would not take revolutionary changes kindly. "There's the fear that Home Depot is changing too much, too fast," said UBS Warburg analyst Aram Rubinson.[13] But Nardelli pointed out that speed was required to bring in positive results faster. He also said that speed in adapting to new conditions was a very critical factor for success in the retail business. "The rate of internal change must be greater than the rate of external change, or we will fall behind," said Nardelli.[14]

Secondly, Nardelli's application of GE's numbers-oriented management did not go down well with executives at Home Depot. Soon after Nardelli joined, many top executives at Home Depot resigned or threatened to resign, as they

were not able to accept the sudden change in orientation at the company. "It was time to infuse some different thinking in the company, but his 'do it my way' style undercut the sense of ownership employees had," said one longtime human-resources manager who left Home Depot for a job at another Atlanta company, taking along several employees. "It was revolution, not evolution," he added.[15]

Thirdly, analysts feared that some of Nardelli's revolutionary policies could alienate customers. For instance, Nardelli's elimination of the "cash return" policy of the company was widely criticized. Home Depot's original cash return policy allowed customers to return any product they bought at Home Depot, to any store, without any time limitations and even without proof of purchase, to claim [a] full refund. In the 2000s, Nardelli and Tome conducted a study to see the efficacy of this policy and realized that it was highly abused. Consequently, Nardelli abolished it and introduced a new policy, which allowed customers to return goods only with a proof of purchase and within 90 days of purchase. It was estimated that the new policy would save Home Depot $10 million annually, but some analysts still felt that it would harm the company's goodwill with customers.

HOME DEPOT VS. LOWE['S] IN THE EARLY 2000S

In the early 2000s, Lowe['s] became a major competitor to Home Depot. Lowe['s], which was initially set up as a regional operator in North Carolina, was the top home improvement retailer in the U.S. in the 1980s, but was overtaken by Home Depot's rapid expansion in the 1990s. Lowe['s] changed its strategy in the 1990s, opening more stores in metropolitan areas, and consequently, grew rapidly in the 1990s and early 2000s.

By 2004, Lowe['s] had over 950 stores in the U.S. (the company's store expansion rate was around 14 percent in the 2000s, while Home Depot had lowered its expansion rate to around 10 percent). It was the second largest home improvement retailer in the U.S. at this time. Lowe['s] planned to open 140 more stores in 2004. Some company insiders and shareholders blamed Nardelli for Lowe's closing in on Home Depot. They said that Lowe['s] had a good chance of overtaking Home Depot, considering that Nardelli had slowed Home Depot's store expansion rate. Lowe['s] was also performing better than Home Depot on the financial front and the company's stock had tripled in the first three years of the 2000s, as against Home Depot's, which fell by 12 percent. Lowe's profits also rose by nearly 40 percent in 2003, while Home Depot's profits were increasing at about 18 percent.

---

[12] "Home Depot Preparing to Expand to China," *The Boston Herald*, June 7, 2004.

[13] Patricia Sellers, Julie Schlosser "Its His Home Depot Now," *Fortune*, September 20, 2004.

[14] Patricia Sellers, "Something to Prove," *Fortune*, June 24, 2002.

[15] Carol Hymowitz, "How One Savvy Executive Led a Winning Revolution," *Career Journal*, March 17, 2004.

Exhibit 4   Stock Price Movement

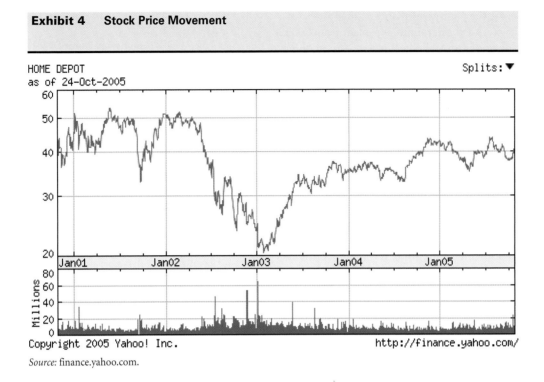

HOME DEPOT
as of 24-Oct-2005   Splits: ▼

Copyright 2005 Yahoo! Inc.   http://finance.yahoo.com/

Source: finance.yahoo.com.

Lowe's entry into city markets led analysts to fear that it would overtake Home Depot in these areas. "Lowe's has the opportunity to grab market share. It's a tight, tough business, but there's definitely room for them," said Mike Porter, an analyst at Morningstar.[16]

Some analysts also said that Lowe['s] had a competitive advantage over Home Depot in that its stores were generally perceived to be better laid out and more appealing, especially to women. Lowe['s] had made a conscious decision to make stores more appealing to women as its research indicated that women made a majority of the purchasing decisions. Executive Vice-President for Merchandising Dale C. Pond said, "Eighty percent of (home) projects are initiated by females."[17] Therefore, Lowe['s] made its stores brighter, cleaner and more spacious, to attract women as well as other non-professional shoppers, who hesitated to buy things in "lumber shops." Sandy Cooper, a homemaker and loyal customer of Lowe['s] said about Lowe['s], "I have to sing their praises, because they were very nice. At Home Depot, you can't find anybody to help—and if you do, they just point."[18]

Home Depot had a practice of employing more part-time staff to operate the stores. Analysts said that part-time staff did not take much interest in closing sales because they did not have a sense of responsibility. On the other hand, Lowe's store assistants, most of whom were permanent employees, were found to be more friendly and helpful. (In 2004, 60 percent of Home Depot's staff was permanent compared to Lowe's 80 percent.) Analysts said that, because store assistants were the main points of contact for the customer with the store, they played an important role in determining the image that customers formed of a store.

THE SHARE PRICE PARADOX

While analysts were speculating about whether Lowe['s] would be able to overtake Home Depot to become the biggest retailer in its segment, Home Depot's executives, especially Nardelli, were trying to analyze the reasons for the fall in the company's share price. The stock, which traded at around $70 in late 1999 and early 2000, fell to an all-time low of around $22 in early 2003 and was trading at around $38 in 2004 (Refer [to] Exhibit 4 for stock price movements). Executives were worried that the market was not responding to the company's growth. Nardelli was reported to have said, "I can understand not getting rewarded, but I don't understand getting punished."[19] It was also said that shareholders

[16] Amy Tsao, "How Home Depot and Lowe Measure Up," *BusinessWeek,* December 5, 2001.

[17] Aixa M. Pascual, "Lowe is Sprucing up Its House," *BusinessWeek,* June 3, 2002.

[18] Aixa M. Pascual, "Lowe is Sprucing up Its House," *BusinessWeek,* June 3, 2002.

[19] Patricia Sellers, "Something to Prove," *Fortune,* June 24, 2002.

blamed Nardelli for the poor performance of the stock, considering that the stock fell by around 50 percent from 2000. "I think there are people on Wall Street who are questioning his ability to make the change and run a retail organization," said Erik Becker, an analyst at Waddell & Reed Financial, an investment fund.[20]

What was even more perplexing was that the price failed to rise despite the improving financial performance of Home Depot. In the first quarter of 2004, same store sales rose 7.7 percent, which was the highest rate of growth experienced in the last five years.

Some analysts explained that although Home Depot had made some changes for the better since 2000, the company was by no means stable in the market. Competition had increased not only from Lowe['s], but also from other smaller companies, which sold home improvement items over the [Internet], at prices much lower than Home Depot's. Of these companies, some were suppliers to Home Depot.

Although Nardelli made some positive changes to Home Depot's operations and strategy, analysts said that most of the steps he took were more relevant to manufacturing than to retail. They said that Nardelli had moved too fast, considering that he had no experience in retail. One example of this was his new inventory management system, which made stores run on leaner inventory. Store managers said that leaner inventory often led to under-stocking of high demand goods, which created a shortfall and led to customer complaints.

However, Nardelli's supporters said that his numbers-oriented and scientific style of management managed to streamline the somewhat haphazard growth path that Home Depot followed until 2000. "They had been in start-up mode for 22 years," said Nardelli soon after becoming CEO.[21] His supporters believed that Nardelli was the right person to shift Home Depot from its startup mode to that of a mature industry leader.

Additional Readings & References:

1. Patricia Sellers, **Can Home Depot Fix Its Sagging Stock?** *Fortune,* March 4, 1996.
2. Nicole Harris, **Home Depot: Beyond Do It Yourselfers,** *BusinessWeek,* June 30, 1997.
3. Jennifer Bresnahan, **Home Depot's Ron Griffin on How IS Benefits from Corporate Values,** *CIO Magazine,* May 1, 1998.
4. Roy Johnson, **Home Depot Renovates,** *Fortune,* November 23, 1998.
5. Lawrence Armour, **Home Depot: Now It Can Be Told,** *Fortune,* May 1, 1999.
6. Katrina Brooker, **E-Rivals Seem to Have Home Depot Awfully Nervous,** *Fortune,* August 16, 1999.
7. Cora Daniels, **To Hire a Lumber Expert, Click Here,** *Fortune,* April 3, 2000.
8. Nicholas Stein, **Winning the War to Keep Top Talent,** *Fortune,* May 29, 2000.
9. Sam Jaffe, **What's Hammering Home Depot?** *BusinessWeek,* October 18, 2000.
10. **Co-Founder Trades Depot's Orange Apron for Family and Community,** www.findarticles.com, March 5, 2001.
11. Patricia Sellers, **Exit the Builder, Enter the Repairman,** *Fortune,* March 19, 2001.
12. Sam Jaffe, **New Tricks in Home Depot's Toolbox?** *BusinessWeek,* June 5, 2001.
13. Patricia Sellers, **Home Depot's Home Defense,** *Fortune,* October 15, 2001.
14. Aixa M. Pascual, **Tidying Up At Home Depot,** *BusinessWeek,* November 26, 2001.
15. Amy Tsao, **How Home Depot and Lowe Measure Up,** *BusinessWeek,* December 5, 2001.
16. Anthony Williams, **What? Now We Have to Make a Profit *and* Be Ethical?** *Business 2.0,* February 1, 2002.
17. Aixa M. Pascual, **Lowe Is Sprucing up Its House,** *BusinessWeek,* June 3, 2002.
18. Amy Tsao, **Reading Home Depot's Fuzzy Blueprint,** *BusinessWeek,* June 4, 2002.
19. Patricia Sellers, **Something to Prove,** *Fortune,* June 24, 2002.
20. Dean Foust, **Home Depot's "Big Disappointment": Sales,** *BusinessWeek,* January 17, 2003.
21. Dean Foust, **The GE Way Isn't Working at Home Depot,** *BusinessWeek,* January 17, 2003.
22. Janice Revell, **Can Home Depot Get Its Groove Back?** *Fortune,* February 3, 2003.
23. Matthew Maier, **How to Revive Home Depot,** *Business 2.0,* May 1, 2003.
24. Dean Foust, **Home Depot Still Hasn't Nailed Lowe's,** *BusinessWeek,* November 20, 2003.
25. Dean Foust, **Home Depot's Remodeling Project,** *BusinessWeek,* January 9, 2004.
26. Carol Hymowitz, **How One Savvy Executive Led a Winning Revolution,** *Career Journal,* March 17, 2004.
27. Janice Revell, **More Room for Improvement?** *Fortune,* March 22, 2004.
28. **Home Depot Preparing to Expand to China,** *The Boston Herald,* June 7, 2004.
29. Jyothi Thottam, **Bob the Builder,** *Time,* June 21, 2004.
30. Rebecca Zicarelli, **Home Depot's Hardware Warriors,** *Fast Company,* September 2004.
31. Chana R. Schoenberger, **House Call,** *Forbes,* September 6, 2004.
32. Elizabeth Lazarowitz, **Home Depot Goes Urban, Opens First Manhattan Store,** news.yahoo.com, September 9, 2004.
33. Patricia Sellers, Julie Schlosser, **Its His Home Depot Now,** *Fortune,* September 20, 2004.
34. Kelvin Taylor, **The Windfall of Hurricanes,** www.fool.com, September 20, 2004.
35. Julie Schlosser, **He'll Take Manhattan,** *Fortune,* September 20, 2004.
36. Karen Jacobs, **Home Depot, Lowe's Sees Strong Post-Hurricane Demand,** about.reuters.com.
37. www.rabble.ca.
38. www.sprawl-busters.com.
39. www.youareworthmore.org.
40. www.hoovers.com.
41. ir.homedepot.com.
42. www.homedepot.com.

[20] Dean Foust, "The GE Way Isn't Working at Home Depot," *BusinessWeek,* January 17, 2003.

[21] Carol Hymowitz, "How One Savvy Executive Led a Winning Revolution," *Career Journal,* March 17, 2004.

"Everyone always says, 'What's your secret?' It's very simple. We're like Wal-Mart in the U.S.—we pile it high and sell it cheap."

–Michael O'Leary, CEO of Ryanair[1]

"Ryanair is the best imitation of Southwest Airlines that I have seen."

–Herbert D. Kelleher, founder of Southwest Airlines[2]

"He (O'Leary) is almost certainly one of the most successful leaders in the industry, with a unique business model, discipline and an extraordinary level of confidence."

–Sir Michael Bishop, chairman, BMI British Midland[3]

"Ryanair has the financial and operational capacity to maintain its position as the dominant player in the low fares, no frills market, and indeed become one of Europe's largest airlines."

–Stephen Furlong, airline analyst, Davy Stockbrokers[4]

Ryanair—The "Southwest" of European Airlines

BSTR059

RYANAIR CHALLENGES EASYJET

In the summer of 2003, Michael O'Leary (O'Leary), the CEO of Ryanair, one of the oldest and most successful low-cost airlines of Europe, outfitted himself in combat gear and led a small army of Ryanair's employees to Luton airport, the base of rival easyJet.[5] An old World War II battle tank was also roped in to complete the effect. This was Ryanair's way of "attacking" the fares of easyJet, which, it claimed, were very high for a low-cost airline. O'Leary said he wanted to "liberate" the public from the high fares of easyJet. Through this unconventional publicity stunt, O'Leary was able to get his message across successfully and create positive media attention for his airline.

Ryanair was one of the first independent airlines in Ireland. Until Ryanair was set up in 1985, the Irish air services were almost exclusively under the control of Aer Lingus, the national carrier. Some other airlines, notably Avair, had been set up in Ireland before Ryanair, but most of them collapsed due to their inability to compete with the more powerful national carrier. The setting up of Ryanair was an important

---

---

[1] Kerry Capell, Carlos Tromben, William Echikson, Wendy Zellner, "Renegade Ryanair," *Business Week,* May 14, 2001.

[2] Kerry Capell, Carlos Tromben, William Echikson, Wendy Zellner, "Renegade Ryanair," *Business Week,* May 14, 2001.

[3] "The Life of Ryan," www.easyprotest2.com.

[4] www.ryanair.com.

[5] easyJet is a low-cost airline based in London. It was set up [by] Stelios Haji-Ioannou, a Greek shipping magnate.

landmark in Irish airline history. Ryanair went through a few turbulent years of operation, but soon it managed to refocus itself successfully as a low-cost no-frills carrier, capturing a large share of the market for air services between England and Ireland. By the late 1990s, it was the largest low-cost airline in Europe. However, it was overtaken by easyJet when the latter took over Go, the low-cost subsidiary of British Airways (BA), to gain a larger market and a bigger combined fleet. (Refer [to] Exhibit 1 for note[s] on low-cost airlines in Europe.)

BACKGROUND NOTE

Ryanair started operations in July 1985, flying between Waterford in the southeast of Ireland and London's Gatwick airport. Three brothers, Catlan, Declan and Shane Ryan, were the founding shareholders of Ryanair, which was set up to offer low-cost, no-frills services between Ireland and London. The airline began operations with a fifteen-seater turbo prop commuter plane which was leased to the company by Guinness Peat Aviation (GPA),[6] of which their father, Tony Ryan, was the chairman.

Ryanair got an early break when, shortly after its formation, the UK and Irish governments signed a new air services agreement that deregulated air traffic between the two countries. In anticipation of the increased air traffic between the two countries, the Irish government decided to license a second Irish operator on the route from Dublin to London. Ryanair happened to be the only airline to apply for the license. It was granted the license to operate on the Dublin (Ireland)–Luton (London) route. By the end of the first year, Ryanair had carried 5,000 passengers and had a staff of 57.

To meet increased operational requirements, Ryanair purchased two more planes (24-year-old 50-seaters) from Dan Air. The airline quickly realized that it could capitalize on the market by offering cheap fares, and set its initial fare at IR£95 (1 Ireland pound was equal to approximately 1.44 U.S. dollars) for a return ticket. The price was 20 percent lower than the cheapest fare of its competitors. Gradually, the airline replaced its old aircraft with newer aircraft purchased from TAROM, a Romanian air transport company.

By the end of 1986, services to London were firmly established. However, further expansion had been blocked because the requisite licenses could not be obtained. To overcome this, Ryanair acquired an 85 percent stake in London European Airways (LEA, a Luton-based airline). LEA had been flying scheduled flights to Amsterdam and Brussels from London, but the flights had been suspended in early 1987. By May 1987, Ryanair had resumed services to both the cities. However, load factors were low on both the routes

---

6 GPA was set up in 1975 as an aircraft leasing company. Tony Ryan was a founder member of GPA.

Exhibit 1   Low-Cost Airlines in Europe

In the mid-1990s, after the European Union deregulated air travel, a number of upstart airlines came up, providing no-frills travel around Europe. easyJet, Ryanair, Buzz,[13] bmibaby[14] and Go[15] were some of the airlines fighting for airspace. Low-cost airlines had a large market in Europe because the number of people traveling between the different countries increased after the formation of the European Union. Train travel was slow and expensive. Therefore, people looked to airlines to meet their travel needs. Low-cost airlines identified the business opportunity and offered tickets which were about half the price of a train ticket. They thrived on volumes rather than profit margins. So successful were the low-cost airlines that some of the national carriers also set up low-cost subsidiaries. (Go was set up by British Airways, Buzz by Dutch carrier KLM, and bmibaby by British Midlands Airlines.)

The low-cost airline industry was characterized by high competition. The standard of service of all these airlines was almost the same and they competed within the same markets. This made rivalry intense. In the early 2000s, the low-cost airline industry began getting consolidated, with Go being taken over by easyJet and Ryanair taking over Buzz.

EasyJet and Ryanair became the biggest low-cost airlines in Europe. Ryanair had the advantage of age and experience, as it had been set up ten years before easyJet. But easyJet, with its fleet of new planes and practice of flying to airports in the main cities (unlike Ryanair) overtook Ryanair to the top position in 2002.

---

13 The low-cost subsidiary of Dutch carrier KLM.
14 The low-cost subsidiary of British Midland [A]irlines.
15 Go was the low-cost subsidiary of British Airways.

Source: Compiled from various sources.

(around 45 percent), and the Amsterdam route had to be dropped later that year. The Brussels route also had problems and had to be more closely integrated with the parent company which was called Ryanair Europe. However, several difficulties cropped up and the scheduled routes had to be abandoned. The company repositioned itself as a charter tour operator flying to various destinations in the Mediterranean and Europe.

In the summer of 1987, Ryanair started its first charter operation to over 65 locations around Europe. By the end of that year, the airline had carried over 400,000 passengers. 1988 started well, with Ryanair getting more licenses on new routes from Dublin, Knock, Cork and Shannon. However, attempts to develop new routes from Dublin to Manchester and Glasgow came up against entrenched competition from Aer Lingus, which slashed prices and increased capacity.

In the face of this competition, Ryanair's losses on the Manchester route rose alarmingly to IR£700,000. In April that year, Eugene O'Neil, who became Chief Executive within a year of the airline's formation, was removed from his post. The company released a statement citing differences with the management. Declan Ryan was named acting chief executive and both the Glasgow and Manchester routes were axed. Shortly afterwards, P.J. McGoldrick (McGoldrick) was brought in from a similar position at Heavylift Cargo Airlines (a UK-based cargo company), to take over as chief executive.

On October 20, 1988, Ryanair carried its 1,000,000th passenger, Jane O'Keefe, on the flight to Dublin from London. She was presented with a golden voucher entitling her and a nominated friend free travel for life on any Ryanair route. By the end of 1988, Ryanair's total fleet had increased to six aircraft. Losses, however, were continuing to mount, reaching IR£6 million in 1988.

In September 1989, the Irish government announced a "two airline policy," which would be valid for three years (till October 1992). The new policy was directed at benefiting both the Irish carriers, Aer Lingus and Ryanair, and eliminating the cut-throat competition between them that was harming both. The new policy ruled that the airlines would not compete on any international route and allotted them separate routes. (Aer Lingus would fly from Dublin to Paris and Manchester and Ryanair, from Dublin to Liverpool and Munich.)

Ryanair continued to expand and carried 100,000 passengers on the Dublin–London route in 1990. Some new routes were also added. However, the Gulf War (1990–1991) caused a general downturn in the market, and at the AGM held in November 1990, the management announced losses of IR£4.5 million for 1989. The situation in 1990 looked even worse. The airline had to cut down some routes, retrench staff and shift its base from central Dublin, to Dublin airport. In 1990, the losses amounted to IR£7 million. Realizing that its position was becoming increasingly weak, Ryanair refocused its activities on providing low-cost, no-frills services. It also moved its base in London from Luton airport to Stansted. Services to regional airports were also reorganized.

In late 1991, senior management changes were announced, with McGoldrick relinquishing his position as chief executive. Patrick Murphy (Murphy), who had earlier worked for Aer Lingus, was brought in to replace him. A few weeks later, Conor Hayes was appointed chief executive and Murphy became non-executive chairman. In financial year 1991, Ryanair made its first profit of IR£300,000 since it was started in 1986. In 1992, a new livery was introduced for the planes in the fleet, with the Ryanair logo and the Irish harp painted on them in a white and blue scheme. In 1992, the airline made a profit of IR£0.8 million. In 1993, O'Leary, who had joined as chief operating officer in 1991, took over as CEO.

Exhibit 2   Summary Table of Results (Irish Gaap)— in Euro

Year ended	March 31st, 2002	March 31st, 2003	% Increase
Passengers	11.09m	15.74m	(+)42%
Revenue	€621.1m	€842.5m	(+)35%
Profit After Tax	€150.4m	€239.4m	(+)59%
Basic EP (euro cents)	20.64	31.71	(+)54%

Source: www.ryanair.com.

In 1994, Ryanair took delivery of its first Boeing 737–204. By 1995, when Ryanair completed 10 years in service, it had become the biggest passenger carrier on the London–Dublin route and the largest Irish carrier on every route it operated. The airline carried a total of 2.25 million passengers in 1995. In 1997, the European Union deregulated the airline business and a number of low-cost airlines (notably easyJet) offering no-frills services were set up. The deregulation of the market enabled Ryanair to open new routes to continental Europe. The same year, the airline also came out with an IPO on NASDAQ and the Dublin Stock Exchange for $500 million. With the money raised from the IPO, it ordered 45 new Boeing planes.

In 2000, the airline opened Ryanair.com, an online booking site. Within three months, the site was taking over 50,000 bookings a week. By the next year, over 75 percent of the bookings were made over the internet. In 2002, Ryanair made Frankfurt-Hahn (Germany) its second continental European base, after Brussels-Charleroi (Belgium). The airline also entered into a partnership with Boeing for the purchase of about 150 new aircraft over the next eight years (till 2008). By the end of 2002, the internet accounted for almost 95 percent of the tickets booked with Ryanair. By the end of 2002, the airline's fleet had 44 aircraft.

In early 2003, the airline took over Buzz, the low-cost subsidiary of Dutch carrier KLM, for £15 million. Until then Ryanair had not gone in for acquisitions, but O'Leary said that this offer was too good to pass over. Ryanair later shut down the operations of Buzz as it undertook a massive restructuring program to make the ailing airline more profitable.

In the financial year ended March 31st, 2003, Ryanair had carried 15.74 million passengers and earned revenues of £842.5m. (Refer [to] Exhibit 2.) O'Leary declared that he would double the numbers of passengers to 30 million in 5 years.

THE RECIPE FOR LOW FARES

Ryanair followed a strategy of cost focus. The airline served a class of flyers who looked for functional and efficient service rather than luxury. It did not aim to satisfy all segments of the market. The airline's operational policies supported its strategy of cost focus. The operational model of the airline included the following components:

Simple Fleet

Ryanair flew a fleet compris[ed] entirely of Boeing 737s. This focus on standardization was a key feature in keeping the costs of the airline low, thus allowing it to offer low fares. Flying a standard fleet had the advantage of simplifying the maintenance function of the planes. The airline did not have to stock spares for different types of planes. As spares and other aircraft parts could be purchased in bulk, it resulted in economies of scale. It also reduced training requirements for the pilots and the cabin crew, as they had to only learn to operate a single type of plane. This ensured interchangeability of crews, spares and furnishings between planes which made operations easier.

Secondary Airports

Ryanair used secondary airports. This was one of the important elements in keeping costs low. Using airports located outside city centers (many of them were former military airfields) saved time and money for the airline, as secondary airports had relatively lower landing charges. Besides, due to lower traffic, there were no delays, allowing the planes to turn around (turnaround is the time required for a plane after landing, to be ready for its next flight) in a very short time. In exchange for bringing in passengers to airports which normally witnessed little or no traffic, Ryanair negotiated 15- [to] 20-year deals on landing fees and other agreements to the advantage of the airline. In these airports, Ryanair negotiated airport fees of as little as $1.50 per passenger (much lower than the average rate of $15 to $22 per passenger charged by Europe's major hubs).

Faster Turnarounds

The turnaround time for Ryanair planes was approximately 25 minutes (the major carriers took about an hour). Most low-cost airlines based on the Southwest model (Refer [to] Exhibit 3) emphasized faster turnaround times to allow a plane to fly more times a day rather than spending time on the ground. This increased the efficiency of the asset. By taking about half the time of the larger airlines like British Airways (BA) or Lufthansa, Ryanair's planes made an average of nine trips per day as [opposed to] the average six of larger airlines. This made Ryanair's planes more productive than the planes of the major carriers.

Higher Productivity

Ryanair used fewer employees per plane than other airlines. This increased the productivity per employee for the airline

and also helped keep the wage bill low. Consequently, Ryanair's revenue per employee was approximately 40 percent higher than that of other airlines. The simple service model also allowed Ryanair to have only two flight attendants per flight, compared to the five attendants that major carriers required.

Ryanair sweated its assets. The airline flew its planes for an average 11 hours per day as [opposed to] the 7 hours of BA. The pilots at Ryanair also clocked in 900 hours a year, which was 50 percent more than the pilots at BA. The airline did not keep many planes on standby to meet unforeseen contingencies. All the assets were put to work, unlike BA which usually kept about ten planes at any given time on standby.

Online Sales

After Ryanair.com was launched in 2000, a large number of tickets began to be booked online. By early 2003, almost 95 percent of the bookings were done through the internet. This allowed the airline to make the booking process cheaper as transaction costs came down considerably. The benefits of lower costs were passed on to customers in the form of lower prices. Although some bookings were done over the telephone and some through agents, the internet brought in the major part of business. So, the airline decided to slash the commissions of agents from 7.5 percent to 5 percent. Analysts estimated that bookings over the internet saved the airline about $6 million a year on an average.

No Freebies

Like other discount airlines, Ryanair did not serve food or drinks on its flights. Snacks, however, could be purchased on the airline. Unlike Southwest, which served drinks and light snacks, Ryanair even charged for water on the flights (a bottle of water cost about $3). Analysts said that Ryanair transformed a cost into a revenue opportunity, as it not only eliminated all expenses on food (which formed a major portion of the expenditure per passenger), but also made additional revenues through the sale of food and drinks. According to a published report of the airline, Ryanair saved $50,000 a year, simply by not serving ice on its flights.

None of the services provided by the airline were free either. Baggage check-in cost the passenger according to the amount of baggage carried. It meant that users paid for what they needed and didn't pay for anything they didn't need. Since Ryanair charged for all the optional parts of a flight, it was able to fix the basic ticket price very low.

Volumes

What was distinctive about Ryanair was its focus on filling its planes to capacity. If tickets did not get sold at a high price, it tried to sell them by lowering prices. It realized that it was more profitable for it to fly its planes full at lowered

Exhibit 3   Southwest Airlines

Southwest Airlines (Southwest) was started in 1967 by Rollin King, John Parker and Herb Kelleher. King, an entrepreneur from San Antonio, Texas, owned a small commuter air service. Parker was his banker, while Kelleher was the legal advisor to King's air service. The airline aimed to provide the best service with the lowest fares for short-haul, frequent-flying and point-to-point "non-interlining"[16] travelers. Over 30 years of operation, Southwest became one of the most successful airlines in the U.S. In fact, it was the only airline that was able to stay profitable even after the September 11th terrorist attacks on the [U.S.] in 2001.

The success of Southwest spawned a number of other airlines which tried to imitate Southwest's model of providing low-cost and high quality services. Some of the components of the Southwest operational model are given below.

1. **Low fares:** Southwest offered one of the simplest and most inexpensive fare structures in the U.S. The low fares were made possible by adopting a number of techniques which brought down the operating expenses of the airline. The airline also had a frequent flyer program which gave a free round trip to a customer who purchased eight round trips on a particular route.

2. **Customer focus:** Southwest geared its operations to the needs of its customers. It therefore developed a flight schedule with frequent departures to meet the customers' need for flexibility. Airports were also conveniently located near city centers to make flying more convenient.

3. **Standard fleet:** To simplify operations, Southwest used only one type of aircraft—the Boeing 737, in an all coach configuration. This simplified the maintenance function and resulted in economies of scale due to bulk purchase of spares and other parts.

4. **Secondary airports:** Southwest flew into less congested, secondary airports. This helped negotiate better landing terms and also save time. This also allowed it to turn around the planes faster.

5. **Turnarounds:** Southwest had one of the fastest turnaround records of all airlines. It turned around planes in about 15 minutes, which was a quarter of the time taken by major airlines. This allowed better utilization of the fleet.

6. **Point-to-point flights:** Southwest flew point-to-point, short haul flights, which made operations simple and inexpensive, and allowed the airline to save time. It could also operate with fewer staff than airlines which adopted a hub-and-spoke system.

7. **No food:** Southwest pioneered the concept of not serving food on short haul flights. Instead of meals, the airline served drinks and light snacks. On the shortest flights, even these were eliminated. This helped the airline save a considerable amount of money and consequently keep fares low.

[16] Southwest did not arrange connections with other airlines; passengers transported their own luggage to recheck themselves onto connecting airlines.

Source: Compiled from various sources.

ticket prices rather than half-empty at its standard rates, as the per unit cost of flying a person came down. Besides, since Ryanair charged for all additional services like food and baggage, it stood to profit even if the ticket was sold at a huge discount.

Simplified Operations

The airline did not assign seat numbers; this simplified the ticketing and administration processes. It helped the airline save time as it ensured that passengers came to the airport on time to be able to sit together or get seats of their choice on the plane. The decision to fly short and medium haul point-

to-point[7] flights also enabled the airline to work with a smaller number of personnel than it would have required if it adopted the more complicated hub-and-spoke system.[8] Transfer of baggage and people from one plane to another is generally considered a vulnerable area for airlines. Flying point-to-point avoided the need for any kind of transfer, thus keeping operations simple and inexpensive. Ryanair

[7] In the point-to-point system the [plane] has a simple flight route and flies from the origin to destination.

[8] A hub-and-spoke system uses a strategically located airport (the hub) as a passenger exchange point for flights to and from outlying towns and cities (the spokes).

had very low operating costs. The $50 average cost of a Ryanair ticket could be broken down into approximately $35 operating costs and $15 profit. Thirty-five dollars as operating cost per passenger was low by any standards.

Partnering

Ryanair entered into partnerships and agreements with car rental companies and hotels so that it could earn commissions by selling these products to passengers. These commissions bridged the gap between the airline's cost and profit, which allowed it to sell its tickets for very low prices. Ryanair viewed each passenger as an opportunity to make money in more ways than just transporting them somewhere by plane. By charging them for additional services and earning commissions through them, the airline could constantly drop ticket prices. Ryanair.com also hooked up with hotel chains, car-rental companies, life insurers, and mobile-phone companies to expand the website's range of offerings.

RYANAIR'S PUBLICITY

Ryanair had a publicity program, which though sometimes unconventional, nearly always achieved its aim. The "attack" on easyJet was one of the typical publicity exercises of Ryanair. The CEO of an airline blatantly waging war against another airline was a topic guaranteed to generate publicity, and Ryanair leveraged the publicity by bringing it to the notice of the public that easyJet's fares were much higher than those of Ryanair.

One ad released by the airline featured the Pope whispering into a nun's ear. Many people felt the ad had gone too far and was in bad taste. The Vatican even sent out a press release accusing the airline of insulting the Pope. The release attracted so much attention that it got reported in newspapers as far away as India, and generated a great deal of free publicity. "I thought I died and went to heaven," said O'Leary.[9] Added David Bonderman, the chairman of Ryanair, "It's hard to think of another CEO of a company with a $4 billion market cap who would run those ads. They accomplished everything he set out to and more."[10]

Ryanair also often released ads comparing its prices to competitors' prices. In 2001, it was involved in a controversy with BA for claiming through an ad that BA's fares were five times higher than those of Ryanair. BA complained to the Advertising Standards Authority that Ryanair was exaggerating the situation and that the fares were, in fact only about three times higher. The advertising standards authority

asked Ryanair to withdraw the ads and behave more responsibly in the future.

RYANAIR'S COMPETITIVE POSITION

Being the oldest low-cost carrier in Europe, Ryanair had some advantages over its competitors. For one thing, it had the advantage of experience, and secondly, its brand enjoyed good recognition. However, after the deregulation of air travel in Europe in the late 1990s, a number of startup airlines came up in the low-cost market. Notable among the competitors was easyJet, the discount airline set up in 1995 by Greek shipping magnate Stelios Haji-Iaonnou. easyJet was based in London's Luton airport and competed on some of the same routes as Ryanair. In 2002, with the takeover of Go, easyJet beat Ryanair to the top position as the biggest low-cost airline in Europe. O'Leary declared that Ryanair would soon bounce back to reclaim its number one position.

Although Ryanair and easyJet both operated in the low-cost segment and had similar operational models, there were some inherent differences between the two airlines. Firstly, Ryanair made a major portion of its profits by flying to secondary airports which were a long distance away from the main cities. For instance, the destination advertised as Frankfurt actually flew to Hahn, 60 miles away from the main city. A trip to Paris meant a flight to Beauvais, 43 miles north of the city, where the terminal looked like a bus depot and the baggage handlers were local firemen. The claimed flight to Copenhagen in Denmark actually landed in Malmo in Sweden. Flying secondary airports gave Ryanair a cost advantage, but put passengers to a lot of trouble as they had to seek other forms of conveyance from the place of landing to their final destination. This resulted in a lot of delay as well as additional expenses for the passengers.

Analysts said that, while leisure travelers may not really mind having to put up with additional travel, business travelers would not appreciate the inconvenience. This might put them off Ryanair. In contrast, easyJet flew to main destination airports around Europe, which made it the favorite of business travelers or people who were pressed for time.

Not flying to main destination airports did not affect the market for Ryanair too much, because, unlike easyJet which sought to serve leisure as well as business markets, Ryanair only targeted leisure travelers. Additionally, analysts said that flying to main destination airports could affect easyJet adversely, because the major carriers which also flew there had begun to defend their positions against low-cost airlines aggressively. The increased aggressiveness of major carriers, who had more resources than low-cost airlines as well as more governmental support, could lead to the withdrawal of easyJet from those airports. Thus, there appeared some doubt as to whether easyJet would be able to withstand the intense competition from flag carriers.

[9] Kerry Capell, Carlos Tromben, William Echikson, Wendy Zellner, "Renegade Ryanair," *BusinessWeek*, May 14, 2001.

[10] Kerry Capell, Carlos Tromben, William Echikson, Wendy Zellner, "Renegade Ryanair," *BusinessWeek*, May 14, 200[1].

Secondly, Ryanair flew older planes than easyJet. Where easyJet emphasized passenger safety by buying and flying new planes, Ryanair had some planes in its fleet which were over 20 years old. The average age of the easyJet fleet was three years, while the average age of Ryanair's fleet was about 15 years. The founder of easyJet, Stelios Haji-Ioannou, publicly expressed doubts about Ryanair's use of 20-year-old aircraft on some of its routes, pointing out that though they flattered profits in the short term, they put the future of the airline at risk in the event of an accident. In response, O'Leary said that easyJet was only trying to harm its rival's reputation. He pointed out that Ryanair had an unblemished safety record in the eighteen years that it had been in operation. Nevertheless it was clear that a single airline accident (even in another airline) could make passengers think twice about an airline with an older fleet. Realizing this, Ryanair had already begun phasing out its older aircraft as it purchased new ones.

In terms of price, however, Ryanair had a distinct advantage over easyJet. easyJet's fares were almost 60–70 percent higher than those of Ryanair. Ryanair's lowest fare, on flights between Glasgow's Prestwick and London's Stansted was $71, round-trip, while easyJet's round-trip flight between Glasgow International and London's Luton was $123. Ryanair's average fares in 2002 were 30% cheaper than easyJet, and its unit costs were 80% less. Ryanair also had [a] better punctuality record than easyJet, taking off and landing on time more often than its rival (Refer [to] Exhibit 4 for punctuality statistics of early 2003).

To steal customers from easyJet, Ryanair announced that it would lower fares 5% a year for the foreseeable future. O'Leary believed that he could launch a new price war and still stay highly profitable, mainly because of the profitable agreements he had with the airports. Ryanair also got a huge discount from plane manufacturer Boeing for the purchase of new planes. Boeing offered Ryanair this discount in order to be able to beat competitor Airbus in the European market. Ireland, where Ryanair was based, was also eligible for U.S. aircraft subsidies as it did not manufacture aircraft domestically. This helped the airline substantially in terms of price. In 1998, the airline ordered 25 737–800 planes for about $30 million each ($15 million below the list price) from Boeing, when it was engaged in a price war with Airbus Industrie.

In addition to this, easyJet's break-even load factor (the percentage of total available seats to be sold each month to break even) was 71 percent compared to Ryanair's 53 percent. This meant that easyJet needed more passengers than Ryanair to break even. The profits of easyJet were correspondingly lower. Ryanair's 27% operating margin (ratio of operating income to sales revenue) was also higher than British Airways 3.8%, easyJet's 8.7%, and the 8.6% of Southwest Airlines. Ryanair had a built-up cash pile of $1 billion and its $5 billion market capitalization exceeded that of BA, Lufthansa,[11] and Air France.

Exhibit 4   Punctuality Statistics

Week ended (2003)		Ryanair	easyJet	Ryanair position
1	06-Jan	81%	72%	1
2	12-Jan	84%	76%	1
3	19-Jan	93%	86%	1
4	26-Jan	97%	88%	1
5	02-Feb	81%	64%	1
6	09-Feb	90%	63%	1
7	16-Feb	89%	73%	1
8	23-Feb	86%	72%	1
9	02-Mar	91%	79%	1
10	09-Mar	88%	81%	1
11	16-Mar	94%	86%	1
12	23-Mar	86%	82%	1
13	30-Mar	93%	78%	1
14	6-Apr	92%	68%	1
15	13-Apr	95%	79%	1
16	20-Apr	93%	78%	1
17	27-Apr	97%	81%	1
18	05-May	91%	75%	1
19	11-May	94%	81%	1
20	18-May	92%	70%	1
21	25-May	91%	NA	1
22	01-Jun	90%	63%	1
23	8-Jun	90%	62%	1
24	15-Jun	95%	77%	1
25	22-Jun	94%	74%	1
26	29-Jun	92%	72%	1

Source: www.ryanair.com.

O'Leary believed that his biggest advantage was that Ryanair did not compete head-on with Europe's biggest carriers. It targeted the discount market which the majors shunned in favor of the business-class traveler. "These [low-cost] companies are opening up new segments of the market without really taking clients from the regular carriers," said Air France CEO Jean-Cyril Spinetta.[12] [Forty-eight percent] of Ryanair's passengers were budget-conscious leisure travelers who did not care about luxury and only wanted the lowest possible fares.

No other low-cost airline managed to replicate Ryanair's results. According to analysts, its "cost per available seat mile," (the yardstick used by the airline industry to measure costs) was 30% lower than the average for Europe's major airlines, and its productivity—as measured by the number of passengers per employee—was 40% higher. As a result, Ryanair could break even when its planes were just over half-full.

---

[11] The national airline of Germany.

[12] Kerry Capell, Carlos Tromben, William Echikson, Wendy Zellner, "Renegade Ryanair," *BusinessWeek*, May 14, 2001.

Exhibit 5	Ryanair vs. Easyjet			

	Ryanair		easyJet	
	March 2002	March 2001	Sept 2002	Sept 2001
Revenue (in dollars)	543.4m	427.2m	861.5m	525.7m
Total Net Income (in dollars)	130.9m	91.6m	76.5m	55.8m

Adapted from www.hoovers.com.

With the acquisition of Go, easyJet may have become the bigger low-cost airline (with 19 million passengers in 2002 to Ryanair's 16 million), but Ryanair was in a better financial position, with net incomes higher than those of easyJet, from lower revenues. (Refer [to] Exhibit 5.) easyJet had reported losses for the first quarter of 2003, due to the acquisition costs of Go for which it paid a phenomenal £374 million; however, Ryanair had made a profit, in spite of the acquisition of Buzz.

Analysts wondered how Ryanair would fare if there was new competition in the European airline market. O'Leary, however, felt that there was unlikely to be any major new competition. "There are huge barriers to entry now, and none of the new airlines are going to be able to find a price point below Ryanair or easyJet," he said. He said that Ryanair was poised to become the counterpart of Southwest Airlines in Europe, while easyJet was imitating the strategy of JetBlue, which flew to major airports and did not cut costs quite as drastically as Southwest. "Air transport is just a glorified bus operation. You get on, you want to get there quickly, with the least amount of delays, and cheaply," said O'Leary. He believed that those who could provide the fastest and cheapest means of transport were likely to survive in the long run.

Questions for Discussion

1. Ryanair is one of the oldest low-cost airlines in Europe. Discuss the growth of Ryanair and comment on its present position in the European low-cost market vis-à-vis rivals.

2. Ryanair offered the lowest airfares across various routes in Europe. The airline was able to do this because of the opera-

tional advantages it enjoyed. Discuss the components of Ryanair's operational model and how they supported the low fares offered by the airline. Also discuss the role of publicity in helping create brand awareness.

3. Examine the competitive advantages Ryanair had over rival easyJet. According to you, which of the two airlines has a higher long-run sustainability? Discuss this in the light of the operational advantages of the two airlines.

Additional Readings & References

1. Kerry Capell, Carlos Tromben, William Echikson, Wendy Zellner, "Renegade Ryanair," BusinessWeek, May 14, 2001.
2. "How Ryanair Keeps the Cost Down," BusinessWeek, May 14, 2001.
3. "Ryanair Brothers Make £33.4m from Shares Sell-Off," The Irish Examiner, July 06, 2001.
4. O'Connell, Patricia, "Full-Service Airlines Are 'Basket Cases,'" BusinessWeek, September 12, 2002.
5. Day, Julia, "Ryanair Sells 1m Seats for Less Than a Tenner," The Guardian Review, September 24, 2001.
6. Tomlinson, Richard, "Europe's Businessman of the Year," Fortune, December 9, 2001.
7. "The Pluck of the Irish," The Economist, January 24, 2002.
8. Peachey, Paul, "Ryanair 'Misled' Public over Flight Destinations," The Independent, March 13, 2002.
9. Eoghan, Nolan, "Good Product, Bad Brand," Marketing Magazine, July 3, 2002.
10. Capell, Kerry, "Ryanair Rising," BusinessWeek, June 2, 2003.
11. Capell, Kerry, "Suddenly, Life Is Hard for easyJet," BusinessWeek, June 2, 2003.
12. Wachman, Richard, "Can Ryanair Soar Higher?" The Observer, June 8, 2003.
13. Smith, V. Kenneth, "easyJet Leads Low Fare Airline Battle in Europe," www.webtravelnews.com, September 27, 1999.
14. "Business Profile: High Flier Who Built a Fortune on Low Fares," www.telegraph.co.uk.
15. Lee, James, "Ryanair: The First Ten Years," www.iol.ie.
16. www.thetravelinsider.info.
17. www.easyprotest.com.
18. www.theolivehouse.it.
19. www.bbc.co.uk.
20. www.legal500.com.
21. www.msnbc.com.
22. www.hoovers.com.
23. www.ryanair.com.

"It is a competitive market—there is absolutely no doubt about it."

–Seth Walker, an Intel Spokesman, in February 1999

"AMD is their (Intel's) worst nightmare."

–Ben Anixter, AMD's Vice-President (External Affairs), in December 2001

"Isn't it odd that for all the years during the early and mid-nineties, Intel was slowly increasing speed about 33 or 50 MHz at a time and prices were rather high? But then, AMD comes along and in two years, we can change 1000 MHz. I really like this competition thing, I just hope it lasts."

–A Microprocessor Customer, quoted on www.geek.com

Advanced Micro Devices—Life Beyond Intel

ENACTING THE DAVID/GOLIATH STORY

In June 2001, the Sunnyvale, California (U.S.) based microprocessor manufacturer Advanced Micro Devices Inc (AMD) launched a new microprocessor, the 1.4GHz Athlon. This was in response to the launch of the Pentium 4 2GHz processor of its archrival, Intel Corporation (Intel) based in the same city (Refer [to] Exhibit 1 for a note on the microprocessor and Exhibit 2 for a note on Intel). AMD's move did not attract much attention initially as Intel had always beaten it on the market share, brand recall and product superiority fronts for decades (Refer [to] Table 1).

ICFAI UNIVERSITY This case was written by **V. Sarvani** under the direction of **A. Mukund,** ICFAI Center for Management Research (ICMR). It is intended to be used as a basis for class discussion rather than to illustrate either effective or ineffective handling of a management situation.

The case was compiled from published sources.

Over the next few months, news spread across the globe that the Athlon processor was much better than Pentium 4 in terms of performance. Intel had to face customer unrest as the usual marketing hype surrounding the launch of Pentium 4 wore off and Athlon was increasingly being accepted as a technically superior product. Analysts observed that Intel's advertisements had made PC users believe that a higher clock frequency resulted in higher performance—something that was reportedly far from the truth (Refer [to] Exhibit 1).

However, this did not come as a major surprise to industry observers who had watched the two companies battle each other for decades. In fact, AMD and Intel were even termed as the "Pepsi and Coca-Cola" of the global microprocessor industry. Every time AMD launched a new chip, Intel brought out a faster chip into the market, thus preventing AMD from gaining any competitive advantage. Due to its financial muscle and successful marketing efforts, Intel had always had the lead in this battle for leadership and most of the leading personal computer (PC) original manufacturers used Intel's chips for their PCs. However, things changed with Athlon.

AMD sought to break this widely accepted "Megahertz Myth" which attributed a microprocessor's superiority to its clock speeds. In Athlon, AMD had a product that challenged Intel's chips not on the basis of clock speeds, but on the overall performance of the processor. Commenting on this, Wee Yep Yin, Product Marketing Manager, SEA, AMD Far East, said, "Ultimately, AMD delivers what is most important to

A microprocessor can be crudely defined as the brain of a PC, not seen by the end-user. Simply put, it is a processor made on a microchip. A microchip is a small unit made of silicon and is [a] package of computer circuitry. It performs operations such as adding, subtracting, comparing two numbers, fetching numbers from one area to the other, etc. The processor can perform these functions as they form a part of the instructions coded at the time of designing the microprocessor. Once a microprocessor of a system is turned on, it fetches the first instruction from the basic input and output system (BIOS, a part of computer memory). Once this is done, the operating system or the application program drives the functioning of the processor by giving it instructions, till the system is switched off.

The efficiency of a processor is judged by the speed with which it carries out the instructions—the greater the speed, the faster the system. The speed of a microprocessor is measured in terms of clock speed. The number of pulses generated by an oscillator is called clock speed (an oscillator is an electronic [device] used in a computer for generating signals). Clock speeds are usually measured in terms of millions of pulses per second (MHz) or billions of pulses per second (GHz). When a microprocessor runs at higher clock speed, it consumes more electricity, which in turn generates a lot of heat. Excessive heat can damage the processor (by melting the circuitry etched in aluminum/copper) as well as the surrounding components. Thus, to keep the system cool, a small fan is attached to the system.

Intel was accused of making users believe that a PC's performance depended (almost) entirely on the kind of microprocessor used. However, there were many other factors such as the cache speed, memory speed and graphics acceleration capabilities that contributed towards providing users a 'better PC experience.' For instance, Intel said that using the Intel Pentium 4 chip would improve their Internet browsing experience. However, this was not entirely true. Given a basic personal computer (PC) configuration, the browsing experience depended primarily on the bandwidth used to access the Internet.

Source: www.whatis.com, ICMR.

business and consumer PC users—superior software performance, higher productivity and platform longevity."

The Athlon/Pentium tussle continued till the end of 2002, and then AMD did something it had never done before. The company launched its first-ever high profile advertisement campaign across the world, on the lines of Intel's high-decibel marketing campaigns. This move attracted comments in media reports that AMD was getting aggressive like never before against Intel. This newfound aggression was attributed

to a host of reasons, most of them rooted deep in the bitter rivalry between the two companies.

BACKGROUND NOTE

AMD was established in 1969, by Jerry Sanders (previously Director [Worldwide Marketing] at Fairchild Semiconductor[1]), along with seven others with a capital of $1,00,000. They identified their mission as "building a semiconductor company that offered products for electronic communication, computation and instrumentation manufacturers" (Refer [to] Exhibit 3 for a brief note on the semiconductor industry). AMD began operating from a room in a co-founder's (John Carey) apartment, shifting later on to a full-fledged office in Sunnyvale, California, which became its headquarters.

Initially, the company produced alternate source devices; that is, they obtained products from other companies and redesigned them to function more efficiently at greater speeds. AMD defined this as "Parametric Superiority," a strategy that it followed for many years. To make its products saleable and also to enhance the quality of the already improvised versions of the products, the company made and tested all its products according to the MIL-STD-833 standards.[2]

In 1970, AMD had 53 employees and launched 18 different products along with its first proprietary product, the Am2501 chip. In 1972, AMD became a publicly traded company and in 1973, it established its first overseas manufacturing facility in Penang, Malaysia. By 1974, AMD had made more than 200 different products and the number of employees had increased to 1500. The company posted $26.5 million in annual sales for the same year. In 1975, AMD launched the 8080A standard processors and introduced the AM2900 processor line. The company posted revenues of $168 million in the financial year 1974–75.

Intel had become a formidable name in the industry by now. Not only were both the companies started by ex-Fairchild employees, they were operating essentially in the same business. However, these initial years were very different in terms of the relationship between the two. In 1976, AMD and Intel entered into a patent cross licensing agreement to benefit from each other's technologies. According to this agreement, both companies could license their patented products to each other for their own use.

In 1977, AMD along with the U.S. based multinational Siemens established Advanced Micro Computers. In 1978, it set up an assembly unit in Manila, [the] Philippines, and opened another manufacturing unit in Austin. It also expanded

[1] Established in 1957, Fairchild was a leading supplier of high performance semiconductor products for logic, analog, mixed logic, optoelectronic, power, interface and configurable product markets.
[2] U.S. military standards that are used by companies to assess the ability of their products/components to perform under expected conditions of transportation, storage and all aspects of operational use. MIL-STD-833 is a commonly used environmental test specification.

Exhibit 2   About Intel

Three engineers, Robert Noyce, Gordon Moore, and Andy Grove, established Intel in 1968. Unhappy with the state of affairs at the company they were working for, Fairchild Semiconductor, the trio decided to start their own company and develop technology for silicon based chips. The result was the establishment of Intel (an abbreviation for Integrated Electronics) at Mountain View, California. Intel invented the microprocessor. Its first microprocessor was called 4004. It was designed to perform the function of 12 silicon chips put together. The specialty of this chip was that it could compute as fast as ENIAC, the fastest computer at that time. Following the success of 4004, Intel launched the next processor, 8008, in 1972, which became the brains of one of the world's first PC[s]. In 1974, Intel launched the 8080 chip and in 1978, it released the chips 8086 and 8088. The 8088 was used by IBM's PC division for making new PCs. It went on to become a huge success in the market and propelled Intel into the ranks of *Fortune* 500 companies.

Intel released the 80286 (286), 386 and 486 chips in 1982, 1985 and 1989 respectively. In 1985, Intel entered into an agreement with Microsoft, according to which every PC that functioned with the Windows operating system would make use of Intel chips. This created the so-called monopoly of "Wintel." It was during these years that Intel signed cross-licensing agreements with AMD and other companies, wherein these companies could make use of Intel's technology and vice-versa. From 1993, Intel changed the processor numbers to names and launched the range of Pentium processors. It launched the Pentium Pro and Pentium II, Pentium III, Pentium 4 and Xeon & Itanium processors in 1995, 1997, 1999, 2000 and 2001 respectively.

However, the company's net profit declined from $10,535 million in 2000 to $1291 million 2001. The drastic decline in the company's profits was due to poor sales because of the sluggish PC economy and increasing competition from rivals like AMD. Intel had often been accused of charging exorbitant prices for its chips. Various antitrust investigations carried out by the European Commission accusing Intel of making use of "abusive marketing practices" were also responsible for this. Intel also faced problems because of the class action suit filed against it regarding the poor performance of the Pentium 4.

Source: www.intel.com, ICMR.

Intel—Consolidated Statements of Income (1999–2001)

	2001	2000	1999
Net revenues	26,539	33,726	29,389
Cost of sales	13,487	12,650	11,836
Research and development	3,796	3,897	3,111
Marketing, general and administrative	4,464	5,089	3,872
Amortization of goodwill and other acquisition-related intangibles and costs	2,338	1,586	411
Purchased in-process research and development	198	109	392
Operating costs and expenses	24,283	23,331	19,622
Operating income	2,256	10,395	9,767
Gains (losses) on equity securities, net	(466)	3,759	883
Interest and other, net	393	987	578
Income before taxes	2,183	15,141	11,228
Provision for taxes	892	4,606	3,914
Net income	1,291	10,535	7,314

Source: www.intel.com.
(in $ million)

the manufacturing facility at Penang. In 1981, AMD set up another factory in San Antonio, California.

In the early 1980s, after leading personal computer (PC) manufacturer IBM used Intel's 86 series of microprocessors for its PCs, IBM persuaded Intel to license its technology to some other company in the market. This way IBM could get a steady [. . .] supply of microprocessors from either of the companies and also put in place price competition between both companies (AMD and Intel). As a result, AMD and Intel entered into a technology sharing agreement in 1982 (referred to as "the 1982 agreement"), which was an extension of the 1976 agreement. According to this agreement, Intel shared the databases for the 8086, 80186, 80286 processors which had information required to produce replicas of Intel processors. Consequently, AMD became the second source for the x86 series and other related computer chips. The agreement was valid till 1996.

In 1983, AMD introduced the INT.STD.1000, which went on to become the highest quality standard for the semiconductor industry. In 1984, the company set up another manufacturing facility in Bangkok. In 1985, AMD was named as one of the best companies to work for in the book *The 100 Best Companies to Work for in America*. In the same year, it entered the *Fortune* 500 list for the first time. In 1986, AMD launched the 29300 32-bit[3] chips and the first 1 million bit Electrically Programmable Read Only Memory (EPROM) in the market. In 1987, Monolithic Memories Inc. merged with AMD.

In the late 1980s, major changes took place in the semiconductor industry. Japanese companies such as NEC, Hitachi, Toshiba, Fujitsu, Mitsubishi, Matsushita and Oki were eating away considerable share of the market including that of AMD and Intel. Moreover, the demand for processors declined due to the decrease in the demand for computers in general. This affected both companies badly. As competitive pressures intensified, relations between both companies began to sour. It was during this phase that trouble started brewing between AMD and Intel.

---

[3]A bit is the smallest unit of data in a computer. Computers are designed to store and execute data in bit multiples called bytes (four eight-bit bytes form a 32bit data). Microprocessors can transmit 32bit data or 64bit data at one time. A processor transmitting 64bit data is faster than a processor transmitting 32bit data.

Exhibit 3	A Brief Note on the Semiconductor Industry

Semiconductors are used widely by a host of industries to automate time consuming and repetitive tasks. Semiconductors refer to a set of integrated circuit chips, which can control everything from PCs, cell phones and elevators to complicated systems like aircraft navigational products. Integrated circuits are used in all electronic equipments. Semiconductors can be broadly classified into two categories—analog and digital. Analog chips are used mainly in amplifiers for telephones, fax machines and scanners. Digital chips can also be further classified into three categories—memory chips, logic chips and microprocessors.

According to the Semiconductor Industry Association, the global semiconductor sales amounted to $204 billion in 2000, a 37% growth since 1999. The U.S. accounted for one third of the world's semiconductor sales with sales of nearly $47.5 billion. According to the U.S. Department of Commerce, the semiconductor industry employed around 280,000 people in the U.S. alone. One of the reasons attributed to the robust growth in the industry was that it had [a faster] rate of technological innovations and product improvements than any other contemporary industry. Some of the major customers for semiconductors are: the military, [a]erospace, [m]aterials and equipment, [i]ndustries, communications and computers. The semiconductor industry can be broadly classified into four categories—memory, microprocessors, commodity integrated circuits and complex SoC (used mostly in consumer applications).

In the past couple of decades, the industry (memory segment) has consolidated to a great extent and memory prices have become very low. Only a few companies like Toshiba, Samsung and NEC could afford to stay in the market. In the microprocessor segment, Intel's legendary success had forced [everybody] out of the game except AMD. Other smaller players had to shift to smaller niches and at times, shift into entirely new market segments. Many players in the semiconductor industry do not opt to stay in the commodity integrated circuits segment because of the poor profit margins. The fourth segment (SoC) is the only segment that offers ample opportunities for most of the companies to operate.

Sources: www.techsectortrends.com, www.synopsys.com.

Marking the first sign of discord in their long association, Intel terminated the "1982 agreement" in 1987. It stopped sharing information [about] the new 86 series processors and other related chips with AMD. However, AMD continued to reverse engineer the microcode (a microprocessor's software code) of Intel's chips and soon launched replicas of the 287 processors. Intel filed a case against AMD alleging that it did not have the license to copy the microcode for its processors. In response to this, AMD initiated an arbitration action against Intel, stating that according to the 1976 agreement, it could make use of Intel's microcode.

Things worsened further in 1981, when AMD launched the Am386 microprocessor on the lines of Intel's 386 range. Intel once again sued AMD, claiming that AMD could not use the number 386, as it was Intel's protected trademark. In response to this, AMD filed another suit against Intel for breach of contract. The legal battle continued for over five years, almost wiping out the professional camaraderie the two companies once shared. AMD's winning the arbitration case in 1992 proved to be the proverbial final nail in the coffin. The courts stated that processor numbers were not trademarks and AMD was awarded full rights to produce and sell the whole line of 287, 386 and 486 microprocessors along with a hefty monetary compensation.

However, this was not the end—allegations and counter allegations, suing and counter suing became regular features of the two companies. An intense war raged between the two companies in the areas of product development, product launch and marketing fronts.

BATTLING IT OUT

In 1993, AMD announced the launch of the K5 project which was to directly compete with Intel's launch of the Pentium (1993) and Pentium Pro (1994) processors. But, by the time AMD came out with the final product in the market (in 1995), it was too late. Pentium had gained immense popularity, due to its superbly crafted marketing campaign and also because at that time there was no other processor which was equally powerful.

In 1994, AMD entered into a long-term alliance with the leading PC manufacturer Compaq Computer Corporation, wherein Compaq agreed to use the Am486 microprocessor for its PCs. In the same year, the Digital Equipment Corporation served as a foundry[4] for the Am486 processors. In the same year, AMD won the ongoing court battle against Intel for the right to use Intel's microcode for the 278 range of processors.

Though it won the legal battle, AMD realized that it would have to work hard in order to strengthen its position in the market. The company strengthened its relationships with various original equipment manufacturers (OEMs) and focused on improving its infrastructure, software and technology. AMD also decided to introduce new products more frequently. Nexgen, a U.S.-based microprocessor manufacturer, was acquired in 1996 with the same objective. The AMD-NexGen alliance led to the introduction of the K6 series of processors which were to compete with Pentium II launched in 1997.

Though the K6 processors gained wide acceptance due to their 'good performance,' AMD was unable to cash in on this as it could not manufacture the required quantities due to inadequate facilities. The company reportedly did not have the required machinery to deal with the complicated manufacturing procedure in large numbers. Moreover, the K6 processors did not follow the same chip format as that of Intel's. AMD's chips could be used only on the socket-7 motherboard whereas Intel made use of another motherboard (socket-370). The socket-7 motherboards were not as widely available as socket-370 motherboard[s]. Thus, even by selling chips as powerful as those of Intel's, and at much cheaper prices, AMD could not beat Pentium II.

In early 1998, AMD introduced a range of much better and more powerful processor[s], the K6-2 processor, to counter Pentium II. The K6-2 ran at 100MHz bus as against Intel's 60MHz bus and was 16% cheaper than Intel's Pentium II. The range was very suitable for programs used for creating graphics. Due to the above aspects, K6-2 started gaining popularity amongst microprocessor customers. (This new range was based on AMD's own chip designs and marked the beginning of innovations at the company.)

Intel retaliated by releasing the Pentium III processors (P3) in the market that were equipped with features that enhanced the graphics capability of the chip (to match the K6 range). However, since P3 was only slightly faster than K6-2 but was four times costlier, it wasn't very popular. Moreover, the K6-2 chips were priced 15%–20% lower than the K6 range. AMD's sales picked up substantially as more and more dealers and customers became aware of the above facts. For the year 1998, K6-2's accounted for 43.9% of the total processor sales in the U.S. market as compared to Intel's 40.3% (Pentium range).

In late 1998, AMD launched the K6III to compete with P3. However, AMD again faced problems on the manufacturing front—there were manufacturing delays that the company could not control as a result of which it could not meet the demand. Moreover, Intel's hugely successful "Stayin' Alive" campaign and its stronghold on the market made the Pentium range the [de facto] choice for consumers. Not surprisingly, AMD posted losses of $125 million in 1997 and 1998 (combined). Also, the company's inability to produce and release chips as fast as Intel rendered it unable to take advantage of the increasing demand for PCs in late 1998 and early 1999.

In 1999, AMD and Intel launched the Duron and Celeron processors respectively, targeted at the lower end of the market. In the same year, AMD entered into a long-term alliance with Motorola to develop the copper interconnect technology[5] and other process technologies. Thus, AMD became the first company to use the copper interconnect technology to make processors that were

---

[4] Foundries are dedicated contract manufacturers that focus on the physical production of chips, thereby sustaining the massive investments needed to keep up with the latest in manufacturing technology. PC major IBM operates the largest foundry service in the U.S.

[5] Making use of copper wires instead of aluminum wires so as to facilitate faster connections.

compatible with Microsoft Windows. AMD also started a factory in Dresden (Germany) to produce its next generation microprocessors.

In 1999, AMD came out with the fastest microprocessor in its history, Athlon. With this, for the first time, AMD was "one up" on Intel by becoming the company to launch the fastest processor in the market (Athlon was the first processor in [the] market to have reached the 1GHz speed). AMD made use of a "cooling system" that kept the processor cool even while running at a speed of 1GHz and more. This dispelled the doubts of OEMs and consumers regarding AMD's processor heating up fast (Refer [to] Exhibit 1).

Athlon's launch seemed to have changed the dynamics of the microprocessor market, as till now Intel never had to follow AMD's lead in releasing faster processors. Commenting on this changed scenario, Kelly Spang, an analyst at Technology Business Research said, "For the first time in this rivalry, AMD has the ability to keep pace with Intel in this speed race. That basically puts a new twist on Intel and how it plans its own strategy in terms of its own product rollout."

Due to the superior performance and lower prices offered by AMD, many OEMs decided to use Athlon chips for their systems. The PC manufacturer Gateway, which had stopped using AMD processors in mid-1999 because of their lower speed, decided to use AMD processors once again. Gateway suffered a loss of around $200–250 million in sales during late 1999 due to a shortage of Celeron and P3 chips. This also prompted Gateway to use AMD chips for its computers.

Another victory came in the form of IBM and Compaq's decision to build more systems with Athlon processors (apart from Dell, almost all major PC OEMs used both AMD and Intel chips). Another favorable move for AMD was when Compaq started using Celeron for its low-cost[6] and low-performance systems. This pushed up AMD's processors to the midrange and the low higher end systems of Compaq's product line.[7]

Due to all the above issues, Intel was forced to launch faster versions of P3 processors, much before their scheduled launch time. Though Intel claimed that better manufacturing yields had resulted in earlier launches, there were few takers for this. Analysts observed that AMD's moves had forced Intel to act swiftly. Commenting on this, Kelly Spang said, "Intel now must play for a worse-case scenario in terms of speed grades. It was always the assumption Intel would be faster than AMD, and that assumption is being discarded in some cases."

THE WAR GOES ON

In 2000, Intel came out with the Pentium 4 processor to compete with Athlon. However, Pentium 4 could neither match Athlon in terms of speed nor performance. The 1.4GHz Athlon processor along with the Double Data Rate (DDR)[8] memory outperformed the 1.7GHz Pentium 4 processor (which ran only on RDRAM) by 40% on various performance measurements (benchmarks) like desktop publishing, digital imaging, multimedia and voice recognition applications.

Intel also faced problems when supply could not keep up with the demand for Pentium 4. Moreover, since Pentium 4 was priced much higher than Athlon, the issue of price-performance anomaly remained unaddressed. Above all, Athlon was priced much cheaper than P3—while a 600 MHz Athlon cost $1429, a similar Pentium processor cost $1849.

Soon, the Intel-AMD battle focused more on the clock-speed issue, especially in the "below gigahertz" market (chips meant for low-end systems). When the Celeron range was released, it was hailed for being the "king" of the low-end, low-performance market. However, this reputation gradually decreased as the company launched new versions of Celeron. Duron always beat Celeron as it ran at the same clock speed and cost [less]. In some cases, Duron even outperformed Celeron chips that were clocked for 100 MHz or more.

For instance, the 600/700 MHz Duron processors could be easily overclocked[9] [up to] 900 MHz. Even though Celerons could be overclocked to 800–900 MHz as well, the fact that they were priced much higher than Durons tilted the battle in the latter's favor. Also, Durons could easily reach up to 85%–90% of the speed of AMD's own higher-end Thunderbird Athlon (TA) processor. While Durons used a 200MHz front side bus,[10] Celerons used the outdated 66MHz front side bus technology. Thus, it was no surprise that Durons went on to become a great hit with the users.

By late 2001, AMD was slowly but steadily gaining market share. Research conducted by Gartner, a market research firm headquartered in Stamford, Connecticut, revealed that about 27% of desktop PCs sold in the market used Athlon. To

---

[6] Cheapest systems sold for under $600.

[7] Prior to this Compaq used AMD chips for its low-end and low-performance systems.

[8] DDR, Rombus Dynamic Random Access Memory (RDRAM) and Dynamic Read Only Memory (SDRAM) are various types of memory devices that are used to enhance the performance of a PC's memory by improving its clock speed. DDR is less costly than SDRAM and RDRAM. In descending order according to their performance, the three can be rated as follows: DDR, RDRAM, SDRAM.

[9] When a chip is overclocked, it means that the computer is reset so that the processor can run at a higher speed than the speed specified by the manufacturer.

[10] A bus is a physical interface that connects the microprocessor with the motherboard and other devices on the motherboard. A front side bus is a data path or a physical interface that connects the microprocessor and the main memory.

further increase its presence in the market, AMD came out with a new chip-numbering scheme and a new marketing campaign to make the public aware of the same. It was targeted at taking away the spotlight from the clock speed and the Megahertz [M]yth. AMD planned to gather consumer advocates and industry groups to develop what it referred to as a "true" performance measurement basis.

Commenting on the need to change the perception of consumers about the measurement of processor performance, Mark Bode, Division Product Marketing Manager [at], AMD said, "At that point, the underlying work component was done differently with each architecture. Before that, the 286, 386 and 486 processors from both Intel and AMD were using the same underlying architecture, so clock speed was a fair measure of performance. You expected that the work per clock cycle (of the processor) was going to go up and the frequency would go up. But with different architectures, clock speed alone does not equal performance."

Under the new scheme, the 1.5MHz processor was renamed 1800+ because AMD claimed that an Athlon 1.5MHz processor could perform as efficiently as a Pentium 4 1.8MHz processor. These claims were also substantiated by tests conducted by Tom's Hardware Guide, a technology [Web site][11] that published hardware reviews and news. The tests revealed that the Athlon processors were indeed faster and performed better than the Pentiums. Commenting on this, Ben Anixter said, "We really have truth in advertising on our side."

In late 2001, while AMD was basking in the glory [of] its Athlon chips, Intel launched the Itanium processor. Itanium was targeted at the high-end enterprise class servers and workstations. It was designed to process data at 64 bits at a time, which was much higher than the prevailing norm of 32 bits. This gave it the capacity to handle large database programs. However, one disadvantage with Itanium processors was that they could not process 32-bit programs without making use of emulation programs[12] especially designed for that purpose. AMD prepared to launch the Hammer[13] series of chips in response to this. Hammer scored over Itanium as it was designed to process 64-bit programs as well as 32-bit programs.

In another competitive move, AMD joined hands with the software giant Microsoft and launched one of its fastest and most powerful chips in the Athlon series, the Athlon XP 2000+ in January 2002. This $339 chip that ran at 1.67GHz was designed to perform at its optimum level when used with Microsoft's latest operating system, Win-

dows XP. Intel shot back soon by launching the fastest Pentium 4's running at 2GHz and 2.2GHz [and] priced at $364 and $562 respectively.

In early 2002, for the first time in its 33-year history, AMD launched its "largest global, integrated branding and advertising campaign." It was called the "AMD me" campaign with a punch line "Challenge me. Surprise me. Free me. AMD me." Designed by McCann Erickson (ME),[14] the "AMD me" campaign was targeted at both home and business markets. Commenting on the new campaign, Executive Vice President, Chief Sales and Marketing Officer [at] AMD, Rob Herb, said, "The 'AMD me' campaign is an excellent expression of our commitment as a business to build deep relationships with customers, and address the real-world needs of the global marketplace."

The advertisements marketed the 64-bit Athlon. AMD laid much emphasis on the fact that their chips could be run both on 32-bit and 64-bit programs in spite of changing the chip's architecture from 32-bit to 64-bit. The campaign was expected to convert a lot of Intel users to AMD users. The Executive Vice President and Director of Client services at ME, Michael McLaren, said, "The campaign is expected to generate over 285 million impressions worldwide. We anticipate a [grassroots]-effect that will positively impact AMD's business and drive demand for the company's already highly-anticipated 64-bit product line."

Apart from this campaign, AMD was once again [trying] to drive home the point that crude numbers do not clearly suggest the speed and performance of a chip. To educate the processor users it also launched a new informative campaign called the "True Performance Initiative" (TPI). Commenting on this Patrick Moorhead, AMD said, "We have seen an incredible response to AMD's ongoing efforts to expose the megahertz myth."

OF WINNERS & LOSERS

The winner in the bitter rivalry between AMD and Intel was the customer. They were getting better and faster processors at a rapid pace, at much cheaper prices. However, analysts claimed that the rivalry was affecting both the companies adversely. While the PC market was rather dull, both AMD and Intel were resorting to price cuts in order to gain a larger share of the market.

Intel usually reduced the price of the existing chips every time it launched a faster chip. Company sources claimed that this was done to clear the inventory of old chips. For instance, when the Pentium 4 2.8GHz was introduced in the market, the price of [the] Pentium 4 2.53GHz

---

[11] www.tomshardware.com.

[12] Emulation programs are used when a hardware [device] has become outdated. They help the [device] to communicate with other programs or devices.

[13] The Hammer series was scheduled to be launched in 2002 fall but due to certain delays in production, the chip's launch was postponed to 2003 summer.

[14] San Francisco based ME is one of the leading advertising agencies in U.S. and across the world.

Table 2   Changes in Intel Processor (Pentium 4) Prices (After the September 2002 Price Cuts)

Processor	Old Price	New Price	% Change
2.40GHz	$400	$193	52%
2.26GHz	$241	$193	20%
2.20GHz	$241	$193	20%
2.0AGHz	$193	$163	16%
1.80GHz	$163	$143	16%

Source: www.geek.com.

Table 3   Changes in AMD Processor Prices (After the November 2002 Price Cuts)

Processor	Old Price	New Price	% Change
Athlon XP 2200+	$183	$157	14
Athlon XP 2100+	$174	$93	47
Athlon XP 2100+	$155	$83	46
Athlon XP 1900+	$139	$76	45
Athlon XP 1800+	$130	$69	47
Athlon XP 1700+	$114	$54	53
Duron 1.3GHz	$64	$47	27
Duron 1.2GHz	$64	$42	34

Source: www.geek.com.

[was] reduced. But analysts stated that Intel was forced to cut down prices only because of severe competition from AMD. In September 2002, Intel reduced prices of its chips by [up to] 52%. The price of [the] Pentium 4 2.4GHz was drastically reduced from $400 to $193 (Refer [to] Table 2).

Though AMD products were cheaper than comparable Intel products, AMD also had to resort to price cuts to retain its share of the market. In November 2002, the company announced price cuts, wherein the prices of Athlon XP processors were reduced by about 53%. The price of [the] Athlon XP 1700+ was drastically reduced from $114 to $53 (Refer [to] Table 3).

Analysts felt that if AMD continued to cut prices the way it had been doing in the past, it might not be able to survive for long. The company posted losses of $60.6 million in 2001 and suffered losses of $184.9 million and $17.6 million in the second and third quarter[s] of 2002 respectively (Refer [to] Exhibit 4 for AMD's financials). However, some analysts were optimistic. Scott Randall of Technology Group said, "The real challenge is growing the business in a flattish market against a tough competitor. AMD has had tough times before and they have in the past proven they've been effective in terms of cost cutting. The question is, how disruptive will it be."

Interestingly, some market observers believed that despite the seemingly "customer-friendly competition," both the companies were taking the microprocessor customer for a ride as there was no significant difference between the performance of their chips and that Intel enjoyed a slight edge over AMD due to its strong brand name. An analyst at IDC, Alan Promisel, commented, "It is basically the same, they both have performance marks that will tell you theirs is better than the other."

It was quite evident that [. . .] AMD was working hard to create its own identity and establish itself in the market. But, the company still had a long way to go. The following comment on the Intel–AMD war made in a 1995 report on www.computerworld.com surprisingly seemed to hold good even in late 2002, "As Intel and AMD sheathed their legal swords, analysts argued that neither side had gained much from the bitter and acrimonious battle. Even so, AMD appears at first glance to be the bigger winner."

Questions for Discussion

1. Analyze the circumstances that laid the foundation of the AMD-Intel rivalry and briefly comment on the various fronts on which the war was fought over the decades. What do you think drives the semiconductor industry—technology, prices or brand equity? Give reasons to support your answer.

2. Intel has the technology as well as the financial and marketing muscle to bring out faster chips in the market than AMD. What

Exhibit 4   AMD—Five Year Financial Summary

Year ended December 31	2001	2000	1999	1998	1997
Net Sales	3,891,754	4,644,187	2,857,604	2,542,141	2,356,375
Operating Income (loss)	(58,258)	888,736	(320,916)	(163,642)	(90,653)
Net Income (loss)	(60,581)	983,026	(88,936)	(103,960)	(21,090)
Total Assets	5,647,242	5,767,735	4,377,698	4,252,968	3,515,271
R&D spending	650,930	641,799	635,786	567,402	467,877
Income Tax provision	(14,463)	256,868	167,350	(91,878)	(55,155)
Effective Tax rate	(15.4)%	20.5%	227.3%	(44.3)%	(54.7)%
Worldwide employment	14,757	14,435	13,354	13,597	12,759

Source: www.amd.com.
(U.S. Dollars in Thousands)

steps should AMD take to increase its market share and consumer interest in its products? Do you think that AMD's marketing strategies will increase its market share in the future?

3. "It is basically the same, they both have performance marks that will tell you theirs is better than the other." As a microprocessor customer, would you agree that AMD and Intel have been taking customers for a ride in terms of limiting technology and inflating prices? Give reasons to justify your stand.

Additional Readings & References

1. Blackwood, Jonathan, **Bargain Chips,** 1998, www.techweb.com.
2. Lemos, Robert, **The Future Looks Bleak for AMD,** February 10, 1999, www.news.zdnet.co.uk.
3. Cringley, X. Robert, **The Aging of Intel,** February 25, 1999, www.pbs.org.
4. Silverman Dwight, **New Chip Has a Speed Edge Over Intel,** August 26, 1999, www.dwightsilverman.com.
5. Kanellos, Michael, Wilcox, Joe, **AMD Counters Intel with 800-MHz Athlon Chip,** January 6, 2000, www.news.com.
6. Stanfield, Heather, **AMD War,** March 6, 2000, www.linux.omnipotent.net.
7. Sam Jaffe, **AMD Is Still Scratching for Respect,** July 25, 2000, www.businessweek.com.
8. Kanellos, Michael, **Intel, AMD Battle for Chip Speed Crown,** July 28, 2000, www.marketwatch-cnet.com.
9. Masse, Cheryl, **Chip Fight,** October 2000, www.computeruser.com.
10. Connolly, Chris, **AMD Duron 800 MHz,** October 10, 2000, www.gamepc.com.
11. Spooner, John, **Best Buy Puts Brakes on Pentium 4,** November 28, 2000, www.znet.com.
12. **Intel and AMD Power Up 64-Bit Processors,** December 2000, www.win2000mag.net.
13. McDonald, Tim, **AMD Trumps Intel in Cheap-Chip Speed Race,** January 8, 2001, www.newfactor.com.
14. Stam, Nick, **Athlon vs. P4: Intel Escalates the Rivalry,** January 16, 2001, www.pcmag.com.
15. Kanellos, Michael, **AMD Chip Name to Echo Pentium,** May 9, 2001, www.marketwatch-cnet.com.
16. **AMD Unveils New Processors,** June 19, 2001, www.blonnet.com.
17. Gray F. Douglas, **AMD Launches Athlon XP Processor,** October 9, 2001, www.pcworld.com.
18. Hagen, Eric, **The Future of the Athlon XP,** October 10, 2001, www.anandtech.com.
19. Neel, Dan, **AMD's Athlon XP Snubs Megahertz Ratings,** October 12, 2001, www.infoworld.com.
20. Mainelli Tom, **Does Anybody Understand AMD's New Chip Names?** October 17, 2001, www.pcworld.com.
21. Hoie W. Oystein, **AMD's Future Plans,** November 21, 2001, www.infosatellite.com.
22. Port, Otis, **The Chip War Moves to Terahertz Terrain,** December 17, 2001, www.businessweek.com.
23. **Recovery Heats Up AMD-Intel Rivalry,** December 27, 2001, www.taipeitimes.com.
24. McDonald, Tim, **AMD Releases Speedy New Athlon,** January 7, 2002, www.newsfactor.com.
25. McDougall, Paul, **Intel, AMD Continue Rivalry with New Superfast Chips,** January 7, 2002, www.informationweek.com.
26. McDonald, Tim, **Mobile Chip Speed Wars Roll On,** January 28, 2002, www.wirelessnewsfactor.com.
27. Magee, Mike, **AMD Outlines Consumer Plans Ahead,** January 29, 2002, www.theinquirer.com.
28. Brown, Spencer Ken, **Chip Rivals Intel, AMD Seek Different Niches In 64-Bit Bout,** June 7, 2002, www.sanjose.bizjournals.com.
29. McDougall, Paul, **Intel, AMD Continue Rivalry with New Superfast Chips,** July 1, 2002, www.commonweb.com.
30. Hughes, Rob, **Complaint Develops Against P4 Marketing,** August 19, 2002, www.geek.com.
31. Popovich, Ken, **AMD, Intel Release Faster Chips, Cut Prices,** August 21, 2002, www.eweek.com.
32. Osborne, Brian, **Intel Slashes Prices Up to 52%,** September 4, 2002, www.geeg.com.
33. **AMD Launches Largest Global, Integrated Branding and Advertising Campaign in Company History,** September 16, 2002, www.biz.yahoo.com.
34. Singer, Michael, **"'AMD Me' Unleashed"** September 12, 2002, www.siliconvalley.internet.com.
35. Rao, L. Prashant, **AMD Plays the x86–64 Card with Opteron and Hammer,** www.express-computer.com.
36. Widowmaker, **Intel 'Back in the Drivers Seat,'** October 8, 2002, www.tswn.com.
37. Dunn, Darrell, **AMD and Intel Turn Up the Heat in Handheld Market,** November 2, 2002, www.ebnonline.com.
38. Abreu, Elinor Mills, **AMD to Take Charge; Cut Costs, Jobs,** November 7, 2002, www.reuters.com.
39. Sigvartsen, Ana Letícia, **AMD, Intel Processors Get Cheaper,** November 13, 2002, www.infosatellite.com.
40. Hodgin, C. Rick, **AMD Lowers Low-end Prices By Up to 53%,** November 15, 2002, www.geek.com.
41. Hachman, Mark, **AMD, Intel Reach Milestone With Debuts of 1-GHz Athlon, Pentium III,** November 19, 2002, www.ebnonline.com.
42. Antonelli, Cesca, **Look Who's Winning the Chip Wars,** www.bloomberg.com.
43. **AMD vs. Intel,** www.cyberaddicts.net.
44. www.intel.com.
45. www.dacs.org.
46. www.amd.com.

"In prior years we found customers somewhat cautious about supporting Airbus. This year it has become acceptable and, frankly, even stylish to laud Airbus and to chastise Boeing."

–Excerpt from Bear Stearns Analyst Report as reported in *Fortune* in August 1999

"We are not here to buy market share."

–Noel Forgeard, Chairman, Airbus Industrie, in August 1999

Airbus—From Challenger to Leader

BSTR/046

BOEING'S NIGHTMARE

In October 2002, *The Seattle Times,* a local newspaper published from Seattle, USA, where Boeing is headquartered, carried a headline story, *Boeing Is Slipping to No. 2.* According to the newspaper report, Boeing's sole competitor, Airbus Industrie (Airbus) had bagged an order from easyJet[1] for 120 A-319 jets. easyJet was one of Boeing's most loyal customers (Refer [to] Exhibit 1 for a profile of Boeing).

Analysts felt that after easyJet's shift away from Boeing, other low-cost airlines would follow suit in opting for Airbus. Airbus seemed all set to take market leadership in the low cost segment from Boeing for the first time. From the mid-1990s onwards, Airbus had steadily increased its market

This case was written by **K. Subhadra,** under the direction of **Sanjib Dutta,** ICFAI Center for Management Research (ICMR). It is intended to be used as a basis for class discussion rather than to illustrate either effective or ineffective handling of a management situation.

The case was compiled from published sources.

share. By the late 1990s, Boeing and Airbus had an equal share in the market.

Rival Boeing accused Airbus of resorting to heavy price cutting in order to beat off the competition. It also accused Airbus of producing aircraft for which it had not received orders and creating a glut in the market. But Airbus rejected the allegations, saying that it was in the market to make money and not to buy market share. Some analysts were of the opinion that Airbus was able to increase its marketshare because of the financial support it received from its consortium partners. However, others attributed Airbus' success to its fuel-efficient jets, which were economical to run.

THE TAKEOFF

The history of Airbus dates back to the late 1960s, when Britain, France and West Germany launched the Airbus Project. Airbus was a desperate attempt by the European governments to end the monopoly of American manufacturers in the aerospace industry. At that time, American manufacturers dominated the global aerospace industry and European aircraft manufacturers were unable to compete with American players.

The big three of Europe—Britain, France and West Germany—came together to salvage European pride and industry. Due to differences with the other partners, Britain quit the project in July 1967, and in 1970 the Airbus Project was reorganized and named Airbus Industrie, a Franco-German company under French law.

In 1971, Spain joined the consortium with [a] 4.2% stake through state-owned Construcciones Aeronautics S.A (CASA).

---
[1] Europe's biggest low-cost airliner.

Exhibit 1   Profile of Boeing

The leading airplane manufacturer in the U.S., Boeing Airplane Company (Boeing), was formed in 1916 by William Boeing (W. Boeing) and George Westervelt (Westervelt). At the time, it was called the Pacific Aero Products Company. The company's name was changed to Boeing in 1917. Boeing began by manufacturing [aircraft] for the U.S. military during the First World War. In 1922, Edgar Scott became the company's president and during his tenure the navy awarded Boeing a contract to build a primary trainer (a plane for test flights). In 1927, the Model 40A mail plane won the U.S. Post Office contract to deliver mail between San Francisco and Chicago. The Boeing Air Transport (BAT) [company] was formed to run the new airmail services. BAT also trained pilots, set up airfields and provided maintenance staff for the new service.

However, Boeing realized that to grow, it needed to design and go in for mass production and sell its own aircraft. After the Second World War, the company shifted its focus from the defense industry to commercial jets. In 1952, Boeing launched its first commercial jet, the Boeing 707, a short-range jet. In 1960, William M. Allen (Allen) became the company's CEO. The same year, Boeing began manufacturing its first jumbo jet—the Boeing 747. During Allen's tenure, Boeing launched one of its most successful jets, the 737. In 1962, Boeing manufactured the Air Force One for the American president's use. In late 1969, Boeing entered the spacecraft manufacturing business by contributing to the Apollo program.

In the early 1970s, Boeing faced a host of problems due to the recession in the aviation industry. When Airbus Industrie was formed in 1970, Boeing's market share (70% in the early 1970s) began to decline. In the mid-1970s, Boeing launched long-range planes (the 757 and the 767). By the mid-1980s, Boeing expanded its presence in the consumer electronics business through joint ventures, mergers and subcontracting. In March 1984, Boeing took over the De Havilliard Aircraft [company] of Canada to enter the commuter planes market. In the early 1990s, Boeing completed the manufacture of the 727 and the 737. By October 1994, the company launched the new 737 series, the 737-800.

In the mid-1990s, Boeing's revenues plunged and it had to retrench around 9,300 employees due to the economic slowdown. The company faced a 10-week strike in the fourth quarter of 1995. In late 1996, Boeing and McDonnell Douglas announced plans to merge. In 1997, Boeing had approximately 70% of the world market for passenger aircraft. By the end of 1997, Boeing was severely affected by the Asian economic crisis[2] that put in doubt over one-third of the $1.1 trillion projected commercial aircraft sales for the next 20 years. The company's internal problems such as excessive bureaucracy, redundant manufacturing processes and an outdated information technology setup further aggravated the situation. Boeing lost 17% of its market value as a result of the Asian crisis.

In 2002, Boeing was a $54 billion company operating in 145 countries with around 112,000 employees worldwide. The company was divided into six major units: Air Traffic Management, Boeing Capital Corporation, Commercial Airplanes, Space and Communications, Military Aircraft and Missile Systems, and Connexion by Boeing. The commercial aircraft division contributed around 60% of the total revenues. Boeing's manufacturing plants were located at Renton, Everett (Washington), Wichita (Kansas) and Long Beach (California).

Source: ICFAI Center for Management Research.

[2] The Asian financial crisis started in early July 1997, when international currency speculators as well as many Thai nationals started selling Thailand's currency, the Baht, to buy U.S. dollars, causing a flight of capital out of the country. As a result, capital became scarce and interest rates on borrowed money rose sharply, leading to the Baht losing about 20% of its value. Then the Thailand stock and real markets collapsed, pushing the country into its worst recession, as production decreased, unemployment rose sharply and businesses went bankrupt. The crisis spread quickly to other countries in the southeast Asian region like Indonesia, South Korea and Japan, significantly damaging the region's economy.

Initially, Airbus had its headquarters in Paris; in 1974, the headquarters were shifted to Toulouse (France). Each partner in the consortium was assigned specific production and assembly tasks, and the consortium was responsible for coordinating designing, development, financing and production activities of the partners.

Airbus' first product was the A-300-B—a widebody twin-jet plane with a capacity of 226 passengers. The next product was the A-300-B2, a 250-seater. By 1975, Airbus was able to garner 10% of market share, and received first time contracts from Eastern Airlines[3] and Thai Airways.[4] By the end of 1975, Airbus had orders for 55 aircraft. By 1978, Airbus' orders had increased to 133, and it had a 26% market share by value. It also launched [the] A-310 with a 218-passenger capacity in the two-class configuration. The A-310 had a two-man cockpit with a six-cathode ray tube display, replacing dials—the first of its kind in the aviation industry. In 1979, British Aerospace Systems (BAE Systems) entered the consortium with a 20% stake, and in the same year, Airbus announced that it would launch a single-aisle aircraft with a seating capacity of 130–170; the aircraft was later called the A-320.

In the early 1980s, Airbus experienced difficulties in financing the A-320 project, since all the Airbus partner governments had not approved the program. While the French government had approved the project, both British and German partner governments wanted more time to measure the market potential for the plane. Another problem was that the consortium had not yet made money on products already in the market.

By 1985–86, Boeing's market share had decreased to 46%, with Airbus having increased its share to 25%. With Airbus' increasing market share, Boeing began to accuse Airbus of using unfair trade practices by getting heavy subsidies from its European governing partners. The U.S. government too started [pressuring] the EU to reduce subsidies to Airbus. The then President of the United States, Ronald Reagan, cited Airbus as a classic example of violation of international trade agreements.

In the late 1980s, [the] U.S. government filed a complaint against Airbus at The General Agreement on Trade and Tariffs (GATT). It complained of unfair competition against two U.S. airline manufacturers, McDonnell Douglas and Boeing, by Airbus. Airbus, it said, had the financial support of four European governments, who provided cheap loans to the consortium with no repayment conditions. Airbus responded by denying that it received heavy subsidies from the governments concerned. The governments of the four European states also stated that U.S. aircraft manufacturers received indirect government subsidies through the U.S. defense department. After protracted discussions, in 1992 a bilateral deal was signed between the European governments on one side and the U.S. government on the other, that limited the financial help that could be given to Airbus to develop any new model, to 33% of its total development costs. The agreement also stipulated that the aid would have to be repaid with interest within 17 years.

In the mid-90s, the main problem for Airbus was to raise finance for its major projects, such as the development of a new super jet. Airbus wanted to bring in more partners; however, no new partner was willing to invest money because of the uncertain financial health of the consortium. Under French law, Airbus was not obliged to publish its annual accounts or reveal cost and revenue details. With no financial data on the consortium, no new partner was forthcoming. Another negative feature of Airbus was its slow decision-making process—every partner (representing [each] different country) tried to safeguard its own interests rather than [make] decisions that would benefit [the] consortium as a whole.

Airbus came under strong pressure to corporatize itself. Despite its success in attracting orders and increasing its market share, many were skeptical about its ability to compete with Boeing with its existing structure.

Airbus announced its decision to restructure itself on the lines of an integrated company. However, the managing partners could not reach agreement on the nature of the restructuring. Around the same time, Boeing announced its decision to take over U.S. aircraft manufacturer McDonnell Douglas. *BusinessWeek* summarized the challenges that Airbus faced: "With 35% of the world jet market, Airbus has so far proved a spirited challenger to Boeing. But to face up the new behemoth, Airbus must change itself from an unwieldy, four-partner consortium into one for-profit company. It must develop planes with more than 400 seats to compete with Boeing's 747 series and develop a next-generation super-jumbo that can carry up to 700 passengers. And it must overhaul its inefficient manufacturing, which is geared more toward making sure each partner gets its share of jobs than it is toward making money."[5]

Reports said that though British Aerospace and DaimlerChrysler Aerospace AG (DASA) were in agreement over the plan for revamping Airbus' organizational structure, the French partner—Aerospatiale—was opposed to it. The French company did not want to pool manufacturing assets, fearing that rationalization of production might lead to massive layoffs. This was politically unacceptable to France, a country with an already high unemployment rate.

In early 1998, the Airbus partners re-started discussions on revamping the organizational structure of the consortium. In the same year Noel Forgeard (Forgeard)[6] was appointed as CEO of Airbus. However, there were serious

---

[3] Eastern Airlines was one of the largest airlines in [the] U.S., which operated on eastern coast routes. It was liquidated in 1991 due to heavy losses.

[4] Thai Airways is an airline company, operating from Thailand.

[5] "Angst at Airbus," *BusinessWeek,* December 23, 1996.

[6] Former CEO of French missile and satellites maker Matra Hautes Technologies.

Table 1　Manufacturing Plants of Airbus

Parts Manufactured	Location
Cabin Interior	Buxtehude, Laupheim (Germany)
Fuselage (forward & aft)	Hamburg, Nordenham, Bremen, Varel (Germany)
Fuselage (cockpit & centre)	Meaulte, Saint Nazaire, Nantes (France)
Wing	Broughton, Filton (England)
Pylon, Nacelle	Toulouse (France)
Empennage—horizontal tail plane	Puerto Real (France), Getafe & Illescas (Spain)
Empennage—vertical tail plane	Stade (Germany)
FINAL ASSEMBLY LINES	
A-320 Family	Hamburg (Germany) & Toulouse (France)
A-300/A-310 & A-330/A-340	Toulouse (France)
A-380	Hamburg (Germany) & Toulouse (France)

Source: www.airbus.com.

Table 2　Turnover of Airbus

Year	Turnover (in billions)
1997	$11.6
1998	$13.3
1999	$16.7
2000	$17.2
2001	€20.5
2002	€24.3

Source: www.airbus.com.

differences between the consortium partners over the valuation of the assets to be pooled in the new corporate structure. The fact that accounting standards differed from country to country was also a hindrance in the valuation of assets.

In 1999, the stumbling blocks to restructuring were finally cleared, when Aerospatiale was merged with Marta Hautes Technologies, and DASA (Germany) [took] over the Spanish partner CASA. Aerospatiale Marta and DASA together formed the European Aeronautic Defense and Space Company (EADS). By 2001, Airbus was incorporated into an integrated company, with EADS and BAE owning stakes of 80% and 20% respectively. In 2002, Airbus employed around 45,000 employees, with manufacturing plants spread all over Europe (Refer [to] Table 1). In 2002, it reported a turnover of 24.3 billion[7] (Refer [to] Table 2).

---
[7] On June 6, 2003, 1 Euro = $1.18.

NOTE ON AEROSPACE INDUSTRY

The history of the aerospace industry dates back to 1917, when the U.S. government built an aeronautics research center in Langley, Virginia. In the subsequent years, there was close private and public sector collaboration in the industry. The U.S. government's investment in the aerospace industry was substantial, before and during the Second World War. After the Second World War, U.S. manufacturers had distinct technological and financial advantages over their European competitors. Prior to the Second World War, Britain had been the leader in the aerospace industry. However, it failed to retain its leadership position due to the lack of a proper corporate and regulatory climate.

The industry continued to be a high priority area for governments after the Second World War. Western governments invested in the industry to an increasing extent after the war. While military aviation received federal funding in the U.S., in Europe, governments provided funds for civil aviation.

The aerospace industry can be broadly divided into three categories: defense contracts, space programs, and commercial aircraft. The aerospace industry is one of the most capital-intensive industries in the world. It is characterized by high labor and research [and] development costs. R&D, apart from developing new commercial aircraft designs, provides technological inputs for the defense and space programs.

Investment in the aerospace industry involves a high degree of risk. The investment risk can be gauged from Airbus' investment in its A-380 aircraft; the investment required was equivalent to the company's net worth. The cost structure of the aerospace industry is also very high. It is estimated that the cost of development of a new aircraft model from designing to launching, is around $4 billion. The cost structure in developing a new aircraft can be broken up as follows:

Development	40%
Tooling	20%
Work-in-progress and overhead expenses	40%

Product development of an aircraft begins with a "paper airplane"—a three-dimensional model, estimating the performance and the operating costs of the aircraft. The manufacturers generally [use] these models to demonstrate new technology and most importantly to assess the response of potential buyers. Generally, before initiating production of new aircraft, companies hold discussions with key airline companies about adaptations and options that need to be incorporated into the prototype. Often, these airlines [become] launch customers, placing initial orders that [guarantee] the minimum volume, while sending signals to potential buyers that the aircraft is worth considering.

One of the important characteristics of the global aerospace industry was the high entry barrier of heavy capital investment required. Another characteristic was the high level of involvement of governments in the industry. Prior to the Second World War, [the] British ruled the aerospace industry. But after the war, the Americans began to dominate the global aerospace industry. Many European aircraft manufacturers became bankrupt, being unable to compete with the American aircraft companies. The main players in the aerospace industry were [the] Boeing, McDonnell, Douglas and Lockheed companies, all [from] the U.S. Over the years, there was strong consolidation in the aerospace industry through mergers and acquisitions. One of the first moves towards consolidation was made in the 1960s, when McDonnell and Douglas merged, forming a new company—McDonnell Douglas. In the late 1960s, in order to challenge American dominance in the industry, the big three of [. . .] Europe joined together, forming the consortium Airbus Industrie. From this point, American and European companies competed for dominance in the global aerospace industry.

In the early 1980s, the American company Lockheed announced that it was stopping production of commercial aircraft to concentrate on the military and space segments. The commercial aircraft market was now divided between the three dominant players—Boeing, McDonnell Douglas and Airbus Industrie. There was further consolidation in the industry when, in the late 1990s, the two American majors, Boeing and McDonnell Douglas, announced their merger. The merger resulted in a situation of duopoly in the commercial aircraft market with only two players—Boeing and Airbus Industrie (Refer [to] Table 3 for market share).

In the late 1990s and early 2000s, the worldwide economic recession compounded by terrorist attacks in the USA resulted in turbulent times for the industry. The September 11, 2001 attacks on the U.S. had a devastating [effect] on [airline] companies all over the world, with a decline in the world air passenger traffic. Many airline companies went broke and filed for bankruptcy. The U.S. government stepped in and announced a bailout package for the U.S. airline industry. The slump in airline services had a very negative impact on aircraft manufacturers, with most airline companies canceling orders for new aircraft.

FLIGHT TO SUCCESS

In 1970, when Airbus Industrie was set up, the commercial aircraft market was totally dominated by U.S. aircraft manufacturers led by Boeing. Boeing dominated the world market with its 747 jumbo jet family of aircraft. Although Airbus had great difficulty in breaking into the market initially, over the years, it managed to attract more and more customers. Though some attributed Airbus' success to the subsidies it received from European governments, others felt that Airbus succeeded because of its production efficiency and innovative product development.

Innovative Product Development

In the 1970s, the aerospace industry was in a transition. The regulatory set-up in the American market restricted price wars among existing carriers and the entry of new carriers. However, existing airlines were allowed to fly any number of flights on [a] route, resulting in an increasing number of flights on the popular routes. Airlines found that the use of Boeing aircraft (Boeing 727s) was expensive for frequent flying. There was a demand for wide-body aircraft with twin engines and twin aisles, and with passenger capacities of 250 passengers.

However, Boeing was not interested in manufacturing such aircraft. Though both McDonnell Douglas and Lockheed came out with the wide-body planes, their aircrafts had three engines and a range of 3,500 miles. Airbus was able to identify the niche left by the U.S. aircraft manufacturers, and decided to launch a wide-body aircraft with twin engines and with a range of 2,100 miles. Thus Airbus launched its first product—[the] A-300—in 1974, a wide-body aircraft with twin engines and twin aisles, which reduced flying costs for the airliners. However, the A-300 model was not as popular as expected and for around 18 months there were no orders for [it].

The first breakthrough for Airbus came in 1978, with Eastern Airlines[8] placing an order for 23 A-300s, and soon Airbus started receiving more orders for the A-300. In the same year, Airbus decided to develop a new model—[the] A-310—an extension of the A-300, with a budget of $1 billion. Till the late 1980s, Airbus had only two aircraft models on the market—[the] A-300 and [the] A-310. Soon it realized that it needed to increase its product range in order to compete with

Year	Boeing	Airbus
1995	69.7	13
1996	64	32
1997	60	35
1998	50	50
1999	45	55
2000	45	55
2001	47	53
2002	43	57

Table 3   Global Aerospace Industry—Market Shares (in %)

Source: Compiled from various articles.

---

[8] Eastern Airlines was one of the largest airlines in [the] U.S., which operated on eastern coast routes. It was liquidated in 1991 due to heavy losses.

Boeing in all product categories. During the 1990s, Airbus focused on introducing new aircraft. It launched 4 product families with nine airplane models during the 1990s; in the same period Boeing launched only two product families— 717[9] and 777—and revamped its old models in other product lines. Commenting on the Airbus products, Ned Laird, managing director of Air Cargo Management Group, said, "Airbus airplanes are newer in design, and in most cases they are cheaper to own than Boeing alternatives."[10] In 1989, Airbus launched the A-321 with increased seating capacity (185 passengers), and in 1992, [the] A-319—a 124-seater—was launched. In 1993, Airbus launched the A-319 with a seating capacity of 124 passengers (Refer [to] Exhibit 2 for [the] Airbus product range).

Airbus was able to emerge as a serious threat to Boeing chiefly because of the success of the A-320 family of aircraft, which included [the] A-318, A-319, A-320 and A-321. Instead of imitating Boeing's products, Airbus came out with product innovations to differentiate itself from Boeing. For instance, Airbus offered similar cockpits across every model, unlike Boeing, which designed the cockpit differently for every plane. The identical cockpit design was an instant hit with airline companies. Similar cockpits meant that airline companies could use the same crew across Airbus aircraft, right from the 107-seat A-318 to the 380-seat A-340. Said Tim Bennett and Alex Hunter, analysts at Morgan Stanley, "Airbus has taken the technological lead by offering a common cockpit configuration. We believe this is helping to consolidate Airbus' position with airlines operating a mixture of short-haul and long-haul aircraft."[11]

Airbus also differentiated itself from Boeing in its aircraft design. For instance, the A-320 was designed with [a] 7½-[inch] wider fuselage than Boeing's 737 (designed during the 1960s), giving the airlines extra space to add more seats in a six-across configuration. Richard Aboulafia, director [of] aviation [at] Teal Group, said, "That inch makes a difference, because North American rear ends aren't getting any smaller."[12]

The wider choice of aircrafts encouraged airlines to switch to Airbus in order to spread their maintenance costs. Commenting on the economies of using Airbus aircraft, Frederic Brace, vice president [of] finance [at] United Airlines, said, "Once you get an Airbus in your fleet, you tend to want more of them. They make a good plane that is very economical to operate."[13]

Exhibit 2   Product Range of Airbus & Boeing

Category	Airbus	Boeing
Single Aisle Family Model	A-319	757
	A-320	757–200
	A-321	767
	A-318	757–300
		717
Wide Bodied Aircraft Model	A-300–600R	767–200ER
	A-330–200	767–300ER
	A-340–200	767–400ER
	A-330–300	
	A-340–200	
	A-340–300	
	A-340–500	
	A-340–600	
Super Jet Jumbo	A-380	747–400

Source: www.airbus.com & www.Boeing.com.

Over the years Airbus has come out with aircraft in line with the market demand, and [has incorporated] technological innovations, unlike Boeing's aircraft, which were extensions of its 747 technology. Boeing had failed to introduce new technology in its commercial jets after its Super Jumbo 747.

Airbus' A-320, launched in 1984, had new technology, resulting in better operating efficiencies and performance. The A-320 was the first commercial jet with 'fly-by-wire'[14] controls and side sticks, and was designed to meet the requirements of short-distance routes. In 1986, Airbus launched the medium capacity A-330/-340 for long-distance routes. While Airbus was coming out with new models, Boeing was offering its existing 747 and 737 product lines only.

Unlike Airbus, Boeing did not use computers for designing its aircraft. Its designing activities were done manually, consuming a huge number of engineering hours, while Airbus used computer software to design its aircraft. The use of computer-aided design reduced the number of engineering hours spent on designing, and also helped Airbus bring out better designs.

Production Efficiency

In 1995, Boeing started offering huge discounts of about 25% on its aircraft in a bid to draw customers back from Airbus. However, though it succeeded in getting more orders than

---

[9] Some analysts pointed out that Boeing inherited [the] 717 aircraft family from McDonnell Douglas, which was acquired by it 1997, so they pointed out that effectively, Boeing came out with only one new product—[the] 777—during the 1990s.

[10] "Upstart Airbus Threatens to Leave Giant Boeing in Its Jet Stream," *The Seattle Times*, May 13, 2002.

[11] "Upstart Airbus Threatens to Leave Giant Boeing in Its Jet Stream," *The Seattle Times*, May 13, 2002.

[12] "Blue Skies for Airbus," *Fortune*, August 2, 1999.

[13] "Blue Skies for Airbus," *Fortune*, August 2, 1999.

---

[14] Fly-by-wire is a means of aircraft control that uses electronic circuits to send inputs from the pilot to the motors that move the various flight controls on the aircraft. There are no direct hydraulic or mechanical linkages between the pilot and the flight controls. Digital fly-by-wire uses an electronic flight control system coupled with a digital computer to replace conventional mechanical flight controls.

Airbus that year, it was unable to stick to its delivery schedule. Two of its production plants were shut down due to shortage[s] of parts and [workers]. As a result of the delays, many clients cancelled their orders with Boeing and returned to Airbus, raising Airbus' market share over that of Boeing.

The main problem for Boeing, as many analysts saw it, was that its production processes dated back to [the] Second World War period, after which the company had never comprehensively revamped its production processes. It followed traditional aircraft manufacturing methods. In Boeing factories, planes were docked in stalls on either side of the factory floor. Each plane was surrounded by ramps and workers found the parts and installed them, and during the night, partly-finished planes were moved into the stall using cranes, for the next stage of assembly.

Compared to Boeing's cumbersome production practices that were decades old, Airbus had very sophisticated production practices. Airbus adopted the line-manufacturing method, which made the process of assembling aircraft easier. Boeing employed 216 workers per aircraft, while Airbus employed only 143 workers. This amounted to a 51% productivity difference between the two companies. Boeing's 119,000 workers manufactured 550 jets, while Airbus manufactured 230 jets with [the] help of 33,000 employees per year.

Airbus also benefited from the transnational element of its organizational structure. It could exploit the expertise of its four partners to the full, resulting in low designing and manufacturing costs. This enabled Airbus to price its aircraft lower than Boeing. The company had manufacturing units (all over Europe) which made cockpits, fuselages and wings.

Airbus also had much fewer HR problems than Boeing. During the mid-1990s, when its orders were up, Boeing hired 38,000 people and trained them. However due to production problems, it was forced to reduce its workforce and lay off around 26,000 employees in late 1998. By the late 1990s, workforce salaries and overhead expenses [at] Boeing were around 30% of total overhead costs—very high for any company. In addition, Boeing had difficulties with its employee unions. Boeing unions went on strike over 4 times between 1998 and 2002, resulting in serious production problems for the company.

Airbus, on the other hand, managed its workforce well. Although Airbus was regularly criticized on the grounds that it was set up to provide jobs for Europeans, Airbus had a lean workforce. Due to Europe's strict lay-off rules, Airbus had, right from the start, relied on contract workers. It could increase or decrease the workers hired on contract on the basis of its order-book position. Further, its sophisticated manufacturing practices enabled it to work with fewer people.

THE GAMBLE

In order to increase its market share, Airbus decided to enter the super jet category (400 seater). In 1998 it announced that it would be developing a super jumbo jet with a planned ini-

tial investment of $10 billion. If it took off, Airbus's A-3XX (later called A-380) would end the monopoly of Boeing's 747 in the over-400-seats category. According to company sources, the A-380 would be a double-decker plane with a seating capacity of 555 passengers (137 more than the Boeing 747). The super jumbo would be priced at $213 million and was expected to fly by 2004 (later the launch date was postponed to 2006). The main challenge for Airbus was to raise the funds required to manufacture [the] A-380. Finally, Airbus was able to split the total costs of development of the project as follows: around 40% would be funded by its suppliers such as Saab (Sweden), 30% would be in the form of government loans [brought] in by partners, and the remaining 30% would be the consortium's own funds.

Boeing questioned Airbus' wisdom in putting funds into the development of a super jumbo. While both Airbus and Boeing were [in agreement about] the expectation that air traffic would increase 5% annually over the next 20 years, they differed in their expectation regarding the type of aircraft the market would absorb. Airbus felt that airlines would opt to buy larger aircraft to accommodate growing consumer demand, whereas Boeing felt that airlines would be buying smaller aircraft such as [the] 777, as there would be increased demand for point-to-point services rather than long-haul flights requiring bigger planes. Said Allan Mullay, head [of the] commercial airplane division [at] Boeing, "We think the lineup we have is what airlines want, and there is no economic justification for a bigger airplane."[15]

Airbus disagreed, saying that with increasing restrictions in airports regarding noise and pollution, airlines would opt for big planes, as they would require few takeoffs and landings. Said Philippe Jarry, head [of] Airbus market development, "Boeing acts as if there are no constraints on airports, runways, or the environment. I'm really surprised that the leading American manufacturer is so concerned about the bottom line that it says, 'Flying is more fun in our smaller planes. You should buy more of them.'"[16]

The Airbus super jet project received further encouragement when airline companies also showed interest in the aircraft. Companies such as Federal Express were reportedly interested in the super jumbo as freight shipments were predicted to grow fast—in fact, faster than passenger volumes. Commenting on their interest in [the] A-380, Don Barber, senior vice president of FedEx air operations, said, "The A-3XX may be an option to increase our capacity per trip."[17]

Airbus consulted more than 60 airports worldwide to ascertain whether or not its super jumbo jet would take off and land easily. To reduce the weight of the aircraft, a crucial element in take-off and landing, Airbus developed a new material called *Glare*.[18] During the design of the aircraft, the

---

[15] "Blue Skies for Airbus," *Fortune*, August 2, 1999.

[16] "Blue Skies for Airbus," *Fortune*, August 2, 1999.

[17] "Blue Skies for Airbus," *Fortune*, August 2, 1999.

[18] Glare was made of aluminum alloy and glass-fiber tape, which reduced the weight of the aircraft.

Airbus staff had to give careful consideration to seating arrangements and arrangements for evacuating 555 people from the aircraft in case of an emergency. Initially, passenger seating [was] on a single deck or in side-by-side fuselages; however, later on designers hit upon double-deck seating arrangements as it would be easier to get passengers off the plane quickly. Another advantage was that double-deck planes would not require more space on runways. In order to avoid the problem of claustrophobia among passengers, Airbus announced that it would create an ambience of leisure on the plane. [The] A-380 would have a staircase connecting both decks, and also exercise rooms, and sleeping rooms with bunk beds. It enlisted 1,200 frequent fliers from eight cities across the world to assess and provide suggestions for its mock cabins.

In response to fears that operational costs of the super jet would be high, Airbus sources said that the use of new technology meant that the A-380 would be 15% cheaper to operate than the Boeing 747. Airbus also said that the 656-seater A-380 would [. . .] reduce operating costs by around 25%. Boeing officials, however, calculated that cost savings through the super jet would amount to half the level claimed by Airbus.

As Airbus went ahead with its super jet plan, Boeing too started considering the manufacture of similar large planes. Although reports came out on Boeing's plans to design a 550-seat aircraft with a wide single deck and three aisles, company officials denied any firm designs. Later the project was dropped due to lack of orders.

Meanwhile, the response to Airbus' super jumbo jet was good. In 2000, the super jet project received a boost with Britain's Virgin Atlantic airline (owned by Richard Branson), and Qantas—Australia's major airliner—placing orders for the A-380 aircraft. Geoff Dixon, CEO [at] Qantas, said, "The aircraft will also enable us to further enhance our onboard customer product consistent with our recognized tradition as a pioneer in the development of long-haul air travel."[19]

A major concern that arose for Airbus was Boeing's decision to extend its 747 family. In March 2001, Boeing announced that it would be extending the family of 747s with its 747-X planes that would be on par with Airbus A-380s[20] and would carry around 522 passengers. It was also reported that Boeing's costs for [the] 747-X would be around a quarter of the A-380's budget. However, by the end of 2001, Boeing abandoned its plans to go for [the] 747-X due to weak market projections for the large super jet. It announced that it would launch a 'Sonic Cruiser' that would travel at 98% of the speed of sound. However, this project too failed to arouse any interest among airline companies due the turbulent conditions in the industry.

After the September 11th (2001) attacks, the airline industry was down and out because of the sharp [fall] in air travel. The worldwide economic slowdown also affected the industry very badly. Both Airbus and Boeing announced declines in their revenues due to recession. However, in October 2002, Airbus had 276 orders, while Boeing had just 186 orders. Analysts felt the lower operational costs of Airbus aircraft might have brought about this situation. However, as far as the A-380 project was concerned, Airbus would need around 100 orders to break even, but it actually had only 50 orders by the end of 2002.

While Airbus was gearing up to consolidate its position through its A-380, Boeing also started re-focusing on operational efficiencies in order to regain market leadership. In June 2003, Boeing announced the launch of a new plane—[the] 7E7, with a seating capacity of 200–250 passengers. Boeing sources said that with the help of new technology and operational processes it would be able to assemble the plane in only 3 days. With Boeing seemingly set to face up to the challenge from Airbus, it remains to be seen how long Airbus will be able to sustain its leadership position.

Questions for Discussion

1. When Airbus was set up, it failed to attract customers and did not get any orders over a period of 18 months. Discuss the problems faced by Airbus initially, and analyze the strategies adopted by the company to overcome them.

2. By the early 2000s, Airbus had acquired market leadership in the aerospace industry. Discuss the nature of the competition between Airbus and Boeing. What differentiating strategies did Airbus adopt in order to survive and succeed over the past few decades? How far do you think the advantages are sustainable in the long run? Justify.

3. Analyze the changes in the structure of the aerospace industry over the years and evaluate [their] effect on competition in the industry.

Additional Readings & References

1. Healy, Tim, **Competition: Battle for Asia,** www.asiaweek.com, March 29, 1996.
2. **Can Airbus Partners Unite?** *BusinessWeek,* July 22, 1996.
3. Edmondson, Gail & Browder, Seanna, **Angst at Airbus,** *BusinessWeek,* December 23, 1996.
4. Edmondson, Gail & Browder, Seanna, **A Wake Up Call for Airbus,** *BusinessWeek,* December 30, 1996.
5. **Peace in Our Time,** *The Economist,* July 24, 1997.
6. Guyon, Janet, **The Sole Competitor,** *Fortune,* January 12, 1998.
7. Henkoff, Ronald, **Boeing's Big Problem,** *Fortune,* January 12, 1998.
8. Edmondson, Gail, **Up, Up, and Away at Last for Airbus?** *BusinessWeek,* February 9, 1998.
9. **Airbus Highflier Grounded,** *BusinessWeek,* February 2, 1998.
10. **Hubris at Airbus, Boeing Rebuilds,** *The Economist,* November 26, 1998.
11. **Boeing Admits It "Let Clients Down,"** www.news.bbc.co.uk, September 8, 1998.
12. **Fearful Boeing,** *The Economist,* February 25, 1999.

---

[19] "Airbus Steals Boeing Ground," www.news.bbc.co.uk, November 30, 2002.
[20] [The] A3XX was renamed [the] A380 in early 2001.

13. Taylor, III Alex, **Blue Skies for Airbus,** *Fortune,* August 2, 1999.

14. Edmondson, Gail, **Overhauling Airbus,** *BusinessWeek,* August 2, 1999.

15. Burgner, Norbert, **The Airbus Story,** www.flugrevue.com, February 2000.

16. **Airbus Gets a Boost,** *The Economist,* April 6, 2000.

17. **Rivals in the Air,** www.news.bbc.co.uk, June 23, 2000.

18. **Airbus Steals Boeing Ground,** www.news.bbc.co.uk, November 30, 2000.

19. Useem, Jerry, **Boeing vs Boeing,** *Fortune,* October 2, 2000.

20. **Airbus Draws First Blood,** www.news.bbc.co.uk, June 18, 2001.

21. Matlack, Carol & Holmes, Stanley, **Trouble Ahead for Airbus?** *BusinessWeek,* October 1, 2001.

22. **Bettering Boeing,** *The Economist,* July 18, 2002.

23. Holmes, Stanley, **Showdown at 30,000 Feet,** *BusinessWeek,* July 22, 2002.

24. **Airbus Just May Win This Dogfight,** *BusinessWeek,* August 5, 2002.

25. **Bashing Boeing,** *The Economist,* October 17, 2002.

26. Matlack, Carol & Holmes, Stanley, **Look Out, Boeing,** *BusinessWeek,* October 28, 2002.

27. **Boeing vs Airbus,** *The Economist,* April 17, 2003.

28. **Boeing Can Assemble 7E7 in 72 Hours,** *The Economic Times,* June 6, 2003.

29. www.flugrevue.com.

30. www.airwise.com.

31. www.aviationnow.com.

32. www.seattletimes.com.

33. www.news.bbc.co.uk.

34. www.airbus.com.

35. www.speednews.com.

36. www.boeing.com.

Case **12**

Moving Tata Consultancy Services into the "Global Top 10"

Rafiq Dossani, Stanford University

Martin Kenney,[1] University of California, Davis

JSME1-2CS2

Abstract. This case study examines three strategic questions that India's largest software services firm, Tata Consultancy Services (TCS), faced in 2003. TCS had pioneered the industry and remained the market leader; of late, its lead over domestic rivals had been slipping, even while much larger multinational rivals were establishing large Indian operations. TCS needed a strategy to move up the software value chain. Meanwhile, a new industry was emerging, namely business process outsourcing, growing at 50 percent per year. There seemed to be synergies between BPO and software services, but also differences. TCS's Indian rivals had made major investments in BPO, while TCS had only a small presence. TCS had to quickly settle on its BPO strategy. The questions are: 1. How may TCS move up the software value chain? 2. Should TCS enter the BPO business? If so, 3. Should it make a major acquisition or grow organically?

Keywords: software, business process outsourcing, India, Tata Consultancy Services, value-chain, strategy.

INTRODUCTION

Flying across the Pacific Ocean on his way to a critical meeting with a large customer, S. Ramadorai (Ram), the current CEO of Tata Consultancy Services (TCS), was thinking back over his 31 years with the firm, and pondering what the strategy for the future should be. He and his predecessors

This case study has been peer reviewed by the editorial board of the *Journal of Strategic Management Education (JSME)*. For further information on this textbook journal please visit the Senate Hall Academic Publishing website at www.senatehall.com.

---

[1] The authors thank Jayashree Rukmani for research assistance, TCS officials for interviews and access to internal documents and Charles Holloway of the Graduate School of Business, Stanford University for comments. We also thank the editor, Peter Neilson, and three anonymous referees for their comments. An Industrial Note, as well as the Teaching Note, is available from Senate Hall Academic Publishing.

had built TCS into India's largest software services outsourcing firm. Begun in 1968 as an in-house division of its parent firm, which was a member of the Tata group, India's largest conglomerate, TCS had grown to a 23,000-person firm by 2002. He remembered how they had been able to evolve with many changes in the global computer industry, and continue their steady and profitable growth. In the process they had developed a client list of global *Fortune* 500 firms, including General Motors, Ford Motor, GE, Citigroup, ChevronTexaco and IBM. Even during the global technology downturn, revenue and profits had grown. As a result, they had become the 19th largest software services provider in the world, and in fiscal 2002–2003, revenues had grown to $1.04 billion.

Their previous success convinced Ram and his management team that even greater growth was possible. The movement to outsourcing was increasing around the world. The difficulties in proving to executives in other nations that India could deliver high-quality software and services had been largely overcome. Further, TCS's own retained earnings and the ability to call on the financial resources of the Tata Group meant that access to capital was not a constraint.

Even as opportunities abounded, dangers lurked. Not surprisingly, TCS's success had not gone unnoticed. Several new and serious Indian competitors, especially Wipro and Infosys, had been growing rapidly and competed with TCS for business. Moreover, multinational technology service providers such as IBM, HP and Accenture had established operations in India during the 1990s to leverage its cheap, skilled and abundant labor pool (see Table 1, page 518). There was no doubt in Ram's mind that competition would become ever more ferocious.

Ram had other concerns. TCS had the lowest revenue per employee of its peers (Table 1). Further, the dramatic downturn in the high-technology business in the Western economies that had begun in late 2000 was continuing. This downturn had had both positive and negative effects. Clients

Table 1   TCS's Strategic Competitors (Local and International)

	Annual Revenue ($million)	Employees	Revenue/ Employee ($)
IBM Global Services	36,129.0	150,000	240,086
EDS (Including A. T. Kearney)	22,193.5	140,000	158,525
Accenture	11,643.0	75,000	155,240
TCS	792.1	19,000	41,689
Infosys	545.0	10,600	51,415
Wipro	491.8	9,500	51,768
Satyam	378.0	8,500	44,470

Source: TCS documents.

Notes: Figures for U.S. firms are as of December, 2001; figures for Indian firms refer to export revenue and are as of March, 2002.

had become more aggressive on rates, but they had also become willing to offshore far more business—potentially, including higher-end work for which firms like IBM and Accenture were better known than Indian firms. TCS had responded by adding staff with new, higher-end capabilities, cutting wages and increasing the automation of its own business processes. But the advent of multinationals would clearly have an impact on the factors for success and could change the industry's structure through the kinds of work done and consolidation.

Given these facts, there was an opportunity for TCS to move to capture some of the higher value-added portions of the software creation process. Management knew this would not be simple. It would have to either purchase these skills overseas or make very competitive bids on projects where it could learn by doing. The final possibility was to wait until these skills emerged in the Indian environment. An acquisition would not be inexpensive and would require TCS'[s] executives to manage an American firm, a challenge but something Ram was convinced he and his managers could do. The second alternative of bidding aggressively on projects would affect profitability negatively, and could lead to other undesirable repercussions if TCS got in too far over its head. Still this offered an excellent learning opportunity. The final alternative of waiting until the skills were available in the Indian market might result in TCS missing opportunities to move upstream and expand.

The question about the future strategic directions for TCS had suddenly become more complicated, because in the late 1990s a new growth opportunity had emerged as foreign firms had begun to look to India as a site for locating business process activities. Undertaking business processes seemed like a natural fit for a firm like TCS. *Business processes* (BPs) is the catchall term used for the myriad white-collar processes that any bureaucratic entity undertakes in servicing its employees, vendors and customers including but not limited to human resources, accounting, auditing, customer care, telemarketing, tax preparation, claims processing, document management and many other chores necessary for firm functioning.[2] In some ways, running a BP resembled software programming in that it was "white-collar" work conducted in an office environment. So even as Ram was working to grow the software business, the question of whether they should enter the BP outsourcing (BPO) industry was vexing him and his advisors.

TCS would not enter the BPO industry without any experience. It [had been] operating a small call center operation in a joint venture with another Indian company since 2001 and in early 2003 had acquired a small provider of BPO services to the airline industry. These were moderately successful businesses. However given the pace of growth, the large number of entrants and rapid consolidation within the BPO industry, TCS's entry would need much management time and capital to catch up. Several of TCS's competitors were rapidly expanding their BPO operations and capturing major contracts. A decision on entry had to be made very soon, along with a concomitant decision as to whether to acquire a significant existing player or grow rapidly organically. Unfortunately, there was no easy answer.

Ram and his advisors had been discussing their options recently. However, his advisors continued to be divided. One group argued that TCS should stick with software-related businesses and work to move up the value chain, so as to better compete with the IBMs and Accentures. They argued that the software arena was their core competency and that it was higher value-added than BPO. Moreover, they felt that TCS had developed its expertise in managing engineering project teams, not the daily routine management that was necessary in the BPO area. Also, they were concerned about the differences in managing social science and commerce graduates as opposed to engineers and scientists. Their concern was that this might change TCS's culture.

Another group of managers countered that BPO was growing extremely rapidly (at 50 percent per annum versus 20 percent per annum for software outsourcing) and currently was quite profitable. They felt that if TCS missed out on this new sector it might fall irrevocably behind its Indian rivals. Moreover, they believed that TCS would be able to use its engineering capabilities to automate some service functions, thereby increasing the value-added TCS could provide its customers.

---

[2] We define a "business process" as a complete service, such as handling a customer complaint, processing a medical claim, or processing a purchase order. Completing a process requires undertaking a set of activities. For example, in handling a customer complaint it is necessary to understand the complaint, decide on a course of action, undertake the action, and follow up to ensure the action solved the complaint. Each of these is an activity that is potentially separable from the others.

Table 2   Selected Financial Data for TCS (fiscal year ends March 31)

	Export Revenue ($m)	Exports Share of Total Revenue (%)	PBT Margin (% of total revenue)	Employment
1990	28.1	70.8	13.2	2,300
1991	45.0	75.6	13.2	2,600
1992	52.3	80.0	16.2	4,761
1993	55.9	80.7	24.3	6,450
1994	64.0	79.2	19.8	5,589
1995	90.1	80.5	22.9	6,071
1996	123.9	81.9	24.7	7,864
1997	169.0	84.2	24.0	9,929
1998	241.8	88.2	25.6	11,176
1999	357.8	89.8	30.0	12,770
2000	417.9	86.1	28.7	15,044
2001	616.2	91.3	24.9	17,607
2002	792.1	92.7	29.3	20,459

Source[s]: Kennedy (1999) 18, Exhibit 9; Dheer and Viard (1997) 32 Exhibit 12; TCS documents.

Notes:

1. 1990–92 exchange rates are average rates for the year, based on the controlled rate of the time; convertibility for export income was introduced on 3/1/92; for 1993 onwards, year-end market rates are used.

2. Average export revenue growth rate in USD for 1990–2002 = 32.1 percent.

TCS, therefore, had several options ahead. Ram believed that TCS was ready to compete with the global giants in the IT outsourcing business. To motivate its employees, the firm had adopted the slogan "Global Top 10 by 2010." The question was what would be the most effective strategy to build TCS into a first-rank global competitor. Ram considered TCS to be well positioned for accessing the resources needed for managing significant strategic change, if it so chose. It was highly profitable and had financed growth internally almost from the beginning (Table 2 above). As noted, its parent, Tata Sons Limited, was a holding company for the Tatas, India's largest and arguably most-respected industrial group. Hence, raising financial resources for internal or acquisition-led growth,[3] or access to the best labor pool in the country, were possible.

The case is organized as follows. In section 2, we review the historical growth of TCS and the industry. In section 3, we pose the case question.

---

[3] TCS had contemplated a stock market listing in 2000, partly to better reward employees in order to help control a growing attrition rate caused by the global Internet boom. However, attrition had declined from its peak of 15% in 2000 to its historical average of 3% by 2002 with the end of the boom, and the decline in stock markets led to a suspension in the listing process. Listing had also been viewed as a way to gain visibility among clients, i.e., as a marketing tactic, although this was a minor reason. As TCS contemplated its foray into BPO in 2003, listing was again viewed as a possibility given the possible need to purchase its way into the business, although stock markets still needed to be cooperative.

THE DEVELOPMENT OF TCS

In every shift in the Indian software industry, TCS had been a pioneer. TCS was established in 1968 to service the in-house data processing requirements of the Tata Group and in 1969 offered data-processing (EDP) services to outside clients. In 1970, it became the exclusive Indian licensee to sell and maintain mainframe computers built by the American firm Burroughs. In an effort to encourage the development of an Indian computer industry in 1973, the government enacted the Foreign Exchange Regulation Act of 1973 forbidding foreign firms from operating fully owned subsidiaries. As a result, IBM, the largest IT firm in India at the time, chose to leave India. However, other foreign firms were willing to establish joint ventures, and the Indian industry grew gradually. During this period, all of these firms, including TCS, sold and maintained the computers and software systems made overseas by their joint venture partner and offered EDP services to local clients. Table 3 on page 520 shows how TCS was able to lead the Indian software industry and keep pace with the evolving needs of its American clients.

TCS's overseas experience in providing software-related services began in 1974 when TCS was asked by Burroughs to install its systems for U.S.-based clients. Burroughs was attracted by the combination of software engineering talent and the English language that it had found in TCS'[s] workforce. This was the beginning of the "body-shopping" business, which entailed the dispatch of Indian programmers to the sites of overseas clients. Typically, these assignments were for a few months at a time. At this time, the Indian firms did little more than recruitment.

Table 3   Comparing Work Done in [the] U.S. and TCS in Common Time Frames

Work Type =>	U.S. Firms	TCS
Up to 1970	Support for in-house IT department (hardware and O/S maintenance).	
1971–80	Applications development, conversion to IBM platforms.	Labor exported to client site to support in-house IT department (O/S maintenance and conversion to IBM platforms).
1981–90	Systems integration (hardware with systems), system design, conversion to Unix platforms.	Offsite conversion work to Unix platforms, onsite and offsite applications development.
1991–2002	Consulting, systems integration (software).	Offsite applications development in large projects, onsite conversion (Y2K).

Source: Authors' compilation.

As the software industry changed and Burroughs continued to lose market share TCS developed a growing competence in "conversion" work, i.e., converting clients' existing Burroughs' systems to work on IBM hardware. To further its growth, in 1979, TCS opened the first overseas office by an Indian software firm in New York. Entering the 1980s, TCS remained the dominant software services firm in India. In 1980, the Indian software industry exports were $4 million shared by 21 firms, of which TCS and a sister Tata firm accounted for 63 percent.[4] By 1984, the number of firms had increased to 35 and export revenues had reached $25.3 million.

In 1984, the Indian government promulgated a New Computer Policy (NCP-1984), and with it the Indian software industry entered a new phase. Import duties on hardware were reduced from 135% to 60% and on software from 100% to 60%. The domestic software business was recognized as an "industry," thus making it eligible for loans from commercial banks. It was also "delicensed," so that no permits were needed to enter the business.[5] Third, wholly-owned foreign firms developing software for export were once more allowed to operate in India provided they received a government license. Simultaneously, a fourth policy change exempted all export revenue from income tax. An unfortunate side effect of this policy was that it made soft-

ware development for the domestic market even more unattractive. The fifth policy initiative was the creation of export processing zones, the first of which (in Mumbai) harbored TCS. Rentals in these zones were low by market standards, procedures for establishing a business were simplified, and power and water were guaranteed.

The policy liberalizations were fortuitous as they coincided with technological changes in the global computer industry. The most important of these was the replacement of mainframes with workstations as the programmer's hardware tool. Moreover, workstations used Unix and C in place of the variety of operating systems and languages used on mainframes (we shall term this adoption of Unix and workstations the "U-W standard"). Towards the end of the 1980s and the early 1990s, the U-W standard would be accompanied by the adoption of standardized database management platforms sold by firms such as Oracle, IBM, and Sybase and this further simplified the writing of applications' software.

These changes set the stage for undertaking work in India rather than overseas at the customer's site. Oddly enough, the change to offsite work was pioneered in 1985 by a multinational, Texas Instruments (TI), whose wholly-owned foreign subsidiary was the first to enter the Indian software industry since IBM's departure in 1978. TI persuaded the government to supply it with scarce satellite bandwidth and used programmers working out of its offices in Bangalore. Soon, several multinational firms imitated TI's delivery model and began to do product development work in India.

According to Suresh Kumar of TCS, "Earlier, firms had been forced to work on the client's site in large part because they could not afford to buy or rent computers locally; they, therefore, needed to offer programming skills that differed with the machines they were working on, be these IBM, Burroughs, VAX, etc. It was not until tariffs were reduced and Unix became an accepted programming standard in the mid-80s that offshore work for clients became feasible."

TCS pioneered the "remote project management model," as it came to be called, which required it to develop the skills to manage projects remotely. By 1988, 10% of the work was done offsite, and this had risen to 40.8% by 2000. An additional benefit of the IT industry's shift to the U-W standard was that it became a new source of conversion work for Indian firms as they found clients for the conversion of installed applications into Unix-compatible programs.

The remote project management model also had another very important benefit. It allowed TCS to hire many less-skilled programmers. Jayant Pendharkar of TCS recalled, "We were able to better match skills with requirements. Earlier, when we sent programmers overseas, we estimated the skill-sets needed and sent a compact team to the client's site. That team was necessarily overqualified since it was expensive to replace team members (if found lacking in skills) once they had been dispatched overseas. By doing work in India, we could use our 'bench': programmers of dif-

[4] Heeks (1996) p 88.

[5] Heeks, ibid., p 44–5.

ferent skill levels and depending on the job could switch to different jobs quickly. Thus, we could substantially increase the use of lower-skilled programmers at much lower costs than before."

In the second half of the 1980s the Indian software industry became established. This coincided with a maturation of the industry globally, and India captured the first-mover advantages in the offshoring business. The number of firms rose to 700 by 1990. Among them were Infosys and Wipro, which had moved their headquarters to Bangalore in the 1980s. Following TI's lead, several other MNCs including HP and Digital opened in-house product development operations in India. Also, a number of the large global banks, which had long-established operations in India, opened Indian software divisions for developing software for in-house use.

Government regulations created some difficulties for the Indian software firms. For example, Ram believed that the absence of a domestic market and tight controls on technology imports to India led to a reliance on overseas clients and made it difficult for the Indian industry to develop and demonstrate the expertise that would prepare it to offer higher value-added services. As he noted, "in the absence of domestic markets, we did not have the opportunity to prove (via domestic work) that we could do more sophisticated work—there was nothing to showcase. Technology was not allowed to flow in. It still took very long for approvals for equipment. Domestic firms that could have been clients of TCS could not access the equipment and complementary technologies that would allow them to take advantage of India's skills in IT services."

Needing global-class domain expertise, the tight controls also forced Indian firms to provide services in those few sectors with a strong foreign presence in India, all of which existed due to historical accidents. In particular, the financial services industry contained several foreign banks. This enabled TCS to recruit financial service expertise of global quality at home. Fortunately, banking was a sector with one of the largest rates of absorption of IT globally. However, other high-growth IT users, such as insurance and telecommunications, would not become important clients until the liberalizations of the 1990s.

The activities undertaken by TCS changed substantially in the 1990s. Conversion work tapered off as most corporations had adopted the common Unix platform. It was replaced with writing applications programs, a more profitable activity. TCS eagerly sought higher value-added work, such as systems integration, and focused considerable effort into bidding for larger projects. According to TCS's K. Ananth Krishnan. "Prior to 1991, the range of projects was from 5 man years to 20 man years, while it rose to a range of 20 man years to 150 man years by the end of the decade." The largest industry serviced by TCS continued to be financial services, although new sectors and service areas also developed.

A feature of the post-1991 reform period was the opening of India-based client-specific offshore development

centers (ODCs) by the large domestic firms. Again, TCS was a pioneer. Combined with their overseas branches, the ODCs enabled firms like TCS to undertake large, turnkey projects that combined India-based and overseas staff (the latter often supplying critical industry expertise otherwise unavailable in India).

A continuing pattern of deregulation meant that from 1991 onward multinational firms could more easily open wholly-owned subsidiaries. They responded more cautiously to the liberalizations than Indian firms, although IBM established a joint venture with the Tatas in 1991.[6] EDS started operations in India in 1996, and Accenture began its IT outsourcing operations in India in 2001. The top 20 MNC software exporters employed 25,204 persons as of March 2002, or 13.1% of the software exporters workforce.[7] With the arrival of the MNCs, it was clear to Ram that the success factors for the industry were set to change. The earlier advantage of cheap talent was now available to the MNCs as well, and success would increasingly depend on other factors, such as credibility for undertaking larger or more complex projects.

As the industry grew, some differentiation among the larger Indian firms appeared. Financial services firms, particularly American banks, were still the largest clients. TCS offered the widest range of services ranging from system integration to the writing of code and the running of the client's systems for the financial services industry (see Figure 1, page 522). In contrast, Infosys specialized in applications software for the financial services industry, while Wipro focused on applications software for the IT industry.

The Year 2000 (Y2K) problem was an unexpected bonanza that increased India's software sales in the years prior to 2000, and introduced several new clients to the capabilities of Indian software companies. Phaneesh Murthy, a Director at TCS's competitor Infosys, said, "Y2K allowed us to expand our target client list. Many medium-sized firms that would not otherwise have considered Indian software firms were forced to get to know them as a result of the shortage of U.S.-based programmers in the run up to Y2K. These software firms were later able to get other business from the medium-sized firms."[8]

In the years following Y2K, a rapid improvement in global and Indian telecommunications capabilities expanded the range of software development services that TCS could offer. In particular, databases located in developed countries could now be accessed remotely to offer new services such as real-time database management, quality assurance and web services.

---

[6] The Tata group disinvested in 1999. Source: http://www.ibm.com/in/ibm/history.html, downloaded Dec. 6, 2002. As of the end of 2002, IBM employed 4373 persons in India. Source: http://www.ibm.com/in/ibm/qfacts.html#IN.

[7] Source: Nasscom (2003), p 43, 138.

[8] Source: Phaneesh Murthy, Director, Infosys, 1/02, personal interview.

Figure 1   TCS's Market Segmentation 2003

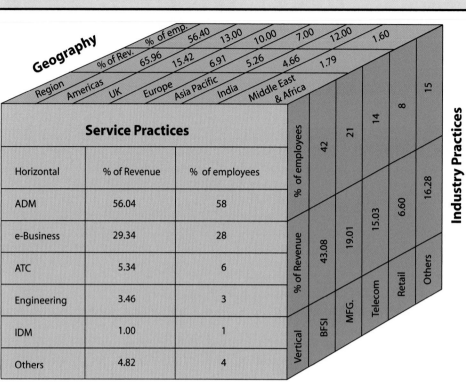

Source: TCS documents.

Acronyms:

ADM—Application Development and Maintenance
ATC—Architecture and Technology Consulting
IDM—Infrastructure Development and Management
BFSI—Banking, Financial Services and Insurance

TCS had previously only grown organically. To accelerate growth, in 2001, it made its first acquisition ever when it acquired CMC, an Indian government-owned firm with 2500 employees, sold under a divestment program. CMC was strong in the fields of infrastructure services and the management of computing hardware and networks, a field hitherto dominated by large American firms such as EDS and CSC and European firms such as Cap Gemini. With the CMC acquisition, TCS was able to develop new capabilities in its core business of financial applications development. In June 2003, TCS acquired Airline Financial Support Services (AFSS), a specialized BPO provider to the airline industry. Thus TCS was becoming comfortable making acquisitions when it made strategic sense.

The BPO Question

TCS already had a small BPO joint venture that was growing and the addition of AFSS increased its experience in the field. However, TCS's BPO operations were smaller than its

major competitors (Table 4 opposite). Wipro and a smaller competitor, HCL, had strengthened their BPO capability through acquisition. Infosys had opened a free-standing subsidiary firm, Progeon, and was increasing its size. The activities of Wipro and Infosys were especially worrisome because these firms were already growing faster than TCS. This concern was even greater because BPO, though admittedly from a low base (in March 2003, the BPO industry employed 175,000 employees in India including those in multinational firms), was growing at 50 percent per year, while software services was only growing at 20 percent a year from a base in March 2003 of approximately 500,000. U.S. outsourcing firms (Accenture, EDS, ADP etc.) were simultaneously announcing ambitious new plans to establish or expand existing Indian operations in both software programming and BPO applications. Having a growth strategy that explicitly addressed BPO was a necessity.

BPO does share some features of the software services industry; however, it does differ on some important dimensions. First, much of what is outsourced, such as call centers

Table 4   Indian IT Firms' Strategies for Entering the BP Outsourcing Industry

Firm	Strategy	BPO Employees (March 2003)	BPO Employees (December 2003)	Primary BPO Location (April 2003)
TCS	Joint venture with HFDC: Intelenet	900	2,500	Mumbai
Infosys	Established a subsidiary, Progeon	3,000	4,000	Bangalore
Wipro Spectramind	Acquired by Wipro in 2002 for approx. $93 million	3,200	10,000	Delhi
HCL eServe	Acquired a British Telecom BP subsidiary, now an HCL subsidiary	2,500	5,000	Delhi
Satyam	Established a subsidiary, Nipuna	Not available	2,000	Hyderabad

Source: Authors' compilation.

and claims processing is, at least initially, low value-added even compared to coding. This was especially difficult for TCS because it had developed such an engineer-focussed culture. Was doing BPO going to mesh well with the culture TCS had worked so hard to create?

The work process in BPO is also different as much of it is in real-time and there is no room for mistakes. The employees, though very capable graduates of Indian universities, were from humanities, social sciences, and commerce backgrounds and would require a very different type of managerial skills. Since they worked in the public eye, especially those in call-centers, politeness and conviviality were as important or more important than technical expertise. Not that his management team could not do this, but it would require a reorientation, although perhaps this could be mitigated by creating a subsidiary.

Another problem with the BPO business was that at this point much of the profit came by increasing the size of the operation. That is, the more workers, the more profit—not exactly in line with Ram's goal of increasing the value-added per employee. The other important way of increasing profit was to better utilize the infrastructure, which most firms only operated 12–14 hours a day, i.e., during business hours in the U.S. and, to a lesser degree, Europe. Could his team find a way to utilize the infrastructure more totally? He did not know, but that would be an important consideration.

There was also the opportunity to create synergies between BPO and the software services operations. One of these was that TCS'[s] blue-chip client list for software projects could be marketed its BPO services. A second was TCS'[s] expertise in managing services remotely without disruption.

If TCS decided to seriously enter the business, it would also have to decide whether to grow the BPO operation organically or make a major acquisition. There were

several independent firms in the 3,000–5,000 range that might be acquired, but such firms would be expensive, probably costing $25,000 per employee (based on similar recent acquisitions). Making such an acquisition would require careful management of the integration process, and though Ram felt confident his team could do it, there was no doubt that this would occupy management bandwidth at the very time when he felt they needed to ramp up their software services business.

On the other hand, building the operation internally would take time, and large contracts were being signed today. Without an acquisition, TCS might be consigned to a second-tier position in an industry that might exhibit important economies of scale and scope. Even TCS's and the Tata Group's deep pockets would not support a long period of losses. Thus the organic growth TCS has so favored also had its own set of pitfalls.

Finally, Ram was concerned about whether the BPO industry might not become a political issue in the U.S. as concern about the offshoring of jobs increased. He did not believe that the U.S. government would intervene. However, no one was entirely certain what the outcome of what appeared to be an increasingly intense controversy would be.

THE QUESTIONS RESTATED

1. What strategy should TCS use to move up the software services value chain?

2. Should TCS enter the BPO business or would it be better to stay with the software services business?

3. If you believe TCS should enter the BPO business, then should it make a major acquisition or grow organically?

SUPPLEMENTARY TABLES AND FIGURES

Table 1   Top 5 IT Firms in India, 2002: Number of Years Behind TCS

Name of Firm	Export Rev, 2002 ($m)	Export Rev, 2001 ($m)	Growth Rate (%)	# of Years Behind[1]
TCS	792.1	616.2	28.5	
Infosys	545.0	405.4	34.4	6
Wipro	491.8	377.1	30.4	24
Satyam	378.0	271.9	39.0	7.5
HCL Tech	332.8	298.4	11.5	N/A

Notes:

1. # of years behind, n, that Firm A is behind TCS is calculated as (an approximation) the nth root of the arithmetic difference in growth rate that equals the ratio of 2002 export revenue of TCS to Firm A.
2. TCS data from company sources.
3. Infosys data from http://www.infy.com/investor/reports.asp downloaded 2/20/03.
4. Wipro data from http://www.wipro.com/investors/annualreport.htm downloaded 2/20/03.
5. Satyam data from http://www.satyam.com/mediaroom/pr1apr02.html downloaded 2/20/03.
6. HCL Tech data from http://www.hcltechnologies.com/artdisplay.asp?cat_id=40 downloaded 2/20/03.

Table 2   Percentage Shares of Revenue of Indian Firm Activities, 2001

Services Provided	All Indian Firms (%)	TCS (%)
Systems Integration/ Large Projects	12.3	22
Architecture/ Technology Consulting	3.9	3
Engineering Services	18.7	0
Applications Programming & Maintenance	46.2	70
e-Business	9.1	0
Other	9.9	5

Source[s]: Akella, R., and R. Dossani (2002); TCS documents.

Table 3   Educational Levels at TCS Relative to the Industry in India (%)

	All Firms	TCS in 2002
Undergraduate in CS/EE	42.9	53.5
Master in CS/EE	7.2	27.9
Ph.D. in CS/EE	0.7	0.46
Certified/Other Graduate	35.3	10.3
MBA	5.2	7.17
Other	8.7	0.52

Sources: Akella, R., and R. Dossani (2002); TCS documents.

Notes:

1. CS/EE refers to computer science/electrical engineering.
2. Certified employees [include] only those with a certificate from a qualified IT-training institute (minimum 6 months full-time equivalent).
3. MBAs may or may not have IT education.

Table 4   Primary Industry Focus Areas at TCS, 2002 and Targets, 2005

Industry Practices	Revenue Share (%) 2002	Targeted Revenue Share (%) 2005
Banking, Financial Services and Insurance	43%	35%
Manufacturing	20%	20%
Telecommunications	14%	15%
Retail	7%	8%
Transportation	5%	8%
Other	11%	14%

Source: TCS documents.

Note:

1. Other includes technology companies, government, and healthcare firms.

Table 5   Primary Service Practice Focus Areas at TCS, 2002 and Targets, 2005

Service Practices	2002	2005
Custom Applications (build and support) and Large projects	52%	40%
Packaged Applications and Systems Integration	31%	23%
Products-based solutions	5%	13%
Consulting	4%	4%
Infrastructure Services	2%	8%
Engineering and other Business Process services	5%	11%
Other services	1%	1%

Source: TCS documents.

Table 6   Employment Designations at TCS, 2002

Staff Category	
Domain Experts	1350
Marketing, sales and relationship management	1000
Delivery	18675
Research and Development	250
Administration	1700
Total	22975

Source: TCS documents.

Figure 1 Interplay between IT and Business Process in a Typical Product Development Scenario

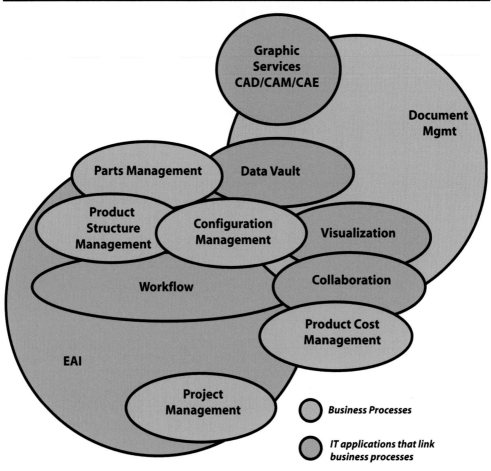

Source: TCS documents.

Figure 2 Organization Chart of TCS

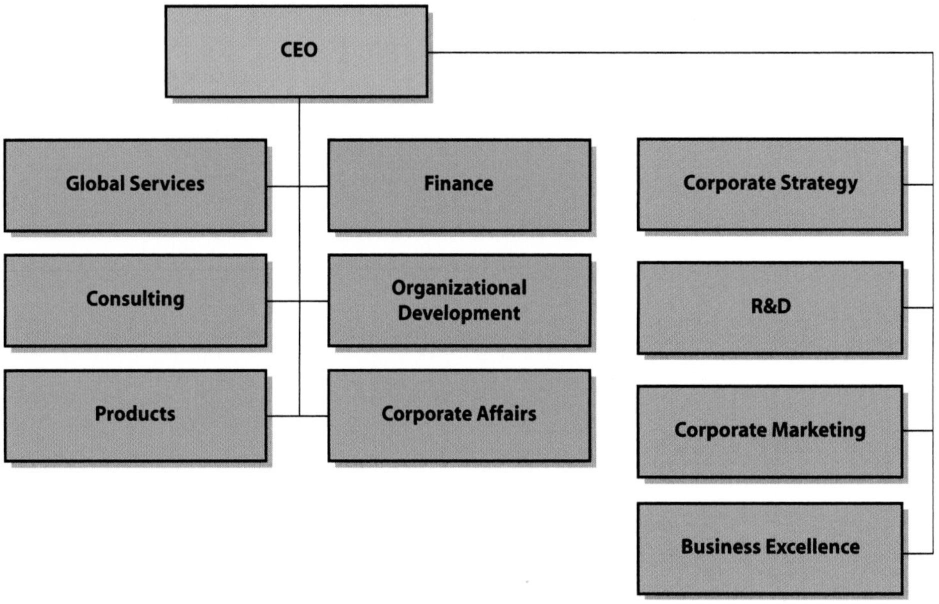

CEO

Global Services

Finance

Corporate Strategy

Consulting

Organizational Development

R&D

Products

Corporate Affairs

Corporate Marketing

Business Excellence

Source: TCS documents.

References

Akella, R. and Dossani, R. (2002), *The Software Value Chain in India*, Stanford University, unpublished manuscript.

Correa, C. M. (1996), "Strategies for Software Exports from Developing Countries," *World Development* 24(1): 171–82.

Dheer, S. and Viard, B. (1997), *Tata Consultancy Services: Globalization of Software Services,* Stanford, CA: Graduate School of Business, Stanford University.

Dossani, R. (2003), *History of the Software Industry in India*, Stanford University, unpublished manuscript.

Dossani, R. and Kenney, M. (2004), "Lift and Shift: Moving the Back-Office to India," *Information Technology and International Development* 1(2) forthcoming.

Heeks, R. (1996), *India's Software Industry*, New Delhi, India: Sage.

Kennedy, R. (1999), *Tata Consultancy Services: High Technology in a Low-Income Economy*, Harvard Business School, Harvard University.

Ministry of Finance, Government of India: various documents.

Mowery, D. (1996), "Introduction," in Mowery, D. (ed.) *The International Computer Software Industry*, New York: Oxford 3–14.

Nasscom (2002), *The IT Industry in India: Strategic Review 2002*, New Delhi, India: Nasscom.

Nasscom (2003), *The IT Industry in India: Strategic Review 2003*, New Delhi, India: Nasscom.

Schware, R. (1992), "Software Industry Entry Strategies for Developing Countries: A 'Walking on Two Legs' Proposition," *World Development* 20(2): 143–164.

Steinmuller, W. (1996), "The U.S. Software Industry: An Analysis and Interpretive History," in Mowery, D. (ed.) *The International Computer Software Industry*, New York: Oxford 15–52.

STPI (2000), *Business Support Center*, Software Technology Parks of India, unpublished manuscript.

Tata Consultancy Services, www.tcs.com: various documents.

Teubal, M. (2002), "The Indian Software Industry from an Israeli Perspective: A Microeconomic and Policy Analysis," *Science, Technology & Society* 7(1): 151–186.

McDonald's and the McCafé Coffee Initiative

9B04M008

Ralph Sgro, on his usual morning tour of the Burlington-area McDonald's restaurants, stopped at a traffic light and counted the number of cars ordering through the Tim Hortons drive-through. The number of cars in his competitor's drive-through had been continually increasing over the last few years. Sgro was concerned that, although McDonald's breakfast sales were increasing, the breakfast market share had declined. As well, the snack business segment of McDonald's sales had not kept pace with industry growth. Sgro attributed the loss of market share predominantly to the growth of strong coffee competitors (including Tim Hortons) and McDonald's poor reputation for coffee. In response, Sgro introduced the McCafé concept to Canada, in May 2001, at restaurants in Burlington, Ontario.

McCafé was a full-service coffee bar located either as an extension of a McDonald's front counter or as a stand-alone restaurant. It had also been introduced in Australia, New Zealand, Brazil and many European countries. While McCafé was well received in Burlington, Sgro wondered if the McCafé concept would help McDonald's regain dominance in breakfast and snack-time sales and rebuild McDonald's competitive advantage.

THE CANADIAN FOODSERVICE INDUSTRY

The Canadian foodservice industry, which includes those businesses that transport, cook and serve prepared foods, grossed $32.7 billion and accounted for 4.3 per cent of Canada's gross domestic product (GDP).[1] Restaurant sales dominated this industry, accounting for 66 per cent of the foodservice industry, and of all the meals services, quick service (commonly known as fast food) accounted for about 60 per cent (see Exhibits 1 and 2). In 2001, Canadians spent $0.41 of every designated food dollar on meals prepared outside the home.[2]

Commercial restaurant growth had been attributed largely to an increase in franchising activity.[3] In the last 10 years, independently owned restaurants decreased by nearly 10 per cent. In the quick service industry, restaurants such as McDonald's, Wendy's and Burger King competed with similar product lines, prices, speed of service and convenience. Industry players often fought for high traffic locations—it was not unusual to see a busy corner with two or three fast food restaurants clustered together.

Ivey

Richard Ivey School of Business
The University of Western Ontario

Lindsay Sgro prepared this case under the supervision of Professor Tima Bansal solely to provide material for class discussion. The authors do not intend to illustrate either effective or ineffective handling of a managerial situation. The authors may have disguised certain names and other identifying information to protect confidentiality.

[1] Kostuch Information Services, *Canada Multi-Unit Report of 125 Foodservice Operators,* International Foodservice Manufacturers Association, Edition Canada, 1997.

[2] Kimberley Noble, "Fast Food Whole in One," *Maclean's,* August 20, 2001.

[3] Kostuch Information Services, *Canada Multi-Unit Report of 125 Foodservice Operators,* International Foodservice Manufacturers Association, Edition Canada, 1997.

Exhibit 1   Who Gets the Foodservice Dollar?

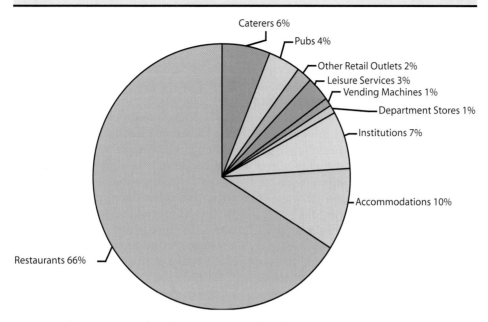

Source: Canadian Restaurant and Foodservices Association (CRFA) and Statistics Canada.

Exhibit 2   Best Product Prospects—Canada

Share of Meal Occasions as a Percentage of Total Services Commercial Foodservice Industry 1996 to 1998

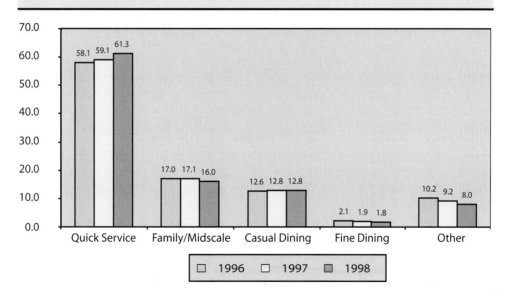

Mergers, acquisitions and alliances were commonplace in this industry. In 1995, Wendy's International acquired Tim Hortons (TDL Group Ltd.) for $542 million. After acquiring some smaller American coffee chains, the Second Cup sold 37 per cent of their shares to Cara Foods (the owner of Harvey's and Swiss Chalet). The Second Cup entered into a distribution contract with The Great Canadian Bagel. In spite of this consolidation of the industry and the co-operative agreements, McDonald's continued to be the Canadian quick-service industry market share leader, second only to the Four Seasons Hotels and Resorts.

Quick-service consumers were both time and value conscious. They demanded low prices, good quality, safe food and fast service. Although Canadian consumption decisions were impacted by brand image and marketing, value and convenience were high on the priority list. While each competitor attempted to provide a unique offering, it was difficult to build customer loyalty, given the large number of restaurant choices.

THE RETAIL COFFEE INDUSTRY IN CANADA

Tim Hortons, McDonald's, Second Cup, Country Style, Coffee Time, Starbucks, as well as many independent coffee retailers, drove the coffee industry. Tim Hortons had the largest share of coffee consumption in Canada at 33 per cent. In Ontario, Tim Hortons lead with a 41.4 per cent market share, followed by independent coffee chains at 22.1 per cent, McDonald's at 7.1 per cent, Second Cup at 4.4 per cent and Starbucks at one per cent. While many competitors focused on brewed coffee, specialty teas and specialty coffees, many were expanding their product lines to offer sandwiches, soups and other gourmet treats. Canadian consumers appeared to receive this product line extension well, as reflected by the 39 per cent increase in Tim Hortons lunch sales in 2000.

Each coffee competitor had a different value proposition. Reliability, quality and service all positively impacted the retailer's brand image. Further, some coffee houses catered to the coffee connoisseur, while others were simply convenient locations to consume good quality coffee. Producing consistent quality and taste in specialty coffee, however, required skill and training. Service was slower for specialty coffee retailers because the specialty coffee production process took approximately three to four minutes, compared to simply pouring a cup of brewed coffee. Specialty coffee customers seemed to accept long queues, long service times, varying quality and high prices.

Although coffee competitors distributed their products primarily through their individual retail outlets, many experimented with unique distribution strategies. For example, the drive-through had traditionally served brewed coffee, but many specialty coffee retailers had started to also offer drive-through service. Also, distribution alliances had formed in the coffee industry. Starbucks had joined with Chapters, and Second Cup with the Home Depot. Tim Hortons had partnered with Wendy's in 1995. Together, they opened Wendy's/Tim Hortons food court–styled restaurants where a customer could order both Wendy's and Tim Hortons products at the same location.

The Canadian retail coffee industry had experienced explosive growth over the last five years. Annual retail coffee consumption had increased by 15 per cent to more than 16 million cups of coffee purchased every week in Canada. Although most Canadians still consumed their coffee in traditional sit-down retail coffee outlets, 29 per cent of the industry's coffee consumed was purchased from drive-throughs. Drive-through coffee consumption had grown almost fourfold since 1995.

Canadians, who consumed on average two or more cups of coffee per day, expected a different experience at different times of the day. Their morning consumption was driven by a "get up and go" ritual that required a convenient, dependable coffee source. In the afternoon, consumers wanted a coffee break—a "pick me up" or reward for their hard work. At night, coffee consumption was often a way to finish the evening meal. While specialty coffee growth had been significant, brewed coffee continued to be the dominant purchase throughout the day.

MCDONALD'S CORPORATION

Ray Kroc, the founder of the McDonald's system, opened the first McDonald's Restaurant in Des Plaines, Illinois, in 1955. Although McDonald's was originally a hamburger restaurant, McDonald's now offered a diverse menu and quick service in 121 countries worldwide. While each country offered a slightly different dining experience to cater to the local culture, food preparation and marketing were standardized across the globe—from Tokyo to Toronto, the Big Mac was the same. According to Tom Peters, the three most recognized brands in the world were McDonald's golden arches, Coca-Cola and Disney.[4] In fact, these three brands often jointly marketed their products, further securing the primacy of their brands.

In the 1980s McDonald's experienced rapid growth, partly attributable to the successful "Big Mac Attack" ad promotion. By 2000, the McDonald's brand represented value and fast service. Through product innovation, McDonald's attracted many customer segments including families, teens and adults. After partnering with Disney, McDonald's Happy Meals revolutionized children's dining. With Ronald McDonald as the spokesperson, no other competitor was able to match the brand equity associated with the McDonald's Happy Meal. Furthermore, the introduction of the "combo meal" made McDonald's another favorite at both lunch and dinner for a variety of adult customers. In 2000, McDonald's in the United States and Canada initiated the "Value Campaign." This promotion slashed the prices of McDonald's small and large sandwiches, to bring "value" to the customer. McDonald's also built its reputation through community activities. Ronald McDonald Children's Charities (RMCC), for example, was established to help fund children's charitable causes.

McDonald's Corporation was a publicly held company based in Chicago, Illinois. The head office established standard marketing, operations and quality practices, but the international subsidiaries could make independent decisions that addressed the needs of their particular customers. International subsidiaries were accountable to the head office for profitability and had to regularly remit their financial statements and strategic positions to the international headquarters.

McDonald's Corporation adopted a growth by acquisition strategy. To leverage the strong McDonald's brand, it

---

[4] www.worklifechoices.org/brandyou.htm, referenced January 12, 2001.

acquired Aroma Café, Boston Market, Chipotle Mexican Grill, Donatos Pizza and Pret A Manger. In 2000, McDonald's Corporation was the quick service industry leader with sales of $14.7 billion and the industry's highest profit margin of 12.4 per cent.

COMPETITION

The discussion below identifies the primary competitors to McDonald's.

Wendy's

Wendy's International, Inc. opened its first restaurant in 1969 and operated, developed and franchised a system of distinctive quick-service restaurants. Wendy's was known for its founder, Dave Thomas, and its unique menu blend of burgers, fries and healthy alternatives. Wendy's flagship products included the introduction of the salad in 1979, the baked potato in 1983 and the Super Value Menu in 1989. Furthermore, the introduction of the late night drive-through window allowed Wendy's customers to "eat great, even late." As of December 31, 2000, there were 5,792 Wendy's restaurants in the United States, Canada and 25 other countries and territories. Of these restaurants, 1,153 were operated by the company and 4,639 by the company's franchisees. The merger with the Canadian coffee and doughnuts icon, Tim Hortons, provided Wendy's the opportunity to expand into the coffee business in the United States, even though Tim Hortons continued to operate as a separate entity. Although Tim Hortons was best known for its coffee and doughnuts, the introduction of deli-style sandwiches, bagels and Tim's Own soups and chili made it a major player in lunch sales. As of December 31, 2000, there were 1,980 Tim Hortons restaurants in Canada and the United States, of which 95 per cent were owned by franchisees.

In 2001, Wendy's International, Inc. enjoyed significant financial success. Its revenues increased by seven per cent as a result of strong domestic and international sales and its net income increased nine per cent largely attributed to improved operating performance at the Tim Hortons restaurants. More recently, Wendy's International focused much of its expansion through "combo units" of Wendy's and Tim Hortons in a food court–style [restaurant].

Burger King

Burger King's reputation was associated with inexpensive food served quickly, in an attractive, clean environment. Founded in 1954, in Miami, Florida, there were more than 11,370 Burger King restaurants in 58 countries and interna-

tional territories worldwide by 2002. The restaurants were owned and operated by independent franchisees. Burger King was best known for its flagship flame-broiled Whopper, its "Have It Your Way" motto (that enabled customers to design their own hamburgers) and its drive-through and take-out services (that accounted for 50 per cent and 15 per cent, respectively, of their sales). In fiscal year 2002, Burger King, part of Diageo (an international food and drinks corporation), had system-wide sales of $11.4 billion.

KFC, Pizza Hut and Taco Bell

Tricon Global Restaurants, through its three brands, KFC, Pizza Hut and Taco Bell, developed, operated, franchised and licensed a worldwide system of restaurants which prepared, packaged and sold a menu of competitively priced food items. The Tricon organization operated more than 30,400 units in more than 100 countries and territories, and was the global leader in the chicken, pizza and Mexican restaurant categories. Tricon was also the leader in multi-branded quick-service restaurants with more than 1,100 locations worldwide. Multi-branding had proven to be a growth vehicle for Tricon in the United States, as consumers appeared to enjoy the variety of two or three dining options at the same location. In 2001, in spite of a three per cent drop in revenues as a result of foreign currency exchange issues and refranchising, net income rose 15 per cent due to restrained corporate and project spending.

McDONALD'S CANADA

McDonald's Canada had approximately 1,200 locations throughout the country with 70 per cent owned and operated by franchisees. McDonald's Canada developed its own strategy, marketing plan and product line, although it was often similar to that of McDonald's USA. Canada based its success on the "three-legged stool": the company, the suppliers and the franchisees. Each leg brought stability to the partnership. Supplier "partners" included Coca-Cola, Disney, Nestlé, Cuddy Foods, Mother Parkers, and Cossette Communications-Marketing.

McDonald's entered the Canadian breakfast industry in April 1976, and for many years, dominated the industry with its flagship Egg McMuffin sandwich and other hand-held product features. Tim Hortons was essentially ignored by McDonald's and was allowed free reign to develop its brand, based on the slogan of "Always Fresh" coffee and doughnuts. Even though the McDonald's breakfast business had grown, Sgro believed that McDonald's Canada did not allocate the necessary operational expertise and marketing drive to develop its coffee equity or breakfast business.

CORPORATE/FRANCHISEE RELATIONSHIP

Franchisees played important roles in the McDonald's system because of their customer contact and their entrepreneurial spirit. Although some franchisees were employees of McDonald's who were promoted through the corporate ladder, most franchisees applied from outside of the system because they saw the tremendous business opportunity. Franchisees were screened and selected for their entrepreneurial drive and prior business success. Franchisees were expected to act as owner-operators, not strictly as investors. They were required to be active in the day-to-day operations of their franchise and assume the responsibility of building the McDonald's system within the community. Franchisees paid a monthly rent and service fee to McDonald's Canada, based on a percentage of top-line sales. In addition, franchisees were required to meet the corporate standards of quality, service and cleanliness. They were obliged to contribute to the marketing fund and take an active involvement in all marketing initiatives. It was the franchisees' responsibility to represent the company well in their community, and to grow the business to the best of their ability. In return, franchisees leveraged McDonald's brand equity and received considerable support for every facet of their business. McDonald's Canada offered support in training, human resources, operations, marketing, construction, purchasing and product development. Through involvement in most of the functional areas of the business, the franchisees played active roles in the strategic direction of McDonald's Canada. Finally, McDonald's corporation and the franchisee shared in the cost of each restaurant. McDonald's owned the land (or the head lease) and the building, while the franchisee owned the equipment and décor package. A strong corporate/franchisee relationship was the cornerstone of the McDonald's philosophy.

OPERATIONS AND TRAINING

In Canada, all operations and training requirements were set and standardized by McDonald's Canada and were followed precisely in the restaurants. Each store was equipped with an operations and training manual that dictated everything from cooking times and temperatures, to drive-through service standards and appearance standards. All products were prepared on the spot, offering "Made for You" service. Using clamshell grills, timed fryers and high-tech holding cabinets, McDonald's restaurants could produce quality products quickly. In recent years, drive-through service had been a priority throughout Canada, with numerous management initiatives focused both on the speed and accuracy of service. The overarching goal was to ensure that customers received the same food and service in Vancouver, B.C., as they did in Tokyo, Japan.

All salaried managers received standardized business training from the McDonald's Institute of Hamburgerology, which was based in Chicago and had affiliate campuses in Vancouver, Montreal and Toronto. McDonald's functioned as a meritocracy. Managers were evaluated through annual performance and compensation reviews based on standardized goals set by McDonald's Canada, goals set by the market franchisee and their ability to attain objectives that they set themselves to enhance personal development. Managers were offered competitive salaries and there existed considerable opportunity for advancement. They received regular feedback through Management Visitation Reports that graded the overall efficiency of their shift. They also received a performance review every six months and a formal wage review once a year.

Outside of the management team, McDonald's restaurants were staffed by part-time employees. These part-time workers were often teenagers looking to build their work experience or adults looking for a flexible job. Management tried to create an environment built on mutual respect, hard work and fun. Managers often organized monthly crew social outings, treat days and crew operational competitions. In addition, McDonald's offered all employees flexible scheduling, regular wage reviews, free uniforms and benefits. All McDonald's crew members were also given a McGold Card that allowed employees McDonald's food at half price, as well as a variety of discounts at local and national retail restaurants. To support their business, all McDonald's crew received an orientation class, at least three training shifts, and were evaluated bi-monthly through a Station Observation Checklist that dictated precisely how to operate their particular station. Crew received a wage review every six months, which evaluated their Station Observation Checklist grades, as well as their versatility, initiative and leadership ability.

BURLINGTON OPERATIONS

Ralph Sgro, the owner-operator of the Burlington market, had more than 30 years of McDonald's experience. He began his career in 1973 as a front line manager in London, Ontario, and advanced through the system to become the senior field service manager of Eastern Canada in 1985. Within the corporate system, Sgro worked in a variety of operational areas, product development and menu management. In 1988, Sgro and his wife purchased the four-store market in Burlington, Ontario. In 2002, the Burlington market was home to seven restaurants. Although Sgro focused on Burlington, he continued to be involved with strategic planning for McDonald's Canada as the Ontario representative on the Partnering Committee. Sgro was recognized throughout the McDonald's for his operational involvement and commitment to the McDonald's system.

McCAFÉ

On a recent vacation to Italy, the Sgros encountered McCafé, a full-service coffee bar located inside a downtown Rome McDonald's. McCafé offered espressos, cappuccinos and lattes, as well as cookies and pastries, complete with a marble countertop. Sgro believed that this European concept could be successful in Canada and could address the issue of Tim Hortons' increasing market share. Looking into the McCafé concept, Sgro discovered that there were more than 300 McCafés in 19 countries worldwide, including the United States.

After discussing the McCafé opportunity with his friend, the McDonald's Canada chief operating officer (COO), Bill Johnson, Sgro was given the go-ahead to introduce it to Canada. The implementation team, led by Sgro, comprised entrepreneurial and experienced corporate employees with diverse backgrounds in operations, marketing and menu management, as well as representatives from Cossette Advertising. The McCafé operational prototype was scheduled to open as an extension of the front counter at the Millcroft location in Burlington, Ontario.

In Canada, McCafé was positioned for working adults who enjoy coffee. McCafé was among the few restaurants that offered specialty coffee conveniently, quickly and relatively inexpensively. Its products included a full selection of specialty coffees and teas, 100 per cent Arabica-brewed coffee, baked goods and tins of the McCafé blend. All products could be purchased at both the front counter and through the drive-through. The McCafé design had a mahogany wood backdrop, stainless steel appliances and dark green accents. The baked goods were presented in a rounded, refrigerated, glass display case. The overall McCafé package was modern, sophisticated.

McCAFÉ BURLINGTON

On May 26, 2001, McCafé Burlington opened its doors. The McCafé prototype restaurant was designed as an addition to the front counter at the Millcroft location in Burlington, Ontario. The purpose of this location was purely operational—an opportunity to work out the operational kinks before taking McCafé public.

Compared to the space requirements of other McDonald's equipment, McCafé equipment was relatively small, inexpensive and easy to fit into an existing counter. McCafé construction took less than four days, and did not significantly disrupt the McDonald's operations during construction. As with other McDonald's operations, McCafés were also standardized. Specialty coffee machinery poured lattes, cappuccinos and espressos at the push of a button, in 22 seconds. The McCafé equipment did not require the expertise of well trained baristas. The brewed coffee was prepackaged to ensure every pot of coffee had the same strength. Other than the cookies and muffins, none of the baked goods was prepared on site. The cakes were delivered in bulk packaging and cut as needed.

Local billboards and newspapers were used to advertise the new Burlington McCafé and in-store samples and promotions allowed customers to sample the new products. Comment cards were distributed to collect customer feedback on the new venture.

THE FUTURE OF McCAFÉ IN CANADA

Sgro and his team were excited about McCafé. The initial customer response was positive; the quantity of coffee sold in the first six months of operation increased over 30 per cent from the previous year. Moreover, McCafé had fit seamlessly into McDonald's operations. However, there was still much to learn about the product lines that were successful and those that were not. Further, the competition had not responded yet to McCafé. While breakfast sales had improved with McCafé, it was not clear whether the increase in sales would be sustained. While Sgro was optimistic about the future of McCafé, he was unsure if McCafé was the white knight needed to stem the loss of McDonald's market share in breakfast sales over the long term.

"Putting cold bottles on shelves is the best marketing we can do, we don't have to ask ourselves if our product will sell, only, how do we get it to the consumer?"

–E. Neville Isdell, Chairman and CEO, The Coca-Cola Company, in a trade publication in 1992[1]

"Any of you with experience operating in China know that to have a shot at success, you've really got to take the time to invest in the country. China is large and diverse and it's a long-term proposition. So you have to make the effort to patiently and diligently build your business over time. That's where our focus was decade after decade and our results today prove the wisdom of this approach."

–Patrick T. Siewert, President, East and South Asia Group, the Coca-Cola Company, at the 8th Annual International Conference on "The Future of Asia" in 2002[2]

Coca-Cola's Re-Entry and Growth Strategies in China

BSTR140

INTRODUCTION

The Coca-Cola Company (Coke) re-entered China in 1979. Today it is recognized as one of China's most trusted brands according to Interbrand.[3] It was voted number 5 of the top 10 multinational companies doing business in Asia in the 2003 Review 200,[4] a survey conducted by *Far Eastern Economic Review* (*FEER*).[5] Since 1990 it has been making profits in China and according to AC Nielsen[6] it had a market share of over 50 percent [. . .] of the Chinese beverages market in 2002.

How did Coke achieve this success in China? Coke's top managers and industry observers too believe that it is the company's winning approach of "Think local, act local" that has enabled it to capture markets outside of the United States. This is particularly true of the Asian markets where the diversity of cultures and income levels makes for a rather diverse consumer base. Coke encourages local man-

[1] "Coke's Big Gamble in Asia: Digging Deeper in China, India," by Leslie Chang in Kunyang, China and Chad Terhune and Bets Mckay in Atlanta, USA, August 11, 2004, *The Wall Street Journal*.

[2] Press center, www.coca-cola.com.

[3] Interbrand is a global brand consultancy firm founded in 1974. It attempts to identify, build and express the right idea for a brand, so that positive business results can be achieved.

[4] Review 200 is a survey designed to identify the companies that Asia's [businesspeople] regard as leaders in their class.

[5] *FEER* is one of Asia's leading business magazines, published every Thursday in Hong Kong. It is fully owned by Dow Jones & Company, the publishers of [the] *Wall Street Journal*. The magazine covers politics, business, economics, technology and social and cultural issues throughout Asia, with a particular emphasis on Southeast Asia and China.

[6] AC Nielsen, a market research company, was established in the United States of America by Arthur C. Nielsen Sr. in 1923. It gradually spread its operations [all over] the world. In 2001, AC Nielsen became part of VNU, a world leader in marketing information, media measurement and information, business media and directories.

agers to develop strategies that are best suited for their areas, and regional offices have the freedom to approve local initiatives.

From the very beginning, Coke's strategy for re-entry into the Chinese market has been based on localization of the entire Coca-Cola system. In order to achieve this, Coke had to work closely with Chinese state-owned enterprises and develop strong relationships with the Chinese government. Since China had just opened up to foreign investment at the time of its re-entry, Coke had to deal with its restrictive policies. It brought its technology and equipment to China and built bottling plants, which it then handed over to the Chinese government. Later it formed joint ventures with state-owned enterprises to set up more bottling plants. Coke formed joint ventures with local Chinese companies as well. Even though initially it had to import certain inputs for the production process, Coke eventually sourced them from Chinese companies. Coke developed its own infrastructure for distribution but gradually came to mainly rely upon state-owned distribution companies and local Chinese distribution companies. This strategy of localization of the Coca-Cola system in China proved to be a success and China grew to be its second largest market in Asia in 2003 (in terms of volume).

BACKGROUND NOTE

In the early 1920s, Coke made its entry into China with bottles imported from its plant in the Philippines. In an effort to localize production, two bottling plants were opened in 1927. These plants were located in Shanghai and Tianjin, and in 1930 another was opened in Qingdao. Coke faced setbacks during [. . .] World War II when the Japanese occupied China and took over its plants. However, in 1946, after the war ended Coke opened a bottling plant in Guangzhou. The Shanghai plant had the distinction of being the most up-to-date and fastest bottling line in China, and in 1948 became the first overseas plant to make annual sales of more than 1 million cases. This was great progress for Coke, even though the customers in Shanghai were mostly expatriates.

When the People's Republic of China (PRC) was formed in 1949, all foreign companies were asked to cease operations and leave the country. Coke shut down operations in China and its bottling plants were nationalized by the government. State-owned companies were formed to produce beverages and some of these companies used the former Coke plants to produce soft drinks. In [the] case of the Shanghai plant, the equipment was shipped to Beijing to be re-installed in a factory there. For almost 30 years after the PRC was formed, foreign direct investment and direct production activity by a foreign company were not allowed. Only the state-owned foreign trade corporations were allowed to have contact with foreign businesses and to carry out exporting and importing of goods.

Coke's Re-Entry in China

In December 1978, Deng Xiaoping (Deng)[7] announced the "open door policy." This policy was part of Deng's larger plan for economic reforms in China. An open door policy meant that China would allow foreign trade and investment. December 1978 was an important time for Coke as well. Soon after China made its announcement, Coke initiated discussions with the Chinese government. Coke expressed its commitment to making long-term investments and to economic development in China.

In 1979, Coke began importing cans from California and bottles from Hong Kong to sell in China. Initially, these were sold only to foreigners through hotels and special stores called friendship stores where only foreigners could shop. Even though Coke made its re-entry into the Chinese market with imported products, its intention was to localize every aspect of the business from sourcing inputs and production to sales and distribution, eventually. Establishing the localized Coca-Cola system in China was a difficult and a long process. China had opened its doors to foreign companies but at the same time, had set in place policies to control and closely monitor the foreign investments. Most areas of business were heavily regulated and needed approvals from various government officials. Nevertheless, Coke was determined to establish itself in China.

LOCALISATION STRATEGIES

Long before Coke was given permission to sell its products to the Chinese people, it began developing production capabilities through various joint ventures with the Chinese government. In sharp contrast to its strategies in the past (in China and other countries as well), initially Coke did not own any bottling plants in China. It imported the concentrate and sold it to bottling plants. The bottling plants (that it sold the concentrate to) had been built by Coke and handed over to the Chinese government. The first of these plants was built in Beijing and was operational in 1981. According to an agreement between Coke and the state-owned China National Cereals, Oils, and Foodstuffs Import and Export Corporation (COFCO) in 1980, Coke agreed to build a plant and hand it over to the government in exchange for approval to expand distribution and sales in China. The second bottling plant was built in Guangzhou and was also handed over to the Chinese government in 1982. However,

---

[7] Deng Xiaoping was the Vice-Chairman of the Central Committee. The Central Committee is the highest authority within the Communist Party of China, the sole political party in the People's Republic of China. He was also the Vice-Premier of the State Council, which is the chief civilian administrative body of the country. The State Council is chaired by the Premier and consists of the heads of each governmental department and agency. There are about 50 members in the Council.

this time it was agreed that both plants would pay for the concentrate supplied to them. This agreement was approved by the Chinese government's Export Committee, of which President Jiang Zemin was also a member.

In 1983, Coke began constructing a bottling plant in the Xiamen SEZ,[8] and on completion in 1984 handed it over to the Ministry of Light Industry. This Ministry later became the State Light Industry Bureau. The year 1984 was a special year for Coke as many significant events took place that year. In 1984, the plant in the Xiamen SEZ, in addition to producing Coca-Cola also started producing Sprite and Fanta. Coke became the first company to air a foreign commercial on China's Central Television station (CCTV). Even though Coke's products were not sold to the Chinese at that time, it decided to advertise in order to develop brand recognition. Coke was allowed to air its commercials in exchange for underwriting CCTV's coverage of the Queen of England's trip to China. In 1984, Coke signed an agreement with the Ministry of Light Industry to establish its first joint venture in China, a bottling plant in the Zhuhai SEZ. Construction of this plant began in 1984 and it became operational in 1985.

In 1984, the Chinese government signed a letter of cooperation with Coke to set up cooperative bottling plants in China. The proposed locations for these plants were Shanghai, Tianjin and Qingdao. Also in 1984, Coke signed proposals to build a wholly owned concentrate plant in Shanghai, and to build a bottling plant as a joint venture close to the proposed concentrate plant. The agreement stated that Coke would be the sole owner of the concentrate plant and the Ministry of Light Industry and the Shanghai Investment and Trust Corporation (SITCO)[9] would own the bottling plant.

Finally, in 1985 the Chinese government gave Coke its approval to sell its products to the Chinese. However, construction work for both plants would not begin until 1986 when President Jiang Zemin gave his approval. Also in 1986, Coke sponsored and organized the first Asian Coca-Cola Cup football tournament in China. In 1988, construction of the Shanghai concentrate plant was completed and it began

production. The opening of the concentrate plant marked the localization of the inputs of Coke's production process, as it began producing the concentrate locally using local inputs. The bottling plant in Tianjin was also completed in 1988 and produced local Chinese brands of soft drinks in addition to Coke's products. Production of local Chinese brands was another feature of Coke's localization strategy.

By 1993 Coke had set up a total of 14 bottling plants in China, and had obtained permission from the Ministry of Light Industry and the State Economic and Trade Commission to build 10 more plants. However, the approval to build bottling plants came with certain stipulations. The provinces in which the bottling plants were to be built were specified by the Chinese government, and in addition the plants had to be located in the capital cities of these provinces. Another stipulation was that Coke should, in addition to Coke's brands, produce local Chinese beverages at these new plants.

Since Coke already had 14 plants and had permission to open 10 more it decided to restructure its bottling operations to form bottling alliances. In 1993, it formed alliances with two Hong Kong–based multinational companies, Swire Pacific (Swire)[10] and Kerry Beverages Group (Kerry).[11] These two firms became its key partners in China. Coke signed an agreement with Swire to produce and distribute its products in southern China and certain interior provinces. Coke also acquired a 12.5 percent stake in Swire. By the year 2000, Coke and Swire [had become] partners in nine joint ventures in China. Also in 1993, Coke bought [a] 12.5 percent stake in Kerry Bottling Company, which is part of the Kerry Beverages Group. Kerry Bottling focused on bottling operations in northern and interior China, and partnered with Coke for ten joint ventures.

In 1995, Coke set up separate production lines for its own products and for the local Chinese brands produced at the Tianjin plant. The existing facility in Tianjin became the Tianjin Jin Mei Beverage Company, which produced the beverage base for all domestic brands and also provided training to professionals in the Chinese soft drink industry. In the same year, the Tianjin Coca-Cola Bottling Company was built in the Tianjin Economic and Technological Development Zone to produce Coke's brands.

When Coke realized that many Chinese consumers preferred non-carbonated beverages with Chinese [flavors], it decided to enter the domestic non-carbonated beverages market. In 1996, Coke launched the "Tian Yu Di"[12] a non-carbonated beverage brand [that] was the first domestic non-carbonated beverage brand to be produced by a multi-

---

[8] In order to promote economic growth and foreign direct investment, the Chinese government began setting up Special Economic Zones (SEZs) in 1980. China has established SEZs in Shenzhen, Zhuhai and Shantou in Guangdong Province and Xiamen in Fujian Province, and the entire province of Hainan. A SEZ is a geographical region that has economic laws that are different from the country's economic laws. A SEZ has special economic systems and policies [that] are designed to promote foreign investment and economic growth in that particular region. SEZs usually have special tax incentives for foreign investments and greater independence regarding international trade activities.

[9] SITCO was established in July 1981, with the Shanghai Municipal Government as the major shareholder. It is an investment and finance company with a presence in real estate, international trading, tendering and consulting. In January 1993, SITCO was renamed Shanghai International Trust & Investment Corporation (SITICO).

---

[10] Swire Pacific is a Hong Kong–based company [that] was established in the 1960s. It is also a partner in Coca-Cola's bottling operations in Taiwan and the United States.

[11] A privately owned Hong Kong–based group. Robert Kouk, a Malaysian Chinese, owns a major share in the company.

[12] The brand name "Tian Yu Di" translates as "Heaven and Earth" in English.

national company. Under this brand, the Tianjin Jin Mei Beverage Company produced fruit juices like mango and lychee (a popular Chinese dessert fruit), ready-to-drink teas in oolong and jasmine flavors, and bottled water. Also in 1996 Coke sponsored the Asian Games in China. In 1997, it also started producing carbonated beverages under the brand name "Xingmu."[13] Once again in an effort to cater to the tastes of the Chinese consumers, this line of domestic beverages came in fruit flavors such as green apple, watermelon, coconut, peach and orange. The flavors were a huge hit and soon the brand's sales had surpassed those of Tian Yu Di. Over the years Coke opened several bottling facilities and by 1999, it had 28 bottling plants and 2 concentrate plants; one for Coke's brands and one for the local brands.

Localizing the Coca-Cola System

The central part of the Coca-Cola system [is comprised] of the concentrate plants and bottling enterprises [that] produce the final product. But many inputs and services go into producing the final product and it also takes a good distribution network to get the product to the consumer. Therefore, the network of suppliers of inputs and services and the distribution network are extensions of the Coca-Cola system.

When Coke re-entered China, it formed local partnerships to open several bottling plants. These bottling plants were owned by bottling enterprises that operated as joint ventures (Refer to Exhibit 1). Typically the joint venture consisted of Coke, one of its key bottlers (either Swire or Kerry) and either a state-owned enterprise or a local Chinese company (based in the city where the joint venture was located), or both the state enterprise and the private local firm. In some cities the bottling enterprise ran more than one bottling plant. Coke also had independent bottling enterprises where its key bottlers were not involved. These bottlers operated under a franchise arrangement with Coke and were allowed to use its trademark. The local bottlers needed to invest in the land, building, machinery, trucks, crates and bottles.

Localization of the Coca-Cola system was not limited to the bottlers and production of the beverages. It extended to the inputs that went into making the final product and the distribution of the product.

The bottling enterprises depended upon local suppliers for various inputs and services and each of these enterprises handled its own procurement of inputs based upon its production schedule. Since bottlers order supplies according to their immediate requirements, they choose suppliers on the basis of how efficiently they can deliver supplies on demand. Bottlers only accepted inputs that met Coke's global standards. Initially, Coke could not find suppliers that met its

standards so it had to import certain inputs. For example, in the early 1980s it had to import PET bottles. However, in 1986 Coke began procuring PET bottles from the Zhong Fu Industrial Group (Zhong Fu).[14] Zhong Fu began manufacturing PET bottles in 1986, after it received technical advice and training from Coke. Zhong Fu went on to become one of China's biggest suppliers of PET bottles to Coke, and also to other beverage companies.

Unlike the bottling enterprises, Coke had no share of ownership in the companies that supplied the inputs for production. The bottling enterprises developed good relationships with their local suppliers as they were usually among the suppliers' biggest customers. [Ninety-eight] percent of the final product consisted of local inputs such as water, sugar, CO_2, PET bottles, glass, paper, closures, crowns and other packaging material. The bottlers relied upon Chinese companies for bottling line machinery, trucks, and lifting machinery as well. Coke also engaged local firms for business services such as legal services, financial services, repair services, accounting services, advertising, design, travel, construction, etc. The services of local construction companies were hired when building new plants or for expansion of existing plants.

During the 1980s, demand for Coke's products far exceeded the supply. However, it had difficulty distributing its products beyond the major cities and towns due to lack of proper infrastructure such as roads and railways, at that time. In most other countries, Coke's main method of distribution is the 'direct store delivery.' It [runs] its own sales centers [and] trucks, and [employs] sales and delivery staff to sell and deliver soft drinks directly to retail outlets and restaurants. But this method of distribution [is] effective only in developed markets and economies. To overcome the challenges of covering a large geographical area and lack of good infrastructure, Coke had to develop a different kind of distribution network in China. Coke based its distribution network on where the demand was and where the consumers could actually buy a Coke product. Since a method that would work for one geographical area might not work for another, Coke had to customize its methods of distribution for each market. It used both wholesalers and the direct store delivery system to distribute products in China.

The Coke bottlers owned and operated direct store delivery systems, but it was not the primary method of distribution. This system accounted for only about 20 percent of its sales while wholesalers accounted for the rest. The bottlers had warehouses, sales centers, fleets of trucks, sales personnel and other staff to manage sales and delivery to retail customers as well as wholesale customers. Depending upon the size of the city and market as well as its proximity to a

---

[13] The brand name "Xingmu" translates as "Smart" in English.

[14] The Zhong Fu Industrial Group was founded by Huang Le Fu, who started out with a small plastics company in 1971. Then in the 1980s he started manufacturing fiber material for the garment industry.

Exhibit 1   Coca-Cola China Ltd.'s List of Bottling Enterprises (as of March 2000)

Name	City/Province	Key Shareholders	Key/Anchor Bottler
Beijing Coca-Cola Beverage Co. Ltd.	Beijing	Kerry Beverages National COFCO Beijing COFCO	Kerry
Swire Guangdong Coca-Cola Ltd.	Guangdong	Swire Coca-Cola HK Ltd. Guangdong Foodstuffs Imp & Export (Group) Corporation COFCO Industries Development Co.	Swire
Guangmei Foods Co. Ltd.	Guangdong (for Xingmu & Meijin)	BFC International (Asia) Ltd. Guangzhou Eagle Coin Enterprise Group Corporation	Swire
Swire Coca-Cola Beverages Xiamen Ltd.	Xiamen, Fujian	Swire Beverages Xiamen Luquan Industrial Co. Ltd.	Swire
Zhuhai Coca-Cola Beverage Co. Ltd.	Zhuhai, Guangdong	Macau Industrial Limitada Zhuhai Food & Beverage Co. Ltd.	Independent
Nanning Coca-Cola Beverage Co. Ltd.	Nanning, Guangxi	Kerry Bottlers (Nanning) Co. Ltd. Nanning Kangle Shareholding Co. Ltd.	Kerry
Dalian Coca-Cola Beverage Co. Ltd.	Dalian, Liaoning	Kerry Beverages Dalian Fruits Co.	Kerry
Shanghai Shen-Mei Beverage & Foods Co. Ltd.	Shanghai	Coca-Cola China Ltd. National COFCO Shanghai SITICO & Shanghai Food Industrial Investment	Independent
Nanjing BC Foods Co. Ltd.	Nanjing, Jiangsu	BCD National COFCO Nanjing Perfumery Factories	Swire
Hangzhou BC Foods Co. Ltd.	Hangzhou, Zhejiang	BC Development Co. Ltd. National COFCO Hangzhou Tea Factory	Swire
Tianjin Jin Mei Beverage Co. Ltd.	Tianjin, Hebei	Coca-Cola (Asia) Holdings Ltd. Tianjin Beverage Factory China National Food Industry Corporation China Light Industrial Corp for Foreign Economic & Technical Cooperation	Independent
Hainan Coca-Cola Beverage Co. Ltd.	Hainan	Coca-Cola China Ltd. National COFCO Hainan COFCO	Independent
Tianjin Coca-Cola Bottling Co. Ltd.	Tianjin, Hebei	Coca-Cola (Asia) Holdings Tianjin Beverages Factory China National Food Industry Corporation	Independent
Xian BC Hans Foods Co. Ltd.	Xian, Shaanxi	BCD Xian Hans Brewery	Swire
Wuhan Coca-Cola Beverage Co. Ltd.	Wuhan, Hubei	Kerry Beverage National COFCO Wuhan Second Beverage Factory	Kerry
Shenyang Coca-Cola Beverage Co. Ltd.	Shenyang, Liaoning	Kerry Beverages Ba Wangshi Beverage Beijing COFCO	Kerry
Harbin Coca-Cola Beverage Co. Ltd.	Harbin, Heilongjiang	Kerry Beverages Harbin Economic & Technology Area Industrial Development Co. Ltd. Beijing COFCO	Kerry

Exhibit 1   (continued)

Name	City/Province	Key Shareholders	Key/Anchor Bottler
Swire Coca-Cola Beverages Zhengzhou Ltd.	Zhengzhou, Henan	BCD, Beijing Beijing Zhong Yin Industrial & Trading Co. Zhengzhou General Food Products Factory	Swire
Qingdao Coca-Cola Beverage Co. Ltd.	Qingdao, Shandong	Kerry Beverages Qingdao Yiqing Industrial Corp.	Kerry
Swire Coca-Cola Beverages Hefei Ltd.	Hefei, Anhui	BCD CITIC Anhui Jiushi Group	Swire
Swire Beverages (Dongguan) Ltd.	Dongguan, Guangdong	Swire Coca-Cola HK Ltd. Dongguan Huaxin Industrial Co.	Swire
Taiyuan Coca-Cola Beverage Co. Ltd.	Taiyuan, Shanxi	Kerry Beverages National COFCO Xishan Coal & Electricity (Group) Co. Ltd.	Kerry
Chengdu Coca-Cola Beverage Co. Ltd.	Chengdu, Sichuan	Kerry Beverages Chengdu Hua Jin Group	Kerry
Kunming Coca-Cola Beverage Co. Ltd.	Kunming, Yunnan	Kerry Beverages COFCO Hong Kong Yuan Tong Investment Co. Ltd.	Kerry

Source: www.moore.sc.edu.

bottling plant, the bottler would have either a warehouse or a sales center or sometimes both. In a large city the bottler had a big warehouse from which it would transport products to its smaller warehouses in other locations and to retailers. In smaller cities the bottlers ran sales centers as well as warehouses. Salesmen from these sales centers visited customers every day to take orders; the turnaround time (the time between placement of an order by the customer and delivery of product) for an order was usually 24 hours. In some cities bottlers ran the sales center at the bottling plant itself instead of at a different location. However, the bottler-owned direct store delivery system was not enough to reach all retail outlets such as restaurants, small stores and vendors.

As mentioned earlier, in addition to selling directly to retail outlets, the bottlers also sold the products to the wholesalers who in turn distributed them to the retail outlets. Therefore, Coke was dependent on the local Chinese distributors to get its products to the final consumer. For various reasons this proved to be an effective method of distribution. Firstly, Coke did not need to invest a large amount of capital in the distribution network. Secondly, the local Chinese companies had more expertise in wholesaling in the area that they were located in, as they were more familiar with the area as well as the requirements of the retailers. Over the years Coke has developed strong relationships with different kinds of wholesalers in China. During the 1980s,

most of Coke's distributors were state-owned enterprises as most of the wholesale sector was state-owned. Later in the 1990s, many state-owned distribution companies were privatized and individual private entrepreneurs were also encouraged to set up their own wholesale companies. So, more and more local Chinese private wholesale companies began to distribute Coke products.

Marketing and Advertising Strategies

Back in 1927 when Coke first entered China, it faced the challenge of communicating with the Chinese. The company needed to transliterate "Coca-Cola" into Chinese characters if it wanted to reach the millions of Chinese consumers. However, finding the nearest phonetic equivalent to Coca-Cola proved to be a difficult task. Not only did the transliteration need to sound like Coca-Cola but it also needed to have an appropriate meaning. Some shopkeepers who made their own transliterations and put up signs, proved how disastrous it could be if the meaning of the characters is not considered. Some of them put up signs that had ridiculous meanings such as "female horse fastened with wax" and "bite the wax tadpole." The Chinese language is made up of thousands of characters and out of these only 200 would even remotely sound like Coca-Cola. Also, most of the characters have more than one meaning. After extensive research the company finalized K'o K'ou K'o Leˆ (the aspirates designated by ' are necessary to approximate the English sounds) in Mandarin, a dialect understood by most Chinese. K'o means to permit, be able, may, can; K'ou means mouth, hole, pass, harbor; and Leˆ means joy, to rejoice, to laugh, to be happy. So, K'o K'ou K'o Leˆ can be interpreted as "to permit [the] mouth to be able to rejoice" or "something palatable from which one derives pleasure."

Coke believed that it needed to use music, color, arts and sports that the Chinese could identify with in order to connect with them. It gave its local managers autonomy over advertising and promotions. During the 1996 Chinese New Year it aired a television commercial using a Chinese dragon, which is something all Chinese would recognize. In the commercial the dragon was decorated with red Coke cans from head to tail and danced in a parade. Towards the end of the commercial a voice said, "For many centuries, the color red has been the color for good luck and prosperity. Who are we to argue with ancient wisdom?" In July 2001, when China announced that it would host the 2008 Olympics, Coke immediately introduced a commemorative gold Coke can in the market.

Recognizing the Chinese people's love for soccer, Coke designed some of its marketing and promotions around the FIFA World Cup. In January 2001, Coke became the official beverage and a main sponsor of the national Chinese soccer team. It also commissioned a special song sung by eight popular Chinese singers during a live telecast of the Chinese team's first match. The song became popularly known as the 'Team China Anthem.' From the time the Chinese team started playing the qualifying matches Coke aired different TV commercials and organized other promotions based on the World Cup. In August 2001, during the World Cup Asian Qualifying Matches, Coke launched "The Dream Never Dies," an advertisement that showed the Chinese soccer fans' enormous support for their national team. Then in October 2001, marking the occasion of the Chinese team qualifying for the finals, Coke introduced a commemorative can and video disc called "The Road to the World Cup."

Later, in early 2002, Coke organized a road show called "Hero Tours" so that soccer fans all over China could meet with the team. It also ran special customized local promotions such as special packaging, World Cup star cards, ticket give-aways, flag bearer selections, and "Finger Soccer"[15] tournaments for school kids. In May 2002, Coke aired another advertisement about the Chinese team and the soccer fans' support to the team. The advertisement, which was called "Home Ground Advantage," showed a Chinese boy giving the players a Coke bottle filled with soil to wish them "home ground advantage" in the World Cup.

Coke also used SMS to run promotions and increase interaction between the company and its consumers. This was an effective method to use in China because, according to Teleconomy, a London-based market research company, China had 176 million mobile phone users in 2002. In 2002, during the end of summer, Coke ran [an] SMS contest for 35 days. The contest, which was called Coke Cool Summer, was announced through a television advertisement. Whoever guessed the correct highest daily temperature in Beijing and sent the reply through SMS, won a year's supply of Coke or Siemens cell phones. According to Coke, it received over 4 million messages during the contest. "We are thrilled with the results, which frankly exceeded expectations; consumers can look forward to Coke adding more fizz on this platform, which is now clearly a key part of our consumers' lifestyle," said Sumanta Dutta, Coca-Cola China's Brand director.[16] In early 2004, Coke introduced "Modern Tea Workshop," a new line of tea drinks. To promote this new line of tea drinks, it hired Hong Kong movie stars Tony Leung and Shu Qi. It also hired Taiwanese pop stars S.H.E. and Will Pan to promote Coca-Cola.

CHINA, COCA-COLA'S SECOND LARGEST MARKET IN ASIA

Coke has enjoyed great success in China and in the Asian markets on the whole. According to the 2003 annual report, Coke's Asian operating segments boosted its revenues when growth in its U.S. market was slowing down. In terms of volume, China was Coke's second largest market in Asia in 2003 (Refer to Exhibit 2) and Coke estimates that China will beat Japan to the top position in 2004. Encouraged by its success in big cities and towns, Coke wants to reach more customers in rural areas. "We'd grown well by reaching the top 100 cities, but how many people were we reaching? Rather than continuing to focus solely on those highly competitive urban areas, Coke must push aggressively into the rest of China and India," said Patrick Siewert, Coke's East and South Asia group president.[17] In early 2004, Coke announced plans to build two new bottling plants in China's western provinces to tap the market potential of China's rural areas. Kerry signed an agreement with Chongqing Economic and Technological Development Zone to build [an] $11 million bottling plant in Chongqing, Western China. COFCO Coca-

---

[15] "Finger Soccer" is a very popular game in Latin America and has been brought to China by Coca-Cola. The soccer match is [. . .] played using fingers instead of feet, with 2 members [on] each team. The game kit consists of a pair of miniature replica soccer boots [that] are slipped onto two fingers of one hand.

[16] "Coke Judges China SMS Campaign a Success," by Brian Morrissey, October 30, 2002, www.boston.internet.com.

[17] "Coke's Big Gamble in Asia: Digging Deeper in China, India" by Leslie Chang in Kunyang, China, and Chad Terhune and Bets McKay in Atlanta, *The Wall Street Journal*. Gabriel Kahn in Hong Kong and Eric Bellman in Kithore, India, contributed to this article, August 11, 2004, www.mlive.com.

Exhibit 2   Percentage-Wise Breakup of Total Unit Case Volume in Asia Operating Segment

Total Unit Case Volume

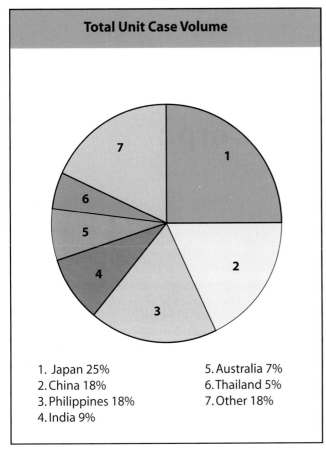

1. Japan 25%
2. China 18%
3. Philippines 18%
4. India 9%
5. Australia 7%
6. Thailand 5%
7. Other 18%

Source: 2003 Annual Report Summary, www.coca-cola.com.

Cola, a Coke bottling enterprise, announced plans to build a bottling plant in Lanzhou, the capital city of Gansu Province in Northwest China. COFCO Coca-Cola also announced plans to build two new plants in Guangdong province in Southern China. These plants will be built in Zhanjiang and Huizhou. The construction of the Zhanjiang plant began in mid-2004 and construction of the Huizhou plant began in September 2004.

Additional Reading & References

1.   **Two Reasons Why Coke Is It: China and Russia**, March 7, 1994, www.businessweek.com.

2.   Mark L. Clifford in Hong Kong and Nicole Harris in Atlanta, with Dexter Roberts in Beidaihe and Manjeet Kripalani in Bombay, **Coke Pours into Asia,** October 28, 1996, www.businessweek.com.

3.   Zeng Min, **Is China the Real Thing for Coca-Cola?** February 18, 2000, www.chinadaily.com.

4.   Anil K Joseph, **Coca Cola to Double its China Business in Five Years, Says Company Official,** August 15, 2000, www.financialexpress.com.

5.   Drake Weisert, **Coca-Cola in China: Quenching the Thirst of a Billion,** July–August 2001, www.chinabusinessreview.com.

6.   **Coca-Cola Eyes Western China,** September 2, 2002, www.peopledaily.com.cn.

7.   Li Heng, **Coca-Cola Has over 50 Percent Market Share in China,** September 4, 2002, www.peopledaily.com.cn.

8.   **Basketball Player Yao Ming Sues Coca-Cola,** May 26, 2003, www.china.org.cn.

9.   **Coca-Cola Launches Its World Cup Marketing Initiative "It's Our Turn,"** March 25, 2002, www.coca-cola.com.

10. **Coca-Cola's First Chinese Majority-Owned Bottling Plant Set Up,** April 16, 2000, www.fpeng.peopledaily.com.cn.

11. **China Seen as Coca-Cola's Largest Market in 10 Years,** February 20, 2003, www.peopledaily.com.cn.

12. **Coca-Cola Tops Again,** 2001, www.bjreview.com.

13. **China Recognizes Coca-Cola for Its Social, Environmental Contributions,** January 19, 2003, www.peopledaily.com.cn.

14. Jane Tian, **Beverage Maker Thirsty: Coca-Cola Rosy About Potentials in China,** November 28, 2000, *Shanghai Star.*

15. Brian Morrissey, **Coke Judges China SMS Campaign a Success,** October 30, 2002, www.boston.internet.com.

16. **Coca-Cola Launches New 2008 Beijing Olympic Games Commemorative Cans,** August 4, 2003, www.coca-cola.com.

17. **First New Chinese Logo for Coca-Cola in 24 Years Marks Start of "Year of Coke" in China,** February 18, 2003, www.coca-cola.com.

18. **Cola War Rages on as Can Suppliers Cut Off Supplies,** Feb 11, 2002, *Asian Economic News,* www.findarticles.com.

19. **Investment of Coca-Cola in China Hit US$1.1b,** July 27, 2001, www.fpeng.peopledaily.com.

20. H.F. Allman, formerly Legal Counsel in China for The Coca-Cola Company, **Transliteration of Coca-Cola Trademark to Chinese Characters,** www.tafkac.org.

21. Ann Chen and Vijay Vishwanath, **Be the Top Pick in China,** January 16, 2004, www.business-times.asia1.com.

22. **Coca-Cola.com.cn Debuts in China,** July 26, 2000, www.chicagopride.com.

23. Geoffrey A. Fowler, Shanghai and Ramin Setoodeh, Hong Kong, **A Question of Taste,** August 12, 2004, www.feer.com.

24. **Is Diet Coke Drugged?** September 7, 2004, www.chinadaily.com.

25. Craig Simmons, **Marketing to the Masses,** September 4, 2003, www.feer.com.

15

Fuji Xerox and the Xerox Corp.: Turning Tables?

03/2005-5097

In the spring of 2000 it became clear to Yotaro "Tony" Kobayashi, chairman of Fuji Xerox, that his company might be facing a watershed not of its making. The Xerox Corporation, which had co-founded Fuji Xerox over four decades ago, was considering selling part or all of its equity to Fuji Xerox's other parent, Fuji Photo Film. There was no doubting the information: Kobayashi had been a member of Xerox's board since 1987, a fact that said a great deal about the unusual respect accorded this joint venture by its U.S. parent. Yet until recently Fuji Photo Film had been a rather passive investor and "sleeping" partner. In contrast, collaboration between the American partner and the Japanese venture had been increasingly active, trusting and successful over the years. Kobayashi could not help wondering: If Fuji Photo Film acquired majority control of the joint venture, what would become of its ongoing collaboration with Xerox? Would Fuji Xerox enjoy the same autonomy of strategy and initiative that Xerox had gradually but steadily permitted?

CONSTRAINTS SHAPE THE VENTURE

Negotiations for the founding of Fuji Xerox began in May 1958, when the Fuji Photo Film company of Japan, interested in xerographic technology as a possible substitute for silver halide photography, inquired into the possibility of licensing it from Rank Xerox, a joint venture of the Xerox Corp. and the Rank Group[1] that held responsibility for operations and rights to copier patents in Asia and the British Commonwealth. Xerox had started making and leasing copiers in the U.S. in the early 1950s, based on comprehensive xerography patents acquired from the Batelle Institute. Rank Xerox refused Fuji a license, but instead suggested a 50-50 joint venture, which Fuji agreed to with some private misgivings, notably that it would lose control. Fuji engineers were already working on photosensitive plates, the core of copier technology, and on a prototype machine, on their own. Recalled former Xerox president and Chairman Paul Allaire:

> "The Xerox and Rank Xerox people wanted to get into the world market very quickly before a competitive technology came along . . . [.] Fuji Photo Film [was seen by them as] nearly equivalent to Rank Xerox, because they had capabilities in optical mechanics, chemical technology, and the competence to manufacture Xerox copiers. [It is] a complex technology from a manufacturing standpoint—toner, developer, drums, making it work in a big unit."[2]

Two years were required to reach agreement between Fuji and Rank Xerox, and another two to get Japanese government approval. Under Japanese law, Fuji could not own less than 49%, and the joint venture had to undertake manufacturing as well as sales.

Four agreements defined Fuji Xerox operations: a Joint Enterprise Contract and Technological Assistance Contract between Fuji Xerox and Rank Xerox, a Manufacturing

---

[1] Xerox controlled 50 percent of Rank Xerox's voting rights at the time, and two-thirds of its profits. In operational terms, Rank Xerox was a 50-50 joint venture with the Xerox group. The Rank Group was involved in industries as diverse as leisure and precision machinery.

[2] Interviewed by telephone, April 9, 2004.

Contract for consumables between Fuji Photo Film and Fuji Xerox, and another manufacturing agreement between Fuji Xerox and Fuji Photo Optical. The new company would sell only Xerox copier products, and only in the Japanese market.[3] Fuji Photo Film could participate in film-related aspects of the venture, but not in the development or sales of office equipment. Directors were drawn equally from each company. Though two of the Xerox side's directors came from the Xerox Corp., Rank Xerox executive T. A. Law, who played a critical role in pushing for an Asian policy for the group, nominated two Japan-based directors.[4] Among Fuji's directors was Nobuo Shono, the leader of the copier development project, while Setsutaro Kobayashi was appointed president. Under the Technical Assistance Agreement, which was to be renegotiated in ten years, Fuji Xerox paid Rank Xerox 5% of sales for licenses of technology and patents. Neither Fuji Photo Film nor Xerox wanted the venture to conduct its own R&D.

The Manufacturing Contract provided for Fuji Xerox to give Fuji Photo Film and its subsidiary, Iwatsuki Optical, the know-how necessary to produce copiers and consumables (like toners and paper), which were sold to Fuji Xerox with a certain markup. Initially, machines were assembled with parts imported from Rank Xerox in London. These locally assembled machines cost Fuji Xerox half the price of imported machines. By 1965, Fuji Xerox sought to manufacture its parts in Japan, despite Rank Xerox's opposition.

FUJI XEROX BEGINS INDEPENDENT PRODUCT DEVELOPMENT

Fuji Xerox broke with traditional sales practices in the Japanese market by relying on its own direct sales force instead of local agents, leasing machines rather than selling them, and charging customers as a function of copy volumes, following Xerox's business model. This enabled the venture to collect detailed information on how its products were actually used. Some of the feedback pointed to costly design changes. For example, in the 1960s, Xerox machines were designed for different paper sizes than those commonly used in Japan, made poor copies from the blue ink used in Japanese offices, and lacked sufficient resolution to print Kanji characters. (Likewise, in the 1970s, the Xerox 7000 copier, designed for American office workers, forced shorter

Japanese workers to stand on a box to reach the print button).[5] Despite close technical cooperation with Rank Xerox, Fuji Xerox noted that "information from Rank Xerox alone was not sufficient" (Xerox Corp. did nearly all the group's R&D work, worldwide) to solve most problems related to copier design.[6] Instead, Fuji Xerox and Iwatsuki Optical solved the problems by trial and error.

In 1966, Fuji Xerox launched the inexpensive Xerox 813 desktop copier, developed in the U.S. onto the Japanese market, and concentrated advertising and marketing on the many small businesses that could not afford, and did not need, high-end machines like the flagship Xerox 914. The 813 and its follow-up, the 660, contributed to rapid growth at Fuji Xerox as the superiority of xerography over electro-fax technologies used by competitors became evident. However, the 813 offered relatively poor resolution, and it could not copy book pages, a fairly serious problem on the Japanese market.

Secretly, in April 1968, Fuji Xerox initiated the development of its own desktop copier, the 2200. It used the key components of the 813, but incorporated a far smaller, lighter developer (the part that sets character images on the printed page). The resulting machine was half the size and one-fifth the weight of the 813, an important advantage in cramped Japanese small business offices. By the time it was first demonstrated in the UK in 1970, it was already written into Fuji Xerox's fiscal planning. Worried about this autonomous development, American executives considered buying out Fuji Photo Film's stake to regain control of the joint venture, but it was not for sale.

Simultaneously, Fuji Xerox lobbied its other parent, Fuji Photo Film, to obtain full control of Iwatsuki Optical's production facilities. The parent wanted Fuji Xerox to remain focused on sales, and to keep production revenues for itself. Fuji Xerox countered that, under its cost-plus arrangement with Iwatsuki Optical, there was no incentive to decrease production costs. Fuji Xerox also believed that it would attract better engineers if it controlled production. With the support of Rank Xerox, which had previously integrated its own manufacturing, the joint venture swayed the argument, and Fuji Xerox acquired Iwatsuki Optical in April 1971.

Under the joint enterprise contract, Fuji Photo Film could not seek other ways of participating in the development of office equipment with Fuji Xerox. Nor was it allowed to enter the field on its own. However, it remained a supplier of paper and other consumables to the joint venture. And, Fuji Photo Film paid close attention to changes in the relationship with Xerox that might affect the venture's growth. Most important, it urged the venture's management

---

[3] However, Fuji Xerox had the right to eventually expand into Southeast Asian territories, subject to the approval of Fuji Photo Film's and Xerox's boards.

[4] Xerox's directors were J. C. Wilson and Sol M. Linowith, respectively president and chairman of Xerox. C. W. Rayden and Goro Inouye, chairman and president of the Rayden company in Japan, served at T. A. Law's request and with Wilson's support.

[5] Reported by David T. Kearns and David Nadler in "Prophets in the dark: How Xerox reinvented itself and beat back the Japanese." New York: HarperBusiness 1993, p. 90.

[6] Anon., "Three decades of Fuji Xerox, 1962–1992." Fuji Xerox 1994, pp. 65–66.

CLAIMING THE LOW-END COPIER NICHE

The model 2200 transformed Fuji Xerox's business. At the beginning of the 1970s, 30,000 large business and government offices accounted for 95% of Fuji Xerox's customer base. In 1976, three years after the introduction of the 2200, such offices accounted for only 57% of installed machines, as low-end customers multiplied by three.[8] The 2200 was also picked up for distribution by Rank Xerox, at the time led by Allaire. He explained: "The U.S. product development organization . . . didn't have the product we thought was right for the rest of the world. The Xerox products were great but not cheap." Thus began an enduring rivalry between product development executives in Japan and the U.S. Said Allaire:

> "There was always a contention between the developers as to the product of one or the other—whether it met market segments, whether Japanese segments were different—why Canon could make one product for the world, and Xerox needed two. It was competitive, and top management arbitrated."

Fuji Xerox's management was increasingly convinced that Xerox Corp., with its focus on the U.S. market, "did not always come up with the kind of products that Fuji Xerox wanted" for Japan. While Xerox targeted large corporate accounts, it was clear that smaller companies were the growth sector in Japan, and that even large companies were buying small copiers from Canon and Ricoh.[9] In 1970, Fuji Xerox discovered that one-fifth of its customers who cancelled their contracts switched to smaller competing machines. Others bought machines outright from competitors rather than fit with Xerox lease policies. That same year, key Xerox patents expired. By 1972, half of Fuji Xerox customers who ended their contracts moved to competitors like Canon and Ricoh, who also seized 50% of new customers through hard discounting. Fuji Xerox's sales growth rates began to decline from an average of 50% annually.[10] It no longer looked as much like "a gold mine for the future," in Tony Kobayashi's phrase.

Top managers, including Kobayashi, concluded that the threat was permanent. He had joined Fuji Xerox in 1963, several years after obtaining his MBA at the Wharton School

of Business in the U.S. He was appointed to the executive board of directors five years later.[11] His American experience left him highly critical of those and many U.S. executives, whom he considered "people who thought only about the short term." (His opinion would change in the late 1970s, when, during a visit to the Aspen Institute, he discovered that some American executives including J. Wilson, then Xerox Chairman and CEO, were well-trained in liberal arts in general, and particularly familiar with the arts and philosophy.) His own business philosophy was that "strength, kindness and fun constitute the three conditions of a good company."[12] An executive who worked closely with him spontaneously recalled that citation, and said admiringly: "He gets to *causes*, the cultural bases of why companies succeed."

In 1976, Kobayashi proposed that Fuji Xerox undertake "Total Quality Control" (TQC) to streamline management and upgrade operations and results. Fuji Photo Film had long since initiated statistical quality control methods—an effort crowned by winning the prestigious Deming Prize for quality management in 1956—and Ricoh began a similarly successful project in 1971. Later renamed the New Xerox Movement, Kobayashi's initiative centered on accelerating new product development and technology research while cutting costs and waste. A year after it started in 1977, on the death of his father, Kobayashi was appointed president of Fuji Xerox.

A crucial early test of his plans came with the creation of the model 3500 console copier, aimed at achieving twice the reliability performance and requiring only half the development and production costs of existing Xerox machines. When Kobayashi first proposed it to Xerox it was turned down, partly because Xerox wanted to promote its own model 3100. The numbers were on Xerox's side—but for the wrong reasons, warned Kobayashi.

> "We faced a tremendous disadvantage in the relationship. Unless products were sold in North America and Europe, they faced a much smaller-sized accessible market. We had lower volumes than Xerox because of market size difference, particularly since Rank Xerox never developed its own products and sold Xerox's products in Europe. So the numbers always showed we had a much smaller potential market . . . We were not taking advantage of our global size, and we did not act as a single global company."

Kobayashi also argued that Xerox's products could not counter new products from Canon and Ricoh in different segments of the Japanese market. He finally "won the day." The 3500 served as a test for a new "overlapping" (as opposed to phased or sequential) development process; it

[7] Interviewed 20 Oct. 2003 in Tokyo.
[8] Op. cit., "Three decades of Fuji Xerox," p. 91.
[9] Op. cit., "Three decades of Fuji Xerox," pp. 141–142.
[10] Op. cit., "Three decades of Fuji Xerox," p. 86.
[11] Anon., "Fuji Xerox head works to humanize his company's working environment." *Japan Economic Journal*, Jan. 14, 1989, p. 12.
[12] Kazunara Yokota, "Fuji Xerox leader pushes for change." *The Nikkei Weekly*, Jan. 25, 1999, p. 1.

became "a key product helping Fuji Xerox to recapture market share" in Japan.[13]

When it was first demonstrated for Xerox president David Kearns, he burst into spontaneous applause. A protégé of former president Peter McCullogh, who had taken a liberal view of the joint venture, Kearns believed that the old system, in which Fuji Xerox took Xerox equipment "and had to redesign it to tailor it to their market . . . was not a way to do business."[14] However, he recalled, Fuji Xerox's arguments aroused widening skepticism, if not suspicion, at Xerox headquarters in Stamford, Connecticut. Said Kearns, "People did not really accept that the cost of developing medium and small sized copiers was so much less for our Japanese competitors than for Xerox."

He added, "There are people in Xerox to this day who see Fuji Xerox as a competitor." The perception was not entirely unfounded. In particular, U.S. and European manufacturers were interested in having as much work as they could to maintain jobs and minimize industrial relations issues, while Japanese executives wanted to build and expand their own factories. A further "block to full cooperation," said Kobayashi, was that Xerox's financial analysts not infrequently emphasized the risks that a given product or initiative by Fuji Xerox might pose to the parent's profits and market valuation. In particular, Fuji Xerox's return on invested capital tended to be lower than some Xerox managers would have liked. In general, Japanese firms enjoy lower costs for capital than American firms do, which encourages investment.

Thus, despite the fact that a "a global partnership mindset, and not that of a parent-subsidiary relationship prevailed among key executives . . . we faced great difficulties in translating this into implementation at the operational level," said Kobayashi. In effect, said Allaire, there were two relationships between Fuji Xerox and Xerox—one at the top, and one at lower levels:

> "There was a lot of stability on the Xerox side at the top—mainly McCullogh, Kearns and me. The trust was transitioned, generation to generation. We were able to meet and talk, share issues and problems. . . . This didn't necessarily happen at lower levels in the organization—you can get quite a bit of mistrust in an organization in Rochester, even without language barriers and different legal systems. Sometimes problems weren't just misinterpretations—people lower down could have objections. But if top management sets objectives and says, 'We'll make this work,' that sets a tone that's effective in sending a message down the organization—'Even if you don't like it, you're gonna cooperate.'"

The technology assistance contract had made no provision for the independent development of products by Fuji Xerox until now. But after 1977, a new clause provided that Rank Xerox would pay half the development costs of Fuji Xerox, up to 1% of sales of products based on Xerox technology.[15] Commented Allaire, "As [Fuji Xerox] spent more on product development . . . they said, 'We now have a patent portfolio and competencies, we should take the [technology-fees paid to Xerox] down, relative to revenues.'"

XEROX'S QUALITY GAP

At Xerox, the dominant opinion was that products made by Fuji Xerox's competitors were no more reliable than those of Xerox, "and generally their quality was worse."[16] But that perception changed as Japanese firms grew out of their domestic market into the U.S. No fewer than 77 new Japanese copiers were introduced to the U.S. market between 1971 and 1978—mainly small desktop models—and this figure nearly doubled by the end of the decade. During this period, Xerox introduced only three new machines, prompting a top sales executive to complain that he was fighting with "a rusty bayonet and an empty rifle."[17]

Although xerographic technology was still in many ways the best of what are called "electrophotographic" reproduction technologies, it was no longer the only one. Ricoh, for example, founded in 1936 to make specialty papers for photographic applications, had moved on to establish fine-tuned competencies in optical imaging, lens and photographic technologies, and finally developed its own electro-photographic technology. A new and highly effective copier technology, named "Savin," after its inventor, emerged in the early 1970s and was adopted by leading Japanese manufacturers. Canon developed its own "NP" analog copying process. By the early 1980s, Ricoh and Canon were challenging Xerox for leadership in copy machines using plain paper, a field Xerox had dominated since 1957.

From 1970 through 1982, Xerox's share of new copier installations in the U.S. fell from 95% to 13%.[18] Though these figures were somewhat deceptive, because Xerox still dominated high-end installations where a single machine could generate several dozen times the revenue of a small device, they revealed Xerox's growing difficulty in competing at the low end. Its first counter-attack, an inexpensive desktop model called the 3300, was so noisy and unreliable that 4,000 machines were recalled soon after its launch in October 1979, becoming Xerox's "first really public disaster."[19] In contrast, in 1979, Fuji Xerox's 3500 set a new record for annual sales of a copier in the Japanese market. As a result, Fuji Xerox won the Deming Prize in 1980. Meanwhile, Tony Kobayashi complained to Xerox Corp.'s president, David Kearns, that his Japanese competition was "just

---

[13] Op. cit., "Three decades of Fuji Xerox," p. 144.

[14] Interviewed May 7, 2004, in Stamford, CT.

[15] Op. cit., "Three decades of Fuji Xerox," p. 193.

[16] Op. cit., "Prophets in the dark," p. 134.

[17] Ibid., p. 93.

[18] Ibid., pp. 134–135.

[19] Ibid., pp. 108–109.

murdering him in the marketplace."[20] Kearns responded by sending a team to study Japanese development and manufacturing techniques. The results, he said, were "nauseating" for Xerox, whose quality, overhead costs, and unit manufacturing costs dramatically lagged best practices in Japan—by "at least 40%," he told a Xerox manager. The manager shot back, "Well, I can't control that!" Kearns replied: "Of course you can't, but how do you deal with it?"

Kearns concluded that "the trends affecting Xerox were so ominous that if something revolutionary weren't done the company would surely go out of business."[21] Paul Allaire, who returned to Xerox at this moment to run Kearns's staff, fully agreed. Simultaneously, Kobayashi proposed the New Xerox Movement as a model for quality management. Said Allaire:

> *"We really learned a lot from Fuji Xerox. They were ahead of us, they'd gone for the Deming Award. The fact that Fuji Xerox was in the homeland of the competition—they had insights that were very important to Xerox. They had relations in Japan—competitors there can be more friendly than in the U.S. and Europe. We would go meet with the Canon executives, get insight into what was happening."*

Among other things, Fuji Xerox served Kearns as "lead user" for practices such as shifting quality controls from finished products to parts and sub-assemblies during the manufacturing process.[22] Xerox's efforts culminated in winning the U.S.'s Malcolm Baldrige National Quality Award in 1989. Meanwhile, collaboration between Fuji Xerox and Xerox steadily deepened. Bi-annual senior management workshops brought together research, product development, manufacturing and planning executives from both companies. Nearly all Fuji Xerox managers had served in English-speaking countries, and spoke excellent English. At the operational level, Fuji Xerox seconded to Xerox several hundred high potential, young engineers and managers for three-year postings. Xerox employees were also seconded to Fuji Xerox, but in much smaller numbers.

WIDENING THE PRODUCT LINE AND TERRITORIES

In 1983, as Xerox's quality drive was underway, the 10-year date for renegotiation of the Technical Assistance Agreement arrived. Fuji Xerox argued that its R&D spending was still less than half that of Canon, and also smaller than the R&D budget of Ricoh. Access to R&D at other firms, or licensing technology to them, through partnerships or development contracts, was limited by the Technology Assistance Agreement,

which constrained disclosure to outside companies. Fuji Xerox saw its royalties to Xerox as cutting into profits and R&D investments.

In the ensuing "Codestiny" discussions, Fuji Xerox widened access to its parent's xerographic technologies, with a license to use product-related information for its own development projects. Xerox agreed that the 5% royalties on the sales of xerographic products would decline annually and cease by 1993, on condition that Fuji Xerox invest the difference in R&D. Xerox also agreed to pay a variable manufacturing license fee on Fuji Xerox products exported as components and assembled in the U.S. by Xerox. The "balance of trade" was such that Fuji Xerox continued to pay small fees to Xerox.

Throughout the 1980s, as Xerox focused on a new generation of upmarket machines, by mutual agreement Fuji Xerox became the group's low-end product developer and manufacturer.[23] By the late 1980s, 94% of the smaller copiers sold worldwide by the Xerox Group were Fuji Xerox designs, up from 30% in 1980. Many of these were exported from Japan. By 1987–88, Fuji Xerox sold over US$600 million of equipment to Xerox and purchased less than US$40 million annually. Between royalties on technology transfers and Xerox's share of profits, Fuji Xerox's contribution to the Xerox Group's profits increased from 5% in 1981 to 22% by 1988. In 1989, the capitalization of Fuji Xerox was doubled to 20 billion yen (about US$160 million), with the Xerox Group (via Rank Xerox) maintaining its 50% ownership share.

Having argued before that Fuji Xerox needed to develop its own products to compete effectively in Japan, Kobayashi now pointed out that amortizing Fuji Xerox's R&D required opening new markets. Moreover, Rank Xerox emphasized sales of high end products, which Fuji Xerox felt were not always appropriate for Asian markets. Fuji Xerox publicly complained that it was "caught between its domestic rivals and the worldwide Xerox group."[24] Most of the Eastern Hemisphere remained the territory of Rank Xerox, while Xerox Corp. covered principally the U.S., Canada and Latin America. The result, acknowledged Paul Allaire, was a loss of global efficiency:

> *"In Singapore and Hong Kong, products came from [Rank Xerox in] Holland, in the Philippines and Thailand products were coming from Tokyo—it wasn't effective . . . As companies started to have a multinational world, if you're an American company with a Philippine subsidiary, you*

[20] Ibid., p. 121.

[21] Ibid., p. 133.

[22] Ibid., p. 283. See also Krista McQuade and Benjamin Gomes-Casseres, "Xerox and Fuji Xerox." *Harvard Business School*, 1991, p. 12.

[23] At Xerox, "low end" meant a print speed of under 20 pages per minute. The firm's upmarket move had begun with the model 9200, introduced in 1972, and accelerated with the 9700 in 1977. Originally conceived as a central printer for large offices, the 9700 missed that market but connected with a huge new one: variable data print jobs like credit card bills. In 1982 the 10 Series of belt-driven high speed copiers paved the path for steady growth; by one estimate it accounted for 90% of Xerox profits through the early 1990s.

[24] Op. cit., "Three decades of Fuji Xerox," pp. 183–85, 214.

might not see why you can't have a regional contract, and why there are two different machines [from different Xerox subsidiaries]."

In 1990, Fuji Xerox was allowed to acquire Rank Xerox subsidiaries in Australia, New Zealand, Singapore and Malaysia. However, Xerox Corp. retained Rank Xerox's subsidiary in Hong Kong. Though willing to sell, Xerox believed that China's value as a source of low-cost components would exceed any sum that Fuji Xerox would pay for the moment.

That issue aside, Kobayashi's team saw the transfer of markets as an essential but insufficient step. It increasingly appeared that digital printers would someday replace copiers. To have a strong presence in printers, Fuji Xerox believed it must build high volumes for low end products, and it could not do so without a global territory. But until now, Fuji Xerox had never sold globally. Management considered many options before proposing a joint venture to Xerox, which accepted on condition that it [retain] a 51% majority.

In 1991, Xerox International Partners was launched to sell low-end digital printers developed in Japan to Xerox, as well as to OEM manufacturers in the North American and European markets. In a joint statement, the chief executives of Xerox and Fuji Xerox announced that the product development, manufacturing, marketing and customer service divisions of both companies would be involved in the new venture.[25] Thus it was officially recognized that Fuji Xerox would participate in the development of products for the world market with Xerox Corp. But to what extent?

IN SEARCH OF A COMMON DESTINY

In one way the cumulative impact of these changes was clear: Fuji Xerox sales more than doubled from 1983 to 1990, as did after-tax profits. But it was less clear why the *growth* rate of sales and profits slowed steadily after 1988. (See Table 1.)

Kobayashi told a reporter that one reason for the slowdown was that total quality control had made his company "a little too structured, and people have lost interest. It's not interesting enough. Not fun. People are saying individualism is being killed off by the so-called quality approach." His contacts with Xerox led him to wonder if his own company was merely "passively caring for people":

"Xerox was more creative in this area. Until twenty years ago they were a small, almost family run and family-owned company in upstate New York. Their tradition was to be very humane, to sincerely care for and honour people. Peter had a rule that any lay off of someone who had been with the com-

pany over eight years he had to sign-off personally . . . I myself had doubts about Japanese management. Do we really care for people, from a really pro-active standpoint?"

In 1988, he instituted the New Work Way, explicitly aimed at encouraging his employees to "have fun" while becoming the kind of risk-takers who ask "why not" instead of just "why."[26] The New Work Way was also an in-house laboratory, whose goal was to experiment with innovative ways of organizing Fuji Xerox's satellite offices in Tokyo and elsewhere, for example to reconcile communication and information flows with mobility.

Kobayashi remained concerned that new digital technologies which made it possible to exchange and print multiple copies of documents without copying them would quickly erode the market for copiers, 80% of Fuji Xerox's sales in 1988. Instead, Fuji Xerox hoped to expand its new Document System Division, "aimed at improving the productivity of knowledge" through digital technologies and systems management services, from 7% of revenues in 1988 to 16% by 1992.[27] These sectors were "expected to grow at a substantially higher rate" than the market for black and white copiers, agreed Xerox Corp.[28] However, said Kobayashi, in the U.S. there was "little reaction" from Xerox's customers, while "in Japan if someone sets a new trend, everybody runs in that direction, no matter what. So solutions and systems gained momentum here as the way of the future." Though top managers at parent and venture alike agreed on future directions, the different paces at which their markets evolved could and did lead to disagreements about the specifics.

To make its digital shift work, Fuji Xerox needed a business model for software, and access to Xerox's applications. That was the backdrop for the second "Codestiny" negotiations, conducted by Allaire and Kobayashi over several years. As negotiations got underway, both Xerox and Fuji Xerox sought to protect their in-house technologies from scrutiny by the other. A key issue was access to Xerox's digital printing software. Fuji Xerox had good low-end color printing technology, but Xerox's software would improve it, and its brand would help to sell the products. Fuji Xerox realized that it could not access or acquire the software skills it needed in Japan. Commented Allaire, "Both sides wanted Fuji Xerox to have that technology, to help the group in total. The question was what they'd give in return."

The issues were resolved progressively. In October 1990, Xerox offered Fuji Xerox a building in Palo Alto, close to the famous PARC research center, for use as an R&D outpost, with the promise of greater cooperation and coordination in developing new products. Later renamed the FX Palo Alto Laboratory (FXPAL), by the mid-1990s the center comprised

[25] Press release, "Xerox, Fuji Xerox form US venture to market printers." Xerox Corp. (Stamford, CT), Oct. 1, 1991. Toshio Arima, at the time Fuji Xerox vice president for strategic development, was later named president of the venture.

[26] Jerry Yoram Wind and Jeremy Main, "Insight: Redefining quality." *Business Line*, Nov. 19, 1998.

[27] Op. cit., "Three decades of Fuji Xerox," pp. 211–212.

[28] Xerox Corp. Annual Report (form 10-K), 1995.

Table 1   Sales and Profits of Fuji Xerox, 1983–1990: Absolute Figures and Growth Rates

Year	Sales	Pre-Tax Profit	After-Tax Profit	Growth in Sales (%)	Growth in AT Profit (%)
1983	263.9	26.3	11.1	—	—
1984	304.5	30.7	12.2	15.4	9.9
1985	347.3	33.5	14.1	14.1	15.6
1986	355.8	29.4	11.9	2.4	(15.6)
1987	427.4	36.8	15.4	20.1	29.4
1988	457.5	48.6	22.2	7.0	44.1
1989	490.3	52.5	22.3	7.1	0.4
1990	539.2	54.2	23.2	9.9	4.0
1991	621.2	48.6	22.3	15.2	(3.9)
1992	681.9	38.9	15.5	9.8	(30.5)
1993	706.6	39.4	16.7	3.6	7.7

(Sales and profits in billions of yen; 125 yen = US$1)

Source: Growth rates calculated from Fuji Xerox sales and profit figures.

two dozen scientists and a dozen assistants. In exchange for open access to PARC technologies—an agreement that caused some initial consternation among managers at PARC—Fuji Xerox agreed to joint ownership of any resulting developments, and to pay a premium for Xerox's digital technologies, in addition to sharing development costs.

FXPAL proved crucial in developing software for control systems and networking of Fuji Xerox's digital print engines. Fuji Xerox also helped Xerox's XSoft division to develop and sell document management software in Japan, where domestic firms were well entrenched in that market via a joint venture. XSoft division's president, Dennis Andrews, noted that Fuji Xerox's strong resources" were of critical importance to penetrating the market.[29]

Increasingly, the Xerox Corp. agreed with Fuji Xerox that it made sense for "the parent company [to] utilize any useful product or technology of its subsidiaries," and that "the whole Xerox Group [should] pursue the same goals and global strategy."[30] In a digital world, said Allaire, it was "insane" to create separate products for different markets. But implementation of that insight required time.

HARD TIMES AT XEROX, BOOM TIMES AT FUJI XEROX

In 1993, the Xerox Corp. embarked on a restructuring that included downsizing 14,000 of its nearly 100,000 workforce worldwide. While revenues remained largely flat for the

Table 2   Xerox Corp. Revenues and Profits, 1992–96

Year	Revenues (US$M)	Profits (US$M)	Profit Margin
1996	17,378	1,206	6.9%
1995	16,588	(472)	—
1994	15,084	794	5.3%
1993	14,229	(126)	—
1992	14,298	(1,020)	—

Source: Hoover's

Xerox Group through 1996, losses were more frequent than profits. (See Table 2.)

In contrast, Fuji Xerox set new profit records in each of these years. By 1994, Fuji Xerox's gross sales reached US$7.2 billion, not far behind the US$8.2 billion of the Xerox Corp. The Xerox Corp.'s revenues from Fuji Xerox grew steadily. (See Table 3.)

Xerox's restructuring revived tensions rooted in the group's territorial structures. Xerox sought to establish more direct, "line of sight" influence over the foreign operations of its business divisions in the U.S. in order to maximize ser-

Table 3   Fuji Xerox Net Income and Parents' Equity in Net Income, 1992–95

	1995	1994	1993	1992
Fuji Xerox net income	224	171	149	122
Rank Xerox's equity in net income	112	86	75	61
Xerox's equity in net income	88	57	50	41

Source: Xerox Corp. Annual Report (form 10-K), 1995, 1996.

[29] Anon., "XSoft Division of Xerox establishes operations in Japan." Xerox (Palo Alto), Feb. 28 1995.

[30] Op. cit., "Three decades of Fuji Xerox," pp. 214–215.

vice revenues service in particular. But as Japanese multinationals moved abroad, Fuji Xerox complained that its provision of "effective technical and service support" was hampered by the necessity to work with and through Rank Xerox or Xerox reps.[31]

The coordination of production that was initiated in the early 1990s remained incomplete, prompting Fuji Xerox to press for "a global manufacturing strategy to improve competitiveness."[32] Fuji Xerox's production was concentrated in Korea, Southeast Asia, Japan and Oceania, while Xerox Corp.'s plants were based mainly in the Americas and China, with some overlap among plants. Fuji Xerox also wished to use China as a production base, and after discussions with Xerox Corp., opened its first Chinese plant in 1995, in a joint venture with Xerox's Chinese subsidiary. Fuji Xerox owned 90% of the new company. Its skills in low cost component manufacturing were critical to the success of Xerox's digital printing strategy.

In 1994, the Xerox Corp. reported that Fuji Xerox's R&D was fully "strategically coordinated" with that of the parent company. In effect, the parent now saw Fuji Xerox as an *essential* strategic partner, if not entirely an *equal* one, as Fuji Xerox would like. The Technology Assistance Agreement was amended and renamed, simply, the Technology Agreement. Fuji Xerox's R&D investments grew steadily, and attained US$537 million in 1996—slightly more than one-half of the Xerox Corp.'s US$1.04 billion.[33] However, the flow of R&D still ran mainly from the U.S. to Japan, where as always Fuji Xerox faced domestic competitors who far outspent it on R&D. For example, Canon, although devoting part of its budget to product lines (such as digital cameras) outside Fuji Xerox's markets, spent nearly as much on R&D in 1996 as Xerox and Fuji Xerox combined. (See Table 4.)

CHANGES IN OWNERSHIP STRUCTURE AND STRATEGY

In 1997, Xerox bought out the Rank Group's interest in Rank Xerox for US$1.5 billion. The Rank Group's CEO, Andrew Teare commented that the sale "will enable us to dispose of a minority interest in an unrelated business over which we could exert little management influence."[34] The purchase coincided with the official recognition that Xerox had changed "from a predominantly black-and-white light lens copier company to a digital, color and document solutions company," in the words of Allaire, now Xerox chairman.[35] That year, 40% of Xerox's revenues came from digital products, including the Docucolor 4040 digital printing engine aimed at small printing shops and developed by Fuji Xerox. Xerox and Fuji Xerox combined brought 75 new products to market in 1997, more than double the number in 1994.[36] Fuji Xerox supplied the engines for all of Xerox's digital printers but the highest-end systems. A decline in the traditional core businesses of copiers and consumables was now fully underway. (See Table 5.)

Sales fell in the first half of 1999 for Xerox and Fuji Xerox, impacting on an ongoing debate over strategy.[37] (See Appendix 1 for more financial data.) Fuji Xerox clearly saw the threat of Canon, Ricoh, Konica and others moving from low-end office products to higher end products and solutions. Kobayashi's successor as president, Toshio Arima, a former Xerox International Partners president, also saw a reorganization as urgent to becoming an increasingly efficient development, design, and manufacturing company. Both Fuji Xerox and Xerox hoped to evolve into a software system solutions and services group. However, copiers still accounted for 30% of Xerox's revenues—a piece too large to drop.

Table 5   Xerox Revenues by Product Line

Year ended December 31 (in US$ billions)	1999	1998	1997
Digital products	10.2	8.6	6.3
Light-lens copiers	5.8	7.4	8.3
Paper, other products, currency	3.2	3.4	3.5
Total revenues (in US$ billions)	19.2	19.4	18.1

Source: Xerox annual reports.

Table 4   Canon R&D Expenditures, 1992–1996 (in millions of yen; 125 yen = US$1)

1992	1993	1994	1995	1996
100,521	104,191	121,273	125,253	150,085

Source: www.canon.com.

---

[31] See Emiko Terazono and Christopher Lorenz, "An angry young warrior," *Financial Times*, Sept. 19, 1994, p. 16.

[32] Ibid.

[33] Xerox Corp. Annual Report (form 10-K), 1996.

[34] Anon., "Rank Group PLC–Disposal of interest." Regulatory News Service, June 6, 1997.

[35] Anon., "Xerox chairman sees momentum accelerating in transformation of Xerox: A leader in digital, color and document solutions." This press release details announcements at Xerox's annual shareholder meeting in Chicago, May 21, 1998. Allaire, president of the company since David Kearns stepped down, introduced a new president and CEO, Richard Thoman, at the meeting.

[36] Ibid.

[37] Fuji Xerox sales in the first half of 1999 fell by 5% to 426.2 billion yen (US$3.7 billion) compared to the previous year, while pre-tax profits dropped by 43%. Reported in Anon, "Fuji Xerox plots course for wholesale transformation; Photocopier maker aims at rebirth as services company." *The Nikkei Weekly*, Sept. 27, 1999, p. 8.

Meanwhile, Fuji Photo Film, a largely silent partner since the 1970s, was considering buying all or part of Xerox's stake in Fuji Xerox, to which Xerox assigned a book value of US$1.5 billion in 1999.[38] For many years Fuji Photo Film had been preoccupied by increasingly severe competition with Eastman Kodak of the U.S. for global market share in films, the two companies' core businesses. Tension between the companies had [become] so high that, at one point, Kodak successfully demanded that a Japanese employee of Fuji Photo Film be excluded from the William E. Simon School of Business in Rochester, Kodak's home.[39] Kodak had also intensified its competition in copiers, mostly in the U.S. with Xerox, as a way of countering Fuji Photo Film, focusing on the more lucrative high-end market. More recently, digital photo equipment (including cameras and printers) had become an increasing share of Fuji Photo Film's business,

and it saw a growing synergy with Fuji Xerox's digital printing and document management solutions. As for Xerox, it needed cash—so much so that it sold its interest in the China joint venture to Fuji Xerox.

Would Fuji Xerox enjoy the same autonomy and mutual comprehension with Fuji Photo Film that it had with Xerox? In any case Fuji Xerox had to play a new role, Kobayashi concluded:

> *"To date, we have developed overseas markets with products that were originally targeted at the Japanese market. Now, however, our thinking has changed, and we plan to begin developing products for the global market from the earliest stages. That way, we can become a base for supplying the entire global market . . . we must determine local needs precisely and then work as an organization to develop and manufacture these products."*[40]

---

[38] Xerox Corp. Annual Report 2000 (form 10-K).

[39] Kenneth Stier, "Eastman-Kodak Fuji photo film rivalry spills into classroom." Japan Economic Newswire, Sept. 16, 1987.

[40] Fuji Xerox Annual Report 1999, p. 15.

APPENDIX 1

Revenues, Profit and Loss for Xerox Corp., 1997–2000

Year	Revenue (US$M)	Net Income	Net Profit Margin
2000	18,751	(273)	–
1999	18,995	844	4.4%
1998	18,777	395	2.1%
1997	17,457	893	5.1%

Revenues, Profit and Loss for Fuji Xerox, 1997–2000

Year	Revenue (US$M)	Net Income	Net Profit Margin
2000	8,398	140	1.7%
1999	7,710	109	1.4%
1998	6,809	108	1.6%
1997	7,415	238	3.2%

Source: Hoover's.

Case 16

Neilson International in Mexico (A)

9A95G003

In January 1993, Howard Bateman, vice-president of International Operations for Neilson International, a division of William Neilson Limited, was assessing a recent proposal from Sabritas, a division of Pepsico Foods in Mexico, to launch Neilson's brands in the Mexican market. Neilson, a leading producer of high quality confectionery products, had grown to achieve a leadership position in the Canadian market and was currently producing Canada's top selling chocolate bar, "Crispy Crunch." In the world chocolate bar market, however, Neilson was dwarfed by major players such as M&M/Mars, Hershey/Lowney and Nestlé-Rowntree. Recognizing their position as a smaller player with fewer resources, in a stagnant domestic market, Neilson in 1990 formed its International Division to develop competitive strategies for their exporting efforts.

Recent attempts to expand into several foreign markets, including the United States, had taught them some valuable lessons. Although it was now evident that they had world class products to offer to global markets, their competitive performance was being constrained by limited resources. Pepsico's joint branding proposal would allow greater market penetration than Neilson could afford. But, at what cost?

Given the decision to pursue international opportunities more aggressively, Bateman's biggest challenge was to determine the distributor relationships Neilson should pursue in order to become a global competitor.

THE CHOCOLATE CONFECTIONERY INDUSTRY[1]

The "confectionery" industry consisted of the "sugar" segment, including all types of sugar confectionery [and] chewing gum, and the "chocolate" segment, which included chocolates and other cocoa based products. Most large chocolate operations were dedicated to two major products: boxed chocolates and bar chocolates, which represented nearly 50 per cent of the confectionery industry by volume.

Competition from imports was significant, with the majority of products coming from the United States (39 percent). European countries such as Switzerland, Germany, the United Kingdom and Belgium were also major sources of confectionery, especially for premium products such as boxed chocolates. (See Exhibit 1 for a profile of chocolate exporting countries.) In order to maintain production volumes and to relieve the burden of fixed costs on operations, Canadian manufacturers used excess capacity to produce goods for exporting. Although nearly all of these products were traditionally exported to the United States, in the early nineties, the world market had become increasingly more attractive.

Firms in the confectionery industry competed on the basis of brand name products, product quality and cost of production. Although Canadian producers had the advantage of being able to purchase sugar at the usually lower world price, savings were offset by the higher prices for dairy

IVEY
Richard Ivey School of Business
The University of Western Ontario

Gayle Duncan and Shari Ann Wortel prepared this case under the supervision of Professors P. W. Beamish and C. B. Johnston solely to provide material for class discussion. The authors do not intend to illustrate either effective or ineffective handling of a managerial situation. The authors may have disguised certain names and other identifying information to protect confidentiality.

---

[1] Some information in this section was derived from: J. C. Ellert, J. Peter Killing and Dana Hyde, "Nestlé-Rowntree (A)," in *Business Policy, A Canadian Casebook*, Joseph N. Fry et al. (Eds.), Prentice Hall Canada Inc., 1992, pp. 655–667.

Exhibit 1	World Chocolate Exports (value as % of total) [1987]–1990			
	1987	1988	1989	1990
Africa	x1.5	x1.0	x1.1	x0.7
Americas	8.1	9.1	9.2	x9.1
LAIC[1]	2.1	1.9	1.4	x1.4
CACM[2]	0.1	x0.1	x0.1	x0.1
Asia	2.5	3.2	3.4	2.9
Middle East	x0.5	x0.5	x0.7	x0.4
Europe	86.4	85.0	84.2	85.4
EEC (12)[3]	73.3	71.8	71.3	73.5
EFTA[4]	12.5	12.7	12.1	11.5
Oceania	x1.5	1.8	x2.1	x1.8

Figures denoted with an "x" are provisional or estimated.

Adapted from: The United Nations' "International Trade Statistics Yearbook," Vol. II, 1990.

[1]LAIC = Latin American Industrialists Association
[2]CACM = Central American Common Market
[3]EEC (12) = The twelve nations of the European Economic Community
[4]EFTA = European Free Trade Association

ingredients used in products manufactured for domestic consumption. Other commodity ingredients, often experiencing widely fluctuating prices, caused significant variations in manufacturing costs. Producers were reluctant to raise their prices due to the highly elastic demand for chocolate. Consequently, they sometimes reformatted or reformulated their products through size or ingredient changes to sustain margins. Three major product types were manufactured for domestic and export sales:

Blocks
These products are molded blocks of chocolate that are sold by weight and manufactured in a variety of [flavors], with or without additional ingredients such as fruit or nuts. Block chocolate was sold primarily in grocery outlets or directly to confectionery manufacturers. (Examples: baking chocolate, Hershey's Chocolate Bar, Suchard's Toblerone.)

Boxed Chocolates
These products included a variety of bite-sized sweets and were generally regarded as "gift" or "occasion" purchases. Sales in grocery outlets tended to be more seasonal than for other chocolate products, with 80 per cent sold at Christmas and Easter. Sales in other outlets remained steady year round. (Examples: Cadbury's Milk Tray, Rowntree's Black Magic and After Eights.)

Countlines
These were chocolate covered products sold by count rather than by weight, and were generally referred to by consumers as "chocolate bars." The products varied widely in size, shape, weight and composition, and had a wider distribution than the other two product types. Most countlines were sold through non-grocery outlets such as convenience and drug stores. (Examples: Neilson's Crispy Crunch, Nestlé-Rowntree's Coffee Crisp, M&M/Mars' Snickers, and Hershey/Lowney's Oh Henry!)

Sweet chocolate was the basic semi-finished product used in the manufacture of block, countline, and boxed chocolate products. Average costs of sweet chocolate for a representative portfolio of all three product types could be broken down as follows:

Raw material	35%
Packaging	10
Production	20
Distribution	5
Marketing/sales	20
Trading profit	10
Total	100% (of manufacturer's selling price)

For countline products, raw material costs were proportionately lower because a smaller amount of cocoa was used.

In value terms, more chocolate was consumed than any other manufactured food product in the world. In the late eighties, the world's eight major markets (representing over 60 per cent of the total world chocolate market) consumed nearly three million [tons] with a retail value close to $20 billion. During the 1980s, countline was the fastest growing segment with close to 50 per cent of the world chocolate market by volume and an average annual rate of growth of seven per cent. An increasing trend towards indulgence in snack and "comfort" foods strongly suggested that future growth would remain strong.

COMPETITIVE ENVIRONMENT

In 1993, chocolate producers in the world included: M&M/Mars, Hershey Foods, Cadbury-Schweppes, Jacobs Suchard, Nestlé-Rowntree, United Biscuits, Ferrero, Nabisco and George Weston Ltd. (Neilson). Chocolate represented varying proportions of these manufacturers' total sales.

For the most part, it was difficult to sustain competitive advantages in manufacturing or product features due to a lack of proprietary technology. There was also limited potential for new product development since the basic ingredients in countline product manufacturing could only be blended in a limited variety of combinations. This forced an emphasis on competition through distribution and advertising.

Product promotion played a critical role in establishing brand name recognition. Demand was typified by high-impulse and discretionary purchasing [behavior]. Since consumers, generally, had a selection of at least three or four [favorite] brands from which to choose, the biggest challenge facing producers was to create the brand awareness necessary to break into these menus. In recognition of the wide selection of competing brands and the broad range of snack food substitutes available, expenditures for media and trade promotions were considerable. For example, Canadian chocolate bar makers spent more than $30 million for advertising in Canada, in 1992, mostly on television. This was often a barrier to entry for smaller producers.

MAJOR COMPETITORS

M&M/Mars

As the world leader in chocolate confectionery M&M/Mars dominated the countline sector, particularly in North America and Europe, with such famous global brands as Snickers, M&Ms and Milky Way. However, in Canada, in 1992, M&M/Mars held fourth place with an 18.7 per cent market share of single bars. (Exhibits 2 and 3 compare Canadian market positions for major competitors.)

M&M/Mars' strategy was to produce high quality products which were simple to manufacture and which allowed for high volume and automated production processes. They supported their products with heavy advertising and aggressive sales, focusing marketing efforts on strengthening their global brands.

Hershey/Lowney

Hershey's strength in North America was in the block chocolate category, in which it held the leading market position. Hershey also supplied export markets in Asia, Australia, Sweden, and Mexico from their chocolate production facilities in Pennsylvania. In Canada, in 1992, Hershey held third place in the countline segment with a 21.6 per cent share of the market.

Hershey's strategy was to reduce exposure to volatile cocoa prices by diversifying within the confectionery and snack businesses. By 1987, only 45 per cent of Hershey's sales came from products with 70 per cent or more chocolate content. This was down from 80 per cent in 1963.

Cadbury Schweppes

Cadbury was a major world name in chocolate, with a portfolio of brands such as Dairy Milk, Creme Eggs and Crunchie. Although its main business was in the United Kingdom, it was also a strong competitor in major markets such as Australia and South Africa.

Cadbury Schweppes diversified its product line and expanded into new geographic markets throughout the 1980's. In 1987, Cadbury International sold the Canadian distribution rights for their chocolate products to William Neilson Ltd.

Exhibit 2   Single Bars Canadian Market Share: 1991–1992

Manufacturer	1992	1991
Neilson	28.1%	29.4%
Nestlé/Rowntree	26.9%	26.2%
Hershey/Lowney	21.6%	21.9%
M&M/Mars	18.7%	19.0%
Others	4.7%	3.5%

Source: Nielson News, Issue #1, 1993.

Exhibit 3   Top Single Bars in Canada: 1991–1992

Top Single Bars	Manufacturer	1992	1991
Crispy Crunch	Neilson	1	1
Coffee Crisp	Nestlé/Rowntree	2	3
Kit Kat	Nestlé/Rowntree	3	2
Mars Bar	M&M/Mars	4	4
Caramilk	Cadbury Schweppes	5	6
Oh Henry!	Hershey/Lowney	6	5
Smarties	Nestlé/Rowntree	7	7
Peanut Butter Cups	Hershey/Lowney	8	8
Mr. Big	Neilson	9	11
Aero	Hershey/Lowney	10	10
Snickers	M&M/Mars	11	9
Crunchie	Cadbury Schweppes	12	12

Source: Nielson News, Issue #1, 1993.

Only in Canada were the Cadbury brands incorporated into the Neilson confectionery division under the name Neilson/Cadbury. In 1988, Cadbury sold its U.S. operations to Hershey.

Nestlé-Rowntree

In 1991, chocolate and confectionery comprised 16 per cent of Nestlé's SFr 50.5 billion revenue, up sharply from only eight per cent in 1987. (In January 1993, 1SFr = $0.88 CAD = 0.69 U.S.) This was largely a result of their move into the countline sector through the acquisition in 1988 of Rowntree PLC, a leading British manufacturer with strong global brands such as Kit Kat, After Eights and Smarties. In 1990, they also added Baby Ruth and Butterfinger to their portfolio, both "Top 20" brands in the U.S. Considering these recent heavy investments to acquire global brands and expertise, it was clear that Nestlé-Rowntree intended to remain a significant player in growing global markets.

NEILSON

Company History

William Neilson Ltd. was founded in 1893, when the Neilson family began selling milk and [homemade] ice cream to the Toronto market. By 1905 they had erected a house and factory at 277 Gladstone Ave., from which they shipped ice cream as far west as Winnipeg and as far east as Quebec City. Chocolate bar production was initiated to offset the decreased demand for ice cream during the colder winter months and as a way of retaining the skilled [labor] pool. By 1914, the company was producing one million pounds of ice cream and 500,000 pounds of chocolate per year.

William Neilson died in 1915, and the business was handed down to his son Morden, who had been involved since its inception. Between 1924 and 1934, the "Jersey

Milk," "Crispy Crunch" and "Malted Milk" bars were introduced. Upon the death of Morden Neilson in 1947, the company was sold to George Weston Foods for $4.5 million.

By 1974, "Crispy Crunch" was the number one selling bar in Canada. In 1977, "Mr. Big" was introduced and became the number one teen bar by 1986. By 1991, the Neilson dairy operations had been moved to a separate location and the ice cream division had been sold to Ault Foods. The Gladstone location continued to be used to manufacture Neilson chocolate and confectionery.

Bateman explained that Neilson's efforts under the direction of the new president, Arthur Soler, had become more competitive in the domestic market over the past three years, through improved customer service and retail merchandising. Significant improvements had already been made in Administration and Operations. All of these initiatives had assisted in reversing decades of consumer share erosion. As a result, Neilson was now in a position to defend its share of the domestic market and to develop an international business that would enhance shareholder value. (Exhibit 4 outlines the Canadian [. . .] confectionery market.)

Neilson's Exporting Efforts

Initial export efforts prior to 1990 were contracted to a local export broker—Grenadier International. The original company objective was to determine "what could be done in foreign markets" using only working capital resources and avoiding capital investments in equipment or new markets.

Through careful selection of markets on the basis of distributor interest, Grenadier's export manager, Scott Begg, had begun the slow process of introducing Neilson brands into the Far East. The results were impressive. Orders were secured for containers of "Mr. Big" and "Crispy Crunch" countlines from local distributors in Korea, Taiwan, and Japan. "Canadian Classics" boxed chocolates were developed

for the vast Japanese gift ("Omiyagi") market. Total 1993 sales to these markets were projected to be $1.6 million.

For each of these markets, Neilson retained the responsibility for packaging design and product formulation. While distributors offered suggestions as to how products could be improved to suit local tastes, they were not formally obliged to do so. To secure distribution in Taiwan, Neilson had agreed to launch the "Mr. Big" bar under the distributor's private brand name "Bang Bang," which was expected to generate a [favorable] impression with consumers. Although sales were strong, Bateman realized that since consumer loyalty was linked to brand names, the brand equity being generated for "Bang Bang" ultimately would belong to the distributor. This put the distributor in a powerful position from which they were able to place significant downward pressure on operating margins.

Market Evaluation Study

In response to these successful early exporting efforts Bateman began exploring the possible launch of Neilson brands into the United States (discussed later). With limited working capital and numerous export opportunities, it became obvious to the International Division that some kind of formal strategy was required to evaluate and to compare these new markets.

Accordingly, a set of weighted criteria was developed during the summer of 1992 to evaluate countries that were being considered by the International Division. (See Exhibit 5 for a profile of the world's major chocolate importers.) The study was intended to provide a standard means of evaluating potential markets. Resources could then be allocated among those markets that promised long-term incremental growth and those which were strictly opportunistic. While the revenues from opportunistic markets would contribute to the fixed costs of domestic production, the long-term efforts could be pursued for more strategic reasons. By the end of the summer, the study had been applied to thirteen international markets, including the United States. (See Exhibit 6 for a summary of this study.)

Meanwhile, Grenadier had added Hong Kong/China, Singapore and New Zealand to Neilson's portfolio of export markets, and Bateman had contracted a second local broker, CANCON Corp. Ltd, to initiate sales to the Middle East. By the end of 1992, the International Division comprised nine people who had achieved penetration of 11 countries for export sales (see Exhibit 7 for a description of these markets). As of January 1993, market shares in these countries [were] very small.

THE U.S. EXPERIENCE

In 1991, the American chocolate confectionery market was worth US$5.1 billion wholesale. Neilson had wanted to sneak into this vast market with the intention of quietly selling off excess capacity. However, as Bateman explained, the quiet U.S. launch became a Canadian celebration:

> Next thing we knew, there were bands in the streets, Neilson t-shirts and baseball caps, and newspaper articles and T.V. specials describing our big U.S. launch!

Exhibit 4   Canadian Confectionery Market—1993

	Dollars (millions)	%
Total Confectionery Category	$1,301.4	100.0
Gum	296.5	22.8
Boxed Chocolates	159.7	12.3
Cough Drops	77.0	5.9
Rolled Candy	61.3	4.7
Bagged Chocolates	30.3	2.3
Easter Eggs	22.0	1.7
Valentines	9.4	0.7
Lunch Pack	3.6	0.3
Countline Chocolate Bars	641.6	49.3
Total Chocolate Bar Market Growth	+ 8%	

Source: Neilson Marketing Department estimates.

Exhibit 5	World Chocolate Imports (value as % of total) [1987]–1990			
	1987	1988	1989	1990
Africa	x0.7	x0.7	x0.7	x0.7
Americas	x15.6	x15.0	x13.9	x13.2
LAIC[1]	0.2	0.4	1.1	x1.3
CACM[2]	x0.1	x0.1	x0.1	x0.1
Asia	11.7	x13.9	x15.6	x12.9
Middle East	x3.5	x3.3	x3.9	x2.8
Europe	70.8	68.9	67.7	71.4
EEC (12)[3]	61.1	59.5	57.7	59.3
EFTA[4]	9.3	9.0	8.9	8.4
Oceania	x1.3	x1.7	x2.1	x1.8

Figures denoted with an "x" are provisional or estimated.

Adapted from: The United Nations' "International Trade Statistics Yearbook," Vol. II, 1990.

[1]LAIC = Latin American Industrialists Association
[2]CACM = Central American Common Market
[3]EEC (12) = The 12 nations of the European Economic Community
[4]EFTA = European Free Trade Association

The publicity greatly increased the pressure to succeed. After careful consideration, Pro Set, a collectible trading card manufacturer and marketer, was selected as a distributor. This relationship developed into a joint venture by which the Neilson Import Division was later appointed distributor of the Pro Set cards in Canada. With an internal sales management team, full distribution and invoicing infrastructures and a 45-broker national sales network, Pro Set seemed ideally suited to diversify into confectionery products.

Unfortunately, Pro Set quickly proved to be an inadequate partner in this venture. Although they had access to the right outlets, the confectionery selling task differed significantly from card sales. Confectionery items demanded more sensitive product handling and a greater amount of sales effort by the Pro Set representatives, who were used to carrying a self-promoting line.

To compound these difficulties, Pro Set sales plummeted as the trading-card market became over-saturated. Trapped by intense cashflow problems and increasing fixed costs, Pro Set filed for Chapter 11 bankruptcy, leaving Neilson with huge inventory losses and a customer base that associated them with their defunct distributor. Although it was tempting to attribute the U.S. failure to inappropriate partner selection, the U.S. had also ranked poorly relative to other markets in the criteria study that had just been completed that summer. In addition to their distribution problems, Neilson was at a serious disadvantage due to intense competition from the major industry players in the form of advertising expenditures, trade promotions and brand proliferation. Faced with duties and a higher cost of production, Neilson was unable to maintain price competitiveness.

The International Division was now faced with the task of internalizing distribution in the U.S., including sales management, broker contact, warehousing, shipping and collections. Neilson managed to reestablish a limited presence in the American market using several local brokers to target profitable niches. For example, they placed strong emphasis on vending-machine sales to increase product trial with minimal advertising. Since consumer purchasing patterns demanded product variety in vending machines, Neilson's presence in this segment was not considered threatening by major competitors.

In the autumn of 1992, as the International Division made the changes necessary to salvage past efforts in the U.S., several options for entering the Mexican confectionery market were also being considered.

MEXICO

Neilson made the decision to enter the Mexican market late in 1992, prompted by its parent company's, Weston Foods Ltd., own investigations into possible market opportunities which would emerge as a result of the North American Free Trade Agreement (NAFTA). Mexico was an attractive market which scored very highly in the market evaluation study. Due to their [favorable] demographics (50 per cent of the population was within the target age group), Mexico offered huge potential for countline sales. The rapid adoption of American tastes resulted in an increasing demand for U.S. snack foods. With only a limited number of competitors, the untapped demand afforded a window of opportunity for smaller players to enter the market.

Working through the Ontario Ministry of Agriculture and Food (OMAF), Neilson found two potential independent distributors:

Grupo Corvi A Mexican food manufacturer, operated seven plants and had an extensive sales force reaching local wholesalers. They also had access to a convoluted infrastructure which indirectly supplied an estimated 100,000 street vendor stands or kiosks (known as "tiendas") representing nearly 70 per cent of the Mexican confectionery market. (This informal segment was usually overlooked by marketing research services and competitors alike.) Grupo Corvi currently had no American or European style countline products.

Grupo Hajj A Mexican distributor with some experience in confectionery, offered access to only a small number of retail stores. This limited network made Grupo Hajj relatively unattractive when compared to other distributors. Like Grupo Corvi, this local firm dealt exclusively in Mexican pesos, historically a volatile currency. (In January 1993, 1 peso = CDN$0.41.)

While considering these distributors, Neilson was approached by Sabritas, the snack food division of Pepsico Foods in Mexico, who felt that there was a strategic fit between their organizations. Although Sabritas had no previous experience handling chocolate confectionery, they had for six years been seeking a product line to round out their portfolio. They were currently each week supplying Frito-Lay type snacks directly to 450,000 retail stores and tiendas.

Exhibit 6   Summary of Criteria for Market Study (1992)

CRITERIA	Weight	Australia	China	Hong Kong	Indonesia	Japan	Korea	Malaysia	New [Zealand]	Singapore	Taiwan	Mexico	EEC	USA
* U.S. Countline	—	4	4	4	4	4	4	4	4	4	4	4	4	4
1 Candy bar Economics	30	20	20	30	20	20	28	20	15	25	15	20	10	10
2 Target Market	22	12.5	14	13	15.5	19	15	10	7	9.5	12.5	21	22	22
3 Competitor Dynamics	20	12	15	8	7.5	11	13.5	10	12	14.5	12	11	20	6.5
4 Distribution Access	10	9	4	4	3.5	5	6	6.5	9	3.5	7.5	9.5	9	9
5 Industry Economics	9	2.5	3.5	6	5.5	2	5	2.5	7	4.5	3	3.5	3.5	4.5
6 Product Fit	8	7	6	6	6	3	7.5	7.5	7.5	8	4	8	5	8
7 Payback	5	4	4	1	2.5	4	5	2.5	4	2	2	5	2	1
8 Country Dynamics	5	5	1	4	3	5	3.5	4.5	4.5	5	4	3	2	4
TOTAL	109	72	67.5	72	63.5	69	83.5	63.5	66	72	60	81	73.5	65

COMPETITOR DYNAMICS	Score	Mexico
Financial Success of Other Exporters	0–8	5
Nature (Passivity) of Competition	0–6	2.5
Brand Image (vs. Price) Positioning	0–6	3.5
SCORE/20	/20	11

Due to Neilson/Cadbury's limited resources, it was not feasible to launch the first western-style brands into new markets. The basic minimum criteria for a given market, therefore, was the presence of major western industry players (i.e., Mars or Hershey). Countries were then measured on the basis of 8 criteria which were weighted by the International Group according to their perceived importance as determinants of a successful market entry. (See above table.) Each criterion was then subdivided into several elements as defined by the International Group, which allocated the total weighted score accordingly. (See table, right.)

This illustration depicts a single [criterion,] subdivided and scored for Mexico.

Source: Company Records.

Exhibit 7   Neilson Export Markets—1993

Agent (Commission)	Country	Brands
Grenadier International	Taiwan	Bang Bang
	Japan	Mr. Big, Crispy Crunch, Canadian Classics
	Korea	Mr. Big, Crispy Crunch
	Hong Kong/China	Mr. Big, Crispy Crunch, Canadian Classics
	Singapore	Mr. Big, Crispy Crunch
CANCON Corp. Ltd.	Saudi Arabia	Mr. Big, Crispy Crunch, Malted Milk
	Bahrain	Mr. Big, Crispy Crunch, Malted Milk
	U.A.E.	Mr. Big, Crispy Crunch, Malted Milk
	Kuwait	Mr. Big, Crispy Crunch, Malted Milk
Neilson International	Mexico	Mr. Big, Crispy Crunch, Malted Milk
	U.S.A.	Mr. Big, Crispy Crunch, Malted Milk

Source: Company records.

(The trade referred to such extensive customer networks as "numeric distribution.") After listening to the initial proposal, Neilson agreed to give Sabritas three months to conduct research into the Mexican market.

Although the research revealed strong market potential for the Neilson products, Bateman felt that pricing at two pesos (at parity with other American style brands) would not provide any competitive advantage. Sabritas agreed that a one peso product, downsized to 40 grams (from a Canadian-U.S. standard of 43 to 65 grams), would provide an attractive strategy to offer "imported chocolate at Mexican prices."

Proposing a deal significantly different from the relationships offered by the two Mexican distributors, Sabritas intended to market the "Mr. Big," "Crispy Crunch" and "Malted Milk" bars as the first brands in the "Milch" product line. "Milch" was a fictitious word in Spanish, created and owned by Sabritas, and thought to denote goodness and health due to its similarity to the word "milk." Sabritas would offer Neilson 50 per cent ownership of the Milch name, in exchange for 50 per cent of Neilson's brand names, both of which would appear on each bar. As part of the joint branding agreement, Sabritas would assume all responsibility for advertising, promotion, distribution and merchandising.

The joint ownership of the brand names would provide Sabritas with brand equity in exchange for building brand awareness through heavy investments in marketing. By delegating responsibility for all marketing efforts to Sabritas, Neilson would be able to compete on a scale not affordable by Canadian standards.

Under the proposal, all "Milch" chocolate bars would be produced in Canada by Neilson. Neilson would be the exclusive supplier. Ownership of the bars would pass to Sabritas once the finished goods had been shipped. Sabritas in turn would be responsible for all sales to final consumers. Sabritas would be the exclusive distributor. Consumer prices could not be changed without the mutual agreement of Neilson and Sabritas.

ISSUES

Bateman reflected upon the decision he now faced for the Mexican market. The speed with which Sabritas could help them gain market penetration, their competitive advertising budget, and their "store door access" to nearly a half million retailers were attractive advantages offered by this joint venture proposal. But what were the implications of omitting the Neilson name from their popular chocolate bars? Would they be exposed to problems like those encountered in Taiwan with the "Bang Bang" launch, especially considering the strength and size of Pepsico Foods?

The alternative was to keep the Neilson name and to launch their brands independently, using one of the national distributors. Unfortunately, limited resources meant that Neilson would develop its presence much more slowly. With countline demand in Mexico growing at 30 per cent per year, could they afford to delay? Scott Begg had indicated that early entry was critical in burgeoning markets, since establishing market presence and gaining share were less difficult when undertaken before the major players had dominated the market and "defined the rules of play."

Bateman also questioned their traditional means of evaluating potential markets. Were the criteria considered in the market evaluation study really the key success factors, or were the competitive advantages offered through ventures with distributors more important? If partnerships were necessary, should Neilson continue to rely on independent, national distributors who were interested in adding Neilson brands to their portfolio, or should they pursue strategic partnerships similar to the Sabritas opportunity instead? No matter which distributor was chosen, product quality and handling were of paramount importance. Every chocolate bar reaching consumers, especially first time buyers, must be of the same freshness and quality as those distributed to Canadian consumers. How could this type of control best be achieved?

"They are two pathetic companies just trying to survive."

–Sanjay Jhaveri, a technology analyst at Zurich-based Vontobel Asset Management[1]

"This will be the biggest hardware company in the world, and that gives them tremendous market power."

–Lawrence J. Ellison, CEO, Oracle in 2001

The HP-Compaq Merger Story

BSTR/027

A SETBACK

On September 4, 2001, leading global computer industry players Hewlett-Packard Company (HP) and Compaq Computer Corporation (Compaq) announced their merger. HP was to buy Compaq for $25 billion in stock in the biggest ever deal in the history of the computer industry. The merged entity was to have operations in more than 160 countries with over 145,000 employees, offering the industry's most complete set of products and services.

Surprisingly, the stock markets reacted negatively to the announcement with shares of both companies collapsing—in just two days, HP and Compaq share prices declined by 21.5% and 15.7% respectively (See Exhibit[s] 5 and 6). Together the pair lost $13 billion in market capitalization. In spite of this, HP's Chairman and CEO, Carly Fiorina (Fiorina) was confident about the merger. In an interview[2] she said, "This is a very tight agreement. You

don't make this kind of move and judge its success by the short-term stock price."

However, in the next two weeks, HP's stock went down by another 17%, amidst a lot of negative publicity. HP's competitors felt that the proposed merger would not work for the company and the combined entity would lose market share. Sun Microsystems President Edward J. Zander said, "When two sick companies combine, I'm not sure what you get. This is a great opportunity for us, IBM, and others to go after market share." Dell CEO Michael S. Dell added that the merger would only confuse customers and benefit HP's competitors.

On November 6, 2001, the merger faced another hurdle in the form of Walter B. Hewlett (Walter), the eldest son of Hewlett-Packard co-founder William R. Hewlett. Though Walter had initially approved the bid, he decided to use his 5.2% stake to oppose the merger. Soon, another relative of HP's founders, David Woodley Packard (David) and The David and Lucile Packard Foundation, HP's largest shareholder, with a 10.4% stake, also decided to oppose the merger. By January 2002, with so much going against the merger, industry observers seemed to have written it off—even though the shareholder meeting for the proposal's approval was yet to be held.

BACKGROUND NOTE

Hewlett-Packard

Stanford engineers Bill Hewlett and David Packard started HP in California in 1938 as an electronic instruments company. Its first product was a resistance-capacity audio oscillator, an electronic instrument used to test sound equipment. During

---

[1] In an interview with *BusinessWeek*, September 2001.

[2] In an interview with *BusinessWeek*, September 5, 2001.

the 1940s, HP's products rapidly gained acceptance among engineers and scientists. HP's growth was aided by heavy purchases made by the U.S. government during the Second World War. During the 1950s, HP developed strong technological capabilities in the rapidly evolving electronics business. In 1951, HP invented the high speed frequency counter, which significantly reduced the time required to measure high frequencies. HP came out with its first public issue in 1957.

HP entered the medical field in 1961 by purchasing Sanborn Company. In 1963, HP entered into a joint venture agreement with Yokogawa Electric Works of Japan to form Yokogawa-Hewlett-Packard. In 1966, the company established HP Laboratories, to conduct research activities relating to new technologies and products. During the same year, HP designed its first computer for controlling some of its test-and-measurement instruments.

During the 1970s, HP continued its tradition of innovation. In 1974, HP launched its first minicomputer that was based on 4K dynamic random access semiconductors (DRAM's) instead of magnetic cores. In 1977, John Young was named HP president, marking a transition from the era of the founders to a new generation of professional managers.

During the 1980s, HP emerged as a major player in the computer industry, offering a full range of computers from desktop machines to powerful minicomputers. This decade also saw the development of successful products like the Inkjet and LaserJet printers. HP introduced its first personal computer (PC) in 1981, followed by an electronic mail system in 1982. This was the first major wide-area commercial network that was based on a minicomputer. HP also introduced its HP 9000 computer with a 32-bit superchip.

HP became a leader in workstations with the 1989 purchase of market leader Apollo Computers. In 1992, HP acquired Texas Instruments' line of UNIX-based computers. HP reinforced its cost cutting efforts and reduced the prices of its PCs. HP also combined its PC, printer, UNIX workstation, and customer support operations in 1995 into an integrated computer division. In 1997, HP acquired electronic transaction company Verifone[3] for nearly $1.2 bn, to strengthen its capabilities in Internet commerce. HP's capabilities in Internet security and Verifone's expertise in handling financial transactions were expected to complement each other. During 1997, lower demand caused a drop in growth to below 20% for the first time in five years, and HP responded by reorganizing printer and other operations.

In the first quarter of 1999, HP spun off its test-and-measurement equipment division, into a new $8 bn business. Analysts felt that the [spin-]off reflected the increasingly [cutthroat] competition in the computer industry. They also felt that HP needed a new leadership to cope with rapidly evolving industry trends. According to an HP employee, "What you are seeing is an end of a class of management. If you look at all the top management, they are all of the same age, they lived through a certain era of HP. We need to refresh the leadership; there will be more youthfulness and spontaneity with the changes." In view of these concerns, the HP board appointed Fiorina[4] as the CEO in July 1999.

By 2001, with net revenues of $48.78 billion, HP ranked 19th in the global *Fortune* 500 list (See Exhibit 3). The company had emerged as the second largest computer manufacturer in the world, and was the market leader in desktop computers, servers, peripherals and services such as systems integration. Besides computer related products and services, which accounted for more than 80% of sales, the company also made electronic products and systems for measurement, computing and communications (See Exhibit 1).

Compaq

Compaq was founded by Joseph R. Canion along with some of his erstwhile Texas Instruments colleagues in February 1982. The seed capital of $1.5 million was arranged by venture capitalist Benjamin Rosen, who became the founder chairman. Compaq initially manufactured and sold IBM compatible computers. The name Compaq was derived from compatibility and quality. Within a year of incorporation, Compaq registered sales of $111 million. In December 1983, the company made an Initial Public Offer (IPO) of six million shares at $11 per share. Compaq soon came to be seen as a major alternative to IBM for the supply of personal computers.

Over the years, Compaq had developed into a full range computer company catering to various segments. Compaq offered three broad categories of products:

- **The Enterprise Computing Group**—The group provided both products and services. Products included mainframes, servers, workstations, fault tolerant business critical solutions, enterprise options and solutions, Internet products and networking products. Compaq provided services fulfilling a wide variety of information technology infrastructure business requirements, both directly and in alliance with third party service providers. Compaq's service offerings included business critical services for multi-vendor software and hardware products. Professional services included information system consulting; technical and application design services; systems integration and project management services; network design, integration and support services; and outsourcing and resource management services.

- **The Commercial PC Group**—The group dealt with products like commercial desktops, portables, [and] small and medium business solutions. PCs products accounted for approximately 30 percent of Compaq's worldwide revenues.

- **The Consumer PC Group**—Products like desktops, mini tower computers, portables, [and] printers [. . .] were included in

---

[3] Verifone, founded in 1981, had strong capabilities in automated credit card transaction systems. Verifone also had expanded into Internet and smart cards, earning net revenues of $472 mn in 1996, and its systems had handled electronic commerce transactions worth $520 bn (market size $800 bn) during 1996.

[4] Fiorina had an experience of 20 years at AT&T and Lucent. During the two years before joining HP, she was president of Lucent's Global Service Provider Business. Prior to Lucent, Fiorina held a number of senior positions at AT&T.

Table 1   HP-Compaq Merger Transaction Summary

Structure	Stock-for-stock merger
Exchange Ratio	0.6325 of an HP share per Compaq share
Current Value	Approximately $25 billion
Ownership	HP shareholders 64%; Compaq shareholders 36%
Accounting	Purchase
Expected Closing	First half of 2002

Key Figures (previous 4 qrts—in $ billion)	HP	Compaq	Combined
Total Revenues	47.0	40.4	87.4
Assets	32.4	23.9	56.4
Operating Earnings	2.1	1.9	4.0
Number of employees	88,500	70,100	158,600
Market Capitalization (as [of] 31/08/01)	45,109	20,995	66,104

Source: HP Press Release, September 5, 2001.

this category. They accounted for approximately 16 percent of Compaq's worldwide revenues.

In 1998, Compaq acquired Digital Equipment Corporation (DEC) for $9.1 billion in an attempt to become a "full services" computer company. However, the integration with DEC did not go as smoothly as planned. Analysts felt that the company's efforts to imitate competitor Dell Computer's (Dell) direct sales strategy were not proving effective. In July 1999, Capellas[5] was appointed as CEO and President.

With revenues of $42.38 billion in 2000, Compaq secured the 27th rank in the 2001 Global *Fortune* 500 list (See Exhibit 4). The company's manufacturing operations were spread across the U.S., Scotland, Singapore, China and Brazil and its products were sold in more than 100 countries across the globe.

In the late 1990s, the PC industry slipped into its worst-ever recessionary phase, resulting in losses of $1.2 billion and 31,000 layoffs by September 2001. According to analysts, with the computer industry commoditizing and consolidating very fast, mergers had become inevitable. The HP-Compaq merger thus did not come as a major surprise to industry watchers.

The details of the merger were revealed in an HP press release issued soon after the merger was announced. The new company was to retain the HP name and would have revenues of $87.4 billion—almost equivalent to the industry leader IBM ($88.396 billion in 2000). Under the terms of the deal, Compaq shareholders would receive 0.6325 share of the new company for each share of Compaq (See Table 1). HP shareholders would own approximately 64% and Compaq shareholders 36% of the merged company. Fiorina was to remain as the Chairman and CEO of the new company while Capellas was to become the President.

The new company would have four operating units:

- A $20 billion Imaging and Printing franchise to be led by Vyomesh Joshi, President, Imaging and Printing Systems, of HP.
- A $29 billion Access Devices business to be led by Duane Zitzner, President, Computing Systems, of HP.
- A $23 billion IT Infrastructure business, including servers, storage and software, to be led by Peter Blackmore, Executive Vice President, Sales and Services, of Compaq.
- A $15 billion Services business with approximately 65,000 employees in consulting, support and outsourcing, to be led by Ann Livermore, President, HP Services.

THE MERGER RATIONALE

After the merger announcement, HP issued a number of press releases in which it claimed that the new HP would become the undisputed worldwide leader in revenues for servers, access devices (PCs and hand-held devices), and imaging and printing. It would also have a leading revenue position globally for information technology services, storage and management software. The merger was expected to yield savings projected to reach $2.5 billion annually by 2004. These savings were expected to come from

- Product rationalization;
- Efficiencies in administration, procurement, manufacturing and marketing; and
- Improved direct distribution of PCs and servers.

According to a *BusinessWeek* report, HP opted for the merger mainly because the size of the new entity would have enabled it to take advantage of volume sales. Fiorina revealed that the two companies bought $65 billion worth of materials a year, which when combined could result in a cost savings of 3% or 4%. She added that post-merger, HP would become more efficient by moving closer to a Dell-like model

---

[5] Capellas had joined Compaq in August 1998 as chief information officer. He was made the chief operating officer in June 1999.

Table 2   Top 5 Vendors, Worldwide PC Shipments: First Quarter 2001

Vendor	Q1 01 Shipments (in 000s)	Market Share (%)	Q1 00 Shipments (in 000s)	Market Share (%)	Market Growth (%)
Dell (1)	4,147	13.1	3,190	10.4	30.0
Compaq (2)	3,768	11.9	3,952	12.8	−4.7
HP (3)	2,380	7.5	2,488	8.1	−4.4
IBM (4)	2,004	6.3	1,876	6.1	6.8
Fujitsu Siemens (5)	1,773	5.6	1,788	5.8	−.8
Others	17,652	55.5	17,486	56.8	.4
All Vendors	**31,633**	**100.0**	**30,781**	**100**	**2.8**

Source: International Data Corporation, April 2001.

Table 3   Top 5 Vendors, U.S. PC Shipments: First Quarter 2001

Vendor (Rank)	Q1 01 Shipments (in 000s)	Market Share (%)	Q1 00 Shipments (in 000s)	Market Share (%)	Market Growth (%)
Dell (1)	2,535	24.2	1,980	17.1	28.0
Compaq (2)	1,509	14.4	1,890	16.3	−20.2
HP (3)	1,075	10.2	1,415	12.2	−24.0
Gateway (4)	924	8.8	1,038	9.0	−11.0
IBM (5)	562	5.4	471	4.1	19.3
Others	3,886	37.0	4,800	41.4	−19.0
All Vendors	**10,491**	**100.0**	**11,594**	**100.0**	**29.5**

Source: International Data Corporation, April 2001.

of direct selling and doing away with middlemen (See Exhibit 2). Compaq was already closer to that model and could help HP make the transition. Former Compaq Chairman Ben Rosen said, "The deal will jump-start both companies in their race for efficiency."

However, many analysts felt that the synergies HP foresaw would not materialize easily. They said that the merged company would have to cut costs drastically in order to beat Dell in PCs, while constantly investing money in research and development and consulting to compete with IBM and Sun Microsystems (See Exhibit 7).

According to a report[6] published by International Data Corporation (IDC), the worldwide PC market grew only 2.8% in the first quarter of 2001, while the U.S. market shrunk by 9.5% (See Table[s] 2 and 3).

For the quarter ended September 30, 2001, Dell gained worldwide [market share][7] while the combined HP-Compaq market share went down from 20.9% (quarter ended March 31, 2001) to 17.7%. Dell's financial performance was much better compared to the industry as well as HP and Compaq (See Exhibit 8). In the same quarter, Compaq reported

a 33% fall in revenues, compared to HP's 18% and Dell's 10%. In the high-end server markets, IBM and Sun Microsystems were constantly introducing new products. Since both companies showed poor results in the quarter ended September 30, 2001, analysts also expected HP's 2001 earnings to come down substantially. Analysts also expressed concerns that since more than half of the new company's sales would be from low-margin PCs and printers, it would not have enough cash to invest in R&D in order to compete in the high end market.

THE PROBLEMS

Doubts were raised about Fiorina's ability to execute the merger successfully. According to some analysts, Fiorina was responsible for the mess the merger had landed in. They contended that if she knew Hewlett was against the deal, she should have scrapped the merger talks, rather than risk a damaging proxy fight. Charles M. Elson, director of the Center for Corporate Governance at the University of Delaware, said, "You have to question her business judgment."

HP was reportedly planning a lawsuit against Walter for improper corporate governance. With this, the company seemed all set for one of the biggest proxy fights in U.S. corporate history. This would adversely affect its corporate image. Moreover, there were fears that Fiorina would be

---

[6] "Dell Takes Lead in Worldwide PC Shipments as Market Slump Deepens," April 20, 2001.

[7] According to a *BusinessWeek* article dated November 19, 2001.

forced to step down as CEO in case the merger did not materialize. Analysts claimed that Fiorina's exit could worsen HP's financial position, as the new CEO would have to figure out new strategies for the company.

Meanwhile, with the Hewlett and Packard Foundation opposing the merger, HP employees began to lose faith in Fiorina's management. According to a *BusinessWeek* report, HP surveys done before November 6, 2001, showed that 84% of the employees supported the acquisition—this fell to 55% after Walter's opposition. HP Vice-President for Human Resources Susan Bowick admitted, "Morale statistics are lower than we've ever seen them. Employees were really with us until Walter did what he did, but he opened up a flurry of doubt."

The report also hinted that there was growing employee resentment over the steps taken by Fiorina to control costs. Some of the cost-cutting measures, including the forced five-day vacation for the workers in December 2000, the postponement of wage hikes for three months and the January 2001 [layoff] of 1,700 employees, were strongly opposed. Things worsened when the HP management announced that it would lay off 6,000 workers in July 2001. This was less than a month after 80,000 employees had willingly taken [pay cuts]. The management also sent memos saying that layoffs would continue and that volunteering for [pay cuts] would not guarantee continued employment. According to company insiders, once the merger was implemented, Fiorina was likely to lay off 15,000 to 30,000 employees as a part of a major cost saving drive.

With Walter, David and The Foundation opposing the deal, Fiorina was relying on the remaining institutional shareholders (with a 67% stake) to vote in favor of the deal. Fiorina hoped to convince investors by the time the merger was to be voted upon. Interestingly enough, while the merger was being seen as potentially harmful for HP and Compaq, observers, including HP insiders and a number of financial and legal experts in [. . .] Silicon Valley, said that if the merger was unsuccessful at this point, it could be equally disastrous for the companies involved.

THE FUTURE

Since HP and Compaq had already initiated the integration process, they were privy to many key facts about each other's business. If the merger did not materialize, both the companies were potentially vulnerable to insider information being misused. Also, the companies, as independent entities, would face extreme skepticism from the stock markets, which had already shown their disapproval of the proposal. Some industry experts were also worried that Fiorina, Capellas and several key board members and senior executives, who had been staunch supporters of the deal, would leave.

The merger's failure would also set back the company formally opting out of the deal by $675 million in [the] form of a breakup fee. Analysts also claimed that Compaq would have an especially tough time in the future, as its credibility in the stock market had been badly affected.

Another cause of concern was the European Commission[8] expressing fears that the deal would allow HP to dominate PC distribution and therefore fix prices for the entire industry. Investigations were also on by the U.S. antitrust[9] authorities. The only ones to gain out of the whole episode seemed to be the stock market arbitrageurs, who were capitalizing on the short-term volatility of HP and Compaq stocks.

Questions for Discussion

1. The HP-Compaq merger [was] met with opposition from various parties. Analyze the reasons for this opposition and critically comment on the pros and cons of the merger.

2. Assuming the merger is completed, do you think the new HP would be able to counter the competition from companies like Dell and IBM? Give reasons for your answer.

Additional Readings & References

1. Popper, Margaret, **The Hewlett-Packard Dilemma,** *BusinessWeek*, August 03, 2001.
2. **HP to Buy Compaq for $25 Billion in Stock,** *Business Standard*, September 05, 2001.
3. Jaffe, Sam, **HP-Compaq's Great Software Challenge,** *BusinessWeek*, September 06, 2001.
4. Hadded, Charles, **Mazel Tov for the HP-Compaq Wedding,** *BusinessWeek*, September 13, 2001.
5. Burrows, Peter, Park, Andrew, Hamm, Steve, and Smith, Geoffrey, **HP-Compaq: Where's the Upside?** *BusinessWeek*, September 17, 2001.
6. Gopinath, C., **Where Are the Synergies?** *Business Line*, September 17, 2001.
7. Taylor, Chris, **Compaq: Fiorina's Folly or HP's Only Way Out?** *Time Magazine*, November 2001.
8. Burrows, Peter, Park, Andrew and Hof, Robert D., **A Stunning Reversal for HP's Marriage Plans,** November 19, 2001.
9. Park, Andrew, **Can Compaq Survive as a Solo Act?** *BusinessWeek*, December 24, 2001.
10. Burrows, Peter, Park, Andrew and Kerstetter, Jim, **Carly's Last Stand?** December 24, 2001.
11. Burrows, Peter and Park, Andrew, **Walter Hewlett: Behind His Big Switcheroo,** December 31, 2001.
12. www.hp.com.
13. www.compaq.com.
14. www.hoovers.com.
15. www.idc.com.
16. HP Annual Report 2000.
17. Compaq Annual Report 2000.

[8] All acquisition/merger deals where the revenue of the combined company exceeds 5 billion euros and where each individual company has revenues of at least 250 million euros in the European Union is investigated by the European Commission.

[9] The U.S. antitrust policy aims at promoting vigorous competition and rivalry in markets and preventing monopolistic practices. Antitrust policies prohibit certain kinds of business conduct such as price fixing.

Exhibit 1   HP's Product Segment Information

Year ended October 31,	2000	1999	% Increase/Decrease
Net Revenues			
Imaging and Printing Systems	20,476	18,550	10
Computing Systems	21,095	17,814	18
IT Services	7,129	6,255	14
Other	1,299	886	47
Total Segments	**49,999**	**43,505**	
Eliminations/Other	(1,217)	(1,135)	
Total HP Consolidated	**48,782**	**42,370**	**15**
Earnings from Operations			
Imaging and Printing Systems	2,746	2,335	18
Computing Systems	960	850	13
IT Services	634	575	10
Other	(108)	(71)	45
Total Segments	**4,237**	**3,689**	
Eliminations/Other	(348)	(1)	
Total HP Consolidated	**3,889**	**3,688**	**5**
Assets			
Imaging and Printing Systems	7,571	7,150	6
Computing Systems	6,686	5,846	14
IT Services	8,455	7,100	19
Other	446	250	78
Total Segments	**23,158**	**20,346**	
Corporate/Other	10,851	11,418	
Total Assets from Continuing Operations	34,009	31,764	7
Net Assets of Discontinued Operations	—	3,533	
Total HP Consolidated	**34,009**	**35,297**	**(4)**

Source: HP Annual Report, 2000.

Exhibit 2   How Would an HP-Compaq Combo Measure Up?

Products	Analysis
PCs	With 19% market share, it would be the world's largest PC maker. But with PC sales and margins at record lows, the companies have lost a total of nearly $500 million this year, while Dell continues to gain.
Printers	HP's dominant 50% market share would grow, as would sales of its hugely profitable printer ink. But margins and sales are weak, and pricing pressure is mounting from Lexmark, Canon and other rivals.
Low-End Servers	Compaq dominates, and the combined companies would have a huge 37% market share in Windows-based machines. But cutthroat competition from Dell and IBM could eat away at sales.
High-End Servers	In this key high-margin market, HP and Compaq are laggards. Compaq will phase out its Alpha servers, while HP's high-end UNIX machines have stagnated against Sun and IBM.
Services	HP and Compaq covet IBM's services business. But 62% of their 65,000 service specialists do basic computer repair, not the lucrative high-end consulting Big Blue specializes in.
Storage	Compaq's $5.2 billion storage business should get a big boost as HP sells Compaq gear to its customers. Still the merger wouldn't help HP take customers from storage giant EMC and others.
Software	Providing complete solutions for big corporations requires specialized software called middleware. But HP badly lags rivals, and Compaq is a no-show.

Source: BusinessWeek analysis, September 17, 2000.

Exhibit 3   HP's Consolidated Statements of Operations

Year ended October 31,	2000	1999	1998
Net Revenues			
Products	41,446	36,015	33,585
Services	7,336	6,355	5,834
Total net revenue	**48,782**	**42,370**	**39,419**
Costs and expenses:			
Costs of products sold	29,727	25,305	24,044
Costs of services	5,137	4,415	3,746
Research and Development	2,646	2,440	2,380
Selling, general and administrative	7,383	6,522	5,850
Total costs and expenses	**44,893**	**38,682**	**36,020**
Earnings from operations	3,889	3,688	3,399
Interest income and other, net	993	708	530
Interest expense	257	202	235
Earning from continuing operations before taxes	**4,625**	**4,194**	**3,694**
Provision for taxes	1,064	1,090	1,016
Net earnings from continuing operations	3,561	3,104	2,678
Net earnings from discontinued operations	136	387	267
Net earnings	**3,697**	**3,491**	**2,945**
Net earnings per share:			
Basic	1.87	1.73	1.42
Diluted	1.80	1.67	1.39
Weighted average shares:			
Basic	1,979	2,018	2,068
Diluted	2,077	2,105	2,144

Source: HP Annual Report 2000.

(In $ million, except per share data)

Exhibit 4   Compaq's Consolidated Statements of Operations

Year ended December 31,	2000	1999	1998
Revenue:			
Products	35,667	31,902	27,372
Services	6,716	6,623	3,797
Total Revenue	**42,283**	**38,525**	**31,169**
Cost of Sales			
Products	27,624	25,263	21,383
Services	4,793	4,535	2,597
Total Cost of Sales	**32,417**	**29,798**	**23,980**
Selling, general and administrative expenses	6,044	6,341	4,978
Research & Development costs	1,469	1,660	1,353
Purchased in Process Technology	—	—	3,196
Restructuring and asset impairment charges	(86)	868	393
Other (income) expense, net	1,664	(1,076)	(69)
Total	**9,091**	**7,793**	**9,851**
Income (loss) before provision for income tax	875	934	(2,662)
Provision for income taxes	280	365	81
Income (loss) before cumulative effect of accounting change	595	569	(2,743)
Cumulative effect of accounting change	(26)	—	—
Net Income (loss)	**569**	**569**	**(2,743)**
Earnings (loss) per common share			
Basic	$0.33	0.35	(1.71)
Diluted	$0.33	0.34	(1.71)
Shares used in computing earnings per common share			
Basic	1,702	1,693	1,608
Diluted	1,742	1,735	1,608
Cash dividends per share	$0.10	0.085	0.065
Financial Position			
Current Assets	15,111	13,849	15,167
Total Assets	24,856	27,277	29,051
Current liabilities	11,549	11,838	10,733
Long-term obligations	575	—	422
Stockholders' equity	12,080	14,834	11,351

Source: Compaq Annual Report 2000.

(In $ million, except per share data)

Exhibit 5 **HP's Stock Price Chart**

Source: www.bigcharts.com.

Exhibit 6 **Compaq's Stock Price Chart**

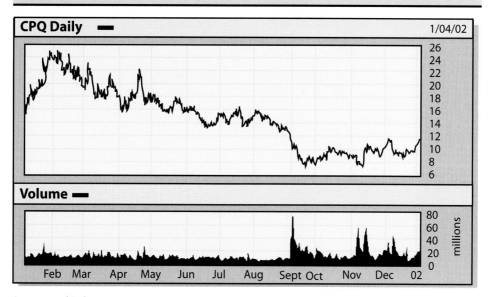

Source: www.bigcharts.com.

Exhibit 7   A Brief Note on Dell and IBM

· Dell Computer

Dell Computer Corporation (Dell), with its headquarters in Round Rock, Austin, is the world's largest direct seller of computer systems. The company is also the largest PC seller in the U.S., having overtaken Compaq in the second quarter of 1999. Dell recorded revenues of $31.88 billion and a net profit of $2.17 billion for the year ended January 29, 2001. As [of] January 16, 2001, the company had a market capitalization of $71.9 billion. Dell sells desktop computers, notebook computers, workstations, network servers and storage products. The company also sells a range of hardware peripherals and third party application software. Besides, it provides services like hardware and software integration, and network installation and support. Dell's customers [include] large corporations, government agencies, educational institutions, small businesses and individuals.

· IBM

With revenues of $88.39 billion in 2000, IBM was ranked 8th in the 2000 *Fortune* 500 list. IBM, popularly referred to as [...] Big Blue, is the largest computer manufacturer in the world. IBM's net earnings rose by 4.9% to $8.09 billion in 2000. As [of] January 16, 2001, the company had a market capitalization of $202 billion. The company ranks #2 in the software business, behind Microsoft, and generates about 35% of revenues from its IT services business, the largest in the world. IBM owns Lotus Development, maker of the Lotus Notes messaging system. About 60% of IBM's revenues come from customers outside the U.S. IBM has divided major operations into different segments—Technology, Personal Systems, Server (hardware), Global Services, Software, Global Financing and Enterprise Investments.

Compiled from various source[s].

Exhibit 8   Key Financial Ratios of Dell Computers

Profitability Ratios	Company	Industry	Market
Gross Profit Margin	21.34%	24.49%	46.18%
Pre-Tax Profit Margin	10.61%	8.04%	8.38%
Net Profit Margin	7.46%	5.58%	5.50%
Return on Equity	36.9%	19.1%	11.7%
Return on Assets	16.8%	9.6%	2.3%
Valuation Ratios			
Price/Sales Ratio	1.96	1.16	1.54
Price/Earnings Ratio	27.67	22.35	37.15
Price/Book Ratio	9.70	4.00	3.29
Price/Cash Flow Ratio	23.88	15.07	13.87
Operating Ratios			
Days of Sales Outstanding	37.01	52.18	52.38
Inventory Turnover	59.2	23.2	8.2
Days Cost of Goods Sold in Inventory	6	16	44
Asset Turnover	2.5	1.9	0.5
Net Receivables Turnover Flow	10.2	7.5	7.8
Effective Tax Rate	29.7%	30.0%	41.5%
Financial Ratios			
Current Ratio	1.45	1.46	1.36
Quick Ratio	1.3	1.2	0.9
Leverage Ratio	2.20	1.98	5.01
Total Debt/Equity	0.08	0.07	1.25
Interest Coverage	—	33.4	2.4
Per Share Data ($)			
Revenue Per Share	11.60	17.46	21.01
Fully Diluted Earnings Per Share from Total Operations	0.82	0.91	0.87
Dividends per Share	0.00	0.03	0.36
Cash Flow per Share	0.95	1.35	2.33
Working Capital per Share	1.07	1.97	(0.62)
Long-Term Debt per Share	0.20	0.27	8.14
Book Value per Share	2.34	5.09	9.83
Total Assets per Share	5.15	10.10	49.27
Growth Rates			
12-Month Revenue Growth	27.0%	15.8%	20.1%
12-Month Net Income Growth	35.2%	41.0%	23.8%
12-Month EPS Growth	32.3%	24.7%	(1.1%)
12-Month Dividend Growth	—	0.0%	9.1%

Source: www.hoovers.com.

(Financial year ended January 29, 2001)

Cisco Systems, Inc.: Acquisition Integration for Manufacturing (A)

David Keller, vice president of manufacturing, new product introduction, and technology at Cisco Systems, Inc. (Cisco), hung up the phone and sat back to think about the challenges that lay ahead. He had just spent the last hour talking with Gary Wilder, director of manufacturing operations, and Dick Swee, vice president of engineering, at Summa Four Inc. (Summa Four)—a systems company which developed and manufactured programmable switches used in the development of telephony applications. Cisco had announced in July 1998 that it had reached an agreement to acquire publicly held Summa Four for $116 million in stock. The conversation had been about the major effort that lay ahead to integrate the two companies' manufacturing organizations. While the deal was not expected to officially close until November 1998, Keller had called Wilder and Swee to give them an overview of how Cisco managed these types of integration projects so that they could begin to prepare the Summa Four organization.

Keller had reviewed the due diligence report on Summa Four written by a team from his department and knew that the integration process would be complex. While Cisco had made 25 acquisitions prior to the Summa Four acquisition, most had been of Silicon Valley–based software or pre-production hardware companies which had small (if any) manufacturing orga-

Nicole Tempest, Associate Director of the HBS California Research Center, and Dean's Research Fellow Christian G. Kasper prepared this case under the supervision of Professor Steven C. Wheelwright and Professor Charles A. Holloway, Kleiner Perkins Caufield and Byers Professor of Management at Stanford University's Graduate School of Business as the basis for class discussion rather than to illustrate either effective or ineffective handling of an administrative situation.

nizations. The Summa Four acquisition had the potential to be different. Summa Four was a 22-year-old hardware company with $42 million in revenues, over 200 employees, one manufacturing plant located in Manchester, New Hampshire, and a full line of products being shipped. Summa Four represented one of Cisco's largest acquisitions to date in terms of current revenues and employees.

Keller was concerned about just how difficult the acquisition integration process would be from a manufacturing standpoint. How would they treat Summa Four's legacy and next-generation products? Where would they be manufactured? How would Cisco deal with Summa Four's suppliers? Did it make sense to keep the Manchester plant operating? If so, for how long? What risks did Cisco face during the integration process and what could be done to help mitigate those risks?

CISCO OVERVIEW

Cisco Systems, founded in 1984 by Leonard Bosack and Sandy Lerner—a husband and wife team of computer specialists at Stanford University—grew out of a project to tie together disparate computer networks on campus. Bosack and Lerner developed the first "multi-protocol" router—a specialized microcomputer that sat between two or more networks (even those with different operating systems) and allowed those networks to "talk" to each other by deciphering, translating, and funneling data between them. As Bosack explained back then: "We network networks."[1] Cisco's technology opened up the potential for linking all of the world's disparate computer networks together in much the same way as different telephone networks were linked around the world. Technology pioneered by Cisco provided the functionality for the World Wide Web.

As the global Internet and corporate Intranets grew in importance, so too did Cisco. With an early foothold in this

---

[1] *The San Francisco Chronicle*, February 17, 1990.

rapidly growing industry, Cisco quickly became the leader in the data networking equipment market—the "plumbing" of the Internet. By 1998, most of the large-scale routers that powered the Internet were made by Cisco. While routers and switches continued to be Cisco's core products, the company's product line had expanded to include a broad range of other networking solutions, including Web site management tools, dial-up and other access solutions, Internet appliances, and network management software. (See Exhibit 1 for a list of Cisco's product categories.) Cisco's broad product line enabled it to offer customers an "end-to-end" network solution—an option which over 50% of *Fortune* 500 companies were actively considering, according to Cisco. By 1998 the company held the number one or number two position in 14 of the 15 markets in which it competed. As a result, Cisco had become a safe decision for large companies. As one industry analyst commented, "I have heard from a number of really large clients: 'It's like IBM in the old days—you won't get fired for choosing them.'"[2]

In 1996 Cisco entered the $250 billion telecom equipment market, which was undergoing significant change due to rapid advances in technology. Whereas historically there had been three separate types of networks—phone networks for transmitting voice, computer networks for transmitting data, and broadcast networks for transmitting video—advances in digitization had allowed voice, data, and video all to be translated into the ones and zeros of computer language. This, in turn, made it possible to transmit all three over *one* network in a more efficient and economical manner. As a result, phone companies were beginning to replace their century-old voice-only networks with new networks capable of carrying voice, data, and video. By positioning its products for this market, Cisco was competing with a far larger group of rivals than it had in the past—including Lucent Technologies and Nortel. In June 1998 Cisco scored a major victory against these rivals when Sprint selected Cisco to be the primary supplier of its new data and telephone network.

Having received its initial funding from the venture capital firm Sequoia Capital, Cisco went public in February 1990, closing its first day of trading with a market value of $222 million. Just 8 years later, Cisco's market value topped the significant $100 billion mark, reaching that mark faster than any company in history and stripping Microsoft of the previous record of 11 years. Between 1989 and 1998 Cisco's revenues grew at a compound annual rate of 89%, from $28 million to $8.5 billion, and with traffic on the Internet doubling every four months, Cisco continued to have significant growth potential. (See Exhibit 2 for Cisco's financials.)

Cisco's Business Strategy

Cisco's business strategy reflected the experience of CEO John Chambers and Chairman John Morgridge. Morgridge, who had been CEO of Cisco from 1988 to 1995, established

[2] *Wired News*, March 1997.

Exhibit 1   Cisco Product Categories

Product Category	Description
High-end routers	Cisco's high-end platforms for the most mission-critical networks
WAN switches	Wide-area networking switching for Frame Relay and ATM, plus network access devices
LAN switches	Local area-networking switching for workgroup networks
Hubs	Devices to link small workgroups in local networks
Access products	Scalable products for remote access
Web scaling products and technologies	Products that provide Internet access, security, scalability, and management
Security products	Comprehensive solutions for network protection and enabling Internet business applications
InterWorks for SNA	Availability, scalability, performance, flexibility, and management for IBM/SNA networks
IOS software	Cisco's Internetworking Operating System software
Network management	Network management solutions that offer end-to-end network management for any Cisco-based network

Source: www.cisco.com.

many of Cisco's core business principles, including the importance of customer satisfaction, time-to-market, and frugality. Chambers, who took over as CEO in January 1995, spent most of his career at IBM and Wang, and watched both companies suffer crippling declines as a result of not adapting to changing market conditions quickly enough. Morgridge, Chambers, and Ed Kozel—then Cisco's chief technology officer—crafted a strategic plan for Cisco in 1993, which was still being executed in 1998. The plan consisted of four main components:

1. assemble a broad product line in order to provide customers one-stop-shopping for networking solutions,

2. systematize the acquisition process,

3. define industry-wide software standards for networking equipment, and

4. pick the right strategic partners.

An inherent part of Cisco's strategy was using acquisitions and partnerships to gain access to new technologies. This strategy was relatively unique in the high-tech world, where many companies viewed looking to the outside for technological help as a sign of weakness. However, Chambers believed that this was just the sort of insular thinking that had led to IBM and Wang's downfall. He viewed partnerships and acquisitions as the most efficient means of offering customers an end-to-end networking solution and developing next-

Exhibit 2   Cisco Financials

Selected Financial Data

Five Years Ended July 25, 1998 (in thousands, except per-share amounts)

	1998	1997	1996	1995	1994
Net sales	$8,458,777	$6,440,171	$4,096,007	$2,232,652	$1,334,436
Net income	$1,350,072[a]	$1,048,679[b]	$ 913,324	$ 456,489[c]	$ 322,981
Net income per common share—basic[d]	$ 0.88	$ 0.71	$ 0.64	$ 0.33	$ 0.25
Net income per share—diluted[d]	$ 0.84[a]	$ 0.68[b]	$ 0.61	$ 0.32[c]	$ 0.24
Shares used in per-share calculation—basic[d]	1,533,869	1,485,986	1,437,030	1,367,453	1,296,023
Shares used in per-share calculation—diluted[d]	1,608,173	1,551,039	1,490,078	1,425,247	1,342,213
Total assets	$8,916,705	$5,451,984	$3,630,232	$1,991,949	$1,129,034

[a]Net income and net income per share include purchased research and development expenses of $594 million and realized gains on the sale of a minority stock investment of $5 million. Pro forma net income and diluted net income per share, excluding these nonrecurring items net of tax, would have been $1,878,988 and $1.17, respectively.

[b]Net income and net income per share include purchased research and development expenses of $508 million and realized gains on the sale of a minority stock investment of $153 million. Pro forma net income and diluted net income per share, excluding these nonrecurring items net of tax, would have been $1,413,893 and $0.91, respectively.

[c]Net income and net income per share include purchased research and development expenses of $96 million. Pro forma net income and diluted net income per share, excluding these nonrecurring items net of tax, would have been $515,723 and $0.36, respectively.

[d]Reflects the three-for-two stock split effective September 1998.

generation products. For example, Cisco's partnership with Microsoft enabled the company to develop a new technology for making networks more intelligent in just 18 months. Cisco insiders estimated that it would have taken Cisco four years to develop the product itself without the Microsoft partnership.

Cisco's Manufacturing Philosophy and Organization

From its beginnings, Cisco was structured as a highly centralized organization. Morgridge believed that too many start-up companies decentralized too quickly, and therefore were unable to benefit from the advantages of scale and control associated with a centralized organization. However, in 1995 Cisco established three separate "lines of business"—Enterprise, Small/Medium Business, and Service Provider—each of which had two to nine separate "business units" reporting to them. Although Cisco had begun to move to a more decentralized structure, most of the company's functional areas still remained centralized as of mid-1998, including manufacturing, customer support, finance, information technology, human resources, and sales. Only engineering and marketing were decentralized at the business unit level.

Cisco operated three manufacturing facilities: two in San Jose, "Tasman" and "Walsh"; and a third in South San Jose, "Silver Creek." Tasman and Walsh were Cisco's first manufacturing plants and they produced most of Cisco's enterprise routers and LAN switches. The Silver Creek facility

was inherited through the 1996 acquisition of StrataCom, Inc., and it produced most of Cisco's high-end Internet backbone products for service providers (e.g., Sprint, MCI). In addition to these three owned and operated manufacturing facilities, Cisco utilized "external factories" to outsource production of some of its high volume products. (See Exhibit 3 for Cisco's manufacturing department organization chart.)

Cisco's manufacturing strategy was heavily dependent on outsourcing. The company outsourced many manufacturing activities, such as board stuffing and board testing, to contract manufacturers since these activities required a significant investment in "bricks and mortar," were less scalable, and generated lower returns relative to Cisco's core business. For example, in the case of Cisco's higher-end, more highly configured products, Cisco would outsource subassembly, bring in completed subsystems, and conduct final testing and assembly in-house, in one of its three manufacturing facilities. At the other end of the spectrum, Cisco utilized external factories to build, test, and ship its less configured, high volume products, such as its low-end routers. Carl Redfield, senior vice president of manufacturing and logistics at Cisco, explained the strategy: "I want my people focusing on the intellectual portion, establishing the supply base, qualifying new suppliers, and developing better processes, not managing direct labor. We supply the intellect; they supply the labor."[3]

Tom Fallon, vice president and plant manager at Cisco, added: "If we can make it cheaper, we do. But even

---

[3] Timothy Laseter, *Balanced Sourcing* (San Francisco: Jossey-Bass, 1998).

Exhibit 3   Cisco's Manufacturing Organization (as of 7/98)

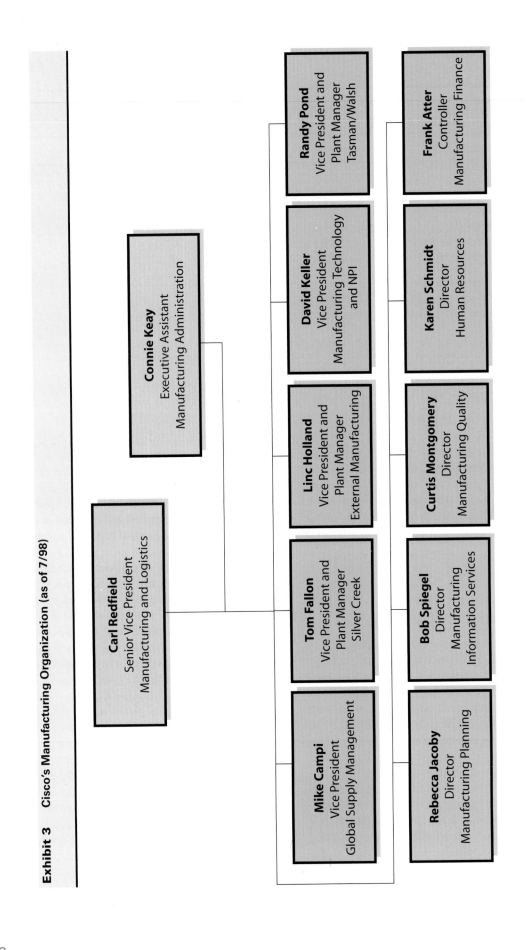

then, we look for suppliers who can match our costs. Strategically we want to outsource."[4]

Approximately 25% of Cisco's revenue and 50% of its unit volume was manufactured and shipped out of external factories. While external factories were not owned by Cisco, and their employees were not Cisco employees, Cisco did supply them with Cisco information systems and test systems to ensure that they met Cisco's standards for quality and customer satisfaction.

CISCO'S ACQUISITION STRATEGY

Cisco regarded acquisitions primarily as a means to secure technology and scarce intellectual assets. As Chambers commented: "Most people forget that in a high-tech acquisition, you really are acquiring only people. That's why so many of them fail. At what we pay, $500,000 to $2 million an employee, we are not acquiring current market share. We are acquiring futures."[5]

Cisco had three primary goals for ensuring the success of its acquisitions. These were, in order of importance: 1) employee retention, 2) follow-up on new product development, and 3) return on investment.

Employee Retention

Since the employees of acquired companies were critical to the success of the acquisition, Cisco went to great efforts to retain them. Cisco itself was basically just the combination of 25 different organizations that had merged over time. Integration success was due in large part to the very organized, methodical approach that Cisco took toward managing the experience of acquired employees. In the words of a senior human resources manager, "Our objective during the acquisition and transition is to make the employees whole." That is, their efforts were focused on ensuring that employees maintained comparable— if not better—financial consideration and benefits as they transitioned to Cisco's policies and plans.

The responsibilities of the human resources department (HR) began even before the acquisition was consummated. A team of HR professionals typically would spend several weeks at the acquisition candidate developing a transition plan. The plan would map the changes and time frame required to smoothly transfer the personnel, benefits, and compensation policies of the acquired company to Cisco. Based on a belief that people don't like change—especially change they can't predict—Cisco's HR professionals went to great lengths to tailor the specifics of the transition plan to the needs of the acquired company's employees. For example, Cisco added a new health care provider to its employee benefit options so that the acquired employees were able to keep their existing doctors.

After the acquisition closed, Cisco's HR team would spend another six to seven weeks on-site executing the transition plan. This would give them the opportunity to review the details of the plan with the acquired firm's management before rolling it out to all the employees. The rollout process typically centered on small group discussions with Cisco's HR team and employees from the acquired company. Furthermore, Cisco usually insisted that the acquired company's management team play an active role in educating their own employees.

For the employees of the acquired firm, working for Cisco required a number of significant changes to their compensation. One of the most significant issues was that Cisco required all employees to waive their rights to accelerated vesting on their existing stock options—an event usually triggered by an acquisition—before the deal closed. In return, employees would receive an equivalent value of Cisco options for all of their company's unvested options. In addition, they offered a retention bonus at the end of the first and second years. Given the historically strong performance of Cisco's stock, there was usually little resistance to the new compensation package.

The employees of the acquired companies also benefited from Cisco's history of explosive growth and need for skilled workers. Of its first 25 acquisitions, only two required layoffs, and every redundant person had the opportunity to apply for any Cisco job opening worldwide. Since Cisco typically had 300–600 job openings available at any one time, this represented an attractive option for redundant employees. Part of this policy stemmed from Chamber's experience as vice president of U.S. operations at Wang where he was given the unpopular and heart-wrenching task of laying off 4,000 of Wang's 10,000-person workforce. He vowed to never face this situation again.

These policies had met with great success in the past. The employee turnover rate for acquisitions was only 8%, the same level as for Cisco's long-term employees. Approximately one in five Cisco employees and one-third of Cisco's top management positions were filled by people who had come from acquired companies, and these individuals continued to promote an environment that welcomed acquired employees into its ranks.

New Product Development

Successful new product development required both technical expertise and management talent in order to understand the market, translate market needs into a product, and deliver that product to market quickly. Cisco's new product introduction (NPI) process required that input from marketing, engineering, and manufacturing was incorporated into the product design to ensure that products were designed for functionality, manufacturability, testability, and cost-effectiveness. Since Cisco viewed acquisitions as a means of introducing new products, it was important for Cisco to accelerate the acquired company's new product development efforts. Cisco had found that the most effective way to do this was for the acquired company to adopt Cisco's cross-functional, systematic NPI process. (See Exhibit 4 for a detailed description of Cisco's NPI process.)

---

[4] Ibid.

[5] *BusinessWeek*, August 31, 1998.

Exhibit 4   Cisco's New Product Introduction Process

Cisco's NPI process involved three phases: strategy and planning, execution, and deployment. The process also included a series of checkpoints between the "strategy and planning" and "deployment" stage to help instill rigor and discipline into the new product introduction process. The multiple checkpoints ensured that there was both a shared vision for the new product and a commitment to allocate sufficient resources to it.

The "concept commit checkpoint" came at the beginning of the strategy and planning phase. This checkpoint ensured that a cross-functional team had approved both the product requirement document (PRD) and the business plan attached to it, and was willing to commit resources sufficient to get to the product design point. By the end of the strategy and planning phase, designers would have developed a definitive design specification for the product.

Next the product had to clear the "execution checkpoint" which ensured that the cross-functional team agreed on both the design specifications and the revised PRD, and was committed to dedicating the resources required to ship the product on a particular date. In the execution phase, the engineering group worked with manufacturing to develop and test prototypes. Manufacturing would conduct a thorough design for manufacturability (DFM) review early in the prototype development process and would help the engineering group develop a product that was easily testable on the Autotest system.

Close to the end of the execution phase—about a month before the first product was shipped—the product had to pass the "orderability checkpoint." This was a manufacturing-driven checkpoint that ensured that the product had passed a rigorous set of [criteria] before being posted on Cisco's Web site. The manufacturing group used the test to ensure they could hit the ship date and meet the expected ramp-up in demand. The check list included questions such as:

Has the product completed and passed its development test?

Has the product been beta tested, and is the feedback good?

Are the results from the software tests positive?

Do we have suppliers lined up? Can they make the parts?

Do we have reasonable yields at the prototype stage?

Once the product passed the orderability check point, it was added to Cisco's price list, and it entered into the deployment phase where it was either slated for "unlimited release" or "controlled release." Products slated for unlimited release were typically those that were in high demand, had completed all the development milestones, and for which Cisco had significant capacity to build, test, ship, and service. Products slated for controlled release were typically those that still faced some degree of design risk. For example, the product could have received compliance approval in some, but not all geographic areas (i.e., approved for the U.S., but not yet for Europe). In these cases, Cisco would restrict output as a way of controlling the risk involved in the product launch.

Two to three months after the first product had been shipped, the product faced yet another manufacturing checkpoint, known as the "time to quality and volume" (TTQV) checkpoint. This checkpoint—which included analyses on yields and costs—was designed to ensure that the manufacturing group could make the product cost-effectively at high volumes. The TTQV checkpoint was conducted two to three months after production had begun so that sufficient run-rate data could be collected and used for analysis. Once the product had passed this checkpoint, it was produced according to its own roll-out plan and lifecycle.

More than simply adding to its list of offerings, Cisco saw product development as a high leverage item. Cisco's goal was to quickly convert newly acquired products to its own NPI process and hopefully reap significant sales volume improvements. This required Cisco to quickly assess where each of the company's products were in the development process. With this information, Cisco could make an informed decision about which products to convert to the NPI process, and which products were too far along in their development to benefit from the change. Although Cisco tried to convert as many new products as possible, typically only the early-stage development products would use the new process.

Return on Investment

Cisco also looked for acquisitions to generate a high return on investment. The key to accomplishing this was to quickly and effectively leverage Cisco's powerful sales organization and third party distributors (value added resellers, or "VARs") to sell the acquired company's products. Charles Giancarlo, vice president for global alliances at Cisco, reiterated Cisco's focus on generating results quickly following an acquisition: "If there are no results in three to six months, people begin to question the acquisition. If you have good short-term results, it's a virtuous cycle."[6]

In order to generate results quickly, Cisco made every attempt to have the acquired company's products appear on Cisco's price list on the day the deal closed so that Cisco's sales force could immediately begin to sell the new products. The power of leveraging Cisco's sales and distribution channels, alone, could result in a two- to five-times ramp up in the acquired company's volume. Effectively leveraging its distribution channels in this manner was one of the key drivers behind the significant growth in Cisco's revenues.

Types of Acquisitions

Cisco made its first acquisition in 1993, when it purchased Crescendo Communications—a LAN-switching company—for $97 million. By mid-1998, Cisco had announced 29 acquisitions worth about $7 billion and had made non-controlling investments in 40 companies—three of which Cisco later acquired.[7] (See Exhibit 5 for a list of Cisco's acquisitions.) Cisco's target was to have 30% of its revenue come from acquisition and development ("A&D") efforts and 70% from internal research and development (R&D) efforts. Proposals for specific acquisition candidates often came directly from Cisco's business units, based on feedback from customers. Cisco would then screen these potential candidates against a well-defined set of criteria (see Exhibit 6).

Cisco's acquisitions spanned a range of companies producing different types of products, at different points in their lifecycles. There were essentially four types of acquisitions: software companies, "pre-production" hardware companies, small hardware companies shipping product, and mature hardware companies. The complexity of the integration process, and the level of resources dedicated to the effort, varied depending on the type of acquisition. From a manufacturing standpoint, software companies and pre-production companies were the least complex to integrate into Cisco, since these types of companies typically did not have a manufacturing organization in place, nor an existing customer backlog to satisfy. At the other end of the spectrum, small hardware companies shipping product and mature hardware companies were the most complex to integrate. In fact, the complexity of the integration process had far more to do with the company's stage of development than with its acquisition price. For example, the manufacturing integration process for a $300 million acquisition of a pre-production company could be far easier than for a $100 million acquisition of a hardware company that was already shipping products. Keller compared the effort involved in integrating pre-production companies to companies already shipping product:

> The integration of pre-production companies tends to be less difficult than integrating companies that are already shipping product, since we can have more influence and add more value on the manufacturing side, and there isn't a lot we have to "undo." We can integrate the company into our operations and set them up on our systems right from the start.

While Cisco had made several acquisitions of software, pre-production hardware, and small hardware companies already shipping product, as of 1998 Cisco had made only one acquisition of a mature hardware company—the acquisition of StrataCom in 1996. (See Exhibit 7 for examples of acquisitions by type.)

CISCO'S ACQUISITION INTEGRATION PROCESS

Before agreeing to the terms of an acquisition, Cisco conducted thorough due diligence on the company. A project manager from Cisco's business development group would coordinate the overall due diligence process, in which a cross-functional team—comprised of representatives from marketing and engineering within Cisco's business units and representatives from Cisco's centralized manufacturing organization—conducted a detailed assessment of the acquisition candidate's business processes. For example, the manufacturing due diligence team reviewed the company's manufacturing processes, identified risks, provided input to valuation discussions, and scoped the work that would be required to integrate the two companies, if the deal were to close. The manufacturing due diligence process centered around a 1 to 2 day visit to the company to see and discuss a number of details regarding their technology, manufacturing and engineering processes, and organization.

---

[6] *BusinessWeek*, August 31, 1998.

[7] *San Jose Mercury News*, October 12, 1998.

Exhibit 5   Cisco's Acquisitions

Date[a]	Company	Business Description	Alignment with Cisco Line of Business	Approximate Acquisition Price ($MM)	Approximate Number of Employees
10/98	Selsius Systems	Supplier of network PBX systems for high-quality telephony over IP networks	Enterprise	$145 (stock + cash)	51
9/98	Clarity Wireless Corporation	Wireless communication technology for computer networking and the Internet service markets	Service Provider	$157 (stock)	39
8/98	American Internet Corporation	Software for IP address management and Internet access	Service Provider	$56 (stock)	50
7/98	Summa Four, Inc.	Open programmable digital switching systems	Service Provider	$116 (stock)	210
5/98	CLASS Data Systems	Network management software	Enterprise	$50 (stock + cash)	34
3/98	Precept Software, Inc.	Multimedia networking software	IOS Technologies[b]	$84 (stock)	50
3/98	NetSpeed, Inc.	Standards-based DSL technology	Service Provider	$236 (stock)	140
2/98	WheelGroup Corporation	Intrusion detection and security scanning software	IOS Technologies	$124 (stock)	75
12/97	LightSpeed International, Inc.	Voice signaling technologies	Service Provider	$160 (stock)	70
7/97	Dagaz (Integrated Network Corporation)	Broadband networking products	Service Provider	$126 (stock)	30
6/97	Ardent Communications Corp.	Combined communications support for compressed voice, LAN, data, and video traffic across public and private Frame Relay and Asynchronous Transfer Mode (ATM) networks	Service Provider	$156 (stock)	40
6/97	Global Internet Software Group	Windows NT security	Small/Medium Business	$40 (cash)	20
6/97	Skystone Systems Corp.	High-speed Synchronous Optical Networking/ Synchronous Digital Hierarchy (SONET/SDH) technology	Service Provider	$102 (stock + cash)	40
3/97	Telescend	Wide area network access products	Service Provider	Terms not disclosed	NA
12/96	Metaplex, Inc.	Network products for the IBM enterprise marketplace	Enterprise	Terms not disclosed	20
10/96	Netsys Technologies	Network infrastructure management and performance analysis software	Service Provider	$79 (stock)	50
9/[96]	Granite Systems, Inc.	Standard-based multi-layer Gigabit Ethernet switching technologies	Enterprise	$220 (stock)	50
8/96	Nashoba Networks, Inc.	Token Ring switching technologies	Enterprise	$100 (stock)	40
7/96	Telebit Corp's MICA Technologies	Modem ISDN Channel Aggregation (MICA) technologies	Service Provider	$200 (cash)	288
4/96	StrataCom, Inc.	ATM and Frame Relay high-speed wide area network switching equipment	Service Provider	$4,666 (stock)	625

Exhibit 5 (continued)

Date[a]	Company	Business Description	Alignment with Cisco Line of Business	Approximate Acquisition Price ($MM)	Approximate Number of Employees
1/96	TGV Software, Inc.	Internet software products for connecting disparate computer systems over local area, enterprise-wide and global computing networks	Small/Medium Business	$138 (stock)	130+
10/95	Network Translation, Inc.	Network address translation and Internet firewall hardware and software	Small/Medium Business	Terms not disclosed	10
9/95	Grand Junction, Inc.	Fast Ethernet (100Base-T) and Ethernet switching products	Small/Medium Business	$400 (stock)	85
9/95	Internet Junction, Inc.	Internet gateway software connecting desktop users with the Internet	Small/Medium Business	$5.5 (stock)	10
8/95	Combinet, Inc.	ISDN remote-access networking products	Small/Medium Business	$132 (stock)	100
12/94	LightStream, Corp.	Enterprise ATM switching, workgroup ATM switching, LAN switching and routing	Service Provider	$120 (cash)	60+
10/94	Kalpana, Inc.	LAN switching products	Enterprise	$240 (stock)	150
8/94	Newport Systems Solutions, Inc.	Software-based routers for remote network sites	Small/Medium Business	$91 (stock)	55
9/93	Crescendo Communications	High-performance workgroup networking products	Enterprise	$97 (stock)	60

Source: www.cisco.com, literature search.

[a]Date of announcement
[b]Internetworking Operating System

Exhibit 6	**Screening Criteria for Potential Acquisition Candidates**
Screening Criteria	**Means of Achieving Criteria**
Offer both short-term and long-term win-wins for Cisco and the acquired company	• Have a complementary technology that fills [...] a need in Cisco's core product space • Have a technology that can be delivered through Cisco's existing distribution channels • Have a technology and products which can be supported by Cisco's support organization • Is able to leverage Cisco's existing infrastructure and resource base to increase its overall value
Share a common vision and chemistry with Cisco	• Have a similar understanding and vision of the market • Have a similar culture • Have a similar risk-taking style
Be located (preferably) in Silicon Valley or near one of Cisco's remote sites	• Have company headquarters and most manufacturing facilities close to one of Cisco's main sites

Prior to the due diligence session, Cisco would send an outline of issues for discussion to the heads of the manufacturing and engineering groups at the company to help prepare for the visit. (See Exhibit 8 for a sample list of manufacturing due diligence issues.)

After the acquisition had closed, Cisco would move forward with its post-acquisition integration process. Although each of Cisco's acquisitions was unique and required a customized integration approach based on a comprehensive understanding of the company, there were ten common steps that were mandatory. The mandatory steps centered on converting the acquired company to Cisco's manufacturing systems, processes, and methodologies. While the time allotted for completing these steps could vary, ultimately the "Cisco way" would be put into place. Cisco described these steps as "stakes in the ground." On the other hand, certain decisions—such as how to handle the integration of an acquired company's employees and manufacturing plants—varied from acquisition to acquisition and required significant management judgment. (See Exhibit 9 for a diagram of the integration process.)

In both cases, Cisco utilized a "scenario planning" approach to make decisions about what to do and how fast to do it. The scenario planning approach took into account Cisco's business objectives for the acquisition, information on the company gathered from the due diligence effort, and projected outcomes under various integration scenarios (e.g., higher volumes, merging plants). The approach was used to help outline alternatives and generate consensus regarding recommendations.

Manufacturing Integration Team

Cisco organized a manufacturing integration team to manage the post-acquisition process. Cisco's approach was to appoint one of the senior managers within the *acquired* company as the integration team leader. Tony Crabb, previously the vice president of manufacturing for StrataCom (before becoming director of manufacturing at Cisco), was chosen to lead the StrataCom integration team. Crabb reflected on the impact of Cisco's approach to leading the integration process:

From the perspective of employees within the acquired company, it's pretty important to see someone they know and trust leading the integration effort. If it were a Cisco person leading the process, they would feel as if it were being imposed upon them, and therefore resent the process. On the other hand, if it's someone they know, it's easier for them to ask questions and feel a part of the process.

The balance of the integration team was comprised of experienced members of both organizations. The overall team was then divided into subteams that were responsible for leading key business process conversion tasks.

Based on experience from several acquisitions, Cisco also had developed an approach called the "buddy system." The buddy system involved appointing an experienced Cisco employee to be the "manager of the intangibles" within both the acquired company's engineering and manufacturing organizations, and swapping a handful of Cisco employees with employees from the acquired company. Both the "managers of intangibles" and the on-site Cisco staff would assist employees from the acquired company with questions regarding how to access information and get things done within the Cisco organization. While the "manager of intangibles" position had no official reporting structure beneath it, the role was considered a critical part of the integration process and was reserved for strong performers within the Cisco organization. Crabb described how the buddy system worked in the StrataCom acquisition:

One of the keys to success in the StrataCom integration process was to have Cisco people within the StrataCom organization, so that we had people on site who knew how to get information from the big Cisco organization. As an outsider you don't know how to get even the most basic things done—like how to get a new ID badge. But, by having a Cisco person sitting in the cube right next to you, he or she can immediately tell you who to call and even give you the person's number. The buddy system de-stresses a lot of angst about how to do things and how to be productive within the Cisco organization. As Cisco does more remote acquisitions, the buddy system will become even more important because you won't have the opportunity to walk down the hall and talk to someone.

Mandatory Integration Steps

As soon as the manufacturing integration team was created, work began on the mandatory components of the integration process. The mandatory steps provided a clearly articu-

Exhibit 7   Examples of Acquisitions by Type

Acquisition Type	Description	Examples of Acquisitions by Type
Software Companies	These were companies that designed and sold software—primarily engineering companies. Since they were not involved in the hardware side of the business, they did not have a manufacturing organization. As a result, this type of acquisition required the least amount of involvement from the Cisco manufacturing organization during the integration process.	American Internet Corporation CLASS Data Systems Precept Software, Inc. WheelGroup Corporation LightSpeed International, Inc. Global Internet Software Group Netsys Technologies TGV Software, Inc. Internet Junction, Inc.
Pre-production Hardware Companies	These were companies that had a technology that Cisco wanted, but they were not yet shipping any product. Frequently these companies had developed a prototype, but the product was not yet designed for manufacturability. This type of acquisition was relatively straightforward from a manufacturing integration standpoint, since there was no existing infrastructure with which to contend and no existing customer order backlog to satisfy.	Clarity Wireless Corporation Dagaz Ardent Communications Corp. Skystone Systems Corp. Telescend Granite Systems, Inc. Nashoba Networks, Inc. Telebit Corp's MICA Technologies
Small Hardware Companies Shipping Product	These were small companies—sometimes private, sometimes public—that were shipping products to a limited installed base of customers. Cisco would typically acquire these companies for their engineering team and the potential they offered for developing next generation products. These companies typically had some sort of enterprise resource planning (ERP) system in place, but often would not have the manufacturing quality standards of a mature company. This type of acquisition proved to be more complex than pre-production companies since the integration process had to proceed without impacting the continuity of supply to existing customers.	Summa Four, Inc. NetSpeed Inc. Network Translation, Inc. Grand Junction, Inc. Combinet, Inc. Kalpana, Inc. LightStream Corp. Newport Systems Solutions, Inc. Crescendo Communications
Mature Hardware Companies	These were large, mature companies that had a substantial customer base. They typically had established manufacturing processes in place and were ISO-certified (International Organization for Standardization). This type of acquisition typically took far longer to integrate due to the complexity of decisions that had to be made. However, in this type of acquisition both companies would typically have significant resources to dedicate to the integration process, thereby facilitating the effort.	StrataCom, Inc.

lated plan for achieving fast and seamless integration. From the customer's perspective, Cisco wanted to make it appear that the acquired company was a part of Cisco from the day the deal closed. Yet, Cisco was very aware that massive and unilateral changes could potentially have enormous disruptive effects. Cisco's mandatory steps drew on the experience gained from numerous previous acquisitions and provided a framework and timeline for the integration team to tackle their job (see Exhibit 10 for more details on the mandatory integration steps).

The mandatory steps effectively broke down into three primary categories: merging information systems, aligning current processes, and implementing ongoing methodologies. The merging of information systems involved both the materials resource planning system (MRP) and the product testing system (Autotest). Due to the large number of acquisitions undertaken, it would have been incredibly complex and redundant for Cisco to main-

tain multiple systems. Thus, the integration team was tasked with transitioning the acquired company to Cisco's MRP and Autotest systems in a staged process that typically achieved full integration within 90 days. Although an aggressive timeline, the rapid implementation of the Autotest system ensured that the product quality would meet Cisco's standards. The move to Cisco's MRP system not only aided the sales staff in placing orders for the new product, but also helped identify opportunities for part consolidation and supplier rationalization.

In aligning the acquired company's current processes with Cisco's, the integration team focused on three areas: evaluating suppliers, assessing outsourcing options, and determining product lifecycles. In the first area, the integration team reviewed the suppliers of the acquired company, with the ultimate goal of transitioning them to Cisco's vendors. Supplier choice was a difficult decision, and factors such as continuity of supply, on-time delivery, quality, customer support, and cost were all taken into consideration. The second area, assessing outsourcing options, examined the role that outsourced manufacturing could play in the acquired company. Cisco Relied heavily upon outsourcing, and mandated that all piece part assembly and board level testing be outsourced. A comprehensive outsourcing plan was crafted to move the acquired company toward optimal use of outsourcing. The third area, determining product lifecycle, was one of the most important tasks of the integration team. The acquired company's products needed to be segmented by development phase so that appropriate decisions could be made about their integration into Cisco's organization. In all, these steps were usually completed within 90 days of the time of the merger.

The last category of mandatory integration steps was the implementation of ongoing methodologies, including defect reduction, forecasting, and new product introductions. To reduce defects, Cisco required the acquired company to immediately implement statistical process controls. While this functionality would later be provided by the Autotest system, quickly reducing and maintaining low defect rates was a crucial driver of financial performance. Cisco also required that the acquired company adopt its forecasting methodology within 30 days of the close of the deal. Forecasting at Cisco stressed joint development of production and sales volume predictions between Cisco's business-unit level marketing group and the management of the acquired company. Cisco believed there was great value in the analytical rigor of a detailed plan with clearly articulated assumptions. Finally, the integration team implemented Cisco's new product introduction methodology. Within 90 days of purchase, the new company would use Cisco's NPI model—including cross-functional teams—on all products that were early enough in their development cycle to benefit.

Situation-Specific Integration Steps

While Cisco had a number of mandatory integration steps, it handled manufacturing facility and employee integration issues on a situation-specific basis. On the manufacturing facility side, the preliminary question was whether to leave the acquired facilities essentially intact, fully integrate them into Cisco's facilities, or any one of many options in between. The time required to reach decisions on these issues and implement a transition plan also varied widely from acquisition to acquisition. A team, made up of staff from Cisco's new product introduction group, considered a number of factors in making their recommendations on how to treat an acquired company's production facilities. These factors included the business plan for the acquired company (e.g., projected volumes, ramp-up timing, product lifecycles), the competencies of the acquired company's production facilities (e.g., quality controls, production processes), an affordability assessment (e.g., how can we maximize the

Exhibit 8   Sample List of Manufacturing Due Diligence Issues

Issues	Sample Questions
Target market dynamics	• What was the demand forecast? • What were the gross margin targets?
Product portfolio	• What was the product set? • What was the development status on new products?
Manufacturing technology	• What was their process for designing products for manufacturability, testability, cost, cycle time, and volume?
Verification process	• How did they conduct internal and external design verification?
Supply base and order fulfillment	• Who was on their approved vendor and subcontractor list? • How did they manage their material pipeline and inventory?
Development, release, and manufacturing process	• What was their philosophy on design? • How much were they influenced by sales versus engineering? • Did they utilize cross-functional teams in the development process?
Manufacturing process competencies	• Did they have any specific manufacturing core competencies that should be taken into consideration?
Organizational structure	• How were they organized? • How many people were in each area?
Leadership/management competencies	• What was the skill level of the work force as a whole? • What were the leadership capabilities of the management team?

value of the company's products?), and an assessment of other intangibles (e.g., how would a plant closure affect the R&D and engineering effort?).

During the period the team was developing the recommendation on whether and when to merge plants, Cisco would continue to operate out of the acquired company's production facility. However, since Cisco was ultimately accountable for the quality of the products coming out of the acquired company's plants, the team would frequently audit the company's quality control processes to ensure that they met Cisco's standards. In addition, Cisco mandated that its acquired companies implement certain of its engineering and manufacturing procedures in their production facilities and go through an ISO (International Organization for Standardization) audit of those procedures within six to twelve months.

In terms of employee integration, Cisco would customize a plan to meet the needs of the acquired company's labor force. Cisco would offer employees flexibility around the transition process (e.g., timing of geographic moves), in addition to the

Exhibit 9   Post-Acquisition Integration Steps

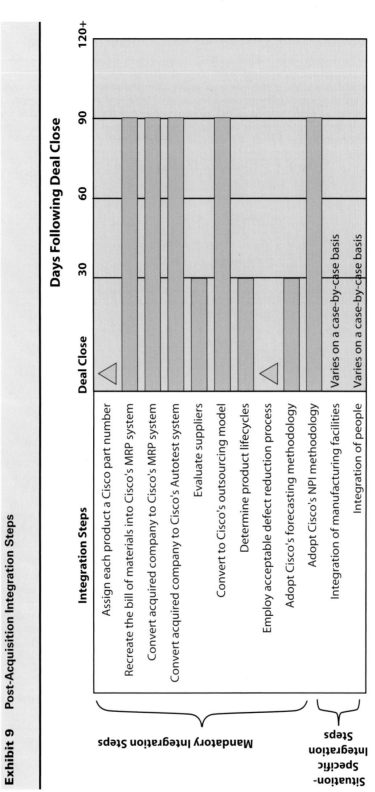

Days Following Deal Close

Integration Steps	Deal Close	30	60	90	120+

Assign each product a Cisco part number

Recreate the bill of materials into Cisco's MRP system

Convert acquired company to Cisco's MRP system

Convert acquired company to Cisco's Autotest system

Evaluate suppliers

Convert to Cisco's outsourcing model

Determine product lifecycles

Employ acceptable defect reduction process

Adopt Cisco's forecasting methodology

Adopt Cisco's NPI methodology

Integration of manufacturing facilities — Varies on a case-by-case basis

Integration of people — Varies on a case-by-case basis

Mandatory Integration Steps

Situation-Specific Integration Steps

Source: Casewriter interviews.

Exhibit 10 Mandatory Manufacturing Integration Steps

Assign each of the acquired company's products a new Cisco product number

Cisco assigned a new product number to each of the acquired company's products that would be entered into Cisco's MRP (manufacturing resource planning) database. At the initial phase, there would be no other details on the product (e.g., parts, cost data) in the database, so a transaction could not be fully conducted electronically through Cisco's MRP database. Instead, if a customer placed an order for one of the acquired company's products, Cisco would transfer the order internally (by phone, email, or fax) to the acquired company's order desk for fulfillment. The acquired company would then make, test, and ship the product from its facilities. However, all of this was done behind the scenes; from the customer's perspective, they were dealing directly with Cisco. (See **Table 2** below.)

Table 2 Order and Product Flow

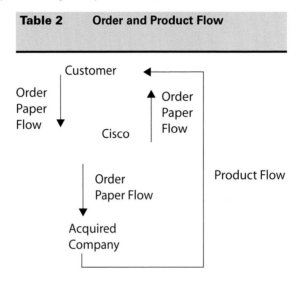

Recreate the bill of materials into Cisco's MRP database

The next step was to recreate the bill of materials for each of the acquired company's products into Cisco's MRP database. This involved a detailed part-mapping process whereby a team from Cisco's component engineering group would analyze each specific part that went into each product to determine if an identical part was already used by Cisco—and therefore, already in the MRP database. The process involved an extensive review of each part's data sheet, since parts that seemed identical on the surface could be ever-so-slightly different in reality. If an exact match were found, then the part would be given the existing Cisco part's number. If no match were found, then the part would be given a new part number. Since it was a detailed and time-consuming process, often taking up to 90 days to complete, the detailed part-by-part mapping would not be done for those products that were slated for short-term production or end of life.

While the primary goal of the part-mapping process was to "get it done," a secondary goal was to identify opportunities to consolidate parts and vendors. Cisco's goal was to utilize existing, pre-approved vendors where possible and minimize the growth of its parts database. In other words, if the acquired company was buying a part that was almost identical to one that Cisco was already buying from another vendor, the team would flag it as an opportunity for near-term substitution. However, since the overarching goal was to integrate the parts data into Cisco's MRP database, only the obvious substitution opportunities were identified during this process. As Crabb described it: "We'll take all the low hanging fruit, but we don't try to do everything at this point."

Convert the acquired company to Cisco's MRP system

Once all the parts had been given Cisco part numbers, Cisco would convert the company over to Cisco's MRP system. Unlike some of its competitors, Cisco did not believe in running multiple MRP systems in parallel; instead, Cisco made it mandatory for acquired companies to convert to Cisco's MRP system. However, in some cases, Cisco would recommend that the acquired company keep its own MRP system in place for its short-term production products or end of life products. Once the company had converted to Cisco's MRP system, Cisco had all the necessary infrastructure required to plan, build, and ship the acquired company's products. Typically conversion to Cisco's MRP system would take place within 90 days of close.

Convert the acquired company to Cisco's Autotest system

Cisco considered its Autotest system—a software-based automated testing system that measured the functionality and configuration of products—to be an essential component of its overall quality control process. The system worked by running data from the manufacturing process through a set of test "scripts." The Autotest system analyzed the data and determined whether the product passed or failed the tests, and under what conditions. The Autotest system was networked to Cisco's MRP system, enabling it also to test final product configuration to ensure that it matched the customer's order. Since Cisco sold many built-to-order, highly configurable products, there were numerous opportunities to make mistakes. The Autotest system gave the operator an almost foolproof way to ensure

Exhibit 10 (continued)

that the right product was being shipped to the customer. Cisco's external factories and sub-assembly contractors were also networked into the Autotest system.

If Cisco decided to continue operating an acquired company's plant for an extended period of time, then Cisco would require that the Autotest system be implemented in the acquired company's manufacturing facility. To set up the Autotest system, the integration team had to first determine whether the company had a set of written diagnostics for each product, since diagnostics were needed to write the test scripts. If the company did not have written diagnostics—which was typically the case—then development engineers from the relevant Cisco business unit would work with engineers from the acquired company to write diagnostics for the Autotest system.

On average it took three months to get the Autotest system up and running in an acquired company; however, it could take longer in cases where the engineering department was making significant changes to product design. During the period in which the Autotest system was being set up, Cisco depended on the acquired company's existing test processes for quality control—usually a set of PC-driven tests that required an operator to enter the script coding, run the test, and watch the results on the computer screen. While these types of tests were adequate for a small company, they were prone to human error, which was why Cisco mandated conversion to the Autotest system. In the best case scenario, the implementation of the Autotest system would coincide with the ramp-up in the acquired company's production volume.

Evaluate suppliers

Cisco's supply operations (supply ops) group evaluated, approved, and managed suppliers for both Cisco and its acquired companies. To qualify as an approved Cisco vendor, the vendor had to meet pre-determined financial and business criteria, such as:

> Cisco could represent no more than 20% of the supplier's business, so that fluctuations in Cisco's demand did not threaten continuity of supply,
>
> The vendor had to be in solid financial standing, and
>
> The vendor had to rate highly on a quarterly scorecard administered by Cisco which measured performance against a series of [criteria], including on-time delivery, lead time, quality level, customer support, and cost.

Cisco's supply ops group began to evaluate an acquired company's suppliers during the due diligence process to identify any risks to continuity of supply following the acquisition. Within 30 days of close the supply ops group was expected to have developed a plan for how to handle the supplier base. The goal was to convert the acquired companies to Cisco suppliers over time. However, the desire to use Cisco vendors had to be weighed against the impact the conversion would have on the continuity of supply and the development time for new products—in addition to the cost of the effort. As a result, Cisco rarely made supplier changes for products slated for short term production or end of life. For products slated for long term production and new products, Cisco's supply ops group evaluated new suppliers using the same criteria used to add suppliers to Cisco's approved vendor list. Marc Beckman, senior manager of global supply management for electronic components at Cisco, explained:

> We want to be able to influence supplier selection decisions just like we do here at Cisco. On the other hand, we don't want to impact the acquired company's business in a negative way. If we can switch to an existing Cisco supplier without having an adverse impact on their business, then we do. If we think it will have a real adverse impact, then we won't make the switch; we'll approve the vendor, but only for that *particular* product. If it's a critical supplier for a new product and we're too far down the road on development to switch, then we'll evaluate the proposed supplier and analyze the risks on a case by case basis.
>
> One thing we are sensitive about is the effect our decisions have on suppliers who have been supporting the acquired company over a period of time. We will often evaluate the impact of switching suppliers on the existing suppliers, and if the impact appears severe, we will try to work out an arrangement whereby they can support the product for a period of time until they can re-address their customer base.

Convert to Cisco's outsourcing model

Cisco required that the companies that it acquired convert to its outsourced manufacturing model as well. There were essentially three levels of outsourcing: piece part assembly, board level testing, and final assembly and testing. As a rule, Cisco always outsourced the first two to contract manufacturers. They also outsourced the third—final assembly and testing—in the case of products fulfilled by external factories. If the acquired company were operating under a highly vertically-integrated production model, Cisco developed a transition plan for outsourcing the piece part assembly and intermediate testing activities, at a minimum. However, for products slated for short-term production or end of life, Cisco would often leave their in-house manufacturing processes in place. Cisco had also explored the possibility of leveraging its contract manufacturers to produce, fulfill, and provide after-sale support for products slated for end of life—but had not yet tested this option. Cisco's goal was to have a comprehensive outsourcing plan in place within 90 days of the close.

Determine product lifecycles

In order to determine how to treat each of the acquired company's products, the manufacturing group first needed to determine how long Cisco planned to manufacture and support each product. Due to their importance, a first pass at these decisions was typically made within 30 days of the close. In order to make these decisions, the manufacturing

Exhibit 10   (continued)

team carefully reviewed the business case underlying the acquisition. In some cases Cisco acquired a company for its current line of products—meaning that most of its products would be slated for long-term production. In other cases, Cisco acquired the company for its potential to develop next generation products, rather than for its existing products—meaning that many of the existing products would be slated for short-term production or positioned for end of life. However, even if a product were slated for end of life, it would be phased out over time, rather than eliminated outright, since Cisco's goal was to assure continuity of supply to the acquired company's customers immediately following the acquisition.

Employ an acceptable defect reduction process

Cisco required that a basic statistical process control [mechanism] be put in place to track yield and failure data on a daily and weekly basis. While the Autotest system would ultimately produce these data, Cisco mandated that the acquired company have an acceptable process in place at the time of the close for charting the data—even if it were a manual process.

Adopt Cisco's forecasting methodology

Following an acquisition, Cisco continued to depend on the acquired company to provide product booking forecasts, since Cisco believed that the acquired company was most familiar with the demands of its own customers and marketplace. However, the acquired company would submit its forecasts to Cisco's business-unit level marketing group to discuss and revise, if needed. Input from Cisco's business-level marketing group was essential since they had the experience to project the implications of leveraging Cisco's sales and distribution channels on an acquired company's production volume. Since the forecast would ultimately be entered into Cisco's MRP system and drive production decisions, it was important to reach consensus on it. As a result, Cisco required that acquired companies adopt Cisco's approach to forecasting within 30 days of the close.

Cisco required both a monthly review as well as a transaction-level forecast, and was just as interested in the assumptions that were used to develop the forecasts as in the forecasts themselves. Cisco required that acquired companies adopt Cisco's "envelope of demand" methodology of monthly forecasting, which entailed providing a set of quantified upside and downside ranges to the forecast. As part of the forecast, the marketing group included detailed assumptions about what would need to happen to achieve the upside and downside forecasts (e.g., three accounts would need to sign contracts to meet the upside forecast) and they provided probability assessments for these scenarios. By providing analytical rigor behind a set of ranges to the forecast, the marketing group helped the manufacturing group determine the types and levels of buffers to set up in manufacturing.

Adopt Cisco's New Product Introduction (NPI) methodology

Cisco required that the companies it acquired adopt Cisco's NPI process for its new product development where feasible (sometimes new products were too far along the development process to convert to Cisco's NPI process). On the day the deal closed, Cisco would make a determination as to which new products were early enough in their development cycle to convert to Cisco's NPI process, and within 90 days of the close, the NPI process would be implemented.

traditional economic incentives. For example, they might be given the option to continue working at the acquired company's plant for as long as the facility was maintained; move to one of Cisco's production facilities in California; or move into another part of the Cisco organization (e.g., quality control, field service). Cisco believed in being open, honest, sensitive, and flexible with the employees of the acquired company during the post-acquisition integration process.

THE SUMMA FOUR ACQUISITION

Founded in 1976, Summa Four had become a leading provider of open programmable digital switching systems, sold primarily to telecommunications service providers worldwide (i.e., AT&T, MCI, Sprint, British Telecom). By 1998, Summa Four had installed over 2,000 switches in over 30 countries. Approximately 50% of its systems were installed outside the United States. Customers used Summa Four's open programmable switching platforms for basic call switching as well as for delivering value-added services, such as voice mail, calling card applications, voice-activated dialing, intelligent 800-call routing, and voice and fax messaging. Summa Four was also developing a next-generation product—code-named Project Alpha[8]—that represented the industry's first standards-based open programmable switch.

Due to the deregulation of the telecommunications industry, service providers were in a fierce, competitive race to develop and deliver these types of enhanced services to their customers. Prior to the advent of open programmable switch-

---

[8] Name has been disguised.

Exhibit 11   Summa Four's Product Line

Product Name	VCO/Series 80	VCO/Series 20	VCO/4K
Introduction Date	February 1995	September 1996	March 1998
Description	High-density open-programmable switch used for application development, highly distributed intelligent peripheral implementations, and scaleable transport deployments in both wireline and wireless networks	Same functionality as VCO/Series 80, but offers a smaller footprint and rack-mountable design, which makes it suitable for turnkey integration with other application systems	World's highest density open-programmable switch
Density	2,048 timeslots	2,048 timeslots	4,096 timeslots
Fully-NEBS Compliant	Yes	No	Yes

Source: www.summafour.com, casewriter interview.

ing technology, service providers typically used large-scale proprietary central office switches. The proprietary nature of these switches made service providers dependent on their switching equipment vendors to help develop new services. However, open programmable switches allowed service providers to develop or purchase their own applications, which reduced development costs and accelerated time to market. Summa Four's company vision was to "provide open, intelligent, standards-based switches to telecom service providers worldwide, fundamentally changing the cost and time-to-market for deploying new networks and services."

Cisco announced it would acquire the Manchester, New Hampshire–based company in July 1998. The acquisition was intended to enable Cisco to offer value-added telephony applications to telecommunication service providers, and extend these services to IP (Internet Protocol) networks, which were able to transmit voice, data, and video.

Summa Four Product Line

Summa Four's product line included the VCO Series/20, the VCO Series/80, and the VCO/4K—all of which were highly configurable and built-to-order. While Project Alpha was still in the development phase at the time of the acquisition, and over a year away from product launch, it was a key reason behind Cisco's interest in Summa Four.

All products in the VCO family shared a similar architecture and many of the same features. (See Exhibit 11 for an overview of Summa Four's products.) The key distinguishing feature among them was their time slot density (the greater the time slots, the more lines could run in and out of the switch). The VCO Series/80—introduced in February 1995—offered a non-blocking switching matrix of 2,048 time slots. In addition, the Series/80 was fully NEBS (Network Equipment Building Systems) compliant—meaning that it conformed to a specific set of environmental compatibility criteria (e.g., physical protection, electromagnetic compatibility, and electrical safety) that most of the large telecommunication service providers required. Smaller telecommunication service providers were often willing to

work with products that were not fully NEBS compliant in order to gain a particular design advantage or reduce costs.

The VCO Series/20—introduced in September 1996—offered the same number of time slots as the Series/80, but was a far smaller unit than the Series/80. Its small footprint and rack-mountable design made it well-suited for turnkey integration with other application subsystems. However, the Series/20 was not fully NEBS compliant, due to tradeoffs in design that would have been required to comply with NEBS standards. Both the VCO Series/20 and VCO Series/80 were considered mature products and the plan was to migrate customers to the VCO/4K over time.

The VCO/4K was Summa Four's newest and most advanced product. Introduced in March 1998, the VCO/4K was the world's highest density programmable switch. It offered a non-blocking switching matrix of 4,096 time slots, was fully NEBS compliant, and included all of the other features common to the Series/20 and Series/80. While the VCO/4K was still in field trial deployment, it was ramping up faster than expected. While the initial signs were positive, Cisco would have to wait to see the market's reaction to the 4K before it could make a determination about its potential lifespan. If the 4K turned out to be a highly successful product and the decision was made to keep its production in Manchester, Cisco would need to invest in both equipment and labor in order to increase the capacity of the Manchester manufacturing facility. Given that Cisco's California manufacturing facilities had additional capacity and had all the key testing infrastructure in place, Cisco was unsure of whether this type of investment into Summa Four's Manchester facility was prudent.

Summa Four Organization

In September of 1998, the idea of being acquired by Cisco was still very new to Summa Four's employees. At the time of the acquisition announcement, Summa Four had 210 employees, including 65 development engineers and 23 employees in the manufacturing organization. While there was a good deal of excitement about the prospect of working for Cisco, a number of employees voiced reservations. One manager said,

"This is an exciting time, but I worry that a number of changes are going to be forced down our throats."

One of the areas that attracted the most concern was the cultural implications of being acquired by a much larger firm. Summa Four's management knew that they were just one of many in a long line of Cisco acquisitions. They had built their business in a simple functional organization, where personal connections and informal processes allowed for quick action. In a larger organization, effective problem solving would likely require a host of specialists and multiple organizational units, resulting in a far more complex process. Some employees worried that the feel of working in the high-energy world of a small business would be lost. Dick Swee captured much of this sentiment when he said, "There is a big difference between a $10 billion organization and a $50 million organization. We've been used to the feel of a small company, and that is certainly going to change."

There was also concern about the level of influence that Summa Four employees would be able to exert within Cisco. It was unclear what [role] their current products would play among the Cisco offerings, and their ability to guide the integration process might be severely limited. With well over 10,000 people working for Cisco, Summa Four employees worried that Cisco would not be very receptive to their input. However, with the New England job market so hot, at least there would be attractive alternatives for most of the experienced engineers if things didn't work out.

Summa Four Manufacturing

Summa Four's headquarters and manufacturing plant shared the same facility in Manchester, which was less than an hour away from one of Cisco's remote R&D facilities, located in Chelmsford, Massachusetts. Cisco's due diligence team found Summa Four's plant to be clean, orderly, and efficient. Summa Four's plant compared favorably to many of the other plants that Cisco had acquired. However, the plant used a home-grown, PC-based test system that was far less automated than Cisco's Autotest system. Summa Four's MRP system was from Symix, a supplier of systems for midrange manufacturers of discrete, configurable products. It did not appear that the Symix software was compatible with Cisco's MRP system.

As for its manufacturing processes, Summa Four had moved toward more and more outsourcing with each generation of products. For example, almost all of the assembly and testing for Summa Four's early VCO Series/20 and Series/80 products was conducted in-house, including power supply assembly and board testing. On the other hand, in the case of its newer VCO/4K product, Summa Four had outsourced most of the piece part assembly.

Suppliers

Summa Four purchased approximately 5,000 individual parts from 250 suppliers, 85 of whom were new to Cisco. While the Summa Four acquisition was far smaller than the $4.6 billion acquisition of StrataCom in 1996, Summa Four had a comparable number of parts and suppliers to StrataCom, reflecting the complexity of the Summa Four integration process. Of some concern was the fact that approximately 200 of Summa Four's parts were sole-sourced, meaning that only one vendor supplied each of those parts, which created a pricing and continuity of supply risk.

Fortuitously, Summa Four had recently contracted with Sanmina—a Cisco approved back-plane and chassis integration company—to do sub-assembly for its VCO/4K product. Sanmina had quickly become one of Summa Four's major suppliers. Cisco considered Sanmina to be a potential candidate for testing the idea of leveraging a contract manufacturer to handle the production, fulfillment, and after-sale support of mature products in the future.

DECISIONS AHEAD

Keller anticipated that the post-acquisition integration of Summa Four would be relatively complex given the company's remote location, its line of legacy products, and its number of employees. In a week's time he would have to present his recommendations on how to integrate Summa Four's products, plant, and people. His initial thoughts were that it would make the most sense to transfer the Alpha generation to the main Cisco facility and leave the other products where they were, to eventually be phased out. While this appeared to be the easiest route to take, would it deliver the type of [. . .] returns that Cisco had come to expect? What would he do with the Manchester plant if expected demand were to increase dramatically? What were the risks inherent in these choices? What would be the impact on retaining Summa Four's key employees?

As Keller sat back to consider these issues, he received a phone call informing him of yet another Cisco acquisition on the horizon, this time of Selsius Systems of Texas— a maker of products which allowed companies to combine voice and data communications on their corporate networks. Keller knew that Summa Four would likely serve as a role model for the Selsius acquisition integration process and potentially many more to come. He knew that he would have to think very carefully about the myriad of integration issues facing Cisco with the Summa Four acquisition.

Multiplication of Best Practices at Holcim: A History of Firsts

403-004-1

1 INTRODUCTION

In August 1998, Holcim, one of the world's largest cement producers,[1] acquired a 25% stake in Thailand's Siam City Cement and, together with key local managers, assumed management responsibility in March 1999. At the time, the country's second largest cement producer was in deep trouble as a result of the Asian Crisis of 1997–1998. Additionally the Thai cement market[2] had suffered a 50% decline in demand, falling from 36 million tons per year in 1997 to only 18 million tons per year in 1999. However, Thailand's total production capacity was 52 million tons—more than twice the annual consumption.

Three years after the acquisition, Siam City Cement posted excellent business results. The company turned a loss

---

This case was written by **Heidi Armbruster, Stefano Borzillo** and **Professor Gilbert Probst,** University of Geneva, HEC. It is intended to be used as the basis for class discussion rather than to illustrate either effective or ineffective handling of a management situation.

The case was made possible by the co-operation of Holcim.

© 2003, H Armbruster, S Borzillo and G Probst, University of Geneva, HEC, Switzerland.

Distributed by The European Case Clearing House, England and USA.

North America, phone: +1 781 239 5884, fax: +1 781 239 5885, e-mail: ECCHBabson@aol.com.

Rest of the World, phone: +44 (0)1234 750903, fax: +44 (0)1234 751 125, e-mail: ECCH@cranfield.ac.uk.

All rights reserved. Printed in UK and USA. Web Site: http://www.ecch.cranfield.ac.uk.

---

[1] For further information about Holcim, please see Figure 1.

[2] See Figure 2 for more details on the Thai cement market.

of 0.6 billion Baht[3] into a profit of 2.2 billion Baht and the market share increased from 25% in 1999 to 30% in 2001.[4]

2 A SUCCESS STORY IN THE MAKING: LAUNCHING WEBSALES IN THAILAND

After the acquisition, the new Siam City Cement management team—comprising Thai and Holcim managers—decided that Siam City Cement needed to make a strategic shift in order to meet the new market situation in Thailand. Siam City Cement had a clear vision:

> "We want to move from being a production-focused company to a customer-centric organization. Our aspiration is to become the leading domestic cement supplier in Thailand through total cost leadership, and superior marketing and distribution approaches, thus achieving above industry profitability."[5]

To achieve these strategic objectives, the setting up of adequate processes and tools and employee training to handle these tools were seen as crucial for the company's future success. Felix Hoechner, Senior Vice President Knowledge & Information Technology,[6] faced the following challenge at Siam City Cement:

> "When I first arrived, there was nothing here and there were no qualified people. We had to find the right people

---

[3] 1,000 Baht are 23 US$ (October 28, 2002).

[4] Company information.

[5] Company information.

[6] As [of] 2002 Felix Hoechner [became] the CEO of Holcim Services (Asia) Ltd. (HSEA) [in 2002].

Figure 1 Geographical Expansion of Holcim 1910–2000

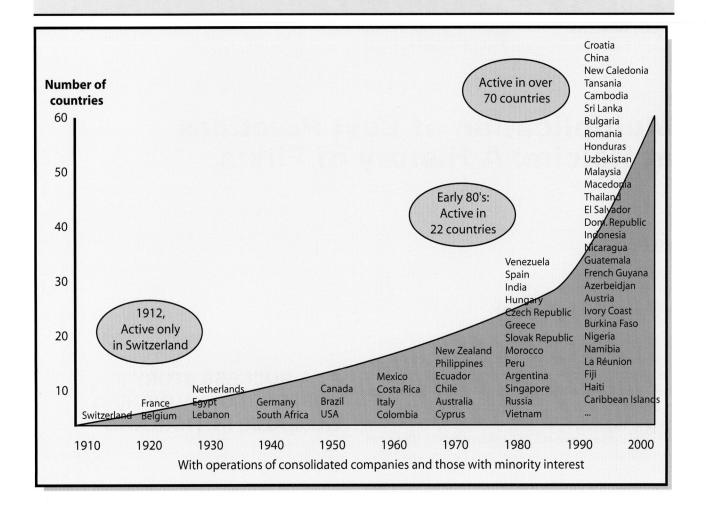

Figure 2 Thai Cement Market in 2001

	Siam Cement	Siam City Cement	TPI Polene	Ciment Français	Cemex Mexico
Market Share 2001	38%	28%	18%	13%	3%
Capacity	19.4 mio tpa	12.3 mio tpa	7.6 mio tpa	5.8 mio tpa	0.6 mio tpa

with the right skills at the right place and implement an IT infrastructure."

The aim was obvious: in order to become a customer-oriented organization, the management team had to implement a radical change in terms of both the company's infrastructure and employee skills. Consequently, to improve the information sharing between customers and employees a technical infrastructure, comprising features such as an integrated telephone exchange, a voice mail system between the three offices in Bangkok and Saraburi, and an e-mail system, was set up. They also implemented a SAP System and trained their employees to handle it. The SAP system went live in May 2000.

2.1 A Customer-Centric Organization: Implementation of webSALES

In May 2000, the executive committee of Siam City Cement decided to launch webSALES, a milestone on the way to a customer-centric organization. In the words of Chantana Sukumanont, Senior Vice-President cement marketing:

> *"Siam City Cement's key strategic objective is to be customer centric throughout the entire organization. WebSALES is one element of our Customer Relationship Management (CRM) activities that are at the heart of our value proposition to our customers."*

WebSALES is a web-based platform that allows customers to order their cement via the Internet. This tool provides a 24-hour, seven days a week and 365 days a year ordering service. Additionally, it offers a 24-hour delivery service for orders placed via the Internet. This day and night service enhances [customer] service as well as offering [customers] a high degree of flexibility.

2.2 The first e-business initiative in Asia

In order to ensure the successful implementation and to supervise the execution of webSALES, the company formed a steering workgroup comprised of executive committee members.[7] The implementation of webSALES was completed within five months following a five-step approach.[8]

Step 1: Evaluation and assessment of webSALES
The first step was the evaluation and assessment of webSALES, which took two weeks. Siam City Cement first had to confirm the compatibility of the project with the sales strategy. A project plan was developed and a project team established. This project team consisted of 60 people, mostly company employees and some external consultants from Price Water-

house Coopers (PwC/IBM). The project was supervised by Felix Hoechner and Chantana Sukumanont.

Step 2: Analysis and definition of webSALES
A closer analysis and definition of the webSALES tool were developed in the second step.

The challenge was to understand the sales environment and client expectations. In order to gain greater clarity, focus groups of pre-selected customers were set up. The project team developed a conceptual "to be" design for webSALES processes and showed how they would integrate the organization and the impacts this would have on its policies. This step took 3 weeks.

Step 3: Design of webSALES
Step three included the design of webSALES, which took 4 weeks.

When the project team designed the actual Web page through which online orders would be placed, the customer focus groups were asked to provide feedback on what they thought was the most "user-friendly" Web page. The project team also designed the webSALES "to be" processes and determined the impacts of these, regarding structure, skills, etc., on the organization.

Step 4: Construction of webSALES
This step entailed the actual construction of webSALES.

The project team finalized webSALES, integrating testing plans and preparing new processes and procedures for documentation, within 5 weeks. The different webSALES tools were tested. Meanwhile, the company staff was being trained by the Training Management Team—they would be ready to use the webSALES software on the day of implementation.

Step 5: Final implementation of webSALES
During the 5-week implementation phase of webSALES, previously selected pilot customers "tested" the new online-purchasing software and provided feedback. This allowed some refinements to be made before its rollout.

Large workshops taught selected customers how to purchase cement via webSALES. During this "teaching-learning phase" customers were formally given access to the manifold services available through webSALES. To additionally support customers, a Customer Call Center was installed that would allow Siam City Cement to help several clients at a time. It would, furthermore, be a useful unit where customers could [ask] their questions and express their needs.

The first online sale of cement was made on 15 September 2000. Not only was this the first online cement order for Siam City Cement, but it was also the first one in Asia.

2.3 Siam City Customer Call Center

A Customer Call Center was established and launched on 15 September 2000—the same day that webSALES went live.

---

[7] For the team structure in the webSALES implementation process, please see Figure 3.

[8] For an overview of the implementation steps, please see Figure 4.

Figure 3   Team Structure at SIAM CITY CEMENT

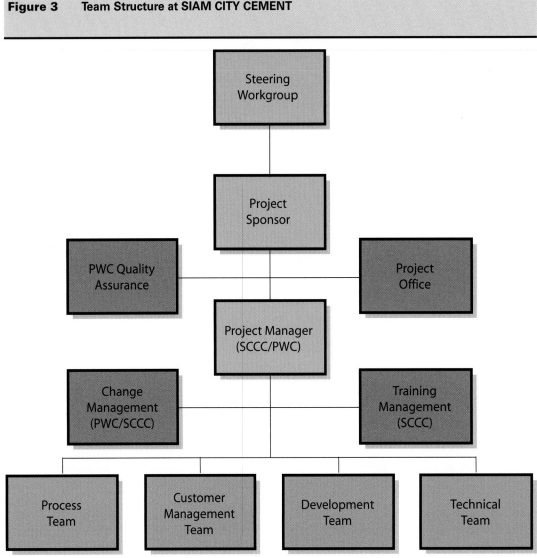

The Call Center's objective was to provide customers with a 24 hours a day, 7 days a week single point of contact for the support of webSALES and for normal customer inquiries. WebSALES customers were especially targeted; here they could ask questions and make requests if they had a problem purchasing cement online. Experts were assigned to assist customers by phone and offer solutions to their purchasing problems, or simply offer them product information. Khun Banjong Jaikam, purchasing officer of Lertwasin Ltd. in Chieng Mai, confirmed:

> *"Whenever I had a problem with the webSALES system I called the Siam City Customer Call Center via a toll-free number, because I knew they would assist me. They are experts on the webSALES system."*

Currently, the Call Center team is building up a database of "frequently asked questions" coupled with "best delivered solutions." This allows them to build up knowledge and offer customers quick "pre-made" solutions, instead of

"re-inventing the wheel" each time a similar request is made or question is asked. At the moment, the Call Center can answer 80% of customer questions immediately.

2.4 Results—webSALES' success in Thailand

Currently, 318 Siam City Cement customers order cement via webSALES, which means that 75% of all sales are placed through webSALES. The remaining 25% are placed by fax. The marketing and sales costs decreased from 3.5% in 1999 to 2.5% in 2002.

Not only the figures prove the success of webSALES; there are also customers such as Paisan Sricharoenchit, one of the larger Siam City Cement customers, who attest to the benefits of webSALES. He remarks:

> *"Before webSALES it was complicated and difficult to place an order. You weren't able to check the credit limit or the*

Figure 4   Steps of webSALES Implementation in Thailand

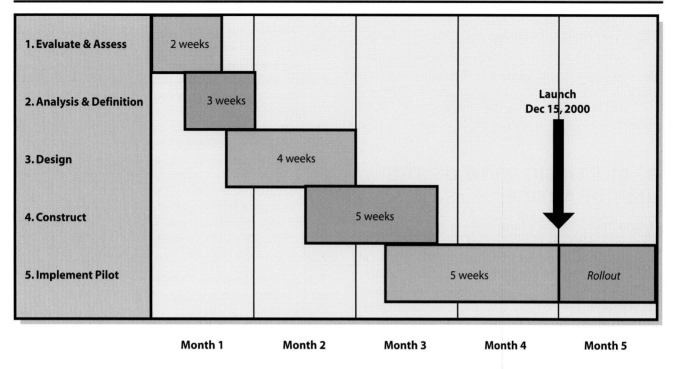

logistic process. Life is much easier with webSALES. It is easy to place an order, we can see when our truck arrives, we can check the credit limit and, if we have a question, we can always call the Customer Call Center. Compared to other providers of cement, Siam City Cement is number one in service and webSALES is by far the easiest tool to use."

Not only the larger clients are convinced of web-SALES' benefits; also the smaller clients, who demand only a few tons per month, have been converted. Their first contact with computers and the Internet was when ordering by webSALES. Pongchai Amornkitja, owner of Bangyai Karwasaduphan Ltd., a small construction material distributor, states:

"At the beginning I was not sure about webSALES, because it was the first time I had used a computer and the Internet. But all the information I got from webSALES, such as prices and promotions, and the speed, accuracy and simplicity of the system, convinced me. Now I completely trust this tool."

Although it is estimated that Internet users will increase by 70% per year, in 2000 there were only 1.8 million Internet users in Thailand, approximately 3% of the Thai population.[9] To encourage its customers to use webSALES and, therefore, the Internet, Siam City Cement provided free

PC[s] and free Internet access for each customer. As Chantana Sukumanont, remarks:

"After the customer training, they got used to webSALES and even became proud of using a PC. This was a driving force."

It was the extensive customer trainings with the help of the Siam City Cement trainers that made webSALES successful in Thailand. The well-educated trainers provided the support and intensive training to facilitate the use of the new technology for webSALES customers. The customers were given step-by-step training on each feature and the benefits of using webSALES were explained in detail.

With this training and belief in the benefits and user friendliness of webSALES, the customers could face the challenge of using the web-based tool.

2.5 Multiplication of webSALES in other Asian companies

Siam City Cement was the cement industry's pioneer in e-commerce in Asia. WebSALES' success also made the executive committee and Paul Hugentobler, at that time Area Manager of Holcim's Asia Pacific Group Region and today EXCO Member responsible for Northern Asean, South Asia, decide to multiply this tool to other Group companies in the region. This would lead to profits from the benefits of

---

[9] Company information.

webSALES and the company's experiences could be shared. In Paul Hugentobler's words:

> "We need to share best practices such as webSALES with other regions to enhance business performance and achieve company growth and profitability goals."

As a first step, they decided to multiply webSALES in Vietnam, where it went online on 1 December 2001. WebSALES is at present in preparation for implementation in Sri Lanka. Next year will see the start of webSALES in Indonesia.

3 MULTIPLICATION OF THE BEST PRACTICE "webSALES"

Holcim Vietnam has a leading position in the South Vietnamese cement market, supplying 1.9 million tons of cement. The company (formerly Morning Star Cement Ltd.) is a Joint Venture by the Holcim Group and Ha Tien 1 Cement Company, a member of the Vietnam Cement Corporation. The invested capital of Holcim Vietnam is US$388 million, in which the Holcim Group has a share of 65% and Ha Tien 1 a 35% share.

Morning Star officially changed its name to Holcim Vietnam in April 2002 to conform [to] Holcim's global branding strategy. Holcim Vietnam employs 600 skilled people at 3 different sites: a) at the Head Office; b) at the Cat Lai Terminal, both located in Ho Chi Minh City; and c) at the cement plant in Hon Chong Kien Giang, 300 km from Ho Chi Minh City.

Currently, in 2002, the South Vietnam cement consumption per capita is 265 kg. It is estimated that in 2007 this will be 454 kg per capita. The growth rate of cement consumption in South Vietnam during the next 3 years is predicted to be 14% (10% for Vietnam as a whole).[10]

3.1 Implementation of webSALES at Holcim Vietnam

To implement webSALES here, the company adopted exactly the same model as the one used for Siam City Cement in Thailand.[11]

3.1.1 Building a good Project Team As was done at Siam City Cement, a project team comprising skilled people was set up.[12] The team was led by a Steering Group consisting of Gerard Letelier, CEO at that time;[13] Felix Hoechner, CEO Holcim Services Asia, who had been part of

the Siam City Cement project; Laurent Houmard (Sales & Marketing Director of Holcim Vietnam), who was appointed "Project Sponsor" and was responsible for the Change Management; and Mr. Lam, a project manager.

The team was also strengthened by 2 Siam City Cement employees, who had come to Vietnam for 3 months to offer their support. One of them was Khun Sukanda, a project manager and member of the process team who had gained experience as part of the process team at Siam City Cement. The other person was Khun Chonlatee, also a member of the process team. At Siam City Cement she is called a "webSALES champion," meaning that she has mastered the software and can teach others to configure, install and use it efficiently. Both these Siam City Cement experts were able to convey their webSALES know-how to Holcim Vietnam.

To ensure that the know-how was properly transferred, Holcim Vietnam received valuable additional support from external PwC/IBM consultants who had also worked on the webSALES project at Siam City Cement.

3.1.2 The implementation process Following the same methodology as that at Siam City Cement, Holcim Vietnam first of all selected 27 of its customers (or distributors; 14 from Ho Chi Minh City, 7 from East Vietnam, 6 from the Mekong Region) and assessed their needs in terms of webSALES. This first evaluation (completed within 24 days) was made during one-to-one discussions with the customers; they were asked about the problems they had frequently encountered during the traditional cement purchasing process and to describe the logistics of this process.

> "My biggest problem used to be that as soon as I had finished placing my cement order by phone, I no longer controlled it. There was absolutely no way of knowing when the cement I had ordered would be placed on the delivery truck and when it would be delivered. This used to be embarrassing, because I myself then had to deliver the cement to my customers whom I could never precisely guarantee when their cement order would be available." (Huynh Tan Dinh, CMID Construction, Vietnamese customer)

These complaints and requests were analyzed by Laurent Houmard and his team and the customers' needs [were] defined. This analysis was followed by webSALES' definition and design phase (lasting 25 days) and thereafter by the construction period (lasting 22 days). During these phases Khun Sukanda and Khun Chonlatee, the two Thai webSALES specialists, coached Holcim Vietnam's employees. When the software was ready for use, it was implemented and went live on [. . .] 1 December 2001. The project had lasted 71 days.

A sophisticated Call Center, such as the one at Siam City Cement, has not yet been installed. Instead, a customer with a question can directly call a webSALES expert who will help him. However, Holcim Vietnam is considering installing a similar Call Center.

3.1.3 Training employees and customers to use webSALES Prior to the installation of webSALES,

---

[10] Company information.

[11] For an overview of the implementation steps, please see Figure 5.

[12] For the Team Structure, see Figure 6.

[13] In charge until 30 November 2001. Since 1 December 2001 Martin Foreman [has been] CEO of Holcim Vietnam.

Figure 5   Steps of webSALES Implementation in Vietnam

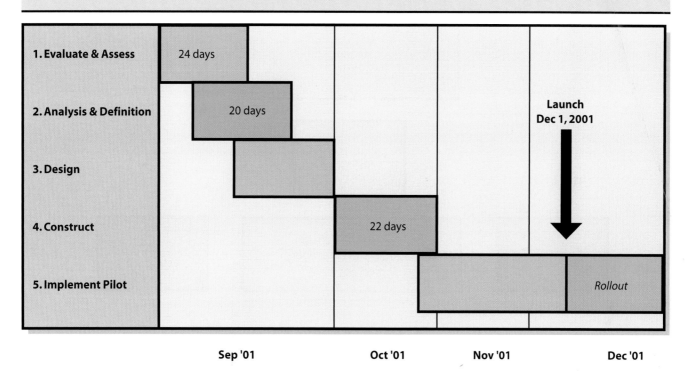

Project Duration: 71 Days

and following the exact Siam City Cement project management model, Holcim Vietnam had taught its employees how to use basic software and SAP. The day webSALES went live, [. . .] the employees were ready to use it efficiently.

Teaching Holcim staff how to use the webSALES software was just one part of the training process: the customers also had to be familiarized with its functioning. For this purpose, and adopting [the] Siam City Cement Thailand method, classroom training with webSALES exercises (using real-life data), enlivened by a webSALES instructor who interacted with the customers and answered their questions, were offered to 27 selected customers.

Since some of these customers had no computer skills, they brought family members (wife, daughter, son, etc.) along to help, bringing the number of participants to 48. Some of the customers delegated the task of placing online cement orders to their family members. The 27 customers each received 1 PC set, a modem and an Internet prepaid card. The training was in Vietnamese, with bilingual training materials being supplied.

"I have never been familiar with computers. As a matter of fact, before Holcim Vietnam provided me with a PC, I had never owned one. My wife and my daughter only use that computer to place cement orders via webSALES. I do not know how to use it, but I tell them when I want the online order to be placed and they do it. So I still have control of

the orders." (Nguyen Nam Cuong, a customer in Ho Chi Minh City, Vietnam)

Holcim Vietnam adopted the same "train the trainers" approach as Siam City Cement had implemented. This meant that the sales executives received special training to be able to explain webSALES whenever they visited a customer.

3.1.4 The first enhancements of webSALES
In Vietnam, new features, which had not been "copy-pasted" from Siam City Cement, were added to webSALES. The first enhancement was the "truck number report": each time a customer places an online cement order, a number is assigned to the truck—belonging to a delivery company—that will deliver the cement. The customer can then check this number on the webSALES site at any time. If the order requires several trucks, several numbers will be allocated. Each order number is linked to a truck number, as is also the case at Siam City Cement.

The second enhancement to be made was the "delivery update": if a truck delivery company has a truck available for Holcim sooner than planned, this truck will take the order instead of the assigned one and webSALES will automatically reflect a new truck number. The new feature allows for more flexibility and facilitates the delivery of cement. This "delivery update" has recently been implemented in Thailand as well, since it has proved to be a good practice in Vietnam.

Figure 6   Team Structure at HOLCIM VIETNAM

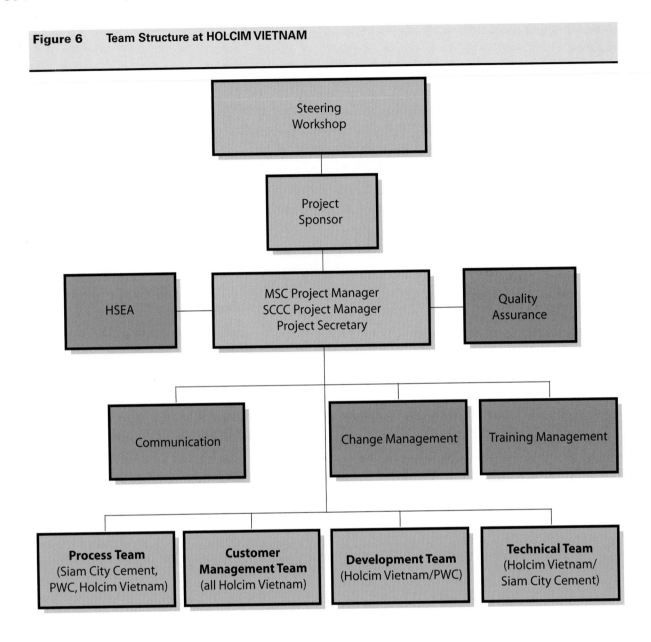

The third feature that was added to webSALES was the "delivery report," which allows customers to check how many tons of cement they have already ordered online from Holcim. The respective dates of order and truck numbers can also be checked.

"I feel more confident if I know exactly which truck is going to deliver the cement. It gives me some control of the situation, because I know that the truck driver will have to deliver on time with the right amount of cement. I also really appreciate being able to check online if the truck has already arrived at Holcim and is being loaded with the cement I ordered. It gives me an approximation of when I should be receiving my cement. Another good thing about webSALES is that I can check the totality of my past cement

invoices and quantities. This keeps me updated on my transactions and gives me an immediate overview of the fluctuations in my commercial activities." (Tram Bua, a customer in Ho Chi Minh region, Vietnam)

3.1.5   The second wave of customers This second phase lasted from 15 May to 31 August 2002. The aim was to get more customers to use webSALES. This time Laurent Houmard selected 36 new customers and processed them through the same training program. Holcim Vietnam financed the purchase of a PC set and a modem from a selected local supplier for each of these customers. Simultaneously, the 27 original PCs were retrieved from the first wave of customers (for licensing reason[s]), who then received an identical financing opportunity.

The training classes were successful and Holcim Vietnam now has 63 Web customers.

3.2 Results—webSALES' success in Vietnam

During December 2001, 18,000 tons of cement were sold via webSALES, which represented 24% of the total cement sales. In September 2002, customers purchased 103,874 tons online, which represented 78% of all sales.

Clearly the 36 new second wave customers contributed to this increase in the volume of online sales; but it is also clear that the general tendency of the 63 Web customers to buy online is increasing.

"Our sales have gone up; however, it is difficult to measure if this is due to webSALES. Nevertheless, since webSALES has been installed, we have greatly improved our customer relationship[s] and our cement market share in Vietnam has improved.

Because of the banking infrastructure in Vietnam, we still can't integrate e-payments into webSALES; payment is made in cash on delivery of the cement." (Laurent Houmard, project sponsor)

Holcim also analyzed the kind of problems with which the customers need support. They discovered two main reasons for these phone calls: 19% relate to webSALES' slow response time and 15% pertain to being disconnected when using webSALES. The company counted 338 support calls in December 2001 (the first month webSALES went live), whereas only 57 were made during the period [from] mid-May to [the] end [of] August 2002. This shows that customers were quickly familiarized with the usage of webSALES.

'Multiplying webSALES from Thailand to Vietnam, using a copy-paste philosophy, went very smoothly. We basically had to apply an appropriate project management model that could-be transferable from one country to another. Very few obstacles were encountered during this process and the Siam City Cement webSALES experts were committed to sharing their know-how with people at Holcim Vietnam. Experience has showed me that webSALES implementation is an easy process to experience and therefore can be copy-pasted throughout our Holcim Asian market.' (Felix Hoechner, CEO Holcim Services Asia)

Holcim Services Asia (HSEA) believe[s] [it] can use the Vietnamese enhancements to webSALES, and transfer them to Thailand. The creation of [ongoing] and transferable enhancements confirms Holcim's philosophy of using a good practice as a basis, developing it until it becomes a best practice and then "copy-pasting" it to other subsidiaries. These enhancements will also be multiplied to the webSALES that will be implemented at Holcim in Sri Lanka and PT Semen Cibinong in Indonesia. In turn, enhancements will be made in these two countries and then be "copy-

pasted" to Vietnam and Thailand, creating a feedback loop. This is an ongoing process that Holcim Services Asia wants to expand to its whole Asian market, making Holcim a faster learning organization.

4 HOLCIM SERVICES ASIA (HSEA) AND ITS ROLE IN THE MULTIPLICATION OF BEST PRACTICES

The implementation of webSALES in Thailand and Vietnam was a success and still is. Not only was it a transfer of a best practice from Thailand to Vietnam, it was more: it was—except for two small enhancements—copy-exactly the tool of webSALES and copy-exactly the implementation process of webSALES. In this instance, copying the same tool and the same implementation process and multiplying them to another Group company in Asia was also very profitable. Holcim Vietnam saved money because Vietnam adopted webSALES and its implementation process, which had already been developed and proved in Thailand.

This was the impetus for outsourcing all Information Technology (IT) services in Asia and creating a department that is responsible for the implementation of standard IT solutions, such as SAP or webSALES, in other Asian Group Companies. These standard IT solutions are all copies of best practice solutions from different Group Companies in Asia. Thus, Holcim Services Asia (HSEA) collects best practices and distributes them to other Group companies. It acts as a central department for the storage and re-implementation of best practices. Before the foundation of Holcim Services Asia, the situation in the Asian Area was very different. Felix Hoechner remembers:

"Everybody developed something. We had a mess of different solutions and practices. People took initiatives, but not in a structured way. This is why Holcim Service Asia was founded. We support Holcim Asia Group Companies in terms of the implementation of best practice IT solutions, such as webSALES or SAP."

He envisages sharing the Asean cluster approach with other Holcim regions. The different regions' cultural differences make the establishing of regional Service Centers an imperative. Hoechner explains:

"Multiplication of best practices is limited by management, culture and language. Owing to the differences in culture and language, we built a Service Center operating only in Asia. As far as the management of the Group company is concerned, you have to have a CEO who fully supports the initiative of taking a best practice, multiplying it and implementing it in his Group company. The success of a multiplication of a solution stands and falls with the local management's support."

The successful multiplication of webSALES in Vietnam—the impetus for the founding of HSEA—will play a major role in future multiplication processes.

5 LESSONS LEARNED FOR ATTEMPTING A MULTIPLICATION PROCESS

At the end of 2002 Holcim Asia, at the request of Paul Hugentobler, initiated a Lessons Learned process and a case write-up for internal use. The results of the processes would form a basis for further learning and the use of best practices in the Holcim Group.

In the process of writing up, the extent to which the sharing of a best practice through the "copy-pasting" of existing knowledge had allowed the company to take advantage of the law of increasing returns was perhaps first fully understood. All those involved in the case also agreed that the whole webSALES multiplication process was successful, because several prerequisites for the transferring of know-how from one subsidiary to another were fulfilled. The argument was raised that multiplication of a best practice, being a socio-technical process, is in general only possible if certain technical prerequisites are in place and employees are willing to cooperate. From their experience, these colleagues could only agree that it was indeed the fulfillment of prerequisites that had allowed them to move beyond possible resistances and make the replication of best practice feasible.

As part of the Lessons Learned, those involved in the case then decided to list the most important elements of their success story.

After much discussion it was decided that the first vector of success was the top management's high degree of commitment during the projects. It was generally agreed that people like Paul Hugentobler, Felix Hoechner, Chantana Sukumanont, Martin Foreman[14] and Laurent Houmard were motivated and extremely convinced sponsors of the two webSALES implementations. They were unanimously declared to be "agents of multiplication," because they had been truly persuaded of the necessity of sharing best practices between subsidiaries and totally convinced that the multiplication process would work.

The question was asked what exactly had made these people of the first hour so successful when promoting the necessity of installing webSALES. The group decided that it had been their strong leadership and management skills that they had specifically used and exhibited at meetings, information sessions, workshops, etc. when vigorously promoting webSALES. These qualities allowed them to transmit their enthusiasm and positivism to the middle management and employees, actions that supported the feasibility of the implementation and, consequently, allowed the accumulated

know-how to be transferred viably from Thailand to Vietnam. This point was concluded with the remark that the named persons' communication and motivational skills, combined with their hard work, contributed to the institutionalizing of a "copy-paste of webSALES" philosophy in Holcim's day-to-day practice in Asia.

Further discussion revealed that the second element that had contributed to the success of the multiplication of webSALES' best practice was the building up of people networks, since those involved had realized that know-how is best transferred through direct contact between individuals. While reminiscing, the group remembered that to prevent problems with the copy-pasting of the best practice, the process of transferring know-how within the people networks had to be done as efficiently as possible. Consequently, only the right people with relevant experience were selected to carry the knowledge from one subsidiary to another when the transfer took place. Felix Hoechner had been appointed to carry the "managerial know-how package" and to transmit it to the Vietnamese colleagues, who then implemented webSALES according to the SCCC project management model.

This led to further discussions on Felix Hoechner's contribution to the clear delimitation of the topic—another prerequisite for multiplication. He had flawlessly fulfilled this prerequisite by from the beginning clarifying what the project was all about and the exact results that he expected from all involved. The group could only reiterate that the success of the project was also due to it having clear borders, which allowed no leeway for divergence from the main topic and a subsequent loss of valuable time.

It was thereafter decided that as a result of Felix Hoechner's valuable work, the very specific and technical knowledge that had been carried to Vietnam via the Thai webSALES champions, Khun Sukanda and Khun Chonlatee, could then be transmitted to the employees via direct contact and close daily collaboration. Martin Foreman and Laurent Houmard had ensured that the transmission of "imported" know-how was essentially targeted at the Vietnamese employees involved in the usage of webSALES.

"It was important for me to identify who the employees at Holcim Vietnam were who really showed an interest in learning about webSALES. When I spotted them, I immediately pushed them to work very interactively with Khun Sukanda and Khun Chonlatee, the actual bearers of know-how. It was an advantage to have this group of motivated employees connected to the carriers of the best practice; their desire to learn assured me that they would absorb the knowledge that was being transmitted to them quicker and more efficiently. By doing so, I knew that I was building a new team of people who would become future know-how bearers, and who would later become 'mobile agents of multiplication' for Holcim's other webSALES implementations in Asia." (Laurent Houmard, project sponsor, Holcim Vietnam)

The next and third point that surfaced during the discussion—one that was used in the projects in both

---

[14] Since 1 December 2001 CEO Holcim Vietnam.

Thailand and Vietnam and that contributed to the successful replication of the best practice—was the "great story" that the management had told the employees in order to motivate them.

The colleagues remembered that in Thailand, the story had been based on the fact that Siam City was the first cement company in Asia to ever install e-commerce. Being part of such a project would therefore provide the employees with modern technological skills and with an unforgettable experience of which they would always be proud. When multiplying the best practice in Holcim Vietnam, it was Martin Foreman and Laurent Houmard who had shown creativity and motivational skills by inventing such a story. Their story had also pointed out the benefits and the reflected pride of being part of a revolutionary e-business project.

Felix Hoechner emphasized that creating a motivating atmosphere around a story is generally easier in developing countries, because there is still so much to be created.

> *"Before any software tool was even installed at Siam City Cement, I had to create an atmosphere around the story I told the employees; this had to be a driving force to lead every employee towards a common goal. When a team spirit had been created, I can remember feeling the enthusiasm that was 'burning them from inside.' They were really excited to participate in an e-commerce project. I think that this 'story technique' has a better chance of working in emerging markets than in the Western World where e-commerce is already very large. In other words, to build up a 'motivational story' that will influence your employees, you must adapt it to the degree of sophistication of the market in which you work." (Felix Hoechner, CEO Holcim Services, Bangkok, Thailand)*

The group all agreed, however, that telling a "great story" to employees was not enough. Convincing arguments about the "greatness" of webSALES also had to be communicated to Holcim's Thai and Vietnamese customers. If the latter had not been convinced of the benefits e-commerce would bring them, the chances were they would never use the tool and the tool, of course, had to deliver the benefits. For this reason, Holcim's management had taken extreme care to communicate in clear and simple terms all the advantages [customers] would enjoy when purchasing online. Only when the customers "had bought the story," did Holcim know that webSALES implementation was feasible.

The group then decided that the fourth point that contributed to facilitating the implementation of webSALES in Thailand and in Vietnam had been the employees' motivation through career promotion. In Siam City Cement, for example, employees who had been appointed "webSALES Champions" were then considered and called "web specialists." Giving them new, challenging responsibilities had been very motivating and an incentive to swiftly learn how to master the webSALES tool.

All were in agreement that the fifth and last prerequisite that absolutely had to be taken into account when multiplying a best practice from Thailand to Vietnam, had been the question of their different cultures. When the project sponsors were deciding on the "great story" with which to motivate the employees in Vietnam, they had known that it would have to be locally adapted to the Vietnamese understanding of "great." What motivated a Thai didn't necessarily appeal to a Vietnamese.

The projects managers had also made a valuable contribution by taking the fact that the Thai and Vietnamese cultures are collectivist in nature, which means that people are used to working together and finding group solutions and consensus, into consideration. This allowed the project management to plan for as much [teamwork] as possible in advance. This, in turn, accelerated the multiplication process, since know-how circulate[d] directly through groups of people, instead of going to individuals first (as in an individualistic culture) before it could be shared.

Holcim's management too had been aware that the Thai and Vietnamese cultures have a high sense of and respect for hierarchy in their working environments. This had been taken into consideration during the project management. The managers had known that the employees were expecting, and perfectly willing, to receive instructions. The managers had been warned that their management style should be adapted, since in countries where employees rely on instructions to a greater extent, the management style differs from the style in those cultures where employees feel free to take initiative. The group emphasized that this aspect should always be taken into account when finding the best project management model for the replication of a best practice.

The discussion was summarized with the words that multiplying a best practice within subsidiaries requires coordination, structure and motivation; however, it remains a simple process which ought to encourage other subsidiaries throughout the world to multiply their best practices as well.

Paul Hugentobler was very satisfied with what the meetings had accomplished, but this was not the end of the line. In future he would have to find answers to follow-up questions in respect [to] the company's multiplication of a best practice. Questions such as: How can the Group Companies, spread over 4 continents, faster and better create and share best practices? Does a case such as the multiplication of webSALES in Asia provide the necessary push and motivation? What else has to be done worldwide for a successful use of Best Practices in general? Can Holcim become a faster learning organization by applying the specific technique?

"We will endeavor to maintain this top position in the future as well. The basic requirement is a continuous increase in the efficiency of all processes and the streamlining of structures."

–Dr. Wendelin Wiedeking, President and CEO of the Porsche AG[1]

Implementation of the Balanced Scorecard as a Means of Corporate Learning: The Porsche Case

903-030-1

An innovative modernization process allowed Porsche to turn around and reconquer its position as one of the world's leading sports car manufacturers, thus recovering from the crisis it had faced in the early 1980s. Since the memory of the past problems was still fresh, there was a general awareness in the company that they could not afford to rest on their laurels if they wanted to stay ahead of the competition. In this spirit of continually striving to hone every single element of the business to perfection, the International Dealer Network Development team at the headquarters in Germany convened with some market representatives in 2000 to discuss new ideas on how to secure Porsche's success story for the future.

At this meeting, project manager for the international dealer development, Andreas Schlegel, presented his idea of implementing a balanced scorecard to measure performance. After long discussions, the participants finally arrived at a common understanding of how to implement this business tool as a means to turn the international dealer network into a learning organization. The goal was to make efficient use of the vast store of knowledge that lay dormant in the different dealerships and subsidiaries of the major markets

around the world, and, eventually, to turn this knowledge into profit. Another significant benefit would be the mass of data on the individual dealerships that the headquarters would acquire in the course of generating the balanced scorecard figures in each reporting cycle. After the senior representatives of the Sales Operations department had been convinced of the idea, a decision was taken in favor of the balanced scorecard and work began in the autumn of 2001.

However, soon after, resistance to the idea began to arise within the company itself. Dr. Andreas Offermann, the director [of] sales, was quick to comprehend the peril of the situation. Knowing that a previous attempt to introduce a balanced scorecard in another department had failed, which meant that the new effort would be met with resistance at all stages, he had the project renamed "Porsche Key Performance Indicators" (KPI).

Andreas Schlegel, who had focused on balanced scorecard research during most of his studies, became the project manager. Together with a capable team of assistants, he accepted the challenge to revolutionize the international Porsche Sales Organization.[2]

DESIGN PHASE

Everyone was aware of the heavy burden they had to bear to make a success of this huge project. Sun-Tzu, the ancient Chinese strategist, once suggested that large enemy armies should be maneuvered and split into small, vincible units. In

This case was written by **Professor Gilbert Probst**, HEC, University of Geneva, and **Jan Dominik Gunkel**, WHU, Otto Beisheim Graduate School of Management. It is intended to be used as the basis for class discussion rather than to illustrate either effective or ineffective handling of a management situation.

The case was made possible by the co-operation of Porsche AG.

[1] Porsche AG, *Annual Report 1999/2000.*

[2] The Porsche Sales Organization includes the Sales Operations department at the headquarters, the subsidiaries in the markets and the dealerships.

Exhibit 1   The Balanced Scorecard[3]

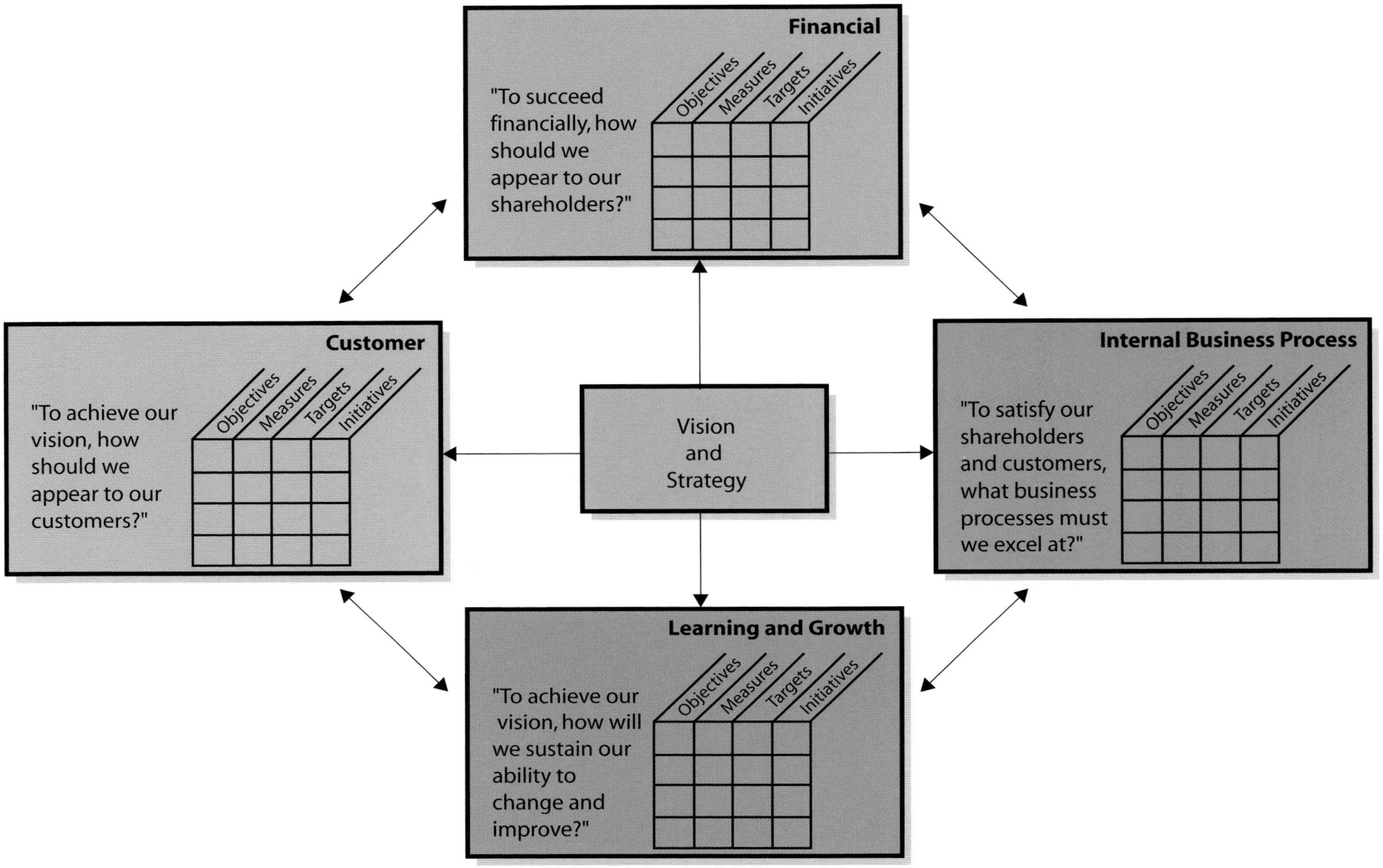

Financial

"To succeed financially, how should we appear to our shareholders?"

Objectives | Measures | Targets | Initiatives

Internal Business Process

"To satisfy our shareholders and customers, what business processes must we excel at?"

Objectives | Measures | Targets | Initiatives

Customer

"To achieve our vision, how should we appear to our customers?"

Objectives | Measures | Targets | Initiatives

Learning and Growth

"To achieve our vision, how will we sustain our ability to change and improve?"

Objectives | Measures | Targets | Initiatives

Vision and Strategy

[3] Robert S. Kaplan, David P. Norton, "Using the Balanced Scorecard as a Strategic Management System," *Harvard Business Review*, January–February 1996, p. 76.

this spirit, the project team decided on a step-by-step approach and started by selecting a few pilot markets in which to kick off the project.

First the members of the project team familiarized themselves with balanced scorecard theory by reading everything they could lay their hands on. After a careful study of all major Porsche markets, the markets in France (POF), Italy (PIT) and the UK (PCGB) were chosen for their proximity to the headquarters. The [German] market was specifically excluded to prevent the impression of a home market bias. In addition, the three markets were on different levels of dealership sophistication, with PIT at the lower and PCGB at the upper end of the scale. But all of them had basic IT infrastructure in their accounting as well as in their communication technologies. PCGB's highly developed internal reporting system was considered the benchmark with which the others had to comply. For instance, PCGB's reports provided almost twice the number of figures than those of Porsche Italia. The project team therefore organized several workshops with representatives of the three markets to discuss their various reporting systems in order to compile a comprehensive list of key issues. It was clear that PIT, which had the largest gap to close in its reporting system, would benefit most, but even PCGB was able to learn from the interesting reporting methods that the PIT management had devised. After all, the Italians invented accounting centuries ago.

By including the markets in the creation process, their full acceptance of the balanced scorecard as part of themselves was ensured.

With extensive input from the markets guaranteed, the project team started to outline its ideas. Once they had a common understanding of their goals, they sought the assistance of an experienced automotive IT consultancy. After a long selection process, a European-based British provider that specialized in complete solutions in respect [to] reporting systems for the automobile industry was chosen. This project was, however, the consultancy's first contract with the headquarters of an automobile group, since it had previously only dealt with national subsidiaries of other renowned car manufacturers. The consultancy appeared highly motivated, presumably because of the chance to add Porsche's good name to its list of clients. It was, furthermore, the company's first balanced scorecard project; therefore its strategic importance was considerable.

In a challenging process, the project team, the consultancy and the markets agreed upon the structure and the content of the balanced scorecard. The idea was to publish the KPIs as a PDF report adapted for the individual markets and thus only showing the data of the respective dealership. [The reports] would contain almost 40 front-page indicators distributed across four categories: "Financial," "Customer/ Market," "Internal Processes," and "Staff and Learning." The dealers would be able to retrieve the underlying detailed data on the following pages through a simple drill-down approach by clicking on a figure. On the first pages the figures would be marked according to a traffic-light scheme, with red lights indicating that urgent action was required. POF and PIT were to receive quarterly reports reflecting fewer figures than the monthly report that PCGB would receive. Yet the goal was to have a common report for the participating markets in the long run.

During the development phase, close contact was maintained with the area sales manager in charge of the communication with the American market (PCNA), whose office was next to that of the project team. PCNA had independently developed a similar, but less evolved system several years previously and had thus acquired a plethora of valuable experiences.

A tool, such as the balanced scorecard, that evaluates several [thousands] . . . figures per dealer has to first retrieve the data from somewhere. Luckily, most of the values could be derived from the multitude of figures already available in every dealership. The consultants therefore developed a software client to retrieve these data from the existing dealer management system on site. The additionally required data were entered by hand. Via the secure Porsche Partner Network phone lines, the data were then transferred to the server that generated the reports. The latter process was supervised by the consultants, who also notified the dealerships once [the reports] were available. The reports were then downloaded via a web-based interface. All the data available on the server could also be accessed by the regional managers—the people in charge of several dealerships. The concept even included a high-end profiling tool to compare dealerships, their performance and development.

The result was a unique system of such sophistication that it had no competitor. The Key Performance Indicator System was recommended to the dealers as a tool with many advantages:

- It focused on long-term strategic action, leading to lasting success instead of invoking shortsighted decisions to improve the annual accounts. Each dealership could evaluate its performance beyond that indicated by financial figures. Values such as customer satisfaction could be monitored constantly. And the KPI could even reveal specific potential for future improvement. Moreover, since warnings regarding critical developments were generated automatically, this allowed countermeasures to be taken to prevent these problems before they arose. All the KPI of the dealership were benchmarked to the national average and averages of groups of selected dealerships. These groups were determined by each of the markets.

- A two-way communication between the dealership and the headquarters during all stages allowed everyone to understand one another and to adapt to the overall strategic objectives of the organization and to adapt these objectives as well.

- In the long run the profitability of the entire sales network would improve.

ROLLING OUT—HITTING THE ROAD

After the development of this revolutionary tool, it was necessary to ensure that the dealerships could and would make appropriate use of it. Unfortunately, a new tool initially always means additional work, and there are rarely immediate payoffs. During the development phase the project team had already laid the foundation for the dealerships' acceptance of the KPI by constantly keeping them informed and included in the process. The early pilot dealerships were proud of their participation and therefore put considerable effort into the system. The project team anticipated that after word about the first positive results had spread, further successes would be ensured.

The project team was fortunate to be able to draw on the previous experiences of either team members or colleagues in the same department, since many other innovations had been rolled out before. The most closely related example was the dealer web platform for pre-owned Porsche cars, whose schedule was only [a] few months ahead of the KPI. The tool itself could not be compared to a balanced scorecard, but it too was a web-based application on the Porsche Partner Network that was distributed to all dealerships and that depended on the active participation of every single dealership to be a success. With its similar structure, much of this innovation's incoming feedback could be directly applied to the KPI rollout process as well.

Another source of experience was the Porsche training department. Here manuals are written and trainings in respect [to] technical issues and sales techniques are provided for dealership employees. As the dealers participating in the project were used to their way of communication, the project team tried to understand the working style of the training department in order to emulate their approach, which would expedite the chances of acceptance by the dealerships. The knowledge transfer between the two departments was arduous at times since the training department had a natural desire to take charge of the training. It was, however, short of training resources due to the introduction of the new SUV: the Cayenne. In addition, knowledge of the KPI was almost exclusively limited to the project team. It was finally agreed to leave the team in charge of training, while continuous communication with the training department would allow the latter to monitor conformity to the Porsche training spirit.

One of the assistants [to] the project team wrote a handbook for the Key Performance Indicator System. This includes an introductory chapter on the motivation behind the KPI, its purposes, background and underlying theories, plus a description of the implementation and installation steps of the system, as well as instructions for its use. The manual moreover includes descriptions of and tips on approximately fifty main indicators. Restricted to the essence, this manual is targeted at general managers, dealership accountants and, in an extended version, at regional managers. The project team furthermore developed initial training sessions for accountants, which were to be conducted by the staff of the external agency and the project manager.

As the project took shape, contact between the headquarters, the external agency, and the markets was maintained. The initial version of the software system itself was basically completed, so process details and roll-out issues became more urgent. In a discussion with the market managers, the well-organized German project team learned that there was a strong tendency by the Italian dealers not to submit their data on time, while the British dealerships, conversely, would most likely submit their data without being reminded at all. This information led to a submission schedule being issued for each market: the official closing dates for PIT were brought forward to several days before the official internal closing date, with the real closing date being made known to PCGB. A series of reminders were also initiated to ensure submissions in a timely fashion, since the generation of the report would be delayed until all data had been collected.

It was very obvious that flawed submissions would disrupt the whole system and, due to the sheer size of the eighty-page report, the submissions were prone to errors. Before submission of the data, the client system would therefore validate it automatically and issue warnings and errors that would have to be removed by the dealer. Dealers were also asked to update their data if they discovered faulty submissions after the submission date. This kept the database accurate and long-term development could be monitored more precisely. If such an update were to occur, new reports would not be issued—neither for all dealerships, nor for the relevant dealership.

The roll-out was planned to start with a connection time of approximately one to 1.5 days per dealer and to arrive at five dealers per week in the long run. On these days a representative of the consultancy would visit the particular dealership and configure the KPI client application to fit the dealer management system. Prior to the roll-out, one of the assistants developed checklists of what would have to be done before and during a dealership's roll-out day. There were checklists for the consultancy, for the project team and for the dealership itself. The consultancy and the dealership had to evaluate each other's performance and suggest improvements. This feedback, which was initially copious, helped to improve the roll-out process dramatically.

In the first dealerships, the roll-out was supervised by the project manager and one of his assistants as well as the market manager in order to have an immediate on-site evaluation of the performance. During these first roll-out sessions many questions were answered and open issues resolved, which were then compiled into an information sheet that could be distributed to the dealerships beforehand. The dealership accountant, or whoever else was responsible for the KPI, had to be present at the roll-out. He was shown how to [set up] the system if a reinstallation or adaptation were ever necessary. In addition, he received a quick introductory training by the consultancy's representative and was given the KPI System Handbook.

On each roll-out day the consultant compiled a list of what had to be done for the dealership to fully comply with the requirements of the KPI System. Many dealerships had to create new accounts and start keeping track of previously ignored figures. These action lists were also passed on to the project team, who then monitored the course of their implementation according to a schedule that had been agreed upon with the dealerships. In general, the headquarters always endeavored to maintain their relationship with the dealerships as one of equal partners, but from time to time decisions had to be taken and thereafter enforced.

Since, despite the comprehensive documentation available, questions were sure to arise when the accountants entered data into the system, or when a general manager analyzed a report, the consultancy set up a hotline in each market. The dealerships were also provided with a small flowchart as a decision aid on when to contact the consultants' support network, or when to contact their particular regional manager. At this stage the dealerships were truly equipped for the first phase.

Approximately a month after the first dealerships had been piloted through the system, data had to be submitted for the first time. Everything went well, although some minor delays occurred on the server generating the reports. Everyone involved was proud to see that things had worked out well and Dr. Offermann was pleased to receive the first report.

HOT PHASE

When the reports were sent to the first dealerships, it became increasingly clear that the planned dedicated training was necessary. The training, which was already in the pipeline, targeted general managers and dealership accountants who had to deal with the tool in their daily business. Regional managers too had to be trained to provide their dealerships with consultation in respect [to] KPI issues. The first training sessions were therefore scheduled as soon as enough dealerships had been connected, which was about two months after the first dealership had been piloted. In order to carry out the trainings, the trainees were summoned to a regional training facility—Porsche-owned or independent— and [. . .] the capabilities and the features of the system [were explained]. Questions were encouraged, and first experiences were exchanged amongst participants from the various dealerships. As many dealerships also handled other automobile brands, they could make use of previous experiences with other, interior, reporting systems. Porsche was utterly convinced that it was the first manufacturer to introduce this type of balanced scorecard in automotive retailing.

In its handbook, the project team suggests a way of dealing with the reports, although the dealerships are not bound to this suggestion. They suggest that on receiving the report, the accountant should analyze it and create a memo of points that require attention. The report and the memo are then to be passed on to the general manager, who should study them and decide which actions to take. A print function allows a selection of pages that refer to a specific job position to be printed for these specific employees. With this personal printout everyone has access to information on issues in his sphere of influence without the inconvenience of receiving data related to other domains. This is thought to raise the awareness of the key factors that really matter for continuous improvement. The project team also stresses that simply handing out the sheets may not suffice—explicit encouragement to review them and information regarding their meaning may be required as well. Conducting a KPI meeting with managers, or putting KPI on the agenda of regular management meetings may further improve the success of the KPI System. During these meetings, all upcoming dangers, obstacles and progress should be examined to decide on how to handle the consequences. The meetings are promoted to focus on strategic questions—not tactical ones.

A regional manager's job is to visit and to provide all the dealers of a region with consultation. In order to facilitate their work, they, too, receive their dealerships' reports. They can analyze the performance with the profiling application and benchmark it to any other dealership, which might help to find the source of problems quicker than with the report alone. This unique profiling tool accelerates many of the regional managers' tasks that they would have to do by hand otherwise. Previously, i.e., before the balanced scorecard, these could only be done on the basis of information that the dealerships wished to provide. However, this profiling tool was not directly given to the dealerships, since the detailed data of other dealerships were kept strictly confidential.

OUTLOOK

For the future, annual or semi-annual meetings, so-called Corporate KPI Conferences with representatives of all connected markets, are planned. The goal of these conferences, which nurture mutual exchange among markets, is to discuss ideas about improvement and future development of the KPI system. A further plan, suggested by the team, is to offer an award for the dealership of the quarter, which would then be presented as a best practice example in a circular. To improve the acceptance and the usage of the Key Performance Indicators by dealership employees, a KPI flyer was also introduced. This flyer summarizes all generally important information on the project plus information specific to various job positions. Employees will accordingly always know to which KPIs they primarily contribute.

Porsche has been committed to *Kaizen*—the Japanese expression for continuous improvement—since Dr. Wiedeking requested Japanese consultants to review all processes. It is therefore clear to everyone that a business tool such as the KPI System cannot be static. It has to keep track of the changes in its environment that can occur in very many ways to undermine core assumptions. For instance, competitors might take unexpected actions, new ones might emerge, major technological innovations could arise, government regulatory or deregulatory actions could change the competitive

Exhibit 2   Porsche Group Highlights

		1992/93	1993/94	1994/95	1995/96	1996/97	1997/98	1998/99	1999/00	2000/01	2001/02
Sales	€ million	978.1	1,194.2	1,332.9	1,437.7	2,093.3	2,519.4	3,161.3	3,647.7	4,441.6	4,857.3
Domestic	€ million	447.6	554.1	569.7	527.7	671.9	735.5	955.6	893.2	1,001.3	1,121.0
Export	€ million	530.5	640.1	763.2	910.0	1,421.4	1,783.9	2,205.7	2,754.5	3,440.2	3,736.3
Vehicle sales (new cars)	units	14,362	18,402	21,124	19,262	32,383	36,688	43,982	48,797	54,586	54,234
Domestic Porsche	units	3,544	5,574	6,420	5,873	9,670	9,174	10,607	11,754	12,401	12,825
Export Porsche	units	8,219	10,269	11,992	13,346	22,713	27,512	33,375	37,043	42,185	41,409
Other Models	units	2,599	2,559	2,712	43	—	—	—	—	—	—
Vehicle Sales Porsche	units	11,763	15,843	18,412	19,219	32,383	36,686	43,982	48,797	54,586	54,234
911	units	7,702	13,010	17,407	19,096	16,507	17,869	23,090	23,050	26,721	32,337
928	units	672	509	510	104	—	—	—	—	—	—
944/968	units	3,389	2,324	495	19	—	—	—	—	—	—
Boxster	units	—	—	—	—	15,876	18,817	20,892	25,747	27,865	21,897
Production											
Porsche total	units	15,082	19,348	20,791	20,242	32,390	38,007	45,119	48,815	55,782	55,050
911	units	7,950	13,771	17,293	20,132	16,488	19,120	23,056	22,950	27,325	33,061
928	units	730	633	470	28	—	—	—	—	—	—
944/968	units	3,803	2,385	316	82	—	—	—	—	—	—
Boxster	units	—	—	—	—	15,902	18,887	22,063	25,865	28,467	21,989
Other models	units	2,599	2,559	2,712	—	—	—	—	—	—	—
Employees	at year-end	7,133	6,970	6,847	7,107	7,959	8,151	8,712	9,320	9,752	10,143
Personnel expenses	€ million	357.4	343.6	363.7	392.1	464.4	528.2	574.9	631.3	709.9	799.4
Balance Sheet											
Total Assets	€ million	769.7	795.6	836.7	951.4	1,249.7	1,490.9	1,916.1	2,205.4	2,891.6	5,408.7
Shareholders' Equity	€ million	197.2	218.2	210.5	239.1	298.1	415.8	587.4	782.0	1,053.3	1,466.8
Fixed Assets	€ million	382.8	351.4	353.2	482.5	565.3	579.6	525.6	577.7	731.8	2,207.7
Capital Expenditures	€ million	90.6	63.0	83.9	213.6	234.8	175.8	155.0	243.7	293.8	1,739.5[3]
Depreciation	€ million	78.2	76.6	55.2	67.7	107.6	157.1	183.7	196.6	132.7	278.8
Cash Flow	€ million	−17.9	17.6	94.8	123.6	205.5	305.0	407.8	424.7	418.4	781.5
Extended Cash Flow	€ million						413.1	592.5	506.5	764.4	1,067.3
Net income/loss before taxes	€ million	−122.3	−73.9	5.8	27.9	84.5	165.9	357.0	433.8	592.4	628.9
Net income/loss after taxes	€ million	−122.1	−76.8	1.1	24.6	71.3	141.6	190.9	210.0	270.5	462.0
Dividends	€ million	—	1.0	1.1	1.8	13.0	21.9	21.9	26.4	46.0	297.0[4]
Dividends per share[1]											
Common stock	€	—	—	—	0.08	0.72	1.23	1.23	1.48	2.54	16.94[5]
Preferred stock	€	—	0.13	0.13	0.13	0.77	1.28	1.28	1.53	2.60	17.00[5]
DVFA/SG earnings per share[2]	€	−8.90	−5.30	0.10	1.10	4.10	4.80	13.00	13.70	17.20	27.80

[1] Fiscal years up to 1999/00 have been retroactively recognized according to the stock split in fiscal year 2000/01.
[2] Deutsche Vereinigung für Finanzanalyse und Anlageberatung/Schmalenbach-Gesellschaft, fiscal years up to 1999/00 have been retroactively recognized according to the stock split in fiscal year 2000/01.
[3] Excluding additions related to initial consolidations.
[4] Thereof special dividend of 245 million Euros.
[5] Thereof special dividend of 14 Euros.

Source: Porsche AG, Online Annual Report, December 1, 2002

circumstances, and macroeconomic conditions could alter. Consequently, the project team emphasized the need for a regular review of the KPI System right from the beginning. The idea is to initiate a process of bilateral exchange in order to develop and improve the KPI System constantly. To keep the participants up to date with the development of the system, dealerships and regional managers will receive a regular circular that will also contain the best practice example mentioned above. It is planned to keep them informed about the news, exceptional successes, problem-solving strategies, and future plans. A questionnaire through which they can provide feedback will also be attached to the circular. Dealerships are also encouraged to let all levels participate in the feedback process, since many important ideas come from frontline employees and not only from general managers. Sufficient feedback could result in the removal or addition of key figures to the balanced scorecard. Additionally, a whole development cycle around the Corporate KPI Conferences, comparable to the initial planning workshops, is under way and will take place in November 2003 to continuously improve the KPI-System.

Despite the satisfying initial results in the piloting markets and the promising future, only the first steps of a long [journey] have been taken.

Blue Whale Moving Company, Inc. (A)

9-496-001

It was a late evening in September 1988 when Blake Miller sat alone pondering the events that had taken place that afternoon. Earlier in the day, Blake met with Brad Armstrong, a local attorney and entrepreneur. The pair discussed the possibility of starting a new business together and Brad wanted to have a firm answer by the next day. Faced with what was undoubtedly the most important decision of his young life, Blake stared into space trying to imagine what success, or failure, would be like. Maybe he would become famous, or rich, or both. Or perhaps he would fail miserably and waste the most important years of his life. Either way, he had 14 hours to decide whether the business concept would work at all and whether Brad Armstrong was the individual with whom he wanted to develop the idea. Two weeks earlier, he never would have imagined the possibilities that lay ahead.

BLAKE MILLER AND BRAD ARMSTRONG

Having just graduated from the University of Texas, Blake Miller, 23, was sure that he wanted to enter a challenging and rewarding career. He had put himself through college by working for Advanced Moving, a local moving company in Austin, and had continued to work there since graduation. He was hard working and motivated, but disliked his current job. He was applying for entry into an MBA program and looked forward to an exciting business career.

Research Associate Adam Friedman and PhD Student Chris Long prepared this case under the supervision of Professors Laura Cardinal and Sim Sitkin as a basis for class discussion rather than to illustrate either an effective or ineffective handling of an administrative situation. Laura Cardinal was at the Fuqua School of Business, Duke University at the time the case was developed. She is currently at Tulane University.

At the age of 29, Brad Armstrong was a successful attorney looking to diversify into different types of businesses. He was passionate about business and had already initiated ventures in a few different industries: a clothing manufacturer that created doctor style scrub shirts out of Hawaiian prints, a federal firearms importing business, and a media company that published a local business newsletter. None of the businesses became an overwhelming financial success, but each turned a small profit.

A few days earlier, Blake had given Brad Armstrong a phone call. Blake thought Brad would be an excellent business reference for his MBA application and planned to ask him for his consent. The two had met a year earlier when Brad hired Advanced Moving for an office move. Brad had been impressed with Blake's energy and requested him by name when he hired Advanced Moving for a residential move a few months later. This time, even more delighted by Blake's commitment to the move, Brad asked Blake to give him a call upon graduation

THE MEETING

When Brad agreed to have lunch with Blake, he was clearly approaching the meeting as a business opportunity. Blake, on the other hand, saw Brad simply as a business contact. The discussion quickly moved toward Brad's agenda. Brad posed the idea of Blake's expanding some of his already established businesses, but Blake was not very excited by any of them. As the empty appetizer plates were removed and the main course was served, conversation turned more toward Blake's current job as a mover.

Blake explained to Brad some of the intricacies of the local moving industry in Austin. The rivalry among firms was fierce. He described how both customers and movers alike were treated as disposable commodities by moving companies. Furthermore, the movers felt a level of dissatisfaction that created a negative experience for the customers and, in turn, for the movers themselves. The vicious circle was made even worse by the financial situation of the industry as a whole. Competitors understood that price was the determining factor in the customer decision, so sales representatives with the responsibility for quoting prices would do anything possible to cut the price of a potential move, which eventually affected how much the movers earned. Morale in the industry was low and customer perceptions were negative.

Blake continued to explain how most of the competitors knew each other because they had worked together at some time in the past. It was common for employees to break away from their old employers and start up competing companies. The capital costs could be kept to a minimum and the necessary know-how was minimal. For this reason alone, new competitors were constantly entering the Austin market. As the competitive situation became more intense, though, competitors would leave as quickly as they entered. The only thing that could be said definitively about the Austin market was that it was in a constant state of turmoil.

As Blake discussed the situation, he found himself getting increasingly excited. He had worked in the industry for four years and had his own personal solutions for each of the problems he had encountered. Brad, too, was intrigued by the vivid description. As the two continued to talk, they began to form the idea for a new company that would do everything "right." At first, it was no more than a chat about a problematic industry, but it soon turned into a discussion of a possible business opportunity.

The pair analyzed the concept by calculating gross profits for a theoretical company. They used the $25,000 that Blake had made the previous year on 18 percent of the price of his moves to estimate the possible revenue for one moving crew. Multiplying by the number of crews at an average local moving company, Advanced Moving for example, Brad and Blake were able to calculate the total possible revenue they could anticipate. Furthermore, they calculated some of the expenses necessary to get the business started: a phone, business cards and stationery, a trailer for Blake's truck and a paint job for the trailer. Based on this set of assumptions, they soon agreed that a new moving company would not only be feasible but also profitable.

The company they envisioned would provide customers with unparalleled service and empower movers to provide that service. Furthermore, the company would compete in the high-end market and differentiate itself not on price but on superior customer service. While this was a far cry from the industry norms, the pair was convinced that a substantial segment of the rapidly growing Austin market of about 1 million people would be willing to pay a premium for the confidence that they and their possessions were being treated with the utmost respect.

By the end of a 90-minute lunch, Blake and Brad had tentatively agreed to form a new local moving company in Austin. Brad would provide the needed capital and Blake would run the moving operation. Each man decided that he needed to think about the decision overnight, so the pair agreed to talk the next afternoon to confirm the decision to form a partnership.

THE LOCAL MOVING INDUSTRY

The United States has the world's most mobile society. More than 42 million Americans—almost 20 percent of the U.S. population—move each year at an average cost per household of more than $3,200. These moves can be classified as either long-haul or short-haul. Long-haul moves are generally between states and are handled by large van-line companies such as Allied Van Lines, Atlas Van Lines, Mayflower Transit Co., and United Van Lines. Short-haul moves, or local moves, are generally within the same city, or at least the same state. While some people choose to move themselves, the majority of these moves are handled by local moving companies in the area. The van-line industry is controlled by a few major carriers and is monitored by national moving associations. Conversely, the local moving industry, while deeply entrenched in every city across the country, is made up of thousands of different players. There are no nationwide local moving companies and no sources of precise competitive information on the industry.

A small metropolitan area of 1 million people may have as many as 80 local moving companies. The smallest of these companies may be a two-person operation where each person has a career other than moving. This company may post advertisements around town, rent a truck and trailer on the weekend, and perform one or two moves a week. On the other hand, the largest of these companies has a well-placed advertisement in the yellow pages, owns their own trucks and trailers, and can perform as many as 200 moves a week. The local moving industry is profitable for both types of movers.

A large moving job may take three or four movers one complete day to finish. An example might be a family moving from a five-bedroom house on one end of town to a larger house on the other. Depending on the number of items, the move may cost anywhere from $2,000 to $5,000. A smaller move, on the other hand, may involve a single person living in an apartment who is moving down the street. This move requires only a few hours and may cost as little as $200. A two-person moving team may perform as many as six apartment moves in one day. The larger move is obviously most preferable to both moving companies and the movers themselves due to higher profit margins and the easier moving situation. One additional type of move is an office relocation. Due to the logistical complexities of these moves, these are low-profit, difficult moves that require many movers. In addition, these relocations almost always need to be performed on the weekends, when higher profit residential moves are most frequent.

The decision to hire a moving company is made almost exclusively on price. Customers will inevitably call, or be visited by, multiple moving companies to obtain and compare price quotes. The key in the moving industry, therefore, is getting the phone to ring. Prospective customers can be brought in through a variety of means. They may have used the company previously and been happy with the results, been referred by a friend or colleague, seen an advertisement in the yellow pages, or noticed one of the company's trucks around town. In addition, moving companies sometimes establish contracts with a large business in the local area, a real estate agency, a housing subdivision, or an apartment complex. Although this generates greater volumes, profits can be undermined because people moving in association with one of these groups are always given a discount.

Equipment

Because the cost of acquiring a new truck or trailer is significant (as high as $60,000), many companies try to buy used equipment. Most of the distances driven are fairly short, so a used vehicle can be driven with relative security. Alternatively, in order to minimize the fixed cost of owning trucks and trailers, many local moving companies have established relationships with truck rental companies like U-Haul and Ryder. The moving companies will enter into a lease agreement for a used truck or trailer in which the maintenance (and sometimes storage) of the vehicle is the responsibility of the rental company.

Movers

Movers are generally treated as independent contractors to keep labor costs as low as possible. In addition, their low salaries are reflective of their respective education and work experiences. Often the only job qualification is physical strength. Most moving companies will have at least one ex-convict or parolee in their ranks. Some movers have attended college and some are not as strong, but these are definitely the exceptions, not the rule. This fact spurred one mover to comment that "Education doesn't mean anything in this business. It's all strength." Although working conditions are good and movers are paid more than they would earn performing similar manual labor elsewhere, turnover in the industry is as high as 50 percent a year. The cited reason is predominantly job dissatisfaction. Movers generally become frustrated by their managers or customers or are simply worn down by the constant strain on their bodies.

Customer Perceptions

Customers generally have negative perceptions of the moving industry. Customers expect the service to be substandard, their goods to be damaged, and their nerves to be frayed. Like a nuclear power plant that avoids accidents or a prison that avoids escapes, customers consider a good move to be one that minimizes damage—positive outcomes are never cited. People generally have these expectations regardless of whether they previously had a good or bad encounter with a moving company. Although some of this bad sentiment may be well-founded, moving company personnel are quick to comment that customers are extremely sensitive to even the most minor errors during a move due to the other stress that they may be feeling at the time. This stress might be caused by the selling or purchase of a home, career changes, marriage, divorce, or other life events. Regardless of the cause, however, negative customer perceptions are prevalent.

THE DECISION

Blake returned home the evening of the meeting to find himself plagued by unanswered questions. Although Blake's concept of a new strategy in the moving industry seemed to make sense, he was unsure whether it was realistic given the harsh industry norms. He worried about alienating his current employer, as well as his peers. Maybe they would ridicule his new concept or, worse yet, exploit him in a competitive situation. In addition, because this new concept was a serious departure from the traditional method of business in the industry, he knew that it would be difficult to both implement and maintain.

In addition, he wondered whether Brad was really the best partner for such a venture. With no experience in the industry, would their visions of the company be the same or would they be destined to split? He thought that Brad, too, must have had some reservations about the venture. Maybe Brad felt uneasy putting his money into an unknown industry with a partner he barely knew. Perhaps he was not committed to the success of the company and would leave Blake without a job if at any time he decided to divest his capital. Blake knew he could make a profit, but was unsure whether it would be enough to justify the financial investment.

Blake called his parents and then his sister to ask their advice. Each of them thought he was crazy for even thinking of the idea. Not only did he know nothing about running his own company, but he also knew nothing of his new "partner." The combination, they felt, was cause for serious concern. Blake hesitantly agreed, thanked them for their advice, and hung up the phone. He truly wanted to join Brad in the venture, but there were so many issues that were either unclear or unknown. As midnight approached, Blake was as uneasy as ever, but he was determined to make a decision before drifting off to sleep.

THE EARLY YEARS

Blue Whale Moving Company was cofounded by Brad Armstrong and Blake Miller in September 1988. Faced with a fast approaching deadline for submission of an advertisement in the yellow pages, the pair was challenged with creating, trademarking, and incorporating a business all within a week of their initial discussion of the business concept. But the first hurdle to climb was deciding on a name. The two founders thought endlessly of names before one of Brad's law partners inspired them to think of a somewhat fanciful name, one that conveyed trust and courage. This spurred the pair to think about animals and when they imagined the biggest animal of them all, the blue whale, the name stuck. They felt that it not only conjured a pleasant image in one's mind but also instilled a feeling of strength and confidence. Later advertisements often referred to the company as the "Gentle Giant," supporting the idea of a large and powerful company that can move household goods safely and effortlessly. Additionally, each truck was painted with a lifelike image of a blue whale (see Exhibit 1). While this was a fairly high-cost proposition, they later found that much of their business stemmed from potential customers seeing their trailers on the street and remembering them vividly.

In a market where moving companies are named Advanced Moving, Apartment Movers, AAA Moving, and Discount Moving, the moniker Blue Whale Moving is a far cry from the norm. But while its competitors assumed a nondescript profile, Blue Whale emphasized that its service, and therefore the company, was discernible from the rest of the competition. Although their competitors often used substandard equipment and labor, Blue Whale stressed the importance of spotless trucks, tidy equipment, and clean-cut personnel—reasoning that if their customers saw Blue Whale take care of its business, they would certainly feel that Blue Whale could take care of their valuables.[1] With the initial investment of $10,000, the company purchased a used trailer (Blake already owned a truck), a cellular phone, and some miscellaneous supplies. Before the yellow pages ad was published, Blake posted fliers around the city and made endless phone calls to drum up business. Blake and one other employee formed the first moving crew. They would perform as many moves as possible, seven days a week, and take calls on the cellular phone to quote or book new moves. In a sense, Blake *was* the business; Brad was not involved in the daily operations of Blue Whale. Eight weeks later, the yellow pages advertisement was published and revenues started to take off. By April 1989, Blue Whale was able to purchase another trailer and hire a second crew with its cash flow from the first seven months of operations. By 1993, revenue soared to $1.7 million (see Exhibits 2 and 3 for specific financial data).

BLUE WHALE'S VISION AND GROWTH

The local moving business that Brad and Blake established was different than other moving companies. The two entrepreneurs constantly stressed the importance of customer service in their organization. While the mainstream at-

tempted to undercut their competition in price wars, Blue Whale targeted the subset of customers who felt that a professional, stress-free move had an intangible value for which they would pay a premium.[2] Brad and Blake recognized that moving meant a transition for most people. As a result, customers were particularly sensitive and responsive to the perceived quality of the move. The entrepreneurs summed up their key notion:

Moving . . . is a stressful time for most customers. You have the potential to ruin this person's day or make it the best day they've ever had.[3]

Blue Whale's vision statement, which every employee recited to each potential customer, further emphasized the importance of customer service:

By 31 December 2000, Blue Whale will have become pre-eminent in the moving and storage industry, with locations in 100 cities worldwide.

Marked by complete commitment and dedication to the highest standards of moral and ethical excellence, Blue Whale will be delivering an exceptional service experience created uniquely for each customer, by radiating positive energy throughout our team, and reflecting this love and respect upon our customers and all those we serve.

Only then will our successful evolution into other markets, products and services be guaranteed.

Brad believed that the Blue Whale vision was the most important thing his customers should know about the company. He remarked,

If a customer just wants a price, I can give him the name of several other companies. We're offering something different.

Our vision statement was built from the bottom up. We all developed it together and we've never known any other way. Then we created a training program for incoming employees so everyone knows right from the start what Blue Whale is all about.[4]

Brad and Blake required that all employees know the vision and demonstrate Blue Whale's values to the customer. This was extremely unusual in an industry best known for rude, belligerent movers and managers. Brad felt that even though the initial investment in developing character was significant, so were the long-term payoffs. He felt that if employees were able to internalize Blue Whale's principles, it would instill pride in the organization and teach employees how to behave when no one was looking over their shoulder.[5] Blue Whale's customers would frequently comment about how professional the Blue Whale movers were compared with their competitors. In addition, movers were given

---

[1] "Austin's Gentle Giant: The Blue Whale Moving Company," *Moving and Storage Times*, March 15, 1993.

[2] "Austin's Gentle Giant."

[3] "This Blue Whale Is on the Move," *Austin-American Statesman*, January 1, 1993, p. E1.

[4] "A Whale of an Idea," *AdInfinitum*, March 1994.

[5] Ibid.

Exhibit 1   Blue Whale Moving Truck and Trailer

the ability to make discretionary decisions regarding certain aspects of the move, such as the application of additional charges or discounts. Other than reinforcing the concept of customer service, Brad and Blake exercised little formal control over their movers.

Brad and Blake's strategy worked. Revenues grew exponentially and the number of employees in the firm swelled.

While competitors initially mocked the company for its fanciful name and vision, these companies were soon copying Blue Whale both in service delivery and style. Some of them began using mission statements in their advertisements that stressed customer service. New competitors began using more imaginative names like Aardvark, American Eagle, and Unicorn. Both Brad and Blake were heralded for the entrepreneurial

Exhibit 2   Blue Whale Moving Co. (Austin) Statement of Earnings (Years Ended December 31, 1989 to 1993)

	1989^A	1990^A	1991	1992	1993
Revenue					
Sales	181,971	388,396	587,708	1,106,586	1,659,108
Less: Refunds/Discounts	0	0	0	453	6,660
Net Sales	181,971	388,396	587,708	1,106,133	1,652,448
Cost of Sales	0	319,309	515,667	489,283	671,624
Gross Profit	181,971	69,087	72,041	616,850	980,824
Expenses					
Operating Expenses	181,840	20,805	43,326	572,972	992,261
Other Income/(Expenses)		(567)	(6)	(27,368)	(33,239)
Total Expenses	181,840	21,372	43,332	600,339	1,025,500
Net Earnings	131	47,714	28,709	16,510	(44,677)

^{A}There was an accounting change in 1990. Much of the information for 1989 was either incomparable or incomplete.

Exhibit 3   Blue Whale Moving Co. (Austin) Balance Sheet (Years Ended December 31, 1989 to 1993)

	1989[A]	1990[A]	1991	1992	1993
Assets					
Cash		3,763	19,133	(4,095)	22,485
Accounts Receivable		1,131	6,356	13,355	25,140
Other Current Assets		775	1,130	776	5,063
Total Current Assets		5,669	26,619	10,036	52,688
Net Fixed Assets		28,083	76,937	90,431	188,932
Other Assets		0	0	4,032	4,307
Total Assets		33,753	103,556	104,500	245,927
Liabilities					
Current Liabilities		14,930	62,523	34,500	133,356
Long-Term Liabilities		9,753	7,753	20,209	107,457
Total Liabilities		24,683	70,276	54,709	240,813
Shareholder's Equity					
Capital Stock		1,000	1,000	1,000	1,000
Retained Earnings		(39,645)	3,570	32,280	48,790
Profit (Loss) for Year		47,714	28,710	16,510	(44,677)
Total SE		9,070	33,280	49,790	5,114
Total Liabilities and SE		33,753	103,556	104,500	245,927

[A] There was an accounting change in 1990. Much of the information for 1989 was either incomparable or incomplete.

spirit in the local and national press, and they were soon the recipients of many esteemed entrepreneurial awards (see Exhibit 4 for a list of Blue Whale honors and awards).

Customers

Blue Whale was devoted to customer service but not only in a traditional sense. A Blue Whale brochure clarifies this by stating, "We don't sell moving services. We sell 'peace of mind.'" According to Brad and Blake, the most important quality that a Blue Whale employee could possess was the ability to make customers relax. This concept was manifest throughout the organization, from the first inquiry to the final payment. Sales representatives were supposed to continuously remind potential customers that "Blue Whale will take care of everything" and it was an explicit goal to have customers "breathe a sigh of relief" when Blue Whale movers arrived at their door. Additionally, each move was followed up with a phone call from a Blue Whale employee during which he/she asked the following questions:

1. *Do you feel that the movers on your job fully executed the Blue Whale vision statement?*

2. *Were you treated with respect and made aware of all the events that occurred on your move?*

3. *Can Blue Whale do anything further for you at this time?*

Exhibit 4   Blue Whale Awards and Honors During the First Six Years of Operation

1992   Best of Austin—"Best Way to Get from Point A to Point B"
Recipient: Blue Whale Moving Company, Inc.
Sponsor: *Austin Chronicle*

1993   Austin Entrepreneurs of the Year—Service Category
Recipients: Blake Miller, CEO, President /
Brad Armstrong, CFO, Secretary, Treasurer
Sponsors: Ernst & Young, *Inc.* Magazine, Merrill Lynch

1993   Best of Austin—"Best Moving Day Companions"
Recipient: Blue Whale Moving Company, Inc.
Sponsor: *Austin Chronicle*

1994   Blue Chip Enterprise/Blue Chip Initiative State Designee—Service Category
Recipient: Blue Whale Moving Company, Inc.
Sponsors: Connecticut Mutual Life Insurance Company, United States Chamber of Commerce, *Nation's Business* Magazine

1994   *Inc.* 500 Listing
Recipient: Blue Whale Moving Company, Inc.
Sponsor: *Inc.* Magazine

Customers were then asked to rate Blue Whale on a scale of 1 to 10. On average, customers rated Blue Whale a 9.5. Brad stated, "As we continue to grow and expand, we take pride in the high customer satisfaction ratings we consistently receive."[6] Each of these scores and comments was recorded and followed up on with managers and movers alike. Brad and Blake reinforced that negative experiences were to be eliminated and positive experiences were to be duplicated. The idea was that this feedback would help produce a positive experience for each and every customer. One clear sign that customers found value in the service they received was that 25 percent of Blue Whale's business was from repeat customers and 41 percent came from personal referrals,[7] far greater than the industry average. Customers became an unpaid but highly credible sales force, reducing Blue Whale's expenses for promoting itself.[8]

Blue Whale often received letters from customers thanking them for the care with which they transported their goods or just commending them for the overall moving experience (see Exhibit 5 for excerpts from customer satisfaction letters). These letters were promptly posted where all employees could see for themselves the difference they could make in a person's life.

Employees

Blue Whale had only 49 employees in 1993 and almost 75 percent of these were movers. The administrative side of the company was very small and could be loosely[9] broken down into operations, sales, accounting, and support staff, all of whom reported to the company vice-president, Jim Traynor. All movers reported to the operations manager, B. "Bernie" Bernard (see Exhibit 6 for the Blue Whale organizational structure), who also reported to Traynor.

Brad Armstrong. As one of the cofounders of the business, Brad Armstrong was the guiding force behind Blue Whale's customer service orientation. While originally having only a small role in the business in 1988, he became increasingly involved as Blue Whale's revenues grew. When he would visit potential customers on his marketing rounds, he would jovially recite the Blue Whale vision and then proceed to impress them with his many tales of customer service. He built relationships with past and potential customers so they felt as if they were part of the Blue Whale "family." Whether at a social or business gathering, he would never fail to discuss the merits of Blue Whale moving. Brad

---

[6] "Blue Whale Moving Company, Update" *Moving and Storage Times,* July 15, 1994.

[7] Blue Whale International, Inc., franchise proposal, 1995.

[8] "A Whale of an Idea."

[9] The term "loosely" is used because employees often covered each other's positions, as necessary.

Exhibit 5   Excerpts from Customer Satisfaction Letters

"I want to extend my thanks to your company's assistance with my grandmother's recent move. Your tremendous capabilities in aiding her during a busy time of the year and on short notice, proved to be very helpful. Your responsiveness and reliability are to be commended. I would be happy to recommend your company to anyone. Thank you again for all your help."

"This team of movers was professional, courteous, careful, and fast."

"The movers were professional, efficient, and sensitive to our concerns, especially with regard to several large and delicate antique pieces. The fellows were very patient, and they had a wonderful attitude, not only toward us but with each other as well. We can say that this was the most stress-free moving experience we have ever had! We would heartily recommend your company to our friends and neighbors. Thanks again."

"You run a business that is second to none. The entire moving event was actually pleasant due to your superior employees."

"The guys were courteous and attentive. I felt like we were friends!"

"The movers' careful handling of all of our furniture made the move a lot less stressful."

"I would definitely recommend Blue Whale to my personal friends and business colleagues."

"Moving is never pleasant especially right before Christmas and on a drizzly day, however, due to two of your employees my move was most pleasant. The movers were hardworking, punctual, polite, and just enjoyable. They should get high marks. I will highly recommend your company anytime due to their service. Blue Whale was recommended to me by several friends and now I can see why. Your company is run extremely efficiently. Keep up the good work."

---

felt that the Blue Whale approach was new and innovative, and was proud of it. In many cases, he made business decisions that sharply contradicted industry norms because he wanted Blue Whale to be built with completely original ideas. He noted,

> . . . if it has been done before by someone else, I tend to reject it. . . .

In addition to the customer focus, he also continuously stressed the importance of employee satisfaction. He talked with managers about employee needs and often asked new employees what they were hoping to achieve both as a part of Blue Whale as well as in their personal life. He tried to build a relationship with each employee and empower him/her to act in the best interest of the customer and, therefore, the company. The idea was that a happy mover was a good mover. While this was extremely uncommon in the industry, Brad felt that it was one of the most important elements of the business.

Most employees, however, felt that Brad was rather unapproachable. Instead of consulting with him on a business or personal issue, they would instead seek out Blake or employ a different approach to solving the problem.

Exhibit 6   Blue Whale Moving Co. Organization Chart, 1994

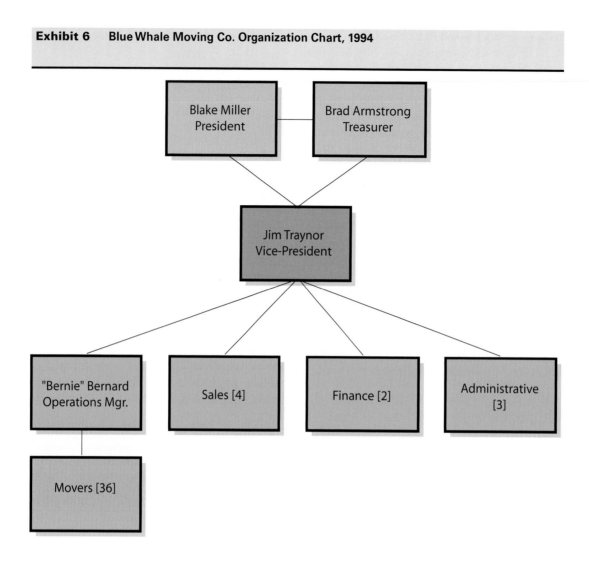

Blake Miller. Because Blake had worked as a mover prior to starting Blue Whale, he was responsible for the general operations of the firm. As profits grew, he shifted out of the "mover" role and into the "manager" role, but still maintained an inseparable tie to the day-to-day operations of the business. He was extremely driven, due in part to a strict upbringing by his father, and worked as many as 110 hours per week making the business run.

To some extent, Blake fit the stereotypical image of a tall, easygoing, friendly Texan. He frequently "visited with" customers during a move and talked with both them and the movers to see how things were going. At the end of a long moving day, when the movers congregated back at the office, he would join them for a beer or a good story. Movers respected him as "one of us" and often sought his help solving personal and professional problems. He established professional relationships with equipment leasing companies, gas stations, mechanics, advertising agents, the phone company, and any other source of external contact. When Brad was asked by a reporter to comment on one of Blue Whale's many awards, he said, "We're thrilled about it . . . but I really

give all the credit to Blake."[10] His comment reflected the general feeling throughout the organization.

Other Managers. Jim Traynor joined Blue Whale in 1992 and was named vice-president of Blue Whale in January 1994. Brad and Blake established the position in order to delegate some of the day-to-day operations of the business. Jim, an ex-mover in his late twenties, was responsible for the bottom line of the Austin office. He was given full authority to act in the best interest of the firm, with the exception of hiring employees, a responsibility that was retained by Brad and Blake. Although Jim was diligent, many employees felt that Brad and Blake still maintained full control of the organization and that Jim was no more than a puppet for the owners.

B. "Bernie" Bernard joined Blue Whale in 1991 as a mover and by 1994 had worked his way up to become the

---

[10] "Austin's Finalists for the 1993 Entrepreneur of the Year Award," *Austin Business Journal*, May 1993.

operations manager of the company. Bernie was responsible for managing all of the movers and scheduling jobs and equipment. Additionally, he often went out on moves on the weekends, when the administrative office was closed. There was no doubt in any employee's mind that Bernie was completely committed to Blue Whale and its values. Movers felt comfortable with him and trusted his ability to communicate their issues and concerns to both Jim and the owners. Where many employees felt that Jim was committed to Brad and Blake, the same individuals agreed that Bernie was committed to helping them.

CONTROL ISSUES

Movers

Blue Whale movers were called *associates* in all of the company's brochures. Brad and Blake felt this more accurately highlighted the caring relationship that the movers were supposed to develop with customers. Within the company, though, movers were called *movers*. Typical for the industry, they were not highly educated, some of them had spent time in jail, and all of them were strong. Movers generally stuck together and had little contact with the administrative office. They were happy just to show up in the morning to pick up a truck and a schedule, work hard all day, and get a paycheck at the end of the week.

Blue Whale movers were all hired as employees, while movers in the rest of the industry were typically hired as contract labor and bonded[11] by the firm. This was an expensive proposition (movers' pay represented about 45 percent of the total revenue of the firm), but Brad was adamant that Blue Whale not engage in a potentially damaging practice. Not only was the industry norm illegal, but it also encouraged movers to "cheat" on their taxes. Since income tax was not deducted from their paychecks, they frequently had no money saved up to pay the IRS when taxes came due. For this reason alone, Blue Whale movers had much more job security than movers employed with other companies.

The movers were paid on a commission (percentage per move) basis. Each mover on a two-man team typically received between 12 percent and 26 percent of the price of a move. If a third man was necessary, each mover would receive two-thirds of their two-man rate. Brad and Blake believed the commission basis created a disincentive for the low productivity typically seen with an hourly pay scheme. Movers under this compensation system were motivated to finish a job as quickly and efficiently as possible. The compensation for a hard working mover at Blue Whale was a little higher than at other companies in the industry. This was a critical factor because money was the most important element of the movers' motivation. When asked for the primary reason they enjoyed working at Blue Whale, each and

every mover responded, "The money." One mover made $52,000 in 1993. While this was extremely unusual (annual mover earnings averaged $25,000 to $30,000), compensation was clearly one of the benefits of working at Blue Whale. As was the case for other moving companies, movers were responsible for the payment of damages out of their own pocket. Although this rarely occurred, it was quite a bone of contention when it did.

Sales

Anywhere from three to five employees worked in a sales capacity. Most of their time was spent providing estimates over the phone, but they would also visit potential customers if the move was large enough or if the individuals wanted a written estimate. Their goal was to secure the move by whatever means possible. Often, this meant reducing the price of a move to be competitive with the industry. As one salesperson commented, ". . . some customers just don't understand our concept of customer service." This often created friction between the movers and the salespeople because the movers' pay was based upon the total dollar value of the job. The salespeople did their best to keep the movers happy, but they were primarily driven by their own needs, which were to book as many moves as possible and earn the small commission (between 3% and 5%) that came with each one. Salespeople earned between $24,000 and $28,000 per year, of which approximately 75 percent was salary-based.

Finance

One part-time clerk performed most of the financial functions within the firm. The clerk was not an accountant but rather an individual who was just "good with numbers." She spent most of her time processing payroll, depositing checks, and keeping the checkbooks balanced. One day a week, a CPA would come to Blue Whale and perform all of the "official"[12] accounting duties like budgeting and financial statement preparation.

BRAD AND BLAKE'S CHALLENGE

The two founders had tried a variety of management structures and controls over the preceding years, yet they remained unsure about which was the most effective. Even though they liked the idea of having a vice-president in charge of day-to-day operations, they wondered whether their direct involvement was essential to the functioning of the firm and were concerned that a vice-president might impede this contact.

---

[11] "Bonded" refers to the insurance that a moving company purchases to cover its contract employees for the damage or theft of goods.

[12] The term *official* is what the part-time clerk used to refer to the accountant's work.

Everything seemed to go so smoothly when the business was smaller and people were guided solely by the Blue Whale vision of customer service. Now the business was more complicated, and control of the business and its employees was much more difficult. Despite the "growing pains," Brad Armstrong and Blake Miller were as excited as ever about the possibilities that lay ahead of them, but they knew one thing for sure, the journey would not be easy. They had to not only get control of their business but also reach the goal of expansion they set forth in their mission statement. As they planned their discussions regarding the actions to be taken on some of the specific labor issues, they each thought individually about what needed to be done to get the entire business moving in the right direction again.

It was important to Blake and Brad that Blue Whale expand in its current markets, as well as in new markets. In the Blue Whale vision statement, they established an aggressive goal of opening 100 Blue Affiliates in different cities by the year 2000. As a first step along this path, they made a concerted effort to expand by opening offices in other Texas cities. Although they were optimistic about their plans, they questioned the timing and implementation of their expansion efforts. They also wondered if they could continue to use the management approach that had made their initial efforts so successful.

"The brilliance of the technology cannot take precedence over the market case. At the end of the day, if you're spending $5 billion on the technology, there better be a market for it. And if there isn't, there will be great humiliation."

–Herschel Shosteck, a Wheaton-based wireless analyst, in March 2000

"Iridium failed to match its system to its mission, which caused too much pressure on the company to get customers quickly."

–Leslie Taylor, a consultant for the satellite industry in Washington, in March 2000

Reviving Iridium

BSTR-031

IRIDIUM'S FAILURE

In August 1999, Iridium LLC[1] (Iridium), the world's largest provider of global mobile satellite voice and data solutions, filed for Chapter 11[2] bankruptcy protection in the United

ICFAI UNIVERSITY This case was written by **V. Sarvani** under the direction of **A. Mukund,** ICFAI Center for Management Research (ICMR). It is intended to be used as a basis for class discussion rather than to illustrate either effective or ineffective handling of a management situation.

The case was compiled from published sources.

To order copies, call 0091-40-2343-0462/63 or write to ICFAI Center for Management Research, Plot # 49, Nagarjuna Hills, Hyderabad 500 082, India or email icmr@icfai.org. Website: www.icmrindia.org.

[1] LLC or limited liability company is a hybrid legal entity that has the characteristics of a corporation and a partnership. An LLC provides its owners with corporate-like protection against personal liability, although it is treated as a non-corporate business organization for tax purposes.

[2] Often referred to as "business reorganization," Chapter 11 bankruptcy is one of the most complex areas of the U.S. bankruptcy law. Organizations/individuals can file for Chapter 11 bankruptcy to deal with their financial problems of a large magnitude. Those who file for Chapter 11 can propose a payment plan and their creditors can vote on this plan. If a stipulated number of creditors vote in favor of the plan, it is approved. Once it is approved, Chapter 11 essentially rewrites many of the contracts the debtor has with the creditors and thereafter both parties act according to the new agreement.

States Bankruptcy Court. The news did not come as a major surprise to the global telecommunications industry since the company's financial trouble was well known. It had defaulted on US$1.55 billion in bank loans.

Considering the company's investment loss of US$5 billion, the bankruptcy court imposed a deadline of March 15th, 2000 to either bring forth a purchaser or to close its operations. In response, Iridium promised that if it couldn't attract a buyer by 5 p.m. that day, it would proceed with plans to liquidate. Despite the company's best efforts, it was not able to convince any party to support its business and it was forced to file for bankruptcy. Following this, many executives in the top management cadre resigned and its satellite services covering an estimated 20,000 subscribers were stopped.

Commenting on the debacle, COO Randy Brouckman said, "I am deeply saddened by this outcome. I particularly regret the impact this will have on our customers. Iridium achieved significant milestones, and I want to thank the more than 160 countries that licensed the service and the distribution partners around the world who helped market Iridium."

A spokesman for Globestar, one of Iridium's major competitors, said, "We think Iridium could very well have succeeded. There's nothing wrong with the concept, but with their execution." Industry analysts commented that Iridium's chances of coming out of this crisis were very bleak. Many of them even stated that Iridium had all the features of a potential failure right from its inception.

BACKGROUND NOTE

The idea of Iridium was conceived in 1987 by three engineers—Ray Leopold, Ken Peterson and Bary Bertiger—who were working for the U.S.-based electronics major Motorola. They pioneered the concept of a satellite-based, wireless personal communications network that could be accessed from anywhere on earth. The engineers worked hard to bring to life the concept of satellite telephones. They launched gateways[3] in 1988 to facilitate the proposed Iridium satellites to communicate with the existing terrestrial telephone systems throughout the world.

In 1991, Motorola incorporated Iridium to develop and deploy the satellite network system. Besides Motorola, which held a 20.1% stake in the venture, some of the other major partners included Germany's Vebacom with 10%, Korea Mobile Telecommunications 4.4%, Sprint Corporation [with] 4.4% and Italy's STET with 3.8% stakes respectively. In 1992, the U.S. Government Federal Communications Commission (FCC) issued an experimental [license] to Iridium. In the same year, the World Administrative Radio Conference (WARC)[4] decided to work towards establishing guidelines to regulate worldwide radio spectrum rights and facilitate the building of Iridium systems.

In 1992, Iridium also signed a US$3.37 billion contract with Motorola for construction, delivery and system development. This made Motorola the prime contractor for supplying satellites, gateways and communication products for Iridium. By the end of 1993, the company had raised US$800 million as equity. After the second round of equity financing in 1994, Iridium's capital increased to US$1.6 billion. In 1995, the Federal Communication Department of the U.S. government granted an operational license to Iridium.

In 1996, Motorola launched the first Iridium satellite. In the same year, Iridium also entered into agreements with various mobile satellite service providers. The agreements were expected to facilitate their cooperation in the company's efforts to secure global authorizations for the use of [the] radio frequency spectrum[5] through "frequency-use plans."[6]

In the same year, it also managed to secure additional investment of US$315 million, bringing the total project capital to US$1.915 billion. Meanwhile, it also arranged for a credit of US$750 million from BZW and Chase banks. The company appointed Edward F. Staiano as CEO and Vice Chairman.

By 1997, Iridium launched 49 of the proposed 66 satellites successfully into [. . .] orbit. The same year, the company entered into strategic agreements with Kyocera to develop and market its wireless phones and with AlliedSignal to develop wireless telecommunication products for aircraft passengers and the crew. In the same year, Iridium came out with its IPO (Initial Public Offering) of $240 million and obtained $800 million in debt financing.

In 1998, Iridium selected Sprint Telecenters[7] to manage its global customer care centers. The company also obtained an additional US$350 million by issuing high yield bonds. All [. . .] 66 satellites were successfully launched by November 1998 and Iridium then launched its global satellite phone paging services. In 1999, Staiano resigned and John Richardson, the then CEO of Iridium Africa Corporation, was appointed the new CEO and Vice Chairman.

Iridium's venture into the upcoming Mobile Satellite Services (MSS) market marked a new beginning in the field of personal communications. In the late 1990s, analysts expected MSS to grow significantly over the next few years. Thus, the company's pathbreaking services were being heralded as the technology that would change the face of the global telecommunications industry.

ABOUT SATELLITE TELEPHONES

Satellite telephone systems work on the concept of wireless technology that uses individual radio frequencies to make and receive calls. These radio frequencies are used over and over again by dividing a service area into different geographic zones called "cells," with each cell having its own transmitter/receiver antenna. These cells could be as small as a building or as big as 50 km across. When a customer makes a call on a wireless phone, the message is transmitted by low energy radio signals to the nearest antenna site, which is connected to the local terrestrial phone networks. These messages are delivered to the receiver via phone lines if the call is made to a landline phone and by radio signals if the call is made to a wireless phone.

Whenever a wireless phone user reaches the boundary of a cell the wireless network immediately senses that the signal is getting weak and automatically passes the call to the antenna of the cell into which the caller is [traveling]. Customers can make/receive calls even when they are out of the accessible geographical area with the help of a wireless carrier. This facility is also known as roaming. The services that make use of wireless telephone technology are:

---

[3] Gateways interconnect a satellite constellation with public switched telephone networks, thus facilitating communication with handheld phones and any other telephone in the world.

[4] WARC was held in 1992 at Torremolinos, Spain, on behalf of the Committee on Radio Astronomy Frequencies (CRAF). CRAF works on behalf of the European Science foundation that is responsible for coordinating the use of frequency bands so as to keep the frequency bands used by astronomers free from interference. It also discusses issues related to the use of radio frequencies by different government organizations as well as corporations.

[5] It is considered a national asset and a scarce resource that had to be used keeping in mind the best interests of all those organizations that use it.

[6] The plan made for radio frequency bands and services in use or intended to be used in a particular frequency band.

---

[7] Sprint is a global communications company, which provides outsourced call center services for many *Fortune* 500 companies and multinational firms. It is the leader in advanced data communications services and also one of the world's largest carriers of Internet traffic. Sprint entered into a long-term multi-million dollar contract with Iridium for [management of the] 24-hour customer service centers named Iridium Global Customer Care Centers.

- Advanced Mobile Phone Service (AMPS): It is a cellular standard that transmits voice as FM radio signals. It is the most widely used system in the U.S.

- Code Division Multiple Access (CDMA): It is also known as the spread spectrum technology. CDMA uses a low-power signal that is spread across a wide bandwidth. Each phone call is assigned a code, which identifies it to the correct receiving phone. A large number of calls can be carried simultaneously on the same group of channels, by making use of the identifying code and a low-power signal.

- Time Division Multiple Access (TDMA): TDMA is a digital air interface technology designed to increase channel capacity by enabling it to handle simultaneous phone calls. Using TDMA, a signal is divided into pieces and each one is assigned to a different time (fraction of a second) slot. This increases channel capacity.

- Global System for Mobile Communications (GSM): This is a type of TDMA that has encryption[8] features. GSM has become a standard in Europe and the U.S. for mobile communications.

- Personal Communications Service (PCS): It is a completely digital, two-way, wireless telecommunications system specifically designed for the U.S. metropolitan areas. PCS networks are CDMA, TDMA and global system for mobile communications (GSM).

Satellite telephones are another kind of wireless telephone service that communicate via satellites circling the earth. There are two types of satellites:

- GeoSynchronous Satellites: These satellites, located 22,300 miles above the earth, revolve [a]round the earth every 24 hours and hence they appear stationary. Two frequency bands are used, one each for uplinking and downlinking. Such satellite systems are excellent for data transmission, but not very good for voice communications. This is because of the distance involved and the time taken for electrical signals to make one Earth-Satellite-Earth round trip. Because of the long time taken to send and receive signals, voice communications are usually not carried via GeoSynchronous satellites.

- Low Earth Orbit (LEO) Satellites: LEO satellites communicate directly with handheld telephones on earth. They are stationed as low as 900 miles above the earth's atmosphere. The communications equipment on a satellite catches the call from earth and passes it to an earth-based switching system. Due to the high speed at which the satellite revolves, it is necessary to hand off a particular call to another satellite that is just rising over the horizon. The process is similar to that of a cellular system, except in this case the cell site moves rather [than] the subscriber.

The demand for wireless cellular services has increased considerably from a mere 10 million subscribers in 1989 to around 520 million in 2001. Yet, using a wireless cellular service was not very convenient to people who were always [traveling]. They could not make calls to their desired places once they were out of their home network. Also, making calls to/from places following different cellular standards or

frequencies was not possible. Moreover, the cost for making international calls was high and GSM users had to use only GSM compatible handsets that [would] rather expensive because of high rental and call charges.

Here, MSS came to the rescue of those customers who required a telephone service that could be used anywhere in the world. The market for MSS has increased steadily in the last couple of years. With MSS, customers did not have to take different connections at different locations and change their handsets from country to country. According to a study,[9] the number of MSS subscribers was projected to increase from 0.5 million in 1999 to 8 million by the end of 2002. Also, the revenues from the business were expected to increase from $4 billion in 1999 to $19 billion by the end of 2002. [The] subscriber base for other services like data and paging was also expected to increase and their revenues were expected to reach around $2 billion by 2002 from $250 million in 1999.

Many players including Globalstar, Odyssey, and Inmarsat-P/ICO entered the MSS market seeing the strong growth potential (Refer [to] Exhibit 1). These companies employed different technologies like LEO, MEO and Geo-Synchronous satellites to deliver MSS services to customers. The Iridium system used a constellation of 66 LEOs (See Exhibit 2 for a detailed description of the working of Iridium's satellite system). However, the success of satellite telephone systems was dependent on a host of factors such as:

- Competition from other forms of service.

- Customer demand.

- Cost and financing.

- The ability of companies to capture different segments of the market.

- Access to critical foreign markets.

- The success of these innovative new technologies in the long run.

THE IRIDIUM VENTURE

Iridium had invested lot of money in R&D [and] building, deploying and [maintaining] its satellite constellation. Though Motorola realized the fact that the venture would involve substantial time and cost outlays and was very risky, it was perturbed when the venture consumed more time and money than expected.

By 1999, Iridium found itself in deep financial trouble with a huge amount of outstanding debt to be repaid to its bankers and creditors. Chase Manhattan, Iridium's lenders, had already given three extensions for repayment of loans by August 1999. Analysts remarked that the company's troubles

---

[8] Encryption is one way of ensuring data security. To read an encrypted file, a user must have access to a secret key or password that enables him to decrypt it.

[9] Leslie A Tailor of Leslie Tailor Associates conducted a study on Market Demand for Mobile Satellite Services, Satellite Statistics in 1999.

Exhibit 1   Players in the MSS Market

Name of System/ Application	Major Investors	Number of Satellites	Estimated Cost of Project/Service	Year of Operation
IRIDIUM [Handheld] dual-mode phones, paging, low-speed data transmission	Motorola, Raytheon, Lockheed Martin, Sprint, Khrunichev State Research (12 small investors)	66 (low-earth orbit)	$5 billion Handset: $2,000–$3,000 Charges: $3.00–$5.00/ minute (retail) Access fee: Varies by country	September 1998
GLOBAL STAR [Handheld] dual-mode phones, fixed ordinary phones, paging, low speed data transmission	Loral Space & Communications, Qualcomm Inc., AirTouch Communications, and others	48 (low-earth orbit)	$2.6 billion Handset: $750 Charges: 35–55 cents/minute (wholesale) Access fee: Service providers set the fees	August 1998 (partial), 1999 (full)
ICO GLOBAL COMMUNICATIONS [Handheld] dual-mode mobile phones; phones for cars, ships, aircraft; fixed phones in developing areas	ICO is a London-based private offshoot of INMARSAT; 47 investors including COMSAT, TRW and Hughes	12 (medium earth orbit)	$4.5 billion Handset: $1,000 Charges: $1.00–$3.50/minute (retail) Access fee: Varies by country	2000 (ICO was executed to launch its first satellite by the end of 1998)
ELLIPSO [Handheld] phones for mobile and fixed uses. Will use smaller satellites in highly inclined and equatorial orbits to provide low-cost service	Mobile Holdings Communications Inc. (Boeing, Spectrum Astro, Lockheed Martin, Israel Aircraft Industries, Vula Communications, and Harris Corp.)	17 (low-earth orbit)	$1.1 billion Handset: $1,000 Charges: 50 cents/minute Access fee: $35/month	2000
ECCO [Handheld]phone for mobile and fixed uses; focus on providing telecom coverage in equatorial countries such as Indonesia and Brazil, with remote villages and low-density populations spread throughout vast geographic areas	Constellations Communications (Orbital Sciences, Bell Atlantic, Raytheon E-Systems, Space Vest, Matra marconi)	12 (low-earth orbit)	$1.2 billion Handset: $750–$1,000 Charges: 60–90 cents/minute Access fee: $20–$40/month	2001

Source: Office of Telecommunications, U.S. Department of Commerce, July 17, 1998.

were not due to the concept of satellite telephones, but due to its faulty strategies.

Iridium had to spend a couple of million dollars every month just to maintain its infrastructure. In addition to the 66 satellites being used, Iridium was incurring heavy expenditure[s] to maintain the spare satellites as well (to be launched in case any of the 66 satellites failed). Moreover, the company planned to offer its services to a broad customer base so as to make the business viable.

The company needed at least a million subscribers to get close to the break-even point. This necessitated the maintenance of a dozen gateways, making the infrastructure involved very complex.

From the very beginning, Iridium faced problems in building up a sizeable subscriber base. Iridium targeted global business travelers and certain high-end customers.

But this market was not large enough. Consequently, in 1999, it had only 20,000 subscribers as [opposed to a projected] 60,000. Customers were not interested in using Iridium's services for various reasons. First, Iridium's subscribers had to essentially buy the specially designed Motorola handsets. They could not use any other handset. Consumers used to sleek and cheaper handsets were not happy with the bulky handsets that weighed almost a kg.[10] They were not only difficult to carry around but awkward to use as well. Second, handsets were also priced on the higher side at about US$2500 to US$3000, which was [. . .] a major deterrent. To

---

[10] The more popular cellular phones weighed less than 100 grams as compared to the heavy satellite phones and were small enough to fit in the customer's pockets.

Exhibit 2   Iridium's Satellite System Configuration

Components	Description
Iridium Satellites	With 66 satellites forming a cross-linked grid above the earth, the Iridium system is a low earth orbit for a wireless telephone service. Just about 700 km (480 miles) high, these satellites work different[ly] than those at a different orbit (36,000 km) in two major ways. They are close enough to receive the signals of a [handheld] device and second they act like cellular towers in the sky where wireless signals can move overhead instead of through ground-based cells.
Aeronautical	Iridium aeronautical services provide essential voice facsimile and data services to travelers on commercial, business, and general aviation aircraft. Compact, lightweight Iridium units are designed to [complement] existing aeronautical communications, offering passengers and crew convenient global access to telecommunications.
Iridium Pager	[Pocket-size] Iridium pagers are capable of receiving alphanumeric messages. For worldwide applicability, the message display will feature an international character set. An off-the-shelf disposable battery will provide an average lifetime of one month.
Iridium Telephone	The Iridium phone is the primary means by which the caller will communicate directly through the Iridium network. One telephone number with the use of a mini subscriber module (SIM) keeps the subscriber connected.
Iridium Gateway	Iridium gateways connect the Iridium constellations with public switched telephone networks, making communications possible between Iridium phones and any other telephone in the world.
Wireless Customer	A person who has signed for the Iridium services.
Terrestrial Wireless Switch	Iridium Gateways interconnect the iridium constellation with public switched telephone networks, making communications possible between Iridium phones and any other telephone in the world.
Wireless Operator	—

Source: www.iridium.com.

attract customers, Iridium reduced the price to $1000. In September 1999, Iridium's main competitor, Globalstar, launched its satellite telephone services with handsets initially priced at $1000 and later reduced to $700. This added to Iridium's problems.

Iridium's initial service charges were $7 per minute, which was later reduced to $2 to $4 per minute depending on the location (depending on the country they were used in—for example, in Japan, users paid an initial fee of $77 and a monthly charge of $50, plus actual call charges that ranged from $2.67 per minute to $6.59 per minute). To address the criticisms of high service charges, Iridium slashed its call rates to $1.50–2.50 per minute for domestic phone calls, and $3 per minute for international calls in June 1999. However, these charges were still very [much] higher than those for telephone calls made using terrestrial or cellular networks, which worked out to less than a dollar. To add to the company's problems, Globalstar priced its service charges on the lower side from 73 cents to $3, depending on the location.

Iridium faced another setback when it encountered technical problems during the launch of its services to customers. These problems were not limited to [one occasion] but [happened] several times. The company also faced delays in delivering handsets to its customers. Customers could not get the services according to the schedules announced by the company.

The service costs and handsets were not the only problems. There were many technical glitches as well. The company's phones did not work indoors, because they could not catch the signals relayed by the satellites. This was very inconvenient for the users who had to go outdoors to answer an incoming call. Moreover, Iridium did not offer any data services[11] initially.

All the above factors landed the company [in] deep financial problems. In the fourth quarter of 1998, Iridium posted a loss of $440 million and in the first quarter of 1999, Iridium reported a higher net loss of $505 million on revenues of only $1.45 million. The company could [sign up] only 10,294 customers as [opposed to their] projection of 57,000, as stipulated in the terms of the $800 million loan taken by the company. The company's sorry state of affairs prompted some of its major investors to file an involuntary Chapter 11 petition against it. Iridium's strategic partners began discussions to work out a financial restructuring plan for the company. However, they were not able to reach a consensus.

Commenting on this development, a member of the Steering Committee[12] that owned about 25% of Iridium's

---

[11] Facilities to connect to the Internet or a corporate network with the help of a satellite phone form anywhere on earth. Using this, the customer can browse the Web, send/receive email and transfer files.

[12] Iridium's major investors formed a steering committee called the "Informal Committee of the Holders of the Senior Notes of Iridium." Members of this committee were called the members of steering committee.

$1.45 billion in outstanding debt said, "Despite the best efforts of the parties involved, consensual agreement could not be reached on a restructuring plan. It became clear to the various parties at interest that a Chapter 11 filing was inevitable and, unless drastic action was taken, the company's assets could be at serious risk."

The company asked its key partners for investments but it did not get any positive replies. Even Motorola refused to invest more money into the failing company. However, it agreed to provide full operational support and a significant amount of technical, sales and marketing support. The company decided to file for Chapter 11 bankruptcy in August 1999.

Iridium also tried to look for some outside buyers, but again in vain. Though Craig McCaw[13] initially showed some interest, eventually he ended up buying one of Iridium's competitors, ICO Global Communications, which was also bankrupt. With even the last bidder turning away, Iridium had no other option but to decommission its network of LEOs and stop offering its services.

RESURRECTING IRIDIUM

Things changed dramatically for Iridium in late 2000 when Dan Colussy[14] came to the rescue of the company. He formed Iridium Satellite LLC (Iridium Satellite) and made a bid of $25 million, out of which $6.5 million was paid in cash, to acquire Iridium's business. This included purchasing all of Iridium's existing assets, its satellites and the satellite control network. In November 2000, the U.S. Bankruptcy Court for the Southern District of New York approved Iridium Satellite's bid to purchase Iridium's operating assets.

Following this, Colussy took many constructive steps towards positioning Iridium as the best mobile satellite service in the market. Iridium Satellite entered into a contract with aviation major Boeing to operate and maintain the 66-satellite constellation instead of Motorola, which now only provided subscriber equipment. He then introduced closely monitored plans to ensure a successful re-launch of Iridium's services.

Having learnt its lessons the hard way, Iridium Satellite was careful not to repeat [the] mistakes Iridium had committed earlier. Since Iridium was bought [...] for [only] $25 million as compared to the $5 billion spent to create it, the new management was not under severe cost pressures.

Iridium Satellite decided to make its satellite communications services affordable to customers and refocused on its target customer base. It decided to target all those industry segments that had a particular need for satellite communications like the government, military, humanitarians, heavy industry, maritime, aviation and adventure. Along with voice communications, Iridium also launched a series of data services, Simple Messaging Service (SMS) and paging services for its customers. The company started offering several value-added features that include:

- Flat rates for calls from/to anywhere in the world.

- Unlike cellular services where customers had to use different phone numbers for different locations, Iridium proposed [giving] its customers the facility of using only one phone number worldwide.

- Introduction of SIM cards[15] and a host of other Internet-enabled features.

In December 2000, Iridium Satellite got [a] much needed boost when the U.S. Department of Defense (DoD), awarded a $72 million contract to the company for providing satellite communications services for the next two years. By the end of March 2001, Iridium Satellite had re-launched its commercial services.

The company also incorporated certain technological improvements in the satellites and handsets, which improved [the] quality of voice and equipment performance. The company's research showed that each satellite could function well for around seven years. Since many of these satellites had already been in orbit for 2–3 years before the launch of the service to customers, they had only 4–5 years of satellite life left. However, with the above improvements, the company ensured longer life for its satellite constellation.

In late 2001, Iridium Satellite also changed the design of its handsets. The company launched handsets weighing less than 400 grams that were as light and small as regular cellular phones. The cost of calls had also become cheaper than that of calls made on GSM mobile phones. Iridium charged a flat rate of $1.50/minute to call any other phone in the world, without any constraint on the duration of the call made. Reportedly, Iridium also claimed to have attained the status of being able to provide 100% global coverage.

The company also took steps to enhance its customer service and support by setting up 24/7-customer support call centers. This improved its acceptance in the market and enhanced its goodwill.

With all these favorable developments, it seemed that Iridium was resurrected and was on the road to success. The

---

[13] A pioneer in the cellular telephone industry and a leading name in the global wireless communications industry. He was the Chairman and Co-CEO of Teledesic, the leading U.S.-based telecommunications company. He initially made a $75 million offer to buy Iridium but later backed off.

[14] An aviation industry businessman who had previously served as Chairman, President and CEO of the U.S.-based aviation major UNC Inc.; Chairman, President and CEO of Canadian Pacific Airlines; and President and COO of Pan American World Airways.

---

[15] [The] Subscriber Identification Module (SIM) card is a "smart" card that allows users to make and receive calls. The SIM card identifies the user to the network and contains a microprocessor chip, which stores unique information about the user account, including [the user's] phone number and security number. SIM cards have many functions like providing memory space to save up to 100 names, phone numbers and 15 short text messages (SMS).

company had come a long way [toward] becoming the most advanced telephone and paging service [to] date.

Questions for Discussion

1. What were the reasons for Iridium's failure during the first phase of its launch despite substantial support from banks, creditors and suppliers? Explain in detail.

2. Identify and explain the critical success factors for a company operating in the mobile satellite services industry. How did Iridium fare on all these counts?

3. Conduct a SWOT analysis for Iridium Satellite LLC. Using this analysis, comment on the future of the company's services.

4. Dan Colussy revived Iridium, which had been written off as a bankrupt company, with his turnaround strategy. What was the turnaround strategy adopted by Colussy? Which elements of the strategy, in your opinion, were critical to the revival of the company and why?

Additional Readings & References

1. Blodgett, Mindy, **Delayed Satellite Launch Hampers Global Network,** www.computerworld.com, February 03, 1997.
2. Fisher, James, **Sprint Telecenters Wins Multi-Million Dollar Contract to Support Global Communications Consortium Iridium LLC,** www3.sprint.com, January 21, 1998.
3. Taylor, A. Leslie, **Market Demand for Mobile Satellite Services: Satellite Statistics Phillips' Satellites 99**, www.ita.com, February 4, 1999.
4. Farmer, Austria Melanie, **Iridium Posts Wider Loss,** www.news.com.com, April 26, 1999.
5. Stewart Fist, **Iridium and the LEOs,** www.electric-words.com, May 1999.
6. Sheridan, H. John, **Bullish on Iridium,** www.industryweek.com, June 21, 1999.
7. **Telecommunication Will Be Wireless,** Government Computerization Newsletter No 13, www.unescap.org, June 1999.
8. **Iridium Files for Bankruptcy Protection,** www.space.com, August 13, 1999.
9. **Iridium Files for Bankruptcy,** www.ustoday.com, August 13, 1999.
10. Goodman, S. Peter, **Without an Angel Iridium's Sky Will Fall,** www.washingtonpost.com, March 16, 2000.
11. Motta, Mary, **Iridium Falls to Earth,** www.space.com, March 17, 2000.
12. **Iridium Announces End of Satellite Telephone Service,** www.floridatoday.com, March 20, 2000.
13. Brown, S. P., **Iridium Eradication,** www.splittrader.com, March 22, 2000.
14. Motta, Mary, **Analysts Say Iridium's Downfall Has Limited Ripple Effect,** www.space.com, August 29, 2000.
15. **Eleventh Hour Bid Rescues Iridium,** www.eham.net, Nov 17, 2000.
16. Weiss, R. Todd, **Pentagon Awards $72M Wireless Contract to Iridium,** www.computerworld.com, December 11, 2000.
17. Weiss, R. Todd, **Iridium Satellite Launches Service Today,** www.computerworld.com, March 28, 2001.
18. Mathewson, James, **Iridium Is Staying Alive. This Is a Deal for the Ages,** www.computeruser.com, August 6, 2001.
19. **For the Consumer—How Wireless Works,** www.wow.com, September 11, 2001.
20. **The World's First Global Handset-Iridium Handset—Our Story,** www.iridium.com.
21. **Corporate [Fact] Sheet,** www.iridium.com.
22. **Falling Prices Hit Operators,** www.specials.ft.com.
23. **Services-Iridium,** www.matrixmaricom.com.
24. Gordon, Masson, Iridium Service Heralds a New Era in **Personal Communications**.
25. **IRIDIUM LLC: Company History,** www.iridium.com.
26. Whatisasimcard, www.travelbuyarc.com.

"We need a new, dynamic global partnership of business and politics. The dust of the trust crisis has settled somewhat. And many national governments have demonstrated their ability to act swiftly within their own territories. Now we should join forces in leading the way towards a wider, increasingly multilateral approach to Corporate Governance rules."

–Jürgen Schrempp, CEO, DaimlerChrysler AG, 2003

DaimlerChrysler: Corporate Governance Dynamics in a Global Company

Ever since the announcement of the merger between Daimler-Benz AG and Chrysler Corporation in May 1998, the company had been in the spotlight. The merged company, DaimlerChrysler (DC) was a full-range provider controlling six car brands and eight truck brands. In addition, DC acquired strategic holdings in Mitsubishi Motors of Japan (37% stake) and Hyundai Motors of Korea (10% stake). Besides this global push, DC divested many of its non-core businesses as recommended by the financial community. Nevertheless, the dividend dropped from €2.35 in the first three years to €1.00 in 2001. By 2002 the turnarounds at Chrysler and Mitsubishi had led to profitability, and the dividend was raised by 50%. However, by 2003, an ongoing price war in North America, with average rebates of $4,500 per vehicle, was proving costly and the outcome was uncertain.

Over the years, DC became an international benchmark for global operations and management. As for all corporations, corporate governance was of special importance. New regulations, a lack of shareholder and public confidence in big business, and general uncertainty increased the pressure on companies to consider their governance structures. How could a company such as DC reconcile regulatory differences and the diverse expectations of various stakeholders around the globe? There was agreement that corporate governance "had to be lived," but how?

Research Associate George Radler prepared this case under the supervision of Professor Ulrich Steger as a basis for class discussion rather than to illustrate either effective or ineffective handling of a business situation.

BACKGROUND: UNDERSTANDING THE DAIMLERCHRYSLER MERGER

When the merger of Daimler-Benz AG and Chrysler Corporation was announced on May 6, 1998, this "merger in heaven" came as a total surprise to everyone in the industry. Both companies seemed to complement each other well on geographic and product dimensions[1] and both had outstanding reputations. *Forbes* had even selected Chrysler as "company of the year 1996":

> *You may think of Chrysler as an old-fashioned metal bender in a mature industry, cyclical as hell. You may think it's just lucky with all those Jeeps and minivans when everyone happens to want a Jeep or minivan. Jeeps and vans go out of fad, Chrysler flops. That's the perception—which is why Chrysler stock sells at less than seven times earnings. But perceptions notoriously lag reality, and we think the reality here is that Chrysler's good luck is being leveraged by a superb management team that has made smart, disciplined decisions.[i]*

Chrysler was perceived as a very efficient producer and thereby earning more cash than any other major carmaker. Daimler-Benz's luxury car division (Mercedes-Benz) was the envy of the industry. This was a "merger of equals" with anticipated synergies of $1.4 billion for a combined revenue

---

[1] See Radler, Neubauer and Steger, *The DaimlerChrysler Merger: The Involvement of the Boards,* Case no. IMD-3–0771, for detailed corporate governance issues during the merger negotiations in 1998. The present case only covers the developments after the deal had taken place.

Figure 1   Overview of Phases

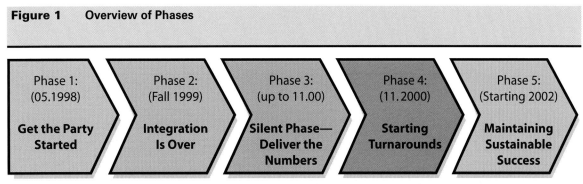

| Phase 1: (05.1998) Get the Party Started | Phase 2: (Fall 1999) Integration Is Over | Phase 3: (up to 11.00) Silent Phase—Deliver the Numbers | Phase 4: (11.2000) Starting Turnarounds | Phase 5: (Starting 2002) Maintaining Sustainable Success |

Note: While reading this case, please keep on referring to *Exhibit 1* for the representation of the phases and the creation/elimination of various committees.

of $132 billion in its first year of operation. The merger of these two icons also caught the attention of the public right from the beginning. This $36 billion merger became a symbol for what is generally described as a complex business environment for global players: total transparency, Wall Street formulating earnings growth, and immense scrutiny of all stakeholders involved.

With hindsight, the merger developments between 1998 and 2003 can be split into five phases. Figure 1 gives an overview of the five phases.

Revenues increased from €132 billion in 1998 to €162 billion in 2000, before falling to €150 for 2002 *(refer to Exhibit 2 for a fact sheet on DaimlerChrysler for the five years up to 2002).*

Exhibit 1   Overview of Phases and the Creation/Elimination of Various Committees

| Phase 1: (05.1998) Get the Party Started | Phase 2: (Fall 1999) Integration Is Over | Phase 3: (up to 11.00) Silent Phase—Deliver the Numbers | Phase 4: (11.2000) Starting Turnarounds | Phase 5: (Starting 2002) Maintaining Sustainable Success |

Management Board
17 Members ────────────────────────→ 11 Members

termination   *pooling*

Committees
Chairmen's Integration Council ──→ Automotive Council
Automotive Integration Teams ──→
Non-Automotive Council ──→ Sales & Marketing Council
→ 2001 EAC established ──→

Supervisory Board
20 Members ────────────────────────→ 20 Members

Committees
Mediation Committee
Presidential Committee
Audit Committee
Labor Committee
Shareholder Committee ────────────→

termination

Additional External Bodies
2001: Chairman's Council established ──→
Alliance Committee with Mitsubishi ──→
International Advisory Board ────────────────────→

Source: IMD Analysis.

Exhibit 2   DaimlerChrysler Fact Sheet 1998–2002 (in € billion)

	1998	1999	2000	2001	2002
Revenues	131.782	149.985	162.384	152.873	149.583
Operating Profit	8.593	11.012	9.752	(1.318)	6.854
Operating Margin	6.5%	7.3%	6.0%	(0.9%)	4.6%
Net Operating Income	6.359	7.032	4.383	1.647	4.335
Net Operating Income as % of Net Assets (RONA)	12.7%	13.2%	7.4%	2.5%	6.7%
Net income (loss)	4.820	5.746	7.894	(662)	4.718
Cash Dividend per Share in €	2.35	2.35	2.35	1.00	1.50
Employees (in 000s)	442	467	416	372	366

Sales and Operating Profit by Division 2002 (in € billion)

	Sales	Operating Profit
Mercedes Car Group	50.170	3.020
Chrysler Group	60.181	0.609
Commercial Vehicles	28.401	(0.343)
Services	15.699	3.060
Other Activities	2.723	0.903

Regional Sales Distribution 2001

	DaimlerChrysler	Global GDP Distribution
NAFTA	53%	36%
Western Europe	31%	27%
Asia	11%	27%
ROW	5%	10%

Source: DaimlerChrysler.

Phase 1: Merger Announcement 1998—"Get the Party Started"

Initially, the rationale for the deal was clear. In an interview on October 5, 1998 Dieter Zetsche, board member of Daimler-Benz AG, explained:

> Our problem has been that costs are high for these new technologies because of our low volume. We always lost the technology to competitors. (. . .) Like with ESP (electronic stability program) we wanted one year of exclusivity [from our suppliers]; but they gave us three months, and we had to fight for it. Chrysler will give us the volume. We can stay No. 1 in developing technology—and take it as soon as possible to Chrysler.[ii]

The synergy target of $1.4 billion (around 1% of gross revenue) was generally seen as low, but there was only a limited overlap of products. Helmut Petri, executive VP Production for Mercedes cars, explained at the time: "There will be no platform sharing. We can share parts and components, but we won't share platforms." However, competitors in the industry considered platforms as the "holy grail" for reaping synergies.

November 17, 1998 marked the first day of stock-trading for the DC share, which rose by around 30% to the high €90s in the spring of 1999. Executives and board members were trying to turn DC into one company, not just a company name. The integration was organized around 17 clusters (Issue Resolution Teams, or IRTs) and dealt with both automotive and non-automotive issues (*refer to* **Exhibit 3** *for an overview of the integration structure and IRT cluster*). A corporate airline was set up to shuttle executives between Stuttgart (home of Daimler-Benz) and Auburn Hills (Chrysler), with video or telephone conferences complementing the integration efforts.

As part of the strategy to become a truly global company, managers at DC continued to develop strategies for Asia. Asia was going to be *the* growth market for automobiles, but it was a missing link for DC. DC identified two possible

Exhibit 3 Integration Structure and IRT Clusters

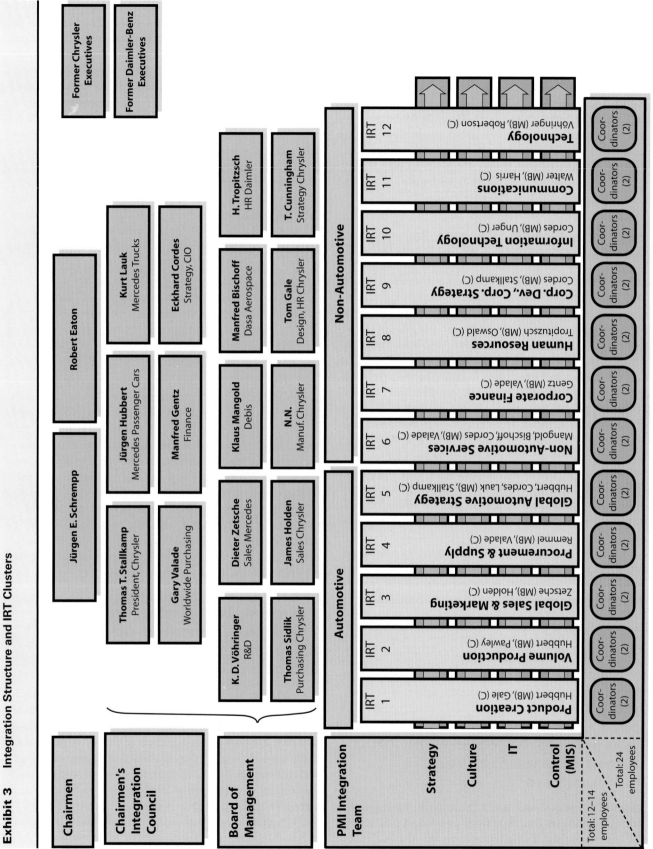

Chairmen

Jürgen E. Schrempp

Robert Eaton

Chairmen's Integration Council

Board of Management

Thomas T. Stallkamp
President, Chrysler

Gary Valade
Worldwide Purchasing

K. D. Vöhringer
R&D

Thomas Sidlik
Purchasing Chrysler

Jürgen Hubbert
Mercedes Passenger Cars

Manfred Gentz
Finance

Dieter Zetsche
Sales Mercedes

James Holden
Sales Chrysler

Kurt Lauk
Mercedes Trucks

Eckhard Cordes
Strategy, CIO

Manfred Bischoff
Dasa Aerospace

Tom Gale
Design, HR Chrysler

Klaus Mangold
Debis

N.N.
Manuf. Chrysler

H. Tropitzsch
HR Daimler

T. Cunningham
Strategy Chrysler

Former Chrysler
Executives

Former Daimler-Benz
Executives

PMI Integration Team

Strategy

Culture

IT

Control (MIS)

Automotive

Non-Automotive

IRT 1	Product Creation — Hubbert (MB), Gale (C)
IRT 2	Volume Production — Hubbert (MB), Pawley (C)
IRT 3	Global Sales & Marketing — Zetsche (MB), Holden (C)
IRT 4	Procurement & Supply — Remmel (MB), Valade (C)
IRT 5	Global Automotive Strategy — Hubbert, Cordes, Lauk (MB), Stallkamp (C)
IRT 6	Non-Automotive Services — Mangold, Bischoff, Cordes (MB), Valade (C)
IRT 7	Corporate Finance — Gentz (MB), Valade (C)
IRT 8	Human Resources — Tropitzusch (MB), Oswald (C)
IRT 9	Corp. Dev., Corp. Strategy — Cordes (MB), Stallkamp (C)
IRT 10	Information Technology — Cordes (MB), Unger (C)
IRT 11	Communications — Walter (MB), Harris (C)
IRT 12	Technology — Vöhringer (MB), Robertson (C)

Coor-dinators (2)

Total: 12–14 employees

Total: 24 employees

Source: Company information Case IMD-3-0771.

625

partners and even performed due diligence for acquiring a stake in Nissan Motors. However, after a lively discussion among the management board, this idea was dropped.

As integration got off the ground, second quarter earnings (1999) failed to meet Wall Street expectations and the stock started to fall. In addition, the share was refused from the American S&P 500 index, a move which took the stock off the shopping list of many funds. By July, the company had to reduce its earnings growth expectations and suddenly synergies became very important. *Automotive News,* an industry journal, stated: "Meanwhile, Wall Street, underwhelmed by the company's performance to date, is expecting much more from DaimlerChrysler."[iii]

Phase 2: September 1999 "Integration Is Over!"

On September 27, 1999 Jürgen Schrempp announced the completion of the integration of both companies. The formal integration with its 17 IRTs was concluded and the Chairmen's Integration Council was abandoned (after two of its eight members left the company). One of them, Tom Stallkamp, the president of North American Chrysler operations and the executive in charge of integrating the company, was replaced by James Holden. Holden was previously executive VP Sales & Marketing.

Following its earlier decision to focus its business lines, DC decided to concentrate on the automotive and trucking business. Non-core activities (Adtranz trains, Debitel telecommunications, European Aeronautic Defense and Space Company [EADS, maker of Airbus]) were either sold, prepared for sell-off or merged with other companies. Selling some of the non-core businesses added financial flexibility for possible acquisitions.

But the geographic expansion continued. Schrempp and his team were convinced that they needed a local partner in Asia in order to participate in the forecasted growth there. In the summer of 2000 DC ultimately bought:

- A 34% equity stake in Mitsubishi Motors of Japan, and later raised it to 37%.

- A 10% equity stake in Hyundai Motors of South Korea.

With this set-up, DC did not need to consolidate these minority stakes, which was an issue given Mitsubishi Motors' debt.

Phase 3: Up to November 2000 "Silent Phase—Deliver the Numbers"

The year 2000 was actually a good year for the car industry. Mercedes-Benz cars benefited from its product line extension and maintained strong financial results. The American market was performing very well and a new record was expected for the whole year. However, Chrysler was no longer able to grow with the market. A flood of new competitive

models was expected in the minivan segment for which Chrysler had up to 55% share (in the U.S.). As a result, Chrysler loaded its new minivan with expensive options and prices rose accordingly. However, sales of the new minivan were below expectations and the vehicles needed sales incentives/price reductions early on. For Chrysler's other pillar of profitability, SUVs, a wide range of competitive products was suddenly eating into Chrysler's market, too.

The results soon became visible: Chrysler's U.S. market share fell from over 16.2% in 1998 to 13.5% in 2000 and no miracle cure was to be expected from international demand. In order to move the vehicles, cash rebates/incentives of up to $3,000 had to be paid. At the same time, production costs spiraled out of control, as production capacity could not be reduced fast enough (*refer to* **Exhibit 4** *for a comparison of manufacturing hours by make*). In late 2000 *Fortune* reported:

> (. . .) after its merger with Daimler-Benz, Chrysler was in the midst of one of its once-a-decade swoons. Having ridden the crest of the 1990s boom with popular minivans and sport-utility vehicles, the company's American managers had allowed costs to career out of control and big gaps to open in Chrysler's new-product program. Despite record U.S. auto sales, the company reported an operating loss.[iv]

Within DC, divisions had to meet prearranged profit and sales targets ("deliver the numbers"). This approach made it relatively easy to compare different divisions and several executives hoped it "would bring back the Chrysler spirit." Holden argued that Chrysler could not make money because of the huge incentives that were bringing down transaction prices. When the Chrysler Group missed a set of prearranged goals (and profit levels), a supervisory board meeting was held on November 17, 2000 and the decision taken to dismiss Holden—after only one year. DC brought in Dieter Zetsche, who had been running the commercial vehicles division, and he started three days later. However, in the fall of 2000, the share price fell below €50.

Phase 4: November 2000 "Starting Turnarounds at Chrysler, Mitsubishi and Freightliner"

The situation facing Zetsche when he arrived was complicated. According to Ward's *Autoworld*, "to say that Zetsche inherited a mess is an understatement." He arrived in Detroit with only his chief operating officer (COO), Wolfgang Bernhard, to a welcome that was anything but friendly. During a press conference, Zetsche was asked how many more Germans they should expect in Detroit. He replied: "Four. My wife and three kids."

Excluding one-time write-offs, Chrysler Group lost $1.8 billion in the last two quarters of 2000. Within DC, the Mercedes Car Group was producing strong cash flows and in Stuttgart, the public opinion was that Mercedes was financing the rest of the Group. After three months, Zetsche pre-

Exhibit 4   Perception vs. Reality at Chrysler

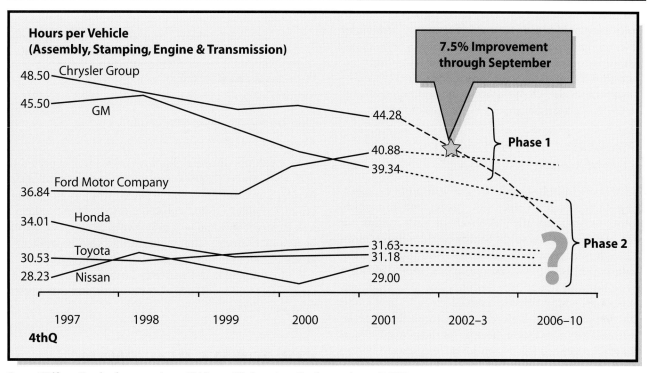

Source: Wolfgang Bernhard, presentation at JP Morgan/Harbour Auto Conference, August 7, 2002.

sented his turnaround plan. *The Economist* reported on February 3, 2001:

> *Chrysler's German overlords this week mounted a dramatic assault on the growing losses at DaimlerChrysler's ailing American subsidiary. At least 26,000 jobs will go [equivalent to 20% of the total workforce] in a reorganization that will close six plants and trim production at seven more. (. . .) Analysts (. . .) noted the absence of any American assembly plants on the list. The plant in Belvidere, Illinois, which produces the slow-selling Neon, seemed a sure bet to be shuttered, but Chrysler inadvertently outsmarted itself two years ago, when it agreed to restrictions on plant shutdowns as part of its contract with the United Auto Workers union.*

The turnaround plan called for lowering the break-even point from 113% of plant capacity in 2001 to 83% in 2003.[v] Zetsche's first quarter (Q1, 2001) finished with an operating loss of €1.4 billion, and the full year saw a loss of $5 billion (including one-time effects) at Chrysler.

The equity stakes in Asia (Hyundai and Mitsubishi) developed differently. While Hyundai was becoming highly profitable due to very successful cars and trucks, Mitsubishi required more management attention. Rolf Eckrodt, formerly CEO of ADTRANZ trains [a DC subsidiary that was sold off in 2001], became COO of Mitsubishi Motors in January 2001 and in summer 2002, he left DC and took over as CEO of Mitsubishi Motors.

Mitsubishi Motors had too many models and no real success. The company was plagued by a set of issues. *Manager Magazin*, a German publication, commented:

> *No controlling, inefficient structures and processes, which killed the company due to excessive harmony. After two failed turnaround attempts, the company was unable to reform itself.[vi]*

The turnaround plan at Mitsubishi was drastic. Within three years, the production capacity was going to be cut by 28% and material cost by 15%. The turnaround was also a test for the DC merger, as it dispatched a group of 35 executives from both companies to Japan. The financial year 2000 ended with a loss of $750 million at Mitsubishi.

Neither of the equity stakes in Asia were limited to cars. In 2002 both Mitsubishi and Hyundai spun off their truck and bus divisions. Soon afterwards, DC announced the acquisition of a 43% share in Mitsubishi Fuso Truck and Bus Corporation for €760 million. In Korea, the "Daimler Hyundai Truck Corporation" was expected to be founded in 2003 with both companies holding equal shares.

DC's truck division, with revenues of €28 billion in 2002, also saw considerable changes. In 2000 DC acquired Detroit Diesel, a highly regarded supplier of heavy-duty engines, and Western Star Trucks of Canada for $877 million. But around the same time, Freightliner, DC's trucking division in North America, was facing problems. The American market for new trucks decreased by 50%. This slump hit Freightliner, as market leader for heavy trucks, especially hard. The demand for new trucks collapsed, and at the same time, leasing models were returned. "Easy credit" and market values dropping below the book values led to a huge loss on each leasing truck returned. In the case of Freightliner, Jim Hebe, the CEO overseeing the leasing deals, was replaced by Rainer Schmückle. Schmückle knew the company quite well from a previous assignment as CFO of Freightliner.

Phase 5: "Maintaining Sustainable Success"

By 2002 both Mitsubishi and Chrysler were profitable again. Chrysler recorded an operating profit, and Mitsubishi Motors recorded an after-tax profit of $290 million for 2002—the highest ever in the history of Mitsubishi Motors! Although budgets were cut in many cases, the number of products increased. In the case of Chrysler, capital spending was reduced by about 30%—while eight additional new models were added. Chrysler even developed a new model with the help of the Mercedes Car Group, the Chrysler Crossfire. Executives had high hopes for the new vehicles, as sales of Chrysler had fallen from 3.2 million units in 1999 to 2.8 million in 2002. Nevertheless, Chrysler set a growth target of one million additional units by 2011.[vii] Table 1 summarizes the results between 1998 and 2002.

However, 2003 remained a challenging year. The *Financial Times* reported on June 5, 2003:

> *Chrysler's incentives for buyers have reached $4,500 per vehicle, almost doubling in a year. . . . The company said Chrysler's second-quarter operating loss would be about €1 billion—against analyst forecasts of a €500 million profit. Most of the difference was accounted for by an estimated $400m–$500m writedown in the value of 500,000 cars in dealers' lots and by a cut in the second-hand value of cars held by rental companies.*

By Q3, 2003, Chrysler was able to rebound into profit, but the focus on controlling cost continued. The share price remained at around €30.

In order to reap the synergies, Chrysler and Mitsubishi also evaluated the development of a joint platform with an annual volume of one million cars. This was expected to enter the market by 2005. For the same year an annual capacity of 1.5 million units was expected from a "global four cylinder engine." Of this, 600,000 units would be made in a new factory that would be jointly owned by Chrysler, Mitsubishi and Hyundai. The engine would also be built in a Hyundai factory in Korea and at Mitsubishi in Japan.

In summary, DC had considerably streamlined its portfolio. Table 2 outlines major acquisitions and divestitures since 2000.

CORPORATE GOVERNANCE AT GLOBAL CORPORATIONS POST-ENRON

Manfred Gentz, DC's chief financial officer, commented as early as 1999 on the corporate governance challenges:

> *The merger of the former Chrysler Corporation and the Daimler-Benz Aktiengesellschaft presented us with a number of integration challenges, including how to combine two different legal systems in such a way as to meet the differing expectations of each company's shareholders and management. With DaimlerChrysler AG's corporate governance, which was already finalized in the Business Combination Agreement of May 6, 1998, we tried to find a solution that combines German and U.S. forms of corporate management.*

While the merger was taking place and requiring considerable management attention, the external environment

Table 1   Financial Summary in € billion (at year-end)

	1998		2002	
	Sales	Operating Profit	Sales	Operating Profit
Mercedes Car Group	32.6	1.9	50.2	3.0
Chrysler Group	56.4	4.2	60.2	0.6

Source: Der Spiegel, September 8, 2003: 117.

Table 2   Major Acquisitions and Divestitures (year, company, value)

	Acquisitions			Divestitures	
2000	Mitsubishi Motors (34%, later 37%)	€2 billion	2000 and 2002	Debis Systemhaus (IT Services)	€5.5 billion
2000	Hyundai (10%)	$428 million	2001	Debitel (mobile phone operator)	€300 million
2000	Detroit Diesel and Western Star	$877 million	2001	ADTRANZ trains	$725 million
2003	Mitsubishi Trucks	€760 million			

Note: DC owns 33% of EADS. This stake was estimated at around €5 billion at the time of the IPO in 2000.

for corporate governance changed dramatically. Although DC was legally based in Germany, it was traded on the New York Stock Exchange (NYSE) and hence had to adhere to many rules and regulations: [the] Sarbanes-Oxley Act, SEC regulations and the German Corporate Governance Code. On top of that, DC had to comply with German codetermination rules and other peculiarities in the different countries where DC operated. The effort and bureaucracy involved were considerable:

■ **The Sarbanes-Oxley Act (SOA)** aimed to improve investor confidence and the accuracy of financial statements. It stated that CEOs and CFOs should certify the "appropriateness of the financial statements . . ." and that the audit committee should be totally independent.

■ **[The] American Securities and Exchange Commission (SEC)** stipulated more detailed requirements for audit committees, e.g., committee members had to prove their familiarity with US-GAAP accounting rules. The chief regulators also wanted a better power balance between managers, board members and shareholders.

■ **The German Corporate Governance Code** (Cromme Code) provided an overview of various existing laws and regulations in order to create transparency for foreign investors (as opposed to creating new laws). This resulted in about 50 recommendations (e.g., deductible of liability insurance for directors and officers, or the need to disclose financial reports within 90 days). By law, publicly traded companies had to state whether they complied with each recommendation (*refer to Exhibit 5 for the main headings of the code*). If not, management was requested to publish reasons for not doing so. In addition, there were several suggestions covering items such as individual salaries of management board members.

    Generally, the code was seen as an opportunity to evaluate control and management structures. Moreover, according to the code, members of the management board could be on a maximum of five different supervisory boards of listed companies if they held executive functions in [other] listed companies. The code also suggested more personal liability (including personal assets) and a maximum of two members could immediately transfer from the management board to the supervisory board. The code also strongly encouraged the creation of different committees. The chairman of the commission, Gerhard Cromme, explained: "[After all], an efficient and confidential discussion is not possible at regular supervisory board meetings."[viii]

■ **Intricacies of the German Corporate Governance System:** The German system had some special features:

    ■ The size of board meetings in this two-tier system was considerable. With 20 members of the supervisory board, plus the board of management, plus staff, there could easily be up to 40 people at the table. As an American board member put it, "A German supervisory board meeting is like an opera."

    ■ Increasingly, the salaries of German supervisory board members were heavily debated among the general public. The lowest paid head of a supervisory board (Lufthansa Airlines) earned €21,000[2]—the highest paid (Schering Pharmaceuticals) received €343,000. Kari-Hermann Baumann, former CFO of Siemens and now on the supervisory boards of six big German companies (Siemens, Deutsche Bank, Eon, Linde, Schering,

---

[2] Salary levels are for 2001 or 2002.

Exhibit 5   **German Code for Corporate Governance**

Chapter 1: Foreword

Chapter 2: Shareholders and the General Meeting

2.1 Shareholders

2.2 General Meeting

2.3 Invitation to the General Meeting, Proxies

Chapter 3: Cooperation Between Management Board and Supervisory Board

Chapter 4: Management Board

4.1 Tasks and Responsibilities

4.2 Composition and Compensation

4.3 Conflicts of Interest

Chapter 5: Supervisory Board

5.1 Tasks and Responsibilities

5.2 Tasks and Authorities of the Chairman of the Supervisory Board

5.3 Formation of Committees

5.4 Composition and Compensation

5.5 Conflicts of Interest

5.6 Examination of Efficiency

Chapter 6: Transparency

Chapter 7: Reporting and Audit of the Annual Financial Statements

7.1 Reporting

7.2 Audit of Annual Financial Statements

Source: Government Commission, German Corporate Governance Code, version May 21, 2003; www.corporate-governance-code.de.

Thyssen-Krupp), earned a total salary of €589,000. In comparison, a board member at Nestlé earned on average €371,000 in 2002 (for one seat). At DC, the 2003 annual assembly voted for an increase from €51,000 to €75,000 for regular members of the supervisory board and from €102,000 to €225,000 for the chairman.

■ German corporate law was written with the aim of protecting creditors and thereby allowed companies to accumulate hidden reserves, using book values rather than market values in accounting, etc. This was in sharp contrast to the American system, where corporate laws were aimed at creating transparency for the shareholders, allowing them to control management, and thereby limiting principal–agent conflicts.

CORPORATE GOVERNANCE AT DAIMLERCHRYSLER

At DC, trying to adhere to the different codes caused regulatory conflicts. While Sarbanes-Oxley increased the personal responsibilities of CEOs and CFOs, in Germany the members of the management board had collective responsibility (*refer to* **Exhibit 6** *for more conflicts*). As part of this collective responsibility, the board met as a "legal entity" rather than as a set of individuals. At the same time, Sarbanes-Oxley also led to considerable organizational adjustments, in order to comply with the comprehensive requirements. Schrempp explained:

> In this context, several international initiatives designed to improve corporate governance and restore public confidence in the corporate sector have been undertaken. (. . .) I can tell you:
>
> 1. There can be no barriers to information.
>
> 2. The whole company has to be as committed to DaimlerChrysler's balance sheet as Manfred Gentz [CFO] and I are. It is obvious that with their signature on those documents, the chairman and the CFO are accepting certain obligations for the company. Therefore, it is also clear that every senior executive must feel this obligation as well.
>
> 3. This means that we will install a cascade signing system. Starting with every General Manager and CFO of every business entity within DC and going to the top via every principal.

Due to the changes in the corporate governance landscape, considerable challenges lay ahead. As Dr. Manfred Schneider, member of the supervisory board at DC, explained: "We have to anticipate that in the future less people will be willing to become members of the supervisory board or even head of the supervisory board."[ix]

For a global company like DaimlerChrysler, corporate governance was centerstage. But corporate governance went far beyond the newly introduced six-page special in the 2002 annual report. This special feature covered the functioning of the annual meeting, a short explanation of the two-tier system and some of the legally non-binding arrangements: Executive Automotive Council (EAC), Chairman's Council and the International Advisory Board (IAB). The implications of the new corporate governance system were far-reaching, as can be seen by the developments on both boards and within various committees.

THE MANAGEMENT BOARD: RUNNING DAIMLERCHRYSLER

Developments

Strong leaders, such as Lee Iacocca, often dominated the board of [the] former Chrysler Corp. Their ability was to get designers to "think outside the box" while getting their managers to meet budgets and cost targets. In 1999 key executives of [the] former Chrysler Corp. left the DC management board, including Stallkamp (President), Gale (Design), Cunningham (Strategy), and co-chairman Bob Eaton followed in March 2000. On the former Daimler-Benz side, two members had left the board: Lauk (Trucks) and Tropitzsch (HR). After Holden's dismissal in November 2000, two former Chrysler executives remained on the board (both in purchasing functions).

Between 1998 and 2003 the board shrank from 17 members to 11, and by 2003 only two members retained their original positions (Hubbert, Mercedes Car Group, and Gentz, CFO). In the process, the structure of the board was also changed. The organizational chart showed clear separations between operating and functional divisions (*refer to* **Exhibit 7** *for the evolution of the organizational chart*). Several former board members remained as advisors to the company (Mangold, Bischoff, Valade). Interestingly, new board members appointed were only "deputy board members," with a

---

Exhibit 6   Managing Conflicts

	Germany	USA
CEO/CFO Certification (Sarbanes-Oxley Act)	Collective responsibility of the board of management	Personal responsibility of CEO and CFO
Disclosure of Deviation to Regulation (German Code, NYSE)	Disclosure of deviation from German Code	Disclosure of significant differences to CG practices*
Audit Committee Appointment of Auditors (Sarbanes-Oxley Act, NYSE)	Annual general meeting of shareholders	Audit committee
Public Company Accounting Oversight Board Inspections	Secrecy agreement between company and auditor	Right to request confidential records from auditor
D&O Insurance Policy	Introduce suitable deductible/excess	Deductible/excess not common

*Not yet in effect.

Source: DaimlerChrysler.

Exhibit 7   Evolution of the Board of Management (1998–2003)

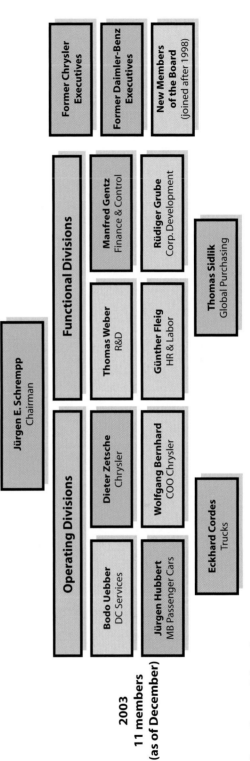

1998
17 members

Former Chrysler Executives
Former Daimler-Benz Executives

Robert Eaton
Chairman

Jürgen E. Schrempp
Chairman

Gary Valade
Global Purchasing

K. D. Vöhringer
R&D

Dieter Zetsche
Sales Mercedes

N.N.
Manuf. Chrysler

Tom T. Stallkamp
President, Chrysler

Eckhard Cordes
Strategy, CIO

Kurt Lauk
Mercedes Trucks

Tom Gale
Design, HR Chrysler

Thomas Sidlik
Purchasing Chrysler

Manfred Gentz
Finance

Manfred Bischoff
Dasa Aerospace

T. Cunningham
Strategy Chrysler

James Holden
Sales Chrysler

H. Tropitzsch
HR Daimler

Klaus Mangold
DC Services

Jürgen Hubbert
MB Passenger Cars

2003
11 members
(as of December)

Former Chrysler Executives
Former Daimler-Benz Executives
New Members of the Board (joined after 1998)

Jürgen E. Schrempp
Chairman

Operating Divisions

Functional Divisions

Bodo Uebber
DC Services

Dieter Zetsche
Chrysler

Thomas Weber
R&D

Manfred Gentz
Finance & Control

Jürgen Hubbert
MB Passenger Cars

Wolfgang Bernhard
COO Chrysler

Günther Fleig
HR & Labor

Rüdiger Grube
Corp. Development

Eckhard Cordes
Trucks

Thomas Sidlik
Global Purchasing

Source: Company information.

631

three-year contract rather than the usual five-year contract for regular board members (the norm in Germany). Company policy generally required board members over the age of 60 to have their contracts renewed on an annual basis.

Working Style

Initially the meetings were held in Stuttgart and Auburn Hills, but most American meetings were soon moved to New York (for travel reasons). English was the management language. Annually, there were between 22—in 2003—and 35—in 2000—meetings (*refer to **Exhibit 8** for the frequency and location of meetings*).

Creation of New Committees

In the first year of the merger, the Chairmen's Integration Council (CIC) was a central point of the integration. However, the overlap between the CIC and the board of management could not be avoided (*refer to **Exhibit 3***) and all members of the management board were also allowed to join the meetings of the CIC. On the CIC, votes had to be unanimous, while on the management board they could be majority-based. The CIC ceased to exist in September 1999, as the integration was officially completed. Instead, two councils (Automotive, and Sales & Marketing) were set up to coordinate possible component sharing, etc. However, both councils were abandoned.

The potential for sharing components and parts increased fundamentally with the addition of partners in Asia. In order to reap "potentially huge synergies" (*Wall Street Journal Europe*) from economies of scale and to improve the decision-making procedure, the Executive Automotive Committee (EAC) was set up. This committee, co-chaired by Schrempp and Hubbert, normally met before each board meeting and prepared recommendations regarding the product portfolio, technology, production capacity, and sales and marketing. The EAC's recommendations were then taken to the board (*refer to **Exhibit 9** for an overview of the EAC*). Besides Hubbert and Schrempp, EAC members included Zetsche (Chrysler), Cordes (Trucks), Bischoff (Head of the Alliance Committee with Mitsubishi) and Grube (corporate development). All of them were board members, too.

Grube's staff members prepared the materials for the EAC. Early on in the process, the team considered corporate governance implications. Grube explained:

> *Strategic initiatives, e.g., our new efforts in China, are discussed on every aspect of our corporate governance system. Strategy depends on feedback and consensus in our governance structure.*

For cultural and legal reasons, a similar EAC structure was set up for the minority stakes in Asia. The "Alliance Committee" functioned in [a] similar way to the EAC. In 2002 a similar structure to the EAC was also created for trucks (Truck Product and Decision Committee).

SUPERVISORY BOARD: KEEPING UP IN A CHANGING INDUSTRY

In the German two-tier system, the main function of the supervisory board was to supervise, advise on and monitor business developments. At the same time, this board was also responsible for hiring board members (for which a two-thirds majority was required). The spoken language was German, but all documents were prepared in both German and English, with simultaneous translation at the meetings. The meetings remained driven by the issues. Lynton Wilson, former board member of Chrysler and current board member of DC, explained the style of these meetings:

> *Schrempp is a very American-style leader. He is open and [knows] he has to make sure to have relationships and support in the company. So the discussions are matter of fact, issue-related and [end with a decision] on what to do.*

The DC supervisory board was led by Hilmar Kopper, former CEO and chairman of Deutsche Bank, who also sat on the boards of Akzo Nobel, Xerox, Solvay and Unilever. The media reported on the close working relationship between Kopper and Schrempp.

The supervisory board had seen few membership changes on the capital side over the years (*refer to **Exhibit 10** for the evolution of the supervisory board*). The supervisory board met six times in 2003, both in the U.S. and in Germany.

CORPORATE GOVERNANCE IN ACTION

DC, like any other global company, had to deal with increasing complexity. However, its corporate governance system

Exhibit 8	**Frequency and Location of Management Board Meetings**				
	1999	2000	2001	2002	2003*
Germany	11	13	17	16	16
USA	17	18	9	7	6
Other	1	4	1	1	—
Total	**29**	**35**	**27**	**24**	**22**

*planned

Note: Some of these board meetings lasted for two days. In this case, they were counted twice. This list also includes meetings of the strategic and planning process.

Source: Company information.

Exhibit 9   Role of the Executive Automotive Committee

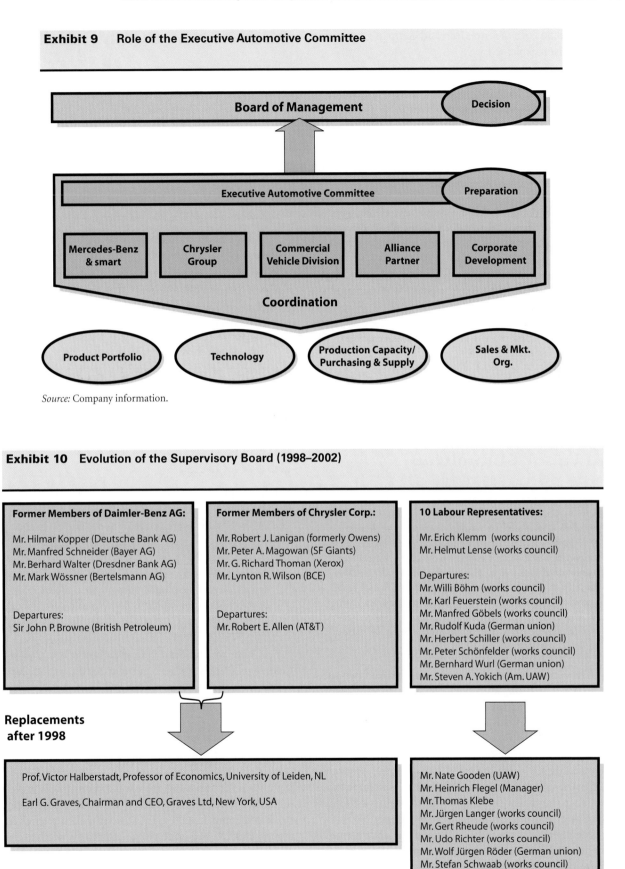

Source: Company information.

Exhibit 10   Evolution of the Supervisory Board (1998–2002)

Former Members of Daimler-Benz AG:	Former Members of Chrysler Corp.:	10 Labour Representatives:
Mr. Hilmar Kopper (Deutsche Bank AG)	Mr. Robert J. Lanigan (formerly Owens)	Mr. Erich Klemm (works council)
Mr. Manfred Schneider (Bayer AG)	Mr. Peter A. Magowan (SF Giants)	Mr. Helmut Lense (works council)
Mr. Berhard Walter (Dresdner Bank AG)	Mr. G. Richard Thoman (Xerox)	
Mr. Mark Wössner (Bertelsmann AG)	Mr. Lynton R. Wilson (BCE)	Departures:
		Mr. Willi Böhm (works council)
		Mr. Karl Feuerstein (works council)
		Mr. Manfred Göbels (works council)
Departures:		Mr. Rudolf Kuda (German union)
Sir John P. Browne (British Petroleum)	Departures:	Mr. Herbert Schiller (works council)
	Mr. Robert E. Allen (AT&T)	Mr. Peter Schönfelder (works council)
		Mr. Bernhard Wurl (German union)
		Mr. Steven A. Yokich (Am. UAW)

Replacements after 1998

Prof. Victor Halberstadt, Professor of Economics, University of Leiden, NL Earl G. Graves, Chairman and CEO, Graves Ltd, New York, USA	Mr. Nate Gooden (UAW) Mr. Heinrich Flegel (Manager) Mr. Thomas Klebe Mr. Jürgen Langer (works council) Mr. Gert Rheude (works council) Mr. Udo Richter (works council) Mr. Wolf Jürgen Röder (German union) Mr. Stefan Schwaab (works council)

Source: Company information.

had to combine both the American and German governance systems. Wilson explained:

> We are talking here about two very different systems. In North America, non-executive directors are much more involved and have certain responsibilities. In the German system, you have co-determination. Nevertheless, both systems work.

Three committees were established, each consisting of two shareholder and two employee representatives.

1. Presidential Committee: Employment terms and remuneration for board members. It also conducted "preliminary discussions on key decisions to be taken by the supervisory board."
2. Audit Committee: Examination of annual and semi-annual statements of accounts. This committee also ensured the independence of the auditors. The committee's work became a lot more important due to Sarbanes-Oxley.
3. Mediation Committee: In case of disagreement between supervisory board members with regard to the nomination of the new board (this was required by law).

Over the years, however, DC developed several legally non-binding committees:

Shareholder Committee and Labor Committee

The shareholder committee was a big change for the German establishment. CFO Gentz explained:

> A shareholder committee modeled on the U.S.-style board of directors was set up alongside the supervisory board. The committee included the two chairmen, all ten shareholder representatives as well as four prominent outsiders. [This committee] has no decision-making powers, which rest solely with the supervisory board, but instead restricts itself to debate and counseling and provides fact-based recommendations to support opinion-forming among the shareholder representatives.

The committee met six times a year and had two sub-committees. The audit sub-committee dealt with the examination of financial accounts and dividend policy, while the nomination & compensation sub-committee dealt with remuneration of board members and senior executives. The aim was to ensure competitive packages on a global scale, for which outside advisors were hired. However, the issues discussed in the shareholder committee were too similar to those discussed in the supervisory board—it was seen as a duplication, and the committee ceased to exist in January 2001.

Members of the workforce formed the labor committee to accommodate the needs of American and Canadian labor unions, which had only one seat on DC's supervisory board. In addition, employees formed various international committees that were independent of the supervisory board; they met around five times in 2003.

ADDITIONAL COMMITTEES
Chairman's Council

A new council was started in the fall of 2001. The *Financial Times* reported in September 2001:

> DaimlerChrysler, the international automotive group, is to become the first German-based company to embrace Anglo-Saxon corporate governance rules by forming an independent chairman's council of non-executive directors. (. . .) Officials describe the project as a "unique hybrid" between Anglo-Saxon corporate governance and the co-determination preferred by most German companies.[x]

The Chairman's Council consisted of six selected members of the capital side of the supervisory board and selected external members, including CEOs from blue chip companies. In a press statement, DC formalized the council:

> The council will provide advice to management on global business strategy issues. Elements of American and European corporate governance structures are combined to meet the specific requirements of a truly global company and the interests of the different stakeholders. The legal rights and responsibilities of the supervisory board will remain untouched. The Chairman's Council is complementary to the current governance structure.

International Advisory Board (IAB)

The IAB replaced the Daimler-Benz International Advisory Board, which was started in 1995. It usually met once a year. The IAB's activities were outlined in the annual report:

> The IAB of DaimlerChrysler advises the DaimlerChrysler Group on questions relating to global economic, technological, and political developments and their effect on the business activities of the group. It supports the DaimlerChrysler Board of Management but is not responsible for making business decisions. The meetings are private to encourage frank and open discussion.

(Refer to **Exhibit 11** for members of the Chairman's Council and IAB.) Figure 2 summarizes the various levels of supervision and management in DC.

OUTSIDE VIEW: FINANCIAL MARKETS

Right from the beginning, there was a strong focus on pleasing the financial markets. DC tried to create awareness about the stock price and installed TV screens showing stock prices around HQ. DC had done a lot to cater to the needs of institutional investors. Even before the merger, both companies had used U.S. GAAP accounting rules; afterwards DC added detailed reporting according to business segments, value-based stock options plans and employee profit sharing based on operating profits. Nevertheless, the base of American share-

Exhibit 11   Members of the Chairman's Council and International Advisory Board

Chairman's Council

Jürgen E. Schrempp	Chairman

Internal Members

Victor Halberstadt	Prof. of Economics, Leiden University
Hilmar Kopper	Chairman of the Supervisory Board DCX
Robert J. Lanigan	Chairman Emeritus of Owens-Illinois
Dr. Manfred Schneider	Chairman of the Supervisory Board of Bayer AG
Lynton R. Wilson	Chairman of the Board of Nortel Networks
Dr. Mark Wössner	Former CEO and Chairman of Bertelsmann

External Members

The Lord Browne	Group CEO of BP Amoco
Louis V. Gerstner, Jr.	Former Chairman and CEO of IBM
Minoru Makihara	Chairman of Mitsubishi Corp.
Dr. Daniel Vasella	Chairman & CEO of Novartis AG
Lorenzo H. Zambrano	Chairman and CEO of Cemex

International Advisory Board (IAB)

Internal Members

DC Board of Management

External Members

12 members with various backgrounds in academia, politics and business.
The members are based in Asia, Europe and the Americas.

Source: Company information.

holders was rapidly decreasing. By December 31, 2002 American shareholders accounted for only 14% of total DC shareholders (down from 44% in 1998). Most shareholders were based in Germany (57%), with 21% in the rest of Europe and 8% in the rest of the world, other than the U.S. The reduction in the number of American shareholders could have been the result of DC's removal from the S&P 500 Index or, as an industry expert explained, "Americans don't trust the two-tier boards." The stock price development was unsatisfactory, but it was in line with that of major competitors (*refer to Exhibit 12 for the share price development of DC and some competitors*).

Deutsche Bank remained the largest shareholder, owning 12%, followed by the Emirate of Kuwait, with 7%. Institutional investors held 54%, private investors 27%.

UNDERSTANDING RISKS

The globalization of DC created many opportunities. However, for corporate governance purposes, it was also essential to understand the business risk. Besides risks originating from *off-balance sheet activities* or *bad debt*, DC and other car companies faced considerable industry-specific risks: Being a global player and consolidating in euros, any drastic *exchange rate fluctuations* could severely impact the financial results. At the same time, large parts of the operating income resulted from *financial services* (e.g., car leasing), a business dependent on many "outside" forces. DC also faced considerable *technology risks* (e.g., fuel cells, fuel efficiency, lightweight materials). Missing one trend could mean suffering for half a decade. The increasing number of brands brought with it the risk of wrong *brand positioning*. Also, because the factory assets were so specific to the industry, the *exit risk* was considerable. And since the merger, the company was also increasingly subject to North American risks such as *product liability* issues or court cases from *disgruntled shareholders*.

In 2003 Schrempp commented on the merger and corporate governance:

> *When Daimler-Benz and Chrysler merged, there was no textbook written on how to do it. I admit, we were not as efficient from day one as we could have [been]. But now the international cooperation and the implementation of the strategy work very well.*[xi]

And they broke new ground in corporate governance, too.

Endnotes

[i] Flint, Jerry. "Company of the Year: Chrysler." *Forbes*, January 13, 1997, p. 82 ff.

[ii] "Merger Details, from 'Autonomy' to 'Zetsche.'" *Automotive News*, October 5, 1998, Vol. 73, Issue 5787, p. 41 ff.

[iii] Kisiel, Ralph. "Gale: D/C Won't Share Platforms." *Automotive News*, October 4, 1999, Vol. 74, Issue 5841, p. 1.

[iv] Taylor, Alex. "Just Another Sexy Sports Car." *Fortune*, March 17, 2003: 32.

[v] Taylor, Alex. "Can the Germans Rescue Chrysler?" *Fortune*, April 30, 2001: 47.

[vi] Hirn, Wolfgang. "Die Revolution von Tokio." *Manager Magazin*, November 2002: 88ff.

[vii] Smith, David C. "Is This the Next Chairman?" *Ward's AutoWorld*, November 2002: 48.

[viii] Wiskow, Jobst-Hinrich. "Beschränkter Durchblick." *Capital*, March 6, 2003.

[ix] "Neue Aufsichtsräte sind nur noch schwer zu finden." *Handelsblatt*, April 1, 2003.

[x] Burt, Tim. "First German-Based Firm to Adopt Anglo-Saxon Corporate Governance Rules." *Financial Times*, September 28, 2001.

[xi] "Ein hartes Stück Arbeit," Interview with Jürgen Schrempp. *Der Spiegel*, September 8, 2003: 120.

Figure 2   Levels of Supervision and Management (scheduled number of meetings in 2003)

Controlling the Management...	Managing the Company...	Advising the Management...
Supervisory Board 6 meetings p.a.	Board of Management 22 meetings p.a.	Chairman's Council 5 meetings p.a.
International Employee Committees 5 meetings p.a.	Executive Automotive Committee 10 meetings p.a.	International Advisory Board 1 meeting p.a.
...according to German Law & Co-Determination Principles	...combining German legal requirements and global business needs	...combining elements of U.S. and European Corporate Governance

Exhibit 12   Share Price Developments of DaimlerChrysler vs. Major Competitors

Source: www.comdirect.de.

"I spend my life being Odysseus. I tie myself to the mast, and I don't listen to the Sirens."

–Michael Eisner, chairman and CEO of Disney in 2002[1]

"Michael has used the shield of corporate governance to get rid of people who were not in his pocket."

–Andrea Van de Kamp, an ex-director of Disney in 2003[2]

"It's almost a religious view, fervently held, that directors (at Disney) don't talk. They don't talk to the press. They don't talk to investors. They don't talk about what goes on in the boardroom. I think that's got to change. They were elected by the shareholders, and they ought to be accountable. As it stands now, the owners have no clue as to who's effective or what's going on."

–Richard Koppes, a corporate governance lawyer with Jones Day in 2003[3]

Trouble in the "Magic Kingdom" — Governance Problems at Disney

BECG-038

DISNEY DIRECTORS RESIGN

At the end of November 2003, Roy Disney (Roy), the vice chairman of the Walt Disney Company (Disney) and the chairman of its animation department, resigned from the company. Roy was the nephew of Walt Disney (Walt), the

ICFAI UNIVERSITY — This case was written by **Sirisha Regani**, under the direction of **Sanjib Dutta**, ICFAI Center for Management Research (ICMR). It is intended to be used as a basis for class discussion rather than to illustrate either effective or ineffective handling of a management situation.

The case was compiled from published sources.

To order copies, call 0091-40-2343-0462/63 or write to ICFAI Center for Management Research, Plot # 49, Nagarjuna Hills, Hyderabad 500 082, India or email icmr@icfai.org. Website: www.icmrindia.org.

founder of Disney, and last surviving member of the Disney family to work at the company. Holding over 17 million shares, he was the company's largest individual stockholder and served on the board of directors. Roy's resignation was said to be prompted by the information that he would not be nominated to the board in the following year. This was because according to the new corporate governance norms adopted by Disney in 2002, he was past the maximum age limit to be a director of the company. Roy, who had served the company throughout his life in various capacities, preferred to avoid such an ignominious exit and chose to resign voluntarily.

Close on the heels of Roy's resignation came the resignation of Stanley Gold (Gold), an investment banker, who was also a director at Disney. Both men wrote lengthy resignation letters outlining their reasons for leaving the company. They laid the major portion of the blame on Disney's CEO and chairman[4] Michael Eisner (Eisner) who, they alleged, did not run the company in accordance with the principles of good governance. They also expressed concern that bad governance would put the future of the company at risk, unless drastic changes were made. They believed that Eisner

---

[1] Marc Gunther, "Has Eisner Lost the Disney Magic?" *Fortune*, January 7, 2002.

[2] Marc Gunther, "Disney's Loss Is Eisner's Gain," *Fortune*, December 22, 2003.

[3] Marc Gunther, "The Directors," *Fortune*, December 27, 2003.

[4] In early March 2004, Eisner was replaced by former U.S. Senator George Mitchell as the chairman of Disney after 43% of shareholders gave him a no-confidence vote.

was the root of all troubles at Disney and that the company would benefit from his departure. In his resignation letter to Eisner, Roy wrote, "It is my sincere belief that it is you that should be leaving and not me."[5]

The company's board was also criticized for being a rubber-stamp to the decisions of Eisner and for not giving sufficient consideration to the benefit of the shareholders. Criticizing the board, Gold wrote, "It is clear to me that this board is unwilling to tackle the difficult issues I believe this company continues to face—management failures and accountability for those failures, operational deficiencies, imprudent capital allocations, the cannibalization of certain company icons for short-term gain, the enormous loss of creative talent over the last years, the absence of succession planning and the lack of strategic focus."[6]

After leaving the company, both men launched a public campaign to oust Eisner ([whom] they had helped appoint in 1984). They said that he held sway over the board and ran the company like a "personal fiefdom." Both were considering meeting with the company's major shareholders to muster support in their campaign.

Well known for its animated films and theme parks, Disney was popularly known as the "Magic Kingdom," because of the entertainment and pleasure it provided to children and adults alike. However, the resignation of two of the company's directors and their bid to oust the CEO made analysts wonder if the Magic Kingdom was losing its magic.

BACKGROUND NOTE

Disney was first set up by Walt and his brother Roy O. Disney (the father of the present Roy Disney) in 1923, as a small studio. The studio was moderately successful, making and selling short animated films and commercials. In 1927, during a train journey from New York to Los Angeles (where the studio was based), Walt created the character of Mickey Mouse. In November 1927, the Disney studio made "Steamboat Willie," the first Mickey Mouse animated film. It was also the first animated film synchronized to sound. The movie was very successful and Mickey Mouse soon became the world's most loved cartoon character.

Over the years, the Disney studio grew and started making several other animated films apart from Mickey Mouse cartoons. In the late 1920s, Disney animators started working on an animation series called "Silly Symphonies." This series featured animation pieces that were set to classical music. One of this series, "Flowers and Trees," won Disney its first Academy Award. In the late 1930s, [the] Disney studio made "Snow White," which was the first ever full length animation film. "Snow White" was extremely successful, receiving critical acclaim as well as commercial success.

Gradually, the studio began making live action movies [without] animation. The first live action movie made by Disney was "Treasure Island."

In the early 1940s, Walt conceptualized Disneyland, which was to be a theme park that would provide entertainment facilities for children as well as their adult companions. To raise money for the development of the park, Walt decided to make a television show, which would yield additional revenues [for] the studio. The first Disney television show, also called "Disneyland," debuted on [the] ABC network[7] in 1954. [The] Disneyland park was opened in 1955 and soon became very popular, attracting millions of visitors every year from all around the world.

In the 1960s, [the] Disney [studio] made films like "Sleeping Beauty," "101 Dalmatians," and "Pollyanna," which did reasonably well, but were not successful enough to make huge profits for the studio. In the mid-1960s, the studio made "Mary Poppins,"[8] a movie that Walt had been trying to make since the 1950s. The movie was a huge success and received 13 Academy Award nominations. In 1966, Walt died of lung cancer. After Walt's death, the company was managed by his brother Roy Disney. Under him, the company opened Walt Disney World, a new theme park in Florida, which was Walt's unrealized dream. (The concept for the park was initially called Experimental Prototype Community of Tomorrow [EPCOT], and was later renamed Walt Disney World.)

Roy Disney died in 1971, and after his death Don Tatum (Tatum) became the chairman and Card Walker (Walker), the president of the company. Ron Miller (Miller), Walt's son-in-law, became the executive producer. According to analysts, the successors lacked the vision of Walt and Roy Disney and almost led the company to bankruptcy. Initially, the company had planned to fund the EPCOT project completely with outside sponsorship. However, as the work progressed, a part of the company's internal surpluses had to be ploughed into the project. This led to a severe resource crunch. Another major problem cropped up in 1979 when 14 of the company's best animators left it. In 1980, after Tatum retired, Walker became the chairman and CEO of the company. In 1982, the EPCOT center was finally opened and plans were made for a new Disney channel on television. The channel was launched in 1983, the same year in which Tokyo Disneyland was opened.

In 1983, Walker resigned from his post and Miller became the CEO. Just a month later, Miller gave up his post to Ray Watson (who was his [right-hand] man in the company). These constant changes in leadership led to a steep fall in the company's share price. The share price fell from

[5] *Corporate Conflict*, www.cbsnews.com, December 1, 2003.

[6] *Corporate Conflict*, www.cbsnews.com, December 1, 2003.

[7] American Broadcasting Corporation. One of the biggest television networks in the U.S. It was taken over by the Disney conglomerate in 1995.

[8] *Mary Poppins* was a book written by Pamela L. Travers, published in 1934. "Mary Poppins" is also the name of the lead character in the book and its sequels.

$84 in 1983 to $45 in 1984. The lowered share prices and the lack of stability in the top management resulted in a number of corporate houses attempting to take over Disney in the early 1980s.

One of the most serious takeover bids faced by Disney was from Saul Steinberg (Steinberg), the chairman of Reliance Group Holdings Inc.[9] Steinberg started making serious bids to acquire stock in Disney. By April 1984, he had acquired 8.3% of the stock and announced his intention to acquire 25% of the company before long. Recognizing the threat, Disney management started making defensive moves. It announced its decision to buy back shares at a premium. Roy and Gold played a very important role at this stage and helped muster shareholder support to prevent Disney from being taken over.[10] They enlisted the support of the Bass family, who were the largest shareholders in Disney, to regain a majority. Steinberg finally agreed to re-sell his stock to the company at a premium of $32 million and an additional $28 million for his expenses. All this added to the huge debt of the company. By the mid-1980s, what was needed was a change in leadership to bring about a turnaround.

Disney's board, led by Roy and Gold, installed Eisner as the chairman and CEO of Disney and Frank Wells (Wells) as its president in 1984. The decision to bring in Eisner proved to be a good one as Eisner and Wells helped Disney reestablish its position in the entertainment industry. They began by revamping the entire internal structure of the company. They brought in 60 executives from Warner Bros. and Paramount Studios, two of the major movie studios in Hollywood, and retrenched over 1000 Disney employees. They developed a new culture among the employees, of complete commitment to the company. The employees were expected to stay late every night and work seven days a week. A new strategic planning department was set up, and focus was on strategic alliances and acquisitions that would help the company move forward.

By the early 1990s, Disney established itself as a diversified media company. It opened another theme park in Paris, called Euro Disney. Disney Stores, which sold Disney [merchandise] exclusively, were opened across the U.S. The company also set up or acquired film studios, which helped it make a foray into adult entertainment. Further, it acquired ABC networks in the mid-1990s and started an Internet portal called Disney.Go.com. In the first thirteen years under Eisner (between 1984 and 1997), Disney's revenues rose from $1.65 billion to $22 billion.

Things began to change after the tragic death of Wells in a helicopter crash in 1994. Analysts had often felt that the success of Disney was primarily due to the fact that Eisner and Wells made a good team. Eisner was an aggressive person who tended to dominate people to get his own way. Wells, on the other hand, was people oriented and could tackle people and situations in more subtle ways. "When people came out of Michael's office wounded, Frank was the emergency room," said a Disney insider.[11] The leadership style of one complemented that of the other and together, the two of them were able to get people to work for the company's growth.

After Wells died however, Eisner's working style reportedly began to fail. He was often criticized for being too aggressive and for not giving people enough importance. Unable to put up with Eisner's overbearing attitude, several key people like Jeffrey Katzenberg (Katzenberg, a former studio chief) Steven Bollenbach (the Chief Financial Officer) and Paul Pressler (the head of Disney's theme parks and resorts) left the company. A series of wrong decisions in the 1990s also increased the strength of Eisner's opposition. The appointment of Michael Ovitz (Ovitz) as the company's president in 1995, the failure of the company's Internet venture, a long-drawn lawsuit with Katzenberg, and the acquisition of the Fox Family Network[12] were counted among the major mistakes made by Eisner. In the early 2000s, ABC began to experience a decline in viewership, due to a rut in the programs and the overexposure of its most popular show, 'Who Wants to Be a Millionaire?'[13]

Problems intensified after the terrorist attacks on the U.S. in September 2001. The attacks led to a drastic fall in theme park attendance due to people's fear of travel. The recession that gripped the U.S. in the late 1990s and early 2000s also affected Disney. The consumer-products division, which had been struggling for years, had to be revamped and Disney closed 50 of its 530 American stores in 2001. In the same year, Disney also closed its web portal, which had been losing money since it was launched in the late 1990s. The closure had cost the company an estimated $900 million. Disney's net result for 2001 was a loss of $158 million, on revenues of $25.2 billion. To meet the requirements of the new situation, the company laid off 400 people in 2001. Disney's share price also began to drop precipitously and was trading around $14 in 2002, as against $40 in 2000. Although the company returned to profit in 2002 with a net income of $1.2 billion, it was a third lower than the profit of $1.8 billion in 1997.

In 2002, Eisner developed a new plan for turning around the company and obtained approval from the board. By 2003, the company started showing signs of a turnaround

---

[9] Reliance Group Holdings Inc. is a New York–based company, which underwrites a broad range of commercial property and provides personal-casualty and automobile insurance. It also provided information technology consulting services.

[10] Roy joined the company in 1954 as an assistant film editor and took over as the chairman of the animation department in 1984. He became a member of the board in 1967. He met Gold in the late 1970s and made him his financial adviser. Gold was later nominated to the Disney board.

[11] Marc Gunther, "Has Eisner Lost the Disney Magic?" *Fortune,* January 7, 2002.

[12] The television channels of Rupert Murdoch's NewsCorp.

[13] A popular game show on which a contestant could win a million dollars by answering certain questions correctly.

and during 2003, the company's share price rose by about 34%. Disney also made a profit of $1.26 billion on revenues of $27 billion (Refer [to] Exhibit 1 for Disney's Income Statement and Exhibit 2 for Disney's performance in relation to the Standard & Poor's Index).

NEW GOVERNANCE NORMS

According to analysts, by the early 2000s, the Disney board had acquired the dubious distinction of being one of the worst boards in the U.S. Analysts believed that the board was

Exhibit 1   Income Statement

Income Statement (all numbers in thousands)

Period Ending	30-Sep-03	30-Sep-02	30-Sep-01
Total Revenue	27,061,000	25,329,000	25,269,00
Cost of Revenue	—	—	—
Gross Profit	27,061,000	25,329,000	25,269,00
Operating Expenses			
Research Development	—	—	—
Selling General and Administrative	24,330,000	22,924,000	21,670,00
Non Recurring	—	(34,000)	1,454,000
Others	18,000	21,000	767,000
Total Operating Expenses	—	—	—
Operating Income or Loss	2,713,000	2,418,000	1,378,000
Income from Continuing Operations			
Total Other Income/ Expenses Net	334,000	495,000	322,000
Earnings Before Interest and Taxes	3,047,000	2,913,000	1,700,000
Interest Expense	793,000	723,000	417,000
Income Before Tax	2,254,000	2,190,000	1,283,000
Income Tax Expense	789,000	853,000	1,059,000
Minority Interest	(127,000)	(101,000)	(104,000)
Net Income from Continuing Ops	1,338,000	1,236,000	120,000
Non-recurring Events			
Discontinued Operations	—	—	—
Extraordinary Items	—	—	—
Effect of Accounting Changes	(71,000)	—	(278,000)
Other Items	—	—	—
Net Income	1,267,000	1,236,000	(158,000)
Preferred Stock and Other Adjustments	—	—	—
Net Income Applicable to Common Shares	**$1,267,000**	**$1,236,000**	**($158,000)**

Source: finance.yahoo.com.

Exhibit 2   Disney's Performance

Disney's Performance in Relation to the Standard and Poor Index

Period Between		Compounded Annual Growth
1984–1995	S&P 500	15.4%
	Disney	28.1%
1995–2003	S&P 500	8.8%
	Disney	2.8%

Adapted from Marc Gunter, "Mouse Hunt," *Fortune*, January 12, 2004.

not powerful enough to oppose Eisner on any matter and that it allowed him to bulldoze all the decisions. In January 2002, the board appointed Ira Millstein (Millstein), a leading corporate governance lawyer, to suggest changes that would improve the governance of the company. Some of Millstein's recommendations included: the expansion of the company's corporate governance committee, the shrinking of the board from 16 to 12 directors and not using the company's auditor for non-auditing consulting work. By the end of 2002, the company had formally adopted the new governance norms [that] were based on Millstein's recommendations.

By early 2003, the company had stopped using its auditor, PricewaterhouseCoopers, for non-auditing consulting work. Disney adopted a policy that two-thirds of the directors be independent, and that all of them hold at least $100,000 in company stock. The size of the board was reduced and the company began making moves towards cutting all business relationships between board members and the company. However, the resignations of Roy and Gold in protest against bad governance raised doubts in the minds of observers about whether the moves towards good governance at the company were just an eyewash.

INSTANCES OF BAD GOVERANCE

Although it was generally acknowledged that Eisner was responsible for making Disney (which was until then known for its children's films and theme parks) into a well recognized and successful global media conglomerate, it was felt that he was assuming too much power in the organization. In the first thirteen years under Eisner, the market value of Disney rose from $2 billion to $67 billion. However, by the late 1990s, analysts began noticing that the company was hinging too much on Eisner.

In 1999 and 2000, Disney [was] featured in *BusinessWeek's*[14] annual survey of corporate boards [as] among the

---

[14] A leading business magazine.

Exhibit 3   Attributes of a Good Board

INDEPENDENCE
Friends and cronies of the CEO are out. Crucial panels like audit should contain no insiders. Cross-directorships are taboo.

QUALITY
Board meetings should include real, open debate. Directors need to be familiar with managers and conditions in the field.

ACCOUNTABILITY
Directors ought to hold serious stakes in the company. They should also be prepared to challenge under-performing CEOs.

Source: "Attributes of a Good Board," *BusinessWeek*, January 24, 2000.

---

worst boards in the U.S. Ever since Eisner took over as chairman and CEO, analysts felt that he exercised an undesirable level of control over the board at Disney. It was alleged that he resorted to nepotism in appointing board members, and tried to make most of the appointments from among his personal friends and acquaintances. This seemed to have increased his clout in the company and the board became a rubber stamp to his decisions. It was alleged that dissenting members on the board were often victimized and prevented from serving on important committees on some pretext. The instances of bad governance at Disney are outlined below (Refer [to] Exhibit 3 for attributes of a good board).

APPOINTMENTS AT DISNEY

While the principles of good corporate governance required that the CEO be accountable to the board, analysts felt that this was not the case at Disney. Eisner was known to appoint his personal friends and acquaintances on the board, whether or not they were Disney shareholders at the time of appointment. As a result, the board ceased to be independent and Eisner held sway over the directors of the company.

The composition of the board also came under criticism. Of the 16 board members in 2002, half were either current or former executives at Disney, or people who did business with the company. Some of the others were the headmistress of an elementary school where one of Eisner's children had studied, Eisner's personal lawyer, his architect and a Hollywood actor. Therefore, the directors were either not independent (working, or having worked at Disney, or doing business with the company), or were dummy appointments. Nell Minnow (Minnow), a corporate governance expert based in the U.S., said that the Disney board was "About as bad a board as we've seen."[15] What was even more

objectionable was that some of these members were serving on critical committees like the compensation committee or the nomination committee.

The method of determining a member's independence was also largely arbitrary. Gold was judged as not independent because he was the financial adviser of Roy, who was a company executive. On this basis he was deprived of the chairmanship of the governance committee. On the other hand, another director, John Bryson, whose wife held a high and well paid position in Lifetime Entertainment cable channel (which was 50% owned by Disney) was judged independent and was appointed as the chairman of the same committee. Patrick McGurn, an analyst with Institutional Shareholder Services, a Rockville-based organization, which advises investors on corporate-governance issues, believed that Bryson could not be judged as independent because of the strong financial links that his family had with Disney (Bryson was later judged as non-independent and replaced on the committee). He also questioned the independence of former Senator George Mitchell (Mitchell), whose law firm used to work for Disney (the firm severed its ties with Disney prior to Mitchell's becoming the board's presiding director). Mitchell was appointed to the governance and nomination committee. Another important issue was that Mitchell was appointed although he was a member of four other boards, when good governance principles mandated that a person should not sit on more than three or four boards in all.

The most controversial appointment made by Eisner, however, was that of Ovitz, who was a personal friend of Eisner. He was brought in as the president of Disney in 1995. By 1996, it was clear that Ovitz was a failure. He himself was not satisfied with his work and wanted to leave. Eisner wanted his friend to leave the company on good terms and, under Eisner's influence, the board approved of a severance package of $38 million in cash as well as stock options valued at $101 million. Analysts felt that this package (which represented 10% of Disney's revenues in 1996) was far too generous. It was also far greater than the amount Ovitz would have made, had he continued to work at Disney for the full five-year period of his contract. The package caused great uproar and triggered a lawsuit by Disney shareholders, demanding that the money be returned to the company.

It was also alleged in the [lawsuit] that Eisner was advised by at least three members of the board that Ovitz was not suitable for the post. Eisner, however, chose to disregard their advice. He also appointed Irwin Russell, his personal lawyer who was also a board member, to negotiate the contract with Ovitz. Russell then sat on the compensation committee that approved Ovitz's hiring based on a summary of the deal. No written contract went before the board for approval and Ovitz's contract was later altered in his favor without board approval. It was said that the board did not try to negotiate with Ovitz to obtain better terms for the company and the shareholders. It simply approved the amount that Ovitz demanded.

---

[15] Marc Gunther, "Has Eisner Lost the Disney Magic?" *Fortune*, January 7, 2002.

EISNER'S COMPENSATION

Corporate governance experts believe that the compensation made to CEOs should be linked to the performance of the company. Under this consideration, the compensation made to Eisner was also severely criticized by analysts. At the time of his appointment in 1984, Eisner was granted a base salary of $75,000 per year and some stock options. Many analysts found this amount a fair one. However, in 1996, when he renegotiated his contract, he was granted 24 million options at the then-current price of $21.10, meaning that if Disney's stock climbed $1 a year, or less than 5%, for the seven years until they vested, Eisner would collect $105 million. Of the 24 million options granted, 19 million were not indexed.[16] During the mid-1990s, when Disney shares were trading at around $40, Eisner had cashed in more than $750 million worth of options, which was one of the highest payments ever made in American corporate history.

The performance of the company also left a lot to be desired. After the performance peaked in 1997, the journey [had] been downhill. Earnings per share fell from 92 cents in 1997 to about 55 cents in 2003. Operating income also fell from $4.3 billion in 1997 to $2.7 billion in 2003. Although Eisner did not receive any bonus in 2002 (because of the loss in 2001), he still had a huge number of options which he could [cash]. Another important reason for criticism was that the compensation committee at Disney was made up largely of Eisner's friends, whom he could manipulate to suit his interests.

LACK OF SUCCESSION PLANNING

The Disney board was further criticized for not making an effort to develop a formal succession plan. Eisner had been the chairman and CEO of Disney since 1984 and analysts believed that it was time he made way for a new person. However, Eisner showed no inclination to leave. It was said that when he underwent a risky bypass surgery in 1994, he called his family to the hospital bed and suggested a few names of those he thought could succeed him in case of [a bad outcome].

Analysts felt that it was not healthy for the company to be overly dependent on a particular person. They expressed concern that if something happened to Eisner, the company would suffer from a lack of leadership. It was said that Eisner had the name of a possible successor in a closed envelope in his desk. This was to be opened in case something happened

to prevent him from continuing with his duty. But analysts felt that this was not a good method and did not constitute succession planning. "This is not an Oscar Award winner. This is the next leader of the company. It's not supposed to be a surprise to the board," said Minnow.[17] Grooming a possible successor was [an] important function of a CEO and not doing so could be risky for the future of the company. Besides, analysts said that it was the duty of the board to select a CEO, and that the current CEO would be exceeding his powers if he chose his successor arbitrarily. They compared the situation at Disney to that at GE,[18] where [long-standing] CEO Jack Welch identified three possible successors and encouraged the board to interact with them long before he was due to retire.

THE FUTURE OF THE MAGIC KINGDOM

Soon after their well publicized resignations, Roy and Gold announced that they would launch a campaign to oust Eisner. Both men were planning to meet major shareholders in the company as well as institutional investors and governance bodies to seek their help in ousting Eisner from Disney. In addition to removing Eisner, they also hoped to get the shareholders to nominate a new body of independent directors at an upcoming board meeting in March 2004.

Their efforts began to yield results when, in December 2003, the corporate governance wing of a major investment firm asked Disney's independent directors to respond to some of the issues raised by Roy and Gold. At the end of December 2003, Herbert Denton (Denton), who ran a firm called Providence Capital and specialized in leading shareholder campaigns, organized a meeting of about 50 investment firms and sent a letter to the Disney board outlining some of their demands.

The letter demanded that the post of chairman be separated from that of CEO, director nominees be solicited from major investors, financial benchmarks and timetables be set, the board develop a succession plan, and make it easier for shareholders to vote changes to company bylaws. "It's our way of seeing whether Michael Eisner's embrace of good governance is for real or for show," said Denton.[19] Several other analysts also favored splitting the positions of chairman and CEO. "It basically provides checks and balances," said Kathy Styponias, an analyst at Prudential Securities.[20]

---

[16] Indexed options are those [that] are linked to performance. They reward only those executives who outperform their peers. For instance, if a company's stock goes up by 10%, when the rest of the stocks in the industry go up by 12%, the options are not paid. They are usually linked to an industry index.

[17] Richard Verrier and James Bates, "No Succession Plan at Disney," *The Herald*, December 10, 2003.

[18] General Electric was the largest and most successful [company] in the world. GE was a conglomerate comprising several mature businesses, from aircraft engines to household and electric appliances.

[19] Marc Gunther, "The Directors," *Fortune*, December 27, 2003.

[20] Marc Gunther, "The Directors," *Fortune*, December 27, 2003.

There was also some speculation that Disney could become a target of takeover bids, considering the vulnerable condition it was in following the threats to remove the CEO. Comcast (a cable firm), Yahoo (a major Internet company) and InterActiveCorp (a multibrand interactive commerce company) were thought to be some of the likely suitors of Disney.[21] There was considerable speculation as well, on who would replace Eisner if the dissidents were successful in overthrowing him. Even if they were not, Eisner's term was due to expire in 2006, and analysts felt that it was time some potential successors were considered.

However, analysts felt that Roy and Gold would require a fair amount of luck to be able to succeed in their intentions to remove Eisner. They felt that it would not be very easy to obtain unconditional support from Disney shareholders, especially in [. . .] light of the company's improved performance in 2003. In 2003, stock [prices] grew by about 35% and analysts expected the earnings per share to increase simultaneously by more than 30%. Another reason for the skepticism was that, when Roy and Gold were not able to convince the board of the need to remove Eisner when they were board members themselves, it would be even more difficult to do so as outsiders. Their [resignations were] perceived by many as an admission of defeat, and the future of the "Magic Kingdom" was in the hands of the shareholders.

Questions for Discussion

1. Roy and Gold alleged that most of the governance problems at Disney could be traced to Eisner. What were the major governance problems at Disney? Is it true that Eisner was responsible for the company's governance problems? Do you think that the new governance norms adopted by the company were an eyewash?

2. Not identifying a successor has been one of the major complaints against Eisner. What could be the reason for this? What are the possible repercussions to the company in case of an emergency? Comment also on the independence issue of the Disney board.

3. Governance problems at Disney were forcefully brought to notice with the resignation of Roy and Gold. Do you think that their resignation from the board was a good move? Discuss the future of Disney in [. . .] light of the criticism it faced regarding governance.

---

[21] In February 2004, Comcast Corp., the No. 1 cable operator in the U.S., made an offer to buy Disney for $54 billion.

Additional Readings & References

1. **"Elbow Power,"** *The Economist*, November 19, 1998.
2. **"Attributes of a Good Board,"** *BusinessWeek*, January 24, 2000.
3. **"The Best and Worst Corporate Boards,"** *BusinessWeek*, January 24, 2000.
4. Marc Gunther, **"The Wary World of Disney,"** *Fortune*, October 15, 2001.
5. Marc Gunther, **"Has Eisner Lost the Disney Magic?"** *Fortune*, January 7, 2002.
6. **"Disney or Doesn't He?"** *The Economist*, January 10, 2002.
7. Ronald Grover, **"Eisner's Challenge: Beat the Buzz,"** *BusinessWeek*, August 16, 2002.
8. Frank Ahrens, **"At AOL and Disney, Uneasy Chairs,"** *Washington Post*, September 18, 2002.
9. **"Disney Top Shareholders Urged to Meet,"** money.cnn.com, September 11, 2002.
10. Dan Milmo, **"Eisner Survives as Disney Board Backs Recovery Plan,"** *The Guardian*, September 25, 2002.
11. David Teather, **"Magic Kingdom May Expel Eisner,"** *The Guardian*, September 25, 2002.
12. **"Peacemaker to Aid Disney Shake-Up,"** news.bbc.co.uk, September 25, 2002.
13. **"Disney Board Backs Eisner's Plan for Growth,"** www.telegraph.co.uk, September 26, 2002.
14. **"Wobbly Kingdom,"** *The Economist*, September 26, 2002.
15. **"The Tragic Kingdom,"** *The Economist*, July 24, 2003.
16. Marc Gunther, **"Boards Beware,"** *Fortune*, November 10, 2003.
17. Ronald Grover and Gerry Khermouch, **"Renovating This Old Mouse,"** *BusinessWeek*, November 10, 2003.
18. Ronald Grover, **"Stalking a Wily Prey at Disney,"** *BusinessWeek*, December 2, 2003.
19. Gary Gentile, **"Gold 2nd to Quit Disney Board,"** *Newsday*, December 2, 2003.
20. **"Wishing Upon a Star,"** *The Economist*, December 4, 2003.
21. **"A Tale of Two Boards,"** *The Economist*, December 4, 2003.
22. Ronald Grover, **"Eisner's Very Repressive Regime,"** *BusinessWeek*, December 4, 2003.
23. Richard Verrier and James Bates, **"No Succession Plan at Disney,"** *The Herald*, December 10, 2003.
24. **"Succession Planning,"** *The Economist*, December 11, 2003.
25. Marc Gunther **"Disney's Loss is Eisner's Gain,"** *Fortune*, December 22, 2003.
26. Marc Gunther, **"The Directors,"** *Fortune*, December 27, 2003.
27. Marc Gunther, **"Mouse Hunt,"** *Fortune*, January 12, 2004.
28. **"Corporate Conflict,"** www.cbsnews.com, December 1, 2003.
29. **"Disney Corporate's Mouse Droppings,"** www.cbsnews.com, December 1, 2003.
30. **"Disney Heir Quits; Blasts Eisner,"** www.cbsnews.com, December 1, 2003.
31. finance.yahoo.com.
32. www.disney.com.

Case Index

Glossary

acquisition Strategy by which one firm acquires another through stock purchase or exchange.

acquisition premium Difference between current market value of a target firm and purchase price paid to induce its shareholders to turn its control over to new owners.

agency problem Separation of its ownership from managerial control of a firm.

agent Party, such as a manager, who acts on behalf of another party.

ambidextrous structure Organizational structure for dynamic contexts in which project teams are organized as structurally independent units and encouraged to develop their own structures, systems, and processes.

arena Area (product, service, distribution channel, geographic markets, technology, etc.) in which a firm participates.

balanced scorecard Strategic management support system for measuring vision and strategy against business- and operating-unit-level performance.

barrier to entry Condition under which it is more difficult to join or compete in an industry.

behavioral controls Practice of tying rewards to criteria other than simply financial performance, such as those broadly identified in the balanced scorecard.

board of directors Group of individuals that formally represents the firm's shareholders and oversees the work of top executives.

bootstrapping Process of finding creative ways to support a startup business financially until it turns profitable.

business strategy Strategy for competing against rivals within a particular industry.

buyer power Degree to which firms in the buying industry are able to dictate terms on purchase agreements which extract some of the profit that would otherwise go to competitors in the focal industry.

CAGE framework Tool that considers the dimensions of culture, administration, geography, and economics to assess the distance created by global expansion.

capabilities A firm's skill at using its resources to create goods and services; combination of

procedures and expertise on which a firm relies to produce goods and services.

causal ambiguity Condition whereby the difficulty of identifying or understanding a resource or capability makes it valuable, rare, and inimitable.

codes of governance Ideal governance standards formulated by regulatory, market, and government institutions.

coevolution Process by which diversification causes two or more interdependent businesses to adapt not only to their environment, but to each other.

commoditization Process during industry evolution by which sales eventually come to depend less on unique product features and more on price.

competitive advantage A firm's ability to create *value* in a way that its rivals cannot.

complementor Firm in one industry that provides products or services which tend to increase sales in another industry.

conglomerate Corporation consisting of many companies in different businesses or industries.

consortia Association of several companies and/or governments for some definite strategic purpose.

co-opetition Situation in which firms are simultaneously competitors in one market and collaborators in another.

core competence Capability which is central to a firm's main business operations and which allow it to generate new products and services.

corporate governance The system by which owners of firms direct and control the affairs of the firm.

corporate new venturing New-venture creation by established firms.

corporate renewal Outcome of successful strategic change in the context of an established business.

corporate strategy Strategy for guiding a firm's entry and exit from different businesses, for determining how a parent company adds value to and manages its portfolio of businesses, and for creating value through diversification.

cross-subsidizing Practice by which a firm uses profits from one aspect of a product, service, or region to support other aspects of competitive activity.

culture Core organizational values widely held and shared by an organization's members.

differentiation Strategic position based on products or offers services with quality, reliability, or prestige that is discernibly higher than that of competitors and for which customers are willing to pay.

differentiator Feature or attribute of a company's product or service (e.g., image, customization, technical superiority, price, quality and reliability) that helps it beat its competitors in the marketplace.

diseconomies of scope Condition under which the joint output of two or more products within a single firm results in increased average costs.

diseconomy of scale Condition under which average total costs per unit of production increases at higher levels of input.

disruptive technology Breakthrough product- or process-related technology that destroys the competencies of incumbent firms in an industry.

distinctive competence Capability that sets a firm apart from other firms; something that a firm can do which competitors cannot.

diversification Degree to which a firm conducts business in more than one arena.

divestiture Strategy whereby a company sells off a business or division.

dominant logic Way in which managers view the firm's competitive activities and make corporate resource-allocation decisions.

due diligence Initial pre-closing screening, analysis, and negotiations for an acquisition.

dynamic capabilities A firm's ability to modify, reconfigure, and upgrade resources and capabilities in order to strategically respond to or generate environmental changes.

economic logic Means by which a firm will earn a profit by implementing a strategy.

economy of scale Condition under which average total cost for a unit of production is lower at higher levels of output.

economy of scope Condition under which lower total average costs result from sharing resources to produce more than one product or service.

entrepreneurial process Integration of opportunity recognition, key resources and capabilities, and an entrepreneur and entrepreneurial team to create a new venture.

entrepreneurship Recognition of opportunities and the use of resources and capabilities to implement innovative ideas for new ventures.

equity alliance Alliance in which one or more partners assumes a greater ownership interest in either the alliance or another partner.

escalation of commitment Decision-making bias under which people are willing to commit additional resources to a failing course of action.

ethnocentrism Belief in the superiority of one's own ethnic group or, more broadly, the conviction that one's own national, group, or cultural characteristics are "normal."

exit barriers Barriers that impose a high cost on the abandonment of a market or product.

exporting Foreign-country entry vehicle in which a firm uses an intermediary to perform most foreign marketing functions.

first mover Firm choosing to initiate a strategic action, whether the introduction of a new product or service or the development of a new process.

five-forces model Framework for evaluating industry structure according to the effects of rivalry, threat of entry, supplier power, buyer power, and the threat of substitutes.

focused cost leadership Strategic position based on being a low-cost leader in a narrow market segment.

focused differentiation Strategic position based on targeting products to relatively small segments.

foreign direct investment (FDI) Foreign-country entry vehicle by which a firm commits to the direct ownership of a foreign subsidiary or division.

functional structure Form of organization revolving around specific value-chain functions.

general resources Resource that can be exploited across a wide range of activities.

generic strategies Strategic position designed to reduce the effects of rivalry, including *low-cost*, *differentiation*, *focused cost leadership*,

focused differentiation, and *integrated positions*.

geographic roll-up Strategy whereby a firm acquires many other firms in the same industry segment but in different geographic arenas in an attempt to create significant scale and scope advantages.

geographic scope Breadth and diversity of geographic arenas in which a firm operates.

global configuration Strategy by which a firm sacrifices local responsiveness for the lower costs associated with global efficiency.

globalization Evolution of distinct geographic product markets into a state of globally interdependent product markets.

goals and objectives Combination of a broad indication of organizational intentions (*goals*) and specific, measurable steps (*objectives*) for reaching them.

greenfield investment Form of FDI in which a firm starts a new foreign business from the ground up.

high-end disruption Strategy that may result in huge new markets in which new players redefine industry rules to unseat the largest incumbents.

horizontal alliance Alliance involving a focal firm and another firm in the same industry.

horizontal scope Extent to which a firm participates in related market segments or industries outside its existing value-chain activities.

hubris Exaggerated self-confidence that can result in managers' overestimating the value of a potential acquisition, having unrealistic assumptions about the ability to create synergies, and a willingness to pay too much for a transaction.

illusion of control Decision-making bias under which people believe that they're in greater control of a situation than rational analysis would support.

illusion of favorability Decision-making bias under which people tend to give themselves more credit for their successes and take less responsibility for their failures.

illusion of optimism Decision-making bias that leads people to underestimate the prospect of negative future events while overestimating the prospect of positive outcomes.

implementation levers Mechanisms used by strategic leaders to help execute a firm's strategy.

importing Internationalization strategy by which a firm brings a good, service, or capital into the home country from abroad.

improvisation Managerial practices that contribute to a culture of frequent change, especially in turbulent or hypercompetitive contexts.

incentive alignment Use of incentives to align managerial self-interest with shareholders'.

industry life cycle Pattern of evolution followed by an industry inception to current and future states.

initial public offering (IPO) First sale of a company's stock to the public market.

institutional investors Pension or mutual fund that manages large sums of money for third-party investors.

integrated position Strategic position in which elements of one position suport strong standing in another.

international configuration The firm leverages key resources and capabilities by centralizing them to achieve economies of scale, but it decentralizes others, such as marketing, so that some activities can be somewhat localized.

international strategy Process by which a firm approaches its cross-border activities and those of competitors and plans to approach them in the future.

intrinsic value Present value of a company's future cash flows from existing assets and businesses.

joint venture Alliance in which two firms make equity investments in a third legal entity.

key success factor (KSF) Key asset or requisite skill that all firms in an industry must possess in order to be a viable competitor.

knowing-doing gap Phenomenon whereby firms tend to be better at generating new knowledge than at creating new products based on that knowledge.

learning curve Incremental production costs decline at a constant rate as production experience is gained; the steeper the learning curve, the more rapidly costs decline.

Level 5 Hierarchy Model of leadership skills calling for a wide range of abilities, some of which are hierarchical in nature.

long-term incentive plans Incentive plan tying future bonus payouts to defined accounting-return targets over a three- to five-year period.

low-cost leadership Strategic position based on producing a good or offering a service while maintaining total costs that are lower than what it takes competitors to offer the same product or service.

low-end disruption Strategy that appears at the low end of industry offerings, targeting the least desirable of incumbents' customers.

managerialism Tendency of managers to make decisions based on personal self-interest rather than the best interests of shareholders.

market for corporate control Phenomenon by which the possibility that corporate control can be shifted to competitors or other buyers encourages management to operate a firm effectively and ethically.

market value Current market capitalization of a firm.

matrix structure Form of organization in which specialists from functional departments are assigned to work for one or more product or geographic units.

merger Consolidation or combination of two or more firms.

minimum efficient scale (MES) The output level that delivers the lowest total average cost.

mission Declaration of what a firm is and what it stands for—its fundamental values and purpose.

monitoring Functioning of the board in exercising its legal and fiduciary responsibility to oversee executives' behavior and performance and to take action when it's necessary to replace management.

multidivisional structure Form of organization in which divisions are organized around product or geographic markets and are often self-sufficient in terms of functional expertise.

multinational configuration Strategy by which a firm is essentially a portfolio of geographically removed business units that have devoted most of their resources and capabilities to maximizing local responsiveness and uniqueness.

network structure Form of organization in which small, semiautonomous, and potentially temporary groups are brought together for specific purposes.

new-venture creation Entrepreneurship and the creation of a new business from scratch.

nonequity alliance Alliance that involves neither the assumption of equity interest nor the creation of separate organizations.

organizational structure Relatively stable arrangement of responsibilities, tasks, and people within an organization.

outcome controls Practice of tying rewards to narrowly defined financial criteria.

outsourcing Activity performed for a company by people other than its full-time employees.

overconfidence bias Decision-making bias under which people tend to place erroneously high levels of confidence in their own knowledge or abilities.

patching Process of remapping businesses in accordance with changing market conditions and restitches them into new internal business structures.

PESTEL analysis Tool for assessing the political, economic, sociocultural, technological, environmental, and legal contexts in which a firm operates.

portfolio planning Practice of mapping diversified businesses or products based on their relative strengths and market attractiveness.

principal Party, such as a shareholder, who hires an agent to act on his or her behalf.

profit pool Analytical tool that enables managers to calculate profits at various points along an industry value chain.

purchase price Final price actually paid to the target firm's shareholders of an acquired company.

real-options analysis Process of maximizing the upside or limiting the downside of an investment opportunity by uncovering and quantifying the options and discussion points embedded within it.

related diversification Form of diversification in which the business units operated by a firm are highly related.

relational quality Principle identifying four key elements (initial conditions, negotiation process, reciprocal experiences, outside behavior) in establishing and maintaining interorganizational trust.

resources Inputs used by firms to create products and services.

reward system Bases on which employees are compensated and promoted.

rivalry Intensity of competition within an industry.

road show Series of presentations in which top management promotes an IPO to interested investors and analysts.

S-1 statement Legal document outlining a firm's financial position in preparation for an initial public stock offering.

second mover (often *fast follower*) Second significant company to move into a market, quickly following the first mover.

self-serving fairness bias Decision-making bias under which people believe that they're fair and want to act in ways that are perceived as fair and just.

serial acquirers Company that engages in frequent acquisitions.

simple rules Basic rules for guiding improvisation by defining strategy without confining it.

specialized resources Resource with a narrow range of applicability.

staging Timing and pace of strategic moves.

stakeholder Individual or group with an interest in an organization's ability to deliver intended results and maintain the viability of its products and services.

stereotyping Relying on a conventional or formulaic conception of another group based on some common characteristic.

stock options Incentive device giving an employee the right to buy a share of company stock at a later date for a predetermined price.

straddling Unsuccessful attempt to integrate both low-cost and differentiation positions.

strategic alliance Relationship in which two or more firms combine resources and capabilities in order to enhance the competitive advantage of all parties.

strategic change Significant changes in resource allocation choices, in the business and implementation activities that align the firm's strategy with its vision, or in its vision.

strategic coherence Symmetric coalignment of the five elements of the firm's strategy, the congruence of functional-area policies with these elements, and the overarching fit of various businesses under the corporate umbrella.

strategic group Subset of firms which, because of similar strategies, resources, and capabilities, compete against each other more intensely than with other firms in an industry.

strategic leadership Task of managing an overall enterprise and influencing key organizational outcomes.

strategic management Process by which a firm incorporates the tools and frameworks for developing and implementing a strategy.

strategic positioning Means by which managers situate a firm relative to its rivals.

strategic purpose Simplified, widely shared mental model of the organization and its future, including anticipated changes in its environment.

strategy Central, integrated, externally focused concept of how the firm will achieve its objectives.

strategy formulation Process of developing a strategy.

strategy implementation Process of executing a strategy.

succession planning Process of managing a well-planned and well-executed transition from one CEO to the next with positive outcomes for all key stakeholders.

superordinate goal Overarching reference point for a host of hierarchical subgoals.

supplier power Degree to which firms in the supply industry are able to dictate terms to contracts and thereby extract some of the profit that would otherwise be available to competitors in the focal industry.

synergy Condition under which the combined benefits of activities in two or more arenas are greater than the simple sum of those benefits.

synergy value Difference between the combined values of the target and the acquiring firm after the transaction and the sum of the values of the two firms taken independently.

takeoff period Period during which a new product generates rapid growth and huge sales increases.

threat of new entry Degree to which new competitors can enter an industry and intensify rivalry.

threat of substitutes Degree to which products of one industry can satisfy the same demand as those of another.

transnational configuration Strategy in which a firm tries to capitalize on both local responsiveness and global efficiency.

unrelated diversification Form of diversification in which the business units that a firm operates are highly dissimilar.

value chain Total of primary and support value-adding activities by which a firm produces, distributes, and markets a product.

value curve A graphical depiction of how a firm and major groups of its competitors are competing across its industry's factors of completion.

value-net model Map of a firm's existing and potential exchange relationships.

vehicle Means for entering new arenas (e.g., through acquisitions, alliances, internal development, etc.).

vertical alliance Alliance involving a focal firm and a supplier or customer.

vertical integration Diversification into upstream and/or downstream industries.

vertical scope The extent to which a firm is vertically integrated.

vision Simple statement or understanding of what the firm will be in the future.

VRINE model Analytical framework suggesting that a firm with resources and capabilities which are valuable, rare, inimitable, non-substitutable, and exploitable will gain a competitive advantage.

willingness to pay Principle of differentiation strategy by which customers are willing to pay more for certain product features.

winner's curse Situation in which a winning M&A bidder must live with the consequences of paying too much for the target.

Name Index

A

Acs, Z., 365n4
Afuah, A., 183n15
Aguirre, Fernando, 390–91
Akbar, Y., 211n10
Aldrin, Edwin Jr., 302
Allaire, Paul A., 26, 27, 28
Allen, Robert E., 381
Almeida, P., 273n21
Altman, Edward I., 356
Amihud, Y., 300n5
Amit, R., 121n5
Amram, M., 183n26
Anders, William, 144
Anderson, P., 121n18, 121nn20–21, 183n19
Andrews, K. R., 24n1, 24n6, 24n8, 333n2
Anfuso, D., 333n1
Argote, L., 121n15, 149n9
Arino, A., 273n26
Armstrong, Lance, 123, 124, 126, 145
Armstrong, Neil, 302
Arregle, J., 245n34
Atkins, Betsy, 40, 41
Audretsch, D., 365n4

B

Baetz, M. C., 59n19, 59n21, 59n25, 334n24
Bagley, C. E., 395n21
Bailey, E., 273n22
Bamford, J. D., 253
Bandler, J., 58n1
Barkema, H., 84n2, 245n34
Barnett, W. P., 121n19
Barney, J. B., 24n19, 24n21, 24n23, 69,
    85nn6–7, 85n12, 85n18, 85n33, 273n12,
    273n24, 334n38
Bart, C. K., 59n19, 59n21, 59n25, 334n24
Bartlett, C. A., 85n35, 235, 335nn51–52
Bayliss, B., 245n20
Baysden, C., 75
Baysinger, B., 395nn18–19
Bazerman, M., 59n35, 59n38, 59n41
Beamish, P. W., 219, 245nn6–8
Becker, B., 334n34
Bell, Charlie, 39
Berkrot, B., 59n30
Berle, A. A., Jr., 395n9, 396n39
Beyer, J. M., 273n34
Bhide, A., 365nn6–7
Bibeault, D. B., 365nn24–25
Birkenshaw, J., 235
Black, J., 241
Blake, J., 365n1
Bleeke, J., 273n5, 273nn29–30, 273n33
Block, Z., 365n11
Bloom, M., 396n38
Bobala, B., 121n6
Boivie, S., 395n6
Bonsall, Jim, 360–61

Boudette, N., 308
Bouton, Garret, 334n30
Bower, J. T., 284–87, 301nn10–11
Bowman, E., 273n22
Bowman, G., 112, 183n16
Bradach, J., 334n32
Brandenburger, A., 121nn10–11, 183n5, 257
Bransen, Sir Richard, 101
Bransten, L., 211n15
Bremner, B., 396n44
Brin, Sergey, 342
Brooks, R., 372
Brown, J. S., 245n31
Brown, S. L., 24n9, 25n27, 175, 183n2, 183n24,
    211n16, 273n23, 301n19, 335n59
Browning, L. D., 273n34
Bruner, R. F., 300n3, 301n9, 301n14, 301n18
Buffet, Warren, 23, 204, 287, 288, 290, 376
Bulkeley, W. M., 58n1, 244n1
Bullock, Frasier, 24n15
Burgelman, R. A., 24nn9–11, 85n29, 334n21
Burke, Richard, 124
Burt, R. S., 334n12
Bygrave, W., 365n2
Byrne, J. A., 395n1

C

Cadbury, Sir Adrian, 374
Calantone, R., 59n36
Callaway, Wayne, 86
Cameron, K., 58n10
Campbell, A., 59n21, 211n14
Cannella, A., 18, 333n3, 334n15, 335n48
Cantalupo, Jim, 39
Cappetta, R., 211n11
Capron, L., 85n9
Carl, T., 24n14
Carpenter, M. A., 59n11, 59n14, 85nn36–37,
    211n6, 241, 334n25, 335n53, 365n22,
    396n24, 396n28, 396n37
Carreyrou, J., 395n16
Casti, J., 183n23
Caves, R. E., 121nn12–13
Chadwick, C., 334n36
Chandler, A., 210n3, 245n9, 309, 334n16,
    334n19
Chatman, J. A., 333n9
Chen, M., 183n4
Chesbrough, H., 365n10, 365n16
Chevalier, J., 183n13
Chi, D., 244n1
Chowdury, N., 244n1
Christensen, C. M., 24n1, 24n16, 25n26, 25n29,
    85n28, 121nn22–23, 149n12, 183n21,
    211n18, 333n2, 335n56
Cioletti, J., 121n6
Clark, D., 211n9
Clark, K. B., 121n19
Clifford, J. D., 210n2

Coff, R. W., 334nn41–42
Collins, J. C., 32, 33, 58nn7–9, 59n20, 59n22, 59n24, 319, 334n31
Conger, J., 41
Connelly, John, 67
Cook, J., 273n4
Cool, K., 85n12, 85nn15–16
Covin, J., 183n14
Coyne, K. P., 210n2
Cummings, L. L., 333n9
Curtin, M., 59n29

D
Dacin, M. T., 245n34
Daems, H., 121n12
Daft, Douglas N., 87, 288
Daft, R. L., 334n17
Dahya, J., 395n20
Darr, E. D., 149n9
Daum, J., 183n27
D'Aveni, R., 183n9
Davidson, W. N. III, 334n35
Davis, G. F., 210n4
Day, D., 365n12
Day, D. L., 149n16, 149n19
Dean, J. W. Jr., 334n37
Deeds, D. L., 149n20
de la Torre, J., 273n26
Dell, Michael, 45, 212, 213, 376
Demos, Steve, 248, 294
der Hovanesian, M., 396n44
Deromedi, Roger, 32
Dial, J., 149n21, 396n36
Diekman, K. A., 210n4
Dierickx, I., 85n12, 85nn15–16
Dixit, A., 121n11
Downing, D., 244n1
Downing, P., 349
Drucker, P. F., 15, 24n18, 59n21, 333n6
Dunlap, Al, 366–69, 370, 380, 385, 386, 388, 395n1
Dybis, K., 361
Dyer, J. H., 258, 265, 268, 269, 273n9, 273n12, 273n19, 273n25, 273n28, 273nn31–32

E
Eckhardt, J., 365n4
Edison, Thomas, 185
Eisenhardt, K., 24n9, 25n27, 84n1, 85nn22–23, 85n26, 175, 183n2, 183nn24–25, 210n5, 211nn16–17, 273n23, 301n19, 334n33, 335n59
Eisenhower, General Dwight D., 72
Elenkov, D., 300n4
Ellis, J. E., 107
Ellison, S., 333n4
Elson, Charles, 368, 369, 380, 395n1
Enrico, Roger, 86
Epple, D., 149n9
Epstein, M. J., 334n28
Ernst, D., 273n5, 273nn29–30, 273n33

Estess, P., 59n17
Evans, P., 67

F
Fama, E. F., 395n3, 395n8
Fanning, Shawn, 150, 151
Fast, N., 365n14
Ferrier, W. J., 156, 183n6
Finkelstein, S., 84n2, 365n23, 365nn27–28
Flamm, K., 273n7
Fox, J. B., 334n35
Fransman, M., 273n7
Fredrickson, J. W., 6, 8, 24n5, 24n12, 149n22, 183n3, 211n6, 280, 396n29
Freeman, R. E., 49
Fulmer, R., 41

G
Gabbay, S. M., 334n12
Gadiesh, O., 198, 211nn7–8
Galunic, C., 210n5, 211nn16–17
Gandossy, R., 59n31
Garvin, D., 347, 365n13, 365n17
Gedajlovic, E. R., 396n42
Gee, R., 365n15
Geletkanycz, M. A., 59n11
Gell-Mann, M., 183n23
Gerhart, B., 334n34, 334n43
Gerstner, Lou, 42–43
Ghemawat, P., 245nn13–14
Ghoshal, S., 85n35, 235, 335nn51–52
Gilbert, J. L., 198, 211nn7–8
Gimeno, J., 25n28
Goizueta, Roberto C., 86, 88
Golden, Hyman, 282
Gomes-Casseres, B., 253, 267
Gong, Y., 335nn54–55
Goold, M., 211n14
Goolsbee, A., 183n13
Gordon, M. E., 121n12
Gore, V., 302
Gore, W. L., 302–5
Gorman, P., 210n2
Govindarajan, V., 228, 244n3, 245n5, 245nn10–12, 245n18, 245n23, 245n26, 245n35, 245n38
Grant, R. M., 273n21
Greenberg, Arnold, 282
Gregersen, H. B., 59n14, 85n36, 241, 335n53
Grimm, C. M., 156, 183n6
Grossman, W., 395n15
Grove, A., 24n1, 60, 149n8
Gupta, A., 228, 244n3, 245n5, 245nn10–12, 245n18, 245n23, 245n26, 245n35, 245n38

H
Haddox, Margaret, 85n19
Hagel, J., 245n31
Haleblian, J., 84n2
Halevy, T., 273nn4–5

Company/Product Index

Subject Index

Photo Credits